The 18th Century

1701-1800

Great Events from History

The 18th Century

1701-1800

Volume 2
1774-1800

Editor

John Powell

Oklahoma Baptist University

SALEM PRESS

Pasadena, California   Hackensack, New Jersey

Editor in Chief: Dawn P. Dawson

Editorial Director: Christina J. Moose	*Production Editor:* Joyce I. Buchea
Acquisitions Editor: Mark Rehn	*Design and Layout:* James Hutson
Research Supervisor: Jeffry Jensen	*Graphics:* William Zimmerman
Research Assistant Editor: Rebecca Kuzins	*Photo Editor:* Cynthia Breslin Beres
Manuscript Editors: Desiree Dreeuws, Andy Perry	*Editorial Assistant:* Dana Garey

Cover photos (pictured clockwise, from top left): Declaration, 1776 (The Granger Collection, New York); Blanchard's Balloon (The Granger Collection, New York); Whitney's Cotton Gin (The Granger Collection, New York); Istanbul mosque (EPA/Landov); California mission (The Granger Collection, New York); Peking barges (The Granger Collection, New York)

Some of the essays in this work originally appeared in the following Salem Press sets: *Chronology of European History: 15,000 B.C. to 1997* (1997, edited by John Powell; associate editors, E. G. Weltin, José M. Sánchez, Thomas P. Neill, and Edward P. Keleher) and *Great Events from History: North American Series, Revised Edition* (1997, edited by Frank N. Magill). New material has been added.

Library of Congress Cataloging-in-Publication Data

Great events from history. The 18th century, 1701-1800 / editor John Powell.

    p. cm.

Includes bibliographical references and index.

ISBN-10: 1-58765-279-X (set : alk. paper)

ISBN-10: 1-58765-308-7 (v. 1 : alk. paper)

ISBN-10: 1-58765-309-5 (v. 2 : alk. paper)

ISBN-13: 978-1-58765-279-0 (set : alk. paper)

ISBN-13: 978-1-58765-308-7 (v. 1 : alk. paper)

ISBN-13: 978-1-58765-309-4 (v. 2 : alk. paper)

1. Eighteenth century. I. Title: 18th century, 1701-1800. II. Title: Eighteenth century, 1701-1800. III. Powell, John, 1954- IV. Chronology of European history, 15,000 B.C. to 1997. V. Great events from history, North American series. 1997.

D286.G74 2006

909.7—dc22

2006005406

First Printing

PRINTED IN THE UNITED STATES OF AMERICA

CONTENTS

1770's *(continued)*

1780's

1790's

CONTENTS

Appendixes

Indexes

KEYWORD LIST OF CONTENTS

LIST OF MAPS, TABLES, AND SIDEBARS

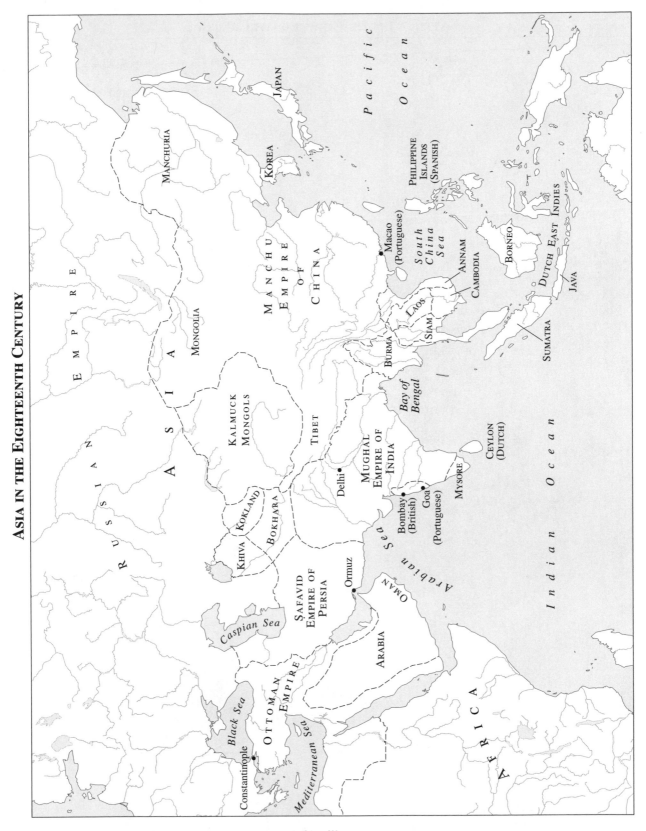

ASIA IN THE EIGHTEENTH CENTURY

Pacific Ocean

JAPAN

MANCHURIA

KOREA

PHILIPPINE ISLANDS (SPANISH)

Macao (Portuguese)

MANCHU EMPIRE OF CHINA

South China Sea

BORNEO

ANNAM

CAMBODIA

DUTCH EAST INDIES

MONGOLIA

LAOS

SIAM

JAVA

SUMATRA

E M P I R E

BURMA

KALMUCK MONGOLS

TIBET

Bay of Bengal

R U S S I A

CEYLON (DUTCH)

KOKLAND

BOKHARA

MUGHAL EMPIRE OF INDIA

Delhi

KHIVA

MYSORE

Indian Ocean

SAFAVID EMPIRE OF PERSIA

Bombay (British)

Goa (Portuguese)

Caspian Sea

Ormuz

Arabian Sea

OMAN

ARABIA

Black Sea

OTTOMAN EMPIRE

A F R I C A

Constantinople

Mediterranean Sea

AFRICA IN THE EIGHTEENTH CENTURY

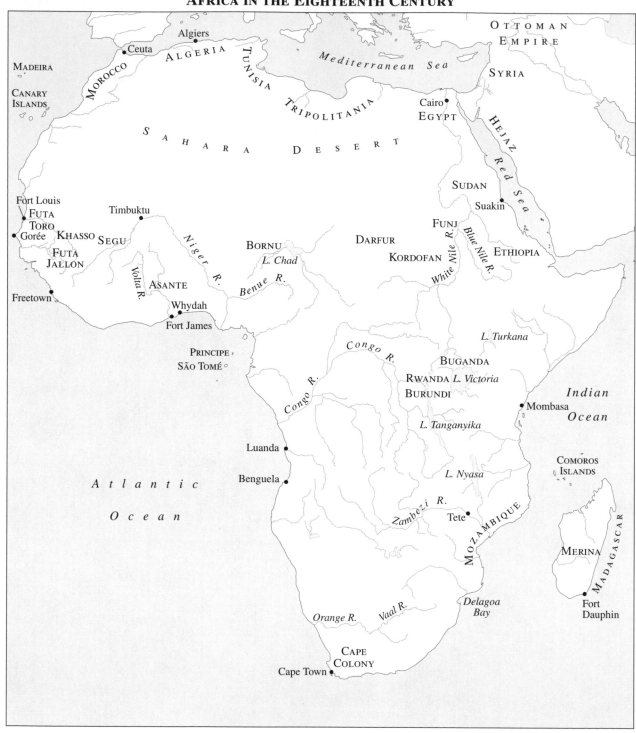

MADEIRA

CANARY
ISLANDS

Ceuta

Algiers

MOROCCO

ALGERIA

TUNISIA

TRIPOLITANIA

Mediterranean Sea

OTTOMAN
EMPIRE

SYRIA

Cairo

EGYPT

HEIAZ

Red Sea

SAHARA   DESERT

SUDAN

Suakin

Fort Louis

FUTA
TORO

Gorée   KHASSO   SEGU

FUTA
JALLON

Freetown

Timbuktu

Niger R.

Volta R.

ASANTE

Whydah

Fort James

BORNU

L. Chad

Benue R.

DARFUR

KORDOFAN

FUNJ

White Nile R.

Blue Nile R.

ETHIOPIA

PRINCIPE

São Tomé

Congo R.

Congo R.

L. Turkana

BUGANDA

RWANDA   *L. Victoria*

BURUNDI

L. Tanganyika

Mombasa

*Indian
Ocean*

Luanda

Benguela

*Atlantic

Ocean*

L. Nyasa

COMOROS
ISLANDS

Zambezi R.

Tete

MOZAMBIQUE

MERINA

MADAGASCAR

Fort
Dauphin

*Delagoa
Bay*

Orange R.

Vaal R.

CAPE
COLONY

Cape Town

SOUTH AMERICA IN THE EIGHTEENTH CENTURY

Porto Bello

Caracas

DUTCH
GUIANA

Paramaribo
Cayenne

FRENCH
GUIANA

= Portuguese South America

= Spanish South America

Santa Fé de Bogota

NEW
GRANADA

Quito

Japurá R.

Negro R.

Amazon R.

Manaus

Amazon

A m a z o n   B a s i n

Madeira R.

Purus R.

B R A Z I L

Lima

Cuzco

A n d e s

Arequipa

Santa Cruz

La Plata

Bahia (Salvador)

M o u n t a i n s

P E R U

Paraná R.

Minas Novas

Rio de Janeiro

Asuncion

Pacific   Ocean

Porto Alegre

Colonia do
Sacramento

Santiago

Buenos Aires

Montevideo

A t l a n t i c

O c e a n

Negro R.

P a t a g o n i a

Malvinas
(Falkland Islands)

NORTH AMERICA, 1775

ALASKA

Kodiak
Island

Alexander
Archipelago

GREENLAND

Baffin Bay

CANADA

Hudson
Bay

Rupert's
Land

James Bay

Newfoundland

Louisbourg

QUEBEC

St. Lawrence R.

Quebec

Nova Scotia

New Hampshire
Massachusetts
Rhode Island
Connecticut
New York
New Jersey
Delaware
Maryland
Virginia

Great Lakes

Penn-
sylvania

Ohio R.

LOUISIANA

San Carlos
San Antonio
San Luis Obispo

San
Gabriel

Colorado R.

Rio Grande

Santa Fe

North Carolina

Mississippi R.

South Carolina

San Diego

El Paso

NEW SPAIN

Georgia

Florida

New
Orleans

Pacific
Ocean

Atlantic
Ocean

Cuba

Belize

Mosquito
Coast

Caribbean Sea

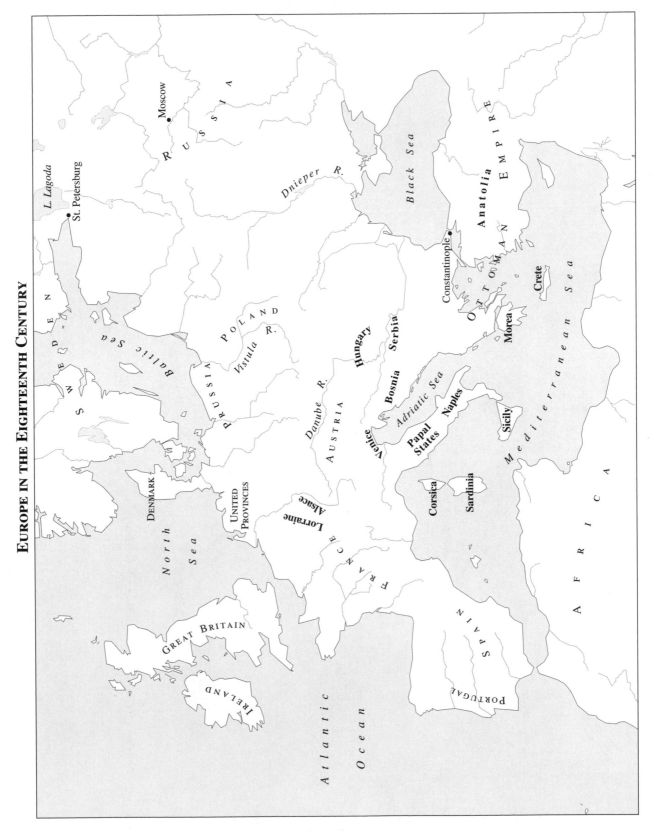

Europe in the Eighteenth Century

Moscow

RUSSIA

L. Lagoda

St. Petersburg

Dnieper R.

Black Sea

Anatolia

OTTOMAN EMPIRE

Constantinople

Crete

Morea

Mediterranean Sea

Baltic Sea

SWEDEN

PRUSSIA

POLAND

Vistula R.

Hungary

Serbia

Bosnia

Adriatic Sea

Venice

Danube R.

AUSTRIA

Papal States

Naples

Sicily

North Sea

DENMARK

UNITED PROVINCES

Lorraine

Alsace

FRANCE

Corsica

Sardinia

AFRICA

GREAT BRITAIN

IRELAND

Atlantic Ocean

SPAIN

PORTUGAL

The 18th Century

1701-1800

December, 1774-February 24, 1783
FIRST MARĀTHĀ WAR

The First Marāthā War was the first of three major conflicts between the British East India Company and the Marāthās in India, wars that were fought intermittently until 1818. Final victory came to the British and led to the disbandment of the Marāthā army, the abolition of the peshwaship, and the incorporation of the Marāthās into the British subsidiary alliance system.

ALSO KNOWN AS: First Anglo-Marāthā War
LOCALE: Central India
CATEGORIES: Wars, uprisings, and civil unrest; expansion and land acquisition; colonization

KEY FIGURES

Raghunath Rāo (Raghoba; 1735-1783), Marāthā pretender to the peshwaship supported by the British
Mahādāji (Madhava Rāo Sindhia; 1727-1794), ruler of Gwalior, r. 1761-1794
Warren Hastings (1732-1818), governor general of the British East India Company, 1773-1785

SUMMARY OF EVENT

The First Marāthā War, the beginning of the Anglo-Marāthā Wars, was part of the expansion of the British in South Asia between the Battle of Plassey (1757) and the capture of Punjab (1849). The Marāthās were Hindu inhabitants of the state of Maharashtra who had been unified and made into a great power under Shivaji Bhonsle and his son and grandson. These rulers forged the Marāthās into a powerful confederation based on Pune, Gwalior, Indore, Berar, and Baroda, and headed by a peshwa, a title first used for the chief of Shivaji's eight ministers. By 1749, the peshwaship had become a hereditary office. United and under good leadership, the Marāthās were a powerful force, but their weaknesses were personal petty jealousy and personal rivalries that often led to civil war. These weaknesses would eventually lead to their defeat by the British. However, in 1775 they remained a powerful enemy, and the wars would be characterized by the capture and loss of territory, its return by treaty, and its subsequent recapture.

As a naval power, the members of the British East India Company were eager to wrest control of the coastline near Bombay, which was a British territory, from the Marāthās. Control of the coast would increase British security and trade opportunities, and it was for this reason

that they had already attacked states in the Carnatic and Mysore. The company had also seized islands near Bombay to secure supplies of teakwood for their ships. Their chance to challenge the Marāthās came when Peshwa Madhav Rāo died in 1773, and his younger brother, Narayan Rāo, became the peshwa. He was murdered nine months later by his uncle, Raghunath Rāo, who declared himself peshwa and attacked Hyderabad.

Raghunath Rāo's campaign against Hyderabad was militarily successful, but it generated no wealth and led to opposition by other Marāthā leaders. They went to the city of Pune to the widow of Narayan Rāo to await the birth of her son, whom they supported as the rightful peshwa. After the birth of this child, they established a regency in his name and controlled Pune and the administration. Raghunath Rāo's principal enemies were Mahādāji of Gwalior, Tukoji Holkar and Ahilyabai Holkar of Indore, Gaikwad of Baroda, and Bhonsle of Nagpur, who all controlled large, valuable, and mostly independent states. In addition, Nana Phadnavis was an able administrator who controlled the revenue administration and became a very powerful figure. Finding himself increasingly isolated and losing the support of one faction after another, Raghunath Rāo fled Pune and turned to the British in Bombay for support in a gathering civil war.

Raghunath Rāo's appeal perfectly suited the British, who throughout India had maintained a successful policy of supporting a candidate in a succession struggle in the hope of acquiring more territory if their candidate won the throne. They agreed to support Raghunath Rāo, and it was this intervention by the British in Marāthā affairs that led to the First Marāthā War. The war consisted of a series of major battles and minor frays spread over a wide area in the states of Maharashtra, Gujerat, and Malwa. In December, 1774, the war began with the British attack on the fort of Salsette, and the war was fought in three phases: December, 1774, until the March, 1776, Treaty of Purandar; Purandar to the February, 1779, convention of Wadgaon; and Wadgaon to the February, 1783, Treaty of Salbai.

Raghunath Rāo agreed to cede to the British large tracts of land in Gujarat and some islands near Bombay and to pay the British East India Company 150,000 rupees per month in order to pay for twenty-five hundred troops and some artillery. In spite of this support, Raghunath Rāo's army had been defeated in March,

1775, by his Marāthā enemies in Gujarat, and he fled to his only ally, the British, at their trading post at Surat. The British East India Company assembled an army from Madras India and Bombay and won a number of skirmishes against the Marāthās in Gujarat. However, Warren Hastings, the first British governor general to control all of British India, opposed this independent action by Bombay and stopped the attack. The troops retreated to their barracks, and Hastings's agent negotiated the Treaty of Purandar in March, 1776, which returned cessions in Gujarat and gave the British Salsette, Bassein, the revenues of Broach, and some money in cash. The company agreed to withdraw its support of Raghunath Rāo and to provide him with a pension.

Neither Bengal nor Bombay approved the Treaty of Purandar, so the British authorized war again in 1777 and sent additional forces from Bengal. They were faced, however, by a Marāthā force strenghtened by Holkar's ten-thousand-man army. The last of Raghunath's supporters in Pune were thrown in prison. At the end of 1778, the British, not yet supported by the forces from Bengal, marched out from Bombay with more than three thousand troops and nineteen thousand bullocks pulling the guns and supplies. They climbed the Ghats Mountains but ran out of supplies en route and decided to retreat. The Marāthā army surrounded the British at Telegaon and, in the convention of Wadgaon (February 12, 1779), the British were forced to sign a treaty promising to give up Raghunath Rāo, to cede all the territory they had acquired since 1773, to pay forty-one thousand rupees, and to leave two hostages behind before they were allowed to return to Bombay.

Hastings repudiated the convention of Wadgaon and renewed hostilities to wipe out the disgrace of defeat. The army from Bengal finally arrived, deliberately attacked the territories of Mahādāji, captured Ahmedabad, and received most of the revenues from south Gujarat. By 1781, the Marāthās had established a grand alliance against the British, but on May 17, 1782, the British and the Marāthās signed the Treaty of Salbai, which was formally ratified on February 24, 1783. The treaty committed the British and Marāthās to friendship. It brought the First Marāthā War to an end with neither side clearly victorious. The treaty contained seventeen articles. The Marāthās received back Bassein and the Gaekwad territories on Gujarat, while the British were allowed to keep the island of Salsette and to aquire the islands of Elephanta, Carranja, and Hog, as well as the city of Broach. The British also had—once again—to cease supporting Raghunath Rāo, but their trade privileges were recognized.

BRITISH INDIA, 1784

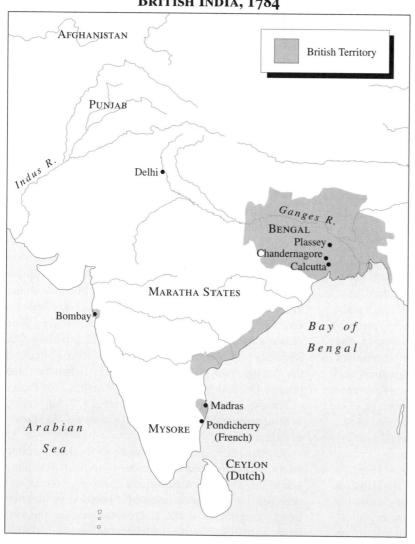

SIGNIFICANCE

The First Marāthā War was of major importance to the history of central India. It was important for the British East India Company, as it established a peace with the Marāthās that lasted for twenty years and enabled the company to expand considerably from its base in Bombay. It also entrenched the British in India, establishing them as the controlling factor in Indian politics. The centrality of the British to Indian politics was demonstrated in their dealings with Mahādāji, who gained control of the Marāthā forces. In the following years, Mahādāji adopted European military training and tactics, then turned on his fellow Marāthās to extend his power, knowing that the British would give him a free hand. Other Marāthās copied him, ending the advantage of their traditional cavalry and enabling the British to meet Marāthā armies who now utilized European methods of warfare. Familiar with these methods and how to counter them, the British were able to establish their military superiority. Thus, it was ironically British lessons in warfare that ensured the ultimate British victory over their pupils. The British alliance with the Marāthās also allowed them to crush Mysore in 1799.

—*Roger D. Long*

FURTHER READING

Fernandes, Praxy. *The Tigers of Mysore: A Biography of Hyder Ali and Tipu Sultan*. New Delhi, India: Viking, 1991. A detailed history of the four Anglo-Mysore Wars that often involved the Marāthās.

Gordon, Stewart. *The Marāthās, 1600-1818*. Part 2, Vol. 4 in *The New Cambridge History of India*. New York: Cambridge University Press, 1993. Offers a comprehensive but short introduction to Marāthā history, administrative practice, and especially Marāthā geopolitics.

Kantak, M. R. *The First Anglo-Marāthā War, 1774-1783: A Military Study of Major Battles*. Bombay, India: Popular Prakashan, 1993. Five of the major battles and sieges are examined in this study.

_____, ed. *The First Anglo-Marāthā War: The Last Phase, 1780-1783 A.D.* Pune, India: Deccan College Post-Graduate and Research Institute, 1989. The first twenty-five pages offer a useful inroduction to various aspects of Marāthā polity and warfare.

SEE ALSO: 1746-1754: Carnatic Wars; Jan., 1756-Feb. 15, 1763: Seven Years' War; June 23, 1757: Battle of Plassey; Aug., 1767-May, 1799: Anglo-Mysore Wars.

RELATED ARTICLES in *Great Lives from History: The Eighteenth Century, 1701-1800*: First Marquess Cornwallis; Warren Hastings; Hyder Ali.

1775
SPANISH-ALGERINE WAR

Responding to a Moorish siege of Spanish Moroccan possessions by Sultan Mohammed III, King Charles III ordered an invasion of Algiers. Led by Alexander O'Reilly, who commanded a combined military and naval expedition of nearly fifty ships and more than twenty thousand troops, the Spaniards were decisively defeated. The campaign proved a humiliating blow to the Spanish military revival, and it further empowered the Moroccan sultanate.

ALSO KNOWN AS: Algerine-Spanish War
LOCALE: Algeria
CATEGORY: Wars, uprisings, and civil unrest

KEY FIGURES

Charles III (1716-1788), king of Naples and Sicily as Charles IV, r. 1734-1759, and king of Spain, r. 1759-1788

Alejandro O'Reilly (1725-1794), Irish-born Spanish military leader and first governor of Spanish Louisiana

Manuel Ventura Figueroa (1708-1783), chief minister of Spain during the Algerine war

Muḥammad III (1710?-1790), sultan of Morocco, r. 1757-1790

Count de Floridablanca (José Moñino y Redondo; 1728-1808), Spanish foreign minister, 1776-1792

SUMMARY OF EVENT

With the final expulsion of the Moors from Spain at the end of the fifteenth century, the Spanish advanced into North Africa itself. They occupied and maintained key enclaves along the coast of this region, the western half of which was known in the Arab world as the Maghreb (land where the sun sets). The coastal area was a notorious region of pirate and slaver activity: Maritime outlaws preyed especially on neighboring ships from Spain, leading the area to be called the Barbary Coast. The coast marked the farthest western extent of the Ottoman Empire, and Islamic potentates in the Maghreb were under relative and varying degrees of Turkish suzerainty. As a result, once the Spanish began to encroach upon it, the entire Mediterranean region witnessed continual Christian and Islamic confrontations.

Two of the most noted Spanish enclaves in Morocco were Ceuta and Mellila, fortified Christian ports on the Mediterranean. Despite chronic conflict between Morocco and Spain over these territories, a treaty securing improved trade relations between the two had been signed in 1767. The treaty was a result of the astuteness of the count of Aranda, chief minister of Charles III, one of the most effective progressive monarchs of the Bourbon Dynasty. Muḥammad III, sultan of Morocco and equally astute, was eager to sign the treaty and improve the financial conditions of his realm. He could thereby advance his plans to control neighboring Algeria, which was nominally under the control of a *dey* and subordinate *beys*, representatives in absentia of the distant Ottoman sultan in Istanbul.

Despite his wish for peace and stability with Spain, internal pressures on Muḥammad forced him to lay siege to Melilla from late 1774 to early 1775. Mountain tribesmen demanded that the Christian infidels be driven from the Maghreb. Moreover, Spanish pirate ships preyed on Islamic traders, disrupting the safe commerce that the treaty was supposed to guarantee. Melilla, nonetheless, withstood the Moroccan advance, receiving powerful reinforcement from the Spanish navy. The sultan did not prevail despite his efforts to strengthen his position by friendly overtures to his Algerian neighbors.

Aranda was no longer in power by 1775, Charles having replaced him with Manuel Ventura Figueroa, a veteran diplomat. Determined to demonstrate to the sultan that Spain would not waver in its resolve to hold onto its Moroccan enclaves, Charles's government decided to send a military and naval expedition to occupy Algiers, a key and supposedly vulnerable Barbary port. A force of more than four dozen ships of war and more than twenty thousand men was organized by late spring. It set course from Cartegena for the Bay of Algiers, reaching its objective by the beginning of July. The expedition was commanded by Alejandro O'Reilly, an Irish officer who at a young age had entered Spanish military service. As head of the royal household guard in 1765, he had protected Charles III from a deadly assault. Gaining the king's gratitude and favor, O'Reilly received numerous appointments, including the later military governorship of Louisiana from 1769 to 1770, when the territory was transferred from French to Spanish control.

O'Reilly's forces for the Algerine expedition included considerable Irish contingents. Many of these were Jacobites, individuals committed to restoring a Catholic Stuart monarch to the British throne. The Stuart pretender, Charles Edward (also known as Bonnie Prince Charlie), had unsuccessfully invaded Britain during 1745-1746. O'Reilly maintained that with England's colonies in North America in revolt, British defenses would be so depleted that with Spanish aid he could successfully occupy Ireland and free it from British control. Charles III's government, however, preferred a less aggressive relation with Britain, mindful of the ancient English alliance with Portugal, a neighbor with which it did not wish debilitating entanglements.

Despite O'Reilly's reputation and the size of the force under his command, the assault on Algiers was a miserable failure. The Spanish troops landed in two waves, overwhelmed by sweltering summer heat. Poorly trained, except for the Irish veterans, they were duped by a feigned retreat by Moorish forces from Algiers. The latter had been massively augmented by warrior tribesmen from the interior, who had been alerted by intelligence from Moorish merchants in Marseilles who had followed the course of Spanish military preparations during the spring.

Unable to hold a line of resistance, the Spanish forces were routed, returning in chaos to their ships. More than 5 percent of the Spanish soldiers were killed, and more than 10 percent were wounded. O'Reilly wanted to retaliate by bombarding Algiers from the sea, but he learned that he had only enough provisions on board to last for an immediate return to Spain.

SIGNIFICANCE

Although in general Charles III's reforms of the Spanish military would enhance his country's military position, O'Reilly's poor preparations and leadership made the Algiers defeat a mockery of the Spanish army. While the Moors had detailed intelligence on the Spanish, the Spaniards had no information about their foes. Where Spain had mostly raw recruits, the Algerians had veteran warriors. The Algerians confronted the Spanish with a united force, whereas O'Reilly and the commander of the Spanish ships despised each other. This bitterness resulted in an extraordinary lack of planning, which in turn left O'Reilly with inadequate provisions and armaments. O'Reilly proved incapable of coordinating the varied elements of his forces. Popular discontent over the humiliating defeat at Algiers forced Charles to save his commander's life by spiriting him away to remote commands.

Further changes occurred when Charles appointed the count de Floridablanca as his foreign minister in 1776. Supervising Spain's foreign affairs for fifteen years, Floridablanca became one of the most effective and respected of Bourbon public servants. Despite the Algiers invasion, in 1780 Spain and Morocco signed a treaty of friendship. Muḥammad III recognized that his own interests in Algeria would move forward only if he had Spanish support. In 1785, the sultan demonstrated the extent of his influence in Algiers by sponsoring a treaty between Spain and Algeria. The tensions Spain had chronically encountered along the Barbary Coast were reduced. Moreover, a year after his appointment, Floridablanca achieved a treaty of mutual neutrality between Spain and Portugal, a document that would restrain their participation in the American Revolution. France, the principal enemy of Britain in Europe, decisively supported the revolt.

—Edward A. Riedinger

FURTHER READING

Beirich, Heidi Ly. "The Birth of Spanish Militarism: The Bourbon Military Reforms, 1766-1808." Unpublished master's thesis. San Diego State University, 1994. Examines the reorganization and revival of Spanish armed forces in the context of general national and colonial administrative reforms under Charles III and Charles IV.

Bennison, Amira K. "Liminal States: Morocco and the Iberian Frontier Between the Twelfth and Nineteenth Centures." In *North Africa, Islam, and the Mediterranean World: From the Almoravids to the Algerian War*. London: Frank Cass, 2001. Reviews the transitional nature of geopolitical relations between Spain and Morocco and their shifting "marcher state" status from the height of Islamic power in Spain to the decline of Ottoman power in the Mediterranean.

Brown, L. Carl. *Imperial Legacy: The Ottoman Imprint on the Balkans and the Middle East*. New York: Columbia University Press, 1996. Places the history of Morocco, Algeria, and the Maghreb during the eighteenth century in relation to the wider historical and regional interests, policies, and limitations of the Ottoman Empire.

Hull, Anthony H. *Charles III and the Revival of Spain*. Washington, D.C.: University Press of America, 1980. Exceptional scholarly study that examines details of the origin, course, and failure of the Algerine war within the scope of the wider objectives and accomplishments of reign of Charles III.

Mantran, Robert. *Great Dates in Islamic History*. New York: Facts On File, 1996. Includes chronological summary of Ottoman hegemony in Morocco from the sixteenth to eighteenth century.

Petrie, Charles. *King Charles III of Spain: An Enlightened Despot*. New York: John Day, 1971. Work by an English scholar that examines Charles III as an exceptionally effective Spanish Bourbon monarch. The author has also written works on the Stuart Dynasty and the Jacobites.

Stein, Stanley J., and Barbara H. Stein. *Apogee of Empire: Spain and New Spain in the Age of Charles III, 1759-1789*. Baltimore: Johns Hopkins University Press, 2003. Authoritative reassessment by noted scholars of the late Spanish imperial revival under Charles III. A sequel to the authors' *Silver, Trade, and War: Spain and American in the Making of Early Modern Europe* (2000).

Wolf, John B. *The Barbary Coast: Algiers Under the Turks, 1500 to 1830*. New York: W. W. Norton, 1979. Examines the Spanish-Algerine conflict of 1775 in the context of centuries-old confrontations between various entities of the Barbary Coast, Spain, and other European powers.

SEE ALSO: c. 1701: Oman Captures Zanzibar; 1750: Treaty of Madrid; 1759: Charles III Gains the Spanish Throne; 1776: Foundation of the Viceroyalty of La Plata; 1779-1803: Frontier Wars in South Africa; June 21, 1779-Feb. 7, 1783: Siege of Gibraltar.

RELATED ARTICLE in *Great Lives from History: The Eighteenth Century, 1701-1800*: Charles III.

1775-1790
JOSEPH II'S REFORMS

Holy Roman Emperor Joseph II instituted a series of judicial, ecclesiastical, and social reforms designed to strengthen the Habsburg monarchy and improve the lives of his subjects. Joseph's actions inspired a liberal tradition that subsequently flowered in the nineteenth century.

LOCALE: Austrian Empire

CATEGORIES: Government and politics; social issues and reform; religion and theology; laws, acts, and legal history

KEY FIGURES

Joseph II (1741-1790), Holy Roman Emperor, r. 1765-1790

Maria Theresa (1717-1780), archduchess of Austria, r. 1740-1780, and mother of Joseph II

Wenzel Anton von Kaunitz (1711-1794), state chancellor of Austria, 1753-1792

Joseph von Sonnenfels (c. 1733-1817), professor at the University of Vienna

Johann Gottfried Herder (1744-1803), German philosopher and theologian

Leopold II (1747-1792), Holy Roman Emperor, r. 1790-1792

SUMMARY OF EVENT

The reforms of the Holy Roman Emperor Joseph II represented a continuation and enlargement of those inaugurated by his mother, Maria Theresa, shortly after the end of the War of the Austrian Succession in 1748. Like other sovereigns of the late eighteenth century, they are referred to as "enlightened despots" because they injected rational-scientific principles into the basic concept of authoritarian government, modernizing the government of the Austrian crown lands while strengthening the absolute authority of the dynasty at the expense of the nobility. This struggle between the forces of absolutistic centralism and historic federalism had been going on ever since the Habsburg rulers of Alpine Austria extended their hereditary claims over Bohemia and Hungary in 1526. The ruthless suppression of revolt in Bohemia in the 1620's and the conquest of Hungary by 1699 enabled the Habsburg rulers simultaneously to reduce the power of the estates in both countries.

The enlightened despotism of Joseph II, known historically as "Josephinism," comprised three basic principles: an absolutist, bureaucratic, centralization of government with German as the state language; an emphasis on the importance of the ordinary citizen and the peasantry with a corresponding diminution of the historically privileged position of the nobility and its diets; and the establishment of a greater measure of state control over the Roman Catholic Church, with increased toleration for Protestants and Jews. Only from the time that Joseph began to take over full control of the state from his mother, around 1775, could he begin to carry out his reforms, and most of his major programs had to be postponed until the death of Maria Theresa in 1780. Assisting Joseph in the implementation of his reforms were, among others, Joseph von Sonnenfels, a leading scholar whose ideas inspired the emperor, and Wenzel Anton von Kaunitz, state chancellor of Austria, who, like the Habsburgs themselves, considered the increased centralization of authority in the hands of the dynasty of the utmost importance for the preservation of the monarchy.

Administratively, the power of the crown-land aristocracy, already reduced by Maria Theresa, was curtailed further by Joseph early in his reign. To centralize authority in Vienna, the "colleges," or committees of estates, which previously had attended to local administrative tasks in financial and military matters, were abolished. The entire provincial administration was transferred to the state bureaucracy, and the twelve provincial units composing the Austrian crown lands were organized into six larger groupings, for each of which new governments, the *Gubernia*, were established in order to reduce the importance of the traditional diets. In 1784 Joseph decreed the use of German as the official language of the central and crown-land administration, an edict designed to facilitate his policies of centralization. In a land of such deep and diverse traditions as the Habsburg monarchy, his act caused great bitterness, especially in Hungary, whose autonomous status was further reduced through the introduction of Austrian laws and the German language.

Additional Josephinist reforms ameliorated the lot of the peasants. Under a decree of 1781, the peasants of alpine Austria and Bohemia were all but freed from the customary feudal obligations to their lords, and they became wards of the state. Four years later, a similar measure was promulgated in Hungary. In 1789, all peasant services and dues were converted into payments of money.

Other acts sought to alter the traditional role of Catholicism in Austrian life. Religious reforms included the

Emperor Joseph II. (Library of Congress)

severing of jurisdictional ties with Rome and a sweeping reorganization of dioceses and parishes with an eye to better pastoral care. The salaries of high churchmen were slightly reduced; those of common clergy were much increased. About a third of the monarchy's monastic institutions, deemed socially useless, were dissolved and their property devoted to education and pastoral ministry. Joseph established seminaries under government control to train clergy for service to the state. The number of holy days was reduced, and many popular liturgical and devotional practices were suppressed or simplified. Under an Edict of Toleration issued in 1781, Joseph extended a wide measure of religious liberty to Protestants. Subsequently, he granted a more limited freedom to Jews. The state assumed from the Church responsibility for care of the sick and the poor and declared marriage a civil contract. Joseph brought censorship under state control and granted unprecedented freedom to the press.

Among Joseph's most significant and lasting achievements was the reform of the law. The judiciary was greatly improved by more extensive legal training and much higher salaries. Vienna received an embryonic modern police force; its streets were lighted, paved, and cleared of prostitutes. In 1787, Joseph issued a new crim-

inal code, the so-called Allgemeines Gesetzbuch. Conforming to the principles of the Enlightenment, it provided for the equality of all persons before the law. Torture was abolished, a measure for which Sonnenfels argued effectively, and traditional barbaric punishments were suppressed. Capital punishment virtually disappeared from the Austrian crown lands, replaced by imprisonment at hard labor.

Joseph's reforms, expected by their author to lead to the creation of a more unified Austria, encountered opposition from virtually every quarter. A successful revolt of the Austrian Netherlands (Belgium) in 1789-1790 paralleled widespread unrest in Galicia. Elsewhere, unrest developed in Bohemia and Hungary among the Czech and Magyar elites, who looked to hostile Prussia for assistance. A witness to these events, Johann Gottfried von Herder, the champion of German and Slav literary revivals and national individualism, criticized those reforms of Joseph that ignored the customs and traditions of the various Habsburg peoples. Thus, Joseph and von Herder, each in his own way, contributed to the genesis of cultural nationalism in east central Europe.

A few days before his death in 1790, Joseph revoked the reforms that had caused so much discontent. His feeling of discouragement over the failure of his policies is reflected in the sad epitaph he composed shortly before his death: "Here lies Joseph II who was unfortunate in all his enterprises."

SIGNIFICANCE

Ultimately, the emperor achieved more than he had realized. His brother and successor, Leopold II (1790-1792), skillfully restored the state's authority in the Austrian Netherlands and Hungary to what it had been under Maria Theresa, making concessions where necessary and playing one dissatisfied group off against another. He abandoned the most radical agrarian and tax reforms and closed the state-controlled seminaries.

Yet Leopold saved Joseph's reforms of the law, education, and censorship and preserved the rights of the Protestant and Jewish minorities. The peasantry in the Austrian crown lands remained personally free. The Catholic Church retained its Josephinian organization and liturgy.

In the long term, Joseph's reforms exercised significant influence on the future course of Habsburg history. As the memory of his shortcomings diminished, he became known and admired as "The People's Emperor" (*der Volkskaiser*), a potent inspiration to the development of Austro-German liberalism of the nineteenth century, based on the Josephinist principle of a centralized government and the corresponding reduction of the influence of the crown-land nobility and ecclesiastical hierarchy.

—*Edward P. Keleher, updated by Charles H. O'Brien*

FURTHER READING

Beales, Derek. *In the Shadow of Maria Theresa, 1741-1780*. Vol. 1 in *Joseph II*. New York: Cambridge University Press, 1987. Authoritative treatment of Joseph's efforts to accelerate the reform of the Habsburg monarchy during the last five years of his mother's reign.

Bernard, Paul. *Jesuits and Jacobins: Enlightenment and Enlightened Despotism in Austria*. Urbana: University of Illinois Press, 1971. Relates the work of Sonnenfels and other enlightened Austrian intellectuals to Joseph II and his reforms.

_____. *Joseph II*. New York: Twayne, 1968. A dependable survey of Joseph's life and work.

Blanning, T. C. W. *Joseph II*. London: Longman, 1994. Focuses on the emperor's struggles to transform his multinational empire into a unified state. Blanning's earlier work, *Joseph II and Enlightened Despotism* (1970), contains an analysis of the monarch's reign, presenting Joseph as a pragmatic ruler who was both Catholic and enlightened.

Ingrao, Charles W. *The Habsburg Monarchy, 1618-1815*. 2d ed. New York: Cambridge University Press, 2000. A concise survey by one of the leading historians of early modern central Europe. It highlights the distinctive elements of the monarchy's development, including the dynasty that provided continuity and pragmatic reforms.

O'Brien, Charles H. *Ideas of Religious Toleration at the Time of Joseph II*. Philadelphia, Pa.: American Philosophical Society, 1969. A comprehensive study of the genesis and the application of one of Joseph's most successful reforms.

Szabo, Franz A. J. *Kaunitz and Enlightened Absolutism, 1753-1780*. New York: Cambridge University Press, 1994. Biography of Wenzel Anton von Kaunitz, state chancellor of the Habsburg monarchy from 1753 to 1972, who helped Joseph II administer and modernize the Habsburg state. The book includes a great deal of information about Joseph II and his reign.

Wangermann, Ernst. *The Austrian Achievement, 1700-1800*. New York: Harcourt Brace Jovanovich, 1973. This brief overview is valuable for the social and cultural context of Joseph's reforms.

SEE ALSO: Mar. 7, 1714, and Sept. 7, 1714: Treaties of Rastatt and Baden; 1715-1737: Building of the Karlskirche; 1736-1739: Russo-Austrian War Against the Ottoman Empire; Nov. 18, 1738: Treaty of Vienna; Oct. 20, 1740: Maria Theresa Succeeds to the Austrian Throne; Dec. 16, 1740-Nov. 7, 1748: War of the Austrian Succession; Oct. 18, 1748: Treaty of Aix-la-Chapelle.

RELATED ARTICLES in *Great Lives from History: The Eighteenth Century, 1701-1800*: Johann Gottfried Herder; Joseph II; Wenzel Anton von Kaunitz; Maria Theresa.

April 14, 1775
PENNSYLVANIA SOCIETY FOR THE ABOLITION OF SLAVERY IS FOUNDED

The first antislavery society in America was formed by, mostly, members of the Society of Friends, or Quakers. The Quakers had formed an abolitionist philosophy that was in line with the religion's belief in equality for all individuals.

LOCALE: Philadelphia, Pennsylvania
CATEGORIES: Organizations and institutions; social issues and reform

KEY FIGURES
Anthony Benezet (1713-1784), a teacher and philanthropist who converted to the Quaker religion

John Woolman (1720-1772), a teacher and Quaker leader

SUMMARY OF EVENT
On April 14, 1775, a group of men gathered at the Sun Tavern on Second Street in Philadelphia to establish the first antislavery society in America. After electing John Baldwin their president and adopting a constitution, they named their organization the Society for the Relief of Free Negroes Unlawfully Held in Bondage. Sixteen of the twenty-four founders were members of the Society of Friends, or Quakers. The creation of this antislavery society was instigated when Philadelphia Quakers Israel

Pemberton and Thomas Harrison aided American Indian Dinah Neville and her children, who were being detained in Philadelphia waiting to be taken to the West Indies to be sold as slaves.

Harrison was fined in a Philadelphia court for giving protection to the Neville family. When this incident gained notoriety, members of the Quaker Philadelphia Meeting came together to form the antislavery society. At its first meeting, the antislavery society enlisted legal counsel to help the Nevilles and five other victims illegally held in bondage and to form a standing committee to investigate any conditions of slavery in the Philadelphia area.

The Revolutionary War interrupted regular meetings until 1784. At this time, Quaker abolitionist Anthony Benezet revived the antislavery society as members learned that two African Americans had committed suicide rather than be illegally enslaved. Benezet increased the membership to forty, including Benjamin Franklin,

James Pemberton, and Benjamin Rush. The society renamed itself the Pennsylvania Society for Promoting the Abolition of Slavery, for the Relief of Free Negroes Unlawfully Held in Bondage, and for Improving the Condition of the African Race. Since the majority of the members were Friends, the group developed directly from Quaker religious beliefs and within the Quaker social structure. To explore the founding of the Pennsylvania Society for the Abolition of Slavery, it is critical to trace events and movements within the Society of Friends in seventeenth century colonial Pennsylvania.

One of the basic principles espoused by Quaker founder George Fox was that all people are created equal. On a visit to the colonies in 1671, Fox spoke at Friends' meetings and encouraged Quaker slaveholders to free their slaves after a specified period of service. In 1676, Quaker William Edmundson, an associate of Fox, published the first antislavery literature in Rhode Island. While Quakers were formulating an antislavery position early in their movement, German Mennonites migrating to America had vowed that they would not own slaves. Several members of the Mennonite community and Dutch Pietists adopted Quakerism and became members of the Friends' Germantown Meeting. These Quakers, their minister Pastorius, and other Friends of the Germantown Meeting delivered a petition to the Philadelphia Meeting in 1688 demanding that slavery and the slave trade be abolished. The protest addressed to slave owners of the Philadelphia Monthly Meeting challenged these Friends to explain why they had slaves and how such a practice could exist in a colony founded on the principles of liberty and equality.

Representing the radical leadership of Philadelphia Friends, George Keith published a tract entitled *An Exhortation and Caution to Friends Concerning Buying or Keeping of Negroes*. He gave several directives: that Friends should not purchase African slaves except for the express purpose of setting them free, that those already purchased should be set free after a time of reasonable ser-

"Am I not a man and a brother?" pleads a slave in chains. The image was adopted originally by England's Society for the Abolition of Slavery in the 1780's, but it is symbolic of the struggles against slavery in the American colonies as well. (Library of Congress)

vice, and that, while in service, slaves should be given a Christian education and taught how to read.

During the early eighteenth century, the conservative, wealthy membership of the Philadelphia Meeting took a somewhat confusing position on slavery. Their inconsistent policies included a separate meeting for African Americans, a request that Quakers in the West Indies stop sending slaves to Philadelphia, and disciplinary measures for members of the meeting who were engaged in antislavery activity. Many prominent Quakers, such as James Logan, Jonathan Dickinson, and Isaac Norris, continued to purchase and own slaves.

The customary procedure of resolving issues at Friends' meetings was to achieve a consensus by gaining a sense of the meeting. Thus, the Quaker drift toward an antislavery sentiment gained momentum with the efforts of a few radicals but achieved success only when the majority bowed to the principles of Quaker conscience.

Unpopular radical member Benjamin Lay was unwelcome at the Philadelphia Meeting because of his unorthodox promotion of the antislavery cause. For example, Lay once had kidnapped a Quaker youth in order to illustrate the tragedy of abduction of African children for the slave trade. In 1738, he outdid himself at the Philadelphia Yearly Meeting, wearing a military uniform to emphasize the connection between slavery and war and concealing under his cloak an animal bladder that he had filled with red juice. Delivering an inflamed speech on the evils of slavery, he concluded by saying that slavery took the very lifeblood out of the slave, simultaneously piercing the bladder and splashing the horrified audience with simulated blood.

By the 1730's, the effects of the antislavery movement were evident among Quakers as more Friends provided for the manumission of their slaves in their wills. In addition, the increased immigration of Germans in need of work eliminated the demand for slave labor in the Middle Colonies.

Much of the credit for the success of the antislavery movement among Quakers must be given to New Jersey Quaker John Woolman. Known for his gentle, persuasive approach as a Quaker minister, he began a series of visitations to Quaker slaveholders in New England, the Middle Colonies, and the South in 1743. In 1754, he published *Some Considerations on the Keeping of Negroes*, which proclaimed the evils of slavery and the absolute necessity for Friends to free their slaves. Meetings throughout the colonies and England effectively used his visitations to pressure Quakers to free their slaves. By 1774, Quaker meetings in England, New England, and Pennsylvania had adopted sanctions to disown any member for buying slaves or for serving as executor of an estate that included slaves. It also required slaveholders to treat their slaves humanely and to emancipate them as soon as possible.

SIGNIFICANCE

Some have argued that Quakers were willing to emancipate their slaves because slavery was not profitable in Pennsylvania in the absence of labor-intensive agriculture. Others claim that Quaker sensitivity to antislavery was aroused not by their own religious ideals but rather by eighteenth century Enlightenment philosophy, which held that liberty is a natural human right. These may be considered arguments; nevertheless, it was the Quakers who first championed the antislavery cause and who organized the first antislavery group in America. The Pennsylvania Society for the Abolition of Slavery served as a model for other antislavery groups. As early as 1794, other states that had formed antislavery societies were asked to send representatives to Philadelphia for annual meetings. As new associations were formed, Friends constituted a majority of the membership. Statesmen such as Franklin, Rush, Alexander Hamilton, John Jay, and Thomas Paine believed that the institution of slavery contradicted the ideals of the Declaration of Independence and joined in support of the Friends' antislavery campaign.

—Emily Teipe

FURTHER READING

Davis, David Brion. *The Problem of Slavery in the Age of Revolution, 1770-1823.* Ithaca, N.Y.: Cornell University Press, 1975. An exhaustive study of the slave question immediately before the American Revolution and in the succeeding federal period, which includes the pioneering efforts of the Quakers.

Frost, J. William, ed. *The Quaker Origins of Antislavery.* Norwood, Pa.: Norwood Editions, 1980. A history of the Quaker antislavery cause that includes a comprehensive collection of Quaker documents.

James, Sydney V. *A People Among Peoples: Quaker Benevolence in Eighteenth Century America.* Cambridge, Mass.: Harvard University Press, 1963. This classic work discusses antislavery as an outreach of Quaker religious piety, along with the Quakers' other efforts for the good of the social order.

Nash, Gary B. *Quakers and Politics: Pennsylvania 1681-1726.* Princeton, N.J.: Princeton University Press, 1968. Places the antislavery cause within the larger framework of troubled politics in colonial Pennsylvania.

_____. *Race and Revolution*. Madison, Wis.: Madison House, 1990. An examination of racial relations during the Revolutionary War. Chapter 2, "The Failure of Abolitionism," includes information on the Pennsylvania Society for the Abolition of Slavery. The book also contains supporting annotated documents, including a petition from the society.

Newman, Richard S. *The Transformation of American Abolition: Fighting Slavery in the Early Republic*. Chapel Hill: University of North Carolina Press, 2002. A history of American abolitionist activities from the 1770's to the 1830's. Newman traces the beginning of the abolition movement to Pennsylvania, and the first four chapters detail the founding and activities of the Pennsylvania Society for the Abolition of Slavery.

Soderlund, Jean R. *Quakers and Slavery: A Divided Spirit*. Princeton, N.J.: Princeton University Press,

1985. A study of the Philadelphia Yearly Meeting and its progression to an antislavery philosophy. Draws parallels with the Civil Rights movement of the 1960's.

SEE ALSO: Sept. 9, 1739: Stono Rebellion; 1760-1776: Caribbean Slave Rebellions; 1773-1788: African American Baptist Church Is Founded; July 2, 1776: New Jersey Women Gain the Vote; Apr. 12, 1787: Free African Society Is Founded; Feb. 22, 1791-Feb. 16, 1792: Thomas Paine Publishes *Rights of Man*; Mar. 16, 1792: Denmark Abolishes the Slave Trade.

RELATED ARTICLES in *Great Lives from History: The Eighteenth Century, 1701-1800*: Benjamin Banneker; Olaudah Equiano; Benjamin Franklin; Alexander Hamilton; John Jay; Ann Lee; Thomas Paine; Benjamin Rush; Samuel Sewall; Granville Sharp; George Whitefield; William Wilberforce.

1770's

April 19, 1775
BATTLE OF LEXINGTON AND CONCORD

The American Revolution began with the Battle of Lexington and Concord, in which the British seriously misjudged the resistance of the American colonists.

LOCALE: Lexington, Massachusetts; Concord, Massachusetts

CATEGORY: Wars, uprisings, and civil unrest

KEY FIGURES

Thomas Gage (1721-1787), governor of Massachusetts and commander in chief of British forces in North America

John Parker (1729-1775), veteran militia officer who commanded the Minuteman company on the Lexington green

John Pitcairn (1722-1775), Francis Smith's second in command

Paul Revere (1735-1818), silversmith-engraver and active patriot who aroused the Massachusetts countryside

Francis Smith (1723-1791), who headed the royal detachment sent to Concord

SUMMARY OF EVENT

In the early morning hours of April 19, 1775, Captain John Parker, forty-five-year-old veteran of the French and Indian War, stood with his single company of Min-

utemen on the village green at Lexington, Massachusetts. Several hours had passed since Paul Revere's word of an approaching column of redcoats had brought them tumbling out of their beds. Revere had been unsure as to how General Thomas Gage would lead his men, quartered in Boston, toward Lexington. The land route across the isthmus to the mainland was long and more obvious; the Charles River was not frozen, and the river route was shorter. A signal from the steeple of Christ's Church provided the answer; the British were coming by sea.

Soon a messenger reported that the royal troops were almost within sight. Earlier, the Minutemen and their neighbors had adopted a resolution that the presence of a British army in their province constituted an infringement upon their "natural, constitutional, chartered rights." They had pledged their "estates and every thing dear in life, yea and life itself" if necessary in opposing the Coercive Acts of 1774. The British were correct in their suspicions that the Americans had hidden arms; gunpowder and shot had been stored all winter for such a moment as this.

The seventy-seven men who answered Parker's call, including sixteen-year-old drummer William Diamond, were hopelessly outnumbered by the approaching British. Many were old for such work; fifty-five were more than thirty years of age. Most of the town's men hoped

Paul Revere woke sleeping militiamen and their families, warning them of massing British troops, in the early hours before the Battle of Lexington. (Library of Congress)

turned volleys of fire, beyond control of their officers. The Americans were quickly driven from the field, leaving eight dead and ten wounded. Lexington was hardly a battle, and yet a war had begun. The United States was born in an act of violence lasting but fifteen to twenty minutes.

British troops had returned to Boston following the Tea Party and the Coercive Acts. With them came a new governor of Massachusetts, General Thomas Gage, longtime military commander in chief in North America. In retaliation, the Massachusetts assembly, now calling itself the Provincial Congress and sitting as an extralegal body, took control of the militia, appointed general officers, and ordered the organizing of one-fourth of all the militia into Minute companies. Massachusetts's firm resolution to fight if pressed was duplicated throughout New England, as well as in the Middle Colonies and in far-off Virginia, where, on March 9, the Virginia convention sat transfixed by the eloquence of Patrick Henry: "The war is inevitable. . . . The war is actually begun. . . . Our brethren are already in the field! Why stand here idle?" The potentially explosive situation was heightened by the struggle over gunpowder in the colonies. In London, the ministry imposed an embargo on the shipment of munitions to America, except for quantities headed for Gage's army. Armed clashes were narrowly averted in Rhode Island, New Hampshire, and Virginia, as patriots and British authorities sought to monopolize the critically low amounts of powder. The capture or destruction of the Massachusetts Provincial Congress's military stores was the assignment of Lieutenant Colonel Francis Smith as he headed down the silent country road that ran through Lexington and on to Concord on the night of April 18, 1775.

Long before reaching Lexington, Smith realized that his assignment was known to the patriots, whose church bells and signal guns were audible to the marchers. Consequently, Smith dispatched Major Pitcairn ahead with

not to provoke the British. Parker kept his men on the green and away from the nearby road the British would follow to the next town of Concord. The captain of the Minutemen intended their presence to serve only a symbolic purpose, an expression of their displeasure at the redcoats' intrusion. British major John Pitcairn nevertheless led his advance companies onto the green. As the British approached, Pitcairn ordered his men to hold their fire. He told the Minutemen to leave their arms and disperse. Seeing they had made their point, some of the Americans broke ranks and walked away, but a shot rang out, its origin unknown. The British immediately re-

"LAY DOWN YOUR ARMS!"

A deadly skirmish between American militiamen in Lexington, Massachusetts, and British troops on their way to seize guns and ammunition stored in Concord marked the start of the American Revolution. An enduring question remains, however: Who fired the first shot? In the following eyewitness account by the Reverend Jonas Clark, a local pastor, it was the British who fired first.

Between the hours of twelve and one, on the morning of the nineteenth of April, we received intelligence, by express, from the Honorable Joseph Warren, Esq., at Boston, "that a large body of the king's troops (supposed to be a brigade of about 12 or 1,500) were embarked in boats from Boston, and gone over to land on Lechmere's Point (so called) in Cambridge; and that it was shrewdly suspected that they were ordered to seize and destroy the stores belonging to the colony, then deposited at Concord. . . ."

Upon this intelligence, as also upon information of the conduct of the officers as abovementioned, the militia of this town were alarmed and ordered to meet on the usual place of parades; not with any design of commencing hostilities upon the king's troops, but to consult what might be done for our own and the people's safety; and also to be ready for whatever service providence might call us out to, upon this alarming occasion, in case overt acts of violence or open hostilities should be committed by this mercenary band of armed and blood-thirsty oppressors. . . .

Immediately upon their [the British troops] appearing so suddenly and so nigh, Capt. Parker, who commanded the militia company, ordered the men to disperse and take care of themselves, and not to fire. Upon this, our men dispersed—but many of them not so speedily as they might have done, not having the most distant idea of such brutal barbarity and more than savage cruelty from the troops of a British king, as they immediately experienced! . . .

Eight [militiamen] were left dead upon the ground! Ten were wounded. The rest of the company, through divine goodness, were (to a miracle) preserved unhurt in this murderous action!

Source: From "Fire! By God, Fire!" in *Living History America*, edited by Erik Bruun and Jay Crosby (New York: Tess Press), pp. 136, 137.

six companies to occupy the bridges over the Concord River, at the same time that he wisely sent a courier to ask General Gage for reinforcements. After routing the Lexington Minutemen, Pitcairn continued on the additional five miles to Concord, entering the village at eight o'clock in the morning. The patriots had managed to cart away part of their supplies. When the British had burned several gun carriages and destroyed flour, they set out about noon on their return journey.

The sixteen miles back to Boston were a nightmare

Colonial militiamen, in the foreground, exchange fire with British troops at Lexington. Historians still have questions about who fired the first shot. (H. Hallet and Company)

for Smith and Pitcairn. The scarlet column proved an inviting target for the swarms of militia and Minute companies that had converged on Concord and Lexington. From trees, rocks, and stone walls, they kept up a steady fire. Smith's force may well have escaped annihilation only because at Lexington they received a reinforcement of nine hundred men under General Hugh, the earl Percy. Even so, the combined column might have been destroyed had the efforts of the various American detachments been coordinated. As it was, the wild, unorthodox battle continued until the British reached Charleston, across the harbor from Boston, where dusk and the protecting guns of the Royal Navy brought an end to the mauling.

SIGNIFICANCE

British losses came to 73 killed, 174 wounded, and 26 missing, while American casualties in all categories totaled 93. The colonists remained to besiege the enemy in Boston. The *Newport Mercury* described the day's events as the beginning of "the American Civil War, which will hereafter fill an important page in History." At least some British papers also reflected the American viewpoint. For example, forty-one days after the fighting, the *London Chronicle* carried a detailed description of the events that had transpired at Lexington. The account included statements from witnesses who reported that the British had indeed fired first, clearly favoring the American version of events. This was followed some weeks later with General Gage's account of the affair. Gage also alluded to the Americans having returned fire, the implication being that the British had fired the first shots.

The British had badly misjudged the extent of American resistance. While at no point in the war were the Americans united in their stand against England, events that transpired at Lexington and Concord had lit a fire in the "belly of the beast." It would be only a short time before the patriots would be unsatisfied with anything but independence.

—*R. Don Higginbotham, updated by Richard Adler*

FURTHER READING

Commager, Henry, and Richard Morris. *The Spirit of Seventy-Six*. 1975. Reprint. New York: Da Capo Press, 1995. Provides an excellent account of events in the war as seen by the participants.

Fischer, David. *Paul Revere's Ride*. New York: Oxford University Press, 1994. Although centered on the famous ride of Paul Revere, the book provides a fine account of the opening engagements at Lexington and Concord.

Forbes, Esther. *Paul Revere and the World He Lived In*. Boston: Houghton Mifflin, 1942. Pulitzer Prize-winning biography and history of events unfolding around the early fighting.

Galvin, John R. *The Minute Men, the First Fight: Myths and Realities of the American Revolution*. Washington, D.C.: Brassey's, 1996. A military history of the initial battles of the American Revolution. Galvin describes the Minutemen's training and preparation for battle.

Langguth, A. J. *Patriots: The Men Who Started the American Revolution*. New York: Touchstone, 1988. An illuminating account of the prominent figures in the war and their evolving role as the revolution proceeded. Takes a humanistic approach.

Morrissey, Brendan. *Boston, 1775: The Shot Heard Around the World*. Westport, Conn.: Praeger, 2004. A pictorial military history of the earliest battles in the American Revolution, including the battles at Lexington and Concord.

Tourtellot, Arthur. *William Diamond's Drum: The Beginning of the War of the American Revolution*. Garden City, N.Y.: Doubleday, 1959. An account of the opening engagements of the war, which led to the creation of the Continental army.

SEE ALSO: Mar. 5, 1770: Boston Massacre; Dec. 16, 1773: Boston Tea Party; Sept. 5-Oct. 26, 1774: First Continental Congress; Apr. 19, 1775-Oct. 19, 1781: American Revolutionary War; May 10-Aug. 2, 1775: Second Continental Congress; July 4, 1776: Declaration of Independence; Mar. 1, 1781: Ratification of the Articles of Confederation; Oct. 19, 1781: Cornwallis Surrenders at Yorktown; Sept. 17, 1787: U.S. Constitution Is Adopted; Dec. 15, 1791: U.S. Bill of Rights Is Ratified.

RELATED ARTICLES in *Great Lives from History: The Eighteenth Century, 1701-1800*: Ethan Allen; Benedict Arnold; Sir Henry Clinton; Thomas Gage; George III; Nathanael Greene; John Hancock; Patrick Henry; Paul Revere; Daniel Shays.

April 19, 1775-October 19, 1781
AMERICAN REVOLUTIONARY WAR

Disaffected American colonists, deciding to wrest their independence from Great Britain, held their own against numerically superior British forces and were able to garner alliances and assistance from France, Spain, and the Netherlands. After more than six years of fighting, the revolutionaries compelled the British government to negotiate the Treaty of Paris of 1783, recognizing the United States of America as an autonomous nation.

LOCALE: North America

CATEGORIES: Wars, uprisings, and civil unrest; government and politics

KEY FIGURES

George Washington (1732-1799), commander of the American Continental army

First Marquess Cornwallis (Charles Cornwallis; 1738-1805), British general

Thomas Gage (1721-1787), commander in chief of British forces in North America

William Howe (1729-1814), commander in chief of British forces in North America, 1775-1778

Sir Henry Clinton (1730-1795), commander in chief of British forces in North America, 1778-1782

Benedict Arnold (1741-1801), general, first in the American and then in the British army

Nathanael Greene (1742-1786), American commander of the Southern Department, 1780-1783

Benjamin Franklin (1706-1790), American diplomatic envoy to Britain and France

Comte de Rochambeau (Jean-Baptiste Donatien de Vimeur; 1725-1807), commander of French troops in North America

Count de Grasse (François-Joseph-Paul de Grasse; 1722-1788), French admiral

SUMMARY OF EVENT

The pent-up frustrations of at least a dozen years were unleashed on April 19, 1775, when the American Revolutionary War began with three skirmishes over the course of a single day. General Thomas Gage—the commander of British forces in North America—ill-advisedly dispatched a small British expeditionary force from Boston into the countryside of Middlesex County, igniting an unexpectedly forceful reaction from the Minutemen militia groups. What had been intended as a quick strike aimed at capturing dissident leaders Samuel Adams and John Han-

cock at Lexington and seizing a store of gunpowder at Concord turned into fiasco as Paul Revere, William Dawes, Samuel Prescott, and others raised the alarm. At Lexington Green, the British under the command of Colonel Francis Smith confronted a crowd of Minutemen and dispersed them, but they were later defeated at Concord Bridge and forced to turn back to Boston. On the march back, the Minutemen waged guerrilla warfare, ambushing and harassing the British all the way back to the Massachusetts capital until, at nightfall, Boston was invested by an estimated sixteen thousand militia.

As news of the Battle of Lexington and Concord spread through the colonies, irregular military units began assuming control over much of the countryside, and a state of rebellion materialized. On the night of May 10, 1775, a Vermont militia called the Green Mountain Boys under the command of Benedict Arnold and Ethan Allen seized the strategic outpost of Fort Ticonderoga in New York. The fait accompli of hostility was recognized by the Second Continental Congress, which convened at Philadelphia on May 10, 1775. The Congress was to give political expression and direction to the uprising and attempted to consolidate the military efforts of the Thirteen Colonies through the appointment on June 15 of George Washington, a colonel in the Virginia militia, to command all the colonial forces. Washington's task was to organize and command a single Continental army. Though there were several officers of higher rank, Washington's choice was strongly dictated by the perceived political advantages of placing a southerner over what were at this stage mainly northern (New England) forces, so as to more readily coax the southern colonies into support for the revolutionary cause.

Before Washington had a chance to assume direction of the Siege of Boston (he would not arrive until July 3), Continental forces under general Israel Putnam fortified the high ground at Breed's Hill overlooking the city. Considering Breed's Hill too strategically important to allow the Continentals to occupy, the British launched a determined assault on June 17, 1775. Two uphill charges were repelled, until a third attempt, launched at a moment when the Continentals had expended their gunpowder, succeeded in dislodging them. The misnamed Battle of Bunker Hill (nearly all the fighting took place on neighboring Breed's Hill) was a very costly and demoralizing British victory. In the end, the noose remained tied around Boston.

HIGHLIGHTS OF THE AMERICAN REVOLUTIONARY WAR

Mar. 5, 1770   BOSTON MASSACRE: British soldiers kill five American civilians and wound several others in a bloody encounter that symbolized colonial unrest.

Dec. 16, 1773   BOSTON TEA PARTY: Group of men calling themselves the "Sons of Liberty" dump forty-five tons of tea into Boston Harbor.

Apr. 19, 1775   BATTLE OF LEXINGTON AND CONCORD: American Minutemen confront British troops in Lexington Common. When someone fires "the shot heard round the world," both Americans and British open fire and the war begins.

May 10-11, 1775   BATTLE OF FORT TICONDEROGA: Colonel Ethan Allen and co-commander Benedict Arnold lead a successful, bloodless victory against a surprised British garrison.

June 17, 1775   BATTLE OF BUNKER HILL: Americans engage British at Breed's Hill near Boston; British win but sustain heavy losses.

Dec. 31, 1775   BATTLE OF QUEBEC: Americans mount two offensives against British Canada but are defeated.

Mar. 17, 1776   BRITISH EVACUATE BOSTON, retreating to Halifax, Nova Scotia.

July 4, 1776   DECLARATION OF INDEPENDENCE approved by Congress.

Aug. 27-30, 1776   BATTLE OF LONG ISLAND: Leading the British, General William Howe and Admiral Richard Howe enter New York harbor, land twenty thousand troops on Long Island, and establish a base of operations. General George Washington retreats to Manhattan Island. British occupy New York City by September.

Sept. 6-7, 1776   SUBMARINE EXPERIMENTATION.

Oct. 11, 1776   BATTLE OF VALCOUR BAY: British commander Guy Carleton attacks American General Benedict Arnold at Lake Champlain, routing the American flotilla.

Oct. 28, 1776   BATTLE OF WHITE PLAINS: British defeat Americans, who take heavy losses. Washington's troops retreat to Peekskill, Ft. Lee, and Trenton, New Jersey.

MAJOR SITES IN THE AMERICAN REVOLUTIONARY WAR

Dec. 26, 1776	BATTLE OF TRENTON: Washington defeats the British after crossing the icy Delaware River in a surprise attack.
Jan. 3, 1777	BATTLE OF PRINCETON: Washington routs British near Princeton, New Jersey, and then establishes headquarters in Morristown.
June-July, 1777	BRITISH ADVANCE FROM LAKE CHAMPLAIN: General John Burgoyne leads British forces up the Hudson River, taking strategic points at Fort Ticonderoga, Mt. Defiance, and Fort Anne.
Aug. 6, 1777	BATTLE OF ORISKANY CREEK: Southeast of Lake Ontario and Fort Stanwix, an Indian force fighting for the British under Chief Joseph Brant ambushes Americans under General Nicholas Herkimer. Native American losses and renewed American efforts force the British to retreat.
Aug. 16, 1777	BATTLE OF BENNINGTON: In Vermont, a German contingent fighting for the British under orders of Burgoyne is routed by Americans under General John Stark.
Sept. 11, 1777	BATTLE OF BRANDYWINE: In Pennsylvania, the British force Washington and his men to retreat to Philadelphia, occupying that city by September 26.
Oct. 4, 1777	BATTLE OF GERMANTOWN: Washington's attack on British forces fails when fog confuses his troops. Americans retreat to Valley Forge, where they will spend a harsh winter.
Sept. 19-Oct. 17, 1777	BATTLES OF SARATOGA: Burgoyne's campaign to capture Albany, New York, is foiled when Benedict Arnold assaults British forces at Bemis Heights; Burgoyne retreats. One week later, Burgoyne and his British forces surrender.
Nov., 1777	ARTICLES OF CONFEDERATION SUBMITTED TO THE STATES: After a year of debate, the Continental Congress devises a plan of government and submits it to the states for ratification, achieved in March, 1781.
Feb. 6, 1778	FRANCO-AMERICAN TREATIES: France agrees to assist Americans against British.
June 28, 1778	BATTLE OF MONMOUTH: After a severe winter at Valley Forge, George Washington and the Americans pursue General Henry Clinton, who had commanded the British campaign in Philadelphia. Under General Charles Lee, the Americans rout the British; Washington later engages Clinton in an ensuing battle, forcing a British retreat.
July-Aug., 1778	ATTACK AT NEWPORT: In Rhode Island, combined American and French forces are repelled after attempting to take a British garrison.
July 15, 1779	BATTLE OF STONY POINT: American General Anthony Wayne takes Stony Point, on the Hudson River, from Clinton.
Aug. 29, 1779	BATTLE OF NEWTOWN: At modern-day Elmira, New York, Americans under John Sullivan defeat British loyalists and Indians who had been terrorizing frontier settlements of Pennsylvania and New York.
Sept. 23-Oct. 18, 1779	SIEGE OF SAVANNAH: In Georgia, American and French forces fail to take Savannah from the British, suffering heavy casualties.
Apr. 1,-May 12, 1780	SIEGE OF CHARLESTON: General Clinton assaults Charleston, South Carolina, capturing the American garrison and four ships—the greatest American losses of the war.
Aug. 16, 1780	BATTLE OF CAMDEN: In South Carolina, Americans under General Horatio Gates move against the British under Lord Cornwallis but are routed, opening the way for a British advance into North Carolina.
Sept., 1780	TREASON OF BENEDICT ARNOLD: After supplying the British with information for more than a year, Arnold is exposed in a plot to hand over the American garrison at West Point. He becomes a British officer and conducts British assaults on Virginia and Connecticut in 1781.
Oct. 7, 1780	BATTLE OF KING'S MOUNTAIN: British troops are repelled by Carolina backwoodsmen, forcing Cornwallis to retreat to Winnsborough.

(continued)

1770's

Jan. 17, 1781	BATTLE OF COWPENS: In South Carolina, American General Daniel Morgan repels the British forces of General Banastre Tarleton.
Mar. 15, 1781	BATTLE OF GUILFORD COURTHOUSE: American General Nathanael Greene engages Cornwallis in North Carolina; Americans are defeated but seriously weaken the British, forcing their retreat.
Sept.-Oct., 1781	BATTLE OF YORKTOWN AND VIRGINIA CAPES.
Oct. 19, 1781	SURRENDER AT YORKTOWN: Having abandoned the Carolinas for Virginia, Cornwallis and the British establish a base at Yorktown, but French ground and naval forces join with the Americans to hem him in, forcing surrender. Despite General Clinton's remaining forces in New York, the British are essentially defeated.
Sept. 3, 1783	TREATY OF PARIS: British and Americans negotiate a peace settlement.

General Gage, who seemed to have been rendered ineffectual by the swift-moving events of the revolution, was relieved of his command and replaced by Major-General William Howe on October 10, 1775, although at first there was no measurable change in policy. From August to December, 1775, however, a two-pronged American invasion of Canada was launched under the command of Benedict Arnold and Richard Montgomery. After enjoying initial success, the expedition ended in disaster at the Battle of Quebec (December 8-31), where Montgomery was killed and Arnold was severely wounded. In May of 1776, the remaining American forces were compelled to leave Canada.

On the political front, the Second Continental Congress at first proposed reconciliation and a negotiated cease-fire. This so-called Olive Branch Petition was rejected out of hand by King George III, and further overtures to Parliament by Benjamin Franklin likewise met with rebuff. These diplomatic setbacks and the publication of Thomas Paine's influential pamphlet *Common Sense* (1776) dramatically shifted public opinion in the colonies. Rather than try to find a basis for compromise, most Americans now began to favor a complete break with Britain.

This tendency was further strengthened by Washington's first military triumph. The American commander had sent General Henry Knox to Fort Ticonderoga to transport the powerful cannon housed there to Dorchester Heights, overlooking Boston. This remarkable engineering feat was accomplished and, faced with destruction, Howe had no choice but to withdraw the British garrison from Boston on March 17, 1776. On July 4, 1776, the Second Continental Congress finalized the document (shortly to be dubbed the Declaration of Independence) officially separating the colonies from Britain

and creating the United States of America.

Howe also returned in July, this time at New York, with a large expeditionary force transported by a war fleet under command of his brother, Admiral Richard Howe. Facing a huge disadvantage once the British took control over the sea lanes and outflanked by General Howe, Washington suffered a crushing defeat at Long Island (August 27, 1776), barely avoiding the destruction of his army, and though he was able temporarily to check the British at Harlem Heights (September 16), he was heavily beaten at White Plains (October 28), Fort Washington (November 16), and Brunswick, New Jersey (December 1). His army rapidly disintegrating, Washington was forced to cede New York City and New Jersey and retreated across the Delaware River.

Unexpectedly, Washington countered the British gains with a dangerous and audacious maneuver, transporting his army at night across the icebound and treacherous Delaware River and surprising the garrison of Hessian mercenaries at Trenton (December 26). This morale-restoring victory was followed by an even more effective coup, as Washington slipped away from the First Marquess Cornwallis to defeat a portion of the British army at Princeton (January 3, 1777). Trenton and Princeton temporarily stabilized the military situation, and both sides retired to winter quarters.

The year 1777 witnessed significant diplomatic initiatives on the part of the United States and military initiatives from the British. Benjamin Franklin was dispatched as special envoy to the court of King Louis XVI of France to elicit supplies, money, volunteers, diplomatic recognition, and even military assistance from the French government. The British grand strategy, meanwhile, revolved around severing New England from the rest of the United States along the line of the Hudson

River. General Howe was to advance northward from New York City, and separate armies from Canada were to move from a southerly and westerly direction under the respective commands of John Burgoyne and Barry St. Leger. The three were to converge near Albany.

The plan began to go awry when Howe changed his mind and secured the permission of War Minister Lord George Germain to transport most of his forces to capture Philadelphia. This left in New York only a remnant under the command of Sir Henry Clinton, who was in the end unable to contribute greatly to the Hudson River expedition. St. Leger's trek was halted at Fort Stanwix, which endured a siege from August 3 to August 22. A pitched battle at Oriskany Creek on August 6 proved inconclusive, though the British withdrew. Energetic relief efforts by Benedict Arnold and stubborn resistance by the Fort Stanwix garrison compelled St. Leger to turn back on August 22. General John Burgoyne, marching down the Hudson Valley from Canada, sustained an initial defeat at the Battle of Bennington (August 16) and, becoming bogged down near Saratoga, New York, was attacked by American forces led by Horatio Gates and Benedict Arnold: A series of pitched clashes from September 19 to October 17 resulted in Burgoyne's surrender. While Arnold was recuperating from a dangerous leg wound, Gates took most of the credit for the victory at Saratoga.

In Pennsylvania, the British were more successful. William Howe landed at Head of Elk, Maryland, and brushed off an attempt by Washington at the Battle of Brandywine Creek (September 11) to halt the British drive on Philadelphia, which fell on September 26. Washington's plan to surprise the British at the Battle of Germantown on October 4 was frustrated by a combination of poor coordination and an unexpectedly thick mist over the battlefield. After a few hours of intense fighting, Washington broke off the engagement, ending the campaign for the winter. The Americans wintered at Valley Forge, and the British encamped in and around Philadelphia.

Saratoga more than offset the disasters in Pennsylvania, because Franklin, persuading King Louis's government that the American army was a substantial military force, convinced France to enter into war against Britain on the U.S. side (February 6, 1778). At this stage, the conflict was no longer localized but became part of an international struggle known as the War of the American Revolution. On June 21, 1779, Spain joined the effort against Britain, and on December 20, 1780, after a dispute over the Caribbean island of St. Eustatius, which

had long been supplying American rebels, the British government opened hostilities against the Dutch, who became America's third ally.

Washington survived a brutal winter at Valley Forge—as well as a plot by disgruntled officers, led by General Thomas Conway, to replace him with Horatio Gates—and emerged with a well-trained army that had been whipped into shape by the Prussian drillmaster Baron Friedrich von Steuben. Howe was replaced on March 7, 1778, by Sir Henry Clinton, who evacuated Philadelphia and was attacked while withdrawing to New York by Washington's rejuvenated troops at Monmouth, New Jersey, on June 28. This, the war's largest engagement, ended in a draw. Thereafter, the more intense military action shifted to the southern colonies.

On December 20, 1778, British forces captured Savannah, Georgia, and successfully withstood determined Continental attempts to recapture the city. In the western territories, American general George Rogers Clark engaged in a seesaw struggle with British lieutenant colonel Henry Hamilton but won the ultimate victory when Hamilton was captured on February 25, 1779, at Fort Vincennes, in what later became Illinois.

Benedict Arnold, disaffected since he had been shortchanged of the credit for Saratoga and probably influenced by his Loyalist wife, Peggy Shippen, plotted through British major John André to hand over the garrison at West Point, New York, but was found out by Washington (September 25, 1780). Arnold fled to become a general in the British army, and André was hanged for espionage.

The British offensive in the south began in earnest in February, 1780, when Clinton and Cornwallis besieged Charleston, South Carolina, which fell on May 12. Thereafter, one American disaster followed another: Gates was heavily defeated at Camden, South Carolina, and murderous partisan warfare broke out in the countryside. The situation began to stabilize when the British were checked at the Battle of King's Mountain (October 7) and Gates was superseded as commander of the Southern Department by Nathanael Greene (October 14). General Daniel Morgan won a resounding victory over Colonel Banastre Tarleton's "British Legion" at the Cowpens in South Carolina (January 17, 1781), and his forces joined with those of Greene. Greene and Cornwallis fought a series of running engagements throughout the Carolinas, culminating in a bloody standoff at Guilford Courthouse, North Carolina (March 15, 1781). Cornwallis advanced into Virginia, while Greene set about liberating much of the Carolinas.

Cornwallis did little of importance in Virginia besides capture the state capital at Richmond, and he withdrew to winter quarters at Yorktown. Washington, encamped near New York, combined his troops with a French expeditionary force led by the comte de Rochambeau, and their consolidated armies marched to Yorktown to surround Cornwallis from the landward side. At the same time, a French fleet under count de Grasse cleared away the British and blocked any escape by water. Cornwallis endured a twenty-day siege before surrendering on October 19, 1781.

SIGNIFICANCE

Yorktown was the final large clash of the American Revolution. The British then opened peace talks, which resulted in the signing of the Treaty of Paris on September 3, 1783, whereby Britain recognized the independence of the United States of America. The American Revolutionary War was the first successful colonial uprising in the Western Hemisphere and resulted in the establishment of a republic based on liberalist principles. This event, which established the United States of America, may well be counted as the most important geopolitical development of the eighteenth century.

—*Raymond Pierre Hylton*

FURTHER READING

Edgar, Walter. *Partisans and Redcoats: The Southern Conflict That Turned the Tide of the American Revolution*. New York: Perennial, 2001. The author believes that atrocities committed by British troops and Loyalists in South Carolina backfired, and tipped the balance in favor of the Continentals.

Galvin, John R. *The Minute Men—The First Fight: Myths and Realities of the American Revolution*. Washington, D.C.: Brassey's, 1996. Gives a detailed account of the April 19, 1775, fighting and argues that the Minutemen were much better organized and more effective than previously thought.

Greenwood, John. *A Young Patriot in the American Revolution, 1775-1783*. Edited by Isaac J. Greenwood. Tyrone, Pa.: Westvaco, 1981. Firsthand account written in 1809 by a veteran who served in both the Continental army and navy, and who was later George Washington's dentist.

Hibbert, Christopher. *Redcoats and Rebels: The American Revolution Through British Eyes*. New York: W. W. Norton, 2002. Despite what the title might indicate, Hibbert offers an impartial rather than pro-British narrative; and this he does in a highly readable style.

Ketchum, Richard M. *Saratoga: Turning Point of America's Revolutionary War*. New York: Henry Holt, 1997. The campaign is meticulously described; though Franklin's diplomatic follow up is not presented in as much detail.

Liell, Scott. *Forty-Six Pages: Thomas Paine, "Common Sense," and the Turning Point to Independence*. Philadelphia: Running Press, 2004. Makes the cogent argument that Paine's pamphlet was an indispensable element in turning the sentiment of the rebellious colonies toward complete separation from Britain.

McCullough, David. *1776*. New York: Simon & Schuster, 2005. Actually covers the period 1775-1777, focusing on Washington's leadership qualities—and weaknesses—during what was arguably the time of his greatest challenge.

Mitchell, Broadus. *The Road to Yorktown: Climax of the American Revolution*. New York: McGraw-Hill, 1971. Though the Carolina campaigns are deemed important, the greater degree of importance is laid on the maneuvers occurring in Virginia in 1781.

Randall, William Sterne. *Benedict Arnold: Patriot and Traitor*. New York: William Morrow, 1990. A refreshingly impartial study of one of the revolution's more controversial figures. Cites new financial and personal records to offer insights behind Arnold's baffling shift in allegiance.

Tuchman, Barbara. *The First Salute: A View of the American Revolution*. New York: Alfred A. Knopf, 1988. An internationally renowned historian focuses on the importance of the little-known factors of rivalry among the major European states, and the crucial role of seapower in the final stages of the war.

SEE ALSO: Mar. 22, 1765-Mar. 18, 1766: Stamp Act Crisis; June 29, 1767-Apr. 12, 1770: Townshend Crisis; Mar. 5, 1770: Boston Massacre; Dec. 16, 1773: Boston Tea Party; Apr. 27-Oct. 10, 1774: Lord Dunmore's War; Sept. 5-Oct. 26, 1774: First Continental Congress; Apr. 19, 1775: Battle of Lexington and Concord; May 10-Aug. 2, 1775: Second Continental Congress; May, 1776-Sept. 3, 1783: France Supports the American Revolution; May 24 and June 11, 1776: Indian Delegation Meets with Congress; July 4, 1776: Declaration of Independence; Sept. 6-7, 1776: First Test of a Submarine in Warfare; Aug. 6, 1777: Battle of Oriskany Creek; Sept. 19-Oct. 17, 1777: Battles of Saratoga; Feb. 6, 1778: Franco-American Treaties; Mar. 1, 1781: Ratification of the Articles of Confederation; Oct. 19, 1781: Cornwallis Surrenders at Yorktown; 1783: Loyalists Migrate to Nova Scotia; Sept. 3, 1783: Treaty of Paris.

RELATED ARTICLES in *Great Lives from History: The Eighteenth Century, 1701-1800*: Samuel Adams; Ethan Allen; Benedict Arnold; Sir Henry Clinton; First Marquess Cornwallis; Benjamin Franklin; Thomas Gage; George III; Nathanael Greene; John Hancock; Richard Howe; William Howe; Louis XVI; Paul Revere; Comte de Rochambeau; George Washington.

April 27-May, 1775
FLOUR WAR

Riots swept the provinces surrounding Paris, caused by the lifting of government controls over the price of grain following the poor wheat harvest of 1774. Ultimately, two French armies quelled the riots. However, the event was indicative of the poverty and poor economic management that would bring about the French Revolution at the end of the following decade.

LOCALE: Paris, France, and its rural environs
CATEGORIES: Wars, uprisings, and civil unrest; economics

KEY FIGURES
Anne-Robert-Jacques Turgot (1727-1781), controller-general of France, 1774-1776
Louis XVI (1754-1793), king of France, r. 1774-1792
Louis XV (1710-1774), king of France, r. 1715-1774
Jacques Necker (1732-1804), French director-general of finances, 1777-1781

SUMMARY OF EVENT
Bread was the staff of life in early modern Europe. In 1775, a French laboring family of four ate 1.2 tons of grain per year, 80 percent of which came from the Paris basin, a rural area extending to a ninety-mile radius around the city. Town workers in France normally spent half their salary for the purchase of bread. While wages for most common laborers were structured to support their basic subsistence, periodic steep rises in the price of grain caused by poor harvests often meant death for family members, particularly in towns and cities. Eighteenth century France was in the midst of urbanization and rapid population growth, leaving it vulnerable to periodic starvation. There was no corresponding growth in new land under cultivation or improved agricultural techniques to increase productivity. Yet with only five exceptions, harvests in France were good prior to 1774.

Royal price control of grain was an integral part of mercantilist economic policies, and France's absolutist monarchy was Europe's leading mercantilist power.

Hence, in times of scarcity the people looked to the monarchy for protection. French aristocrats too welcomed stable grain prices, because they led to social stability and protection of their privileged position in society. When the government was slow to respond, local grain riots did occur, but these were sporadic and usually led to angry protesters intimidating merchants to absorb a short-term lowering of prices. Such disturbances did take place from 1763 to 1770, following a partial lifting of price controls, an act that helped to make Louis XV one of France's most detested monarchs.

With the coming to power of the twenty-year-old Louis XVI in May, 1774, expectations for reform reverberated among the population. Louis's appointment of Anne-Robert-Jacques Turgot as controller-general of France seemed to underline a commitment to promoting economic efficiency by cutting unnecessary expenditures, reducing the nation's debt, and reestablishing its credit. One of Turgot's plans, hailed by Enlightenment writers such as Voltaire (who viewed physiocratic policies as inherently progressive), was to stimulate agricultural production by establishing free trade in grain. Unfortunately, Turgot's policy, instituted on September 13, 1774, came at exactly the wrong time, since all indices pointed to the fact that the autumn harvest would be poor. The price of grain rose steadily over the winter. By Spring, 1775, when grain reserves had to be apportioned for spring planting, the cost of grain had skyrocketed.

Disturbances began on April 27, 1775, with a riot in the market town of Beaumont-sur-Oise. Rioters, consisting of common townspeople, dunked the leading grain merchant in a fountain, seized his grain, and paid about one-third of the asking price. Local authorities did not intervene. Instead of being contained, riots spread over the next three weeks to more than three hundred separate locales in the Île de France and the four adjacent provinces. While rioters often paid what they defined as a fair price, in other instances grain was just looted in market towns. As town markets closed, crowds of rioters from diverse towns attacked grain shipments on overland routes and waterways.

Grain was seized from granaries located both in towns and in the countryside, from mills and bakeries, from rural monasteries, from stocks held in farms, and even from flour merchant's homes. Within a week of the first incident at Beaumont-sur-Oise, the royal family had to be evacuated, as mobs seized half of the grain supply of Versailles. The prince de Poix, commander of the Royal Guard, permitted the mob to set their own fair price for grain, rather than risk escalation of the rioting. The following day, more than one thousand bakeries were raided in Paris. In response, on May 4 two armies consisting of twenty-five thousand troops were ordered to restore order in town markets and the countryside, while a third army was garrisoned in Paris to restore order there. The sweeping nature of the events led to their popular appellation, the Flour War (*guerre de farines*).

Turgot's strong stand in using the army did result in suppression of the disturbances by mid-May. Of 548 rioters arrested, only 2 received the death sentence. There appear to have been no fatalities among the 447 individuals classified as having been victimized by mob action. With his official coronation set for early September, Louis XVI was most interested in establishing order. Moreover, conditions over the late spring and summer of 1775 pointed to a bumper grain crop and a dramatic lowering of prices.

Other factors, too, argued for a policy of leniency. Many French aristocrats advocated government grain price regulation and viewed Turgot's physiocratic policies as the cause of public disorder. Moreover, rioting was directed mainly at merchants, not aristocrats, and appeared symptomatic of the immediate distress of the working poor. Women concerned about the survival of their children formed a large part of the rioting mobs. Ironically, no connection was seen at the time to any looming threat to the given social order: What the common people seemed to want were the traditional paternalistic policies of the Old Order, not new reformist free market policies, when it came to purchasing food staples. This desire was answered in 1776 by the unceremonious firing of Turgot and the reversal of free trade policies by his successor, the Swiss banker Jacob Necker.

SIGNIFICANCE

While the bread issue took backstage for more than a decade, other aspects of the French economy, such as the national debt and international credit, continued to deteriorate. By 1789, the French monarchy was threatened with bankruptcy. With the failure of the grain crop over two successive years (1788-1789), the French capital and its environs were faced with a situation even more volatile than that of 1775. Government policy again came under public scrutiny, as the price of bread rose to record heights. Grain riots began in April, 1789, and continued throughout the summer.

As is seen in the list of grievances (*cahiers*) brought by individual delegates to the Estates-General convened by Louis XVI to remedy France's economic problems, the king was held responsible for both the price and availability of bread. When the early months of the French Revolution did not resolve the grain issue, a mob of several hundred whose main core was the women of Paris marched to Versailles and demanded that Louis resolve the bread issue. The event, known as the Women's Bread March (October, 1789), resulted in the king's permanent return to Paris. Along the return route, the mob is reported to have sung "We have the baker, the baker's wife, and the baker's son. Now we will have bread."

The Flour War and the French Revolution are linked through the price and supply of bread and the potential social upheaval that can occur when people are deprived of a basic staple of life. Similar links between inflationary bread prices or bread shortages and revolution can be seen in the revolutionary storm that swept across Europe in 1848 and in the Russian Revolution of 1905. The Russian Revolution of February, 1917, which toppled czarism, also originated in bread riots which got out of control. It is no coincidence that along with "peace and land," Lenin promised the people of Russia "bread" if his Bolsheviks ever obtained power. This came to pass in October, 1917.

—*Irwin Halfond*

FURTHER READING

Bouton, Cynthia A. *The Flour War: Gender, Class, and Community in Late Ancien Regime French Society.* University Park: Pennsylvania State University Press, 1993. A scholarly in-depth sociohistorical analysis, with copious footnotes, extensive bibliography, index, and appendicies

Doyle, William. *Oxford History of the French Revolution.* New York: Oxford University Press, 2003. An excellent background to the French Revolution and its major events. Index and bibliography.

Fagan, Brian. *The Little Ice Age: How Climate Made History, 1300-1850.* New York: Basic Books, 2000. An interesting steady of the relationship between climatic changes, food supply, and major events. Chapter 9 deals with the issue of revolution. Index and bibliography.

Kaplan, Steven L. *The Bakers of Paris and the Bread Question, 1770-1775*. Durham, N.C.: Duke University Press, 1996. An extensive analysis of the political policies and implications of the bread issue in prerevolutionary France. Illustrations, tables, appendices, footnotes, bibliography, and index.

SEE ALSO: 1720: Financial Collapse of the John Law System; Sept., 1720: Collapse of the South Sea Bub-

ble; Nov. 1, 1755: Great Lisbon Earthquake; 1763-1767: Famine in Southern Italy; Oct. 10-18, 1780: Great Caribbean Hurricane; 1786-1787: Tenmei Famine; May 5, 1789: Louis XVI Calls the Estates-General; Mar., 1796-Oct. 17, 1797: Napoleon's Italian Campaigns.

RELATED ARTICLES in *Great Lives from History: The Eighteenth Century, 1701-1800*: Louis XV; Louis XVI; Jacques Necker; Anne-Robert-Jacques Turgot; Voltaire.

May 10-August 2, 1775
SECOND CONTINENTAL CONGRESS

The second congress of colonial delegates, now a revolutionary body, formed an army, managed the Revolutionary War, began the process of issuing paper money, and took the first steps toward creating a federal government that would bind the individual colony-states in common cause.

LOCALE: Philadelphia, Pennsylvania
CATEGORIES: Government and politics; wars, uprisings, and civil unrest

KEY FIGURES

John Adams (1735-1826), delegate from Massachusetts, who urged Washington's election

Benjamin Franklin (1706-1790), delegate from Pennsylvania, who was experienced in military affairs

John Hancock (1737-1793), delegate from Massachusetts and first president of the Second Continental Congress

Thomas Jefferson (1743-1826), delegate from Virginia and coauthor of the Declaration of Causes of Taking up Arms

George Washington (1732-1799), delegate from Virginia, who was appointed commander in chief of the Continental army

SUMMARY OF EVENT

The Second Continental Congress began its deliberations at the state house in Philadelphia on May 10, 1775. It was, like the First Continental Congress, an extralegal body, until the ratification of the Articles of Confederation in 1781. However, it continued to meet throughout the Revolutionary War, exercising whatever authority the colony-states permitted. Although it was weak in

terms of legal jurisdiction and state pressures, and it lacked material resources for waging war, the Second Continental Congress accomplished much. Out of a bond forged by a common threat from Great Britain, a bond often frustrated by local politicians more interested in state sovereignty than in wartime efficiency, there emerged a cluster of American political leaders, nationalists who echoed the plea of New York's John Jay that the "Union depends much upon breaking down provincial Conventions."

Forging a national identity was a delicate task that was much discussed among the delegates. Wary of a strong national government that had plagued the colonies, pushing them into war with the mother country, the delegates recognized that a united effort would be the only solution to the problems with Great Britain. The delegates to the congress knew also that a central government would be necessary long after the current feud and revolution ended, and that actions taken at the congress would dictate whether a central government could be formed and survive. Through the judicious coordination of individual events and the selection of military commanders from one section of the colonies to lead in other sections, the delegates at the Second Continental Congress were able to form a central government that bound the individual states in common cause and made the idea of a federal government acceptable to independent-minded Americans.

Delegates came to Philadelphia from all the colonies except Georgia, which was not represented until the second session of the Congress, held that fall. An extraordinary task faced the delegates: The First Continental Congress had hammered out agreements on constitutional principles, but the Second Continental Congress had to unite for military action. Fortunately, the new congress contained men of distinction, such as John Hancock, who became its president. There were familiar faces from the preceding year, including the Adams cousins of Massachusetts, George Washington and Richard Henry Lee of Virginia, Edward Rutledge of South Carolina, John Jay of New York, and John Dickinson of Pennsylvania. They were joined by talented newcomers, such as the youthful Thomas Jefferson, the venerable Benjamin Franklin, and the scholarly James Wilson of Pennsylvania.

Although realizing that the chances of securing an amicable reconciliation might suffer if the delegates involved themselves in the confrontation between New England and British General Thomas Gage's redcoats, this congress was in no mood to turn the other cheek. In their Declaration of Causes of Taking up Arms, the legislators solemnly announced that the American people had two choices: submission to tyranny or resistance by force. They preferred the latter. The colonies, moreover, looked to the Continental Congress for advice and direction. Connecticut asked what should be done with munitions captured at Ticonderoga and Crown Point. New York inquired whether it should resist a landing by British troops. Massachusetts sought approval for establishing a civil government and urged the congress to assume responsibility for the New England forces besieging Boston. "Such vast Multitude of Objects, civil, political, commercial and military, press and crowd upon us so fast, that we know not what to do first," exclaimed John Adams.

The congress nevertheless moved resolutely to put America in a state of defense, calling upon the colonies to prepare themselves and voting to take charge of the New England troops outside Boston. In selecting a commanding general, the congress rejected Massachusetts' ranking officer, General Artemas Ward, as well as John Hancock, both of whom desired the post. It was "absolutely Necessary in point of prudence," wrote Eliphalet Dyer of Connecticut, "to pick a non-New Englander to head the Continental army; it removes all jealousies [and] more firmly Cements the southern to the Northern" colonies. One important reason for the subsequent appointment of George Washington as commander in chief was to demonstrate to Americans everywhere that the war transcended the interests of a particular section, a step that would arouse support for the military effort in the middle and southern parts of America. Washington, bearing the proper regional credentials, also hailed from the "right" colony, prosperous and populous Virginia. Equally or more important, Washington possessed certain qualities as a man, a patriot, and a soldier requisite for the high of-

fice bestowed upon him. The congress, in picking a ranking general, had taken an accurate measure of its man. Aware of the congress's limitations and cognizant of state jealousies, he remained unflinchingly deferential to the civil authority.

Washington was a rare combination of soldier and statesman who understood, however maddening it might be at times, that the revaluation was a peculiar kind of coalition war. It is doubtful whether his accomplishments could have been equaled by any other general officer appointed at the time—men such as Major Generals Artemas Ward, Charles Lee, Philip Schuyler, and Israel Putnam, or Brigadier Generals Seth Pomeroy, William Heath, John Thomas, David Wooster, Joseph Spencer, John Sullivan, Nathanael Greene, and Richard Montgomery.

Along with problems of state, the conduct of war, and the development of philosophies for a new kind of nation, the delegates to the congress dealt with the problems of personalities and special interests. Strong personalities such as John Adams, Richard Henry Lee, and Thomas Jefferson often conflicted with more tempered personalities such as Benjamin Franklin, James Wilson, and John Hancock. Only because of their strong sense of duty and their belief in the future of a new nation could such men as Jefferson withstand the constant haggling over committee reports that had been laboriously written or the parliamentary tactics that were used to give one group an advantage in the various debates. Regional squabbles, especially over the issues of trade and slavery, were obstacles to the formation of a central government that would be capable of leading yet flexible enough to accommodate turning over many powers and privileges to individual states.

SIGNIFICANCE

The first session of the Second Continental Congress came to an end on August 2, with the legislators agreeing to reconvene six weeks later. The delegates had accomplished much in less than three months. Besides calling the colonies to defensive preparations, adopting an army, providing for its regulation, and appointing its general offices, they had taken steps to issue paper money, encourage limited foreign trade, and bolster the militias. The congress was no longer a temporary council of American dignitaries sitting to articulate constitutional doctrines and draft remonstrances; it was the central government of a people at war, a revolutionary body in the fullest sense.

*　　　　　　　　　　　—R. Don Higginbotham, updated by Kay Hively*

British, and they attempted to stabilize the region in the wake of this foreign invasion, but it was too little, too late. The bourgeoisie of Buenos Aires took to the streets, and in 1810 they became the driving force behind a revolution that echoed the bourgeois revolutions of the late eighteenth century in France and the United States. The last viceroy, Baltasar de Cisneros, was overthrown, and the region became independent of Spanish control.

Six years after gaining functional independence, however, the official sovereignty of La Plata was still unclear: Its citizens had not produced a document like the Declaration of Independence or any other announcement of autonomy. Representatives from the region's various provinces therefore met to discuss what kind of relationship they should have with Spain. On July 9, 1816, the delegates proclaimed independence from Spain's rule and formed a loose national government with limited authority over the people of the region. After considerable discussion, the region was renamed the United Provinces of South America.

A director was named to head the new state, but the governmental body of representatives could not agree as to the form of government they desired. Agreement was hard to reach, because there were two distinct groups of citizens, urbanites from Buenos Aires and inhabitants of rural communities and smaller cities. Those from Buenos Aires favored a constitutional monarchy, similar to the government of the United Kingdom. The opposition wanted a federal system closer in philosophy and structure to that of the United States.

These two factions continued to disagree, the situation escalated, and by 1819 a civil war had broken out. A tentative peace was reestablished the following year, but the form of the region's government was still not decided. As a result, amid general unrest and a lack of any formal governmental institutions being created, local, authoritarian dictatorships slowly came to rule the provinces.

Ten years after the civil war, General Juan Manuel de Rosas was appointed governor of the province of Buenos Aires, the most heavily populated province in what had come to be called the Argentine confederacy. He gained increasing popular support, and his authority grew accordingly. Opposition groups were hushed and driven underground. As his power grew, enforced loyalty became the norm in Buenos Ares, and disloyalty resulted in death. He even dictated the appearance of his citizens, instituting a uniform dress code in public for both men and women.

In 1852, Rosas was overthrown by Justo José de Urquiza. Urquiza became the first president of the Argentine Republic. Buenos Aires did not support the president at first and attempted to secede from the new republic, but it was rapidly defeated and brought under the control of the new government. After several conflicts were resolved and mutual respect was reestablished, governmental representatives made the city of Buenos Aires the capital of Argentina.

The region continued to be unstable, however. Many factors contributed to the unrest, but the primary one was simply uneasiness over governmental power—after the excesses of the previous dictatorship, the populace was loathe to allow any centralized government to control too many facets of their lives. Moreover, Agentina's borders were insecure: Turmoil in Uruguay led to an invasion of Argentina by Paraguay in 1865. The resulting War of the Triple Alliance ended in 1870 with Argentina, Brazil, and Uruguay victorious. The War of the Desert, fought at the end of the decade by General Julio Argentino Roca and others, established the dominance of the republics over Native Americans who had resisted Argentina's territorial expansion. As a result, vast agricultural lands were wrested from the indigenous peoples and added to the possessions of the republic. Roca became president following the war.

SIGNIFICANCE

The establishment of the Spanish viceroyalty of La Plata was a crucial step in the evolution of Latin America. Charles III's decision to shift resources and authority to Buenos Aires paid off in the short term, as the British invasion of 1806 was defeated. However, Spain lost control of the colony shortly thereafter, and it could not prevent the United Kingdom from seizing the Falkland Islands in 1833, which had been one of the purposes of the new viceroyalty.

It took little more than one hundred years for the provinces of the viceroyalty to become separate, sovereign republics. During that time, these colonial provinces evolved rapidly through several forms of government, struggling—ultimately successfully—to establish stable borders and international relations, as well as stable internal political structures.

—*Earl R. Andresen*

FURTHER READING

Brown, Jonathan C. *A Brief History of Argentina*. New York: Facts On File, 2003. Covers Argentine history from precolonial times to the late twentieth century, with substantial discussion of La Plata, Spain's attempts to retain control, and the aftermath of the revolution.

1770's

Nouzeilles, Gabriela, and Graciela Montaldo, eds. *The Argentina Reader: History, Culture, Politics*. Anthology of essays on the history and culture of the nation that arose out of the viceroyalty of La Plata.

Reynal, Gualberto. *La Plata y su historia enterrada*. La Plata, Argentina: Editorial Martin, 2001. Brief monograph on the history of the region. In Spanish.

Rivera, Kenneth T., ed. *Argentina: Issues, History, Bibliography*. New York: Nova Science, 2002. Anthology

focusing especially on the economic history of the region.

SEE ALSO: May, 1735-1743: French Scientists Explore the Amazon River; 1759: Charles III Gains the Spanish Throne; 1780-1781: Rebellion of Tupac Amaru II.

RELATED ARTICLES in *Great Lives from History: The Eighteenth Century, 1701-1800*: Charles III; Tupac Amaru II.

January 10, 1776
PAINE PUBLISHES *COMMON SENSE*

Thomas Paine, who argued against monarchy and for American independence from Britain in a pamphlet that sold out its first edition in a matter of days, became the talk of the American colonies. Many of the American revolutionaries credited the persuasiveness and passion of Paine's arguments for their decision to declare independence.

LOCALE: Philadelphia, Pennsylvania
CATEGORIES: Government and politics; literature; philosophy

KEY FIGURE
Thomas Paine (1737-1809), English-born American political philosopher

SUMMARY OF EVENT

In the summer of 1775, in spite of British troops firing on American colonists at Lexington and Concord the preceding April, very few colonists felt that the English oppression should be answered by taking up arms and forging an independent nation. Even George Washington argued as late as May, 1775, that such ideas were "wicked," and that reconciliation was still possible. In June of the same year, Thomas Jefferson expressed a hope to remain with England. Half a year later, however, both Washington and Jefferson prepared to risk everything to wage war against British rule, and both cited a small pamphlet as changing the minds of their countryfolk, if not their own: Thomas Paine's fifty-six-page *Common Sense* (1776), first published anonymously.

Paine had arrived in America only a little more than thirteen months before his pamphlet appeared, fleeing scandal in England for infractions he had committed as an excise officer. He was guilty of the minor charge of signing for shipments he had not inspected, but British authorities were mainly interested in stopping his protests against what he considered unfair labor practices in the excise offices. Thus, Paine came to America already set against what he saw as an abuse of authority by the government of King George III. Because he had made his case in an eloquent and widely distributed pamphlet, *Case of the Officers of Excise* (1772), friends in London supplied him with a letter of introduction to Benjamin Franklin before Paine sailed to Philadelphia, in the hope that the American editor and publisher could find a use for his skills.

Only a few months after landing in Philadelphia, Paine took over as editor of *Pennsylvania Magazine* and lost no time in becoming an outspoken advocate of political freedom, especially denouncing the practice of slavery. Paine's antislavery convictions led to the essay "African Slavery in America" (wr. 1774, pb. 1775), in which he denounced New World slavery as another instance of the British crown's suppression of human freedom. Paine's argument became part of Jefferson's first draft of the Declaration of Independence, which argued that slavery was an unjust British imposition. However, delegates to the two Continental Congresses who were from slaveholding states threatened to withdraw unless all references to slavery were removed. Paine's second pamphlet of 1775, *A Serious Thought*, included most of the other major points of the declaration one year before it was written.

The stage was set for the appearance of the most important essay of Paine's career. Near the end of 1775, friends arriving from England told him of a provocative speech England's king George III had made before Parliament, denouncing as treasonous American complaints about not being allowed to choose governors and being taxed without representation. George added that the complainers needed to be silenced by force. Paine had been about to publish his call to armed resistance to British authority, but he decided to wait until the transcript of the speech reached America. As it turned out, Paine guessed the moment correctly, to the day, and both the belligerent speech and *Common Sense* appeared in Philadelphia bookshops on January 10, 1776. Within days, it had been read throughout the Thirteen Colonies. Within a week the first printing of one thousand copies had sold out.

Instead of rushing out a second printing from the same plates, Paine took a few days to enlarge the essay with additional arguments and produce a second edition, taking advantage of the enthusiastic responses of his readers. On January 20, Paine published six thousand copies of *Common Sense*, and this edition, too, sold out in days. At the end of three months, Paine had sold an unprecedented 120,000 copies of *Common Sense*.

A facsimile of the title page of Thomas Paine's Common Sense *(1776).*

Common Sense begins with an iteration of what later became known as a "social contract" theory of government, derived from the writings of Thomas Hobbes (1588-1679) and, more directly, John Locke (1632-1704). Societies, Paine argued, begin as mere conglomerations of people, but soon develop laws and means of protecting individual freedoms—in short, a government, which Paine calls a "necessary evil." The original formation of government according to this theory occurred in prehistoric times, but, Paine suggested, the process could be seen more recently in the case of colonies, such as those in North America.

In contrast to this "natural" development of government, Paine begins the second section of *Common Sense* with a description of the "unnatural" notion of monarchy, the false exaltation of one group of people over another. In his third section, Paine invokes the title of the essay, insisting that common sense and plain language will convince the reader that reconciliation with England is a vain wish. In the fourth and final section, Paine overcomes objections to armed struggle with England. Concerns about the English navy being the most powerful in the world are answered by Paine as a nonissue because very little of any American-British confrontation would take place at sea. There also were concerns about the major financial burden that a war would place on the colonies. Paine answers that this, too, should be of no concern because, if necessary, the valuable frontiers could be sold for more money than what any war would cost.

So eloquent was Paine's rhetoric in this anonymous pamphlet that readers were certain that one of their favorite orators had written *Common Sense*. The most common guess was Benjamin Franklin, but both Samuel Adams and John Adams were suspected. Ironically, neither Adams could have persuaded the American public the way *Common Sense* did, largely because they were formally educated, and the middle-class tradesman Paine was self-educated, much as Franklin was. Paine's appeal to ordinary reason, everyday language, and "common sense" went straight to the heart of the average American the way a learned treatise on political philosophy never could.

For all that Paine's express purpose was to appeal to common sense and plain truth, the success of *Common Sense* was due in no small part to his masterful appeal to human emotions. To the American willing to forgive British slights in the name of peace, Paine rubbed their noses in those slights, creating vivid pictures of the worst enormities, real or hypothetical, perpetrated by British soldiers. The result was the mass persuasion of Americans teetering on the edge of a decision.

SIGNIFICANCE

The rhetoric of Thomas Paine's *Common Sense* was pivotal to America's embracing the idea of independence from England. Not only is the pamphlet an enduring part of American literary history, its very publication also was a carefully orchestrated political event, consciously timed to coincide with the appearance in American periodicals of King George III's inflammatory speech before Parliament. A reading of the correspondence of the leaders of the American Revolution in the first six months of 1776 makes clear that it is not too much of an exaggeration to suggest that Paine's pamphlet was the greatest motive force impelling American patriots to war with England.

Yet as tied to the moment as *Common Sense* was, it is still read not just because it is an important founding document but also because it eloquently and persuasively presents a political philosophy of absolute egalitarianism, echoing the more densely intellectual theories of John Locke, but doing so in a popular style that appeals not to the intellect alone but to, as the title suggests, common sense.

Half a year before the Declaration of Independence, Paine had already outlined the declaration's principles in *Common Sense*: the origin of governmental authority in the people governed, the consequent right of the governed to set aside a bad government, and a demonstration that the current colonial government was indeed bad.

—*John R. Holmes*

FURTHER READING

Aldridge, A. Owen. *Thomas Paine's American Ideology*. Newark: University of Delaware Press, 1984. A thorough analysis not only of Paine's writings in America but also of the earlier writings and events that shaped his thought.

Fish, Bruce, and Becky Durost Fish. *Thomas Paine: Political Writer*. Philadelphia: Chelsea House, 2000. A brief, readable overview of Paine's political writings for the Revolutionary War Leaders series.

Foner, Eric. *Tom Paine and Revolutionary America*. New York: Oxford University Press, 1976. A bicentennial celebration of Paine's contributions to the intellectual background of the American Revolution.

McCarthy, Pat. *Thomas Paine: Revolutionary Patriot and Writer*. Berkeley Heights, N.J.: Enslow, 2001. A brief, nonacademic summary of Paine's life, including a detailed discussion of the role of *Common Sense* in the American Revolution.

McCartin, Brian. *Thomas Paine: Common Sense and Revolutionary Pamphleteering*. New York: Power-Plus Books, 2002. At 112 pages, this book is a short examination of Paine's work as a pamphleteer.

Paine, Thomas. *The Complete Writings of Thomas Paine*. Edited by Philip S. Foner. New York: Citadel Press, 1945. A classic, accessible, and well-prepared edition of Paine's works. Also available online at http://www.thomaspaine.org. Accessed August, 2005.

Williamson, Audrey. *Thomas Paine: His Life, Work, and Times*. London: Allen & Unwin, 1973. A study of Paine's revolutionary thought and activities from a British point of view.

Wilson, Jerome D., and William F. Ricketson. *Thomas Paine*. Boston: Twayne, 1989. A revised edition of a volume in the standard Twayne's U.S. Authors series. A good starting point for studying Paine.

SEE ALSO: Mar. 22, 1765-Mar. 18, 1766: Stamp Act Crisis; Dec. 16, 1773: Boston Tea Party; Sept. 5-Oct. 26, 1774: First Continental Congress; Apr. 19, 1775: Battle of Lexington and Concord; May 10-Aug. 2, 1775: Second Continental Congress; July 4, 1776: Declaration of Independence; Mar. 1, 1781: Ratification of the Articles of Confederation; Sept. 17, 1787: U.S. Constitution Is Adopted; Oct. 27, 1787-May, 1788: Publication of *The Federalist*; Feb. 22, 1791-Feb. 16, 1792: Thomas Paine Publishes *Rights of Man*; 1792: Wollstonecraft Publishes *A Vindication of the Rights of Woman*.

RELATED ARTICLES in *Great Lives from History: The Eighteenth Century, 1701-1800*: John Adams; William Blake; Edmund Burke; First Baron Erskine; Benjamin Franklin; George III; William Godwin; Thomas Jefferson; Guillaume-Thomas Raynal; Jean-Jacques Rousseau; George Washington; Mary Wollstonecraft.

March 9, 1776
ADAM SMITH PUBLISHES *THE WEALTH OF NATIONS*

The Wealth of Nations marked the culmination of Enlightenment political economy and the advent of modern economics. It became one of the most influential works on capitalism, being used variously as a practical guide, a theoretical description, a defense, and a critique of industrialization and the market.

LOCALE: London, England
CATEGORIES: Economics; philosophy

KEY FIGURES
Adam Smith (1723-1790), Scottish economist and philosopher
Francis Hutcheson (1694-1746), Scottish philosopher
William Pitt the Younger (1759-1806), prime minister of Great Britain, 1783-1801, 1804-1806
François Quesnay (1694-1774), French economist

SUMMARY OF EVENT
Adam Smith's *Inquiry into the Nature and Causes of the Wealth of Nations* (1776; commonly known as *The Wealth of Nations*) exerted greater influence in the systematization and development of economic theory than any other single work. In this volume, as in his lectures, Smith extracted economic theory from the broad field of moral philosophy and offered a comprehensive theory of economic value and of the operation of the market system. Although Smith was clearly dependent on others for many of the insights in *The Wealth of Nations*, the importance of his work has led many to call him the father of political economy.

Smith was reared by his widowed mother in the Scottish village of Kirkcaldy in Fifeshire and attended the University of Glasgow, where he studied moral philosophy under Professor Francis Hutcheson, who taught an optimistic natural philosophy. He subsequently studied classics at Oxford and lectured on rhetoric and belles lettres in Edinburgh. In 1751, he became professor of logic at Glasgow University, and he was made professor of moral philosophy in the following year. In 1759, he published his *The Theory of Moral Sentiments*, in which he emphasized that mutual regard—sympathy—binds the members of society together in a Providential harmony. The pursuit of esteem was an important part of an individual's status; as Smith would argue in *The Wealth of Nations*, the economy was one of the major realms where esteem and status were realized and discovered.

In 1763, Smith resigned his position to become tutor to the young duke of Buccleuch, and with his pupil he traveled on the Continent for two years. In France, he met Anne-Robert-Jacques Turgot and François Quesnay, whose economic ideas impressed him. Smith returned to Kirkcaldy in 1766 and spent most of the following decade there writing *The Wealth of Nations*. He subsequently received a post as customs commissioner in Edinburgh and died there in 1790.

The Wealth of Nations reveals Smith as widely read in the political and economic theory of the seventeenth and eighteenth centuries, and as indebted to many individuals and schools of thought for his insights. Yet Smith also shows that he is more than a mere systematizer or popularizer of the ideas of others. *The Wealth of Nations* breaks new ground, and its comprehensiveness is far superior to many of its nineteenth century successors as well as its physiocratic and other predecessors.

Smith's work commences with a discussion of the importance of labor as the source of the annual wealth of a nation, and the division of labor as a means for increasing its productivity and the nation's wealth. Division of labor results in exchanges, which leads Smith into a discussion of money as the medium of exchange, and to problems of value, where he sharply distinguishes between value in exchange and value in use. Accepting labor as a measure of value, Smith defines prices in terms of component costs of production including wages, profit, and rent. Natural price is the long-run, competitive, equilibrium price determined by the cost of production, while market price is a short-run price determined by supply and demand. Smith points out the self-regulating nature of the market system and insists that artificial regulations of a legislative or monopolistic type are unnecessary and unwise. He then considers wages, profits, and rent and the effects of economic progress on these three types of income.

In the second book of *The Wealth of Nations*, Smith turns to a consideration of the nature, accumulation, and employment of capital. Here he explains the importance of banking and paper money, and distinguishes productive from unproductive labor. In his distinction he recognizes the productive quality of nonagricultural labor and thus moves beyond the position of the Physiocrats. He defines saving as investment and relates private saving to the national welfare, thus providing encouragement for thrift and capital investment. Smith traces a natural

1770's

course of development in all nations whereby the capital of the society is first directed to agriculture, then to manufacturing, and finally to foreign commerce, unless interrupted by legislation or other unwise interference.

In the third book, Smith reveals his historical account of the progress of wealth in different nations. This served the purpose of explaining the transition from agricultural to commercial societies, and of the historical basis of his later critique of mercantilism. In the fourth book of his study, Smith offers a critique of the mercantile system and of the agricultural system of the Physiocrats. Smith's major attack on mercantilism is directed against restrictive monopolistic regulations and practices that interfere with the free operation of the natural laws of the market. He argues for free trade domestically and internationally, and urges the abolition of duties, bounties, and the monopolistic privileges of chartered companies. Smith was not, however, a doctrinaire opponent of all economic restrictions. He grants the appropriateness of certain exceptions, as well as the wisdom of moving gradually in the adoption of a free trade policy. He insists that as individuals pursue their own best interest, they unknowingly but effectively promote the best interest of society.

Smith considers the economic functions of the state in the fifth book of *The Wealth of Nations*. He recognizes three duties of the state according to his system of natural liberty: defense against foreign states, protection of every citizen against every other citizen, and the building and maintenance of public works and institutions that are advantageous to society but unprofitable as public investments. He also recognizes the necessity for restraint in situations where the exercise of natural liberty by a few individuals might endanger the security of the whole society. Thus, while Smith generally encourages the free economic action of individuals under the impulse of self-interest, he is not an advocate of an unqualified laissez-faire doctrine.

As a moral philosopher, Smith recognized in issues such as the division of labor and the pursuit of self-interest particular challenges to civic morality. Smith was particularly concerned that the laboring poor have the education and moral instruction necessary to retain their psychological independence and wholeness in the face of pursuit of self-interest upon their part and that of their employers. Commerce and liberty had in Britain enjoyed a general mutually rewarding relationship. Yet Smith was concerned that commerce created increasingly complex social relationships that could endanger civic liberty; therefore, the statesman must carefully monitor commercial progress with an eye to legislation that will protect liberty.

MEASURING THE WEALTH OF FOREIGN LANDS

In The Wealth of Nations, *Adam Smith begins his discussion of the mercantile system by examining common conceptions of the relationship between wealth and money, or other things taken to stand for wealth as such. In the following passage, he compares the Spanish and Tatar methods of measuring the wealth of other nations.*

A rich country, in the same manner as a rich man, is supposed to be a country abounding in money; and to heap up gold and saver [sic] in any country is supposed to be the readiest way to enrich it. For some time after the discovery of America, the first inquiry of the Spaniards, when they arrived upon an unknown coast, used to be, if there was any gold or silver to be found in the neighbourhood. By the information which they received, they judged whether it was worth while to make a settlement there, or if the country was worth the conquering. Plano Carpino, a monk, sent ambassador from the King of France to one of the sons of the famous Genghis Khan, says that the Tartars used frequently to ask him if there was plenty of sheep and oxen in the kingdom of France? Their inquiry had the same object with that of the Spaniards. They wanted to know if the country was rich enough to be worth the conquering. Among the Tartars, as among all other nations of shepherds, who are generally ignorant of the use of money, cattle are the instruments of commerce and the measures of value. Wealth, therefore, according to them, consisted in cattle, as according to the Spaniards it consisted in gold and silver. Of the two, the Tartar notion, perhaps, was the nearest to the truth.

Source: Adam Smith, *An Inquiry into the Nature and Causes of the Wealth of Nations.* 5th ed. (London: Methuen, 1904). Book 4, chapter 1, paragraph 2. http://www.econlib.org/library/Smith/smWN.html. Accessed November 15, 2005.

SIGNIFICANCE

The economic system of natural liberty advocated in *The Wealth of Nations* had many prominent advocates in the eighteenth and nineteenth centuries. A notable disciple of Adam Smith was the British prime minister William Pitt the Younger, who sought to introduce free trade principles in British economic policy. The Manchester School later depended on Smith's theories in its legislative proposals. *The Wealth of Nations* had advocates outside Britain as well; Smith even influenced opponents of capitalism such as Karl

A 1790 engraving of Adam Smith. (Library of Congress)

Marx. Smith's greatest achievements in *The Wealth of Nations* were his successful definition of a science of economics, his explanation of wealth, and his emphasis on the division of labor. From his work, readers were able to see clearly the operation of the market as a self-regulating system.

—*Samuel C. Pearson, updated by Michael Kugler*

FURTHER READING

Campbell, R. H., and A. S. Skinner. "General Introduction." In *An Inquiry into the Nature and Causes of the Wealth of Nations*, by Adam Smith. New York: Oxford University Press, 1979. This scholarly edition of *The Wealth of Nations* provides a very useful outline of Smith's major work and of his earlier works as well.

Dougherty, Peter J. *Who's Afraid of Adam Smith? How the Market Got Its Soul*. New York: J. Wiley, 2002.

Analyzes two of Smith's books: *The Wealth of Nations*, with its ideas about the free market, and the more obscure *A Theory of Moral Sentiments*, expressing Smith's belief that free markets can flourish only in societies with social capital and strong institutions of civil society.

Fleischaker, Samuel. *On Adam Smith's "Wealth of Nations": A Philosophical Companion*. Princeton, N.J.: Princeton University Press, 2004. Fleischaker explains Smith's economic ideas within the context of Smith's moral theory and philosophies of science and social science. He also relates Smith's ideas to the thoughts of his contemporaries, including David Hume and Francis Hutcheson.

Heilbroner, Robert L. *The Worldly Philosophers: The Lives, Times, and Ideas of the Great Economic Thinkers*. New York: Simon & Schuster, 1953. Still a very useful and readable introduction to the history of the discipline of economics, in which Smith plays a formative role.

Hont, Istvan, and Michael Ignatieff, eds. *Wealth and Virtue: The Shaping of Political Economy in the Scottish Enlightenment*. New York: Cambridge University Press, 1983. This collection of essays offers compelling accounts of the historical background of Smith's political-economic thought.

Raphael, D. D. *Adam Smith*. New York: Oxford University Press, 1985. A short, clear work by an expert, with a good introduction to Smith's writings.

Ross, Ian Simpson. *The Life of Adam Smith*. New York: Oxford University Press, 1995. A comprehensive and scholarly biography of Smith.

Skinner, Andrew S., and Thomas Wilson, eds. *Essays on Adam Smith*. Oxford, England: Clarendon Press, 1975. A full and wide-ranging set of scholarly essays on Smith in his capacities as moral philosopher and political economist.

SEE ALSO: 1720: Financial Collapse of the John Law System; Sept., 1720: Collapse of the South Sea Bubble; 1763-1767: Famine in Southern Italy; Apr. 27-May, 1775: Flour War; Jan., 1790: Hamilton's *Report on Public Credit*; May 6, 1795: Speenhamland System; 1798: Malthus Arouses Controversy with His Population Theory.

RELATED ARTICLES in *Great Lives from History: The Eighteenth Century, 1701-1800*: David Hume; William Pitt the Younger; Adam Smith; Anne-Robert-Jacques Turgot.

March 28, 1776
FOUNDING OF BOLSHOI THEATRE COMPANY

Since it was founded by Catherine the Great, the Bolshoi Theatre Company has been a preeminent opera and ballet, and it has staged significant works by Russian playwrights. Its influence has been global, and its name is familiar to most, if not all, arts enthusiasts.

LOCALE: Moscow, Russia
CATEGORIES: Organizations and institutions; dance; music; theater

KEY FIGURES

Peter Urusov (fl. late eighteenth century), Russian theater owner and manager
Mikhail Medoks (Michael Maddox; b. 1747), Urusov's English partner
Catherine the Great (1729-1796), empress of Russia, r. 1762-1796
Christian Roseberg (fl. late eighteenth century), Russian architect
Osip Bovet (Joseph Beauvais; fl. late eighteenth century), Russian architect

SUMMARY OF EVENT

Before the Bolshoi Theatre Company was founded in 1776, the Znamensky Theater served as Moscow's opera house. Catherine the Great, an ardent supporter of the arts, had encouraged artistic development both in St. Petersburg and throughout Russia. She also wrote several operas, some of which were eventually performed at the Bolshoi Theatre.

On March 28, 1776, Catherine granted Prince Peter Urusov the exclusive right for a period of ten years to operate a private theater in Moscow and also obliged him to build within five years "a stone building of a theater that would decorate the city and also serve as the premises for public masquerades, comedies, and comic operas." Urusov, an educated aristocrat who served as Moscow's public prosecutor, had the connections to secure the grant, but he needed help. Mikhail Medoks, his partner, was an English entertainment entrepreneur who had come to Russia to demonstrate clever scenic illusions. He supplied the funds for the building, which was erected on Petrovka Street and named for the street. The Bolshoi ("big" in Russian) Theatre now stands at the site where the Petrovsky Theatre, which was burned to the ground in 1805, was built.

In 1776, Medoks and Urusov owned the Znamensky Theater, where they were soon staging performances. On

January 8, 1777, D. Zorin's *La Renaissance*, the first Russian one-act comic opera derived from original Russian songs, was staged and was a great success. Urusov's troupe consisted of thirteen actors, nine actresses, four dancers, three ballet dancers with a ballet master, and thirteen musicians. Performers from Moscow University and the troupe of Nikolay Titov augmented Urusov's company. The troupe performed ballets, operas, and plays, although initially opera was the most important. Eventually, all the best performing artists in Moscow, in addition to the dancers and actors who were trained at the Moscow Orphanage, worked with the Medoks troupe. (The orphanage, whose members were serfs, was established in 1764 and began ballet instruction in 1773. Medoks acquired the ballet school of the orphanage in 1784.)

Before the partners began construction of the Petrovsky Theater, they began adapting the Stroganov mansion for the company's purposes. When the Znamensky Theater, which had housed all the stage properties and costumes, was destroyed by fire in 1780, Urusov, who lost most of his funds, gave his privileged grant to Medoks. Medoks devoted his money and energy to the construction of the Petrovsky Theater, an unattractive red-brick structure designed by Christian Roseberg. It seated eight hundred and had three tiers of boxes, a gallery for poorer patrons, and several rows of armchairs in the front of the orchestra for privileged customers. It was one of the best-equipped theaters in Europe, and its orchestra floor could be raised and converted to a ballroom.

Aleksandr Onisimovich Ablesimov wrote *The Wanderers* (pr. 1780), a prologue, for the opening performance of the completed Petrovsky Theater in 1780. In the prologue, two characters, representative of the arts, wander in search of a venue, because their previous home (the Znamensky Theater, regarded by Natalia Roslavleva as the "cradle" of Russian national opera) was destroyed by fire. Apollo descends to Earth to tell them that they have a new venue, the Petrovsky Theater, created by a mortal (Mikhail Medoks) at Apollo's command. During Apollo's speech, the scenery changes and the backdrop features Moscow and Medoks's theater.

The prologue was followed by *The Magic School* (pr. 1780), a pantomime ballet, and by some operatic works by Russian writers. Initially, most operas were written by Russians, such as Vasily Pashkevich, about scenes from everyday life, but works of such foreign composers as

Antonio Salieri, Luigi Cherubini, and Giovanni Pergolesi were also included. Ballet scenes were used as *divertissements* (diversions) for operas and dramatic productions. The Petrovsky Theater, unlike many other theaters, had an advisory council composed of actors, dramatists, and art critics who made decisions about what to perform and whom to cast. In 1805, the Petrovsky Theater met the fate of it predecessor: It was destroyed by fire. This time, it was Medoks who was financially ruined, and in 1806 the theater in Moscow was taken over by the imperial government, and the serf actors were freed.

The troupe continued to perform in various venues until January 6, 1825, when the new Bolshoi Theatre was completed. One of the largest theaters in Europe, eclipsed only by La Scala in Milan, the Bolshoi was designed by Professor Alexander Mikhailov and constructed by architect Osipe Bovet. Mikhail Dmitriyev wrote the lyrics and Alexei Vertovsky and Alexander Alyabyev wrote the score for *Torzhestvo muz* (pr. 1825; the triumph of the muses), which was performed opening night. Under Vertovsky's and dramatist Fyodor Kokoshkin's leadership, the Bolshoi established a primarily Russian operatic repertoire derived from traditional songs and melodies. Moreover, the ballet sequences in the operas, which had been incidental, became integral parts of the operas.

SIGNIFICANCE

Since 1776, the Bolshoi Theatre has occupied several structures and taken several forms. It was damaged by fire again in March, 1853, and extensively reconstructed. It remains synonymous with Russian opera and especially ballet, although it has had its low points, such as the period when it was under the control of the imperial theaters in St. Petersburg. In the late nineteenth century, an Italian company performed at the theater four or five times a week, leaving the Bolshoi Theatre Company only one day a week to perform. Before 1900, Russian nationalism prevailed. Peter Ilich Tchaikovsky's opera *Eugene Onegin* (1878) was staged at the Bolshoi and was followed by three Russian classics: Petrovich Mussorgsky's *Boris Godunov* (1889), Nikolay Rimsky-Korsakov's *Snegurochka* (the snow maiden; 1882), and Yevgeniy Borodin's *Prince Igor* (1898). In the same period, Tchaikovsky's classic ballet *Swan Lake* (1877) was staged at the Bolshoi.

Russian opera dominated the theater, but the operas of Wolfgang Amadeus Mozart, Gioacchino Rossini, Giuseppe Verdi, Richard Wagner, and Giacomo Puccini were also performed. Russian nationalism and Western art operated in a kind of tenuous balance. Because the Bolshoi troupes tour frequently, they have had a tremendous influence on the arts, particularly in ballet. So dominant was Russian ballet that non-Russian dancers assumed Russian names to give themselves more credibility. Lilian Marks, for example, adopted the name Alicia Markova and became a famous English ballerina.

The Bolshoi Theatre operates on a ten-month schedule, allowing the ballet and opera troupes to tour, and foreign companies and outstanding performers have appeared at the Bolshoi, considering it one of the premier venues in the world.

—*Thomas L. Erskine*

FURTHER READING

Bocharnikpva, Yelena, and Mikhail Gabovich. *Ballet School of the Bolshoi Theatre*. Translated by K. Danko, edited by D. Ogden. Moscow: Foreign Languages, n.d. The chapter "A Peep into History" discusses the origins of Russian ballet at the Orphanage Theatrical School, which was turned over to the Petrovsky Theatre, site of the Bolshoi Theatre.

Lushin, Stanislav, ed. *The Bolshoi Theatre of the USSR: History, Opera, Ballet*. Translated by Sally Patterson. Moscow: Planeta, 1987. Short introductory chapter about the origins of the Bolshoi Theatre. Includes a synopsis and a production history. Color photographs.

Pokrovsky, Boris Alexandrovich, and Yuri Nikolayevich Grigorovich. *The Bolshoi: Opera and Ballet at the Greatest Theater in Russia*. New York: William Morrow, 1979. History of the ballet and opera in Russia, supplemented by photographs of the actors, singers, dancers, and scenes from lyric operas and ballets staged at the Bolshoi.

Roslavleva, Natalia. *Era of the Russian Ballet*. New York: E. P. Dutton, 1966. First chapter focuses on the origins of Russian ballet and the contributions of Mikhail Medoks, Prince Urusov, and others in the creation of the Bolshoi Theatre.

SEE ALSO: 1724: Foundation of the St. Petersburg Academy of Sciences; May 15, 1738: Foundation of St. Petersburg's Imperial Ballet School; Aug. 10, 1767: Catherine the Great's Instruction; Aug. 3, 1778: Opening of Milan's La Scala; Nov., 1796: Catherine the Great's Art Collection Is Installed at the Hermitage.

RELATED ARTICLES in *Great Lives from History: The Eighteenth Century, 1701-1800*: Catherine the Great; Jean Dauberval; Wolfgang Amadeus Mozart.

1770's

May, 1776-September 3, 1783
FRANCE SUPPORTS THE AMERICAN REVOLUTION

French military and financial support proved indispensable to the United States during the Revolutionary War, and the French played a vital role in the Battle of Yorktown, at which the British surrendered. French diplomacy, however, was less helpful during peace treaty negotiations.

LOCALE: France; United States
CATEGORIES: Wars, uprisings, and civil unrest; diplomacy and international relations

KEY FIGURES

Charles Gravier de Vergennes (1719-1787), French foreign minister, 1774-1787
Comte de Rochambeau (Jean-Baptiste Donatien de Vimeur; 1725-1807), commander of the French army in the United States
Marquis de Lafayette (Marie-Joseph-Paul-Yves-Roch-Gilbert du Motier de Lafayette; 1757-1834), French volunteer during the American Revolution
Comte de Grasse (François-Joseph-Paul de Grasse; 1722-1788), French naval commander
Benjamin Franklin (1706-1790), American diplomat in Paris, 1776-1785
John Adams (1735-1826), American diplomat in Europe, 1778-1788, and later president of the United States, 1797-1801
John Jay (1745-1829), American diplomat in Europe, 1780-1784, and later chief justice of the U.S. Supreme Court, 1789-1795

SUMMARY OF EVENT

The French government watched attentively as disputes between the British and their American colonies intensified during the 1770's, hoping to exploit the conflict to impair Britain's position in the European balance of power and to gain revenge for their defeat in the Seven Years' War. The French foreign minister, Charles Gravier de Vergennes, believed loss of the American colonies would gravely weaken the British Empire, thereby enhancing France's position in Europe.

In September, 1775, Vergennes sent an unofficial agent to Philadelphia who encouraged the Continental Congress to apply to Paris for military aid. Vergennes in May, 1776, secretly provided funds to a fictitious company that bought military supplies at low cost from French armories and shipped them on credit to the Americans. Vergennes expected France ultimately to enter the conflict, but he could not risk a British declaration of war by openly helping the Americans, since the French navy would not be ready to fight before 1778. During the next few years, 90 percent of the arms and ammunition reaching the United States were surreptitiously supplied by France. Despite angry protests from Britain, France permitted American privateers attacking British shipping to bring in prizes and refit in French ports.

After the Declaration of Independence in 1776, many unemployed European officers volunteered for service in America, hoping to advance their fortunes. Unique among them was the Marquis de Lafayette, who arrived at Philadelphia in July, 1777, with a shipload of munitions, purchased at his own expense, which he donated to the Americans. Commissioned a major-general, Lafayette proved an effective commander of American forces and a useful advocate for the United States with the French court.

News of the surrender of an entire British army at Saratoga reached Paris on December 3, 1777, providing the occasion for Vergennes to offer formal recognition of the United States. On February 6, 1778, Benjamin Franklin signed a Treaty of Amity and Commerce that acknowledged the independence of the United States and granted each country most-favored-nation status. In a secret Treaty of Alliance, signed the same day, which would not become operational until war broke out between Britain and France, each country pledged not to conclude a truce or peace with Great Britain without consent of the other.

Protesting recognition of the United States, Britain recalled its ambassador from France in March, 1778. When British warships attacked the French on June 17, France openly entered the war, sending a naval squadron to help the Americans. Although the fleet failed to capture New York City, arrival of French ships in American waters led the British to evacuate Philadelphia and move troops to New York.

French loans and subsidies were indispensable to the United States, especially in 1781, when the American currency collapsed and only substantial grants Franklin obtained from Vergennes permitted Congress to restore the monetary system. When Vergennes in June, 1781, requested replacement of John Adams, who had infuriated Vergennes with his ignorance of and open contempt for European diplomatic protocol, Congress revoked Adams's mandate to conduct peace negotiations with Britain and reduced him to one member of a five-member commission. Dependence on French help explains Congress's instructions to the peace commissioners to do nothing without the knowledge and concurrence of the French.

Direct French military activity made possible the successful 1781 campaign. In 1780, Lafayette convinced the French that the war could be won only if they established a continuous military presence in America. The comte de Rochambeau arrived at Newport, Rhode Island, in August, 1780, with fifty-five hundred troops, who served under General George Washington's command. The comte de Grasse led a French fleet that campaigned mostly in the West Indies. When Lafayette, commanding a Virginia militia contingent, notified Washington in September, 1781, that a British army was fortifying the Yorktown peninsula, the Americans and French coordinated a joint attack. Washington's army, which had been besieging New York, was joined by Rochambeau and his French troops, and they moved stealthily south to join Lafayette. De Grasse arrived from the Caribbean with his fleet, preventing the British from relieving their army by sea. The First Marquess Cornwallis's surrender on October 19, 1781, effectively ended the Revolutionary War.

When the British sent an informal agent in the spring of 1782 to sound out the Americans on peace terms, Franklin was the only American peace commissioner in Paris. John Adams was in the Netherlands winning recognition of America and would not arrive until negotiations were in their final stage; John Jay, who would play the major role in the actual negotiations, was on his way from Madrid. Franklin told the British what he considered necessary and advisable concessions. Among the necessary articles (which included all the major points of the final peace treaty, except for access to Newfoundland

A print dated 1779 and published in London. "Brittanias Ruin" shows Brittania, or Great Britain, lamenting the state of the nation: "What a Situation I am in sold by an American & purchased by France & Spain," referring to French and Spanish support for American independence. (Library of Congress)

fisheries) were full recognition of American independence and a western boundary on the Mississippi River. As an "advisable" gesture, to restore American goodwill toward Britain, Franklin suggested ceding Canada to the United States.

After Franklin came down with a severe case of kidney stone, Jay took over bargaining detailed peace terms and precise boundaries. A descendant of Huguenot refugees from France, Jay disliked and distrusted Catholics and Frenchmen; he suspected Vergennes of plotting to strike an agreement with Britain at American expense. With Franklin's reluctant consent, Jay ignored Congress's instructions to do nothing without French knowledge and proceeded to negotiate a separate peace with Britain. A provisional treaty was signed November 30, 1782.

Jay's suspicions may have been founded upon prejudice, but they were not unrealistic. Vergennes understood that France's interests in America were better served by a weak United States, dependent upon French support and subservient to French direction, than by a strong, self-reliant country. He therefore encouraged the British and Spanish to establish protectorates over the trans-Appalachian Indians, confining the Americans to the coastal plain, and he suggested that Britain bar American ships from Newfoundland waters, where they competed with French fishermen.

Historians have described Vergennes as unpleasantly surprised when he learned of the agreement, which seems unlikely, given how thoroughly spies permeated the American delegation. He was somewhat astonished by Britain's generosity to its former colonies, commenting that they bought rather than made peace. Despite the displeasure Vergennes expressed after Franklin informed him of the American achievement, he responded to Franklin's request for more financial aid by arranging a loan of another six million livres.

SIGNIFICANCE

French help made the American victory in the Revolutionary War possible. When final treaties were signed on September 3, 1783, France and the United States considered themselves the clear victors. The United States had its independence and extensive territorial boundaries; France enjoyed revenge for its defeats in 1754-1763. The British House of Commons reluctantly accepted peace-treaty terms considered so humiliating that the government had to resign. Over the next decades, however, Britain emerged stronger than before, while the economic expense of the war proved a major disaster for France.

Vergennes hoped that France would replace Britain as the major trading partner of the United States, but Britain soon regained its dominance of the American market. As the Industrial Revolution created increasing wealth and Britain became the world's foremost financial power, its influence in European grew at the expense of France. Despite the nominal boundaries of the United States, the British maintained a de facto protectorate over western Indians; it would take a decade of negotiations to remove the British army from western forts and another war to reduce their influence over the Indians.

Within five years of the war's end, in part due to wartime expenditures, the French government was bankrupt, necessitating recall of the Estates-General in 1789. The ensuing French Revolution convulsed France, set off decades of European war, and left France in 1815 impoverished, with many of its young men dead.

In the short run, the United States struggled, but in the long run it was the major beneficiary of the war. After the Constitution created an effective government, the rich territory won by the United States with French help provided the foundation for economic developments that created the leading world power of the twentieth century and into the twenty-first century.

—*Milton Berman*

FURTHER READING

Brecher, Frank W. *Securing American Independence: John Jay and the French Alliance.* Westport, Conn.: Praeger, 2003. Poorly organized, but very informative on peace negotiations.

Dull, Jonathan R. *A Diplomatic History of the American Revolution.* New Haven, Conn.: Yale University Press, 1985. A brief scholarly history of American and European diplomacy, 1763 to 1783.

McCullough, David. *John Adams.* New York: Simon & Schuster, 2001. Defends Adams against criticism of his diplomatic activities.

Morgan, Edmund S. *Benjamin Franklin.* New Haven, Conn.: Yale University Press, 2002. A concise biography with an excellent account of Franklin's diplomatic role.

SEE ALSO: May 28, 1754-Feb. 10, 1763: French and Indian War; Jan., 1756-Feb. 15, 1763: Seven Years' War; Sept. 5-Oct. 26, 1774: First Continental Congress; Apr. 19, 1775-Oct. 19, 1781: American Revolutionary War; May 10-Aug. 2, 1775: Second Continental Congress; July 4, 1776: Declaration of Independence; Sept. 19-Oct. 17, 1777: Battles of Saratoga; Feb. 6, 1778: Franco-American Treaties;

Oct. 19, 1781: Cornwallis Surrenders at Yorktown; Sept. 3, 1783: Treaty of Paris; Oct. 22, 1784: Fort Stanwix Treaty; Sept. 17, 1787: U.S. Constitution Is Adopted; May 5, 1789: Louis XVI Calls the Estates-General.

RELATED ARTICLES in *Great Lives from History: The Eighteenth Century, 1701-1800*: John Adams; First Marquess Cornwallis; Benjamin Franklin; John Jay; Comte de Rochambeau; Charles Gravier de Vergennes; George Washington.

May 24 and June 11, 1776
INDIAN DELEGATION MEETS WITH CONGRESS

Representatives of the Iroquois Confederacy attempted to secure neutrality during the Revolutionary War. They believed they had succeeded, but secret American plans to recruit Iroquois mercenaries, as well as a British alliance with the Mohawks, led not only to Iroquois involvement but also to warfare between Iroquois tribes, ultimately causing the dissolution of the confederacy.

LOCALE: Philadelphia, Pennsylvania (now in the United States)

CATEGORIES: Diplomacy and international relations; wars, uprisings, and civil unrest

KEY FIGURES

Joseph Brant (Thayendanegea; 1742-1807), Mohawk chief and military leader

William Johnson (1715-1774), British commissioner of Indian affairs, 1756-1774

John Johnson (1742-1830), son of William and British commissioner of Indian affairs, 1782-1830

Samuel Kirkland (1741-1808), first American-born missionary to the Iroquois

SUMMARY OF EVENT

The withdrawal of the French in 1763 from the New World was a watershed event for the Iroquois Confederacy (the Six Nations). Between 1640, when the Iroquois established their hegemony over the fur trade, and the end of the French and Indian War in 1763, the Iroquois were profoundly involved in the imperial rivalries between the English and the French and were pivotal in the balance of power in the New World. When the French left, the Iroquois lost the fulcrum on which they had kept the balance.

The British government's Proclamation of 1763 provided that all territory between the crest of the Alleghenies and the Mississippi River and from Florida to 50 degrees north latitude were closed to settlers and land speculators and reserved "for the present" to American Indians. This proclamation, however, served the British

agenda, not the needs of either natives or settlers. Britain wished to protect valuable furbearing animals' habitats from encroaching colonists. Guaranteeing boundaries, moreover, did not guarantee sovereignty.

In fact, the British were less accommodating to the Iroquois than the French had been. Native resistance flared with Pontiac's Resistance (1763-1766), in which the Senecas—one of the Iroquois Nations—fought on the side of Pontiac, while the Mohawks supported the British. When that rebellion failed, the Senecas were punished by William Johnson, the commissioner of Indian affairs, and were forced to cede some of their land to the British. In 1775, the Senecas successfully negotiated with the Americans at Pittsburgh to remain neutral in the frontier battles and the impending Revolutionary War, as long as the Americans stayed out of Iroquois territory. This negotiation was approved by the full governing council of the Six Nations. It was the last significant action to exhibit the council's control over its warriors.

In that Pittsburgh agreement, American settlers who encroached on Mohawk territory were supposed to be punished by American authorities. However, encroachment of the farmers and frontiersmen called the Albany Group near the Mohawk River Valley never abated. Since the Americans failed to police their own settlers, the Mohawks, led by Joseph Brant, grew more dependent on the British to help defend against American encroachment.

During 1775 and into the spring of 1776, the British expended considerable effort to create military alliances with all the tribes of the Iroquois Confederacy. So great was their influence among the Mohawks that Joseph Brant and several other warrior chiefs sailed to England in November, 1775, professedly to secure Iroquois sovereignty in exchange for allegiance to the British during the war. By 1776, the Continental Congress wanted desperately for the Iroquois to join the fight on the side of the colonies but did not have the financial wherewithal to dispense the gifts of food, ammunition, clothing, and other necessities that the Iroquois expected when asked to fight as mercenaries. The American alternative was a proclamation of friendship and the stated desire that the Iroquois remain neutral.

In England, King George III guaranteed Joseph Brant that the boundaries of the Iroquois homelands would remain unchanged, but this was no concession of sovereignty over those homelands. It is believed that Joseph Brant misunderstood the distinction drawn by the British between territorial *sovereignty* and territorial *occupancy*. It is known that Brant believed the Americans' goal was to overrun the continent at the expense of all American Indians. Brant decided the Iroquois' future lay with the British. In England, Joseph Brant was commissioned a colonel in the British colonial militia.

Up to this time, the Americans had done no violence to the Iroquois and, with the exception of the Albany Group, were careful to avoid trespassing on Iroquois territory. This situation changed when the patriot missionary Samuel Kirkland traveled to Oriskany, a stronghold of the Oneidas. Acting Indian commissioner John Johnson attempted to arrest Kirkland, and the Albany Group responded by entering Mohawk territory to arrest Johnson. Both actions failed in their objectives, although Kirkland was momentarily muzzled and Johnson had to flee to Canada with a significant force of Mohawk warriors.

These events formed the background against which an Iroquois delegation of twenty-one members, representing four of the Six Nations, traveled to Philadelphia to be presented to the Continental Congress on May 24, 1776, and again on June 11. Brant was still in England. The delegates were presented to "the great warrior chief" George Washington on May 24 and to the full congress on June 11. While in Philadelphia, they boarded in a room directly above the meeting room of the congress.

Washington had spent the previous two weeks persuading the Continental Congress to break the Pittsburgh agreement and allow him to recruit an Indian militia. On May 25, the congress resolved that it would be expedient to engage American Indians in the service of the colonies. The significance of this decision was twofold: The congress was ignoring or nullifying the sovereignty of the Council of the Confederacy that had approved the Pittsburgh agreement, and the congress was ignoring the purpose of the Iroquois delegation, which was to assure the sincere and serious effort by the Iroquois to hold fast to the neutrality agreement.

Washington knew the path to either a British or an American victory led through Iroquois land. The strategic importance of that land could not be ignored. The congress was clever enough not to tell the Iroquois delegates that Washington was about to recruit Iroquois as soldiers, as the minutes of June 11 show:

> We shall order our warriors not to hurt any of your kindred, and we hope you will not allow any of your young brothers to join with the enemy . . . we desire you accept these few necessaries as tokens of our good-will . . . we hope the friendship between us will be firm as long as the sun shall shine and the waters run, that we be as one people.

While saying these words, the congress did not understand the disastrous implications of its conniving efforts to recruit American Indians.

The order to recruit Native Americans, including Iroquois, was passed through patriot channels to the Reverend Kirkland and the Oneida and Tuscarora, and also to General Philip Schuyler of the Albany Group. Schuyler was asked to recruit two thousand Iroquois, who were to be paid a reward of one hundred dollars for every British officer killed or taken prisoner and thirty dollars for every enlisted man. Schuyler was dubious not only of the policy but also of the numbers—there were not two thousand Iroquois men available, much less warriors, who were not already aiding the British. The Oneida, however, decided to send five hundred warriors to help protect the American Fort Stanwix near Utica, New York. This unilateral action by the Oneida breached the Iroquois Confederacy.

SIGNIFICANCE

The Iroquois delegation to Philadelphia was one of a set of events and commitments that entangled the Iroquois nation at the time of the American Revolution. The delegation made promises to the Continental Congress that several Iroquois Nations felt bound to honor. Other nations, however, allowed their warriors to fight as mercenaries on behalf of the Americans or formally allied themselves with the British.

The Revolutionary War thus brought about an event that had heretofore seemed impossible to the Iroquois Nations: Their Covenant Chain broke. In 1777, the league chiefs "covered their fire." For the first time within living memory, Iroquois fought and killed Iroquois, and their league shattered. The Treaty of Paris in 1783 said nothing about the American Indians. Those who had allied with Britain were abandoned to the care of the Americans. Joseph Brant's pledge to the king, made, he thought, in exchange for a pledge of Mohawk sovereignty, ended particularly bitterly, as he discovered that the British had ceded all Mohawk land to the Americans. That the Mohawks were given a reserve in Canada was little consolation.

—Glenn Schiffman

FURTHER READING

Fenton, William N. *The Great Law and the Longhouse: A Political History of the Iroquois Confederacy*. Norman: University of Oklahoma Press, 1998. A survey of Iroquois history and culture from the mid-sixteenth century until 1794. Includes information about Brant, Kirkland, Johnson, and the Continental Congresses.

Graymont, Barbara. *The Iroquois*. New York: Chelsea House, 1988. A useful book by a recognized expert on the subject.

_____. *The Iroquois in the American Revolution*. Syracuse, N.Y.: Syracuse University Press, 1972. The author is considered to be the foremost authority on the Iroquois and the Revolutionary War.

Jennings, Francis. *The Founders of America*. New York: W. W. Norton, 1993. This exceptional history of the events around the American Revolution is accessible to both casual readers and scholars.

Josephy, Alvin M., Jr. *Five Hundred Nations: An Illustrated History of North American Indians*. New York: Alfred A. Knopf, 1994. Companion book to the CBS television series *Five Hundred Nations*, written by one of America's foremost authorities on American Indian culture.

Richter, Daniel K., and James H. Merrell. *Beyond the Covenant Chain: The Iroquois and Their Neighbors in Indian North America, 1600-1800*. Preface by Daniel K. Richter and James H. Merrell. Foreword by Wilcomb E. Washburn. University Park: Pennsylvania State University Press, 2003. A new edition of the book originally published in 1987. This collection of essays examines diplomatic and military relations among the Iroquois in seventeenth and eighteenth century North America.

Stone, William L. *Life of Joseph Brant*. Albany, N.Y.: J. Munsell, 1864. A source for quotations of early colonial documents. Contains some historical inaccuracies; for example, this is the source of the erroneous information that Brant was in North America at the time of the Philadelphia meeting.

Wise, Jennings C. *The Red Man in the New World Drama*. Edited by Vine Deloria, Jr. New York: Macmillan, 1971. The key words "New World drama" provide a clue to the American Indian perspective of this author and editor.

SEE ALSO: May 28, 1754-Feb. 10, 1763: French and Indian War; May 8, 1763-July 24, 1766: Pontiac's Resistance; Oct. 7, 1763: Proclamation of 1763; Dec. 16, 1773: Boston Tea Party; Apr. 27-Oct. 10, 1774: Lord Dunmore's War; Sept. 5-Oct. 26, 1774: First Continental Congress; Apr. 19, 1775: Battle of Lexington and Concord; May 10-Aug. 2, 1775: Second Continental Congress; July 4, 1776: Declaration of Independence; Aug. 6, 1777: Battle of Oriskany Creek; Sept. 19-Oct. 17, 1777: Battles of Saratoga; Feb. 6, 1778: Franco-American Treaties; Oct. 19, 1781: Cornwallis Surrenders at Yorktown; Sept. 3, 1783: Treaty of Paris; Oct. 22, 1784: Fort Stanwix Treaty.

RELATED ARTICLES in *Great Lives from History: The Eighteenth Century, 1701-1800*: Joseph Brant; George III; Pontiac; George Washington.

1770's

July 2, 1776
NEW JERSEY WOMEN GAIN THE VOTE

More than a century before national woman suffrage was secured, women in New Jersey briefly exercised the right to vote after being given the right in the state's new constitution. In 1807, however, the state legislature changed the suffrage clause to include only white, taxpaying men.

LOCALE: New Jersey

CATEGORIES: Women's rights; social issues and reform; government and politics; laws, acts, and legal history

KEY FIGURES

Elias Boudinot (1740-1821), lawyer and Federalist orator

John Cooper (fl. 1776), Quaker and Federalist legislator in the New Jersey Provincial Congress

SUMMARY OF EVENT

New Jersey was unlike other states of the early republic in that its first constitution allowed its female inhabitants the right to vote. It has been said that this instance, even though it lasted just thirty-one years, was one of the most important, early, opportunities women have had to vote in the United States. Yet, after being the center of a political struggle between male politicians, the right to vote was taken from women. Women did not regain it until the Nineteenth Amendment to the U.S. Constitution was ratified in 1920.

On the recommendation of the Second Continental Congress, several New Jersey legislators of the Provincial Congress met from May 26 to July 2, 1776, to draft their first constitution to formalize their revolutionary government. That first draft of the New Jersey constitution included the clause that allowed, albeit indirectly, women the right to vote. The clause states that all residents worth at least £50 "shall be entitled to vote."

Few records remain from the eight days it took to draft the document at the highly secretive forum, making it difficult to determine the drafters' motives. Scholars have debated whether it was the framers' intention from the beginning to include women or if, in their haste to draw up the document, they inadvertently included the rights of some women to vote. Such women would have included only young women not yet married and women who were widowed, as well as African Americans of both genders; few African Americans, however, would have been able to meet the economic qualifications.

The Quakers, a religious group known for embracing gender equality, likely played a substantial role in the drafting of New Jersey's constitution. In the Quaker religion, women could hold positions of power, although they could not hold all the same positions as men. John Cooper, a Quaker, created a draft of the constitution that entitled women to vote, a move of which many members approved. It was not until 1790 that Cooper openly expressed his belief that women should be able to vote and that a law was drafted to specifically include women. The law became effective November 18, 1790, and it cleared up any misconceptions of the suffrage clause by replacing "he" with "he or she" in the clause.

ALL INHABITANTS SHALL BE ENTITLED TO VOTE

The framers of the New Jersey constitution included certain women among those who have the right to vote in the state. Scholars have debated whether or not this right came by way of exclusion. That is, was the right implied, and extended deliberately, because the term "man" was not used in the document to refer to the voter, thereby extending the right to vote to both genders, or was the omission of gender pronouns accidental? The following excerpt comes from the New Jersey constitution of 1776.

We, the representatives of the colony of New Jersey, having been elected by all the Counties, in the freest manner, and in congress assembled, have, after mature deliberations, agreed upon a set of charter rights and the form of a Constitution, in manner following, . . .

That all inhabitants of this Colony, of full age, who are worth fifty pounds proclamation money, clear estate in the same, and have resided within the County in which they claim a vote for twelve months immediately preceding the election, shall be entitled to vote for Representatives in Council and Assembly; and also for all other public officers, that shall be elected by the people of the County at large.

Source: New Jersey Constitution (1776), in Living History America: The History of the United States in Documents, Essays, Letters, Songs, and Poems, edited by Erik Bruun and Jay Crosby (New York: Tess Press), p. 147.

New Jersey was the first state in which women were allowed to vote. That right did not last long, however, because the New Jersey legislature changed its suffrage clause in 1807, barring all persons except white, taxpaying males from voting. (North Wind Picture Archives)

The year 1790 also marks the point when Federalists, many of whom were Quakers, wanted to expand their electorate in hope of gaining control of the legislature. In 1790, east Jersey controlled the legislature and west Jersey needed to find more support, and women were an eligible group. The pinnacle of the Federalist campaign to include women in the electorate came in 1793. On July 4 of that year, Elias Boudinot, a friend of Federalist Alexander Hamilton, gave a speech expressing his desire for more women to become involved in public affairs. Boudinot, aware of the criticisms women would receive, reminded the audience that if it were not for Spain's Queen Isabella, Christopher Columbus would not have been able to make his discoveries in the Americas during the late fifteenth century.

As the decade progressed, the Federalists began to change their opinion of woman suffrage because of the influence of French émigrés who were strongly affected by the French Revolution. These émigrés believed New Jersey was giving women too much credit in the political scene. The emergence of the Republican Party also created concern for women voting. Despite their hesitancy, the Federalists continued to seek the support of women voters in the elections.

In Essex County, New Jersey, in October, 1797, John Condit, a Republican from Newark, and William Crane, a Federalist from Elizabethtown, were both candidates for the legislature. Condit was able to win by a narrow margin, but only after a large group of women went to the polls to vote in the last hours, swaying the outcome. Immediately after the election, the local newspaper reported the seemingly rare occurrence of women voting. For the first time, women voting became a fiercely debated issue for many people of New Jersey.

The Federalists had needed the votes of women to win the elections of 1797 and 1798. At the same time they sought the women's vote, however, they feared that women's votes would benefit the Republican cause more than their own; therefore, they altered their position on woman suffrage and began to discourage women from

613

voting. Also, it became increasingly necessary to revise the constitution of New Jersey so that it reflected the federal Constitution, which many believed did not allow for woman suffrage.

The next several years saw continued debate over whether the U.S. Constitution actually provided for the franchise for women. In 1800, a presidential election year, Republican officials suggested an amendment to the election law to guarantee the rights of women to vote at the polls. The amendment was rejected on the basis that the constitution already provided the right. Republican politicians advertised this ruling prior to the election.

With the Republican politicization of women, the Federalists were again forced to seek the female vote. The Republican politicization did not help in the 1800 election, because more women supported the Federalist candidate than the Republican candidate. Republicans made a swift change of position and presented a bill to Congress that would allow only free white males to vote. At this time, the Federalists saw no need to support the plan when the votes were already on their side.

In 1804, a third party of liberal Republicans emerged. The party succeeded in placing itself directly in the middle of Republican and Federalist ideology, gaining support from both sides, with the larger share coming from the more moderate Republicans. The 1806 election for the building of a new courthouse in the heavily populated Republican county of Essex created a great deal of intraparty conflict. The moderate Republicans lost the fraudulent election and petitioned for its annulment. The Republican leadership saw the strain and embarrassment the third party was creating so close to the 1808 presidential elections and began to make amends. Newark would receive the courthouse in return for the vote of moderate Republicans on the bill to limit the vote to white, taxpaying, male citizens. Federalists also agreed to the passage of the bill.

SIGNIFICANCE

In 1807, New Jersey would change the suffrage clause of its constitution to include only adult taxpaying white males, thereby taking away women's voting rights. As 1808, a presidential election year, approached, it became necessary to create a unified Republican Party in order to win the election in the light of President Thomas Jefferson's unpopular embargo in New Jersey. Little was heard from the women who lost their right to vote. They were not able to arrange a formidable group as a result of laws that denied married women, the largest single group of women, a voice in politics. The young Federalist

women who could vote declined to speak out for fear of association with African Americans and others who were disenfranchised. The law of 1807 eliminated female representation for political reasons, much as women had been granted suffrage for political reasons. It would be 1920, more than a century later, before women won the right to vote on a national level.

—Jeri Kurtzleben

FURTHER READING

Baker, Paula. "The Domestication of Politics: Women and American Society, 1780-1920." *American Historical Review* 89 (June, 1984): 620-647. Discusses the politicization of women for the advancement of male candidates and their political parties.

Dodyk, Delight W. "Education and Agitation: The Woman Suffrage Movement in New Jersey." Unpublished Ph.D. dissertation. Rutgers University, 1997. Traces the complex history of the New Jersey suffrage movement from 1776, when landed women were given the vote, to 1807, when it was taken away, and throughout the nineteenth and early twentieth centuries.

Flexner, Eleanor. *Century of Struggle.* Cambridge, Mass.: Belknap Press, 1959. Demonstrates the importance of New Jersey women in the suffrage movement.

Klinghoffer, Judith Apter, and Lois Elkis. "The Petticoat Electors: Women's Suffrage in New Jersey, 1776-1807." *Journal of the Early Republic* 12, no. 2 (Summer, 1992): 158-193. Sheds new light on what once was considered a hastily drawn draft of New Jersey's first constitution.

Lurie, Maxine N., ed. *A New Jersey Anthology.* Newark: New Jersey Historical Society, 1994. Collection of seventeen essays by historians covering the full range of the state's history, including the Revolutionary War, feminism, and movements for women's rights.

Pomfret, John. *Colonial New Jersey: A History.* New York: Charles Scribner's Sons, 1973. Describes in detail the events surrounding the drive to gain votes for representation.

Trager, James. *The Women's Chronology.* New York: Henry Holt, 1994. Demonstrates the activities of women in the early republic.

Turner, Edward Raymond. "Women's Suffrage in New Jersey: 1790-1807." *Smith College Studies in History* 1 (1916): 165-187. Explores the early conception of the anomaly concerning women voting in New Jersey.

1770's

July 4, 1776
DECLARATION OF INDEPENDENCE

The Declaration of Independence announced the beginning of the United States of America to Great Britain and the world, justifying the colonies' decision to secede from Britain and setting forth the political philosophy of the new republic.

LOCALE: Philadelphia, Pennsylvania
CATEGORIES: Government and politics; wars, uprisings, and civil unrest

KEY FIGURES

Thomas Jefferson (1743-1826), Virginia delegate to the Continental Congress and principal author of the declaration
Richard Henry Lee (1732-1794), Virginia delegate to the Continental Congress
Thomas Paine (1737-1809), English-born colonist whose pamphlet *Common Sense* crystallized thoughts of independence
Benjamin Franklin (1706-1790), Pennsylvania delegate to the Continental Congress
John Adams (1735-1826), Massachusetts delegate to the Continental Congress

SUMMARY OF EVENT

The Declaration of Independence was the culmination of a gradual, ten-year shift by the colonies from active participants in the British Empire to rebellious advocates of a total break with the mother country. This decade of accelerating estrangement was fueled by fundamental disagreements over the Proclamation of 1763, the Sugar Act and Currency Act (1764), the Stamp Act and Quartering Act (1765), the 1766 Declaratory Act, and the 1767 Townshend Revenue Act, as well as the Boston Massacre (1770), the Tea Act and Boston Tea Party (1773), the 1774 Coercive Acts, and the 1775 Battle of Lexington and Concord.

In the opening months of 1776, the colonists faced a momentous decision. Should they content themselves with a return of British authority as it existed prior to 1763, or should they irrevocably sever all political ties with and dependence upon Great Britain? Since Great Britain was unwilling to give them that choice, offering instead only abject surrender to parliamentary sovereignty, Americans in increasing numbers concluded that complete independence, not merely autonomy within the British Empire, must be their goal.

Many of the undecided colonists were won over to defiance of the Crown as a result of Parliament's Prohibitory Act, which called for a naval blockade of the colonies, the seizure of American goods on the high seas, and the dragooning of captured provincial seamen into the Royal Navy. For many colonists, news of the British ministry's decision to employ German mercenaries for use in America was the last straw. The requirements of the struggle itself lent weight to the idea of complete separation. People would not do battle wholeheartedly for vaguely defined purposes, nor would French or Spanish aid, deemed essential to military success, be forthcoming if the colonies fought merely for a greater freedom within the empire.

In January, 1776, these colonial issues were the subject of Thomas Paine's *Common Sense*. Although it may be doubted that Paine's widely read pamphlet was the immediate impetus for the break, and although he advanced no new arguments, Paine expressed cogent and compelling arguments for a free America that would pursue its own destiny. Although Americans of almost every persuasion were already disputing the right of Parliament to rule over the colonies, there remained among the colonists a strong attachment to the British crown and to King George III. Monarchy in general, and the Hanoverian king in particular, received a scathing denunciation

Signing the Declaration of Independence. (Francis R. Niglutsch)

from Paine, who asserted that kings were frauds imposed upon people capable of governing themselves. George III, Paine reasoned, was no exception and had engaged in oppressive acts that had destroyed every claim upon American loyalties. Paine held that the break should come immediately, while Americans were in arms and sensitive to their liberties. Independence, he argued, was inevitable for a wealthy, expanding continent that could not long be tied to a small and distant island controlled by "a Royal Brute."

One by one, the Southern and New England colonial assemblies authorized their delegates to the Continental Congress, meeting in Philadelphia, to vote for independence. On June 7, 1776, Richard Henry Lee, obeying instructions from Virginia, introduced at the congress a resolution declaring the colonies independent. Temporarily, the Middle Colonies hesitated to make such a drastic decision, causing a delay in acting on the matter; but on July 2, with only New York abstaining, the vote was twelve to nothing in favor of Lee's resolution declaring that "the United colonies are, and of right ought to be, free and independent States."

Anticipating this outcome, the congress had earlier formed a committee, composed of Thomas Jefferson, John Adams, Benjamin Franklin, Robert R. Livingston, and Roger Sherman, to prepare a statement concerning independence. The now famous document was drafted by Jefferson with some assistance from Adams and Franklin. Congress, after first making some revisions, such as deleting Jefferson's passage denouncing the king for not ending the slave trade, adopted it on July 4.

The purpose of the Declaration of Independence was not to change the legal status of America; on July 2, the Continental Congress had voted to sever the colonies from the British Empire. The intent of Jefferson and his colleagues was rather to explain and justify the action of the congress in terms meaningful to Americans and Europeans alike. In doing so, Jefferson drew heavily upon Enlightenment thought. Besides a preface and a conclusion, the Declaration of Independence consists of a statement of the right of revolution based upon the philosophy of natural rights, a list of grievances against the king, and an account of the colonists' inability to obtain redress of grievances within the structure of the British Empire.

Some modern scholars consider the barrage of accusations heaped upon the king to be lacking in dignity and significance in relation to the rest of the document. They point out that George III was a strict constitutionalist whose conduct in the political arena was in accord with the practices and traditions of the earlier Hanoverian monarchs. Moreover, most of the programs and policies held to be reprehensible by the colonists hardly originated in the mind of the king. Still, George III favored a rigid policy of government, and he consistently turned a deaf ear to the remonstrances of the American assemblies and congresses. To counter the public mood of the times, it was essential for Jefferson to lay America's troubles at the feet of the king. Since the time of the First Continental Congress in 1774, patriot leaders had denied that there was any legitimate parliamentary authority to cast off; it was only the lingering loyalty to the Crown that held many colonists to the empire, and the portions of the declaration dealing with George III's performance as king were designed to undo that loyalty.

SIGNIFICANCE

The enduring significance of the Declaration of Independence transcends the British-American conflict. The statement that "all men are created equal"—that they have certain unalienable rights under God that governments may not destroy—not only inspired people at the time but also has moved people in the United States and elsewhere ever since. The phrase, applied narrowly at first, came to be the focus of debate as women, people of color, the young, and the poor—excluded de facto from the document's guarantees—began to fight for full equality. Women were denied the right to vote in federal elections until ratification of the Nineteenth Amendment in 1920; African American men received this right in the Fifteenth Amendment, ratified in 1870; persons between eighteen and twenty-one years of age were given the right to vote by the Twenty-sixth Amendment in 1970.

Rights and liberties other than voting—due process of law, fair housing and public accommodations, equal opportunity in employment and college admissions—have all been fought for and gradually won by groups previously discriminated against. The force that sparked the emergence of this powerful movement was the burning desire of the supporters of the Declaration of Independence to be free to shape their own destiny. The message they conveyed has left a lasting imprint on the conscience of the world.

—*R. Don Higginbotham,*
updated by Joseph Edward Lee

FURTHER READING

Bailyn, Bernard. *The Ideological Origins of the American Revolution.* Cambridge, Mass.: Belknap Press,

---

DECLARATION OF INDEPENDENCE

The Declaration of Independence is remarkable for being at once a work of theoretical political philosophy and an eminently practical document that announced and brought about the independence of the American colonies from Great Britain. The first two paragraphs, excerpted here, establish the theoretical foundation for the practical act that follows.

When in the Course of human events, it becomes necessary for one people to dissolve the political bands which have connected them with another, and to assume among the powers of the earth, the separate and equal station to which the Laws of Nature and of Nature's God entitle them, a decent respect to the opinions of mankind requires that they should declare the causes which impel them to the separation.

We hold these truths to be self-evident, that all men are created equal, that they are endowed by their Creator with certain unalienable Rights, that among these are Life, Liberty and the pursuit of Happiness.—That to secure these rights, Governments are instituted among Men, deriving their just powers from the consent of the governed, —That whenever any Form of Government becomes destructive of these ends, it is the Right of the People to alter or to abolish it, and to institute new Government, laying its foundation on such principles and organizing its powers in such form, as to them shall seem most likely to effect their Safety and Happiness. Prudence, indeed, will dictate that Governments long established should not be changed for light and transient causes; and accordingly all experience hath shewn, that mankind are more disposed to suffer, while evils are sufferable, than to right themselves by abolishing the forms to which they are accustomed. But when a long train of abuses and usurpations, pursuing invariably the same Object evinces a design to reduce them under absolute Despotism, it is their right, it is their duty, to throw off such Government, and to provide new Guards for their future security.—Such has been the patient sufferance of these Colonies; and such is now the necessity which constrains them to alter their former Systems of Government.

Source: Declaration of Independence. The National Archives Experience, National Archives and Records Administration. http://www.archives.gov/national-archives-experience/charters/declaration_transcript.html. Accessed November 15, 2005.

1967. An intellectual history of the revolution based on a close reading of the ideas that found their way into the era's pamphlets.

Becker, Carl L. *The Declaration of Independence: A Study in the History of Political Ideas*. 2d ed. New York: Harcourt, Brace, & World, 1951. The classic study of the power of the ideas embodied in the document.

Gerber, Scott Douglas, ed. *The Declaration of Independence: Origins and Impact*. Washington, D.C.: CQ Press, 2002. Contains primary documents and twelve essays about the declaration, including essays describing the document's drafting; its political theory; its relation to the Articles of Confederation, Constitution, and Bill of Rights; and its reception.

Maier, Pauline. *American Scripture: Making the Declaration of Independence*. New York: Random House, 1997. Examines the evolution of the Declaration of Independence, placing it within the context of similar British and state documents, describing its drafting and editing, and exploring how the document has been redefined over the years.

Middlekauf, Robert. *The Glorious Cause: The American Revolution, 1763-1789*. New York: Oxford University Press, 1982. A comprehensive history of the revolution.

Norton, Mary Beth. *Liberty's Daughters: The Revolutionary Experience of American Women, 1750-1800*. Boston: Little, Brown, 1980. A pioneering study of women's contributions to the revolution.

Wills, Garry. *Inventing America: Jefferson's Declaration of Independence*. Garden City, N.Y.: Doubleday, 1978. Links Jefferson to the ideas argued by the Scottish Enlightenment figures.

Wood, Gordon S. *The Radicalism of the American Revolution*. New York: Alfred A. Knopf, 1992. Asserts that the move toward independence was radical in nature.

SEE ALSO: Oct. 7, 1763: Proclamation of 1763; Mar. 22, 1765-Mar. 18, 1766: Stamp Act Crisis; June 29, 1767-Apr. 12, 1770: Townshend Crisis; Mar. 5, 1770: Boston Massacre; Dec. 16, 1773: Boston Tea Party; Apr. 27-Oct. 10, 1774: Lord Dunmore's War; Sept. 5-Oct. 26, 1774: First Continental Congress; Apr. 19, 1775: Battle of Lexington and Concord; May 10-Aug. 2, 1775: Second Continental Congress; Jan. 10, 1776: Paine Publishes *Common Sense*; May, 1776-Sept. 3, 1783: France Supports the American Revolution; May 24 and June 11, 1776: Indian Delegation Meets with Congress; July 2, 1776: New Jersey Women Gain the Vote; Aug. 6, 1777: Battle of Oriskany Creek; Sept. 19-Oct. 17, 1777: Battles of Saratoga; Mar. 1, 1781: Ratification of the Articles of Confederation; Oct. 19, 1781: Cornwallis Surrenders at Yorktown; Sept. 3, 1783: Treaty of Paris; Sept. 17, 1787: U.S. Constitution Is Adopted; Oct. 27, 1787-May, 1788: Publication of *The Federalist*.

RELATED ARTICLES in *Great Lives from History: The Eighteenth Century, 1701-1800*: Abigail Adams; John Adams; Benjamin Franklin; George III; Thomas Jefferson; Thomas Paine.

September 6-7, 1776
FIRST TEST OF A SUBMARINE IN WARFARE

The first submarine, called the Turtle, *was built in an effort to blow up a British navy ship in the waters of New York Harbor by attaching underwater explosives to the ship's hull. The test marked not only the first submarine journey but also the first time such a vessel, and underwater explosives, had been used in warfare.*

LOCALE: New York
CATEGORIES: Science and technology; wars, uprisings, and civil unrest

KEY FIGURES
David Bushnell (1742-1824), inventor of the first submarine

Ezra Bushnell (fl. late eighteenth century), David's brother, who assisted him in building the submarine
Ezra Lee (fl. late eighteenth century), sergeant who piloted history's first combat submarine attack
Israel Putnam (1718-1790), a major general of the Continental army, who secured government financing for Bushnell's endeavor
Jonathan Trumbull (1710-1785), governor of Connecticut, 1769-1783, who supported Bushnell

SUMMARY OF EVENT
David Bushnell was known throughout his native Connecticut for his inventive mind. While on his father's farm, he had developed a harrow with flexible teeth,

which farmers could use in the stony New England fields without the teeth breaking constantly. As a student at Yale College, he became interested in exploding kegs of black powder under water. Traditional theories of the time held that such an explosion would not work, because the water would dissipate its force. Through experiments, Bushnell proved that this theory was wrong and developed the forerunner of the naval mine.

With the onset of the American Revolution, Bushnell decided that his mine would be useful against the blockading British fleet, but he needed an accurate method of placing his explosives under a ship's keel without being seen by naval gunners. His solution was a submarine vessel he called the *Turtle*, which he designed early in 1775 while a student at Yale. During the college's spring vacation that year, Bushnell went home to Saybrook, Connecticut, where he and his brother Ezra spent more than a month constructing the world's first submarine. They built no model; the *Turtle* was built full-sized from the start.

According to its inventor, the submarine "bore some resemblance to two upper tortoise shells of equal size joined together." The boat was 7.5 feet long, 4 feet wide, and 8 feet deep. Made of carefully fitted oak timbers caulked with cork and tar, Bushnell's craft was driven by a screw propeller, the first one ever used to power a ship. The contraption included a short, primitive "snorkel," through which the navigator could obtain fresh air. The tube was equipped with valves that automatically closed when the submarine submerged to greater depths. The operator navigated the vessel by looking through a glass conning tower and by checking his compass and depth gauge, which were illuminated by fox fire.

Although many accounts of David Bushnell and his *Turtle* do not indicate that he piloted the vessel, Robert F. Burgess in *Ships Beneath the Sea* (1975) reveals that he did. Once Bushnell graduated from Yale in June, 1775, he returned to Saybrook to make some adjustments to the boat. The maiden voyage of the *Turtle* took place in Long Island Sound, where Bushnell stayed submerged for a rather uneventful forty-five minutes. He nearly fainted, however, and based on this initial experience, realized he was not physically capable of piloting the submarine for extended periods. From then on, his brother Ezra practiced maneuvering the *Turtle* in the sound and prepared for its ultimate mission.

In subsequent months, several devices were added to assist in navigation, including a compass and a barometer. At this point, Benjamin Gale, a family friend of the Bushnells, brought Benjamin Franklin to see the *Turtle*.

Franklin encouraged Bushnell to take his vessel to New York, where the British fleet had set up a blockade. Franklin then told General George Washington about the submarine. Washington was doubtful, however, about the boat's potential in his endeavors.

Through the influence of Governor Jonathan Trumbull of Connecticut in late 1775, Bushnell demonstrated the *Turtle* for Major General Israel Putnam of the new Continental army. Putnam was impressed and secured government financing for further development of the submarine. The army wanted to use the submersible to break the British blockade of Boston, but the British squadron departed before Bushnell could fully assemble the ballast pumps.

The next opportunity to strike at the British fleet was in 1776 in New York City. The *Turtle* was hauled overland and launched into the harbor from Manhattan Island. Ezra Bushnell was to have navigated the submarine in its first real combat mission; he was well prepared after a year's training in the sound. Unfortunately, he became seriously ill with a fever and had to be hospitalized for several weeks. The mission could not wait. General Putnam provided three volunteers, whom Bushnell trained to navigate the vessel. It was twenty-seven-year-old sergeant Ezra Lee who proved to be the most capable replacement.

Just after midnight on the night of September 6, 1776, Lee slipped into the *Turtle* and, after two hours of tediously maneuvering the boat with hand cranks, guided it under the sixty-four-gun HMS *Eagle*, the British flagship. Lee was supposed to attach an explosive charge to the flagship by screwing it to the hull. Some historians speculate that Lee might have hit an iron bar connecting a part of the rudder to the stern, because each time he attempted to twist the bit into the metal of the ship, it would not engage. The hull of the *Eagle* was sheathed in copper, but Bushnell had anticipated this and had made the auger strong enough to penetrate the weaker metal. While Lee tried to maneuver the submarine to another spot on the hull, the *Turtle* rose to the surface in broad daylight.

At the mercy of the tide and without the aid of a compass—which, for some reason, was not working—Lee remained four miles from safety. Although he submerged every few minutes, he finally had to remain on the surface to see his way. Lee's craft was spotted by English sentries on Governor's Island, and the sentries quickly launched their own boat in a chase. Lee reported that the sailors came within fifty yards of the *Turtle* but were frightened of what they saw and turned away. Lee released the keg of powder, which drifted harmlessly into the bay and later exploded. Heading back to New York Harbor, Lee was spotted by his own people and towed to shore by a whaleboat.

Lee made several other attempts to destroy British ships in New York Harbor, but all were unsuccessful. When the British advanced up the Hudson River in October, 1776, Bushnell placed his invention aboard a small sloop. A British warship sank the sloop as it fled up the river in an effort to avoid capture. Although Bushnell reportedly recovered his submarine from the depths, its actual fate remains unknown. After the loss of the *Turtle*, Governor Trumbull had Bushnell commissioned as an officer in the Sappers and Miners Corps of the Continental army, and Bushnell served during the remainder of the war as a demolition expert. After the American Revolution, the reticent inventor moved to Georgia, where he practiced medicine and taught school. He died in obscurity in 1824.

SIGNIFICANCE

Although David Bushnell's submarine failed to sink any enemy vessels, he was responsible for several notable achievements. He invented the first practical submarine. In so doing, he solved several basic engineering and nautical problems: constructing a watertight and pressure-proof hull with vertical and horizontal propulsion mechanisms, achieving vertical stability and steering control, and developing the means of using variable ballast systems. Furthermore, he was the first to prove that gunpowder could explode underwater with sufficient force to disable and sink a surface ship, and he developed floating and submerged mines. Bushnell's inventions were rapidly improved upon by other American inventors who continued to develop the submarine for use in subsequent U.S. naval conflicts.

—*William L. Richter, updated by Liesel Ashley Miller*

FURTHER READING

Abbot, Henry L. *Beginning of Modern Submarine Warfare Under Captain Lieutenant David Bushnell*. Edited by Frank Anderson. Hamden, Conn.: Archon Books, 1966. A facsimile reproduction of an 1881 pamphlet containing the earliest accounts and descriptions of the *Turtle*, Bushnell, and Sergeant Ezra Lee. Includes biographical appendices and a bibliography by the editor.

Burgess, Robert Forrest. "The *Eagle* and the *Turtle*." In *Ships Beneath the Sea: A History of Subs and Submersibles*. New York: McGraw-Hill, 1975. A superior description of Bushnell, his design, and the construction of the *Turtle*. One of the most thorough accounts of the events surrounding the first combat submarine attack.

Coggins, Jack. *Ships and Seamen of the American Revolution*. Harrisburg, Pa.: Stackpole Books, 1969. A colorful, well-illustrated book on virtually all aspects of the numerous naval engagements of the Revolutionary War.

Gunton, Michael. *Submarines at War: A History of Undersea Warfare from the American Revolution to the Cold War*. New York: Carroll & Graf, 2003. Focuses on the use of submarines during World War I and subsequent wars. The first chapter provides information about the development of the submarine, with a brief description of Bushnell and the *Turtle*.

Hoyt, Edwin P. *Submarines at War: The History of the American Silent Service*. Briarcliff Manor, N.Y.: Stein & Day, 1983. Commencing with the unsuccessful attack of Bushnell's *Turtle* on the British Royal Navy, this work chronicles the development of American submarines and submarine warfare into the 1980's.

Hutchinson, Robert. *Jane's Submarines: War Beneath the Waves from 1776 to the Present Day*. London: HarperCollins, 2001. Traces the development of the submarine as a weapon of warfare from its earliest designs in the sixteenth century through 2000. Includes information about Bushnell's *Turtle*.

Macintyre, Donald G. F. W. "The Pioneers." In *Fighting Under the Sea*. New York: W. W. Norton, 1966. One of the most complete accounts of the *Turtle*'s attempt to sink the English warship *Eagle*. Proves details of Ezra Lee's efforts, using Lee's own words.

Parrish, Thomas. *The Submarine: A History*. New York: Viking, 2004. This history begins with a description of Bushnell's *Turtle* and continues through the year 2000. Includes information on submarine technology and combat operations.

Perlmutter, Tom, ed. *War Machines: Sea*. London: Octopus Books, 1975. Contains one of the few detailed diagrams of the *Turtle*.

Van der Vat, Dan. *Stealth at Sea: The History of the Submarine*. Boston: Houghton Mifflin, 1995. An invaluable reference source on the history of submarines and submarine warfare. Illustrations, bibliography, and index.

January 1, 1777
FRANCE'S FIRST DAILY NEWSPAPER APPEARS

The Journal de Paris, *France's first daily newspaper, was launched on January 1, 1777, and remained in print for sixty-three years. Its pages offered concise information on developments in local and national politics, administrative and police matters, science, health, fashion, art, music, dance, and literature.*

LOCALE: Paris, France
CATEGORY: Communications

KEY FIGURES

Guillaume Olivier de Corancez (1734-1810), French
  journalist
Jean de Romilly (1714-1796), Swiss watchmaker and
  journalist
Antoine-Alexis Cadet de Vaux (1743-1828), French
  pharmacist and journalist
Louis d'Ussieux (1744-1805), French writer and
  journalist
Jean-Baptiste-Antoine Suard (1732-1817), French
  journalist and royal censor
Jean-Michel Xhrouet (fl. late eighteenth century),
  French journalist

SUMMARY OF EVENT

The expansion of journalism in prerevolutionary France was slower than in most other major European nations during the same period. The highly centralized French government granted monopolies on the dissemination of local, national, and foreign news to a limited number of presses. Domestic nondaily newspapers such as the *Gazette* (pb. 1631-1792), the *Journal des savants* (pb. 1665-1792; journal of scholars), and *Mercure galant* (pb. 1672-1710; gallant Mercury) all held monopolies but were closely monitored by an obedient caste of royal censors and had to compete with independent newspapers published abroad. Studies point to the decades after 1750 as a period of significant growth in the French press, when an increasing number of available journals found their way into the hands of an increasing number of literate and interested readers. The nation's earliest daily newspaper, the *Journal de Paris* (pb. 1777-1840; Paris journal), was founded well after the establishment of daily newspapers in Germany and England.

Official permission to publish and distribute the *Journal de Paris* as a daily periodical was granted on September 11, 1776. Its first issue appeared on January 1, 1777. From 1777 to 1782, the advertised annual subscription price was fixed at £24 for Paris and £31, 4 shillings for the provinces—about what a skilled laborer in the Paris region might earn in two weeks. In 1782, the newspaper absorbed into its pages the well-established *Necrologe des hommes célèbres* (pb. 1767-1782; necrology of famous men) and raised its price accordingly to £30 for Paris and £33 for the provinces. In its first year of publication, the journal reached more than 2,500 subscribers, and it had as many as 5,000 subscribers in 1782. Reportedly, more than 12,000 readers subscribed in 1791, but their numbers declined dramatically as the new millennium drew closer and as competition between journals increased.

The *Journal de Paris* was founded by four men of bourgeois origins: Guillaume Olivier de Corancez, Jean de Romilly, Antoine-Alexis Cadet de Vaux, and Louis d'Ussieux. As a journalist, Corancez specialized in literary criticism. Coproprietor of the newspaper from 1777 to 1799, he frequented the salons of Parisian aristocracy and enjoyed friendly commerce with Jean-Jacques Rousseau and the French poet Jean-Antoine Roucher. He wrote a series of articles on Rousseau for the *Journal de Paris*, which later appeared as a monograph titled *De J. J. Rousseau* (1788; *Anecdotes of the Last Twelve Years of the Life of J. J. Rousseau*, 1798).

Corancez's father-in-law and the cofounder and coproprietor of the newspaper, de Romilly, was a famous watchmaker from Geneva, Switzerland, who had contributed articles on clocks and clock making to Denis Diderot's *Encyclopédie: Ou, Dictionnaire raisonné des sciences, des arts, et des métiers* (1751-1772; partial translation *Selected Essays from the Encyclopedy*, 1772; complete translation *Encyclopedia*, 1965). He took charge of the newspaper's meteorological reports from 1777 to 1799. The newspaper's third cofounder, Cadet de Vaux, was a pharmacist and chemist close to the Parisian milieu of freemasons and was probably responsible for a good portion of the newspaper's coverage of scientific news. Moreover, his friendly ties to the lieutenant-general of police, Jean Charles Pierre Le Noir (1732-1807), gave him convenient access to newsworthy items through government agencies.

The newspaper's fourth cofounder, d'Ussieux, wrote articles on the various theatrical arts from 1777 to at least 1786. In 1786, he sold his share in the newspaper to Jean-Michel Xhrouet, who then assumed its management until 1991. Historians remember d'Ussieux as the author of

1770's

popular historical novellas and translator of literary works from German and Italian into French. Like his colleague Cadet de Vaux, he was closely linked to the intellectual circles of the Parisian freemasons.

From its inception, the *Journal de Paris* was a conservative newspaper intended for the general literate public. Each issue consisted of four in-quarto pages (not counting the inclusion of occasional supplements); after 1777, pagination was consecutive, so at year's end, all pages could be bound together as a book. Columns in the newspaper covered such topics as weather, events in the arts and sciences, new publications, administrative announcements of various sorts, community service announcements, advertisements, theater, fashion, clever anecdotes, commodity prices, exchange rates, lottery results, and a regular necrology.

The newspaper published letters to the editors and miscellaneous pieces written by celebrated individuals, such as the American envoy to France, Benjamin Franklin; French chemist Antoine-Laurent Lavoisier; and German physician Franz Anton Mesmer. Illustrations were too expensive to reproduce, however, and only a handful were included in the journal's pages, such as a depiction of women's hair fashion (February 20, 1777), a likeness of Rousseau (January 1, 1780), surgical instrument designs (October 27, 1782), and a drawing of a hot-air balloon (September 19, 1783). Excerpts from musical scores were frequently included as part of an ongoing discussion of the era's leading operatic performances in the French capital.

Journalists associated with the newspaper discreetly endorsed Enlightenment ideals but, for the most part, limited their discussion of controversial topics to art, music, literature, and science. Their writing style was simple; their coverage of politics was limited and cautious. Jean-Baptiste-Antoine Suard, a royal censor and writer for the journal, ensured that offensive material seldom made its way into print. A substantial amount of the newspaper's information came from local administrative sources in Paris and Versailles. Such news tended to support the monarchy by projecting a positive view of the Catholic Church and the government. The editorial staff's compliant sense of journalism, at least during its early years, was perhaps best expressed in the following description of *le bon ton* (the proper tone) reproduced in its pages:

> The proper tone, is the tone of high society. It is better felt than defined. It requires a flair for noble sentiment, an adherence to polite expression, decency of conduct, decorum in all matters, a manner of reporting which confounds neither ranks, titles, estates nor individuals.

Adherence to the dictates of *bon ton* helped ensure the newspaper's survival, not only under the Old Regime's strict censorship laws but also during the chaotic years of the French Revolution and beyond.

SIGNIFICANCE

One of the express goals of the *Journal de Paris* was to serve as an instrument of the Enlightenment. Its founders and contributing writers used the journal's pages to promote discussion of art, science, and literature. However, as a government-sanctioned periodical in a tightly controlled industry, the newspaper also served as an organ of the Old Regime monarchy, diffusing official announcements while advocating conservative social and political reforms. Closely monitored by censors, it avoided sensitive political, philosophical, and religious issues. Its general coverage of politics and societal conditions, nonetheless, helped bring policy-making out of the secretive chambers of government ministries and into the arena of public opinion, thus contributing to the notion of accountability in government.

"BELLES-LETTRES"

The Journal de Paris *regularly published commentary upon the state of contemporary French thought. A representative passage, produced here, commented on moral philosophy and the need for vibrant new ideas.*

A crowd of Authors has published some detached thoughts, but most of them have done nothing but add to the glory of *la Bruyere* and *la Rochefoucauld*, and in the present century, we know almost no point in the Works of this genre that has preserved its reputation. It seems that one is more demanding of consideration from those who practice it. If one dispenses with them for tracing a plan and reading their ideas in their transitions, one wants the majority of these ideas to contain either new views or novel combinations, or, at the very least, they should be presented in a delicate and provoking manner. In a word, we can no longer pardon a Morality for being erected upon tired old truths. It is all we can do to allow them to pass to some Philosophers of antiquity. In that case, the truths would not be so old.

Source: "Belles-Letters." *Journal de Paris* no. 31 (January 31, 1783). Translation by Andy Perry.

Sections of the newspaper containing letters to the editors as well as community service announcements provided a convenient forum for public expression and encouraged involvement among the middle and upper bourgeoisie in matters of local governance. In addition to being France's first daily newspaper—a model and testing ground for future journalism—the *Journal de Paris* was also the first major news source to embrace paid advertising. Scholars of French history now look to early newspapers such as the *Gazette*, the *Journal des savants*, the *Mercure galant*, and *Journal de Paris* as precious mirrors of the science and mores of prerevolutionary France.

—*Jan Pendergrass*

FURTHER READING

Censer, Jack Richard. *The French Press in the Age of Enlightenment*. New York: Routledge, 1994. A comprehensive study of eighteenth century journalism.

Darnton, Robert, and Daniel Roche, eds. *Revolution in Print: The Press in France, 1775-1800*. Berkeley: University of California Press, 1989. A collection of articles by specialists in the history of eighteenth century print culture.

Feyel, Gilles. *L'Annonce et la nouvelle: La Presse d'information en France sous l'ancien régime, 1630-1788*. Oxford, England: Voltaire Foundation, 2000. An in-depth look at prerevolutionary journalism. In French.

Harris, Bob. *Politics and the Rise of the Press: Britain and France, 1620-1800*. New York: Routledge, 1996. Chapter 3 concentrates on the development of prerevolutionary journalism in France.

Sgard, Jean, ed. *Dictionnaire des journalistes, 1600-1789*. 2 vols. Oxford, England: Voltaire Foundation, 1999. Articles on the major French journalists of the prerevolutionary era, including Corancez, Romilly, Cadet de Vaux, d'Ussieux, and Suard. In French.

_____. *Dictionnaire des journaux, 1600-1789*. Vol. 1. Paris: Universitas, 1991. Articles on 1,267 French-language periodicals of the prerevolutionary era, including the *Journal de Paris*. In French.

Thogmartin, Clyde. *The National Daily Press of France*. Birmingham, Ala.: Summa, 1998. A survey of French journalism from the early seventeenth century to the present.

SEE ALSO: Mar. 1, 1711: Addison and Steele Establish *The Spectator*; 1736: *Gentleman's Magazine* Initiates Parliamentary Reporting; Mar. 20, 1750-Mar. 14, 1752: Johnson Issues *The Rambler*; Sept. 10, 1763: Publication of the *Freeman's Journal*; 1774: Hansard Begins Reporting Parliamentary Debates; Jan. 4, 1792-1797: The *Northern Star* Calls for Irish Independence.

RELATED ARTICLES in *Great Lives from History: The Eighteenth Century, 1701-1800*: Benjamin Franklin; Antoine-Laurent Lavoisier; Jean-Jacques Rousseau.

1770's

July 2, 1777-1804
NORTHEAST STATES ABOLISH SLAVERY

Eight northeastern states emancipated their slaves and ended slavery during and in the wake of the American Revolution. Most of the states chose to phase out slavery gradually, and the slave population of the North decreased during the next few decades until abolition was accomplished.

LOCALE: Northeastern United States
CATEGORIES: Laws, acts, and legal history; social issues and reform

KEY FIGURES

Moses Brown (1738-1836), Rhode Island abolitionist
Aaron Burr (1756-1836), United States senator, 1791-1797, and leader of the fight against slavery in New York
Caleb Cushing (1800-1879), Massachusetts judge who ruled that slavery was illegal
Quork Walker (fl. 1781-1783), Massachusetts slave who successfully sued for freedom

SUMMARY OF EVENT

In 1775, Pennsylvania's Provincial Congress called for an end to the importation of slaves and the gradual emancipation of all slaves in the colony. Two years later, on July 2, 1777, Vermont became the first state to abolish slavery fully. Its 1777 Constitution outlawed "holding anyone by law to serve any person" as a servant, slave, or apprentice after he or she reached twenty-one years of age.

Despite the earlier call of its Provincial Congress, Pennsylvania waited until 1780 to pass a law gradually ending the slave system, because some leaders argued that abolishing slavery during the Revolutionary War would divide the colonies and hamper the war effort: Any radical attack against human bondage would antagonize the South, where slavery was a deeply embedded institution. Pennsylvania, like the other Northern states, had allowed slavery since its beginning as a colony, but slaves had never become an important part of the workforce there. In 1780, only 3,761 of Pennsylvania's 435,150 inhabitants were slaves, and most of them were household servants. White workers argued successfully that free labor cost less than slavery, because slave masters had to take care of their slaves even if they were not working.

Pennsylvania's 1780 law called for a gradual end to slavery. Property rights were respected, and children born slaves in 1780 would remain in service to their owners until they were twenty-eight years of age. This length of service was to compensate masters for the cost of raising slave children. The law required owners to register their slaves by the end of the year. Any African Americans not registered would be freed immediately. The law also ended years of discrimination against people of color: They could now testify against Caucasians in courts, the separate courts established for them were abolished, and interracial marriage became legal. Pennsylvania became the only Northern state to provide for this kind of equality. Conservatives, who could not accept the idea of equality for African Americans, resisted all these measures and successfully defeated a proposal granting freed slaves the right to vote.

Massachusetts acted slowly on the slavery question. In 1777, opponents defeated a gradual emancipation bill, arguing as they had in Pennsylvania that such a bill would divide the new nation by antagonizing the South. Three years later, voters turned down a new constitution that declared all men free and equal and provided voting rights for free blacks. In 1781, however, a slave named Quork Walker sued for his freedom in a state court because his owner had severely abused him. The trial judge, Caleb Cushing, instructed the jury that the idea of slavery conflicted with state law, so Walker was ordered freed. Although the legislature refused to act, by 1790, as a result of similar court actions in dozens of other cases, slavery no longer existed in Massachusetts.

More than six hundred slaves lived in New Hampshire prior to the American Revolution. During the war, the state legislature granted freedom to any slave who volunteered for the militia. Other slaves gained their liberty by running away and joining the British military, which also promised freedom to slaves who fought with them. Thus, when the state's 1783 constitution declared all men equal and independent from birth, only fifty slaves remained the property of masters in New Hampshire. Although slavery was never abolished legally, slave property was removed from tax rolls in 1789, and eleven years later only eight slaves remained in the state.

Rhode Island acted in 1783, after Moses Brown and five other Quakers petitioned its assembly for the immediate liberation of all human beings kept as property. The cautious legislators passed a gradual emancipation bill instead. Under its provisions, all slave children born after March 1 would be apprentices. Girls became free at the age of eighteen years, while boys could be kept until they reached twenty-one years of age. Until then, the apprentices would get food and economic support from the towns in which they lived. After slaves were freed, their masters were required to post bonds with the state guaranteeing that the former slaves would never require public assistance.

Connecticut, the New England state with the largest population of African Americans, granted freedom to slaves who fought against England, but three times—in 1777, 1779, and 1780—the legislature rejected gradual emancipation. Some lawmakers feared a race riot if blacks were freed. In 1784, however, the legislature finally declared an end to slavery. The law declared that African American and mulatto (mixed-race) children would become free at twenty-five years of age. Persons being held as slaves at the time would be freed by the end of the year. At the same time, discriminatory colonial laws similar to those found in Massachusetts became part of the state legal code. Free people of color could not vote, could not serve on juries, and could not marry Caucasians. African Americans were free but not equal.

New York and New Jersey were the last Northern states to act on the slavery question. Both of these states freed African Americans who served in the army, but opponents of emancipation warned against doing anything more, so as to respect property rights. Some opponents used openly racist arguments, saying that free blacks would not work unless forced to do so. They argued that blacks were lazy, ignorant, and criminal, and that slavery protected whites from an onslaught of savagery. New York's legislature rejected gradual emancipation in 1777. Eight years later, a freedom bill supported by the New York Manumission Society, whose membership included Alexander Hamilton, John Jay, and Aaron Burr, went down to defeat. Although proposals to discriminate legally against blacks failed, the legislature did agree to deny African Americans the right to vote.

In 1785, New York prohibited the sale and importation of slaves and allowed masters to manumit (free) their slaves, but only if they guaranteed that they would not require public assistance. The next year, New Jersey passed similar laws. In 1788, New York declared that slaves would no longer be judged or punished under standards different from those used to judge whites.

Still, freedom did not come. In the 1790's, the New York Manumission Society fought a constant war against the slave system. It sent petitions with thousands of signatures to the state legislature. The Society for Promoting the Abolition of Slavery in New Jersey conducted a similar campaign. In both states, antislavery groups organized boycotts of businesses that had any connection with slavery, such as newspapers that advertised slave auctions and companies that built slave ships. Auctions of slaves ended in both states by 1790. Only in 1799, however, did New York pass an emancipation bill. Owners could free their slaves regardless of age or condition, although children could still be kept as property—boys until twenty-eight years of age and girls until the age of twenty-five. In 1804, New Jersey became the last of the original Northern states to end slavery legally. Neither New York nor New Jersey allowed free African Americans to vote.

SIGNIFICANCE

The 1810 census found that the five New England states—Vermont, New Hampshire, Massachusetts, Connecticut, and Rhode Island—had 418 slaves out of an African American population totaling more than 20,000. New York and New Jersey, on the other hand, had nearly 18,000 slaves, because their laws provided longer time periods for emancipating children and were passed much later. Pennsylvania, the first state to provide for gradual emancipation, had fewer than 50 slaves.

Thus, despite racist attitudes and the desire of many legislators to protect property rights, slavery was close to an end in the North by the second decade of the nineteenth century. It would take a bloody civil war to end slavery in the South fifty years later. Emancipation in the North did not mean equality for African Americans, however. Laws discriminating against free people of color were passed, usually alongside or shortly after bills calling for the end of slavery. Prejudice remained high in Northern states, although they had very small African American populations—less than 1 percent in most cities and towns. Efforts to end slavery did not eliminate racism and belief in white supremacy.

—*Leslie V. Tischauser*

FURTHER READING

Horton, James Oliver, and Lois E. Horton. *In Hope of Liberty: Culture, Community, and Protest Among Northern Free Blacks, 1700-1860*. New York: Oxford University Press, 1997. A study of the first free African Americans, tracing their lives from the colonial slave trade through the antebellum era. Includes information about the American Revolution and the abolition of northern slavery. Features biographical sketches and describes how the freed Northern blacks struggled to assimilate yet maintain a unique cultural identity.

Litwack, Leon F. *North of Slavery: The Negro in the Free States, 1790-1860*. Chicago: University of Chicago Press, 1961. Describes prejudice against African Americans in the Northeast, but points out that free blacks, despite second-class status in the North, were at least free and not someone's property.

Nash, Gary B., and Jean R. Soderlund. *Freedom by Degrees: Emancipation in Pennsylvania and Its Aftermath*. New York: Oxford University Press, 1991. Describes the movement toward gradual freedom for slaves; discusses the racism underlying opposition to complete abolition.

Newman, Richard S. *The Transformation of American Abolition: Fighting Slavery in the Early Republic*. Chapel Hill: University of North Carolina Press, 2002. History of the American abolition movement from the 1770's through the 1830's. Focuses on antislavery activities in Pennsylvania and Massachusetts.

White, Shane. *Somewhat More Independent: The End of Slavery in New York City, 1770-1810*. Athens: University of Georgia Press, 1991. Demonstrates that freedom did not lead to equality.

Zilversmit, Arthur. *The First Emancipation: The Abolition of Slavery in the North*. Chicago: University of Chicago Press, 1967. An excellent general survey, which provides a state-by-state account of the movement toward abolition. Describes supporters and opponents of abolition.

SEE ALSO: 18th cent.: Expansion of the Atlantic Slave Trade; Apr. 6, 1712: New York City Slave Revolt; Nov. 23, 1733: Slaves Capture St. John's Island; Sept. 9, 1739: Stono Rebellion; 1760-1776: Caribbean Slave Rebellions; Apr. 14, 1775: Pennsylvania Society for the Abolition of Slavery Is Founded; July 4, 1776: Declaration of Independence; Mar. 16, 1792: Denmark Abolishes the Slave Trade; Feb. 12, 1793: First Fugitive Slave Law.

RELATED ARTICLES in *Great Lives from History: The Eighteenth Century, 1701-1800*: Olaudah Equiano; Alexander Hamilton; John Jay.

1770's

August 6, 1777
BATTLE OF ORISKANY CREEK

At Oriskany Creek, American troops coming to break Britain's siege of Fort Schuyler were ambushed by a force of Native Americans and Tories. Although ultimately forced to retreat, the Americans inflicted heavy casualties on the Iroquois, weakening their resolve and laying the groundwork for a British retreat from Benedict Arnold's reinforcements.

LOCALE: Oriskany Creek, New York
CATEGORY: Wars, uprisings, and civil unrest

KEY FIGURES

Nicholas Herkimer (1728-1777), general in the
    American militia
Joseph Brant (Thayendanegea; 1742-1807), Mohawk
    chief and commander of Iroquois and Tory forces
    allied with the British
Barry St. Leger (1737-1789), British military
    commander
John Burgoyne (1722-1792), British general
Horatio Gates (c. 1728-1806), American military
    commander

SUMMARY OF EVENT

The strategy of the British for suppressing the rebellion in their American colonies during 1776 and 1777 was twofold: They sought to defeat George Washington's rebel army and to invade through New York State to cut the colonies in two. If they succeeded in their strategy, the British would cut off New England, the center of the rebellion, allowing for its conquest and occupation by British troops. The remaining colonies, bereft of leadership, would fall under British control.

In the summer of 1776, a British army of thirty thousand soldiers under General William Howe was to move west from New York City, to be met by a smaller force advancing from Canada under Sir Guy Carleton, British general and governor of Canada. Although an American initiative into Canada led by Colonel Benedict Arnold and General Richard Montgomery was stopped at the gates of Quebec, it disrupted this strategy. Carleton, knighted for his success at Quebec, was nonetheless unable to press on into New York.

The British lieutenant general John "Gentleman Johnny" Burgoyne, so named for his appearance and manner, had been in the colonies since the beginning of the revolution. Burgoyne had accompanied Carleton in the attempt to invade New York during the summer of

1776. Returning to England the following winter, Burgoyne presented to King George III a paper called "Thoughts for Conducting the War from the Side of Canada," arguing the soundness of the strategy for an invasion from Canada. Burgoyne felt that more aggressive leadership (provided by himself) would render another invasion attempt more successful than the earlier one.

Burgoyne's plan called for the invasion to begin from Montreal, cross Lake Champlain, and follow the Hudson River. A second force would proceed from Oswego down the Mohawk Valley, along a tributary of the Hudson River; a third force, under Howe, would move from New York City up the Hudson River. The three armies would converge at Albany, cutting off the northern colonies and isolating Washington's army. The British ministry accepted Burgoyne's plan as its war strategy for the following year, and in March, 1777, Burgoyne was given command of the forces from Canada. Lieutenant Colonel Barry St. Leger was given the temporary rank of brigadier general and command of the force moving down the Mohawk Valley.

On May 6, 1777, Burgoyne arrived in Quebec, where he was met by Carleton. Burgoyne's army of eighty-three hundred men included thirty-seven hundred regulars and four hundred Iroquois Indians. On June 20, Burgoyne and his forces assembled and set sail from Lake Champlain, heading for Crown Point, eight miles north of Fort Ticonderoga. The second arm of the British strategy, four hundred troops under St. Leger, arrived at Oswego in western New York on July 25. There St. Leger was joined by one thousand Iroquois under the command of Joseph Brant. St. Leger planned to advance along the Mohawk River to the Hudson River, brushing past Fort Schuyler on the way.

Opposing the British was the Northern Department of the Continental army. Ostensibly under the leadership of General Philip Schuyler, the Americans actually regarded Horatio Gates as their commander. Schuyler was a New York patroon, autocratic, and less than successful in earlier campaigns. Many of his troops were New Englanders. They had not excelled as soldiers to date, and Schuyler despised them for it. Gates, although a plantation-owning Virginian, was much like the New Englanders he hoped to lead. He was a man of plain appearance and, although a veteran of the French and Indian War, not a strict disciplinarian. He admired the New Englanders and was admired in return.

Burgoyne's first target was Fort Ticonderoga. The fort had been seized two years earlier by Americans under the command of Benedict Arnold and Ethan Allen. The fort straddled the northern tip of Lake George and was virtually indefensible if the British occupied a nearby hill. They took that hill on July 5, and the commander at Fort Ticonderoga, General Arthur St. Clair, evacuated his army south. Burgoyne spent the next three weeks advancing toward the Hudson River, which he reached on July 30. On August 4, Gates replaced Schuyler as commander of the northern Continental army.

Meanwhile, St. Leger was about to march toward the Hudson River, 150 miles east. Only Fort Schuyler stood in the way. Built during the French and Indian War, the fort had only recently been reoccupied. Its commander, Colonel Peter Gansevoort, had strengthened its defenses during the previous three months. When his allies, local Oneida Indians, warned him of St. Leger's approach, Gansevoort evacuated the women and children, leaving about 750 men to oppose St. Leger. The British commander began an encirclement of the fort, preparing to lay siege. Meanwhile, General Nicholas Herkimer and eight hundred volunteers of the Tryon County militia began marching to relieve the fort and break the siege. On August 5, Herkimer approached Oriskany Creek, eight miles from Fort Schuyler.

That night, Herkimer sent messengers to the fort requesting that guns be fired as a diversion to cover his men. St. Leger, however, was well aware of the American arrivals. Herkimer's column included four hundred oxcarts full of supplies, strung out for more than a mile. In addition, Molly Brant, Joseph Brant's sister, had learned of Herkimer's approach and warned St. Leger.

St. Leger laid a trap along a ravine on the road to the fort. At ten o'clock, Herkimer reached the ravine, where a waiting Tory detachment and Native Americans commanded by Brant opened a cascade of fire. Herkimer charged the source of the gunfire and was badly wounded

American militia general Nicholas Herkimer, wounded during battle, died ten days after the Battle of Oriskany Creek. (North Wind Picture Archives)

in the leg. He propped himself by a tree, lit his pipe, and directed his men in the ensuing battle.

Refusing to panic, the American officers assembled their men into a defensive perimeter from which they held off the British and their Native American allies for an hour, until rain interrupted the battle, wetting the troops' gunpowder and preventing their guns from firing. When fighting resumed, Herkimer directed his men to fight in pairs, so an Iroquois soldier could not tomahawk a man while he was reloading. Brant's troops were reinforced by some of the British soldiers, who had remained to hold the Siege of Fort Schuyler. Hoping to fool the Americans, they disguised themselves as fellow militiamen. However, an actual militiaman recognized one of the imposters as his neighbor, a Tory who was known to have sided with the British, and the ruse failed.

The battle continued for six hours, evolving into bitter hand-to-hand combat. Losses among the attacking force approached 25 percent, and finally they withdrew. More than two hundred Americans were killed or wounded. Herkimer was carried to his home and died ten days later. He never reached the fort or broke the siege.

SIGNIFICANCE

Despite Herkimer's failure to relieve the fort directly, casualties among St. Leger's Native American allies were so heavy that they lost interest in the campaign. Furthermore, General Schuyler was determined that the Americans would retain control of the Mohawk Valley; he directed reinforcements under General Arnold to come to Gansevoort's aid. When St. Leger learned these American reinforcements were approaching, he lifted the siege, ending his role in Burgoyne's campaign. Burgoyne himself would receive no reinforcements. Trapped by General Gates in Saratoga a month later, he surrendered his army.

Following the Battle of Oriskany and the defeat of Burgoyne, fighting became increasingly bitter, as each side revenged itself on its opponent's allies. In July, 1778, Colonel John Butler, leading four hundred Tories and five hundred Senecas, burned and murdered his way through Pennsylvania's Wyoming Valley. In response, Washington ordered General John Sullivan to destroy the country of the Iroquois Confederacy, comprising much of western New York and northern Pennsylvania. During the spring and summer of 1779, Sullivan's four thousand men marched through the Mohawk Valley. They destroyed more than forty Seneca, Cayuga, Onondaga, and Mohawk towns. Similarly, Iroquois warriors under Joseph Brant worked devastation on tribes allied with the Americans, burning Oneida and Tuscarora villages. This period not only marked an escalation in the bitterness and the extent of fighting but also heralded the disintegration of the once neutral Iroquois Confederacy. The union of the Six Nations did not survive the revolution.

—*Richard Adler*

FURTHER READING

Hibbert, Christopher. *Redcoats and Rebels: The American Revolution Through British Eyes*. New York: W. W. Norton, 1990. Examines the revolution from the British perspective.

Middelkauff, Robert. *The Glorious Cause: The American Revolution, 1763-1789*. New York: Oxford University Press, 1982. An excellent general narrative on the history of the American Revolution.

Scheer, George, and Hugh Rankin. *Rebels and Redcoats*. New York: World, 1957. A scholarly account of the American Revolution, with emphasis on first-person narratives.

Smith, Page. *A New Age Now Begins: A People's History of the American Revolution*. 2 vols. New York: Penguin Books, 1976. Depicts the revolution as a people's rebellion; analyzes actions and feelings.

Watt, Gavin K. *Rebellion in the Mohawk Valley: The St. Leger Expedition of 1777*. Toronto, Ont.: Dundurn Press, 2002. Military history of the failed St. Leger expedition, including an account of the Battle of Oriskany Creek.

Wood, W. J. *Battles of the Revolutionary War, 1775-1781*. New York: Da Capo Press, 1995. A detailed history of the major campaigns and skirmishes of the war.

SEE ALSO: May 28, 1754-Feb. 10, 1763: French and Indian War; Sept. 5-Oct. 26, 1774: First Continental Congress; Apr. 19, 1775: Battle of Lexington and Concord; May 10-Aug. 2, 1775: Second Continental Congress; May 24 and June 11, 1776: Indian Delegation Meets with Congress; July 4, 1776: Declaration of Independence; Sept. 19-Oct. 17, 1777: Battles of Saratoga; Oct. 19, 1781: Cornwallis Surrenders at Yorktown; Sept. 3, 1783: Treaty of Paris.

RELATED ARTICLES in *Great Lives from History: The Eighteenth Century, 1701-1800*: Ethan Allen; Benedict Arnold; Joseph Brant; Sir Guy Carleton; George III; William Howe; George Washington.

September 19-October 17, 1777
BATTLES OF SARATOGA

Britain's defeat at Saratoga marked the end of any realistic prospect of British victory in the Revolutionary War. It represented the failure of Britain's plan to divide the colonies in half, isolating New England from the rest of America, and it began the series of events that would culminate with the British defeat at Yorktown.

LOCALE: Upper New York State
CATEGORY: Wars, uprisings, and civil unrest

KEY FIGURES

Horatio Gates (c. 1728-1806), commander of the American troops at Saratoga
John Burgoyne (1722-1792), British commander of the expedition from Canada
Benedict Arnold (1741-1801), subordinate commander of American troops at Saratoga
Sir Henry Clinton (1730-1795), commander of the British garrison in New York
William Howe (1729-1814), commander in chief of the British forces in America in 1777

SUMMARY OF EVENT

For the 1777 campaign of the American Revolution, the British devised a bold strategy designed to bring the war to an immediate end. The strategy involved military action in three different locales. The British navy was to transport William Howe and a large invasion force to Philadelphia, the seat of the Continental Congress, which they were to seize and occupy. Lieutenant General John Burgoyne would attack New York State from Canada, leading his troops down the Lake Champlain-Lake George waterway to assault and seize Albany. Finally, British forces would set out from their base in New York City up the Hudson River, meeting Burgoyne at Albany. The effect would be to split the colonies in two—in particular to seal off New England, where revolutionary fervor was greatest, from the colonies to the south. Although all participants agreed on the plan, the exact role each was to play and especially their coordination with one another was never made clear.

George Washington, the American commander in chief, realized early the nature of the British plan but was powerless to do much about it. He felt compelled to try to protect Philadelphia, but his efforts led only to defeat by Howe. Recognizing the significance of the Burgoyne expedition, Washington sent Colonel Daniel Morgan's detachment of sharpshooters north to join the American

army defending Albany. Morgan's unit at Saratoga helped to neutralize the Native American forces fighting on the British side and played a vital role in overcoming the British officers.

General Burgoyne's army, about eighty-three hundred strong, was successfully advancing toward Albany. A large flotilla had been assembled, able to proceed by water down the Richelieu River to Lake Champlain, where it defeated American attempts to halt it. The British disembarked at the foot of Lake George and successfully seized the lightly guarded Fort Ticonderoga, from which the American force was compelled to withdraw. Burgoyne then proceeded overland toward the Hudson River, but the terrain, the weather, and the lack of adequate oxen and horses to draw his supplies slowed his advance substantially.

Foreseeing the need for more supplies and especially more animals, Burgoyne detached a force of Germans serving under him to invade Vermont and capture any supplies and animals they could find. This force was wiped out by the Americans at the Battle of Bennington on August 16. The American victory did much to enhance American morale and to motivate recruits to join the American army defending Albany.

The American army, previously under the command of General Philip Schuyler, was now turned over to General Horatio Gates. Gates's talent was organization, not battlefield tactics, and he has been much criticized for taking a defensive posture against Burgoyne's advancing army. However, he did realize the importance of a strong defensive position, and this led him to move the American forces northward, to a position above Stillwater on Bemis Heights, overlooking the Hudson River. The American forces heavily fortified their position.

On September 19, 1777, the opposing forces came face to face with each other. Burgoyne, recognizing the folly of attempting to advance further on the road to Albany, deployed his forces, by now reduced to about five thousand men. His plan was to attack the American left wing, on the heights, with his British troops, leaving the Germans to anchor the position on the road and along the river. The attack on the heights was fought largely in the woods, but partly in a clearing around an isolated farm called Freeman's Farm. As a result, it is known as the Battle of Freeman's Farm, or the First Battle of Saratoga. The American sharpshooters shot down the officers; the British suffered heavy casualties.

British lieutenant general John Burgoyne and his troops surrender to Horatio Gates, commander of American forces, at Saratoga. (C.A. Nichols & Company)

Burgoyne regrouped his forces to consider what to do next. He had received little news of the cooperating army, under Sir Henry Clinton, that was supposed to advance up the Hudson River and meet him at Albany. He did learn that many of the supplies he had left behind at Fort Ticonderoga had been seized by American forces, leaving him with only enough supplies to last until mid-October. Burgoyne therefore staged a second, hotly contested attack on the American positions at Bemis Heights on October 7. This became known as the Battle of Bemis Heights, or the Second Battle of Saratoga. Benedict Arnold again led the Americans in battle, and the British were unable to overcome the American forces. Unable to advance, Burgoyne on October 8 ordered his army to retreat toward Saratoga.

Meanwhile, American forces had seized more of the territory along the British line of retreat to Canada. Burgoyne's army was effectively surrounded. On October 13, Burgoyne began to negotiate terms of surrender with Gates, negotiations that were completed on October 16. Under the terms of the Convention of Saratoga, the British troops laid down their arms on October 17. They were to be marched to a port of embarkation and sent back to Europe, on condition that they would take no fur-

ther part in the conflict. In the end, the Continental Congress reneged on this commitment, and the captured troops spent the rest of the war in prisoner-of-war camps in America.

SIGNIFICANCE

Burgoyne's invasion of New York represented the heart of Britain's military strategy in the colonies in 1777 and its only hope to bring the war to a swift conclusion. When Gates defeated Burgoyne at Saratoga, this hope came to an end. The British were forced to regroup while they strove to find a new strategy for success. At the same time, the Americans—although they did not know the extent to which Britain's plans had relied upon Burgoyne's success—sensed that a turning point had been reached, and their hopes for victory greatly increased. France, meanwhile, impressed by the colonists' success, officially recognized the United States of America as an independent nation, opening the door for its support of the revolution. This support led eventually to the American victory at Yorktown and the end of the Revolutionary War.

         —Nancy M. Gordon

FURTHER READING

Fuller, J. F. C. *The Decisive Battles of the Western World*. Vol. 3. London: Eyre & Spottiswode, 1955. Chapter 9 discusses Saratoga. Credits Burgoyne for honesty and courage and notes his popularity with his troops, but blames him for some tactical errors. Asserts that Benedict Arnold, Gates's subordinate, should receive credit for the U.S. victory.

Glover, Michael. *General Burgoyne in Canada and America: Scapegoat for a System*. London: Gordon & Cremonesi, 1976. An exoneration of Burgoyne that lays the blame for Burgoyne's defeat on General Clinton, for his failure to communicate effectively with Burgoyne, and on the British ministers.

Hargrove, Richard J., Jr. *General John Burgoyne*. Newark: University of Delaware Press, 1983. A balanced judgment, noting Burgoyne's virtues and his weaknesses. Contains a first-rate account of the battles of Bennington and the two at Saratoga, making clear the reasons for the outcome.

Howson, Gerald. *Burgoyne of Saratoga: A Biography.* New York: Times Books, 1979. A scholarly attempt to rescue Burgoyne's reputation. Asserts that Burgoyne was a competent, careful officer. Attributes Burgoyne's defeat to inadequate appreciation of American capabilities and terrain, coupled with poor strategic planning and coordination on the part of the British military authorities.

Ketchum, Richard M. *Saratoga: Turning Point of America's Revolutionary War.* New York: H. Holt, 1997. This popular history recounts Burgoyne's military campaign, using participants' diaries, letters, and memoirs to provide detailed descriptions of the battles. Includes an account of the feud between Horatio Gates and Benedict Arnold.

Lunt, James. *John Burgoyne of Saratoga.* New York: Harcourt, Brace, Jovanovich, 1975. A popular account with a balanced judgment on Burgoyne. Describes Burgoyne's attempt to rescue his reputation and transfer the blame to the contemporary British ministry and, to some degree, to Howe.

Mintz, Max M. *The Generals of Saratoga: John Burgoyne and Horatio Gates.* New Haven, Conn.: Yale University Press, 1990. Depicts the Saratoga battle as a competition between Generals Burgoyne and Gates, and asserts that Gates was the hero. Stresses the numerical superiority of the American army.

Morrissey, Brendan. *Saratoga, 1777: Turning Point of a Revolution.* Illustrated by Adam Hook. Oxford, England: Osprey, 2000. Illustrated military history of what many historians believe was the decisive battle in the Revolutionary War.

SEE ALSO: Apr. 19, 1775: Battle of Lexington and Concord; May 10-Aug. 2, 1775: Second Continental Congress; May 24 and June 11, 1776: Indian Delegation Meets with Congress; July 4, 1776: Declaration of Independence; Aug. 6, 1777: Battle of Oriskany Creek; Feb. 6, 1778: Franco-American Treaties; Oct. 19, 1781: Cornwallis Surrenders at Yorktown.

RELATED ARTICLES in *Great Lives from History: The Eighteenth Century, 1701-1800*: Benedict Arnold; Sir Henry Clinton; William Howe; George Washington.

November, 1777-January 1, 1781
CONSTRUCTION OF THE FIRST IRON BRIDGE

The area around Coalbrookdale was one of the foremost iron-producing centers of the world in the eighteenth century. The construction of an iron bridge over the River Severn proved just what could be achieved with the material.

LOCALE: Coalbrookdale, Shropshire, England
CATEGORIES: Architecture; science and technology; transportation

KEY FIGURES
Thomas Farnolls Pritchard (1723-1777), Shrewsbury architect, proposer, and designer of the iron bridge
Abraham Darby III (1750-1789), English ironmaster and manager of the bridge's construction
Abraham Darby (c. 1678-1717), English foundry worker and ironmaster
Abraham Darby II (1711-1763), English ironmaster

SUMMARY OF EVENT
The county of Shropshire, lying in the English East Midlands toward the Welsh border, has always been one of the more rural counties of the country. There is one notable exception, however: the district known today as Telford, in the northeastern part of the county. There, the River Severn, England's longest river, runs through a gorge. Coal mining and iron-ore smelting had been carried out extensively in the area around Coalbrookdale from the sixteenth century. Until the mid-eighteenth century, the iron had been smelted by the use of charcoal, a process demanding a large amount of lumber. As lumber became scarcer and demand for iron increased, it occurred to a young ironmaster, Abraham Darby, to experiment with the locally available coal as a replacement fuel. Darby, a Quaker, gained iron-foundry experience in Bristol and Sweden before moving to Coalbrookdale in 1708 and buying a derelict blast furnace.

By converting coal into coke by heating off its sulphur content, Darby was able to smelt iron ore into so-called pig iron. However, because of its high phosphorous content, the iron was brittle and needed reheating with charcoal and further hammering to strengthen it. By 1750, his son, Abraham Darby II, had been able to refine smelting methods to obviate the need for such reworking, and iron production increased rapidly. Other local ironmasters, such as Richard Reynolds and William Reynolds, also Quakers, and John Wilkinson, also experimented and advanced iron production, so that the area could rightly be called the birthplace of the Industrial Revolution, which, of course, relied heavily on iron for its machinery.

By the 1780's, one-third of the pig iron produced in Britain was being smelted in the district. Abraham Darby III took over the Coalbrookdale works in 1768, after his father's death. He and other local iron makers developed "cast" and "wrought" iron in the 1770's and 1780's, using the steam engines newly developed by James Watt and others to do this. Demand for wrought-iron products for domestic purposes increased rapidly, but even more greater was the demand for cast iron, particularly for steam engines, machine frames, cooking ranges and stoves, and grates.

It was in this context that Thomas Farnolls Pritchard, an architect from the county town of Shrewsbury, proposed to John Wilkinson the building of an iron bridge to span the Severn gorge near Coalbrookdale. Pritchard had started life as a joiner, moved into designing wrought-iron domestic appliances, and had then supervised some bridge building. He went on to design some bridges, using iron and wood, though the designs had never been accepted. A public meeting was called in 1775. There was a legitimate practical need for a bridge to replace the existing ferries, but the real concept behind the bridge was to show practically what a large cast-iron structure could do. The weight-bearing capacity of a single-span iron bridge had yet to be proven.

Pritchard was commissioned to design the bridge. His design was for a single 100-foot span to be sited at the narrowest part of the gorge, using stonework only for piers and abutments, which were to rise above the height of the gorge. Darby, together with Wilkinson, was commissioned to build the bridge to Pritchard's plan after a separate act of Parliament had been passed in 1776 to set up a commercial and legal basis for it. Differences between the various proprietors led to delays, and construction did not begin until November, 1777. Pritchard died the next month. Work progressed very slowly throughout 1778, and not until the summer of 1779 were the iron ribs in place. Finally, on New Year's Day, 1781, the bridge opened to traffic.

The original estimate for construction had been £550. In the end, the bridge alone cost £2,737, using 378 tons of iron. The cost of land, abutment, and ironwork brought the final total to about £3,200. A tollhouse was constructed to help pay for the bridge, which is still in use for nonvehicular traffic. The bridge also carried two water pipes under the sidewalk. Gradually a small town, Ironbridge, sprang up around the bridge, which is now the site of a series of museums: The area has been designated a World Heritage Site and includes the eldest Abraham Darby's house of 1715.

Abraham Darby III used the project to advertise his own skills, commissioning paintings and engravings of the bridge even before its completion. Thomas Jefferson, while a minister to France, purchased one of these engravings, which became a veritable icon of the Industrial Revolution. In 1788, Darby was awarded the gold medal of the Royal Society of Arts for a mahogany model of the bridge. However, despite meticulous bookkeeping, Darby lost a considerable sum of money on the overspend, and the firm's fortunes declined for a while.

SIGNIFICANCE

The bridge became a nationwide sensation. It proved iron bridges and other large-scale edifices could be constructed safely. Its success encouraged another local architect, Thomas Telford, to design a new London Bridge as a single-span iron bridge. Another local engineer, Richard Trevithick, built the earliest high-pressure steam locomotive at Coalbrookdale in 1802, based on the experience of more than two hundred steam engines at work by 1800 in the local coal shafts, and by the local production of iron rails. Earlier in 1787, John Williams launched the first iron boat, *The Trial*, to be used for commercial purposes. In 1796, Charles Bage built an iron flax mill in nearby Shrewsbury, and the following year William Reynolds built the first iron aqueduct. John Wilkinson went on to construct iron pipes for the Paris water supply in 1788.

The iron bridge over the River Severn could be considered symbolic of the coal-iron symbiosis foundational to the Industrial Revolution. Interestingly, the district never became urbanized as did most of the other industrial areas of Britain, but it still managed to remain highly productive and innovative throughout the nineteenth century. The fortunes of the Darby family declined under Francis Darby in the first half of the nineteenth century but revived under two of Abraham Darby III's great-nephews, peaking during the time of the 1851 Great Exhibition.

—*David Barratt*

FURTHER READING

Cossons, Neil, and Barrie Trinder. *The Iron Bridge: Symbol of the Industrial Revolution*. London: Moonraker, 1979. A focused account on the significance of the bridge.
Muter, Grant. *The Buildings of an Industrial Community: Coalbrookdale and Ironbridge*. Chichester,

Shropshire, England: Phillimore, 1979. An account of the factories, mines, houses, and bridges of the area.

Ruddock, E. C. *Arch Bridges and Their Builders, 1735-1835*. New York: Cambridge University Press, 1979. One of the fullest accounts of the technical aspects of the bridge. Includes an index and a bibliography.

Smith, Stuart. *A View from the Bridge*. Ironbridge, Shropshire, England: Ironbridge Gorge Museum Trust, 1979. A brief introduction produced by the local museum.

Trinder, Barrie. *The Darbys of Coalbrookdale*. 4th ed. Chichester, Shropshire, England: Phillimore, 1993. A full account of this illustrious Quaker family of iron-masters spanning well over a century.

_____. *The History of Shropshire*. Chichester, Shropshire, England: Phillimore, 1998. A more general account of the area's history, with index and bibliography.

_____. *The Industrial Revolution in Shropshire*. 3d ed.

Chichester, Shropshire, England: Phillimore, 2000. An authoritative study by the leading local historian of the industrial history of the county. Full index and bibliography.

_____, ed. *The Most Extraordinary District in the World*. Shropshire, England: VCH Press, 1988. A collection of essays for the general reader.

Vialls, Christine. *Coalbrookdale and the Iron Revolution*. New York: Cambridge University Press, 1980. Considers the area the cradle of the first nation to become industrialized.

SEE ALSO: 1705-1712: Newcomen Develops the Steam Engine; 1709: Darby Invents Coke-Smelting; 1765-1769: Watt Develops a More Effective Steam Engine; 1783-1784: Cort Improves Iron Processing.

RELATED ARTICLES in *Great Lives from History: The Eighteenth Century, 1701-1800*: Abraham Darby; Thomas Jefferson; Thomas Newcomen; James Watt; John Wilkinson.

February 6, 1778
FRANCO-AMERICAN TREATIES

In the wake of the American victory at the Battle of Saratoga, which suggested that the rebelling colonies had a substantial chance of victory in the Revolutionary War, France recognized the United States and allied with the emerging nation against Great Britain.

LOCALE: Paris, France

CATEGORIES: Diplomacy and international relations; wars, uprisings, and civil unrest

KEY FIGURES

Charles Gravier de Vergennes (1719-1787), French minister of foreign affairs

Benjamin Franklin (1706-1790), American ambassador to France

Thomas Paine (1737-1809), English-born American political philosopher

Silas Deane (1737-1789), American commissioner at the French court

Louis XVI (1754-1793), king of France, r. 1774-1792

Count de Floridablanca (José Moñino y Redondo; 1728-1808), Spanish minister of foreign affairs and prime minister of Spain, 1776-1792

Chevalier de La Luzerne (Anne-César de La Luzerne; 1741-1791), French minister to the United States, 1778-1784

SUMMARY OF EVENT

The American revolutionaries did not believe that their war of independence would go unnoticed by the outside world. With the conclusion of the Seven Years' War in 1763, the balance of power in Europe had swung decisively toward Great Britain, largely because of its defeats of France and Spain in battles fought in the Western Hemisphere. Americans and Europeans both knew that the scales would remain tipped in favor of the island kingdom only so long as it retained its New World possessions. At first, colonial writers warned that the Bourbon monarchies might attempt to seize several of George III's American provinces while his house was divided against itself: This fear represented the most compelling reason for the colonies and the mother country to patch up their quarrel. As the imperial crisis deepened, however, American opinion of the Catholic European states gradually shifted from fear to the hope that they would assist the colonies in case of war with Great Britain.

That change of sentiment was one of the radical features of the American Revolution. Bred on a hatred of Catholicism and the political absolutism associated especially with France, American publicists for decades had called for the permanent removal of the French peril from North America. The elimination of France from

Canada in 1763, however, meant that France no longer represented the threat that it had previously. France and its ally, Spain, were now more tolerable from afar than in the day when the *fleur-de-lis* loomed over the back door of the mainland settlements. Moreover, France's nearly total elimination from mainland North America did not mean that the striving colonies were destined to lose a potentially valuable international trading partner. A thriving market for import-export trade had grown between Atlantic seaboard ports and the Spanish and French colonial possessions in the Caribbean. The American colonists' desire to keep this trade free from British control was as much a factor in their feelings toward France as was their interest in political independence.

The need for foreign assistance, so ably expressed in Thomas Paine's *Common Sense* (1776), was a powerful catalyst for independence. Anticipating the final break, the Continental Congress in March, 1776, dispatched Silas Deane to Paris to purchase military stores and to explore the possibilities of a commercial alliance. Even before Deane's arrival, French leaders decided to provide the patriots with covert aid. The British-American war gave France a long-awaited opportunity to gain revenge for its humiliation in 1763. However, Charles Gravier de Vergennes, French minister of foreign affairs, was cau-

tious and prudent, a tough-minded career diplomat, and no messenger of Enlightenment idealism. Fearful of American defeat or a compromise settlement between the colonies and Great Britain, Vergennes plotted a judicious course until the likely outcome of the war became more clear.

The attitude of Spain, which feared an independent America as a threat to its overseas dominions, also served to restrain Vergennes and his countrymen. Nevertheless, the year 1777 marked France's increasing commitment to the American patriots: The growing stream of supplies bought with royal funds or taken surreptitiously from military arsenals, the opening of French ports to rebel privateers and warships, the procession of French officers bound for Washington's army, the unremitting pressures of Silas Deane, and the subtler blandishments of his colleague, Benjamin Franklin, all combined to move France toward the patriots' orbit.

News of the British capitulation of General John Burgoyne at Saratoga in October, 1777, dispelled any lingering doubts as to the patriots' ability to continue the struggle. Vergennes now feared that the American victory might give rise to a spirit of conciliation in Great Britain, leading to some form of reunion between the English-speaking people on opposite sides of the Atlan-

Benjamin Franklin, American ambassador to France, at the court of King Louis XVI. (Francis R. Niglutsch)

tic. The minister notified Franklin and his fellow commissioners that the government of Louis XVI was ready to establish formal ties with the United States.

Prior to and after final agreement on the treaties that were signed on February 6, 1778, Vergennes had French agents in America contact (and contract) willing propagandists to support a Franco-American alliance. The best-known of these agents, until American leaders' political differences led to his alienation, was Thomas Paine. Another supporter of the French, this one in Massachusetts, was the Reverend Samuel Cooper, whose brother was active in the politics of independence both before and after 1776. Cooper not only wrote articles calling for closer Franco-American relations but also gathered key information from the American emissary in Paris, Benjamin Franklin. His activities actually earned for him a salary from the French foreign ministry.

Shortly after the French and Americans signed the 1778 treaties, Cooper and a number of other Francophiles opened a literary and social salon in Boston, to which French officers, including the famous Marquis de Lafayette, were invited. Although Cooper was among a small number of American patriots who corresponded regularly with French officials (including Foreign Minister Vergennes and France's chief minister in America, the chevalier de La Luzerne), Lafayette did not know of their semiofficial propagandistic functions. Lafayette even wrote to Vergennes in May, 1780, urging Paris to "especially put Dr. Cooper at the head of the list of our friends." Cooper's service to the cause of closer Franco-American relations continued until he died in 1784. Another patriot propagandist who maintained close ties with La Luzerne was Hugh Henry Brackenridge, a Philadelphia Presbyterian minister and attorney who in 1779 edited *United States Magazine*. Although the magazine did not print specific articles backing the French treaties, it was assumed that French pay for other propagandistic pieces helped finance Brackenridge's publication.

For both parties, the Franco-American Alliance was the child of necessity. If the patriots in the beginning hoped for massive French aid and the entrance of the Bourbon nation into the war, they wanted only a temporary relationship; too intimate a formal connection would mean becoming involved in the future strife of the Old World, whose peoples mirrored a society and way of life incompatible with free, republican institutions. While the patriots offered only a commercial treaty to France, Vergennes successfully demanded more, a "conditional and defensive alliance."

The French minister of foreign affairs and his sovereign, King Louis XVI, were not enthusiastic about revolution against kings. Their willingness to recognize the United States of America and to sign treaties with the infant nation was based upon a desire to humiliate France's ancient foe. Officially titled the Treaty of Amity and Commerce, the document signed on February 6, 1778, contained most of the proposals made by Congress for liberalization of trade according to principles foreign to mercantilism.

The Treaty of Alliance, signed the same day, stipulated that, in case of war between Great Britain and France—which the two treaties made inevitable—neither America nor France would make peace without the approval of the other. France renounced forever any claims to British territory on the continent of North America and agreed to recognize the United States' right to any such territory seized by patriot armies. The two nations also guaranteed each other's territorial boundaries in the New World as they would be drawn at the end of hostilities.

SIGNIFICANCE

Once news of the Franco-American Treaties spread, an inevitable division of opinion over their presumed positive or negative significance surfaced among American clerics. Although not all Anglican and Methodist ministers denounced the treaties, their denominational closeness to England caused schisms among parishioners. Many loyalists among the clergy had already left their pulpits as early as 1775 and 1776. The dissenting clergy that took over such ministerial posts tried to combine support for independence with some form of justification for the expediency of a formal alliance between the secularist Continental Congress and monarchical, Catholic France.

Among non-Anglicans, some pastors, such as the Reverend Cooper (already committed, for pay, to the French cause), defended the treaties openly. Others, including James Dana of Wallingford, Connecticut, recognized the need for international political alliances to help the struggling former colonies defeat Great Britain but insisted that more extensive ties with "popery" would run counter to American principles of free government. A striking example of denunciation of the alliance as mere camouflage to hide presumed French Catholic propagandistic intentions came from John Zulby, a Swiss-born cleric and anti-independence member of the Continental Congress. Zulby was ultimately banished for referring to American patriots as preferring "Independancy and papist Connections" over "the Gospel and . . . former acknowledged happy Connections" with Great Britain.

Great Britain's international difficulties continued to mount after hostilities opened with France in the summer of 1778. The next year, Spain entered the fray after Prime Minister Count de Floridablanca secured a promise from Vergennes to continue hostilities until Gibraltar was regained. Although Spain did not join the Franco-American Alliance, the United States, through its tie with France, found itself committed to fight until Gibraltar fell to Spain. In 1780, British-Dutch commercial friction brought the Netherlands into the war. Great Britain was also confronted by the League of Armed Neutrality, organized by several nonbelligerent nations in protest against British practices of search and seizure on the high seas. Unlike the circumstances of earlier wars of the eighteenth century, Great Britain was isolated both diplomatically and militarily. Its defeat was therefore all but inevitable.

—R. Don Higginbotham,
updated by Byron D. Cannon

FURTHER READING

Corwin, Edward S. *French Policy and the American Alliance of 1778*. Princeton, N.J.: Princeton University Press, 1916. A revisionist and realistic look at the motives of France in supporting the American Revolution, concluding that the alliance reflected a desire to reverse the effects of France's defeat in 1763 and reestablish its position as an international power.

Gottschalk, Louis. *Lafayette Comes to America*. Chicago: University of Chicago Press, 1935. This first installment of Gottschalk's multivolume biography tears away much of the myth surrounding Lafayette and reveals attitudes of the French Court toward America.

Kennedy, Roger G. *Orders from France: The Americans and the French in a Revolutionary World, 1780-1820*. New York: Alfred A. Knopf, 1989. An excellent study of repercussions—social, economic, and cultural (particularly in art and architectural styles)—that followed the political and military aid links between France and the United States during the American Revolution. Concentrates on major biographies.

Liss, Peggy K. *Atlantic Empires: The Network of Trade and Revolution, 1713-1826*. Baltimore: Johns Hopkins University Press, 1983. Ties North and South America to eighteenth century European commerce. The chapter on the Thirteen Colonies shows a number of economic links between the North American colonists and French colonies in the Caribbean just before and during establishment of the Franco-American Alliance.

Morris, Richard B. *The American Revolution Reconsidered*. New York: Harper & Row, 1967. Explores misconceptions about the diplomatic history of the American Revolution.

Morton, Brian N., and Donald C. Spinelli. *Beaumarchais and the American Revolution*. Lanham, Md.: Lexington Books, 2003. Comprehensive biography of Pierre-Augustin Caron de Beaumarchais, with information about his experiences as an arms dealer to the American revolutionaries and his dealings with Louis XVI, Benjamin Franklin, and the Continental Congress.

Schiff, Stacy. *A Great Improvisation: Franklin, France, and the Birth of America*. New York: Henry Holt, 2005. Examines the seven years Benjamin Franklin spent in Paris, including his negotiations with Vergennes to secure the Franco-American Treaties in 1778. Schiff depicts Franklin as an improvisational diplomat who created foreign policy as he went along.

Stinchcombe, William C. *The American Revolution and the French Alliance*. Syracuse, N.Y.: Syracuse University Press, 1969. A comprehensive examination of the process that led to the Franco-American Alliance, beginning with the conclusion of the Seven Years' War and the Peace of Paris in 1763. Valuable, extensive bibliography.

Varg, Paul A. *Foreign Policies of the Founding Fathers*. East Lansing: Michigan State University Press, 1963. A provocative book that deals with the relationship between commerce and foreign policy, a factor that many historians believe operated in the Franco-American Alliance.

SEE ALSO: Jan., 1756-Feb. 15, 1763: Seven Years' War; June 8-July 27, 1758: Siege of Louisbourg; Feb. 10, 1763: Peace of Paris; Apr. 27-Oct. 10, 1774: Lord Dunmore's War; Sept. 5-Oct. 26, 1774: First Continental Congress; Apr. 19, 1775-Oct. 19, 1781: American Revolutionary War; May 10-Aug. 2, 1775: Second Continental Congress; May, 1776-Sept. 3, 1783: France Supports the American Revolution; July 4, 1776: Declaration of Independence; June 21, 1779-Feb. 7, 1783: Siege of Gibraltar; Oct. 19, 1781: Cornwallis Surrenders at Yorktown; Oct. 4, 1797-Sept. 30, 1800: XYZ Affair.

RELATED ARTICLES in *Great Lives from History: The Eighteenth Century, 1701-1800*: Pierre-Augustin Caron de Beaumarchais; Benjamin Franklin; George III; Louis XVI; Thomas Paine; Charles Gravier de Vergennes.

August 3, 1778
OPENING OF MILAN'S LA SCALA

Crowning the already-rich theatrical life of Italy's most cosmopolitan city, La Scala confirmed Milan as the most important operatic center in Italy.

LOCALE: Milan (now in Italy)
CATEGORIES: Music; theater

KEY FIGURES
Giuseppe Piermarini (1734-1808), Italian architect
Antonio Salieri (1750-1825), Italian composer

SUMMARY OF EVENT
Milan's theatrical traditions ran through the court life of the Sforza dukes and the Habsburg archdukes (first Spanish, then Austrian). In 1598, the Salone Margherita was opened in the Ducal Palace. Though soon complemented by the adjacent Teatro Ducale, as well as smaller theaters, the Salone Margherita set the city's highest performance standards through the seventeenth century. It also established structural patterns for theaters: They were to incorporate a hall in horseshoe shape with "stalls," or movable seating, at the front and standing space behind. This floor area, or *parterre*, was surmounted by tiers of boxes rented or owned privately by noble families, seating them apart from the lesser orders.

After it was damaged by fire, the Salone Margherita was enlarged and refurbished in 1699. Renamed the Regio Ducal Teatro Nuovo, it operated until its destruction by fire in 1708. Only in 1717 was it replaced, when a group of Milan's noblemen agreed to build a new house out of their own money, on condition that they own the boxes and in effect control the theater. This structure was named the Regio Ducal Teatro (or Teatro Regio Ducale). For more than half a century, it was the most important opera house in Italy, presenting the best singers of the day in Italian operas by composers both Italian and Austrian. The young Wolfgang Amadeus Mozart composed and directed three of his early operas for it in the consecutive years 1770-1772.

On February 24, 1776, the Regio Ducal Teatro was completely destroyed by fire. Pending a replacement, a temporary theater, the Teatro Interinale, was built on the grounds of an old palace of Duke Bernabò Visconti (1323-1385). The theater's designer was Giuseppe Piermarini. Foligno-born, he had recently built the Palazzo Reale and other important structures in and around Milan, establishing himself in the process as the city's dominant architect during the latter decades of the eighteenth century.

In the summer of 1776, the committee of box-holders of the old Regio Ducal Teatro received authorization to build a proper, permanent replacement. Piermarini was again to be the architect, and leading painters were assigned the decoration. Its location was the site of a derelict and decommissioned church neighboring the old Visconti gardens, at the beginning of the narrow but important street, the Contrada del Giardino—now the major Via Manzoni. The church had been known as Santa Maria della Scala, from its fourteenth century patron, Beatrice della Scala, daughter of the Scaliger (or della Scala) family of Verona, who had married Bernabò Visconti. The new building thus became known as the Regio Ducal Teatro alla Scala (the name refers to the old church, rather than to any "stair," or *scala*, as might be supposed).

As designed by Piermarini, the building had a neoclassical facade, which it still maintains. A spacious lounge and foyers, now removed, allowed places for the gambling and refreshment concessions. Those antechambers gave access to the house, whose hall was only slightly deeper than the ample stage. Up until 1907, there was no pit for the orchestra. Instead, the seventy-member ensemble played on the same level as the parterre audience. On the parterre, movable chairs provided the forward stalls, leaving standing room behind. (Fixed seating was installed only in 1891.)

The theater's horseshoe held five tiers of boxes for the social elite. There were 36 boxes in each of the first three tiers (plus the Royal Box) and 39 boxes in each of the other two tiers (added to 8 boxes on the stage itself, removed only in 1921), for a total of 194 boxes. Above all that was a gallery, or balcony, for paying ticket-holders. Each box had an antechamber and wardrobe, and in a nearby kitchen servants could prepare food for the box patrons. The theater's construction had been financed by the sale of the boxes: They were officially owned by the box-holders, for whom, as a body, the theater was an investment. The total seating capacity of twenty-five hundred made La Scala (as it was soon commonly called) one of the larger theaters in Europe at the time.

For the opening on the evening of August 3, 1778, the inaugural opera was provided by the court composer of Habsburg Vienna, the then-illustrious Italian-born master, Antonio Saleri. His *L'Europa riconosciuta* (Europa recognized) called for all sorts of spectacular effects, intended to show off the house's advanced stage mecha-

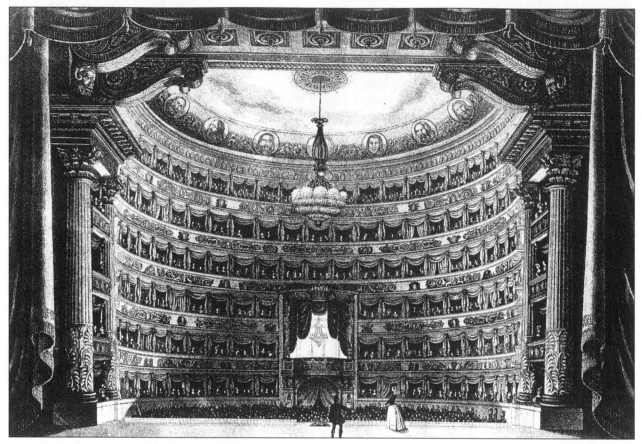

The interior of Milan's La Scala Theater, c. 1900. (Library of Congress)

nisms and facilities. In accord with Milanese taste and established theatrical practice, two ballets were performed between the acts, with music also by Salieri.

Barely a year after La Scala opened, it was given a partner, the Teatro della Cannobiana, named for its location adjacent to a school built in the sixteenth century by Paolo Cannobio. The Cannobiana was also designed by Piermarini and was inaugurated on August 21, 1779, with the performance of another opera by Salieri.

SIGNIFICANCE

As with any Italian opera house, La Scala was the city's social arena: Its leading citizens on display in their boxes, lording it over the lesser types in the stalls or galleries. Struggles over what classes of people might be admitted to what parts of the seating became a symbolic social issue by the mid-nineteenth century. Above all, the theater served the city of Milan, Italy's metropolis of international importance. It immediately provided the setting for festivities marking important moments of the

day, such as Napoleon Bonaparte's arrival there in 1797 to replace the Austrian rulers, as well as his celebratory appearance there as Emperor Napoleon I in 1805. La Scala's stage served the presentation of a variety of patriotic and politically motivated spectacles for decades, as political circumstances allowed.

In addition to its location, La Scala's size and splendor certified it as the leading opera house in Italy. It was scarcely challenged by the Teatro San Carlo in Naples or Venice's Teatro La Fenice, much less smaller houses in Rome. Its managers and impressarios over the decades aggressively sought the best singers and brand new works from the leading Italian composers of the day. The names in each category are a "who's who" of musicians of the next two centuries. For La Scala, Gioacchino Rossini composed five of his operas, Gaetano Donizetti composed seven, Vincenzo Bellini composed three, Giuseppe Verdi composed ten, and Giacomo Puccini composed three—to name only the most eminent among Italian operatic composers. La Scala also led Italian opera houses in staging (sometimes even commissioning) operas by non-Italian composers, from Richard Wagner onward, through the twentieth century. One of the engines of Italian opera, it remains among the handful of leading opera houses in the world today.

Ownership of the theater varied. After 1806, the box-holders and patrons shared rights with alternating state and municipal involvement, plus commitments to successive impresarios. In 1897, with the end of municipal subsidies, an independent syndicate was formed, and it was reestablished in 1920, at both points with Arturo Toscanini as the key artistic figure. Today, the theater enjoys a balance of private ownership and public subsidies.

Inevitably, the house has undergone physical alterations. There were extensive renovations in 1830, while there were further efforts to enlarge the seating space. Electric lighting was installed in 1881, replacing gas light (which had previously replaced candles). Demolition of the houses opposite its facade enhanced its external situation. Across the newly created Piazza della Scala, the theater then faced the entrance to the subsequently built Galleria Vittorio Emmanuele II and, through that, stood on an axis with the great Duomo, stressing the more La Scala's place in the heart of central Milan. Then it suffered terrible bomb damange on August 13, 1943, during World War II. Rebuilding it became the city's first postwar priority, and it was reopened on May 11, 1948, with a concert conducted by Arturo Toscanini.

—*John W. Barker*

FURTHER READING

Arruga, Lorenzo. *La Scala*. Translated by Raymond Rosenthal. New York: Praeger, 1976. Though a "popular" work in coffee-table format, lavishly illustrated, this book traces the theater's history and glories quite thoroughly.

Donnà, Mariangela. "Milan." In *The New Grove Dictionary of Opera*, edited by Stanley Sadie. Vol. 3. New York: Grove, 1992. Thorough survey of the city's history in lyric theater, with bibliography (most titles in Italian).

Ferrari, Luigi, et al. *Duecento anni alla Scala, 1778-1978*. Milan, Italy: Electa Editrice, 1978. A lavishly

illustrated catalog to an exhibition covering all aspects of the theater's history and traditions; text in Italian, but still easy to use.

Museo Teatrale alla Scala. *La Scala Theatrical Museum Guide*. Milan, Italy: La Scala, 1992. Nicely illustrated introduction to the theater and its richly stocked archives and collections.

Norwich, John Julius, ed. *The Italians: History, Art, and the Genius of a People*. New York: Abrams, 1983. Chapters by six distinguished scholars, including good coverage of the epoch and contexts of La Scala's contributions.

Pistone, Danièle. *Nineteenth-Century Italian Opera from Rossini to Puccini*. Translated by E. Thomas Glasow. Portland, Oreg.: Amadeus Press, 1995. Discussion of the idiom for which La Scala was so crucial, somewhat more analytical than Weaver's book below.

Rosselli, John. *The Opera Industry in Italy from Cimarosa to Verdi: The Role of the Impresario*. New York: Cambridge University Press, 1984. A leading historian of Italian opera analyzes the operation of lyric theaters in the era that comprehends the early decades of La Scala's history.

Rossi, Nick. *Opera in Italy Today: A Guide*. Portland, Oreg.: Amadeus Press, 1995. Systematic survey which includes a good section on La Scala's history and status (pp. 84-103).

Weaver, William. *The Golden Age of Italian Opera: From Rossini to Puccini*. London: Thames & Hudson, 1980. Handsomely illustrated and attractively written, a survey of the literature in whose creation La Scala played so important a role.

SEE ALSO: Jan. 29, 1728: Gay Produces the First Ballad Opera; Dec. 7, 1732: Covent Garden Theatre Opens in London; Oct. 5, 1762: First Performance of Gluck's *Orfeo and Euridice*; Nov. 12, 1766: First American Theater Opens in Philadelphia; Apr. 27, 1784: First Performance of *The Marriage of Figaro*.

RELATED ARTICLES in *Great Lives from History: The Eighteenth Century, 1701-1800*: Christoph Gluck; Wolfgang Amadeus Mozart.

1779
CROMPTON INVENTS THE SPINNING MULE

To invent the spinning mule, Crompton drew on the concepts of James Hargreaves and Richard Arkwright in spinning machinery to create a machine that not only vastly increased the output of yarn relative to its predecessors but also was well adapted to the application of mechanical power and the advent of the Industrial Revolution.

LOCALE: England
CATEGORIES: Inventions; science and technology; manufacturing

KEY FIGURES

Samuel Crompton (1753-1827), English inventor of the spinning mule
Sir Richard Arkwright (1732-1792), English inventor of the water frame
James Hargreaves (1720-1778), English inventor of the spinning jenny
Sir Robert Peel (1750-1830), English industrialist

SUMMARY OF EVENT

The area around Bolton, in Lancashire, England, was the center of the yarn-spinning industry in the last third of the eighteenth century. It was there that both James Hargreaves and Sir Richard Arkwright were located and carried through their innovative ideas on how to speed up the spinning of yarn from cotton, and it was there that Samuel Crompton, a member of the next generation, created the machine that dominated the British textile industry for the next century.

Crompton's mother, a widow when her son was five years old, was a stern disciplinarian who taught her son perseverance. At an early age, he learned to spin yarn, but found the then-prevailing method, the spinning jenny invented by James Hargreaves, to be a less than satisfactory mechanism. He devoted five years of his life, between 1774 and 1779, to crafting a machine that did not suffer from the defects of the jenny, incorporating into his machine also some of the ideas that had inspired Richard Arkwright in his development of the water frame.

Crompton's machine was built initially on a frame somewhat like that used by Hargreaves, who, in turn, had apparently derived it from a loom frame. In addition to mounting multiple spindles on the device and utilizing the more advanced rollers of Arkwright's water frame to simulate the twisting motion of the spinner's fingers, Crompton's machine incorporated a movable segment

that enabled him to adjust the roving (a loose rope of fibers that was created from the raw cotton once it was cleaned) so that its tension did not vary. By using the movable carriage, Crompton's machine was able gradually to increase the tension on the roving as it was spun ever tighter. Thus, he was not restricted to the rather loose and easily broken yarn created by the spinning jenny but was rather able to produce tightly woven yarn that withstood all the tensions placed upon it in the weaving process.

Where the jenny had produced yarns that added up to no more than a 20 count (the number of yarns to the inch in the woven fabric) and were of variable thickness, the yarn produced by Crompton's mule was of uniform thickness and could add up to a 300 count. This method of designating the fineness of a weave is still in use. Crompton's machine in fact duplicated the work of the finger and thumb of the hand spinner, holding the material tightly and gradually lengthening the fibers as it wound them together.

Crompton did not attempt to patent his new machine, which was ready for use in 1779. Perhaps he was disheartened by the difficulties of Hargreaves and Arkwright in maintaining and enforcing the patents they had initially acquired against the intense copying then going on in the spinning business. Instead, he dedicated his machine to the public and went into the spinning business himself. He turned down an offer from Sir Robert Peel, the first of that name, an active and prosperous manufacturer of yarn using largely Hargreaves's machines. Crompton, using his machine, became in fact the instructor of others in the business, and those who had had the advantage of being tutored by Crompton were much in demand. Crompton himself was not particularly successful in business, however.

Though Crompton had not sought a patent for his machine, he was inspired by the success of Edmund Cartwright, inventor of the power loom, to seek payment from the government for his achievement. Parliament had awarded Cartwright £10,000 for his invention in 1809, and Crompton sought a similar reward for his accomplishment. Parliament appointed a committee to investigate Crompton's claim, and, with the support of many Lancashire businessmen, he was rewarded in 1812 with a grant of £5,000. Crompton used the funds thus acquired to underwrite several businesses in the textile field, but none was financially successful.

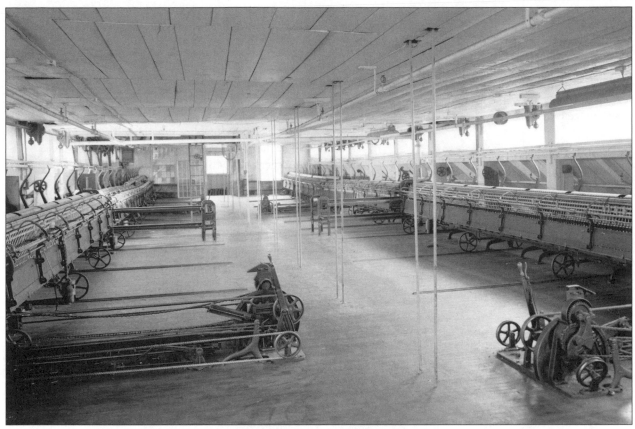

A line of spinning mules. (Library of Congress)

Crompton's achievement, however, especially combined with Cartwright's power loom, had profound consequences. Hitherto the production of lightweight cotton fabrics had been almost entirely confined to India, though over the course of the eighteenth century such materials became increasingly popular in Europe. Hargreaves and Arkwright's inventions had not changed that, because the yarns produced by their machines were too coarse and, in the case of Hargreaves's jenny, too fragile to be used in weaving the finer, lightweight cotton fabrics. Instead, in weaving such fabrics, the loose yarns produced by the jenny were combined with yarns in which linen fibers were used to strengthen the cotton, or, as in the case of yarns produced by Arkwright's frame, they were used in the manufacture of stockings. With Crompton's mule, the English textile industry could take over the manufacture of lightweight cotton textiles.

Moreover, the mule was adapted for use in large factories, requiring, as had Arkwright's water frame, an outside source of power to move the components of the machine. The mule was not superseded for at least a century

in the British textile business, becoming the core piece of equipment not only in Lancashire, the center of textile manufacture, but even in Scotland and in the United States as well, where it was not replaced until at least the middle of the nineteenth century by ring spinning. The factories using Crompton's mule spread very rapidly in the last decades of the eighteenth century. Between 1788 and 1811, the number of spindles on mules grew from fifty thousand in the earlier year to 4.6 million in 1811. The cost of yarn for weaving dropped to one tenth what it had been in the first half of the eighteenth century, thus revolutionizing the textile industry.

SIGNIFICANCE

In a sense, Crompton's mule can be said to have reversed the situation that inspired Hargreaves's spinning jenny, in which the demand for yarn from the weavers led to his invention. With the mule, the supply of yarn greatly outpaced the demand, leading to the invention of the power loom by Edmund Cartwright, who took out a patent in 1785-1787, but whose patent likewise did not lead to

641

prosperity. Other inventions followed too, including carding machines to replace the laborious process of turning the bulk cotton into usable fibers, new processes for finishing the fabric, and new methods for printing and dyeing. The resulting enormous expansion of the output of textiles in its turn led to the introduction of the steam engine into factories, and the Industrial Revolution began.

—*Nancy M. Gordon*

FURTHER READING

Cardwell, D. S. L. *Turning Points in Western Technology*. New York: Neale Watson Science History, 1972. Gives a concise description of the new textile technologies, with some illustrative line drawings.

Chapman, S. D. *The Cotton Industry in the Industrial Revolution*. London: Macmillan, 1972. A compact history of the textile industry.

Floud, Roderick, and Paul Johnson. *The Cambridge Economic History of Modern Britain*. Vol. 1. New York: Cambridge University Press, 2003. The best concise description of the new technologies, complete with line drawings of the important machines.

Mann, Julia de L. "The Textile Industry: Machinery for Cotton, Flax, Wool, 1760-1850." In *A History of Technology*, edited by Charles Singer. Vol. 1. New York: Oxford University Press, 1958. In this classic multivolume history of technology, a considerable degree of detail about the new textile inventions is provided, also with some line drawings.

Mokyr, Joel. *The Lever of Riches: Technological Creativity and Economic Progress*. New York: Oxford University Press, 1990. A brief section describes, along with a few line drawings, the major innovations of the eighteenth century in textile machinery. In another work Mokyr refers to the spinning inventions as "macroinventions."

SEE ALSO: 1701: Tull Invents the Seed Drill; 1705-1712: Newcomen Develops the Steam Engine; 1709: Darby Invents Coke-Smelting; 1733: Kay Invents the Flying Shuttle; 1764: Invention of the Spinning Jenny; 1765-1769: Watt Develops a More Effective Steam Engine; 1767-1771: Invention of the Water Frame; Apr., 1785: Cartwright Patents the Steam-Powered Loom; Dec. 20, 1790: Slater's Spinning Mill; 1793: Whitney Invents the Cotton Gin; 1795: Invention of the Flax Spinner.

RELATED ARTICLES in *Great Lives from History: The Eighteenth Century, 1701-1800*: Sir Richard Arkwright; James Hargreaves; John Kay.

1779
INGENHOUSZ DISCOVERS PHOTOSYNTHESIS

By studying the relationship between green plants, oxygen, carbon dioxide, and light, Ingenhousz discovered the major, externally observable structures that contribute to the process of photosynthesis. It would remain for later scientists to understand the internal chemical reactions at the heart of the process.

LOCALE: London, England
CATEGORIES: Biology; science and technology; chemistry

KEY FIGURES

Jan Ingenhousz (1730-1799), Dutch-born English physician and chemist
Joseph Priestley (1733-1804), English clergyman and chemist
Jean Senebier (1742-1809), Swiss clergyman and naturalist
Antoine-Laurent Lavoisier (1743-1794), French chemist

SUMMARY OF EVENT

The understanding that green plants synthesize their own food is relatively recent, as is an appreciation of the importance of this process. In photosynthesis, a plant uses two simple, inorganic raw materials, water and carbon dioxide, and, in the presence of light, produces carbohydrate (which constitutes plant food), releasing oxygen gas as a waste product. Light provides the energy for this process. At the time of Jan Ingenhousz's discoveries, photosynthesis was only beginning to be understood.

Aristotle and other ancient Greeks had believed that plants obtain all of their nutrition from the soil, analogously to the way animals ingest their food. This belief persisted until the Enlightenment, in the seventeenth and eighteenth centuries, when intensive experimentation and discoveries led to a series of insights into photosynthesis. In the early seventeenth century, Jan van Helmont concluded from an experiment that water rather than soil was the source of the gain in dry weight by growing plants. He was correct that water played a role but incorrect in concluding that water was the sole factor. In the early eighteenth century, Stephen Hales correctly surmised that some of a plant's nutrition was derived from "air."

Ingenhousz's discoveries came later in the eighteenth century, as scientists were making great advances in the understanding of chemistry, especially the composition of air. Chemists of the time, such as Joseph Priestley and Antoine-Laurent Lavoisier, were replacing old ideas with new concepts and terminology. Their chemical dissection of the air revealed that it was composed of various gases, including carbon dioxide, oxygen, hydrogen, and nitrogen. These gases were as yet imprecisely understood, however, and they were given names such as "pure air," "dephlogisticated air," or "vital air" (oxygen) and "impure air," "vitiated air," or "fixed air" (carbon dioxide). Advances in the understanding of photosynthesis both benefited from and contributed to the growing knowledge of gases and their roles in chemical reactions.

Ingenhousz's research on plants was inspired by experiments conducted by Priestley. In 1771, Priestley had discovered that air that had been made "impure" (oxygen-poor, in modern terms) by the burning of a candle or the respiration of a mouse could be "restored" by a sprig of mint so that it was again capable of supporting combustion and respiration. By showing that animals inhale "pure air" and plants release it, Priestley had discovered the interdependence of plants and animals, mediated by gases. Priestley was troubled by inconsistency in his results, however.

During the summer of 1779, Ingenhousz conducted more than five hundred experiments on plants. He repeated and extended the work of Priestley, performing many trials on detached leaves immersed in water. Substitution of leaves for the whole plants used by Priestley allowed Ingenhousz to draw conclusions that would have been elusive using whole plants, which are composed of both green and nongreen parts. Ingenhousz analyzed the gas composition of the bubbles that collected on the surfaces of the submerged leaves to determine whether they were "pure air" (oxygen) or "impure air" (carbon dioxide).

Ingenhousz confirmed Priestley's observations and demonstrated, in addition, that light is required for plants to produce oxygen. Ingenhousz showed that, under brilliant illumination, plants could restore "impure air" within several hours, rather than the several days that Priestley had often found. Ingenhousz attributed Priestley's inconsistent results to variation in the degree of illumination of Priestley's plants from experiment to experi-

ment. Ingenhousz also identified leaves as the portion of plants affected by light and showed that the part of the Sun's radiation that affects them is visible light, not heat.

In addition, Ingenhousz discovered that, although the green parts of plants give off oxygen in sunlight, they emit carbon dioxide in shade and at night and that the nongreen parts of plants emit carbon dioxide in both dark and light conditions. Thus, he provided evidence that plants, like animals, perform respiration. In a modern, cellular sense, respiration is the process whereby plants, animals, and some other organisms use oxygen to break down organic compounds in order to obtain energy and molecular building blocks. In the process, they release carbon dioxide, the raw material for photosynthesis, and

The title page of Jan Ingenhousz's Experiments upon Vegetables, *in which he published his findings relating to photosynthesis.* (Library of Congress)

thus they complete what is now known as the "oxygen cycle." Ingenhousz showed that, overall, the amount of oxygen taken up by green plants in respiration is far smaller than the amount released through photosynthesis.

Ingenhousz immediately published the results of his summer's work in *Experiments upon Vegetables: Discovering Their Great Power of Purifying the Common Air in the Sunshine and of Injuring It in the Shade and at Night* (1779). Subsequently, Priestley claimed that he had discovered the light requirement before Ingenhousz had. Thus began a long-running quarrel between the two men over the priority of their claims. Most scholars, however, credit Ingenhousz with the breakthrough.

Working at about the same time as Ingenhousz, Swiss naturalist Jean Senebier repeated and extended Ingenhousz's experiments. Senebier showed that plants must have access to carbon dioxide in order to liberate oxygen and that the amount of oxygen liberated is related to the amount of carbon dioxide available to the plant. Using Senebier's findings, Ingenhousz subsequently established that plants retain weight from the carbon in the carbon dioxide they absorb. Ingenhousz thereby disproved the idea that the carbon in plants is absorbed through the roots, from humus in the soil. His finding explained the disappearance of carbon dioxide during photosynthesis. He published these research results in the second of his two works on photosynthesis, *An Essay on the Food of Plants and the Renovation of Soils* (1796).

SIGNIFICANCE

Ingenhousz's work laid the groundwork for further research on photosynthesis. In 1804, Nicholas de Saussure discovered that a growing plant gains more in dry weight than just the weight of the carbon dioxide it absorbs. He correctly reasoned—in a throwback to van Helmont—that water also contributes to the increase in dry matter of the plant during photosynthesis.

Although Ingenhousz discovered the requirement for light, he did not determine the function of light in photosynthesis. Robert Mayer, a physicist, demonstrated in the mid-nineteenth century that the amount of energy that is liberated by the combustion of the organic matter produced in photosynthesis is equivalent to the amount of light energy that the plant has absorbed. This finding showed that photosynthesis is a mechanism for converting the radiant energy of the Sun into a stored, chemical form of energy. The organic molecules produced in photosynthesis are used for energy and as building blocks for other organic molecules, both plants and the animals that

eat them. The oxygen released by photosynthesis is essential to plant and animal respiration, making photosynthesis critical to life on Earth.

Late in the nineteenth century, the overall chemical equation for photosynthesis was formulated, stating that carbon dioxide and water, in the presence of light, yield glucose and oxygen. The early twentieth century brought the insight that the oxygen released in photosynthesis is derived from the splitting of water, not from carbon dioxide as Ingenhousz had thought. As of the early twenty-first century, at least fifty intermediate steps in photosynthesis had been identified, and the discovery of many more was fully anticipated.

—*Jane F. Hill*

FURTHER READING

Galston, Arthur W. *Life Processes of Plants*. New York: Scientific American Library, 1994. Chapter 1 of this easy-to-read volume includes historical material. Illustrations, index, bibliography.

Gest, Howard. "A 'Misplaced Chapter' in the History of Photosynthesis Research: The Second Publication, 1796, on Plant Processes by Dr. Jan Ingen-Housz, M.D., Discoverer of Photosynthesis." *Photosynthesis Research* 53 (1997): 65-72. Describes Ingenhousz's final publication on photosynthesis, which shows how his original concepts were modified by intervening breakthroughs in chemistry.

Govindjee, J. T. Beatty, H. Gest, and J. F. Allen, eds. *Discoveries in Photosynthesis*. Berlin, Germany: Springer, 2005. Details the entire history of photosynthesis research.

Ingenhousz, Jan. *An Essay on the Food of Plants and the Renovation of Soils*. 1796. Reprint. Oquawka, Ill: J. Christian Bay, 1933. Ingenhousz's final publication on plant physiology.

_____. *Experiments upon Vegetables: Discovering Their Great Power of Purifying the Common Air in the Sunshine and of Injuring It in the Shade and at Night*. London: P. Elmsly and H. Payne, 1779. Ingenhousz's first publication on plant physiology.

Nash, Leonard K. *Plants and the Atmosphere*. Cambridge, Mass.: Harvard University Press, 1952. A detailed analysis of the complex history of the discovery of basic photosynthetic processes, from circa 1650 to 1804.

Raven, Peter H., Ray F. Evert, and Susan E. Eichhorn. *Biology of Plants*. 6th ed. New York: W. H. Freeman, 1999. Comprehensive botany textbook; chapter 7, on photosynthesis, includes historical material.

1779-1803
FRONTIER WARS IN SOUTH AFRICA

Three major conflicts occurred when white settlers and indigenous peoples fought over the frontier lands northeast of the South African Cape Colony. Antagonisms had intensified since Dutch farmers first claimed Africans' territory, and war broke out when aggressive settlers and military commandos attempted to seize more land from the Xhosa and other tribes.

ALSO KNOWN AS: Kaffir Wars
LOCALE: South Africa
CATEGORIES: Wars, uprisings, and civil unrest; expansion and land acquisition; colonization

KEY FIGURES
Joachim van Plettenberg (1739-1793), governor of the Cape Colony, 1774-1785
Adriaan van Jaarsveld (fl. late eighteenth century), Dutch commandant
Rharhabe (1722-1787), Xhosa chief, r. 1773-1787
Tshaka (d. 1793), Xhosa chief, r. 1793
Langa (fl. later eighteenth century), Xhosa chief
Ndlambe (c. 1740-1828), Rharhabe's son and Xhosa chief, r. 1787-1797

SUMMARY OF EVENT
After Dutch East India Company officials established a South African port in 1652, they encouraged some company employees to farm in frontier areas northeast of the Cape Colony. Indigenous Africans, however, relied on that territory for agricultural and hunting activities to feed their communities. The Xhosa and Khoikhoi were agriculturists. The San, sometimes called Bushmen, were hunters. Soon after Dutch colonists began migrating to the frontier, some settlers clashed with Khoikhoi and San over territory and livestock issues. Seeking more land, the colonists moved north, disregarding Africans' land claims and extending the colony's area. The Dutch settled huge farms, measuring six thousand acres. Conflicts between colonists and Africans resulted in a war from 1673

to 1677, in which European weapons overwhelmed the resisters. Deprived of farmland, many Khoikhoi worked for colonists as herders or left the frontier.

Because most frontier soils were poor, colonists concentrated on raising livestock for meat, milk, skins, and wool: Instead of growing crops, they accumulated grazing land. The Zuurveld, bordered by the Fish River, offered rich soils and grassland. In the mid-eighteenth century, Xhosa had seized the Zuurveld from the Gonaqua Khoikhoi, who had lived there, and integrated them in their communities. These African tribes encountered colonists desiring their Zuurveld land, despite Dutch company officials' attempts to set borders and their assurances that settlers were not allowed to move east of the Fish River. Those officials, however, were too far away to enforce their rules.

Colonists moved livestock across the river, perceiving most local peoples as hindering expansion. The Xhosa and colonists both valued cattle herds, which represented wealth and prestige, and needed adequate grazing areas. Some Xhosa traded cows and indigenous products to Dutch farmers for European goods, even though the company outlawed colonists bartering directly with Xhosa.

Regarding themselves as superior, many colonists demanded that African laborers perform work with minimal compensation. Colonists sometimes prevented the laborers access to water sources. The workers responded by ruining crops and stealing livestock. Colonists complained that officials several hundred miles away did not understand the frontier situation or provide guards to prevent frontier raids. Arming themselves, groups of commandos guarded crops and herds in frontier districts and also retaliated against Africans. Commandos' weapons and horses assured them advantages over most Africans.

Upset by colonists hunting for sport on the frontier, San injured or killed the colonists' livestock and their Khoikhoi herders. They also assaulted vulnerable colonists and their families. Farmers loaded weapons for protection to perform chores. Many fled to safer places in the frontier. Unable to control San marauders, commandos requested government troops, but officials refused, demanding that colonists resolve the issue themselves. As conditions worsened by 1774, leaders appointed Godlieb Rudolph Opperman as commandant in the northern frontier. He attempted to secure a peace resolution, but military action was necessary for colonists to reclaim farms. Colonists and Khoikhoi allied to fight the San.

Relations between colonists and the Xhosa worsened as the amount of available pasture land declined and cultural misunderstandings occurred. Reports of farmers flogging African servants increased the hatred felt by the tribesmen. In 1778, Cape Colony governor Joachim van Plettenberg and several Xhosa chiefs, particularly Rharhabe, agreed that only the Xhosa could settle the Zuurveld. Hoping to prevent war with the Xhosa, van Plettenberg placed beacons to mark the boundary at the Fish River, ordering Dutch farmers to remain west of that river. Despite diplomatic efforts, however, some Xhosa moved west of the Fish River to secure land, and some colonists crossed the river to the east.

By 1779, skirmishes between the colonists and the Xhosa concerning land and water resources escalated into the First Frontier War. Some Khoikhoi fought with Dutch commandos. A 1780 policy council emphasized the river border and approved commandos forcing Xhosa east of the Fish River. Eastern frontier field commandant Adriaan van Jaarsveld focused on that goal. He committed one of the most inflammatory acts in the war, when he threw tobacco toward a group of Xhosa then ordered his men to shoot them when they retrieved it. The First Frontier War lasted until 1781, but distrust and resentment festered afterward.

Frontier tensions simmered for the next decade, as less land was available for everyone who wanted to live on the frontier. Xhosa chiefs, including Langa and Tshaka, brought their people and cattle into the Zuurveld, because droughts in the mid-1780's reduced available grazing areas. Also, after Rharhabe died, his successor, Ndlambe, forced many enemy Xhosa, including the Gqunukhwebe, to flee west into the Zuurveld. Colonists encountered hostile Xhosa, especially those following Langa, and they lost cattle and supplies to raiders. In 1793, militia officer Barend Lindeque and Ndlambe started the Second Frontier War when their troops ambushed a group of Xhosa who refused to abandon lands in the Zuurveld. The ambushed Xhosa fought back. Colonists fled, and Xhosa seized horses, cattle, and sheep. Commandos

chased the disruptive Xhosa across the river, where Ndlambe's troops slew Tshaka and apprehended Langa.

The commandos were unable to remove targeted Xhosa, and more Africans moved into the Zuurveld. Local Dutch East India Company representatives stated that the Xhosa could retain disputed lands. Feeling betrayed that their officials had not helped them and had sided with Xhosa instead, colonists in the Graaff-Reinet frontier district revolted in 1795. They expelled the local magistrate and declared Graaff-Reinet an autonomous republic. British forces occupied the Cape Colony that year, protecting from Napoleon the port and shipping routes to India. Uninterested in acquiring additional frontier land, the British attempted to prevent wars between Europeans and Africans and dispatched forces to control colonists on the frontier.

In 1799, the Third Frontier War began after the Van Jaarsveld Rebellion in Graaff-Reinet. When van Jaarsveld was arrested for fraud, rebels rescued him. British and Khoikhoi soldiers caught the rebels, instigating chaos. Natives raided farms, and terrorized colonists fled. Sensing an opportunity, the Xhosa and the Khoikhoi allied in an attempt to recover and secure desired frontier territory, end settler interference, and become autonomous. Colonists in the Zuurveld rebelled against the British government. During this revolt, many Khoikhoi servants stole farmers' guns and horses to use to attack and destroy colonists' property. The natives seized an estimated fifty thousand Dutch cows and fifty thousand sheep. They razed approximately 470 farms, forcing colonists to abandon property. Reduced agricultural supplies resulted in high market prices.

Political changes affected war strategies, especially when the 1802 Treaty of Amiens returned the Cape to Dutch leadership under the Batavian administration. Realizing the frontier was crucial to the Cape's economy, Cape officials agreed to a peace treaty in 1803 that permitted both Xhosa and colonists to keep their property.

SIGNIFICANCE

After the Third Frontier War ended in 1803, the Xhosa stayed on disputed lands for almost a decade before British troops and commandos forced them east of the Fish River in 1812. The British government had resumed control of the Cape Colony from the Dutch in 1806 and pursued efforts to dominate the Xhosa. During the nineteenth century, frontier hostilities continued, with Xhosa and whites attempting to secure permanent authority. The British wanted political power to enhance their international strength. The Xhosa wanted independence to protect their homeland from foreign destruction.

Hostilities ended with the Xhosa's defeat in 1878. Conflict between white settlers and Xhosa in the frontier regions had endured with minimal interruption for more than a century, affecting trade, the economy, and culture. A total of nine Frontier Wars resulted in the Cape Colony annexing Xhosa land and peoples. Historians emphasize the significance of long-term African resistance to European interference and domination in the eighteenth and nineteenth century Frontier Wars. Sometimes referred to by Europeans as the Kaffir Wars, emphasizing their view of Africans as infidels, the Frontier Wars represented how foreign colonialism altered indigenous populations and politics, reshaping South Africa's geographical and socioeconomic boundaries. Exclusionary and racist tactics in eighteenth century Zuurveld lingered in divisive social and ethnic restrictions, which the indigenous, like their ancestors, challenged.

—*Elizabeth D. Schafer*

Further Reading

Giliomee, Hermann B. *The Afrikaners: Biography of a People*. Charlottesville: University of Virginia Press, 2003. Discusses warfare between Xhosa and colonists, providing details regarding how those groups interacted and became enemies and their strategies to gain control of territory.

Maclennan, Ben. *A Proper Degree of Terror: John Graham and the Cape's Eastern Frontier*. Johannesburg, South Africa: Ravan Press, 1986. Discusses the eigh-

teenth and nineteenth century Frontier Wars, particularly the Fourth Frontier War, and explains how the three prior conflicts led to continued hostilities. Includes Xhosa perspectives.

Omer-Cooper, J. D. *History of Southern Africa*. 2d ed. London: James Curry, 1994. Two chapters focus on events relevant to the Frontier Wars and their impact on the Cape Colony, the indigenous, and Europeans. Well illustrated with contemporary images and maps indicating territorial changes.

Thompson, Leonard. *A History of South Africa*. Rev. ed. New Haven, Conn.: Yale University Press, 1995. One chapter analyzes how wars erupted between Africans and white settlers in the eighteenth century and the military aftermath continuing into the next century. Maps show lost Xhosa territories and the dates of those losses.

Van der Merwe, P. J. *The Migrant Farmer in the History of the Cape Colony, 1657-1842*. Translated by Roger B. Beck. Athens: Ohio University Press, 1995. An Afrikaner scholar describes the agricultural aspects of eighteenth century South African life and practices and ideas that intensified cultural antagonisms.

See also: c. 1701: Oman Captures Zanzibar; Dec., 1768-Jan. 10, 1773: Bruce Explores Ethiopia; 1775: Spanish-Algerine War.

Related articles in *Great Lives from History: The Eighteenth Century, 1701-1800*: James Bruce; Mentewab; Mungo Park.

June 21, 1779-February 7, 1783
Siege of Gibraltar

During the American Revolutionary War, Spain and France declared war on Great Britain, and for three and one-half years they laid siege to the British fortress at Gibraltar. However, three convoys loaded with supplies managed to run the blockade, enabling the British on Gibraltar to hold firm, and the "Great Siege" failed.

Locale: Rock of Gibraltar
Categories: Wars, uprisings, and civil unrest; diplomacy and international relations

Key Figures

George Augustus Elliott (1717-1790), British lieutenant general and governor of Gibraltar, 1775-1790
Sir Robert Boyd (1710-1794), British major general and lieutenant governor of Gibraltar, 1769-1790

Sir William Green (1725-1811), British colonel and senior engineer at Gibraltar
George Rodney (1718-1792), British admiral
George Darby (c. 1720-1790), British vice-admiral and commander of the Channel fleet, 1780-1782
Richard Howe (1726-1799), British admiral and commander of the Channel fleet, 1782-1783
Louis des Balbes de Berton de Crillon (1718-1796), French commander in chief of the combined French-Spanish forces at Gibraltar, 1782-1783

Summary of Event

Positioned as it was at the western entrance of the Mediterranean, the Rock of Gibraltar was one of the major fortresses in Great Britain's ever-increasing empire. Historically, however, the peninsula had been attached to

Spain. It had been captured by the British in 1704, during the War of the Spanish Succession, and ceded to Great Britain by the Treaty of Utrecht in 1713. The Spanish wanted Gibraltar back. Moreover, they agreed with the French in viewing Great Britain as the most dangerous threat to their colonial endeavors. Word of successes by the rebelling American colonists persuaded France and Spain in 1779 that the British were now vulnerable, and the two countries decided to join forces against Great Britain. After an abortive attempt to invade the British Isles, they turned their attention to Gibraltar. The only way to win it, they decided, was to starve its inhabitants into submission.

The siege began on June 21, 1779. During the summer, the Spanish rearmed their batteries on the isthmus and stationed ships and gunboats in Algeciras, Spain, and in Ceuta, their base in North Africa. In August, Gibraltar's tough, battle-hardened governor, Lieutenant General George Augustus Elliott, and his highly respected second in command, Major General Sir Robert Boyd, began preparing for a long siege. Civilians were urged to leave, and rationing was instituted. On September 12, when Elliot gave the order "Britons strike home," an officer's wife fired the first shot of the siege, targeting Span-

ish working parties that were erecting new batteries on the isthmus side of Gibraltar.

Two major factors contributed to the ultimate triumph of the British. One was the fact that in 1769 Gibraltar's chief engineer, Sir William Green, had obtained permission from a governmental commission to rework the long-neglected defenses of the fortress. By the time the siege began, Green had the defenses in superb condition. Second, as the siege went on, the British gunners kept improving their techniques. They learned how to adjust their fuses so that they would burst high in the air, scattering shrapnel on the workers in the Spanish lines; they invented illuminating shells for use at night; and they produced new mixtures for the filling of firebombs, which were effective against both wooden fortifications and the floating batteries that were later introduced by their enemies. The British also developed better ways of heating shot red-hot and launching it against floating targets. Their engineers blew out apertures in the face of the rock and installed guns there, placing them on carriages that a junior artillery officer had devised to stand the shock of being fired downward.

Clearly, the British had the technical capability to hold off the enemy. However, they soon ran short of food

The Rock of Gibraltar. (R. S. Peale and J. A. Hill)

and supplies. In January, 1780, a relief convoy was dispatched to Gibraltar, escorted by twenty-one ships of the line under the command of Admiral George Rodney. A Spanish fleet of twenty-six ships was waiting for the British off Cape St. Vincent, but Rodney defeated it soundly, capturing the Spanish admiral, and arrived in Gibraltar with his convoy augmented by a Spanish convoy that he had captured along the way.

Although Gibraltar was now restocked, its defenders had to remain vigilant. Early in 1780, British sailors managed to keep Spanish fire ships from reaching the harbor. That summer, however, Spanish gunboats began making nightly attacks on the city. Meanwhile, there was a smallpox epidemic, and scurvy broke out. In 1781, bribed by the Spanish, the sultan of Morocco expelled the British, making it more difficult for the forces on Gibraltar to obtain intelligence about Spanish movements and also putting a stop to the fortress's best hope of obtaining fresh food.

On April 12, 1781, the second relief convoy arrived, under the command of Vice-Admiral George Darby. Despite constant bombardment by the Spanish, the ships managed to unload. However, the cannonballs and shells destroyed many homes and sent the inhabitants fleeing, leaving their stores of wine undefended. For three days, soldiers indulged in a drunken orgy; it ended only after Elliott imposed the death penalty on looters.

The summer of 1781 was relatively quiet, because Spanish troops had been sent to join the Louis des Balbes de Berton de Crillon in his attack on the British at Minorca. The hiatus enabled the defenders of Gibraltar to make repairs and to plan a sortie against the Spanish on the isthmus. On a dark night in November, the British silently stole out of the Land Port and blew up the Spanish land batteries.

In February, Minorca fell to Crillon, freeing him to focus on taking Gibraltar. A French engineer named Jean-Claude-Éléonore Le Michaud d'Arçon came up with a design for floating batteries that he insisted could be made incombustible. By April, 1782, ten of them had been completed. However, it was September before Crillon was ready to attack. Early on September 13, the bombardment of Gibraltar began. Within a matter of hours, however, the floating batteries were on fire and British gunboats were rescuing their Spanish crews.

The combined French-Spanish fleet now lay in wait for Richard Howe, who they knew was on the way with a relief convoy. Lord Howe was outnumbered, for he had only thirty-four line ships, compared to the forty-five French and Spanish battleships in the bay. However,

when Howe arrived in October, 1782, the winds were on his side. He was able to drop off his convoy at Gibraltar, evade the other fleet, and sail safely for home. Recognizing that the siege would not succeed, an agreement to end it was drawn up in January of 1783. The siege officially ended on February 7.

SIGNIFICANCE

In a sense, Crillon's failure to take Gibraltar leveled the playing field. Britain, France, and Spain had all had their losses. Britain had lost its North American colonies, as well as Minorca, while France and Spain had invested so heavily in the various struggles that they were both in serious economic trouble. With no one emerging victorious from the struggle, the three countries could enter negotiations for peace on equal terms. When the preliminary agreements were signed on January 30, 1783, Britain ceded East and West Florida to Spain. However, because of the heroic efforts of Elliott and his men, as well as of the three fleets of ships that brought them supplies, Great Britain did not have to relinquish Gibraltar.

Ironically, the Spanish later become Britain's ally in the war against Republican France and in the later conflict with Napoleon I. During the Napoleonic Wars, Gibraltar was both a convenient supply depot and an observation post from which the British could track the movements of enemy ships. The Britons who were on Gibraltar during what came to be known as the Great Siege have been credited by history with a highly significant achievement: by keeping the Rock for their country, they made possible the British victory over the French at the Battle of Trafalgar and the eventual defeat of Napoleon.

—Rosemary M. Canfield Reisman

FURTHER READING

Dull, Jonathan R. *The French Navy and American Independence: A Study of Arms and Diplomacy, 1774-1787*. Princeton, N.J.: Princeton University Press, 1975. A detailed study. Appendices, bibliography, and index.

Gardiner, Robert, ed. *Navies and the American Revolution, 1775-1783*. Annapolis, Md.: Naval Institute Press, 1996. Chatham Pictorial Histories Series. Maps, charts, and paintings of ships in action are accompanied by explanatory text. Invaluable.

Hills, George. *Rock of Contention: A History of Gibraltar*. London: Robert Hale, 1974. Three chapters are devoted to the Great Siege. A useful chart shows the disposition of forces. Illustrated.

Jackson, William G. F., Sir. *The Rock of the Gibral-*

tarians: A History of Gibraltar. Rutherford, N.J.: Fairleigh Dickinson University Press, 1987. A former governor discusses the siege in detail. Includes maps, charts, and numerous illustrations.

Mahan, Alfred Thayer. *The Influence of Sea Power upon History, 1660-1783*. New York: Barnes & Noble Books, 2004. A standard text, first published in 1890. Sums up the reasons the Great Siege failed.

Syrett, David. *The Royal Navy in European Waters During the American Revolutionary War*. Columbia: University of South Carolina Press, 1998. Discusses the

first relief of Gibraltar, though the author focuses primarily on the inadequacies of the British navy.

SEE ALSO: May 26, 1701-Sept. 7, 1714: War of the Spanish Succession; Apr. 11, 1713: Treaty of Utrecht; 1775: Spanish-Algerine War; Apr. 19, 1775-Oct. 19, 1781: American Revolutionary War; May, 1776-Sept. 3, 1783: France Supports the American Revolution; Feb. 6, 1778: Franco-American Treaties.

RELATED ARTICLES in *Great Lives from History: The Eighteenth Century, 1701-1800*: Richard Howe; George Rodney.

1780-1781
REBELLION OF TUPAC AMARU II

Motivated by a long tradition of economic and social oppression at the hands of the Spanish, Tupac Amaru II led the last great indigenous uprising in Peru before independence from Spain in 1821.

LOCALE: Viceroyalty of Peru (now Peru); Upper Peru (now Bolivia)

CATEGORIES: Wars, uprisings, and civil unrest; government and politics; social issues and reform; colonization; economics

KEY FIGURES

Tupac Amaru II (José Gabriel Condorcanqui; c. 1740-1781), indigenous-Peruvian rebel leader

Francisco de Toledo (1515-1584), Spanish viceroy and the creator of the colonial system in Peru

Tupac Katari (1750-1781), leader, with his brothers, of the revolt in Upper Peru

Antonio de Arriaga (d. 1780), a Spanish *corregidor* who was executed by Tupac Amaru II

SUMMARY OF EVENT

The most serious challenge to Spanish rule in colonial Latin America during the eighteenth century drew its strength not from the European Enlightenment, but from a resurgence of Inca resistance in Peru from the 1740's to the early 1780's. This flare-up had its roots in the forty-year indigenous struggle against the conquistadores of the sixteenth century in the Andes. While the Aztecs of Mexico quickly crumbled before Hernán Cortés and his men in the early sixteenth century, the Inca of Peru held out much longer, as the Spanish turned on their leader, Francisco Pizarro, and then on each other. Exploiting these divisions, Manco Inca Yupanqui, the emperor after

the duped Atahualpa, initially tried to retake his capital of Cuzco, but he was forced to retreat to a smaller area of indigenous control around Vilcabamba. He was brutally murdered there in 1544, but his two successors kept up the fight until 1572. In that year, the Spanish viceroy, Francisco de Toledo, captured Tupac Amaru II's great-grandfather, Tupac Amaru, who was the last indigenous sapa Inca (emperor), and publicly executed him in 1572 after a humiliating trial. More than two hundred years later, the leader of the Andean fight for dignity, if not for outright independence, was José Gabriel Condorcanqui, who would fight under the name Tupac Amaru II ("royal or resplendent serpent").

The viceroyalty of Peru under Toledo began to use Inca institutions against the Incas and for the profit of the Spanish crown and the Creole (colonial-born Spanish) elite. The *mita*, the rotational labor system designed for local sustenance before conquest, became forced labor for the dreaded silver mines of Potosí as well for the mining of mercury at Huancavelica that made the processing of silver possible. This now-mandatory draft and the accompanying resettlement or reduction of many South American Indian villages to a few Spanish towns disrupted traditional extended families, or *ayllus*, and severely strained the ability of those left in the villages to fend for themselves. Recurrent epidemics of plague and smallpox until the 1720's led to further agricultural labor shortage, while Inca men and their families were diverted to servicing the colonial economy and society. These abuses of the *mita* and forced migrations would only deepen in the eighteenth century, especially as the Andean populations would finally rebound in number and, thus, in confidence.

While the persistence and acceleration of the *mita* was the most significant factor perpetuating Andean revolts from the 1740's through 1780, other exploitative arrangements fed Inca resentment leading to violence. The *repartos* system was particularly galling, forcing the Inca to trade with the Spanish for artificially high-priced Spanish goods that they neither wanted nor needed. Also, Inca producers of coca, ponchos, and blankets had to sell their wares at far below market prices. Local Spanish bureaucrats, particularly *corregidores* and *alcades mayors*, regulated and enforced this coercive monopoly, profiting from its exploitation. Accordingly, the officials personally became the targets of Andean rebels seeking to get rid of greedy parasites.

The Bourbon reforms, intended to bring rational efficiency and mercy to the notoriously arbitrary and cruel colonial bureaucracy, only made the situation for Andean peoples worse. As more bureaucrats and experts were hired to professionalize the government, taxes, particularly the sales tax, or *alcabala*, went up. For the first time ever, in the 1770's, the Inca became subject to the *alcabala* on basic products such as dried meat and coca that they had made for themselves. Tax collection became more efficient and regular, and the *repartos* became official imperial policy in Peru rather than an ad hoc policy affecting the indigenous only.

Cultural and ethnic divisions also magnified and complicated Andean resistance. The Catholic Church's orthodoxies about monogamy and premarital sex clashed with more flexible and permissive practices among the Inca. However, petty disputes between priests and bureaucrats over land and perquisites could lead to some priests siding with the indigenous against the state. Furthermore, a growing *casta* (mixed-race) population faced discrimination from whites and suspicion from the indigenous. In addition to his claims about being the legitimate biological heir to the last sapa Inca, Tupac Amaru was a mestizo who was proud of being a mestizo. He even had friends and sympathizers among the Creoles and Catholic priests, who resented the new intrusions and higher taxes imposed by Madrid. In contrast, some Andean rebels wanted a separatist utopia without any European, African, and mixed-race peoples, whom they viewed as surrogates for the Spanish. On top of that, preconquest tensions and hatred between Andean peoples remained, allowing the Crown to divide and conquer as always.

In 1780, ancient and new enmities among the oppressed were pushed to the side, as a number of revolts against Spanish rule broke out in different parts of the viceroyalty. Most of these rebels, however, took the standard premodern stance of fighting on behalf of and in the name of their distant king, Charles III of Spain, and against his evil counselors on the ground in Peru, who were exposed as the real traitors because of their venality. Tupac Amaru, in particular, portrayed himself as a Christian crusader upholding the faith against hypocrites and usurpers. He also saw himself as a divine Inca emperor and observed Andean religious customs. Like most *naturales* (indigenous), Tupac Amaru saw no problem in combining Catholic and polytheistic beliefs. He wrapped himself in various clothes of legitimacy, appealing to a wide coalition of the disaffected.

Tupac Amaru's revolt centered in the Quechuan-speaking, southern areas around the old imperial capital of Cuzco; in upper Peru, Tomas Katari and Tupac Katari led the Aymara-speaking areas to fight. They differed in the inclusive nature of Tupac Amaru's broad coalition versus the exclusive and separatist message of the northern groups. Yet neither group hesitated to take out centuries of frustration against officials or royalists. A particularly egregious *corregidor*, Antonio de Arriaga, was executed in November of 1780 under Tupac Amaru's orders, and 22,000 pesos of tribute were seized to underwrite the insurgency in the south. Posing as the true representative in Peru of both God and Charles III, the Inca pretender claimed that the Bourbons themselves had sanctioned both the execution of Arriaga and the redistribution of tribute as necessary and appropriate. Invoking Andean traditions about humiliating the immoral in the afterlife at the same time, rebel armies refused to bury royalists murdered or killed in action because those Inca or Spanish loyal to the Crown were deemed criminals. Various outliers within Tupac Amaru's coalition went further in their vengeance, ritually mutilating the corpses of enemies by drinking their blood and extracting their hearts.

The Spanish did not hold back either. Both the northern and southern uprisings were put down relatively quickly and brutally. In Upper Peru, the Katari brothers were hunted down and executed. As for Tupac Amaru, his whereabouts were relayed to Spanish authorities by a loyalist indigenous wife whose family had been killed by the rebels. On May 18, 1781, Tupac Amaru, his wife, his oldest son, his uncle, his brother-in-law, and high-ranking comrades were executed. His family members had their tongues cut out before they were hanged, and Tupac Amaru had his tongue cut out before he was drawn and quartered and beheaded. The leader's nine-year-old son, Fernando, was spared, but he was forced to watch the killing and dismemberment of the bodies of his family. Their body parts were strewn about the viceroyalty as an example for any future rebels. Tupac Amaru's group continued to fight under his cousin Diego Cristobal, but they soon accepted the viceroyalty's offer of pardon by early 1782. The Spanish authorities remained wary of the sapa Inca's remaining family members, so in 1783 they rounded up Diego and his mother and killed them. Then, they forced nearly ninety members of Tupac Amaru's family to go to Lima in chains; many of them were then deported to Spain, only to be lost in a shipwreck along the way.

SIGNIFICANCE

The revolts culminating with Tupac Amaru II's death were especially gory. More than eighty thousand people died on both sides (far more, for example, than the number of Americans killed in the American Revolution). Even though the uprisings were futile failures from a military perspective, they did lead to some overdue reforms. Colonial officials quickly agreed to at least two of Tupac Amaru's demands: the end of the *repartos* and the creation of an *audiencia* (high court) of Cuzco that would hear Andean complaints in a more timely manner.

Yet, in the interim, the rebellions stalled any momentum toward independence in Peru. The rebellion led by Tupac Amaru ironically persuaded most of the Creole elite there to remain loyal to the Spanish crown. The overt hints of a race war in which the Spanish could have been annihilated, magnified by the successful slave uprising on French Saint Domingue in the 1790's, particularly haunted Creoles in Peru, which became a bastion of loyalism during the drives for independence during the 1810's and 1820's. Those Creoles insisted on the hated Potosí *mita* until the bitter end, keeping the most hated patterns of subordination and dependency going long after Tupac Amaru II's death.

—*Charles H. Ford*

FURTHER READING

Burkholder, Mark, and Lyman L. Johnson. *Colonial Latin America*. 4th ed. New York: Oxford University Press, 2001. This textbook is the most detailed and the best synthesis of the history of colonial Latin America in the eighteenth century. Provides comparative context with other colonies in relation to the viceroyalty of Peru.

Cahill, David Patrick. *From Rebellion to Independence in the Andes: Soundings from Southern Peru, 1750-1830*. Amsterdam: Aksant, 2002. This work studies the social context of subversive political activity from the period preceding the rebellion of Tupac Amaru to the independence of Peru.

Campbell, Leon G. *The Military and Society in Colonial Peru, 1750-1810*. Philadelphia: American Philosophical Society, 1978. This work details the military campaigns and counterinsurgency tactics used by the Spanish crown.

Fisher, Lillian Estelle. *The Last Inca Revolt, 1780-1783*. Norman: University of Oklahoma Press, 1966. A classic account of the circumstances of the insurrection of Tupac Amaru.

Hemming, John. *The Conquest of the Incas*. New York: Harcourt Brace Jovanovich, 1970. This work provides the best chronological account of the forty-year struggle of the Incas against the Spanish in the sixteenth century, a struggle that inspired Tupac Amaru more than two centuries later.

Robins, Nicholas A. *Genocide and Millennialism in Upper Peru: The Great Rebellion of 1780-1782*. Westport, Conn.: Praeger, 2002. Analyzes Tupac Amaru's insurrection within the context of Peruvian and Bolivian indigenous millennial movements, evaluating policies for eliminating enemies.

Stavig, Ward. *The World of Tupac Amaru: Conflict, Community, and Identity in Colonial Peru*. Lincoln: University of Nebraska Press, 1999. This work brings alive the lives of ordinary Andean peoples and their mestizo and Creole counterparts.

Tandeter, Enrique. *Coercion and Market: Silver Mining in Colonial Potosi, 1692-1826*. Albuquerque: University of New Mexico Press, 1993. This work exposes the exploitative Potosí *mita* and its economic and social effects.

Thomson, Sinclair. *We Alone Will Rule: Native Andean Politics in the Age of Insurgency*. Madison: University of Wisconsin Press, 2002. Traces the history of Aymara and Quechuan politics, government, and warfare during the eighteenth century and the insurrection of Tupac Amaru within that context.

Valcárcel, Carlos Daniel. *La rebelión de Túpac Amaru*. Lima, Peru: Comisión Nacional del Sesquicentenario de la Independencia del Perú, 1972. A four-volume collection of original documents that examine the events before, during, and after Tupac Amaru's rebellion.

SEE ALSO: 18th cent.: Expansion of the Atlantic Slave Trade; Apr. 6, 1712: New York City Slave Revolt; Aug., 1712: Maya Rebellion in Chiapas; 1730-1739: First Maroon War; Jan. 24, 1744-Aug. 31, 1829: Dagohoy Rebellion in the Philippines; 1760-1776: Caribbean Slave Rebellions; 1776: Foundation of the

Viceroyalty of La Plata; Aug. 22, 1791-Jan. 1, 1804: Haitian Independence; July, 1795-Mar., 1796: Second Maroon War.

RELATED ARTICLES in *Great Lives from History: The Eighteenth Century, 1701-1800:* Nanny; Toussaint Louverture; Tupac Amaru II.

June 2-10, 1780
GORDON RIOTS

The Gordon Riots, which were caused by anti-Catholicism and resentment over the state of the British economy, were inadvertently instigated by Lord George Gordon and illustrated the depths of resentment felt by disenfranchised Londoners toward the wealthy. They also demonstrated the need for better means of controlling mobs.

LOCALE: London, England

CATEGORIES: Wars, uprisings, and civil unrest; government and politics

KEY FIGURES

Lord George Gordon (1751-1793), English member of Parliament and rebel leader

Frederick Bull (fl. late eighteenth century), English alderman

Lord Amherst (Jeffrey Amherst; 1717-1792), British military commander

Lord North (Frederick North; 1732-1792), prime minister of Great Britain, 1770-1782

First Baron Erskine (Thomas Erskine; 1750-1823), English barrister

George III (1738-1820), king of England, r. 1760-1820

Brackley Kennett (c. 1713-1782), lord mayor of London

SUMMARY OF EVENT

At the time of the Gordon Riots, England was enmeshed in the American Revolutionary War, and Lord North's government was in a precarious position. Since France and Spain, Catholic countries, had sided with the American colonists, England was virtually isolated. The Gordon Riots, moreover, were not without precedent. There had been other riots, albeit on a much smaller scale, not only in England but also in France. There was also a great deal of anti-Catholic prejudice, stemming from past conflicts between Protestants and Catholics relating to the throne. The Irish who had emigrated to London to find work and had subsequently taken low-paying jobs from the English lower class, were specifically targets of anti-Catholic feeling. Given these conditions, the time was ripe for an individual to spearhead a Protestant movement against the Catholics.

Lord George Gordon, who had left the British navy after a less than distinguished short career, led the Protestant revolt against the Catholics. At the age of twenty-two, he took a seat in Parliament and became a follower of Edmund Burke, whose democratic principles brought him in conflict with North's government, which was as unpopular as the dull and stubborn King George III. Gordon was upset by Parliament's passage of the Catholic Relief Bill (June 3, 1778), which effectively repealed King William III's act requiring army enlistees to take an oath swearing that they were Protestants. Since the war in America was not going well, the British governement thought that repeal of the anti-Catholic act might bring them more soldiers, but Gordon believed that the repeal was designed to trick Catholics into participating in the war against the American colonists, whose cause he supported.

Gordon was not alone in his opposition to the repeal. Many Methodist and Dissenting ministers, including John Wesley, as well as Protestant associations, adept at keeping antipapal feelings alive, voiced their displeasure with the Catholic Relief Bill. When he became president of the London Protestant Association, Gordon took on the leadership role, and, despite Lord North's attempts to dissuade him, called a meeting of dissidents for 10:00 A.M., June 2, at St. George's Fields.

When the march to the House of Commons began, the crowd—many of them wearing blue cockades, which became a symbol for the protesters—was peaceful. The composition of the marchers was altered, however, by the unwelcome addition of toughs, pickpockets, street urchins, and prostitutes. By the time the crowd reached the House of Commons, some of the original marchers had dropped out, and the mood became violent. The crowd accosted members of the Commons and Lords and attempted to break into the House of Commons. Gordon, inside and presenting a petition to the Commons, which was seconded by Alderman Frederick Bull, to repeal the Catholic Relief Bill, kept in touch with the rioters outside, informing them of their friends and enemies. Elated by his sudden acquisition of power, akin to a kind of megalomania, Gordon at first did not realize that he was not in control of what he had started. The Foot and Horse

1780's

THE TRIAL OF LORD GEORGE GORDON

Lord George Gordon stood trial for his part in the riots that have come to bear his name. While the members of the lower classes who participated in the riots were punished for their crimes with sentences up to and including death, Gordon himself was eventually acquitted. Reproduced here is a portion of the charge sheet from Gordon's trial.

Middlesex.—The Jurors for our Lord the King upon their Oath present that George Gordon late of the parish of Saint Mary le Bone otherwise Marybone in the County of Middlesex Esquire commonly called Lord George Gordon being a Subject of our said Sovereign Lord George the Third by the Grace of God of Great Britain France and Ireland King Defender of the faith etc . . . not having the Fear of God before his Eyes nor weighing the duty of his Allegiance but being moved and seduced by the Instigation of the Devil and entirely withdrawing the Love and true and due Obedience which every subject of our said Sovereign Lord the King should and of right ought to bear towards our said present Sovereign Lord the King and wickedly devising and intending to disturb the peace and public Tranquility of this Kingdom on the second day of June in the Twentieth Year of the Reign of our said Sovereign Lord the now King at the Parish of Saint Margaret within the Liberty of Westminster in the said County of Middlesex unlawfully maliciously and traiterously did compass imagine and intend to raise and levy War Insurrection and Rebellion against our said Lord the King within this Kingdom of Great Britain and to fulfil and bring to Effect the said traiterous compassings Imaginations and Intentions of him the said George Gordon He the said George Gordon afterwards that is to say on the said second day of June in the twentieth Year aforesaid with Force and Arms etc at the said Parish of Saint Margaret within the Liberty of Westminster in the said County of Middlesex with a great Multitude of Persons whose names are at present unknown to the Jurors aforesaid to a great Number to wit to the Number of Five hundred persons and upwards armed and arrayed in a warlike manner that is to say with Colours flying and with Swords Clubs Bludgeons Staves and other Weapons as well offensive as defensive being then and there unlawfully maliciously and traiterously assembled and gathered together against our said present Sovereign Lord the King most wickedly maliciously and traiterously did ordain prepare and levy public War against our said Lord the King his supreme and undoubted Lord contrary to the Duty of his Allegiance against the peace of our said Lord the King his Crown and Dignity and also against the form of the Statute in such Case made and provided.

Source: "The Gordon Riots, 1780." The National Archives: Records of the UK Government from Domesday to the Present. http://www.nationalarchives .gov.uk/pathways/citizenship/rise_parliament/docs/thunderer.htm. Accessed November 7, 2005.

Guards were summoned, but they were ineffective, since they did not have the support of the civil authorities. Although the violence abated, just before midnight the mob attacked the chapel of the Sardinian ambassador. It then proceeded to ransack other Catholic chapels.

By Saturday noon, the hostilities seemed to be over, but they resumed at 9:00 P.M., when the mob attacked the Irish workers at Moorfields. In the course of the next two nights, the mob burned every Catholic chapel to the ground, and unless people wore blue cockades, they were in danger. Houses were spared if they had anti-papal signs on their doors, and prominent businessmen, like Bull, attempted to save their warehouses. In response to the violence, the House of Commons passed resolutions encouraging the identification and prosecution of those responsible for the burning of houses and chapels.

Gordon voted for all the resolutions and did attempt unsuccessfully to quell the violence, which no longer seemed to be related to Catholicism, but rather was directed against all persons in authority. The mob also turned its attention to the prisons, starting with the hated Newgate Prison but also encompassing Fleet, Bridewell, and New Prison. They destroyed what they could and freed a total of sixteen hundred convicts, some of them hardened criminals and some debtors. It was estimated that the accumulated debt of the escaped prisoners was £700,000. There were also three unsuccessful attacks on the Bank of England. In addition to the destruction, there was a great deal of looting, especially of liquor, and many of the rioters were drunk.

The government responded by enforcing the Riot Act, which gave soldiers the right to fire on unruly mobs, and some rioters were killed when it was first used, but there arose disagreement about whether or not the assent of a civil authority was necessary to authorize gunfire. The Attorney General ruled that the approval of civil authorities was not necessary. Despite the objections of opposition leaders Burke and Charles James Fox, martial law was enacted in London. In addition, seven thousand soldiers from the Home Counties arrived in London, and others were on their way.

Lord Amherst assumed control and sent men to the

London and Blackfriars Bridges to protect them, and civilian volunteer bands and the London Military Association helped reestablish order. By June 10, the government had regained control and many of the escaped prisoners were recaptured. During the riots, about sixty Catholic houses were destroyed, and more than two hundred people were killed by the military. Almost one hundred others died in the hospitals, and almost two hundred were treated for wounds. These numbers can be documented, but other people doubtless died and were unceremonially dumped in the Thames.

Lord George Gordon was arrested and sent to the Tower, and Brackley Kennett and James Fisher were brought in for questioning but soon released. Gordon's trial was twice postponed, and by the time it was held feelings had cooled enough that he was able to elicit sympathy from some members of the establishment. Defended in court by Thomas Erskine (later first baron) and Lloyd Kenyon, Gordon was acquitted. While the instigator of the riots was freed, however, the lower-class rioters were not as fortunate. At the Old Bailey and Southwark

Sessions, sixty-two rioters were sentenced to death, and twenty-five were eventually hanged. Twelve others received lighter sentences.

SIGNIFICANCE

Because the rioters' actions were directed not against the poor Catholics, but against Catholics of substance, it seems clear that the riots reflected not only dislike of Catholics, but also of the wealthy, providing an outlet for the smoldering anger of the lower classes. The riots also made it apparent that the civil authorities were unwilling or unable to control mobs. As a result, there was increased pressure for a professional police force. The riots also brought attention to conflicts between the national government and the City of London, which had impeded, rather than helped, efforts to control the riots. Finally, by successfully controlling the mob, which represented a threat to law and order, the conservative administration of Lord North was able to retain control of the government for another two years.

—*Thomas L. Erskine*

FURTHER READING

DeCastro, John Paul. *The Gordon Riots*. London: Oxford University Press, 1926. Early account of the riots, with a discussion of their implications.

Dickens, Charles. *Barnaby Rudge and the Riots of 'Eighty*. London: Oxford University Press, 1841. Novel focusing on the riots.

Hibbert, Christopher. *King Mob and the Story of Lord George Gordon and the Riots of 1780*. London: Longmans, Green, 1959. Account of the riots with biographical details about Lord George Gordon and transcripts from his trial.

Rudé, George F. E. *Paris and London in the Eighteenth Century: Studies in Popular Protest*. New York: Viking, 1971. Focuses on the victims of the riots, correcting popular accounts about the extent of the anti-Catholic victimization.

A portrait of rebel leader Lord George Gordon. The scroll to his left reads, "Protestants Petition against Popery," referring to the Gordon Riots. (Library of Congress)

SEE ALSO: July 24, 1702-Oct. 1, 1704: Camisard Risings in the Cévennes; Mar. 23-26, 1708: Defeat of the "Old Pretender"; Sept. 6, 1715-Feb. 4, 1716: Jacobite Rising in Scotland; Aug. 19, 1745-Sept. 20, 1746: Jacobite Rebellion; Sept., 1773-Sept., 1774: Pugachev's Revolt; July 14, 1789: Fall of the Bastille; May-Nov., 1798: Irish Rebellion.

RELATED ARTICLES in *Great Lives from History: The Eighteenth Century, 1701-1800*: Lord Amherst; Edmund Burke; First Baron Erskine; George III; Lord North; John Wesley.

October 10-18, 1780
GREAT CARIBBEAN HURRICANE

One of the deadliest storms in history struck the eastern Caribbean Islands, killing tens of thousands of people, mostly black slaves. Many of England's and France's lucrative sugar-producing colonies on the islands were severely damaged or destroyed as well. The two European countries had been at war with each other in the Caribbean, and the storm's aftermath affected naval warfare in the region into the following year.

LOCALE: Caribbean Islands

CATEGORIES: Environment; trade and commerce; wars, uprisings, and civil unrest

KEY FIGURES

Luc Urbain de Bouexic (Count de Guichen; 1712-1790), French admiral, and commander of the French fleet in the Caribbean Sea

George Rodney (1718-1792), British admiral, and commander of the British fleet in the Caribbean Sea

SUMMARY OF EVENT

English and French Caribbean sugar plantations of the eighteenth century were economic alternatives to Spain's silver mines. A changing European diet had created a growing market for sugar in tea, coffee, jams, and confections. Caribbean sugarcane thrived in the region's tropical climate and fertile volcanic and limestone soils. The importation of African slave laborers made sufficient production of the crop possible. However, hurricanes posed a greater risk than usual to the enterprise during the century; a cluster of the tempests occurred from the mid-1760's to 1780, with 1780 being the most terrible hurricane season of the lot. Eight different storms hit the Caribbean region that year; four of the storms arrived in October alone.

In October, 1780, a great hurricane's path of destruction focused on the Lesser Antilles, a teardrop chain of small islands that forms the eastern boundary of the Caribbean Sea. The islands stretch from Puerto Rico (which is part of another Caribbean Islands chain, the Greater Antilles) to South America. The archipelago sits astride routes taken by tropical storms that form over the equatorial Atlantic Ocean. These low-pressure troughs push westward toward the Lesser Antilles. Each year, fueled by evaporating tropical waters, a few of these storms grow to become hurricanes. Some hurricanes miss the islands entirely or brush by closely. When a hurricane hits the island chain, it usually affects a few unlucky islands that are directly in its path.

The great Caribbean hurricane of 1780 took the worst route possible for the islands. On October 10, 1780, the storm hit Barbados, Saint Vincent, and Saint Lucia near the southern end of the chain. At this stage, the diameter of the storm was so great that reports from Granada and even Tobago, which is 250 miles southeast of Barbados, had described damage to shipping from the storm. The storm then turned north and traveled slowly along the length of the archipelago, leaving no island north of Barbados unscathed. After passing over St. Eustatius at the north end of the chain, the hurricane jogged west to brush against the southern coast of Puerto Rico. On October 15, it moved through Mona Passage (the strait between Puerto Rico and the island of Hispaniola) and headed north into the open waters of the North Atlantic. On October 18, after eight terrible days, the storm dissipated over cooler waters near Bermuda in the middle Atlantic. As if guided by the hand of a merciless god, the storm ravaged the entire Lesser Antilles chain, left tens of thousands of people dead, and earned its reputation as the "great hurricane."

No one knows the exact number of human deaths caused by the hurricane. Estimates appear in letters, diaries, and newspaper articles written by islanders who witnessed the storm and by visitors who saw the aftermath. The estimates range between 20,000 and 26,000 lost lives. The British colonial government of Barbados conducted the only precise census and counted 4,326 deaths on the island. The highest figures for the other islands are estimated at 9,000 deaths in Martinique, 6,000 in Saint Lucia, and 5,000 in Eustatius. The majority of the dead were on land and were mostly black slaves, who outnumbered whites by more than ten to one on most islands. A large proportion of the victims starved to death after the storm, as the hurricane's ferocious winds and floods destroyed most of the food crops. The dead included sailors and passengers aboard ships that sank offshore.

The Lesser Antilles had been the center of operations for the British and French navies in the Western Hemisphere when the storm struck in 1780. The two countries were at war over control of the Caribbean region's sugar production. The primary mission of the fleets was to protect merchant vessels involved in the sugar trade. Tobago, Barbados, Saint Lucia, Montserrat, Nevis,

St. Kitts, and Antigua were under British control. Granada, Saint Vincent, Dominica, Guadeloupe, and Martinique were French possessions at the time. The Dutch (who would be at war against the British beginning in 1781) held St. Eustatius. France and England were also at odds in the American War of Independence. France was giving moral support and financial backing to the American rebels and using its Caribbean fleet to harass the British in American waters. The Spanish had possessions in the Greater Antilles (for example, Cuba), and their Caribbean fleet was fighting on the side of France and the American rebels.

Until July, 1780, the English and French fleets, of equal strength, had been engaged in operations around the island of Martinique, but nothing decisive occurred. As in previous years, the fleet commanders kept part of their navies out of harm's way during the most dangerous part of the hurricane season (September to November) by sending most of the ships of the line out of the region. England would use part of its Caribbean fleet to bolster an effective blockade of its rebellious American colonies. The British fleet commander, George Rodney, sailed for North America, reaching New York on September 14. At about the same time, the commander of the French fleet, Luc Urbain de Bouexic, arrived in Brest, France, with the ships that were most in need of repairs.

Admiral Rodney had left some of his fleet behind at Gros Islet Bay in Saint Lucia. The great hurricane sank and killed the crews of three key battleships: HMS *Beaver's Prize*, HMS *Cornwall*, and HMS *Vengeance*. HMS *Experiment* sank nearby at Saint Vincent. The crews of perhaps one hundred smaller British merchant vessels in the region were lost as well. The storm did not spare de Bouexic's ships either, as four thousand French troops perished when a convoy of forty transports sank off Port Royal, Martinique. No large French warships sank, however. The Spanish fleet was in Havana, Cuba, and out of reach of the hurricane.

SIGNIFICANCE

Relief efforts from outside the region were slow to materialize largely because relief convoys bearing troops and supplies were at risk of attack in time of war. In December, 1781, France attempted to send a relief convoy under the command of Bouexic to the Lesser Antilles from Brest, but a British squadron intercepted and defeated the convoy in the Bay of Biscay. The closest major food-producing area for British-held islands were the thirteen American colonies, but the ongoing American War of Independence barred organizing relief shipments to the Lesser Antilles. Eventually, small donations of private and government funds trickled in, and church sermons and newspaper advertisements in England and France called for aid to the islands, making British Barbados one of the first European colonies to have received money from its government for natural disaster relief. The Caribbean Islands' agricultural economy would remain vulnerable to hurricanes, but, as in other parts of the world, government agencies dedicated to disaster relief were nonexistent until the second half of the twentieth century.

The great Caribbean hurricane's widespread destruction in the Antilles, in addition to killing thousands, jeopardized the investments of colonial planters and merchants by shattering thousands of hectares of sugarcane. Local plantation managers and merchants had to rely on credit from merchants in their home countries to finance repairs. The purchase and transport of thousands of new slaves also were costly. Debts were so great that many planters sold their holdings to creditors or to owners of larger plantations. It took more than two years for sugar production to return to levels seen before the hurricane.

In the short term, the hurricane had influenced as well the course of the war between the French and British in the Caribbean. In February, 1781, Rodney was back in the region. His fleet overwhelmed the storm-damaged defenses of the Dutch island of St. Eustatius. However, because the British fleet was battered by the hurricane, the French and Spanish naval forces were able to take the British islands of Tobago, Montserrat, St. Kitts, and Nevis in 1781. The British would eventually replace the warships lost in the great hurricane and take control of most of the Lesser Antilles islands and the sugar trade before the Treaty of Paris ended the conflict in 1783.

—*Richard A. Crooker*

FURTHER READING

Ludlum, David. *Early American Hurricanes*. Boston: American Meteorological Society, 1963. Ludlum details the 1780 storm's track and includes several quotations from primary sources describing the impacts of the hurricane.

Mulcahy, Matthew. *Melancholy and Fatal Calamities: Hurricanes and Society in the British Greater Caribbean*. Baltimore: Johns Hopkins University Press, 2005. A thorough account of how inhabitants and governments of the Caribbean region have dealt with hurricanes.

Reclus, Elisée. *The Ocean, Atmosphere, and Life*. New York: Harper and Brothers, 1873. This older work by

1780's

a French geographer is often quoted for its description of the death and destruction caused by hurricanes.

SEE ALSO: 18th cent.: Expansion of the Atlantic Slave Trade; Nov. 23, 1733: Slaves Capture St. John's Island; Nov. 1, 1755: Great Lisbon Earthquake; 1760-1776: Caribbean Slave Rebellions; 1763-1767: Fam-

ine in Southern Italy; May, 1776-Sept. 3, 1783: France Supports the American Revolution; Sept. 3, 1783: Treaty of Paris; 1786-1787: Tenmei Famine.

RELATED ARTICLES in *Great Lives from History: The Eighteenth Century, 1701-1800*: George Rodney; Toussaint Louverture.

1781
KANT PUBLISHES *CRITIQUE OF PURE REASON*

Immanuel Kant revolutionized philosophy by asking and answering the seemingly simple question, "How is knowledge possible?" His Critique of Pure Reason *is among the most important texts in the history of philosophy, as it is the starting point for both the analytic and continental traditions that followed.*

ALSO KNOWN AS: Kant's First Critique
LOCALE: Königsberg, East Prussia (now Kaliningrad, Russia)
CATEGORIES: Philosophy; literature

KEY FIGURES

Immanuel Kant (1724-1804), German philosopher
Alexander Gottlieb Baumgarten (1714-1762), German philosopher and aesthetician
René Descartes (1596-1650), French mathematician and philosopher
Johann Gottlieb Fichte (1762-1814), German philosopher
Georg Wilhelm Friedrich Hegel (1770-1831), German philosopher
David Hume (1711-1776), Scottish philosopher
Gottfried Wilhelm Leibniz (1646-1716), German philosopher
Friedrich Wilhelm Joseph von Schelling (1775-1854), German philosopher
Christian Wolff (1679-1754), German philosopher

SUMMARY OF EVENT

The continental rationalism that René Descartes pioneered in the 1630's culminated in the elaborate philosophical vision of Gottfried Wilhelm Leibniz. Starting around 1709, Christian Wolff built an internally coherent and overarching philosophical system based mainly on Leibniz's principle of sufficient reason, the idea that anything that exists must necessarily have some reason why it exists. Wolff intended this system to be the last word in philosophy, and for a time he was successful.

By the mid-eighteenth century, the Leibniz-Wolff system had become the standard curriculum in German universities and secondary schools. Its effect on German thought was at once stimulating, because of its wide scope, and smothering, because of its pretensions of inclusiveness, closure, and finality. Among the Leibniz-Wolffians was Alexander Gottlieb Baumgarten, whose metaphysics and philosophy of art strongly influenced Immanuel Kant.

Kant claimed in 1783 that reading David Hume in the 1760's or 1770's had awakened him from the "dogmatic slumber" that had been induced by immersion in the Leibniz-Wolff school of metaphysics. Kant's new doubts about Leibniz-Wolff pushed him toward unprecedented critical inquiry. He began to ask questions that were more fundamental and potentially more unsettling than any questions asked by the continental rationalists. Kant published his answers to these questions about the very nature of knowing as *Kritik der reinen Vernunft* (1781; *Critique of Pure Reason*, 1838). His purpose in this massive, difficult, and supremely important book was to determine which logical, metaphysical, or transcendental conditions are absolutely necessary for any knowledge, especially a priori knowledge, to arise. He called the book *Critique of Pure Reason* because pure reason is supposed to be that faculty which alone is capable of a priori knowledge.

Kant's philosophy, although systematic, is critical and exploratory rather than dogmatic and didactic. He attacked rationalism by saying that concepts without percepts are empty, attacked empiricism by saying that percepts without concepts are blind, and sought a synthetic middle ground in which rationalism and empiricism would take each other seriously. He considered his inquiry "transcendental," that is, concerned not with the knowledge of the usual objects of knowledge, but with the a priori knowledge of how the knowledge of objects is possible. Accordingly, the book is divided into sections such as "Transcendental Aesthetic," considering how sensation is possible; "Transcendental Logic," considering how concepts, intuitions, and thinking itself are possible; "Transcendental Analytic," considering how understanding is possible; and "Transcendental Dialectic," considering how the generation of new ideas is possible.

The transcendental aesthetic posits the two forms of intuition, space and time, through which all perception must occur. The transcendental analytic, as part of the transcendental logic, offers an exhaustive table of twelve kinds of judgments in four groups of three. Under "Quantity" are universal, particular, and singular judgments; under "Quality" are affirmative, negative, and infinite; under "Relation" are categorical, hypothetical, and disjunctive; and under "Modality" are problematic, assertive, and certain. This table corresponds to the twelve "pure concepts" or categories of the understanding, also divided into four groups of three. Under "Quantity" are unity, plurality, and totality; under "Quality" are reality, negation, and limitation; under "Relation" are substance/accident, cause/effect, and community; and under "Modality" are possibility/impossibility, existence/nonexistence, and necessity/contingency. Rational consciousness, and therefore human understanding, is internally coherent through what Kant calls "the transcendental unity of apperception." This self-consciousness defines not only the human self, but also any other possible rational selves of any other species that may exist anywhere in the universe.

The transcendental dialectic, as the other part of the logic, examines some of the consequences and paradoxes of pure reason. Central to this section are the antinomies, four examples of how conflicts in dogma, when argued out to their logical conclusions, result in unresolvable contradictions. The dialectic also examines difficult questions about God, freedom, and immortality, and challenges the traditional theistic proofs.

For Kant as for the continental rationalists, mathematics is the epitome of clear and rational knowledge. All that

---

KANT RECONCEPTUALIZES DESCARTES'S *COGITO*

The central part of Immanuel Kant's Critique of Pure Reason *is the Transcendental Deduction of the Categories, in which Kant claims to provide an objective proof that the phenomenal world really appears as perceived by the human mind. The ground upon which this proof is based is what Kant calls "transcendental apperception," or what René Descartes called the "I think." In the passage excerpted here, Kant explains that without the "I think"—without the ability to withdraw from any given experience and understand that the experience belongs to an "I" that exists independently of its experiences—human experience itself would be impossible.*

This original and transcendental condition is no other than *transcendental apperception*. Consciousness of self according to the determinations of our state in inner perception is merely empirical, and always changing. No fixed and abiding self can present itself in this flux of inner appearances. Such consciousness is usually named *inner sense*, or *empirical apperception*. What has *necessarily* to be represented as numerically identical cannot be thought as such through empirical data. To render such a transcendental presupposition valid, there must be a condition which precedes all experience, and which makes experience itself possible.

There can be in us no modes of knowledge, no connection or unity of one mode of knowledge with another, without that unity of consciousness which precedes all data of intuitions, and by relation to which representation of objects is alone possible. This pure original unchangeable consciousness I shall name *transcendental apperception*. That it deserves this name is clear from the fact that even the purest objective unity, namely, that of the *a priori* concepts (space and time), is only possible through relation of the intuitions to such unity of consciousness. The numerical unity of this apperception is thus the *a priori* ground of all concepts, just as the manifoldness of space and time is the *a priori* ground of the intuitions of sensibility.

Source: Immanuel Kant, *Critique of Pure Reason*, translated by Norman Kemp-Smith (New York: Humanities Press, 1929), p. 136.

1780's

is empirically knowable is phenomenon or appearance, that is, the way that things appear to perceivers. Appearances are not true reflections of reality. Kant posited that behind every appearance is an unknowable and unreachable noumenon or thing-in-itself. However, the truths of mathematics are knowable, reachable, and synthetic a priori because they emerge from the application of pure reason alone without recourse to experience. Kant aimed in the *Critique of Pure Reason* to establish synthetic a priori knowledge for other fields besides mathematics. Philosophers continue to debate whether he achieved this goal.

Kant published two other critiques, *Kritik der praktischen Vernunft* (1788; *Critique of Practical Reason*, 1873), which grounds social, ethical, and political philosophy, and *Kritik der Urteilskraft* (1790; *The Critique of Judgment*, 1892), which develops a philosophy of art. Philosophers typically refer to these books as Kant's First, Second, and Third Critiques. Kant's other major work, *Grundlegung zur Metaphysik der Sitten* (1785; *Fundamental Principles of the Metaphysics of Ethics*, 1895; better known as *Foundations of the Metaphysics of Morals*, 1950), introduced to ethics the concept of the categorical imperative, or an objectively valid moral law that holds in all circumstances. All three of these later works, especially the *Foundations of the Metaphysics of Morals*, depend upon the principle of freedom as established in the First Critique. Kant defines freedom as the ability of an agent to be an unconditioned cause of some event, which makes freedom an absolutely necessary precondition for any human thought, action, judgment, morality, or ethics.

SIGNIFICANCE

Kant's influence on philosophy is immeasurable. Along with Plato, Aristotle, Thomas Aquinas, Descartes, Baruch Spinoza, Hume, Georg Wilhelm Friedrich Hegel, Friedrich Nietzsche, Martin Heidegger, and Ludwig Wittgenstein, he is acknowledged as one of the greatest philosophers of all time. Greatness in philosophy involves innovation, intelligence, coherence, discernment, and relevance. Kant's writings all show these qualities in abundance.

It is not an exaggeration to argue that, without Kant's insights, the course of subsequent philosophy would not have been possible. Within two decades after the publication of his first critique, reaction against his concept of the thing-in-itself had sown the seeds of German Idealism in Johann Gottlieb Fichte, Friedrich Wilhelm Joseph von Schelling, and Hegel. German Idealism was the first major post-Kantian movement in philosophy that would not have been possible without Kant.

Kantians generally divide into two camps, those who see him as essentially a metaphysician and those who use his thought as the foundation of analytic philosophy. We might call these camps rationalist and empiricist, respectively, but, like most philosophical labeling, this is problematic. Kant aimed to synthesize rationalism and empiricism, and perhaps to some extent succeeded, but the point is that neither rationalism nor empiricism could have proceeded into the nineteenth century without considering Kant. Continental European speculative thinkers who are concerned with overarching truths and British-American philosophers who prefer the minute analysis and clarification of language and logic equally take their direction from Kant.

—*Eric v.d. Luft*

FURTHER READING

Adorno, Theodor. *Kant's "Critique of Pure Reason."* Stanford, Calif.: Stanford University Press, 2001. An engaging work by a major twentieth century German philosopher that tells as much about Adorno as it does about Kant.

Dicker, Georges. *Kant's Theory of Knowledge: An Analytical Introduction.* New York: Oxford University Press, 2004. A useful aid for first-time readers of the transcendental aesthetic, logic, and analytic.

Gardner, Sebastian. *Kant and the "Critique of Pure Reason."* New York: Routledge, 2000. A well-reviewed basic introduction to Kant in Routledge's popular Philosophy Guidebooks series.

Hanna, Robert. *Kant and the Foundations of Analytic Philosophy.* New York: Oxford University Press, 2004. Defends Kant against several kinds of criticism.

Hartnack, Justus. *Kant's Theory of Knowledge: An Introduction to the "Critique of Pure Reason."* Indianapolis, Ind.: Hackett, 2001. A classic short introduction.

Kant, Immanuel. *Critique of Pure Reason.* Translated by Norman Kemp Smith. New York: St. Martin's Press, 1965. The standard English translation.

Kuehn, Manfred. *Kant: A Biography.* New York: Cambridge University Press, 2001. A commendable focus on the chronological development of Kant's ideas, rather than on his uneventful life.

Sassen, Brigitte, ed. *Kant's Early Critics: The Empiricist Critique of the Theoretical Philosophy.* New York: Cambridge University Press, 2000. Even though fixed on the empiricist contribution to the philosophical dialogue, Sassen identifies three strains of German comment on Kant during his lifetime: empiricist, rationalist, and idealist.

Savile, Anthony. *Kant's "Critique of Pure Reason": An Orientation to the Central Theme.* Malden, Mass.: Blackwell, 2005. A penetrating analysis by a renowned expert on Kant, continental rationalism, and eighteenth century aesthetics.

Sedgwick, Sally S., ed. *The Reception of Kant's Critical Philosophy: Fichte, Schelling, and Hegel.* New York: Cambridge University Press, 2000. A solid collection of new interpretations by world-class scholars.

Smith, Norman Kemp. *A Commentary to Kant's "Critique of Pure Reason."* New York: Palgrave Macmillan, 2003. The standard commentary and an important key to Kant's difficult work.

SEE ALSO: 1721-1750: Early Enlightenment in France; 1739-1740: Hume Publishes *A Treatise of Human*

1781-1784
CAVENDISH DISCOVERS THE COMPOSITION OF WATER

After discovering "inflammable air," or hydrogen, Cavendish investigated its properties and found that pure water formed when hydrogen burned in "dephlogisticated air," or oxygen.

LOCALE: Clapham Common, London, England
CATEGORIES: Science and technology; chemistry; biology

KEY FIGURES

Henry Cavendish (1731-1810), English natural philosopher who is best known for his research on gases and the nature of water

Joseph Priestley (1733-1804), English scientist and Unitarian minister who discovered oxygen and several other gases

James Watt (1736-1819), English inventor of an improved steam engine who gave an interpretation of water's nature

Antoine-Laurent Lavoisier (1743-1794), French chemist who interpreted water as a compound of hydrogen and oxygen

Sir Charles Blagden (1748-1820), Cavendish's assistant during the years that he studied hydrogen and the nature of water

SUMMARY OF EVENT

Although Henry Cavendish lived and worked largely as a recluse, his greatest discoveries cannot be understood apart from the community of scientists to which he belonged. This certainly was the case with his discovery of "inflammable air" and his related research on the composition of water.

Scientists such as Robert Boyle had noticed that a flammable gas was generated when acids were added to metals, but Cavendish was sufficiently intrigued by this gas to study it comprehensively. He prepared it with various metals (iron, zinc, and tin) and acids (what we now call hydrochloric and sulfuric acids). Using two different methods, he determined the gas's specific gravity, find-

ing it was nearly nine thousand times lighter than water and about one-fourteenth the weight of common air. When he introduced a flame into a mixture of this gas and ordinary air, the gas burned bright blue, and so he called it "inflammable air from the metals," which was later shortened to "inflammable air" (its modern name is hydrogen). Because he believed in the phlogiston theory, which posited that every combustible material contained a substance called phlogiston, and because inflammable air burned with no residue, Cavendish believed that this new gas ("inflammable air") was phlogiston.

In 1766, Cavendish published his findings in a tripartite paper in which each part dealt with a specific gas prepared by a certain process: one, inflammable air from metals and acids; two, fixed air (carbon dioxide) from alkalis and acids; and three, "mixed airs" from organic materials by fermentation or putrefaction. Cavendish's report on inflammable air stimulated Joseph Priestley, who, in 1781, put an electric spark through a mixture of inflammable air and common air and noticed that the inside of the dry glass container became coated with moisture. Neither Priestley nor a colleague who helped him understood what they had done, but Cavendish did understand after he repeated their experiment in a systematic and quantitative way. During the summer of 1781 he found that all the inflammable air and about one-fifth of the ordinary air had ceased being gases in forming what he discovered was pure water.

Cavendish and Priestley routinely interacted, so Cavendish was aware of a new gas, "dephlogisticated air" (oxygen), discovered by Priestley in 1774. Cavendish was therefore curious about what would happen if he sparked various mixtures of inflammable air and dephlogisticated air. After several trials he established that a two-to-one ratio of inflammable to dephlogisticated air led to the complete conversion of these gases to water. Although he was the first scientist to establish this experimental fact, his interpretation of the results was confusing. The obvious explanation was to see water as the union of these two gases, but Cavendish was a phlogistonist and still tied, in a way, to the old idea of water as an element (that is, a basic, indivisible substance rather than a combination of other substances). For him, inflammable air was either phlogiston or "phlogisticated water" (water united to phlogiston). Dephlogisticated air, on the other hand, was water deprived of its phlogiston. Therefore, Cavendish saw water as preexisting in the combining gases, and the spark-induced reaction simply revealed what had previously been hidden.

Even though Cavendish did not publish his experimental results and interpretation until 1784, scientists in England and France learned about them. For example, in 1783, Sir Charles Blagden, Cavendish's assistant, made a trip to Paris and met Antoine-Laurent Lavoisier, whom he informed of how Cavendish, with his assistance, had made pure water from two new gases. Antoine-Laurent Lavoisier quickly realized the implications of their results for his new theory of chemistry. In November, 1783, Lavoisier reported to the French Academy of Sciences on experiments that he and Pierre Simon de Laplace had performed, which demonstrated that water was not an element but instead was a compound of hydrogen and oxygen. Lavoisier failed to mention the stimulus he had received from the research of Cavendish, who did not publish his results until 1784. In this later publication, Cavendish was able to complete his earlier studies by showing that the gas that was left behind when dephlogisticated air was removed from common air was a colorless gas in which mice died and a candle would not burn (this gas was what Lavoisier called azote and others called nitrogen).

Because the discovery of the compound nature of water was so significant, and because so many people contributed in one way or another to that discovery, a "water controversy" soon developed. It was basically a priority dispute. Both Priestley, who could have made a claim but never did, and Cavendish, whose introverted personality ill suited him to controversy, stayed on the sidelines. The contending parties in the first phase of the water controversy were James Watt and Lavoisier. Watt became involved because Priestley told him about his dew-forming experiments and Watt then circulated his interpretation of Priestley's results to Royal Society members. When Watt learned of Cavendish's and Lavoisier's reports on water's nature, he accused Cavendish of plagiarizing his ideas and Lavoisier of plagiarizing Cavendish's experiments. For his part, Cavendish was willing to give credit to Lavoisier for interpreting the composition of water in terms of the oxygen theory. Al-

though most historians of science appreciate Lavoisier's contributions, they criticize him for neglecting to credit Cavendish. These scholars also find Watt's claims confused and his interpretation derivative. Indeed, they bestow on Cavendish, the least contentious of the claimants, the lion's share of the honor for finding water's true nature.

SIGNIFICANCE

Some scholars consider Henry Cavendish to be Britain's preeminent eighteenth century scientist, who lived and worked between the time of Sir Isaac Newton in the seventeenth century and James Clerk Maxwell in the nineteenth century. Cavendish's studies of what he called "factitious airs" (those contained in solids) were models of a rigorously quantitative approach to chemistry. Future chemists would use his methods for generating, collecting, transferring, and measuring gases and for determining their unique characteristics. He used these methods to help discover the composition of water but also to help clarify the nature of compounds such as nitric acid. His quantitative studies of the specific combining volumes of the gases necessary to form water constituted an important step toward the law enunciated by Joseph-Louis Gay-Lussac in 1809, which states that the ratios of the volumes of reacting gases are always small, whole numbers. Cavendish's experimental contributions were much more important than his theoretical contributions, and his adherence to the phlogiston theory hampered his understanding of his experimental results almost to the end of his life, when he finally began to see some value in the new chemistry of Lavoisier.

The water controversy was significant because of what it revealed about the changing nature of science. Before the eighteenth century scientists tended to work alone, and their discoveries were often seen as a consequence of their individual genius. In the eighteenth century scientific discoveries increasingly involved many talented individuals working in concert with others or working with the knowledge that many others were working on the same or similar projects. Inevitably, more than one scientist would make the same conclusion or discovery simultaneously.

Some scholars attribute the water controversy to the casual way in which scientific data were then gathered, dated, and reported. Other scholars point to nationalism as a factor in the water controversy, especially as it continued in the nineteenth century after the deaths of the original contenders. French and British scholars, using newly available primary sources, argued about the credit that should be given to Watt and Cavendish. One significant by-product of the study of Cavendish's papers was the role that some of his data played in the discovery of a new element in 1894. When Cavendish had removed oxygen and nitrogen from ordinary air, he found a small bubble of gas still remaining. In the late nineteenth century this bubble of gas was shown to be argon, a new noble gas, a belated testimony to the meticulousness of Cavendish's experimental prowess.

—*Robert J. Paradowski*

FURTHER READING

Jaffe, Bernard. *Crucibles: The Story of Chemistry*. New York: Dover, 1998. This popular history of chemistry told through the lives and achievements of the great chemists has a chapter on Cavendish. Includes a section of sources and an index.

Jungnickel, Christa, and Russell McCormmach. *Cavendish: The Experimental Life*. Lewisburg, Pa.: Bucknell, 1999. This biography is an extensive revision of the authors' earlier biography published by the American Philosophical Association. With updated primary and secondary sources, this edition offers an extremely rich view of the context and contributions of Cavendish to physics and chemistry. Illustrated, with an extensive bibliography and a detailed index.

Miller, David Philip. *Discovering Water: James Watt, Henry Cavendish, and the Nineteenth Century "Water Controversy."* Burlington, Vt.: Ashgate, 2004. Describes how Cavendish's (and Watt's and Lavoisier's) discovery that water was a compound of "airs," and not a combination of elements, became an issue of controversy among nineteenth century scientists.

Partington, J. R. *A History of Chemistry*. Vol. 3. London: Macmillan, 1962. The eighth chapter of this comprehensive history of chemistry is on Cavendish's life and contributions to chemistry. The chapter's footnotes include many references to both primary and secondary sources. Illustrated, with indexes of names and subjects.

Strathern, Paul. *Mendeleyev's Dream: The Quest for the Elements*. New York: Berkeley Books, 2000. This popular history of chemistry treats Cavendish's achievements in chapter 5, "Trial and Error." Illustrated, with a further-reading section and an index.

SEE ALSO: 1718: Geoffroy Issues the *Table of Reactivities*; 1723: Stahl Postulates the Phlogiston Theory; 1738: Bernoulli Proposes the Kinetic Theory of Gases; 1742: Celsius Proposes an International Fixed Temperature Scale; 1745: Lomonosov Issues the First Catalog of Minerals; 1771: Woulfe Discovers Picric Acid; Aug. 1, 1774: Priestley Discovers Oxygen; 1781-1784: Cavendish Discovers the Composition of Water; 1786-1787: Lavoisier Devises the Modern System of Chemical Nomenclature; 1789: Leblanc Develops Soda Production; c. 1794-1799: Proust Establishes the Law of Definite Proportions.

RELATED ARTICLES in *Great Lives from History: The Eighteenth Century, 1701-1800*: Joseph Black; Henry Cavendish; Antoine-Laurent Lavoisier; Joseph Priestley; Georg Ernst Stahl; James Watt.

1780's

March 1, 1781
RATIFICATION OF THE ARTICLES OF CONFEDERATION

The Articles of Confederation represented the first attempt of the thirteen American colonies to band together as a single political unit. The articles, however, represented a treaty between thirteen sovereign entities more than they created a new, single sovereign entity. The states of the Confederation soon discovered that they had retained too much sovereignty for themselves to the detriment of the new country, and they set about creating the U.S. Constitution to correct their mistake.

LOCALE: Philadelphia, Pennsylvania
CATEGORIES: Government and politics; laws, acts, and legal history

KEY FIGURES

John Dickinson (1732-1808), principal author of the first draft of the Articles of Confederation
Thomas Jefferson (1743-1826), Virginia delegate to the Continental Congress and later president of the United States, 1801-1809
Thomas Burke (1747?-1783), North Carolina delegate to the Continental Congress
Chevalier de La Luzerne (Anne-César de La Luzerne; 1741-1791), French envoy to the United States

SUMMARY OF EVENT

The American experience with nationalism ran counter to developments that had led to nationhood throughout much of the modern world. A sense of American nationalism scarcely existed during the colonial period. Nor did nationalism produce a revolution aimed at the creation of a single, unified American government. Slowly, almost imperceptibly, Americans' sense of oneness grew as the colonies stood together in opposition to Great Britain's post-1763 imperial program. As Americans traveled the long road to 1776 and became more aware of their shared principles and interests, they began to think simultaneously about independence and union. Because the independent states realized they must work cooperatively or perish, American patriots turned to the task of creating a confederacy of states.

In June, 1776, while Thomas Jefferson and his committee worked on the Declaration of Independence, a second committee was appointed by the Continental Congress. Including one representative from each colony, the committee was instructed to draft a series of articles that would set forth the principles and structure of a cooperative union between the states, thus linking the thirteen self-governing states into a "league of friendship." With John Dickinson from Pennsylvania as chairman, the committee quickly proposed a plan for union, but in late July, opponents of such a union convinced the Continental Congress to reject Dickinson's document.

Nearly five years elapsed before all agreements and compromises could be reached both within the Continental Congress and at the state level. The exigencies of the Revolutionary War slowed the process as the Continental Congress grappled with enlistments, supplies, finances, and foreign aid. The lawmakers were also forced to flee Philadelphia twice in the face of approaching British armies; once they fled to Baltimore and once to York, Pennsylvania. State governments were similarly distracted, which further slowed the process, since each state legislature had to agree on instructions to its delegate to the congress.

Political clashes in and out of the Continental Congress about the contents of the proposed document added yet another obstacle to approval of the Articles of Confederation. Historians have differed sharply over the nature of these struggles. Some contend that they were ideological in substance, between so-called radicals and conservatives; others contend that they were rivalries between the small and large states. However, few scholars deny that the conflicts over questions concerning local authority versus central authority were conditioned by the colonists' previous experience with remote, impersonal government control from London. Nor should it be forgotten that creating a central administrative authority

for all thirteen states and participating in government beyond the colony level were experiences largely foreign to Americans.

Although the committee report, of which John Dickinson was the primary architect, was placed before the Continental Congress as early as July 12, 1776, it languished, as attention was focused on questions about administering the western frontier and apportioning representation and financial burdens among the states. Most delegates favored a loose confederation, as opposed to a highly centralized and powerful national government. Sometimes explicitly, but more often implicitly, it seemed that the Dickinson draft left too much authority in the hands of Congress. Finally, in November, 1777, the Continental Congress agreed upon the Articles of Confederation and submitted the agreement to the states for ratification.

Under the Articles, the confederated Congress became the only branch of the central government. Each state would have one vote to cast, regardless of population, by a delegate selected by the legislature of that state. A simple majority of states was required for most votes, except in explicitly specified matters that required the consent of nine of the thirteen. Each state had the sole power to tax its population, although each state also was expected to contribute its share of money (based upon improved lands) to the upkeep of the Confederation. States also retained exclusive power to regulate their own commercial activities.

Each state claiming territory in the trans-Appalachian region was allowed to keep its possessions instead of turning them over to the United States. Individually, the states were to retain their sovereignty, freedom, and independence, as well as all rights not specifically granted to Congress. In turn, the Articles gave the confederated Congress the authority to make war and peace, make military appointments, requisition men and money from the states, send out and receive ambassadors, and negotiate treaties and alliances. Management of postal affairs and the authority to coin money, decide weights and measures, and settle disputes between states were also responsibilities that the Articles gave to the confederated administration.

Although the Articles of Confederation vested momentous responsibilities in the confederated Congress, the agreement did not give Congress the authority to discharge those responsibilities. Without the ability to tax or regulate trade and lacking powers of enforcement, Congress could only hope that the states would meet their assigned requisitions and cooperate with the confederated administration in other vital areas. Despite the limits on power built into the Articles of Confederation, some states were reluctant to give their consent to the proposed confederated Congress. Opponents continued to question jurisdictional responsibilities assigned to the central government.

By 1779, all states except Maryland had endorsed the Articles. Maryland's continuing opposition was driven largely by avaricious land speculators. Colonial charters had given Connecticut, Massachusetts, and all states south of the Potomac River land grants extending westward to the Pacific Ocean. Many people from the "landless" states felt that regions beyond the settled areas should be turned over to the Confederation, so that states with extensive western claims would not enter the union with distinct natural advantages over states without western claims. Likewise, "landless" representatives maintained that the western frontier eventually would be won through the combined military efforts of all states working in tandem.

If Maryland land speculators (who hoped to fare better from Congress than from the Commonwealth of Virginia in having prewar claims recognized) had exercised a decisive role in their state's refusal to ratify, their stand did not invalidate the reasoning of others who demanded an equitable solution to the western land problem. To break the impasse, Congress reversed itself and recommended that the landed states relinquish generous portions of their tramontane territories. Virginia, with vast claims, held the key.

Prompted by Thomas Jefferson, on January 2, 1781, Virginia offered the Confederation its rights to all lands north of the Ohio River. Equally important and far-reaching were Virginia's stipulations (ultimately accepted) that speculators' claims be canceled and that new states be created and admitted to the union on terms of equality with the original thirteen. New York responded, abandoning its tenuous claims, as Connecticut abandoned its more solid ones. In time, the remaining landed states followed suit. Maryland, which had requested French naval protection, was prodded into ratification by the French envoy, the Chevalier de La Luzerne, and on March 1, 1781, Congress finally announced the formal creation of a "perpetual union."

CONFEDERATION CONGRESS

The Articles of Confederation created a relatively loose affiliation of states, as is attested by the fact that section 2, the first substantive section of the document, immediately addresses the powers of the states before the powers of the Confederation have been enumerated or discussed. Section 5 of the document establishes the federal legislature, stipulating that each state gets one vote regardless of population and that congressional representatives cannot receive salaries from the government for their service or for any other job.

I.

The Stile of this Confederacy shall be "The United States of America".

II.

Each state retains its sovereignty, freedom, and independence, and every power, jurisdiction, and right, which is not by this Confederation expressly delegated to the United States, in Congress assembled.

[. . .]

V.

For the most convenient management of the general interests of the United States, delegates shall be annually appointed in such manner as the legislatures of each State shall direct, to meet in Congress on the first Monday in November, in every year, with a power reserved to each State to recall its delegates, or any of them, at any time within the year, and to send others in their stead for the remainder of the year.

No State shall be represented in Congress by less than two, nor more than seven members; and no person shall be capable of being a delegate for more than three years in any term of six years; nor shall any person, being a delegate, be capable of holding any office under the United States, for which he, or another for his benefit, receives any salary, fees or emolument of any kind.

Each State shall maintain its own delegates in a meeting of the States, and while they act as members of the committee of the States.

In determining questions in the United States in Congress assembled, each State shall have one vote.

Freedom of speech and debate in Congress shall not be impeached or questioned in any court or place out of Congress, and the members of Congress shall be protected in their persons from arrests or imprisonments, during the time of their going to and from, and attendence on Congress, except for treason, felony, or breach of the peace.

Source: "Transcript of Articles of Confederation." Our Documents, National Archives and Records Administration. http://www.ourdocuments.gov/doc.php?doc=3&page=transcript. Accessed November 15, 2005.

1780's

SIGNIFICANCE

The Articles of Confederation created a relatively loose union of thirteen sovereign states, characterized as a league of friendship far more than a collection of subordinate provinces within a single sovereign nation. Time and circumstances during the 1780's, however, would demonstrate the inherent flaws in the Articles. By the end of the decade, it had become apparent to many Americans that the Articles were not adequate for the needs of the thirteen member states. Instead, the states consented, for the first time, to create a national government, and they produced a new document, the Constitution of the United States, to bring about that government.

—*R. Don Higginbotham, updated by Paul E. Doutrich*

FURTHER READING

Berkin, Carol. *A Brilliant Solution: Inventing the American Constitution.* New York: Harcourt, 2002. Chapter 1 contains information about the Articles of Confederation and how the inadequacies of that document spurred creation of the U.S. Constitution. Includes an appendix with the full text of the Articles.

Callahan, Kerry P. *The Articles of Confederation: A Primary Source Investigation into the Document That Preceded the U.S. Constitution.* New York: Rosen Primary Source, 2003. Aimed at young adults, this book describes the drafting and ratification of the Articles, their significance, and the eventual drafting of the U.S. Constitution.

Douglas, Elisha P. *Rebels and Democrats: The Struggle for Equal Political Rights and Majority Rule During the American Revolution.* Chapel Hill: University of North Carolina Press, 1955. Demonstrates that the fortunes of the prerevolutionary ruling class varied from state to state.

Henderson, H. James. *Party Politics in the Continental Congress.* New York: McGraw-Hill, 1974. Focuses on the various interests that separated and then united members of the Continental Congress.

Jameson, J. Franklin. *The American Revolution Considered as a Social Movement.* Princeton, N.J.: Princeton University Press, 1926. Stimulating and suggestive, although the degree of immediate change produced by the American Revolution may be exaggerated.

Main, Jackson T. *The Social Structure of Revolutionary America.* Princeton, N.J.: Princeton University Press, 1965. Describes the era as one of relatively little social change, although few Americans were frozen in a lower-class status.

Miller, John C. *Triumph and Freedom, 1775-1783.* Boston: Little, Brown, 1948. Provides a somewhat detailed account of the events involved in the American Revolution.

Morris, Richard B. *Forging of the Union, 1781-1789.* New York: Harper & Row, 1987. The evolution of U.S. national government is described in some detail.

Wood, Gordon. *The Creation of the American Republic, 1776-1787.* New York: W. W. Norton, 1969. Presents a thorough analysis of the motives and goals of American political theory between independence and the creation of the nation in 1787.

SEE ALSO: Oct. 7, 1763: Proclamation of 1763; Sept. 5-Oct. 26, 1774: First Continental Congress; Apr. 19, 1775: Battle of Lexington and Concord; May 10-Aug. 2, 1775: Second Continental Congress; July 4, 1776: Declaration of Independence; Feb. 6, 1778: Franco-American Treaties; Oct. 19, 1781: Cornwallis Surrenders at Yorktown; Sept. 3, 1783: Treaty of Paris; May 20, 1785: Ordinance of 1785; July 13, 1787: Northwest Ordinance; Sept. 17, 1787: U.S. Constitution Is Adopted; Oct. 27, 1787-May, 1788: Publication of *The Federalist.*

RELATED ARTICLES in *Great Lives from History: The Eighteenth Century, 1701-1800*: John Dickinson; Thomas Jefferson.

October 19, 1781
CORNWALLIS SURRENDERS AT YORKTOWN

The entire British field army surrendered to combined American and French forces, marking the military end to the Revolutionary War and confirming once and for all American independence.

LOCALE: Yorktown, Virginia
CATEGORY: Wars, uprisings, and civil unrest

KEY FIGURES

Second Earl of Cornwallis (Charles Cornwallis; 1738-1805), ranking British general in the American South and later first Marquess Cornwallis, 1792-1805

Comte de Rochambeau (Jean-Baptiste Donatien de Vimeur; 1725-1807), commander of French land forces at Yorktown

Nathanael Greene (1742-1786), commander of the American Southern Department

George Washington (1732-1799), commander in chief of the Continental army and later president of the United States, 1789-1797

Sir Henry Clinton (1730-1795), British commander in chief in America, 1778-1781

SUMMARY OF EVENT

The surrender of the second earl of Cornwallis at Yorktown made immortal the name of that sleepy village at the tip of a Virginia peninsula. The roots of the Yorktown debacle are to be found in a train of events that followed from the British decision in 1778 to shift the focus of the war to the region below the Potomac. French intervention and failure to win in the North led the British to campaign in the South. Although their southern campaign would see royal military forces dispersed from Manhattan to the West Indies, the policymakers in London based their decision on two crucial assumptions: first, that the southern Loyalists were exceedingly numerous, and second, that Great Britain could maintain its naval superiority against the combined Bourbon forces of France and Spain. Although the Loyalists were not so numerous as anticipated and a British garrison at Savannah almost fell to French admiral Jean-Baptiste-Charles-Henri-Hector d'Estaing in October, 1779, when he caught the British fleet napping, those two basic assumptions of the British government were never altered.

The war in the South went extremely well for the British up until 1781. Georgia fell in 1779 and South Carolina in 1780. In major actions in the latter state—at

Charleston on May 12, 1780, and at Camden on August 16, 1780—the Continental Congress entrusted to Major General Nathanael Greene, a former Quaker from Rhode Island, the task of rallying the scattered and dispirited American forces. His antagonist was Major General Lord Charles Cornwallis, who headed the British field army when Lieutenant General Sir Henry Clinton returned to New York.

Cornwallis displayed none of the caution or timidity that many of the British senior officers had shown during the American Revolutionary War. Determined to overrun North Carolina and, he hoped, Virginia as well, he refused to allow the annihilation of two of his detached units—at King's Mountain on October 7, 1780, and at Cowpens on January 17, 1781—to dampen his ambitions. Nor did the failure of the Loyalists, whose numbers he exaggerated, alter his thinking. Greene, a master of harassment tactics, severely mauled still more of Cornwallis's irreplaceable redcoats at Guilford Court House, North Carolina, on March 15, 1781. In April, Greene and Cornwallis went opposite ways—Greene south to pick off British outposts in South Carolina, Cornwallis north to invade Virginia.

Greene's brilliant campaign eventually cleared the enemy from all points except Charleston, South Carolina, and Savannah, Georgia, while Cornwallis, far from his supply depots, took the road to disaster. Although Clinton had favored the establishment of a naval base on the Chesapeake and had sent the turncoat Brigadier General Benedict Arnold to Virginia on a raiding expedition, he had been more concerned about the welfare of British interests in the lower South. Consequently, he had instructed his restless subordinate to undertake nothing that might endanger "the tranquility of South Carolina." After limping to Wilmington, North Carolina, to rest his troops, Cornwallis wrote to Clinton, who previously had been in the dark as to Cornwallis's whereabouts, that "a serious attempt upon Virginia . . . would tend to the security of South Carolina and ultimately to the submission of North Carolina."

On May 20, Cornwallis joined Arnold at Petersburg, Virginia, and assumed direction of the combined force of seventy-two hundred men. Apprehensive about the possible arrival of a French fleet in Chesapeake Bay, Clinton disapproved of Cornwallis's abandonment of South Carolina and voiced his reluctance to turn Virginia into a prime military theater. Clinton, an able strategist but an insecure commander in chief, failed to deal decisively with Cornwallis, a personal rival who, he feared, might be appointed to succeed him at any moment. Cornwallis, meanwhile, idled away vital weeks skirmishing in the Old Dominion before retiring to Yorktown in the late summer to erect fortifications.

In New York, Clinton fretted and George Washington, the American commander in chief, awaited a large French fleet. Approximately five thousand French troops under Brigadier General the comte de Rochambeau were already at Newport, Rhode Island, but the comte de Barras's escorting ships had been quickly blockaded inside the harbor by a superior British squadron. Finally, word came that Admiral Françoise-Joseph-Paul de Grasse had sailed from France to the West Indies with plans to detach part of his fleet later to assist a mainland campaign. Although Washington preferred to attack New York City, after hearing on August 14 that

Grasse was bound for the Chesapeake, he recognized that his better prospect would be to trap Cornwallis. Accordingly, Washington and Rochambeau hurried southward with seven thousand men, while Barras, loaded with siege guns for the allied armies, slipped out of Newport.

It was scarcely the British navy's finest hour: Not only had the navy permitted Barras to elude the Newport blockade, but also the West Indian squadron had been equally lax, because Admiral Sir George Rodney had assumed erroneously that Grasse would not sail to Virginia with his entire fleet of twenty-eight ships. Rodney consequently sent only fourteen vessels northward under Admiral Sir Samuel Hood, who united with the seven ships of Admiral Sir Thomas Graves at New York. Unaware of Grasse's strength, Graves hastened down the coast and met the French admiral at the mouth of Chesapeake Bay on September 5. The ensuing contest was indecisive, but

British general Charles Cornwallis surrenders at Yorktown to American and French troops, marking the end of British control of the colonies and the end of the Revolutionary War. (C. A. Nichols & Company)

Graves felt compelled to return to New York, leaving the French in control of the ocean approaches to the Middle Colonies. The fate of Cornwallis at Yorktown was then all but sealed.

Franco-American land operations began on September 7, when soldiers carried by Grasse and Lafayette's Americans took up positions on the land side of Yorktown. By September 28, after the arrival of Washington and Rochambeau, the entire allied force was in siege position. The force numbered more than sixteen thousand men, about half French and half American. Once the first parallel was opened and allied siege guns were emplaced, the firing was incessant, forcing the British to withdraw to their inner fortifications.

At this point, the British were closely invested by land and completely isolated by sea. With their supplies and morale dangerously low, the British recognized the hopelessness of their position. On October 17, when Cornwallis asked for terms, the allies demanded complete surrender. Two days later, his seven thousand scarlet-uniformed veterans marched out between rows of white-coated Frenchmen and ill-clad Americans and stacked their arms, while the British bands played "The World Turned Upside Down." News of Yorktown convinced responsible leaders on both sides of the Atlantic that Great Britain's American empire had been permanently rent asunder.

SIGNIFICANCE

The defeat of Cornwallis and the surrender of his army by no means automatically resulted in an American victory in the Revolutionary War. In fact, had the British Empire chosen to do so, it could have mounted renewed thrusts against the rebellious colonies, either from forces in New York or with reinforcements from the British Isles. However, the effect of a major military setback in the Americas, in conjunction with Great Britain's precarious position in a worldwide struggle against Spain, France, and Holland, as well as the newly formed United States, combined to force George III and his ministers to accept American independence as the best possible solution left to them under the circumstances. Peace was formally established in the Treaty of Paris (1783), and the new republic was officially recognized by its former mother country.

—*R. Don Higginbotham, updated by Michael Witkoski*

FURTHER READING

Cook, Don. *The Long Fuse: England and America, 1760-1785*. New York: Atlantic Monthly Press, 1995. Because it covers the entire period of the American Revolution, including the gradual but persistent growth of opinion in favor of independence among the colonies, this work is especially helpful in explaining why Cornwallis's surrender proved such a devastating blow to the British will to continue the contest.

Hallahan, William H. *The Day the Revolution Ended: 19 October, 1781*. John Wiley & Sons, 2004. Popular, accessible history recounting events during the final year of the Revolutionary War. Includes information on the siege at Yorktown and Cornwallis's surrender.

Hibbert, Christopher. *Redcoats and Rebels: The American Revolution Through British Eyes*. New York: W. W. Norton, 1990. Presents a subtler and more complicated story than is often told. Places Cornwallis's surrender, and its impact, in a fresh light.

Ketchum, Richard M. *Victory at Yorktown: The Campaign That Won the Revolution*. New York: Henry Holt, 2004. A military history covering the final period of the Revolutionary War, from the autumn of 1780 to the American victory at Yorktown. The book uses numerous anecdotes to provide a detailed recreation of colonial life.

Lumpkin, Henry. *From Savannah to Yorktown: The American Revolution in the South*. Columbia: University of South Carolina Press, 1981. Persuasively advances the thesis that the American Revolution was actually won during the Southern phase of the struggle, and that Greene's campaigns against Cornwallis—along with the efforts of partisans such as Francis Marion—were the decisive factor in gaining American independence.

Mackesy, Piers. *The War for America, 1775-1783*. Cambridge, Mass.: Harvard University Press, 1964. For the British, the struggle in America was part of a worldwide war that ranged from the colonies to the West Indies to Europe and India. For example, troops under Clinton in New York were also expected to defend British possessions in the Caribbean. Reveals the larger pattern of which Cornwallis's surrender was but a part.

Tebbel, John. *Turning the World Upside Down: Inside the American Revolution*. New York: Orion Books, 1993. An excellent introduction that underscores how the decision at Yorktown was a final blow to Great Britain's efforts to subdue the rebellious colonies while simultaneously maintaining a global conflict.

Tuchman, Barbara. *The First Salute: A View of the American Revolution*. New York: Alfred A. Knopf, 1988. An excellent historian presents a survey of the entire

1780's

669

struggle, placing Yorktown and its impact into its contemporaneous setting and significance. Invaluable in helping the reader understand the causes as well as the events of the American Revolution.

SEE ALSO: Oct. 7, 1763: Proclamation of 1763; Mar. 22, 1765-Mar. 18, 1766: Stamp Act Crisis; June 29, 1767-Apr. 12, 1770: Townshend Crisis; Mar. 5, 1770: Boston Massacre; Dec. 16, 1773: Boston Tea Party; Sept. 5-Oct. 26, 1774: First Continental Congress; Apr. 19, 1775: Battle of Lexington and Concord; May 10-Aug. 2, 1775: Second Continental Congress; Jan. 10, 1776: Paine Publishes *Common Sense*; May,

1776-Sept. 3, 1783: France Supports the American Revolution; July 4, 1776: Declaration of Independence; Aug. 6, 1777: Battle of Oriskany Creek; Sept. 19-Oct. 17, 1777: Battles of Saratoga; Feb. 6, 1778: Franco-American Treaties; Mar. 1, 1781: Ratification of the Articles of Confederation; Sept. 3, 1783: Treaty of Paris.

RELATED ARTICLES in *Great Lives from History: The Eighteenth Century, 1701-1800*: Benedict Arnold; Sir Henry Clinton; First Marquess Cornwallis; George III; Nathanael Greene; Comte de Rochambeau; George Washington.

1782-1798
PUBLICATION OF ROUSSEAU'S *CONFESSIONS*

Rousseau's Confessions *created a new tradition in autobiography, the telling of one's life from a subjective point of view for the purpose of introspective revelation. It was thus influential on all subsequent works, both of fiction and of nonfiction, in which the main drama occurs in the mind of the storyteller.*

LOCALE: France
CATEGORIES: Literature; philosophy

KEY FIGURE
Jean-Jacques Rousseau (1712-1778), French writer and philosopher

SUMMARY OF EVENT
The tradition of autobiography reaches back to the narratives of St. Augustine and St. Teresa of Avila, of Abelard's *Historia calamitatum* (c. 1132; *The Story of My Misfortune*, 1922), Dante's *La vita nuova* (c. 1292; *Vita Nuova*, 1861; better known as *The New Life*), and Benvenuto Cellini's *La vita di Benvenuto Cellini* (wr. 1558-1562, pb. 1728; *The Life of Benvenuto Cellini, a Florentine Artist*, 1771; better known as *Autobiography*). These works are of two kinds, those that describe the writer's quest for a spiritual relationship with God and those that explore the self in this world. Michel Eyquem de Montaigne challenged the older tradition in his *Essais* (1580-1595; *The Essays*, 1603), injecting subjectivity into personal writing.

By the eighteenth century, Jean-Jacques Rousseau would take a step that would influence the writing of autobiography ever after and would give the Romantic movement its core precept. The publication of Rous-

seau's *Les Confessions de J.-J. Rousseau* (1782, 1789; *The Confessions of J.-J. Rousseau*, 1783-1790; better known as *Confessions*) was indeed a great event, one that has been seen as promulgating a new era in human consciousness. We might see Rousseau's life up until 1782 as a preparation for that moment in literary history.

In 1749, on his way to visit Denis Diderot, then imprisoned in Vincennes, Rousseau read about a competition sponsored by the Académie de Dijon. The subject matter was whether or not progress in the arts and sciences had contributed to progress in morals. Rousseau's essay, *Discours sur les sciences et les arts* (1750; *The Discourse Which Carried the Praemium at the Academy of Dijon*, 1751; better known as *A Discourse on the Arts and Sciences*, 1913), won the competition. Its argument contested the idea that ancient civilization surpassed the contemporary. It was, however, his contribution to the 1753 Dijon prize, *Discours sur l'inégalité* (1754; *A Discourse on Inequality*, 1756), that may be seen as the genesis of the *Confessions*, for in this argument, amid his ideas of the goodness of "natural man," Rousseau established *himself* as the locus of truth in the world. Subsequently, in *Émile: Ou, De l'éducation* (1762; *Emilius and Sophia: Or, A New System of Education*, 1762-1763), Rousseau advocated the individual conscience as the "divine instinct," the source of moral truth, further elaborating his evolving doctrine of subjectivity. Later, his publisher, Marc-Michel Rey, who had been planning to publish an edition of Rousseau's works, asked for an autobiographical note for the introduction (for Rousseau had by then become an enigmatic figure).

The first part of the *Confessions* discusses the first

thirty years of his life. The second part, covering the next twenty-four years, was written during the course of his growing persecution mania when he thought he was being defamed by friends and colleagues, by Voltaire, Diderot, Friedrich Melchior von Grimm, and Madame d'Épinay. Believing that his work and reputation would survive his death, he sought to justify his life to posterity. So it was that after November, 1762, when the Parlement of Paris issued a warrant for his arrest for his *Émile*, that he began the *Confessions*.

Rousseau wrote part 1 of the *Confessions* in 1766-1767 and part 2 in 1769-1770. Due to its frank nature, he wished to prohibit its publication until 1800, when all parties mentioned in it would have passed away. Despite his wishes, an abridged part 1 came out with his *Les Rêveries du promeneur solitaire* (1782; *The Reveries of the Solitary Walker*, 1783); an abridged part 2 surfaced in 1789, and a complete edition was published in 1798.

Rousseau's work is an autobiography, like many autobiographies to which we have become accustomed today, a life story, written by the author, telling the readers and posterity what the author wants others to know, in terms not only of what happened but of how the writer *felt* while events were occurring. It is the latter aspect of the text that in 1782 was novel and distinctively modern. The modern autobiography is, generally speaking, not, as with St. Augustine, about one's relationship with God, and not, as with Cellini in Renaissance Italy, about one's daily affairs, but, as with Rousseau, about the relationship of the self with the self. It is an exploration of the interior country of the mind. The mode of introspective revelation led not only to the shift in sensibility of the Romantic era, but eventually, to Sigmund Freud's exploration of interior mental worlds through depth psychoanalysis.

Rousseau reviewed his life—having taken himself as his subject—and confessed. When, in 1770, he first read the book to an audience of seven for approximately fifteen hours, he was presenting a new genre to his listeners:

> I have resolved on an enterprise which has no precedent, and which, once complete, will have no imitator. My purpose is to display to my kind a portrait in every way true to nature, and the man I shall portray will be myself.

Reactions were mixed, ranging from admiration to outrage: Madame d'Épinay received an injunction to restrain him from further performances. The ground that Rousseau broke in *Confessions*—the focus on the subjective life—helped earn him the title "the Father of

Romanticism," influencing autobiographers such as François Auguste René, the vicomte de Chateaubriand, William Hazlitt, Thomas De Quincey, and William Wordsworth.

Rousseau editorialized his past, as most autobiographers do—it is in the nature of the project—but his selection of what to represent was different, and the very personal aspects he presented may be seen as making possible such works as Casanova's *Aus den Memoiren de Venetianers Jacob Casanova de Seingalt* (1822-1828; *The Memoirs of Jacques Casanova de Seingalt*, 1894), which provided intimate details of the author's private life, no matter how depraved those details seemed. Rousseau wrote, for instance, of incidents in his childhood and youth, of belatedly rejecting the advances of a male "Moor" while in a monastery approaching conversion to Catholicism, of having enjoyed corporal punishment at the hands of an attractive thirty-year-old woman, and of thieving and the circumstances under which he began, the theft of a pin which he blamed on a blameless girl, an event he claimed to regret his entire life.

It is the very frankness with which Rousseau discussed issues, both detrimental and beneficial, and their effects on the developing character that make the *Confessions*, along with *Émile*, a primer in child psychology. In *Émile*, Rousseau—building on primitivist ideas circulating at the time—propounded a philosophy of education founded on the principle that the judgment and character of a child could be formed only when he or she was kept from the deleterious influence of a jaded civilization. In the *Confessions*, Rousseau employs a narrative of causal analysis to reflect upon how events affect a child's psyche and form the character that evolves in adulthood. Rousseau in effect forced into the genre of life-writing a serious and intensive consideration of many aspects of childhood experience, including parents and guardians, friends and enemies, general social situations, and education.

Rousseau's focus on the child as an individual worthy of in-depth examination undermined the eighteenth century's notion of children as miniature adults. It did not take much of a leap from this to the Romantic adulation of the innocence of childhood as a state to be protected. This concept existed in tandem with Rousseau's notion of the "Noble Savage," that individuals are innocent and pure when uncontaminated by adult life in the civilized world.

Rousseau's influence is seen everywhere in Romanticism. In "Lines Composed a Few Miles Above Tintern Abbey" (1798), William Wordsworth takes as his starting point his own childhood, reflecting on who he was when he first visited the ruined abbey and its pristine environs on the banks of the river Wye, and the changes wrought in him by time and circumstance. Wordsworth's "My Heart Leaps Up" (1802) and "Ode on Intimations of Immortality" (1807) state "The child is father of the man," while Samuel Taylor Coleridge's "Dejection: An Ode" (1802) addresses a child as "thou best philosopher" and comments with melancholy on the effects that living in society will have on a child's psyche.

Rousseau's influence on Romanticism is by no means limited to the concept of childhood. *Confessions* so influenced the worldview of the educated classes that it contributed to the florescence of Romanticism—imagination and dream, the fascination with the distant and remote past, the Romantic antihero, the flawed Titan, self-authenticating experience, the cult of personality, the revolutionary spirit—these and other qualities of the Romantic worldview were prefigured in the *Confessions*.

The seeds of other Romantic ideas may be found in the *Confessions* as well. When Rousseau declaims his preference for sublime forms of Nature, he gives voice to ideas propounded by Edmund Burke in his *A Philosophical Enquiry into the Origin of our Ideas of the Sublime and Beautiful* (1757). Rousseau writes: "I need torrents, rocks, firs, dark woods, mountains . . . abysses beside me to make me afraid." The Romantic vision of grand nature runs through all art forms, from Caspar David Friedrich's paintings to George Gordon, Lord Byron's *Childe Harold's Pilgrimage* (1812-1818) and Percy Bysshe Shelley's *Mont Blanc* (1817). The antihero emerges nearly contemporary with the first performances of the *Confessions*, with Johann Wolfgang von Goethe's *Die Leiden des jungen Werthers* (1774; *The Sorrows of Young Werther,* 1779), and continues with Alexander Pushkin's protagonists and the Byronic hero and the "superfluous hero" of the great nineteenth century Russian novelists. The subject matter of dream and imagination permeate literature and culture from his time to ours.

SIGNIFICANCE

Rousseau is widely seen as a progenitor of contemporary educational reform, the first person who effected lasting change in our perceptions of childhood, bringing into being changes such as the institution of children's literature as a vehicle for entertainment rather than instruction. His influence on autobiography as a subjective art can be seen from Goethe's *Aus meinem Leben: Dichtung und Wahrheit* (1811-1814, 3 volumes; *The Autobiography of*

ROUSSEAU RECALLS HIS AUNT

Jean-Jacques Rousseau's Confessions *is an extremely personal work that relates his thoughts, emotions, and private experiences. The following characteristic passage includes Rousseau's imperfect recollection of the songs his aunt sang to him in his youth, along with meditations on the lasting impact of his youthful experiences on his mind and character.*

The charms of her voice had such an affect [sic] on me, that not only several of her songs have ever since remained on my memory, but some I have not thought of from my infancy, as I grow old, return upon my mind with a charm altogether inexpressible. Would any one believe that an old dotard like me, worn out with care and infirmity, should sometime surprise himself weeping like a child, and in a voice querulous, and broken by age, muttering out one of those airs which were the favorites of my infancy? There is one song in particular, whose tune I perfectly recollect, but the words that compose the latter half of it constantly refuse every effort to recall them . . .

I have endeavored to account for the invincible charm my heart feels on the recollection of this fragment, but it is altogether inexplicable. I only know, that before I get to the end of it, I always find my voice interrupted by tenderness, and my eyes suffused with tears. I have a hundred times formed the resolution of writing to Paris for the remainder of these words, if any one should chance to know them: but I am almost certain the pleasure I take in the recollection would be greatly diminished was I assured any one but my poor aunt Susan had sung them.

Such were my affections on entering this life. Thus began to form and demonstrate itself a heart at once haughty and tender, a character effeminate, yet invincible; which, fluctuating between weakness and courage, luxury and virtue, has ever set me in contradiction to myself; causing abstinence and enjoyment, pleasure and prudence, equally to shun me.

Source: Jean-Jacques Rousseau, *The Confessions of Jean-Jacques Rousseau*, translated by W. Conyngham Mallory. University of Wales, Swansea, Politics Hypertext Library. http://www.swan.ac.uk/poli/texts/rousseau/confa.htm. Accessed November 15, 2005.

Goethe, 1824; better known as *Poetry and Truth from My Own Life*) to Edmund Gosse's *Father and Son: A Study of Two Temperaments* (1907) and in the novel as a vehicle for the exploration of psychological realism.

By shifting the locus of truth from the world-out-there, from objective reality, to the world-in-here, or subjective reality, Rousseau provided, in a work of imaginative literature, what theorists had been expostulating: He articulated the paradigm for a new way of seeing.

—*Donna Berliner*

FURTHER READING

France, Peter. *Rousseau: "Confessions."* New York: Cambridge University Press, 1987. Examines the *Confessions* in the genre of autobiography, its themes and meaning.

Havens, George R. *Jean-Jacques Rousseau.* Boston: Twayne, 1978. Accessible introduction to Rousseau's life and works.

Kelly, Christopher. *Rousseau's Exemplary Life: The Confessions as Political Philosophy.* Ithaca, N.Y.: Cornell University Press, 1987. Discusses the *Confessions* in the context of Rousseau's political system.

Stelzig, Eugene L. *The Romantic Subject Autobiography: Rousseau and Goethe.* Charlottesville: University Press of Virginia, 2000. Comparative study; places the *Confessions* in literary history.

SEE ALSO: 1721-1750: Early Enlightenment in France; 1726-1729: Voltaire Advances Enlightenment Thought in Europe; 1743-1744: D'Alembert Develops His Axioms of Motion; 1748: Montesquieu Publishes *The Spirit of the Laws*; 1749-1789: First Comprehensive Examination of the Natural World; 1751: Maupertuis Provides Evidence of "Hereditary Particles"; 1751-1772: Diderot Publishes the *Encyclopedia*; 1754: Condillac Defends Sensationalist Theory; July 27, 1758: Helvétius Publishes *De l'esprit*; Jan., 1759: Voltaire Satirizes Optimism in *Candide*; Apr., 1762: Rousseau Publishes *The Social Contract*; July, 1764: Voltaire Publishes *A Philosophical Dictionary for the Pocket*; 1770: Publication of Holbach's *The System of Nature*.

RELATED ARTICLES in *Great Lives from History: The Eighteenth Century, 1701-1800*: Denis Diderot; Johann Wolfgang von Goethe; Jean-Jacques Rousseau; Voltaire.

1780's

1782-1810
WARS OF HAWAIIAN UNIFICATION

From 1782 to 1810, the rulers of the various Hawaiian Islands clashed in a struggle for power until King Kamehameha I consolidated rule over Hawaii into a single kingdom. As a united kingdom, Hawaii was able to remain independent in the next century, while the other Pacific islands fell to the European imperial powers.

LOCALE: Hawaii
CATEGORIES: Wars, uprisings, and civil unrest; expansion and land acquisition; government and politics

KEY FIGURES

Kamehameha I (c. 1758-1819), warrior and chief who unified the Hawaiian Islands
James Cook (1728-1779), English explorer
Kahekili (d. 1794), ruler of Maui, r. 1758-1794, and Oahu, r. 1782-1794
Kaumauli'i (d. 1824), ruler of Kauai who ceded his authority to Kamehameha in 1810

SUMMARY OF EVENT

Before the European discovery of Hawai'i (Hawaii) by Captain James Cook, the islands were loosely governed by chiefs who controlled various parts of the archipel-

ago. Warfare was common, aimed at establishing political boundaries and clarifying succession after the deaths of local chiefs. Raids were conducted from time to time, though truces were often declared, usually in order to allow time to harvest crops.

In 1738, the islands were nearly unified by Alapainui, ruler of the southernmost island of the archipelago, the island of Hawaii, and his brother Kamehamehanui, who was the chief on Maui, when they joined forces to seize control of Molokai and took their armies to Oahu for a bloody encounter with the powerful forces of Peleioholani. Rather than pursuing what might have been a pyrrhic victory, the rivals concluded the Treaty of Naonealaʿa, in which Molokai was returned to Peleioholani, who also controlled a portion of Kauai, the northernmost inhabited island in the archipelago. As a result, a peaceful era ensued.

After both Alapainui and Kamehamehanui died, war broke out between their successors, Kalaniopu'u and Kahekili respectively, in the Battle of Kapalipilo of 1758, which resulted in a draw. In 1759, Kalaniopu'u invaded Maui and succeeded in controlling the southern part.

The situation changed dramatically after Captain Cook arrived in 1778 with modern instruments of war, including muskets, pistols, and four-pound cannon; his ships also brought iron, which could be fashioned into superior spears. When Cook died at the hands of the local population in 1779 while demonstrating the power of his muskets, local military leaders lusted to possess more of the advanced technology. Traders from abroad set up shop on the major islands, offering modern goods and weapons for sale; in exchange, island chiefs provided such commodities as sandalwood, the forests of which were soon exhausted.

When 1782 began, Kalaniopu'u ruled the island of Hawaii and south Maui, Kahekili controlled north Maui and Lanai, Peleioholani remained in charge of Oahu and Molokai, and Kaeokulani unified rule on Kauai as well as Ni'ihau. Kahekili then attacked the forces of Kalaniopu'u, successfully expelling them from Maui. When

A statue of King Kamehameha I, who united the Hawaiian islands to form one strong kingdom that repelled European imperial powers for a century. (Library of Congress)

Kalaniopu'u died in 1782, Kahekili turned his sights in the opposite direction; after seizing Molokai, he defeated the ruler of Oahu, his foster son. Ruling most of the islands of the archipelago, he then moved to establish an alliance with his half brother Kaeokulani, ruler of Kauai, and might well have unified the islands at that point.

Meanwhile, the island of Hawaii was convulsed in a civil war that arose as rivals sought to become Kalaniopu'u's successor. One faction, headed by Kiwalao, controlled the Kau and Puna districts; Kalaniopu'u had designated him as his heir. Keawemauhili, ruler of the Hilo and Puna districts, refused to accept Kiwalao's authority. Kamehameha, whom Kalaniopu'u had named as the protector of the war god Kukailimoku, refused to recognize Kiwalao as his leader; he maintained the loyalty of the people in the Kona and Kohala districts. To gain the upper hand, Kamehameha captured and married both Kiwalao's daughter, Keopuolani, and his prospective wife, Ka'ahumanu. In the Battle of Mokuohai (1786), Kamehameha's forces killed Kiwalao. He was succeeded by Keoua, who sustained the rivalry with Kamehameha. Fighting between the three factions continued inconclusively on the island until 1795.

After Kahekili relocated his residence from Maui to Oahu while suppressing a revolt there, Kamehameha took advantage of the power vacuum to subdue Maui in the Battle of Kapaniwai and Kauwau-pali (1790); among Kamehameha's allies were Isaac Davis and John Young, both from Britain. On the third day of the battle, Kamehameha prevailed by deploying a cannon for the first time. He devastated the opposing army, which tried to escape down a steep cliff.

In February, 1794, Captain George Vancouver, midshipman with Cook, landed on the island of Hawaii. Kamehameha soon offered to cede the archipelago to Great Britain, an offer never acted upon by the British parliament, in exchange for a supply of muskets and for the construction of a warship. Meanwhile, muskets had been supplied in 1793 to Kahekili by William Brown, a trader who had taken up residence on Oahu. When Kamehameha returned to Hawaii to deal with Keoua, Kahekili thought that he could wipe out his main opponent by sending a gunboat. However, the first naval battle in the history of the islands was inconclusive.

In mid-1794, Kahekili died, leaving his son Kalanikupule in control of Oahu and Kahekili's half brother Kaeokulani in control of Kauai, Lanai, Molokai, and Ni'ihau. The two rivals then fought, with Kalanikupule the victor, thanks in part to men and munitions supplied by Brown. However, Kalanikupule then overpowered the commanders of one of the ships in port, ordering the boat to sail for new conquests, but his crew soon mutinied and ignominiously forced Kalanikupule and his men off the ship.

In 1795, Kamehameha sailed his army to Oahu, overwhelming Kalanikupule's depleted forces, which were forced up the Pali precipice in the Battle of Nu'uanu. Those who escaped plunging to their deaths over the precipice did not regroup, so Kamehameha I became the ruler of the central islands of the archipelago as the successor to Kalanikupule's control over Lanai and Molokai. He then returned to the island of Hawaii to defeat the remaining faction, killing his cousin Keoua by the end of 1795. He also managed to put down a rebellion by Namakeha in 1796.

Only Kauai and Ni'ihau, now ruled by Kaumauli'i, were independent of the power of Kamehameha I. In 1796, Kamehameha launched warships toward Kauai, but a heavy storm turned them back. He then ordered construction of a fleet of fourteen hundred vessels to maintain authority on the various islands; the armada was completed by 1802. He readied the fleet to attack Kauai in 1804 but relented when his sailors were stricken with an epidemic, possibly typhoid fever. In 1809, Kaumauli'i went to Oahu; when he voluntarily surrendered his island to Kamehameha in 1810, the latter in turn named him governor of the island. Kamehameha had also named loyalists as governors of other islands, so as of 1810, the islands were effectively unified under a single ruler, Kamehameha I, who had established a stable hereditary monarchy.

SIGNIFICANCE

While the rest of the South Pacific was gobbled up by European imperial powers in the nineteenth century, the unification of Hawaii by Kamehameha I served to preserve the archipelago as an independent country that was recognized diplomatically by the major powers as a sovereign state throughout most of the nineteenth century. The rulers, who had outfitted armies in the wars of unification with some modern weaponry, continued to adopt progressive innovations—notably the world's first sys-

tem of compulsory public elementary education and the world's first ministry of public health—to develop a literate, healthy population. The monarchs also encouraged expatriate entrepreneurs from Britain, Germany, and the United States to cultivate coffee, pineapple, and sugarcane, thus developing exports that brought much wealth to the islands.

With the introduction of the export crops, the monarchy sought ever-closer trade relations with the United States, leading ultimately to the decision in 1887 to grant the United States a naval leasehold of Pearl Harbor. Mindful of the dominant position of military forces at Pearl Harbor, Congress voted in 1898 to annex Hawaii as a territory without first conducting a plebiscite of the native population, some of whom today believe that the annexation was contrary to international law and that the sovereign status of the Kingdom of Hawaii, as established by Kamehameha in 1810, should be restored.

—*Michael Haas*

FURTHER READING

Brantly, Chris. "Hawaiian (1100-1785 AD) DBA IV/ 12c." http://www.fanaticus.org/dba/armies/IV/12c, 2004. A detailed account of the wars of unification.

Daws, Gavin. *Shoal of Time: A History of the Hawaiian Islands*. New York: Macmillan, 1968. Chapters 1-2 describe issues involved in the internecine warfare from 1779.

Grant, Glen. *Fornander's Ancient History of the Hawaiian People*. Honolulu: Mutual, 1996. The definitive work on the early history of Hawaii.

Kuykendall, Ralph S., and A. Grove Day. *Hawaii: A History from Polynesian Kingdom to American State*. Rev. ed. Englewood Cliffs, N.J.: Prentice-Hall, 1961. The definitive work on the modern history of Hawaii.

SEE ALSO: Sept., 1720: Collapse of the South Sea Bubble; Apr. 5, 1722: European Discovery of Easter Island; Aug. 25, 1768-Feb. 14, 1779: Voyages of Captain Cook.

RELATED ARTICLES in *Great Lives from History: The Eighteenth Century, 1701-1800*: James Cook; George Vancouver.

1780's

1783
LOYALISTS MIGRATE TO NOVA SCOTIA

The settling of the Loyalists in Nova Scotia helped to preserve Great Britain's remaining North American colonies and played a pivotal part in the establishment of Canada as a separate nation.

LOCALE: Nova Scotia (now in Canada)
CATEGORIES: Wars, uprisings, and civil unrest; expansion and land acquisition; diplomacy and international relations

KEY FIGURES

Sir Guy Carleton (1724-1808), British representative to the North American colonies
John Parr (1725-1791), governor of Nova Scotia
Stephen Blucke (1752-1796), leader of the Black Loyalist community in Birchtown, Nova Scotia

SUMMARY OF EVENT

In the United States, historical accounts of the American Revolution often slight a significant aspect of the struggle for independence: the story of the Loyalists, who remained faithful to the British crown and continued to support a united empire. The Loyalists questioned the effectiveness of a democratic government, feared the collapse of social order, and believed that a continued affiliation with Great Britain would provide safety, prosperity, and continuity. It is estimated that more than 200,000 people—approximately 10 percent of the population in the Thirteen Colonies—resisted the revolution. Many remained silent to protect their property and to ensure their livelihoods. Others voiced their objections and received harsh treatment from the Patriots, including public ridicule through tarring and feathering. The Patriots also seized the Loyalists' property, removed them from positions of authority, and threatened their livelihood.

As well as spying and providing aid to the British troops, the Loyalists formed about fifty regiments to fight against their fellow colonists. In addition, approximately thirty thousand African slaves escaped behind British lines, where they served as soldiers, laborers, cooks, and musicians. Because the British were greatly outnumbered, their generals promised the slaves freedom if they would help swell the dwindling ranks of the imperial army.

The conflict between the Patriots and the Loyalists started in the mid-1760's, when the British government levied heavy taxes on its North American colonies and

attempted to tighten control over its farflung subjects—acts that served as a prelude to the Revolutionary War. Breaking out in 1775, the war continued until the defeat of a British regiment at Yorktown forced the government into peace negotiations with its rebellious colonists. In 1783, the Treaty of Paris recognized the United States as an independent nation.

Shortly after the Continental Congress issued the Declaration of Independence in 1776, the first band of Loyalists migrated to the maritime province of Nova Scotia. The major migration occurred following the treaty in 1783, however, when approximately fourteen thousand British sympathizers were evacuated to Nova Scotia. Considered enemies of the state, the Loyalists were unwelcome in the newly independent nation, as the popular rhyme declared "That Tories, with their brats and wives,/ Should fly to save their wretched lives." It is estimated that more than fifty thousand Loyalists moved to the remaining British North American colonies, with a large number settling in Quebec. While others returned to England or moved to other parts of the British Empire, many remained in the new nation and adjusted to life under a democratic government.

The British representative in Quebec, Sir Guy Carleton, who had received the title Lord Dorchester for his loyalty to the Crown, faced countless problems settling the influx of Loyalists fleeing to Lower Canada. While accommodating many of the new arrivals in Quebec, Carleton looked toward Nova Scotia as an alternate place for settlement. Nova Scotia, along with Cape Breton, Prince Edward Island, and smaller islands, formed the Maritime Provinces. An inhospitable landscape with brutal winters and short summers, Nova Scotia had first been colonized in the early seventeenth century by the French, who called the land Acadia. After the Seven Years' War (1756-1763), British, Scots, Irish, and other European immigrants came to the port city of Halifax. In 1783, the city's population nearly doubled when shiploads of Loyalists arrived. The influx placed immense strains on Nova Scotia's basic administrative structure, on the supply of provisions, and on the availability of housing. Expecting a hero's welcome, the destitute newcomers were disgruntled to be treated as refugees. Many did not survive the first winter as a result of lack of food and makeshift housing in tents, warehouses, and sheds.

Appointed governor of Nova Scotia in 1782, John Parr was inundated with problems. The longtime residents of Halifax resented the fractious Loyalists, who demanded improved living conditions and land grants. To resolve these mounting difficulties, Parr encouraged the newcomers to take up land in uninhabited parts of the province. Under his sometimes inefficient supervision, communities sprang up along Nova Scotia's rocky coast and on its barren terrain. In 1784, the appeals of settlers on the St. John River led to the division of Nova Scotia and the establishment of New Brunswick. Within a few years, the settlements outside Halifax lost population as discontented Loyalists moved to more amenable places in the British Empire. For example, the township of Shelburne boasted eight thousand residents in 1784, but the number gradually dwindled to a few hundred with the departure of those who found Nova Scotia undesirable.

Around three thousand former slaves who had been enticed to join the British forces also made their way to Nova Scotia. Expecting equality and freedom, they were disillusioned to find themselves in conditions that differed little from slavery. Many settled in the segregated community of Birchtown, which was headed by an intriguing figure named Stephen Blucke, a well-educated mulatto from Barbados and a man with a mysterious past. He would act as a liaison between the black and white communities, help obtain land grants, and set up a school to educate the town's children. Yet he was something of an opportunist. In 1791, when the Sierra Leone Company offered Birchtown residents the chance to move to Africa, Blucke headed an unsuccessful effort to boycott the operation. Over half of the population departed, thus diminishing Blucke's influence. Accused of stealing funds, he disappeared without a trace in 1796.

According to tradition, all Loyalists were upper-class, educated, and English. Although some did fit this category, the migration comprised people from every social, economic, and national background, including Irish, Scots, Welsh, and Germans.

SIGNIFICANCE

Had it not been for the Loyalists' presence and influence, the remaining North American colonies most likely would have been the target of the American Republic's expansionist ambitions, and Canada as a separate nation would not exist. The Loyalists' opposition to republicanism helped to assure that Canada preserved its ties with Great Britain and eventually emerged as an independent nation.

In spite of the hardships and setbacks, many of the Loyalists remained in Nova Scotia, New Brunswick, and Quebec, out of which the province of Ontario was formed in 1891. Although initially considered intruders, the original settlers and their descendants carved out a venerable place in Canadian history. In 1789, Carleton announced that he wanted "to put the mark of Honour upon the Families who had adhered to the Unity of the Empire." An order was issued permitting those who "joined the Royal Standard" in 1783, their children, and their descendants of either sex "to be distinguished by the following Capitals, affixed to their names: U.E. Alluding to their great principle, The Unity of the Empire." Today, the United Empire Loyalists Association of Canada and the Black Loyalist Society preserve, promote, and celebrate the Loyalists and their role in Canadian history.

—Robert Ross

FURTHER READING

Brown, Craig, ed. *The Illustrated History of Canada*. Toronto: Key Porter Books, 2003. Sweeping account of the Canadian experience from early times to the present. Provides material on the Loyalists. Excellent illustrations.

Bruce, Harry. *The Illustrated History of Nova Scotia*. Halifax, N.S.: 1997. Records the founding of Nova Scotia, the role of the Loyalists, and the province's subsequent history.

Chidsey, Donald Barr. *The Loyalists: The Story of Those Americans Who Fought Against Independence*. New York: Crown, 1974. Tracks the activities of Loyalist leaders in the colonies before and during the Revolutionary War.

Fillmore, Cathleen. *The Life of a Loyalist: A Tale of Survival in Old Nova Scotia*. Canmore, Alta.: Altitude, 2004. Reveals the difficulties Christiana Margaret Davis and her family faced on their trek from upstate New York to Nova Scotia. Sheds light on the plight of the Loyalists.

MacKinnon, Neil. *This Unfriendly Soil: The Loyalist Experience in Nova Scotia, 1783-1791*. Montreal: McGill-Queen's University Press, 1989. Traces the arrival of the Loyalists in 1783 and the opposition they faced from the existing community, the neglect they experienced from the British government, and their eventual settlement.

Treanor, Nick, ed. *Canada*. San Diego, Calif.: Greenhaven Press, 2003. Comprehensive history of Canada, which includes discussion of the Loyalists and their influence.

Walker, James W. *The Black Loyalists: The Search for a Promised Land in Nova Scotia and Sierra Leone*. To-

1780's

ronto: Toronto University Press, 1993. Documents the black loyalists' harsh experience in Canada and follows them to Sierra Leone after their disillusionment with life in Nova Scotia.

Winks, Robin W. *The Blacks in Canada: A History*. 2d ed. Montreal: McGill-Queen's University Press, 1997. Provides a detailed and lively account of the former slaves who became Loyalists in order to gain freedom, only to find a new form of bondage in Canada.

SEE ALSO: 1713: Founding of Louisbourg; July, 1755-Aug., 1758: Acadians Are Expelled from Canada; Jan., 1756-Feb. 15, 1763: Seven Years' War; Apr. 19, 1775-Oct. 19, 1781: American Revolutionary War; May 10-Aug. 2, 1775: Second Continental Congress; July 4, 1776: Declaration of Independence; Sept. 3, 1783: Treaty of Paris; 1791: Canada's Constitutional Act.
RELATED ARTICLE in *Great Lives from History: The Eighteenth Century, 1701-1800*: Sir Guy Carleton.

1783-1784
CORT IMPROVES IRON PROCESSING

Henry Cort developed an economical and quick method for making bar iron (wrought iron) that allowed Britain to go from being an importer to an exporter of this important material needed for industrialization and the military.

LOCALE: Fareham, England
CATEGORIES: Science and technology; trade and commerce

KEY FIGURES
Henry Cort (1741?-1800), English iron manufacturer
Abraham Darby (c. 1678-1717), English iron manufacturer
Adam Jellicoe (d. 1789), dishonest father-in-law of Cort's partner

SUMMARY OF EVENT

Iron was an important industrial and strategic material in the eighteenth century for Britain. Existing technology and available resources restricted Britain to the commercial production of pig iron (cast iron) using charcoal fuel early in the century. The resulting cast iron with its high carbon content was too brittle for many uses, and the forests needed to provide the charcoal were depleting rapidly. Bar iron used to make the purer and malleable wrought iron had to be imported form Sweden and Russia. Henry Cort's development of the "puddling" process associated with a grooved rolling mill provided a solution to these problems.

Henry Cort was born around 1741 in Lancaster, England, where his father worked in construction and as a brick maker. Cort spent ten years as a young adult working in London as a purchasing agent for the Royal Navy. In this job, Cort would have become very knowledgeable about the problems with British iron. The Royal Navy

had rejected the British-produced wrought iron of the day as of too poor quality for use. Cort left this job in 1775 to take over the Fontley (Funtley) ironworks near Fareham on Portsmouth Harbour that had been inherited by his wife from her uncle, William Attwick. Samuel Jellicoe joined him as a partner.

Cort's aim was to develop a commercial method of producing good-quality wrought iron from British pig iron and coal. Cort put a great deal of effort and money into experiments to determine the best way to achieve this goal. Cort's efforts were the next step in a process that had been ongoing during the 1700's. Abraham Darby of Shropshire had made the vital discovery of how to smelt iron with a coal in 1709. The process was improved over time at the Darby family ironworks at Coalbrookdale, but the next step of using coal successfully to refine pig iron to wrought iron was yet to be taken.

In 1766, Thomas and George Cranage of Coalbrookdale incorporated the use of a reverberatory (air) furnace to try to refine pig iron into wrought iron in order to prevent contaminants from the coal fuel from getting into the iron. Another important step was the invention of the steam engine first patented by James Watt in 1769. The steam engine would allow the whole process to use mechanical power. Nor was Henry Cort the only person working on the problem. A patent recorded in 1783 for Peter Onions of Merthyr Tydvil, Wales, describes a "puddling" process similar to Cort's. There is no evidence that the two had any contact, and Onions's work was not generally known by the iron industry.

Cort patented the grooved rolling mill process in 1783 and the "puddling" furnace in 1784. "Puddling" is the method that Cort developed to convert pig iron into wrought iron. The pig iron from a blast furnace is heated in a coal-fired reverberatory furnace. The flames and smoke of the furnace can be directed away from the iron to avoid adding more carbon to the iron. The molten iron is stirred with an iron rod to expose as much of the iron as possible to the air. The carbon is oxidized and separated from the malleable iron mass. The iron mass is then removed from the furnace and is hammered and rolled at the proper constant temperature to force out the slag (waste material) mixed within the iron and to give the iron product the desired shape and properties. Cort's addition of a grooved rolling mill significantly reduced the need for hammering and provided a big saving in time and effort.

The resulting wrought iron from the Cort process is of good quality. The process is wasteful of iron in that as much as 20 percent of the iron can be lost, but the process is also able to produce significant amounts of wrought iron quickly. The blast furnaces of Britain were capable of producing large amounts of pig iron, and the ability to keep up was more important for the iron refiners than the concern about wasting iron.

After some initial skepticism, the Cort process was rapidly accepted by the major ironworks of Britain and became the dominant iron-refining technology in Britain. The Royal Navy soon approved its product for use. There was more debate about how much credit Cort should be given for the technology. However, prominent individuals like James Watt and Lord Sheffield (John Baker Holroyd) praised his accomplishment. The importance of Cort's technical achievement is not really based on new discoveries. Most of the methods used in his patents were already known. The true achievement was in how the methods were improved and united into one simple, continuous process from iron ore to bar iron that could be used commercially.

Despite the importance of Cort's technical achievements, he was not able to benefit from them financially. Cort had borrowed money from his partner's father, Adam Jellicoe, who was the deputy paymaster of seamen's wages. The loans were secured with Cort's patents. When Adam Jellicoe died in 1789, it was discovered that he had embezzled public funds. Since some of the money had gone to Cort for his work, Cort was held immediately liable for the debt by the court and lost his patent rights and property in lieu of payment. Cort was financially ruined. Protests on behalf of Cort led to a small government pension in 1794. Cort died in 1800 and was buried in Hampstead, England.

SIGNIFICANCE

Before Cort's improvements in iron processing, Britain's ability to produce domestic iron products was limited.

The domestic ironworks had to be located in remote, forested areas to make use of the available charcoal. Iron production was limited to cast iron. The brittleness of cast iron makes it unsuitable for many important uses, and large quantities of bar iron to make wrought iron had to be imported from Sweden and Russia at high cost. Cort's iron processing improvements allowed the economical and large-scale production of wrought iron in Britain while using domestic coal and iron resources. In 1780 before the introduction of Cort's processing improvements, the annual production of iron in Britain was 90,000 tons. By 1820, with eighty-two hundred Cort furnaces in operation, the annual iron production was 400,000 tons.

The quick spread of Cort's iron processing improvements was vital for Britain's early industrial development and strategic position. The improvements freed the iron industry from its dependence for fuel on the rapidly depleting forests of Britain. Building ironworks near coal mining districts instead reduced the overall transportation costs of the industry. Britain no longer had to depend on imports of bar iron from Sweden and Russia. Trying to import bar iron during the approaching Napoleonic Wars would have represented a significant strategic liability for Britain. The availability of large amounts of affordable wrought iron was an important factor in the success of important sectors like the railroad system and the navy, as well as the British Industrial Revolution in general.

—*Gary A. Campbell*

FURTHER READING

Deane, Phyllis. *The First Industrial Revolution*. London: Cambridge University Press, 1965. Examines the economic development of Britain during 1750-1850. Chapter 7 is on the iron industry and includes a discussion on the impact of Cort's improvements.

Mantoux, Paul. *The Industrial Revolution in the Eighteenth Century: An Outline of the Beginnings of the Modern Factory System in England*. Chicago: University of Chicago Press, 1983. An economic history of the rise of manufacturing in England. Chapter 3 examines the coal and steel industry. Section 3 of this chapter is about Cort's technology.

Mokyr, Joel, ed. *The British Industrial Revolution: An Economic Perspective*. 2d ed. Boulder, Colo.: Westview Press, 1999. A series of essays on the economic history of the British Industrial Revolution.

More, Charles. *Understanding the Industrial Revolution*. New York: Routledge, 2000. A good economic overview of the Industrial Revolution. Cort is discussed in Chapter 5 on inventors and entrepreneurs.

1780's

Smiles, Samuel. *Industrial Biography: Iron Workers and Tool Makers*. Reprint. McLean, Va.: IndyPublish .com, 2002. An electronic-book reprint of the classic 1863 work. Henry Cort and his inventions are topics of chapter 7.

SEE ALSO: 1705-1712: Newcomen Develops the Steam Engine; 1709: Darby Invents Coke-Smelting; 1765-

1769: Watt Develops a More Effective Steam Engine; Nov., 1777-Jan. 1, 1781: Construction of the First Iron Bridge.

RELATED ARTICLES in *Great Lives from History: The Eighteenth Century, 1701-1800*: Abraham Darby; John Wilkinson.

September 3, 1783
TREATY OF PARIS

The Treaty of Paris brought the American Revolution to a formal conclusion, as Great Britain officially recognized the United States as an independent, sovereign nation.

LOCALE: Paris, France

CATEGORY: Diplomacy and international relations; wars, uprisings, and civil unrest; expansion and land acquisition; colonization

KEY FIGURES

Benjamin Franklin (1706-1790), U.S. minister to France

John Jay (1745-1829), U.S. minister to Spain and later chief justice of the Supreme Court, 1789-1795

John Adams (1735-1826), U.S. minister to the Netherlands and later president of the United States, 1797-1801

Second Earl of Shelburne (William Petty-Fitzmaurice; 1737-1805), prime minister of Great Britain, 1782-1783

Richard Oswald (1705-1784), British negotiator

Charles Gravier de Vergennes (1719-1787), French minister of foreign affairs

Count de Aranda (Pedro Pablo Abarca de Bolea; 1719-1798), Spanish ambassador to France

Joseph Mathias Gérard de Rayneval (1736-1812), Vergennes's secretary and diplomatic courier

Lord North (Frederick North; 1732-1792), prime minister of Great Britain, 1770-1782

Second Marquess of Rockingham (Charles Watson-Wentworth; 1730-1782), prime minister of Great Britain, 1765-1766, 1782

SUMMARY OF EVENT

The United States' ultimate success in winning the Revolutionary War did not immediately translate into an easy peace. The new nation's primary objective in the years

following the first Marquess of Cornwallis's surrender at Yorktown was to gain formal recognition of its independence from Great Britain. It also needed agreements related to tangential issues, such as boundaries and fishing rights off Newfoundland and Nova Scotia.

It quickly became evident that the United States could not expect altruistic generosity from either its friends or its former adversaries. France, an ally of Spain, hesitated to support U.S. interests against the wishes of its Bourbon neighbor. Madrid also objected to any new rising empire in the Western Hemisphere, fearing possible instability within its own Latin American colonies. If Great Britain appeared conciliatory toward the United States, its motives were dictated by a desire to weaken the Franco-American Alliance and maintain remaining North American interests. At the same time, as events later revealed, Great Britain and France were willing to cooperate surreptitiously to limit the territorial aspirations of the United States when it proved to be in the interest of either power.

The U.S. diplomats at the peace conference were a match for their French and English counterparts, despite problems in undertaking their important task. Of those appointed by the Continental Congress to negotiate a peace, Thomas Jefferson did not serve because of the fatal illness of his wife, and Henry Laurens was a prisoner in England during the most crucial period of the peacemaking discussions. Two other appointees were serving in previous diplomatic assignments—John Jay at Madrid and John Adams at the Hague—and did not reach Paris until months after Benjamin Franklin began discussions with the British in April, 1782. (Jay reached Paris in late June, while Adams did not arrive until the end of October.)

In London, Lord North had been prime minister throughout the entire war, but King George III largely had dictated government policy. The revolt of the Ameri-

The United States' Territory Following the Treaty of Paris

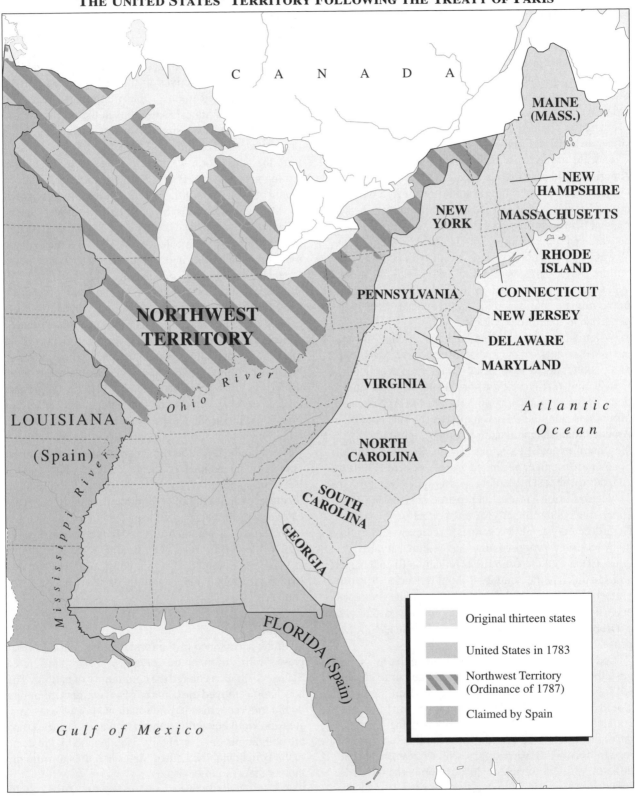

C A N A D A

MAINE
(MASS.)

NEW
HAMPSHIRE

NEW
YORK

MASSACHUSETTS

RHODE
ISLAND

PENNSYLVANIA

CONNECTICUT

NEW JERSEY

DELAWARE

MARYLAND

NORTHWEST
TERRITORY

VIRGINIA

Atlantic
Ocean

Ohio River

LOUISIANA

NORTH
CAROLINA

(Spain)

Mississippi River

SOUTH
CAROLINA

GEORGIA

FLORIDA (Spain)

Gulf of Mexico

1780's

Original thirteen states

United States in 1783

Northwest Territory
(Ordinance of 1787)

Claimed by Spain

can colonies and their probable loss from the British Empire led to North's resignation in March, 1782. The second Marquess of Rockingham succeeded him but died several months later. The second earl of Shelburne, the home secretary in Rockingham's cabinet, had been assigned the responsibility of dealing with the Americans. Shelburne sent to Paris a Scottish merchant named Richard Oswald, an elderly acquaintance of Franklin, to start conversations aimed at luring the venerable commissioner away from France.

Oswald argued that the former British colonies in America could gain more by dealing separately with the mother country, but while Franklin revealed a willingness to speak with the British representatives, he remained firmly committed to the Franco-American military alliance created in 1778. He did, however, assure Oswald that a generous peace would go far toward rebuilding ties between the English-speaking nations. When Rockingham died in July, Shelburne became prime minister but was reluctant to concede total independence to the former colonies.

When Jay finally arrived in Paris in June, he expressed his deep suspicion of French intentions, correctly believing that Charles Gravier de Vergennes, French minister of foreign affairs, favored Spanish ambitions in the disputed region between the Appalachian Mountains and the Mississippi River. The count de Aranda, Spanish ambassador to France, informed Jay of the unwillingness of Charles III, the Bourbon king of Spain, to recognize the United States' western claims to all lands to the east bank of the Mississippi River north of 31 degrees north latitude and to free navigation of the entire river. Subsequently, Aranda and Joseph Mathias Gérard de Rayneval, Vergennes's secretary and diplomatic courier, proposed that the region between the Great Lakes and the Ohio River remain in British hands and that much of the Southwest should become a Spanish protectorate. When he learned that Gérard de Rayneval had slipped away to London, Jay suspected that the Bourbons might negotiate with Great Britain at U.S. expense.

Led by Jay, who personally took the initiative in August, the U.S. commissioners assured Shelburne of their willingness to deal directly with the British if London would change Oswald's instructions to permit him to negotiate openly and with full authority with the representatives of the United States. This would be an implicit recognition of U.S. sovereignty, which Great Britain had hitherto refused to acknowledge. Shelburne now responded positively, believing that the patriots could be separated from France and would be more cooperative with Great Britain in the future. Oswald received his increased authority in September, and the negotiations rapidly clarified the details of an agreement.

Franklin was disappointed at not gaining Canada, one of his personal objectives in the negotiations, but the boundaries agreed upon in the preliminary treaty did meet the United States' aspirations in the northwest and southwest. The Mississippi River was designated as the primary western boundary of the United States. In addition, the new nation was given access to the Canadian fishing grounds, and British forces would be evacuated from U.S. soil. In return, the U.S. commissioners agreed to validate prewar debts owed to British subjects and to recommend to the states that they return confiscated Loyalist property. On balance, the United States gained more than the British in the concessions each side made to reach a satisfactory conclusion.

The preliminary articles, signed on November 30, 1782, although without the advice or consent of Vergennes, did not technically violate the letter of the Franco-American Alliance, for the treaty was not to go into effect until France and Great Britain also had come to terms. What the commissioners had violated, however, were the instructions given by Congress in June, 1781, that they do nothing without the knowledge and consent of France. At that time, Congress had even withdrawn the requirement that the Mississippi River be the nation's western boundary, ordering its commissioners to insist only upon independence. The negotiators' coup enabled Vergennes, never really eager to keep fighting until Spain recovered Gibraltar from the British, to persuade Charles III's ministers to settle instead for the acquisition of the island of Minorca in the Mediterranean Sea, as well as the two Floridas. The final treaties were signed at Paris on September 3, 1783, confirming the detailed British-American understanding of the previous November.

SIGNIFICANCE

With the acceptance of the formal agreement and Congress's ratification of the Treaty of Paris, the United States of America entered the community of nations. The new nation enjoyed the benefits of sovereignty, attaining boundaries recognized by international law whose transgression would constitute an act of war. It also assumed the obligations of sovereignty, as indicated by the debts to the British that the United States had to bear from the moment it officially existed.

—*R. Don Higginbotham, updated by Taylor Stults*

FURTHER READING

Bemis, Samuel Flagg. *The Diplomacy of the American Revolution.* Reprint. Washington, D.C.: American Historical Association, 1957. A pioneering assessment by one of the United States' most distinguished diplomatic historians.

Brecher, Frank W. *Securing American Independence: John Jay and the French Alliance.* Westport, Conn.: Praeger, 2003. Examines the United States' diplomatic efforts to end the Revolutionary War, focusing on the activities of John Jay and Charles Gravier de Vergennes.

Burt, Alfred L. *The United States, Great Britain, and British North America from the Revolution to the Establishment of Treaty After the War of 1812.* Reprint. New Haven, Conn.: Yale University Press, 1968. A detailed account of the controversies and negotiations of the period.

Cohen, Warren, ed. *Cambridge History of American Foreign Relations.* Vol. 1. New York: Cambridge University Press, 1993. Discusses the 1782-1783 peace negotiations from a point of view highly critical of Jay's role in the affair.

Darling, Arthur B. *Our Rising Empire, 1763-1803.* Reprint. New Haven, Conn.: Yale University Press, 1972. Contributes sound chapters on the peacemaking negotiations and the postwar period.

Dull, Jonathan R. *A Diplomatic History of the American Revolution.* New Haven, Conn.: Yale University Press, 1985. Places the Revolutionary War and subsequent peacemaking in the context of European power politics.

Hoffman, Ronald, and Albert, Peter J., eds. *Treaty and the Treatymakers: The Treaty of 1783.* Charlottesville: University Press of Virginia, 1986. Essays cover specific diplomatic issues of the period.

Morris, Richard. *The Treatymakers: The Great Powers and American Independence.* Reprint. New York: Harper & Row, 1983. Widely respected as a comprehensive description and analysis of this subject.

Schiff, Stacy. *A Great Improvisation: Franklin, France, and the Birth of America.* New York: Henry Holt, 2005. Examines the seven years Benjamin Franklin spent in Paris, securing an alliance with the French and eventually helping to negotiate the Treaty of Paris. Schiff depicts Franklin as an improvisational diplomat who created foreign policy as he went along.

SEE ALSO: Apr. 19, 1775-Oct. 19, 1781: American Revolutionary War; May 10-Aug. 2, 1775: Second Continental Congress; July 4, 1776: Declaration of Independence; Feb. 6, 1778: Franco-American Treaties; Mar. 1, 1781: Ratification of the Articles of Confederation; Oct. 19, 1781: Cornwallis Surrenders at Yorktown; Oct. 22, 1784: Fort Stanwix Treaty; Sept. 17, 1787: U.S. Constitution Is Adopted; Nov. 19, 1794: Jay's Treaty; Oct. 27, 1795: Pinckney's Treaty.

RELATED ARTICLES in *Great Lives from History: The Eighteenth Century, 1701-1800*: John Adams; Charles III; Benjamin Franklin; George III; John Jay; Thomas Jefferson; Lord North; Charles Gravier de Vergennes.

1780's

November 21, 1783
FIRST MANNED BALLOON FLIGHT

On November 21, 1783, Pilâtre de Rozier and the Marquis d'Arlandes ascended from the Château de la Muette in a hot-air balloon created by the Montgolfier brothers. Their journey over Paris lasted for twenty-six minutes and marked the beginning of piloted lighter-than-air flight in Europe.

LOCALE: Château de la Muette, near Paris, France
CATEGORIES: Inventions; science and technology; transportation

KEY FIGURES
Joseph-Michel Montgolfier (1740-1810), French inventor
Jacques-Étienne Montgolfier (1745-1799), French inventor and brother of Joseph-Michel
Jean-François Pilâtre de Rozier (1756-1785), pilot of the Montgolfiers' hot-air balloon on its first ascension
Marquis d'Arlandes (François Laurent d'Arlandes; 1742-1809), a passenger on the first manned balloon flight
Louis XVI (1754-1793), king of France, r. 1774-1792

SUMMARY OF EVENT
On November 21, 1783, the people of Paris cheered as they watched the slow passage of the hot-air balloon created by Joseph-Michel Montgolfier and Jacques-Étienne Montgolfier. With the technology of hot-air ballooning nearly perfected, the Montgolfiers had been testing their

invention since the preceding June, first with empty teth- ered flights and then with farm animals aboard. On No- vember 21, they attempted the first piloted free flight, carrying François Pilâtre de Rozier and the Marquis d'Arlandes. Departing from the garden of the Château de la Muette in the northwest of Paris, the balloon sailed through the air for twenty-six minutes before landing safely.

Joseph-Michel Mongolfier was born in Vidalon-les- Annonay in Ardêche in 1740. He was the twelfth child of a family of sixteen children, of which only five survived childhood. He was five years older than his brother Jacques-Étienne. Their father, Pierre Montgolfier, owned a very successful paper factory in Dauphiné, a re- gion near the Alps. Jacques-Étienne was a serious and disciplined student who excelled in mathematics and studied architecture with the famous French architect Jacques-Germain Soufflot. Joseph-Michel, on the other hand, was an indifferent student. Sent to a Jesuit college in Toumon to study for the priesthood, he showed little interest in theology or Latin, soon leaving his studies and migrating to Paris. There, he met and was fascinated by many of the great scientists and mechanics of his day, in- cluding Benjamin Franklin, the naturalist Louis Jean- Marie Daubenton, Jean le Rond d'Alembert, and Jacques Vaucanson, who was engaged in creating automatons.

Jacques-Étienne was given charge of the family busi- ness in 1772, where he industriously began attempting to perfect the papermaking process. Joseph-Michel like- wise became the manager of a paper factory in Voiron, Dauphiné, but lacked his brother's commitment to the profession and his business sense. Though he was a born inventor, gifted in mechanics and the sciences, he was also an absent-minded romantic and dreamer who had been known to walk home from a tavern, forgetting that he had come on his horse.

Though their personalities were so different, the brothers got on well together, forming an alliance be- tween dreamer and diligent mechanic that made them an ideal team. Having read a physics treatise on the laws of gases, they began experimenting with lighter-than-air flight in 1782, designing and building small silk or paper balloons they filled with hot air. Modest successes prompted them to continue their work. On June 5, 1783, the brothers' latest hot-air balloon rose to about 2,000 meters, landing in a vineyard 2.5 kilometers from Annonay.

The Montgolfiers were not, however, the only ones experimenting with flight. Jacques-Alexandre Charles and Marie-Noel Robert developed a hydrogen balloon

Two individuals in a balloon flying above Paris and its envi- rons, staying aloft for twenty-six minutes to mark the first pi- loted balloon flight. (Harper & Brothers)

that, on August 27, 1783, rose from the Champ de Mars, an open grassy area in the center of Paris, and came to rest in Gonesse, 25 kilometers away. Though Charles and Robert's balloon was attacked and destroyed by peas- ants, frightened by its sudden and mysterious descent from the heavens, it had beaten the Montgolfiers' record.

Fostering the competition that led to scientific ad- vances and engineering breakthroughs, the French Acad- emy of Sciences encouraged the Montgolfiers to con- tinue their experiments. A presentation of their work before King Louis XVI and Marie-Antoinette at Ver- sailles was arranged on September 19, 1783. As the king watched, the brothers placed a sheep, a rooster, and a duck in the basket suspended from their balloon. When the craft sailed into the air, landing eight minutes later and 3 kilometers away in the woods of Vaucresson, the king was delighted. Soon thereafter, he ennobled Joseph- Michel and Jacques-Étienne, who were henceforth called de Montgolfier.

A month later, on October 15, the brothers were ap- proached by Jean-François Pilâtre de Rozier as they pre- pared for a flight in a park in Paris. Pilâtre de Rozier, intrigued by the preparations that he had observed, offered to take the place of the domestic animals, becoming the first person to rise 20 meters in a tethered balloon. On October 20, he reached 60 meters. Discovering that sustained flight was almost impossible because of the difficulty of maintaining the fire that provided the hot air, Pilâtre de Rozier suggested that a second passenger would be useful. A few hours later, Giroud de Villette accompanied Pilâtre de Rozier on a flight that reached 80 meters and lasted for ten minutes. Though the problems of sustaining flight had been solved, if not the considerable danger involved in maintaining an open fire so near to a canopy composed of silk and paper, still, free flight had not been achieved.

The Montgolfiers announced that the first free flight of a piloted balloon would take place on November 21, 1783. As the population of Paris awaited the spectacle, at 1:54 P.M. Pilâtre de Rozier, accompanied by an infantry officer, the Marquis d'Arlande, rose from the field surrounding the Château de la Muette at the northwest boundary of Paris. A strong wind blowing from the northwest pushed the balloon over the roofs of Paris, as both aeronauts worked diligently to feed their fire with straw. When they reached the Seine River, the air in contact with the water was colder, and the balloon dropped steadily toward the ground. Feeding more straw into the furnace brought the balloon back up to 1,000 meters, however. The flames from the larger fire ignited the balloon envelope in scattered areas, threatening disaster until Pilâtre de Rozier extinguished the flames with a wet sponge. After flying near Notre Dame Cathedral and the windmills of Montmartre, the balloon landed safely at 2:20 P.M. on the Butte-des-Cailles, near the present-day Place d'Italie. For twenty-six minutes, and for the first time in history, two people had traveled freely in the air.

Soon after the Montgolfiers' success, on December 1, 1783, Charles and Robert flew for fifty-six minutes in their hydrogen balloon and reached an altitude of 3,500 meters carrying meteorological instruments—a thermometer and a barometer. Joseph-Michel de Montgolfier finally flew in his own balloon on January 19, 1784. The dangers that the early balloonists faced became clear when, on June 15, 1785, Pilâtre de Rozier decided to cross the English Channel with Pierre Ange Romain. Soon after taking off, their balloon caught fire and both aeronauts were killed.

SIGNIFICANCE

The key to the success of the Montgolfiers resided in the complementarity of their characters. The empirical

method and imagination of Joseph-Michel was tempered by the order, method, and conservatism of Jacques-Étienne. Their discoveries were integral to the explosion of scientific theory and application resulting from the Enlightenment's faith in the power of rational thought. Like Benjamin Franklin in the United States, they were a convincing demonstration of the ability of intelligent people to make an understanding of the nature of the physical world useful.

The hot-air balloons that they pioneered provided the technological basis for most lighter-than-air flight in the nineteenth century. Used for scientific observation, hot-air balloons also were adapted to military use, primarily for observation and communication. They were successfully employed during the U.S. Civil War, in the 1870-1871 Siege of Paris during the French-Prussian War, and during World War I.

Charles and Roberts's hydrogen balloon was the predecessor of the dirigibles and blimps of the early twentieth century. Though hot-air ballooning has become to a great extent merely the hobby of a community of dedicated enthusiasts, it has led to more efficient and dependable technologies that are still employed whenever modern meteorological balloons are launched to study atmospheric pressure, humidity, and the ozone layer.

—Denyse Lemaire and David Kasserman

FURTHER READING

Christopher, John. *Riding the Jetstream: The Story of Ballooning, from Montgolfier to Breitling*. London: John Murray, 2001. The author examines the invention of the first balloon and its evolution until the present.

Gillipsie, Charles Coulston. *The Montgolfier Brothers and the Invention of Aviation, 1783-1784: With a Word on the Importance of Ballooning for the Science of Heat and the Art of Building Railroads*. Princeton, N.J.: Princeton University Press, 1983. A good introduction to the methods by which Joseph-Michel and Jacques-Étienne Montgolfier invented their balloon, and the science that made it work.

Rosenband, Leonard N. *Papermaking in Eighteenth-Century France: Management, Labor, and Revolution at the Montgolfier Mill, 1761-1805*. Baltimore: Johns Hopkins University Press, 2000. An excellent description of the Montgolfier family papermaking business. Its success gave the Montgolfier brothers the means to develop their balloon.

SEE ALSO: 1714-1762: Quest for Longitude; 1738: Bernoulli Proposes the Kinetic Theory of Gases;

1780's

1759-1766: Construction of the Bridgewater Canal; 1765-1769: Watt Develops a More Effective Steam Engine; Oct. 23, 1769: Cugnot Demonstrates His Steam-Powered Road Carriage; Jan. 7, 1785: First Cross-Channel Flight.

RELATED ARTICLES in *Great Lives from History: The Eighteenth Century, 1701-1800*: Jean le Rond d'Alembert; Benjamin Franklin; Louis XVI; Marie-Antoinette; Jacques-Étienne and Joseph-Michel Montgolfier.

1784
LEGENDRE INTRODUCES POLYNOMIALS

Legendre found, in the course of trying to solve a differential equation, a family of polynomials that satisfied the same kind of properties that ordinary polynomials did. This suggested the use of those polynomials to represent all functions that had certain features, and similar families have been studied by mathematicians and physicists ever since.

LOCALE: Paris, France
CATEGORIES: Mathematics; science and technology

KEY FIGURES
Adrien-Marie Legendre (1752-1833), French mathematician and textbook writer
Pierre-Simon Laplace (1749-1827), French mathematician and astronomer
Leonhard Euler (1707-1783), Swiss mathematician
Joseph Fourier (1768-1830), French mathematician and physicist

SUMMARY OF EVENT
The introduction of differential equations by the founders of calculus led to the formulation of problems about the natural world in mathematical terms. For the earliest workers in the field, there was a limited repertoire of possible solutions to such equations. When none of those solutions seemed to work for equations that were needed to analyze changes in the physical world, new kinds of functions had to be introduced. One of the central groups of equations lacking solutions was orthogonal polynomials, and Legendre's efforts to solve a problem about the solids of revolution brought a particular family of such polynomials to the fore.

Polynomials had been known in mathematics for centuries by the time that Legendre was undertaking his investigations. They are expressions involving combinations of whole-number powers of the variable, and the solution of general equations involving polynomials of the third and fourth degree had been part of Renaissance mathematics in the sixteenth century. One of the central features of polynomials that made them crucial in alge-

bra was the principle of undetermined coefficients. This principle states that if two polynomials are equal for all values of the variable, then the coefficients of like powers of the variable have to be equal. This was taken for granted in the seventeenth century but investigated more rigorously in the eighteenth century.

In view of the centrality of polynomials in algebra, they played an important role in the new field of calculus as well. The field of differential equations involves taking a mathematical statement about the rate at which a quantity is changing and trying to figure out an expression for the original quantity. If it was possible to get the original quantity as a simple polynomial, then the solver could use everything that was known about polynomials to analyze the solution. The earliest differential equations, however, already involved functions that were more complicated than polynomials, like the trigonometric and exponential functions. It seemed as though the background from polynomials was not going to be useful in analyzing such solutions.

Leonhard Euler made an immense contribution to understanding the analysis of such solutions by treating even complicated functions as a kind of polynomial with no limit to the highest power of the term. Such a polynomial of "infinite" degree is called an infinite series, and Euler was a master of manipulating infinite series for many kinds of functions. Once Euler could demonstrate that a function could be represented uniquely as an infinite series, he was able to put information about polynomials to use in talking about complicated functions, although subsequent generations have sometimes found a lack of rigor in his treatment. Nevertheless, his intuition sufficed to get remarkable formulae connecting the solutions of differential equations.

Adrien-Marie Legendre managed to carry the work of Euler further with the help of his colleague Pierre-Simon Laplace. Both men were interested in the question of how to simplify the problem of gravitational attraction by a body that was spread over space, and the work of the founders of calculus, Sir Isaac Newton and Gottfried

Wilhelm Leibniz, indicated that the attraction could be expressed as a differential equation. Solving such differential equations was quite difficult, especially if it was not clear what form the solution was going to take. It was clear that the result was not going to be a simple function, but the problem facing Legendre was to figure out some kind of expression.

Legendre came up with the idea of representing the solution of the differential equation in which he was interested as a series involving powers of the cosine of the angle made at the center of the solid he was studying by two lines connecting the center with the surface. Each of the coefficients of the series would be a polynomial, and from that he could obtain an expression that could be evaluated. If it were possible to determine properties of the polynomials in question, then the solutions for a whole family of differential equations could be evaluated.

In his 1784 paper on celestial mechanics, Legendre generated a number of results about the polynomials that he had derived in the course of working on the solution to the differential equation. In particular, he could derive properties of the polynomials without having to write down their explicit forms (which could be quite complicated). He could figure out how the polynomials interacted with one another. Most important, he was able to show that functions of certain kinds could only be represented in one way as expressions involving his polynomials.

This combination knowledge—of both how the Legendre polynomials (as they came to be known) interacted with one another and how the representation of certain kinds of functions was unique in series involving those polynomials—led to the study of similar classes of polynomials called "orthogonal." The evaluation of the expressions that arose in Legendre's paper required the help of Laplace, and Legendre polynomials are sometimes also called "Laplace coefficients." Legendre did not himself develop the study of such polynomials in detail, as he continued to move about in branches of mathematics like geometry and number theory in addition to differential equations. Nevertheless, the use of orthogonal polynomials as a kind of series offered a solution technique for differential equations that would attract engineers as well as mathematicians and physicists. Even when it might be hard to justify the application of techniques on rigorous grounds, the ability to compute a solution as needed enabled defects in rigor to be overlooked.

SIGNIFICANCE

One of the major subjects for study in physics in the early nineteenth century was the behavior of waves. Regular trigonometric functions like the sine function had simple graphs, but observation found plenty of more complicated curves. Trying to analyze them in terms of ordinary trigonometric functions did not seem helpful, but they also did not fit in with standard polynomials.

The mathematician Joseph Fourier recognized that the waves could be analyzed by using a series of trigonometric functions, using the same kind of approach that Legendre had with his polynomials. These Fourier series enabled mathematical physicists to represent the waves uniquely, and the coefficients could be calculated on the basis of the experimental data. Without Legendre's study of the earlier kind of orthogonal polynomials, Fourier's results (which were still regarded with suspicion by members of the mathematical community with a concern for rigor) would have been even harder to swallow.

The importance of orthogonal series continued to be demonstrated in the twentieth century. One way of interpreting the results of quantum mechanics is in terms of a certain kind of infinite-dimensional space. While this is clearly beyond what Legendre would have envisaged, the notion that one could still be using the properties of polynomials even in such a remote setting was a guide for those who sought to analyze mathematically the behavior of waves in nature.

—*Thomas Drucker*

FURTHER READING

Dunham, William. *The Calculus Gallery: Masterpieces from Newton to Lebesgue*. Princeton, N.J.: Princeton University Press, 2005. A specialist on Euler ties Legendre's work into Euler's.

Freud, Geza. *Orthogonal Polynomials*. Oxford, England: Pergamon Press, 1971. Not much history but an exposition of the ideas underlying Legendre's creation.

Itard, Jean. "Adrien-Marie Legendre." In *Dictionary of Scientific Biography*, edited by Charles C. Gillispie. Vol. 8. New York: Charles Scribner's Sons, 1970. Survey of Legendre's mathematical work.

James, Ioan. *Remarkable Mathematicians: From Euler to Von Neumann*. New York: Cambridge University Press, 2002. Looks forward to Legendre's influence on Fourier.

Kline, Morris. *Mathematical Thought from Ancient to Modern Times*. New York: Oxford University Press, 1972. Most detailed analysis of the text in which

1780's

Legendre introduces his polynomials and the problem they were intended to solve.

SEE ALSO: 1718: Bernoulli Publishes His Calculus of Variations; 1733: De Moivre Describes the Bell-Shaped Curve; 1748: Agnesi Publishes *Analytical In-* *stitutions*; 1748: Euler Develops the Concept of Function; 1763: Bayes Advances Probability Theory.

RELATED ARTICLE in *Great Lives from History: The Eighteenth Century, 1701-1800*: Leonhard Euler.

1784-1791
HERDER PUBLISHES HIS PHILOSOPHY OF HISTORY

Herder's Outlines of a Philosophy of the History of Man *set the stage for the dialectical thinking of Georg Wilhelm Friedrich Hegel. This dialectical thinking—a fundamental aspect of nineteenth century German philosophy—would be taken up by Friedrich Engels and emerge as well in the political philosophy of Karl Marx.*

LOCALE: Germany
CATEGORIES: Philosophy; historiography; cultural and intellectual history

KEY FIGURES
Johann Gottfried Herder (1744-1803), German philosopher
Voltaire (François-Marie Arouet; 1694-1778), French philosopher and writer
Isaak Iselin (1728-1782), German philosopher
Georg Wilhelm Friedrich Hegel (1770-1831), German philosopher
John Locke (1632-1704), English political and social philosopher

SUMMARY OF EVENT
Johann Gottfried Herder's philosophy of history was a reaction against the eighteenth century European Enlightenment, which was based upon an ultrarationalist worldview. Most accurately represented by Newtonian physics, Enlightenment intellectuals thought that every aspect of the universe was governed by natural laws. These laws were believed to be universal and unchanging, and through the use of reason humankind could discover and understand their operations. In turn, this knowledge could be used to improve the quality of life by creating social structures that were compatible with these universal truths.

Over time, this newfound rationalist optimism was challenged by an alternative philosophical school that rejected what it believed was an overemphasis on reason. The Romantics viewed the ultrarationalist approach as severely limiting the scope of humanity. These intellectuals also questioned the ability of Enlightenment philosophers to create a structure solely based upon reason that would bring peace and stability to the human community.

Herder's *Ideen zur Philosophie der Geschichte der Menschheit* (1784-1791; *Outlines of a Philosophy of the History of Man*, 1800) is an important example of the Romantic movement's rejection of the concept of a totally rational, scientific civilization. Romantics believed the Enlightenment limited not only the definition of what it meant to be human but also the parameters of human creativity. They disagreed with the empiricism of John Locke, which stated that people came into the world a blank slate, or tabula rasa, and were then molded by the impact of experience. Romantics believed that human beings were far more complicated and spiritual than the tabula rasa image described by many Enlightenment intellectuals. Romantics also emphasized the importance of the individual, stressing the significance of inherited cultural characteristics in the development of a particular personality.

Herder saw in the Enlightenment the emergence of a secular orthodoxy whose followers believed that they had discovered the pathway to universal truth. These European intellectuals attempted to create a modern utopia based upon conformance to natural law. Instead of focusing on the Judeo-Christian Ten Commandments, Enlightenment orthodoxy directed people to follow universal scientific and secular truth. Herder considered this new worldview as a reflection of humankind's first sin, that of pride. He believed the rationalist philosophers had discovered a scientific tree of knowledge in the workings of the market economy, in Newtonian physics, and in the philosophy of history. Herder feared that human reason unrestrained by traditional religion, in fact hostile to Judeo-Christian theology, would in the end become as authoritarian as the cultural structures it wanted to replace.

Voltaire best describes the Enlightenment view of history in his work *Philosophie de l'histoire* (1765; *Phi-*

losophy of History, 1965). Enlightenment historians believed history should be very skeptical of long-accepted beliefs, especially those concerning the history of Christianity. Voltaire perceived most of these cultural traditions as nothing more than a support system for the superstitious and autocratic actions of organized religion. He wanted to use history as an intellectual scalpel to expose and discredit what he believed to be a corrupt and domineering institution that was preventing European society from realizing true progress and freedom. Voltaire also used the platform of history to attack the period of Christian ascendancy known as the Middle Ages. He popularized the term "medieval" and used it as a derogatory description of the period between the greatness of the Classical era and the "rebirth of learning" of the European Renaissance. Voltaire and his contemporaries emphasized the idea that the Middle Ages was an intellectually stagnant period dominated by the superstitious, dominating power of the Church of Rome.

This idea was extended by the Swiss historian Isaak Iselin in his work *Philosophical Conjectures on the History of Mankind* (1764). Iselin described human history as an inevitable drive toward progress. That history showed the most powerful civilizations, from Mesopotamia and Egypt to Greece and Rome, had been based upon the pursuit of scientific knowledge and the acquisition of political power. He believed that all truly great civilizations constructed a rational cause-and-effect view of nature, and that the Enlightenment was the next great extension of human development.

It was to challenge this worldview that Johann Gottfried Herder began to develop his philosophy of history. He believed historical investigation should reflect the spiritual, psychological, geographical, and cultural side of the human condition. This focus on the impact of cultural history on the evolution of society would form the basis of the Romantic belief in the importance of the nation-state to human history. Historians and philosophers such as Herder thought that people developed their basic worldview and sense of who they are from their national identity. This connection between the nation and its culture formed the intellectual foundation for Herder's concept of the *Volk* or people, which would eventually evolve into the German idea of *Volksgeist*, or the cultural consciousness of a particular ethnic group. According to Herder, cultural history and the national traditions it fostered were the adhesive that held a society together.

Herder believed that to understand the history of a people, the scholar must investigate all the forces that had affected their development, starting with geography and climate. Differences in geographic setting, whether it be maritime, steppe, or a mountainous location, determined a civilization's yearly cycle of activity, its economic focus, and its relationship to other states. Landlocked countries would be oriented toward an agricultural perspective, and their historical experience would reflect the impact of the cycle of the seasons on their economic well-being and a more isolationist cultural worldview. Conversely, nations that were located near large bodies of water would have an economic and political history influenced by trade and a cultural history that was more open to diversity.

All of these factors combined to create a unique historical culture that was represented and understood in a nation's material art, folktales, and literature as well as its religious beliefs and philosophical models. According to Herder's *Outlines of a Philosophy of the History of Man*, cultures are not stagnant but evolve with the changing circumstances of scientific discovery, technological innovation, and historical experience. As a historian, Herder was also the first to suggest that the traditional political and military focus of history was counterproductive. He believed that the glorification of both political intrigue and the relentless quest for domination ultimately did nothing to promote the ethical evolution of a society.

The investigation of the world's great cultures and intellectual diversity would create, according to Herder, a societal model that would emphasize the protection of the freedoms of thought and speech. He also believed that because many different civilizations had developed their own unique and sophisticated moral systems, a strong argument could be made for widespread religious freedom. Herder thought that intellectual and religious freedom were a moral right because they fostered intellectual growth. He, like all Romantics, feared anyone who believed he or she had found universal and unchanging truth. His *Outlines of a Philosophy of the History of Man* firmly supported the idea that it was only through the struggle or dialectic of opposing viewpoints that the continued evolution toward truth would occur. He believed it was this continued intellectual growth that was the true definition of progress.

SIGNIFICANCE

Herder's *Outlines of a Philosophy of the History of Man* and his emphasis on the importance of the continuing struggle between opposing points of view and its connection to human progress set the stage for the philosophical

1780's

work of Georg Wilhelm Friedrich Hegel. His philosophy was based upon the idea that every stage in the evolution of mind incorporated a useful aspect and a false aspect. As each stage was overcome, the false aspect was left behind, and the useful aspect was preserved in an evolution toward the truth.

Friedrich Engels also developed a dialectical philosophy. In his version, every theory (thesis) gave rise to an opposite concept (antithesis), and the intellectual struggle between opposites that ensued ended in the combination of the best of both theories (synthesis). The continuous intellectual and evolutionary struggle, taking different forms in Hegel and Engels, was a model of progress central to nineteenth century German thought. In the middle of the nineteenth century, Karl Marx would use the Hegelian dialectic as his model for the inevitability of communism.

Herder's historical worldview also set the stage for the onset of the most powerful intellectual, cultural, and political force in modern history: nationalism. His theory that every cultural group had a unique past that deserved recognition and respect would form the foundation of the modern political right of self-determination. Every ethnic group had the right to form an independent political structure that would guarantee and protect its cultural worldview.

—*Richard D. Fitzgerald*

FURTHER READING

Adler, Hans, and Ernest A. Menze. *On World History: Johann Gottfried Herder*. New York: M. E. Sharpe, 1997. This book is the most respected work on Herder's philosophy of history. Index.

Evrigenis, Ioannis, and Daniel Pellerin. *Johann Gottfried Herder: Another Philosophy of History and Selected Political Writings*. Indianapolis, Ind.: Hackett, 2004. This book allows the reader to investigate how Herder's political philosophy influenced his philosophy of history. Index.

Forster, Michael. *Johann Gottfried Von Herder: Philosophical Writings*. New York: Cambridge University Press, 2002. This book is an excellent overview of Herder's philosophical thought. Index.

SEE ALSO: 1726-1729: Voltaire Advances Enlightenment Thought in Europe; 1743-1744: D'Alembert Develops His Axioms of Motion; 1748: Montesquieu Publishes *The Spirit of the Laws*; 1749-1789: First Comprehensive Examination of the Natural World; 1751: Maupertuis Provides Evidence of "Hereditary Particles"; 1751-1772: Diderot Publishes the *Encyclopedia*; 1754: Condillac Defends Sensationalist Theory; July 27, 1758: Helvétius Publishes *De l'esprit*; Jan., 1759: Voltaire Satirizes Optimism in *Candide*; Apr., 1762: Rousseau Publishes *The Social Contract*; July, 1764: Voltaire Publishes *A Philosophical Dictionary for the Pocket*; 1770: Publication of Holbach's *The System of Nature*; 1782-1798: Publication of Rousseau's *Confessions*.

RELATED ARTICLES in *Great Lives from History: The Eighteenth Century, 1701-1800*: Johann Gottfried Herder; Voltaire.

April 27, 1784
FIRST PERFORMANCE OF *THE MARRIAGE OF FIGARO*

The first performance of The Marriage of Figaro, *a work that reflected the ideals of the Enlightenment and of the impending French Revolution, came after years of struggle with the French court and has remained a symbol of the freedom of the human spirit. One of Beaumarchais's crowning literary creations, the title character has sometimes been identified with the author.*

LOCALE: Paris, France
CATEGORIES: Theater; literature

KEY FIGURES
Pierre-Augustin Caron de Beaumarchais (1732-1799), French dramatist

Louis XVI (1754-1793), king of France, r. 1774-1792
Charles Gravier de Vergennes (1719-1787), French foreign minister, 1774-1787
Wolfgang Amadeus Mozart (1756-1791), Austrian composer
Gioacchino Rossini (1792-1868), Italian composer
Lorenzo da Ponte (1749-1838), Italian poet and opera librettist

SUMMARY OF EVENT
La Folle Journée: Ou, Le Mariage de Figaro (wr. 1775-1778, pr. 1784, pb. 1785; *The Marriage of Figaro*, 1784) by Pierre-Augustin Caron de Beaumarchais was very much a reflection of the stormy political era in France

during which the drama was written. Beaumarchais began work on the play in 1775, following the success of his *Le Barbier de Séville: Ou, La Précaution inutile* (pr., pb. 1775; *The Barber of Seville: Or, The Useless Precaution*, 1776). Beaumarchais was a man of many talents, ranging from watchmaker, painter, and political activist to writer. Despite his numerous gifts, it is *The Marriage of Figaro* and *The Barber of Seville*, the first two plays in a trilogy along with the less successful *L'Autre Tartuffe: Ou, La Mère coupable* (pr. 1792, pb. 1797; *Frailty and Hypocrisy*, 1804), to which he owes a permanent place in history.

The revolutionary spirit that pervaded France in the late 1700's had a large role in Beaumarchais's life. He was an active supporter of both the French and American Revolutions and spent time in prison for his political activity. He was twice married to wealthy women, who were also well connected politically and socially. Close to the aristocracy, he taught music lessons to the daughters of Louis XV. At times, he even had the attention of Madame de Pompadour and Marie-Antoinette. Charles Gravier de Vergennes, the French foreign minister, engaged him in foreign spy activities. During the war, he was a major shareholder in a periodical named *Le Courier de l'Europe*, which not only publicized his literary works but also contained articles that he authored to help shape public political opinion. There were also articles concerning the workings of democracy and parliamentary procedure that ignited the tempers of the leaders of the French monarchy. As a result, his work was considered suspect by the crown and not easily granted stage privileges, as in the case of *The Marriage of Figaro*.

Beaumarchais was preoccupied by the plight of the social classes and their treatment by the court and addressed these issues in his writing. Paradoxically, he was pleading the case for the lower classes against the nobility of which he had become a member; however, his status informed him of the issues from the viewpoints of both the court and the public. In 1772, Beaumarchais wrote the first of the two dramatic works that bought him lasting literary fame. *The Barber of Seville*, which began the story continued later in *The Marriage of Figaro*, was rejected by the Théâtre Italien. Although in 1773 and 1774 the Comédie Française accepted the play for production, Beaumarchais's questionable political involvements brought recriminations from the court and prohibited the openings.

In 1775, after Beaumarchais was finally granted royal permission for *The Barber of Seville* to be premiered, the opening was a complete failure. In three days, he cut the

The Marriage of Figaro, *act 4, scene 9, "It renders you chaste and pure in the hands of your husband."* (Library of Congress)

play from five acts to four, and it was produced the second time to great applause. The story is of a clever servant (Figaro, the barber) who impertinently spoils the marriage plans of Dr. Bartholo, Rosine's elderly guardian, in order to advance the love affair between Rosine and a Spanish nobleman, Count Almaviva. Clear glimpses of the revolution that is beginning in the middle class in France are revealed, as the servant is cast as superior in wit and cunning to the nobility he serves.

In his sequel, Beaumarchais continued the crafty assault on the upper classes that he had begun in *The Barber of Seville*. In *The Marriage of Figaro*, the barber himself is seeking permission to marry the maidservant to the countess. The same group of characters from *The Barber of Seville* constitutes the cast for *The Marriage of Figaro*. The four central characters are the Count and Countess Almaviva, Figaro, and Susanna. At the center of the plot

691

is the wily Figaro, the barber of Seville. Figaro, although a servant to the count, is feisty and rebellious. Unfortunately, the philandering Count also has designs on Susanna and it is up to the servants again, as in *The Barber of Seville*, to outwit the nobility.

The count's admiration of Susanna enrages the young, hot-blooded Figaro, who puts his own ruses into motion to defend his honor and that of Susanna. His cunning is responsible for thwarting the desires of the count in order to fulfill his own wishes, and the play is not subtle in its ridicule of the aristocracy, including the royalty. After much intrigue by all concerned to bring the count to justice, in the end the countess forgives the count and all couples are happily reunited.

In spite of the fairy-tale ending, the overall attitude of the play is reflective of the rise of the middle class that was at the heart of the French Revolution. The not-so-subtle attacks on French nobility did not escape the notice of King Louis XVI, and the play was banned for six years. Despite the king's objections, once the French censors finally approved the play, Marie-Antoinette requested that it be performed at Versailles. The premiere was set for June 13, 1783, but the king again prohibited the performance until Beaumarchais had more some alterations to the script. *The Marriage of Figaro* finally opened on April 27, 1784, and received tremendous acclaim from the public. The number of performances given rarely had been surpassed by even the most successful eighteenth century plays: With sixty-eight consecutive performances, it broke previous records at the Comédie Française.

SIGNIFICANCE

The drama of the eighteenth century played an important role in the perpetuation of the ideals of the Enlightenment. Although the importance that *The Marriage of Figaro* itself had in the encouragement of the French Revolution has been sometimes exaggerated, it must be recognized for the sense of equality and liberty that it promoted in the society in which it was created. It is even said that Napoleon considered it to be "the revolution in action." Its acclaim by the general public and even by the aristocracy was tremendous, despite the ridicule of the upper classes.

Beaumarchais's mastery of the comedic drama made him able to use his writing to further his political agendas, carefully working his points into the plot in a humorous way. In these works, he freely expressed his love of independence and passion for the liberated human soul. The character of Figaro in some ways represents many aspects of Beaumarchais's own personality. His plays were influential beyond France and became the basis for opera librettos for several famous composers. Giovanni Paisiello (1740-1816) had already written an opera based on *The Barber of Seville* prior to Beaumarchais's writing of *The Marriage of Figaro*. In 1816, Gioacchino Rossini (1792-1868) wrote his operatic version of *The Barber of Seville*, which was produced in Rome and eventually eclipsed Paisiello's earlier opera.

In 1786, Wolfgang Amadeus Mozart used the *The Marriage of Figaro* as the basis for his opera *Le Nozze di Figaro*, produced in Vienna. The librettist for the opera was Lorenzo da Ponte, with whom Mozart later collaborated on two more operas, *Don Giovanni* (1787) and *Così fan tutte* (1790). The opera was immediately successful and gained a huge following, much to Mozart's delight. *Le Nozze di Figaro* has remained one of the best known and most beloved operas in the repertory worldwide. The operatic stories borrowed from both *The Marriage of Figaro* and *The Barber of Seville* are somewhat altered from their source material, and they have lives of their own, but they have been largely responsible for keeping the spirit of Beaumarchais's life and writing alive.

—*Sandra C. McClain*

FURTHER READING

Beaumarchais, Pierre-Augustin Caron de. *The Figaro Trilogy*. New York: Oxford University Press, 2003. Includes all three plays in a new English translation by David Coward, whose introduction gives helpful historical context and chronology of Beaumarchais's life and work

Howarth, W. D. *Beaumarchais and the Theatre*. New York: Routledge, 1995. Provides excellent information about prevailing scholarship on Beaumarchais and French theater, some of which was not previously available in English translation.

Jacobs, Arthur, and Stanley Sadie, eds. *The Limelight Book of Opera*. 4th ed. New York: Limelight Editions, 1996. Provides a comprehensive, easy-to-understand plot synopsis and commentary on Mozart's opera *Le Nozze di Figaro*.

Morton, Brian N., and Donald C. Spinelli. *Beaumarchais and the American Revolution*. Lanham, Md.: Lexington Books, 2003. Detailed historical account of Beaumarchais's revolutionary activities in France and America.

Ratermanis, J. B., and W. R. Irwin. *The Comic Style of Beaumarchais*. Seattle: University of Washington Press, 1961. Analyzes Beaumarchais's style in the context of eighteenth century French theater and his use of literary comic conventions to make aesthetic points. Beaumarchais's works are discussed in detail, but introduction and conclusion chapters provide succinct point summaries.

SEE ALSO: Jan. 29, 1728: Gay Produces the First Ballad Opera; Dec. 7, 1732: Covent Garden Theatre Opens in London; 1739-1742: First Great Awakening; Aug.,

1763-Apr., 1765: David Garrick's European Tour; Nov. 12, 1766: First American Theater Opens in Philadelphia; Aug. 3, 1778: Opening of Milan's La Scala.

RELATED ARTICLES in *Great Lives from History: The Eighteenth Century, 1701-1800*: Pierre-Augustin Caron de Beaumarchais; Louis XV; Louis XVI; Marie-Antoinette; Wolfgang Amadeus Mozart; Madame de Pompadour; Charles Gravier de Vergennes.

September 29, 1784
HALL'S MASONIC LODGE IS CHARTERED

Hall's Masonic Lodge became a pillar organization in the African American middle-class community. Serving many of the same functions that mainstream Freemasonry has served among upper-class white communities, members of the so-called African Lodge have helped one another in countless ways for more than two centuries.

LOCALE: Boston, Massachusetts
CATEGORIES: Organizations and institutions; social issues and reform

KEY FIGURES
Prince Hall (c. 1735-1807), African American former slave, leather worker, and Boston community leader
John Marrant (1755-1791), African American minister and missionary to American Indians

SUMMARY OF EVENT
Prince Hall, a former slave living in Boston, perceived the many benefits of belonging to the fraternal group called the Freemasons. In the Thirteen Colonies, many of the most prominent and respected citizens were Masons, including George Washington, Samuel Adams, and Benjamin Franklin. As in the mother country, Masonic lodges in America stressed religion, morality, and charity to members in need and to all humankind. Many members developed business ties with their Masonic associates.

Prince Hall was born a slave around 1735. When Hall was twenty-one years of age, he was granted his freedom by his master. Hall entered into the trade of leather work. He pursued this calling for the rest of his life, although later, his Masonic leadership and his catering business occupied increasing amounts of his time. Tradition holds that Prince Hall fought against the British in the American Revolution. This is almost certainly true, but since

several Massachusetts soldiers were named Prince Hall, details of this Prince Hall's army career are not clear.

In 1775, just before the outbreak of the American Revolution, a white Mason named John Batt initiated Hall and fourteen other free black Bostonians into the Masonic order. The fifteen initiates soon organized the first black Masonic lodge in America, calling it African Lodge. They continued to meet, but under the strict hierarchy of Masonry, a local group such as the African Lodge must be subordinate to a Grand Lodge, making regular reports as well as payments into the Grand Lodge charity fund. The American Masonic hierarchy was still evolving, and Prince Hall and his associates knew that many white Masons in the new country did not approve of black lodges or even black members.

On March 2, 1784, and again on June 30 of that year, Prince Hall wrote to the Grand Lodge of England asking for an official charter. This charter would confer added legitimacy on African Lodge and would give it a powerful ally. Difficulties in getting letters and money between Boston and England slowed the process of obtaining the charter, but Hall's group finally got the requisite fees to the Grand Lodge of England, and in 1787 African Lodge received its charter. The document, dated September 29, 1784, gave African Lodge the right to initiate new members and the duty of reporting regularly to the English Grand Lodge.

Some of the activities of African Lodge related directly to race. In 1787, three free African Americans from Boston were kidnapped by men who took them to the Caribbean island of St. Bartholomew and prepared to sell them into bondage. One of the three was a member of African Lodge. Prince Hall and the other black Masons of Boston agitated actively for release of their brother Mason, and for law enforcement officers to protect free African Americans from kidnapping. The petition circu-

1780's

lated by Prince Hall helped goad the Massachusetts legislature into passing a law to punish slave traders and kidnappers. The three men won their release when the one who was a member of African Lodge gave a Masonic sign that was recognized by a white Mason living on St. Bartholomew, and the white Mason had the captors arrested and the three men returned to Boston.

Although the records of the early meetings of African Lodge are scarce, copies of two addresses by Prince Hall and one sermon by the lodge chaplain have survived. All three documents exhibit a strong degree of racial pride and solidarity. In his first charge to the African Lodge, delivered and published in 1792, Hall chided white Masons who claimed that the existence of black Masons would somehow make the order too common. He pointed out that that had not been the feeling during the recent Revolutionary War, when white and black soldiers had fought shoulder to shoulder. Prince Hall concluded by saying that any man who rebuked an African American man because of his skin color actually was rebuking God, who had made all people in his own image.

Hall's second charge to his lodge was delivered and published in 1797. In this address, the Masonic leader painted a baleful picture of the barbaric cruelties of slavery, and used the Bible to prove that the institution was not part of God's will. On a more optimistic note, Hall lectured his brother Masons about the nation of Haiti, where six years earlier the slaves had revolted and thrown off the yoke of French government and of slavery itself. Hall saw the revolt in Haiti as a first step by African Americans in ending the hated system of slavery.

John Marrant, a free African American minister living in Boston, became the chaplain of African Lodge. One of Marrant's sermons to the lodge was delivered and printed in 1789. As was the case with Hall's addresses, Marrant's sermon stressed what later writers would call black pride. Marrant said that African Americans should not be ashamed that their race was enslaved, since nearly every great people had been enslaved at one time or another, and such enslavement had often been the prelude to a great flourishing of that people. Marrant dipped into the Bible and into ancient history to prove that Africa had produced at least as many great civilizations as had any other region on Earth.

On at least one occasion, members of the African Lodge put their pride in Africa into action. In 1787, Prince Hall circulated a petition asking the Massachusetts government to aid in returning men and women of color to Africa. Seventy-three persons signed the petition, including most members of African Lodge. The petition is one of the earliest documents in American history associated with a back-to-Africa movement. On most other occasions, however, members of African Lodge preferred to work to improve their standing within the United States.

SIGNIFICANCE

As the free black population in the northern states continued to grow, African Lodge responded to requests to bring Masonry to African Americans in other areas. A number of residents of Providence, Rhode Island, were initiated into African Lodge and later began their own lodge with the blessings of Prince Hall and his followers. African Lodge also helped found new lodges in Philadelphia and New York. Meanwhile, all the Masonic lodges in the United States that were chartered by one of the British Grand Lodges began to have less contact with the Grand Lodges across the ocean. African Lodge was no exception. In 1827, African Lodge declared its independence of the English Grand Lodge and of any other Grand Lodge. It became the Grand Lodge for all chapters of African American Masons it founded in the United States.

The so-called Prince Hall Masonry continued to flourish long after the death of Hall in 1807. In 1995, the order boasted 300,000 members in the United States. For more than two hundred years, Prince Hall Masonry has provided moral teachings, aid to members in need, and even business contacts for the millions of African American men who passed through the ranks of the order. For most of that time, white Masons attacked the Prince Hall Masons for claimed irregularities in the latter's organizational history, including the history of the Prince Hall Masons' charters. Yet any alleged irregularities were also part of the history of early white lodges in the United States. While attacks on Prince Hall Masonry are less common today than they were previously, Masonry remains a highly segregated area of American life.

—*Stephen Cresswell*

FURTHER READING

Crawford, George W. *Prince Hall and His Followers.* 1914. Reprint. New York: AMS Press, 1971. The classic defense of Prince Hall Masons to the charges of irregularity made by white Masonic groups.

Dillard, Thomas Henry. "History of Calumet Lodge #25 Free and Accepted Masons, Prince Hall Affiliation." *Journal of the Afro-American Historical and Genealogical Society* 10, no. 1 (1989): 22-28. A rare glimpse into the history of a single lodge of Prince Hall Masons.

Grimshaw, William H. *Official History of Freemasonry Among the Colored People in North America*. 1903. Reprint. Freeport, N.Y.: Books for Libraries Press, 1971. For many years, this book was considered the basic history of Prince Hall Masonry. Readers should be aware that it contains a vast number of unsubstantiated statements and should be used with care.

Horton, James Oliver, and Lois E. Horton. *In Hope of Liberty: Culture, Community, and Protest Among Northern Free Blacks, 1700-1860*. New York: Oxford University Press, 1997. A history of the Northern freed blacks, tracing their lives from the colonial slave trade through the antebellum era. The founding of the first African American Masonic Lodge is described in chapter 6. The book features additional information about Prince Hall's life efforts to immigrate to Africa.

Muraskin, William A. *Middle-Class Blacks in a White Society: Prince Hall Freemasonry in America*. Berkeley: University of California Press, 1975. Sociological and historical examination of Prince Hall Masonry as a foundation of the African American middle class.

"Ten Most Important Figures in African-American History." *Ebony* 57, no. 4 (February, 2002): 88. Prince Hall is among the ten people listed in this historical overview of significant achievements by African Americans.

Wallace, Maurice O. *Constructing the Black Masculine: Identity and Ideality in African American Men's Literature and Culture, 1775-1795*. Durham, N.C.: Duke University Press, 2002. Focuses on seven episodes that illustrate African Americans' efforts to create a positive male identity; one of the episodes is the founding of the first black Masonic Lodge in 1775.

Wesley, Charles H. *Prince Hall: Life and Legacy*. 2d ed. Washington, D.C.: United Supreme Council, 1983. A careful history that does a good job of separating earlier myths about the origins of Prince Hall Masonry from documented fact.

SEE ALSO: Apr. 6, 1712: New York City Slave Revolt; Sept. 9, 1739: Stono Rebellion; 1773-1788: African American Baptist Church Is Founded; Apr. 14, 1775: Pennsylvania Society for the Abolition of Slavery Is Founded; July 2, 1777-1804: Northeast States Abolish Slavery; Apr. 12, 1787: Free African Society Is Founded; Feb. 12, 1793: First Fugitive Slave Law.

RELATED ARTICLES in *Great Lives from History: The Eighteenth Century, 1701-1800*: Benjamin Banneker; Olaudah Equiano.

1780's

October 22, 1784
FORT STANWIX TREATY

The Iroquois tribes that had sided with the British in the Revolutionary War were forced to cede their lands to the United States and move westward. The dismissive negotiating strategy of the American government at Fort Stanwix marked the beginning of its tendency to treat Native American tribes as conquered occupants of the United States, rather than as equal, sovereign nations.

LOCALE: Fort Stanwix, New York
CATEGORIES: Expansion and land acquisition; diplomacy and international relations

KEY FIGURES
Joseph Brant (Thayendanegea; 1742-1807), Mohawk chief allied with the British during the Revolutionary War
James Madison (1751-1836), American statesman and later president of the United States, 1809-1817

Arthur St. Clair (1734-1818), governor of the Northwest Territory and negotiator of the Treaty of Fort Harmar

SUMMARY OF EVENT
The Treaty of Fort Stanwix, signed October 22, 1784, was a product of the American Revolution that involved colonists and the Iroquois Confederacy. Because several Iroquois tribes had fought alongside the British during the war, the victorious Americans maintained that they had won lands occupied by "defeated" Iroquois. The Treaty of Fort Stanwix marked the beginning of negotiations with Native Americans that dealt with them as a conquered people rather than as equals. The Revolutionary War and resulting treaty negotiations irreparably split the Iroquois Confederacy.

At the outbreak of the American Revolution, the Six Nations of the powerful Iroquois Confederacy were divided over whether to support the English, to side with the American rebels, or to remain neutral. The confederation had traded and fought alongside the English for many years and considered the English and colonists as the same. Both British and American Indian agents encouraged Native Americans throughout the colonies to remain neutral. Initially, the Iroquois remained nonpartisan. This decision allowed the Iroquois to deal with both the British in Canada and the Americans in the colonies, playing one against another as they had the French and British prior to the French and Indian War.

As the Revolutionary War progressed, however, both the British and the Americans saw the advantages of including American Indians in their ranks, and they courted Native Americans as potential allies. The pressure to choose sides exerted by British and American agents split the six-nation Iroquois Confederacy into three groups. The Oneidas and Tuscaroras fought for the rebels. American attacks on Mohawk settlements encouraged the Mohawks to support the British; they were joined by Onondagas, Cayugas, and Senecas. These tribes were effective in British attacks on frontier locations, especially in the Mohawk Valley around Fort Stanwix. Other tribal members attempted to remain neutral throughout the war, although they were still subject to retaliatory pillaging and burning in response to the actions of their fellow tribesmen.

During the war, British officers had made promises of land to Native Americans who fought with them, but during the peace negotiations in Paris, the defeated British ignored the interests of their Native American allies. The Treaty of Paris surrendered all the land east of the Mississippi River to the former colonists. Some of this land belonged to various Native American tribes and was not England's to grant.

New York State granted Iroquois lands to American soldiers as compensation for their services during the war. New York tried to negotiate land sales with the Iroquois that would directly benefit the state. The Confederated Congress and several American statesmen admonished New York officials; James Madison, then a member of the Virginia legislature, was particularly demonstrative in his criticism. The Congress appointed Indian commissioners Oliver Wolcott, Richard Butler, and Arthur Lee to negotiate peace and land cessions for the United States with the Mohawks, Onondagas, Cayugas, and Senecas.

A peace conference was called and held in New York at Fort Stanwix near Oneida Lake. A number of Iroquois could not attend because of illness and other factors, and only a quickly formed, irregular group of Iroquois representatives was present. The commissioners arrived at Fort Stanwix with an intimidating military escort. Rather than negotiating with the Iroquois as equals, as the English had done previously, American commissioners asserted political sovereignty over all tribal natives on American soil. Iroquois speeches were cut short and credentials challenged.

The commissioners insisted that the Iroquois tribes that fought on the side of the British were a conquered people. All lands held by those tribes, therefore, were forfeit to the United States as spoils of war. America would allow them to retain some of their lands but demanded land cessions in reparation for injuries inflicted on Americans during the war. The Iroquois contended (1) that England had had no right to cede tribal lands to America; (2) that if the Iroquois were to surrender their lands to Americans, they expected something in return; and (3) that they had not, in any event, been defeated in battle and therefore were not party to peace negotiations.

As part of the resulting Treaty of Fort Stanwix, the attending Iroquois ceded a strip of land that began at the mouth of Oyonwaye Creek on Lake Ontario, four miles south of the Niagara portage path. The boundary line ran south to the mouth of the Tehosaroro, or Buffalo Creek, to the Pennsylvania line, and along its north-south boundary to the Ohio River. In effect, the treaty took all Iroquois lands west of New York and Pennsylvania and all of Ohio.

The United States released any claim it may have had by right of conquest to tribal lands west of that boundary. Iroquois property in the western region of New York State east of the Oyonwaye remained unaffected. The treaty assured that the Oneida and Tuscarora who had fought on the side of the Americans continued peaceful possession of their lands. The United States agreed to protect the remaining Iroquois territories against encroachments, seizures, and other possible violations and guaranteed the right of the Six Nations of the Iroquois Confederacy to independence.

Representatives for the Iroquois Confederacy agreed to peaceful relations with the United States. The tribes who had fought against the colonies promised to deliver up all prisoners, black and white, whom they had taken during the war. As guarantee of that promise, six Iroquois would be taken as hostages to Fort Harmar by General Arthur St. Clair, governor of the Northwest Territory.

Immediately after the congressional commissioners concluded their negotiations, commissioners from Pennsylvania negotiated for large land grants in their state. In return, the Iroquois received five thousand dollars in goods and supplies. Soon after, New York State, in defiance of Congress, negotiated land sales with the Oneida and Tuscarora. Additional land treaties quickly ensued. Congress's inability to prevent New York State from negotiating separate land sales and to uphold other aspects of the Treaty of Fort Stanwix highlighted the weaknesses in central government under the Articles of Confederation and served as a reminder that each state considered itself a sovereign nation.

In 1786, the Iroquois Confederacy held a council meeting at Buffalo Creek, New York. Disappointed and upset with their delegates, they refused to ratify the Treaty of Fort Stanwix and offered to return gifts presented to the delegates at the negotiations. Congress, however, considered the terms of treaty to be valid and acted on them accordingly.

After the American Revolution, British officials did little to discourage continued relations with northern Native American tribes. The English traded with and provided provisions to local tribes and allowed large councils to be held at British forts. After the council of Buffalo Creek, the Iroquois sought support from the British in their effort to denounce the treaty and continue their war against the United States. The Iroquois Confederacy soon discovered that the British had no intention of militarily supporting their former allies in defense of their land rights. Lacking the desire to go to war against the Americans alone, the Iroquois let the treaty stand.

On January 9, 1789, St. Clair negotiated the Treaty of Fort Harmar with a group of Senecas. The treaty reaffirmed the terms and boundaries set forth in the Treaty of Fort Stanwix. The Iroquois were given permission to hunt in their old lands "as long as they were peaceful about it."

SIGNIFICANCE

The treaties of Fort Stanwix and Fort Harmar further fractionalized the Iroquois Confederacy's six tribes, a process that had begun in 1777, when the Six Nations had split in choosing sides during the Revolutionary War. Joseph Brant led a group of Mohawk, Cayuga, and other tribe members out of the country and into Ontario, Canada, thereby splitting the confederacy in half. Those who remained in the United States were divided over other issues between the American Indians and the settlers. There was no single chief or council that could speak for the entire Iroquois Confederacy, and the Iroquois Confederacy was never again united.

—*Leslie Stricker*

FURTHER READING

Downes, Randolph C. *Council Fires on the Upper Ohio: A Narrative of Indian Affairs in the Upper Ohio Valley Until 1795*. Pittsburgh, Pa.: University of Pittsburgh Press, 1940. Discusses the relations between settlers and various tribes in the Ohio Valley, including those at Fort Stanwix.

Fenton, William N. *The Great Law and the Longhouse: A Political History of the Iroquois Confederacy*. Norman: University of Oklahoma Press, 1998. Chapter 38, "Bitter Medicine at Fort Stanwix, 1784," describes the treaty within the context of Iroquois politics and law.

Graymont, Barbara. *The Iroquois in the American Revolution*. Syracuse, N.Y.: Syracuse University Press, 1972. Chapters 6 and 7 describe Iroquois warfare, diplomacy, decline, and removal.

Jennings, Francis, ed. *The History and Culture of Iroquois Diplomacy: An Interdisciplinary Guide to the Treaties of the Six Nations and Their League*. Syracuse, N.Y.: Syracuse University Press, 1985. Extensive discussion of treaty negotiations, terms, and results.

Richter, Daniel K., and James H. Merrell. *Beyond the Covenant Chain: The Iroquois and Their Neighbors in Indian North America, 1600-1800*. Preface by Daniel K. Richter and James H. Merrell; foreword by Wilcomb E. Washburn. University Park: Pennsylvania State University Press, 2003. A new edition of the book originally published in 1987. This collection of essays examines diplomatic and military relations among the Iroquois in seventeenth and eighteenth century North America.

Trigger, Bruce G., ed. *Northeast*. Vol. 15 in *Handbook of North American Indians*, edited by William C. Sturtevant. Washington, D.C.: Smithsonian Institution, 1978. Discusses Native Americans from the Northeast in considerable detail, including language, history, customs, culture, and religion.

Washburn, Wilcomb E., ed. *History of Indian-White Relations*. Vol. 4 in *Handbook of North American Indians*, edited by William C. Sturtevant. Washington, D.C.: Smithsonian Institution Press, 1988. Extensive coverage of relations between American Indians and whites across the United States, from first contact to 1987.

SEE ALSO: May 28, 1754-Feb. 10, 1763: French and Indian War; May 8, 1763-July 24, 1766: Pontiac's Resistance; Sept. 5-Oct. 26, 1774: First Continental

Congress; Apr. 19, 1775: Battle of Lexington and Concord; May 10-Aug. 2, 1775: Second Continental Congress; May 24 and June 11, 1776: Indian Delegation Meets with Congress; July 4, 1776: Declaration of Independence; Aug. 6, 1777: Battle of Oriskany Creek; Mar. 1, 1781: Ratification of the Articles of Confederation; Oct. 19, 1781: Cornwallis Surrenders at Yorktown; Sept. 3, 1783: Treaty of Paris.

RELATED ARTICLES in *Great Lives from History: The Eighteenth Century, 1701-1800*: Joseph Brant; James Madison.

1785
CONSTRUCTION OF EL PRADO MUSEUM BEGINS

On the orders of King Charles III, the renowned neoclassical architect Juan de Villanueva began construction of a building for a museum of natural history. After years of intervening war, the structure was rehabilitated and inaugurated as the Royal Museum of Painting and Sculpture, popularly known as El Prado, in 1819. It became the repository of much of the artistic wealth gathered by the Spanish monarchs of the seventeenth and eighteenth centuries.

LOCALE: Madrid, Spain
CATEGORIES: Organizations and institutions; art; architecture

KEY FIGURES
Charles III (1716-1788), king of the Two Sicilies, r. 1734-1759, and king of Spain, r. 1759-1788
Juan de Villanueva (1739-1811), royal architect to Charles III
Maria Isabel de Bragança (1797-1818), queen consort of Spain, r. 1816-1818
Anton Raphael Mengs (1728-1779), court painter to Charles III

SUMMARY OF EVENT
November 19, 1819, marks the inauguration of the Royal Museum of Painting and Sculpture, better known as El Prado (the meadow) because of the meadow surrounding the building. With one of the world's most renowned collections of European Renaissance and neoclassical art, the museum building itself also was hailed as a masterpiece, impressively echoing the architecture of classical antiquity.

The inauguration of the museum came after many years of tumult in Spain. Construction began at the end of 1785 by order of King Charles III. However, numerous crises intervened to delay the eventual opening. In 1808, Napoleon I invaded Spain and installed his brother as king. The rightful Spanish monarch, Ferdinand VII, was imprisoned in France. A bloody war to liberate Spain from French control soon followed, lasting until 1814; Ferdinand then returned to Spain. Two years later, he married the Portuguese princess, Maria Isabel de Bragança, who became an advocate for establishing a museum to consolidate and display the royal collections of artworks.

El Prado was initially intended as a museum not for the fine arts but for the natural sciences. Charles III, the Spanish monarch who was the most assiduous follower of the Enlightenment, was committed to establishing institutions that fostered scientific and cultural activities. Thus, he supported academies, schools, museums, gardens, and an astronomical observatory. As king in Naples, he had established a museum for the recently discovered ruins of Pompeii. As king of Spain, he came to be known as "the best mayor of Madrid" because of the many urban amenities he contributed to the city.

To carry out his many construction projects, Charles engaged the most illustrious architects of Spanish neoclassicism. Most prominent among these was architect Juan de Villanueva, born into a family of noted artists: His father was a sculptor, and his older brother was an architect. Villanueva's career advanced when he became architect for repairs and maintenance of the historical Hieronymite church and monastery, situated then just outside the city. Affiliated with the royal court, the monastery gave Villanueva access to King Charles III, who recognized his talent and designated him chief architect.

The Hieronymite monastery housed the hermit monks of the order of St. Jerome and had been built in isolated meadowland. The monastery was an austere retreat from the daily cares of the world. However, the area around it came to be considered a place of bucolic refuge for the court at the royal palace just over a mile away. It was near the Hieronymite, therefore, that King Philip IV built a luxurious new palace, the Palácio de Buen Retiro (Palace of Pleasant Retreat), in the seventeenth century.

Mounted in architectural splendor, it was filled with sumptuous collections of art and surrounded by alluring gardens, fountains, and promenades.

When Charles III entered Madrid as king in 1759, it was in this city that the enlightened monarch would decide to lay out a complex of buildings and grounds for scientific research and study. Along with his advisers, he planned botanical gardens for living nature, a science museum for nonliving nature, and an astronomical observatory. Villanueva completed his designs for the science museum in 1785, and they were quickly approved by Charles; construction began the same year.

Villanueva envisioned a building that continues to impress its visitors. He laid it out on a north-south axis. The west entrance brought one to the central portion, a domed basilica, from which cascaded abundant natural light flooding the heart of the building. From this center, two galleries extend north and south, their ceilings arched, admitting a further flow of light and prompting a subtle play of shadows. Each of the galleries ends in an elegant salon.

The aesthetic balance of the environment was achieved not only by the integrated flow of light but also by the serene, austere design. Using stone and brick, Villanueva followed strict standards of structure and motifs from classical antiquity. Visitors, advancing through the building, encounter an environment both luminous and tranquil, monumental and intimate.

Construction progressed until 1788, when Charles III died. Villanueva became occupied with numerous other commissions and responsibilities, including the observatory. The independence wars at the beginning of the following century ruined most of what had been impressively completed of the building until then. The structure became a stable and storehouse, and many of the building's parts were vandalized or stolen.

In this lamentable state and with the return of Ferdinand VII, the building received the attention of his second wife, Maria Isabel de Bragança. She encouraged the building's housing the royal collections of paintings and sculptures, since they were now being retrieved, restored, and augmented after years of war and exile. In

1780's

The south facade of the El Prado Museum, c. 1860-1880. (Library of Congress)

1819, a year after her death, the royal art museum opened to the public (initially on Tuesdays only) with a stunning collection of more than three hundred works.

SIGNIFICANCE

El Prado Museum arose during an eighteenth century filled with enlightened monarchs, and even despots, who called for neoclassical architecture and design as a secular aesthetic representing social harmony and balance. The courts displayed their wealth and power to the public, and their subjects, through these spaces. By sponsoring art academies that would produce painters, sculptors, and scholars trained in and committed to this cultural wealth, it also became necessary to assemble collections of art to support such study. The holdings of El Prado derived from a monarchy that from the sixteenth century through the eighteenth century attracted and sustained the leading artists of Western Europe.

Nonetheless, it is not the quantity of works in El Prado but the extraordinary quality of its holdings and its elegant setting that have drawn the most admiration. El Prado is dense with iconic masterpieces, including Titian's stalwart portrait of Emperor Charles V, Pieter Brueghel's minuscule drama of *The Triumph of Death*, the chaste sensuality of *Adam* and *Eve* by Albrecht Dürer, the diminutive intricacy of *The Maids of Honor* by Diego Velázaquez, and the luminous horror of Francisco de Goya's war paintings.

El Prado and its collections have survived a harrowing history. The three decades from the museum's construction to its inauguration included the savage battles for Spanish independence. Further tumult threatened during the Carlist Succession Wars in the nineteenth century, and the Spanish Civil War and World War II in the twentieth. Only in recent decades, nestled now in the heart of the city that has expanded well beyond El Prado's walls, has the museum come to enjoy an environment of stability and renown.

—*Edward A. Riedinger*

FURTHER READING

Alcolea i Blanch, Santiago, and Gabriel Martín. *The Prado Museum*. 2d rev. ed. Barcelona, Spain: Ediciones Polígrafa, 2002. A sumptuous illustrated catalog of holdings of El Prado Museum, with a masterful historical essay by scholars of Spanish art.

Herr, Richard A. *The Eighteenth-Century Revolution in Spain*. Princeton, N.J.: Princeton University Press, 1969. A reissue of a detailed scholarly analysis of intellectual life in Spain under the Bourbon Dynasty and during the Enlightenment. Includes an authoritative bibliography.

Hull, Anthony H. *Charles III and the Revival of Spain*. Washington, D.C.: University Press of America, 1980. Exceptional scholarly study that examines the details of the interrelated cultural, socioeconomic, political, and military objectives and accomplishments of the reign of Charles III.

López Torrijos, Rosa. *Mythology and History in the Great Paintings of the Prado*. London: Scala, 1999. Examining El Prado masterpieces of Spanish, Italian, and Flemish painting during seventeenth and eighteenth centuries, this work analyzes themes of classical mythology and portrayals of history. Includes color illustrations.

Petrie, Charles. *King Charles III of Spain: An Enlightened Despot*. New York: John Day, 1971. Work by an English scholar that examines Charles III as an exceptionally effective Spanish monarch, particularly his role in determining intellectual, cultural, and educational developments.

Stein, Stanley J., and Barbara H. Stein. *Apogee of Empire: Spain and New Spain in the Age of Charles III, 1759-1789*. Baltimore: Johns Hopkins University Press, 2003. Recent authoritative reassessment by noted scholars of late Spanish imperial revival under Charles III. The sequel to the authors' *Silver, Trade, and War: Spain and America in the Making of Early Modern Europe* (2000).

SEE ALSO: 1712: Philip V Founds the Royal Library of Spain; Aug. 3, 1713: Foundation of the Spanish Academy; 1737: Revival of the Paris Salon; 1759: Charles III Gains the Spanish Throne; 1762: *The Antiquities of Athens* Prompts Architectural Neoclassicism; Dec. 10, 1768: Britain's Royal Academy of Arts Is Founded; Nov., 1796: Catherine the Great's Art Collection Is Installed at the Hermitage.
RELATED ARTICLES in *Great Lives from History: The Eighteenth Century, 1701-1800*: Charles III; Francisco de Goya.

1785
FIRST STATE UNIVERSITIES ARE ESTABLISHED

Increased governmental support for secular higher education, which, it was believed, would ensure a knowledgeable electorate and an educated leadership, made a college education available to a growing middle class.

LOCALE: Southern and midwestern United States
CATEGORIES: Education; organizations and institutions; cultural and intellectual history; government and politics

KEY FIGURES

Abraham Baldwin (1754-1807), state legislator, lawyer, and author of the charter of the University of Georgia

Manasseh Cutler (1742-1823), clergyman and lobbyist before Congress for the Ohio Company

Thomas Jefferson (1743-1826), third president of the United States, 1801-1809, and founder of the University of Virginia

John Marshall (1755-1835), chief justice of the United States and author of the opinion rendered in the Dartmouth College case

Daniel Webster (1782-1852), representative of Dartmouth College to the Supreme Court

SUMMARY OF EVENT

For most Americans, state universities may be defined as publicly supported and controlled nonsectarian, degree-granting institutions of higher learning, designed to discover, conserve, and disseminate knowledge. The concept, if not the realization, is at least as old as the republic. In 1779, Thomas Jefferson proposed a comprehensive educational plan, part of which involved converting his alma mater, William and Mary College, into the State University of Virginia. Even earlier, North Carolina's founding fathers drafted a constitution that authorized the creation of one or more publicly controlled and endowed universities for that state. They also barred clergymen from holding office in the general assembly. Although neither Jefferson nor the Carolinians succeeded in the 1770's, their schemes to create state universities reflected the strongly republican and secular sentiments prevalent among many of America's revolutionary leaders. They also illustrated the firm conviction of many public servants that no self-governing people could long endure without making provision for an informed electorate and an educated leadership.

The University of North Carolina, Chapel Hill, the first state university, shown in a 1939 photograph. (Library of Congress)

During the colonial period, the principle of the separation of church and state was not yet widely accepted. After the beginning of the U.S. republic, it thus proved more difficult for legislatures to create universities in states where colonial colleges already existed. The first state universities created in the original thirteen states were concentrated in the South, where only one of the nine sectarian colleges founded in the colonial period was located. Under the leadership of a recent immigrant from Connecticut, Abraham Baldwin, Georgia chartered its state university in 1785, although the institution did not admit students until 1801. By that time, North Carolina and South Carolina also boasted state universities. Created in 1789, the University of North Carolina began classes at Chapel Hill in January, 1795. South Carolina's legislature acted in 1801, and the state university opened its doors four years later.

Maryland, Virginia, and Delaware followed Georgia and the Carolinas in chartering state universities. Admitting its first entering class in 1825, the University of Virginia was the only state university founded before the Civil War in a state where a college had existed prior to the American Revolution. On the grounds that any state university needed to reflect basic principles of religious and academic freedom, Jefferson refrained from establishing a professorship of divinity at the university, institutionalized lifetime appointments for the faculty, and gave students more latitude than was customary in deciding which lectures to attend.

From the beginning a successful model of nonsectarian education, the University of Virginia operated

1780's

701

without interruption or significant change in legal status before the Civil War.

Among the new states added to the Union before 1861, at least a dozen chartered state universities, largely as a result of the westward movement and federal largesse. In 1787, lobbying for a group of New England land speculators organized as the Ohio Company of Associates, Massachusetts-born clergyman Manasseh Cutler persuaded Congress to award two free townships to the land company for the purpose of creating a university. Otherwise, Cutler argued, New Englanders would not emigrate. From these grants came Ohio University (1802) and, after another land sale, Miami University at Oxford (1809). By the outbreak of the Civil War, the land grant pattern set by Congress in Ohio had been applied to twenty-one of the twenty-four states admitted to the Union following ratification of the Constitution.

As the American population expanded into the West, the common perception that civic order needed to be established as quickly as possible helped in this region to fuel the rapid growth of state universities. These institutions, it was assumed, would provide their students with an education in civic virtue so, once graduated, they might take on the roles of responsible citizens of a republican nation. They also took the lead in the development of coeducation at the state university level, with the University of Iowa in 1855 becoming the first state university to admit women, followed by the University of Wisconsin in 1863. Early advocates of state-supported, nonsectarian education, despite their initial successes in the South and on the frontier, made almost no headway where denominational schools were well entrenched or where, as in Massachusetts and Connecticut, separation of church and state did not occur until well into the nineteenth century. In any case, by the time Jefferson had left office in 1809, the strongly secular spirit regarding higher education, so widespread immediately following the Revolution, had largely disappeared in a wave of evangelicalism that has been called the Second Great Awakening.

Another obstacle to the early establishment of state universities was the Dartmouth College case of 1819. In 1816 the New Hampshire legislature, influenced by the results of a recent election, sought to bring Dartmouth College, a Congregational institution founded in 1769, under state control. The board of trustees sued to retain the college's charter as a private institution, but the New Hampshire high court upheld the state law. Undaunted, the board appealed to the U.S. Supreme Court. Persuaded by the passionate appeal of Daniel Webster, himself a Congregationalist and alumnus of Dartmouth College, to preserve the institution's autonomy, Chief Justice John Marshall reversed the lower court in a precedent-setting opinion, holding that a charter granted to a private corporation constituted a contract, and a contract, under Article I, section 10 of the Constitution, could not be impaired by the action of a state. Dartmouth College, therefore, was immune from legislative tampering. More important, the Dartmouth decision killed efforts in other states to make public universities out of private colleges. It also unleashed what one authority on higher education has called a Protestant counterreformation; that is, it spurred the creation of innumerable inferior denominational colleges, all secure in the knowledge that their charters, once obtained, placed them beyond state control.

SIGNIFICANCE

America's first state universities, never very well supported from public funds, came under increasing attack after the turn of the century, especially following the War of 1812. While sectarians accused them of "godless atheism," an upwardly mobile electorate suspected them of promoting aristocratic privilege at the expense of the common people. Timid legislators responded predictably. They refused to support state universities altogether, diverted university funds to the common schools, or parceled out meager resources among a host of inferior denominational colleges. In some instances, lawmakers blunted popular criticism by naming representatives of the most powerful sects to state university faculties or boards of trustees. The net effect was that true state universities were almost stifled in their infancy.

Not until the Civil War would state universities begin to break free from the crippling effects of sectarianism, local boosterism, political demagoguery, and stingy legislative appropriations. By the time of the Civil War, new forces were active in American society. The Industrial Revolution and the political coming-of-age of the middle and lower classes combined to bring about a concerted drive for what contemporaries called a more "practical education," one that would stress the agricultural and mechanical arts so necessary to a progressive and developing materialist society.

—Germaine M. Reed,
updated by Diane P. Michelfelder

FURTHER READING

Hoeveler, J. David. *Creating the American Mind: Intellect and Politics in the Colonial Colleges*. Lanham, Md.: Rowman & Littlefield, 2002. Examines nine colleges and universities that were created by the time of the American Revolution (including Dartmouth,

William and Mary, Harvard, and Yale) to determine their role in developing an American intellect, theology, and politics.

Lucas, Christopher J. *American Higher Education: A History*. New York: St. Martin's Press, 1994. Chapter 4, "The American Colonial and Antebellum College," describes the creation of state universities in the late eighteenth century.

Marsden, George M. *The Soul of the American University: From Protestant Establishment to Established Nonbelief.* New York: Oxford University Press, 1994. A captivating account of the history of the relationship between church and state in the development of higher education in America, with a focus on the diminishing role of religious values in publicly supported universities.

Pangle, Lorraine Smith, and Thomas L. Pangle. *The Learning of Liberty: The Educational Ideas of the American Founders.* Lawrence: University Press of Kansas, 1993. An illuminating study of the beliefs held by George Washington, Benjamin Franklin, Thomas Jefferson, and others concerning the role of education in a republican nation. Chapter 8, "Higher Education," concentrates on the development of the University of Virginia.

Rudolph, Frederick. *The American College and University: A History*. New York: Alfred A. Knopf, 1962. Reprint. Athens: University of Georgia Press, 1990. One of the earliest comprehensive histories of higher education in America. Rudolph draws on numerous histories of specific institutions to create an engaging study ranging over a number of topics, including the development of coeducation in higher education and the movement to create land grant colleges. This reprint contains an introductory essay.

Tewksbury, Donald G. *The Founding of American Colleges and Universities Before the Civil War*. New York: Archon Books, 1965. A valuable source of information related to the chronological development of state universities. Includes tables.

Thelin, John R. *A History of American Higher Education*. Baltimore: Johns Hopkins University Press, 2004. A comprehensive history, with chapter 2 focusing on higher education and college-building between 1758 and 1860.

Westmayer, Paul. *A History of American Higher Education.* Springfield, Ill.: Charles C Thomas, 1985. While similar to other histories of American higher education in the material and topics covered, this book also covers the relation of the development of the United States to the development of its colleges and universities.

SEE ALSO: June 20, 1732: Settlement of Georgia; July 4, 1776: Declaration of Independence; Sept. 17, 1787: U.S. Constitution Is Adopted; 1790's-1830's: Second Great Awakening.

RELATED ARTICLES in *Great Lives from History: The Eighteenth Century, 1701-1800:* Abigail Adams; Mary Astell; Johann Bernhard Basedow; Hester Chapone; Claude-Adrien Helvétius; Thomas Jefferson; Benjamin Rush; John Witherspoon.

1785
RITES CONTROVERSY

Shortly after the introduction of Roman Catholicism to Korea, the government cracked down when Catholics refused to practice traditional Confucian religious rituals. Many of those who persisted in practicing the banned Catholic faith became martyrs.

LOCALE: Korea
CATEGORIES: Religion and theology; government and politics; social issues and reform

KEY FIGURES
Chŏng Yak-jong (1760-1801), Korean Christian scholar and leader
Peter Yi Sŭnghun (1756-1801), cofounder of the first Roman Catholic Church in Korea
John-Baptist Yi Byŏk (1754-1785), cofounder of the first Roman Catholic Church in Korea
Francis Xavier Kwŏ Ilsin (1752-1801), Korean Christian scholar
Thomas Kim Bomu (d. 1787), Korean Christian who held services at his home
Chŏngjo (1752-1800), king of Korea, r. 1777-1800

SUMMARY OF EVENT
After the introduction of Roman Catholicism in China, some Korean tributary envoys, who were regularly sent to Beijing four times a year or on special occasions, visited Catholic churches and met Jesuit priests. The priests gave Catholic books to the Korean diplomats, who in

703

turn brought them back to Korea. Some Korean scholars became so interested in the books that in 1779 Chŏng Yak-jong formed a study group at Ganghakdang to compare the new religion with Neo-Confucianism, which was the state religion in Korea; the group included Yi Byŏk, Kwŏ Ilsin, Yi Gahwan, and two of Chŏng Yak-jong's brothers. Chŏng Yak-jong was interested in reforming governance in Korea, notably by a system of land distribution based on egalitarian principles and by the placement of people in professions in accordance with their ability, and he drew philosophical strength for his ideas from the Christian faith.

The reigning monarch, Chŏngjo, was open to Western ideas, which offered new ways of thinking. However, there was factional rivalry among the political elites. Study group member Yi Byŏk, an aristocrat who belonged to the faction out of favor, found much wisdom in the high moral standards of the Christian philosophy that he encountered in the Jesuit missionary books. Accordingly, some of the scholars decided in principle to convert to Christianity, though they knew that they first needed to learn more about the faith.

One of Yi Byŏk's friends was the twenty-seven-year-old Yi Sŭnghun. In December, 1783, Yi Sŭnghun's father, Yi Tonguk, was scheduled to go to Beijing as a chancellor of Korea's winter solstice delegation. Yi Byŏk decided to encourage Yi Sŭnghun to accompany his father so that he could obtain more books about Roman Catholicism. Yi Sŭnghun then went along on the trip, accepted the Catholic faith while in Beijing, and was baptized by a French priest in early 1784, taking the Christian name Peter.

Upon returning to Seoul, Peter Yi Sŭnghun announced that he was a Christian. He carried out the first baptism in Korea when he performed the ritual on Yi Byŏk, who took the Christian name John-Baptist; later, he baptized Kwŏ Ilsin with the Christian name Francis-Xavier. Known as the "three apostles" of the Korean Catholic Church, Peter Yi Sŭnghun, John-Baptist Yi Byŏk, and Francis-Xavier Kwŏ Ilsin spread Catholicism among intellectuals of the noble class as well as the middle and lower classes, including women. As a result, there were more conversions, so recent convert Thomas Kim Bomu allowed Catholic services to be conducted each Sunday at his residence in the Myongdong district of Seoul, now the site of the Catholic Cathedral. The Christian community developed rapidly, with some four thousand adherents by 1794, and scholars continued to translate books on Catholic doctrine from Chinese into Korean. Under the lay leadership, they chose their own

priests and began to celebrate mass and administer the sacraments.

Catholic missionaries were quite eager to spread Christianity in Asia. On encountering local religious practices, some Jesuit priests pragmatically decided to respect the rituals of other faiths. In 1742, when the pope was aware that Christians were performing Chinese and Indian rites, which he deemed idolatrous, he recalled three thousand errant Jesuit priests and missionaries and issued a directive banning Christians from celebrating non-Catholic rituals. Chinese Catholics were thus prohibited from carrying out offerings to their ancestors, and the newly converted Korean Catholics followed suit.

Henceforth, the Catholic faith was in conflict with Korean traditional culture. In March, 1785, Korean police and government officials learned that the Catholic community was meeting at Thomas Kim Bomu's residence. Catholic doctrine prohibited the ancestral rites that Confucian custom considered as important expressions of filial piety to parents, so the government viewed Catholicism as "profane." Catholics believed that politics should be separate from religion, but the rulers considered Catholic beliefs as a direct challenge to the authority of the king. The Catholics also rejected the social hierarchical system and the gender discrimination that placed women in subordinate roles. Christians of all classes were also openly in contact with the Church in China and French missionaries there, whereas the government prohibited or controlled strictly any contacts of the common people with foreigners.

Accordingly, Kim Bomu was arrested in 1785 for his role in providing a place for Catholics to congregate; after being tortured, he was exiled, and he died abroad in 1787. All Catholics were termed criminals by the state for practicing an immoral religion that did not perform Confucian mourning rituals and memorial services for parents. Indeed, most Koreans were shocked that the Catholics even burned ancestral tablets. The persecution of 1785 involved the royal court in banning not only the practice of Catholicism but also the importation of Christian literature from China.

SIGNIFICANCE

Korea is the only country in the world where the Catholic Church was formed by laity: No priest came until 1794, when the early Christians learned from the bishop of Beijing that only members of the clergy could perform the sacraments. The Chinese priest who was then sent secretly to Korea was caught up in the persecution of 1801 and beheaded. The second priest to be smuggled into Korea arrived in 1836, and two followed in 1839, but all three were arrested, tortured, and executed. Consequently, there is a strong democratic tradition within the Korean Catholic Church, as many of the earliest leaders and members included commoners, notably pottery makers, and women seeking their own salvation; nobles who refused to renounce their Catholic faith were stripped of their privileges and titles. Ironically, Korean Christians are now allowed to practice Confucian ancestral rituals.

The crackdown of 1785 was relatively light, but it opened the way for the authorities to up the ante. In waves of persecution during 1791, 1801, 1839, 1846, and 1866, the government arrested and executed about ten thousand Christians, including one Chinese and twelve French missionaries. Governmental hostility to Christianity prevented Protestant missionaries from spreading the faith as well. In 1984, Pope John Paul II visited Korea and canonized 103 of the martyrs as saints for preferring to die as Christians rather than recanting their faith. Among countries in the world, Korea holds the distinction of having the fourth largest number of canonized saints. Today, Christians outnumber adherents of all other religions in Korea, accounting for nearly one-fourth of the population, though Protestants outnumber Catholics.

The persecution of the early Catholics has had a profound influence on Korean history. In 1882, the Korean-American treaty of trade and amity had a clause ending the persecution of Christians, so the churches began to flourish as never before. However, Christians who rejected Shinto rituals during the era of Japanese occupation (1910-1945) were also persecuted. Because of their history of persecution, Christians have been in the forefront of the struggle for Korean democracy and human rights, and some have sought refuge from political repression inside Myongdong Cathedral.

—*Michael Haas*

FURTHER READING

Chung, David. *Syncretism: The Religious Context of Christian Beginnings in Korea*. Albany: State University of New York Press, 2001. Asks why Christianity was accepted successfully in a society previously exposed to Buddhism and Confucianism, the latter of which was the state religion when the first Koreans converted to Catholicism; answers that all foreign religious beliefs were assimilated into Korea's indigenous shamanism, though Roman Catholicism soon opposed other religions and thus brought about a sharp conflict over ideas.

Grayson, James Huntley. *Korea: A Religious History*. New York: Routledge, 2002. Chronological description of Korean religions, from shamanism, Buddhism, Confucianism, Roman Catholicism, Protestantism, and Islam, to Korean New Religions.

Yu, Chai-Shin, ed. *The Founding of Catholic Tradition in Korea*. Mississauga, Ont.: Korean and Related Studies Press, 1996. Essays pointing out that Catholicism entered Korea from the laity, rather than the clergy or church administration, and has grown despite or perhaps because of conflict with secular authorities.

SEE ALSO: Sept. 8, 1713: Papal Bull *Unigenitus*; May, 1727-1733: Jansenist "Convulsionnaires" Gather at Saint-Médard; Oct. 2, 1792-Apr. 12, 1799: Christian Missionary Societies Are Founded.

RELATED ARTICLES in *Great Lives from History: The Eighteenth Century, 1701-1800:* George Macartney; William Wilberforce.

1780's

1785-1788
HUTTON PROPOSES THE GEOLOGICAL THEORY OF UNIFORMITARIANISM

James Hutton's theory that Earth's formation was the result of a cyclic process of erosion and uplift—which, in turn, was the result of the compounding of the ordinary action of water and heat in deep time—was the intellectual precursor of Charles Lyell's uniformitarian geology and a fundamental premise of Charles Darwin's evolutionary theory.

LOCALE: Edinburgh, Scotland
CATEGORIES: Geology; science and technology

KEY FIGURES

James Hutton (1726-1797), Scottish natural philosopher
John Playfair (1748-1819), Scottish geologist, mathematician, and chief popularizer of Hutton's theory
Sir James Hall (1761-1832), Scottish geologist and chemist
Abraham Gottlob Werner (1750-1817), professor at Freiburg Mining Academy
Comte de Buffon (Georges-Louis Leclerc; 1707-1788), French naturalist

SUMMARY OF EVENT

On March 7, 1785, members of the Philosophical Society of Edinburgh assembled to hear a much anticipated paper. Its author, James Hutton, was ill that day and had chosen his closest friend, the renowned philosophical chemist Joseph Black, to deliver the first part of a new theory in a work titled "Concerning the System of the Earth, Its Durability and Stability." Four weeks later, on April 4, Hutton had recovered sufficiently to present the second part of his theory. In July, he privately printed and circulated an abstract of the paper. Eventually, in 1788, the full ninety-five-page manuscript from which Hutton's papers had been drawn was published in the first volume of the *Philosophical Transactions* of the society as "Theory of the Earth: Or, An Investigation of the Laws Observable in the Composition, Dissolution, and Restoration of Land upon the Globe."

Hutton's paper was written in the context of a well-established consensus in eighteenth century geological science. The French naturalist the comte de Buffon had provided a general framework for the consensus in the initial volumes of his *Histoire naturelle, générale et particulière* (1749-1789; *Natural History, General and Particular*, 1781-1812) and again in his *Époques de la nature* (1778; epochs of nature). According to Buffon, the Earth originated as solar matter. As Earth cooled, a universal ocean covered its surface. Sedimentation of materials suspended in this primitive ocean produced rock strata, which were exposed as the ocean receded.

In the 1780's, Abraham Gottlob Werner, a professor at the Freiburg Mining Academy in Saxony, supplemented Buffon's cosmogony with a stratigraphy that distinguished four mineralogical groups according to the order in which they had settled out of the universal ocean. Most primitive were chemical precipitates such as granite. Settling out next at lower elevations were heavier materials such as limestone, followed by basalts at still lower elevations and sand and other alluvial deposits. Werner's stratigraphy would potentially accommodate a great variety of geological phenomena and gain widespread acceptance. Indeed, when professor of natural history John Walker offered the first series of lectures in geology at the University of Edinburgh in 1781, it was Werner's stratigraphy that he introduced.

What the audience for Hutton's society paper heard was an audacious departure from the Wernerian consensus. To be sure, Hutton's theory acknowledged that water was one of the primary agents in geological change. During the 1750's and 1760's, Hutton had been a highly innovative agricultural improver on his Berwickshire estate and knew well the power of erosion. However, for Hutton, water's geological effect was destructive. The action of water could not explain dramatic features of the Earth's topography such as mountain ranges, nor could it adequately explain the presence of unconformities in rock strata.

For these phenomena, Hutton required a more constructive force. A graduate of the University of Edinburgh in 1743, Hutton had had a longtime interest in chemistry and, during the 1740's, he had even invented an improved method of producing the ammonium chloride used in soldering metals. In 1768, Hutton leased his farm and returned to Edinburgh. It was at this time that Hutton developed his friendship with Joseph Black, a pioneer in the study of heat, and Black's former student, James Watt, the inventor of the modern steam engine. These friendships soon suggested to Hutton a second agency in geological change. Subterranean heat, he began to argue, drove the terrestrial machine.

Hutton was combining the so-called Neptunian consensus with a new Plutonism: Like the sea, the underworld could rise and fall. The origins of this conception of dynamic equilibrium again lay in Hutton's own past. As an undergraduate at the University of Edinburgh, Hutton had studied with Colin Maclaurin, one of the eighteenth century's most effective popularizers of Sir Isaac Newton's ideas. In the autumn of 1744, Hutton had begun to study medicine at Edinburgh, in 1747 he transferred to the University of Paris, and in 1748 he enrolled in the center of medical Newtonianism at the University of Leiden, where he completed his medical degree with *Dissertatio physico-medica inauguralis de sanguine et circulatione microcosmi* (1749; *James Hutton's Medical Dissertation*, 1980). Just as in Newtonian astronomy, in which a balance of centrifugal and gravitational forces produced the solar system, and just as systolic and diastolic forces circulate the blood (or just as the piston pushes and pulls in Watt's double-acting steam engine), uplift complemented erosion in Hutton's system of the Earth. As water dissolved rock, the products of sedimentation accumulated, generating intense heat and pressure. The intense heat and pressure, in turn, caused rapid expansion and uplift. Even as old continents become new oceans, old oceans become new continents.

Hutton's argument had profound implications for eighteenth century geology. Whereas Buffon conceived the history of the Earth proceeding in one direction of greater cooling and erosion, Hutton did for matter in time what Newton had done for matter in space and conceived the laws of motion in terms of reciprocal action and reaction. Whereas Neptunism implied catastrophism, the assumption that the geological processes of the past were of a qualitatively greater magnitude than the geological processes of the present, Hutton's dynamic equilibrium implied a uniformitarianism, in which the observed geological processes of the present were the key to understanding the geological processes of the past. Also, whereas catastrophism offered a way to reconcile biblical accounts of the Creation and the Flood, Hutton entirely ignored Genesis as a source of geological knowledge.

Finally, Hutton undercut Werner's stratigraphy. In the years after 1785, Hutton traveled to sites across Scotland—most famously, to the unconformity at Siccar Point—to gather evidence for his theory. This evidence indicated that granite had not originated as an aqueous precipitate but had crystallized from molten magmas. It also revealed that granite, which Werner had made the oldest rock, was in some cases intruded upward into sedimentary strata. Conversely, the evidence also showed the ancient volcanic origin of basalts. By recognizing the igneous origin of many rocks, Hutton reconfirmed that the forces of geological change acted uniformly in past and present. He also reconfirmed that geological processes did not work in one direction and, therefore, no inherent limit could be set regarding Earth's geological history. In short, Hutton had discovered deep time. "We find," Hutton famously concluded in his 1788 paper, "no vestige of a beginning, —no prospect of an end."

SIGNIFICANCE

James Hutton extended the Scottish tradition of conjectural history to the economy of nature. From the perspective of deep time, cycles of dissolution and composition succeeded one another in a spontaneous and, ultimately, benevolent order. As if by an invisible hand, the nearly imperceptible action of heat and water shaped the grandest features of the physical environment. Yet, for all the assurance of durability and stability, Hutton's theory faced intense criticism in the years after 1788. The specter of the French Revolution rendered Hutton's defense of design an invitation to atheism, his understanding of nature's uniformity an incitement to political turbulence.

In 1795, a very ill Hutton attempted to rebut these charges in the two sprawling volumes of "Theory of the Earth." Most responsible for keeping Huttonian geology before a scientific public, however, were his two companions on the trip to Siccar Point in 1788, the chemist and geologist James Hall and the mathematician John Playfair. Under the pressure of criticism, Hutton's geology underwent its own reconstruction. In a series of ingenious experiments between 1798 and 1805, Hall proved aspects of Hutton's theory, demonstrating, for example, the thermal metamorphosis of limestone into marble. In 1802, geologist John Playfair published *Illustrations of the Huttonian Theory of the Earth*. Beautifully presented in compelling prose, Playfair's illustrations were no longer organized as mere proofs of an a priori theory but as the empirical foundation for a historical narrative. It was Hall's experimental and Playfair's empirical Huttonianism that, in 1830, provided the precedent for the scientific uniformitarianism of British geologist Charles Lyell's *Principles of Geology* (1830-1833). It was the same Huttonianism that, in 1859, provided two crucial elements to the variational evolution of Charles Darwin's *On the Origin of Species by Means of Natural Selection: Or, The Preservation of Favoured Races in the Struggle for Life* (1859): the notion that evolutionary change could take place by an incremental accumulation of small variations and the discovery of time that allowed this slow agency to work.

—*Charles R. Sullivan*

FURTHER READING

Dean, Dennis R. *James Hutton and the History of Geology*. Ithaca, N.Y.: Cornell University Press, 1992. An extensively documented scholarly guide to Hutton's writings. Less successful on the natural philosophical origins of Hutton's theory of the Earth.

Gould, Stephen Jay. *Time's Arrow, Time's Cycle: Myth and Metaphor in the Discovery of Geological Time*. Cambridge, Mass.: Harvard University Press, 1987. Argues that Hutton developed uniformitarianism more as a deduction from his Deism than as an induction from field observations.

Hutton, James. *System of the Earth, 1785, Theory of the Earth, 1788, Observations on Granite, 1794, Together with Playfair's Biography of Hutton*. Darien, Conn.: Hafner, 1970. Facsimiles of Hutton's papers presented to the Philosophical Society of Edinburgh and then published in the society's journal, compiled here in book form. Includes an introduction by Victor A. Eyles and a foreword by George W. White.

McIntyre, Donald B., and Alan McKirdy. *James Hutton: The Founder of Modern Geology*. Edinburgh: Her Majesty's Stationery Office, 1997. A well-illustrated short introduction to Hutton for the general reader.

Repcheck, Jack. *The Man Who Found Time: James Hutton and the Discovery of the Earth's Antiquity*. Cambridge, Mass.: Perseus Books, 2003. A fine popular account of Hutton's life and scientific achievement. Contains a good bibliography of the extensive literature on Hutton.

SEE ALSO: 1749-1789: First Comprehensive Examination of the Natural World; 1754: Büsching Publishes *A New System of Geography*; Nov. 1, 1755: Great Lisbon Earthquake; 1781-1784: Cavendish Discovers the Composition of Water.

RELATED ARTICLES in *Great Lives from History: The Eighteenth Century, 1701-1800:* Joseph Black; Comte de Buffon; Henry Cavendish; Colin Maclaurin; Lazzaro Spallanzani; James Watt.

January 7, 1785
FIRST CROSS-CHANNEL FLIGHT

Jean Blanchard and John Jeffries successfully crossed the English Channel in a balloon, demonstrating that travel by air was practical and opening the door to military and scientific observations using balloons.

LOCALE: Dover, England; English Channel; Calais, France
CATEGORY: Science and technology

KEY FIGURES

Jean-Pierre-François Blanchard (1753-1809), a French pioneer in aviation and ballooning
John Jeffries (1745-1819), a Boston medical doctor who accompanied Blanchard on the first piloted balloon flight across the English Channel
Jacques-Alexandre-Cesar Charles (1746-1823), a French chemist who developed the first hydrogen-filled balloon
Joseph-Michel Montgolfier (1740-1810) and
Jacques-Étienne Montgolfier (1745-1799), brothers who demonstrated the first unpiloted balloon flight in 1783
Jean-François Pilâtre de Rozier (1756-1785) and
Marquis d'Arlandes (1742-1809), the first humans to fly in a balloon
Pierre Romain (d. 1785), who, with Pilâtre de Rozier, died in an attempt to fly the first hydrogen-filled balloon across the English Channel

SUMMARY OF EVENT

The balloon, the simplest of all flying machines, consists of a fabric envelope that is filled with a gas that is lighter than air. If the entire balloon, including a suspended basket used to carry instruments or passengers, is less dense than the surrounding air, then the balloon and its payload rise to a height where their density equals the density of the air.

The first balloon that carried humans into the sky used hot air to provide the lifting force. In September of 1783, brothers Joseph-Michel Montgolfier and Jacques-Étienne Montgolfier demonstrated a hot-air balloon for the king and queen of France, but it carried aloft only animals—a sheep, a duck, and a rooster. On November 21, 1783, Jean-François Pilâtre de Rozier and the Marquis d'Arlandes flew above Paris for twenty-five minutes, becoming the first human "aeronauts" in a balloon designed by the Montgolfier brothers.

Also in 1783, Jacques-Alexandre-Cesar Charles, a

French chemist who studied the properties of gases, experimented with using hydrogen instead of hot air in balloons. Hydrogen has two advantages over hot air. First, hydrogen is the lightest gas, so it provides more lifting force than an equal volume of hot air; a smaller balloon filled with hydrogen would be able to lift the same payload, that is, the weight of the basket and its contents, as would a larger balloon filled with hot air. Second, hydrogen does not cool in the same manner as hot air, so it retains its lifting capacity, allowing for a much longer flight. On December 1, 1783, Charles, accompanied by Nicolas Robert, took off from the gardens of the Tuileries in Paris before a crowd of 400,000 people and flew 27 miles in a hydrogen balloon. Hydrogen, however, also has one serious disadvantage: It can burn or explode when combined with oxygen.

Jean-Pierre-François Blanchard and John Jeffries were the first to fly across the English Channel in a balloon. Their journey took them from Dover, England, to Calais, France, a distance of about nineteen miles. (North Wind Picture Archives)

A worldwide interest in ballooning developed quite rapidly after these two successful flights. Showmen began to stage balloon ascents and charged fees to the crowds of spectators. A flight across the English Channel, the body of water that separates England from continental Europe (in this case, France), was considered to be the flight-distance challenge for early balloonists. If the English Channel could be crossed, they believed, it would be proven that balloons were practical for long-distance flight.

One person who developed an interest in ballooning was Jean-Pierre-François Blanchard. Blanchard began inventing mechanical devices as a boy, including a rat trap, a hydraulic pump, and a "velocipede," which was a predecessor of the bicycle that was driven simply by walking while sitting on it. Blanchard also constructed his own balloon, which he flew for the first time on March 2, 1784, from Champ de Mars Park in Paris. His balloon measured 27 feet in diameter, had a parachute in case it burst, and was filled with hydrogen rather than hot air.

Since ballooning was developing rapidly in France, Blanchard decided to move to England, where he would have fewer competitors for fame. Blanchard's first flight demonstrated that he had perfected the basic components of his balloon, so he began a series of experiments to improve the design. Ballooning, however, was expensive, so Blanchard needed financial support for his efforts. He publicized his experiments and found a group of wealthy sponsors. An American medical doctor, John Jeffries of Boston, provided £700. On November 30, 1784, Blanchard and Jeffries made their first flight together, taking off from Rhedarium Garden, London, and landing in Kent, England.

On January 7, 1785, Blanchard and Jeffries became the first to cross the English Channel by air. Jeffries paid Blanchard an additional £100 for the flight across the Channel, but Blanchard did not want Jeffries to share in the glory. He said that Jeffries's weight might keep the balloon from completing the crossing, so, before Blanchard agreed to take him, Jeffries had to promise he would jump overboard into the Channel if the balloon could not stay aloft.

Before their flight began, a slight breeze started to blow toward France from the cliffs of Dover, a city located on the Channel. The flight got off to a good start at about 1:00 P.M., but after only eight miles, the balloon began to descend. Blanchard and Jeffries jettisoned the ballast, the extra weight carried for the balloon's ascent, but, still, they continued to settle toward the water. According to Jeffries's account, the two men had been arguing about

1780's

FIRST CROSS-CHANNEL FLIGHT: DOVER TO CALAIS

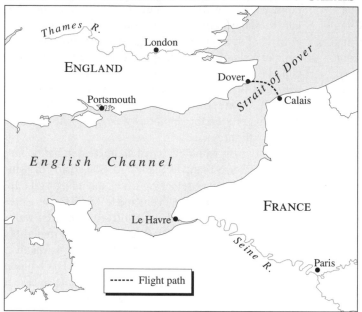

Flight path

bringing with him several balloons and the apparatus for generating hydrogen gas. On January 9, 1793, Blanchard made the first balloon flight in North America, from a prison yard in Philadelphia to Gloucester County, New Jersey. U.S. president George Washington attended the ascent, and Blanchard carried a letter from Washington in the balloon, possibly the world's first "airmail" delivery.

SIGNIFICANCE

Balloons did not emerge as practical methods of transportation because their flight paths are subject to the changing directions of the wind. However, the success of the earliest balloons led to the development of blimps and dirigibles, which use motor-driven propellers to direct the flight path.

The military quickly recognized the utility of balloons for observation. In 1793, the French government began using balloons for reconnaissance. Hot-air balloons were used during the American Civil War. Flying over the battlefield, military observers directed Union Army gunners to fire on Confederate positions without the gunners being able to see the enemy position. Hydrogen-filled observation balloons were widely used during World War I to detect troop movements and direct artillery fire. During World War II, gas-filled barrage balloons were used to intercept low-flying aircraft in the Battle of Britain. The Japanese launched thousands of balloon bombs toward the United States and Canada. The military's use of balloons has continued into the twenty-first century, as surveillance balloons, equipped with high-tech optics, have observed enemy movement from many miles away; surveillance balloons were used during the American invasion of Iraq in 2003.

Long-distance balloon flights continue to challenge adventurers. It was not until 1978, though, nearly two hundred years after the first successful piloted balloon flight across the English Channel, that the *Double Eagle II*, carrying three passengers, was able to cross the Atlantic Ocean, the first balloon to do so with humans aboard. The first crossing of the Pacific Ocean was accomplished in 1981, when the *Double Eagle V* flew from Japan to California.

—*George J. Flynn*

FURTHER READING

Blanchard, Jean-Pierre. *First Air Voyage in America.* Bedford, Mass.: Applewood Books, 2002. A sixty-

what they should throw overboard when the basket bounced on the water. Neither could swim, so they finally threw ropes, anchors, seats, and scientific instruments overboard. With the balloon skimming just above the water, Blanchard and Jeffries tossed their clothes, except their underwear, into the sea.

As they crossed the coast, the natural updraft that occurs as warm air rises from ground heated by the Sun caused the balloon to climb. Because they had thrown their landing ropes and anchors into the Channel, Jeffries grabbed some treetops to slow the balloon, but the balloon continued to rise. When they got over a field, Blanchard released some of the hydrogen and the balloon sank to a landing. A group of men, who had watched the landing, rode up on horseback. The adventurers were given clothes and taken to the nearby town of Calais, where they were greeted by cheering crowds. French king Louis XVI awarded Blanchard about $12,000 as well as a lifetime pension.

On June 15, 1785, Pierre Romain and Pilâtre de Rozier, who had flown on the Montgolfier balloon, also attempted a crossing of the Channel, ascending from Boulogne, France, in a hydrogen-filled balloon. About thirty minutes into the flight, however, at an altitude of about three thousand feet, Pilâtre de Rozier's balloon exploded, killing both men.

In 1792, Blanchard traveled by ship to Philadelphia,

four-page paperback that provides an account of the first American ascent in a balloon. Includes a facsimile of Blanchard's journal describing the flight and its preparations.

Jeffries, John. *A Narrative of Two Aerial Voyages.* 1786. Reprint. New York: Arno Press, 1971. A sixty-page description by Jeffries of two balloon flights with Blanchard. Part of the Physician Travelers series. Illustrated.

Marion, Fulgence. *Wonderful Balloon Ascents: Or, The Conquest of the Skies.* Whitefish, Mont.: Kessinger, 2004. A 218-page paperback reprint of an 1874 book describing the early days of ballooning.

Owen, David. *Lighter than Air: An Illustrated History of the Development of Hot-Air Balloons and Airships.* Lancaster, England: Chartwell Books, 1999. A 128-

page account that begins with the early "Race for the Skies" and continues through the modern "Rebirth of the Hot-Air Balloon."

SEE ALSO: 1733: Du Fay Discovers Two Kinds of Electric Charge; 1735: Hadley Describes Atmospheric Circulation; 1738: Bernoulli Proposes the Kinetic Theory of Gases; Oct. 23, 1769: Cugnot Demonstrates His Steam-Powered Road Carriage; Aug. 1, 1774: Priestley Discovers Oxygen; Sept. 6-7, 1776: First Test of a Submarine in Warfare; Nov. 21, 1783: First Manned Balloon Flight.

RELATED ARTICLES in *Great Lives from History: The Eighteenth Century, 1701-1800*: Louis XVI; Jacques-Étienne and Joseph-Michel Montgolfier; George Washington.

April, 1785
CARTWRIGHT PATENTS THE STEAM-POWERED LOOM

The production of a working power-operated loom was a key step in the mechanization of textile manufacture. Although power looms did not come into general use in England until after 1822, Cartwright's original model paved the way for future refinements, and the basic design remained unchanged until the middle of the twentieth century.

LOCALE: Northern England

CATEGORIES: Inventions; science and technology; manufacturing

KEY FIGURES

Edmund Cartwright (1743-1823), English priest, poet, and inventor

John Cartwright (1740-1824), radical political reformer and Edmund's brother

William Radcliffe (1761?-1842), English mill owner and inventor

Sir Richard Arkwright (1732-1792), English inventor of the water frame

SUMMARY OF EVENT

Early in 1785, Edmund Cartwright, an Anglican clergyman with no connection whatsoever to textile manufacture, was dining with some friends at Malden, near the center of the Lancashire cotton industry. A few years previously, the introduction of Sir Richard Arkwright's cotton spinning frame had enabled manufacturers to pro-

duce high-quality cotton thread very cheaply. The friends worried that the products of this burgeoning mechanized cotton spinning industry would be increasingly exported to the Continent, where labor was cheaper, and that English handloom weavers and their employers would suffer. The owners of weaving mills proposed petitioning Parliament to ban exporting cotton thread. When Cartwright suggested mechanizing weaving as an alternative, the mill owners were skeptical, reasoning based on their experience that weaving was too complex and skilled a process to be accomplished by machine.

Cartwright returned home to his parsonage in Leicestershire and set to work to prove them wrong. Working with a local blacksmith, he was able to produce a working power-operated loom. The first model, patented in April, 1785, was a cumbersome affair. Worked by means of a hand-crank, it required the strength of two men to operate. Warping and cloth uptake were still done by hand, and machine-spun yarn was not strong enough for the warp threads. Although this first power loom realized no savings in labor or production time relative to contemporary hand looms, it proved that mechanization of weaving was possible. It set the stage for further refinements by Cartwright and others, which over the ensuing two decades resulted in a commercially viable mechanism.

Not long after Cartwright obtained the patent, his wife Alice died, leaving him with six children to support and a substantial inheritance, including two houses in Doncaster, in the center of the Yorkshire wool industry. Living now among wool makers, he consulted with weavers and loom-builders, made many modifications to his original design, and in 1790 persuaded his brothers, John and George Cartwright, to provide the startup capital for a loom manufacturing concern. The owner of Knott's Mills in Manchester contracted to purchase and run up to four hundred of the new looms and had actually installed two dozen of them when his mill burned to the ground. Arson was suspected, and no other manufacturer was willing to take a risk on the new technology.

Cartwright also set up a cotton mill of his own in Doncaster, with twenty power looms run first by a bull and later (1789) by a steam engine. The mechanized looms produced high-quality cotton cloth at about four times the rate of a skilled hand-loom weaver, not a sufficient savings in labor to compensate for increased startup costs. The concern never repaid its investment, and it closed in 1793, leaving Cartwright in severe financial difficulties. A power-operated wool-combing system, which initially was expected to be more commercially profitable, likewise proved disappointing, realizing a tremendous saving in labor, but only for the coarsest grades of wool. Patent royalties brought in some income, but a combination of patent infringement and the slow rate of adoption meant that Cartwright never realized much profit from his invention. The original loom patent expired in 1803, just as commercially viable models were beginning to come on the market.

Though Cartwright never prospered as a direct result of the invention for which he is best remembered, the remainder of his long life was hardly a failure. In 1809, a consortium of Manchester manufacturers successfully petitioned Parliament to award him a grant of £10,000 for his services to the British nation. With this substantial sum he purchased a farm and devoted the ensuing years to experimental agriculture. He produced several minor inventions related to agricultural machinery. His home became a meeting place for inventors and innovators. He experimented with steam engines and engaged in a lengthy correspondence with the American inventor Robert Fulton, who credited him with having valuable input in the development of the first steamship.

Cartwright's original loom was ahead of its time. The art of machining had not progressed to the point where all of the delicate mechanisms required for coordinating the many separate processes that go into weaving could be mass-produced. The invention of the screw-lathe (1796) helped facilitate all branches of machine manufacture. William Radcliffe, founder of Manchester's first commercially successful power weaving establishment, contributed the dressing frame, a mechanical method of setting up warps, and an improved cloth uptake mechanism. Together with William Horrock's variable batten-speed motion (1813) and Robert Miller's cam-driven shedding principle (1796), the catalog of improvements to looms finally resulted in the first truly practical power loom, built by Richard Roberts in 1822.

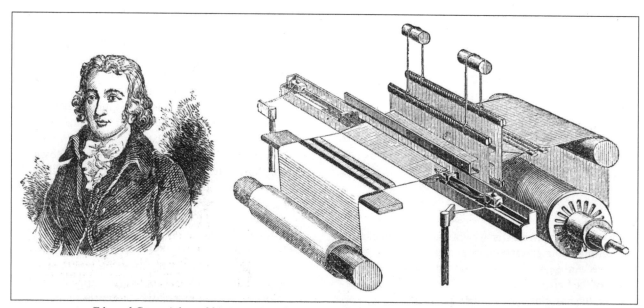

Edmund Cartwright and his invention, the steam-powered loom. (Hulton Archive/Getty Images)

The introduction of power weaving in Britain was hampered by social as well as technological factors. A burgeoning population, growing export markets, the tremendous expansion of cotton cultivation, and the mechanization of cotton cleaning, combing, and spinning, created thousands of skilled jobs for hand-loom weavers, who served a lengthy apprenticeship and expected to earn (by eighteenth century standards, at least) high wages. Though barred from forming unions and in most constituencies unable to vote, the hand-loom weavers, some 200,000 strong in 1812, constituted a potent political force.

The introduction of power looms potentially signaled a decrease in total employment in the industry and certainly meant that skilled male workers could be replaced by women and children. Workmen fought back by attacking machines and establishments that introduced them. Faced with the threat of sabotage, a technology whose labor-saving abilities were more potential than actual, and a surplus of skilled workers, employers found it easier to reduce wages than to introduce machines. The worst outbreaks of machine-breaking occurred during a wartime crisis in 1812-1813 and targeted several other inventions in addition to the power loom; however, the problem was sporadic in the 1790's and continued until about 1820. Industrial sabotage was one reason for the longer lag time between invention and wholesale adoption of technology in weaving, as compared to spinning, a less skilled occupation that had always been the provenance of women and children.

SIGNIFICANCE

Of the many literal and figurative revolutions that convulsed Europe and North America in the last quarter of the eighteenth century, the Industrial Revolution arguably had the most profound effect on the mass of people who experienced it, and it reshaped the political, economic, and social life of subsequent generations. In its earlier stages, it was a revolution primarily of textile manufacture. Cartwright's power loom played a key role in the process, notwithstanding the slow rate of adoption. Had a working power loom not existed, there would have been little incentive for the refinements that followed.

During the protracted Napoleonic Wars (1793-1815) and the depression that followed (1815-1821), incentives for expanding textile production were few, but the stage was set. In 1812, fewer than 2,000 power looms operated in Britain; by 1833, their number had expanded to more than 100,000. The average power loom's output then exceeded that of a hand-loom weaver by a factor of twelve to one, ensuring British supremacy in the manufacture of cheap cotton fabric against all competitors except the United States, where mechanization, piggybacking on and improving upon British inventions, proceeded very rapidly after 1814.

Britain's appetite for raw cotton and search for markets for the finished product helped drive imperial expansion. Supplying the mills of Lowell and Manchester fueled expansion of slavery in the United States, as an institution declining due to economic factors in the 1790's abruptly became immensely profitable.

The immediate social impact of mechanized weaving was largely negative. Mechanization concentrated the textile industry in large industrial towns plagued by pollution generated by coal-fired steam engines. Machines allowed a child to do the work of an adult, and increasingly it required the combined wages of all of the members of a family, working long hours, to sustain that family at a bare subsistence level. The economic advantages to manufacturers and the nation at large were well established by 1833; it took several more decades before the social costs began to be addressed through legislation and individual business practice.

—*Martha A. Sherwood*

FURTHER READING

Dunwell, Steve. *The Run of the Mill*. Boston: David R. Godine, 1978. The focus of this illustrated account is the early history of the textile industry in Massachusetts; it contains a thorough account of the mechanical challenges and the various designs of early power looms.

Mathew, H. C. G., and Brian Harrison, eds. *Oxford Dictionary of National Biography: From the Earliest Times to the Year 2000*. New York: Oxford University Press, 2004. This multivolume set includes detailed biographies of Edmund and John Cartwright and William Radcliffe. It is an invaluable source for biographies of obscure British historical personages.

O'Brien, Patrick. "The Micro Foundations of Macro Invention: The case of Reverend Edmund Cartwright." *Textile History* 28, no. 2 (1997): 201-233. Good for describing the process of invention and the complexities of capitalizing technology in nineteenth century Britain.

Reid, Robert William. *Land of Lost Content: The Luddite Revolt, 1812*. London: Heinemann, 1986. Aimed at the general reading public. Describes the social consequences of the mechanization of weaving, and some of the barriers to industrialization.

1780's

SEE ALSO: 1701: Tull Invents the Seed Drill; 1705-1712: Newcomen Develops the Steam Engine; 1709: Darby Invents Coke-Smelting; 1733: Kay Invents the Flying Shuttle; 1764: Invention of the Spinning Jenny; 1765-1769: Watt Develops a More Effective Steam Engine; 1767-1771: Invention of the Water Frame; 1779: Crompton Invents the Spinning Mule;

Dec. 20, 1790: Slater's Spinning Mill; 1793: Whitney Invents the Cotton Gin; 1795: Invention of the Flax Spinner.

RELATED ARTICLES in *Great Lives from History: The Eighteenth Century, 1701-1800*: Sir Richard Arkwright; James Hargreaves; John Kay; Eli Whitney.

May 20, 1785
ORDINANCE OF 1785

The Ordinance of 1785 established a system for surveying and selling the vast lands outside the former colonies that were then the property of the U.S. government. It set out the framework for the creation of new states and territories in the newly independent United States.

LOCALE: New York
CATEGORIES: Laws, acts, and legal history; expansion and land acquisition; government and politics

KEY FIGURES

Thomas Jefferson (1743-1826), member of the Confederation Congress and later president of the United States, 1801-1809
Winthrop Sargent (1753-1820), member of the Ohio Company of Associates and later secretary of the Northwest Territory
Rufus Putnam (1738-1824), member of the Ohio Company of Associates
Manasseh Cutler (1742-1823), lobbyist for the Ohio Company of Associates
John Cleves Symmes (1742-1814), organizer of the Symmes Purchase

SUMMARY OF EVENT

By 1779, twelve of the thirteen American states, engaged at that time in the Revolutionary War, had ratified the Articles of Confederation. The recalcitrant state, Maryland, ostensibly refused to ratify the document until the states with land claims in the West ceded those lands to the new government. Pressure from the landless states and the exigencies of the war finally compelled the landed states, particularly New York and Virginia, to cede their western claims to the revolutionary government. Maryland then ratified the Articles of Confederation early in 1781, and the confederation government came into existence as the owner of a vast public domain. Although little was

done by that government to dispose of these lands during the war, in October, 1780, Congress passed an act declaring its intent to sell the public lands and create states out of the new territories.

After the Treaty of Paris had been signed in 1783, the Confederation Congress turned to the formulation of a national land policy. To implement the intentions expressed in the Act of 1780, three problems had to be met. First, security against the natives was necessary before the new lands could be established, and some measure of success in this direction was later achieved with General Anthony Wayne's victory at the Battle of Fallen Timbers (1794). Second, some procedure had to be devised for the political organization of the new regions; this problem would be resolved with the Northwest Ordinance in 1787. Third, a system for the survey and sale of the lands had to be established, and this was the purpose of the Ordinance of 1785.

The debate over disposal of the public domain brought into view two divergent approaches that persisted into the nineteenth century. There were those who desired rapid settlement of the land and who therefore favored a policy that would attract settlers by the cheapness of the land. Others, moved by a variety of motives, advocated less liberal terms to settlers. Some of this latter group were concerned about the grave financial situation of the government. The Articles of Confederation did not provide the government with an independent and reliable source of revenue. Proceeds from the sale of public lands might alleviate this situation. Some from eastern (tidewater) areas feared that the rapid growth of the West would quickly diminish the political power of the older states. Others, interested in the possibilities of land speculation, looked upon liberal policies as dangerous competition.

There was also disagreement as to the method of land disposal. Two basic forms were available. The more systematic approach was the New England practice of township settlement, which provided for concentrated patterns of ownership, security in communities, and such community institutions as schools and churches. The other approach, generally referred to as the southern method, resulted in dispersed settlement with each individual staking out a claim to hitherto unsettled lands. In the New England plan, survey preceded sale and the possibility of conflicting claims was considerably lessened.

The matter was debated through 1784 and 1785, and when the Ordinance of 1785 was passed, it appeared to incorporate the basic features of the New England practice. The principle that survey should precede sale was adopted, as the act provided for rectangular surveys that divided the land into townships of six square miles. Townships were divided into tracts of 640 acres, or sections, which were to be sold at public auction for a minimum price of one dollar per acre. In each township, one lot was set aside for the support of public schools and four for the federal government. A provision giving similar support for religion was narrowly defeated.

This ordinance, with its minimal purchase requirement of 640 acres and its prohibition against indiscriminate settlement, seemed to favor the needs of speculators more than bona fide settlers. Few people of the type willing to carve a farm out of the wilderness in an area open to attack by American Indians had $640 in cash. Moreover, the disposition of the people who moved west was to settle where they lit, regardless of surveys, which were unable to keep up with settlement during the nineteenth century.

Congress itself, in its desperate need for ready money, compromised the intent of the act by disposing of vast tracts of land to private land companies for purposes of sale to settlers at a profit. The most famous of these companies was the Ohio Company of Associates, whose members included Winthrop Sargent, Rufus Putnam, and Manasseh Cutler. In 1787, Congress agreed to sell one and a half million acres of land to this group and another three and a half million to the Scioto Company. This latter speculative venture included many of the most important men in Congress, and their inclusion in the speculation made possible the passage of the Ohio Company grant. Also in 1787, the Symmes Purchase of two million acres—organized by John Cleves Symmes—was made at about sixty-six cents per acre.

SIGNIFICANCE

The confederation government did not realize much money from the sales authorized under the Ordinance of 1785, nor did these sales greatly stimulate settlement. Conditions were too precarious in the Ohio Country. The Land Act of 1796, which raised the minimum price to two dollars per acre, did little to advance settlement. The change to a more liberal policy began with the Harrison Land Act of 1800.

Nevertheless, the ordinance established an orderly method of disposing of public lands into private hands—a method that solved several problems simultaneously. First, it brought settlers and farmers into the national effort to repay the Revolutionary War debts. Even if the sales did not achieve what Thomas Jefferson hoped, the concept showed that all the nation's citizens would be called upon to shoulder part of the price of independence. Second, the principle of organized and methodical settlement—although, again, far from perfect in reality—reflected a clear understanding about the importance of keeping populations reasonably dense for purposes of defense and development. Third, and perhaps most significant, the ordinance ratified the fundamental property rights that undergirded the entire economic system. Land, once held only by nobility, was available to anyone for a tiny sum. Along with Jefferson's Northwest Ordinance, the Ordinance of 1785 allowed people to settle new land, bring it into the Union, and participate as equals in the polity.

—*John G. Clark, updated by Larry Schweikart*

FURTHER READING

Atack, Jeremy, and Peter Passell. *A New Economic View of American History*. 2d ed. New York: W. W. Norton, 1994. Contains an excellent chapter on land, land policies, agriculture, and productivity. Another chapter gives a good review of relevant material on the colonial economy.

Harris, Marshall D. *Origin of the Land Tenure System in the United States*. Westport, Conn.: Greenwood Press, 1953. Evaluates the influence of colonial precedents on the Ordinance of 1785.

Hibbard, Benjamin H. *A History of the Public Land Policies*. New York: Peter Smith, 1960. A good treatment of the adoption and implementation of the Ordinance of 1785. Emphasizes political policies more than Robbins's book.

Linklater, Andro. *Measuring America: How an Untamed Wilderness Shaped the United States and Fulfilled the Promise of Democracy*. New York: Walker, 2002. Recounts how the land west of the Ohio River was purchased by the United States, surveyed, and opened up to settlement. Linklater describes how the the concept of private land ownership originated in the United States and is a crucial component of American democracy.

1780's

Morris, Richard B. *The Forging of the Union, 1781-1789*. New York: Harper & Row, 1987. Touches only briefly on the ordinance itself, but sets the political stage for land policies under the Articles of Confederation.

Pattison, William D. *Beginnings of the American Rectangular Land Survey System, 1784-1800*. Chicago: University of Chicago Press, 1957. Focuses far more on the principles behind the surveys—such as how land should be divided and what land reserved for public uses—than on the ideals behind Jefferson's acts.

Robbins, Roy M. *Our Landed Heritage: The Public Domain, 1776-1936*. New York: Peter Smith, 1962. A general survey of land laws and their application.

Treat, Payson Jackson. *The National Land System, 1785-1820*. New York: E. B. Treat, 1910. Reprint. Buffalo, N.Y.: W. S. Hein, 2003. A detailed analysis of the land acts in the early republic. Praises the survey system and details its problems in collecting money for the land.

SEE ALSO: Apr. 19, 1775-Oct. 19, 1781: American Revolutionary War; Mar. 1, 1781: Ratification of the Articles of Confederation; Sept. 3, 1783: Treaty of Paris; Oct. 22, 1784: Fort Stanwix Treaty; July 13, 1787: Northwest Ordinance; Aug. 20, 1794: Battle of Fallen Timbers.

RELATED ARTICLE in *Great Lives from History: The Eighteenth Century, 1701-1800*: Thomas Jefferson.

1786
DISCOVERY OF THE MAYAN RUINS AT PALENQUE

Spanish colonial officials uncovered the spectacular Mayan ruins at Palenque, which had been abandoned in the tenth century. Historians first believed that the technical and artistic abilities of ancient European travelers had inspired and influenced the building of the complex by local peoples. However, the Mayan origins of the site were revealed after the ruins were found, and the origins themselves have been uncovered and celebrated by the Mexican indigenous movement of the twentieth century.

LOCALE: Chiapas, Mexico
CATEGORIES: Anthropology; architecture; cultural and intellectual history

KEY FIGURES

Antonio del Rio (1745-1789), a Spanish artillery officer in Guatemala

Ricardo Almendariz (fl. c. 1787), a Spanish artist active in late-colonial Guatemala

Ramón de Ordoñez y Aguiar (d. c. 1840), a clerical official at the cathedral in San Cristobal de las Casas, Chiapas

Pacal (603-683), lord of Palenque, r. 615-683

Charles III (1716-1788), king of Naples and Sicily, r. 1734-1759, as Charles VII, and king of Spain, r. 1759-1788

SUMMARY OF EVENT

Flourishing during the middle to late centuries of the first millennium, Mayan civilization left a commanding architectural legacy throughout southern Mexico and regions of Guatemala, Belize, El Salvador, and Honduras. Among the most awesome remnants of this heritage was the complex of temples and a palace at Palenque in the Mexican state of Chiapas. Shadowed and framed by tropical verdure, the buildings rose in stony splendor along mountain slopes arching up from the blue crescent of the Gulf of Mexico. The city, which occupied more than six hundred acres, had approximately two hundred buildings at its height. The original inhabitants referred to the locale as Houses of Stone or Big Water.

Dominating the western region of Mayan territory, the later rulers of Palenque, the principal one being Lord Pacal, documented their lineage and accomplishments through elaborate inscriptions carved on temple walls, the primary texts of Mayan history. The buildings at Palenque reflected the cumulative refinement of Mayan architectural and sculptural skills, the elegance of arched mansards, and the richness of layers of detailed carving. The city peaked during the seventh and eighth centuries, then collapsed precipitously in the early ninth century. As the forest reclaimed the site, Palenque subsided from view and memory, even among descendants of those who had formed the complex. The Spanish conquest of Mexico during the early sixteenth century, however, was accompanied by myths and rumors regarding the hidden wealth of indigenous ruins, nurturing prospects for their rediscovery.

A question particularly intriguing to the Spanish was the origin of the indigenous population. The question intrigued even the king of Spain, Charles III, an Enlightenment monarch curious about philosophical and scientific issues. In 1786 the king ordered the governor of Guatemala to confirm speculations regarding the existence of singular indigenous ruins that might lie within the governor's jurisdiction (*audiencia*) in the province of Chiapas. Earlier findings in the previous decade by a local cleric, Ramón de Ordoñez y Aguiar, had confirmed the existence of ruins near the village of Santo Domingo de Palenque. In 1785 the existence of the ruins was confirmed when the village mayor and a government architect examined them and reported their existence.

In the spring of 1786, the governor of Guatemala sent to the site one of his senior military adjutants, Captain Antonio del Rio, to explore it more thoroughly. The captain was instructed to recover treasures or other items of historical importance. Arriving at Palenque and aided by the mayor, del Rio assembled a crew of several dozen local Mayan laborers and set about removing the tropical overgrowth, burning and hacking it away. As evidence of what he had found, he dispatched carvings to Guatemala, which were then shipped to Spain. In addition, he wrote a report, the first detailed study of Palenque, which inaugurated a series of analyses that attempted to interpret the site. Accompanying this report were the first drawings of the site, produced by Ricardo Almendariz, an artist who accompanied del Rio.

Del Rio and Almendariz were singularly impressed by the extent, complexity, and refinement of the architecture and sculpture that del Rio's crew had exposed, the first time the site had been uncovered in centuries. However, the Spanish captain did not consider that the site might have originated from the ancestors of the local Mayans, a demoralized people who had been subordinated and marginalized by the Spanish for nearly two centuries. He speculated that the site was a product of the influence of ancient Western cultures, possibly the seafaring Phoenicians of three millennia earlier or of classical Greece and Rome. Spain, too, had been settled by Phoenicians, Carthaginians, and Romans, who had traded and explored westward across the Mediterranean Sea.

The Spaniards believed that these voyagers may have ventured into the Atlantic Ocean, thereby reaching the Americas and influencing indigenous populations. Catholic clergy even assumed that indigenous religion was a corruption of Christianity, speculating that the region

1780's

Mayan ruins at Palenque in Chiapas, Mexico. (Corbis)

could have been evangelized in apostolic times by Saint Thomas through missionary travels eastward from India over the Pacific Ocean. It was assumed that Quetzalcóatl, the feathered serpent god and prophet of the Aztecs and Mayans, had originated out of confusion with the apostle.

SIGNIFICANCE

Antonio del Rio and Ricardo Almendariz's illustrated report was sent to Spain in 1787, and another copy was archived in Guatemala. Both documents, however, were then forgotten. Charles III died at the end of the following year, and del Rio died in 1789.

The report reemerged in 1822. An English traveler visiting Guatemala came across a study by Pablo Felix Cabrera, a scholar from Spain who had resided in Guatemala during the last decade of the eighteenth century. Cabrera, who had been convinced that the Americas had been settled by the Phoenicians, found the del Rio and Almendariz report and drawings. Cabrera incorporated these findings into a study he wrote on the origin of American Indians, printed in London in 1822 and titled *Description of the Ruins of an Ancient City, Discovered Near Palenque, in the Kingdom of Guatemala*. The authors are listed as Antonio del Rio and Paul Felix Cabrera. The following decade, an American periodical in New York serialized extensive parts of the report.

Throughout the nineteenth century, researchers failed to recognize that Palenque and other marvels of Mayan architecture had indigenous origins. Researchers continued to speculate that in addition to voyagers from the Mediterranean across the Atlantic, the lost continent of Atlantis could be the origin of indigenous culture in the Americas. Also, Mormonism has used such speculation as the rationale for its tenets regarding the ancient subsidiary roots of Christianity in the Americas.

Not until the Mexican Revolution at the beginning of the twentieth century did the true origins of Palenque begin to emerge. The movement known as *indigenismo*, focusing on the accomplishments of indigenous peoples, prompted a renaissance of study and artistic production focusing on native Mexican culture. Especially important in this regard was the establishment in 1939 of the Instituto Nacional de Antropología e Historia (the National Institute of Anthropology and History). Advancing professional standards in anthropology and archaeology, the institute has sponsored projects conducted within an environment of respect for indigenous culture. By the latter half of the twentieth century, these efforts had achieved two significant goals in relation to

Palenque: discovery of the splendid temple tomb of Lord Pacal and the decipherment of Mayan writing, revealing a detailed Mayan chronology and historiography.

—*Edward A. Riedinger*

FURTHER READING

Chouinard, Jeffrey. *Mouths of Stone: Stories of the Ancient Maya from Newly Deciphered Inscriptions and Recent Archaeological Discoveries*. Durham, N.C.: Carolina Academic Press, 1995. Accompanied by maps and illustrations, this work examines the deciphering of ancient Mayan written language at Copan, Palenque, and Tikal, providing clues in narrative form.

Hughes, Nigel. *Maya Monuments*. Woodbridge, England: Antique Collectors' Club, 2000. A study with maps and illustrations of Palenque and numerous other Mayan sites, placing Palenque in architectural, geographical, and historical context.

Palenque Round Table Series. San Francisco, Calif.: Precolumbian Art Research Institute, 1973- . Scholarly papers from a series of conferences conducted since 1973 on Palenque, Mayan antiquities, and indigenous peoples and cultures of Mexico and Central America.

Ringle, William M., and Thomas C. Smith-Stark. *A Concordance to the Inscriptions of Palenque, Chiapas, Mexico*. New Orleans, La.: Middle American Research Institute, Tulane University, 1996. A Mayan hieroglyphic catalog of inscriptions at Palenque, with an accompanying compact disc.

Romer, John, and Elizabeth Romer. *The History of Archaeology*. New York: Checkmark Books, 2001. Relates the intellectual, professional, and social context for the historical development of archaeology, placing Palenque's rediscovery within this phenomenon.

Sandoval, Roberto Romero. "Travelers in Palenque, Eighteenth and Nineteenth Centuries: A Historical Study Through Their Bibliography." *Boletín del Instituto de Investigaciones Bibliográficas*, n.s., 2, no. 1 (1997): 9-40. Provides a chronology of expeditions by more than one dozen travelers who believe the origin of Palenque is Mayan and not of ancient Europe.

Schele, Linda and David Freidel. *A Forest of Kings: The Untold Story of the Ancient Maya*. New York: Morrow, 1992. An extensively illustrated work about temples, palaces, and monuments of Mayan rulers, including the complex at Palenque. Includes numerous linguistic, historical, and archaeological studies by noted scholars of the Maya.

SEE ALSO: Aug., 1712: Maya Rebellion in Chiapas; 1719-1724: Stukeley Studies Stonehenge and Avebury; 1748: Excavation of Pompeii.

RELATED ARTICLES in *Great Lives from History: The Eighteenth Century, 1701-1800*: Charles III; William Stukeley.

1786-1787
LAVOISIER DEVISES THE MODERN SYSTEM OF CHEMICAL NOMENCLATURE

As an important part of the chemical revolution he fathered, Lavoisier, collaborating with other French scientists, devised a rational system of chemical nomenclature in which each substance's name reflected its chemical composition.

LOCALE: Paris, France
CATEGORIES: Chemistry; science and technology

KEY FIGURES
Antoine-Laurent Lavoisier (1743-1794), French natural philosopher and chemist
Louis Bernard Guyton de Morveau (1737-1816), French lawyer and amateur chemist
Claude Louis Berthollet (1748-1822), French physician and chemist
Antoine François de Fourcroy (1755-1809), French chemist

SUMMARY OF EVENT
Before Antoine-Laurent Lavoisier and his collaborators created a rational system of chemical nomenclature, a variety of methods existed for naming chemical substances, resulting in a very confused set of names. For some chemical substances, alchemical names were still in use, and often these bore no relationship to the actual makeup of the material. For example, "powder of Algaroth" was actually a compound of antimony and chlorine. Previous chemists had named some substances after persons (Glauber's salt) and others after a place (Epsom salt). "Oil of vitriol" was named after its appearance, since sulfuric acid was an oily liquid. Sometimes the very same substance had multiple names: Quicksilver and hydrargyrum were both designations for mercury. "Sugar of lead" (lead acetate) was named for its effect on the senses, since it tasted sweet, but it was also very poisonous, revealing the danger in some of these confusing names.

Louis Bernard Guyton de Morveau became concerned about the contradictions and confusions in traditional chemical nomenclature, and in 1782 he wrote a paper whose purpose was to propose a new terminology for chemistry. He believed that chemical substances should have names that indicated their constituents. Like Carolus Linnaeus, who had systematized botanical nomenclature using Latin names, Guyton de Morveau felt that new chemical names should be based on Latin or Greek roots, so their meaning could be easily understood. He made many specific suggestions in his paper; for instance, he derived the names of salts from their respective acids, as in *vitriol de cuivre* (copper sulfate), derived from sulfuric acid. Some of his suggestions found their way into the *Encyclopédie* of 1786, but his ideas really gained wide recognition when he converted from the phlogiston theory to Lavoisier's oxygen theory and when he collaborated with Lavoisier, Claude Louis Berthollet, and Antoine François de Fourcroy in a detailed revision of chemical nomenclature.

Beginning in 1786 and continuing through 1787, Lavoisier, Guyton de Morveau, Berthollet, and Fourcroy met almost daily for discussions about their reform of chemical nomenclature. They collected information, consulted with other scientists, and read extensively, including such works as *La Logique: Ou, Les Premiers Développmens de l'art de penser* (1780; *The Logic of Condillac*, 1809) by Étienne Bonnot de Condillac, who stressed the connection between clear language and clear thinking. On April 17, 1787, Lavoisier read a paper before the French Academy of Sciences in which he used Guyton de Morveau's earlier work and Condillac's ideas in advocating a new language for chemists based on new principles. He wanted a straightforward relationship between the facts and ideas of chemistry and the words in which these facts and ideas were expressed.

By this time in Lavoisier's career, he had rejected the alchemical theory of the four elements (earth, air, fire, and water) and the phlogiston theory of Georg Ernst Stahl (who believed that a weightless fluid called phlogiston was responsible for combustion). Lavoisier held that burning was actually a reaction in which oxygen combined with the combustible substance. Therefore, the "Group of Four" chemists desired not only to reform chemical nomenclature but also to reform chemistry itself. When their *Méthode de nomenclature chimique* (1787; *Method of Chymical Nomenclature*, 1788) was published in Paris, they understood that it would most likely be accepted by disciples of their new theory of chemistry and rejected by phlogistonists.

In *Method of Chymical Nomenclature*, the authors begin by attacking traditional chemical names. They point out that in some cases, one substance had more than ten different names, and even when there was only one name for a substance, its name bore no relationship to its chemical nature. The basic principle of the new nomenclature was that there should be a single name for each chemical substance and that the name should describe its composition in terms of its simple constituents. For example, acids were named for the element from which they were made, as in sulfuric acid from sulfur. Salts made from acids all took the suffix "-ate," for example, sodium sulfate. Since the new system was so simple to use and its powers of clarification were so great, it was quickly adopted by many French chemists, and later, when *Method of Chymical Nomenclature* was translated into other languages, by chemists in other countries as well.

In France, *Method of Chymical Nomenclature* had only a few editions, since two years after its publication its principal methods and ideas were incorporated by Lavoisier into his *Traité élémentaire de chimie* (1789; *Elements of Chemistry*, 1790), often called the first modern textbook of chemistry. This book, with its new nomenclature and new chemical ideas, became the principal vehicle by which young scientists around the world learned of and often were converted to the new chemistry of Lavoisier.

The new nomenclature was not enthusiastically received by all groups, even in France. French phlogistonists objected to it, and they had such a strong hold on the French Academy that, though *Method of Chymical Nomenclature* was approved for publication, its system was not officially adopted. In England, such prominent scientists as Joseph Black expressed disapproval, and as late as 1802, Thomas Thomson, whose textbook of chemistry was highly influential, was very critical of the new chemical names. Nonetheless, with the increasing popularity of Lavoisier's *Elements of Chemistry*, resistance to the new nomenclature declined, though pockets of recalcitrance remained. As late as 1870, the "new" nomenclature was attacked in a French pharmacopoeia. By this time, however, Lavoisier's

---

WATER AND CHEMICAL ELEMENTS

Until the late eighteenth century, water was considered to be a chemical element rather than a compound. This 1783 report prepared for the Royal Academy relates how Antoine-Laurent Lavoisier advanced Henry Cavendish's experiments to identify water as a compound of hydrogen and oxygen.

M. Cavendish . . . observed that if one operates in dry vessels a discernible quantity of moisture is deposited on the inner walls. Since the verification of this fact was of great significance to chemical theory, M. Lavoisier and M. [Pierre-Simon] de la Place proposed to confirm it in a large-scale experiment. . . . The quantity of inflammable air burned in this experiment was about thirty pints [pintes] and that of dephlogisticated air from fifteen to eighteen.

As soon as the two airs had been lit, the wall of the vessel in which the combustion took place visibly darkened and became covered by a large number of droplets of water. Little by little the drops grew in volume. Many coalesced together and collected in the bottom of the apparatus, where they formed a layer on the surface of the mercury.

After the experiment, nearly all the water was collected by means of a funnel, and its weight was found to be about 5 gros, which corresponded fairly closely to the weight of the two airs combined. This water was as pure as distilled water.

A short time later, M. Monge addressed to the Academy the result of a similar combustion . . . which was perhaps more accurate. He determined with great care the weight of the two airs, and he likewise found that in burning large quantities of inflammable air and dephlogisticated air one obtains very pure water and that its weight very nearly approximates the weight of the two airs used. Finally . . . M. Cavendish recently repeated the same experiment by different means and that when the quantity of the two airs had been well proportioned, he consistently obtained the same result.

It is difficult to refuse to recognize that in this experiment, water is made artificially and from scratch, and consequently that the constituent parts of this fluid are inflammable air and dephlogisticated air, less the portion of fire which is released during the combustion.

Source: "Report of a Memoir Read by M. Lavoisier at the Public Session of the Royal Academy of Sciences of November 12, on the Nature of Water and on Experiments Which Appear to Prove That This Substance Is Not Strictly Speaking an Element but That It Is Susceptible of Decomposition and Recomposition." *Observations sur la Physique* 23 (1783): 452-455. Translated by Carmen Giunta.

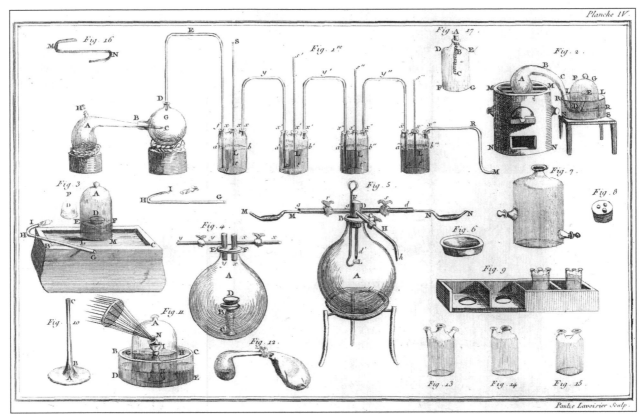

An illustration from the 1789 French edition of Elements of Chemistry *showing the various apparatuses Lavoisier used in his studies of combustion.* (Library of Congress)

ideas and the clear language in which they were expressed had proved their superiority to most of the chemical world.

SIGNIFICANCE

Some scholars have stated that it is "almost impossible" to exaggerate the importance of the new chemical nomenclature for the progress of chemistry. Other scholars have compared the significance of what Lavoisier did at the end of the eighteenth century to what Dmitry Ivanovich Mendeleyev accomplished in the nineteenth century with his periodic table of elements. Both scientists provided a scheme for classifying elements and compounds, and both schemes were productive of important new chemical discoveries. Just like the periodic table, Lavoisier's nomenclature became a tool for discovery; for example, when the names of chemical reactants were clearly expressed, the products of the reaction often became obvious.

The reform of chemical nomenclature developed by Lavoisier and his colleagues was inextricably inter-

twined with his new system of chemistry. Revolutions, be they political or scientific, are disturbing events, and the chemical revolution was no exception. Those who accepted Lavoisier's oxygen theory saw the significance of his reform of nomenclature. Those chemists who clung to the phlogiston theory regarded his nomenclature as barbaric. Revolutions do not bring about the conversion of all those who believed in the old system. A good example is Joseph Priestley, who ironically went to his grave in 1804 still convinced of the value of the phlogiston theory, despite having discovered oxygen. Both the new nomenclature and Lavoisier's new system of chemistry were the province of the young, and their numbers kept multiplying through the nineteenth century. With the new generation of chemists came the nearly complete acceptance of Lavoisier's new names and ideas.

—*Robert J. Paradowski*

FURTHER READING

Guerlac, Henry. *Antoine Laurent Lavoisier: Chemist and Revolutionary.* New York: Scribner, 1975. This short biography, which derives from a long article on Lavoisier the author wrote for the *Dictionary of Scientific Biography*, provides an excellent introduction to Lavoisier's life and achievements. Illustrated, critical bibliographic guide to both primary and secondary sources, and an index.

McKie, Douglas. *Antoine Lavoisier: Scientist, Economist, Social Reformer*. New York: Da Capo, 1980. This reprint of a work originally published in 1952 offers the general reader a biography of Lavoisier that includes his activities in politics and economics as well as in science. Some have called it the best-written account of Lavoisier's life in English, but some reviewers were upset by its lack of footnotes and critical documentation.

Partington, J. R. *A History of Chemistry*. Vol. 3. London: Macmillan, 1962. Chapter 9 of this comprehensive history of chemistry is devoted to Lavoisier, with many references to primary and secondary sources in the footnotes. An index of subjects and an index of names.

Poirier, Jean Pierre. *Lavoisier: Chemist, Biologist, Economist*. Philadelphia: University of Pennsylvania Press, 1996. This biography, translated from the 1993 French version, was well received by American chemists, though American historians of science had some criticisms. Nevertheless, the author, who read and absorbed many new manuscript sources, has produced a vivid portrait for the general reader.

SEE ALSO: 1723: Stahl Postulates the Phlogiston Theory; Beginning 1735: Linnaeus Creates the Binomial System of Classification; Aug. 1, 1774: Priestley Discovers Oxygen.

RELATED ARTICLES in *Great Lives from History: The Eighteenth Century, 1701-1800*: Joseph Black; Étienne Bonnot de Condillac; Antoine-Laurent Lavoisier; Carolus Linnaeus; Joseph Priestley; Georg Ernst Stahl.

1786-1787
TENMEI FAMINE

The Tenmei era saw the most devastating famine in early modern Japan, a nationwide disaster that took as many as 130,000 lives. Many farming villages were abandoned, and large areas became depopulated. Shogunate officials provided little assistance, and they aggravated the situation through corruption and incompetence. Popular uprisings forced the officials out of office, bringing not only greater repression but also needed reforms.

LOCALE: Japan
CATEGORIES: Health and medicine; agriculture; economics; wars, uprisings, and civil unrest; government and politics

KEY FIGURES
Hasegawa Heizo (1745-1795), the shogunate court official in charge of quelling unrest in 1787
Matsudaira Sadanobu (1758/1759-1829), Tokugawa Ienari's chief councilor, who carried out many needed reforms
Tanuma Okitsugu (1719-1788), the shogun's chief councillor, who was regarded by many as responsible for corruption, aggravating famine and social unrest
Tokugawa Ieharu (1736-1786), shogun, r. 1760-1786, who delegated power to Tanuma

Tokugawa Ienari (1773-1841), shogun, r. 1787-1837, initially a reformer, who was advised by Matsudaira

SUMMARY OF EVENT
The Tenmei Famine of 1786-1787, along with the Kyoho Famine of 1732 and the Tempo Famine of 1832 to 1837, were three major famines during the two and a half centuries of the Edo period. Though the Kyoho Famine of 1732 was of shorter duration, it affected close to one million people in forty-six feudal domains in Western Japan. The effects of the Kyoho Famine were mitigated, however, by active efforts by the shogunate and the regional feudal lords to provide food and financial assistance to people in distress, and loans to farm communities so that they could plant new crops. Active relief efforts like these were largely neglected by the shogunate during the Tenmei Famine. This neglect prolonged the intensity and severity of hardship and famine among the people, creating disorders that undermined the power and authority of the shogunate. According to modern historians, the Tenmei Famine was the greatest nationwide disaster to occur in early modern Japan.

In 1782, persistent frost and rain led to an estimated 25 percent crop loss. This was followed in 1783 by an even more disastrous crop loss of 75 percent. There had been heavy rains and floods in the middle of June, which washed out many crops. This was followed by a huge eruption of Mount Asama in July, which killed more than twenty thousand people and produced great quantities of volcanic ash. The ash killed crops over a large area of central Honshu and blocked sunlight so that surviving crops were diminished.

In the spring of 1786, another extended spell of frost destroyed many crops in the Kanto and Tohoku regions of Honshu. More heavy rains followed, which not only ruined crops but also overwhelmed the beginnings of an ambitious Kanto drainage project planned by the shogun's chief councillor, Tanuma Okitsugu, causing large-scale flooding. The widespread famine that followed was reported to have caused severe illness and starvation, leading to the death of as many as 130,000 people.

Many of the starving wandered from place to place in search of food, resulting in a general depletion of food supplies even in communities unaffected by crop failures. The general exodus of farmworkers also resulted in local labor shortages that hindered the planting of new crops, in turn extending and compounding the famine. Many farming villages were abandoned, and people tried to survive by gathering and eating wild vegetation. There were also reported cases of the eating of corpses.

In many locations, the authorities set up shelters, where food such as rice gruel was doled out to the hungry and homeless, but the shogunate provided little substantial financial assistance to help farmers plant new crops, even in the most desperately impoverished communities. Instead, the government under Tanuma tried to set up forced loan schemes, in which loan money would be levied from landholders and merchants and loan interest would be paid to the shogunate. Tanuma also tried to manipulate the rice market, ostensibly to keep prices down, but rice prices continued to rise as food grew scarcer. Having nowhere to turn, desperate people began to resort to violence to get food and shelter.

By late summer, 1786, the national situation had worsened to such an extent that Chief Councillor Tanuma was forced to resign, in August. Shogun Tokugawa Ieharu's untimely death followed in September, and the next six months the government lacked clear control. Riots and uprisings had started to break out all over the country, creating a situation of nationwide chaos. By late spring, 1787, more than thirty major disorders had developed in twenty different locations around the country, including in the cities of Nara, Osaka, Hiroshima, Hakata, Nagasaki, and Edo. This seventh year of the Tenmei era was plagued by the greatest degree of civil strife ever to take place during the entire two and a half centuries of the Edo period.

In mid-April, 1787, fourteen-year-old Tokugawa Ienari began his fifty-year reign as shogun, taking advice from Matsudaira Sadanobu, a feudal lord whose policies of local government austerity and aid to people in distress had made the famine less of a disaster in his domain in northeastern Honshu. In May, Hasegawa Heizo, a shogunate adviser whose father had been in charge of national civil security before him, was given the job of suppressing the disorders. Hasegawa succeeded in this role, and he spent the remaining eight years of his life modernizing shogunate policing methods, which had been designed to prevent civil unrest by keeping displaced and unemployed people under supervision and control.

In the case of the subsequent Tempo Famine of 1832 to 1837, the shogunate and the domain lords adopted relief measures similar to those originally undertaken during the Kyoho Famine, but years of repeated crop failures exhausted relief resources, and rice hoarding in less-affected areas continuously inflated the price of rice. As in the Tenmei Famine, the resultant regional disorders developed into urban uprisings as well. The largest of these occurred in Osaka in 1837, led by the retired official and neo-Confucian scholar Oshio Heihachiro. Oshio and his followers lost their lives in this abortive effort, while Ienari, who had begun as shogun following the peak of the Tenmei Famine in 1787, retired from office following the Osaka uprising.

SIGNIFICANCE

The Tenmei Famine, along with the Tempo Famine, contributed significantly to the depopulation of rural areas and to limited population growth in general because of the deaths of so many people from starvation and malnutrition.

Ienari's successor Ieyoshi followed the example of his father's work in 1787, and subsequently supported advisers who attempted to combine sweeping reforms with stricter policing of the people. As with Ienari, these reforms ended in failure because of the lack of sustained effort to carry them through, though authoritarian rule continued. Ieyoshi died soon after Commodore Matthew Galbraith Perry arrived in 1853 to secure a trade and commerce treaty between Japan and the United States, an event that disrupted Ieyoshi's own reign quite as much as the Tenmei Famine and Tempo Famine had undermined the reigns of his two predecessors.

During the seven decades between the start of the Tenmei Famine in 1782 and Perry's arrival in 1853, the

1780's

military and civil power of the shogunate were progressively weakened by popular discontent aroused by corruption, aggravated by a total of more than ten years of major famine and disorder. Beginning in 1853, the weakened shogunate attempted to maintain its control by a series of grudging compromises with Japanese regional enclaves and encroaching Western power, but the final result was the fall of the last Tokugawa shogun in 1867.

—Michael McCaskey

Further Reading

Cuny, Frederick C. *Famine, Conflict, and Response: A Basic Guide.* Bloomfield, Conn.: Kumarian Press, 1999. A handbook on the nature of famine by a caseworker who devoted his life to its elimination.

Hall, John Whitney. *Tanuma Okitsugu, 1719-1788: Forerunner of Modern Japan.* Cambridge, Mass.: Harvard University Press, 1955. A classic study of a controversial and frequently criticized statesman.

Screech, Timon. *The Shogun's Painted Culture: Fear and Creativity in the Japanese States, 1760-1829.* London: Reaktion Books, 2000. A study of Japanese life and culture, with a focus on the influence of Matsudaira Sadanobu on Japanese society. Extensive bibliography.

Vlastos, Stephen. *Peasant Protests and Uprisings in Tokugawa Japan.* Berkeley: University of California Press, 1990. This study focuses on records of social conditions among the peasants in Fukushima prefecture.

Walthall, Anne, ed. *Peasant Uprisings in Japan: An Anthology of Peasant Histories.* Chicago: University of Chicago Press, 1991. Study and translations of five Tokugawa era peasant narratives.

White, James W. *Ikki: Social Conflict and Political Protest in Early Modern Japan.* Ithaca, N.Y.: Cornell University Press, 1995. Sociological study of cases of peasant rebellion in Tokugawa Japan, based on original sources.

See also: May, 1720-Dec., 1721: Last Major Outbreak of Plague; 1753: Lind Discovers a Cure for Scurvy; 1763-1767: Famine in Southern Italy.

Related articles in *Great Lives from History: The Eighteenth Century, 1701-1800*: Honda Toshiaki; Tokugawa Yoshimune.

January 16, 1786

Virginia Statute of Religious Liberty

Virginia was the first state to legislate religious liberty, which influenced the First Amendment's provision for separation of church and state.

Locale: Richmond, Virginia

Categories: Civil rights; laws, acts, and legal history; religion and theology

Key Figures

Isaac Backus (1724-1806), leader of the fight for the disestablishment of religion in Massachusetts

Patrick Henry (1736-1799), leader of the effort to enact the General Assessment Bill

Thomas Jefferson (1743-1826), author of the "Bill for Establishing Religious Freedom," and president of the United States, 1801-1809

James Madison (1751-1836), leader of the fight to enact Jefferson's bill, and president of the United States, 1809-1817

Roger Williams (c. 1603-1683), founder of Rhode Island

Summary of Event

The adoption by the state of Virginia of the Statute of Religious Liberty was a pivotal episode in the long struggle for separation of church and state in the United States. The American colonies had inherited from England an organic concept of society that had predominated in the Middle Ages and survived the Protestant Reformation. In England, the church and the state had been regarded ideally as parts of a greater and divinely sanctioned social order and so owed mutual support to each other.

While the Puritans and other sects had emigrated partly to practice their particular faiths without harassment, few were committed to religious freedom for others. The legal toleration of all Christians in Maryland and Pennsylvania, and the complete toleration offered in Rhode Island, were exceptional in the seventeenth century, and even those colonies had begun to impose penalties on Catholics by the time of the Revolutionary War. Whereas, in the later colonial period, toleration of dissenting sects was often a practical necessity, connections between church and state persisted. The Church of England was established legally in the Southern colonies, and Protestant churches were supported by public funds in most of New England. Catholics and Jews remained under civil disabilities in some states until well into the nineteenth century.

During the period of the American Revolution, there was a sudden acceleration in the ongoing development of a concept of society in which political and religious life existed in separate compartments and in which religion withdrew, theoretically, into the private sphere of activity. Part of the impetus behind this new desire for a separation of church and state was religious. Some originally radical Protestant sects were committed to separation early, either because of their own experience with persecution or out of more abstract considerations. Some agreed with Roger Williams that a church would be corrupted only by connection with the state. The Baptists were particularly energetic advocates of separation. Isaac Backus, Baptist leader of the fight for religious disestablishment in Massachusetts, has been characterized as the leading American advocate of religious liberty after Williams.

In addition to these strains within American Protestantism, the philosophy of the Enlightenment, emphasizing the sanctity of the individual conscience, was influential, most notably among Thomas Jefferson and other leaders of the disestablishment struggle in Virginia. Perhaps the overriding factor in deciding the general issue in the United States, however, was a practical consideration: Because of the extreme multiplicity of sects in the country, in the long run it was not politically feasible to establish any one of them or even a combination.

The American Revolution, bringing new state constitutions and the withdrawal of British support for the Anglican establishment, provided an occasion for the reform of relationships between church and state. Virginia's action in the period following the Declaration of Independence was particularly significant. Virginia—one of the largest and most important states in the new republic and the seat of the most deeply rooted of the Anglican establishments—took the lead in moving toward religious liberty and the complete separation of church and state. Only Rhode Island offered comparable liberty among the original states, although, despite its early toleration, Catholics and Jews had been barred from citizenship there in the late colonial period.

Revolutionary Virginia inherited a strongly antiestablishment sentiment, marked historically by disputes over clerical salaries and the long struggle by Baptists and Presbyterians against Anglican domination. The Decla-

ration of Rights, adopted by the Virginia legislature three weeks before the Declaration of Independence, asserted that "all men are equally entitled to the free exercise of religion, according to the dictates of conscience. . . ." James Madison had suggested this liberal phrasing in preference to a more narrow statement of religious toleration. Later in 1776, penalties against those of dissenting religious persuasion were repealed, and Dissenters (as they had been called in Great Britain) were exempted from contributing to the support of the still-established Church of England. In 1779, the legislature moved in the direction of disestablishment by discontinuing the payment of salaries to clergy of the Church of England in Virginia.

The conclusive debates in Virginia took place in 1784 and 1785. Patrick Henry led a move in Virginia's legislature to establish a general assessment for the support of Christian worship, which would have substituted a general Christian establishment for the Anglican establishment. Initially passed in November, 1784, this General Assessment Bill was sharply attacked by Madison and defeated on its final reading in October, 1785. Madison followed up this victory by securing a vote on the "Bill for Establishing Religious Freedom," proposed by Thomas Jefferson and originally introduced in the legislature in 1779. It was adopted and became law as the Statute of Religious Liberty on January 16, 1786. With a preamble asserting that God had "created the mind free" and that attempts to coerce it "tend only to beget habits of hypocrisy and meanness, and are a departure from the plan of the Holy Author of our religion," Jefferson's statute provided "that no man shall be compelled to frequent or support any religious worship, place or ministry whatsoever, nor shall be enforced, restrained, molested, or burthened in his body or goods, nor otherwise suffer on account of his religious opinions or belief. . . ."

SIGNIFICANCE

There remained some vestigial connections between church and state, but their separation had been completed by 1802. Few other states immediately followed Virginia's lead. Officeholders under many of the original state constitutions were required to be believers in God, Christians, or even Protestants. It was not until 1818 that Connecticut did away with compulsory public support of churches, and not until 1833 was a similar establishment completely eliminated in Massachusetts. The First Amendment to the federal Constitution, which prohibited religious establishment or infringement of religious liberty on the national level, helped to commend the ex-

1780's

ample of Virginia to its sister states. Moreover, with the passage of the Fourteenth Amendment to the Constitution (1868) and its subsequent interpretation by the Supreme Court, the provisions of the First Amendment were extended to apply to state legislatures and not merely to the federal government. Thus, in the twentieth century, separation of church and state became mandated for all state legislatures.

—*Michael D. Clark, updated by Daniel A. Brown*

FURTHER READING

Drakeman, Donald L. "Religion and the Republic: James Madison and the First Amendment." *Journal of Church and State* 25, no. 3 (1983): 427-445. Provides a historical appraisal of Madison's evolution on this issue.

Howe, Mark De Wolfe. *The Garden and the Wilderness: Religion and Government in American Constitutional History*. Chicago: University of Chicago Press, 1965. Discusses the church and the world in the unfolding drama connecting them.

Lambert, Frank. *The Founding Fathers and the Place of Religion in America*. Princeton, N.J.: Princeton University Press, 2003. Explains how and why the United States became the first modern state committed to separating church and state. Includes information about the triumph of religious freedom in Virginia, including adoption of the statute.

Mapp, Alf J., Jr. *The Faith of Our Fathers: What America's Founders Really Believed*. Lanham, Md.: Rowman & Littlefield, 2003. Describes the religious beliefs of several of the Founding Fathers, including the faiths of three men central to the struggle for reli-gious freedom in Virginia—Thomas Jefferson, Patrick Henry, and James Madison.

Noll, Mark A., ed. *Religion and American Politics: From the Colonial Period to the 1980's*. New York: Oxford University Press, 1990. A collection of historical articles with a comprehensive section on the time of the Founding Fathers.

Peterson, Merrill D., and Robert C. Vaughan, eds. *The Virginia Statute for Religious Freedom: Its Evolution and Consequences in American History*. New York: Cambridge University Press, 1988. A rich collection by historians, philosophers, lawyers, and religion scholars on the impact of the Virginia statute in the late eighteenth century and after.

Stokes, Anson P., and Leo Pfeffer. *Church and State in the United States*. Rev. ed. New York: Harper & Row, 1964. A useful abridgment of the standard, monumental survey of legal development of church and state issues in the United States.

Wald, Kenneth D. *Religion and Politics in the United States*. 2d ed. Washington, D.C.: Congressional Quarterly Press, 1992. A reliable primer on the history, law, and sociology involved in the relationship of church and state in the United States.

SEE ALSO: 1739-1742: First Great Awakening; Oct. 30, 1768: Methodist Church Is Established in Colonial America; 1773-1788: African American Baptist Church Is Founded; Sept. 17, 1787: U.S. Constitution Is Adopted; July 28-Oct. 16, 1789: Episcopal Church Is Established; 1790's-1830's: Second Great Awakening.

RELATED ARTICLES in *Great Lives from History: The Eighteenth Century, 1701-1800*: Patrick Henry; Thomas Jefferson; James Madison.

February 2, 1786
JONES POSTULATES A PROTO-INDO-EUROPEAN LANGUAGE

Sir William Jones stunned scholars in Europe and inspired them to review the origin of Western civilization when he suggested that an unknown prehistoric language was the source of classical languages, such as Greek and Latin, as well as Sanskrit.

LOCALE: Calcutta (now Kolkata, India)

CATEGORIES: Anthropology; cultural and intellectual history; literature; historiography

KEY FIGURE

Sir William Jones (1746-1794), British judge and amateur classicist and linguist

SUMMARY OF EVENT

Sir William Jones, a barrister and an Orientalist, arrived in India in September, 1783. Jones had been knighted the same year for his legal knowledge of Oriental (Asian) societies. This unique aptitude had secured for him the judgeship on the Bengal Supreme Court. Months after his arrival in Calcutta, Jones founded the Asiatic Society of Bengal to promote Oriental studies among British expatriates serving in the colonial administration. He himself began to learn Sanskrit to study Hindu laws, the primary reason being that the pundits hired by the court often gave confusing and conflicting opinions on legal issues involving the Hindus. However, soon Jones realized that his interest in Sanskrit had much broader implications in the realms of linguistics and social anthropology than in Indian jurisprudence. In an address to his society on its third anniversary, he outlined his theory of a proto-language predating all known ancient languages.

Since the founding of the Asiatic Society, Jones, its president, had delivered several papers, on topics as varied as elephantiasis and the gods of Greece, Italy, and India. Though by the time of the singular "Third Anniversary Discourse" his knowledge of Sanskrit was not remarkable (he had studied it only for four months or so), what modest exposure he had to the vedic language convinced him of its excellence and astounded him by its similarities to Greek and Latin. He found the phonetic and morphemic systems of Sanskrit not unlike those of the classical languages.

Such structural likenesses overwhelmed him, which is why, early in the address, Jones discounts the etymological approach in studying languages, instead preferring the a posteriori method, because it enables him to be empirical and ground his findings on evidence rather than speculation. It is also clear that the scope of his findings extends far beyond philology. His project appears to be no less than an account of the origin of humanity. The present address, Jones declares, is the first in a series of five on the origins of the five peoples of Asia: the Indians, the Chinese, the Tatars, the Arabs, and the Persians. In the last address, he intends to discuss whether all five had a common origin. He begins with India not because he thinks it is the center of all but because it is the country of his current residence and affords him the advantage of studying the others. However, that India indeed is the center of these civilizations he strongly implies when next he compares it to the rising Sun in the Zodiac.

Indians, though they have suffered many conquests, are still rich, according to Jones. He reminds his audience that Indians still make the best cotton and that Indians still possess the same features they had many centuries ago. While he pronounces the Indians of his time "degenerate and abased," he showers those of yore with praise because of their talents in many fields. Since Indians have left no clear record of their history for about nineteen centuries prior to his time, Jones names four areas through which ancient India can be known: languages and letters, philosophy and religion, sculpture and architecture, and sciences and arts.

Jones's famous passage on the possibility of a proto-language now lost appears in his discussion India's languages and literature. Jones expresses strong admiration for Sanskrit because it is "of a wonderful structure, more perfect than *Greek*, more copious than *Latin*." He credits Sanskrit with higher refinement than either, but also suggests that in its verbs and grammar, Sanskrit has a strong resemblance with both. Such a remarkable similarity could not have occurred fortuitously; the fact compels one to surmise that all three have "sprung from some common source, which, perhaps, no longer exists." On a similar note, Jones declares that languages as remote as Gothic, Celtic, and Old Persian share the same root.

The rest of the address illustrates Jones's thesis with examples from disciplines other than philology. His aim is no less than to provide a common origin for all known civilizations, the Indian being the closest to the prime source. Jones indicates that the script used in Indian writing is called *nagari*. *Nagari* letters are used in as many as twenty Indian kingdoms. However, they are not as old as those recently found in a cave in India, which derive from

727

the same root whence came Hebrew, Greek, Roman, and Arabic alphabets. Jones is convinced that the Indian deities are the same as those in Greek myths; he shows similar figures in the two mythologies. The six schools of Indian philosophy, on the other hand, "comprise all the metaphysics of the old *Academy*, the *Stoa*, the *Lyceum*."

Next, Jones proclaims that his study of the Vedanta irrefutably suggests to him "Pythagoras and Plato derived their sublime theories from the same fountain with the sages of India." He also finds evidence of the dissemination of Buddhist and Hindu ideas in ancient Greek thought and mentions "*an* Universal Deluge" that Indian myths surrounding the *avatars* suggest. An interesting conjecture that Jones presents is that the Peruvian Inca festival known as *Ramasitoa* that honored the Sun god might have derived from the Indian Rama and his wife Sita. There is no doubt in Jones's mind that South American Indians are part of the same race and civilization to which belong the Indians. Based on the worship of fire and sun, these belief systems had "one great spring and fountain of all idolatry in the four quarters of the globe."

Jones's theory of a proto-Indo-European language appeared at a time when other European scholars were taking a great deal of interest in Asia, particularly in India and its people. Samuel Johnson, whose Literary Club Jones had joined before coming to India, was curious about Asiatic literature and urged colonial officials working in India to make inquiries into Indian literature. Edmund Burke, a member of the same club, who as a member of Parliament eloquently spoke in the British parliament on upholding justice in India, had similar interests. Charles Wilkins, a contemporary Sanskrit scholar of Jones and a member of the Asiatic Society, translated the *Bhagavadgītā* (c. 200 B.C.E.-200 C.E.; *The Bhagavad Gita*, 1785) in 1885, to which Warren Hastings, then governor general of Bengal, gave a rousing ovation when he compared it to Homer's epics.

SIGNIFICANCE

Garland Cannon, the noted Jones scholar, observes that the paragraph in the "Third Anniversary Discourse" in which Jones presents his idea of an *ur* language "is one of the most quoted formulations among all scholarly formulations in all disciplines." What gives the brief passage such a unique distinction is Jones's ability to view languages as members of a family—more specifically, the languages of India and Europe as the group known as "Indo-European." Certainly, the theory helped dismantle European images of Indians and other Asians as savages with monstrous deities and perverse religious customs.

The consequence was profound in its impact. Interest in India grew in seats of learning in the entire Continent and resembled no less than a cultural revolution. The enthusiasm led Friedrich von Schlegel even to think that Sanskrit was the parent of Greek, German, and Latin. Jones's own translation of Kālidāsa's *Abhijñānaśākuntala* (c. 395 C.E.; *Śakuntalā: Or, The Lost Ring*, 1789) became a favorite of Johann Wolfgang von Goethe, and interest in and influence of ancient Indian literature and philosophy could be seen for centuries in authors such as Georg Wilhelm Friedrich Hegel, Samuel Taylor Coleridge, Arthur Schopenhauer, Ralph Waldo Emerson, Max Müller, T. S. Eliot, and V. S. Naipaul.

In India, Jones's scholarship has received its due recognition. The Asiatic Society he founded centuries ago still continues to function and has an Internet Web site. On the second centennial of the society's founding, the then prime minister of India, Indira Gandhi, gave the inaugural speech and lavished praise upon Jones, testifying to the esteem he enjoys in the country he once served as a judge and enriched through his scholarship.

In the wake of Edward Said's anti-Orientalist work *Orientalism* (1978), however, Jones has come under attack, in particular in British-American colleges and universities. In his defense, Jones admirers often point out the distinctions between an Orientalist such as Jones and one such as James Mill, who wrote a voluminous history of India without ever being in the country, or Lord Macaulay, who recommended English to be the only medium of instruction in Indian education and infamously claimed "a single shelf of a good European library was worth the whole native literature of India and Arabia." Publications on Jones upon the bicentenary of the Asiatic Society in 1984 and of his death in 1994 demonstrate that his contributions to philology and Sanskrit studies continue to draw worldwide regard.

—*Farhad Idris*

FURTHER READING

Cannon, Garland. *The Life and Mind of Oriental Jones: Sir William Jones, the Father of Modern Linguistics.* Cambridge, England: Cambridge University Press, 1990. A biography from an avid Jones scholar with a fine bibliography and an appendix containing five new letters.

Cannon, Garland, and Kevin Brine, eds. *Objects of Enquiry: The Life and Contributions of Sir William Jones, 1746-1794.* New York: New York University Press, 1995. A selection of essays by several scholars. Has a useful introduction and bibliography.

Franklin, Michael J., ed. *Sir William Jones: Selected Poetical and Prose Works*. Cardiff: University of Wales Press, 1995. Introduction is more keen on disproving Edward Said's critique of Orientalism and Jones than providing a background to Jones. Contains useful notes to the selections.

Lamb, Sydney M., and Douglas Mitchell, eds. *Sprung from Some Common Source: Investigations into the Prehistory of Languages*. Palo Alto, Calif.: Stanford University Press, 1991. A scholarly work of 411 pages. Extends Jones's hypothesis beyond the languages Jones mentioned in his Third Anniversary Discourse to other less common languages.

Murray, Alexander, ed. *Sir William Jones, 1746-1794: A Commemoration*. New York: Oxford University Press, 1998. Selection of essays based on a conference held to honor Jones on the bicentenary of his death. Presents Jones as a "polymath" and emphasizes his multiple talents.

Sharpe, Jenny. "The Violence of Light in the Land of Desire: Or, How William Jones Discovered India." *Boundary 2* 20, no. 1 (1993): 26-46. Uses Edward Said's analysis of Orientalism to study Jones. Links current interest in multiculturalism with a resurgent Orientalism.

SEE ALSO: 1762: *The Antiquities of Athens* Prompts Architectural Neoclassicism; Aug., 1767-May, 1799: Anglo-Mysore Wars; Dec., 1774-Feb. 24, 1783: First Marāthā War.

RELATED ARTICLES in *Great Lives from History: The Eighteenth Century, 1701-1800*: Edmund Burke; Johann Wolfgang von Goethe; Warren Hastings; Samuel Johnson.

1787

DAVID PAINTS *THE DEATH OF SOCRATES*

In 1787, the celebrated artist Jacques-Louis David painted The Death of Socrates, *which epitomized neoclassicism, an artistic movement that grew in reaction to the frivolous and decorative rococo style. Neoclassical art also reflected the philosophical and moral values of the Enlightenment and the Age of Reason.*

LOCALE: Paris, France
CATEGORY: Art

KEY FIGURES
Jacques-Louis David (1748-1825), French painter
Charles-Michel Trudaine de la Sablière (1766-1794), member of the Parlement of Paris
Joseph-Marie Vien (1716-1809), French painter
Pierre Peyron (1744-1814), French painter
Charles-Louis Trudaine de Montigny (1765-1794), noble and brother of Charles-Michel Trudaine de la Sablière

SUMMARY OF EVENT
On August 30, 1748, Jacques-Louis David was born into an affluent Parisian family. From 1766 to 1774, he studied with the renowned neoclassical painter Joseph-Marie Vien. After winning the Prix de Rome in 1774, David traveled to Italy with his teacher. From 1774 to 1780, David drew from models from antiquity and was inspired by the neoclassical experimentation in Rome. After returning to Paris in 1780, his favorite subjects became mythology and ancient history. In 1787, he painted *The Death of Socrates*, which was the quintessential neoclassical expression.

The painting had been commissioned in 1786 by a wealthy patron, Charles-Michel Trudaine de la Sablière, for the generous sum of 10,000 livres. David frequently attended literary and artistic salon meetings at the home of Charles-Michel and his brother, Charles-Louis Trudaine de Montigny. At these Trudaine Society meetings, David met prominent eighteenth century Enlightenment writers, liberal nobility, and the intellectual elite. These meetings helped shape his artistic, social, and political development.

During the eighteenth century, an important shift occurred in European culture. Intellectuals emphasized the possibility of improving society through the use of reason and began to challenge the political power of the aristocracy as well as the moral authority of the Church. Eventually, trends toward democracy and rationality resulted in political and social changes, especially in France, where a violent revolution succeeded in overthrowing the monarchy. At the same time, the flowery, decorative style of art known as rococo, which had been popular earlier in the century, was associated with the frivolity, wastefulness, and idleness of those who merely

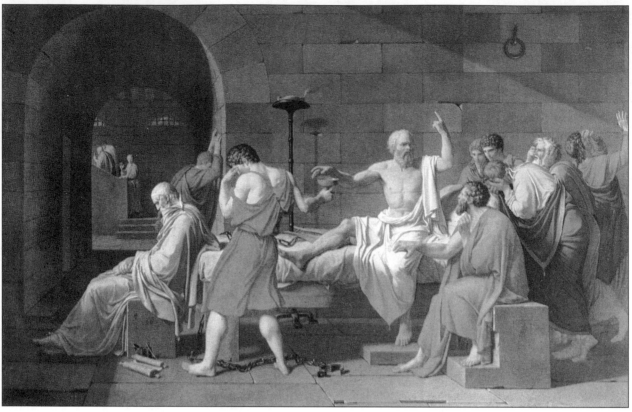

The Death of Socrates *by Jacques-Louis David.* (Courtesy, Metropolitan Museum of Art, New York)

inherited wealth and power rather than earning it through their own merits and labors. Artists, architects, and musicians began to place more value on clarity and simplicity of line, dropping the excessive ornamentation that had characterized the preceding styles.

Sponsorship of art began to shift, so that the middle class played a larger role in supporting art and defining its values. For inspiration, many turned to the ancient Greco-Roman heritage, especially sculpture and architecture. This trend, which was later called the neoclassical movement, also included the use of art to promote moral action, self-sacrifice, and heroism. Although the ancient Greeks and Romans were idealized at this time, and many formal elements were borrowed from them, the eighteenth century movement was essentially secular and democratic, reflecting the values of the French Revolution and its struggle to survive in the face of significant military, political, and economic challenges.

Both the visual and political dimensions of the neoclassical style can be seen in the paintings of David, who is regarded as the most prominent artist of the genre, and of David's many paintings, the clearest and most well-

known example of the neoclassical style is his *Death of Socrates*. The choice of this subject matter in 1787 had a special resonance with the Enlightenment and revolutionary ideas of the time.

Socrates (469-399 B.C.E.) was a great philosopher who emphasized rationality over unquestioned belief, as did the Enlightenment thinkers of David's time. Socrates' respect for the law and truth had turned the ruling factions against him. In 399 B.C.E., he was sentenced to death for corrupting the youth of Athens and for not acknowledging the state's gods. As a prominent historical figure, Socrates was easily associated with an idealized notion of ancient Greece. Socrates' heroic sacrifice could provide a psychological substitute for the martyrdom of Christ and the saints. Also, Socrates' uncompromising morality, his unflinching sense of duty to the state, and his calm fearlessness could be viewed as models for desirable behavior, just two years before the French Revolution. By drinking the cup of poison provided for the completion of his death sentence, Socrates showed that he was willing to die cheerfully for his values, that he would never stop teaching and questioning those around him.

Although the painting quotes from classical Greek sculpture in the poses, musculature, treatment of fabric, and other features of the characters being represented, it also makes use of a full range of techniques from previous generations of Renaissance and Baroque painters, especially the use of dramatic lighting. The bright light on Socrates and his disciples contrasts sharply with the gloomy atmosphere of the prison; it is an almost literal representation of the "light of reason" shining forth in the darkness.

The seriousness of the figures' expressions and the lack of ornamentation in the painting reinforce the sense of purpose and economy of content favored by the neoclassical artists. In their statuesque poses, Socrates and his students are frozen in a moment of glory, and David himself shares in this glory by painting his own initials as if they are carved into the block that supports Plato, Socrates' most illustrious follower. Although he was taking historical liberty by including Plato in the scene, David uses the image of Plato and the block on which he sits to affirm an ongoing, timeless connection between his own culture and the existence of the revered philosophers.

When *The Death of Socrates* was first exhibited at the Salon of 1787, it received phenomenal critical acclaim by both the art world and the public. David's chief rival, Pierre Peyron, exhibited a painting on the same subject, and the general consensus was that David's painting was far superior.

As a result, Peyron withdrew from public life and the art world, and David became the preeminent French artist. Admirers of David's painting included the print publisher John Boydell, the prominent English artist Sir Joshua Reynolds, and Thomas Jefferson. With its message of stoic self-sacrifice and resistance to unfair authority, the *Death of Socrates* was in complete harmony with the sentiments of the imminent French Revolution.

SIGNIFICANCE

David became the leading artist of the French Revolution, supported Robespierre, and voted for the execution of King Louis XVI. When Napoleon rose to power in 1799, David became his painter. After Napoleon's fall, David was exiled to Brussels, Belgium, in 1815 and died in 1825.

David had been a remarkable teacher who influenced a generation of artists, including Anne-Louis Girodet-Trioson (1767-1824), François Gerard (1770-1837), Baron Antoine-Jean Gros (1771-1835), and Jean-Auguste-Dominique Ingres (1780-1867). These students carried on David's neoclassicist legacy, but their individ-

ual styles or expanded palette provided the transition to Romanticism, which succeeded neoclassicism in the mid-eighteenth century and was in vogue from about 1789 to 1832 in both Europe and North America. In their paintings, Girodet-Trioson and Gerard anticipated the dreamlike, imaginative Romantic style. Ingres painted exotic, non-European subjects, such as odalisques (concubines in a harem). Gros, who was one of David's favorite pupils and administered the studio after David was exiled, became a leader in the development of Romanticism. In the early 1800's, Gros was France's most celebrated artist. His bright palette and the dynamic, emotional tone of his paintings greatly impressed the early Romantics, especially Eugene Delacroix (1798-1863) and Jean Louis André Théodore Gericault (1791-1824).

After David's patron, Charles-Michel Trudaine de la Sablière, and his brother Charles-Louis Trudaine de Montigny were executed by guillotine in 1794, ownership of *The Death of Socrates* passed to Louise Trudaine de Montigny (d. 1802) and subsequently to various relatives and descendants. In 1931, *The Death of Socrates* was purchased by the Metropolitan Museum of Art in New York City.

—*Alice Myers*

FURTHER READING

Crow, Thomas. *Emulation: Making Artists for Revolutionary France*. New Haven, Conn.: Yale University Press, 1995. A scholarly political and aesthetic study, focusing on David and two of his pupils. Includes a section on David's *Death of Socrates*. Illustrated. Extensive notes, bibliography, and index.

Einecke, Claudia. *Final Moments: Peyron, David, and "The Death of Socrates."* Omaha, Neb.: Joslyn Art Museum, 2001. Catalog of an exhibition at Joslyn Art Museum, February 3-April 1, 2001, with essays on the fierce competition between the two artists and their paintings on the same theme. Illustrated.

Eitner, Lorenz. *Nineteenth Century European Painting: David to Cezanne*. Boulder, Colo.: Westview Press, 2002. Includes studies of the classical revival, the arts in France at the end of the eighteenth century, and David and his school. Illustrated. Bibliography and index.

Lee, Simon. *David*. London: Phaidon, 1999. This in-depth analysis of David's art, politics, and values asserts that David was the most significant painter of his time. Illustrated. Bibliography, glossary, and index.

Monneret, Sophie. *David and Neo-classicism*. Paris: Pierre Terrail, 1999. More than 160 color illustrations, many full-page. A well-documented study that maintains that David's art was a turning point in history and reflected the paradoxes of his time. Bibliography.

SEE ALSO: 1721-1750: Early Enlightenment in France; 1737: Revival of the Paris Salon; Dec. 10, 1768: Britain's Royal Academy of Arts Is Founded; May 5,

1789: Louis XVI Calls the Estates-General; July 14, 1789: Fall of the Bastille; Nov. 9-10, 1799: Napoleon Rises to Power in France.

RELATED ARTICLES in *Great Lives from History: The Eighteenth Century, 1701-1800*: Louis XVI; Sir Joshua Reynolds; Robespierre.

1787
HERSCHEL BEGINS BUILDING HIS REFLECTING TELESCOPE

William Herschel's 40-foot-long reflecting telescope was used to discover two of Saturn's moons and to observe nebula, identified as galaxies such as the Milky Way. The telescope, functional in 1789, remained the largest such instrument for more than fifty years.

LOCALE: Slough, England
CATEGORIES: Astronomy; science and technology

KEY FIGURES

William Herschel (1738-1822), a German-born astronomer and telescope maker
Caroline Lucretia Herschel (1750-1848), a self-taught German-born astronomer and William's sister
George III (1738-1820), king of England, r. 1760-1820, who funded construction of Herschel's telescope

SUMMARY OF EVENT

William Herschel learned to play a musical instrument as a child, but he also developed a keen interest in observing the sky with his father. From 1757 to 1772, while achieving success as a musician, he continued studying mathematics and made naked-eye observations of the sky. It was in 1773 that William's interest in astronomy intensified. He read books on astronomy and purchased a quadrant, an instrument used to measure angles between the stars, as well as some lenses and mirrors. His first telescope is believed to have been a small, compact reflector of the type designed by the Scottish astronomer James Gregory, but this telescope was too small to be of any significant help. Herschel wanted a bigger, more powerful instrument, one that would gather more light and allow him to see fainter stars. However, large lenses, or mirrors, were very expensive at the time, so he had to make his own mirrors.

By 1774, Herschel had developed techniques to cast and polish mirrors superior to any that had been made previously. He constructed more than four hundred tele-

scopes and observed the planets and their moons, the stars, and unusual objects called nebula, which are luminous patches in the night sky. His large telescopes could resolve the individual stars in nearby nebula, but even with this telescopic power, the nebula could not be separated into individual stars and therefore looked like clouds. This led him to theorize that nebula were groups of stars, gathered together over long periods of time by the force of gravity; the Milky Way, he added, was one of these galaxies.

Herschel's sister, Caroline Lucretia Herschel, became his assistant, recording his observations and helping him grind and polish the mirrors for his new telescopes. She would become a noted astronomer as well—discovering eight comets and three nebulae—and is frequently referred to as the first woman astronomer of lasting significance. William and Caroline, still active musicians, gave their last public musical performance in 1782, after which they devoted themselves to astronomy.

Between 1786 and 1802, William Herschel published three catalogs noting the positions and characteristics of nebulae. These observations were performed mostly using his 20-foot telescope, an instrument with a focal length of 20 feet and a diameter of 18.8 inches. Herschel, however, was not satisfied with the magnifying power of this 20-foot telescope, so, in 1784, he decided to build a much larger one, with a tube having a length of 40 feet and a mirror with a diameter of 48 inches. This project was far more expensive than he could afford. However, he was able to begin construction at his home and observatory in Slough, England, in 1785, upon receiving from King George III of England a £2,000 grant and an annual stipend of £200.

Constructing the 40-foot telescope was a major project, involving as many as forty workers, who removed trees, dug and prepared the ground, and laid a brick foundation. Another group prepared the tools for shaping and polishing the telescope's mirror. During this time, Wil-

William Herschel and Caroline Lucretia Herschel, shown with William's 40-foot reflecting telescope. (Premier Publishing)

liam and Caroline made nighttime observations using the smaller telescopes and supervised construction of the giant telescope during the day.

After about two years of work, it seemed that Herschel's largest telescope was complete. In early 1787, he tried to use the new telescope for the first time, but the quality of the mirror was not satisfactory. It weighed about one thousand pounds and was so thin that it distorted under its own weight, compromising the quality of the image. To take care of the problem, he ordered the casting of a new mirror disk, but this one broke while it was cooling. The third mirror disk proved successful. This mirror, 3.5 inches thick—twice as thick as the first mirror—was free of significant distortion.

The telescope had "first light," an astronomer's term for the first attempt to observe through a new telescope, on August 28, 1789. The extraordinary power of Herschel's telescope was immediately apparent. That first evening, Herschel quickly discovered Saturn's sixth moon, named Enceladus. On September 17, 1789, he discovered Saturn's seventh moon, called Mimas.

Even with all its power and reach, the 40-foot telescope was not Herschel's favorite, for two reasons. First, it required a lot of maintenance and the mirror needed frequent polishing. Second, and even more problematic, the mounting that allowed the telescope to be aimed at different spots on the sky was difficult to handle. Herschel, therefore, continued to make most of his observations with the 20-foot telescope, using it to discover two moons of Uranus, named Titania and Oberon. The 40-foot telescope remained the world's largest for more than fifty years, possibly because of the difficulties using it. It was not until 1845 that William Parsons, the third earl of Rosse, built a larger telescope, which Parsons called the Leviathan. Had Herschel's 40-foot telescope been easier to maintain and aim, he might have discovered even more cosmic phenomena, such as the spiral nebulae, a discovery made by Parsons.

In recognition of his achievements, William Herschel was knighted in 1816. He had helped to start the Astronomical Society of London in 1820, which later became the Royal Astronomical Society. A piece of the tube of the 40-foot telescope is displayed in the garden of Greenwich Observatory in London, but the mirror has been lost.

SIGNIFICANCE

William Herschel's 40-foot reflecting telescope allowed him, along with his sister Caroline, to make significant astronomical discoveries. He located the planet Uranus as well as two moons of Saturn, determined the rotational period of Saturn, used the same techniques to study the rotation of other planets, observed the motion of double stars, and concluded that stars are held together by gravitation. Thus, he was able to confirm the universal nature of Newton's laws of gravity.

The telescopes aided his nebular research as well, which suggested that there existed more than the one hundred known nebulae in the universe. His catalog of nebulae was completed by Caroline after his death and published by Caroline's nephew (and William's son) John Herschel. *General Catalogue of Nebulae and Clusters of Stars* (1864) listed about twenty-five hundred nebulae. The nebular research also suggested that new worlds might begin from gaseous matter, which remains the accepted origin of solar systems. Herschel also concluded that the known solar system is moving through space, and he was able to determine the direction of its motion.

—*George J. Flynn*

FURTHER READING

Armitage, Angus. *William Herschel.* Garden City, N.Y.: Doubleday, 1963. A 158-page account of Herschel's life and scientific contributions, with a chapter focusing on the construction of his large telescope and the discoveries he made with it.

Crawford, Deborah. *King's Astronomer William Herschel*. New York: Julian Messner, 2000. A 191-page biography of Herschel, discussing both his musical and scientific careers, including his development of the high-powered telescope.

Dreyer, John Louis Emil, ed. *The Scientific Papers of Sir William Herschel*. Dorset, England: Thoemmes Continuum, 2003. A massive, 1,441-page collection of Herschel's papers, containing detailed descriptions of his astronomical observations and discoveries.

Hoskin, Michael A. *The Herschel Partnership: As Viewed by Caroline*. Cambridge, England: Science History, 2003. A biographical work that focuses on the partnership between Caroline and William.

_____. *William Herschel and the Construction of the Heavens*. New York: Norton, 1964. A nearly 200-page discussion of Herschel's discoveries, with notes on their astrophysical significance by D. W. Dewhirst.

Lubbock, Constance A. *The Herschel Chronicle: The Life-Story of William Herschel and His Sister, Caroline Herschel*. Cambridge, England: Cambridge University Press, 1933. A biography of William and Caroline with material drawn from their own records.

Sidgwick, J. B. *William Herschel: Explorer of the Heavens*. London: Faber & Faber, 1953. An account of Herschel's life, including his career as a musician and his later work as an astronomer.

SEE ALSO: 1704: Newton Publishes *Optics*; 1704-1712: Astronomy Wars in England; 1705: Halley Predicts the Return of a Comet; 1725: Flamsteed's Star Cata-·log Marks the Transition to Modern Astronomy; 1796: Laplace Articulates His Nebular Hypothesis.

RELATED ARTICLES in *Great Lives from History: The Eighteenth Century, 1701-1800:* Jean-Sylvain Bailly; Benjamin Banneker; George III; George Frideric Handel; Caroline Lucretia Herschel; William Herschel; Joseph-Louis Lagrange; Colin Maclaurin.

April 12, 1787
FREE AFRICAN SOCIETY IS FOUNDED

The Free African Society, the first major secular institution with a mission to aid African Americans, paved the way for later institutions such as the National Association for the Advancement of Colored People (NAACP). The society existed for less than a decade, however, before its membership merged with African American churches and other religious organizations with similar agendas.

LOCALE: Philadelphia, Pennsylvania
CATEGORIES: Organizations and institutions; social issues and reform

KEY FIGURES
Richard Allen (1760-1831), African American former slave, religious leader, and social reformer
Absalom Jones (1746-1818), leader of the Free African Society
Benjamin Rush (1746-1813), American physician and member of the Continental Congress

SUMMARY OF EVENT
Both the origins of the Free African Society and the long-term repercussions of its founding form an essential part of the religious history of African Americans. The origi-

nal organization itself was of short duration: About seven years after it was organized, it disappeared as a formal body. In its immediate wake, however, closely related institutions emerged that tried to take over its proclaimed mission.

Generally speaking, prior to the 1790's, people of African slave origins who managed to obtain their individual freedom had only one option if they wished to practice Christianity: association, as subordinate parishioners, in an existing white-run church. Several churches in the American colonies before independence, including the Quakers and Methodists, had tried to identify their religious cause with that of the black victims of slavery.

Richard Allen, born in 1760 as a slave whose family belonged to Pennsylvania's then attorney general, Benjamin Chew, was destined to become one of the earliest religious leaders of the black segment of the American Methodist Church. As a youth, Allen gained extensive experience with Methodist teachings after his family was separated on the auction block in Dover, Delaware. Allen was encouraged by his second owner, Master Stokeley, to espouse the religious teachings of the itinerant American Methodist preacher Freeborn Garrettson. Allen's conversion to Methodism was rewarded when Stokeley freed him at age twenty to follow the calling of religion. His freedom came just as the Revolutionary War ended.

For six years, Allen worked under the influence of Methodist evangelist Benjamin Abbott and the Reverend (later Bishop) Richard Whatcoat, with whom he traveled on an extensive preaching circuit. Allen's writings refer to Whatcoat as his "father in Israel." With Whatcoat's encouragement, Allen accepted an invitation from the Methodist elder in Philadelphia to return to his birthplace to become a preacher.

At that time, Philadelphia's religious environment seemed to be dominated by the Episcopal Church. This church had been active since 1758 in extending its ministry to African Americans. It was St. George's Methodist Episcopal Church, however, that, in the 1780's, had drawn the largest number of former slaves to its rolls. Once the circumstances of blacks' second-class status became clear to Allen, he decided that his leadership mission should be specifically dedicated to the needs of his people. Within a short time, he joined another African American, Absalom Jones, in founding what was originally intended to be more of a secular movement than a formal denominational movement: the Free African Society.

Absalom Jones was older than Allen and had had a different set of life experiences. Born a slave in Delaware in 1746, Jones served for more than twenty years in his master's store in Philadelphia. He earned enough money to purchase his wife's freedom, to build his own home, and finally, in 1784, to purchase his own freedom. He continued to work for his former master for wages and bought and managed two houses for additional income.

Portraits of African Methodist Episcopal Church bishops, including Richard Allen, who cofounded the Free African Society in Philadelphia. Surrounding the portraits are scenes depicting Methodist education (Wilberforce University), the AME Church book depository, and mission work in Haiti. (Library of Congress)

His success earned him great respect among other free blacks and opened the way for him to serve as lay leader representing the African American membership of St. George's Methodist Episcopal Church.

Traditional accounts of Jones's role in the founding of the Free African Society assert that, when Jones refused to comply with the announcement of St. George's sexton that African American parishioners should give up their usual seats among the white congregation and move to the upper gallery, he was supported by Richard Allen, in particular. The two then agreed that the only way African Americans could worship in an environment that responded to their social, as well as religious, needs would be to found an all-black congregation. Some sources suggest that Jones's reaction to the reseating order was the crowning blow, and that Allen previously had tried to organize several fellow black parishioners, including Doras Giddings, William White, and Jones, to support his idea of a separate congregation, only to have the idea rejected by the church elders.

Whatever the specific stimulus for Allen's and Jones's actions in 1787, they announced publicly that their newly declared movement would not only serve the black community's religious needs as a nondenominational congregation but also function as a benevolent mutual aid organization. The latter goal involved plans to collect funds (through membership fees) to assist the sick, orphans, and widows in the African American community. Other secular social assistance aims included enforcement of a code of temperance, propriety, and fidelity in marriage. It is significant that a number of the early members of the Free African Society came to it from the rolls of other Protestant churches, not only St. George's Methodist Episcopal congregation.

The dual nature of the organization's goals soon led to divisions in the politics of leadership. Apparently, it was Allen who wanted to use the breakaway from St. George's as a first step in founding a specifically black Methodist Church. Others wished to emphasize the Free African Society's nondenominational character and pursue mainly social and moral aid services. Within two years, therefore, Allen resigned his membership, going on to found, in July, 1794, the Bethel African Methodist Episcopal Church. Although this move clearly marked the beginnings of a specifically African American church with a defined denominational status, Allen's efforts for many years continued to be directed at social and economic self-help projects for African Americans, irrespective of their formal religious orientation.

By 1804, Allen was involved in founding a group whose name reflected its basic social reform goals: the Society of Free People of Color for Promoting the Instruction and School Education of Children of African Descent. Another of Allen's efforts came in 1830, when Allen, then seventy years of age, involved his church in the Free Produce Society in Philadelphia. This group raised money to buy goods grown only by nonslave labor to redistribute to poor African Americans. It also tried to organize active boycotts against the marketing and purchase of goods produced by slave-owning farmers, thus providing an early model for the grassroots organizations aimed at social and political goals that would become familiar to African Americans in the mid-twentieth century.

SIGNIFICANCE

The Free African Society passed through several short but key stages both before and after Richard Allen's decision to remove himself from active membership. One focal point was the group's early association with the prominent medical doctor and philanthropist Benjamin Rush. Rush helped the Free African Society to draft a document involving articles of faith that were meant to be general enough to include the essential religious principles of any Christian church. When the organization adopted these tenets, in 1791, its status as a religious congregation generally was recognized by members and outsiders alike.

More and more, its close relationship with the Episcopal church (first demonstrated by its "friendly adoption" by the Reverend Joseph Pilmore and the white membership of St. Paul's Church in Philadelphia) determined the society's future denominational status. After 1795, the Free African Society per se had receded before a new church built by a committee sparked by Absalom Jones: the African Methodist Episcopal Church. This fact did not, however, prevent those who had been associated with the Free African Society's origins from integrating its strong social and moral reform program with the religious principles that marked the emergence of the first all-black Christian congregations in the United States by the end of the 1790's.

—Byron D. Cannon

FURTHER READING

Conyers, James L., Jr., ed. *Black Lives: Essays in African American Biography*. Armonk, N.Y.: M. E. Sharpe, 1999. A collection of fifteen biographies of African Americans, including Richard Allen.

George, Carol V. R. *Segregated Sabbaths: Richard Allen and the Emergence of Independent Black Churches,*

1760-1840. New York: Oxford University Press, 1973. A scholarly account that includes discussion of the African American churches' eventual abolitionist activities.

Mukenge, Ida Rousseau. *The Black Church in Urban America.* Lanham, Md.: University Press of America, 1983. A comprehensive historical account, emphasizing changes that came by the nineteenth and twentieth centuries.

Mwadilitu, Mwalimi I. [Alexander E. Curtis]. *Richard Allen: The First Exemplar of African American Education.* New York: ECA Associates, 1985. This short volume focuses on the career of Richard Allen, including his functions after 1816 as the first bishop of the African Methodist Episcopal Church.

Nash, Gary B. *Forging Freedom: The Formation of Philadelphia's Black Community, 1720-1840.* Cambridge, Mass.: Harvard University Press, 1988. An examination of Philadelphia, which by the late eighteenth century had become an urban black center. Describes relations between whites and blacks, the Quaker antislavery movement, and the creation of black institutions. Contains a great deal of information on Richard Allen, Absalom Jones, the Free African Society, and the African Methodist Episcopal Church.

_____. *Race and Revolution.* Madison, Wis.: Madison House, 1990. Three essays focusing on the Northern states' failure to abolish slavery after the Revolutionary War. Describes how free blacks responded to this failure, including the creation of separate African American churches. Contains supporting documents, including a text by Absalom Jones.

Phillips, C. H. *The History of the Colored Methodist Episcopal Church in America.* 1898. Reprint. New York: Arno Press, 1972. Written by the editor of the church's official newspaper.

Raboteau, Albert J. "Richard Allen and the African Church Movement." In *Black Leaders of the Nineteenth Century,* edited by Leon Litwack and August Meier. Urbana: University of Illinois Press, 1988. A scholarly account of the Free African Society's origins, suggesting that Allen and Jones had discussed the special need for a separate African American church well before the "gallery event" so frequently cited.

SEE ALSO: Apr. 6, 1712: New York City Slave Revolt; Sept. 9, 1739: Stono Rebellion; 1773-1788: African American Baptist Church Is Founded; Apr. 14, 1775: Pennsylvania Society for the Abolition of Slavery Is Founded; July 2, 1777-1804: Northeast States Abolish Slavery; Sept. 29, 1784: Hall's Masonic Lodge Is Chartered; Feb. 12, 1793: First Fugitive Slave Law.

RELATED ARTICLES in *Great Lives from History: The Eighteenth Century, 1701-1800*: Benjamin Banneker; Benjamin Rush.

1780's

July 13, 1787
NORTHWEST ORDINANCE

The Northwest Ordinance established the framework for the addition of new states, politically equal to the existing states, to the United States. It marked the rise of federal involvement in the organization of Western lands and the first sectional compromise over the extension of slavery.

LOCALE: New York

CATEGORIES: Laws, acts, and legal history; expansion and land acquisition; government and politics

KEY FIGURES

Nathan Dane (1752-1835), American lawyer
Timothy Pickering (1745-1829), American politician
Arthur St. Clair (1734-1818), president of the Confederation Congress and first governor of the Northwest Territory

SUMMARY OF EVENT

In March, 1784, the Congress of the Confederation accepted the cession of lands Virginia had claimed west of the Appalachian Mountains. A congressional committee headed by Thomas Jefferson, delegate from Virginia, then took steps to provide for the political organization of the vast area south of the Great Lakes, west of the Appalachians, and east of the Mississippi River. The committee's task was to draft legislation for the disposal of the land and the government of its settlers. The proposal of Jefferson's committee met the approval of Congress as the Ordinance of 1784.

The Ordinance of 1784 divided the West into eighteen districts. Each district would be admitted to the Union as a state when its population equaled that of the least populous of the original states. In the meantime, when the

LAND CESSIONS BY THE STATES AFTER THE REVOLUTIONARY WAR, 1783-1802

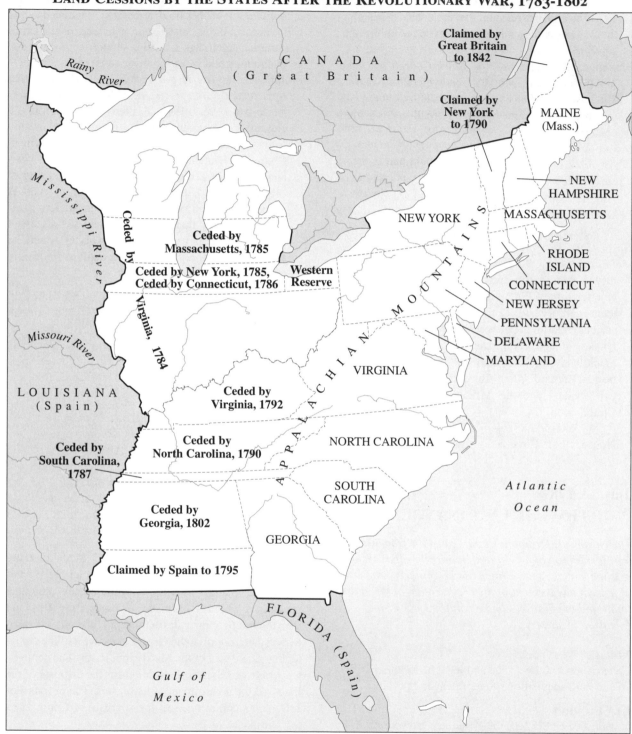

Before the end of the Revolutionary War, the original thirteen colonies had laid claim to lands west of the Appalachian Mountains—formerly reserved as Indian Territory in the Proclamation of 1763, although exploited by white settlers. After the revolution, Congress began to organize these western territories for future settlement, passing the Ordinance of 1784 and the Ordinance of 1787 (the Northwest Ordinance). The former colonies gradually, if reluctantly, ceded their claims.

population of a district reached twenty thousand, it might write a constitution and send a delegate to Congress. As Jefferson envisaged it, as many as ten new states might be carved from the new lands, many of them provided with mellifluous classical names. In Jefferson's original version, slavery was to be excluded after 1800, but this was stricken from the ordinance when it was adopted in 1784. The Ordinance of 1784 was to become effective once all Western lands claimed by the states had been ceded to the government. Before the states ceded their lands, however, a new ordinance was adopted that superseded that of 1784.

The Ordinance of 1787, known as the Northwest Ordinance, was passed, according to some historians, at the insistence of land speculators and politicians such as Timothy Pickering who opposed the liberality of the Ordinance of 1784. The new ordinance, whose final draft was prepared by Nathan Dane, did indeed slow down the process by which a territory might become a state, but it also added certain important features and provided for the more orderly creation of new states. While the Northwest Ordinance may have been less liberal than its predecessor, it was not undemocratic.

The Northwest Ordinance established government in the territory north of the Ohio River. The plan provided for the eventual establishment of a bicameral assembly, the creation of three to five states equal to the original thirteen states, freedom of religion, the right to a jury trial, public education, and a ban on the expansion of slavery. To accomplish these goals, legislation provided that the whole Northwest region should be governed temporarily as a single territory and administered by a governor, a secretary, and three judges appointed by Congress. When the population of the territory reached five thousand free, adult, male inhabitants, the citizens might elect representatives to a territorial assembly. Property qualifications for voting were established, but they were small. The general assembly was to choose ten men, all of whom owned at least five hundred acres, from whom Congress would choose five men to serve as the upper house of the legislature. The governor would continue to be selected by Congress and have an absolute veto over all legislation.

The territory was to be divided into not fewer than three nor more than five districts. Whenever the population of one of the districts reached sixty thousand free inhabitants, it would be allowed to draft a constitution and submit it to Congress. If the constitution guaranteed a republican form of government, Congress would pass an enabling act admitting the district into the Union as a state on an equal basis with those states already in the Union.

The ordinance guaranteed certain basic rights to citizens who moved into the new lands. A bill of rights provided for freedom of religion and guaranteed the benefits of writs of habeas corpus, the right of trial by jury, bail, and the general process of law. The third article read, "Religion, morality and knowledge being necessary to good government and the happiness of mankind, Schools and the means of education shall forever be encouraged. The utmost good faith shall always be observed towards the Indians." The first of these moral injunctions was implemented as the inhabitants obtained the means to do so. The second, regarding the American Indians, has still to be achieved. The fourth article established the basis for relations between the general government and the territories and states that might be formed from them.

The fifth article of the ordinance provided for equitable taxation and the free navigation of the waters leading into the Mississippi and St. Lawrence Rivers. The sixth article was epoch-making. It read, "There shall be neither Slavery nor involuntary Servitude in the said territory otherwise than in the punishment of crimes, whereof the party shall have been duly convicted." This provision determined that the society that developed north of the Ohio River would eventually be free. Influenced by the French slaveholders inhabiting the region, the interpretation of Article VI forbade the further introduction of slavery but did not abolish slavery or affect the rights of those holding slaves prior to 1787. No such provision was written into the act establishing the Southwest Territory, in 1790.

The pattern established by the Northwest Ordinance was more or less followed in the later admission of states into the Union. Some, such as Texas and California, came in without a territorial period. Others, such as Michigan, caused trouble because of boundary disputes with neighboring states. As for the Ohio Country, Arthur St. Clair, president of the Confederation Congress in 1787, was appointed first governor of the territory. Indiana Territory was organized in 1803, the same year in which Ohio entered the Union. Indiana entered as a state in 1816, Illinois in 1818, Michigan in 1837, and Wisconsin in 1848. Statehood was delayed for Indiana and Illinois territories as a result of their repeated petitions seeking repeal of the restrictions in the ordinance against the expansion of further slavery in the territory. Congress refused to repeal or revise the section, making slaveholders reluctant to move into the area. The predominant settlement by nonslaveholders eventually led to strengthening of the antislavery movement in the region.

SIGNIFICANCE

The Northwest Ordinance proved to be a crowning legislative achievement of the otherwise lackluster confederation government. However, while Congress was debating the Northwest Ordinance, the Constitutional Convention was under way in Philadelphia. It has been argued that the antislavery provisions influenced the debates of the Constitutional Convention over congressional representation. Since each state won two seats in the Senate, Southern states acceded freedom to the Northwest Territory by limiting the number of free states formed from the region. In turn, the Southern states hoped for dominance in the House of Representatives through the three-fifths clause counting slaves for congressional representation. Under the new Constitution, Congress reenacted the Ordinance of 1787 as a model of territorial government.

—*John G. Clark, updated by Dorothy C. Salem*

FURTHER READING

Cayton, Andrew R. L. *The Midwest and the Nation: Rethinking the History of an American Region*. Bloomington: Indiana University Press, 1990. Provides an overview of the historical significance of the Northwest Ordinance for the Midwest and its influence on that region.

Finkelman, Paul. *Slavery and the Founders: Race and Liberty in the Age of Jefferson*. 2d ed. Armonk, N.Y.: M. E. Sharpe, 2001. Examines the status of slavery in the newly created republic, including the Northwest Ordinance's ambiguous provisions on the issue.

Johnson, Andrew J. *The Life and Constitutional Thought of Nathan Dane*. New York: Garland, 1987. The best biographical account of the major author of the Northwest Ordinance and his place in the history of the new nation.

Konig, David Thomas. *Devising Liberty: Preserving and Creating Freedom in the New American Republic*. Stanford, Calif.: Stanford University Press, 1995. Examines the role of the Northwest Ordinance within the framework shaping modern U.S. freedom.

Onuf, Peter S. *Sovereignty and Territory: Claims Conflict in the Old Northwest and the Origins of the American Federal Republic*. Baltimore: Johns Hopkins University Press, 1973. Analyzes the land speculation conflicts and their role in shaping the powers of the state.

_____. *Statehood and Union: A History of the Northwest Ordinance*. Bloomington: Indiana University Press, 1987. A comprehensive study of the framing and impact of the Northwest Ordinance and the competing forces that shaped the document.

Williams, Frederick D., ed. *The Northwest Ordinance: Essays on Its Formulation, Provisions, and Legacy*. East Lansing: Michigan State University Press, 1988. Collection of essays addressing the ambiguities of the Ordinance, and slavery, missionary activity, and higher eduction in the Old Northwest.

SEE ALSO: Apr. 19, 1775-Oct. 19, 1781: American Revolutionary War; Mar. 1, 1781: Ratification of the Articles of Confederation; Sept. 3, 1783: Treaty of Paris; Oct. 22, 1784: Fort Stanwix Treaty; May 20, 1785: Ordinance of 1785; Aug. 20, 1794: Battle of Fallen Timbers.

RELATED ARTICLE in *Great Lives from History: The Eighteenth Century, 1701-1800*: Thomas Jefferson.

September 17, 1787
U.S. CONSTITUTION IS ADOPTED

The Constitution of the United States of America replaced the failed Articles of Confederation, creating a new, unified nation under a tripartite federal government. Designed to create a balance of power between the government's branches, the Constitution instituted a system of checks and balances for those branches, and while the states ceded their sovereignty to the nation, they were understood to retain all powers not explicitly granted to the nation.

LOCALE: Philadelphia, Pennsylvania

CATEGORIES: Government and politics; laws, acts, and legal history

KEY FIGURES

Benjamin Franklin (1706-1790), delegate to the Constitutional Convention

James Madison (1751-1836), American statesman and president of the United States, 1809-1817

Gouverneur Morris (1752-1816), author of the final draft of the Constitution

William Paterson (1745-1806), sponsor of the New Jersey Plan

Roger Sherman (1721-1793), mediator between factions at the Constitutional Convention

George Washington (1732-1799), presiding officer at the Constitutional Convention and president of the United States, 1789-1797

James Wilson (1742-1798), American lawyer and constitutional framer

SUMMARY OF EVENT

By the middle of the 1780's, dissatisfaction with government under the Articles of Confederation had became evident throughout the United States. Many of those prominent in the political life of the United States—George Washington, Thomas Jefferson, John Jay, Alexander Hamilton, and Noah Webster, among others—in papers, letters, and conversations criticized the functioning of the Confederation Congress. Specific concerns included Congress's lack of power to tax, to regulate interstate commerce, and to force states to cooperate more effectively with the central government. All efforts to improve the Articles of Confederation seemed doomed to failure, because amendments required unanimous approval by the states. It became evident to many concerned persons that changes might best be accomplished by abandoning the Articles altogether.

In March, 1785, a meeting of delegates from Virginia and Maryland initiated a series of meetings that culminated in the replacement of the Articles. At the March meeting, the two states worked out an agreement involving commercial regulations on the Potomac River. After the success of the meeting, Virginia called for another meeting to be held in Annapolis, Maryland, during the following year. It was hoped that the convention would provide an opportunity for those attending to discuss common problems and possible solutions. Nine states were invited, but only five sent delegates. The most important result of the Annapolis Convention was the publication of a report, probably drafted by Alexander Hamilton, that called for yet another convention. This one, scheduled for May, 1787, in Philadelphia, was to include delegates from all states. The purpose of the convention was to address and correct the defects in the Confederation government. Copies of the report were sent to each state legislature with a request that delegates be appointed and sent to Philadelphia.

Every state except Rhode Island honored the request and sent representatives. Seventy-four delegates were appointed to the convention, although only fifty-five attended. Thirty-nine signed the final document. The Virginia delegation was among the first to reach Philadelphia, arriving two weeks before the scheduled start of deliberations. The Virginians brought with them the outline of a plan of government that they intended to offer to the convention. The plan, considered quite controversial at the time, proposed creating a new national government. The Virginians sought a strong government that would include three branches and a sophisticated system of checks and balances. During the days before the convention began, several of the Virginia delegates, particularly James Madison, conferred with other early arrivals to hone their plan.

The convention first met on May 25 and appointed George Washington as the presiding officer. The selection was significant, because Washington was held in high regard by the American people. The presence of Benjamin Franklin, who at eighty-one years of age was the oldest delegate, also added prestige to the gathering. With two such notable figures participating, the American public anticipated notable results.

On May 29, with the convention only four days old, the Virginia delegation proposed a series of resolutions that immediately were known as the Virginia Plan.

Debate, revision, and other work continued for nearly four months at the Constitutional Convention in Philadelphia. Delegates adopted a finished U.S. Constitution in September of 1787. (C. A. Nichols & Company)

Drafted largely by James Madison and introduced by Edmund Randolph, the plan argued that, rather than merely revise the Articles of Confederation, the convention should discard them altogether and create a constitution that embodied an entirely new frame of government. The proposed government would have far more authority than did the confederated administration, and it would not be subordinate to each state government. The proposals set off a fierce debate that dominated the convention throughout most of June. On one side were delegates who endorsed the Virginia Plan. On the other side were delegates who feared that a powerful national government might jeopardize many of the rights and liberties won during the Revolutionary War.

As the debate intensified, delegates from several of the smaller states devised a series of resolutions designed to counter the Virginia Plan. Introduced by William Pat-

erson from New Jersey, the resolutions became known as the New Jersey Plan. These proposals rejected the need for a new national government and called instead for the convention to retain, but significantly revise, the existing confederated government.

Among the more active delegates in favor of establishing a strong federal government were James Madison and George Mason from Virginia, James Wilson and Gouverneur Morris from Pennsylvania, John Dickinson from Delaware, John Rutledge and Charles Pinckney from South Carolina, and Oliver Ellsworth from Connecticut. In addition to Paterson, the leading supporters of the New Jersey Plan included Roger Sherman from Connecticut, Elbridge Gerry from Massachusetts, and Luther Martin from Maryland.

For almost a month, delegates intensely deliberated over the two plans. In late June, with the convention on the verge of dissolution, Benjamin Franklin implored the delegates to find a common ground. Spurred on by Franklin's pleas, the convention agreed to discard the Articles of Confederation and create a constitution that would embody a strong national government. With the initial differences resolved, other aspects of both the Virginia and New Jersey Plans were debated throughout the summer.

Central to the discussions was the concern of less populated states, such as Connecticut and Maryland, that they would lose all power and authority to the national government if representation within the new government were determined exclusively according to population. Responding to these concerns, proponents of the national government agreed to create a dual system of representation within Congress: Membership in the House of Representatives would be determined according to population; in the Senate, each state, regardless of the size of its population, would be given two members. It also was agreed that before a bill could become a law, both houses of Congress would have to approve it.

The agreement concerning representation within the legislative branch, sometimes referred to as the Great Compromise, reflected the spirit of concession that marked convention proceedings during the late summer months. Many other issues, including the length of presidential terms, the electoral procedure, the responsibilities of the judicial branch, the amendment process, and slavery within the new nation, tested the delegates' ability to negotiate and cooperate. In the end, the document could not be considered the work of any one group or faction of delegates. It had become a synthesis of the plans of all the delegates.

In September, Gouverneur Morris, an outspoken Pennsylvania delegate, became chair of a committee that was instructed to write a final draft of the Constitution. After some preliminary discussions about style and content, the document was formally presented to the convention on September 17. Although few delegates agreed to all revisions, a large majority found the document as a whole acceptable. Signed by thirty-nine delegates, the Constitution was declared adopted "by unanimous consent." Upon endorsement by the convention, the Constitution was submitted to each state legislature for ratification. In late June, 1788, approval by nine states, the number required for ratification, was reached and implementation of the new national government began.

SIGNIFICANCE

Since its ratification, the U.S. Constitution has formed the highest law in the nation it created. Its system of checks and balances, designed to ensure that no portion of the government is capable of exercising power tyrannically or dominating another portion, is complemented

---

CONSTITUTIONAL CHECKS AND BALANCES

One of the most famous aspects of the government created by the U.S. Constitution is the system of checks and balances that it instituted within and between the three branches of government: executive (the president), legislative (Congress), and judicial. One such set of checks and balances is to be found in Article I, section 7, which establishes the rules for presidential vetoes and congressional overrides of vetoes.

Every Bill which shall have passed the House of Representatives and the Senate, shall, before it become a Law, be presented to the President of the United States: If he approve he shall sign it, but if not he shall return it, with his Objections to that House in which it shall have originated, who shall enter the Objections at large on their Journal, and proceed to reconsider it. If after such Reconsideration two thirds of that House shall agree to pass the Bill, it shall be sent, together with the Objections, to the other House, by which it shall likewise be reconsidered, and if approved by two thirds of that House, it shall become a Law. But in all such Cases the Votes of both Houses shall be determined by yeas and Nays, and the Names of the Persons voting for and against the Bill shall be entered on the Journal of each House respectively. If any Bill shall not be returned by the President within ten Days (Sundays excepted) after it shall have been presented to him, the Same shall be a Law, in like Manner as if he had signed it, unless the Congress by their Adjournment prevent its Return, in which Case it shall not be a Law.

Every Order, Resolution, or Vote to which the Concurrence of the Senate and House of Representatives may be necessary (except on a question of Adjournment) shall be presented to the President of the United States; and before the Same shall take Effect, shall be approved by him, or being disapproved by him, shall be repassed by two thirds of the Senate and House of Representatives, according to the Rules and Limitations prescribed in the Case of a Bill.

Source: Constitution of the United States. The National Archives Experience, National Archives and Records Administration. http://www.archives.gov/national-archives-experience/charters/constitution_transcript.html. Accessed November 15, 2005.

by the Bill of Rights, ratified December 15, 1791, which helps to ensure that a majority of the people of the United States cannot rule tyrannically over a minority. These safeguards against tyranny, especially against the tyranny of the majority, form the central philosophical impetus of the Constitution and are the primary reason for its continued standing as a model for such documents throughout the world.

—*Edward J. Maguire,*
updated by Paul E. Doutrich

FURTHER READING

Berkin, Carol. *A Brilliant Solution: Inventing the American Constitution*. New York: Harcourt, 2002. A history of the Constitutional Convention of 1787, describing the conflicts and compromises among delegates, the disagreements between federalists and advocates of states' rights, and the development of the document itself. Contains one hundred pages of appendices, including the full text of the Constitution and brief biographies of convention delegates.

Conley, Patrick, and John Kaminski, eds. *The Constitution and the States: The Role of the Original Thirteen in Framing and Adoption of the Federal Constitution*. Madison, Wis.: Madison House, 1988. A unique look at how each state reacted to the proposed Constitutional Convention.

Farrand, Max. *The Records of the Federal Convention of 1787*. 4 vols. New Haven, Conn.: Yale University Press, 1966. The definitive set of primary source documents for the convention.

Jensen, Merrill. *The Making of the American Constitution*. Princeton, N.J.: Van Nostrand, 1964. A brief but excellent account of the creation of the Constitution.

Kammen, Michael. *A Machine That Would Go of Itself*. New York: Alfred A. Knopf, 1986. Examines the cultural impact of the U.S. Constitution.

McDonald, Forrest. *"Novus Ordo Seclorum": The Intellectual Origins of the Constitution*. Lawrence: University Press of Kansas, 1985. Discusses the traditions and attitudes from which the Constitution was conceived.

Peters, William. *A More Perfect Union: The Making of the United States Constitution*. New York: Crown, 1987. A narrative account of the events involved in the creation of the U.S. Constitution.

Rakove, Jack N. *Original Meanings: Politics and Ideas in the Making of the Constitution*. New York: A. A. Knopf, 1996. Examines the concerns that shaped constitutional decision making in the late 1780's, exploring federalism, representative, executive power, rights, and other issues confronting delegates.

Wood, Gordon. *The Creation of the American Republic, 1776-1787*. New York: W. W. Norton, 1969. A definitive work that explores the ideological foundations of the Constitution.

October 27, 1787-May, 1788
PUBLICATION OF *THE FEDERALIST*

Three American statesmen published a series of essays both advocating and interpreting the newly adopted Constitution in an attempt to convince delegates from the state of New York to ratify the document. While the papers had little effect upon New York's vote, they have since become fundamental documents in the explication of American constitutional law and history.

ALSO KNOWN AS: The *Federalist* papers
LOCALE: New York City, New York
CATEGORIES: Government and politics; literature

KEY FIGURES
Alexander Hamilton (1755-1804), American statesman and coauthor of *The Federalist*
John Jay (1745-1829), coauthor of *The Federalist* and first chief justice of the U.S. Supreme Court
James Madison (1751-1836), coauthor *The Federalist* and president of the United States, 1809-1817

SUMMARY OF EVENT
The Federalist (1788; also known as the *Federalist* papers) comprises eighty-five essays that were first published anonymously by Alexander Hamilton, John Jay, and James Madison between October, 1787, and May, 1788, urging ratification of the United States Constitution. That constitution, drafted by the Philadelphia Convention of 1787, sought to increase the power of the national government at the expense of the state governments. The national debate over ratification began almost immediately after the Philadelphia Convention sent the proposed constitution to Congress on September 17 and its contents became known.

Before the Constitution could take effect, it had to be ratified by specially elected conventions in at least nine of the thirteen states. Throughout the nation, critics of the document (Antifederalists) battled its supporters (Federalists) in campaigns to elect men to the state conventions. The debate was particularly tense in New York, which was sharply divided over the Constitution. Federalists dominated New York City and the surrounding areas, but the rural upstate areas were strongly Antifederalist, as was the state's popular and powerful governor, George Clinton.

Late in September, 1787, the *New York Journal* began printing a series of antifederal essays by "Cato" (who may have been Governor Clinton). In order to refute these and other antifederal tracts, Alexander Hamilton and John Jay, two of New York's most prominent Federalists, agreed to write a series of newspaper essays under the name "Publius." The first essay, *The Federalist* No. 1, written by Hamilton, appeared in the *New York Independent Journal* on October 27. In it, Hamilton outlined the purpose of the entire series: The essays would explain the necessity of the union for political prosperity, the "insufficiency of the present Confederation to preserve that Union," the need for a more energetic government than that which existed under the Articles of Confederation, the "conformity of the proposed constitution to the true principles of republican government," and the security that the Constitution would provide to liberty and property.

John Jay wrote the next four installments before ill health forced him to quit. In November, James Madison, who was in New York representing Virginia in Congress, took Jay's place. Madison and Hamilton produced all but one of the remaining eighty essays; Jay wrote No. 64.

Madison's first contribution to the series, *The Federalist* No. 10, is the most famous of all the essays. In it he discussed the origins of parties, or "factions" as he called them, and argued that they sprang inevitably from the unequal distribution of property. "Those who hold, and those who are without property," he continued, "have ever formed distinct interests in society." In any nation, "a landed interest, a manufacturing interest, a mercantile interest, a monied interest, [and] many lesser interests, grow up of necessity" and divide people into different classes. Some Antifederalists had argued that the nation was much too large and too diverse to be governed effectively by a powerful central government without sacrificing people's liberties and freedoms in the process; in *The Federalist* No. 10, Madison used his ideas about factions to reverse their argument. The nation's size, he wrote, and the great variety of its people and their interests were sources of strength, not weakness. There were so many different groups or factions, so many different interests that would be represented in the new government, that no one faction, no one group, no lone demagogue could ever capture control of the national government. Far from inviting tyranny, he argued, the nation's size and diversity, when coupled with the federal republican form of government proposed by the Constitution, would provide a strong check against tyranny.

Addressed to "the People of the State of New York," the essays of *The Federalist* were intended primarily as

New York ratification campaign tracts, but they also were reprinted by newspapers in other states and cities, particularly in Philadelphia and Boston. Hamilton had the first thirty-six numbers published as a book in March, 1788, and some of these books were sent to Virginia, where they arrived in time to be useful to Federalists at the Virginia ratifying convention. A second volume, containing the remaining forty-nine essays, appeared the following May.

SIGNIFICANCE

It is hard to estimate the impact of *The Federalist* on the campaign to ratify the Constitution even in New York, much less nationally. Certainly, the articles were not as successful as their authors had hoped, for New York voters sent twice as many opponents of the Constitution to the New York ratifying convention as they sent supporters. By the time the convention balloted, however, ten states had already ratified the document, and New York did so too on July 26, 1788, by a narrow three-vote margin. It is unlikely that *The Federalist* contributed much to the result.

Whether or not the essays in *The Federalist* were effective political tracts in 1788, they long have been considered important keys to understanding the intentions of the members of the Philadelphia Convention. Historians and even Supreme Court justices have studied the papers as a guide to the intent of the Framers, even though they were written as election tracts, and in spite of the fact that one author (Jay) did not attend the Philadelphia Convention, another (Hamilton) played a very small role there and was dissatisfied with the Constitution, and the third (Madison) came to have serious doubts about the meaning of the Constitution and the kind of government it created within a few years after he wrote his essays for *The Federalist*.

The reputation of *The Federalist* has grown steadily since 1788. The work has been widely republished around the world in several languages and is regularly reprinted in the United States. The essays have been brought into many public political debates since 1789, particularly during times of constitutional crisis, such as the states' rights debates that preceded the Civil War, the public discussion over the constitutionality of President Franklin D. Roosevelt's New Deal policies, the debate over states' rights and civil liberties in the 1950's, and the proposals during the 1990's to reduce the federal deficit by shifting to the states the responsibility for—and, often, the financing of—many of the social programs enacted in Washington during and after the New Deal. Apart from its partisan

---

THE JUDICIARY DEPARTMENT

Throughout The Federalist, *theoretical arguments had been made concerning the importance of the judiciary to the functioning of the new government contemplated in the U.S. Constitution. In* The Federalist *No. 78, Alexander Hamilton addressed the practical questions concerning the creation and functioning of that judiciary. In the following paragraph, Hamilton discusses the need for judges to remain independent while on the bench.*

This independence of the judges is equally requisite to guard the Constitution and the rights of individuals from the effects of those ill humors, which the arts of designing men, or the influence of particular conjunctures, sometimes disseminate among the people themselves, and which, though they speedily give place to better information, and more deliberate reflection, have a tendency, in the meantime, to occasion dangerous innovations in the government, and serious oppressions of the minor party in the community. Though I trust the friends of the proposed Constitution will never concur with its enemies, in questioning that fundamental principle of republican government, which admits the right of the people to alter or abolish the established Constitution, whenever they find it inconsistent with their happiness, yet it is not to be inferred from this principle, that the representatives of the people, whenever a momentary inclination happens to lay hold of a majority of their constituents, incompatible with the provisions in the existing Constitution, would, on that account, be justifiable in a violation of those provisions; or that the courts would be under a greater obligation to connive at infractions in this shape, than when they had proceeded wholly from the cabals of the representative body. Until the people have, by some solemn and authoritative act, annulled or changed the established form, it is binding upon themselves collectively, as well as individually; and no presumption, or even knowledge, of their sentiments, can warrant their representatives in a departure from it, prior to such an act. But it is easy to see, that it would require an uncommon portion of fortitude in the judges to do their duty as faithful guardians of the Constitution, where legislative invasions of it had been instigated by the major voice of the community.

Source: Alexander Hamilton, *The Federalist* No. 78 (June 14, 1788). Constitution Society. http://www.constitution.org/fed/federa78.htm. Accessed November 15, 2005.

political value, past and present, many historians and political scientists consider *The Federalist* to be the best existing defense of federal republicanism in general and of the American Constitution in particular.

—*Robert A. Becker, updated by Joseph R. Rudolph, Jr.*

FURTHER READING

Allen, W. B., and Kevin A. Cloonan. *The Federalist Papers—A Commentary: "The Baton Rouge Lectures."* New York: P. Lang, 2000. The authors describe how the *Federalist* papers are the foundation for the current principles and practices of American government.

De Pauw, Linda G. *The Eleventh Pillar: New York State and the Federal Constitution.* Ithaca, N.Y.: Cornell University Press, 1966. An outstanding examination of *The Federalist* in the context of its time and as campaign literature aimed at the citizens of New York.

Dietze, Gottfried. *"The Federalist": A Classic on Federalism and Free Government.* Baltimore: Johns Hopkins University Press, 1960. Still one of the best examinations of the work as a statement of the Framers' thoughts and a part of the constitutional heritage that has continued to affect the political process in the United States.

Epstein, David F. *The Political Theory of "The Federalist."* Chicago: University of Chicago Press, 1984. A well-indexed, outstanding analysis of the topic.

Hamilton, Alexander, John Jay, and James Madison. *The Federalist.* Annotated by Jacob E. Cooke. Middletown, Conn.: Wesleyan University Press, 1961. Among the many editions of *The Federalist*, this is one of the best annotated.

Kenyon, Cecelia M., ed. *The Antifederalists.* Indianapolis, Ind.: Bobbs-Merrill, 1966. An excellent collection of essays illustrating the Antifederalist arguments against the Constitution.

Kesler, Charles, ed. *Saving the Revolution: The Federalist Papers and the American Founding.* New York: Free Press, 1987. Published on the two-hundredth anniversary of *The Federalist*, these essays are for advanced research.

Lewis, John D., ed. *Anti-Federalists Versus Federalists: Selected Documents.* San Francisco, Calif.: Chandler, 1967. A well-balanced selection of often hard-to-find documents, including the minority reports from the constitutional convention.

McWilliams, Wilson Carey, and Michael T. Gibbons, eds. *The Federalists, the Antifederalists, and the American Political Tradition.* New York: Greenwood Press, 1992. This brief collection of solid essays provides excellent introductory reading on the constitutional debate.

Potter, Kathleen O. *"The Federalist's" Vision of Popular Sovereignty in the New American Republic.* New York: LFB Scholarly, 2002. Examines Publius's views on the social compact and the role of virtue in the founding of the American Republic to determine how *The Federalist* established the principle of popular sovereignty.

White, Morton Gabriel. *Philosophy, "The Federalist," and the Constitution.* New York: Oxford University Press, 1987. Focuses on the impact of *The Federalist* on U.S. constitutional history. An excellent work.

SEE ALSO: Sept. 5-Oct. 26, 1774: First Continental Congress; May 10-Aug. 2, 1775: Second Continental Congress; Jan. 10, 1776: Paine Publishes *Common Sense*; July 4, 1776: Declaration of Independence; Mar. 1, 1781: Ratification of the Articles of Confederation; Sept. 17, 1787: U.S. Constitution Is Adopted.

RELATED ARTICLES in *Great Lives from History: The Eighteenth Century, 1701-1800*: Alexander Hamilton; John Jay; James Madison.

1780's

1788-September, 1809
RUSSO-SWEDISH WARS

As at the beginning of the eighteenth century, Russia and Sweden battled for supremacy in northern Europe at century's end. Russia was victorious, preserving and expanding its imperial ambitions.

LOCALE: Northern Europe
CATEGORIES: Wars, uprisings, and civil unrest; expansion and land acquisition

KEY FIGURES

Napoleon Bonaparte (1769-1821), French military leader and emperor as Napoleon I, r. 1804-1814, 1815
Alexander I (1777-1825), czar of Russia, r. 1801-1825
Gustavus IV Adolphus (1778-1837), king of Sweden, r. 1792-1809

SUMMARY OF EVENT

The Russo-Swedish Wars were directly linked to the larger Europe-wide historical epoch of the French Revolution and Napoleonic Wars. Most important, both Russia and Sweden were caught in the middle of an early nineteenth century geopolitical "cold war" that pitted Europe's most dominant land power, France, against its strongest naval power, Great Britain: Napoleon Bonaparte's major obstacle to creating his new empire was the British Royal Navy. His hopes of destroying Britain's naval strength ended at the Battle of Trafalgar (1805). There, off the coast of Spain, Admiral Lord Nelson defeated the combined navies of Spain and France. This decisive British victory both ended the hopes of a French invasion of the British Isles and ensured that Great Britain would continue to dominate the sea lanes for years to come.

The strategic situation between England and France continued to become more complex when Napoleon's armies won decisive victories in 1805 against the Austrian and Russian armies at Austerlitz. The string of victories continued in 1806, when the French military defeated the formidable Prussian army at Jena and Auerstadt. As Napoleon's armies occupied the Prussian capital, he issued the Berlin Decrees forbidding his allies from importing British products. The following year, in 1807, France defeated the Russian army at Friedland, placing all of Germany under Napoleon's control. Unable to continue to engage the French military, Czar Alexander I agreed to meet with Napoleon to discuss the future of the two nations. The two emperors met on a raft

in the middle of the Nieman River, and on July 7, 1807, they signed the famous Treaty of Tilsit, which created a Russian-French alliance against Great Britain.

The most important aspect of this agreement was the Continental System. Unable to defeat the British navy, Napoleon decided to expand the Berlin Decrees and declare economic warfare on the British Empire. By cutting off trade with Britain, Napoleon hoped to cripple the British economy, which he believed would eventually lead to domestic unrest and revolution. Czar Alexander I and Napoleon agreed that Russia would use military force to make Sweden comply with the Continental System.

The king of Sweden, Gustavus IV Adolphus, harbored great animosity toward Napoleon for his brutal kidnapping and execution of a member of the Bourbon royal family. International tensions grew when Sweden refused to join the blockade and England responded by giving financial aid to its newfound ally. Russia took advantage of the situation by announcing that it was going to annex Finland to the Russian Empire. The Finnish people had enjoyed a four-hundred-year relationship with the nation of Sweden. Politically, they were under the control of the Swedish government but had always been allowed to keep their own cultural identity. Czar Alexander I looked upon this action against Finland as a win/win situation. The Russian nation would not only add important territory to its empire but would also have another opportunity to degrade the international standing of its most important rival in northern Europe.

The contrast between the two nations' militaries reflected the vast differences in the political and social makeup of the two countries. The Swedish army consisted mostly of free men who joined the military in exchange for the opportunity to become independent yeoman farmers. Sweden's landowning class was directed by the royal family to provide each soldier with land, seed, and the implements needed to cultivate their farms. The vast majority of these farmer/soldiers regarded themselves as agriculturalists first and warriors second. Neither the government nor the landed gentry provided these men with quality military training, so for the most part the Swedish army was totally unprepared for combat. The officer corps was not much better and reflected a lack of confidence and aggressive attitude that would be needed to fight a successful war against Russia.

The Russian officer corps, on the other hand, had the

confidence and esprit de corps of a military organization that, though it had been defeated by a superior French force, had learned the lessons of modern warfare and were ready to put these new skills to the test. The Russian high command had modified the structure of its tactical formations based upon the French model of dispersing light artillery and cavalry among large infantry formations. This early nineteenth century combined arms model allowed commanders to exploit weak spots in their opponent's formations through the firepower of their artillery and the speed of their cavalry.

In addition, most of the members of both the officer and noncommissioned officer corps had experienced the reality of battle and were ready to engage the Swedish military. The major weakness in the Russian forces lay in their enlisted personnel. The ranks of the common infantry platoon were made up of serfs. These illiterate Russian peasants led a slave-like existence and had been placed in the army by the landed aristocracy who owned them. They were not fighting for their own land or freedom but for the imperial expansion of the Russian Empire; thus, their morale was extremely low.

The initial strategy of the Swedish forces in Finland was to fight a defensive, delaying action against what they perceived to be superior Russian forces. This tactical approach was based upon belief in the impregnability of a series of fortifications at Sveaborg. The Swedish general staff planned to retreat behind and reinforce this defensive position and wait until reinforcements arrived from Sweden. The general staff hoped the Russian forces would become bogged down, expending significant amounts of men and material in an unsuccessful attempt to capture the fortification. The final part of the plan called for the Swedish navy to initially gain control of the waterways using their boats as floating platforms to shell Russian troop emplacements. In addition, these boats would be used to deliver Swedish troops behind Russian lines, attacking their avenues of supply.

The fortunes of the Swedish military began to decline almost immediately. When the Russian forces started to probe Sveaborg for possible weak points of attack, the commander misinterpreted the strength of the Russian army, and within a few days the panicked Swedish general surrendered the most extensive set of fortifications in northern Europe. The Russians, without launching one serious attack, captured Sveaborg along with 110 ships and almost seven thousand troops. Most important, the southern portion of Finland, which was the key to the military operation, was now completely open to a Russian military advance. Within a short period of time Hel-

sinki, the ancient capital of Finland, was under the control of the Russian Empire.

As the Russian forces moved into the Finnish heartland, the Swedish soldiers began to gain some confidence and were able to inflict some serious casualties on their overaggressive opponents. The Russian troops were also battered by guerrilla tactics used against them by Finnish civilians who were becoming increasingly angry at the Russian occupation of their homeland. Unfortunately, the Swedish high command was never able to organize a comprehensive strategy. The Swedish king, Gustav IV, had made a series of incompetent decisions and was constantly at odds with his general staff. Every time it seemed as if the Swedes had a chance to knock their opponents out of the war, the Russian military would dig in and outfight their Swedish counterparts. In the end the Russian Empire was willing to take the necessary action and fight with more intensity than the Swedish military. The last decisive Russian victory came at the Battle of Oravais, and from that point on the Swedish forces lost all hope of success. A group of military officers led a successful coup against Gustav IV and the government eventually sued for peace.

SIGNIFICANCE

The immediate impact of the Russian victory was that Alexander I acquired the geopolitical strength necessary for the immediate survival of his empire. The annexation of Finland provided Russia with the buffer zone it needed against any future military action by Sweden.

In the long run, the survival of Russia would be one of the primary reasons for the defeat of Napoleon. The French emperor's Machiavellian diplomatic style began to undermine his alliance with Russia when he proposed to Sweden an offer to regain Finland if in fact it would help enforce the Continental System against Britain. This diplomatic maneuver created a sense of unease in the courts of both Russia and Sweden. Great Britain capitalized upon this situation and made offers of friendship to both nations. The French emperor would eventually turn on his Russian allies in an attempt to control the entire European continent. Russia, Sweden, and Great Britain would be part of a continent-wide alliance that would defeat the armies of France and restore order to the region.

—*Richard D. Fitzgerald*

FURTHER READING

Chaliand, Gerard. *The Art of War in World History.* Berkeley: University of California Press, 1994. The best one-volume military history available to date. Index.

1780's

Nordstrom, Byron. *Scandinavia Since 1500*. Minneapolis: University of Minnesota Press, 2000. This book is an excellent overview of modern Scandinavian history. Index.

Rothenberg, Gunther E. *The Art of Warfare in the Age of Napoleon*. Bloomington: Indiana University Press, 1980. This book is an excellent account of strategy, tactics, and battles during the Napoleonic Wars. Index.

SEE ALSO: c. 1701-1721: Great Northern War; June 27, 1709: Battle of Poltava; Nov. 20, 1710-July 21, 1718: Ottoman Wars with Russia, Venice, and Austria; 1736-1739: Russo-Austrian War Against the Ottoman Empire; Oct., 1768-Jan. 9, 1792: Ottoman Wars with Russia; Aug. 5, 1772-Oct. 24, 1795: Partitioning of Poland.

RELATED ARTICLES in *Great Lives from History: The Eighteenth Century, 1701-1800*: Catherine the Great; Peter the Great.

January 26, 1788
BRITAIN ESTABLISHES PENAL COLONY IN AUSTRALIA

Great Britain established a penal colony in Australia at Sydney Cove not only to overcome inadequate prison facilities at home but also to secure naval resources and create an economic route to Asia.

LOCALE: Sydney Cove, Australia

CATEGORIES: Colonization; expansion and land acquisition; government and politics

KEY FIGURES

James Cook (1728-1779), English explorer and navigator

Sir Joseph Banks (1743-1820), English naturalist and botanist on Cook's expedition

George III (1738-1820), king of Great Britain, r. 1760-1820

Arthur Phillip (1738-1814), English naval commander and governor of Australia, 1788-1792

SUMMARY OF EVENT

During the eighteenth century, a time of increasing economic and political expansion, European countries sent numerous expeditions to the Southern Hemisphere in search of the fabled *terra australis incognita*, and to discover new trading routes to Asia and establish watering and refurbishing stations for trans-Pacific shipping, particularly for the flourishing China tea trade. As early as 1596, the first Dutch commercial fleet reached the East Indies, after Abel Tasman and Dutch seamen had charted approximately two-thirds of Australia's coastline; their observations revealed that the Australian Aborigines possessed no marketable goods, there existed no navigable rivers, and the coastal plains grew nothing of value. It was, therefore, concluded that Australia was of no economic significance. Eventually, a small permanent Dutch refreshment port was established at Cape Town in 1625. In 1629, the first criminals to be exiled to Australia

were two mutinous murderers from the Dutch trading vessel *Batavia*, cast ashore on western Australia shores, approximately 150 years prior to the establishment of the first British penal colony at Sydney Cove.

There remains one major question still debated by historians: Why did Great Britain want to establish Botany Bay as the first British settlement in the Pacific, and as a penal colony when it was isolated from Britain by approximately fourteen thousand miles, or eight months of arduous and even dangerous sea travel? It is now assumed that there were four major reasons for this decision. First, the British government needed to alleviate the ever-growing problem of prison overcrowding. Second, it wanted to secure a dependable source of flax for the manufacture of rigging, hausers, and sails as well as pine for planking, spars, and masts as traditional sources were jeopardized by the Napoleonic Wars and loss of the American colonies. Third, Great Britain was seeking to establish a trade route to Asia. Fourth, Botany Bay could be used as a maritime base and refitting port for commercial shipping. It was assumed the colony would develop its own export trade.

The problem of overcrowded prisons was only too apparent during the reign of George III and into early Victorian England, when many rural people commenced migrating in great numbers to east London and other large industrial centers for work, which along with a rising trade in pauper children and orphans, secured from parish workhouses, helped create an alarmingly increasing "criminal class." In London, approximately one of eight persons was living off crime, in a city with no centralized or organized police force. As a consequence, the profitable practice of thief-taker developed, the predecessors of later detectives who would track down and eventually inform upon the increasing number of felons. The best-

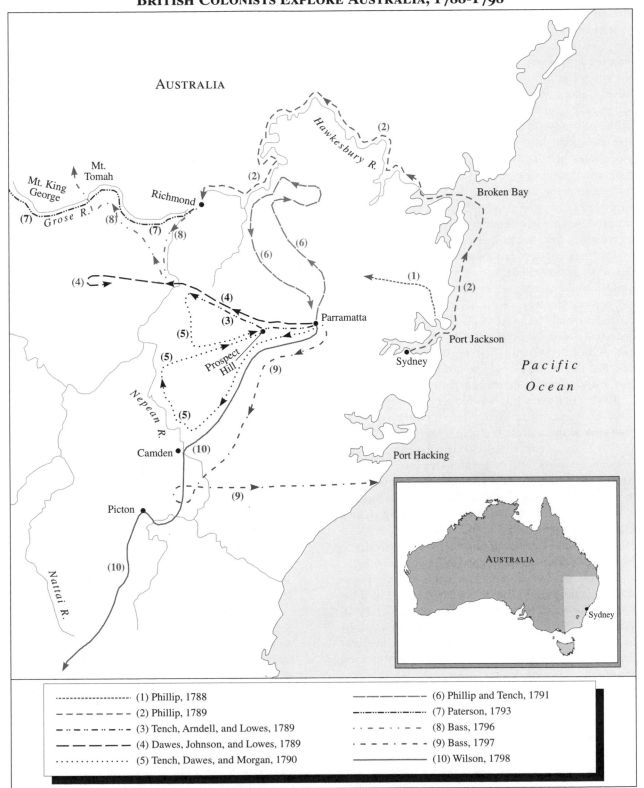

BRITISH COLONISTS EXPLORE AUSTRALIA, 1788-1798

AUSTRALIA

Mt. King George

Mt. Tomah

Grose R.

Richmond

Hawkesbury R.

Broken Bay

Parramatta

Prospect Hill

Nepean R.

Camden

Picton

Nattai R.

Port Jackson

Sydney

Port Hacking

Pacific Ocean

AUSTRALIA

Sydney

1780's

---------- (1) Phillip, 1788

– – – – – – (2) Phillip, 1789

–··–··–··– (3) Tench, Arndell, and Lowes, 1789

— — — — (4) Dawes, Johnson, and Lowes, 1789

·············· (5) Tench, Dawes, and Morgan, 1790

– – – – – – (6) Phillip and Tench, 1791

–·–·–·–· (7) Paterson, 1793

·–·–·–· (8) Bass, 1796

– · – · – · (9) Bass, 1797

———— (10) Wilson, 1798

known informant and thief-taker was Jonathan Wild, himself a noted criminal.

It was not until Peel's Police Act of 1829 that an effective constabulary was established. Convicted felons were usually hung at great public spectacles, some for the slightest of infractions, their bodies often given to the Royal College of Surgeons for dissection. Despite the hangings, prison ship-hulks, privately owned jails, and public prisons were overcrowded and proved unprofitable even though prisoners often had to pay for their food, water, bedding, and drink. Prisons were not segregated by age, sex, or type of crime. Many convicts were sold to shipping contractors, who then sold them to American and Caribbean plantation owners. The prison situation became intolerable by 1776, when the American colonies were lost as a place to transport convicts.

The first search for a prison colony, in 1785, by the sloop *Nautilus*, recommended Das Voltas Bay, near the mouth of the Orange River, in temperate southwest Africa. After actual exploration, this site was rejected because it lacked water, had sandy soil, and was barren of vegetation. The decision to colonize Botany Bay was based on the journals of Sir Joseph Banks, writings that gave the impression that Botany Bay would be an environment conducive to settlement, an impression that later proved false.

The use of Botany Bay was further encouraged by the relatively close proximity of Norfolk Island (one thousand miles to the east) about which Captain James Cook's 1774 account accurately described the abundance of flax (*Phormium tenaxk*) and impressive stands of tall spruce Norfolk pines. This offered a solution to the problem of the British possessing a sustained supply of flax, superior to Baltic flax, and abundant pine. Unfortunately, despite their stately appearance, the Norfolk pines were later found to be internally rotten, good only for firewood; and the flax was discovered to be too difficult to process.

On May 13, 1787, the First Fleet of eleven vessels, under the command of Captain Arthur Phillip, sailed for Botany Bay with 736 adult male, female, and child convicts, "all guilty of crimes against poverty." This was the first shipment of more than 160,000 convicts to be transported. Commencing with the fleet's arrival at an open and protected Botany Bay on January 18, 1788, the expedition experienced difficulty with an inhospitable environment, albeit one that adequately supported the Aborgines. Consequently, Captain Phillip and a complement of marines sailed seven miles north to explore an area more conducive for establishing a penal colony.

The new site, later to be called Sydney Cove, had adequate fresh water and an excellent deep harbor bordered by fertile soil. After five days, Captain Phillip returned to Botany Bay only to see on the horizon what later proved to be *La Boussole* and *L'Astrolabe*, commanded by the French explorer Jean-François de la Pérouse. The following day, after a cordial exchange with the French commander, the British set sail for Sydney Cove, but only after an embarrassing show of poor seamanship when the *Friendship* rammed the *Prince of Wales*, and the *Charlotte* nearly ran onto the rocks. Finally, after a four-hour journey, on January 26, 1788, the fleet cleared South Head, passed into Fort Jackson, and landed at Sydney Cove, later to be called Sydney Harbour. The presence of French ships forced Captain Phillip to colonize the more fertile Norfolk Island as well.

SIGNIFICANCE

January 26, 1788, is now celebrated as Founder's Day or Australia Day, marking the beginning of Australia's existence as a commonwealth nation. From the point of view of aboriginal peoples, however, the day marks the beginning of the British invasion of their home. After the colony was founded, British convicts began to pour in from the mother country. These convicts, after building basic structures for protection, living, and administration, were, according to their offense, assigned to the construction of roads, bridges, and buildings and later assigned to private settlers as servants or laborers. Violent criminals were assigned to chain gangs to work in coal mines or build roads, or were sent to more distant penal colonies. Good behavior could earn a convict a ticket-of-leave and a conditional or full pardon.

—*John Alan Ross*

FURTHER READING

Blainey, Geoffrey. *The Tyranny of Distance*. Melbourne, Vic.: Sun Books, 1970. Explores the various historical and contemporary theories as to why Great Britain decided to colonize such a distant country as Australia, particularly Botany Bay.

Erickson, Carrolly. *The Girl from Botany Bay*. Hoboken, N.J.: John Wiley & Sons, 2005. Erickson, who has written numerous popular histories, tells the tale of Mary Broad, who was arrested for robbery in England in 1786 and transported to a penal colony in Australia. She recounts the squalid conditions aboard ship and in the penal colonies and describes Broad's escape and eventual recapture.

Frost, Alan. *Botany Bay Mirages: Illusions of Australia's Convict Beginnings*. Carlton, Vic.: Melbourne University Press, 1994. Frost examines newly discovered documents and other sources to refute many of the myths regarding the first twelve years of Australian settlement. He argues that previous histories have not accurately described conditions aboard ship, Britain's relations with the colony, and the colonists' treatment of Aborigines, among other aspects.

Hughes, Robert. *The Fatal Shore: The Epic of Australia's Founding.* New York: Vintage Books, 1988. The most authoritative and comprehensive historical account as to why and how Botany Bay was selected as a penal colony.

King, Jonathan. *The First Fleet: The Convict Voyage That Founded Australia, 1787-1788.* London: Secker & Warburg, 1982. Uses the original diaries of British officials to suggest why Great Britain wanted to establish a British base in the South Seas.

Martin, Ged, ed. *The Founding of Australia: The Arguments About Australia's Origin.* Rev. ed. Sydney: Hale & Iremonger, 1981. Collection of papers and articles that present differing theories on the reasons for the founding of Australia.

Rudé, George. *Protest and Punishment: The Story of the*

Social and Political Protestors Transported to Australia, 1788-1868. Oxford, England: Clarendon Press, 1978. A critical examination of the myth that all prisoners were innocent, crushed by an unjust society and a harsh penal code.

Shaw, A. G. L. *Convicts and the Colonies: A Story of Penal Transportation from Great Britain and Ireland to Australia and Other Parts of the British Empire.* London: Faber & Faber, 1966. An account of demographic origins of convicts, their alleged crimes, and legal interpretations and sentences.

Taylor, Peter. *Australia: The First Twelve Years.* Boston: Allen & Unwin, 1982. How an isolated community survived, and how after twelve years Sydney developed.

SEE ALSO: Dec. 5, 1766-Mar. 16, 1769: Bougainville Circumnavigates the Globe; Aug. 25, 1768-Feb. 14, 1779: Voyages of Captain Cook; July 22, 1793: Mackenzie Reaches the Arctic Ocean.

RELATED ARTICLES in *Great Lives from History: The Eighteenth Century, 1701-1800*: Sir Joseph Banks; James Cook; George III; Arthur Phillip.

February 14, 1788

MEIKLE DEMONSTRATES HIS DRUM THRESHER

Meikle innovated agricultural engineering implements and techniques. He improved mechanical threshing methods by creating a machine that enabled farmers to harvest grain crops efficiently. His invention occurred at a time when demand for agricultural goods increased dramatically to feed and clothe growing urban populations employed in industrial positions.

LOCALE: Scotland
CATEGORIES: Inventions; agriculture; science and technology

KEY FIGURES

Andrew Meikle (1719-1811), Scottish millwright
George Meikle (d. 1811), Scottish inventor and Andrew Meikle's son
Sir Francis Kinloch (fl. seventeenth century), Scottish agriculturist
John Rennie (1761-1821), Scottish apprentice to Andrew Meikle and civil engineer

SUMMARY OF EVENT

As British urban populations expanded in the eighteenth century due to industrialization, the demand for food ur-

gently increased. British agriculture required intensive labor to cultivate fields and harvest crops during most of that century. Farmers attempted to grow greater yields to feed nonagricultural populations and supply raw fibers to textile mills. They had fewer laborers to help them, because many people abandoned rural work for urban employment. Enclosure laws forced many agricultural workers from land. Farmers sought to produce large quantities of foodstuffs with minimal labor. In order to do so, they needed technological assistance.

Most people considered agricultural work tedious and time-consuming. For centuries, engineers and inventors had experimented with implements and tools, attempting to create machinery to ease agriculturists' workloads. Jethro Tull's 1701 seed drill inspired innovation. Farmers read agricultural guidebooks recommending ways to achieve success. Some agriculturists tested new methods and tried different equipment, adapting and designing tools suitable for their specific fields and needs.

Scottish inventor Andrew Meikle envisioned a machine to ease the labor- and time-intensive threshing process usually performed by hand. Trained as a millwright by his father, James Meikle, Andrew Meikle understood mechanical processes. James Meikle had traveled to Holland in 1710 to examine Dutch agricultural technology and brought a winnowing machine to remove chaff from grain to the Meikles' East Lothian home. Andrew Meikle probably saw that equipment and gained experiences with his family's mill, grinding barley and corn, prior to building and repairing textile mills in Scotland from the 1740's through the 1760's with his brother, Robert Meikle. They also traveled throughout England, examining mills.

The Meikle brothers worked as consultants for the Scottish mills' board of trustees for manufactures. They advocated that the board provide money to educate apprentices. Andrew Meikle arranged for his neighbor, John Rennie, later a prominent civil engineer, to serve as his apprentice in the mid-1770's, while Meikle worked on threshing machine designs at his Houston Mill, close to East Linton on Haddingtonshire Tyne. He also taught future engineer William Playfair. The Meikles' experiences inspired them to improve technology used in both grain and textile mills. Aware of other people's inventions, they adjusted designs and created new versions of commonly used devices. By 1768, the pair received patent number 896 for a grain winnowing machine to remove husks.

Meikle's related inventions, prior to concentrating on threshing, strengthened his imagination. Intrigued by wind movement, Meikle focused his inventive talents on redesigning windmills. In 1750, Meikle created fantails to keep windmill sails at right angles to wind. By 1772, he secured a patent for windmill sails incorporating springs to permit hinged shutters to vent gusty winds, preventing damage to the sails and ensuring power generation crucial for milling needs was not disrupted.

Aware of farmers' concerns about labor shortages, Meikle considered designing better devices to help agriculturists profitably supply crops to markets. Farmers stated that threshing, the process of stripping grain from plant stalks, required the most time. Before they had access to dependable mechanized threshing, most eighteenth century agricultural laborers beat stalks with flails to remove grain. Meikle knew how equipment worked and wanted to make tools easier to use and more efficient to help farmers.

Meikle probably had seen mechanized devices used to beat flax with internal flails and knew of several models other inventors had designed to thresh grain. In 1636, Sir John Christopher had patented a simple threshing machine. A century later, Meikle might have been inspired by Michael Menzies's 1734 machine, built in East Lothian. Meikle might have learned about the machine Scottish farmer Michael Stirling created in the 1750's, which had wood beaters, often called scrutchers, that revolved like those sometimes used in lint mills to process flax. Sir Francis Kinloch redesigned a machine built by a Mr. Elderton and gave a model to the London Board of Agriculture and another to Meikle.

Meikle contemplated these prior attempts to mechanize threshers, studying varying designs and investigating why machines worked or failed to achieve their tasks satisfactorily and reliably. He noted that rubbing processes removed grain from stalks, but the pressure caused bruising to kernels. Eager to apply his ideas for improvements, Meikle designed, built, and tested prototypes for a threshing machine in the 1770's and 1780's. He adjusted and rejected several designs until he realized what mechanisms would be most effective.

After approximately ten years of trials, sometime around 1787, Meikle envisioned using a revolving drum to remove grain from stalks. He placed rigid iron scrutchers around a drum cylinder. Meikle fed stalks through long, grooved rollers like those utilized in lint mills. Meikle's experience with flax machinery, which beat fiber out of flax, possibly inspired this idea. The drum spun quickly—more than two hundred revolutions per minute—to remove grain, as stalks were pounded against the concave metal container walls securing the drum. This machine met Meikle's expectations, because the drum design beat grain and did not rub it. He added devices to collect grain and remove chaff and debris. Andrew's son George Meikle constructed a threshing machine for a farmer and received orders to build more. When he told Kinloch his father would apply for a patent, Kinloch argued that Meikle's design was unoriginal.

On February 14, 1788, Andrew Meikle exhibited his water-powered machine at Knowes Mill, near Haddingtonshire. Observers told the area's board of trustees for manufactures what they had seen, praising Meikle's machine. Meikle received English patent number 1645 for that machine but was unable to secure a Scottish patent because he had demonstrated the machine and threshed grain in public. Aspiring to help farmers and earn income from machinery sales to consumers, Meikle built a factory in 1789.

Although many farmers were receptive to his machine and purchased it, Meikle did not profit from his invention. In the eighteenth century, patents rewarded inventors and were considered an honor not necessarily a guarantee of property rights. People, including Kinloch, claimed they had invented Meikle's design and ignored his patent. Neither Meikle nor legal authorities enforced it. Copying Meikle's design, craftsmen built and sold hundreds of unlicensed machines. That competition hindered Meikle's sales. Despite his machine's importance and widespread use, Meikle earned minimal income. By 1809, Sir John Sinclair directed Meikle's friends to collect £1,500 to support him.

SIGNIFICANCE

Meikle's pioneering drum thresher represented a significant technological component of the late eighteenth century Agricultural Revolution in Great Britain. His practical, effective design revealed how engineering and scientific inventiveness and applications aided the industrialization and commercialization of agriculture. Meikle's thresher enabled farmers to process crops in less time, especially as farm sizes increased and labor sources decreased. That machine became the basis for future threshing technology, as some innovators improved his design. Since the 1780's, engineers have incorporated Meikle's design in combined harvesters used to cut, thresh, and winnow crops with one machine. Modern machines retain principles of Meikle's invention. Inspired by Meikle's threshing machine, inventors devised such related related tools as reapers to process agricultural produce mechanically.

Most farmers in northern England and Scotland accepted Meikle's thresher because those regions lacked workers due to industrialization employment demands. The Lowland Clearances had forced many rural Scots to relocate to urban areas or emigrate. Although technology usually advanced agriculture, many agricultural workers were impacted negatively. In southern England, where more corn grew, thus increasing threshing demands, farm laborers resented Meikle's machine because they could not compete with mechanization's efficiency. Denied threshing jobs they had relied on to earn income, human threshers suffered unemployment and poverty because factories could not hire all available labor or those jobs did not appeal to rural residents. Workers' frustration and anger grew over the following decades as more farmers used threshing machines. Large farms expanded, and investors, often absentee, embraced technology to gain profits. Those owners were usually uninterested in the welfare of rural communities and laborers. Displaced workers rioted in 1830, damaging threshing machines and burning agricultural buildings and supplies while praising fictional renegade Captain Swing.

—*Elizabeth D. Schafer*

FURTHER READING

Blaxter, Sir Kenneth, and Noel Robertson. *From Dearth to Plenty: The Modern Revolution in Food Production.* New York: Cambridge University Press, 1995. Explores how eighteenth century innovations in technology and science revolutionized agriculture, establishing precedents for later inventions, practices, and ongoing transformations, which industrialized agriculture. Glossary, bibliographical resources.

Fussell, George E. *The Farmer's Tools, 1500-1900: The History of British Farm Implements, Tools, and Machinery Before the Tractor Came.* London: Andrew Melrose, 1952. Comprehensive discussion of agricultural technology, including a chapter about early threshing developments, especially in Scotland, before Meikle's work and his role in improving designs. Illustrations, chronology.

Handley, James E. *Scottish Farming in the Eighteenth Century.* London: Faber and Faber, 1953. Discusses Andrew Meikle, his father, and his son and their contributions to agriculture technology. Based on primary sources and inventors' accounts. Bibliography.

Hobsbawm, Eric, and George Rudé. *Captain Swing.* London: Phoenix Press, 2001. Analyzes the 1830 rebellion of agriculturists reacting to industrialization, examining how agricultural mechanization affected rural employment and conditions and caused poverty and despair.

Mokyr, Joel, ed. *The British Industrial Revolution: An Economic Perspective.* 2d ed. Boulder, Colo.: Westview, 1999. Includes a chapter discussing agriculture advances that coincided with Industrial Revolution technological innovations. States threshing machinery reduced labor but did not increase yields.

SEE ALSO: 1701: Tull Invents the Seed Drill; 1705-1712: Newcomen Develops the Steam Engine; Jan. 7, 1714: Mill Patents the Typewriter; 1733: Kay Invents the Flying Shuttle; 1747: Marggraf Extracts Sugar from Beets; 1760's: Beginning of Selective Livestock Breeding; 1764: Invention of the Spinning Jenny; 1765-1769: Watt Develops a More Effective Steam Engine; 1767-1771: Invention of the Water Frame; 1779: Crompton Invents the Spinning Mule; 1790: First Steam Rolling Mill; 1793: Whitney Invents the Cotton Gin; 1795: Invention of the Flax Spinner.

RELATED ARTICLES in *Great Lives from History: The Eighteenth Century, 1701-1800*: Jethro Tull; Eli Whitney.

1789
LEBLANC DEVELOPS SODA PRODUCTION

Instead of using organic sources, Leblanc discovered an artificial method of making soda (sodium carbonate) from salt (sodium chloride), and his method led to widespread use of soda in industries making soap, glass, and paper, as well as in the bleaching and dyeing industries.

LOCALE: Paris and Saint Denis, France
CATEGORIES: Chemistry; science and technology; manufacturing; environment

KEY FIGURES
Nicolas Leblanc (1742-1806), French physician and industrial chemist
Duc d'Orléans (Philippe Égalité; 1747-1793), French nobleman
Michel Jean Jacques Dizé (1764-1852), French apothecary and Leblanc's assistant

SUMMARY OF EVENT

From antiquity, the compound now known as sodium carbonate was important to alchemists as a reactive alkali and to artisans for its role in making such substances as glass. It was found as a mineral, natron, in desert regions, and it could also be made from the ashes of seaweed or the barilla plant. During the medieval period, other alkaline substances were discovered, but by the eighteenth century soda, or "soda ash," had become the alkali with the greatest practical value, because it was essential to the manufacture of glass, paper, and soap, and it was also used in bleaching and dyeing. France obtained most of its soda from Spain, where the coastal barilla plants were harvested and burned to an ash rich in soda. However, this soda was expensive, varied in quality, and was subject to blockade during conflicts.

Because French industries were increasingly dependent on vulnerable supplies of soda, the French Academy of Sciences, in 1775, announced a substantial monetary prize to be given to the person who invented a commercial process for making soda from common salt. This prize caught the attention of Nicolas Leblanc, a physician with an interest in chemistry who was then employed by the duc d'Orléans, an aristocrat who was willing to support Leblanc's chemical research.

Contrary to what some scholars have described as the "Leblanc legend," Leblanc was not the first person to convert salt into soda. Other chemists had discovered more than a dozen laboratory procedures to bring about

this important conversion. Furthermore, before Leblanc set up his factory, several small industries were actually making artificial soda, but this soda was expensive, and it was not economically competitive with imported natural soda. Leblanc's achievement was to find an efficient method of making artificial soda that was able to outcompete its barilla-based manufacture in quantity, quality, and price.

Scholarly consensus exists that Leblanc began work on the "soda problem" in the 1780's, but disagreements exist over precisely when his work started and when he actually discovered his new process. In his patent application Leblanc stated that he began his research in 1784. Since no evidence in his personal and published papers exists to support this date, some scholars have cast doubt on this early date, preferring instead a time in the late 1780's. J. R. Partington, the distinguished historian of chemistry, thinks that Leblanc discovered his process in 1787, but many scholars choose 1789 as a date "beyond dispute," since Leblanc definitely made soda crystals by his new method in that year.

Controversy also exists about who actually made the discovery and how it was made. According to Leblanc, he got the idea for his method by reading about a trip that a French journalist made to England and Scotland to study their industries. This journalist, Jean Claude Delamétherie, who edited a physics journal, reported, albeit erroneously, on how the British were manufacturing soda. This discussion occurred after his description of British ironmaking. Some scholars think that this serendipitous juxtaposition of garbled chemical reactions helped Leblanc arrive at his idea about the use of limestone and coal to transform salt into soda.

In the late 1780's, while still in the employ of the duc d'Orléans, Leblanc used the laboratory facilities of the Collège de France in Paris to repeat the work of earlier researchers. He reacted common salt with concentrated sulfuric acid to form what he called "salt-cake" (sodium sulfate). He then went beyond the work of others by finding how to make soda from this salt-cake. He did this by using a furnace to heat a crucible containing the salt-cake and a mixture of powdered coal and limestone (calcium carbonate). This reaction resulted in what he called "black ash" (today we know it was a mixture of sodium carbonate and calcium sulfide, along with unreacted coal and limestone). He obtained the desired soda from the black ash by using water to dissolve the soda (the other materials were insoluble). Evaporation of the solution left him with "white ash," which turned out to be soda (sodium carbonate).

The French Revolution was under way while Leblanc, with the assistance of Michel Jean Jacques Dizé, completed his research. Since the duc d'Orléans, the funder of this research, had fled to England, Leblanc and Dizé traveled there in October of 1789 to discuss the commercialization of their artificial soda process. On February 12, 1790, Orléans and his agent, along with Leblanc and Dizé, signed an agreement whose principal provisions were that Leblanc would patent his soda-making process and Orléans would furnish 200,000 livres to enable Leblanc and Dizé to set up a factory to start manufacturing soda. On March 27, 1790, Leblanc deposited a document that included a detailed description of his process with a notary in Paris (this document, discovered in 1856, clearly established Leblanc's priority over Dizé).

In 1791, with money supplied by Orléans, Leblanc built a pilot plant at Saint Denis, north of Paris. The Committee of Public Safety allowed him to obtain a secret patent for his process on September 25, 1791. In scaling up his process from the laboratory to the factory level, Leblanc built three furnaces, the first to make salt-cake, with a chimney to convey a poisonous by-product, hydrogen chloride gas, into the atmosphere. On the site, a horse-driven mill pulverized coal and limestone for use in the second furnace, where the reaction producing the black ash took place. With water, he leached out the soda, which the final furnace evaporated into soda ash.

In his plans, Leblanc hoped that this factory would produce 275,000 pounds of soda annually, but throughout its early years it averaged only a bit more than 10 percent of this theoretical amount. On January 28, 1794, political authorities confiscated the plant and made the details of the Leblanc process public. This nationalization of the plant failed to solve France's soda shortage, and it led to the economic devastation of Leblanc and his family. Leblanc had already become disheartened when the duc d'Orléans, who had returned to France under the name of Philippe Égalité, was guillotined on November 6, 1793. Even though Napoleon Bonaparte returned the factory to Leblanc in 1802, Leblanc was never able to raise the capital to make it a successful enterprise. Burdened with financial problems and desperate to shock the authorities into granting his family the rewards that the state had previously promised him, he shot himself through the head in 1806. Unfortunately, his family's troubles continued, and, to make matters worse, Dizé began making claims that he, not Leblanc, was the real in-

ventor of the process. Based on a study of various documents, modern scholars have declared the contention of Dizé and his family spurious, and Leblanc has been posthumously recognized as the true inventor of the process that is now inextricably tied to his name.

SIGNIFICANCE

James Muspratt, an important nineteenth century English chemical manufacturer, once wrote that the Leblanc process had a greater impact on society, commerce, and chemical technology than any other discovery. Although evaluations of the Leblanc process's significance by modern historians of technology are less sweeping than Muspratt's, they nevertheless recognize the great influence of his method in facilitating the development of many modern chemical industries. Within a generation of Leblanc's death, his method had proved its worth and, especially after the remission of the salt tax, its economic profitability.

The process quickly spread to England and other European countries, where soda was sold in ever-increasing amounts to the textile and soap industries. Inexpensive soap resulted in its increased use, with concomitant health benefits, for example, a decline in infant mortality. On the other hand, the multiplication of soda plants increased environmental degradation, especially because of the vented hydrogen chloride gas. So severe were the problems in England that an Alkali Act was promulgated in 1863 that required factories to recover and not release their hydrogen chloride.

Despite these and other problems, the Leblanc process dominated the industrial production of soda for nearly a century, when it was replaced by a more efficient method developed by Ernest and Alfred Solvay in Belgium. The last Leblanc soda works closed in 1923, but the sodium carbonate that it and many other factories had produced spurred the growth of important industries that were vital in creating our modern technological society.

—*Robert J. Paradowski*

FURTHER READING

Brock, William H. *The Chemical Tree: A History of Chemistry*. New York: Norton, 2000. This reissue of a book originally published in England as *The Fontana History of Chemistry* makes available to American readers the best thematic history of chemistry. Brock discusses the Leblanc process in chapter 8, "Chemistry Applied to Arts and Manufactures." Extensive bibliographical essay for each of the chapters. Index.

Gillispie, Charles C. "The Discovery of the Leblanc Process." *Isis* 48 (1957): 152-170. This article by a distinguished historian of science seeks to demythologize traditional accounts of how Leblanc made (and suffered from) his discovery. Extensive footnotes with references to primary and secondary sources.

Hall, Nina, ed. *The New Chemistry*. New York: Cambridge University Press, 2000. Although this book's emphasis is on twentieth century developments, Colin Russell, in his chapter on "Chemistry in Society," analyzes the Leblanc process and its social impact on the nineteenth century. Each of the chapters ends with a further reading section. Index.

Partington, J. R. *A History of Chemistry*. Vol. 3. Reprint.

New York: Martino, 1996. Chapter 11 contains a section on "The Leblanc Process" in which Partington, basing his treatment largely on original sources, gives a factual rather than analytic account of Leblanc and the development of his process. Name and subject indexes.

SEE ALSO: 1718: Geoffroy Issues the *Table of Reactivities*; 1722: Réaumur Discovers Carbon's Role in Hardening Steel; 1771: Woulfe Discovers Picric Acid.

RELATED ARTICLES in *Great Lives from History: The Eighteenth Century, 1701-1800*: Nicolas Leblanc; Duc d'Orléans.

April 30, 1789
WASHINGTON'S INAUGURATION

As the first president of the United States, George Washington set lasting precedents for future leaders, helping to define both the qualities befitting a president and the appropriate conduct of presidents while in office.

LOCALE: Federal Hall, New York City
CATEGORY: Government and politics

KEY FIGURES
George Washington (1732-1799), president of the United States, 1789-1797
John Adams (1735-1826), vice president of the United States, 1789-1797, and president, 1797-1801
Robert R. Livingston (1746-1813), chancellor of the state of New York
Samuel Allyne Otis (1740-1814), secretary of the Senate

SUMMARY OF EVENT
Early on the afternoon of April 30, 1789, George Washington took the oath of office of president of the United States as prescribed by the new Constitution. Standing on a small portico at Federal Hall, New York City, Washington repeated the solemn words administered by Robert Livingston, chancellor of the state of New York, and then added his own suffix: "So help me God." Bending forward, the first president of the United States kissed the Bible held for him by Samuel Otis, secretary of the Senate. Livingston then declared, "It is done!" and, turning to the multitudes on the rooftops, in the street, and at the windows of Broad and Wall Streets below, he shouted: "Long live George Washington, president of the United

States." The crowd roared back, "God bless our president," and the flag was jubilantly raised to the cupola of the great hall while gun salutes and church bells resounded.

The fifty-seven-year-old Washington took office in a newly formed nation of four million people, citizens and noncitizens, living in thirteen states. He came to the presidency without previous experience in any elected executive office, despite a lifetime of dedicated public service. Influenced as were many men of his generation by the principles of the Enlightenment, Washington believed in the republican ideal, with its emphasis on self-sacrifice and the public good.

Washington's long career had begun in 1758 with his election to the Virginia Assembly. He served as a colonel in the Virginia militia under the British in the French and Indian War. As commander in chief of the Continental army, he wielded more authority—and perhaps commanded more respect—than had the Continental Congress that appointed him. In 1787, he was unanimously chosen as president of the Constitutional Convention, which ultimately would produce the new Constitution. In taking office as president of the nation under that new constitution, Washington provided the fledgling nation with a model of simple dignity—the soul and air of a hero-leader. Earnest and sincere, he evoked memories of the victorious American Revolution and offered unity and confidence to the citizens in their new government. As such, he had been unanimously chosen by the electoral college under the new Constitution.

The anxieties of war, his labor for the Constitution, his desire for retirement from public life, and his love for his family and his home at Mount Vernon made Washington's decision to accept the presidency a difficult one. He wrote: "My movements to the chair of government will be accompanied by feelings not unlike those of a culprit who is going to the place of his execution, so unwilling am I, in the evening of a life nearly consumed in public cares, to quit a peaceful abode for an ocean of difficulties, without that competency of political skills, abilities and inclination which is necessary to manage the helm."

Thus, it was with mixed emotions that Washington set out for New York on April 16, 1789. Acclamations met him on each stage of his journey. In Alexandria, Georgetown, Baltimore, Wilmington, and Philadelphia, grateful citizens welcomed their acknowledged leader, who traveled by carriage, horseback, and flotilla. One week before his inauguration, Washington arrived at the end of Wall Street by barge from Elizabeth Town Point, New Jersey, to be met by thousands of cheering New Yorkers, a great display of boats and festooned ships, and the loud roar of cannon.

Washington represented for the people who cheered him the last great hope for unity. Americans had been made wary by the revolution, the inadequacy of the Articles of Confederation, and the Federalist and Antifederalist factions that had developed as the Constitution underwent the difficult process of ratification. The young nation looked to the new Constitution for the leadership that would set its government in motion and make it endure. Washington took stewardship of the Constitution, which provided for a strong central government while strictly defining the powers of that government. His calm, purposeful presence during the contentious debates, and his refusal to side with any party, would sound the keynote to his new administration. Washington's inauguration marked the delivery of the Constitution and the start of a new era.

That Washington keenly felt the need for unity was apparent in his inaugural address, although the event was marred somewhat by factional debate over what title Washington should take as president. Federalists were concerned their new president would not receive sufficient respect without a dignified title, especially from emissaries from foreign nations. They proposed "His Most Benign Excellency" and "His Highness, the Presi-

Crowds gather outside Federal Hall in New York City to witness the inauguration of the first president of the United States, George Washington. (C. A. Nichols & Company)

dent of the United States and Protector of their Liberties" as likely titles. These received loud and derisive complaints from the Antifederalist members of Congress, already worried that a too-powerful executive would bring a return of the tyranny many recalled under British rule. Eventually, the designation of "President of the United States" was determined, and Washington was pleased to be addressed simply as Mr. President.

After taking the oath of office, the new president entered the Senate Chamber, where both houses of Congress and various dignitaries took seats. On the canopied dias with the president were Vice President John Adams, Chancellor Livingston, and New York governor George Clinton. President Washington modestly delivered the well-fashioned phrases of his first presidential address. In his opening remarks, he spoke of his inner conflict, his consciousness of his "inferior endowments," and his lack of experience in civil administration. He paid homage to God, whose provident hand had guided the people through their struggles and deliberation.

Recognizing his duty under the Constitution to make recommendations to the Congress, Washington expressed his trust that the legislators would rise above the local pledges or attachments and petty animosities. In the only specific suggestion of the address, Washington urged Congress to quell "inquietude" by deciding to what extent it would advocate constitutional amendments. He expressed confidence in Congress's ultimate wisdom in pursuit of the public good. Washington concluded on the theme of unity, trusting that God had

> been pleased to favor the American people, with opportunities for deliberating in perfect tranquillity, and dispositions for deciding with unparalleled unanimity on a form of government for the security of their Union and the advancement of their happiness; so his divine blessing may be equally conspicuous in the enlarged views, the temperate consultations and the wise measures on which the success of the Government must depend.

From Federal Hall, the president walked triumphantly with congressmen and guests through streets lined with militia to services at St. Paul's Chapel.

SIGNIFICANCE

Washington believed that his inauguration as president represented the consummation of the revolution. The political experiment should have a fair trial, and the new president vowed to do his best to support it. Deeply conscious that he was setting the pattern that future presidents would follow, Washington brought the same dig-

nity and modesty he had demonstrated throughout his career to the office of the presidency. Because he was the first president, the specific virtues he displayed in office became the virtues that Americans would expect of all their presidents for generations. Moreover, as the leader of the new nation, Washington projected an international image that became the image of American leadership in the eyes of the world at large.

—*Emory M. Thomas, updated by Kelley Graham*

FURTHER READING

Alden, John R. *George Washington: A Biography*. Baton Rouge: Louisiana State University Press, 1984. A comprehensive, interesting biography that bypasses the common mistake of lionizing the subject.

Burns, James MacGregor, and Susan Dunn. *George Washington*. New York: Times Books, 2004. Concise biography, one in a series of books on the American presidents. Much of the book describes how Washington carefully created a public image emphasizing self-sacrifice and dignity. The authors also praise Washington's presidency, lauding his ability to establish a strong executive branch and to develop the most effective style of collective leadership of any American president.

Ellis, Joseph J. *His Excellency: George Washington*. New York: Alfred A. Knopf, 2004. Best-selling and highly acclaimed biography, based in large part on Washington's newly cataloged letters and papers at the University of Virginia. Ellis provides a complete account of Washington's life and career, placing it within the context of the eighteenth century United States. He describes how Washington, who skillfully crafted his public personality, was equally adept at crafting a political system for the newly created United States.

Langston, Thomas S., and Michael G. Sherman. *George Washington*. Washington, D.C.: CQ Press, 2003. One in a series of books about the American presidents published by the Congressional Quarterly. The authors, who are political scientists, examine Washington's life, election campaigns, his presidential policies, and the political crises that occurred during his administration. Each of the book's six chapters includes a brief bibliographic essay.

Schwartz, Barry. *George Washington: The Making of an American Symbol*. New York: Free Press, 1987. An exploration of the iconization of Washington, a process influenced by public events such as Washington's inauguration.

Smith, Richard Norton. *Patriarch: George Washington and the New American Nation*. Boston: Houghton Mifflin, 1993. Beginning with an account of Washington's inauguration, this book explores the ways in which Washington defined the presidency.

Washington, George. *April-June, 1789*. Vol. 2 in *The Papers of George Washington: Presidential Series*, edited by W. W. Abbot and Dorothy Twohig. Charlottesville: University Press of Virginia, 1992-1995. Includes the full text of Washington's address, as well as the fragmentary text discarded.

Zagarri, Rosemarie, ed. *David Humphreys' "Life of General Washington" with George Washington's "Remarks."* Athens: University of Georgia Press, 1991. A newly edited version of the authorized biography of Washington, which includes his feelings about the presidency and the difficulties of life in public office.

SEE ALSO: Apr. 19, 1775-Oct. 19, 1781: American Revolutionary War; Sept. 17, 1787: U.S. Constitution Is Adopted; Sept. 24, 1789: Judiciary Act; 1790's: First U.S. Political Parties; Jan., 1790: Hamilton's *Report on Public Credit*; Oct., 1790: Nootka Sound Convention; Oct. 18, 1790-July, 1794: Little Turtle's War; Dec. 15, 1791: U.S. Bill of Rights Is Ratified; Aug. 20, 1794: Battle of Fallen Timbers; Nov. 19, 1794: Jay's Treaty; Oct. 27, 1795: Pinckney's Treaty; Sept. 19, 1796: Washington's Farewell Address.

RELATED ARTICLES in *Great Lives from History: The Eighteenth Century, 1701-1800*: John Adams; Thomas Jefferson; George Washington.

May 5, 1789
LOUIS XVI CALLS THE ESTATES-GENERAL

King Louis XVI called the Estates-General, the supreme French legislative body, to meet for the first time in more than 150 years. The disastrous fiscal condition of the French government required new taxes that only the Estates-General could authorize, but those same fiscal problems had caused significant unrest among the bourgeois members of the Third Estate, who were poised to take control of the government.

LOCALE: Versailles, France
CATEGORY: Government and politics

KEY FIGURES
Louis XVI (1754-1793), king of France, r. 1774-1792
Emmanuel-Joseph Sieyès (1748-1836), French clergyman, pamphleteer, and reforming political theorist
Jacques Necker (1732-1804), French minister of finance, 1777-1781, 1788-1789, 1789-1790
Charles-Alexandre de Calonne (1734-1802), French minister of finance, 1783-1787

SUMMARY OF EVENT
When Louis XVI became king of France in 1774, he inherited a wealthy kingdom but an empty treasury and a government deeply in debt. Following a traditionally anti-British policy, France entered the American War of Independence on the side of the colonies. In order to continue this war the government had to borrow even more, thereby plunging the country into deeper financial trouble.

By 1788, the government was on the verge of bankruptcy. Expenses for that year were estimated at 629 million livres, while revenues were expected to bring in only 503 million livres. The deficit of 126 million livres would have to be made up by loans at the usual high rate of interest. Charles-Alexandre de Calonne, the minister of finance, attempted to introduce financial reform without success, as had his predecessors Jacques Necker and Anne-Robert-Jacques Turgot. Now it even became evident to the king that reform was imperative.

France was economically prosperous but its government was financially poor because of inequities in the tax structure and inefficient methods of collecting tax. The French Government had negotiated a free trade treaty with Britain in 1787. As a result France in the short term did not compete well with Britain, and French farmers and manufacturers suffered. Poor weather and harvests in 1787 had led to food shortages, even famine in some areas. Increased pressure was put upon the Crown and its ministers to relieve such distress. Neither the First Estate (the clergy) nor the Second Estate (the nobility) paid any taxes at all; the entire burden of taxes fell upon the Third Estate (the commons). Even within the Third Estate there was inequity; the wealthy bourgeoisie paid a lower percentage of the total taxes than did the poorer peasants; those who were least able were required to pay most.

In an attempt to balance the budget in 1787, Calonne

suggested several major reforms. His most revolutionary suggestion was a "territorial subvention" to be paid by all landowners without distinction or exception. Since the largest owners of land were the nobility and the clergy, Calonne was in effect proposing to tax the two privileged orders. The king realized that reform was necessary, but he did not give Calonne his full support. Calonne therefore turned elsewhere, and with the approval of Louis he convened an Assembly of Notables. Because this gathering was dominated by the higher nobility, the notables rejected the proposed reforms.

Calonne then turned to the Parlement of Paris. This body, judicial rather than legislative, registered royal decrees to make them the law of the land. Calonne prevailed upon the king to hold a "royal session" (*Lit de justice*) in which the king appeared before the parlement and ordered it to register the decrees proposed. This action was taken on August 4, 1787, but the following day, the Parlement of Paris declared its actions of the previous day null and void. This tactic was symptomatic of the struggle between the king and his government, on one side, and the nobility, on the other.

The basic issues became clearer during the following twelve months. The nobility would allow themselves to be taxed only if the king would share his powers with them. They envisaged a form of government similar to that of Great Britain, where the nobility could control the king without losing their cherished feudal rights. To gain this end, the Parlement of Paris took full advantage of the financial embarrassment of the Crown; it declared that it did not have the authority to register new tax decrees, which was the prerogative of the Estates-General. The last time the Estates-General had met was in 1614, and the privileged orders had then dominated the proceedings. Traditionally, the three estates met separately, and each voted as an order. The will of the estates was then expressed by each order casting one vote, with the majority view prevailing. In this manner, the clergy and the nobility were always able to prevent the Third Estate from tampering with their privileges.

In August of 1788, Louis called for a meeting of the Estates-General, to take place the following May. In the months leading up to that meeting, the fruits of Enlightenment political debate appeared in print throughout France, especially in Paris. Discussion of political representation, limits on monarchic power and the balance of power, the

The first meeting of the Estates-General, May 5, 1789. (Harper & Brothers)

ideas of citizenship and nationhood, and the models of republicanism found in the ancient republics, in Britain, and the United States, all salted the discussion of what the Estates-General should or would do when it met.

During the second half of 1788, the Third Estate agitated to have the number of their representatives doubled so that they would be equal in numbers to the First and Second Estates combined. This request was granted by royal decree in December of 1788, although no mention was made about how the voting would take place. The subsequent election of the members of the Third Estate, the most democratic that Europe had seen and would see for many years to come, had for many in France the hallmarks of the election of representatives to a national assembly, though no official status as such had been given it. Such elections required the compilation of local *cahiers* (grievance lists), provoking further debate about reform. Combined, this raised expectations that the coming meeting of the Estates-General signified a fundamental change in French political culture. The nobility believed that it would make little difference how many representatives sat with the Third Estate since they had only one collective vote.

The greatest theoretical challenge to the traditional powers of both Crown and First and Second Estates came in February of 1788. In his pamphlet *Qu'est-ce que le tiers état?* (1789; *What Is the Third Estate?* 1963), the Abbé Emmanuel-Joseph Sieyès argued that the true political nation of France was the Third Estate alone. This work, and others in a similar vein, would provide the script for the rise of the Third Estate from one of three orders to conceiving of itself as representing the French nation.

SIGNIFICANCE

The Estates-General met on May 5, 1789, and from then until June 27, when the First and Second Estates joined the third, the conflict grew in intensity. Necker, who had been recalled as finance minister, was charged by the king with communicating the fiscal situation to the legislature, but he was largely ignored as unrest grew. Louis decided to dismiss Necker once again, call in troops, and disperse the Estates-General by force. The move backfired and led directly to the storming of the Bastille, beginning the French Revolution.

—*John G. Gallaher, updated by Michael Kugler*

FURTHER READING

Baker, Keith Michael. *Inventing the French Revolution.* Chicago: University of Chicago Press, 1990. A com-

plex though compelling discussion of the political theories and debates which helped shape the revolution; includes an explanation of Sieyès's contributions to the discussion of representation.

Doyle, William. *Origins of the French Revolution.* 3d ed. New York: Oxford University Press, 1999. Chapter 13, "The Estates-General, May and June, 1789," recounts the events of this period.

_____. *The Oxford History of the French Revolution.* 2d ed. New York: Oxford University Press, 2002. Doyle's clear narration draws together recent research while covering the economic, political, and cultural facets of the revolution.

Furet, François. *Revolutionary France, 1770-1880.* Translated by Antonia Nevill. Malden, Mass.: Blackwell, 1992. Written by the major revisionist historian of the French Revolution, this work is particularly strong on French politics and political culture.

Jones, P. M. *Reform and Revolution in France: The Politics of Transition, 1774-1791.* New York: Cambridge University Press, 1995. An analysis of governmental, social, and economic conditions in prerevolutionary France. Chapter 5 includes information about Necker and the Estates-General.

Lefebvre, Georges. *The French Revolution: From Its Origins to 1793.* Translated by Elizabeth Moss Evanson. New York: Columbia University Press, 1962. This remains one of the best accounts of the revolution and is particularly strong on France's social ills preceding the calling of the Estates-General.

Rudé, George. *The French Revolution: Its Causes, Its History, Its Legacy After Two Hundred Years.* New York: Grove Weidenfeld, 1988. A noted expert in social history offers a readable account with a particularly helpful introduction to the continuing historiographic debate about the French Revolution.

SEE ALSO: June 20, 1789: Oath of the Tennis Court; July 14, 1789: Fall of the Bastille; Oct., 1789-Apr. 25, 1792: France Adopts the Guillotine; Apr. 20, 1792-Oct., 1797: Early Wars of the French Revolution; Jan. 21, 1793: Execution of Louis XVI; July 27-28, 1794: Fall of Robespierre.

RELATED ARTICLES in *Great Lives from History: The Eighteenth Century, 1701-1800*: Georges Danton; Louis XVI; Marie-Antoinette; Jacques Necker; Robespierre; Emmanuel-Joseph Sieyès; Anne-Robert-Jacques Turgot.

1780's

June 20, 1789
OATH OF THE TENNIS COURT

The representatives of the French Third Estate swore to accomplish major governmental reform and not to separate—nor to allow themselves to be separated—until their goals were achieved. Their oath forced King Louis XVI to accept a truly national assembly, thereby precipitating the French Revolution.

LOCALE: Versailles, France
CATEGORY: Government and politics

KEY FIGURES

Emmanuel-Joseph Sieyès (1748-1836), French
    clergyman and leader of the Third Estate
Jean-Joseph Mounier (1758-1806), member of the
    Third Estate who proposed the Oath of the Tennis
    Court
Louis XVI (1754-1793), king of France, r. 1774-1792
Martin Dauch (fl. 1789), member of the Third Estate
    who refused to take the Oath of the Tennis Court

SUMMARY OF EVENT

King Louis XVI of France was forced to call the Estates-General in 1789 because the nobility and the higher clergy had been unwilling to cooperate with him in an attempt to introduce financial reforms. Although France was one of the most prosperous nations in Europe at the time, the royal government was on the verge of bankruptcy. An inept system of collecting taxes and the inefficient management of royal monopolies contributed to the financial distress of the government, but the real cause was the inequity of the tax system.

Neither the nobility nor the clergy paid taxes to the crown, and exclusion of this substantial portion of the nation's wealth placed an increased burden on the remainder of the population. Furthermore, the tax structure was such that the wealthy bourgeoisie paid a much smaller percentage of their income in taxes than did the peasants. In order to avoid bankruptcy, the government attempted to introduce new taxes that would fall upon the nobility and clergy, hitherto untouched. This attempt led to a struggle between the Crown and the privileged classes in 1787 and 1788. Louis XVI finally gave in to the demands of the Parlement of Paris, which reflected the views of the aristocracy, and announced that the Estates-General would meet in May, 1789.

This body had not been called since 1614. It was an advisory assembly made up of three orders: the First Estate (the clergy), the Second Estate (the nobility), and the

Third Estate (the remainder of the population). The three orders had traditionally met separately and voted within their own assemblies. The consensus of the Estates-General was then expressed by the majority vote of two of the three estates. It was the intention of the aristocracy, declared by the Parlement of Paris, that the Estates-General would meet in the traditional manner in 1789. The First and Second Estates could then dominate the Third Estate and outvote it if their privileges were called into question. Furthermore, the aristocracy hoped that by dominating the Estates-General, they could force the king to share some powers of government with them, thereby creating a system similar to that which had been established in Great Britain through the English parliament.

The Third Estate received the news that the Estates-General had been called with even more eager anticipation than the nobility. Louis XVI was asking his loyal people for advice, and the hope was raised that reform to benefit the bourgeoisie and the peasantry would be introduced. During 1788, the Third Estate asked the king to double their numbers so that they would be numerically equal to the First and Second Estates. In December, Louis agreed so that he could secure the support of the Third Estate in the forthcoming assembly. If votes were still to be taken by the three orders acting separately, nothing had really changed, but the Third Estate had never accepted the idea of each order voting separately. To them, the increase of numbers implied the idea of voting by numbers of heads, even though the king in his decree had made no mention of the method of voting. The Estates-General opened its first session on May 5, 1789, without the Third Estate agreeing to the "legal" voting regulation.

In accordance with the king's instruction, the clergy and the nobility met in their designated halls and began to organize as separate orders. The Third Estate, however, decided to force the three orders to meet as one body and vote as one body, and so it employed the delaying tactic of refusing to organize itself. The nobility ignored the Third Estate and declared themselves organized, but the clergy, displaying sympathy with commoners, postponed its own organization.

During May, the principal means used by the Third Estate to delay its organization was verification of credentials of all members of the Estates-General. It demanded that credentials of all three orders be verified at a

The members of the Third Estate swearing the Oath of the Tennis Court. (The Granger Collection, New York)

joint meeting. The nobility refused to accept this demand, so the Third Estate did not verify its own credentials and therefore could not declare itself organized. Various attempts at compromise failed, and when the clergy began to show increasing sympathy for the Third Estate, the latter became bolder.

On June 10, 1789, the Abbé Emmanuel-Joseph Sieyès, leader of the Third Estate, proposed that the Third Estate summon the two privileged orders to join them and that a roll be called of all members of the Estates-General. Those not answering when their names were called would be declared eliminated. This measure was passed by the Third Estate, and the roll call began on June 12. On June 17, after considerable debate, the Third Estate assumed the name National Assembly. The issue was be-

ing forced, and when many of the clergy voted to join the Third Estate, the king decided to call a royal session on June 23. In order to prevent the Third Estate from continuing to meet until then, the king closed their hall under the pretext of having it prepared for the next meeting. When members of the Third Estate arrived on June 20 for their regular session, they found themselves locked out. As a result, they decided to meet at a nearby indoor tennis court.

There was much excitement at the meeting. The commoners realized that the king was preparing to oppose their recent acts, and when Jean-Joseph Mounier proposed that they bind themselves together in a common oath, they agreed to do so. The oath declared that the National Assembly had been summoned to effect the regeneration of public order and that nothing could prevent it from continuing its deliberations. It went on to assert that where the members gathered they naturally constituted the National Assembly. To give this resolution force, the members of the Third Estate vowed not to separate until their ends had been met and, in language reminiscent of the American Declaration of Independence, bound themselves through their individual signatures.

All members signed the declaration except Martin Dauch. They reaffirmed their determination to stand by their acts of June 12-17. They no longer considered themselves to be merely one order of the Estates-General; instead, they became the National Convention representing the entire French nation. Although he at first resisted, Louis XVI gave way on June 27 and ordered the nobility and clergy to join with the Third Estate in the National Assembly.

SIGNIFICANCE

Marking a decisive shift in the events that would eventually be known as the French Revolution, the Oath of the Tennis Court was the first open expression of solidarity by the Third Estate with what might be termed the "general will" of the French people. From that point on, popular opinion, especially as shaped and directed by first tentative reformers and then outright revolutionaries, became a prime mover in domestic affairs. Louis XVI had challenged the Third Estate and had been decisively defeated. The Oath of the Tennis Court was the irreversible first step to the guillotine for Louis and toward a republic for France.

—*John G. Gallaher, updated by Michael Witkoski*

FURTHER READING

Bosher, J. F. *The French Revolution.* New York: W. W. Norton, 1988. One of the volumes in the "Revolutions in the Modern World" series, this study places the Oath of the Tennis Court in the context of the escalating conflict that developed into the Revolution.

Cobb, Richard, ed. *Voices of the French Revolution.* New York: Simon & Schuster, 1988. Contemporary accounts give an indication of what the participants and outside observers felt the Oath meant and why events unfolded as they did.

Doyle, William. *The Oxford History of the French Revolution.* 2d ed. New York: Oxford University Press, 2002. A sturdy, dependable study of the actions and actors involved in the Oath. Good in placing the event in the context of its times.

Hibbert, Christopher. *The Days of the French Revolution.* New York: Quill/William Morrow, 1999. Each chapter of this book covers the significant events that occurred on a single day or other designated time period during the French Revolution. Chapter 1 recounts "The Day of the Tennis-Court Oath, 20 June 1789."

Paxton, John. *Companion to the French Revolution.* New York: Facts On File, 1988. The expanded dictionary entries of this work help the student keep track of the numerous figures involved during the early period of the revolution.

Schama, Simon. *Citizens: A Chronicle of the French Revolution.* New York: Alfred A. Knopf, 1989. An expansive, at times impressionistic view of the tumultuous events of the times, this volume evokes the intense emotions that led to and resulted in the Oath of the Tennis Court.

Sutherland, D. M. G. *The French Revolution and Empire: The Quest for a Civic Order.* Malden, Mass.: Blackwell, 2003. Chapter 1, "The Origins of the Revolution in France," includes information about the Oath of the Tennis Court.

SEE ALSO: May 5, 1789: Louis XVI Calls the Estates-General; July 14, 1789: Fall of the Bastille; Oct., 1789-Apr. 25, 1792: France Adopts the Guillotine; Apr. 20, 1792-Oct., 1797: Early Wars of the French Revolution; Jan. 21, 1793: Execution of Louis XVI; July 27-28, 1794: Fall of Robespierre.

RELATED ARTICLES in *Great Lives from History: The Eighteenth Century, 1701-1800*: Georges Danton; Louis XVI; Marie-Antoinette; Robespierre; Emmanuel-Joseph Sieyès.

July 14, 1789
FALL OF THE BASTILLE

In the first overt violent act of the French Revolution, a crowd stormed the Bastille, freeing its prisoners and seizing the armaments stored there as well. The Bastille's fall signaled the emergence of the Parisian crowd as a potent political force—a force that not only was central to the Revolution but also defined French political life for centuries after its conclusion.

LOCALE: Paris, France

CATEGORIES: Wars, uprisings, and civil unrest; government and politics

KEY FIGURES

Jean-Sylvain Bailly (1736-1793), French astronomer, statesman, and mayor of Paris, 1789-1793

Jacques de Flesselles (d. 1789), head of the municipal government of Paris

Bernard-René de Launay (1740-1789), French commander of the Bastille

Louis XVI (1754-1793), king of France, r. 1774-1792

Marquis de Lafayette (Marie-Joseph-Paul-Yves-Roch-Gilbert du Motier de Lafayette; 1757-1834), French military officer and member of the National Assembly

Jacques Necker (1732-1804), French minister of finance, 1777-1781, 1788-1789, 1789-1790

SUMMARY OF EVENT

The storming of the Bastille was the climax of the events of July, 1789, a time marked by the determination of Paris crowds to defend the French Revolution against perceived royalist threats to disband the National Assembly, which had been meeting since June at Versailles, and restore absolutism. Composed of the original three estates which the king had summoned in May, 1789, to deal with the government's financial problems, the National Assembly represented the hopes and aspirations of most Frenchmen for extensive political, social, and economic reform.

During the early part of July, Parisians began to fear that King Louis XVI was planning to use mercenary troops to carry out a military coup d'état. The people of Paris became alarmed when they learned that the king was moving Swiss and German mercenary soldiers, whose loyalty was thought to be more dependable than French troops, from the provinces to positions around Versailles and the capital. Ostensibly, Louis XVI claimed that he wanted only to protect the National Assembly against possible disruption and prevent a recurrence of the April Révellion Riots, which local authorities had been unable to quell. To most Parisians and members of the National Assembly, however, Louis's action posed a clear threat to the revolutionary movement in general and the National Assembly in particular.

Louis's determination to confront the Assembly became clear on July 11 when he suddenly dismissed Jacques Necker, the popular and self-righteous minister of finance who personified reform in the public mind. Necker's association with reform had been making him progressively more unpopular at court. The news of Necker's dismissal reached Paris on July 12 and caused crowds of people calling for Necker's reinstatement to take to the streets.

The Paris uprising lasted from July 12 through July 14. This uprising differed from others that had gone before it because of its clear sense of direction. Mainly, its participants were determined to acquire weapons with which to defend themselves, Rumors that Louis's Swiss and German mercenaries were massacring civilians flew. The *gardes françaises* (French guard), a military body that traditionally supplemented the police, confronted the mercenaries and forced them to withdraw.

In the face of mounting disorder, the more conservative, bourgeois elements in the city realized that steps had to be taken to preserve order. Consequently the electoral assemblies of the sixty districts of Paris, which had remained active after fulfilling their appointed task of choosing representative of the Third Estate of Paris to the Estates-General, took charge of the city and elected a central committee. This body then went to the Hôtel de Ville (City Hall), where it fused with the old city council to form a new government in Paris. As chairman of the central committee, the assemblies chose Jacques de Flesselles, the head of the old municipal council. In one of its first moves, the new committee created a National Guard, which together with the French guard was supposed to combat royal oppression and keep order within the capital.

Nevertheless, crowds continued to roam the streets in search of arms. Some people sought arms to protect themselves from the king's mercenaries, who, it was feared, would perpetrate a "St. Bartholomew's Day" massacre of patriots. Others wanted arms simply to protect themselves against the lawless elements unleashed by the uprising. The search for arms met with success on

The liberation of prisoners from the Bastille. (Francis R. Niglutsch)

the morning of July 14 when a huge crowd of some eighty thousand people stormed the Invalides armory and took the thirty thousand muskets that had been stored there. Gunpowder, however, was lacking. It had been moved from the Arsenal to the Bastille several days earlier. The Bastille was an old fortress-prison in the center of Paris that had been built in the 1300's to guard the city's eastern gates, but which had been used for a prison since the seventeenth century. It had largely fallen into disuse, however, and in 1789 housed only seven prisoners—five criminals and two madmen.

Although the Bastille was all but impregnable if properly defended, the crowd decided to march on it on the afternoon of July 14 to demand gunpowder. The crowd did not march on the Bastille with the intention of releasing the prisoners incarcerated there or even of attacking it. Spokesmen for the crowd and the new committee governing the city simply demanded that the Bastille's military governor, Bernard-René de Launay, withdraw his cannon from their menacing position along the citadel's walls and turn over the stores of powder to the people.

De Launay complied with the first demand. During negotiations on the second demand, however, the besiegers managed to push their way from the outer court into the inner court of the fortress, whereupon de Launay panicked and opened fire on them. The fighting raged from about one to three o'clock in the afternoon, with the people suffering most of the losses. At three o'clock, the French guard brought up cannon. De Launay now reluctantly decided to surrender. Shortly after his capture, he was murdered along with Jacques de Flesselles, whom the people accused of misdirecting them in their search for arms. The mob then turned its wrath upon the Bastille itself and proceeded to destroy it. The Paris insurrection for all practical purposes was now over. Royal troops had been driven from the capital. The National Guard eventually succeeded in disarming those rioters who still roamed the streets.

SIGNIFICANCE

The Paris Revolution, highlighted by the storming of the Bastille, had important results of an immediate and long-range nature. On July 15, the king went before the National Assembly to announce the dismissal of his troops and the recall of Necker. The National Assembly then dispatched a delegation to Paris, including its president, Jean-Sylvain Bailly, and the Marquis de Lafayette. The governing committee of the city named Bailly mayor of the Paris Commune, which had been officially organized as such on July 15, and appointed Lafayette to be commander of the National Guard. Lafayette soon afterward bestowed upon the National Guard a cockade of red and blue, the colors of Paris, between which he placed a white band, the king's color. The tricolor thus became the new national flag of France. Louis, in a visit to Paris on July 17, accepted the tricolor, thereby giving formal recognition to his own inability to control the city and to the victory of the people of Paris.

More significant were the long-range effects of the fall of the Bastille. The event resulted in the first emigration of the reactionary nobles, who encouraged their host states to intervene politically against the Revolution. Politically, it completed the transfer of the king's remaining authority to the National Assembly. Also, some of the larger cities throughout France, such as Lyon, Bordeaux, and Marseilles, imitated the example of Paris by establishing new city governments, appointing citizen's guards, and capturing local royal fortresses. Socially, the fall of the Bastille encouraged the spread of peasant unrest, the so-called Great Fear, thereby paving the way for the formal abolition of feudalism in an all-night session of the National Assembly on August 4. Thus, the storming of the Bastille, which had been undertaken with the purpose of protecting the political gains made in May and June, contributed to creating a climate conducive to extensive social transformation.

—*Edward P. Keleher, updated by C. James Haug*

FURTHER READING

Doyle, William. *The Oxford History of the French Revolution.* 2d ed. New York: Oxford University Press, 2002. An authoritative and comprehensive account of French history between 1774 and 1802, written by a prominent historian. Includes information on the fall of the Bastille and its significance within the context of the French Revolution.

Godechot, Jacques. *Taking of the Bastille, July 14, 1789.* New York: Charles Scribner's Sons, 1970. A vivid account of the taking of the Bastille.

Hibbert, Christopher. *The Days of the French Revolution.* New York: Quill/William Morrow, 1999. Each chapter of this book covers the significant events that occurred on a single day or other designated time period during the French Revolution. Chapter 2 recounts "The Day of the Vainquers de la Bastille, 14 July 1789."

Lefebvre, George. *The Coming of the French Revolution.* Translated by R. R. Palmer. Bicentennial ed. Princeton, N.J.: Princeton University Press, 1989. First published in 1947, this is a classic introduction to the causes of the revolution written from a sociological perspective.

Roche, Daniel. *The People of Paris: An Essay in Popular Culture in the Eighteenth Century.* 2 vols. Translated by Marie Evans and Gwynne Lewis. Berkeley: University of California Press, 1987. A social history of the revolution describing the complexity of the Parisian milieu.

Rudé, George. *The Crowd in the French Revolution.* Oxford, England: Clarendon Press, 1959. A valuable work that refutes the idea that the Paris revolutionaries were nothing more than an unruly mob.

Schama, Simon. *Citizens: A Chronicle of the French Revolution.* New York: Alfred A. Knopf, 1989. An epic and exceptionally vivid account of the French Revolution, its antecedents, and its impact, with special emphasis on the central role of violence in the revolution and the revolutionaries' failure to realize their idealistic goals.

Soboul, Albert. *The French Revolution, 1789-1815: Storming of the Bastille to Napoleon.* Translated by Alan Forrest and Colin Jones. New York: Random House, 1975. A standard history of the French Revolution written from a leftist perspective.

SEE ALSO: May 5, 1789: Louis XVI Calls the Estates-General; June 20, 1789: Oath of the Tennis Court; Oct., 1789-Apr. 25, 1792: France Adopts the Guillotine; Apr. 20, 1792-Oct., 1797: Early Wars of the French Revolution; Jan. 21, 1793: Execution of Louis XVI; July 27-28, 1794: Fall of Robespierre.

RELATED ARTICLES in *Great Lives from History: The Eighteenth Century, 1701-1800*: Jean-Sylvain Bailly; Georges Danton; Louis XVI; Marie-Antoinette; Jacques Necker; Robespierre.

1780's

July 28-October 16, 1789
EPISCOPAL CHURCH IS ESTABLISHED

In the wake of the American Revolution, a group of former Anglicans created a church based upon Anglicanism but no longer associated with Great Britain. The general convention of the Protestant Episcopal Church adopted a church constitution, canons, and liturgy that shaped a uniquely American Episcopal church, independent of its mother Church of England.

LOCALE: Philadelphia, Pennsylvania
CATEGORIES: Organizations and institutions; religion and theology

KEY FIGURES
Samuel Provoost (1742-1815), bishop of New York
Samuel Seabury (1729-1796), first presiding bishop of the Episcopal Church in the United States
William White (1748-1836), architect of the Ecclesiastical Constitution

SUMMARY OF EVENT

Although the Episcopal Church in the United States was officially established by the General Convention of 1789, circumstances prior to that event were crucial in laying its foundation. Before the American Revolution, the Anglican Church in America (the Church of England) was in a tenuous position. Early in the eighteenth century, the English Society for the Propagation of the Gospel sent out missionaries to establish parishes in the American colonies. The parishes were under state jurisdiction. Each royal governor supported the Church financially by taxing all community members, regardless of whether they belonged to the Church of England. Because the majority did not belong to the Church of England, this practice caused resentment among the general population. Also, the Church in America had no bishops and was governed by the bishop of London. The close ties between church and state produced mistrust in many colonists.

During the American Revolution, the Anglican Church was almost destroyed. Because of their religious practices, Episcopalians were rebel targets. For example, upon ordination, the clergy were required to take a loyalty oath to the king. They also used the English Book of Common Prayer, which contained prayers for the welfare of the monarch. In spite of these customs, many clergy, such as William White, a leading Episcopal priest in Philadelphia and later chaplain to the Continental Congress, sided with the rebels. In New York, all the clergy were loyal to the king except Samuel Provoost. In

contrast to White and Provoost, Samuel Seabury from Connecticut, a high churchman and a Tory, represented the sentiments of the majority of the people of his state.

When the revolution ended in 1783, the Episcopal Church in America was disestablished and seeking a new direction. The English church no longer provided either economic or spiritual support. Where there had been a unity of sorts with the king as the focal point, there was no single tie to bind the parishes in the various states together. There were no bishops to oversee the Church. In order to survive, the Church in the United States had to reorganize, address the issue of unity, and establish a U.S. episcopate.

Some efforts were made toward these goals even before the Revolutionary War ended. A conference of clergy and laity met in Maryland in 1780 and adopted the name Protestant Episcopal Church. At a larger convention in Annapolis in 1783, the name was officially embraced and the vision of a United States identity began to be realized. The question of a national church was addressed by William White in his essay "The Case of the Episcopal Churches in the United States Considered," written in 1782. In this document, White proposed a democratic church organized along lines similar to those of the federal Constitution.

The quest for a United States episcopate proved elusive. Because a bishop was considered a state official in England, the Church in the United States was ambivalent concerning an American bishop. Because of the separation between church and state mandated by the federal Constitution, U.S. Anglicans were unsure of how the office of bishop would function in their church.

The first step in establishing an American episcopate was taken when the Church in Connecticut sent Samuel Seabury to England to be consecrated by English bishops. To retain episcopal succession, it was important that Seabury be consecrated by bishops whose orders were valid. He left America for England in 1783 and attempted to persuade the English church to consecrate him. The English bishops refused, because Seabury was no longer loyal to the king and because he was not a state official approved by the Connecticut legislature. Seabury then went to Scotland and, in 1784, was consecrated by three nonjuring bishops.

Three important events further shaped the Church in America before the general convention of 1789. First, on May 24, 1784, William White led a convention of clergy and laity in Philadelphia that established a set of basic principles that were later incorporated into the final constitution. These precepts dictated that the American church would remain independent of all foreign authority, that its liturgy would conform to that of the Church of England, and that there would be three orders of ministers: bishops, priests, and deacons.

Second, the first general convention of the Protestant Episcopal Church in the United States of America met on September 27, 1785. This convention addressed the issues of the episcopate, the liturgy, and the church constitution. The delegates decided that they would appeal to the Church of England to reconsider the consecration of U.S. bishops.

Third, in 1786, Parliament passed an act that allowed the English church to consecrate bishops who did not take an oath of loyalty to the king. White and Provoost were elected by their states to travel to England and were consecrated bishops in 1787. The church in the United States then had three bishops, a proposed liturgy, and a constitution, but was not yet unified. Each state (later known as a diocese) was an independent entity. Disagreement resulting from political differences continued to exist between the bishops. There was ill will between Seabury, a former Tory, and Provoost, a former revolutionary. Also, Seabury believed that bishops should control all aspects of church government, while White and Provoost believed that the clergy and laity should have a voice in church affairs.

The general convention of 1789, convened on July 28 at Christ Church in Philadelphia, was vital in organizing and redefining the Anglican Church in the United States. Representatives from New England did not attend the first session, because delegates from other states questioned the validity of Bishop Seabury's Episcopal orders. In order to achieve union with the churches in New England, the delegates voted unanimously to accept Bishop Seabury as equal to Bishops Provoost and White. The absence of Bishop Provoost due to illness was fortuitous. Provoost resented Seabury's political views and would have prevented a decision in Seabury's favor. Another issue addressed during the summer session was the creation of a House of Bishops and a House of Deputies. This structure mirrored the House of Representatives and Senate of the United States government.

The second session of the 1789 General Convention began September 30 and ended October 16. Bishop Seabury, with two clerical deputies plus representatives from Massachusetts and New Hampshire, joined the delegates who had attended the previous session. The House of Bishops, consisting of White and Seabury, met separately without Bishop Provoost. Although he attended the convention, Provoost refused to participate because of Seabury's presence.

Three concerns were addressed during the fall session: the constitution, the prayer book, and canonical law. The church constitution was formally adopted and echoed the democratic principles recently presented in the federal Constitution. The Church would consist of a collection of independent dioceses, each headed by a bishop; church policy would be formulated at a triennial general convention made up of laity and clergy. The central canon of the Church was, and still is, that bishops, priests, and deacons make up the three orders of ministry. The constitution also made the use of the American Book of Common Prayer compulsory.

The revision of the prayer book was an important task, which also conveyed a political message. The liturgical committee decided to retain the text of the English Book of Common Prayer with some revisions. The most important change was the deletion of any reference to the king. The preface to the U.S. prayer book made it clear that the intent of the U.S. church was to remain in communion with the English church but retain its independence to govern its own affairs.

SIGNIFICANCE

The establishment of an American version of the Anglican Church was both practically and symbolically significant. After all, it was not solely the association of Anglicanism with the tyrannical behavior of the British Empire that caused problems for American Episcopalians: Many of the first English immigrants to the Americas came specifically to escape the Anglican Church and to find a place where they could practice Puritanism in peace. With the establishment of the Protestant Episcopal Church, Anglicanism was officially Americanized. It was transformed from the state religion of an imperial power into one form of Protestantism among many and incorporated into what would become arguably the most religiously diverse society on Earth.

—*Pegge A. Bochynski*

FURTHER READING

Addison, James Thayer. *The Episcopal Church in the United States, 1789-1931*. New York: Charles Scribner's Sons, 1951. A narrative of the search of the Episcopal church in the United States for a new identity during the convention of 1789. Addison credits both Seabury and White with strong leadership during the proceedings but calls White "the Madison of the Church's constitution."

1780's

Chorley, E. Clowes. *Men and Movements in the American Episcopal Church*. New York: Charles Scribner's Sons, 1950. A brief profile of Bishop Samuel Seabury, capturing the essence of his personality and exploring his career as a priest, his consecration by the Scottish Church, and his influence on the early Episcopal Church in the United States.

Hatchett, Marion J. *The Making of the First American Book of Common Prayer, 1776-1789*. New York: Seabury Press, 1982. Examines the evolution of the American Book of Common Prayer and details the various editions that eventually led to the revised book of 1789.

Holmes, David L. *A Brief History of the Episcopal Church*. Valley Forge, Pa.: Trinity Press, 1993. A concise account of the sociological, economic, and political factors that shaped the young Episcopal Church in the United States.

Marshall, Paul Victor. *One Catholic, and Apostolic: Samuel Seabury and the Early Episcopal Church*. New York: Church, 2004. An academic biography describing how Seabury adapted Anglicanism for American congregants. Includes a compact disc with Seabury's correspondence, historic documents, and primary sources.

Rhoden, Nancy L. *Revolutionary Anglicanism: The Colonial Church of England Clergy During the American Revolution*. New York: New York University Press, 1999. Examines the experiences of more than three hundred Anglican ministers in America during the Revolutionary War. These ministers faced the dilemma of remaining loyal to the church or repudiating their oaths and altering the liturgy. Rhoden describes how this conflict facilitated creation of an American Episcopal church.

White, William. "The Case of the Episcopal Churches in the United States Considered." In *Readings from the History of the Episcopal Church*, edited by Robert W. Prichard. Wilton, Conn.: Morehouse-Barlow, 1986. This 1782 document explores the democratic concepts eventually incorporated into the U.S. Episcopal Church constitution of 1789. Among its chief ideas is that the laity be given a voice in church government.

SEE ALSO: 1739-1742: First Great Awakening; Oct. 30, 1768: Methodist Church Is Established in Colonial America; 1773-1788: African American Baptist Church Is Founded; Jan. 16, 1786: Virginia Statute of Religious Liberty; 1790's-1830's: Second Great Awakening.

RELATED ARTICLES in *Great Lives from History: The Eighteenth Century, 1701-1800*: Patrick Henry; James Madison; Charles Wesley; John Wesley.

September 24, 1789
JUDICIARY ACT

The Judiciary Act created a federal court system independent of the legislative and executive branches of the U.S. government. Beyond filling a practical need, the act created the third branch of the American three-branch system and began to apportion power to the judiciary, providing it with a role in the day-to-day conducting of the national government.

LOCALE: New York City
CATEGORIES: Government and politics; laws, acts, and legal history

KEY FIGURES
Oliver Ellsworth (1745-1807), U.S. senator from Connecticut, 1789-1796, and later chief justice of the U.S. Supreme Court, 1796-1800
William Paterson (1745-1806), U.S. senator from New Jersey, 1789-1790, and later governor of New Jersey, 1790-1793, and associate justice of the U.S. Supreme Court, 1793-1806
Caleb Strong (1745-1819), United States senator from Massachusetts, 1789-1796, and later governor of Massachusetts, 1800-1807, 1812-1816
John Jay (1745-1829), chief justice of the U.S. Supreme Court, 1789-1795
George Washington (1732-1799), president of the United States, 1789-1797

SUMMARY OF EVENT
The Constitution of the United States created the basic framework for a national government. It remained for the First Congress, meeting in New York in April, 1789, to implement the document. Few congresses have been of greater importance than the first. Virtually every act set a precedent. The vagueness of the Constitution added to the significance of congressional activity. The document

contained many obscure clauses and unanswered questions regarding the powers and responsibilities of the various branches of the federal government. These so-called Silences of the Constitution left Congress with much discretionary power to deal with the problem of judicial authority.

The Constitution, in Article III, sections 1 and 2, provided for an independent judiciary to consist of a Supreme Court and inferior courts. The general jurisdiction of the court system was defined in section 2. The Constitution did not deal with the question of judicial review—the power of the federal courts to determine the constitutionality of federal or state legislation. Nor did the Constitution address itself to the responsibility of the federal courts to interpret the meaning of the Constitution.

Most members of the Philadelphia Convention apparently agreed that the judiciary should possess the power to determine the constitutionality of legislation. The convention's members did not intend that the courts should interpret the document. However, neither of these issues was settled definitively, and much was left to the discretion of Congress.

Work on a federal judicial system began in April, 1789, when a Senate committee was formed and directed to bring in a bill. Its fundamental significance to the new nation was evident. Ten senators from ten different states were chosen, ensuring a committee broadly representative of the new nation's divergent points of view on a federal judiciary. The leading role, however, was played by the Federalist senators Oliver Ellsworth of Connecticut, Caleb Strong of Massachusetts, and William Paterson of New Jersey. To ensure a workable plan, the committee conferred widely with other senators, members of the House of Representatives, and various lawyers and judges.

The principal struggle was over the need for a level of lower federal courts. Antifederalist opponents of a strong central government argued for the use of the state courts as the first instance in federal questions. Federalists contended that lower national courts were necessary in order to safeguard the contract and property rights of merchants engaged in interstate commerce and foreign nationals doing business in the United States.

The First Congress was uncertain as to the proper relationship between the federal courts that they were to create and the already functioning state judicial systems. Although most members of the Congress had been ardent supporters of the Constitution, and therefore nationalist in sentiment, they were fearful that too powerful a federal judiciary would invade the rights of the states. The Judiciary Act of 1789 was a compromise between those who desired a truly national court system and those fearful for the integrity of the state courts. It passed the Senate by a vote of 14 to 6 and the House of Representatives by 29 to 22. President George Washington signed it into law on September 24, 1789.

The Judiciary Act created a Supreme Court, fixing its membership at six justices—a chief justice and five associates. It established a middle tier of three circuit courts, each comprising two Supreme Court justices, who rode circuit, and a district judge from within the circuit. The lowest tier of the federal system was the thirteen district courts, one in each state, with original jurisdiction in both criminal and civil cases. District judges were to be chosen from among residents of the state in which they served. The act also created the office of United States attorney general and provided U.S. attorneys for each federal judicial district. The federal courts were given marshals, serving four-year terms, to attend court, execute precepts directed to them under the authority of the United States, and take custody of prisoners.

The state courts were allowed a limited concurrent jurisdiction with the national courts. Cases arising under the Constitution, laws, and treaties of the United States were first heard in the state courts. The nationalists achieved a significant victory in providing, in Section 25 of the Judiciary Act, for appeals from the state courts to federal courts in all instances where it could be shown that the state courts had failed to give full recognition to the U.S. Constitution, federal laws, or treaties to which the United States was a party—these three constituting the supreme law of the land, according to the Constitution. This appellate jurisdiction implied the power of the federal courts to review the constitutionality of state and federal legislation. In later years, a great controversy arose over the constitutionality of Section 25 of the Judiciary Act.

SIGNIFICANCE

The influence and prestige of the Supreme Court grew slowly during the first decade of its existence. Precedents were established that defined the powers of the Court and its relationship with other branches of the government. In 1793, President Washington requested that the Court advise him concerning certain questions of international law. The Court under Chief Justice John Jay declined to involve itself in extrajudicial or nonjudicial matters. This firmly established the separate and independent existence of the Supreme Court.

1780's

In certain decisions, the Supreme Court did assume the power of judicial review. In *Ware v. Hylton* (1796), the Supreme Court invalidated a Virginia statute sequestering the pre-Revolutionary War debts of British creditors. These debts were guaranteed by the Treaty of Paris of 1783. According to the Constitution, treaties were part of the law of the land and therefore superior to state laws. In *Hylton v. United States* (1796), upholding a Virginia law taxing carriages, the Court not only applied the power of judicial review but also, in deciding whether this tax was direct or indirect, interpreted the Constitution. The lower federal courts were also involved in reviewing state laws.

The decision in the case of *Ware v. Hylton* aroused considerable opposition to the Supreme Court from the Republican Party, which accused the Court of being pro-British. Even more serious opposition was engendered by the decision in *Chisholm v. Georgia* (1793). In that case, two citizens of South Carolina, as agents for a British subject, brought suit in the Supreme Court for the recovery of confiscated property. The Court found in favor of the British creditor. Opponents of this decision immediately launched a campaign to curtail the power of the Supreme Court. The result was the Eleventh Amendment, ratified in 1798, which denied to the Court the authority to decide cases "commenced or prosecuted against one of the United States by Citizens of another State, or by Citizens or Subjects of any Foreign State." States could not be brought into federal courts to be sued without their consent.

In spite of the Eleventh Amendment, the Supreme Court was firmly established by 1800. The Supreme Court, under the dynamic leadership of Chief Justice John Marshall of Virginia, survived an attack by the Republican Party on its independence during the Thomas Jefferson administration and definitively asserted its right of judicial review in *Marbury v. Madison* (1803). The Court became the most effective force for nationalism in the federal government.

—*John G. Clark, updated by Charles H. O'Brien*

FURTHER READING

Brown, William G. *The Life of Oliver Ellsworth*. 1905. Reprint. New York: Da Capo Press, 1970. The biography of a powerful Federalist leader whose judicial experience in Connecticut helped prepare him to draft the Judiciary Act of 1789.

Casto, William R. *The Supreme Court in the Early Republic: The Chief Justiceships of John Jay and Oliver Ellsworth*. Columbia: University of South Carolina Press, 1995. A history of the court during the eighteenth century, describing the court's creation, its members, and its decisions. Chapter 2 focuses on the Judiciary Act of 1789.

Corwin, Edward S. *The Doctrine of Judicial Review*. Princeton, N.J.: Princeton University Press, 1914. A classic study, by one of the foremost students of the Constitution, of the intent of the Founding Fathers regarding judicial review.

Goebel, Julius, Jr. *Antecedents and Beginnings to 1801*. Vol. 1 in *History of the Supreme Court of the United States*. New York: Macmillan, 1971. Chapter 11 offers an exhaustive scholarly examination of the act's evolution.

McCloskey, Robert G. *The American Supreme Court*. 4th ed., revised by Sanford Levinson. Chicago: University of Chicago Press, 2005. A chronological history of the Supreme Court, with information on its creation and the Judiciary Act of 1789.

Marcus, Maeva, ed. *Origins of the Federal Judiciary: Essays on the Judiciary Act of 1789*. New York: Oxford University Press, 1992. Nine substantial essays offering a fresh scholarly appraisal of the act.

Ritz, Wilfred. *Rewriting the History of the Judiciary Act of 1789*. Norman: University of Oklahoma Press, 1990. A major study of the act and its significance in its political context, challenging the work of Warren and Goebel on many points.

Schwartz, Bernard. *A History of the Supreme Court*. New York: Oxford University Press, 1993. An excellent narrative history of the Supreme Court, clarifying complex legal issues with engaging style.

Warren, Charles. *The Supreme Court in United States History*. 2 vols. Boston: Little, Brown, 1932. Revised edition of the most influential scholarly work on the evolution of the Supreme Court.

SEE ALSO: July 4, 1776: Declaration of Independence; Mar. 1, 1781: Ratification of the Articles of Confederation; May 20, 1785: Ordinance of 1785; July 13, 1787: Northwest Ordinance; Sept. 17, 1787: U.S. Constitution Is Adopted; Apr. 30, 1789: Washington's Inauguration; 1790's: First U.S. Political Parties; Dec. 15, 1791: U.S. Bill of Rights Is Ratified; June 25-July 14, 1798: Alien and Sedition Acts.

RELATED ARTICLES in *Great Lives from History: The Eighteenth Century, 1701-1800*: John Jay; Thomas Jefferson; George Washington.

October, 1789-April 25, 1792
FRANCE ADOPTS THE GUILLOTINE

The invention of the guillotine made decapitation more "humane" and gave equality of punishment to all classes. It also made decapitation "easier" and faster, facilitating the mass executions of the Reign of Terror.

LOCALE: Paris, France

CATEGORIES: Inventions; laws, acts, and legal history; social issues and reform; science and technology; wars, uprisings, and civil unrest

KEY FIGURES

Joseph-Ignace Guillotin (1738-1814), French physician, politician, and humanitarian

Antoine Louis (1723-1792), French surgeon and secretary of the Academy of Surgery

Charles-Henri Sanson (1739-1806), French executioner

Louis XVI (1754-1793), king of France, r. 1774-1792

SUMMARY OF EVENT

The guillotine was invented to make execution less painful and to provide one means of execution for all who received the death penalty, regardless of their social class or the crime they had committed. Methods of execution in France, as elsewhere at this time, were cruel and brutal, causing considerable physical suffering to the executed. They were also varied in regard to the type of crime being punished and to the social class of the condemned individual. Only the nobility and upper bourgeoisie had the privilege of being decapitated. The poor were usually hanged in the public square. For certain crimes, however, there were extremely painful methods of execution. Highwaymen were broken on the wheel, those who had committed regicide or crimes against the state were drawn and quartered, heretics were burned alive, and counterfeiters were boiled alive.

In October, 1789, the National Assembly began a debate on the penal code of France. In an effort to make executions more humane and to minimize the suffering of the condemned, Joseph-Ignace Guillotin, a noted physician and member of a small movement that sought the eventual elimination of the death penalty, proposed the use of a decapitation machine as a means of execution. Guillotin's proposal consisted of six articles intended to minimize the suffering of the person condemned to death and to assure the same treatment to all individuals as well as protection of the family of the accused from persecution and stigma. He proposed that all offenses be punished by the same penalty, and that in the case of the death penalty, the means of execution should be decapitation by use of a machine, not by sword or axe. He also recommended that the body of the offender be given to the family at their request, that there should be no confiscation of property, that the family should not be censured or excluded from any public office or profession, and that anyone who reproached a family member for the crime should be publicly reprimanded.

In 1791, the National Assembly passed a law stating that all who received the death penalty would be beheaded. Following this decree, Antoine Louis, a renowned surgeon and secretary of the Academie de Chirurgie et de Medecine de sa Majeste (His Majesty's Academy of Surgery and Medicine) was chosen to oversee the development and construction of a decapitation machine. This type of device was not a new idea. Louis was able to consult drawings of similar machines that had been used occasionally in England, Scotland, and Italy from the twelfth century. He designed a machine that rested upon a platform or scaffold.

Tobias Schmidt, a German harpsichord maker, was hired to do the actual construction of the machine with the assistance of Charles-Henri Sanson, chief executioner of France. The machine was first set up near Schmidt's workshop in the Cour de Commerce and tried out on sheep and calves. It was then taken to the hospital at Bicetre, where it was tested on three human corpses. It was after this experiment with the machine that the blade was modified and rendered oblique. Schmidt is credited with suggesting the oblique blade.

The device was tested again at Bicetre, using three corpses of well-built men, who had died from accidents or short illnesses, to be certain that the blade severed the head quickly and completely. This device, which was now ready for use in the execution of those condemned to death, could be described in the following manner: It was composed of two upright planks of wood that measured fourteen feet and were connected at the top by a wooden crossbeam. The oblique blade, which was weighted and operated by pulleys, traveled down through greased grooves in the sides of the uprights when it was released. The device was placed on a platform with a stair of twenty-four steps.

In March of 1792, King Louis XVI had signed the law adopting the machine. On April 25, 1792, Jacques Nicolas Pelletier, a highwayman, was executed with the

1780's

device, which was operated by Sanson. The machine was then moved to the Place de Carrousel, where political offenders were executed. It was subsequently moved to the Place de la Revolution (the present-day Place de La Concorde), where Louis XVI was executed on January 21, 1793. By this time, people were referring to the machine as the "louison" or "louisette." (There is some controversy as to whether this name made reference to Antoine Louis or to Louis XVI.) Eventually, in spite of Guillotin's protests, the machine became known as the guillotine. It also acquired other descriptive names

THE MARTYRDOM of LOUIS XVI, KING of FRANCE.

DESCRIPTION
OF A
Correct Reprefentation of the GUILLOTINE,
PUBLISHED by S. W. FORES, No. 3, PICCADILLY,
Called, The MARTYRDOM of LOUIS XVI. KING of FRANCE,
With which Print this is given.

The mechanical workings of the guillotine are described in this 1793 etching that represents Louis XVI as a martyr declaring, "I forgive my enemies; I die innocent!!!" (Library of Congress)

among the populace, such as Madame la Guillotine, la Veuve (the Widow), and la Becane (the Machine).

It is ironic that an invention that was the result of a humanitarian's strong desire to alleviate suffering and eventually to eliminate the death penalty should be the instrument of so many deaths and come to inspire fear and trepidation. Such, however, was the fate of the guillotine. The Reign of Terror began in September of 1793 with the rise to power of Robespierre and escalated into the Great Terror with the passage of the Law of 22 Prairial (June 21, 1794), which gave the Revolutionary Tribunal the right to condemn to death whomever they pleased. The Great Terror lasted until Robespierre's fall from power in July of 1794.

This period witnessed the guillotining of approximately twenty thousand French citizens, including nobility, clergy, and commoners. The guillotine deprived the nation of many of its best thinkers and scientists, such as the chemist Antoine-Laurent Lavoisier. It also took the lives of many of the promulgators of the Revolution, including Georges Danton and Robespierre. Although Guillotin was arrested and imprisoned, his neck did not come under the machine's blade. After Robespierre's demise, Guillotin was released. He died in 1814. The guillotine continued to be used as the means of execution in France until 1981, when capital punishment was outlawed.

SIGNIFICANCE

The thought and philosophy of the Enlightenment brought about the invention of the guillotine. It was a physical representation of the period's efforts to improve the life of the individual. Montesquieu, Denis Diderot, Voltaire, and their fellow philosophes (philosophers) believed that humans had the ability to improve the conditions of their lives by the use of reason. To achieve this end, they spoke out against superstition, brutality, violence, and prejudice, including that prejudice that privileged one class over another. They believed in the perfectibility of humans and the right of the individual to dignity and respect. Joseph-Ignace Guillotin, a humanitarian as well as a physician and politician, applied these principles to his medical and political activities. Thus, he proposed the device named after him to minimize human suffering, to eliminate privilege before the law, and to maintain the dignity of the condemned. The quick severing of a head lessened the horror of execution as it replaced long torturous methods of breaking and rending the victim's body.

Guillotin believed that establishing mechanical de-

The guillotine quickly acquired a symbolic import throughout Europe. This 1798 cartoon portrays the British pro-French politician George Tierney as an executioner, standing before a guillotine dripping with blood and gore. (Library of Congress)

capitation as the only means of execution would lead eventually to abolishment of the death penalty. It is ironic that the French Revolution would turn the invention into a diabolical and bloody symbol of death. The revolutionaries unable to maintain control over the political change that they had put into motion fell into a violent frenzy of killing. Either the Enlightenment's beloved reason had left them or they had abandoned it, for they were no longer thinking, just acting brutally, violently, and without respect for human dignity.

The guillotine played an important role in execution from its invention until the last years of the twentieth century. It was adopted by several countries, including Belgium, Switzerland, and Greece. In Nazi Germany, it was used for at least as many executions as during the French Revolution. In 1939, a French law was passed requiring that executions not be done in public. Thus, Guillotin's hope that execution should be private, and not a public spectacle, finally became a reality. The last execution in France actually took place in 1977.

—*Shawncey Webb*

FURTHER READING

Burke, Edmund. *Reflections on the Revolution in France.* Edited by L. G. Mitchell. New York: Oxford University Press, 1999. Treats the mismanagement of change during the Revolution, which turned into violence and terror.

Doyle, William. *The Oxford History of the French Revolution.* New York: Oxford University Press, 1989. Good, comprehensive presentation.

Hardman, John. *The French Revolution Sourcebook.* New York: St. Martin's Press, 1982. English translations of original French documents pertaining to the Revolution (1785-1795).

Hershaw, Alister. *A History of the Guillotine.* London: John Calder, 1958. The best, most-detailed book on the guillotine.

Popkin, Richard, ed. *The Columbia History of Western Philosophy.* New York: Columbia University Press, 1999. Chapter 6 provides an overall view of Enlightenment philosophy, its origins, and its results.

Sutton, Geoffrey V. *Science for a Polite Society: Gender, Culture, and the Demonstration of Enlightenment.* Boulder, Colo.: Westview Press, 1995. Examines the popularization of science, the use of demonstration lectures, and the century's interest in inventions.

SEE ALSO: 1721-1750: Early Enlightenment in France; July 14, 1789: Fall of the Bastille; Jan. 21, 1793: Execution of Louis XVI; July 27-28, 1794: Fall of Robespierre.

RELATED ARTICLES in *Great Lives from History: The Eighteenth Century, 1701-1800*: Georges Danton; Denis Diderot; Antoine-Laurent Lavoisier; Louis XVI; Marie-Antoinette; Montesquieu; Robespierre; Voltaire.

1780's

1790's
FIRST U.S. POLITICAL PARTIES

Philosophical and practical differences led leaders of the United States to form the first political parties—the Federalists, who generally opposed the Constitution, and the Republicans, who mostly supported the Constitution—to advance their interests and ideals.

LOCALE: Philadelphia, Pennsylvania

CATEGORIES: Government and politics; organizations and institutions

KEY FIGURES

John Adams (1735-1826), vice president, 1789-1797, and president, 1797-1801

Albert Gallatin (1761-1849), a congressman from Pennsylvania and Republican leader

Alexander Hamilton (1755-1804), a secretary of the treasury, 1789-1795

Thomas Jefferson (1743-1826), secretary of state, 1790-1793, and later vice president and president, 1801-1809

James Madison (1751-1836), a congressman from Virginia, a Republican leader, and later president, 1809-1817

George Washington (1732-1799), first president of the United States, 1789-1797

SUMMARY OF EVENT

The Founding Fathers did not anticipate the development of political parties in the United States, and the Constitution made no provision for them. James Madison, in writing *The Federalist* number 10, discussed factions (parties) in detail and considered them to be a disease in the body politic. Madison feared the rise of factions, stating, "When a majority is included in a faction, the form of popular government . . . enables it to sacrifice to its ruling passion or interest both the public good and the rights of other citizens." He clearly believed that parties were sources of turbulence, oppression, and corruption. Madison argued that one of the blessings of the Constitution would be its applicability to the control of factions. He believed that a federal and representative form of government operating in a country of vast size would make it impossible for permanent majorities to form. Ironically, within four years Madison became the congressional leader of one of the two political parties contending for power in the United States.

Parties arose in the United States in response to the economic and foreign policies of the Washington admin-

istration. By the end of the debate over Jay's Treaty (1794) in 1796, parties were operating. In tracing their origin, it is necessary to begin with the debate over ratification of the Constitution.

Although there are certain exceptions, those who supported ratification of the Constitution generally became Federalists, and those who opposed the Constitution became Republicans. The most important exception was Madison himself, the "father of the Constitution" and also a founder of the Republican (now Democratic) Party. Patrick Henry, who opposed the Constitution, became a firm Federalist during the Washington administration. For the most part, Washington appointed men who had strongly advocated ratification, while congressional support for Washington's programs derived from the same source.

The debates over Alexander Hamilton's economic programs provided the first serious indication that a strong and vocal opposition existed in Congress. The nucleus for a party was to be found in this opposition, composed mainly of men from the South. Madison opposed the funding of the national debt, the assumption by the federal government of the states' war debts, and the creation of a national bank for two reasons: The legislation favored the North more than it did the South, and, because the power to charter the bank was not one of the enumerated powers of Congress in the Constitution, it was unconstitutional. Madison and others were able to unite their sectional fears with strict construction of the Constitution into a general states' rights philosophy that became the ideological arm of the Republican Party. At this stage of development, although factions existed in Congress supporting or opposing Hamilton's program, parties in a national sense did not exist.

Progress in the organization of parties at the national level and the growth of support at the local level came basically from two sources: implementation and funding of Hamilton's program, and divisions arising from the outbreak of the French Revolution and the ensuing revolutionary wars.

First, paying off the national debt placed an enormous burden on the nation, requiring a tax policy that caused complaints. In particular, the excise tax on whiskey sparked a small uprising in western Pennsylvania. Troops were sent in to crush the rioting, men were arrested, and popular indignation drew many into opposition to Washington's administration. The government was criticized as oppressing the poor to aid the rich.

FEDERALISTS VS. ANTIFEDERALISTS, 1788

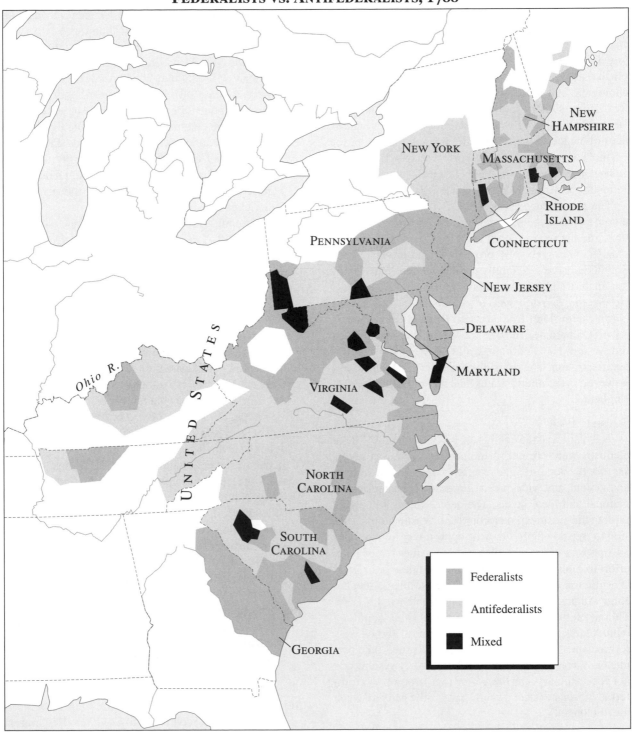

The ratification of the U.S. Constitution was controversial, splitting Federalists—those in favor of a strong central government and ratification of the Constitution—and Antifederalists—those who preferred a weaker central government and greater state powers. This division laid the groundwork for the first political parties in the United States: Federalists versus Jeffersonian, or Democratic, Republicans. Former Antifederalists provided the base for the Democratic Republicans' constituency.

Second, these domestic tensions were coupled with differences that appeared as the French Revolution emerged in Europe and soon plunged the Continent into war. Americans, while basically neutral, openly expressed preferences for either the French or the British. Many people in the United States immediately experienced a psychological association with the idealism of the French Revolution. Others, more conservative, looked to Great Britain as the last bulwark of stability and order against the turbulence of the democratic masses. Hamilton, for example, was outspoken in his preference for Great Britain and his abhorrence of the French Revolution. Thomas Jefferson, however, openly sympathized with the French.

The coincidence of his opposition to Hamilton's economic policies, his attitudes toward the French Revolution, and his sectional residence was striking. New Englanders were generally pro-British and pro-Hamilton. Southerners were generally pro-French and anti-Hamilton. In the middle states, where sectional feeling was less strong, the division was often East-West rather than North-South. Men from western Pennsylvania, such as Albert Gallatin, fell into the anti-administration ranks, as did western New Yorkers, while the seaboard was pro-administration. The divisions were much less clear-cut, however, in the middle states than in the South or in New England.

SIGNIFICANCE

Jay's Treaty was the catalyst of party formation. All the elements were present. A momentous issue was necessary for the bonding. The reaction to the treaty was sharp and violent, and widespread opposition appeared at both national and local levels. The debate raged in the year prior to the presidential election, and Washington's decision to step down provided the opportunity for individuals opposed to his administration to gather forces in an effort to replace those in power. Opposition to the great Washington was dangerous and almost impossible, but John Adams presented no such problems. In 1796, Thomas Jefferson, running as a Republican, contested with Adams for the nation's first position. Parties were formed but, as the next four years would prove, their permanency was not guaranteed. A two-party system was not yet customary, and there were men in power who preferred the existence of a single party—the party to which they belonged.

—*John G. Clark, updated by Michael Witkoski*

FURTHER READING

Aldrich, John H. *Why Politics? The Origin and Transformation of Political Parties in America*. Chicago: University of Chicago Press, 1995. A history of politics and parties in the United States. Chapter 3 focuses on the founding of the first political parties.

Banning, Lance. *Conceived in Liberty: The Struggle to Define the New Republic, 1789-1793*. Lanham, Md.: Rowman & Littlefield, 2004. Analyzes the dispute among Adams, Hamilton, Madison, and Jefferson about the future direction of American government that led to the creation of the first political parties.

Ben-Atar, Doron, and Barbara B. Oberg, eds. *Federalists Reconsidered*. Charlottesville: University Press of Virginia, 1998. Collection of essays about federalism. Part two examines federalism and the origins of American political culture.

Brenner, Lenni. *The Lesser Evil*. Secaucus, N.J.: Lyle Stuart, 1988. Traces the history of the Democratic Party, the oldest continuous political institution in the world, from its beginnings under Jefferson and Madison during the first Washington administration. The study is not entirely favorable, but it does reveal the party's enduring strengths.

Cunningham, Nobel. *In Pursuit of Reason: The Life of Thomas Jefferson*. New York: Ballantine Books, 1988. The public career of Jefferson, founder of the Democratic Party, is explored and presented in a manner accessible to the general reader.

Ellis, Joseph. *Passionate Sage: The Character and Legacy of John Adams*. New York: W. W. Norton, 1993. John Adams, a leading figure of the Federalist Party, is one of the enigmatic figures of U.S. history. This work presents his career in a sympathetic light.

Hoadley, John F. *Origins of American Political Parties, 1789-1803*. Lexington: University Press of Kentucky, 1986. An evenhanded, comprehensive review of the turbulent period that saw the emergence of political parties ("factions," as Madison termed them) and their enduring influence on public life in the United States.

Reichley, A. James. *The Life of the Parties: A History of American Political Parties*. New York: Free Press, 1992. A popular review of the party system in the United States with an informative section on its origins during the early years of the republic.

SEE ALSO: May, 1776-Sept. 3, 1783: France Supports the American Revolution; July 4, 1776: Declaration of Independence; Sept. 17, 1787: U.S. Constitution Is Adopted; Oct. 27, 1787-May, 1788: Publication of *The Federalist*; Apr. 30, 1789: Washington's Inauguration; Dec. 15, 1791: U.S. Bill of Rights Is Ratified;

July-Nov., 1794: Whiskey Rebellion; Nov. 19, 1794: Jay's Treaty; Sept. 19, 1796: Washington's Farewell Address; June 25-July 14, 1798: Alien and Sedition Acts.

RELATED ARTICLES in *Great Lives from History: The Eighteenth Century, 1701-1800*: John Adams; Alexander Hamilton; Thomas Jefferson; James Madison; George Washington.

1790's-1830's
SECOND GREAT AWAKENING

Beginning in the 1790's, the United States witnessed a spiritual reawakening that gave expression to the new social, political, and economic realities of the late eighteenth century. The Second Great Awakening, coinciding with the first decades of the new nation's existence, established a long-standing American tradition of charity and humanitarianism.

LOCALE: United States, particularly the Western frontier
CATEGORIES: Religion and theology; social issues and reform

KEY FIGURES
Francis Asbury (1745-1816), English-born American Methodist bishop
Peter Cartwright (1785-1872), American Methodist circuit rider
Timothy Dwight (1752-1817), president of Yale College
Charles Grandison Finney (1792-1875), American evangelist
James McGready (1758?-1817), American Presbyterian minister and religious leader
Nathaniel William Taylor (1786-1858), member of the Yale Divinity School
Theodore Dwight Weld (1803-1895), a leader of the American Anti-Slavery Society

SUMMARY OF EVENT
The upsurge of religious feeling that began at the end of the eighteenth century constituted one of several major revivals in U.S. history. Designated the "Second Awakening" in reference to the First Great Awakening of the 1730's and 1740's, the revival of the 1790's and beyond followed a period of relative religious laxity. The Protestant clergy complained of the decay of morality, particularly in the West, where access to organized religion was difficult. The spread of Deism, not entirely an elite doctrine in the United States, was viewed as a dangerous threat by orthodox believers.

By the late 1790's, stirrings of revived religious consciousness were apparent in all regions of the United States. Revival among the Congregationalists (Puritan denominations) of New England was precipitated in 1802 by a series of chapel sermons by Yale's president, Timothy Dwight, who sought to arrest "freethinking" among the students at his college. The results were impressive, and revival soon spread to other colleges in New England and then to villages and towns. Lyman Beecher, Nathaniel William Taylor, and others soon were enlisted in the cause of revival of faith. To the south, in Virginia, the Presbyterian colleges of Hampden-Sidney and Washington had already experienced renewed religious concern and would provide a significant part of the Congregationalists' evangelical leadership during the Second Awakening. Western New York, which became one of the most fertile areas of spiritual zeal, knew the winter of 1799-1800 as the time of the Great Revival.

The most spectacular of the early manifestations came on the Western frontier. James McGready, a Presbyterian minister, played the leading role in bringing about the Logan County, or Cumberland, revival in Kentucky, which culminated in 1800, and helped spark revivalism throughout the West. The Cane Ridge, Kentucky, camp meeting that attracted between ten thousand and twenty-five thousand people in the following year has been described as the largest and most emotional revival of early U.S. history.

The Second Awakening affected all the major Protestant denominations, although the more evangelical among them gained the most in strength. The Congregationalists and Presbyterians contributed some of the outstanding revivalists, but their participation in the more emotional phases of the revival was inhibited by their more staid Calvinist traditions. Working together in their Western endeavors, the two sects sanctioned "rational" revivalism, a stand that was rejected by such schismatic groups as the Stonite, or New Light Presbyterian, church. Frontier awakening also saw the birth of new churches such as the Disciples of Christ, a church that advocated Christian unity, a radical doctrine of free grace, and a restoration of New Testament Christianity. Mormonism and Adventism also arose in connection with the Great Revival.

1790's

Quantitatively, Baptists and Methodists dominated the Second Awakening, being the leaders of frontier revivalism. The Methodists, however, were most successful in the West, and by the 1830's constituted the largest religious group in the United States. The Methodists saw notable growth among African Americans and Native Americans, whose membership in the church by the 1930's numbered fifteen thousand and two thousand, respectively.

Like the Baptists, whose numbers also swelled dramatically during the Second Awakening, Methodists were advocates of a free-will theology that complemented the frontier's independent and optimistic character. Emphasis on a simple gospel and comfort with an uneducated clergy also contributed to this remarkable growth. However, the circuit rider, a familiar frontier figure adapted to the American scene by the United States' first Methodist bishop, Francis Asbury, and by charismatic preachers such as Peter Cartwright of Illinois, may have equipped Methodism best to minister to a population at once widely scattered and in motion. The Methodists also enthusiastically adopted the system of protracted outdoor revival service known as camp meetings. By 1825, the camp meeting had become almost exclusively a Methodist institution.

Methodist acceptance of the doctrine that individuals have free will to attain salvation was in accord with a general shift of theological emphasis within American Protestantism in the early nineteenth century. Calvinist sects, including Congregationalists, Presbyterians, and certain Baptists, had traditionally adhered to the doctrine of predestination. In the early phase of the Second Awakening, predestinarian Calvinism and free-will Arminianism were preached side by side.

After 1810, Calvinism was modified by such theologians as Timothy Dwight and Nathaniel William Taylor; later, the revivalist Charles Grandison Finney took the lead in establishing what was clearly an Arminian brand of evangelism within the traditionally Calvinist sector of U.S. Protestantism. The ascendancy of Arminianism appears to have reflected the social and political climate of the country. Although historians have found affinities between Calvinist revivalism and political radicalism in the eighteenth century, by the Jacksonian period the message of free will seemed to many the spiritual counterpart of suffrage and laissez-faire.

Perhaps more significant for the future of revivalism in the United States was the conviction that revivals could be provoked and that methods for creating religious conviction could be cultivated by revivalist preach-

ers, whose ministry shifted from that of a pastor to a winner of souls. Unlike the revivalists of the First Great Awakening—who believed that revivalism was the consequence of a gracious outpouring of God's Spirit, patiently to be awaited—the new revivalists tended to regard revivalism instrumentally as a means or a technique for precipitating religious conviction, inculcating moral principles, or even the restitution of civic life.

At their most successful, these soul-winners became professional mass evangelists, such as Finney, who did much to create the style of modern revivalism represented subsequently by Dwight L. Moody, Billy Sunday, and Billy Graham. With Finney, the preoccupation with theology (exemplified in the Great Awakening by Jonathan Edwards) began to yield to a more one-sided concern with religious experience; revivalism increasingly purveyed a simple religion of the heart.

Another consequence of this emphasis on method and experience was its empowerment of women. Women at revival meetings were encouraged to testify and pray in public. They were emboldened to speak openly of the preacher's opinions and to quote scripture. They formed themselves into voluntary societies that organized and promoted the work of revivalism. In short, revivalism created a psychological and social space for women, within which they could validate their own experience, give voice to their own views, become practiced in organizational ability, and exercise leadership.

SIGNIFICANCE

The tide of religious feeling had begun to ebb by the early 1830's, but the social effects of the Second Awakening were pervasive and lasting. Voluntary societies had been formed to promote religious education and Sunday schools, distribute Bibles, and advance charitable efforts. Moral and humanitarian crusades were launched. A crusade for the abolition of slavery was entered upon by revivalists such as Theodore Dwight Weld, who employed Finney's revival techniques in opposing slavery. Colleges and seminaries were founded which, like Oberlin in Ohio, were dedicated to "universal reform" and the education of women and African Americans. Thus, despite the inherent revivalist concern with individual salvation and the reluctance with which evangelists such as Finney embraced social causes, Finney's own "postmillennialism" involved the belief that the world could be made better in preparation for the Second Coming of Christ.

—*Michael D. Clark, updated by Thomas E. Helm*

FURTHER READING

Cleveland, Catherine C. *The Great Revival in the West, 1797-1805*. 1916. Reprint. Gloucester, Mass.: Peter Smith, 1959. A significant study of the early phase of the revival, with discussion of the social, economic, and psychological factors that shaped it.

Cross, Whitney W. R. *The Burned-Over District: The Social and Intellectual History of Enthusiastic Religion in Western New York, 1800-1850*. Ithaca, N.Y.: Cornell University Press, 1950. Examines the revivals that swept western New York State, with attention to social and religious factors.

Fitzmier, John R. *New England's Moral Legislator: Timothy Dwight, 1752-1817*. Bloomington: Indiana University Press, 1998. Biography, examining Dwight's role as a preacher, theologian, historian, and moralist. Fitzmier argues that an understanding of "godly federalism," the religious system Dwight created, is the key to understanding his life.

Johnson, Charles A. *The Frontier Camp Meeting: Religion's Harvest Time*. Reprint. New introduction by Ferenc M. Szasz. Dallas, Tex.: Southern Methodist University Press, 1985. The first major scholarly study on the frontier camp meeting, with a balanced description of the camp meeting's character, development and role as a social and religious institution.

Luchettik, Cathy. *Under God's Spell: Frontier Evangelists, 1722-1915*. New York: Harcourt Brace Jovanovich, 1989. Captures the flavor of frontier evangelists' experience with excerpts from diaries and journals of eighteenth and nineteenth century evangelists. Includes selections from women and African Americans.

McLoughlin, William G. *Revivals, Awakenings, and Reform: An Essay on Religion and Social Change in America, 1607-1977*. Chicago: University of Chicago Press, 1978. Examines the relationship between the United States' religious awakenings, periods of cultural stress, and social reform.

Perciaccante, Marianne. *Calling Down Fire: Charles Grandison Finney and Revivalism in Jefferson County, New York, 1800-1840*. Albany: State University of New York Press, 2003. Examines the cultural and social influence of Jefferson County, New York, where Finney was a preacher, on the creation of Finney's theology and revival methods.

Posey, Walter B. *Frontier Mission: A History of Religion West of the Southern Appalachians*. Lexington: University Press of Kentucky, 1966. Explores Southwestern revivalism and discusses African Americans, Native Americans, and Roman Catholic expansion.

Thomas, George W. *Revivalism and Cultural Change: Christianity, Nation Building, and the Market in Nineteenth-Century United States*. Chicago: University of Chicago Press, 1989. Explores the structural consequences and causal links among revival religion, Republican politics, Prohibition morality, and economic realities. Decided sociological orientation.

Wigger, John H. *Taking Heaven by Storm: Methodism and the Rise of Popular Christianity in America*. New York: Oxford University Press, 1998. According to Wigger, the number of Methodists in the United States skyrocketed from 1,000 in 1770 to more than 250,000 in 1820. Wigger explains the reasons for this growth, focusing on the church's circuit riders, the role of women and African Americans, and the enthusiastic nature of Methodist worship. He also describes how Methodism influenced American evangelicalism.

SEE ALSO: 1739-1742: First Great Awakening; July 17, 1769-1824: Rise of the California Missions; 1773-1788: African American Baptist Church Is Founded; Jan. 16, 1786: Virginia Statute of Religious Liberty; July 28-Oct. 16, 1789: Episcopal Church Is Established; Oct. 2, 1792-Apr. 12, 1799: Christian Missionary Societies Are Founded.

RELATED ARTICLES in *Great Lives from History: The Eighteenth Century, 1701-1800*: Francis Asbury; Jonathan Edwards; Cotton Mather; Increase Mather; Charles Wesley; John Wesley; George Whitefield.

1790's

1790

BURKE LAYS THE FOUNDATIONS OF MODERN CONSERVATISM

The first year of the French Revolution provoked a scathing denunciation in England by the Whig politician Edmund Burke. Although his lengthy Reflections on the Revolution in France *was not aimed at establishing a systematic political philosophy, Burke nevertheless produced what is widely thought to be the manifesto of modern political conservatism.*

LOCALE: England
CATEGORIES: Philosophy; government and politics

KEY FIGURES

Edmund Burke (1729-1797), Irish parliamentarian and
   writer
Thomas Paine (1737-1809), English-born American
   political philosopher
Charles James Fox (1749-1806), English Whig leader
Mary Wollstonecraft (1759-1797), English philosopher
   and writer

SUMMARY OF EVENT

In *Reflections on the Revolution in France* (1790), a 150-page letter purportedly sent to a very young gentleman at Paris, the British parliamentarian Edmund Burke shared his reflections on the first year of the revolution in France (1789) and, by doing so, established the intellectual framework for modern political conservatism. At the time, conservatism did not even exist as a political term or concept, so it was not Burke's intention to found a new political philosophy (as the French were doing).

Burke was also an unlikely individual to write a polemic against the French Revolution. He had defended the English Glorious Revolution of 1688 and had advocated a policy of reconciliation when Britain's American colonies launched a revolution in 1775. Moreover, as a Whig member of Parliament, he championed many liberal and reform causes of the day, such as granting religious toleration to all but atheists, gradual abolition of slavery, reform of the British East India Company, curbing royal patronage because it contributed to corruption, and liberalization of British policies in Ireland.

Burke's diatribe against the French Revolution also came at an unlikely time. In 1790, the French Revolution was controlled by moderates. France became a constitutional monarchy with a parliament and bill of rights (much like England). In addition, neither Burke nor most other Englishmen had any liking for the Bourbon monarchy or appreciated the almost continual warfare between

England and France that spanned the past century. Besides, the leader of Burke's own party, Charles James Fox, and even Burke's close political friends were enthusiastic about the changes in France. In their minds, France was merely trying to institute reforms that were already part of England's history.

Nevertheless, Burke chose a lengthy letter to denounce the French Revolution while in its infancy and to assert English values. His powerful use of written words and the fact that the French Revolution became increasingly radical after the publication of his letter—leading to regicide, general warfare, and the Reign of Terror—cast Burke in the role of a prophet. He had articulated in the most sinister tones the horrors of a new order, springing from Enlightenment rationalism, which challenged the entrenched interests of an aristocrat-dominated old regime. The themes embedded in the lengthy letter were organized after the end of the French Revolution in 1815 as the basis of a new political concept termed conservatism.

What particularly infuriated Burke, as is seen in the early part of his letter, was the misplaced universalistic belief that Britain had anything to learn from France and that the French Declaration of the Rights of Citizen and Man had any sort of relationship to new liberties to be enjoyed by Englishmen. This Burke attributed to the unrestricted rationalism in human affairs spread by French Enlightenment thinkers—principles that had absolutely nothing to do with English laws, values, or beliefs. Burke argued that the French philosophes and their mediocre political offspring brought to power by the revolution, had no wisdom to offer. Free from all past restraints, and believing they could remodel society any way they wanted, these rationalists had nothing but destruction to offer. In contrast, Britain had its own tradition of order and liberty passed down through the ages as a national inheritance. In turning away from the universal and toward the particular and in stressing English national pride, Burke established an important pillar of later conservative belief, and he dramatically portrayed this belief by arguing that real people are not abstractions but Englishmen, Frenchmen, and Indians. He argued that human beings love their kin above strangers and their nationals above foreigners.

In place of revolution, Burke praised the importance of continuity in political experience. The specific form of a particular society at any given time represented the wisdom of the ages. The present was always composed of a complex mesh of institutions, laws, and mannerisms that moved society over time from primitive savagery to increasingly higher levels of culture. Even strange British habits and prejudices existed for a reason. For Burke, change was slow and organic, like the passing of seasons.

In this argument, Burke established the basis of modern conservatism as the acceptance of slow, organic change. Liberals might move too quickly into the future and stumble along the way; however, absolute disaster would befall revolutionaries who blindly plunged into the darkness of the future without the light of the past. The simple message was that the past provided a solid foundation for the present. The complex theory that Burke used to tie his invectives, sarcasms, and allegories together was that the past, present, and future were one. For Burke, society was composed of those who had lived and those yet to be born, with those living in the present having the imperative of transmitting a slightly improved present as a solid legacy for the future. Hence, he put the "conserve" in conservatism, but he did not make the future a static re-creation of everything from the past. For Burke, the nation was a permanent body composed of transitory parts.

An important part of a nation's legacy was its religious beliefs, which were transmitted through the ages. For Burke and many later conservatives, values flowed from religion and not from the egoistic and opportunistic attempts by individuals to institute new systems of morality. Those in power were there for a reason, evolving from a long and tested historical past. Kings ruled through powers evolving from a nation's historic past and could not be viewed as popularly elected officials in a nation's present.

Those who had power, authority, and wealth (the aristocracy, in other words) had obtained this position from the wisdom of the past, which cast them in the role of the leadership elite. They could not be replaced in the present, as was the attempt in France, by mediocre hairdressers and shoemakers who used demagoguery and chicanery to gain power in the present. The worst chicanery for Burke in his view of the French Revolution was the concept of equality, which he viewed as against nature and subversive to the very existence of order in society. Later conservatives would embrace Burke's elitism and view the stratification of society in terms of power and wealth as an integral part of the natural order.

SIGNIFICANCE

Burke's ideas were embraced first by French émigrés (those who left France in opposition to the revolution) and then by a wide spectrum of Europeans revolted by

the increasing excesses of the revolution. He encountered much wrath for his early opposition in England, including well-publicized denunciations by Thomas Paine and Mary Wollstonecraft. His own Whig Party turned against him.

Burke retired from politics in 1795, at a time when the Jacobin Reign of Terror reached its height, thus validating his prophecies about what happens when a nation cuts its ties to traditional restraints. He fell victim to stomach cancer on July 9, 1797, yet his conservative beliefs were firmly planted in the Congress of Vienna (1815), which attempted to restore Europe (following nearly a quarter century of conflict against the military forces of the French Revolution) to the stability it had had before the revolution.

After 1815, antirationalist thinkers would attempt to return their individual societies to some romanticized point in the past and form movements designated by historians as "reactionary." However, Burke as a conservative would have criticized a rapid leap back into the past as being as dangerous as a radical plunge into the future. Those who equate Burkean conservatism with reactionary doctrines miss entirely the basic difference in attitude toward the direction and rate of societal change.

During the second half of the nineteenth century and the breakup of the Tory and Whig Parties in England, Burke's philosophy became embedded in the newly formed Conservative Party, which competed for power with the Liberal Party. Conservative and centrist political parties formed throughout Europe, trying to maintain stability and slow evolutionary change in the midst of threatening revolutionary upheavals produced by the Industrial Revolution.

—*Irwin Halfond*

FURTHER READING

Ayling, Stanley Edward. *Edmund Burke: His Life and Opinions*. New York: St. Martin's Press, 1988. A scholarly biography and study of the evolution of Burke's political views. Index and bibliography.

Freeman, Michael. *Edmund Burke and the Critique of Political Radicalism*. Chicago: University of Chicago Press, 1980. A study of Burke's role in the reaction against the radicalism of the French Revolution. Index and bibliography.

Kirk, Russell. *Edmund Burke: A Genius Reconsidered*. Wilmington, Del.: Intercollegiate Studies Institute, 1997. An assessment of the life and influence of Burke on conservatism by a leading conservative. Bibliography.

Sack, James J. *From Jacobite to Conservative*. New York: Cambridge University Press, 2002. An interpretive study of the formation of British conservative thought in the pre-1832 world, before the term was part of any political vocabulary. Index and bibliography.

SEE ALSO: May 5, 1789: Louis XVI Calls the Estates-General; July 14, 1789: Fall of the Bastille; Feb. 22, 1791-Feb. 16, 1792: Thomas Paine Publishes *Rights of Man*; 1792: Wollstonecraft Publishes *A Vindica-* *tion of the Rights of Woman*; Apr. 20, 1792-Oct., 1797: Early Wars of the French Revolution; Jan. 21, 1793: Execution of Louis XVI; July 27-28, 1794: Fall of Robespierre; Nov. 9-10, 1799: Napoleon Rises to Power in France.

RELATED ARTICLES in *Great Lives from History: The Eighteenth Century, 1701-1800*: Edmund Burke; Charles James Fox; Thomas Paine; Mary Wollstonecraft.

1790
FIRST STEAM ROLLING MILL

By the late eighteenth century, steam had begun to replace waterwheels as the source of power for English mills. Applicable to ironworks, textile mills, and grain processing, the steam-powered rolling mills would transform England's manufacturing industries during the eighteenth century. Steam power resulted in larger mills, greater efficiency, higher production rates at lower cost, and more flexibility in transportation than the small-scale cottage industries could achieve.

LOCALE: England
ALSO KNOWN AS: Steam roller mill
CATEGORIES: Inventions; science and technology; manufacturing; agriculture

KEY FIGURES

Sir Richard Arkwright (1732-1792), developer of the factory system in England
Edmund Cartwright (1743-1823), British inventor of the steam-powered loom
Henry Cort (1741?-1800), English ironmaster and inventor of the grooved-roller machine
James Hargreaves (1720-1778), English inventor of the steam-powered spinning jenny
Thomas Highs (Thomas Heyes; 1718-1803), English inventor of roller-drafting spinning machines
John Kay (1704-c. 1780/1781), English inventor of the flying shuttle
Thomas Newcomen (1663-1729), English inventor of a steam engine for pumping water
James Watt (1736-1819), Scottish inventor of the rotary steam engine

SUMMARY OF EVENT

The creation of the steam rolling mill in 1790 was a major technological advance that gave impetus to the Industrial Revolution in England during the eighteenth century. The steam-powered roller (or rolling) mill proved useful in iron manufactures, spinning and weaving textiles, and milling of grain—all major industries that placed England in the forefront of Europe's Industrial Revolution.

The invention of the roller mill was made possible by the development of the steam engine in the early eighteenth century. In 1705, Thomas Newcomen invented a steam engine that proved useful for pumping water out of flooded coal mines. Though Newcomen's engine was useful in pumping water from coal mines, however, it could not generate enough power to drive machinery. In the early 1760's, James Watt designed a rotary steam engine that could generate power by burning coal instead of wood, a scarce resource in England. In 1784, Henry Cort, English ironmaster, developed and patented the first steam-powered grooved-roller mill, which allowed the production of finished iron in different shapes and forms. Cort also developed the steam-powered puddling process for decarburizing iron. The steam roller mill led to increased production and use of iron in constructing railroads and industrial machinery, thereby generating a revolution in transportation.

The roller mills not only revitalized the iron industry but also led to the development of steam-powered technologies for the textiles industry. In 1733, John Kay had invented the flying shuttle, which increased the speed of production and generated increasing demand for spun cotton. The market in England was further increased by continental and American factory demands, and faster spinning and weaving technologies became essential to sustain growth of the industry. The steam roller mills answered the need.

In 1763, Thomas Highs teamed with clockmaker John Kay to develop a high-speed spinning machine. They worked secretly in Highs's house while under threats from hand wheel spinners, who feared that steam-powered machinery would put them out of work. Discouraged by their lack of progress and threats of destruction, Highs and Kay tossed their invention out the window, and Kay walked away. Highs decided not to give up and gathered up the pieces to reassemble what became known as the spinning jenny. Evidently, Highs gave his machine to James Hargreaves, who received credit for inventing the spinning jenny in 1767. Highs returned to the development of roller-drafting equipment, again enlisting the aid of John Kay.

In 1767, Highs and Kay finished their model of a water frame. Where the jenny stretched the thread by trapping it in a wooden vice and pulling it out, the water frame achieved a stronger thread by passing the roving through two sets of gripping rollers. The second set of rollers rotated at five times the speed of the first, so the thread was stretched to five times its original length before being twisted by the bobbin and flyer. Kay, at Highs's request, made a working model of the roller-drafting water frame

Workers roll sheets of iron in a steam rolling mill. (North Wind Picture Archives)

for demonstration, but in 1767, Sir Richard Arkwright persuaded Kay to make another model, which Arkwright patented as his own invention. By the same devious method, Arkwright stole ideas from other inventors, and in 1775, he patented models of all the different machines used in manufacturing textiles, claiming them as his own inventions. However, in 1785, based on the testimony of Highs, Kay, Kay's wife, and Hargreaves's widow, the courts set aside Arkwright's patents.

In 1785, Watt's rotary steam engine was adapted for use in spinning machines, and textile mills began to convert to steam power and the use of roller mills. Although Arkwright's reputation as an inventor was tainted, he is credited with developing the factory system that changed industrial England into a workshop of laborers, including children, in automated factories that brought wealth to the owners but impoverished the workers.

During the last decade of the eighteenth century, the cotton mills in the industrial center of Lancashire more than tripled production using steam-powered machinery at every stage of production. The power scutcher was used for opening and preparing the bales of cotton, rotating at high speeds while a fan blew out impurities and mixed the cotton fibers. The cotton lap formed at the back of the scutcher was passed on rollers through the carding machine, then on to the spinning jenny, and then on to the power looms.

In 1787, Edmund Cartwright was granted a patent for the first power loom, which used drafting rollers to take the cloth off the loom automatically. Cartwright built a factory in Doncaster for his looms, but poor understanding of commerce, patent infringements, and public distrust of the steam engine all led to the failure of that factory. He built a new factory that would house four hundred power looms but had installed only twenty-four when anti-industrial agitators burned down the factory. Cartwright abandoned the textile industry in 1793 and moved to London, where he turned his attention to other inventions.

Steam-powered textile machinery boosted England's production of cotton, linen, and woolen cloth. For example, the eight-storied Murray's Mills, established in Ancoats in 1798, included the spinning machinery, warehouses, offices, and a shipping area that linked to the Rochdale Canal via a tunnel beneath the mills. This direct shipping link between the mill and the port at Liverpool was a crucial asset to the success of the mills.

In 1786, James Watt's rotary steam engine was used successfully to power roller mills in the Albion Corn Mill in London. During 1780-1800, England imported large quantities of grain from North America. The grain merchants decided to build new roller mills beside the docks in order to process these grain shipments as soon as they arrived. With improved transportation systems, the processed grain was moved from the dockside mills to destinations throughout the country. The new steam roller mills were particularly attractive to large merchant millers. At first, traditional millers refused to exchange their millstones for metal rollers for grinding grain into flour. Instead, they tried to improve output by increasing the number of furrows or quarters on the millstones. The roller mills were faster, however, and soon were accepted by progressive millers who wanted to improve the quality and quantity of their product.

In the steam roller mills, grain was broken up between two adjustable metal cylinders. Then, another set of rollers or a pair of millstones would be used to regrind the grain particles into flour. Soon, metal rollers were used exclusively, as millers learned how to extract almost all the bran and produce fine white flour with the roller mills. Not only did the roller mills speed up the process, but they also increased the amount of marketable flour produced. Roller mills and added equipment, such as bolting reels, purifiers, and aspirators, required higher capital investment and therefore were more profitable for large urban mills than for small rural mills. Even after the improved transport systems made commercially milled flour widely available, some small water-powered stone-grinding mills continued to serve the local markets. Even commercial roller mills would retain a pair of millstones for processing marketable stone-ground products.

SIGNIFICANCE

The invention of the steam roller mill made possible the transportation revolution that was an essential part of the eighteenth century Industrial Revolution in Europe. The steam roller mill was useful in all three of England's top industries—iron and steel production, textile manufactures, and milling grain: It allowed England to dominate these markets and to become the leading industrial power in Europe.

—Marguerite R. Plummer

FURTHER READING

Ashton, T. *Iron and Steel in the Industrial Revolution*. 3d ed. Manchester, England: Manchester University Press, 1963. Discusses changes in the iron industry brought about by the use of the steam roller mill.

Williams, Robert B. *Accounting for Steam and Cotton: Two Eighteenth Century Case Studies*. New York: Garland, 1997. Provides insight into management, costs of production, and comparative output of steam- and powered cotton mills.

Williams, Trevor I. *The History of Invention: From Stone Axes to Silicon Chips*. New York: Facts on File, 1987. Features brief biographies of inventors and inventions.

SEE ALSO: 1701: Tull Invents the Seed Drill; 1705-1712: Newcomen Develops the Steam Engine; 1709: Darby Invents Coke-Smelting; 1733: Kay Invents the Flying Shuttle; 1764: Invention of the Spinning Jenny; 1765-1769: Watt Develops a More Effective Steam Engine; 1767-1771: Invention of the Water Frame; 1779: Crompton Invents the Spinning Mule; Apr., 1785: Cartwright Patents the Steam-Powered Loom; Dec. 20, 1790: Slater's Spinning Mill; 1793: Whitney Invents the Cotton Gin; 1795: Invention of the Flax Spinner.

RELATED ARTICLES in *Great Lives from History: The Eighteenth Century, 1701-1800:* Sir Richard Arkwright; James Hargreaves; John Kay; Thomas Newcomen; James Watt; Eli Whitney.

January, 1790
HAMILTON'S *REPORT ON PUBLIC CREDIT*

Alexander Hamilton's report to the U.S. Congress on public credit—which gave high priority to paying interest and principal on the securities constituting the national debt—became the basis for the federal government's economic policy.

LOCALE: Philadelphia, Pennsylvania
CATEGORIES: Economics; government and politics

KEY FIGURES

Alexander Hamilton (1755-1804), U.S. secretary of the treasury, 1789-1795
William Duer (1747-1799), New York merchant and assistant U.S. secretary of the treasury
Thomas Jefferson (1743-1826), U.S. secretary of state, 1790-1793, and president, 1801-1809
James Madison (1751-1836), U.S representative, 1789-1797, and later secretary of state, 1801-1809, and president, 1809-1817

SUMMARY OF EVENT

The United States government, operating under the Articles of Confederation, had incurred large debts in the successful Revolutionary War, but the Articles of Confederation provided no tax resources for the national government. The securities issued to borrow money declined in value after the war. Desire to provide a stronger fiscal system and pay off these securities was one of the motives for adopting the new federal Constitution.

When the newly formed Congress convened, one of its first acts was a resolution in September, 1789, instructing the secretary of the treasury to "prepare a proper plan for the support of the Public Credit." Secretary of the Treasury Alexander Hamilton submitted his plan in January, 1790. The *Report on Public Credit* touched off a vigorous congressional debate and was the basis for the Funding Act of August, 1790. This act gave high priority to the payment of the principal of and the interest on the securities constituting the public debt. As a result, investors came to regard United States government securities as a high-grade investment with no significant risk of default.

The *Report on Public Credit* was the first of three classic reports emanating from Hamilton's fertile mind. In December, 1790, he submitted his *Report on a National Bank*, virtually an auxiliary to the funding program. A year later came his *Report on Manufacturers*. Taken together, the reports outlined a comprehensive system of economic

nationalism. They were intended to strengthen the newly formed federal government by enlisting the political support of wealthy entrepreneurs and to promote the economic and industrial development of the new nation.

It was urgent that the new government take steps to provide for the government debt, which amounted, according to Hamilton's calculations, to $77 million. This included debts incurred by individual state governments of $25 million and interest in arrears of more than $14 million. Hamilton proposed that holders of securities and claims against the government could turn them in and receive new securities in exchange. (At the time, these were called stocks; eventually, they would be called bonds.) Payment of these securities' interest and, ultimately, the principal would be given high priority in the government's fiscal program.

The funding of this enormous debt would serve several purposes, according to Hamilton. The credit of the nation would be restored at home and abroad, security prices would increase, and the government would able to borrow on favorable terms in the future, if necessary. Interest rates would be lowered, which would promote investments in land, commerce, and industry. Hamilton believed the new securities would serve somewhat as money, stimulating business.

Hamilton's credit proposals ran into immediate opposition in Congress. Leading the opposition was Hamilton's former ally, James Madison of Virginia. There was no opposition to the funding of the foreign debt, amounting to $11.7 million. It was also agreed that the debt contracted by the Continental Congress and Confederation should be funded. There was considerable debate, however, about Hamilton's proposal to pay off the holders of this debt at its full specie value.

Most of the original holders of the debt had sold their holdings to speculators such as William Duer, often at greatly depreciated prices. If Hamilton's proposal were carried, speculators would receive large benefits. Some members of Congress believed that part of this windfall should go to the original owners. The secretary of the treasury rejected this idea, arguing that such discrimination violated the terms of the implied contract between the government and those who had sufficient faith in it to buy its bonds.

Hamilton's plan for the assumption of the states' debts encountered even more strenuous opposition. Southern states were especially hostile, because many of them had made substantial progress toward paying their debts. New England states, in contrast, had large debts outstanding. Furthermore, large portions of the remaining debts of Southern states were owned in the North. For the states of Virginia, North Carolina, and South Carolina, it has been estimated that nonresident owners, largely Northern, held 53 percent of the total combined debt.

Because of such opposition, Hamilton's measures suffered four successive defeats in Congress. Then occurred one of the classic political deals in U.S. history. Hamilton agreed to support locating the new national capital on the Potomac River. In turn, Secretary of State Thomas Jefferson promised to use his influence to gain Madison's support for the Funding Act, which passed by a narrow margin and was signed into law August 4, 1790. The law authorized issue of three new types of federal securities in exchange for old ones. One component would pay 6 percent interest immediately, while a second (deferred stock) also would pay interest only from 1801. Owners of these securities would receive redemption payments by scheduled installments. A third issue of securities would pay only 3 percent per year and could not be redeemed until all other parts of the national debt were paid off.

A crucial question concerned the willingness and ability of the government to make the payments that the Funding Act promised. One important step was creating a federal tax system, the most important part of which was achieved by imposing tariff duties on imports beginning in 1789. The second step was the consistent commitment of Congress and the successive administrations to scrupulous dedication of federal funds to debt service as promised, even when this required new borrowing, and even when some of the bondholders resided in enemy countries (as during the War of 1812).

SIGNIFICANCE

The funding program got under way in late 1790. In December of that year, Hamilton proposed that the federal government charter a national bank. The proposal was designed in part to make the newly issued federal securities more attractive to investors. Those securities could be used to buy stock in the new bank, stock that was expected (correctly) to pay generous dividends. Thus began a pattern whereby United States government securities became a customary investment for banks, providing them with a low-risk asset that could be sold to raise cash if necessary—a pattern that has continued to exist.

The political accommodation between Hamilton and the two Virginia statesmen, Madison and Jefferson, soon dissolved. Within a year, Jefferson and Hamilton were embroiled in a dispute without hope of compromise over the constitutionality of Hamilton's proposed national bank. Ironically, one of Jefferson's greatest achievements, the purchase of Louisiana Territory in 1803, was made financially possible by the excellent credit standing of the United States government resulting from the adoption of Hamilton's funding plan.

—John G. Clark, updated by Paul B. Trescott

GOOD FAITH AND PUBLIC CREDIT

Alexander Hamilton's Report on Public Credit *functioned as a crash course in national finance and debt to the new Congress, which had little experience in such matters. In the passage below, Hamilton has just finished explaining why credit is important for a nation, and he begins to explain how this vital resource is to be achieved and preserved.*

If the maintenance of public credit, then, be truly so important, the next inquiry which suggests itself is, by what means is it to be effected? The ready answer to which question is, by good faith, by a punctual performance of contracts. States, like individuals, who observe their engagements, are respected and trusted; while the reverse is the fate of those who pursue an opposite conduct.

Every breach of the public engagements, whether from choice or necessity, is in different degrees hurtful to public credit. When such a necessity does truly exist, the evils of it are only to be palliated by a scrupulous attention, on the part of the Government, to carry the violation no further than the necessity absolutely requires, and to manifest, if the nature of the case admits of it, a sincere disposition to make reparation whenever circumstances shall permit. But with every possible mitigation, credit must suffer, and numerous mischiefs ensue. It is therefore highly important, when an appearance of necessity seems to press upon the public councils, that they should examine well its reality, and be perfectly assured that there is no method of escaping from it, before they yield to its suggestions.

Source: Alexander Hamilton, *Report of the Secretary of the Treasury: With His Plan for Supporting Public Credit.* In *A Century of Lawmaking for a New Nation: U.S. Congressional Documents and Debates, 1774-1875* (Washington, D.C.: Library of Congress, 1998-), p. 2042. http://memory.loc.gov/cgi-bin/ampage?collId=llac&fileName=002/llac002.db&recNum=382. Accessed November 15, 2005.

FURTHER READING

Beard, Charles A. *Economic Origins of Jeffersonian Democracy*. New York: Macmillan, 1915. A provocative study that tries to identify the roots of the political split between Hamilton and Jefferson in the economic interest groups strongly affected by policies regarding the national debt and national bank.

Chernow, Ron. *Alexander Hamilton*. New York: Penguin Press, 2004. A comprehensive and meticulously detailed biography, offering new information about Hamilton's ancestry, personality, and relationships with other Founding Fathers. Includes information about the *Report on Public Credit*.

Ferguson, E. James. *The Power of the Purse: A History of American Public Finance, 1776-1790*. Durham: University of North Carolina Press, 1961. Corrects many of Charles Beard's errors and shows how important Hamilton's measures were in saving the country from "currency finance" and creating an environment favoring economic growth and stability.

Gordon, John Steele. *Hamilton's Blessing: The Extraordinary Life and Times of Our National Debt*. New York: Walker, 1997. Gordon argues that the accumulation of the American national debt is not a new development. Instead, it has a long history, originating with Hamilton's ideas that a national debt could create a vital American economy. The first chapter of the book examines Hamilton's theories about debt.

Mitchell, Broadus. *Alexander Hamilton*. 2 vols. New York: Macmillan, 1957-1962. Hamilton's colorful life and political career are fully explored. Volume 2 contains extensive discussion of public debt policy.

Nettels, Curtis P. *The Emergence of a National Economy, 1775-1815*. New York: Holt, Rinehart and Winston, 1962. Chapters 5 and 6 of this traditional economic history present Hamilton's program in economic and political contexts.

SEE ALSO: Apr. 19, 1775-Oct. 19, 1781: American Revolutionary War; Mar. 1, 1781: Ratification of the Articles of Confederation; Sept. 3, 1783: Treaty of Paris; July 13, 1787: Northwest Ordinance; Oct. 27, 1787-May, 1788: Publication of *The Federalist*; Apr. 30, 1789: Washington's Inauguration; Sept. 24, 1789: Judiciary Act; 1790's: First U.S. Political Parties; Dec. 15, 1791: U.S. Bill of Rights Is Ratified; Nov. 19, 1794: Jay's Treaty; Oct. 27, 1795: Pinckney's Treaty. RELATED ARTICLES in *Great Lives from History: The Eighteenth Century, 1701-1800*: Alexander Hamilton; Thomas Jefferson; George Washington.

October, 1790
NOOTKA SOUND CONVENTION

After a prolonged dispute over competing Spanish and British claims to the Canadian Northwest, Spain abandoned all settlements there, ceding the region to the British Empire.

LOCALE: Vancouver Island (now in Canada)
ALSO KNOWN AS: Nutka Sound Convention
CATEGORIES: Diplomacy and international relations; expansion and land acquisition

KEY FIGURES

George Vancouver (1757-1798), British navigator and explorer
Juan Bodega y Quadra (c. 1740-1794), Spanish explorer
John Meares (c. 1756-1809), British trader
Esteban José Martinez (1742-1798), Spanish military commander
Maquinna (fl. 1778-1806), chief of the Nootkas
James Cook (1728-1779), British explorer
Juan Pérez (c. 1725-1775), Spanish explorer

SUMMARY OF EVENT

Nootka Sound is an inlet on the western coast of Vancouver Island, approximately 170 miles northwest of Vancouver, British Columbia. Indigenous peoples have inhabited the island for several thousand years. The first European expedition known to have entered the sound was under the command of Juan Pérez, a Spanish explorer who had made his way north from California in 1774. Pérez's mission was to challenge Russian claims in the northwest. The Russians, who had staked claims in Alaska, had begun exploring down the northwest coast, and the Spanish feared they would encroach on Spanish territories. Pérez traded with Native Americans who came out to meet his ship, but he did not land.

Captain James Cook of England was sent to the Pacific northwest coast in 1778 to try to find the elusive Northwest Passage, a hypothetical all-water route through North America. Cook gave the excellent natural harbor on Vancouver Island the name King George's

Sound but later changed it to Nootka, which he believed was the natives' name for the place. Cook landed and spent almost a month trading for furs with the local people. He did not take formal possession of the area for his king. Captain Cook was killed in 1779 while his expedition was in the Sandwich Islands (Hawaii), but his crew transported the sea-otter furs they had obtained at Nootka to China, where they traded them for enormous prices. For the next several years, traders from many countries sailed the northwest coast and traded with the natives for beaver and sea-otter pelts.

As trade expanded, British businessmen desired a trading base on the northwest coast. In 1788, Captain John Meares, a British trader, obtained permission from a local tribal chief to erect a small building to be used as a house and trading post. Joining him that year at Nootka were several U.S. ships, as well as other English ships. Meares took his furs to China and returned to Nootka in 1789.

Meanwhile, French traders had informed the Spanish government in Mexico of the English presence at Nootka Sound. Esteban José Martinez was sent to assert the Spanish claim to the region. He entered Nootka Sound in May of 1789 and took possession of the region in the name of the king of Spain, with "visible demonstrations of joy" from the local people. He negotiated with them and purchased land on which to build his fort.

The U.S. and Portuguese ships at Nootka quickly agreed they would acknowledge Spanish sovereignty as long as they were allowed to leave with their furs. However, the English ships that Meares had left at Nootka refused to accept the Spanish claims. Martinez promptly seized two of them and sailed them, with their crews, to Mexico.

When Meares learned, early in 1790, of the seizure of his ships by the Spanish, he called immediately for his government to protest the action and asked for $500,000 in compensation for his losses. Spain was prepared to pay restitution, but the British government chose to demand more and to challenge exclusive Spanish claims to territory in the northwest. The British government prepared for war. Spain sought help from France, but the French were embroiled in a revolution and refused to come to Spain's aid. This potential conflict between Britain and Spain was the occasion for the first foreign policy debate of the government of the United States under its new constitution. President George Washington and his cabinet decided not to interfere. Because they were in no position to fight a war with the British, the Spanish soon pressed for a diplomatic settlement. The document re-

sulting from their negotiations, the Nootka Sound Convention, was signed in October, 1790.

The Nootka Sound Convention favored British interests. The British government agreed to forbid British subjects to trade with Spanish settlements or to fish in Spanish waters. Spain agreed to give the British rights to trade freely at Nootka and to restore Meares's property. It also recognized Britain's right to explore, trade, and settle "in the Pacific Ocean or in the South Seas." Both sides agreed to send commissioners to meet at Nootka Sound and work out details for the conduct of trade at Nootka.

Early in 1790, the Spanish sent ships with supplies, soldiers, and artillery to set up a trading settlement and fort at Nootka. By 1792, Cala de los Amigos (Friendly Cove) had about fifty houses and two hundred Spanish inhabitants. During the summer of 1792, Spanish, English, Portuguese, French, and U.S. ships all stopped to trade at Nootka. In August, Juan Bodega y Quadra, the Spanish representative, and George Vancouver, the British representative, met in the Spanish village on the sound and conducted diplomatic negotiations. Bodega y Quadra entertained the many captains of the various trading vessels lavishly. On one occasion, fifty-four people sat down to a dinner served on solid silver plates. Vancouver got along well with the Spanish representative; together they charted the island, which they agreed to call Quadra and Vancouver Island.

In spite of the fact that the two men got along well personally, they could not agree on terms for the formal settlement of the rival claims. Vancouver understood that Spain was to give up all its claim to Nootka Sound, while Bodega y Quadra understood that Spain was to cede only the plot of land on which Meares's building had stood. Bodega y Quadra continually stressed the fact that the Spanish had been given complete title to the land by the local chief.

The two commissioners made some effort to make the great chief of the Nootka, Maquinna, feel that he was a part of the negotiations. They received him on board their ships, invited him to dinner, and made an elaborate state visit to his home. Maquinna's people entertained the Europeans with demonstrations of dancing. The mysterious death of a young Spanish sailor caused a rift between the Europeans and Maquinna's people. The Nootkas withdrew and took no further part in the negotiations. Vancouver and Bodega y Quadra completed their talks and parted as friends, but the real issues between their two governments remained unresolved.

Negotiations between Spain and Britain continued in Europe. In February, 1793, another document, the

Nootka Claims Convention, was signed. This gave Meares $210,000 in compensation, and both Spain and Britain agreed to give up exclusive claim to trade in the northwest. In January of 1794, the third Nootka Convention tied up loose ends and both sides agreed not to establish any permanent settlements at Nootka.

SIGNIFICANCE

In 1795, commissioners from both countries once again arrived at Nootka Sound to oversee the withdrawal of the settlements. By that time, the Spanish had already decided to abandon all claim to the northwest and concentrate their efforts in California and Mexico. Both countries had abandoned their settlements by March of 1795. While they continued to trade with the natives of Nootka, neither country again attempted settlement there. This withdrawal marked the end of Spanish dominance in the Pacific and the beginning of the end of their great empire.

The British government eventually gave exclusive trading rights in the northwest to the Hudson's Bay Company, which competed with various U.S. commercial enterprises for the furs of the northwest. By 1840, the furbearing animals were virtually gone from coastal waters and interior areas. In 1846, after thirty years of joint occupation of the northwest by U.S. and British interests, the Oregon Treaty formally gave possession of Vancouver Island to the British, and it has remained part of the Canadian province of British Columbia.

—*Deborah D. Wallin*

FURTHER READING

Clayton, Daniel W. *Islands of Truth: The Imperial Fashioning of Vancouver Island*. Vancouver, B.C.: UBC Press, 2000. Describes the encounters between the island's natives and Europeans in the late eighteenth and early nineteenth centuries. Includes information on the Nootka Sound controversy.

Gough, Barry M. *Northwest Coast: British Navigation, Trade, and Discoveries to 1812*. Vancouver, B.C.: UBC Press, 1992. Describes how Cook's arrival at Vancouver Island in 1778 initiated a fierce maritime fur trade, setting off a heated competition among several nations, including a rivalry between Britain and Spain for control of the Nootka Sound.

Hays, H. R. *Children of the Raven: The Seven Indian Nations of the Northwest Coast*. New York: McGraw-Hill, 1975. Gives history, culture, stories, and legends of the natives of the northwest coast, including the Nootka. Many photographs.

Johansen, Dorothy O. *Empire of the Columbia: A History of the Pacific Northwest*. New York: Harper & Row, 1967. Presents a detailed account of the Nootka controversy.

Meany, Edmond S. *Vancouver's Discovery of Puget Sound*. 1935. Reprint. Portland, Oreg.: Binfords & Mort, 1957. An annotated transcription of a portion of Vancouver's journals from 1792. Provides an account of his time at Nootka.

Moziño, José Mariano. *"Noticias de Nutka": An Account of Nootka Sound in 1792*. Seattle: University of Washington Press, 1991. An extensively annotated translation of the account of a member of Bodega y Quadra's expedition. Contains a wealth of information about the Nootka people, including a brief dictionary of the Nootka language. Illustrations.

Pethick, Derek. *The Nootka Connection: Europe and the Northwest Coast, 1790-1795*. Vancouver, B.C.: Douglas & McIntyre, 1980. Gives a detailed account of the events and controversies of the time. Maps, illustrations, notes, bibliography, and a detailed chronology.

SEE ALSO: 1713: Founding of Louisbourg; July, 1755-Aug., 1758: Acadians Are Expelled from Canada; June 8-July 27, 1758: Siege of Louisbourg; 1783: Loyalists Migrate to Nova Scotia; 1791: Canada's Constitutional Act.

RELATED ARTICLES in *Great Lives from History: The Eighteenth Century, 1701-1800*: James Cook; George Vancouver; George Washington.

1790's

October 18, 1790-July, 1794
LITTLE TURTLE'S WAR

A coalition of Native Americans in the Ohio Country fought the United States to retain control of their territory. The coalition inflicted the worst battlefield defeat on U.S. Army troops of any Native American force in history, and it prevented the United States from controlling or developing Ohio for four years.

LOCALE: Ohio Valley
CATEGORIES: Wars, uprisings, and civil unrest; expansion and land acquisition

KEY FIGURES
Little Turtle (Michikinikwa; c. 1752-1812), Miami war chief
Anthony Wayne (1745-1796), U.S. general
Blue Jacket (Weyapiersenwah; c. 1745-c. 1810), Shawnee war chief
Tecumseh (1768-1813), Shawnee warrior and leader
Arthur St. Clair (1734-1818), U.S. military commander
Josiah Harmar (1753-1813), U.S. military commander

SUMMARY OF EVENT
On November 4, 1791, Little Turtle was one of the principal chiefs among a coalition of Shawnees, Miamis, Lenni Lenapes (Delawares), Potawatomis, Ottawas, Chippewas, and Wyandots in the Old Northwest (Ohio Country) that defeated an army of fourteen hundred soldiers under General Arthur St. Clair. About 1,200 warriors rallied by Little Turtle, aided by the element of surprise, killed or wounded nearly 950 of St. Clair's force, the largest single battlefield victory by an American Indian force in U.S. history. The victory was short-lived, however; in 1794, "Mad Anthony" Wayne's forces defeated Little Turtle and his allies at the Battle of Fallen Timbers. On August 3, 1795, the American Indians gave up most of their hunting grounds west of the Ohio River, by signing the Treaty of Greenville.

Little Turtle was known as a master of battlefield strategy. Born to a Miami chief and a Mahican (or Mohican) mother, Little Turtle became a war chief of the Miamis because of his extraordinary personal abilities; under ordinary circumstances, the matriarchal nature of the culture would have prohibited a leadership role for him. In 1787, the hunting grounds of the Miamis and their allies had been guaranteed in perpetuity by the U.S. Congress. The act did not stop an invasion of settlers, and by the early 1790's, Little Turtle had cemented an alli-

ance that foreshadowed later efforts by Tecumseh, who assembled an alliance of several native nations a generation later.

Little Turtle's principal allies in this effort were the Shawnee Blue Jacket and the Lenni Lenape Buckongahelos. This alliance first defeated a force of a thousand troops under Josiah Harmar during October, 1790. Harmar dispatched an advance force of 180 men, who were drawn into a trap and annihilated on October 18. On October 19, Harmar dispatched 360 more troops to punish the natives, but the Americans were drawn into a similar trap, in which about one hundred of them were killed. The remainder of Harmar's force then retreated to Fort Washington, on the present-day site of Cincinnati.

Harmar's defeat stunned the Army, whose commanders knew that the Old Northwest would remain closed to settlement as long as Little Turtle's alliance held. General Arthur St. Clair, who had served as president of the Continental Congress in the mid-1780's, gathered an army of two thousand troops during the summer of 1791 and marched into the Ohio Country. About a quarter of the troops deserted en route; to keep the others happy, St. Clair permitted about two hundred soldiers' wives to travel with the army.

On November 4, 1791, Little Turtle and his allies lured St. Clair's forces into the same sort of trap that had defeated Harmar's smaller army near St. Mary's Creek, a tributary of the Wabash River. Thirty-eight officers and 598 enlisted men died in the battle; 242 others were wounded, many of whom later died. Fifty-six wives also lost their lives, bringing casualties close to 950—nearly four times the number killed at the Little Bighorn in 1876 and the largest defeat of a U.S. Army force in all of the Indian wars. After the battle, St. Clair resigned his commission in disgrace. Dealing from strength, Little Turtle's alliance refused to cede land to the United States.

In 1794, General "Mad Anthony" Wayne was dispatched with a fresh army, which visited the scene of St. Clair's debacle. According to Wayne,

> Five hundred skull bones lay in the space of 350 yards. From thence, five miles on, the woods were strewn with skeletons, knapsacks, and other debris.

Little Turtle had more respect for Wayne than he had had for Harmar or St. Clair, calling Wayne "the chief who never sleeps." Aware that Wayne was unlikely to be defeated by his surprise tactics, Little Turtle proposed that the Indian alliance talk peace.

A majority of the warriors rebuffed Little Turtle, so in late June or early July he relinquished his command to a Shawnee, most likely Blue Jacket (although some scholars say it was Turkey Foot). In April, 1790, Blue Jacket had refused to attend treaty councils that he feared would cost his people their lands. His forces were defeated by Wayne at the Battle of Fallen Timbers. Afterward, Blue Jacket signed the Treaty of Greenville and the Treaty of Fort Industry (1805), ceding millions of acres of native land.

SIGNIFICANCE

Stripped of their lands, many of Little Turtle's people sank into alcoholic despair. The aging chief continued to lead them as best he could. In 1802, Little Turtle addressed the legislatures of Ohio and Kentucky, urging members to pass laws forbidding traders to supply natives with whiskey. He said that whiskey traders had "stripped the poor Indian of skins, guns, blankets, everything—while his squaw and the children dependent on him lay starving and shivering in his wigwam." Neither state did anything to stop the flow of whiskey, some of which was adulterated with other substances, such as chili peppers and arsenic.

Little Turtle died July 14, 1812, at his lodge near the junction of the St. Joseph River and St. Mary Creek. He was buried with full military honors by Army officers who knew his genius. William Henry Harrison, who had been an aide to Wayne and who later defeated Tecumseh in the same general area, paid Little Turtle this tribute:

> "A safe leader is better than a bold one." This maxim was a great favorite of [the Roman] Caesar Augustus . . . who . . . was, I believe, inferior to the warrior Little Turtle.

For almost two centuries, local historians placed the site of the Battle of Fallen Timbers along the Maumee River floodplain near U.S. Highway 24, near present-day Toledo, Ohio. A monument was erected at the site, even as Native Americans contended that the battle had really occurred a mile away, in what had become a soybean field. In 1995, to settle the issue, G. Michael Pratt, an anthropology professor in Ohio, organized an archaeological dig in the soybean field. Teams of as many as 150 people excavated the site, which yielded large numbers of battlefield artifacts, indicating conclusively that the Native American account of the site was correct.

—*Bruce E. Johansen*

FURTHER READING

Carter, Harvey Lewis. *The Life and Times of Little Turtle: First Sagamore of the Wabash*. Urbana: University of Illinois Press, 1987. Includes a detailed description of the battle with St. Clair's troops from Little Turtle's perspective.

Edel, Wilbur. *Kekionga! The Worst Defeat in the History of the U.S. Army*. Westport, Conn.: Praeger, 1997. Focuses on a crucial battle of Little Turtle's War— the Miami Indians' devastating attack on American soldiers at the Kekionga Indian village in 1791. Edel chronicles the two-centuries-long conflict between Native Americans and European settlers that led to the battle and describes the settlers' eventual revenge.

Gaff, Alan D. *Bayonets in the Wilderness: Anthony Wayne's Legion in the Old Northwest*. Norman: University of Oklahoma Press, 2004. Military history recounting Wayne's campaign against the Indians in the Ohio River Valley. Includes information about the Battle of Fallen Timbers and the Treaty of Greenville.

Hamilton, Charles, ed. *Cry of the Thunderbird*. Norman: University of Oklahoma Press, 1972. Extensive quotations from some of Little Turtle's speeches.

Porter, C. Fayne. *Our Indian Heritage: Profiles of Twelve Great Leaders*. Philadelphia: Chilton Books, 1964. Little Turtle is one of the twelve leaders discussed.

Sword, Wiley. *President Washington's Indian War: The Struggle for the Old Northwest, 1790-1795*. Norman: University of Oklahoma Press, 1985. Discusses the battles that the U.S. Army fought with Little Turtle's alliance, in the context of United States politics of the time.

Winger, Otho. *Last of the Miamis: Little Turtle*. North Manchester, Ind.: O. Winger, 1935. Concise sketch of Little Turtle's life and his attempts to forge a Native American confederation in the Ohio Valley.

Young, Calvin M. *Little Turtle*. 1917. Reprint. Fort Wayne, Ind.: Public Library of Fort Wayne and Allen County, 1956. A sketch of Little Turtle's life, including the St. Clair battle.

SEE ALSO: Sept. 22, 1711-Mar. 23, 1713: Tuscarora War; Summer, 1714-1741: Fox Wars; Sept. 19, 1737: Walking Purchase; May 28, 1754-Feb. 10, 1763: French and Indian War; Oct. 5, 1759-Nov. 19, 1761: Cherokee War; May 8, 1763-July 24, 1766: Pontiac's Resistance; Apr. 27-Oct. 10, 1774: Lord Dunmore's War; May 24 and June 11, 1776: Indian Delegation

1790's

Meets with Congress; Oct. 22, 1784: Fort Stanwix Treaty; Aug. 20, 1794: Battle of Fallen Timbers; 1799: Code of Handsome Lake.

RELATED ARTICLES in *Great Lives from History: The Eighteenth Century, 1701-1800*: Little Turtle; George Washington; Anthony Wayne.

December 20, 1790
SLATER'S SPINNING MILL

Slater's mill was the first modern industrial mill in the Americas. It introduced both modern textile-manufacturing techniques and modern business management practices to the fledgling United States.

LOCALE: Pawtucket, Rhode Island
CATEGORIES: Manufacturing; science and technology; economics

KEY FIGURES
Samuel Slater (1768-1835), English-born American mechanic and manufacturer
Sir Richard Arkwright (1732-1792), English inventor and manufacturer
Moses Brown (1738-1836), Rhode Island merchant and manufacturer
Jedediah Strutt (1726-1797), English textile manufacturer and former partner of Arkwright

SUMMARY OF EVENT
On December 20, 1790, the waters of the Blackstone River surging through Sargeant's Trench in the tiny village of Pawtucket, Rhode Island, began to turn a waterwheel outside Ezekiel Carpenter's clothier shop. The wheel transmitted power to America's first successful textile machinery built on the Arkwright pattern. A new style of doing business, as well as a great American industry, had been established.

Both were imported from England, results of the ambitious plans of Samuel Slater and Sir Richard Arkwright. Born in 1768 in Belper, Derbyshire, England, Slater had grown up near the banks of the Derwent, a river that powered the world's first water-driven spinning mill. In the same year, Arkwright finally succeeded in organizing the elements of cotton preparation for the spinning industry that was destined to change the course of world history. Within the next two years, Arkwright received patents for his various machines and built his first mill.

When one of Arkwright's partners, Jedediah Strutt, required land and a water privilege to build a new mill in nearby Milford, it was William Slater, Samuel's father and well-to-do farmer and landowner, who arranged the deal. As a result, Samuel was apprenticed to Strutt for the usual seven-year indenture. Because of his father's position and his own aptitude, however, Samuel's apprenticeship was not as a laborer or mechanic but as a trainee in bookkeeping, mathematical calculations, and administration. From Strutt, Samuel learned that the secret to proper management of a water-powered mill was to establish and maintain a continuous flow of materials at the pace at which machines could process them, and to maintain the proper configuration of machines so that no part of the manufacturing process created a bottleneck to hinder that flow.

During this period, England was depending on the American colonies to provide many of the raw materials used in clothmaking; the colonies were not seen as a site for the manufacturing process itself. However, during this period America was acquiring mechanics and a nucleus of small industries centered on shipbuilding. A number of skilled American craftspeople were experimenting in building textile machines, including versions of the Arkwright models. By 1786, two brothers from Scotland, Thomas and Alexander Barr, had produced a carding machine and a spinning frame of the Arkwright design through a subsidy from the Massachusetts General Court, the state's general assembly. Although most of these early machines were never productively operated, they were placed on display in East Bridgewater, Massachusetts, to serve as teaching models. Merchants in adjoining Rhode Island were among those experimenting in textile manufacturing.

Meanwhile, in England, Samuel Slater came to the end of his apprenticeship. Seeing that his country was rapidly becoming saturated with textile manufacturers, he determined that his chances for success would be better in the young United States. On September 1, 1789, Slater left Derbyshire for London, and in November he landed in New York. He secured employment immediately with the New York Manufacturing Company in lower Manhattan, but he was soon disillusioned and sought out Moses Brown, a Rhode Island Quaker who had been experimenting for some years, without success, to mechanize textile production.

In January, 1790, Slater inspected the Pawtucket works of Smith Brown, Moses' nephew, and Moses' son-in-law William Almy and advised the partners that their machinery was un-workable. After some negotiations and a trial period, Slater signed a partnership agreement with Almy and Smith Brown, persuaded them and Moses to write off the machinery they had optimistically collected, and with other craftsmen either rebuild the machinery or build new units. Among those involved were Sylvanus Brown (no relation to Moses), who cut the wooden parts, and David Wilkinson, who did the metal work, assisted by Pliny Earle, a Quaker from Leicester, Massachusetts, who made the hand cards, and an elderly African American named Samuel Brunius Jenks. By the end of the year, the machinery was installed in Ezekiel Carpenter's fulling mill.

The next several years were a time of frustration for Slater, who tried unsuccessfully to introduce modern management methods into the new concern. He considered his responsibility to deliver the most yarn possible and that of his partners to develop markets in which to sell this yarn. Slater's partners, however, were reluctant to manufacture anything until orders had been secured. In 1793, a 49-by-29-foot building containing two floors and an attic was constructed about 20 rods up the Blackstone River from Carpenter's mill, and there Slater organized the machinery for maximum production. Slater also encouraged narrowing the scope of manufacture so that the mill specialized in producing a great volume of a few basic items, thereby functioning as a wholesale outlet for shops along the entire eastern seaboard. Still frustrated by his partners' conservatism, Slater in 1797 constructed the White Mill, directly across the river from the Old Slater Mill, in partnership with his father-in-law and several brothers-in-law.

SIGNIFICANCE

By 1827, Slater held no fewer than thirteen separate partnerships throughout New England. Soon, some 165 cotton mills were working to full capacity in New England.

The Slater Mill in 1927. (Library of Congress)

America had entered the Industrial Age, and Samuel Slater's contribution fully justified the title bestowed on him by Andrew Jackson, Father of American Manufactures.

—*James E. Fickle, updated by Erika E. Pilver*

FURTHER READING

Gordon, John Steele. "Technology Transfer." *American Heritage* 41, no. 1 (February, 1990): 18. Recounts how Slater brought the textile industry to America in the late eighteenth century.

Pursell, Carroll W. *The Machine in America: A Social History of Technology*. Baltimore: Johns Hopkins University Press, 1995. This history of the Industrial Revolution includes information about Slater and changes in the American and British textile industries.

Rivard, Paul E. *Samuel Slater: A Short, Interpretive Essay*. Pawtucket, R.I.: Slater Mill Historic Site, 1974. Although brief (twenty-nine pages), this booklet provides a comprehensive interpretive essay on Slater's role in the birth of the American textile industry.

Thompson, Mack. *Moses Brown: Reluctant Reformer.*

1790's

Chapel Hill: University of North Carolina Press, 1962. Contains a chapter on the Pawtucket story, with emphasis on Moses Brown.

Ward, Nathan. "1790." *American Heritage* 41, no. 8 (December, 1990): 42. Commemorates the opening of the Pawtucket mill in December, 1790. Describes Slater's role in opening the mill and his adaptation of Arkwright's spinning machine.

White, George S. *Memoir of Samuel Slater: The Father of American Manufactures.* 1836. Reprint. New York: Augustus M. Kelley, 1967. Still the most definitive source of factual information, White's work assembles and preserves much personal detail, including a wide selection of Slater's correspondence and other primary documents concerning his life and career.

SEE ALSO: 1733: Kay Invents the Flying Shuttle; 1764: Invention of the Spinning Jenny; 1767-1771: Invention of the Water Frame; 1779: Crompton Invents the Spinning Mule; Apr., 1785: Cartwright Patents the Steam-Powered Loom; 1790: First Steam Rolling Mill; 1793: Whitney Invents the Cotton Gin; 1795: Invention of the Flax Spinner.

RELATED ARTICLES in *Great Lives from History: The Eighteenth Century, 1701-1800*: Sir Richard Arkwright; James Hargreaves; John Kay; Eli Whitney.

1791
CANADA'S CONSTITUTIONAL ACT

One of a series of acts that created a constitution for Canada, the Constitutional Act of 1791 divided the territory into Lower Canada and Upper Canada and created a system that attempted to appease the very different political desires and expectations of British and French Canadians.

LOCALE: Great Britain; Canada

CATEGORIES: Government and politics; laws, acts, and legal history

KEY FIGURES

Sir Guy Carleton (Lord Dorchester; 1724-1808), governor of Quebec, 1786-1791, and of Lower Canada, 1791-1796

William Pitt the Younger (1759-1806), British prime minister, 1783-1801, 1804-1806

SUMMARY OF EVENT

England's defeat of France during the Seven Years' War (known in North America as the French and Indian War) resulted in Great Britain's acquisition, in 1763, of New France, the former holdings of France on the North American continent. This acquisition posed an immediate problem for Britain: how to govern the newly acquired territory. After a series of failed experiments, the British parliament adopted the Canada Constitutional Act of 1791.

The principal difficulty posed to Britain in governing its newly acquired territory was that the two primary groups of inhabitants, French colonists and Canadian Indians, had no previous experience with British methods of colonial government, had cultures that differed profoundly from that of the British, and had been at war intermittently for two centuries with the inhabitants of the British colonies to the south. For France, Canada had been a colony of exploitation, but Great Britain had never practiced direct governance of colonies of exploitation. The British favored privatization of colonies of exploitation, as was the case in India.

The task of governing Canada was profoundly influenced by developments in the British colonies to the south. These were colonies of settlement, and under British rule, Canada became converted from a colony of exploitation to a colony of settlement. Britain's task, then—at least as it appeared to the governmental leaders in Great Britain—was to determine the best way to assimilate a new acquisition so different from those colonies to the south that had been British from the outset (or almost so, in the case of New York). The constitutional development of Canada in this period was an outstanding example of the famous British pragmatism at work.

The first Canadian constitutional document, the Proclamation of 1763, had been issued as a royal proclamation following earlier precedents establishing that government of the colonies arose from royal prerogative. It separated Quebec from the other conquests of 1763. For Quebec, it established a rudimentary system of government by a royal governor assisted by a general assembly to be drawn from the inhabitants. Such an assembly would have the authority to pass laws, subject to approval by the governor and the government in Great Britain, which were to conform with existing British law as far as possible. In actuality, this assembly never met.

Nevertheless, even this rudimentary attempt to assimilate the new conquests to the prevailing system of government in the older British colonies proved unworkable. It took no account of the profound cultural differences between the inhabitants of Quebec, the French-speaking "habitants," and their semifeudal superiors, the seigneurs. Roman Catholics could not participate in any general assembly because they would have had to deny their adherence… to the Roman Catholic Church. All disputes among the French Canadians previously had been settled by French civil law; laws similar to British common law were wholly unfamiliar and unacceptable to them.

Accordingly, the British parliament intervened with the Quebec Act of 1774, ending in the process the old concept that government in the colonies arose from royal prerogative. This act (heavily promoted by the governor, Guy Carleton) recognized the right of the French inhabitants to continue to practice their religion and stipulated that their priests were to continue to receive the payments to which they had formerly been entitled. French civil law was to govern in the province, but English criminal law was to prevail. The act pacified the French Canadians but infuriated the colonists to the south and played a role in arousing the Americans to declare independence.

When that declaration came, sparking the American Revolution, the Canadians did not join the dissidents to the south. Their decision perhaps resulted from the fact that their right to continue in the old ways had been recognized by the Quebec Act. The American Revolution nevertheless had a profound effect on Canada, for it brought a large influx of loyalists into the territories, individuals whose background was wholly British. Although these settlers refused to renounce their allegiance to Great Britain, many shared with the American revolutionaries a desire for self-government. The need to meet this aspiration resulted in the creation of the third British constitutional document, the Constitutional Act of 1791, passed by the ministry of William Pitt the Younger.

This act began by recognizing the difficulty of having the same system of government for the French Canadians as for settlers of British origin. Accordingly, Quebec was divided into two parts: Lower Canada, comprising the lower St. Lawrence lands inhabited by the French Canadians, and Upper Canada, including the upper St. Lawrence River Valley and a corridor west to Lake Huron. Upper Canada's inhabitants were overwhelmingly of British origin. The French Canadians again were guaranteed the free exercise of their religion and, as in the Quebec Act, were provided with an oath to be administered upon taking public office that did not violate their adherence to the Roman Catholic Church.

The act provided that both provinces would be governed by an executive appointed by the British government, with the advice of a legislative council and a legislative assembly. The council was to be appointed by the British government on the advice of the governor, and those appointed would hold office for life. The legis-

---

CANADA'S CONSTITUTIONAL ACT OF 1791

The Constitutional Act of 1791 not only divided Quebec into two provinces and constituted two legislative councils but also set forth the principles under which the counties and municipalities of Upper Canada and Lower Canada were to govern themselves. Section 20 of the act sets forth the basic financial requirements for Canadian subjects to be eligible to vote in elections of local governing bodies.

And be it further enacted by the Authority aforesaid, That the Members for the several Districts, or Counties, or Circles of the said Provinces respectively, shall be chosen by the Majority of Votes of such Persons as shall severally be possessed, for their own Use and Benefit, of Lands or Tenements within such District, or County, or Circle, as the Case shall be, such lands being by them held in Freehold, or in Fief, or in Roture, or by Certificate derived under the Authority of the Governor and Council of the Province of Quebec, and being of the yearly Value of forty Shillings Sterling, or upwards, over and above all Rents and Charges payable out of or in respect of the same; and that the Members for the several Towns or Townships within the said Provinces respectively shall be chosen by the Majority of Votes of such Persons as either shall severally be possessed, for their own Use and Benefit, of a Dwelling House and Lot of Ground in such Town or Township, such Dwelling House and Lot of Ground being by them held in like Manner as aforesaid, and being of the yearly Value of five Pounds Sterling, or upwards, or, as having been resident within the said Town or Township for the Space of twelve Calendar Months next before the Date of the Writ of Summons for the Election, shall bona fide have paid one Year's Rent for the Dwelling House in which they have so resided, at the Rate of ten Pounds Sterling per annum, or upwards.

Source: The Constitutional Act, 1791. The Solon Law Archive. http://www.solon.org/ Constitutions/Canada/English/PreConfederation/ca_1791.html. Accessed August 1, 2005.

1790's

lative assembly was to be elected by the inhabitants. The legislative assembly passed all laws, which however became operative only with the assent of the governor, the council, and the British government.

The act retained for the British government the final authority to approve or disapprove legislation passed by the assembly. The executive remained wholly independent of the legislature, even though in Great Britain at that time the executive was formed by the majority in Parliament. Although the act went part of the way toward satisfying the demands of the settlers of British or American origin for self-government, as the numbers of this group increased it became less and less acceptable to them. Not a few settlers were Americans who took advantage of the favorable terms on which land could be acquired in Canada but who brought with them the same attitudes toward self-government as had prevailed in the United States they had left. They demanded full self-government.

SIGNIFICANCE

The Canada Constitutional Act of 1791 effectively bifurcated Canada, both territorially and, more important, culturally and politically. In Lower Canada, as the number of inhabitants of British origin increased, the division between those settlers and the French Canadian majority became more evident. The governor and legislative council were almost entirely of British origin, although some governors, such as Guy Carleton, sought to balance the picture by protecting the interests of the French Canadians against economic exploitation by the British contingent. The legislative assembly, by contrast, was almost wholly French Canadian in its makeup.

Perhaps one of the most divisive issues in the years following 1791, until the Constitutional Act was suspended in 1840, was the question of access on the part of the executive to funds not controlled by the legislative assembly. The lack of the "power of the purse" meant that the popular representatives in the legislative assembly lacked the ultimate weapon to control the actions of the executive. This lack represented the continued refusal of the British government to allow all taxation to be based upon the consent of the governed. In time, it sparked the revolt of 1837, which shook Canada to its roots and brought about the replacement of the Constitution of 1791 by a system of genuine self-government.

—*Nancy M. Gordon*

FURTHER READING

Creighton, Donald Grant. *Dominion of the North: A History of Canada*. Cambridge, Mass.: Riverside Press, 1944. A history of Canada from the earliest French explorations to 1940. Although it treats constitutional developments only as they arise historically, it gives a good overall view.

Lower, Arthur M. *Colony to Nation: A History of Canada*. Toronto: Longmans, 1946. One of the best accounts of Canadian history. The background of constitutional developments is explored in greater detail than in Creighton's work.

Mallory, J. R. *The Structure of Canadian Government*. Toronto: Gage, 1984. Although this is a description of modern Canadian government, the introduction provides historical background.

Manning, Helen Taft. *British Colonial Government After the American Revolution*. 1933. Reprint. Hamden, Conn.: Archon Books, 1966. Sets Canadian developments in the broader picture of an evolving system of imperial governance.

Nelson, Paul David. *General Sir Guy Carleton, Lord Dorchester: Soldier-Statesman of Early British Canada*. Madison, N.J.: Fairleigh Dickinson University Press, 2000. Comprehensive biography of Carleton, examining his administration of Canada between 1759 and 1796.

Tanguay, J. Fernand, ed. *Canada 125: Its Constitutions, 1763-1982*. Introduction by Gerald A. Beaudoin. Montreal: Éditions Méridien, 1992. The primary source for Canadian constitutions; the texts of all of them are reprinted. The introduction is by Canada's primary constitutional scholar.

February 22, 1791-February 16, 1792
THOMAS PAINE PUBLISHES *RIGHTS OF MAN*

Thomas Paine's Rights of Man *was a response to Edmund Burke's* Reflections on the Revolution in France, *in which the French Revolution and revolutionary causes were heavily criticized. Paine gave a theoretical defense of democracy and republican principles as the ideals of the French Revolution and advocated a remarkably modern welfare state program whose fundamental function was to abolish poverty.*

LOCALE: London, England
CATEGORIES: Philosophy; government and politics

KEY FIGURES

Thomas Paine (1737-1809), English-born American
    political philosopher
Edmund Burke (1729-1797), Irish political philosopher
    and member of Parliament
John Locke (1632-1704), English political philosopher
Jean-Jacques Rousseau (1712-1778), Swiss-born
    French social and political philosopher

SUMMARY OF EVENT

The advent of the French Revolution in 1789 and the subsequent turmoil and erosion of established authority in France precipitated the publication of Edmund Burke's highly critical *Reflections on the Revolution in France* (1790). Burke's hostility stemmed from his conservatism, which was rooted in the idea that the past must be valued for providing a workable and stable framework for all future progress—a principle that was being flagrantly flouted by the French revolutionaries. Thomas Paine, already a champion of the American Revolution and independence, was moved to defend the ideals of French Revolution in his iconoclastic *Rights of Man*, published in two parts on February 22, 1791, and February 16, 1792.

To appreciate the intent and impact of the *Rights of Man*, it has to be examined within the context of Paine's life and intellectual itinerary. After an inconspicuous start in life as a corset maker and customs officer, in 1774 Paine emigrated from England to America, carrying a letter of recommendation from Benjamin Franklin. Immediately, he was caught up in the upheavals of the developing revolution, which launched his radical journalism, and he became a prominent political activist on behalf of American independence and served in the Continental army. Thereafter, he spent some time constantly

on the move between America and France, followed by a trip to England. He then shuttled back and forth between England and France several times, before he settled for ten years in France. In 1802, Paine finally returned to America, where he died seven years later.

Paine himself once said that he was a wanderer, and wandering was indeed emblematic of his lifestyle, but Paine was also an intellectual wanderer: His political and social ideas developed in ways that mirrored his roving lifestyle. From his arrival in Philadelphia in 1774 until his death in New York in 1809, Paine's intellectual itinerary took him through four stages of political and social development. Initially he fell under the sway of the liberal ideas of John Locke and classical republican thought. In France, he encountered and embraced Jean-Jacques Rousseau's notions of community, virtue, and social democracy. Paine's third phase came at the end of the Reign of Terror in the French Revolution, when he found a new spirituality in seeking God's wholeness and oneness in the universe. However, the Deistic spirituality faded away during his final years in America, which marked the fourth and the most despondent phase of Paine's personal life and intellectual standing.

It was in the first phase, under the influence of Lockean liberalism and classical republicanism, that Paine elaborated his ideas about American separation from Britain. They were considered radical at the time, but he had the courage to advocate American independence openly, when others only thought or discussed it privately. Paine was well acquainted with Lockean concepts of human rights and liberties, particularly the obligation to resist tyranny. These ideas permeated Paine's thinking, especially in his influential *Common Sense* (1776), which was his great call for America to separate from Britain and established him as an inveterate vanguard of independence. Paine argued that it was the Americans' duty to demand and win independence from the empire, as well as arguing for his pioneering diplomatic doctrine of avoiding European entanglements.

Paine also used the language of virtue and corruption, which was distinctive of classical republicanism. His contemporary, Burke, who is considered the founder of modern conservative thought, used the same language, but his usage was drastically different from Paine to such an extent that they lost their friendship and became adversaries in the debates over the French Revolution. The classical republicans searched for a virtuous citizenry to overcome corrupt governors. Often, it was the virtuous who sought to achieve public goals that were in everyone's interest, as opposed to corrupt politicians who sought only to attain their own ends and interests.

Paine spoke the language of classical republicanism to argue for the creation of an appropriate structure of good government—the republic. The republic guaranteed that government sought the common good for all rather than the individual interests of a corrupt few. This could presumably be done by ensuring that a virtuous citizenry participated in governmental decision making, which in turn entailed that elections were of utmost significance. When the people elected their representatives, then the governing institutions were based on the balance of the one (executive), the few (the upper house of government), and the many (the lower house). This model was an effective system of checks and balances, and in 1789 the new American government took on this structure with its president, Senate, and House of Representatives.

Intellectually, however, Paine went on to draw upon not only the traditions of both liberalism and republicanism but also the framework of social democracy. With the gathering pace of revolutionary events on the Continent, Paine moved to France, where social and political debates were very much informed by the concept of social democracy articulated through the works of Rousseau. Paine incorporated Rousseau's political philosophy into his thinking, as a result of which he managed to lay the foundations for the most radical and economic proposals in eighteenth century England and America. Although Paine had devoted part 1 of the *Rights of Man* to a direct rebuttal of Burke's assault on French Revolution ideals, the second part ignored him and focused instead on formulating a welfare state project within a Rousseauist social democratic worldview. The astonishing fact is that Paine argued for these policies 150 years before the rise of the social welfare state.

In December, 1792, Paine was tried and condemned in absentia for seditious libel in England, for having written and published part 2 of *Rights of Man*. He was declared an outlaw, and had he returned to England again, he would have been imprisoned for life or even executed. Many publishers and booksellers of his work were taken to court and suffered prison terms from one to seven years, as well as being subjected to heavy financial penalties.

SIGNIFICANCE

Paine has long been a controversial figure, attracting both scholarly and popular interest as a result of his spir-

ited participation in the major social and political issues of his time. His original contributions have managed to transcend time and space and are still relevant to contemporary concerns. In the *Rights of Man*, Paine presented two central arguments that have influenced discussions of governance and social justice.

In part 1, he argued that government should be founded on reason rather than on tradition or precedent and that a democratic society, in which all individuals have equal rights and in which leadership depends on talent and wisdom, is far superior to aristocracy, monarchy, or any type of hereditary governance. In part 2, he argued that political leaders acquired social virtue only when all people were properly cared for, when the needs of the poor became the responsibility of government to alleviate, and when everyone participated in maintaining the health of the community.

Paine's advocacy of social and liberal democracy, with its universalistic orientation, had a great intellectual impact not only on his contemporaries but also on subsequent generations of thinkers worldwide. His ideas were incorporated into the nineteenth and twentieth century internationalist movements, antislavery and anticolonial struggles, and social welfare theories and campaigns. Undoubtedly, Paine irritated many but equally inspired many others.

—*Majid Amini*

FURTHER READING

Ayer, Alfred Julius. *Thomas Paine*. Chicago: University of Chicago Press, 1990. Analytical account of Paine's life, travels, and travails, with a critical examination of his philosophical, political, and religious thoughts.

Blakemore, Steven. *Intertextual War: Edmund Burke and the French Revolution in the Writings of Mary Wollstonecraft, Thomas Paine, and James Mackintosh*. Cranbury, N.J.: Associated University Presses, 1997. A comparative study of Paine's response to Burke in relation to other contemporary reactions by Mary Wollstonecraft and James Mackintosh.

Claeys, Gregory. *The Political Thought of Thomas Paine*. Winchester, England: Unwin Hyman, 1989. A comprehensive commentary on Paine's political thought, especially in the *Rights of Man*.

Fennessey, R. R. *Burke, Paine, and the Rights of Man: A Difference of Political Opinion*. The Hague, the Netherlands: Martinus Nijhoff, 1963. A meticulous account of the relationship between Burke's *Reflections on the Revolution in France* and Paine's response in his *Rights of Man*.

Foner, Eric, ed. *Thomas Paine: Collected Writings*. New York: Library of America, 1995. A convenient collection of Paine's important publications and several essays and letters.

Fruchtman, Jack, Jr. *Thomas Paine: Apostle of Freedom*. New York: Four Walls Eight Windows, 1994. A reader-friendly but rigorous chronological review and reappraisal of Paine's life and thought.

Kaye, Harvey J. *Thomas Paine and the Promise of America*. New York: Hill and Wang, 2005. A thorough tracing of Paine's influence, from the formation of America to the early twenty-first century, on the collective American political psyche.

Keane, John. *Tom Paine: A Political Life*. New York: Grove Press, 2003. An encyclopedic biography of Paine's public and private life.

Woodcock, Bruce, and John Coates. *Combative Styles: Romantic Prose and Ideology*. Hull, England: University of Hull Press, 1995. A literary study of the writing styles of Burke, Paine, and other leading participants in the revolution controversy.

SEE ALSO: May 5, 1789: Louis XVI Calls the Estates-General; July 14, 1789: Fall of the Bastille; 1790: Burke Lays the Foundations of Modern Conservatism; 1792: Wollstonecraft Publishes *A Vindication of the Rights of Woman*; July 4, 1776: Declaration of Independence; Sept. 17, 1787: U.S. Constitution Is Adopted; Dec. 15, 1791: U.S. Bill of Rights Is Ratified.
RELATED ARTICLES in *Great Lives from History: The Eighteenth Century, 1701-1800*: Edmund Burke; Benjamin Franklin; Thomas Paine; Jean-Jacques Rousseau; Mary Wollstonecraft.

August 22, 1791-January 1, 1804
HAITIAN INDEPENDENCE

A massive slave revolt initiated an anticolonial struggle and resulted in the first black republic in modern times and the second successful revolution for independence in the Western Hemisphere.

LOCALE: Haiti (Western Hispaniola)
CATEGORIES: Wars, uprisings, and civil unrest; social issues and reform

KEY FIGURES

Toussaint Louverture (1743-1803), revolutionary military and political leader who fought for Haitian independence

Henri Christophe (1767-1820), Toussaint Louverture's lieutenant, who crowned himself king of Haiti, r. 1811-1820

Jean-Jacques Dessalines (c. 1758-1806), Toussaint Louverture's lieutenant and, as Jacques I, the first ruler of an independent Haiti, r. 1804-1806

Charles Le Clerc (1772-1802), commander of the French expeditionary force that invaded Haiti

Alexandre Pétion (1770-1818), mulatto leader who became president of southern Haiti

André Rigaud (1761-1811), mulatto leader whose forces were crushed by Toussaint Louverture

SUMMARY OF EVENT

On August 22, 1791, a major slave uprising ignited a long, bloody rebellion in Haiti that would ultimately break both the shackles of slavery and the constraints of French colonial rule. Following more than twelve years of continuous revolt, including attacks directed at the might of Napoleon's forces, French Haiti became the first independent nation in Latin America. Having concluded the second successful revolution in the Western Hemisphere, the Haitians established the first black republic in modern times.

In 1697, France had gained control of the western third of Hispaniola (now Haiti) from Spain as part of the Treaty of Ryswick. Long neglected by Spain as a backwater, Haiti rapidly became France's most productive colony. During the eighteenth century, economic activity accelerated, as Haiti became a major exporter of sugar, coffee, indigo, cocoa, and cotton. The high productivity was based on a slave plantation economy. By 1789, more than 500,000 African slaves, often working under abysmal conditions, provided prosperity for approximately forty thousand white planters and twenty-five thousand people of mixed ancestry (mulattoes) who, although officially accorded French citizenship rights, were subject to social and political inequalities.

Brutal plantation conditions led to a high mortality rate and the need to replace slaves, on an average, after twenty years. To escape the ravages of the plantation, many slaves fled to the remote forests and mountains of Haiti to attempt to find freedom by founding their own communities. From these scattered bases the runaways,

1790's

803

Haiti's movement toward independence began with Maroons and slaves demanding freedom from bondage. An estimated ten thousand blacks were killed during a massacre at the port city of Cap François, depicted in this engraving, leading to twelve years of fighting between French colonialists and the black population of Haiti. (The Granger Collection, New York)

called Maroons, launched attacks on the hated plantations to secure supplies and weapons. The most intensive Maroon attacks in Haiti (1751-1757) were led by legendary figure François Macandal and were only repressed after concerted efforts of the white planter and mulatto classes. To set an example, Macandal was burned at the stake in 1758, yet Macandal's revolt was, in many respects, a harbinger of what was to occur in 1791.

The French Revolution of 1789, and its rationale of "Liberty, Equality, Fraternity," shook the already unstable political foundations of Haiti and led to a series of events that culminated in the slave rebellion of 1791. For the white planter class, the French Revolution opened strong possibilities for greater local autonomy. For the mulattoes, it offered hopes of greater social equality and a share in the political power structure. The decision of the National Assembly to grant voting rights to all landed taxpaying mulattoes, and the efforts of the white colonists to repeal these rights, set into motion tensions between the two top classes. A mulatto demonstration for voting rights in March, 1791, led to the seizure of two demonstration leaders, who soon were executed publicly by being broken on the wheel. Also broken were any hopes for peaceful resolution of differences. Ironically, in their dispute, both sides were blind to the revolution-

ary storm brewing among the 85 percent of the population that formed the slave class.

On August 22, 1791, more than 100,000 slaves rose to make their own nonnegotiable demands for liberty. After a week-long planning session in the Bois Cayman (Alligator Woods), presided over by a voodoo priest named Boukman, Maroon and slave leaders decided to unleash the pent-up fury of the exploited majority. In the ensuing carnage, an estimated one thousand plantations were burned and two thousand white settlers were killed. Destruction in the northern settlements was particularly widespread. Survivors fled to the heavily armed and fortified port city of Cap Français to make a stand. Using superior firepower against a motivated attacking force of superior numbers, they fought a fierce battle that exacted a heavy toll from the attackers. It is estimated that ten thousand blacks were killed during the rebellion. However, what might have appeared to be a terminal event to the colonial militia was the initial phase of a thirteen-year revolution for independence and majority rule.

As black forces began to regroup under new, although often divided, leadership, the mulattoes, led by André Rigaud and Alexandre Pétion, continued sporadic action against the colonial militia. Meanwhile, in France, the Bourbon king, Louis XVI, was deposed. The newly formed French Republic soon found itself involved in a European war with two of its adversaries, Spain and Great Britain, eager to intervene in Haitian affairs.

In a highly factionalized and complex political atmosphere, leadership of the black forces was established by Toussaint Louverture, an educated slave and remarkable revolutionary leader who had served as a strategist in the 1791 revolt. He decided to side with republican France after the February, 1794, decree abolishing slavery in French territory. Toussaint Louverture's main goal was the creation of an independent state under black leadership; to achieve this end, he struggled against all foreign parties during the succeeding decade. Lack of mulatto cooperation with his nationalist plans led to open conflict and ultimately to the defeat of Rigaud's forces in 1800.

By 1800, Toussaint Louverture had emerged as undisputed leader of a Haiti still technically under French control. By the constitution of 1801, he became governor general for life. Attempting to reverse a decade of anarchy and destruction, he reinstituted the plantation system and ruled through a military dictatorship. To achieve his goal of prosperity, Toussaint Louverture needed a period of peace. However, revolutionary France had fallen under the command of an individual who favored military dictatorship and a militant colonial policy.

Late in 1801, Napoleon Bonaparte, then first consul of France, decided to return Haiti to more direct French control. In January, 1802, he sent an expedition of between sixteen thousand and twenty thousand troops under the command of his brother-in-law, General Charles Le Clerc. The invading force was joined by both white colonists and mulatto forces under Pétion. Toussaint Louverture's armies were equal in size to the French forces, a situation that may have caused him to decide not to arm the general populace, who could have wreaked havoc on the French in a guerrilla war. Because Napoleon had already reinstituted slavery on Martinique, it would not have been difficult to rally the populace by manipulating the fear that Haiti would be next.

Within three months, Le Clerc was able to wear down Toussaint Louverture's forces. After two of his lieutenants, Jean-Jacques Dessalines and Henri Christophe, deserted his cause, on May 5, 1802, Toussaint Louverture was forced to surrender to Le Clerc. Promised a peaceful retirement, he instead was seized and shipped in chains to a French prison, where he died on April 7, 1803. Le Clerc, his betrayer, died of yellow fever in November, 1802, a victim of the disease that would decimate French forces.

Anger over the betrayal of Toussaint Louverture and the French restoration of slavery caused Dessalines, Christophe, and Pétion to unite with other leaders to drive out the French. Their combined strength, and the tremendous toll taken by yellow fever, undermined Napoleon's efforts to maintain control. Moreover, the resumption of war with Britain in 1803, and the decision to sell Louisiana to the United States, made continuation of the Haitian campaign no longer feasible.

SIGNIFICANCE

On January 1, 1804, Haitian independence was proclaimed, and Dessalines—a former field slave and military commander of Haitian forces during the last phases of the war—was named the new country's first leader. The successful revolution stands as a symbol of the power of antislave sentiment and the desire for independent self-government. Yet, after 1804, Haiti continued to suffer from continued factional struggles between Dessalines, Christophe, and Pétion. Succeeding decades of unstable and ineffective government continued to cloud Toussaint Louverture's vision of a stable, prosperous, and independent state.

—*Irwin Halfond*

FURTHER READING

Bellegarde-Smith, Patrick. *Haiti: The Breached Citadel.* Boulder, Colo.: Westview Press, 1990. A highly readable presentation of major themes and events in the historical development of Haiti.

Brown, Gordon S. *Toussaint's Clause: The Founding Fathers and the Haitian Revolution.* Jackson: University Press of Mississippi, 2005. Examines the reaction of the United States to the Haitian revolution. Some Americans wanted to intervene in support of Toussaint and the rebels, but Southern slave holders, including Thomas Jefferson, rejected intervention because they were alarmed by Toussaint's rise to power and leadership ability.

Dubois, Laurent. *Avengers of the New World: The Story of the Haitian Revolution.* Cambridge, Mass.: Belknap Press, 2004. A chronicle of the Haitian revolution. Describes the initial victory of Toussaint and other rebels, Toussaint's defense of France against British and Spanish invaders, and his imprisonment by Napoleon.

Fick, Carolyn E. *The Making of Haiti: The Saint Domingue Revolution from Below.* Knoxville: University of Tennessee Press, 1990. A detailed study of the influence of popular movements on the course of the Haitian revolution.

James, Cyril L. R. *The Black Jacobins: Toussaint Louverture and the San Domingo Revolution.* New York:

1790's

Vintage Books, 1989. An updated revision of the classic study of the leadership of the Haitian revolution.

Moran, Charles. *Black Triumvirate: A Study of Louverture, Dessalines, Christophe, the Men Who Made Haiti*. New York: Exposition Press, 1957. A short, highly readable study of the roles of the three revolutionary leaders.

Nicholls, David. *Haiti in the Caribbean Context: Ethnicity, Economy, and Revolt*. New York: St. Martin's Press, 1985. A major work in comparative history, which provides an understanding of Haitian affairs from the wider context of Caribbean developments.

Ott, Thomas O. *The Haitian Revolution, 1789-1804*. Knoxville: University of Tennessee Press, 1973. A well-researched, detailed study of the events involved in the Haitian revolution.

Ros, Martin. *Night of Fire: The Black Napoleon and the Battle for Haiti*. Translated by Karin Ford-Treep. New York: Sarpedon, 1994. Originally published in Dutch in 1991, this popular biography of Toussaint is aimed at general readers who desire an understanding of him and of Haitian history.

SEE ALSO: 18th cent.: Expansion of the Atlantic Slave Trade; 1730-1739: First Maroon War; Nov. 23, 1733: Slaves Capture St. John's Island; 1760-1776: Caribbean Slave Rebellions; Oct. 10-18, 1780: Great Caribbean Hurricane; Sept. 29, 1784: Hall's Masonic Lodge Is Chartered; July, 1795-Mar., 1796: Second Maroon War.

RELATED ARTICLES in *Great Lives from History: The Eighteenth Century, 1701-1800*: Joseph Boulogne; Louis XVI; Nanny; Guillaume-Thomas Raynal; Granville Sharp; Toussaint Louverture; Tupac Amaru II.

December 15, 1791
U.S. BILL OF RIGHTS IS RATIFIED

With the ratification of the first ten amendments to the U.S. Constitution, significant limitations were placed upon the powers of the federal government and specific rights and freedoms were granted to individuals and to the states.

LOCALE: United States

CATEGORIES: Government and politics; social issues and reform; laws, acts, and legal history

KEY FIGURES

Roger Sherman (1721-1793), U.S. representative, 1789-1791, senator, 1791-1793, and mayor of New Haven, 1784-1793

James Madison (1751-1836), U.S. representative, 1789-1797, and later secretary of state, 1801-1809, and president, 1809-1817

George Mason (1725-1792), Virginia delegate to the Constitutional Convention who opposed the Constitution

Elbridge Gerry (1744-1814), U.S. representative, 1789-1793, and later governor of Massachusetts, 1810, 1811, and U.S. vice president, 1813-1814

Richard Henry Lee (1732-1794), U.S. senator, 1789-1792

James Wilson (1742-1798), U.S. Supreme Court justice, 1789-1798

SUMMARY OF EVENT

The first ten amendments to the United States Constitution are known collectively as the Bill of Rights. These amendments were added two years after the adoption of the Constitution because of demand from prominent people in the states. Their omission from the original document was not a mistake or an oversight. No such list of rights or privileges was included in the original Constitution because majority opinion held that it was unnecessary to guarantee rights that were already commonly accepted and, in most cases, were already guaranteed by the various state constitutions.

When the Constitution was approved by the Constitutional Convention in Philadelphia in 1787 and sent to the states for ratification, a movement to append a bill of rights immediately was evident. Richard Henry Lee, George Mason, Patrick Henry, Elbridge Gerry, and many other prominent state leaders announced opposition to the ratification of the Constitution because it contained no bill of rights. There is no doubt that these Antifederalists objected to several different parts of the document. They chose, however, to concentrate their attack on the absence of a bill of rights. They correctly reasoned that this issue would bring them popular support.

As the various state conventions met to discuss ratification of the Constitution, it became apparent that the Antifederalists had gathered support for their demands for a bill of rights. The Federalists, who staunchly supported the Constitution, began to show concern and worry. James Madison from Virginia, Alexander Hamilton from New York, James Wilson from Pennsylvania, Roger Sherman from Connecticut, and many other Federalist leaders stepped up their campaign for a quick ratification. Better organized than the Antifederalists and equipped with power and persuasive arguments favoring ratification, Federalists in all states put party machinery into operation and worked hard to promote their cause. A study of the ratification struggle state by state shows that the Federalists prevailed, but the demand for some kind of a bill of rights remained strong.

Pennsylvania, the second state to ratify the Constitution, did so by a vote of forty-six to twenty-three. However, twenty-one of the opponents met afterward and drew up a manifesto demanding the addition of a bill of rights. In Massachusetts, a close vote favoring ratification was preceded by a heated debate on the question of a bill of rights. A compromise was reached by which the state's ratification was accompanied by a recommendation for the addition of a bill of rights. Ratification passed narrowly in Virginia (eighty-nine to seventy-nine) and in New York (thirty to twenty-seven), and both states sent with their ratifications strong demands for changes in the Constitution that would protect personal liberties. Sev-

---

BILL OF RIGHTS

AMENDMENT I
Congress shall make no law respecting an establishment of religion, or prohibiting the free exercise thereof; or abridging the freedom of speech, or of the press; or the right of the people peaceably to assemble, and to petition the Government for a redress of grievances.

AMENDMENT II
A well regulated Militia, being necessary to the security of a free State, the right of the people to keep and bear Arms, shall not be infringed.

AMENDMENT III
No Soldier shall, in time of peace be quartered in any house, without the consent of the Owner, nor in time of war, but in a manner to be prescribed by law.

AMENDMENT IV
The right of the people to be secure in their persons, houses, papers, and effects, against unreasonable searches and seizures, shall not be violated, and no Warrants shall issue, but upon probable cause, supported by Oath or affirmation, and particularly describing the place to be searched, and the persons or things to be seized.

AMENDMENT V
No person shall be held to answer for a capital, or otherwise infamous crime, unless on a presentment or indictment of a Grand Jury, except in cases arising in the land or naval forces, or in the Militia, when in actual service in time of War or public danger; nor shall any person be subject for the same offence to be twice put in jeopardy of life or limb; nor shall be compelled in any criminal case to be a witness against himself, nor be deprived of life, liberty, or

property, without due process of law; nor shall private property be taken for public use, without just compensation.

AMENDMENT VI
In all criminal prosecutions, the accused shall enjoy the right to a speedy and public trial, by an impartial jury of the State and district wherein the crime shall have been committed, which district shall have been previously ascertained by law, and to be informed of the nature and cause of the accusation; to be confronted with the witnesses against him; to have compulsory process for obtaining witnesses in his favor, and to have the Assistance of Counsel for his defence.

AMENDMENT VII
In Suits at common law, where the value in controversy shall exceed twenty dollars, the right of trial by jury shall be preserved, and no fact tried by a jury, shall be otherwise re-examined in any Court of the United States, than according to the rules of the common law.

AMENDMENT VIII
Excessive bail shall not be required, nor excessive fines imposed, nor cruel and unusual punishments inflicted.

AMENDMENT IX
The enumeration in the Constitution, of certain rights, shall not be construed to deny or disparage others retained by the people.

AMENDMENT X
The powers not delegated to the United States by the Constitution, nor prohibited by it to the States, are reserved to the States respectively, or to the people.

Source: The National Archives Experience, National Archives and Records Administration. http://www.archives.gov/national-archives-experience/charters/bill_of_rights_transcript.html. Accessed November 15, 2005.

eral other states followed this pattern, and by the time that Constitution was ratified, it was admitted by all but a few die-hard Federalists that a bill of rights would have to be adopted.

A Federalist in 1788 and a strong supporter of the Constitution from the beginning, James Madison was at first only lukewarm toward a bill of rights, but he assumed leadership of the Antifederalists, who were determined that the first Congress should produce a bill of rights. Although it was believed for many years that Madison himself was the author of the first draft of the Bill of Rights, opinion changed in 1987 as the result of the discovery of a handwritten letter to Madison from Representative Roger Sherman of Connecticut. This manuscript, which was found in the Library of Congress's collection of Madison's papers, actually contains the first draft of the Bill of Rights.

The House of Representatives assembled early in April, 1789, and soon turned its attention to the problem of raising money for the operation of the new government. Madison announced that he would introduce the subject of amendments before the congressional session ended, which he did early in June. Up to that point, a wide variety of opinions had been expressed concerning the manner in which a bill of rights could be incorporated into the Constitution. Some had suggested that the body of the Constitution be amended in different places in order to weave a bill of rights into the original document. Others preferred

a declaration of rights as a preface. Still others thought one inclusive amendment would solve the problem.

As a result of Madison's introduction of separate amendments (slightly modified from Sherman's draft), it was agreed to place the Bill of Rights in a series of amendments. There followed more discussion concerning the subject matter of the amendments. In September, 1789, a conference committee composed of three senators and three representatives worked out a compromise agreement consisting of twelve amendments. The Senate and the House of Representatives both passed these amendments and sent them to the president to be presented to the states for ratification. Two of the twelve amendments were rejected by the states, but the other ten were ratified by the necessary three-fourths of the states by December 15, 1791. In March, 1792, Secretary of State Thomas Jefferson announced to the governors that these amendments, now known as the Bill of Rights, were in effect.

SIGNIFICANCE

The ten amendments that were accepted by the states constitute a powerful charter of liberties, although their effect on many of the most important relations of individuals and government was not potentiated fully until the last third of the twentieth century. It is important to note that the Bill of Rights was designed to limit only the federal government's powers. Because it did not pertain to state governments, it did not provide protection for people in such domains as slavery, domestic relations, law, discrimination, or state criminal procedures. Only with the ratification of the Fourteenth Amendment in 1868, just after the Civil War, did it become possible for courts to apply the Bill of Rights to state and local legal questions.

—*Edward J. Maguire, updated by Robert Jacobs*

FURTHER READING

Amar, Akhil Reed. *The Bill of Rights: Creation and Reconstruction.* New Haven, Conn.: Yale University Press, 1998. A history of the Bill of Rights, analyzing the Founding Fathers' intentions in creating the ten amendments. Amar argues that the Bill of Rights was adopted to protect a majority of citizens against a self-interested government; protection of individual rights was not an issue until the Fourteenth Amendment was adopted after the Civil War.

Broadus, Mitchell, and Louise P. Mitchell. *A Biography of the Constitution of the United States: Its Origin, Formation, Adoption, Interpretation.* New York: Oxford University Press, 1965. Strongly emphasizes the role of public demand in forcing a not altogether enthusiastic Congress to move ahead with the Bill of Rights.

A scanned image of the U.S. Bill of Rights.

Jensen, Merrill. *The Making of the American Constitution*. Princeton, N.J.: Van Nostrand, 1964. Includes a section on the Bill of Rights and a copy of the Virginia amendments of June 27, 1788, which show the kind of rights that were being demanded by the states.

Levy, Leonard W., and Dennis J. Mahoney. *The Framing and Ratification of the Constitution*. New York: Macmillan, 1987. Useful essays describing the intent and politics of the Constitution and Bill of Rights.

Lewis, Thomas T., ed. *The Bill of Rights*. 2 vols. Pasadena, Calif.: Salem Press, 2002. A collection of almost four hundred articles. Volume 1 contains articles on the Bill of Rights, its individual amendments, and issues related to the document. Volume 2 features articles on court cases, the Declaration of Independence, and the U.S. Constitution.

Rutland, Robert A. *Birth of the Bill of Rights, 1776-1791*. Chapel Hill: University of North Carolina Press, 1955. Complete history of the Bill of Rights. Excellent except for the omission of Roger Sherman's contribution, which was not known when this book was written.

Weinberger, Andrew D. *Freedom and Protection: The Bill of Rights*. San Francisco, Calif.: Chandler, 1962. Takes a broader view of the Bill of Rights than most books. Includes in the Bill of Rights the first ten amendments, amendments Thirteen, Fourteen, Fifteen, and Nineteen, and those parts of the original Constitution that deal with personal liberty.

SEE ALSO: Sept. 5-Oct. 26, 1774: First Continental Congress; Apr. 19, 1775-Oct. 19, 1781: American Revolutionary War; May 10-Aug. 2, 1775: Second Continental Congress; July 4, 1776: Declaration of Independence; Mar. 1, 1781: Ratification of the Articles of Confederation; Sept. 17, 1787: U.S. Constitution Is Adopted; Oct. 27, 1787-May, 1788: Publication of *The Federalist*; Sept. 24, 1789: Judiciary Act; June 25-July 14, 1798: Alien and Sedition Acts.

RELATED ARTICLES in *Great Lives from History: The Eighteenth Century, 1701-1800*: Elbridge Gerry; Alexander Hamilton; John Jay; Thomas Jefferson; James Madison; George Mason; Roger Sherman; George Washington; James Wilson.

1792
WOLLSTONECRAFT PUBLISHES *A VINDICATION OF THE RIGHTS OF WOMAN*

English writer and feminist Mary Wollstonecraft wrote and published the first recognized political work advocating gender equality, especially in education.

LOCALE: England
CATEGORIES: Women's rights; social issues and reform; literature

KEY FIGURES
Mary Wollstonecraft (1759-1797), an English writer and feminist
Edmund Burke (1729-1797), British statesman and conservative philosopher
William Godwin (1756-1836), a British political writer and novelist, husband of Wollstonecraft, and father of novelist Mary Shelley

SUMMARY OF EVENT

In 1791, the second edition of Mary Wollstonecraft's *A Vindication of the Rights of Man* appeared—the first edition was published without her name. This book-length response to Edmund Burke's attack on the French Revolution, *Reflections on the Revolution in France* (1790),

which focused upon the living conditions of the British lower class, was an immediate success and provided a place for Wollstonecraft among the London literati, which included such luminaries as publisher Joseph Johnson, poet William Blake, and Swiss-born painter Henry Fuseli.

A year later, in 1792, Wollstonecraft highlighted underprivileged women in her most popular work, *A Vindication of the Rights of Woman*. In this radical pioneering work, produced in an amazing six weeks time, Wollstonecraft analyzes the social conditions of the period, painting women as an oppressed class, repudiated of any sort of rights, political and domestic. As a result of this oppression, women, she maintains, have no chance to develop into responsible and reasonable human beings:

> Hapless woman! what can be expected from thee when the beings on whom thou art said naturally to depend for reason and support, have all an interest in deceiving thee!

Since they must depend totally on men for sustenance, she argues, women are forced to be deceptive. Therefore, marriages cannot be truly happy unions. Primarily, she attacks the educational restrictions, that "grand source of misery," that keeps women in "ignorance and slavish dependency." A feminine weakness of character is brought about by a "confined education," she strongly asserts.

Upper-class women, she also argues, do not have enough physical and mental stimulus. They are kept in a perpetual state of idleness, like hothouse flowers, with beauty their only purpose. This passivity instills in women an overblown sense of vanity and an insistent need to please. The protecting and sheltering of women, she maintains, in an effort to keep them "innocent," results only in keeping them childish and enfeebles them with a sense of "false refinement." As a result, she argues, women's "minds are not in a healthy state." This social situation oppresses not only women but also men. Women should not be placed on thrones, she admonishes, but should be educated to enable them to become "more respectable members of society." In short, young women should be educated in the same manner as young men. In an effort to improve the lives of both genders and to provide happier marriages, boys and girls—rich and poor—should be educated together and, in order to avoid vanity, dressed in uniforms. She breaks new ground by strongly advocating sex education: "truth may always be told to children," she writes, "if it be told gravely, but it is the immodesty of affected modesty, that does all the mischief." The author believed that true freedom could only occur with gender equality.

Wollstonecraft's early life experiences provide an effective backdrop for her famous treatise *A Vindication of the Rights of Woman*, which includes in particular the concurring themes of women's lack of education, resultant poverty, and "unhealthy minds." Her own personal history provided her with firsthand observations of the impediments and indignities suffered by women. This sense of injustice, coupled with an indomitable spirit and gifted writing ability, furnished the fuel for this first classic on equal rights.

Born in Spitalfields, London, the second of seven children born to a middle-class weaver and his wife, Mary Wollstonecraft received little education. The family lived in a variety of places, falling down the social ladder with each new move. As the oldest girl, Wollstonecraft tried to protect her mother from the physical abuse of a drunken tyran-

---

PROPERTY AND WOMEN'S OPPRESSION

Mary Wollstonecraft, like many of the most famous and influential feminists, did not limit her analysis of patriarchal society solely to a discussion of gender. She produced, rather, a synthesis of all the social imbalances and inequities that she observed and explained the relationship of gender oppression to other social problems. In the ninth chapter of A Vindication of the Rights of Woman, *excerpted here, she discusses the overly materialistic nature of British society, and the connection between the distribution of private property and women's oppression.*

From the respect paid to property flow, as from a poisoned fountain, most of the evils and vices which render this world such a dreary scene to the contemplative mind. For it is in the most polished society that noisome reptiles and venomous serpents lurk under the rank herbage; and there is voluptuousness pampered by the still sultry air, which relaxes every good disposition before it ripens into virtue.

One class presses on another; for all are aiming to procure respect on account of their property: and property, once gained, will procure the respect due only to talents and virtue. Men neglect the duties incumbent on man, yet are treated like demigods; religion is also separated from morality by a ceremonial veil, yet men wonder that the world is almost, literally speaking, a den of sharpers or oppressors. . . .

It is vain to expect virtue from women till they are, in some degree, independent of men; nay, it is vain to expect that strength of natural affection, which would make them good wives and mothers. Whilst they are absolutely dependent on their husbands they will be cunning, mean, and selfish, and the men who can be gratified by the fawning fondness of spaniel-like affection, have not much delicacy, for love is not to be bought, in any sense of the words, its silken wings are instantly shrivelled up when any thing beside a return in kind is sought. Yet whilst wealth enervates men; and women live, as it were, by their personal charms, how can we expect them to discharge those ennobling duties which equally require exertion and self-denial. Hereditary property sophisticates the mind, and the unfortunate victims to it, if I may so express myself, swathed from their birth, seldom exert the locomotive faculty of body or mind; and, thus viewing every thing through one medium, and that a false one, they are unable to discern in what true merit and happiness consist. False, indeed, must be the light when the drapery of situation hides the man, and makes him stalk in masquerade, dragging from one scene of dissipation to another the nerveless limbs that hang with stupid listlessness, and rolling round the vacant eye which plainly tells us that there is no mind at home.

Source: Mary Wollstonecraft, *A Vindication of the Rights of Woman.* Chapter 9. University of Wales, Swansea, Politics Hypertext Library. http://www.swan.ac.uk/poli/texts/wollstonecraft/vindij.htm. Accessed November 15, 2005.

nical father. After her mother's death and her sister Eliza Bishop's marriage, she lived with her friend, Fanny Blood, and helped to support the faltering Blood family through needlecraft. Wollstonecraft found her sister Eliza mentally irrational after the birth of a daughter, and suspecting the nervous breakdown to be the result of ill treatment by the husband, removed her sister to safety.

Women at this time had no political rights: Wives were prohibited from leaving their husbands and mothers from gaining custody of their children. Eliza's child died before age one while her mother, in hiding, awaited a legal separation. Penniless, Wollstonecraft, Bishop, and Blood started a school at a time when women's occupations were limited to nurses, servants, and minor shop-clerk positions. The school, however, was short-lived because of Blood's marriage and move to Portugal, her subsequent death after childbirth, and Wollstonecraft's absence from the school during these crises. Wollstonecraft resided briefly at Eton, where she observed one of the oldest private schools, before taking a job as a governess to an aristocratic family in Ireland. After ten months there, she returned to London in 1788, determined to make a living through her pen.

After the publication of *A Vindication of the Rights of Woman*, Wollstonecraft traveled to France, where she became deeply involved in the French political cause and lived through the French Revolution, reported later in her *A Historical and Moral View of the French Revolution* (1794). While in Paris, Wollstonecraft became passionately involved with the American businessman Gilbert Imlay, with whom she had a daughter, Fanny, in 1794. Despondent over Imlay's decision to end their affair, Wollstonecraft twice attempted suicide in 1795. Concerned about Wollstonecraft's health, Imlay encouraged her to travel to Scandinavia as his business representative; her journals and letters to him were later published as *Letters Written During a Short Residence in Sweden, Norway, and Denmark* (1796). In 1797, she married William Godwin. She died soon after giving birth to their daughter Mary.

Wollstonecraft's *Vindication of the Rights of Woman* was not the first book advocating equal rights. Wollstonecraft herself was inspired by, and indeed, very favorably reviewed, Catherine Macaulay's *Letters on Education with Observations on Religious and Metaphysical Subjects* (1790). Wollstonecraft's passionate work, however, originating in firsthand knowledge, cried out to a readership deeply aware of social injustice. It was both acclaimed and denigrated. On one hand, popular poets Robert Southey and William Blake wrote poems prais-

ing her: "To Mary Wollstonecraft" and "Mary," respectively. On the other hand, she was castigated for her masculine attitude and roughness and, in particular, for her views that women should receive sex education.

SIGNIFICANCE

Soon after her death, Wollstonecraft's husband Godwin published *Memoirs of the Author of "A Vindication of the Rights of Woman,"* in which he divulged details of the author's life including her affair with Gilbert Imlay, her subsequent suicide attempts, and her religious doubts. As a result of Godwin's publication, Wollstonecraft's reputation suffered severely, with more attention being paid to her scandalous life than to her written work. As a result, *A Vindication of the Rights of Woman* was mostly neglected during the Victorian era. In the United States, however, Wollstonecraft's tract played an important role in the nineteenth century women's movement. Although she was acknowledged by Elizabeth Cady Stanton and Susan B. Anthony in the 1881 *History of Women Suffrage* as someone who demanded for women "the widest opportunities of education, industry and political knowledge, and the right of representation," her treatise did not receive full recognition as a classic in feminist literature until the late twentieth century.

—*M. Casey Diana*

FURTHER READING

Flexner, Eleanor. *Mary Wollstonecraft*. New York: Coward, McCann & Geoghegan, 1972. An approachable analysis and discussion of Wollstonecraft's life and philosophy.

Franklin, Caroline. *Mary Wollstonecraft: A Literary Life*. New York: Palgrave Macmillan, 2004. Describes the influences that led Wollstonecraft to become a writer. For Franklin, Wollstonecraft exemplifies many women of her time who spread literacy and used print culture to advocate reform. By the 1790's, the role of women as educators and reformers assumed a more political dimension.

Gunther-Canada, Wendy. "The Politics of Sense and Sensibility: Mary Wollstonecraft and Catherine Macaulay Graham on Edmund Burke's *Reflections on the Revolution in France*." In *Women Writers and the Early Modern British Political Tradition*, edited by Hilda L. Smith. New York: Cambridge University Press, 1998. Analyzes Wollstonecraft's and Macaulay's rhetorical and argumentative strategies in response to Edmund Burke's classic conservative treatise.

_____. *Rebel Writer: Mary Wollstonecraft and Enlightenment Politics*. Dekalb: Northern Illinois Uni-

1790's

versity Press, 2001. Places Wollstonecraft's writing within the context of the political writing of her time. Describes her interpretation of women's images in the works of Jean-Jacques Rousseau and other eighteenth century writers, her views of women's place in society, her relation to the work of Edmund Burke, and how *A Vindication of the Rights of Woman* exemplifies women's writing on education.

Jacobs, Diane. *Her Own Woman: The Life of Mary Wollstonecraft*. New York: Simon & Schuster, 2001. A comprehensive biography, generally more sympathetic toward Wollstonecraft than many other biographies. Jacobs relates Wollstonecraft's personal shortcomings to her frustration with society's limited expectations for women.

Paulson, Ronald. *Representations of Revolution*. New Haven, Conn.: Yale University Press, 1983. Chapter 3 of this scholarly work provides an in-depth discussion of Wollstonecraft's work in relation to the French Revolution.

Sherwood, Frances. *Vindication*. New York: Farrar, Straus & Giroux, 1993. A novel based on Wollstonecraft's life and work, with many excerpts.

Taylor, Barbara. *Mary Wollstonecraft and the Feminist Imagination*. New York: Cambridge University Press, 2003. Examines how Wollstonecraft's ideas about feminism were influenced by British Enlightenment theories on universal equality and moral perfection.

Todd, Janet. *Mary Wollstonecraft: A Revolutionary Life*. New York: Columbia University Press, 2000. A well-crafted and comprehensive biography, providing an analysis of Wollstonecraft's life and writing. Despite Wollstonecraft's rational feminist ideas, Todd portrays her subject as a creature of sensibility—as someone needy, self-absorbed, and self-dramatizing.

Wollstonecraft, Mary. *A Vindication of the Rights of Woman*. Edited by Carol H. Poston. New York: W. W. Norton, 1988. Part of the Norton Critical Edition series, this authoritative text includes historical background from such sources as John Locke and Mary Astell; contributions to the Wollstonecraft debate from (among thirteen sources) William Godwin, George Eliot, and Virginia Woolf; and seven critical essays.

SEE ALSO: Apr., 1762: Rousseau Publishes *The Social Contract*; Apr. 19, 1775: Battle of Lexington and Concord; Jan. 10, 1776: Paine Publishes *Common Sense*; 1790: Burke Lays the Foundations of Modern Conservatism; Feb. 22, 1791-Feb. 16, 1792: Thomas Paine Publishes *Rights of Man*; Apr. 20, 1792-Oct., 1797: Early Wars of the French Revolution.

RELATED ARTICLES in *Great Lives from History: The Eighteenth Century, 1701-1800*: Mary Astell; William Blake; Edmund Burke; Hester Chapone; William Godwin; Sophie von La Roche; Catherine Macaulay; Mary de la Rivière Manley; Mary Wortley Montagu; Hannah More; Thomas Paine; Jean-Jacques Rousseau; Mary Wollstonecraft.

1792-1793
FICHTE ADVOCATES FREE SPEECH

Swept up in the ideals of the French Revolution, Johann Gottlieb Fichte and several other young German philosophers argued in the 1790's for increases in individual liberty, including relaxations of censorship.

LOCALE: Germany

CATEGORIES: Philosophy; social issues and reform; government and politics

KEY FIGURES

Johann Gottlieb Fichte (1762-1814), German philosopher

Carl Friedrich Bahrdt (Karl Friedrich Bahrdt; 1741-1792), German theologian

Edmund Burke (1729-1797), Irish statesman and political philosopher

Georg Wilhelm Friedrich Hegel (1770-1831), German philosopher

Friedrich Hölderlin (1770-1843), German poet

Immanuel Kant (1724-1804), German philosopher

Ernst Ferdinand Klein (1744-1810), German jurist and social philosopher

Thomas Paine (1737-1809), English-born American political philosopher

Karl Leonhard Reinhold (1757-1823), German philosopher

Jean-Jacques Rousseau (1712-1778), French social and political philosopher

Friedrich Wilhelm Joseph von Schelling (1775-1854),
   German philosopher
Voltaire (François-Marie Arouet; 1694-1778), French
   political philosopher and satirist

SUMMARY OF EVENT

Johann Gottlieb Fichte was a child of his time, and that
time was revolutionary on unprecedented levels. Recent
revolutions in America and France had overthrown centuries of monarchic tradition, encouraged common citizens with expectations of increased liberty, and inspired
philosophers the world over. The French Revolution especially colored the German philosophy of the 1790's
with speculations of personal freedom and social and political reform in the wake of Immanuel Kant's 1784 brief
manifesto of free thought, *Beantwortung der Frage: Was
ist Aufklärung?* (*An Answer to the Question: What Is Enlightening?*, 1798; better known as *What Is Enlightenment?*). Kant—in *Kritik der reinen Vernunft* (1781; *Critique of Pure Reason*, 1838), *Kritik der praktischen
Vernunft* (1788; *Critique of Practical Reason*, 1873), and
especially *Grundlegung zur Metaphysik der Sitten*
(1785; *Fundamental Principles of the Metaphysics of
Ethics*, 1895; better known as *Foundations of the
Metaphysics of Morals*, 1950)—laid a solid philosophical foundation for the reality of personal freedom and
suggested that to deny such freedom would be contrary
to rational nature.

Modern ideas of civil freedom originated with Jean-
Jacques Rousseau, who claimed that humans are born
free but restricted artificially, and Voltaire, who famously offered to defend to the death the right of anyone
to disagree with him. Both Rousseau and Voltaire
strongly influenced Kant and his followers. Karl Leonhard Reinhold, in his popular simplification of Kant's
philosophy in the late 1780's and early 1790's, emphasized the centrality of the free will for both metaphysics
and ethics. Two influences permeated German ethical
thought in the 1790's: the Kantian philosophy of individual responsibility, autonomy, duty, and freedom and the
practical ideals of radical or romantic freedom, which
emanated chiefly from the social philosophy and political reality of France. These two influences were not at all
at odds with each other.

The spirit of the time included such progressive writings as Ernst Ferdinand Klein's *Über Denk und Druk-
freiheit* (1784; *On Freedom of the Press and of Thought:
For Princes, Ministers, and Writers*, 1996), Carl Friedrich Bahrdt's *Über Pressfreyheit und deren Gränzen*
(1787; *On Freedom of the Press and Its Limits*, 1996),

and Thomas Paine's *Rights of Man* (1791-1792). Even
Edmund Burke, despite his opposition to the French
Revolution, was a champion of individual rights, as
is seen in his sympathy for the American Revolution.
Georg Wilhelm Friedrich Hegel, Friedrich Hölderlin,
and Friedrich Wilhelm Joseph von Schelling, school-
mates at Tübingen during the French Revolution, were
three of the most confident and eloquent German student
voices in support of its ideals of liberty, equality, and fraternity. Hölderlin's poetry between 1789 and 1793 frequently expressed revolutionary sentiments.

A bold and precocious youth from a poor background,
Fichte was impatient to advance his career as a philosopher. In 1791, he made a pilgrimage to Königsberg, East
Prussia, where Kant held his professorship. Fichte managed on July 4 to gain an audience with Kant. Shortly
thereafter, Fichte submitted to Kant a manuscript that interpreted Kantian ethical concepts within a philosophy
of religion. Kant was favorably impressed and arranged
for his own publisher, Hartung, to print it as *Versuch
einer Kritik aller Offenbarung* (*Attempt at a Critique of
All Revelation*, 1978) in the spring of 1792. The book appeared anonymously, as was not unusual in those days
for the first works of young academic authors. Many of
its earliest readers assumed that it was the work of Kant
himself, and Fichte's reputation was instantly and solidly
established among German intellectuals as soon as its
true authorship was publicized.

In 1793, Fichte published anonymously in Danzig
two books on social and political philosophy and topical
issues: the eighty-six-page *Zurückforderung der Denk-
freiheit* (reclamation of freedom of thought) and the two-
volume *Beitrag zur Berichtigung über die französische
Revolution* (contribution to the rectification of the public's judgment of the French Revolution). These two
books laid out a clear philosophy of the individual expression of human freedom. While some of his similarly
inclined contemporaries, notably Bahrdt, claimed that
the right to free speech was ordained by God, Fichte instead regarded the justification of free speech as social.
That is, any civilized society requires that its citizens
be educated. Education requires that ideas be freely
available for discussion and evaluation. Therefore, free
speech is the linchpin of any society that aspires to develop its culture to the highest possible level.

Mainly on the strength of the general praise given to
his *Attempt at a Critique of All Revelation* and despite the
two polemical and radical works of 1793, Fichte was appointed to succeed Reinhold as professor of philosophy
at the University of Jena in May, 1794. He remained in

that post until dismissed in 1799, amid charges, probably true, that his Kantian humanism was a thinly disguised atheism.

Napoleon I's aggressive actions between 1804 and 1807 alienated many of the liberal German intelligentsia, who had formerly supported him as an exponent of revolution and human rights. Feeling betrayed, Ludwig van Beethoven angrily erased his dedication of the Eroica symphony to Napoleon after Napoleon crowned himself emperor in 1804. Hegel remained loyal to Napoleonic ideals, even if disgusted by the emperor's human faults.

Fichte, on the other hand, became a fervent German nationalist and increasingly conservative. In 1806, he offered personal encouragement to Prussian troops defending the homeland against the French invaders. In 1808, he published *Reden an die deutsche Nation* (*Addresses to the German Nation*, 1922), advocating the Prussian militaristic ethic, proclaiming German cultural superiority, and generally abandoning his progressive social and political ideals of fifteen years earlier—except his principle of free speech. He continued to believe that the people, by their free and uncensored public deliberations of anything that concerned them, would act as de facto advisers to the king, enabling the king to make better decisions. In the final version of Fichte's philosophy of individual freedom, the right of the people to free speech was for the benefit of the king, not the people, and the people were always bound to obey all royal commands, regardless of what they were allowed to say about them.

SIGNIFICANCE

With the fall of Napoleon in 1815, the consequent return to conservative values in the German states, and especially the Carlsbad Decrees of 1819, most of the revolutionary prospects for personal liberty and individual freedom of speech came to nought. They would not be revived until the short-lived Young Hegelian movement from about 1835 to 1848. Between 1819 and 1848, throughout the various German-speaking states dominated by Prussia and Austria, governments severely censored the press, restricted public speech and the power of the people to assemble, subverted dissent, and exercised absolute control over the universities.

Many professors were fired or persecuted during this reactionary era. Even Hegel, the most prominent philosopher of the 1820's, suddenly found that he had to be very careful about what he said and even more careful about what he wrote. For example, in his *Grundlinien der Philosophie des Rechts* (1821; *The Philosophy of Right*, 1855), the main locus of his social and political phi-

losophy and his philosophy of history, Hegel wrote that the rational is actual and the actual is rational, which can be interpreted as a conservative endorsement of the current Prussian regime. However, in the lectures that he gave to his students at about the same time on the same topics, he said that the rational *becomes* actual and the actual *becomes* rational, which can be interpreted more nearly along the lines of Hegel's own progressive social theory.

Hegel, a lifelong constitutional monarchist, remained as liberal as one could be in Prussia and still keep an academic job, and he never turned as far toward the conservative end of the spectrum as did Fichte. Nevertheless, Hegel's respect for Fichte remained so high that he requested to be buried next to him. The two philosophers and their wives lie side-by-side in Dorothea Cemetery in Berlin.

—Eric v.d. Luft

FURTHER READING

Ameriks, Karl. *Kant and the Fate of Autonomy: Problems in the Appropriation of the Critical Philosophy*. New York: Cambridge University Press, 2000. Includes interpretations of Kant's, Fichte's, Reinhold's, and Hegel's respective concepts of freedom, placing them within the context of one another.

La Vopa, Anthony J. *Fichte: The Self and the Calling of Philosophy, 1762-1799*. New York: Cambridge University Press, 2001. Biographical study of the young Fichte.

Rockmore, Tom. *Fichte, Marx, and the German Philosophical Tradition*. Carbondale: Southern Illinois University Press, 1980. An account of Marx's appropriation of Fichte's theory of the human self as a free and active moral agent.

Schmidt, James, ed. *What Is Enlightenment? Eighteenth-Century Answers and Twentieth-Century Questions*. Berkeley: University of California Press, 1996. Part 1 is a collection of key texts from the German 1780's and 1790's pertaining to personal reason and autonomy; parts 2 and 3 provide the perspectives and interpretations of seventeen important twentieth century thinkers.

Smith, Lindsley Armstrong. "Johann Gottlieb Fichte's Free Speech Theory." *American Communication Journal* 4, no. 3 (Spring, 2001). Available at http:\\www.acjournal.org/holdings/vol4/iss3/articles/lsmith.pdf. A clear exposition written by a lawyer from the perspective of a philosophy of law, in a peer-reviewed, online-only scholarly journal.

SEE ALSO: 1721-1750: Early Enlightenment in France; 1739-1740: Hume Publishes *A Treatise of Human Nature*; 1754: Condillac Defends Sensationalist Theory; July 27, 1758: Helvétius Publishes *De l'esprit*; July, 1764: Voltaire Publishes *A Philosophical Dictionary for the Pocket*; 1770: Publication of Holbach's *The System of Nature*; 1781: Kant Publishes *Critique of Pure Reason*; 1784-1791: Herder Publishes His Philosophy of History.

RELATED ARTICLES in *Great Lives from History: The Eighteenth Century, 1701-1800*: Edmund Burke; Johann Gottlieb Fichte; Immanuel Kant; Thomas Paine; Jean-Jacques Rousseau; Voltaire.

January 4, 1792-1797
THE *NORTHERN STAR* CALLS FOR IRISH INDEPENDENCE

The Northern Star *became the mouthpiece of Protestant Irish discontent, fanning the flames of nationalism in the years leading up to the Irish Rebellion.*

LOCALE: Belfast, Ireland (now in Northern Ireland)
CATEGORIES: Communications; government and politics; wars, uprisings, and civil unrest

KEY FIGURES
Samuel Neilson (1761-1803), Irish nationalist cofounder and editor of the *Northern Star*
James Porter (1752/1753-1798), Irish journalist, satirist, and editor
Thomas Russell (1767-1803), Irish writer, social critic, and revolutionary
Wolfe Tone (1763-1798), United Irishman who used the *Northern Star* as his mouthpiece

SUMMARY OF EVENT
In October of 1791, two years after the outbreak of the French Revolution, a small group of Belfast radicals banded together to form the Society of United Irishmen, a political club differing from its parent organization, the Northern Whig Club, chiefly in the strong emphasis it put on Roman Catholic participation and the importance of Catholic emancipation. Shortly afterward, twelve of the city's businessmen joined forces to found a newspaper, the *Northern Star*, to disseminate the principles of the United Irishmen. The first issue appeared on January 4, 1792. Thereafter, the paper appeared biweekly until its eventual suppression in 1797. It was distributed all over Ireland, achieving a maximum circulation in 1795 of five thousand copies per issue, the largest circulation of any paper in Ireland and comparable to the largest London papers.

Several circumstances combined to make Belfast, the so-called Athens of the North, a fertile ground for radi-calism. Both the business community and the working class were predominantly Presbyterian, and until 1793 Protestant Dissenters did not enjoy the electoral franchise in Ireland. The large, literate middle class was deprived of participation in civic affairs, which were entirely under the control of the marquess of Donegal and the twelve burgesses he appointed. These burgesses also elected Belfast's two representatives to Irish parliament.

The eighteenth century Irish nationalism expressed in the *Northern Star* had found its first coherent expression in the Volunteer movement of the 1770's and 1780's. This movement, which at its height boasted 100,000 active members throughout Ireland, created a paramilitary force to protect Ireland from invasion by France or Spain after England removed most of Ireland's standing militia force to the American colonies to fight in the Revolutionary War. Organized specifically to prevent invasion by foreign Catholic nations, the Volunteer movement was emphatically Protestant. It left a legacy of armed Protestant extremists in Northern Ireland, against whom the Catholic minority armed themselves. Something resembling a low-level internal civil war was the result. By seeking to enlist the support of the emerging Roman Catholic middle class and pinning their hopes on aid from the now secular government of revolutionary France, the United Irishmen hoped to create a new Irish identity. They were remarkably unsuccessful.

From the outset, the tone of the *Northern Star* was markedly Francophile, with translations from the French revolutionary press occupying large chunks of column space. With respect to local news, the paper was uneven, making no attempt to be comprehensive. For several months in 1793, the main topic of interest was a dispute between the ultraconservative marquess of Downshire and one of his tenants over violations of the game laws. After the emergence of the Reign of Terror, the execution of Louis XVI, and especially the outbreak of war between England and France in October of 1793, pro-French sympathies became increasingly marginalized in the British Empire, and people who espoused them were subjected to official sanctions. By 1796, the United Irishmen had evolved into a paramilitary organization whose avowed purpose was achieving complete Irish independence from England by force of arms, and their mouthpiece could justly be convicted of disseminating sedition.

The *Northern Star*'s first brush with the authorities arose from the publication, on December 15, 1792, of Wolfe Tone's "Declaration and Resolutions of the Society of United Irishmen in Belfast." This manifesto claimed that there existed no national government in Ireland and spoke of "a constitution falsely called free." Although the complaints of parliamentary corruption and the untenability of continued discrimination against Catholics were valid and legal, the terms in which they were couched and the intemperance of the language led to the arrest and prosecution of the editor, Samuel Neilson, on charges of seditious libel. The charges were dropped after it was pointed out that the long-established and more moderate *Belfast News-Letter* had also published Tone's declarations.

The *Northern Star* owed some of its popularity to publication of a series of satires by the Reverend James Porter, a Presbyterian clergyman of radical sympathies. "Billy Bluff and Squire Firebrand" consisted of dialogues between an oafish informer and a paranoid magistrate who saw in every piece of public-house banter evidence of antigovernment conspiracies. The series, which made fun of various local personalities, was often performed in amateur theatricals. Because of his literary celebrity, Porter became a popular lecturer; not surprisingly, he was suspected of traveling for other than literary purposes and was closely watched.

Another frequent contributor of editorial commentary on Irish issues was Thomas Russell, who together with Neilson wrote most of the pieces on economic issues and social inequality. Russell also wrote extensively against the African slave trade and was chided by his fellow United Irishmen for failing to concentrate on Ireland. In Belfast, which was emerging as a center of cotton manufacture, slavery was more than an armchair issue.

On September 16, 1796, militia under the command of Downshire's son raided the offices of the *Northern Star*, searching for materials implicating the United Irishmen in collaboration with France. They arrested Neilson and Russell for sedition and transported them to Dublin, where the journalists remained in Kilmainham jail, awaiting trial, until armed rebellion broke out in Ul-

ster in June of 1798. Meanwhile, Porter assumed the role of acting editor of the *Northern Star* in Neilson's absence, publishing the paper until May of 1797, when a contingent of the Monaghan Militia appeared, demanding that the paper print a loyal declaration. When Porter refused, the militia smashed the presses. This action is presumed to have been engineered by the central Irish government.

Porter was arrested for participating in a rebel attack on a mail coach during the Irish Rebellion. Though his proven actions consisted only of reading dispatches to the illiterate attackers, he was found guilty of treason by a military court-martial and executed during the brief period of savage repression following the hostilities. Neilson remained in prison until 1802, when, broken in health, he was permitted to emigrate to the United States. He died shortly after his arrival. Russell, released at the same time, returned to Ulster, where he was executed in 1803 for his role in the abortive rebellion led by Robert Emmett.

SIGNIFICANCE

In retrospect, the long-term influence of the *Northern Star* was rather slight, despite its large circulation and contemporary popularity. In nearly every case in which progress was made on those social and economic fronts where the United Irishmen led the vanguard, the actual agents of reform were staunchly loyal Whigs or even Tories. The armed rebellion in Ulster in 1798 was a flash in the pan. By the time the uprising got under way, most of the United Irish leaders still committed to separation had either been imprisoned or fled the country. In their absence, the contest became a conflict between desperately poor, illiterate Catholic peasants and anyone connected with the Protestant establishment.

The resulting carnage firmly convinced moderates on both sides of the Irish Sea that Ireland was unfit for even the partial legislative independence it had won in 1782. The Irish parliament dissolved itself and merged with that of Britain in 1801. In the process, representation was substantially reformed but at the cost of relinquishing control over Irish affairs to the larger, imperial legislature. Catholic emancipation, begun in 1793, was not fully achieved until 1828, by which time stalled reform had fueled a resurgence of nationalism and separatism.

—*Martha A. Sherwood*

FURTHER READING

Budge, Ian, and Cornelius O'Leary. *Belfast—An Approach to Crisis: A Study of Belfast Politics, 1613-1970.* London: Macmillan, 1973. Clear explanation of the Volunteer movement and the crucial role local

Belfast politics played in the early stages of the United Irishmen movement.

Carroll, Denis. *The Man from God Knows Where.* Blackrock, Ireland: Columbia Press, 1995. A biography of Thomas Russell, good for accounts of his literary career and role in the *Northern Star.*

McDowell, Robert Brendan. *Ireland in the Age of Imperialism and Revolution, 1760-1801.* Oxford, England: Clarendon Press, 1979. A clear, well-balanced account of Irish politics in the latter part of the eighteenth century; places the *Northern Star* in its historical and cultural context.

_____. "The Late Eighteenth Century." In *Belfast: The Origin and Growth of an Industrial City,* edited by J. C. Beckett and R. E. Glasscock. London: British Broadcasting Corporation, 1967. Contains a good chronological account of the publication history of the *Northern Star,* and of its relationship to the *Belfast News-Letter.*

Mathew, H. C. G., and Brian Harrison, eds. *Oxford Dictionary of National Biography: From the Earliest Times to the Year 2000.* New York: Oxford University Press, 2004. This multivolume set includes detailed biographies of Neilson, Porter, and Russell. It is an invaluable source for biographies of obscure British historical personages.

Quinn, James. "The United Irishmen and Social Reform." *Irish Historical Studies* 31 (1998): 188-201. Cites the *Northern Star* on landlord-tenant issues, combinations, and the electoral franchise.

SEE ALSO: 1726: Swift Satirizes English Rule of Ireland in *Gulliver's Travels*; Sept. 10, 1763: Publication of the *Freeman's Journal*; May-Nov., 1798: Irish Rebellion.

RELATED ARTICLES in *Great Lives from History: The Eighteenth Century, 1701-1800*: First Marquess Cornwallis; William Pitt the Younger; Wolfe Tone.

March 16, 1792
DENMARK ABOLISHES THE SLAVE TRADE

Denmark was the first European nation to outlaw the trade in slaves. Other nations soon followed suit, but neither Denmark nor the other nations outlawed slavery itself at this time. They merely put an official end to their colonies' importation of slaves from Africa and elsewhere.

LOCALE: Denmark; Danish West Indies
CATEGORIES: Laws, acts, and legal history; social issues and reform

KEY FIGURES
Christian VII (1749-1808), king of Denmark, r. 1766-1808
William Pitt the Younger (1759-1806), prime minister of Great Britain, 1783-1801, 1804-1806
William Wilberforce (1759-1833), English member of Parliament, 1780-1825, and abolitionist

SUMMARY OF EVENT

On March 16, 1792, King Christian VII of Denmark signed an ordinance banning the slave trade in his country and its colonies. Slave owners would be allowed ten more years to transport slaves from Africa, however, so that they might have an adequate supply of slaves on hand once the ban went into effect. Despite this provision, the king's order represented a major step forward in the movement to ensure better treatment for slaves and an eventual end to the brutal system altogether.

European involvement in the slave trade had begun in the early 1500's. Portuguese and Spanish traders inaugurated the system and enjoyed a monopoly in the business for the next century. Their ships brought thousands of Africans to sugar plantations in Cuba, Colombia, and Brazil. Beginning in the early 1600's they were joined by Dutch, French, and English slaving vessels.

The Danes became involved in the New World in 1640, when they annexed the uninhabited island of St. Thomas, part of the Virgin Islands chain. Not until 1671, however, did Danish ships transport slaves to their tiny colony. That year, the Royal Chartered Danish West India and Guinea Company was granted a monopoly on the slave trade by King Frederick III. During the next ten years, Danish planters established forty-seven sugar plantations and brought 175 slaves onto St. Thomas to work the land. Eventually, the small group of white settlers, who numbered only 156 in 1680, built a small town called Charlotte Amalie and sent tobacco and cotton to their homeland, though they continually experienced financial problems.

The island's economy had grown a bit by 1708, when a

free trade ordinance signed by the king gave St. Thomas planters permission to ship and sell goods anywhere in North America and Europe, rather than just in the mother country. Ten years later, the Danish government annexed the neighboring island of St. John and a few small plantations were established on it. The third and final Danish possession in the New World, St. Croix, was purchased from the French in 1733. Slavery and sugar were prominent features of all three outposts. A small slave revolt broke out on St. Thomas that year, although it was quickly quelled and slaveholders restored the peace.

By the 1750's, the Danish West India Company was bringing about one thousand slaves a year to its colonies from Danish Guinea, a very tiny outpost located on the west coast of Africa (modern Ghana). Danish Guinea had been established in 1659. It included one town, Frederiksborg, the port from which most slaves were exported to the colonies. Danish merchants traded with the Assante, Accra, and Akim tribes in Africa. Slaves were the most important "product." They were customarily prisoners of war or criminals, as was true with most slaves in traditional African societies. Only rarely did Danes or other Europeans abduct Africans themselves. Most were bought from African rulers for guns, jewelry, or tools.

The Danish share of the slave trade amounted to no more than a small percentage of the total European traffic. Total numbers are hard to estimate, but most experts believe that between 1500 and 1870, approximately fifteen million to twenty million Africans were carried out of their homelands and brought to the New World as slaves. The first calls for abolition of the slave trade and eventually of slavery itself came from religious groups in Europe, especially the Society of Friends (Quakers) in England and Lutheran Pietists in Scandinavia and the German states. Members of these fervently religious communities argued that since all human beings had the light of God within them, all were equal. For human beings to hold other humans as property violated the idea of equality and was therefore sinful and immoral.

Opponents of the slave trade wrote several books beginning in the 1750's that denounced the horrors found on slave ships heading out of Africa to the New World. These accounts depicted cruel captains, bloodthirsty crew members, and nothing but sickness, death, and disaster for the unfortunate people condemned to a lifetime of bondage. Many of these charges were true, although historical scholarship has found some instances of exaggeration in the anti-slave-trade accounts. Death rates on the infamous Middle Passage, that part of the trip where

slaves crossed the Atlantic Ocean after their capture in Africa and before they embarked on the last part of their journey, were high. Most of the deaths resulted from diseases, such as dysentery, measles, smallpox, and scurvy.

On Danish ships life for slaves was monotonous, perilous, and severely restrictive. Male slaves were shackled together in pairs and were allowed no more than fifteen minutes a day for exercise. Their food consisted of beans boiled in lard provided twice a day, along with water. Revolts on ships were few but there were many suicides. Some mothers threw their infants into the sea rather than have them face the horrors that awaited them in the New World. On an average voyage, approximately 8 to 10 percent of the slaves died before reaching the West Indies, and death rates for crew members were equally high. Africa was considered "the white man's grave" by Europeans because of the many communicable tropical diseases to which they had no immunity.

William Pitt the Younger, the British prime minister, called the slave trade "the greatest practical evil that ever afflicted the human race." Other opponents of slavery, such as William Wilberforce, the leading English reformer, argued that ending the slave trade would lead to improved conditions for existing slaves. Planters would realize that they would have to provide proper care for slaves they already owned because they would no longer be able to import more slaves from abroad. Improved conditions would encourage slaves to have more children, thus increasing the domestic slave population and making further importation unnecessary. Opponents of the slave trade even suggested that slave owners might eventually come to recognize the evils associated with enslaving others and end the institution of slavery itself. The first consideration, however, was to abolish the slave trade by making traffic in human beings illegal.

Christian VII, king of Denmark, thus issued his decree to end the slave trade on March 16, 1792. The first European monarch to abolish the slave trade, Christian VII considered himself to be an enlightened despot who looked out for the welfare of his subjects. Informed of the cruelties of the voyage from Africa to Danish possessions in the New World, the Danish king was convinced to ban the slave trade forever. Believing that an immediate end would increase the burden on the existing slave population and cause economic ruin for many planters, however, Christian agreed that planters in the Danish West Indies would be given ten years to build up their supply of slaves before the trade would cease. As a result, slaves were allowed to be imported to the Danish West Indies until 1802.

SIGNIFICANCE

With Christian's decree, Denmark became the first European nation to abolish the slave trade. Great Britain followed in 1807, the Netherlands abolished the trade in 1814, and Spain and Portugal finally eliminated the trade to their overseas possessions in the late 1820's. In 1807, the United States passed legislation that prohibited the importation of slaves beginning in 1808.

The slave trade had never been especially profitable for any of the nations involved; the deaths of crew members and captives and the constantly fluctuating prices paid for slaves kept profits for Danish slave traders to less than 10 percent per year. Sugar plantations, which generated the largest demand for slaves, also faced economic challenges. Prices for sugar fell substantially each year because of increasing production and the introduction of sugar beets that could be grown in more temperate regions such as Europe, thus eliminating the costs of importation. Sugar and tobacco crops also took a heavy toll on the soil, thus exhausting the resources of islands such as St. Croix and St. Thomas by the early 1800's. These conditions curtailed some of the demand for imported slaves.

It was not until 1848, however, that the Danish government abolished slavery itself in its West Indian possessions. By that time, the African population of the islands outnumbered the European population by a ratio of ten to one. Thus, it appeared that the abolition of the slave trade had accomplished the aims of Christian VII. With Africa cut off as a source of supply, planters were forced to pay more attention to the care and living conditions of their own slave labor force.

—Leslie V. Tischauser

FURTHER READING

Curtin, Philip D. *The Atlantic Slave Trade: A Census.* Madison: University of Wisconsin Press, 1969. One of the finest statistical studies of the transatlantic slave trade.

Davis, David Brion. *The Problem of Slavery in Western Culture.* Ithaca, N.Y.: Cornell University Press, 1966. Examines the full story of the crusade against the slave trade, placing the Danish abolition decree in a larger historical context.

Derry, T. K. *A History of Scandinavia.* Minneapolis: University of Minnesota Press, 1979. Includes a brief discussion of the campaign waged in Denmark against the slave trade.

Gobel, Erik. "Danish Trade to the West Indies and Guinea, 1671-1754." *Scandinavian Economic History Review* 31 (1983): 21-49. A scholarly assessment of the history of Danish involvement in the slave trade.

Jespersen, Knud J. V. *A History of Denmark.* Translated by Ivan Hill. New York: Palgrave Macmillan, 2004. Chronicles five hundred years of Danish history, beginning with the Reformation in 1500.

Rawley, James A. *The Transatlantic Slave Trade: A History.* New York: Alfred A. Knopf, 1981. Rawley provides an objective, balanced view of the transatlantic slave trade that assesses the participation of various European nations.

Thomas, Hugh. *The Slave Trade: The Story of the Atlantic Slave Trade, 1440-1870.* London: Picador, 1997. Massive, nine-hundred-page examination of the slave trade includes information about Denmark's participation in, and eventual abolition of, the trade.

SEE ALSO: 18th cent.: Expansion of the Atlantic Slave Trade; Apr. 6, 1712: New York City Slave Revolt; Nov. 23, 1733: Slaves Capture St. John's Island; 1760-1776: Caribbean Slave Rebellions; Apr. 14, 1775: Pennsylvania Society for the Abolition of Slavery Is Founded; July 2, 1777-1804: Northeast States Abolish Slavery; Feb. 12, 1793: First Fugitive Slave Law.

RELATED ARTICLES in *Great Lives from History: The Eighteenth Century, 1701-1800*: William Pitt the Younger; William Wilberforce.

1790's

April 20, 1792-October, 1797
EARLY WARS OF THE FRENCH REVOLUTION

During the French Revolutionary Wars, the French government, which was committed to spreading antiaristocratic principles, fought against conservative European powers that supported traditional social inequalities and royalist institutions.

LOCALE: Western Europe

CATEGORIES: Wars, uprisings, and civil unrest; government and politics

KEY FIGURES

Louis XVI (1754-1793), king of France, r. 1774-1792

Napoleon Bonaparte (1769-1821), French military commander and later emperor of France as Napoleon I, r. 1804-1814, 1815

Charles-François Dumouriez (1739-1823), French field general who defected to Austria

Lazare Carnot (1753-1823), French revolutionary leader

Comte de Custine (Adam-Phillipe de Custine; 1740-1793), French general

Duke of Brunswick (Charles William Ferdinand; 1735-1806), Prussian field marshal

Jean-Baptiste Jourdan (1762-1833), marshal of France

Archduke Charles (1771-1847), Austrian field marshal and brother to Emperor Francis II

Charles Pichegru (1761-1804), French commander of the armies of the Rhine, the Moselle, and the North

Jean Moreau (1763-1813), French general

SUMMARY OF EVENT

The French Revolution, which began in 1789, horrified monarchs, nobles, and conservatives throughout Europe, for they feared the spread of republican and antiaristocratic ideas. French émigrés, mostly from the privileged classes, did their best to persuade foreign governments to oppose the revolution. In June, 1791, after King Louis XVI of France failed in his attempt to flee, his execution appeared likely. In August, the Austrian and Prussian monarchs, hoping to help Louis's chances, issued the Declaration of Pillnitz, which threatened military intervention if joined by the other European powers. Instead of having a sobering effect on the French radicals, however, the prospect of a foreign invasion pushed the revolution in an even more radical direction.

In the French Legislative Assembly, many of the revolutionaries, especially members of the Girondin Party, wanted a foreign war, because they believed it would rally the nation to their cause. On April 20, 1792, the Assembly declared war on Austria. Prussia joined the Austrian side, as did Sardinia somewhat later. The French army, however, was disorganized and unprepared for warfare. When French forces marched into the Austrian Netherlands, they were quickly pushed out by better-trained imperial forces.

In July, 1792, a large army of fifty thousand Austrian and Prussian troops, led by the duke of Brunswick, crossed the frontier and marched toward Paris. On July 25, Brunswick issued a manifesto threatening to annihilate Paris if the royal family were harmed. This unwise threat rallied much of the French population and contributed to the suspension of the king in August. French prospects improved as bad weather slowed Brunswick's movement, which allowed two outstanding commanders, Charles-François Dumouriez and François Christophe de Kellerman, to join forces and meet the invaders at Valmy. After an inconclusive battle on September 20, Brunswick, now outnumbered, withdrew his forces to the Rhine.

With the imminent thread to Paris eliminated, Dumouriez returned to the Austrian Netherlands. On November 6, by surprising Austrian troops at Jemappes, he won an overwhelming victory, which allowed him to capture the capital city of Brussels. Meanwhile in Germany, the comte de Custine captured Mainz and advanced toward Frankfurt. Late in 1792, the revolutionary Convention, reflecting a new confidence, offered assistance to all people wanting to "recover their liberty." This international decree, followed by the execution of Louis XVI in January, 1793, provoked Britain, Spain, and the Netherlands to join with Austria, Prussia, and Sardinia in a war alliance called the First Coalition.

The first part of 1793 was disastrous for the French cause. On March 18, Dumouriez was defeated by the Austrians at Neerwinden, and he defected to the other side. Then Custine was forced to retreat from the Rhine, leaving behind twenty thousand troops in Mainz. Conservative French peasants and royalists revolted in the provinces of the Vendée and Brittany. Royalists took control of the French cities of Toulon and Lyon. At this time, the allies probably could have defeated France, except that Austria, Prussia, and Russia were preoccupied with the partition of Poland.

On April 6, 1793, the Convention, in a state of panic, established the dictatorial Committee of Public Safety. In August, the Convention ordered a draft of all able-bodied men, called a *levée en masse*. Supervised by

A British cartoon of 1798, in which French soldiers declare "We explain de Rights of Man to de Noblesse," as they pillage the House of Lords. (Library of Congress)

Lazare Carnot, the draft soon produced a huge revolutionary army of some 700,000 troops. The Committee attached revolutionary commissioners to each commander. Under the Reign of Terror, unsuccessful officers suspected of disloyalty, such as General Custine, were sent to the guillotine "to encourage the others."

Republican forces gained firm control of France in late 1793. On October 9, they captured Lyon from the royalists. On December 19, Napoleon Bonaparte's strategy of bombardment convinced the British to withdraw their fleet from the harbor of Toulon, and republican troops entered the city. Napoleon was promoted to brigadier general. On December 23, the royalist revolt in the Vendée was crushed in the Battle of Savenay. That month, moreover, allied troops retreated east of the Rhine.

During 1794-1795, French forces were usually victorious. Marshal Jean-Baptiste Jourdan won a decisive victory against the Austrians at Fleurus and took control over much of the Rhineland, including Cologne. General

Charles Pichegru was even more successful in the Netherlands. After he captured Amsterdam in early 1795, the Dutch, now reconstituted into the Batavian Republic, agreed to peace in the first Treaty of Basel, signed on April 5, 1795. Later that year, Prussia and Spain also withdrew from the First Coalition.

France was now able to concentrate on fighting Austria and Sardinia. The newly formed Directory approved a three-pronged attack: Jourdan would march southeastward from the Netherlands, General Jean Moreau would attack southern Germany, and Napoleon was to capture strategic parts of northern Italy and then cross the Alps into Austria. Initially, the French were successful on all fronts. In 1796, however, the outstanding Austrian commander Archduke Charles outmaneuvered Generals Jourdan and Morea, both of whom were forced to retreat to the Rhine by September, 1796.

In the Italian campaign, meanwhile, Napoleon was amazingly successful with his strategy of using speed and surprise attacks by small units. In May, Sardinia agreed to enter into a separate peace. After major victories at Lodi, Arcole, and Rivoli, Napoleon entered Mantua in February, 1797, but as he began to cross the Alps, he faced the possibility of being outflanked by the Austrians, and he decided to negotiate a settlement.

In mid-October, 1797, Napoleon, ignoring the Directory's instructions, signed the Treaty of Campo Formio, which recognized French possession of Belgium, Savoy, Nice, most of the west bank of the Rhine, and the Ionian islands. In return, Austria obtained additional lands in northern Italy and the Balkans. Given Napoleon's great popularity, the Directory had little choice but to ratify the treaty. Napoleon then began to devise strategies to defeat Britain.

SIGNIFICANCE

The early French Revolutionary Wars profoundly affected the societies of Western Europe. Many thousands of soldiers and civilians died in every country involved. Although no accurate statistics are available, it is known that more soldiers died in hospitals than on the battlefield. The violent fighting also destroyed farms and disrupted international commerce. Economic conditions deteriorated almost everywhere, and countless Europeans lacked the basic necessities of life.

Even though thousands of conservative Frenchmen actively opposed the revolution, most historians agree that the majority of French soldiers, coming primarily from the peasantry and the lower classes of the cities, supported the aims of the revolution. Thus, French soldiers often fought harder and were willing to endure greater hardships than the First Coalition's troops. The nationalistic spirit of the French army anticipated important characteristics of military organizations under democratic governments in later centuries.

As a result of the revolutionary wars, the boundaries of France expanded significantly. By 1797, France had annexed almost all of the regions that earlier French expansionists had considered their "natural borders." Although French revolutionaries believed that they were bringing "liberation" to the places they annexed, many of the affected people looked upon the French as foreign occupiers. In all these lands, nevertheless, the French instituted progressive reforms, such as the abolition of seigniorial dues and special privileges of the nobility. Thus, the wars helped diffuse the democratic ideas of the French Revolution—powerful ideas that would resonate into the next centuries.

—*Thomas Tandy Lewis*

FURTHER READING

Asprey, Robert. *The Rise of Napoleon Bonaparte*. New York: Basic Books, 2000. Includes highly detailed accounts of the Siege of Toulon, the Italian campaign, and the Treaty of Campo Formio.

Banning, T. C. W. *The French Revolutionary Wars, 1787-1802*. New York: Arnold, 1996. Emphasizes the devastation inflicted by the revolutionary armies and the negative, destructive aspects of the French Revolution.

Bertaud, Jean-Paul. *Army of the French Revolution: From Citizen-Soldiers to Instruments of Power*. Translated by Robert Palmer. Princeton, N.J.: Princeton University Press, 1989. Highly respected book that emphasizes the major changes within the French army during the period.

Cobb, Richard. *The People's Armies*. New Haven, Conn.: Yale University Press, 1987. A scholarly work about the civilian forces that were an instrument of the Reign of Terror, emphasizing the clash between reluctant rural peasants and urban revolutionaries.

Fremont-Barnes, Gregory. *French Revolutionary Wars*. Botley, England: Osprey, 2001. A balanced introduction in ninety-six pages.

Gardiner, Robert. *Fleet Battle and Blockade: The French Revolutionary War, 1793-1797*. London: Chatham, 1997. From a British perspective, tells how the Royal Navy in 1793 embarked on an almost unprecedented era of victories at sea.

Griffith, Paddy. *Art of War in Revolutionary France, 1789-1902*. London: Greenhill Books, 1998. Award-winning account of how the French won decisive victories because of a combination of competent leaders and revolutionary morale by citizen-soldiers.

Hague, William. *William Pitt the Younger*. New York: Alfred A. Knopf, 2005. Excellent source of information about the prime minister's strategic and military policies.

Lynn, John A. *Bayonets of the Republic: Motivation and Tactics of Revolutionary France, 1791-94*. Urbana: University of Illinois Press, 1984. Argues that the French triumphed because they created a new kind of army with a spirit of patriotic devotion.

Palmer, Robert T. *Twelve Who Ruled: The Year of the Terror in the French Revolution*. Princeton, N.J.: Princeton University Press, 1988. Dramatic narrative of the leaders and policies of the Committee of Public Safety, from a pro-revolutionary point of view.

SEE ALSO: May 5, 1789: Louis XVI Calls the Estates-General; June 20, 1789: Oath of the Tennis Court; July 14, 1789: Fall of the Bastille; Sept. 20, 1792: Battle of Valmy; Jan. 21, 1793: Execution of Louis XVI; Mar. 4-Dec. 23, 1793: War in the Vendée; July 27-28, 1794: Fall of Robespierre; Mar., 1796-Oct. 17, 1797: Napoleon's Italian Campaigns; Apr. 12, 1798-Sept. 2, 1801: Napoleon's Egyptian Campaign; Nov. 9-10, 1799: Napoleon Rises to Power in France.

RELATED ARTICLES in *Great Lives from History: The Eighteenth Century, 1701-1800*: Lazare Carnot; Louis XVI; Marie-Antoinette; William Pitt the Younger; Robespierre.

September 20, 1792
BATTLE OF VALMY

This first battle of the wars of the French Revolution might have also been the last had a hastily assembled French army succumbed to a large Prussian-led invading force. Though a minor skirmish, Valmy is considered an important political turning point in history, because a French defeat might have ended the French Revolution.

LOCALE: Valmy, northeastern France
CATEGORY: Wars, uprisings, and civil unrest

KEY FIGURES
François Christophe de Kellerman (1735-1820),
    commander of the French Center Army at Valmy
Charles-François Dumouriez (1739-1823),
    commander of the French Northern Army at Valmy
Duke of Brunswick (Charles William Ferdinand; 1735-1806), commander of Prussian forces at Valmy
Count von Clerfayt (Charles Joseph de Croix; 1733-1798), Austrian field marshal

SUMMARY OF EVENT
In the issuance of the Declaration of Pillnitz in August, 1791, Austria and Prussia defined their own monarchical interests to be directly related to those of King Louis XVI of France. One year later, it was evident that both the position of Louis and the general international situation had dramatically worsened. In August, 1792, the French royal family was brought to the Temple prison to be kept under guard. In addition, France was in its fourth month of a declared war on Austria over Austrian refusal to cease being a haven for counterrevolutionary French nobles (émigrés). French armies were unsuccessfully attempting to invade the Spanish Netherlands, which served as an émigré base. These events caused the Prussian military commander, the duke of Brunswick, to threaten to occupy Paris if any further disrespect should befall the French royal family.

In command of an army composed of thirty-five thousand seasoned Prussian infantry and forty-two thousand Austrian, Hessian, and émigré troops, Brunswick invaded France on August 18, 1792. Adding stature to the venture, Brunswick was accompanied by the Prussian king, Frederick William II. Brunswick was assured by leading émigrés that much of France would welcome him as a liberator and that the undisciplined raw recruits populating the French army were a mere rabble that would run from the initial salvos of battle. Such had been the case in the French invasion of Belgium during previous months.

Meanwhile, French officers, many of whom sprang from aristocratic backgrounds and were disgusted with the increasing radicalization of the French Revolution, were leaving the army in great numbers. By September, 1792, two-thirds of French army officers had either quit or deserted to the émigrés. In a French army composed of a merger of remaining regular army units, national guardsmen, and recent volunteers, the places vacated by the officers had to be taken by noncommissioned officers. In contrast, Prussian officers and infantry were considered to be the best in Europe and capable of instilling fear in any opposing force.

Although heavy August rains slowed Brunswick's invasion, he was able, by September 3, easily to capture the French fortresses at Longwy and Verdun. In despair at the performance of his raw troops, the French commander of Verdun, Lieutenant Colonel Nicolas François Beaurepaire, shot himself. Brunswick was now in position to move through the Argonne Forest to Paris. Although his troops encountered problems getting supplies, circumstances seemed to point to a "parade march" to Paris. However, marching through Argonne was the Army of the North, commanded by General Charles-François Dumouriez. Although heavily saturated with recent recruits, the Dumouriez's army had gained experi-

1790's

ence in the Belgian campaigns in addition to benefiting from Dumouriez's own extensive military training.

Dumouriez was able to move his forces down from Sedan, behind the Argonne, beating Brunswick to the strategic pass of Les Islettes, on the road to Paris. There, he entrenched defensive positions and awaited the arrival of reinforcements from the Army of the Center,

The Battle of Valmy was touted as a first step in the wars of the French Revolution, as in this poster exhorting French citizens to buy war bonds "so that France will be victorious as at Valmy!" (Library of Congress)

marching from Metz under the command of François Christophe de Kellerman. Serving under Kellerman in command of his right wing was a young army officer, Louis-Philippe, who would later become the last king of France (r. 1830-1848). Dumouriez was able to keep at bay an Austrian and émigré force moving from the west under the command of the count von Clerfayt, who was attempting to prevent the two French armies from meeting. The tables were turned, however, as Austrian forces would be checked by Dumouriez throughout the upcoming battle.

Kellerman headed an army of forty-seven thousand infantry, composed mostly of regular army units and containing experienced heavy artillery batteries. France had long been the rival of Prussia as the leading power in artillery technology and tactics. The two French generals met at Sainte-Menehould, a protected marshland area, on September 19, 1792. They both knew that they were all that stood between Brunswick and Paris. Also on September 19, a third French general, the marquis de Lafayette, deserted to join the émigré forces. For him, the French Revolution was spinning out of control. Hysteria about treason in the wake of the invasion of France had just caused Parisian mobs to round up and often gruesomely execute more than twelve hundred prisoners in an event known to history as the September Massacres (September 2-11).

By the evening of September 19, Brunswick's forces had marched through the upper passes of the Argonne, having successfully made a flanking movement to attack French forces from the East. The Prussians deployed on the heights of La Lune, opposite the high ground held by Kellerman. In response, Kellerman moved his left wing toward the heights of Valmy with artillery positioned near the large Valmy windmill. Ironically, the Prussian positions were further along the road to Paris than the French positions. Had he chosen to, Brunswick could have rapidly moved west through the Marne to Paris. However, the threat of a large French army to his rear and uncertainties in his fore made such a gambit too risky to attempt.

The battle opened on the foggy and overcast morning of September 20 with an intense Prussian barrage intended to take out French cannon positioned near the windmill. Splinters flew from shot smashing into the windmill, becoming shrapnel and forcing the French to tear down the building in the midst of battle. As Prussian infantry and cavalry swarmed up the heights, they were met with intense and well-placed French artillery fire. French infantry forces held their lines, shouting "Vive la nation!" (long live the country) and other revolutionary slogans at the Prussians.

Faced with continuing artillery barrages and determined resistance from French forces, the Prussian lines stopped and withdrew, first downhill then back uphill, to reach their camp on La Lune. The Prussians left 184 dead on the battlefield, while the toll of French dead numbered about 300. The confrontation was not about body count, however: The allied effort to take control of Paris and restore Louis XVI to power had been checked. A demoralized Prussian army, plagued from the beginning by inadequate food supplies, disease, and injury caused by heavy, late-summer rainstorms, limped out of France and back to Prussia.

The Austrian army under the count von Clerfayt arrived near Valmy on the evening of September 20, many hours after the battle had ended. They too reversed course and headed out of France. Had Clerfayt and Brunswick managed to meet up before the battle, or had Clerfayt succeeded in preventing Dumouriez and Kellerman from combining forces, the outcome at Valmy might have been very different. As it was, a Prussian army of thirty-five thousand had faced a French army more than twice its size.

SIGNIFICANCE

On the same day as the Battle of Valmy, the newly created National Convention met for the first time. Emboldened by news of the French victory, the convention created the First French Republic the next day. Thus, a millennium of monarchy in France came to an end. September 21, 1792, would become day one of year one in the new revolutionary calendar. For one of Germany's greatest poets, Johann Wolfgang von Goethe, who had witnessed the battle from Brunswick's camp on the heights of La Lune, the French victory at Valmy began a new era in human history.

Historically, Valmy stands as the first significant French victory in the wars of the French Revolution. It is also regarded as a historical turning point, because an Austrian-Prussian victory most likely would have brought the French Revolution to an abrupt end. Instead, the radical development of the revolution continued to accelerate over the next two years, reaching a climax in the Reign of Terror. The wars of of the French Revolution continued for twenty-three years after Valmy. Volunteerism and conscription continued to fill the army's ranks, as green recruits became seasoned veterans. The once-feared Prussian military machine was replaced by that of the French. French revolutionary armies went on to change the face of Europe and the course of world history.

—Irwin Halfond

FURTHER READING

Doyle, William. *Oxford History of the French Revolution*. New York: Oxford University Press, 2003. An excellent background to the French Revolution and the wars fought to contain it.

Price, Munro. *The Fall of the French Monarchy: Louis XVI, Marie Antoinette, and the Baron de Breteuil*. New York: Pan Macmillan, 2002. A graphic narration of the events leading to the fall of Louis XVI from power, including an excellent description of the Battle of Valmy. Index and bibliography.

Scott, Samuel F. *From Yorktown to Valmy*. Boulder: University Press of Colorado, 2003. A study of the training and performance of the French army from the American Revolution to the beginning of the French revolution. Index and bibliography.

1790's

October 2, 1792-April 12, 1799
CHRISTIAN MISSIONARY SOCIETIES ARE FOUNDED

The evangelical effects of the First Great Awakening and its revival in the Second Great Awakeing of the 1790's were widely felt in the establishment of organizations committed to the "conversion of the heathen," most notably the Baptist Missionary Society, the London Missionary Society, and the Church Missionary Society.

LOCALE: England; Serampore, India
CATEGORIES: Religion and theology; organizations and institutions

KEY FIGURES
William Carey (1761-1834), first Baptist missionary in northern India
Andrew Fuller (1754-1815), British Baptist pastor and secretary of the Baptist Mission Society
William Wilberforce (1759-1833), British abolitionist member of Parliament
Thomas Scott (1747-1821), British biblical scholar and secretary of the Church Mission Society
John Venn (1759-1813), first president of the Church Mission Society

SUMMARY OF EVENT

Protestantism was relatively late in its involvement in the missionary movement. Throughout the seventeenth and early eighteenth centuries, continental Europe was still engaged in religious wars and the solidifying of religious positions. The Thirty Years' War had established the position of *cuius regio eius religio* (whoever rules sets the religion), which led to an attitude of contentment with the status quo. Among Calvinists, the belief in predestination led many to reject the need for evangelism. On the other hand, the rationalist movements of the eighteenth century led to growing secularism.

The Counter-Reformation, however, led the Catholic Church to a renewed interest in missions, especially among the Franciscans, Dominicans, and Jesuits. In 1622, Pope Gregory XV established the Congregation of the Propagation of the Faith. Since Spain and Portugal led the way in global exploration, they found success in India, Japan, China, and the Americas already in the seventeenth century.

In the second half of the eighteenth century, the population explosion in the Protestant countries of northern Europe served as an impetus to move outward. This was soon facilitated by the invention of the steam engine, which increased the speed of travel, yet, for a time, there remained reluctance to engage in mission activity by trade organizations, especially in England. The official policy of the British East India Company was not to disturb the local population, lest such a disturbance jeopardize the commercial venture. The trading companies did take chaplains along but mainly to support the European traders.

The missionary societies were a natural outgrowth of the Pietism movement led by Philipp Jacob Spener at Halle in Germany. His goal was not to create a new, competing church but a movement within the established Church of like-minded individuals in groups for mutual edification and fellowship, with a focus on personal conversion and holiness. The influence of Pietism spread through Europe. In England, the Society for the Propagation of Christian Knowledge (SPCK) was formed in 1698 and the Society for the Propagation of the Gospel three years later.

When the king of Denmark took control of the Danish settlement of Tranquebar on the southeast coast of India, he turned to Spener's successor, August Francke, to train the first missionaries at Halle. Francke selected Bartholomew Ziegenbalg and Henry Plütschau, sent in 1705 as the first Protestant missionaries to India. Their success in a missionary approach that included education, Bible translation, and local leadership development provided a model for future missionaries. Just as important, they developed a communications network with interested persons back home. This included annual missionary letters and furlough visits. As a result, lay people in London, members of the SPCK, were able to participate, purchasing the printing press for the first Bible translation in India. By 1728, this Anglican society had taken over responsibility for the Tranquebar mission. This was the seed that developed into the missionary society movement at the end of the eighteenth century.

When the missionary efforts of Ziegenbalg and Plütschau spread from the small Danish territory in India to British-dominated soil, English clergy and lay people sought to be involved in the missionary effort. There were also changing attitudes among Protestants in England, partly due to the influence of Jonathan Edwards and the Great Awakening of New England. Edwards believed that this movement was a sign that the last days of history were upon the Church, an era that would be marked by the spread of the Gospel throughout the world. This led to new evangelical fervor and openness among a number of Calvinist Baptists, among them ministers John Ryland, John Sutcliff, and Andrew Fuller. When they were joined by William Carey, a young shoemaker who had recently become a minister, their local gatherings began to debate the propriety of missions.

On October 2, 1792, meeting in the back parlor of a private home in Kettering, Northampton, England, the Baptist Missionary Society was founded with Andrew Fuller as its first secretary. As its first missionary, the society sent William Carey to Bengali in 1793. He had impressed the society with his message, "Expect great things from God and attempt great things for God." The society sought to expand its base through contributions from congregations throughout England. By 1799, four additional missionaries were sent to Serampore, a small Danish colony near Calcutta, to join Carey in a successful missionary enterprise.

Among the English there were still obstacles to mission work. Carey and his colleagues had not been allowed to sail on British ships, and they continued to feel the harassment of the British East India Company. This seemed to fire their enthusiasm for mission all the more. In 1795, a group of Congregationalists, Anglicans, Presbyterians, and Methodists joined together to establish the London Missionary Society. A year later, they sent their first group of twenty-nine missionaries to Tahiti and other Pacific islands. As a united effort, they agreed to a basic principle that no form of denominationalism was to be preached by their members. The emphasis was on the development of a local leadership that would make all decisions about church governance.

Others chose a denominational focus: The establishment of the Methodist Mission Society (1796), the Glasgow Presbyterian Missionary Society (1796), and the Scottish Missionary Society (1796) soon followed. Within the Anglican Church, the impetus for missionary activity was closely intertwined with social action. The nucleus for this group lived in a wealthy suburb of London called Clapham, already active in the movement for the abolition of slavery. Among them were Granville Sharp, who had been responsible for the founding of Sierra Leone for freed slaves, and William Wilberforce, who led the abolition movement in Parliament. On April 12, 1799, a group of sixteen clergy and nine laymen, with the rector of Clapham, John Venn, as chair, met at an inn on Aldersgate Street in London to organize the Church Missionary Society to begin missionary work in Africa—their original name had been the Society for Missions in Africa and the East. With the well-known biblical scholar Thomas Scott serving as the society secretary for the next two decades, the society became the most effective arm for missions in the Anglican Church, expanding into numerous countries and becoming a leader in biblical translation.

SIGNIFICANCE

The organization of mission societies in the 1790's bore fruit in the following century, characterized by church historian Kenneth Scott Lautourette as "The Great Century." Numerous other societies sprang up. In England, these included the British and Foreign Bible Society in 1804 and the London Society for Promoting Christianity Among the Jews in 1809. The American churches followed suit with the American (Congregationalist) Board of Commissioners for Foreign Missions in 1810 and the American Baptist Missionary Board in 1814. On the continent of Europe, these developments were paralleled by the founding of the Basel Mission in 1815, the Berlin Society in 1824, and societies in Denmark (1821), France (1822), Sweden (1835), and Norway (1842).

While the early missionary efforts included education and biblical translation, the primary focus had been on evangelism. The focus of the missionary societies soon broadened, however, into a more holistic approach that included medical missions and economic development. This is not surprising, since many of those active in the initial organization of the mission societies were involved also in social reforms, especially in the movement to abolish slavery.

Already in 1810, Carey had proposed a general missionary conference at the Cape of Good Hope in Africa. Although his "pleasing dream" did not materialize, it did demonstrate a new global outlook for Protestantism. The initial work of these mission societies in India, the Pacific islands, and coastal countries of Africa would soon be expanded to include China, Japan, Korea, Indonesia, New Guinea, Latin America, and the interior of Africa.

—*Fred Strickert*

FURTHER READING

Hiney, Tim. *On the Missionary Trail: A Journey Through Polynesia, Asia, and Africa with the London Mission Society*. New York: Grove Press, 2001. This book traces the work of several early nineteenth century missionaries rather than presenting the founding of the organization.

Latourette, Kenneth Scott. *A History of Christianity*. San Francisco, Calif.: Harper, 1953. Still considered a classic. Latourette presents the history of the church with a special focus on expansion through mission.

1790's

Murray, Jocelyn. *Proclaim the Good News: A Short History of the Church Missionary Society.* London: Hodder & Stoughton, 1985. A popular history of nearly two hundred years of mission activity within the Anglican Church.

Neill, Stephen. *A History of Christian Missions.* 2d ed. Harmondsworth, England: Penguin Books, 1994. Originally published in 1964, this remains the standard work on the history of the missionary movement.

Stanley, Brian. *The History of the Baptist Missionary Society, 1792-1972.* Edinburgh: T & T Clark, 1992. Written on the two hundredth anniversary of the founding of this society. Chapters concerning mission activities in various countries are interspersed with a running survey of the work of the society at home.

Ward, Kevin, and Brian Stanley, eds. *The Church Mission Society and World Christianity, 1799-1999.* Grand Rapids, Mich.: W. B. Eerdmans, 2000. Written to commemorate the two hundredth anniversary of the founding of the Anglican Church Mission Society. Not replicating the thorough history written one hundred years earlier by Eugene Stock, this is a collection of essays concerning various aspects of the society's work.

SEE ALSO: 1739-1742: First Great Awakening; July 17, 1769-1824: Rise of the California Missions; 1773-1788: African American Baptist Church Is Founded; July 28-Oct. 16, 1789: Episcopal Church Is Established; 1790's-1830's: Second Great Awakening.

RELATED ARTICLES in *Great Lives from History: The Eighteenth Century, 1701-1800*: Jonathan Edwards; Granville Sharp; William Wilberforce; Graf von Zinzendorf.

1793
WHITNEY INVENTS THE COTTON GIN

Eli Whitney invented a machine to separate the useful portion of the cotton plant from its seeds and other extraneous materials. The gin revolutionized methods of agricultural production and increased the demand for slave labor in the American South.

LOCALE: Georgia, United States

CATEGORIES: Inventions; manufacturing; agriculture; science and technology

KEY FIGURES

Eli Whitney (1765-1825), American inventor

Catherine Greene (1753-1814), friend of Whitney

Phineas Miller (1764-1803), Whitney's business partner

Sir Richard Arkwright (1732-1792), English inventor of the water frame for spinning cotton

Edmund Cartwright (1743-1823), English inventor of the power loom

Samuel Crompton (1753-1827), English inventor of the spinning mule

J. D. B. De Bow (1820-1867), editor of *De Bow's Review* in New Orleans and apostle of southern diversification

James Hargreaves (1720-1778), English inventor of the spinning jenny

Edmund Ruffin (1794-1865), American advocate of scientific farming

James Watt (1736-1819), English developer of the steam engine

SUMMARY OF EVENT

Eli Whitney was born December 8, 1765, in Westborough, Massachusetts. The eldest of four children in a middle-class farming family, he had exceptional manual dexterity and a very inquisitive mind. The young Whitney particularly enjoyed dismantling mechanical devices and putting them back together. He also liked to build things in his father's workshop. This early curiosity continued to manifest itself throughout his teenage years and led to a degree from Yale College in 1792.

Following his graduation from Yale, Whitney decided to take a position in South Carolina as a tutor. On his journey south, he became acquainted with Catherine Greene, who persuaded him to visit her home near Savannah, Georgia. Whitney decided to stay at the Mulberry Grove plantation. It was there that Greene first suggested to Whitney that he invent a machine to clean the seeds from cotton. According to Whitney's personal account, he built that first small-scale model of the cotton gin in about ten days. He showed it to Greene and her plantation manager, Phineas Miller, who encouraged Whitney and financed the gin's development. Whitney made several adaptations to the already existing machines (which he had never seen), and the completed model of the cotton gin took months to finish.

Whitney's genius did not bring him the financial rewards he expected. The gin was of such great general utility that the South refused to allow anyone a monopoly on production of the machine and, as a result, there was much pirating. Whitney's problems with the gin and the patent struggles in which he engaged affected his approach to the rest of his industrial career. He was willing to improve the efficiency of his shop only if it did not threaten his security. He designed a musket-barrel-turning machine, for example, but did not build it for fear that competitors would use it to lure away his trained workmen. Whitney's business abilities were not outstanding. He was primarily interested in the mechanics and efficiency of production, but in those early days an entrepreneur had to be his own chief engineer, foreman, salesperson, and public relations expert. Only in the latter part of the nineteenth century did industrial specialization become common.

The invention of the cotton gin by Whitney was one of several important technological advances during the eighteenth century that revolutionized methods of production and habits of consumption throughout Europe and the United States. Whitney did for the cotton planter what Sir Richard Arkwright, James Hargreaves, Edmund Cartwright, and Samuel Crompton had done for the cotton manufacturer in Great Britain. The cumulative result of the water frame, the spinning jenny, the power loom, and the spinning mule was to increase the demand in England for raw cotton, and the cotton gin made it possible for U.S. planters to meet that demand. The application of steam to these machines greatly increased the output of yarn and cloth, thus serving to intensify the demands made upon cotton plants in the United States.

SIGNIFICANCE

The growth of the cotton industry in the United States was a major force in the rapid economic development of the nation, and much credit for this fact must go to the invention of the cotton gin. The period of the industry's greatest growth followed hard upon the end of the War of 1812, in 1815. Cotton production in the United States rose from 364,000 bales in 1815, of which 82 percent was exported, to 4,861,000 bales in 1860, of which 77 percent was exported. By 1860, Great Britain was consuming one quarter of the entire U.S. crop. Cotton was the United States' leading domestic export. In 1860, the total value of U.S. exports reached $334 million, 57 percent of which was from cotton. If the value of exports of other southern staples, notably tobacco, sugar, and rice,

Eli Whitney's cotton gin not only made cotton production more efficient but also, and most significantly, led to increased demand for slaves and slave labor in the American South. (C. A. Nichols & Company)

is added to this figure, the contribution of the South to the nation's export trade approached 65 percent. In spite of these impressive statistics, southerners complained that the fruits of their labor were gathered by other sections of the country.

To a large degree, this charge was accurate. Southern planters sold their crops abroad or to the northeastern states. The market was erratic, varying according to demand and supply; it was sensitive to international incidents and almost impossible to predict. Communications were slow. Planters shipped according to one set of prices, only to find a different set of prices operative when their cargoes arrived in port. Risks at sea were great. The costs of shipment were large and paid in the form of commissions to agents of the planters. These men, called factors, handled every detail of the shipment, in addition to making purchases for, and offering credits to, the planters.

These problems were common to all the participants of the staple trade, but they fell with greater impact, especially after 1830, on the older cotton-producing regions along the South Atlantic coast. There, constant plantings without attention to soil conservation reduced yields per acre while increasing costs of production per unit of crop. South Carolina planters found it extremely difficult to compete with planters on Mississippi's lush and virgin lands. Economic stagnation and nullification inevitably followed. Another result was an effort on the part of some farsighted southerners to stimulate economic diversification in the region. J. D. B. De Bow of New Orleans and Edmund Ruffin of Virginia were among those who preached the virtues of scientific agriculture, industrialization, and transportation improvements.

The dramatic growth of the cotton plantation was more than a matter of production statistics and marketing problems. It was the story of great movements of population into the lush lands of the lower Mississippi River Valley. It was also the story of the master and the slave. To some historians, particularly those from the South, it was the story of the evolution of a culture distinct from that of other regions. Most historians, including those who deny the concept of cultural distinctiveness, agree that by the 1850's—according to most economic indices—the South was in a manifestly inferior position, perhaps in a colonial position, relative to the North. Most also would agree that the institution of slavery was a major cause of this inferiority.

The North was not an industrial area in 1860, although strong beginnings had been made in some parts. The North was basically agrarian but was more industrialized than the South. This meant that the North offered more nonagricultural opportunities for economic advancement. The agricultural sector in the North was based on the small farm. In the South, by contrast, small farmers found it increasingly difficult to compete with the plantation.

The size of individual landholdings increased markedly in the South after 1840, while farms became smaller in the North. The population of the North was compact; the plantation system dispersed population in the South, retarding southern town and city development. Fewer urban areas meant there were fewer commercial and banking facilities in the South, which, in turn, meant a slow rate of capital formation and presented difficulties to those wishing to diversify or undertake transportation improvement. Fewer inducements were available to attract skilled labor, and the fear of competing with slaves was also an obstacle. At the same time, the need for unskilled labor—specifically African American slave labor—was increasing as the South struggled to meet the growing demand for cotton made possible by the new technology.

The effect of all these factors was to make the South economically weaker than the North, although the South was integrated in the budding national economy. The South was neither distinct nor unique, but as pressures on, and criticism (particularly abolitionist criticism) of, the South accumulated, southerners created the myth of their cultural uniqueness. Whitney's invention had done much to make this myth—and a growing North-South schism—possible.

—*John G. Clark, updated by Liesel Ashley Miller*

FURTHER READING

Aitken, Hugh G. J., ed. *Did Slavery Pay? Readings in the Economics of Black Slavery in the United States*. Boston: Houghton Mifflin, 1971. Essays consider the effects of slavery on the southern economy. Provides examples of the traditional perspective on the economic dimensions of slavery.

Andrews, Mildred Gwin. *The Men and the Mills: A History of the Southern Textile Industry*. Macon, Ga.: Mercer University Press, 1987. Chronicles the development of the southern textile industry from the 1800's to the later 1980's. Glossary of terms, illustrations, photographs, and comprehensive bibliography.

Batchelder, Samuel. *Introduction and Early Progress of the Cotton Manufacture in the United States*. Boston: Little, Brown, 1863. Reprint. Clifton, N.J.: August M. Kelley, 1972. This study is considered to be an economic classic.

Britton, Karen Gerhardt. *Bale O'Cotton: The Mechanical Art of Cotton Ginning*. College Station: Texas A&M University Press, 1992. Chronicles the history of the American cotton ginning industry from its origins in 1793 to the late twentieth century. Examines the folklore associated with the industry.

Fogel, Robert William. *Without Consent or Contract: The Rise and Fall of American Slavery*. New York: W. W. Norton, 1989. A thorough interpretation of the institution of slavery in the United States. Fogel supports his analyses with almost one hundred pages of notes and references.

Fogel, Robert William, and Stanley L. Egnerman. *Time on the Cross: The Economics of American Negro Slavery*. Boston: Little, Brown, 1974. A controversial but important revisionist look at the economic and social foundations of slavery in the U.S. South, using quantitative methods and previously neglected sources of information.

Green, Constance McLaughlin. "The Invention of the Cotton Gin." In *Eli Whitney and the Birth of American Technology*. Boston: Little, Brown, 1956. One of the best accounts of the events leading up to and surrounding Whitney's invention of the cotton gin.

Lakwete, Angela. *Inventing the Cotton Gin: Machine and Myth in Antebellum America*. Baltimore: Johns Hopkins University Press, 2003. Places the invention of the cotton gin within a historical and global context. Lakwete describes early gins invented in Africa and Asia, the earliest gins used in the United States, and the innovations of Whitney and other inventors. She refutes the argument that the slavery-based antebellum southern states had a primitive economy, maintaining that the use of the cotton gin provides proof of innovation, industrialization, and modernization.

Stapleton, Darwin H. "Eli Whitney and the American System of Manufacturing." In *Technology in America: A History of Individuals and Ideas*, edited by Carroll W. Pursell. 2d ed. Cambridge, Mass.: MIT Press, 1990. Summarizes Whitney's contributions to U.S. technology.

SEE ALSO: 1733: Kay Invents the Flying Shuttle; 1764: Invention of the Spinning Jenny; 1767-1771: Invention of the Water Frame; 1779: Crompton Invents the Spinning Mule; Apr., 1785: Cartwright Patents the Steam-Powered Loom; 1790: First Steam Rolling Mill; 1793: Whitney Invents the Cotton Gin; 1795: Invention of the Flax Spinner.

RELATED ARTICLES in *Great Lives from History: The Eighteenth Century, 1701-1800*: Sir Richard Arkwright; James Hargreaves; John Kay; James Watt; Eli Whitney.

1793-January, 1794
MACARTNEY MISSION TO CHINA

Great Britain sent British diplomat Macartney to the court of the Qianlong emperor, who regarded Britain as a vassal state and its people as barbarians. Macartney was to establish diplomatic relations with mainland China and to open new trade opportunities. Although negotiations led to promises, none of them were put into effect, and historians have deemed Macartney's mission a failure.

LOCALE: Guangzhou, Chengde, and Beijing, China
CATEGORIES: Diplomacy and international relations; trade and commerce

KEY FIGURES
George Macartney (1737-1806), British diplomat, colonial governor, and envoy to Beijing, 1792-1794
Qianlong (1711-1799), emperor of China, r. 1735-1796

Heshen (Ho-Shen; 1750-1799), grand secretary to Qianlong
Sir George Leonard Staunton (1737-1801), secretary to the Macartney embassy

SUMMARY OF EVENT
Between 1662 and 1796, China had two rulers who served sixty years or more, Kangxi and Qianlong. The extremely long reigns of these two emperors produced a monolithic sense of permanence in the empire, and the emperors themselves gained an aura of authority even beyond the typical Chinese emperor: They encountered great deference and little opposition. Functioning within strict rules of ceremony to preserve an agrarian culture and persistently avoiding the advances of the Industrial Revolution that European nations experienced, Kangxi and Qianlong also by and large avoided the warfare be-

tween nations that characterized eighteenth century Europe. Thus, China and its rulers felt themselves superior to the "barbarians" of the West and sought to prevent contact between mainland China and the Western world. Western traders, known as "supercargoes" (merchants trading a ship's cargo), were allowed access to the Chinese markets only through the *hoppos* (merchants) of the port of Guangzhou (Canton).

In 1793, George Macartney embarked on a mission on behalf of the British government to seek an audience with the Qianlong emperor. The British were dissatisfied with their limited access to Chinese trade and to the Chinese government, both of which were filtered through Guangzhou. They sought, therefore, to expand both their commercial and their diplomatic contact with the Chinese Empire. Macartney was instructed to seek permission to establish a permanent diplomatic headquarters at the court of Qianlong, to be occupied by a British minister of state. He was also to seek access for British merchants to other ports—to northern ports, where they could trade woolen goods, as well as to centers of the trade in tea and silk. The British also sought access through China to the potential markets of neighboring countries, such as Japan. Most of these terms were transmitted to Heshen, grand secretary to Qianlong, who formed a buffer between Macartney and the emperor and prevented trading concessions or reforms.

Efforts to change Chinese trading habits were thwarted by the established Chinese system of commerce, which placed many layers of intermediaries between the Chinese imperial court and foreign traders. Members of each layer profited from their function within the system. *Hoppos*, regional governors, and the emperor himself all gained great wealth through the existing system. The emperor thus had little incentive to allow the British to circumvent the established system, and the *hoppos* and governors certainly would have resisted any change. Efforts to alter the system were thus doomed to failure.

As was traditional in diplomacy, Macartney brought gifts to the Chinese emperor. The emperor, however, regarded these offical gifts from the nation of Great Britain as tributes from a vassal, rather than gifts from an equal. Qianlong had only to look at a world map to understand that the small European countries that sought to deal with him should be regarded as vassal states, destined to pay homage to the larger, omnipotent Chinese Empire.

In Qianlong's view, the barbarians of Europe could never achieve the high level of Chinese culture. Furthermore, he did not need the scientific or technological advances of the West, such as the steam engine or the spin-

ning jenny, to sustain the culture over which he ruled. Meeting with Qianlong meant performing the kotow ceremony, which required kneeling before the emperor three separate times and, while lying prostrate, knocking the ground three times with one's head. Macartney, accustomed to bowing only before the ruler of England, refused to participate in this ceremony, though his diary entry of September 14, 1793, records that he knelt on one knee before the emperor out of respect when he gave Qianlong a box encrusted with diamonds that bore the letter of George III to the emperor.

Trade between Great Britain and China was restricted to Guangzhou and carried out by the British East India Company. Westerners were not welcome on the mainland. One exception was the presence of Jesuit priests, who were permitted into mainland China by Kangxi's 1692 Edict of Toleration. Their influence, however, was minimal. An estimated 200,000 Catholics resided in China by 1800; they appear to have offered the primary source of contact between the East and the West. Even had they been willing to offer their services, however, Great Britain would have been unwilling to depend upon Roman Catholics as formal or informal diplomatic links to the imperial court.

Macartney's written record of his embassy included speculations about the meaning of his experience in China and extensive comments on all the phases of Chinese life that he observed firsthand. Macartney reported that British trade in Guangzhou in 1793, including both the British East India Company and private traders, amounted to £1,527,775. Trade through India on British ships amounted to another £943,632. He stated that trade between Holland, France, the United States, Denmark, and Sweden had declined, as the Danes and Swedes had given up trade with China, leaving a larger potential marketplace for the British. He felt that the balance of trade was unfavorable to Western merchants, since foreign nations desired Chinese goods, but the Chinese seemed uninterested in purchasing Western commodities. Indeed, they seemed to look upon English technological equipment as mere trinkets.

Macartney recorded his impressions of the imperial city of Chengde (Jehol) in his diary entries for September 14-18, 1793, when he met with the emperor on three occasions. He commented on the vigorous health of the emperor, who seemed to the diplomat to be about sixty years of age (he was actually more than eighty). The emperor presented Macartney with a scepter carved of greenish stone; Macartney presented the emperor with a gift from George III, consisting of a set of watches encrusted with diamonds. Macartney on that occasion likened Qianlong to King Solomon. On September 17, Macartney attended a birthday celebration in honor of Qianlong, including entertainments by acrobats and other carnival performers. The entire court prostrated themselves before Qianlong, whom Macartney then likened to the Babylonian king Nebuchadnezzar, though he was hidden behind a screen during the entire celebration. It does not appear that Qianlong himself, on any of these occasions, discussed official diplomatic business with Macartney, leaving such discussions to his state officers. Macartney returned to England in January of 1794, having accomplished very little.

SIGNIFICANCE

Heshen had the task of sloughing off Macartney's concerns about trade and commerce in his meeting with Qianlong, and he subverted promises made in negotiation with Qianlong's appointees, including Sir George Leonard Staunton, secretary to the Macartney embassy. The Cantonese merchants at court sought to protect their interests and the lucrative profits they afforded the emperor. In one of his "speculations," written upon his return voyage to England in early 1794, Macartney complains directly of the *hoppos'* extortion.

It is the common consensus of historians that Macartney's embassy achieved none of the goals it sought. The failure of the Macartney embassy meant that relations between Great Britain and China continued to be conducted mainly through the British East India Company and that they were therefore filtered through the interests of that company. The failure of the Qing Dynasty to deal with issues of modernization, meanwhile, and the growing corruption of the court led to a series of nineteenth century battles that saw the United Kingdom lay claim to Hong Kong in the Treaty of Nanjing (1842). The subsequent collapse of the Qing Dynasty (1912) may be related to the failure of Qianlong to recognize and respond to the world's industrialization and to his inability to combat the corruption of his own court.

Macartney's embassy returned to England with considerable information that had not been previously available in Europe, including topographical and geographical maps of the Chinese coastline and descriptions of key sites and "factories" (buildings housing merchants and traders identified as "factors") that provided new insight into Chinese life and industry. The botanist on the voyage, David Stronach, compiled lists of Chinese plants and brought back with him tea plants in the hope of developing a British tea industry.

—*Irving N. Rothman*

FURTHER READING

Macartney, George. *An Embassy to China: Lord Macartney's Journal, 1793-1794*. Edited by J. L. Cranmer-Byng. Vol. 3 in *Britain and the China Trade, 1635-1842*, edited by Patrick Tuck. Reprint. New York: Routledge, 2000. Macartney's journal is supplemented by introductory essays on a wide range of topics.

Pritchard, Earl H. *Anglo-Chinese Relations During the Seventeenth and Eighteenth Centuries*. Reprint. New York: Octagon Books, 1970. A history of the commercial development of English trade with China from 1497-1793; includes an account of the cultural differences between China and England and a comprehensive set of tables related to trade between the nations.

_____. *The Crucial Years of Early Anglo-Chinese Relations, 1750-1800*. Reprint. New York: Octagon Books, 1970. An economic history of the efforts of England to gain trading rights to mainland China, with a report and assessment of diplomatic relations, containing statistical appendices and a bibliography of manuscript and published sources.

SEE ALSO: Oct. 21, 1727: Treaty of Kiakhta; 1750-1792: China Consolidates Control over Tibet.

RELATED ARTICLES in *Great Lives from History: The Eighteenth Century, 1701-1800*: George III; Qianlong.

1790's

January 21, 1793
EXECUTION OF LOUIS XVI

The trial and execution of Louis XVI placed the Jacobin faction in ascendancy in the French revolutionary government. It helped discredit the revolution among both moderates and conservatives in France and stiffened resistance to the revolution abroad.

LOCALE: Paris, France

CATEGORIES: Government and politics; wars, uprisings, and civil unrest; laws, acts, and legal history

KEY FIGURES

Louis XVI (1754-1793), king of France, r. 1774-1792

Robespierre (1758-1794), leading member of the Jacobin faction of revolutionaries

Chrétien-Guillaume de Lamoignon de Malesherbes (1721-1794), Louis XVI's principal defense counsel at his trial by the National Convention

Romain de Sèze (1748-1836), one of the king's defense counsels at his trial

François Denis Tronchet (1726-1806), one of the king's defense counsels at his trial

Duke of Brunswick (Charles William Ferdinand; 1735-1806), commander of allied army that invaded France in 1792

Pius VI (Giovanni Angelo Braschi; 1717-1799), Roman Catholic pope, 1775-1799

SUMMARY OF EVENT

The execution of Louis XVI was a personal as well as national tragedy. A decent, well-meaning monarch, he was unable to reconcile the revolutionary changes introduced into the fabric of French government by the National Assembly. Despite concessions that he made during the summer of 1789, despite his acceptance of the constitutional reforms instituted between 1789 and 1791, and despite his consent to the reform of the Catholic Church in France, the king never ceased to look for means of annulling the French Revolution. Throughout the summer and early fall of 1789, he gave serious thought to, and some outward manifestation of, the use of force against the National Assembly. This possibility was eliminated when both the king and the National Assembly moved from Versailles to Paris in October, 1789, but Louis continued to resist.

The constitution of 1791 created a constitutional monarchy in which the king played a major role. The strongest weapon that Louis could use against the Legislative Assembly was the king's veto power. The army was still theoretically under his control, but it was unreliable because the soldiers were becoming sympathetic to the revolution. Moreover, the assembly held the purse strings and with the support of most of the nation, prevented the king from dominating the new government. Louis might have made gradual adjustments to become a constitutional monarch, but he was unable to convince his conscience that reform of the Church was not evil.

When in March and April, 1791, Pope Pius VI solemnly denounced the religious enactments of the revolutionary government (which the king had reluctantly accepted), Louis decided to act. On June 20-21, the French royal family attempted to escape from Paris and flee to

Louis XVI and his family, including Marie-Antoinette, are caught at Varennes attempting to flee the country. (Francis R. Niglutsch)

The execution of Louis XVI, with the remains of Louis XV's statue in the background. (Library of Congress)

1790's

the eastern border, where, with loyal French supporters and with the aid of Austria and Prussia, they hoped to move against the government in Paris. The king was recognized and stopped at Varennes. Forced to return to the capital, he became a virtual prisoner in his own palace.

France drifted toward war during the second half of 1791. Neither the king nor the principal political faction in the Legislative Assembly, the Girondins, made any attempt to avert the calamity. Both believed that a foreign war would consolidate the nation in their respective camps. Louis allowed his wife to persuade him that war between France and the allied powers would result in a French defeat. He would then intercede with the victors, save France from the consequences of its revolutionary folly, and recover the traditional powers of the French monarchy. The Girondins believed France would win an easy and glorious victory that would redound to their credit. The war had an effect, however, which neither the monarchists nor the Girondins desired. It led to the rise of the Jacobins and their own destruction. The king fell first, but the Girondin leaders soon followed.

War was declared on April 20, 1792, but neither France nor its enemies, Austria and Prussia, were prepared for the conflict. Through the summer of 1792, a Prussian army under the command of the duke of Bruns-

wick marched slowly but steadily toward Paris. By the end of July the capital was on the verge of panic. On July 25, the duke of Brunswick issued a manifesto which in substance stated that it was his aim to put an end to anarchy in France and to stop the attacks directed against throne and altar. Furthermore, he stated that if any harm came to the king or members of the French royal family, he would deliver up the city of Paris to military execution and complete destruction. Louis realized the consequences of this manifesto and tried in vain to disassociate himself from it. To the people of Paris and the supporters of the revolution throughout France, the Brunswick Manifesto was the proof needed to convince them that the king was allied with the enemies of the nation.

On August 10, the Tuileries, where the king resided, was attacked by the people, and the king, who took refuge with the Legislative Assembly, was deposed. A temporary government was set up and elections were held for a new constituent assembly. On September 21, 1792, the National Convention met and the following day proclaimed France to be a republic. The representatives were now faced with the problem of what to do with the king. Robespierre preferred simply executing him. A trial might occasion public unrest. Louis also wished to avoid a trial, for that would make the entire nation culpable of regicide, rendering a restoration of the monarchy more difficult. After much debate the Assembly decided that the king should be tried for treason.

The trial dragged on for more than a month. The king was ably defended by three distinguished barristers, Chrétien-Guillaume de Lamoignon de Malesherbes, François Denis Tronchet, and Romain de Sèze. It was a political trial, marked by trivial or vague accusations not susceptible to legal proof. Nevertheless, a large majority of the Convention convicted Louis of conspiring against liberty and the safety of the state. Fearing an adverse reaction to regicide, Girondins attempted to spare Louis. Jacobins, who had led the attack against him, demanded the death penalty.

Robespierre was one of the most outspoken opponents of the king. He summed up the position of those advocating the death penalty by declaring that if Louis were not guilty of treason, then each member of the Assembly, which had unanimously proclaimed France to be a republic, was guilty of a crime against the king and so deserved to be executed. Finally, in January, 1793, the crucial vote was taken, and the king was condemned to death by 387 votes to 334, although 26 of those voting for the death penalty did so with reservations. On January 21, 1793, "Citizen Louis Capet" was executed in the place de la Révolution. There was now no turning back, for the 361 regicides leading the revolution would certainly be executed if it failed.

SIGNIFICANCE

The political significance of Louis's execution was bound to the political struggle for power between the Girondins and the Jacobins. The Girondins, supported by the bourgeoisie and the provinces, had emerged as the dominant faction in the National Convention in October and November, 1792. The Jacobins, supported by the "sansculottes" of Paris, were fighting for their political lives if not for their very existence. Both factions wanted the king out of the way, and each knew that the outcome of the trial meant political victory or defeat. The fight was not waged over the guilt or innocence of Louis XVI, nor over whether he should be executed, but over which political faction would be discredited once the king's fate had been decided.

During this struggle, the power bases of the Girondins and the Jacobins were polarized, and the groundwork was laid for the struggle of both factions to the death. The two years following the king's death were the bloodiest period of the revolution.

—*Charles H. O'Brien*

FURTHER READING

Allison, John M. S. *Lamoignon de Malesherbes: Defender and Reformer of the French Monarchy, 1721-1794*. New Haven, Conn.: Yale University Press, 1938. A perceptive study of Louis XVI's principal defender at his trial.

Doyle, William. *The Oxford History of the French Revolution*. Oxford, England: Clarendon Press, 1989. Impartial and thorough, one of the best single-volume works on the French Revolution.

Dunn, Susan. *The Deaths of Louis XVI: Regicide and the French Political Imagination*. Princeton, N.J.: Princeton University Press, 1994. Explores the transformation of Louis XVI's death into a powerful modern myth of a martyred king.

Hardman, John. *Louis XVI*. New Haven, Conn.: Yale University Press, 1993. A thoughtful, well-balanced biography of the king.

Jordan, David P. *The King's Trial: The French Revolution vs. Louis XVI*. 25th anniversary ed. Berkeley: University of California Press, 2004. Chronicles the period from August 10, 1792, when Louis was deposed, until his execution, including his trial and sentencing. In a preface to this new edition, Jordan considers the previous twenty-five years of scholarship and places his book in an updated context.

Lefebvre, Georges. *The French Revolution: From Its Origins to 1793*. Translated by Elizabeth Moss Evanson. New York: Columbia University Press, 1962. The author, an eminent Marxist historian of the revolution, argues the king was the victim of a power struggle between Girondins and Jacobins.

Padover, Saul K. *The Life and Death of Louis XVI*. 1939. Reprint. New York: Taplinger, 1963. This biography of Louis XVI is sympathetic to the king and also to the aims of the revolutionaries, both headed for inevitable conflict from the beginning.

Price, Munro. *The Fall of the French Monarchy: Louis XVI, Marie Antoinette, and the Baron de Breteuil*. London: Pan, 2002. Recounts the baron's diplomatic efforts to gain European support for the French royal family. Discusses the trial and assassination of Louis and the execution of Marie-Antoinette. Published in the United States under the title *The Road from Versailles: Louis XVI, Marie Antoinette, and the Fall of the French Monarchy*.

Walzer, Michael, ed. *Regicide and Revolution: Speeches at the Trial of Louis XVI*. Translated by Marian Rothstein. New York: Cambridge University Press, 1974. Includes the editor's lengthy introduction, together with eleven speeches by Jacobin opponents of monarchy attempting to justify the king's execution.

SEE ALSO: May 5, 1789: Louis XVI Calls the Estates-General; June 20, 1789: Oath of the Tennis Court; July 14, 1789: Fall of the Bastille; Oct., 1789-Apr. 25, 1792: France Adopts the Guillotine; Apr. 20, 1792-Oct., 1797: Early Wars of the French Revolution;

Mar. 4-Dec. 23, 1793: War in the Vendée; July 27-28, 1794: Fall of Robespierre; Nov. 9-10, 1799: Napoleon Rises to Power in France.

RELATED ARTICLES in *Great Lives from History: The Eighteenth Century, 1701-1800*: Georges Danton; Louis XVI; Marie-Antoinette; Pius VI; Robespierre.

February 12, 1793
FIRST FUGITIVE SLAVE LAW

The U.S. Congress passed a law establishing a procedure for southern slave owners to recover slaves who fled north, aggravating the sectional conflict between free states and slave states.

LOCALE: Philadelphia, Pennsylvania
CATEGORIES: Laws, acts, and legal history; social issues and reform; government and politics

KEY FIGURES

George Cabot (1752-1823), U.S. senator, 1791-1796
Theodore Sedgwick (1746-1813), U.S. representative, 1789-1796, 1799-1801, senator, 1796-1799, and Speaker of the House of Representatives, 1799-1801
Samuel Johnston (1733-1816), governor of North Carolina, 1787-1789, and U.S. senator, 1789-1793
George Read (1733-1798), U.S. senator, 1789-1793, and chief justice of Delaware, 1793-1798
Roger Sherman (1721-1793), U.S. representative, 1789-1791, senator, 1791-1793, and mayor of New Haven, 1784-1793
John Taylor (1753-1824), U.S. senator, 1792-1794, 1803, 1822-1824
George Washington (1732-1799), president of the United States, 1789-1797

SUMMARY OF EVENT

In colonial America, the return of fugitives within and between jurisdictions was a common practice. These fugitives were usually felons escaping from jails; persons charged with crimes; apprentices and indentured servants fleeing from their employers; or black, white, or Native American slaves running away from their masters. Their rendition between jurisdictions depended on comity among colonial authorities. The articles of the New England Confederation of 1643 included a provision for the return of fugitive slaves and servants. Like all

subsequent American legislation on the topic, it did not provide for a trial by jury.

In the late eighteenth century, with the growth of antislavery sentiment in the North and the settlement of territory west of the Appalachian Mountains, a uniform method for the return of fugitive slaves became necessary. Article VI of the Northwest Ordinance of 1787 excluding chattel slavery provided that persons escaping into the territory from whom labor or service was lawfully claimed in any one of the original states might be returned to the person claiming their labor or service. The provision did not distinguish between slaves and indentured servants.

The United States Constitution of the same year incorporated the provision, without limiting the claimants to residents of the original states of the union. One of several concessions intended to win support from the slaveholding states, Article IV, section 2, states that

> no person held to service or labor in one state, under the laws thereof, escaping into another, shall, in consequence of any law or regulation therein, be discharged from such service or labor, but shall be delivered up on claim of the party to whom such service or labor may be due.

In 1793, Congress decided to set federal rules for the rendition of alleged fugitives. This action was prompted by Pennsylvania's attempt to recover from Virginia several men accused of having kidnapped John Davis, a free black man. Unable to receive satisfaction, the governor of Pennsylvania brought the matter to the attention of President George Washington, who referred it to the Congress.

A committee of the House of Representatives, led by Theodore Sedgwick of Massachusetts, reported a rendition bill on November 15, 1791, but no action was taken. A special Senate committee, consisting of George Cabot of Massachusetts (who chaired the committee), Samuel

Johnston of North Carolina, and George Read of Delaware, submitted a bill on December 20, 1792, establishing a ministerial procedure for the extradition of judicial fugitives. It also provided a system for the recovery of fugitives from labor or service. A claimant had to present a written deposition from one or more credible persons to a local magistrate who would order officers of the court to seize the fugitive and turn him or her over to the claimant. The bill set penalties for harboring a fugitive, neglecting a duty, or obstructing an arrest. After debate, the bill was recommitted with instructions to amend, and John Taylor of Virginia and Roger Sherman of Connecticut were added to the committee.

January 3, 1793, a revised bill was reported to the Senate by Johnston, allowing the claimant or his agent to seize a fugitive and bring that person to a federal court or a local magistrate. Oral testimony or an affidavit certified by a magistrate of the master's state sufficed to establish a claim. To guard against the kidnapping of free African Americans, residents of the territory or state in which they were seized, the new bill included a proviso assuring them their rights under the laws of that territory or state. This meant they were entitled to a judicial inquiry or a jury trial to determine their status. They were also to be presumed free, until proven otherwise, and allowed to testify on their own behalf.

After two debates, during which the proviso was dropped, the bill passed the Senate on January 18. It was entitled "An act respecting fugitives from justice and persons escaping from their masters." The House passed it with little discussion, February 5, by a vote of forty-eight to seven. Seven days later, President Washington signed the bill into law.

The first two sections of the act, known popularly as the Fugitive Slave Act of 1793, dealt with the interstate rendition of fugitives from justice. The third section provided that when a person held to labor escaped into any state or territory of the United States, the master or a designated agent could seize that individual and bring him or her before a judge of the federal courts in the state or before any magistrate of a county, city, or incorporated town. Title was proven by the testimony of the master or the affidavit of a magistrate in the state from which the escapee came, certifying that the person had escaped. The judge or magistrate then had to provide a certificate entitling the petitioner to remove the fugitives.

The act applied to fugitive apprentices or indentured servants as well as to slaves, a provision important at that time to representatives of the northern states. The act did not admit a trial by jury, and it contained no provisions for the alleged fugitives to offer evidence on their own behalf, although they were not prevented from doing so if the presiding judge or magistrate agreed.

Section 4 provided criminal penalties, a fine of five hundred dollars, in addition to any civil action the owner might have under state law, for obstructing the capture and for rescuing, harboring, aiding, or hiding fugitives.

Although many attempts were made to amend the act, it remained the law of the land until the abolition of slavery, its constitutionality repeatedly upheld by the Supreme Court. It was amended and supplemented, not replaced, by the Second Fugitive Slave Act of 1850, part of the Compromise of 1850.

SIGNIFICANCE

The Fugitive Slave Act of 1793 contributed significantly to the growth of sectional conflict within the United States. Efforts to enforce its provisions encountered immediate resistance in northern states, isolated and scattered at first but increasingly well organized and vigorous (for example, the Underground Railroad), as slavery prospered in the Old South and spread to western lands. Many northern states passed personal liberty laws (Indiana in 1824, Connecticut in 1828, New York and Vermont in 1840). Designed to prevent the kidnaping of free African Americans, these laws provided for trial by jury to determine their true status.

The effectiveness of the statute was further diminished by the Supreme Court's decision in *Prigg v. Commonwealth of Pennsylvania* (1842) that state authorities could not be forced by the national government to act in fugitive slave cases. Subsequently, Massachusetts (1843), Vermont (1843), Pennsylvania (1847), and Rhode Island (1848) forbade their officials to help enforce the law and refused the use of their jails for fugitive slaves. Because the Fugitive Slave Act of 1793 provided no federal means of apprehending fugitive slaves, owners had to rely on the often ineffectual and costly services of slave catchers. With the outbreak of the Civil War, the law ceased to apply to the Confederate states. It was considered valid in the loyal border states until it was repealed June 28, 1864.

—*Charles H. O'Brien*

FURTHER READING

Campbell, Stanley. *The Slave Catchers: Enforcement of the Fugitive Slave Law, 1850-1860*. Chapel Hill: University of North Carolina Press, 1970. Although the book focuses primarily on the 1850 act, chapter 1 deals with attempts to enforce the Fugitive Slave Act of 1793.

Finkelman, Paul. "The Kidnapping of John Davis and the Adoption of the Fugitive Slave Law of 1793." *The Journal of Southern History* 56, no. 3 (August, 1990): 397-422. Discusses the incident that led Congress to take up the issue of fugitive slaves; thoroughly examines the legislative progress of the law.

_____. *Slavery and the Founders: Race and Liberty in the Age of Jefferson.* 2d ed. Armonk, N.Y.: M. E. Sharpe, 2001. Examines the status of slavery in the newly created republic, including the adoption of the Fugitive Slave Law of 1793.

_____. *Slavery in the Courtroom: An Annotated Bibliography of American Cases.* Washington, D.C.: Library of Congress, 1985. Presents a detailed description of judicial decisions, as well as other documents pertaining to the enforcement of the Fugitive Slave Act of 1793.

McDougall, Marion G. *Fugitive Slaves, 1619-1865.* 1891. Reprint. New York: Bergman, 1969. Appendix includes the text of the Fugitive Slave Act of 1793 and many other relevant legislative and judicial documents.

Morris, Thomas D. *Free Men All: The Personal Liberty Laws of the North, 1780-1861.* Baltimore: Johns Hopkins University Press, 1974. A definitive account of the efforts of northern states to secure individual liberty against the harsh implications of the Fugitive Slave Law of 1793.

Newman, Richard S. *The Transformation of American Abolition: Fighting Slavery in the Early Republic.* Chapel Hill: University of North Carolina, 2002. A history of American abolitionist activities from the 1770's to the 1830's. Newman traces the beginning of the abolition movement to Pennsylvania and discusses the movement's reaction to the Fugitive Slave Law of 1793.

Wiecek, William M. *Liberty Under Law: The Supreme Court in American Life.* Baltimore: Johns Hopkins University Press, 1988. Discusses the Supreme Court's interpretation of the Fugitive Slave Act of 1793 in *Prigg v. Commonwealth of Pennsylvania* (1842).

_____. *The Sources of Antislavery Constitutionalism in America, 1760-1848.* Ithaca, N.Y.: Cornell University Press, 1977. Detailed exposition of the fugitive slave provisions of the Northwest Ordinance and the U.S. Constitution, 1787.

SEE ALSO: 18th cent.: Expansion of the Atlantic Slave Trade; Apr. 6, 1712: New York City Slave Revolt; Nov. 23, 1733: Slaves Capture St. John's Island; 1760-1776: Caribbean Slave Rebellions; Apr. 14, 1775: Pennsylvania Society for the Abolition of Slavery Is Founded; July 2, 1777-1804: Northeast States Abolish Slavery; Mar. 16, 1792: Denmark Abolishes the Slave Trade.

RELATED ARTICLES in *Great Lives from History: The Eighteenth Century, 1701-1800*: Benjamin Banneker; Roger Sherman; George Washington.

1790's

March 4-December 23, 1793
WAR IN THE VENDÉE

Angered by the execution of Louis XVI, the sale of confiscated Church and émigré lands to the middle classes, the deportation of village priests who did not support the revolution, and the institution of a national draft, the peasantry in western France revolted. A counterrevolution developed, threatening to topple the First French Republic during the first year of its existence.

LOCALE: Western France
CATEGORIES: Wars, uprisings, and civil unrest; government and politics

KEY FIGURES
François Charette (1763-1796), French counter-revolutionary leader

Jacques Cathelineau (1759-1793), first commander of the Royal and Catholic Army of the Vendée
Maurice Gigost d'Elbée (1752-1794), second commander of the Royal and Catholic Army of the Vendée
Jean Nicolas Stofflet (1751-1796), peasant rebel leader
Comte de La Rochejaquelein (Henri du Vergier; 1772-1794), noble rebel leader
Louis-Marie Turreau de Garambouville (1756-1816), French Republican general
Jean-Baptiste Carrier (1756-1794), French Republican general

SUMMARY OF EVENT
By March, 1793, there was much about the French Revolution to infuriate a typical peasant living in the Vendée

The Comte de La Rochejaquelein leading a group of peasants during the war in the Vendée. (Francis R. Niglutsch)

(then known as Bas-Poitou), an administrative district in western France noted for its extensive marshlands, forests, and small farming communities. For the average resident of this rural area, the French Revolution, which had begun almost four years before, may have benefited the middle class and urban population, but it had instituted few policies to improve his or her daily life.

The typical peasant of the Vendée seriously resented the reorganization of the Catholic Church in France, which forced clergy to take a civil oath to the constitution and serve under the direction of the French government. In general, two-thirds of the clergy in France refused to take the oath, thus becoming refractory (nonjuring) clergy. In August, 1792, those priests who did not take the oath were removed from their positions and replaced by government appointees. By an order of March, 1793, all churches that did not have a priest who took the civil oath (a juring priest) were closed. Instead of attending mass under their unpopular government-assigned priests, many Vendéans attended secret open-air masses conducted by nonjuring priests.

In the Vendée, village priests were home grown and had long-standing family ties to their communities. More-

over, the peasants could well understand that the confiscation of church lands and the creation of a new money system (*assignats*) was benefiting the same petit bourgeois townsmen who served as renters and financiers, while *assignats* placed more land under the control of outsiders to the detriment of the members of rural communities. Nor were the Vendéans happy about the imprisonment of the king and the establishment of the First French Republic, which taxed them at an even higher rate than had the former monarchy. In other words, it was abundantly clear to the peasantry of the Vendée that the French Revolution was a revolution of the bourgeoisie against the aristocracy, a revolution that would not benefit the lowest classes of French society and that seemed very likely to harm them.

The execution of King Louis XVI in January, 1793, was viewed in the traditionalist Vendée with shock. It was, however, the institution of a national draft the following month that caused cumulative Vendéan rage to explode. The revolutionary government needed to raise an army of 300,000 to protect France's eastern frontiers against invasion by the First Coalition powers, but the announcement of the draft was met with vows of noncooperation, scattered protests, and finally a riot.

The riot broke out at Cholet, a large textile town, on March 4, 1793. Thereafter, draft riots continued throughout the Vendée. Government officials, new priests, and national guard leaders were murdered. It was immediately evident that there were too few Republican troops garrisoned to prevent the riots. Rioting bands joined together on March 11 to seize the large town of Machecoul. Some 40 prorepublicans were immediately stabbed to death in the streets, while an estimated 450 others were marched out of town, forced to dig ditches, and shot. Within two days, the *tocsin*, or alarm bell, was rung and the whole of the Vendée exploded in a revolt so widespread that it has been termed a counterrevolution.

By mid-March, the Vendéans had taken control of most of the towns in western France. Peasant leaders were selected, including Jacques Cathelineau (a carter) and Jean-Nicolas Stofflet (a gamekeeper). Leadership positions were also taken by Vendéan noblemen, such as the comte de La Rochejaquelein and the Duke Maurice Gigost d'Elbée. Refractory priests aided in recruitment, casting the uprising as a spiritual crusade against the forces of evil. By May, an army of thirty thousand was created, carrying flags into battle embroidered with the motto "God and King" and banners featuring the Virgin Mary. A white cockade was worn as a sign of attachment to the Bourbon monarchy, along with a cross covering the sacred heart as a sign of religious devotion. The army adopted the name the Royal and Catholic Army. Vendéans terrorized Republican forces with a screech-owl sound, leading to their nickname of the Chouans (owls). Peasants originally armed with pitchforks, axes, pikes, scythes, and shotguns were now armed with rifles and cannon seized from town arsenals and many undermanned garrisons.

The slowness of the government in Paris to react to the uprising permitted expanding Vendéan forces easily to take over the towns of Bressuire, Parthenay, Thouars, Saumur, and then Angers on June 18. Their efforts were aided by town royalists and nonjuring clergy. However, integral to Vendéan strategy was taking control of the major city of Nantes, which was to be the base of a new government that would be allied to England. Nantes would be a center where émigré forces could return and operate to restore the Bourbon monarchy.

Unfortunately for Vendéan hopes, the conquest of Nantes did not happen. The general population, aligning its interests with those of the revolution, rallied behind the Republic. A formidable force of forty-five thousand under the command of General Jean-Baptiste Kléber was dispatched from the German frontier to aid local forces in successfully blocking a Vendéan takeover on June 28. On August 1, Kléber was replaced by General Jean-Baptiste Carrier, who was ordered to pacify the Vendée by any means necessary. Carrier was given command of a large army swelled by a major national draft. By October 18, he was able to defeat a Vendéan force numbering sixty-five thousand and take control of Cholet, the place where the first significant Vendée riots occurred. In a desperate move, approximately 100,000 soldiers and their families fled across the Loire River on a 120-mile northern march, in hopes of seizing the channel port city of Granville, where they could receive long-promised British and émigré support. Ony a few thousand men under François Charette remained behind to continue resistance in the Vendée.

The siege failed in November, leaving the Vendéans with little choice but to head south and once again cross the swift-running Loire River. The passage was blocked by a large and well-armed Republican army. At the Battle of Le Mans (December 12), at least fifteen thousand died on the field. Many more died in the subsequent Battle of Savenay (December 23) or of drowning, starvation, or sickness. The counterrevolution of the Vendée had been smashed. However, for the population of the Vendée itself, death and destruction were still in their infancy.

By 1794, the Jacobins were firmly in power in France and were determined to institute a Reign of Terror to liquidate all elements hostile to the revolution. The so-called Fiery Columns under the command of General Louis-Marie Turreau de Garambouville were sent to the Vendée to lay waste to the countryside and wreak havoc on the population. The Jacobin revolutionary tribunal ordered mass executions of Vendéans, who were guillotined in large numbers and, when this proved too slow, placed in barges at Nantes that were then sunk in the river. At Les Lucs-sur-Boulogne more than five hundred Vendéans were locked in a church and killed. Such reprisals convinced the remaining Vendée leader Charette to continue fighting a guerrilla war.

The destruction of the Vendée stopped in 1795, after the coming to power of the Directory. A general amnesty and even some reparations were given. Minor royalist uprisings dotted the future history of the Vendée (1796, 1799, 1815, 1832) but lacked the backing of the exhausted and depleted general population.

SIGNIFICANCE

The civil war in the Vendée reflected conflicts in French society that preceded and long proceeded the French Rev-

1790's

olution. The pressures of urbanization upon traditional rural farming, the emerging bourgeoisie's conflicts with the peasantry and landed aristocratic interests, tensions between Enlightenment rationalism and traditional religious values, the struggle between the drive to centralize political power and the desire to maintain regional control, the choice between nationalism and strictly local interests—all these conflicts came to a head during the French Revolution, and their outcomes were determined by a preponderance of power and the use of violence.

These issues would resurface in France in the Revolution of 1830, which brought the bourgeois King Louis-Philippe to power; the Revolution of 1848 and the counterrevolution in June by Parisians; the Paris Commune of 1870-1871; the battles taking place throughout the Third French Republic (1871-1940), leading to a final showdown in the Dreyfus affair (1898); and the establishment and operation of Vichy France during World War II (1939-1945). In each of these conflicts, the deep divisions which marked French political life are visible.

In the Vendée today, the uprising of 1793 and the vengeance of 1794 remain deeply etched in the minds of its inhabitants. Numerous historic sites, museums, and memorials dot the region to remind a nation of an event that many would find convenient to forget.

—*Irwin Halfond*

FURTHER READING

Doyle, William. *Oxford History of the French Revolution.* New York: Oxford University Press, 2003. An excellent background to the French Revolution; Chapter 10, "Revolt of the Provinces," has a clear and concise discussion of the Vendée

Secher, Reynald. *A French Genocide: The Vendée.* Notre Dame, Ind.: University of Notre Dame Press, 2003. A scholarly study of the causes and events of the Vendée conflict using unpublished archival sources and statistical data stressing the policy choices of the First French Republic in enraging Vendéans to revolt. Index and bibliography.

Tilly, Charles. *The Vendée.* Cambridge, Mass.: Harvard University Press, 1964. A sociohistoric and statistical analysis stressing rural peasant animosity toward bourgeois dominance in an increasingly urbanized France as a root cause of the Vendée. Index, bibliography, and appendices.

SEE ALSO: May 5, 1789: Louis XVI Calls the Estates-General; June 20, 1789: Oath of the Tennis Court; July 14, 1789: Fall of the Bastille; Apr. 20, 1792-Oct., 1797: Early Wars of the French Revolution; Sept. 20, 1792: Battle of Valmy; Jan. 21, 1793: Execution of Louis XVI; July 27-28, 1794: Fall of Robespierre; Mar., 1796-Oct. 17, 1797: Napoleon's Italian Campaigns; Apr. 12, 1798-Sept. 2, 1801: Napoleon's Egyptian Campaign; Nov. 9-10, 1799: Napoleon Rises to Power in France.

RELATED ARTICLES in *Great Lives from History: The Eighteenth Century, 1701-1800:* Lazare Carnot; Georges Danton; Louis XVI; Robespierre.

July 22, 1793
MACKENZIE REACHES THE ARCTIC OCEAN

Alexander Mackenzie, searching for an inland water route to the Pacific Ocean, instead found a river that took him to the Arctic coast of North America. This journey, as well as a subsequent trek across the Rocky Mountains, convinced Mackenzie that there was no commercially viable overland route from the Atlantic Ocean to the Pacific Ocean.

LOCALE: Arctic coast (now near Inuvik, Northwest Territories, Canada)

CATEGORIES: Exploration and discovery; expansion and land acquisition

KEY FIGURES

Sir Alexander Mackenzie (c. 1764-1820), Scottish trader and explorer

Aw-gee-nah (English Chief; fl. 1771-1821), Chipewyan guide to Mackenzie's 1789 expedition

Peter Pond (1740-1807), American trader and explorer

Samuel Hearne (1745-1792), English explorer

SUMMARY OF EVENT

At the close of the eighteenth century, three hundred years after European discovery of the North American continent, very little was known of the geography of its western reaches. Both commercial interests and empire builders wanted to find a water route across the continent from the Atlantic to the Pacific Ocean. The British government had offered a prize of £20,000 to the first person to discover such a passage.

It was well known that on the eastern side of the continent, the rivers that flowed west from the Appalachian Mountains to the Mississippi River had sources close to those of the rivers emptying into the Atlantic Ocean. Geographers theorized that a similar arrangement of river systems existed for the west; therefore, it should be possible to discover a transcontinental waterway. This theory was supported by information garnered by explorers. Samuel Hearne, the first European to travel north across the continent to the Arctic coast, reported that there were mountains in the West beyond which all rivers flowed to the Pacific.

In 1787, a twenty-three-year-old, Scottish-born fur trader, Alexander Mackenzie, traveled west from Montreal to a remote North West Company post in what is now northern Alberta. There, at Fort Chipewyan, he met a veteran of the wilderness, Peter Pond.

Pond had spent more than a decade as a fur trader in the northern prairies and had a better-than-average understanding of the geography of the region. He shared with Mackenzie his knowledge of a great river flowing west from Great Slave Lake. Pond had not traveled this river himself and most likely learned of it from the Native Americans with whom he traded. Pond speculated that the Rocky Mountains ended well south of the Arctic coast, and that this great river, therefore, emptied into the Pacific Ocean.

On June 3, 1789, Alexander Mackenzie set off from Fort Chipewyan to find and follow this river to its mouth. His party included a German, four voyagers and two of

Scottish explorer Alexander Mackenzie and his expedition crew reached the Arctic Ocean from a remote outpost in northwest Canada. Upon their return to Fort Chipewyan, they had traversed more than 3,000 miles round trip in 102 days. (The Granger Collection, New York)

843

MACKENZIE'S NORTHWESTERN EXPLORATIONS, 1789-1793

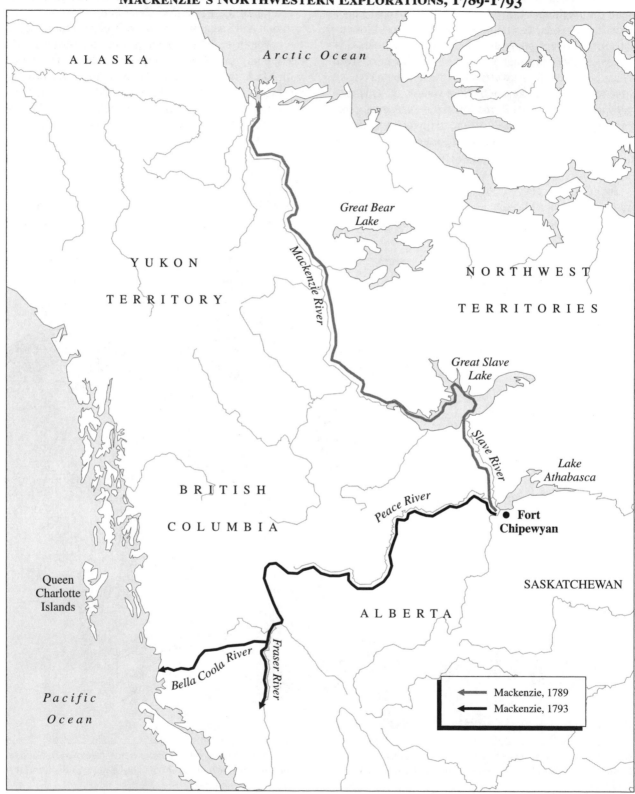

ALASKA

Arctic Ocean

*Great Bear
Lake*

YUKON

TERRITORY

Mackenzie River

NORTHWEST

TERRITORIES

*Great Slave
Lake*

Slave River

*Lake
Athabasca*

BRITISH

COLUMBIA

Peace River

● **Fort
Chipewyan**

Queen
Charlotte
Islands

SASKATCHEWAN

ALBERTA

Bella Coola River

Fraser River

*Pacific
Ocean*

⟵ Mackenzie, 1789
⟵ Mackenzie, 1793

their wives, three Chipewyan Indian men, and two Indian women. Serving as guide and translator was the leader of the Chipewyans, Aw-gee-nah, whom the Europeans called English Chief.

From Fort Chipewyan on Lake Athabasca, this small party descended the Slave River in four birchbark canoes. Nearly a week later, they reached Great Slave Lake and found it too icy for them to proceed by canoe. They portaged along the southwest shore of the lake for twenty days and found the entrance to the "Big River" on June 29, 1789.

At first the river flowed west, raising hopes that they would soon reach the Pacific, but then its course turned north and continued in that direction. Mackenzie realized that this was not the route he wanted and wrote in his journal that "it was evident that these waters emptied themselves into the Hyperborean Sea [Arctic Ocean]."

Rain, cold, and mosquitoes plagued the expedition. Native Americans whom they met along the way (first Slave and Dogrib, later Loucheaux and Hare) reported that it would take several years to reach the ocean. They told tales of dangerous waterfalls, monsters, murderous Inuit, and a shortage of game downstream. A Dogrib man was unwillingly employed to guide the party. He was extremely fearful and repeatedly tried to escape. By July 10, Mackenzie's companions were so discouraged that they begged him to turn back, and he promised to do so if they did not reach the ocean within a week.

On July 12, 1789, the party came to what they thought was another large lake covered with ice. They camped on an island in the mouth of the river and were awakened the next day by the rising tide. Soon afterward, they noticed beluga whales in the water and knew then that they had reached the Arctic Ocean.

The return trip upstream was even more difficult than had been the one downstream, often requiring a great deal of walking while towing the canoes. Although members of the party saw many Inuit campsites throughout the river delta, they encountered no Inuit. Through English Chief, Mackenzie encouraged the natives he met to begin trading beaver, marten, and other furs. He continued to inquire about a great river flowing west beyond the Rocky Mountains. The reports he received were that such a river existed, but that it was protected by giants and other monsters.

Mackenzie soon realized that English Chief, in his desire to conclude the journey, was withholding information. This led to an argument between Mackenzie and English Chief, in which the latter threatened to leave the expedition. Realizing he could not continue without his

guide and interpreter, Mackenzie was forced to back down. They reached Fort Chipewyan on September 12, 1789. They had traveled more than 3,000 miles by canoe and on foot in 102 days.

The discovery of the Mackenzie River, as it is now called, received scant notice at the annual meeting of the North West Company traders the following year at Grand Portage. Mackenzie prepared to undertake another exploration. After a sojourn in England to study surveying and navigation, Mackenzie mounted an expedition across the Rocky Mountains and down the Fraser River, which he mistakenly thought was the Columbia River. The group then proceeded on foot to the Bella Coola River and the Pacific Ocean, arriving there on July 22, 1793.

The route traversed steep ridges and dangerous cataracts. Food was difficult to obtain, and the single large canoe with which the expedition started the journey was smashed on rocks in the white water of the Fraser River. Mackenzie had made it to the Pacific Ocean, but his journey did not present obvious opportunities to expand the fur trade. Mackenzie left Fort Chipewyan and retired from the North West Company the following year.

Significance

Mackenzie's voyages greatly increased knowledge of the geography of the West, and for this he was knighted by King George III. His journals, which were published in 1801, may have provided the United States Congress and President Thomas Jefferson with the impetus to fund the Lewis and Clark expedition, lest the territory of the West be lost to Great Britain.

Although Alexander Mackenzie was the first European known to travel from east to west across the North American continent, his experience helped prove that no commercially viable overland route existed. A dozen years later, Meriwether Lewis and William Clark confirmed this finding. Mackenzie referred to the river that bears his name as the River of Disappointment and considered it to have little commercial potential. It was not until years later that the Mackenzie River became a primary route of travel and commerce between the Subarctic and the Arctic. The search for a Northwest Passage to Asia shifted back to the Arctic waters abandoned two centuries earlier.

—Pamela R. Stern

Further Reading

Allen, John L. "To Unite the Discoveries: The American Response to the Early Exploration of Rupert's Land." In *Rupert's Land: A Cultural Tapestry*, edited by

1790's

Richard C. Davis. Waterloo, Ont.: Wilfred Laurier University Press, 1988. Analysis of the relationship between Mackenzie's explorations and the funding of the Lewis and Clark Expedition.

Francis, Daniel. *Discovery of the North: The Exploration of Canada's Arctic*. Edmonton, Alta.: Hurtig, 1986. Chapter 3 discusses the explorations of Hearne and Mackenzie.

Gough, Barry M. *First Across the Continent: Sir Alexander Mackenzie*. Norman: University of Oklahoma Press, 1997. Comprehensive biography, portraying Mackenzie as an intrepid explorer and practical businessman, with a large ego and a talent for self-promotion.

Hayes, Derek. *First Crossing: Alexander Mackenzie, His Expedition Across North America, and the Opening of the Continent*. Seattle: Sasquatch Books, 2001. Uses journals by Mackenzie and other eighteenth century explorers to chronicle Mackenzie's voyage across North America. Includes drawings, photographs, and maps.

McGoogan, Ken. *Ancient Mariner: The Arctic Adventures of Samuel Hearne, the Sailor Who Inspired Coleridge's Masterpiece*. New York: Carroll & Graf, 2004. Accessible, comprehensive biography, recounting Hearne's exploration of northern Canada, his relations with the Inuits, and his participation in the fur trade.

Mackenzie, Alexander. *Voyages from Montreal on the River St. Laurence Through the Continent of North America to the Frozen and Pacific Oceans in the Years 1789 and 1793*. Ann Arbor, Mich.: University Microfilms, 1966. Facsimile edition of the explorer's 1801 description of the fur trade and his travels.

Newman, Peter C. *Caesars of the Wilderness*. Vol. 2 in *Company of Adventurers*. New York: Penguin Books, 1988. Rich description of the history of the fur trade in Canada. Chapter 3 is devoted to Mackenzie.

Nuffield, Edward W. *Samuel Hearne: Journey to the Coopermine River, 1769-1772*. Vancouver, B.C.: Haro Books, 2001. Uses Hearne's journal of his voyage as the basis for a re-creation of his trip across northern Canada.

Sloan, W. A. "Aw-gee-nah (English Chief)." In *Dictionary of Canadian Biography*. Vol. 6. Edited by Francess G. Halpenny. Toronto: University of Toronto Press, 1987. Brief but comprehensive discussion of the available information on Mackenzie's guide.

SEE ALSO: July, 1728-1769: Russian Voyages to Alaska; Aug. 25, 1768-Feb. 14, 1779: Voyages of Captain Cook; July 16, 1799-July 9, 1804: Humboldt and Bonpland's Expedition.

RELATED ARTICLES in *Great Lives from History: The Eighteenth Century, 1701-1800*: Vitus Jonassen Bering; James Cook; Sir Alexander Mackenzie; George Vancouver.

c. 1794-1799
PROUST ESTABLISHES THE LAW OF DEFINITE PROPORTIONS

Through a series of meticulous experiments, Proust proved that all chemical compounds, whether found in nature or prepared in the laboratory, consist of elements in definite ratios by weight.

LOCALE: Madrid, Spain
CATEGORIES: Chemistry; science and technology

KEY FIGURES
Joseph-Louis Proust (1754-1826), French chemist
Claude Louis Berthollet (1748-1822), French chemist
Antoine-Laurent Lavoisier (1743-1794), French chemist
John Dalton (1766-1844), English chemist

SUMMARY OF EVENT

In the late eighteenth century, the idea that chemical compounds were composed of stable ratios of elements was not uncommon. In fact, many analytic chemists based their work on just such an idea. However, the attitude of chemists toward what came to be called definite proportions was complex, since such distinguished scientists as Claude Louis Berthollet questioned definite proportions and backed this skepticism with experiments that seemed to demonstrate varying compositions of alloys, glasses, and solutions. Although Antoine-Laurent Lavoisier, the founder of the oxygen theory of combustion, made use of compounds with fixed weight ratios, he admitted that some substances might have degrees of oxygenation. Lavoisier had helped establish that true chemical compounds possessed uniform properties, but the claim by some modern scholars that the constancy of components in these compounds was a common assumption in the eighteenth century has been refuted by the de-

LAW OF DEFINITE PROPORTIONS

During the early nineteenth century, the concept of a chemical compound was still being defined and discovered, and Joseph-Louis Proust's chemical theories were not yet accepted. While he held that the chemical elements in a true compound must combine in certain definite proportions to one another, others, such as Claude Louis Berthollet, held that a compound could be composed of elements combined in any proportion. In 1806, during this period of controversy, Proust summarized his law of definite proportions, presented here.

Everything in mineralogy is not a compound [*combinaison*]. . . . [T]here is a large number of substances to which this name should not be applied indiscriminately, as some authors do for want of having thought sufficiently about what is understood by this word in chemistry. Because they have not noticed that the science has made a rule of reserving its use, they have applied it indifferently to substances which it deliberately avoids describing thus. They therefore confuse compounds with certain concrete solutions, certain combinations, certain systems of compound bodies to which it attaches a quite contrary idea. Nature, for example, presents us with compounds of elements, but also with combinations formed by a multiple aggregation of these same compounds. . . .

Let us stop for a moment to satisfy an objection which d'Aubuisson certainly addresses to me, when he says in a memoir in which he so justly sees the futility of certain definitions, "The analyses of the copper ore [cuivre gris], which Klaproth has just published, are a new example of compounds formed in variable proportions." I would reply that the copper ore does not belong at all to the order of compounds which chemists are examining at the moment in order to unravel the principles of their formation. A compound according to our principles, as Klaproth would tell you, is something like sulphide of silver, of antimony, of mercury, of copper; it is an acidified combustible substance, etc.; it is a privileged product to which nature assigns fixed proportions; it is in a word a being which she never creates, even in the hands of man, except with the aid of a balance, *pondere et mensura*.

Source: The Science of Matter: A Historical Survey, edited by Maurice Crosland (Harmondsworth, Middlesex, England: Penguin, 1971). Excerpt translated by Crosland.

stant saturation proportions" influenced Proust. Many chemists had established that a certain amount of acid neutralized a specific quantity of base, and some posited that such reacting substances had a unique property of combination, which was sometimes called the "saturation proportion." Proust knew of these unique combining ratios, but these previous efforts did not result in the broad conclusion that all chemical substances combine in only a small number of fixed proportions. Proust knew that the French mineralogist René-Just Haüy had discovered a relationship between chemical composition and fixed crystal form, and this discovery influenced his thinking on definite proportions. Proust also researched specific chemical compounds of interest to pharmacists, physicians, metallurgists, and painters, and these studies deepened his knowledge of the differences between true chemical compounds and mere physical mixtures.

Precisely when Proust first formulated his famous law has been controversial. Some scholars argue for 1794, others for 1797, and still others for 1799. Proust did publish a paper in 1794 in which he clearly recognized that iron not only had two oxides but also two sulfates, and he went on to state that all metals follow the same natural law regulating their definite combinations with other elements. By 1797, Proust had shown that antimony, tin, mercury, lead, cobalt, nickel, and copper formed distinct oxides with constant proportions. The oxides of these metals had specific physical and chemical characteristics, and Proust responded to those who claimed that metal oxides had variable proportions by showing that these chemists were confusing "maximum and minimum" oxides with their mixtures. He was able to separate mixtures of these maximum and minimum oxides according to the solubilities of the compounds in alcohol or other solvents.

Proust was by now a firm believer that nature's "invisible hand" bound together elements into real combi-

tailed historical analyses of other scholars.

The person who did more than any other chemist to establish and authenticate the principle of constant composition was Joseph-Louis Proust. He pursued the profession of his father, an apothecary, and he worked for several years in the pharmaceutical department of the Saltpêtrière Hospital in Paris. With this background, it is understandable why Proust tended to approach chemical problems pragmatically. With the help of Lavoisier, Proust was able, during the 1780's, to obtain academic positions in Spain, first at Madrid, then at the Royal Artillery College in Segovia. After a stay in Salamanca, he returned to Madrid in 1791, when he began to study the issue of definite proportions.

Scholars differ on how much such early ideas as "con-

1790's

847

nations. In 1799, in a series of painstaking analyses, he demonstrated that the copper carbonate he prepared in his laboratory was identical in composition to the compound found in nature. The artificial and natural copper carbonate each contained identical proportions by weight of copper, carbon, and oxygen. Proust concluded that natural laws governed these proportions, and these laws were the same in the Earth's depths as in a chemist's flask.

Proust explained the immutability of true compounds as a function of nature's ordering power, which he called "election" or "affinity." This stable rate of attraction between certain substances was responsible for the fixity of composition. On the other hand, in France, Berthollet—a Newtonian—assumed that affinity, like gravity, brought about continuous attractions between substances, and he opposed Proust's "elective" characterization of chemical affinity. He interpreted affinity not as a determinative force but as a physical power that could be influenced by the relative concentrations of reactants. In this way, he asserted, the products of chemical reactions were conditioned to have indefinite compositions.

During the first decade of the nineteenth century, Proust and Berthollet, in a series of journal articles, debated whether compounds had fixed or variable compositions. In this gentlemanly dispute, Berthollet argued that variable compositions were exhibited not only by alloys, glasses, and solutions but also by oxides, sulfates, and other salts. For example, he produced experimental evidence that mercury sulfates exhibited a continuous range of combinations between two extremes. Proust, however, refuted Berthollet's interpretation of his observations by showing that he was actually dealing with a mixture of two distinct compounds. Similarly, Proust proved that tin had two oxides and iron two sulfides, and all of these compounds had fixed compositions.

When Proust was unable to disprove that a given complex substance had a variable composition, as in the case of alloys and solutions, he declared the substance to be a mixture, an argument that Berthollet found circular. Although Proust was not correct in all particulars, and although he demeaned Berthollet's valid observations about the effects of "active masses" on the direction of chemical reactions, his principal conclusion that true compounds have properties that are as "invariable as is the ratio of their constituents" was not only true but also important for the future of chemistry.

SIGNIFICANCE

Proust's law of definite composition ultimately became a fundamental principle of modern chemistry, but it took the work of many experimenters to establish it as a law. In a way, the debate between Berthollet, an insightful theoretician, and Proust, a meticulous experimenter, continued through their disciples. Proust's followers certainly had the early victories, when they established that the constituent elements of many specific chemical compounds always exhibited fixed weight ratios.

Proust's law was also important in helping to establish the modern atomic theory of John Dalton, even though Dalton himself made only cursory references to Proust in his publications. More important for Dalton was the law of multiple proportions, which he discovered when he showed that two elements could combine in more than one set of definite proportions. Proust, an empiricist and not an atomist, came close to finding this law himself, because he had recognized cases in which the same elements formed two combinations, each with definite compositions, but he expressed his relationships in percentages, whereas Dalton expressed them in atomic weights. Both Proust and Dalton saw the same regularities, but Dalton creatively envisioned a new way of interpreting them. Indeed, Dalton was able to answer a question that Proust could not: Why should chemical compounds have definite compositions and exist in multiple proportions? Dalton's answer was simple: Matter is atomistic, and when atoms combine with each other, their distinctive weights naturally result in definitely composed compounds or series of compounds.

The significance of some of Berthollet's arguments in the Proust-Berthollet debate did not become obvious until late in the nineteenth century, when the new disicpline of physical chemistry was founded. Berthollet had believed that chemical reactions are influenced by the masses of the reacting substances and that these "active masses" prescribed the reaction's speed as well as the nature and amounts of the products. Although Berthollet was wrong about mass affecting the nature of the products of chemical reactions, he was right about mass affecting the reaction rates. The law of mass action, in which physical chemists quantitatively detailed how chemical reactions are influenced by the quantities of reacting substances, became a basic principle of chemical kinetics.

Like many controversies in the history of science, the Proust-Berthollet debate was not simply an instance of truth (Proust's law) triumphing over error (Berthollet's variable composition). Berthollet, who emphasized how compounds were formed, grasped, albeit inchoately, the law of mass action. Proust, who emphasized the empirical study of the nature of compounds, grasped the law of definite proportions, but not the law of multiple proportions. Furthermore, neither Proust nor Berthollet fully understood the significance of Dalton's atomic theory, which would ultimately, in the hands of future chemists, make sense not only of definite and multiple proportions but also of most of chemistry.

—*Robert J. Paradowski*

FURTHER READING

Ihde, Aaron J. *The Development of Modern Chemistry*. New York: Dover, 1984. This edition, a corrected version of a book originally published in 1964, analyzes Proust's life and contributions in the fourth chapter, "Chemical Combination and the Atomic Theory." Chapter bibliographic notes, indexes of names and subjects.

Nye, Mary Jo. *Before Big Science: The Pursuit of Modern Chemistry and Physics, 1800-1940*. New York: Twayne, 1996. This book, part of Twayne's History of Science and Society series, analyzes Proust's work in the second chapter, "Dalton's Atom and Two Paths for the Study of Matter." Chronology, bibliographical essay, name and subject indexes.

Partington, J. R. *A History of Chemistry*. Vol. 3. London: Macmillan, 1962. Partington, in his comprehensive

treatment of the history of chemistry, deals with Proust's life and achievements in chapter 14, "Foundations of Stoichiometry." Many references to primary and secondary sources in the footnotes. Indexes of names and subjects.

Pullman, Bernard. *The Atom in the History of Human Thought*. New York: Oxford University Press, 1998. This intellectual history of the atom analyzes Proust's contributions in the chapter on the nineteenth century. Extensive chapter notes and an index.

SEE ALSO: 1718: Geoffroy Issues the *Table of Reactivities*; 1722: Réaumur Discovers Carbon's Role in Hardening Steel; 1745: Lomonosov Issues the First Catalog of Minerals; June 5, 1755: Black Identifies Carbon Dioxide; 1771: Woulfe Discovers Picric Acid; Aug. 1, 1774: Priestley Discovers Oxygen; 1781-1784: Cavendish Discovers the Composition of Water; 1786-1787: Lavoisier Devises the Modern System of Chemical Nomenclature; 1789: Leblanc Develops Soda Production.

RELATED ARTICLES in *Great Lives from History: The Eighteenth Century, 1701-1800*: Joseph Black; Henry Cavendish; Antoine-Laurent Lavoisier; Joseph Priestley; Georg Ernst Stahl.

June 1, 1794
ALLGEMEINES LANDRECHT RECODIFIES PRUSSIAN LAW

The Allgemeines Landrecht, which codified Prussian civil and criminal laws on the basis of traditional social stratification, contributed to the unification of the various Prussian regions under absolute monarchy. It was thus an important aspect of the growth of Prussia as the central German power and the establishment in the nineteenth century of a German Empire.

LOCALE: Potsdam, Prussia (now in Germany)
CATEGORY: Laws, acts, and legal history; government and politics

KEY FIGURES
Frederick the Great (1712-1786), king of Prussia, r. 1740-1786
Samuel von Cocceji (1697-1755), Prussian minister of justice and grand chancellor
Johann Heinrich Casimir von Carmer (1721-1801), Prussian grand chancellor
Carl Gottlieb Svarez (1746-1798), Prussian legal expert and von Carmer's legal assistant

Ernst Ferdinand Klein (1744-1810), Prussian legal expert and chamber court official
Frederick William I (1688-1740), king of Prussia, r. 1713-1740
Frederick William II (1744-1797), king of Prussia, r. 1786-1797

SUMMARY OF EVENT
The Allgemeines Landrecht represented the culmination of legal efforts during the eighteenth century in Prussia to collect and codify various royal edicts and laws in order to establish greater unity among the diverse Prussian provincial laws and legal practices. The code also reflected and made clear the tensions between enlightened concepts of natural rights, which were advocated by the code's principal legal authors, and the traditional, stratified society of an absolute monarchy.

In the early eighteenth century, Brandenburg-Prussia was composed of more than twenty different territories, ranging from the Rhine in the west to Memel in the east, a distance of more than eight hundred miles. Each province had its own legal system. Moreover, lords of the manor exercised seigneurial justice, while royal justice was divided between ordinary justice and administrative justice (*Kammer*), serving the interests of the army and royal domains.

To create more legal unity, King Frederick William I in 1714 ordered the law faculty of the University of Halle to collect a law codex for his kingdom. Frederick William I was not successful in creating such a Landrecht for Prussia, but he did introduce an inquisitional process in criminal cases. Under his successor, Frederick the Great, however, judicial reform was pursued much more vigorously in order to increase efficiency and to affirm the king's authority over the various provinces. Frederick, who was influenced by Montesquieu, the author of *De l'esprit des loix* (1748; *The Spirit of the Laws*, 1750), argued that a comprehensive code would reflect the best accomplishments of human reason. On December 31, 1746, the king ordered professor Samuel von Cocceji to collect the royal edicts and prepare a German Landrecht based on reason. Cocceji's draft, "Projekt des Corporis Juris Fridericiani" (1749-1751; project of Frederick's body of law), did not become law, although some provinces adopted its provisions on marriage and guardianship.

The Seven Years' War (1756-1763) interrupted further efforts at legal reform. By the 1770's, though, the king was receiving increasing complaints about slow court proceedings. The major impetus for legal reform came in 1779, when Frederick the Great intervened on behalf of the miller Christian Arnold, who had lost a legal case against his landlord. The king dismissed his ineffective grand chancellor, Carl Joseph von Fürst and Kupferberg, and appointed Johann Heinrich Casimir von Carmer as both justice minister and grand chancellor. Von Carmer, president of the Prussian government in Breslau, Silesia, had increased the efficiency in civil trials in Silesia. From Silesia, he brought with him to Berlin two legal assistants, Carl Gottlieb Svarez and Ernst Ferdinand Klein, who played key roles in preparing the civil and criminal sections of the Landrecht. All three were children of the Enlightenment and had solid practical legal backgrounds.

Frederick the Great issued a cabinet order on April 14, 1780, charging von Carmer with the task of producing a code in German that the ordinary Prussian subject could understand. Legal concepts based on Roman law (Justinian's Code) and Saxon law were to be revised to meet the changing times. For example, slavery was forbidden in Prussia. Frederick the Great never saw the completion of the work he commissioned, but work on the project continued after his death under the new and more conservative king, Frederick William II. The code Allgemeines Gesetzbuch (general lawbook) was completed in March, 1791, and was to go into effect on June 1, 1792. However, the radicalization of the French Revolution after 1791 enabled the new king's conservative advisers to convince him to suspend the code on April 18, 1792. Only in November, 1793, did the king order a revision of the Allgemeines Gesetzbuch, which would eliminate legal limitations placed on the absolute monarch. Finally, fourteen years after the 1780 cabinet order, the new code was accepted on February 5, 1794, and became effective on June 1, 1794, under a new name, Allgemeines Landrecht.

The Allgemeines Landrecht, which was praised by Alexander de Tocqueville, was a collection of both civil and criminal law. Organized in more than nineteen thousand paragraphs, the code required 734 double-column pages of print. The Landrecht was intended to supplement the provincial codes. In cases where the provincial codes did not address an issue, the Landrecht would take precedence. However, since most of the provincial laws were not codified, judges in many regions increasingly relied on the Landrecht for their judgments.

The introduction to the code includes the liberal statement that the general rights of humans are based on their natural freedoms to further their well-being without harming the rights of others. However, the introduction also makes it clear that special rights and obligations of members of the state depend on their personal relations with each other and with the state. The rights of a person are created by his or her birth, estate, and actions.

Frederick the Great had decreed in 1780 that the Landrecht could not affect the social reality of estates and provincial legal practices. The Landrecht made it clear that each major social group or estate, ranging from nobles and the *Bürgerstand* (bourgeoisie) to peasants, had special privileges and obligations. Nobles were classified as the first estate, were authorized to own land, and could be judged only by the highest courts in the province. Peasants could not engage in bourgeois activities or trades without the permission of the state or their lords. They were considered free subjects only outside the nobles' estates, and they could be punished by their lords for laziness or misbehavior. The *Bürgerstand* included everyone who did not belong to the nobility or peasantry.

Like the Allgemeines Gesetzbuch of 1791, the Allgemeines Landrecht allowed religious freedom, but not public disrespect for religion, for both Christians and Jews. It also stipulated that new laws could not be applied retroactively (or *ex post facto*). Private property was protected, and the state had to compensate property owners if land was taken. The Landrecht strengthened the rights of the monarch. The rights to issue and repeal all laws and police and to make war and peace were reserved for the monarch as a "right of Majesty." Laws would go into effect even without the participation of law commissions in cases of disputes. Compared to the 1791 draft, individual rights were reduced in the Landrecht. Eliminated were clauses recognizing the natural freedoms and rights of citizens, which could not be limited by law more than was required by the goals of communal union.

SIGNIFICANCE

The Prussian legal reforms were similar to those carried out in other eighteenth century European countries. French legal reforms in the later part of the century failed because of the opposition of the *parlements*, and successful reforms had to wait until the introduction of the Napoleonic Code. Within Germany, the kingdom of Bavaria was the first state to introduce a new code in 1756. The Austrian Empire began work on a legal code in 1753, but the civil code was not completed until 1808 (effective 1811). In most of these countries, judicial reforms, although influenced by concepts of natural law, were used to modernize and rationalize laws in order to increase the power of the monarch and the state.

Many parts of the civil code of the Allgemeines Landrecht remained in effect in several provinces of Prussia throughout much of the nineteenth century, but the impact of the French Revolution and Napoleon on Prussia modified many provisions of the code within a generation. The Prussian reforms after 1807 freed the serfs and removed restrictions on property ownership based on estates.

The French introduced the Napoleonic Code on the left bank of the Rhine, and it, not the Landrecht, remained in effect after 1814. Because Napoleonic reforms in Germany eliminated many traditional provincial laws, the Allgemeines Landrecht became the primary law in those areas reunited with Prussia after 1814 (except Kleve). In new areas occupied by Prussia after 1814, ranging from the Rhineland to Saxony and Westphalia, either old law or French law remained in effect. After 1848, the Allgemeines Landrecht was no longer introduced in newly annexed provinces. After German unification in 1871, German national civil laws culminating in the German Civil Code of 1900 replaced the Prussian Landrecht. By 1931, when the last edition of the Allgemeines Landrecht was published, it had been reduced to only two hundred pages.

—Johnpeter Horst Grill

FURTHER READING

Behrens, C. B. A. *Society, Government, and the Enlightenment: The Experiences of Eighteenth-Century France and Prussia*. New York: Harper and Row, 1985. Includes an informative chapter on the administration of justice in Prussia and France from Frederick William I to Frederick the Great.

Fay, Sidney B. *The Rise of Brandenburg-Prussia to 1786*. Edited by Klaus Epstein. New York: Holt, Rinehart and Winston, 1964. A detailed and reliable administrative history of the state.

Gothelf, Rodney. "Frederick William I and the Beginning of Prussian Absolutism, 1713-40." In *The Rise of Prussia, 1700-1830*, edited by Philip G. Dwyer. New York: Longman, 2000. Helpful for understanding the polymorphic nature of the Brandenburg-Prussian states.

Koch, H. W. *A History of Prussia*. New York: Longman, 1978. A short but insightful section, which often quotes Alexis de Tocqueville, evaluates both the theoretical basis and the practical application of the 1794 code.

MacDonogh, Giles. *Frederick the Great: A Life in Deed and Letters*. London: Weidenfeld and Nicolson, 1999. Includes a short discussion of the miller Johannes Arnold case, which helped accelerate judicial reforms.

Rosenberg, Hans. *Bureaucracy, Aristocracy, and Autocracy: The Prussian Experience, 1660-1815*. Boston: Beacon Press, 1966. Includes a short section on Samuel von Cocceji's judicial reforms.

Weill, H. *Frederick the Great and Samuel von Cocceji*. Madison: University of Wisconson Press, 1961. Summary of Frederick the Great's legal reforms, particularly useful since most works on von Cocceji are in German.

SEE ALSO: May 31, 1740: Accession of Frederick the Great; Jan., 1756-Feb. 15, 1763: Seven Years' War.

RELATED ARTICLES in *Great Lives from History: The Eighteenth Century, 1701-1800*: Frederick the Great; Frederick William I.

July-November, 1794
WHISKEY REBELLION

A group of dissidents in western Pennsylvania, unwilling to pay a tax on whiskey, engaged in violent protests and attacks upon tax collectors. The response of the federal government demonstrated its willingness and ability to use military force to enforce unpopular laws.

LOCALE: Western Pennsylvania
CATEGORIES: Wars, uprisings, and civil unrest; government and politics; economics

KEY FIGURES

James Wilson (1742-1798), antiexcise leader in Pennsylvania
George Washington (1732-1799), president of the United States, 1789-1797
Alexander Hamilton (1755-1804), U.S. secretary of the treasury, 1789-1795
Thomas Mifflin (1744-1800), governor of Pennsylvania, 1790-1799
Thomas McKean (1734-1817), Pennsylvania's chief justice, 1777-1799, and governor, 1799-1808

SUMMARY OF EVENT

Two of the more pressing and difficult problems that confronted George Washington's administration involved paying the nation's debt and maintaining the loyalty of the West to the United States. These two issues became one during the Whiskey Rebellion crisis.

Problems in the West were largely the product of inadequate security and defense against the resident Native American nations and their European allies. Prior to Jay's Treaty with Great Britain and Pinckney's Treaty with Spain in the mid-1790's, much of the Ohio and Mississippi River Valleys was claimed or occupied by Great Britain and Spain. Both nations apparently encouraged constant Native American attacks against American settlers in the vast region, and Washington's government seemed incapable of containing the hostilities. Settlement was thus retarded, western dissatisfaction was aggravated, and foreign powers were encouraged to bring about the separation of the American West from the United States.

Economic conditions also played an important role in the western problems. High transportation costs compelled Western farmers to ship their bulky produce down the Ohio and Mississippi river systems to the Gulf of Mexico. The overland freight rates charged for hauling goods eastward over the mountains were prohibitive. If the western portions of the nation were to grow economically, not only would the federal government have to exert itself militarily against the Native Americans but also it would have to secure from European governments free navigation as far as the mouth of the Mississippi River.

The economic program proposed by Alexander Hamilton, secretary of the Treasury, compounded the western problems. His plan called for the national government to assume and fund all remaining federal and state Revolutionary War debts. Despite stiff southern opposition, Hamilton successfully steered his program through Congress. However, upon assuming the debt, Hamilton had to devise a way to pay the enormous new liability. The solution included levying a tax. Upon Hamilton's advice, one of the first taxes legislated was an excise tax on distilled whiskey.

Although the excise legislation was quickly approved by Congress, Hamilton's political adversaries immediately launched a campaign against the tax. Southern reaction was particularly negative. Critics of the plan, including Thomas Jefferson, protested that the tax would reward special interests at the expense of small farmers in the West. One Georgia congressman predicted that violence would follow if federal officials attempted to collect the tax.

The proposed tax also was vigorously censured by many settlers west of the Appalachians. Whiskey was an important source of income and a major export product in the West, especially in western Pennsylvania. Farmers found it almost impossible to haul grain to eastern markets because of transportation costs. Instead, grain had to be converted into a form less bulky and more valuable in proportion to its weight. One such form was livestock, which could be driven to market, but this was an arduous and risky business. Another, less difficult form to transport was grain converted into distilled spirits. Whiskey could be carried profitably from western farmsteads to eastern markets. For many west of the Appalachians, Hamilton's tax threatened to eliminate whiskey profits. The excise equaled 25 percent of whiskey's retail value, which was more than enough to wipe out a frontier farmer's whiskey earnings.

Western resentments were further aroused by the appointment of federal tax collectors. Of particular concern were stipulations within the tax legislation that distillers charged with evading the excise were to be tried in federal courts located in the East. Westerners resented the interference in their economic life and were especially antagonistic toward the excise agents. Western settlers placed no special trust or faith in the national government, located as it was in the East and representing, in the minds of many westerners, a challenge to individual freedoms won during the Revolutionary War.

The most threatening protest to the legislation came in western Pennsylvania. Upon learning that the whiskey tax had been passed by Congress, some western Pennsylvanians, led by men such as James Wilson, initiated a series of meetings designed to organize resistance. Local protest groups similar to those created during the American Revolution soon were established. Although most opposition was limited to petitions and demonstrations, in a few instances violence erupted. In one episode in September, 1791, shortly after passage of the tax, an eager excise inspector in the Pittsburgh area was tarred and feathered by a mob of protesters. Several other states also encountered minor disturbances during the first months after passage of the whiskey tax. However, between late 1791 and mid-1794, the resistance, for the most part, remained peaceful.

In July, 1794, after almost three years of protest, peaceful resistance erupted into open rebellion. In one encounter, an armed mob, after a shoot-out with federal troops, attacked and burned the home of the excise inspector of Allegheny County, Pennsylvania. This act of defiance was followed in August by a mass meeting at Braddock's Field and a march to Pittsburgh. In another incident, approximately one hundred angry farmers assaulted a U.S. marshal as he attempted to serve summonses to delinquent taxpayers. In the days that followed, other tax collectors were assaulted, several buildings were burned, and mobs openly roamed through the western Pennsylvania countryside, threatening all who supported the tax.

The turmoil in western Pennsylvania was of grave concern to many, but especially to President Washington. Adding to his alarm was his government's general ineffectiveness at resolving other western problems. Federal efforts to pacify local Native Americans had usually been thwarted, while the British and Spanish influence over the tribes grew stronger. The United States remained no closer to securing the evacuation of the British from the Northwest than it had been immediately after the Revolutionary War. Nor was Washington's administration any closer to freeing navigation along the Mississippi River than it had been five years earlier. With so little success at resolving the western issues, some feared that if left unattended, the West might attempt to leave the union of states and create a country of its own. Such a turn of events would be disastrous for the nation as a whole.

To end the rebellion, President Washington, acting upon reports from state and federal authorities in Pennsylvania, moved swiftly. After issuing a presidential proclamation, Washington called upon several neigh-

1790's

Angry whiskey distillers in the American West, especially western Pennsylvania, protested against a federal government excise tax on whiskey, setting off three years of action that culminated in open rebellion and physical attacks in July of 1794. U.S. president George Washington responded by amassing more than twelve thousand troops to quell the rebellion, which faded upon seeing the force. (C. A. Nichols & Company)

boring states to furnish the federal government with a combined force of more than twelve thousand men. Leading the army as far as the Appalachians, the president prepared to do battle with the rebels if necessary. However, the anticipated opposition disappeared at the sight of Washington's troops. The army encountered only citizens who pronounced themselves loyal to the United States. Even a few known protest leaders reversed themselves when confronted by Washington and his men. With the situation apparently under control, the president placed Alexander Hamilton in command and returned east. In short order, Hamilton rounded up 150 suspected rebels and sent 20 back to Philadelphia for trial. Two of Hamilton's captives were convicted of treason, but both soon were pardoned by the president.

SIGNIFICANCE

While the potentially explosive episode ended with a whimper, effects of the rebellion were profound. For the first time in the nation's history, the federal government had used force to ensure that its laws were obeyed. The rebellion also generated important philosophical opposition to the Washington administration and to Federalists, specifically. By 1796, Jefferson's Democratic-Republican Party was deeply entrenched in western Pennsylvania. In 1799, the Republican chief justice, Thomas McKean, was elected governor, unseating Governor Thomas Mifflin, who had governed the state during the rebellion.

—*John G. Clark, updated by Paul E. Doutrich*

FURTHER READING

Brunhouse, Robert L. *The Counter-revolution in Pennsylvania, 1776-1790.* Harrisburg: Pennsylvania Historical and Museum Commission, 1942. Writing from an economic perspective, the author describes the partisan struggles within Pennsylvania immediately prior to the Whiskey Rebellion.

Clouse, Jerry A. *The Whiskey Rebellion: Southwestern Pennsylvania's Frontier People Test the American Constitution.* Harrisburg: Bureau of Historic Preservation, Pennsylvania Historical and Museum Commission, 1994. A brief history of the rebellion and a description of the buildings associated with it.

Ferguson, Russell J. *Early Western Pennsylvania Politics.* Pittsburgh, Pa.: University of Pittsburgh Press, 1938. Describes Pennsylvania politics and party development.

McDonald, Forrest. *Alexander Hamilton: A Biography.* New York: W. W. Norton, 1979. Focuses on the Hamiltonian and Jeffersonian philosophies as they applied to the Whiskey Rebellion.

Miller, John. *The Federalist Era, 1789-1801.* New York: Harper and Brothers, 1960. Provides a concise description of the Whiskey Rebellion, paying particular attention to the effects of U.S. foreign policy.

Slaughter, Thomas. *The Whiskey Rebellion: Frontier Epilogue to the American Revolution.* New York: Oxford University Press, 1986. Provides a thorough analysis of the events and motives involved in the Whiskey Rebellion.

Wallace, Chris. *Character: Profiles in Presidential Courage.* New York: Rugged Land, 2004. Describes sixteen notable acts of presidential courage, including George Washington's response to the Whiskey Rebellion.

SEE ALSO: Mar. 22, 1765-Mar. 18, 1766: Stamp Act Crisis; Dec. 16, 1773: Boston Tea Party; July 4, 1776: Declaration of Independence; Sept. 17, 1787: U.S. Constitution Is Adopted; Apr. 30, 1789: Washington's Inauguration; 1790's: First U.S. Political Parties; Jan., 1790: Hamilton's *Report on Public Credit*; Oct. 18, 1790-July, 1794: Little Turtle's War; Aug. 20, 1794: Battle of Fallen Timbers; Nov. 19, 1794: Jay's Treaty; Oct. 27, 1795: Pinckney's Treaty.

RELATED ARTICLES in *Great Lives from History: The Eighteenth Century, 1701-1800*: Alexander Hamilton; Thomas Jefferson; George Washington.

July 27-28, 1794
FALL OF ROBESPIERRE

The fall of Robespierre ended the Reign of Terror and allowed the army, until then not used against the populace, to become the primary force of the French Revolution.

LOCALE: Paris, France

CATEGORIES: Government and politics; wars, uprisings, and civil unrest

KEY FIGURES

Robespierre (1758-1794), Jacobin member of the Convention and Committee of Public Safety

Jean-Nicolas Billaud-Varenne (1756-1819), Hébertist member of the Convention and the Committee of Public Safety

Georges Couthon (1755-1794), Robespierrist member of the Convention and the Committee of Public Safety

Paul-François-Jean Nicolas de Barras (1755-1829), revolutionary general

Joseph Fouché (c. 1758-1820), member of the Convention, later minister of police under the Directory and Napoleon I

Jean-Lambert Tallien (1767-1820), member of the Commune, the Convention, and the Committee of General Security

Jacques-René Hébert (Père Duchesne; 1757-1794), French journalist and politician

Jean-Marie Collot d'Herbois (1794-1796), Jacobin member of the Convention and Committee of Public Safety

SUMMARY OF EVENT

The Jacobin Club's advantage over other Parisian political clubs lay in its network of five hundred affiliated provincial clubs. Robespierre came to dominate this organization through the expulsions of the Feuillants in 1791 and the Girondins in 1793. The Jacobins controlled the National Convention through their affiliation with the Commune (the Paris city government and focus of its forty-seven sections).

In the spring of 1793, defeats of French revolutionary armies in the Netherlands and Rhineland and internal rebellion in the department of the Vendée (monarchist, Catholic, and against military conscription) combined with fear of espionage and hunger in Paris to cause the establishment of the Reign of Terror and the Committee of Public Safety, which dominated the Convention in

1793-1794. Robespierre strengthened his position in Paris and the Committee through his image as "incorruptible," a protector of the people's interests. Agencies of the Terror (the Revolutionary Tribunal, surveillance committees in Paris sections, and "representatives on mission" acting for the Convention in the provinces) helped France to regain the offensive abroad and control insurrection at home. Popular leaders, such as Jacques-René Hébert of the Commune and Georges Danton of the Cordeliers Club (and the Jacobin Club), worked with Robespierre in the fall of 1793 to eliminate the Girondins (who represented the Right) and the Enrages (who represented the Left). The Convention also established controls on prices of basic commodities.

As part of this deal, the Cordeliers placed Jean Nicolas Billaud-Varenne and Jean-Marie Collot d'Herbois on the Committee of Public Safety. Afterward, these men allowed the execution of their sponsors, the Hébertists on March 21, 1794, and the Dantonists on April 5. Issues in these purges included de-Christianization and atrocities of representatives on mission; at the same time, a struggle for control—or survival—was as important. Danton's crony, Camille Desmoulins, had challenged Robespierre in print, calling for an end of the Terror and identifying him as its perpetrator. Elimination of these rivals marked the triumph of Robespierre and the Jacobins, but it frightened other Convention members.

The high point of the Terror came in 112 days between the execution of Danton and that of Robespierre. Yet Robespierrists now modified some extremist policies. They called back to Paris notoriously brutal and venal representatives on mission, including Joseph Fouché, Collot, and Jean-Lambert Tallien, and they counteracted Hébertist atheism with the Festival of the Supreme Being, an elaborate public pageant led by Robespierre. On the other hand, Georges Couthon drew up the Law of 22 Prairial (June 10), under which the Revolutionary Tribunal judged crimes against the nation without presentation of defensive evidence and with mandatory death sentences. Executions in Paris tripled—up to 354 each month. (Provincial prisoners had begun to be sent to Paris for trial, which somewhat skews figures.)

The men who overthrew Robespierre acted to get him before he could get them; at the Convention on July 26, "the Incorruptible" had threatened his enemies. Fouché spread the rumor that Robespierre intended to make himself king; after all, when fanatical Catherine Théot had

1790's

proclaimed Robespierre as the Messiah, he had blocked her prosecution. Robespierre was attacked at the Convention on July 27 by Collot and Billaud, his rivals on the Committee of Public Safety, and by Marc Guillaume Vadier and Tallien of the rival Committee of General Security; the Convention refused to hear his self-defense. Confident in his control of the Jacobin Club, the Commune (after Hébert's execution), and the National Guard, Robespierre accepted arrest, hesitating to challenge the Convention's rule of law.

A confrontation followed. The Commune ordered Paris prisons not to incarcerate Robespierre and his friends who assembled at City Hall. The Commune called on National Guard contingents to defend City Hall and issued orders for the arrest of Convention leaders. The Jacobin Club declared that it would remain in session. Only thirteen sections, however, sent troops to defend Robespierre, and these had dwindled by 2:00 A.M., when Convention troops under Paul-François-Jean Nicolas de Barras arrived. As a result, the Robespierrists were arrested a second time without a struggle. On the afternoon of July 28, Robespierre, his brother Augustin,

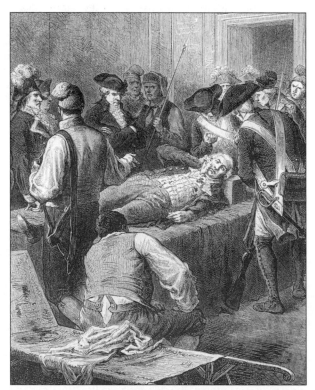

Robespierre is seized by the troops of the National Convention in Paris's City Hall. He is portrayed as wounded, having shot himself in the jaw earlier that night. (R. S. Peale and J. A. Hill)

Couthon, Louis Antoine de Saint-Just, and seventeen associates were condemned by the Revolutionary Tribunal and guillotined. On the following two days, eighty-four additional adherents were executed.

The Thermidorians, victors over Robespierre but themselves terrorists, had not intended to end the Terror; nevertheless, enthusiasm for it had clearly waned. (The conspirators are called "Thermidorians" because Robespierre fell on July 27-28, which was 9-10 Thermidor according to the revolutionary calendar.) After the execution of public prosecutor Antoine Quentin Fouquier-Tinville and other agents of the Terror, few persons volunteered to fill their places. It proved convenient to justify the coup by blaming Robespierre for the Terror. Thus the Revolutionary Tribunal, Committee of Public Safety, and Jacobin Clubs were shut down. On March 8, 1795, surviving Girondins were recalled to the Convention. The Law of 22 Prairial was repealed, and the Thermidorians Collot and Billaud were imprisoned in Cayenne for their terrorism.

SIGNIFICANCE

Lack of popular enthusiasm for Robespierre had stemmed from recently announced wage controls, and on December 24, 1794, the Convention repealed price controls. A bad harvest in 1794 meant terrible prices and food shortages in Paris. In April and May of 1795, hunger riots became insurrection, with people complaining that under Robespierre—and the king—they had had enough to eat. Led by regular army officers, militiamen from conservative neighborhoods pacified Paris, but provincial antirevolutionary atrocities ("White Terror") now equaled those of the earlier "Red Terror"; Jacobins became prime targets. On October 5, 1795, General Napoleon Bonaparte, at the Convention's behest, repressed a Rightist insurrection in Paris protesting a new constitution under which two-thirds of the old Convention would continue to serve. Many Thermidorians (Barras, Tallien, and Fouché among them) figured as leaders of the new regime, the Directory, which proved notoriously corrupt.

Robespierre's fall provides a reliable talisman for discovering a historian's viewpoint: Positivists, Marxists, monarchists, Dantonists, and Robespierrists all view not only the event but also the entire revolution differently. Historians continue to debate, for example, whether Robespierre's fall ended the French Revolution. The term "Thermidor" has become generally used in the idiom of revolutions to denote an inevitable, conservative reaction following revolutionary extremism and freedom.

—John G. Gallaher, updated by Paul Stewart

FURTHER READING

Backzo, Branislaw. *Ending the Terror: The French Revolution After Robespierre*. Translated by Michel Peteram. New York: Cambridge University Press, 1994. Details intrigues and rumors that brought about Robespierre's fall and also dicusses Thermidorian corruption.

Bienvenu, Richard T., ed. *The Ninth of Thermidor: The Fall of Robespierre*. New York: Oxford University Press, 1968. Bienvenu tells the story through a series of contemporary documents connected by his judicious commentary.

Doyle, William. *The Oxford History of the French Revolution*. 2d ed. New York: Oxford University Press, 2002. An authoritative and comprehensive account of French history between 1774 and 1802, written by a prominent historian. Includes information on Robespierre and the events of Thermidor.

Hardman, John. *Robespierre*. New York: Longman, 1999. Biography focusing on Robespierre's political career and the political situation during the French Revolution. Chapter 11 recounts the fall of Robespierre."

Hibbert, Christopher. *The Days of the French Revolution*. New York: Quill/William Morrow, 1999. Each chapter of this book covers the significant events that occurred on a single day or other designated time period during the French Revolution. Chapter 9 recounts the days of Thermidor.

Palmer, Robert R. *Twelve Who Ruled: The Year of the Terror in the French Revolution*. Princeton, N.J.: Princeton University Press, 1941. The inner workings and infighting of the Committee of Public Safety make clear the pressures and confusion at the top.

Rudé, George. *The Crowd in the French Revolution*. New York: Oxford University Press, 1959. Rudé analyzes in depth the great revolutionary "days." Chapter 9 of his work treats the events of 9 Thermidor.

Schama, Simon. *Citizens: A Chronicle of the French Revolution*. New York: Alfred A. Knopf, 1989. Of the plethora of reliable one-volume histories of the revolution, this one catches the bicentennial spirit and is highly anecdotal.

Thompson, J. M. *Robespierre*. Reprint. New York: Basil Blackwell, 1988. Its detail and objectivity make this biography, first published in 1935, the standard work on Robespierre in English.

SEE ALSO: May 5, 1789: Louis XVI Calls the Estates-General; June 20, 1789: Oath of the Tennis Court; July 14, 1789: Fall of the Bastille; Oct., 1789-Apr. 25, 1792: France Adopts the Guillotine; Apr. 20, 1792-Oct., 1797: Early Wars of the French Revolution; Jan. 21, 1793: Execution of Louis XVI; Mar. 4-Dec. 23, 1793: War in the Vendée; Nov. 9-10, 1799: Napoleon Rises to Power in France.

RELATED ARTICLES in *Great Lives from History: The Eighteenth Century, 1701-1800*: Georges Danton; Louis XVI; Marie-Antoinette; Robespierre.

August 20, 1794
BATTLE OF FALLEN TIMBERS

In the Battle of Fallen Timbers, the U.S. Army decisively defeated the Native Americans of the Ohio Territory. The resulting Treaty of Greenville secured U.S. control over much of Ohio, as the indigenous peoples of the area were forced to abandon their territory.

LOCALE: Ohio, south of present-day Toledo
CATEGORIES: Wars, uprisings, and civil unrest; expansion and land acquisition

KEY FIGURES

Anthony Wayne (1745-1796), major general and commander of the Legion of the United States
Blue Jacket (Weyapiersenwah; c. 1745-c. 1810), Shawnee war chief
Little Turtle (Michikinikwa; c. 1752-1812), Miami war chief
James Wilkinson (1757-1825), brigadier general and Wayne's second in command

SUMMARY OF EVENT

In the 1783 Treaty of Paris, which ended the Revolutionary War, the British acknowledged the United States' claims to territory west of the Appalachians and made no effort to protect American Indian lands in the Ohio Valley. Incursions by settlers there led to serious problems, because American Indian leaders refused to acknowledge U.S. authority north of the Ohio River. Between 1784 and 1789, U.S. government officials persuaded some chiefs to relinquish lands in southern and eastern

Major General Anthony Wayne celebrates a U.S. Army victory over the Miami Indians in the Battle of Fallen Timbers in the Ohio Territory. (Henry Francis du Pont Winterthur Museum)

Ohio, but most American Indians refused to acknowledge the validity of these treaties.

Encouraged by the British, the Miami and Shawnee tribes insisted that the Americans fall back to the Ohio River. When the settlers refused, the Miami attacked them. In 1790 and again in 1791, U.S. troops and militia were sent against American Indians along the Maumee River.

The 1790 expedition, the first for the U.S. Army, ended in disaster. In October, Brigadier General Josiah Harmar set out with a poorly trained force of some twelve hundred men. Harmar divided his troops into three separate columns, enabling the Miami and Shawnee, led by Miami chief Little Turtle, to win the battle, inflicting three hundred casualties on U.S. troops.

In November, 1791, Arthur St. Clair, governor of the Northwest Territory and a commissioned major general, led a second expedition, which included the entire six-hundred-man regular army and fifteen hundred militiamen. At present-day Fort Recovery, Ohio, Little Turtle and his warriors administered the most overwhelming defeat ever by American Indians on the British or Ameri-

cans. Some 650 U.S. troops and 250 civilians died; another 300 were wounded. American Indian losses were reported as 21 killed and 40 wounded.

In December, 1792, Congress authorized establishment of a five-hundred-man Legion of the United States. Despite misgivings, Washington recalled General "Mad Anthony" Wayne from retirement to command the legion. Wayne found his first training camp, near Pittsburgh, too distracting and marched his men 25 miles downriver to a site he named Legionville. Utilizing Baron Friedrich von Steuben's Revolutionary War drill manual, Wayne carried out rigorous training. In May, Wayne moved the legion to Cincinnati and then a few miles north to a new camp, Hobson's Choice.

Wayne issued a call for Kentucky mounted militia and in early October, moved north to Fort Jefferson with two thousand regulars. When Kentucky militiamen arrived, Wayne moved a few miles farther north and began a camp to accommodate his larger force. He named it Fort Greeneville (now Greenville, Ohio) in memory of his Revolutionary War commander, Nathaniel Greene. In December, 1793, Wayne ordered a detachment to the site of the previous massacre. On Christmas Day, 1793, U.S. troops reoccupied the battlefield. After burying human remains still in evidence, they constructed a fort on high ground overlooking the Wabash.

Wayne's timetable for the campaign was delayed because of unreliable civilian contractors, attacks on his supply trains, the loss of some of his men to other campaigns, and a cease-fire that led him to believe peace might be at hand. Little Turtle, Blue Jacket, and other tribal chiefs rejected peace negotiations, however.

In February, the British commander ordered construction of Fort Miamis, a post on the Maumee River, to mount cannon larger than those that Wayne might be able to bring against it. By mid-April, work on the fort was well along. This further delayed Wayne's advance, then rescheduled for June.

On June 29, Little Turtle struck first, at Fort Recovery, Wayne's staging point for the invasion. A supply train had just arrived and was bivouacked outside the walls when two thousand warriors attacked. They hoped to take both the supplies and fort in one bold stroke, but Fort Recovery's commander, Captain Alexander Gibson, was ready. Although many soldiers were killed outside the walls, the attackers were beaten back with heavy casualties. After two days with no success, the tribal warriors withdrew. The attack was the high-water mark of their cause; never again would they be able to assemble that many warriors. Defeat at Fort Recovery led some of the smaller tribes to quit the coalition and also caused the eclipse of Little Turtle, who was replaced as principal war leader by the less effective Blue Jacket.

Wayne now had two thousand men. In mid-July, the Kentucky militia, ultimately sixteen hundred men, began to arrive. Wayne also had one hundred American Indians, mostly Choctaws and Chickasaws. On July 28, the men left Fort Greenville for Fort Recovery. Much was at stake, and Washington had warned that a third straight defeat would be ruinous to the reputation of the government.

The two principal American Indian concentrations were Miami Town, the objective of previous offensives, and the rapids of the Maumee River around Fort Miamis. The two were connected by a 100-mile Maumee River Valley road. Wayne vowed to cut it at midpoint, forcing his enemy to split his forces and defend both possible objectives. By August 3, he had established both Fort Adams and Fort Defiance. Wayne then sent the chiefs a final offer for peace. Little Turtle urged its acceptance, pointing out the great numbers of the enemy and expressing doubts about British support. Blue Jacket and British agents urged war, however, which a majority of the chiefs approved.

Having learned that the American Indians were congregating near Fort Miamis, Wayne decided to move there first. On August 15, Wayne's men still were 10 miles from the British fort. Sensing an impending fight, Wayne detached unnecessary elements from his column at a hastily constructed position, Fort Deposit. Staffed by Captain Zebulon Pike and two hundred men, it would serve as a refuge in case things did not go well.

On August 20, Wayne again put his column in motion. More than a thousand American Indian warriors, along with some sixty Canadian militiamen, were lying in wait. They hoped to ambush the U.S. troops from the natural defenses of what had been a forest before it had been uprooted by a tornado. The attack plan was sound but based on the assumption that their enemy would either remain in place or run away. Not expecting the daylong delay to build Fort Deposit, Blue Jacket had thought that Wayne would arrive on August 19. The natives had begun a strict fast on August 18 and continued it the next day. When the Americans did not arrive, many of the natives, tired and half-starved, left for Fort Miamis.

Wayne marched his men so as to be ready to meet an attack from any quarter. His infantry were in two wings; well out in front was a select battalion, led by Major William Price, to trigger the enemy attack and allow Wayne time to deploy the main body. When the American Indians opened fire, Price's men fell back into James Wilkinson's line. Wayne's troops shattered the ambush with an infantry frontal attack driven home with the bayonet, while cavalry closed in on the flanks. The killing went on to the very gates of the fort, while the British looked on. Of Wayne's troops, only thirty-three were killed and one hundred wounded (eleven of whom later died of their wounds); tribal losses were in the hundreds.

Wayne disregarded Fort Miamis but destroyed American Indian communities and British storehouses in its vicinity. His troops then marched to Miami Town, occupied it without opposition on September 17, and razed it. They then built a fort on the site of Harmar's 1790 defeat, naming it Fort Wayne.

SIGNIFICANCE

On August 3, 1795, after six weeks of discussions, chiefs representing twelve tribes signed the Treaty of Greenville. The treaty set a definite boundary in the Northwest Territory, forcing the American Indians to give up most of the present state of Ohio and part of Indiana. All hostilities were to cease, prisoners were to be exchanged, and

1790's

the United States agreed to pay an eight-thousand-dollar-per-year annuity for the loss of hunting lands and twenty thousand dollars in commodities.

The brief Battle of Fallen Timbers broke forever the power of the American Indians in the eastern region of the Northwest Territory. It also led the British to evacuate their garrisons below the Great Lakes. The victory did much to restore the prestige of the U.S. Army; Wayne, justifiably, is known as its father.

—*Spencer C. Tucker*

FURTHER READING

Dowd, Gregory Evans. *A Spirited Resistance: The North American Indian Struggle for Unity, 1745-1815*. Baltimore: Johns Hopkins University Press, 1991. A useful short survey of American Indian affairs.

Edel, Wilbur. *Kekionga! The Worst Defeat in the History of the U.S. Army*. Westport, Conn.: Praeger, 1997. Focuses on a crucial battle of Little Turtle's War—the Miami Indians' devastating attack on American soldiers at the Kekionga Indian village in 1791. Edel chronicles the two-centuries-long conflict between Native Americans and European settlers that led to the battle and describes the settlers' eventual revenge at the Battle of Fallen Timbers.

Gaff, Alan D. *Bayonets in the Wilderness: Anthony Wayne's Legion in the Old Northwest*. Norman: University of Oklahoma Press, 2004. Military history recounting Wayne's campaign against the Indians in the Ohio River Valley. Includes information about the Battle of Fallen Timbers and the Treaty of Greenville.

Nelson, Paul D. *Anthony Wayne: Soldier of the Early Republic*. Bloomington: Indiana University Press, 1985. The best biography of Wayne.

Palmer, Dave r. *1794: America, Its Army, and the Birth of the Nation*. Novato, Calif.: Presidio Press, 1994. A helpful study of early U.S. military policy.

Sword, Wiley. *President Washington's Indian War: The Struggle for the Old Northwest, 1790-1795*. Norman: University of Oklahoma Press, 1985. Discusses the struggle for the northwest frontier.

Tebbel, John W. *The Battle of Fallen Timbers, August 20, 1794*. New York: Franklin Watts, 1972. Useful history of the battle.

Wilson, Frazer. *The Treaty of Greenville*. Pigua, Ohio: Correspondent Press, 1894. The only work specifically devoted to the treaty ending the campaign.

SEE ALSO: Sept. 22, 1711-Mar. 23, 1713: Tuscarora War; Summer, 1714-1741: Fox Wars; Sept. 19, 1737: Walking Purchase; May 28, 1754-Feb. 10, 1763: French and Indian War; Oct. 5, 1759-Nov. 19, 1761: Cherokee War; May 8, 1763-July 24, 1766: Pontiac's Resistance; Apr. 27-Oct. 10, 1774: Lord Dunmore's War; May 24 and June 11, 1776: Indian Delegation Meets with Congress; Oct. 22, 1784: Fort Stanwix Treaty; May 20, 1785: Ordinance of 1785; July 13, 1787: Northwest Ordinance; Oct. 18, 1790-July, 1794: Little Turtle's War; 1799: Code of Handsome Lake.

RELATED ARTICLES in *Great Lives from History: The Eighteenth Century, 1701-1800*: Little Turtle; George Washington; Anthony Wayne.

November 19, 1794
JAY'S TREATY

Jay's Treaty resolved outstanding financial, territorial, and commercial conflicts between Britain and the United States. The treaty led to large-scale settlement of the Northwest Territory, but it opened a rift with France.

LOCALE: Philadelphia, Pennsylvania, and London, England

CATEGORIES: Diplomacy and international relations; expansion and land acquisition; trade and commerce

KEY FIGURES

William Wyndham Grenville (1759-1834), British foreign secretary

Alexander Hamilton (1755-1804), U.S. secretary of the treasury

John Jay (1745-1829), chief justice of the U.S. Supreme Court, 1789-1795

Thomas Jefferson (1743-1826), U.S. secretary of state, 1790-1793, and president, 1801-1809

James Madison (1751-1836), U.S. representative, 1789-1797, and later secretary of state, 1801-1809, and president, 1809-1817

James Monroe (1758-1831), U.S. minister to France, 1794-1796, and later secretary of state, 1811-1817, and president, 1817-1825

Thomas Pinckney (1750-1828), U.S. minister to Great Britain, 1792-1794, and special commissioner to Spain, 1795-1796

William Pitt the Younger (1759-1806), prime minister
of Great Britain, 1783-1801, 1804-1806
George Washington (1732-1799), president of the
United States, 1789-1797

SUMMARY OF EVENT

After Great Britain's recognition of the United States as
an independent nation in the 1783 Treaty of Paris, the
United States had to make that independence meaningful
and permanent. For the next three decades, the new nation struggled to maintain its integrity by achieving security against hostile forces facing it to the north and south.
The southern and western boundaries were in dispute
with Spain. There also existed many outstanding problems in British-American relations after 1783, a number
of which stemmed from the apparent unwillingness of either side to abide fully by the Treaty of Paris. The British
in Canada, for example, refused to evacuate military
posts in the Northwest Territory, which the Treaty of
Paris recognized as belonging to the United States. Disputes over exact boundaries and fishing rights of Americans along the Grand Banks created further tensions.

To compound this unstable situation, Britain and other
European powers went to war in 1793 with France to put
down the subversive doctrines evolving from the French
Revolution and the later military ambitions of Napoleon
Bonaparte. The war between France and the rest of Eu-
rope continued from 1793 to 1815, with only brief pause,
and the United States was buffeted first by one belliger-
ent and then by the other. The 1794 treaty negotiated by
John Jay of New York is an episode in the struggle of the
United States to cope with these difficulties.

The United States and Great Britain by 1793 found
themselves competing in commercial affairs. In an effort
to secure trade for British vessels, Great Britain prohibited American vessels from carrying goods to British colonial ports. At the same time, Great Britain enjoyed a
virtual monopoly of American markets for manufactured
goods. Even though it became evident that Great Britain
could best supply credit and merchandise to the United
States, many Americans resented their economic subser-
vience to Great Britain. The administration of President
George Washington only with difficulty prevented the
passage of commercial legislation designed to retaliate
against alleged British discriminatory practices. The
United States therefore attempted to increase its trade
with France.

When war between France and Great Britain broke
out in 1793, new grievances added to the old, and relations between Great Britain and the United States took a
rapid turn for the worse. The position of the United States
as the major maritime neutral was critical. There was also
residual hostility toward Great Britain in contrast to a generally favorable attitude toward France, the United States'
important military ally during the Revolutionary War.

The British quickly gained mastery of the oceans,
which substantially isolated the French West Indies.
These islands could no longer trade with France in French
ships. Into this vacuum flowed the merchant fleet of the
United States, which gained great profits from this opportunity. The British realized that their naval and commercial supremacy was being weakened. In November,
1793, a British Order in Council ordered British naval
commanders to seize all neutral vessels trading with the
French islands. So suddenly was this order implemented
that approximately 250 U.S. ships were seized and about
half of them condemned to be sold as lawful prizes.

Such action led to widespread anti-British opinion in
the United States. James Madison, congressman from
Virginia, led a vigorous campaign to pass retaliatory legislation. Secretary of the Treasury Alexander Hamilton
successfully thwarted this effort, with Washington's
blessing. To blunt Madison's attack further, the president sent John Jay to London as envoy extraordinary to
negotiate with the British government. Jay met with the
foreign secretary, William Wyndham Grenville, and
Prime Minister William Pitt the Younger, among others.
Washington apparently believed that war with Britain
was inevitable unless Jay, at that time chief justice of the
United States, returned with an acceptable settlement.

The treaty that Jay negotiated in London struck many
contemporary observers as barely acceptable. Nevertheless, parts of the agreement do show Jay's success. It required the British to surrender the military posts that they
held on American soil in the Northwest Territory by June
of 1796. It also provided for the creation of a joint commission to settle the claims of British citizens for unpaid
prerevolutionary U.S. debts, to settle the claims of Americans for the illegal seizures of their ships, and to determine the disputed boundary between Maine and Canada.
The rest of the treaty dealt with commercial matters and
was to be in force for twelve years. It stated that the "most
favored nation" principle was to operate between the
United States and Great Britain. American vessels were
promised the same privileges as British vessels in both
Great Britain and the East Indies.

Jay failed, however, to gain British acceptance of several important U.S. objectives. American trading rights
with the British West Indies were so restricted that the
United States struck out that part of the treaty when it was

1790's

submitted to the Senate. The agreement included a broad definition of contraband, but said nothing on the important matters of the rights of visit and search and impressment. Other issues were not resolved or included. A number of these issues later contributed to the underlying causes of the War of 1812.

The agreement was signed on November 19, 1794, in London, and Jay returned to the United States satisfied with his efforts. When the terms of the treaty became known, however, advocates of U.S. commercial rights and anti-British opinion criticized Jay for his apparent failure to obtain complete success in the London negotiations. The Republicans charged the Washington administration with selling the nation out to the British. Effigies of Jay were burned throughout the country. Political pamphleteers and journalists entered the fray.

Congress debated the controversial treaty. The Senate ratified it June 24, 1795, by a vote of 20 to 10, barely meeting the two-thirds minimum required under the Constitution. After ratification by the Senate in a strictly partisan vote (Federalists for, Republicans against), the arguments continued both in Philadelphia and elsewhere. Secretary of State Edmund Randolph was forced to resign in a scandal related to the treaty's adoption. Washington, disappointed by the unevenness of the treaty, reluctantly signed it because he believed its acceptance the only alternative to war. Only an intense effort by his administration prevented the Republicans in the House of Representatives from undercutting the treaty by their threat to refuse to appropriate the funds necessary for its implementation. The essential legislation passed the House in 1796 by a narrow margin of only three votes (51 to 48).

SIGNIFICANCE

The effects of Jay's Treaty were significant. Most important, it kept the peace between the United States and Great Britain. It also induced Spain to conclude a treaty the following year (Pinckney's Treaty) that was very favorable to the United States, and it prepared the way for the large-scale settlement of the Northwest Territory. The disagreements over the treaty completed the organization of the opposition Republican Party, intensified by Thomas Jefferson's and Madison's antagonism to Hamilton and his policies. The Federalists also were divided and weakened. Washington's invulnerability to political attack was breached.

The restraining influence of the British on the Indians along the northwestern frontier was withdrawn, creating further problems in that region. Most significant, the French First Republic was incensed at this apparent repudiation by the United States of the Franco-American Treaties of 1778. While relations with Great Britain improved temporarily, the United States and France drifted apart, despite the best efforts of James Monroe and other diplomats. This rift between the only republican governments in the world culminated in an undeclared war and proved to be the dominant issue during the administration of President John Adams (1797-1801). Positive relations with Great Britain eventually deteriorated as well, culminating in the War of 1812.

—*John G. Clark, updated by Taylor Stults*

FURTHER READING

Bemis, Samuel F. *Jay's Treaty: A Study in Commerce and Diplomacy*. 2d ed. New Haven, Conn.: Yale University Press, 1962. The classic account of the treaty.

Cohen, Warren, ed. *Cambridge History of American Foreign Relations*. New York: Cambridge University Press, 1993. Volume 1 contains coverage of Jay's Treaty in the context of the diplomacy of the 1790's.

Combs, Jerald A. *The Jay Treaty: Political Battleground of the Founding Fathers*. Berkeley: University of California Press, 1970. Covers the domestic debate.

Ellis, Joseph J. *His Excellency: George Washington*. New York: Alfred A. Knopf, 2004. Best-selling and highly acclaimed biography. Includes information about the events occurring during Washington's presidency.

McColley, Robert, ed. *Federalists, Republicans, and Foreign Entanglements, 1789-1815*. Englewood Cliffs, N.J.: Prentice-Hall, 1969. Includes the text of Jay's March, 1795, statement defending the agreement.

Monaghan, Frank. *John Jay*. 1935. Reprint. Indianapolis, Ind.: Bobbs-Merrill, 1972. An old but solid biography.

Reuter, Frank T. *Trials and Triumphs: George Washington's Foreign Policy*. Fort Worth: Texas Christian University Press, 1983. Admiring assessment of Washington's leadership.

Stahr, Walter. *John Jay: Founding Father*. London: Hambledon and London, 2005. Comprehensive biography based, in part, on previously unavailable information. Stahr describes Jay's influence and importance in the early years of the American republic, examining his public career as well as his personal life.

SEE ALSO: Sept. 3, 1783: Treaty of Paris; Oct. 22, 1784: Fort Stanwix Treaty; May 20, 1785: Ordinance of 1785; July 13, 1787: Northwest Ordinance; 1790's: First U.S. Political Parties; Oct., 1790: Nootka Sound Convention; Oct. 18, 1790-July, 1794: Little Turtle's

War; July-Nov., 1794: Whiskey Rebellion; Aug. 20, 1794: Battle of Fallen Timbers; Oct. 27, 1795: Pinckney's Treaty; Oct. 4, 1797-Sept. 30, 1800: XYZ Affair.

RELATED ARTICLES in *Great Lives from History: The Eighteenth Century, 1701-1800*: Alexander Hamilton; John Jay; Thomas Jefferson; James Madison; William Pitt the Younger; George Washington.

1795
INVENTION OF THE FLAX SPINNER

While visiting Great Britain, Robert Fulton invented a flax-spinning machine that would significantly advance the American textile industry, although it would ironically be used for spinning cotton and wool rather than flax. The steam-powered spinning machine built upon the legacy of English inventors and contributed to the rapid growth of textile mills during the Industrial Revolution in the United States.

LOCALE: England; United States
CATEGORIES: Inventions; science and techonlogy; agriculture; manufacturing

KEY FIGURES
Robert Fulton (1765-1815), American engineer and inventor
Sir Richard Arkwright (1732-1792), English inventor
Samuel Crompton (1753-1827), English inventor
James Hargreaves (1720-1778), English inventor
John Marshall (1765-1845), English owner of a steam-powered flax mill
James Watt (1736-1819), Scottish inventor

SUMMARY OF EVENT
In 1795, American engineer Robert Fulton invented a steam-powered flax-spinning machine that could run multiple spinning frames from the same engine. Fulton drew upon the technology invented by English engineers that enabled England's textile production to move from rural cottage industries to urban industrial factories. These inventions, collectively, expanded the capacity of textile mills in terms of workers and production, leading to the factory system in England and, by 1800, the entry of the United States into the world textile market.

Several eighteenth century inventions prepared the way for the flax spinner. In 1765, James Hargreaves, of Blackburn, England, had invented the spinning jenny, a device that could twist and spin as many as one thousand threads at once on a single spinning frame. Thus, one person using a spinning jenny could spin as much yarn as twenty to one hundred workers using spinning wheels. Hargreaves took out a patent in 1770 to protect his inven-

tion, but copiers made free use of the easily built spinning jenny.

In 1769, Sir Richard Arkwright of Preston, England, invented a water-powered spinning frame, with rollers and flying spindles, that could spin flax, cotton, or wool. Arkwright's water frame was an improvement over Hargreaves's spinning jenny in that it could both twist rovings (carded fiber) and spin finished yarn. In 1771, Arkwright founded the first great cotton mill in Cromford, Derbyshire, England, thereby becoming the father of the factory system in England. His was the first mill to employ children, which became standard practice in English textile factories as devices such as the water frame made it possible for workers with less strength than an adult male to operate heavy machinery.

In 1774, Samuel Crompton combined the rollers of Arkwright's water frame and the carriage of Hargreaves's spinning jenny and created his spinning mule (thus named because it was a hybrid). Crompton's mule ran up to thirty spindles and could spin both warp and weft threads. Crompton's machine was adopted throughout the world. In 1785, James Watt's steam engine was applied to spinning machinery, and the shift from water-power to steam power began.

In 1788, John Marshall and his two partners, draper Samuel Fenton and linen merchant Ralph Dearlove, leased Scotland Mill, near Leeds, and established the first flax mill there. The machines in Marshall's mill did not work well at first, and Marshall asked engineer Matthew Murray to help him. By 1790, the firm was producing good quality yarn, and Marshall was ready to terminate his lease at Scotland Mill and build a new steam-powered factory. He moved to Holbeck, just outside Leeds, and built Temple Mill. He installed a twenty-horsepower Boulton and Watt steam engine, twenty-eight handlooms, fourteen spinning frames, and fourteen carding engines. By 1793, the mill employed two hundred workers and produced eighty-five tons of cloth for sale annually. Marshall established a second mill at Castle Foregate, and his business grew rapidly over the next two decades, becoming a major producer of linen fabrics. With the exception of Marshall's mill, however, flax mills were rare until the nineteenth century.

In 1787, coincidental with the rise of steam-powered textile mills in England, American engineer Robert Fulton arrived in that country. Even before he left Philadelphia, Fulton had become interested in the idea of using steam engines to power boats. Fulton's genius was in seeing what the market needed, looking at what had been invented by others, and seeking ways to improve upon those devices and to market his improvements. For seven years, however, Fulton ignored these talents and worked instead to become a gentleman artist. He became adept in charming noblemen, becoming a guest in their households and making valuable contacts.

In 1793, Fulton returned to engineering. He was intrigued by the idea of applying James Watt's rotary steam engine to power sailing vessels and focused on improving England's canal system. In 1794, Fulton patented his double-inclined plane for canals, which he believed would do away with the need for water cisterns to raise and lower canal levels. In 1794, he patented steam-powered machines for sawing marble, dredging canals, and making rope, and in 1795 he patented a steam-powered flax-spinning machine. Apparently, Fulton's flax-spinning machine was patented only in England and never in the United States. The manuscripts containing descriptions of Fulton's 1794-1796 inventions were lost in a shipwreck in transit from Paris to the United States in 1804.

After the American Revolution, textile manufacturers in the United States adopted the Arkwright machine, expanding textile production and establishing new mills in the northeastern and southern coastal states. Despite England's law of 1774 forbidding export of its textile machinery, the new inventions reached America. In 1789, one of the earliest American factories to make use of the spinning jenny was that of Hugh Templeton at Stateburg, Sumter District, South Carolina. Waterpower propelled the ginning, carding, and spinning machines at Templeton's factory, the latter of which drove eighty-four spindles each. In 1790, Rhode Island's first textile mill was established by Samuel Slater and Moses Brown. With the advent of steam power, mills in the Northeast and the South were set for explosive growth early in the next century.

Flax mills, as in Britain, were virtually nonexistent in the United States in the late eighteenth century. Settlers from Europe had brought flax seed for planting, and most farmers and planters raised flax for their own use, but converting flax to linen was labor intensive, and there

were no large commercial producers of flax. Flax fiber had to be harvested by hand-pulling the plants completely out of the ground, as the fiber extended into the roots. It was then dried in the field, the seeds were removed by combing, and the fiber was then submerged in a pool or lake, weighed down with stones, where it rotted. The process could take up to three weeks, depending on the method and temperature of the water. After rotting, the flax would be sent to the mill, where scutching rollers would break up and separate the usable fiber from the woody portions of the stalk. Next, the fibers were cleaned and straightened by combing. Then the flax fiber was ready for carding, drawing, roving, and spinning, in the same manner as cotton. The final treatment before spinning depended on the finish desired for the linen cloth and its use.

The availability and relative ease of production of cotton and wool and the absence of commercial cultivation of flax for fiber in the United States led to a concentration of wool and cotton mills in the American textile industry. Flax was cultivated for fiber mostly in Spain, France, the Netherlands, Belgium, Ireland, and on several English estates. In the United States, flax was cultivated commercially for harvesting the seed, a source of flax oil and linseed oil. Fulton's steam-powered flax-spinning machine was therefore used primarily in cotton and wool mills in the United States.

SIGNIFICANCE

The advances made in spinning technology during the last quarter of the eighteenth century led to the rapid rise in industrial textile mills in England. Steam power applied to new inventions had an immediate effect upon the textile industry, ushering in the urban factory system and marking the rapid decline of cottage textile production. Fulton's steam-powered spinner was one of the last such inventions of the century, and it built upon and improved all the devices invented previously. After the American Revolution, the steam-powered flax-spinning machine, which could spin cotton and wool as well, enabled the fledgling textile industry of the United States to grow rapidly and enter the world textile market in the late eighteenth and early nineteenth centuries, beginning the rise of the United States as a great industrial power that would culminate in the twentieth century.

—*Marguerite R. Plummer*

FURTHER READING

Editors of American Fabrics Magazine. *AF Encyclopedia of Textiles*. 2d ed. Englewood Cliffs, N.J.: Prentice-Hall, 1972. Lists fibers, fabrics, inventions and inventors related to textile industry. Does not include Robert Fulton.

Morgan, John S. *Robert Fulton*. New York: Mason/ Charter, 1977. Candid biography of Fulton, focusing on the late eighteenth century inventions and his schemes for making money in France and England. Bibliography.

Raistrick, Arthur. *Industrial Archaeology: An Historical Survey*. London: Eyre Methuen, 1972. A survey of historic textile mills and machinery in England.

Thurston, Robert H. *Robert Fulton: His Life and Its Results*. New York: Dodd, Mead, 1891. Available at http://www.history.rochester.edu/steam/thurston/fulton/index.html. An overview of Fulton's life and inventions.

SEE ALSO: 1701: Tull Invents the Seed Drill; 1705-1712: Newcomen Develops the Steam Engine; 1709: Darby Invents Coke-Smelting; 1733: Kay Invents the Flying Shuttle; 1764: Invention of the Spinning Jenny; 1765-1769: Watt Develops a More Effective Steam Engine; 1767-1771: Invention of the Water Frame; 1779: Crompton Invents the Spinning Mule; Apr., 1785: Cartwright Patents the Steam-Powered Loom; Dec. 20, 1790: Slater's Spinning Mill; 1793: Whitney Invents the Cotton Gin.

RELATED ARTICLES in *Great Lives from History: The Eighteenth Century, 1701-1800*: Sir Richard Arkwright; James Hargreaves; John Kay; Thomas Newcomen; James Watt.

1795
MURRAY DEVELOPS A MODERN ENGLISH GRAMMAR BOOK

Lindley Murray produced a simple-format English grammar book that was widely adopted by schools in both England and the United States. It proved to be an acceptable compromise between proponents of rules of usage and a universal grammar, and those who wanted language presented and described as it actually was used.

LOCALE: Holdgate, York, England
CATEGORIES: Education; cultural and intellectual history

KEY FIGURES
Lindley Murray (1745-1826), grammarian, lawyer, and merchant
Samuel Johnson (1709-1784), writer and lexicographer
Robert Lowth (1710-1787), scholar, bishop of London, and poetry professor
Joseph Priestley (1733-1804), scientist, Unitarian minister, and lecturer in language and literature

SUMMARY OF EVENT

During the eighteenth century in Britain, great attempts were made to codify the English language and to determine how it should be taught. The century saw the first major English dictionaries and grammar books. A rising middle class was eager to educate its children to the level of the upper classes, and there were concerns over language norms. Lindley Murray's grammar book (or, simply, grammar), which was published at the end of the

eighteenth century, took into account earlier efforts and produced a focused, eclectic, fairly prescriptive grammar for children of the middle classes.

Until the end of the seventeenth century the term "grammar" had applied only to the study of Latin and, to a lesser extent, Greek. Indeed, "grammar school" originally meant a school where Latin and Greek were taught. Between 1612 and 1669, no fewer than 169 editions of Latin grammars were printed. By contrast, only a few English grammars were produced, modeled on the Latin. The dramatist Ben Jonson's *The English Grammar* of 1640 was one of the first grammars in English.

By the beginning of the eighteenth century, however, there was a new confidence in the elegance and potentialities of the English language. As part of the Enlightenment philosophy of codifying the natural world, languages, too, were believed worthy of codification. In some countries, academies had been set up to perform this type of work, but the English believed these academies were too restrictive. In England, therefore, individuals, and not the government, were left to codify the language. One major landmark in the study of English was the systematic production of *A Dictionary of the English Language* by Samuel Johnson, which he began in 1746 and published in 1755. The dictionary attempted to include both etymologies (origins of words) and meaning distinctions with quotations to show meanings in use. Another major landmark was the English grammar of Robert Lowth, *A Short Introduction to English Grammar* (1762), who sought an "elevated style" with prescriptive rules, as in Latin grammar, and a fixed universal grammar.

By contrast, Joseph Priestley, a Unitarian scientist and linguist, had argued in his *The Rudiments of English Grammar* (1761) that the job of a grammar book was to describe the language as it was actually used, not to make it conform to an abstract set of rules. This view was reinforced by George Campbell's *The Philosophy of Rhetoric* (1776), in which language, as varied and fluid, requires that grammars be descriptive, not prescriptive. Campbell's view prevails in linguistic studies. The problem with determining current usage, however, was the question, Whose usage? In the end, the descriptionists chose the usage espoused in liberal education, with the criteria that it be reputable, national, and current. Murray preferred a descriptive grammar.

An American Quaker who had come to live in York, England, after the Revolutionary War, Murray had been trained as a lawyer but ultimately made his wealth in trade and speculative commerce, the career path of the rest of his family. There are several different accounts of why he settled in England in 1784 on his accumulated wealth. One account cites health reasons; another, that family members were British loyalists, and although they did not suffer confiscation, it was expedient for Murray to leave the country. For whatever reason, he settled in the Quaker community of York, where he was approached by a local Quaker girls' school to develop its English curriculum. He wrote *The Power of Religion on the Mind* in 1787, which was in its sixth edition by 1795, the year in which he published *An English Grammar: The Principles and Rules of the Language.*

Murray believed that the existing grammars, some two hundred of them, were unsuitable for girls. Some were written specifically for sons of tradespeople; others for grammar school students; others included the study of logic and rhetoric. Many were not for school use at all. Although Murray agreed with the usage based on liberal education, his main influence was Lowth, whose prescriptive approach he modified. However, he also acknowledged the work of others, including James Beattie's *Of Accent: Its Nature and Use* (1783), on phonology, and Thomas Sheridan's *A Rhetorical Grammar of the English Language* (1781), on spoken as well as written expression.

Murray's grammar comes in two volumes. The first volume has four parts: orthography, etymology, syntax, and prosody and pronunciation. The second and shorter volume has three parts: words and phrases, sentences and figures of speech, and usage and criticism. The orthog-

raphy section is brief, with a set of fairly arbitrary spelling rules. In etymology, he discusses, mainly, parts of speech, and includes very short chapters on word derivation and vocabulary. One significant aspect of this chapter is the running argument Murray conducts in small print with other grammarians (the large print is for student use). For example, while rejecting full Latinate case declension for the noun, he is uncertain as to precisely how many cases should be employed in English. He also argues for a "potential" mood for verbs, whereas modern linguists would speak of modal auxiliaries ("may," "must," "ought to," and so on). These arguments are part of the historical development of English grammar, which—like a good deal of eighteenth century science—was conducted by amateur scholars rather than professional academics.

The section on syntax, in volume 1 of the grammar, presents twenty-two rules to govern the correct writing of sentences. One of the suggested exercises for students is "parsing," which requires a word in a sentence to be given a full grammatical analysis, an exercise borrowed from Latin grammars. The sentences Murray uses are of a morally edifying nature. The grammar was not written simply for the acquisition of linguistic skills; it also intended to inculcate moral principles. Good language and good morality typically were considered two sides of one coin during the eighteenth and nineteenth centuries.

The other exercise employed is the correction of sentences, an exercise that was used by Lowth and many contemporaries, though not without controversy. Some had argued against the correction of sentences, claiming it was better to work with actual mistakes made by the students, for example, in their own letters or compositions.

In the second volume, which covers sentence stylistics, a number of key words are repeated as a type of Enlightenment mantra: "perspicacity," "purity," "propriety," and "precision." The criteria are both logical and moral. "Low" expression is considered morally as well as stylistically reprehensible.

After the initial and quite unexpected success of the grammar's first edition in 1795, Murray produced a shorter version that omitted the initial work's theoretical discussion. He also produced a reader as well as a series of exercises with a key, both of which were combined in various ways with other works. For example, the shorter grammar was combined not only with the exercises but also with other authors' work, such as John Entick's *The New Spelling Dictionary* of 1765. Murray's grammar was criticized by other grammarians, so every new edition either had modifications or added points of debate.

What Murray did not include is also significant. He made no attempt at rhetoric or composition. He addresses the grammar of the single sentence only. He does not examine the swelling eighteenth century paragraph or the heavily embedded complex periodic sentence. Prose style was kept simple and plain, which anticipated a more general shift.

SIGNIFICANCE

Lindley Murray's *An English Grammar*, together with the exercises and reader, outsold every grammar book during the fifty years that followed its first edition in 1795, including its competitors on both sides of the Atlantic. Eventually, more than three hundred editions would appear. Murray outsold even his great American contemporary, Noah Webster, whose *A Grammatical Institute of the English Language* had appeared in 1784. In the long run, however, Webster had the greater influence as a lexicographer.

Murray's grammar worked above all as a school textbook, one that fairly unqualified instructors could use, because it required no prior knowledge of Latin. Its sets of rules, its exercises and passages with their keys, its moral sentiments, and its sense of propriety made it "safe" for teachers and parents alike. Its outline and approach became the template of school grammars for the next hundred years.

—*David Barratt*

FURTHER READING

Mitchell, Linda C. *Grammar Wars: Language as Cultural Battlefield in Seventeenth and Eighteenth Century England*. Burlington, Vt.: Ashgate, 2001. A thorough background survey of the battle of ideas over grammar being fought in Murray's time. Lists all the grammars produced in the eighteenth century.

Monaghan, Charles. *The Murrays of Murray Hill*. Brooklyn, N.Y.: Urban History Press, 1998. The first part of this work examines the Murray family; the second part looks at Lindley Murray's propagation of Enlightenment ideals through his school textbooks.

Romaine, Suzanne, ed. *The Cambridge History of the English Language*. Vol. 4. New York: Cambridge University Press, 1998. Chapter 6 examines English grammar and usage, and discusses Murray's work and that of his contemporaries.

Tieken-Boon van Ostade, Ingrid, ed. *Two Hundred Years of Lindley Murray*. Münster, Germany: Nodus, 1996. This work traces the popularity of the various versions of Murray's school textbooks.

SEE ALSO: 1746-1755: Johnson Creates the First Modern English Dictionary; 1751-1772: Diderot Publishes the *Encyclopedia*; July, 1764: Voltaire Publishes *A Philosophical Dictionary for the Pocket*.

RELATED ARTICLES in *Great Lives from History: The Eighteenth Century, 1701-1800:* Denis Diderot; Samuel Johnson; Joseph Priestley; Voltaire.

1795-1797
PAGANINI'S EARLY VIOLIN PERFORMANCES

The violin prodigy Niccolò Paganini, who undertook his first concert tour at the age of fifteen, amazed audiences with his feats of agility, as well as his passionate stage presence, and became one of the Romantic era's most famous examples of the emotionally absorbed artist.

LOCALE: Northern Italy
CATEGORY: Music

KEY FIGURES
Niccolò Paganini (1782-1840), Italian violinist and composer
Alessandro Rolla (1757-1841), Italian violinist, conductor, and composer
Ferdinando Paer (1771-1839), Italian opera composer
Pietro Locatelli (1695-1764), Italian violinist and composer

Napoleon Bonaparte (1769-1821), French general and later emperor, r. 1804-1814, 1815

SUMMARY OF EVENT

During the early stages of Niccolò Paganini's career, an important transformation was occurring in the lives of musicians, mirroring changes in politics, economics, and other dimensions of life at this time. As power structures shifted, merit and individual initiative became more important, and social status became more fluid. Rather than remaining humble servants of the aristocracy and the Church, musicians such as Paganini struck out boldly on their own and were supported to some extent by members of the rising middle class who attended their concerts, as well as by more traditional, aristocratic sponsors.

There was already an established tradition of solo violin performance in Italy during the time of Paganini's first concerts, and it is quite likely that Italian audiences were more demanding than the foreign concert attendees who would be so amazed by his technique in the early decades of the nineteenth century. Many of the musicians active in Paganini's early years were little more than entertainers, however, hoping to attract an easily bored, casual audience with musical acrobatics and tricks to hold their attention. In his earliest concerts, the young Paganini imitated animal sounds as part of his act. As an adult, he dropped these more theatrical gimmicks, but he always retained a dramatic persona.

There were some parallels between Paganini's early experiences and those of other great musicians. Like the young Ludwig van Beethoven, he was forced to practice long hours by his father, Antonio Paganini. Paganini's father also arranged for the first concerts to be given by his son, as Leopold Mozart had done for the young Wolfgang Amadeus Mozart and his sister Nannerle a generation before.

Antonio Paganini was an amateur mandolinist who worked on the docks of Genoa, one of Europe's major seaports. He gave Niccolò his first lessons in music and, seeing that his son was gifted, made sure that he received lessons from capable Genovese musicians, such as violinists Giovanni Cervetto (Giovanni Servetto) and Giacomo Costa and the opera composer Francesco Gnecco. Antonio demanded a return on this investment, insisting that Niccolò maintain a grueling practice schedule, and he did not allow the sickly young boy much time to run and play. Giacomo Costa, one of Paganini's violin teachers, was active in both sacred and secular music and suggested that the boy begin playing in church on Sundays in order to gain experience playing in public. In this way, a lifetime of performance began when Paganini was about twelve years old.

Although he received professional training on the violin, Paganini retained a fondness for the guitar, which was very popular in Italy, and his first composition, "Variazioni sulla Carmagnola," which he performed at the Teatro di S. Agostino in Genoa in 1795, was a duet for violin and guitar. This piece, written when he was only twelve or perhaps even earlier, also showed Paganini's interest in the "theme and variations" structure common to both the elite and vernacular musical styles that he inherited. By repeating a harmonic structure within a strict metrical framework, a musician could create increasingly complex melodic patterns, and for a virtuoso like Paganini, the possibilities were infinite. The fourteen

Niccolò Paganini in 1819. (Hulton Archive/Getty Images)

variations of Paganini's first composition were built on the structure of a well-known song that reflected the cultural links between northwestern Italy and France. Named after a town in the Piedmont region, which like Genoa is geographically close to France, "Carmagnola" was a favorite song of the French revolutionaries who had gained power earlier in the decade.

Paganini learned rapidly and developed some of his own musical techniques, including sound effects such as blowing across the ridge of the violin to imitate the sound of an organ. He was very independent artistically and had benefited both from the intuitive rote learning of the vernacular music he learned from his father and from the notation-centered approach of the trained musicians under whom he studied. His teachers recommended that he study with Alessandro Rolla, a well-known violinist and conductor in the town of Parma. His father agreed, and in 1795, at the age of thirteen, Paganini gave a special fundraising concert in order to support the endeavor. He traveled to Parma and met Rolla, and the older musician was deeply impressed when he heard Paganini sight-reading one of Rolla's own pieces. Rolla accepted him as an equal and introduced him to Ferdinando Paer and other musicians, who gave lessons to the young prodigy. Paganini returned to Genoa in 1796 and continued giving concerts to enthusiastic audiences.

Events in the region soon led to more travel and to Paganini's first concert tour. Napoleon Bonaparte invaded Italy in 1796, and his troops occupied Genoa. In 1797, Napoleon abolished the state's existing government and absorbed Genoa into his Ligurian Republic. When the British fleet blockaded Genoa's harbor, Paganini's family, which still depended on Antonio's income from the docks, was under economic pressure, and Antonio decided to move south to Livorno to look for work. This move resulted in new opportunities for his son as well. Paganini played concerts not only in Livorno, where he played for the British consul, but also in other cities in northern Italy. Audiences loved his playing, and his confidence as a performer grew significantly.

SIGNIFICANCE

The confidence and experience gained from Paganini's early performances shaped his later career. In 1801, Paganini decided to move to Lucca, where he would live for the next decade, while continuing to travel to other cities to give concerts. By this time, he was earning enough money to become financially independent and was no longer under the authority of his overbearing father. In contrast to the incredible discipline of his childhood, his personal life as a young adult was extremely chaotic and impulsive. This period coincided with the rule of Napoleon, who appointed his sister Elisa as princess of Lucca in 1805. Paganini served in her court during this time and dedicated an orchestral composition to Napoleon. However, in 1810, Paganini left the court and returned to touring as an independent musician.

For his remaining thirty years of life, Paganini continued to explore the frontiers of technique on his instrument as a performer and composer. Eventually, he played outside Italy in most of the major cities throughout Europe, and he became almost a cult figure. He promoted his performances with a flair for publicity and showmanship and cultivated an air of mystery. Although he may have amazed international audiences who had never heard such playing, and who even gossiped about possible supernatural connections, all of it was built on the solid foundation of skills he had acquired through his years of rigorous practice as a young boy and the centuries of tradition preceding him. This tradition included the compositions of Pietro Locatelli, whose twenty-five caprices for solo violin probably were the models for Paganini's own twenty-four caprices, which took the use of special techniques even further.

Paganini had a unique background that reflected both elite and folk traditions, and his music was accessible to many kinds of listeners, making him an ideal figure to participate in the social transition from elite and church sponsorship of musicians to a wider and more middle-class audience. With time, disillusionment over political idealism led to a general recognition of the suffering and passion associated with the creative spirit. The role of the virtuoso soloist became associated with voluntary self-sacrifice, emphasizing the intense concentration and emotional expression required for these performances. For popular audiences, the gaunt figure of Paganini became associated with magic and the occult, but to the Romantic intellectuals, he personified the struggles of the heroic individual.

Musically, Paganini made extensive use of special effects, including many kinds of harmonics, bouncing the bow on the strings, scordatura (alternate tunings of the strings), unusual left-hand fingerings and stretches, use of the left-hand fingers to pluck the strings, use of a single string (usually the thickest G-string) for entire pieces, and others. In his later years, his compositions became part of standard curriculum for aspiring violinists, and the precedents he set for solo performers of all instruments have inspired many generations of musicians.

—*John Myers*

FURTHER READING

Borer, Philippe. *The Twenty-Four Caprices of Niccolò Paganini: Their Significance for the History of Violin Playing and the Music of the Romantic Era*. Zurich, Switzerland: Stiftung Zentralstelle der Studentenschaft der Universität Zürich, 1997. Dissertation exploring the characteristics, background, and context of these important solo works.

Connelly, Frances S. *Modern Art and the Grotesque*. Cambridge, England: Cambridge University Press, 2003. Cultural and historical analysis, including a section on Paganini and the aesthetics of the Romantic period.

Kolneder, Walter. *Amadeus Book of the Violin: Construction, History, and Music*. Pompton Plains, N.J.: Amadeus Press, 1998. Updated English translation from German of a monumental work on the violin, its players, and its composers, with appropriate attention to Paganini. Includes music examples, full references, and index.

Metzner, Paul. *Crescendo of the Virtuoso: Spectacle, Skill, and Self-Promotion in Paris During the Age of*

1790's

Revolution. Berkeley: University of California Press, 1998. Includes coverage of Paganini and others in the context of the cultural influence of the French Revolution, resulting in an emphasis upon personal accomplishments instead of traditional power structures.

Roth, Henry. *Violin Virtuosos from Paganini to the Twenty-First Century*. Los Angeles: California Classics Books, 1997. While its second chapter is completely devoted to Paganini, the book also includes frequent references to him throughout the later chap-

ters, showing his continued influence on subsequent generations of eminent solo violinists.

SEE ALSO: c. 1701-1750: Bach Pioneers Modern Music; c. 1709: Invention of the Piano; Apr. 13, 1742: First Performance of Handel's *Messiah*; Jan., 1762-Nov., 1766: Mozart Tours Europe as a Child Prodigy.

RELATED ARTICLES in *Great Lives from History: The Eighteenth Century, 1701-1800*: Johann Sebastian Bach; George Frideric Handel; Joseph Haydn; Wolfgang Amadeus Mozart.

May 6, 1795
SPEENHAMLAND SYSTEM

The county magistrates of Berkshire, England, modified an existing system to help poor farmworkers. They linked the amount of money given to the poor to the price of bread, so workers would automatically be given more money as bread became more expensive. Such "index-linking" schemes became widely adopted and remained in place until a new Poor Law was enacted in 1834.

LOCALE: Speenhamland, near Newbury, Berkshire, England

CATEGORIES: Economics; agriculture; government and politics; social issues and reform

KEY FIGURES

Thomas Gilbert (1720-1798), English reformist member of Parliament

Samuel Whitbread (1764-1815), English reformist member of Parliament

William Pitt the Younger (1759-1806), British prime minister, 1783-1801, 1804-1806

SUMMARY OF EVENT

By the end of the eighteenth century, there had been a poor law in England since late in the reign of Elizabeth I (1601). A "poor law" is legislation designed to aid the poor, whether their poverty arises from disability, unemployment, or low wages. The Elizabethan Poor Law raised money for such aid from local parish rates (taxes), which were supervised by local magistrates.

By the second half of the eighteenth century, the system was beginning to break down in certain, mainly rural, areas. As a result of agricultural reforms, landowners were enclosing land, thereby preventing farmworkers from grazing animals on "common" land. Nor did all

farmers supply their workers with housing that included yards in which animals could graze. From 1760 onward, the pace of enclosing land increased. It is reckoned that 95 percent of enclosure legislation injured the poor, as the increase in the number of completely landless laborers increased the level of poverty. Poverty was also exacerbated by increases in seasonal unemployment. Contemporary observers demonstrated that it was no longer possible for an agricultural worker to subsist on the wages he earned.

Some politicians, for example Member of Parliament Thomas Gilbert, saw the need to reform the Poor Law to take account of these changes. He had been a land agent for the second earl of Gower—the future marquess of Stafford and one of the nation's wealthiest landowners—and he had seen for himself the effects of enclosure. In 1765, he began a campaign for the better organization of parish relief and for more accountable oversight. His efforts were consistently defeated until 1782, when he introduced three bills into Parliament. The first two bills passed and became law, enabling local parishes to supplement low wages from the rates and to create work for the unemployed. Infirm paupers were to be kept in workhouses. Guardians were to be appointed to administer relief.

The Gilbert Act helped the British poverty level, but it did not fix a national system of supplementing income. In the north of England, agricultural workers were paid better than in the south or the Midlands, because there was a shortage of such workers in that area. The Industrial Revolution was beginning, and the mills and factories that had begun springing up and draining the potential labor pool were centered in the north. Industrial rates of pay were typically higher than rural wages, so northern farms had to increase their wages to compete. Elsewhere, though, wages were kept low, despite the beginnings of the Napoleonic Wars in 1793 and a series of bad harvests, which drove up food prices. Taxation also rose sharply. Food riots occurred in 1795 to protest the growing disparity between wages and prices.

In the county of Berkshire in the south of England, eleven local magistrates—five landowners and six clergymen—met at the Pelican Inn in the village of Speen, near Newbury, on May 6, 1795, to consider the plight of the farmworkers and to discuss the problem of parish relief. They decided to set a standard for the amount of relief, or supplemental wages, to be paid to poor workers out of parish funds. They based their standard on the assumptions that a man consumed twenty-six pounds of bread per week and a woman or child consumed half that amount.

The magistrates agreed to fix the index at the cost of a "gallon loaf" of bread, that is, one weighing eight pounds and eleven ounces, made of second-grade-quality flour. Thus, if such a loaf cost one shilling, then each laborer in the county was to receive a total income of three shillings a week plus one and one-half shillings each for his wife and children. If the price of bread rose to one and one-half shillings per loaf, then the total minimum income would increase to four and one-quarter shillings per laborer and two shillings per dependent (wife or child). The difference between a worker's actual income and his minimum permissible income according to the index was to be paid to each household from money raised through the parish rates.

This payment of supplemental wages based on the price of bread came to be known as the Speenhamland system. It was a practical solution arrived at by local authorities, not a piece of legislation, and there were other systems already in practice elsewhere in England. Indeed, Prime Minister William Pitt the Younger opposed any further government intervention in the form of national poor laws or wage regulation. In 1796, Samuel Whitbread, the son of a millionaire brewer, attempted to introduce a parliamentary measure for a minimum national wage, and it failed in the face of Pitt's opposition. In the absence of such a national measure, most parishes in the south and the Midlands of England quickly adopted the Speenhamland system.

The system did not prevent further unrest: Food riots took place in 1796, 1800, and 1801. Moreover, larger landowners tended to profit by the system. Although they contributed more to the rates, their workers also received more from them. Smaller farmers had less need of laborers, but they still had to contribute substantially to the parish rates. For example, a farmer in 1816 holding three hundred acres of land had to pay £380 per annum in rates and taxes, plus one-tenth of his income as a tithe to the Anglican Church. A number of smaller farmers went bankrupt.

The price of wheat fluctuated enormously as a result of poor harvests and the wars, rising from a little more than fifty-two shillings per quarter in 1794 to 119.5 shillings per quarter in 1801. The restrictive Corn Laws of 1791, 1804, and 1815 kept the price of wheat high, so the Speenhamland system became increasingly difficult to budget for and expensive to operate. Farmers refused by and large to raise wages. A typical farm laborer's wage was twenty-six pounds per annum (ten shillings per week), while women and children would only receive five shillings and three and one-half shillings per week, respectively. After the Napoleonic Wars, taxes shifted from direct to indirect, so the tax burden fell disproportionately on the poor, as many necessary items for living came to be taxed. In the 1830's, a series of riots called the Swing Riots broke out in the southern counties, as living conditions there deteriorated even further.

SIGNIFICANCE

The success of the Speenhamland system is hard to assess. Some social historians believe it worked against the working classes by keeping wages low, by demoralizing them, and by keeping them dependent upon handouts. Under the system, however hard a man worked, he ended up receiving the same amount of money each week. Other historians, however, believe the Speenhamland system prevented starvation and revolution in a time of massive social change and in fact acted in the same way as a minimum wage.

During the period in question, there was a change away from the eighteenth century philosophy of patronage and humanitarian duty on the part of the landowning classes to a nineteenth century philosophy of *laissez-faire* economics. Proponents of the new economics suggested that the Speenhamland system encouraged large families and thus rural overpopulation, while it prevented market forces from operating properly. There was general contemporary agreement that if the laboring classes were not kept fractionally above the starvation level, they would not work hard. Even enlightened reformers like William Wilberforce subscribed to such views. Thus, ideological opposition to the system grew.

In addition to theoretical and philosophical opposition, there was growing dissatisfaction with the system on a practical level. The amount spent nationally on poor law relief was growing dramatically. For example, in

1790's

1784, £2 million was spent annually; by 1813 this figure was £6.5 million; and in 1818 it had reached £8 million. The result was that in 1832 a royal commission was set up to look into the workings of the Poor Law, under the able direction of Nassau Senior and Edwin Chadwick. The commission's eight-thousand-page report was published in 1834, and in that year Parliament passed the Poor Law Amendment Act, setting up a nationally administered system and bringing the Speenhamland system to an end. Thus, the system could best be seen as an evolutionary transition in social reform, as local parishes moved to take action in an arena that would later be seen as the necessary purview of the nation.

—*David Barratt*

FURTHER READING

Boyer, George R. *An Economic History of the English Poor Law, 1750-1850*. Cambridge, England: Cambridge University Press, 1990. A very full account of the old and new poor laws, fully indexed. Bibliography.

Chambers, J. D., and G. E. Mingay. *The Agricultural Revolution, 1750-1880*. London: B. T. Batsford, 1966. Links the plight and fortunes of agricultural workers with wider aspects of the Agricultural Revolution.

Hammond, J. L., and Barbara Hammond. *The Village Labourer, 1760-1832*. Reprint. London: Longmans, 1978. One of a classic series of studies on the British working classes.

Marshall, J. D. *The Old Poor Law, 1795-1834*. New York: Macmillan, 1968. The fullest study of the fortunes of the Speenhamland system.

Neeson, J. M. *Commoners: Common Right, Enclosure, and Social Change in England, 1700-1820*. Cambridge, England: Cambridge University Press, 1993. Focuses on the effect of the various enclosure acts. Index and bibliography.

Rule, John. *The Vital Century: England's Developing Economy, 1714-1815*. New York: Longman, 1992. Sets the system in the wider context of English economic history. Index and bibliography.

Snell, K. D. M. *Annals of the Labouring Poor: Social Change and Agrarian England, 1660-1900*. Cambridge, England: Cambridge University Press, 1985. A full and modern overall history of the agricultural worker. Bibliography.

Thompson, E. P. *The Making of the English Working Class*. 2d ed. Harmondsworth, England: Penguin, 1982. Argues the disadvantages of the Speenhamland system.

SEE ALSO: 1720: Financial Collapse of the John Law System; Sept., 1720: Collapse of the South Sea Bubble; 1763-1767: Famine in Southern Italy; Apr. 27-May, 1775: Flour War; Mar. 9, 1776: Adam Smith Publishes *The Wealth of Nations*; 1786-1787: Tenmei Famine; 1798: Malthus Arouses Controversy with His Population Theory.

RELATED ARTICLES in *Great Lives from History: The Eighteenth Century, 1701-1800*: William Pitt the Younger; William Wilberforce.

July, 1795-March, 1796
SECOND MAROON WAR

Jamaica's largest community of Maroons—rebellious and escaped slaves—battled British forces for nine months in an uprising prompted by local grievances. The conflict ended when the Maroons agreed to a peace treaty, the terms of which were violated when Jamaica's British governor deported the Maroons to Nova Scotia in Canada. The war marked the last significant Maroon rebellion in Jamaican history.

LOCALE: Jamaica
CATEGORIES: Wars, uprisings, and civil unrest; social issues and reform

KEY FIGURES
Sixth Earl of Balcarres (Alexander Lindsay; 1752-1825), governor of Jamaica and British military officer who served in the American Revolutionary War
Leonard Parkinson (fl. 1795-1796), Maroon captain and last of the rebels to surrender during the Second Maroon War
George Walpole (1758-1835), British major general who led British forces in the Second Maroon War

SUMMARY OF EVENT
In the Second Maroon War (1795-1796), Maroon combatants battled a British force that numbered about five times that of the Maroons. Jamaica was Britain's chief sugar colony, and Trelawney Town was the largest of Jamaica's five officially recognized Maroon communities. The British government granted Maroons legal status in

the 1739 treaties that ended the First Maroon War, which accorded the Maroons more than fifteen hundred acres of land and a quasi-autonomous state in exchange for their aid in tracking and returning fugitive slaves. The causes of Jamaica's second and final Maroon war involved local concerns as well as larger ideological and political developments that accompanied the French and Haitian revolutions.

Alexander Lindsay, the sixth earl of Balcarres, became governor of Jamaica when his predecessor was sent to command British forces intended to quell the revolution in Saint Domingue (or Hispaniola, the island now occupied by Haiti and the Dominican Republic). Many ruling-class Jamaicans feared that the thousands of émigrés and fugitives arriving from Saint Domingue intended to arm Jamaica's slaves and incite them to revolution. In August, 1795, a French royalist confirmed the ruling class's fears when he asserted (but later recanted) that French Jacobin commissioner Victor Hughes had sent Afro-Caribbean infiltrators to Jamaica (Hughes had recently reclaimed Guadeloupe and Saint Lucia and inspired rebels in Grenada). In this climate of heightened anxiety regarding slave insurrection, Jamaica's substantial, semiautonomous, and armed Maroon communities may have seemed especially dangerous to some.

Despite the fears and rumors linking French and Haitian revolutionary activity to Jamaican insurrection, it was a confluence of local resentments that prompted the actions of the Trelawney Maroons. As the population grew, the Maroon communities found the original land allotment from the 1739 treaty to be inadequate, and by the 1790's, Trelawney Town was suffering from a land shortage. At the same time, the town was experiencing a weakening of local authority. Many members of the community were aggrieved by the British appointments of town superintendents in 1792 and 1794; the latter superintendent, Thomas Craskell, was thought to be particularly inept.

The immediate spark of the war occurred in July, 1795, when two Trelawney Maroons were convicted of stealing pigs in Montego Bay in St. James Parish. Parish magistrates, rather than Trelawney authorities, sentenced the offenders, which was a breach of the 1739 treaty. Furthermore, for the fiercely independent Maroons, what was exceptionally offensive was that their punishment, flogging, was administered by a slave (who had been a runaway recovered by the Maroons) and administered before an audience of slaves. In the furor that began with the news of the flogging, Superintendent Craskell was forcibly ejected from Trelawney Town.

In an effort to address Trelawney grievances regarding concerns about land and about the flogging, Craskell, numerous magistrates, local property owners, and a former, well-respected superintendent met with Trelawney authorities for discussion and to offer redress. Despite the initial success of these negotiations, Governor Balcarres sent a letter to Britain's secretary for war suggesting that the French may have prompted the Maroon insurrection. Balcarres opposed the conciliatory efforts of the magistrates and pressed for military suppression of what, he claimed, was an imminent threat. Balcarres declared martial law and demanded the surrender of all Trelawney Maroons capable of bearing arms. The thirty-seven men who complied were imprisoned. Soon after, approximately three hundred Maroons attacked and defeated the St. James Parish militia, marking the opening battle of a nine-month engagement with British troops. Fighting against the British were not only military regulars but also local residents, including slaves and Accompong Maroon mercenaries. Free Afro-Jamaicans made up about one-third of the Jamaica militia.

While numerous slaves were pressed into British service, roughly 100 to 250 defected to the Trelawney side. Some free Afro-Jamaicans joined the Maroon warriors as well. The combined force of Trelawney Maroons, slaves, and Afro-Jamaicans, totaling approximately 500 persons, sustained a successful guerrilla war against the much larger British force (approximately 2,500). Unable to secure a military victory, Balcarres proposed peace in late October, 1795. In December, British major general George Walpole wrote to Balcarres of a truce he had reached with the Trelawney Maroons on the condition that they would not be deported.

On December 28, Balcarres declared that the treaty would be ratified when the Trelawney Maroons met at his headquarters on January 1, 1796. Balcarres may have once again deliberately manipulated circumstances, given that the conditions of communication and travel made the three-day time frame infeasible. When only three Trelawney men arrived on the first of the year, Balcarres issued chasseurs, the handlers of Cuban bloodhounds used throughout the Caribbean (including the First Maroon War), to track Maroons, rebel slaves, and criminals. Many Trelawney Maroons were en route, in good faith, to Balcarres's headquarters, while others, remotely situated, may not have even learned of the treaty for several weeks. Some 150 fugitive slaves refused to surrender. Several Maroon bands continued to rout their opponents, most notably, the 36 combatants led by Maroon captain Leonard Parkinson, whose exploits became

1790's

legendary and whose surrender at the end of March signaled the de facto end of the war.

By March, 1796, large numbers of Trelawny Maroons had complied with the conditions of the treaty (excepting the January 1 date) and surrendered their arms. Like those who had acquiesced to Balcarres at the start of war, the Trelawny Maroons were imprisoned in warships off the coast of Montego Bay. Recaptured rebel slaves, free blacks, and many of the Maroons were sentenced to whipping and imprisonment. In express violation of the terms of the treaty, Balcarras deported nearly six hundred Maroons to Nova Scotia in 1796. Many individuals, including Major General Walpole, were outraged by Balcarres's patent breech of trust. As a result, Walpole resigned his post in Jamaica and rejected the disbursement offered to him and Balcarres by the Jamaican assembly. Discontented in Canada, the Trelawny Maroons petitioned the British government and, as did many of the African American loyalists who emigrated to Nova Scotia after the American Revolutionary War and the War of 1812, they ultimately settled in Sierra Leone, Africa.

SIGNIFICANCE

Second only to Brazil, Jamaica experienced more slave insurrections than any other colony in the Americas, and Jamaica's Maroons were among the most powerful Maroon communities in the New World. The Maroons were independent, unvanquished societies made up of or descended from fugitive slaves. As such, they were a constant symbol of successful slave resistance in the face of the colonial state and plantation society. In Jamaica, after the 1739 and 1740 treaties ending the First Maroon War, the Maroons found themselves at odds with rebellious and runaway slaves, whom they were thus required to subdue (yet upon whom they often relied for provisions, intelligence, and mates). An important episode of colonial resistance, the Second Maroon War was not a slave uprising per se, as the Trelawny Maroons were recognized as free subjects of the British crown and as a semiautonomous state (though their rights granted in the 1739-1740 treaties were not infrequently curtailed). Despite antagonism between slaves and Maroons, many slaves switched allegiances during the course of the war.

Whether or not in earnest, Governor Balcarres presented the 1795 Maroon uprising as the work of French subversives. During the course of the conflict, Balcarres consistently rejected reconciliation and seized every opportunity to eliminate the Trelawny Maroons. While the Maroons' military success was an embarrassment to the

plantocracy, their deportation was for many planters a victory and a relief. The Second Maroon War signaled the last significant Maroon uprising in Jamaican history. Jamaica would be free of large-scale slave insurrection from the end of the Second Maroon War until 1831, when Jamaican slaves rose up in the Christmas Rebellion (or Baptist War), the largest slave revolt in the Americas after Saint Domingue.

—*Christina Proenza-Coles*

FURTHER READING

Campbell, Mavis C. *The Maroons of Jamaica, 1655-1796: A History of Resistance, Collaboration, and Betrayal*. Trenton, N.J.: Africa World Press, 1990. Colonial history of Jamaican Maroons, focusing on both their collaboration with and their resistance to the British Empire.

Cranton, Michael. *Testing the Chains: Resistance to Slavery in the British West Indies*. Ithaca, N.Y.: Cornell University Press. 1982. Gives a detailed, chapter-length description of the war and its consequences.

Dallas, Robert. *The History of the Maroons*. Vols. 1-2, London: Longman and Rees, 1803. An account of Jamaican Maroon history including the Second Maroon War and settlement in Sierra Leone by a contemporary historian.

Furness, A. E. "The Maroon War of 1795." *Jamaican Historical Review* 5 (May, 1965): 30-49. A comprehensive account of the war and its causes.

Geggus, David. "The Enigma of Jamaica in the 1790's: New Light on the Causes of Slave Rebellion." *William and Mary Quarterly*, 3d series, 44, no. 2 (April, 1987): 274-299. Challenges scholarship linking French agents with the Second Maroon War and analyzes larger processes surrounding resistance in late eighteenth century Jamaica and the colonial Atlantic.

Hart, Richard. *Slaves Who Abolished Slavery*. Vol. 2. Kingston, Jamaica: Institute of Social and Economic Research, University of the West Indies, 1985. Contains two chapters dedicated to the Second Maroon War based on contemporary correspondence.

Jamaica Assembly. *Proceedings in Regard to the Maroon Negroes*. London: John Stockdale, 1796. Reprint. Westport, Conn.: Negro Universities Press, 1970. Documentation of the Jamaica Assembly's deliberations over the Second Maroon War with an introduction by contemporary historian Edward Long.

Robinson, Carey. *The Iron Thorn: The Defeat of the British by the Jamaican Maroons*. Kingston, Jamaica: Kingston, 1993. Examination of Jamaican resistance, beginning with the 1509 Spanish colonization and focusing on the Second Maroon War.

SEE ALSO: 18th cent.: Expansion of the Atlantic Slave Trade; Apr. 6, 1712: New York City Slave Revolt; Aug., 1712: Maya Rebellion in Chiapas; 1730-1739: First Maroon War; Nov. 23, 1733: Slaves Capture St. John's Island; Sept. 9, 1739: Stono Rebellion; 1760-1776: Caribbean Slave Rebellions; 1780-1781: Rebellion of Tupac Amaru II; Aug. 22, 1791-Jan. 1, 1804: Haitian Independence.

RELATED ARTICLES in *Great Lives from History: The Eighteenth Century, 1701-1800*: Joseph Boulogne; Nanny; Guillaume-Thomas Raynal; Granville Sharp; Toussaint Louverture; Tupac Amaru II.

October 27, 1795
PINCKNEY'S TREATY

Wars in Europe prompted Spain to sign Pinckney's Treaty, recognizing the United States' western boundary claims and ensuring free navigation of the Mississippi River.

LOCALE: Spain
CATEGORIES: Diplomacy and international relations; expansion and land acquisition; trade and commerce

KEY FIGURES
Manuel de Godoy (1767-1851), prime minister of Spain, 1792-1798, 1801-1807
John Jay (1745-1829), chief justice of the U.S. Supreme Court, 1789-1795
Thomas Pinckney (1750-1828), U.S. minister to Great Britain, 1792-1794, and special commissioner to Spain, 1795-1796
George Washington (1732-1799), president of the United States, 1789-1797
James Wilkinson (1757-1825), U.S. military commander

SUMMARY OF EVENT
The negotiation of Pinckney's Treaty clearly demonstrates how European conflicts contributed to American diplomatic success and facilitated the nation's territorial growth and expansion during its formative years. With Spain, France, and Great Britain involved in yet another series of wars during the French Revolution, the European powers found it extremely difficult to maintain control over their empires in North America. Further complicated by the expanding westward moving population of the United States, Spain quickly realized that it needed to settle its dispute with the United States in the West in order to sufficiently mobilize all of its resources for the European war. Once again, as the historian Samuel Flagg Bemis concluded, the United States benefited from European distress.

One of the most pressing diplomatic problems facing the United States after 1783 was Spanish occupation of, and claims to, a large portion of the southern and southwestern United States. The Spanish had enjoyed undisputed possession since 1763 of the territory that had been French Louisiana. They had also regained Florida in 1783, after Great Britain had temporarily obtained control over this region between 1763 and 1783. Spanish power rested solidly along the entire Gulf Coast of North and Central America, both banks of the Mississippi River from its mouth to a point midway between present-day Baton Rouge, Louisiana, and Natchez, Mississippi, and the west bank of the river north to the Missouri River and west to the Pacific Ocean. In addition to these vast holdings, the Spanish claimed by right of conquest during the American Revolution a large portion of the present-day states of Alabama, Mississippi, and Tennessee. In other words, Spain held or claimed both banks of the Mississippi from its mouth to the mouth of the Ohio River and east to the western slopes of the Appalachian Mountains. Yet with American settlers and commerce expanding rapidly into this disputed territory, a potentially volatile diplomatic dispute erupted between the Washington administration and Spain.

The United States had received the right to navigate the Mississippi from Great Britain in the Treaty of Paris in 1783. Since Spain, however, had not been a party to this treaty, it refused to accept this settlement and closed the Mississippi to all but Spanish commerce. This action directly threatened both the commercial and political success of the American settlers crossing the Appalachians.

In an attempt to thwart American westward expansion, the Spanish, as did the English in the north, manipulated Native American antagonism toward the settlers and encouraged Indian raids in this region. At the same time, the Spanish intermittently schemed with dissident western Americans who were dissatisfied with the lack-luster western policies of the federal government. Looking to strengthen its position within the southeastern region of North America, Madrid tried to convince the settlers to abandon their ties with the United States and form a new republic aligned with Spain. The Spanish were desperately seeking a face-saving solution to its problem in America because of its inability to control and manage its affairs in the region. Aggressive and lawless in nature, the frontiersmen threatened the Spanish with an invasion because of the closure of the Mississippi River and Spanish-sponsored Indian raids on American settlements.

Military conflicts, separatist sentiments, and navigation rights posed grave problems for the United States. The administration of George Washington, fearful over the potential establishment of an independent republic on its southern border, recognized that the right to free navigation of the river was an absolute necessity to the West, since the river was the only economically feasible route to the market. The federal government was also under pressure by western speculative interests whose landholdings suffered in value as a result of Spanish-supported Indian attacks. Washington realized that failure to mollify western interests could significantly undermine American territorial growth.

Little progress was made in solving the disputes until 1794. Until that time western intrigues, Spanish fears of a French-American invasion, and Indian wars were recurrent themes along the southern border. The Spanish attempted, with the aid of the American major-general James Wilkinson and others, to stimulate disunion in the West. The Spanish, in an attempt to generate momentum for the separatist movement, opened up trade on the Mississippi to Americans on payment of a 15 percent duty. This somewhat mollified the West but failed to produce any meaningful support for separation. Then, in 1794-1795, the French revolutionary wars brought relations to a crisis. In this instance, as has often been the case throughout American history, European wars provided the United States with the opportunity to achieve a striking diplomatic victory without surrendering any of its initial demands.

Spain had joined with Great Britain in the war against the French First Republic. In 1794-1795, when the war turned against Spain, the Spanish began to look for a way out. In 1794, even before Spain made its decision relative to the war, it indicated willingness to negotiate with the United States. As a result of this offer, President Washington dispatched Thomas Pinckney, minister to Great

Britain, as envoy extraordinary and minister plenipotentiary to Madrid. Pinckney arrived in 1795, and since Spain's military position had so deteriorated that it had decided to make a separate peace with France, the delay worked to America's advantage. Spain was also apprehensive concerning John Jay's diplomatic mission to Great Britain. These negotiations convinced the Spanish prime minister, Manuel de Godoy, that a possible British-American rapprochement was about to take place and that a joint attack on Spain's overseas empire might coincide with the signing of Jay's Treaty. Furthermore, Spain was about to abrogate its alliance with Great Britain and reenter the war allied with France. Thus, de Godoy feared British retaliation.

Pinckney was able to capitalize on Spain's anxieties in negotiating the Treaty of San Lorenzo, or Pinckney's Treaty, signed on October 27, 1795. The Spanish conceded point after point, while the United States gave up virtually nothing in return. Spain recognized American sovereignty to the east bank of the Mississippi north of the 31st parallel; granted permission to Americans to navigate the river; established a place to deposit American goods for transfer to oceangoing vessels; and recognized the American definition of neutral rights. Both

A nineteenth century portrait of Thomas Pinckney. (The Granger Collection, New York)

powers promised to restrain the Native Americans. This was a tacit admission by Spain that it had incited them in the past. In addition, the treaty did not affect the drive of westward expansion.

SIGNIFICANCE

The Spanish implementation of the treaty came slowly. However, because of Spain's unfavorable situation in Europe, de Godoy's government had little choice but to acquiesce to Washington's demands. Spain pulled out of the disastrous war with the French First Republic in the secret Treaty of Basel in 1795. The following year, in the secret Treaty of San Ildefonso, Spain plunged into an equally disastrous war as an ally of the French against Great Britain. With Spain preoccupied with the war in Europe, the United States emerged from Pinckney's negotiations completely victorious. Thus, as historian Samuel Flagg Bemis concluded, this treaty represents an excellent example of how "America's advantage" resulted from "Europe's distress."

For the second time the possibility of an British-American alliance against Spain compelled Spain to placate the United States. The Treaty of San Lorenzo was executed in full by 1798. In negotiating the Treaty of Greenville (1795) with Native Americans, Jay's Treaty, and Pinckney's Treaty, the Washington administration had achieved much in the field of diplomacy. The separatist movement was dead, and the West was secured to the Union.

—*John G. Clark, updated by Robert D. Ubriaco, Jr.*

FURTHER READING

Bemis, Samuel Flagg. *Pinckney's Treaty: A Study of America's Advantage from Europe's Distress*. Baltimore: Johns Hopkins University Press, 1926. This classic work in American diplomacy reveals how the United States was able to secure favorable concessions from Spain because of Spanish fears over a British-American alliance and a potential French invasion.

Clarke, Thomas D., and John D. W. Guice. *Frontiers in Conflict: The Old Southwest, 1795-1830*. Albuquerque: University of New Mexico Press, 1989. Reprint. *The Old Southwest, 1795-1830: Frontiers in Conflict*. Norman: University of Oklahoma Press, 1996. Examines the almost unending conflict in the states between present-day South Carolina and Louisiana during the early years of the American republic. Includes information about the Pinckney Treaty.

Darling, Arthur B. *Our Rising Empire, 1763-1803*. New Haven, Conn.: Yale University Press, 1940. A readable synthesis of American diplomatic history from the French Alliance of 1778 to the Louisiana Purchase.

DeConde, Alexander. *Entangling Alliances: Politics and Diplomacy Under George Washington*. Durham, N.C.: Duke University Press, 1958. This source outlines how foreign trade issues and the American relationship with Great Britain shaped American diplomacy during the Washington administration.

Lewis, James E., Jr. *The American Union and the Problem of Neighborhood: The United States and the Collapse of the Spanish Empire, 1783-1829*. Chapel Hill: University of North Carolina Press, 1998. Describes how leaders of the new American nation sought to preserve the union against challenges from foreign nations or from divisions among states within the union. Focuses on the United States' relations with Spain, providing some information on the Pinckney Treaty.

Tucker, Robert W., and David C. Hendrickson. *Empire of Liberty: The Statecraft of Thomas Jefferson*. New York: Oxford University Press, 1990. Places Pinckney's Treaty in the context of the Hamiltonian-Jeffersonian debate over the direction of American foreign policy during the early national period.

Young, Raymond A. "Pinckney's Treaty: A New Perspective." *Hispanic American Historical Review* 43, no. 4 (1963): 526-535. This article highlights Pinckney's decisive role during the negotiations.

SEE ALSO: Sept. 3, 1783: Treaty of Paris; Oct. 22, 1784: Fort Stanwix Treaty; Oct., 1790: Nootka Sound Convention; Apr. 20, 1792-Oct., 1797: Early Wars of the French Revolution; July-Nov., 1794: Whiskey Rebellion; Aug. 20, 1794: Battle of Fallen Timbers; Nov. 19, 1794: Jay's Treaty; Oct. 4, 1797-Sept. 30, 1800: XYZ Affair.

RELATED ARTICLES in *Great Lives from History: The Eighteenth Century, 1701-1800*: John Jay; George Washington.

1790's

1796

LAPLACE ARTICULATES HIS NEBULAR HYPOTHESIS

Laplace published The System of the World, *in which he put forward a theory of the origins of the solar system. He demonstrated mathematically that Newton's laws of motion and gravity could result in a simple cloud of dust transforming over time into the Sun and planets.*

LOCALE: Paris, France; Beaumont-en-Auge, France
CATEGORIES: Astronomy; mathematics; science and technology

KEY FIGURES

Pierre-Simon Laplace (1749-1827), French mathematician, astronomer, and physicist
Jean le Rond d'Alembert (1717-1783), French mathematician and encyclopedist
Claude Louis Berthollet (1748-1822), French chemist
Napoleon Bonaparte (1769-1821), first emperor of France as Napoleon I, r. 1804-1814, 1815

SUMMARY OF EVENT

Pierre-Simon Laplace revolutionized astronomy in 1796, when he published his *Exposition du système du monde* (*The System of the World*, 1809), in which he first promulgated his now famous nebular hypothesis on the origin of the solar system. According to Laplace, the solar system derived from a cloud of gas and dust, a gaseous nebula he designated the *nébuleuse primitive*. In this hot and rotating cloud, the condensation of the material, caused by gravitational attraction, formed the planets. This condensation, according to Laplace, began at the outskirts of the cloud, forming the planets most distant from the Sun first and progressing inward.

Laplace was born on March 23, 1749, in Beaumont-en-Auge, Normandy. The second of the three sons in a family of five children, Laplace enjoyed a comfortable childhood. His father was a wealthy farmer who augmented his income by running a relay station on a busy stagecoach line, where he sold fermented cider to weary travelers. His mother, Marie-Anne Sochon, came from a comfortably wealthy agricultural family as well.

The Laplace family's economic security provided Pierre-Simon with educational opportunities that allowed him to develop his considerable intellect. He was sent to a Benedictine priory school for his primary education, and at the age of seventeen, he advanced to the University of Caen, where he discovered his passion and aptitude for mathematics. After two years at the university,

he spent the next two years teaching mathematics at his former priory school while he saved enough money to finance a trip to Paris. In the city, he met the famous mathematician Jean le Rond d'Alembert. D'Alembert was immediately interested in Laplace and, in 1770, recommended him as a mathematics teacher at the École Royale Militaire in Paris.

Turning his attention and mathematical skills to astronomy, Laplace came to the attention of the scientific community in 1773, when he produced a groundbreaking essay titled "Sur le principe de la gravitation universelle, et sur les inégalites séculaires des planètes qui en dépendent" (on the principle of universal gravitation, and on the age-old inequalities of the planets that depend upon it). In this paper, he used his mathematical skills to solve a problem in celestial mechanics that had puzzled many scholars, including the famous Leonhard Euler and Joseph-Louis Lagrange: There were apparent variations in the speeds at which the planets revolved around the Sun that seemed to have no reasonable explanation and that seemed to indicate a worrisome instability in the solar system. Indeed, Sir Isaac Newton himself had responded to this instability by saying that the solar system required intermittent divine intervention to keep it going.

Laplace demonstrated that this planetary instability was only apparent; in fact, the variation in the speed of the planets was a periodic phenomenon that could be predicted. Saturn and Jupiter speed up and slow down because of the gravitational effects they have on each other, with a periodicity of 919 years. Laplace thus demonstrated that Newton's laws alone were sufficient to explain the mechanics of the solar system, and divine intervention was not necessary. The tables that Laplace created to track and predict the effect that the planets have on one another's orbits remained in use through the end of the nineteenth century. This work was the basis for his admission as an adjunct in mechanics to the French Academy of Sciences (Académie des Sciences), where he would rise to become president in 1812.

In 1785, Laplace was an examiner at the Royal Artillery Corps (mathematical skill was essential to effective artillery fire) when sixteen-year-old Napoleon Bonaparte underwent examination to achieve the rank of second lieutenant. Many years later, Bonaparte was instrumental in advancing his examiner's career, making him a count and naming him a minister in the government.

The transformational zeal of the French Revolution

Illustration of a spiral nebula cyclone. (Premier Publishing)

extended beyond politics and into science. Laplace's scientific reputation placed him in a intellectual, social, and political position in which he was able to help effect profound changes. In 1790, the French National Assembly wished to replace the more than seven hundred different units of measure employed in the country. Laplace was instrumental in developing the metric system, giving elegant coherence to what had been a chaotic situation. In 1795, Laplace was a cofounder and first director of the Bureau of Longitudes. He also served as the director of the Paris Observatory.

One year later, in 1796, he published *Exposition du système du monde* (*The System of the World*), the work that revolutionized astronomy. It was a huge accomplishment, a series of five books in two volumes devoted to the analysis of the apparent motions of celestial bodies, the movement of the sea, the actual movements of celestial bodies, and the formation of the solar system. Extremely well written and targeted at a semipopular audience, the work not only disseminated Laplace's theories and analyses but also helped bring Newtonian astrophysics to a wider audience.

Laplace noticed in *The System of the World* that the planets known at the time (only the seven innermost planets had been discovered) had elliptical trajectories and were almost all in the same plane. Also noting the relatively slow rotation of the Sun itself, Laplace proposed that the solar system had been formed out of a rotating cloud of dust and gas, the *nébuleuse primitive*. Very hot, this nebular cloud flattened as its rotation increased in speed over time, ejecting small amounts of its particles that would become the planets and their moons. The condensing center of the cloud became the Sun.

In 1806, Napoleon named Laplace a *comte d'empire* and gave him the position of minister of the interior in his government. Much more a scientist than an administrator, Laplace kept his ministerial position for only six weeks before gracefully withdrawing. In an endeavor more to his liking, in 1807, Laplace, along with the well-known chemist Claude Louis Berthollet, organized a group of famous scientists and young researchers called Société d'Arcueil (Society of Arcueil). Housed in a property neighboring that of Berthollet and provided with laboratory facilities built for their needs, the group was designed to encourage promising young scientists by enabling them to continue their research under the supervision and mentoring of established and reputable scientists.

Among the significant scientists mentored by the society were physicists Joseph Louis Gay-Lussac and Jean-Baptiste Biot and naturalist and explorer Alexander von Humboldt. Laplace was elected to the French Academy in 1816, and, in 1817, Louis XVIII named him Marquis de Laplace. During his very long career, Laplace distinguished himself because of his genius, method, analysis, and extraordinary mathematical knowledge. When he died in 1827, at seventy-eight years of age, not only had he revolutionized astronomy, but he had made profound transformations in the field of probability, weights and measures, and mathematics.

SIGNIFICANCE

Pierre-Simon Laplace's nebular hypothesis is still broadly accepted today as the most probable origin of the solar system. When combined with his demonstration that the solar system is stable and its motion is fully self-perpetuating without divine intervention, Laplace's work represents the first rigorous, mathematically precise, and fully secular description of both the creation and the functioning of the solar system. Laplace perfected the Newtonian theory of mechanics and gravitation and applied it in ways of which Newton himself was incapable. *The System of the World* was the springboard for the apotheosis of his work, *Traité de mécanique céleste* (1798-1827; partial translation as *A Treatise upon Analytical Mechanics*, 1814; full translation as *Mécanique Céleste*, 1829-1839), a five-volume set on which he would labor for the rest of his life.

In a eulogy presented at the French Academy on November 13, 1827, Laplace's successor, Pierre-Paul Royer-Collard, said that

> Laplace was born to perfect everything, to deepen everything, to push back the limits, and to solve all of the things people believe unsolvable. He would have completed the study of astronomy if this science could be completed.

Though the hyperbole of his eulogy was probably extravagant, Laplace did demonstrate the power of combining scientific and mathematical skills in the attempt to understand the workings of the physical universe. His scientific creativity, extraordinary mathematical ability, curiosity, and discipline not only unlocked the secrets of the solar system's origins but also provided a model of synthesis of disciplines for future scientists to follow.

—Denyse Lemaire and David Kasserman

FURTHER READING

Bell, E. T. "From Peasant to Snob: Laplace." In *Men of Mathematics: The Lives and Achievements of the Great Mathematicians from Zeno to Poincaré*. New York: Simon and Schuster, 1986. Bell provides a brief biography of Laplace from his humble origins in the country side of Normandy to the high status he achieved in the sciences and in politics.

Crosland, Maurice. *Society of Arcueil: A View of French Science at the Time of Napoleon*. Boston: Harvard University Press, 1967. Details the work of Laplace and Berthollet, founders of the Society of Arcueil, in encouraging the development of young scientists.

Gillipsie, Charles Coulston, Robert Fox, and Ivor Grattan-Guinness. *Pierre-Simon Laplace, 1749-1827: A Life in Exact Science*. Princeton, N.J.: Princeton University Press, 2000. Describes the life and achievements of Laplace.

Hershel, Sir John Frederic William, and Pierre-Simon, Marquis de Laplace. *Essays in Astronomy*. Honolulu, Hawaii: University Press of the Pacific, 2002. The editor has collected and translated into English many of Laplace's original articles in this volume.

SEE ALSO: 1704: Newton Publishes *Optics*; 1704-1712: Astronomy Wars in England; 1705: Halley Predicts the Return of a Comet; 1714-1762: Quest for Longitude; 1725: Flamsteed's Star Catalog Marks the Transition to Modern Astronomy; 1740: Maclaurin's Gravitational Theory; 1743-1744: D'Alembert Develops His Axioms of Motion; 1748: Bradley Discovers the Nutation of Earth's Axis; 1748: Euler Develops the Concept of Function.

RELATED ARTICLES in *Great Lives from History: The Eighteenth Century, 1701-1800*: Jean le Rond d'Alembert; Jean-Sylvain Bailly; Leonhard Euler; Joseph-Louis Lagrange.

1796-1798
JENNER DEVELOPS SMALLPOX VACCINATION

English physician Edward Jenner was the first person to establish the scientific legitimacy of smallpox vaccinations through his experiments and research publications. His campaign to popularize the procedure led to its worldwide use and effectively protected millions from the often fatal disease.

LOCALE: Berkeley, Gloucestershire, England
CATEGORY: Health and medicine

KEY FIGURES
Edward Jenner (1749-1823), English physician
Lady Mary Wortley Montagu (1689-1792), writer and
    wife of Britain's ambassador to the Ottoman
    Empire, who observed the practice of variolation
    and helped introduce it into England
James Phipps (1788-1808), first person to be
    vaccinated by Edward Jenner
Benjamin Jesty (1736-1816), English farmer who
    vaccinated his family against smallpox in 1774
William Woodville (1752-1805), head of the London
    Smallpox and Inoculation Hospital
George Pearson (1751-1828), a physician at
    St. George's Hospital in London

SUMMARY OF EVENT
In eighteenth century England, smallpox was a leading cause of death, and traditional methods of treating it were largely ineffective. The practice of variolation was introduced to England from the Ottoman Empire in 1721 by Mary Wortley Montagu and gained general acceptance after some successful trials. This procedure involved inoculating patients with pus from smallpox sores in the hope of giving them a mild case of the disease and future immunity. However, the risks of a patient developing a serious, possibly lethal, case of smallpox and even creating an epidemic were significant, and there was a clear need for a safer and more effective method of protection from the disease.

Edward Jenner, a physician in Berkeley, England, in the county of Gloucestershire, began variolating patients using a refined procedure developed by Robert Sutton in 1768. Jenner found that his patients who had previously contracted cowpox, a relatively mild disease, did not react to the smallpox virus. This finding was consistent with the conventional wisdom in rural areas that cowpox conferred an immunity to smallpox, which had been supported in reports to the Medical Society of London in

the mid-1760's by several physicians, including at least two from Gloucestershire. In fact, in 1774 a farmer in Yetminster, England, named Benjamin Jesty successfully protected his wife and two sons from a smallpox epidemic by vaccinating them with the pus from the udders of cows suffering from cowpox. Jenner, however, always maintained that he was unaware of these earliest documented smallpox vaccinations.

By the early 1780's, Jenner's interest in the connection between cowpox and smallpox immunity led him to distinguish between two similar but distinct diseases, "spontaneous," or genuine, cowpox, which created an immunity to smallpox, and "spurious," or false, cowpox, which did not. In May of 1796, a young woman named Sarah Nelmes came to Jenner to be treated for cowpox. On May 14, Jenner vaccinated James Phipps, an eight-year-old boy, by placing fluid from a sore on Nelmes's hand into two small incisions on the boy's arm. A week later, Phipps developed the symptoms of cowpox, including infected sores, chills, head and body aches, and loss of appetite. The child recovered quickly, and, on July 1, 1796, Jenner variolated Phipps using fluid from smallpox pustules, and he had no reaction. Jenner inoculated the boy several more times in this manner with the same results.

In late 1796, Jenner submitted a paper to be considered for publication in *Philosophical Transactions of the Royal Society*, England's premier scientific journal. The manuscript described the cases of thirteen former cowpox sufferers who exhibited no reaction when variolated by Jenner, as well as his experiments with James Phipps. The Council of the Royal Society rejected the article and berated Jenner in scathing terms, characterizing his findings as unbelievable and "in variance with established knowledge," and advising him that advancing such wild notions would destroy his professional reputation. Jenner was undaunted and began experimenting again in the spring of 1798, when cowpox broke out again in Gloucestershire. Through these studies he learned that cowpox could be transferred from one patient to another by using the pus from the sores of one vaccinated person to vaccinate another, and so forth. This discovery of "arm-to-arm vaccination" made a natural outbreak of cowpox unnecessary as a source of vaccine.

In June of 1798, Jenner independently published the findings from his research to date, including reports of the cases from his first manuscript and nine other patients

1790's

A caricature showing a frightened woman receiving a vaccination from Edward Jenner at the "Smallpox and Vaccination Hospital at St. Pancras." The illustration reads, "The Cow Pock—or—the Wonderful Effects of the New Inoculation." (Library of Congress)

he had vaccinated besides Phipps. This seventy-five-page book was titled *An Inquiry into the Causes and Effects of the Variolae Vaccinae, a Disease Discovered in Some of the Western Counties of England, Particularly Gloucestershire, and Known by the Name of the Cow Pox*. The word *variolae* means "smallpox" in Latin, and *vaccinae* is from *vaca*, which is Latin for "cow." In his inquiry, Jenner described the process now called "anaphylaxis," the body's allergic reaction to a foreign protein after a previous exposure, and coined the term "virus" to describe the mechanism of cowpox transmission.

The London medical establishment's initial reaction to Jenner's publication was extremely negative. Just as in 1796, some prominent physicians questioned the validity of Jenner's findings. Others, who were profiting handsomely from variolation, attacked Jenner for fear of losing their lucrative monopoly on protecting the public from smallpox. Jenner had rejected the suggestion that

he could become personally wealthy from his discovery, and he planned to share it with all of England and the world. After the publication of his findings, Jenner tried for three months to find people who would agree to be vaccinated in order to demonstrate the effectiveness of the procedure. He did not find a single volunteer because of the public attacks on his professional competence.

Instead, Jenner pursued his goal of popularizing vaccination indirectly, through London physicians to whom he provided vaccine. For example, the director of the London Smallpox and Inoculation Hospital, William Woodville, vaccinated some six hundred people in the first half of 1799. Based on vaccinations that he performed in 1799, George Pearson of St. George's Hospital replicated Jenner's findings and tried to take credit for the procedure. Woodville, who caused several cases of smallpox and at least one death by inadvertently contaminating some vaccine with the smallpox virus, blamed

Jenner's procedure in order to protect his own reputation. However, a nationwide survey conducted by Jenner, which documented cases of immunity to smallpox by former cowpox sufferers, clearly validated his work.

By late 1799, vaccination had gained widespread acceptance, and the procedure was being performed not only by physicians but also by schoolteachers, ministers, gentleman farmers, and others in all parts of the country. Jenner continued to report the results of his research on vaccination through publications such as *The Origin of the Vaccine Inoculation* (1801). In recognition of his achievements, Parliament awarded Jenner £10,000 in 1802 (the equivalent of more than $500,000 today) and an additional £20,000 in 1807. Oxford, Harvard, and Cambridge Universities honored him as well.

SIGNIFICANCE

Edward Jenner's work on refining and promoting the use of smallpox vaccinations, before the development of antibiotics, was a major breakthrough in preventive medicine. Countless lives were undoubtedly saved in Great Britain during the years immediately following Jenner's efforts, given the high mortality rates during earlier smallpox epidemics.

Jenner's method of preserving vaccine for up to three months enabled him to share his vaccination procedure with the world. As a result, an estimated 100,000 people had been vaccinated worldwide by the end of the eighteenth century. Shortly thereafter, Benjamin Waterhouse, a professor at the Harvard School of Medicine, used vaccine from England to perform the first vaccinations in the United States on his young son and servants. Jenner also shipped vaccine to President Thomas Jefferson, who had eighteen of his relatives vaccinated and established the National Vaccine Institute, with Waterhouse as its director, to spread vaccination throughout the country. In addition, mass vaccination programs were initiated in all Spanish colonies in North and South America and Asia by King Charles IV of Spain, in India by the British governor general, for the French army by Napoleon, and in numerous other countries. These programs were all undertaken in the early 1800's using Jenner's vaccine.

Jenner's successful lobbying for a government-sponsored national vaccination program eventually led to the passage of the Vaccination Act in 1840, which provided for the free vaccination of infants and made the riskier practice of variolation illegal. Subsequent laws made vaccination mandatory, with severe penalties for noncompliance. By 1871, 97.5 percent of England's population reportedly had been vaccinated.

By 1967, although smallpox had completely disappeared from North America and Europe, there were still 10 to 15 million cases reported in the world annually. The World Health Organization initiated an effort to eradicate smallpox worldwide. The campaign was declared a success in 1980. Jenner's work is credited not only with the defeat of smallpox but also with being the foundation of the science of immunology, which has produced vaccines against numerous lethal and debilitating diseases.

—Jack Carter

FURTHER READING

Barquet, Nicolau, and Pere Domingo. "Smallpox: The Triumph over the Most Terrible of Ministers of Death." *Annals of Internal Medicine* 127 (1997): 635-742. A detailed account of Edward Jenner's vaccination experiments and their immediate and long-term impacts, starting with a concise history of the global spread of smallpox, the resulting epidemics, and variolation techniques.

Baxby, Derrick. "The End of Smallpox." *History Today* (March, 1999) 14-16. Explains how high smallpox mortality rates in England and the dangers of variolation practices motivated Jenner to refine vaccinations and promote their use.

Fisher, Richard B. *Edward Jenner, 1741-1823*. London: Andre Deutsch, 1991. A complete biography, including an account of Jenner's experiments with smallpox vaccinations and the widespread application of this technology, at his urging.

Plotkin, Susan L., and Stanley A. Plotkin. "A Short History of Vaccination." In *Vaccines*, edited by Stanley A. Plotkin and Walter A. Orenstein. Philadelphia: W. B. Saunders, 2004. Discuses the migration of smallpox variolation practices to England from the Ottoman Empire in the early eighteenth century to Jenner's work, which led to modern vaccination techniques.

1790's

March, 1796-October 17, 1797
NAPOLEON'S ITALIAN CAMPAIGNS

Napoleon's lightning strike into Italy secured the region for France; provided a source of revenue, manpower, and resources for the French armies; and reduced the Austrian forces' ability to stand against the French hegemony in Europe.

LOCALE: Italy
CATEGORIES: Wars, uprisings, and civil unrest; expansion and land acquisition

KEY FIGURES

Napoleon Bonaparte (1769-1821), French military commander and later emperor of France as Napoleon I, r. 1804-1814, 1815
Lazare Carnot (1753-1823), French minister for war
Louis-Alexander Berthier (1753-1815), Napoleon Bonaparte's chief of staff
Johann Peter Beaulieu (Jean Pierre Beaulieu; 1725-1819), commander of the Austrian forces in Italy
Dagobert Wurmser (1724-1797), commander of Austrian relief forces
Pius VI (Giovanni Angelico Braschi; 1717-1799), Roman Catholic pope, 1775-1799

SUMMARY OF EVENT

In 1793, the French revolutionary government had decided to use force to spread its bourgeois ideals abroad. It had accordingly declared war on Great Britain, Holland, and Spain. By 1796, however, the Directory, the governing body of France, found that, while its armies had met with success in the early years of this struggle, it was becoming increasingly difficult simultaneously to finance military operations and satisfy domestic obligations. The solution to this problem, the Directory decided, could be achieved by conquering Italy, a region rich in resources that consisted of eleven semi-independent states. The states had often been in conflict with one another over the centuries, so it seemed unlikely that the entire region could band together effectively to resist an external invasion.

The Directly accordingly placed Napoleon Bonaparte in charge of an army of invasion and sent him to conquer Italy. Unfortunately for the French, though, the Austrian empire had already established a foothold in the northern sections of Italy. War there meant facing a strong Austrian force that had been deployed for two purposes: to guard Austrian possessions in Tyrol, as well as the Piedmont and other sections of northern Italy, and to pre-

vent a French advance from the south on Vienna, the capital of the Austrian empire.

To lead the French army against the combined forces of the Piedmontese and Austrians, the French minister of war, veteran general Lazare Carnot, chose a brilliant young officer who had risen meteorically in the French army during the early years of the revolution. Although only twenty-seven, Napoleon Bonaparte had demonstrated exceptional military skills, especially in handling artillery, both in the defense of Paris and in early battles during France's wars with Austria. Bonaparte had commanded France's interior defense forces and spent time at the war ministry, helping to plan his country's grand strategy.

Carnot took a chance in assigning this rising military star to command an army whose division commanders were substantially older and more experienced than Bonaparte, but Bonaparte, a brilliant strategist who was equally adept at selecting key subordinates, assembled a staff that included Louis-Alexandre Berthier. Berthier's ability to manage the administrative aspects of major conflicts made him invaluable as Bonaparte's chief of staff. The Italian campaign gave the two men their first chance to maneuver large forces against enemies that relied on outmoded military tactics to protect their interests. Bonaparte's reliance on the offensive and his flair for bold action against forces that sometimes outnumbered his own would prove to be too much for commanders such as General Johann Peter Beaulieu, the commander of Austria's forces in northern Italy.

Violating both conventional wisdom and the instructions of his superiors in the Directory, Bonaparte arrived in Italy in March, 1796, and immediately sent his forces against the Piedmontese army, effectively dividing his enemy but risking a counterattack that could pin his troops between two forces that collectively enjoyed numerical superiority. In a single month, April, 1796, the French divisions routed opposing forces in battles at Montenotte, Dego, and Mondovi. By the end of the month, after defeating the Piedmontese at Cherasco, Bonaparte signed an armistice with them that allowed him to turn his attention against the Austrians and to move southward against the Papal States.

Bonaparte was able to drive his army relentlessly, because he had quickly established himself as a commander who cared for troops. He badgered the Directory for supplies and back pay for his soldiers and arranged for them to share in the spoils of war. At the same time, he was able to maintain discipline within the ranks, preventing the kind of reckless pillaging that often turned locals against invading forces. His boldness was best exhibited at Lodi, where he drove a small force across the Po River against a larger Austrian army: The soldiers' bravery, inspired by the presence of their commander, resulted in victory when reinforcements arrived. Meanwhile, the Austrians had consolidated forces in the north and sent a garrison to relieve Mantua, the fall of which would permit Bonaparte to march virtually unimpeded toward Vienna. Unfortunately for them, the relief force, commanded by Field Marshal Dagobert Wurmser, was trapped inside the city when Bonaparte placed it under siege.

After his victory at Lodi, Bonaparte entered the northern city of Milan, which fell easily. Establishing Italians loyal to him as rulers in the north, Bonaparte threatened the Papal States and in June, 1796, extracted humiliating concessions from Pope Pius VI; the French treasury was enriched immensely in the process. Attack and counterattack against the Austrians continued in the region for another six months, but the French army's success at the Battles of Arcola (November, 1796) and Rivoli (January, 1797) left the Austrians penned up in the north. When Mantua fell in February, Bonaparte sent his army north toward Vienna. Two months later at Leoben, on April 18, the Austrians requested an armistice.

During the summer of 1797, Bonaparte began to consolidate his power in Italy, becoming more statesman than soldier. Although he had no authority from the French government to interfere in political affairs, he established the Cisalpine Republic in northern Italy and overthrew the governments of Genoa and Venice. In Oc-

A cartoon from 1797 depicts Napoleon auctioning off the art treasures of Italy to a group of Frenchmen. The caption reads, "Well, sirs! Two million." (Library of Congress)

tober, 1797, Bonaparte met with representatives of the Austrian emperor to negotiate a formal end to hostilities. The terms he offered to the Austrians required them to cede Belgium and territories west of the Rhine to France; in exchange, Bonaparte returned Venice to Austrian control. The Treaty of Campo Formio, a compromise document that favored the French while allowing the Austrians some concessions to save face, was signed on October 17 and brought peace between the countries for the next eighteen months.

SIGNIFICANCE

The Treaty of Campo Formio provided the French needed respite from campaigns in the Alpine region of Italy, secured the government a foothold in an area whose resources would prove vital to the expansion of French hegemony—especially in later years, when Bonaparte replaced the Directory and made himself sole ruler of France—and freed the young French general for further adventures in Egypt. The terms of the treaty were drafted by Bonaparte rather than by the Directory, however, and politicians in Paris were furious that their field commander had usurped the role of diplomat.

Under Napoleonic rule, the political construct of Italy as a group of semi-independent states was transformed, as systems of national government were instituted by ministers appointed by the French. Many of Italy's human and natural resources were devastated, however, through conscription and heavy taxation, as well as transference of food and manufactured products to the French armies throughout Europe. In 1815, at the Congress of Vienna, the European powers that had defeated Bonaparte at Waterloo attempted to restore some independence to the Italian states. They found it impossible, however, to turn back the clock and re-create the political landscape as it had existed before the country became a vassal state in the French empire.

Perhaps the greatest significance of the Italian campaigns, however, was the opportunity they afforded to Bonaparte to demonstrate his abilities as both a general and a statesman. He gave notice to his own countrymen and to all of Europe that he could command large forces, negotiate successfully with local politicians and other governments, and exert his will over others to gain the ends he sought. In this sense, Italy was the crucible in which the young general was transformed into a leader to be reckoned with, both in his own country and across the Continent.

—*Laurence W. Mazzeno*

FURTHER READING

Esdaile, Charles J. *The French Wars, 1792-1815*. New York: Routledge, 2001. A chapter on Napoleon's venture into Italy offers insight into the general's military prowess. Other chapters describe Napoleon's other military operations, from his rise to power to his defeat at Waterloo.

Gregory, Desmond. *Napoleon's Italy*. Cranbury, N.J.: Associated University Press, 2001. A lengthy chapter details Napoleon's military operations in Italy during the campaign of 1796-1797; subsequent chapters outline the political situation that developed in Italy as a result of the French occupation.

Johnson, Paul. *Napoleon*. New York: Viking, 2002. This brief biography of Napoleon places the Italian campaign in the larger context of Napoleon's systematic conquest of Europe and North Africa.

Marshall-Cornwall, James. *Napoleon as Military Commander*. London: B. T. Batsford, 1967. This extensive analysis of Napoleon's military career by a retired British general provides insight into the strategy used in the Italian campaign, and suggests how Napoleon's military background affected his ability as a politician.

Rothenberg, Gunther E. *Napoleon's Great Adversaries: The Archduke Charles and the Austrian Army, 1792-1814*. Bloomington: Indiana University Press, 1982. Rothenberg offers extensive analysis of the Austrian forces that opposed Bonaparte for two decades, and explains why the French general was successful against larger ground forces.

Wilkinson, Spenser. *The Rise of General Bonaparte*. Brookfield, Vt.: Ashgate, 1991. This study provides details about Napoleon's military career, detailing troop movements for the various battles in the Italian campaign.

SEE ALSO: July 14, 1789: Fall of the Bastille; Apr. 20, 1792-Oct., 1797: Early Wars of the French Revolution; Sept. 20, 1792: Battle of Valmy; July 27-28, 1794: Fall of Robespierre; Apr. 12, 1798-Sept. 2, 1801: Napoleon's Egyptian Campaign; Aug. 1-2, 1798: Battle of the Nile; Nov. 9-10, 1799: Napoleon Rises to Power in France.

RELATED ARTICLES in *Great Lives from History: The Eighteenth Century, 1701-1800*: Lazare Carnot; Georges Danton; Pius VI; Robespierre.

September 19, 1796
WASHINGTON'S FAREWELL ADDRESS

George Washington published his final address as the first president of the United States, articulating foreign and domestic policy for the young nation.

LOCALE: Philadelphia, Pennsylvania
CATEGORIES: Diplomacy and international relations; government and politics

KEY FIGURES

George Washington (1732-1799), first president of the United States, 1789-1797

John Adams (1735-1826), U.S. vice president and president, 1797-1801

Pierre Adet (1763-1832), French minister to the United States in 1796

Edmond-Charles-Édouard Genet (Citizen Genet; 1763-1834), French minister to the United States

Alexander Hamilton (1755-1804), secretary of the U.S. Treasury and principal adviser to Washington, who helped Washington write his Farewell Address of 1796

John Jay (1745-1829), a Federalist who negotiated the unpopular Jay's Treaty with Great Britain

Thomas Jefferson (1743-1826), a leading Antifederalist, former secretary of state, and U.S. president, 1800-1809

James Madison (1751-1836), a leading Federalist who prepared a farewell address for Washington in 1792, and U.S. president, 1809-1817

SUMMARY OF EVENT

On September 19, 1796, Claypoole's *Daily American Advertiser*, a Philadelphia newspaper, published the valedictory remarks of retiring president George Washington. The speech promptly became known as Washington's Farewell Address. In publishing the address rather than reading it before Congress, Washington demonstrated that his words were intended for the entire nation. These were not merely the concluding remarks of an outgoing politician, but the final advice of a much beloved and respected leader of more than twenty years, now retiring to private life. As such, the words of the Farewell Address had great impact and weight, and have been recalled by politicians and policymakers into the twenty-first century.

Four years earlier, when Washington had thought seriously of retiring from office, James Madison had prepared a final address for him. In 1796, however, Washington asked Alexander Hamilton, his closest adviser

and a leading Federalist theorist, for assistance in writing a final political testament. Historians differ over the nature of Washington's contribution, but it is generally agreed that the Farewell Address represents the joint labor of Hamilton and Washington. It embodies ideas to which Washington had long subscribed, but it is written in an elegant fashion that was Hamilton's special talent.

Washington's Farewell Address is remembered as a classic statement of U.S. foreign policy, but, in fact, it concerned mostly domestic issues rather than foreign affairs. Although Washington deeply desired retirement for personal reasons, he seems to have felt keenly that the nation was potentially facing a crisis. In particular, Washington feared that sectionalism and extreme allegiance to political parties would wreck the national unity that he had worked so long to achieve. Washington had entered the presidency when there were no identifiable political parties in the United States. By 1796, he was witnessing the formation of opposing factions in U.S. politics, a development he felt boded ill for the future. The "baneful effects of the spirit of party generally," he warned, "open the door to foreign influence and corruption." Clearly, Washington was upset by the formation of organized opposition to the policies of his own administration, in particular Thomas Jefferson's Antifederalists. His Farewell Address was intended in part to explain the necessity of a Federalist victory in the upcoming presidential election of 1796, which would, he felt, preserve the unity of the nation.

Washington's remarks about a suitable foreign policy for the United States have come to be known as his "Great Rule of Conduct." His general comments were based on recent severe problems in Franco-American relations. In 1778, the United States had concluded a Treaty of Amity and Commerce with France, providing support that would be vital to American success in the revolution against Great Britain. In 1789, as Washington began his first term as president, France began its own revolution, receiving widespread approval from the United States. By 1793, however, successive revolutionary governments in France had replaced the monarchy and executed the king, who had approved funding for the American Revolution in 1778.

France was at war with most of Europe and demanded U.S. assistance, just as the French king had aided the colonies during their revolution against Great Britain. Events in France and the wars in Europe inspired partisanship in the United States. The Federalists, with their heavy commercial ties to Great Britain, had grave reservations about supporting the French in a European war. Jefferson and the Antifederalists charged that Washington had an obligation to support revolution in France because of the treaty of 1778. The arrival in 1793 of the French minister, Edmond-Charles-Édouard Genet, initially produced a wave of popular support for the French Revolution. For a time, Genet even actively recruited soldiers for that revolution. As a Federalist, Washington issued a proclamation of neutrality—which renounced U.S. obligations to France as having been contracted under a former government—and supported Jay's Treaty, which was quite favorable to France's bitter enemy, England.

Thus, when Washington, in his address, warned "against the insidious wiles of foreign influence [to which] the jealousy of a free people ought to be constantly awake," his readers knew it was France that he had in mind. When the president, in the most frequently quoted passage from the address, suggested that "the great rule of conduct for us in regard to foreign nations is, in extending our commercial relations to have with them as little political connection as possible," he justified his decision that the United States should not honor its obligation to France. The dispassionate tone of his remarks may obscure their unmistakable Federalist bias from the unwary modern reader. Washington considered some political alliances, such as Jay's Treaty, to be legitimate. He wrote, "So far as we have already formed engagements let them be fulfilled with perfect good faith." The 1778 treaty with France was, quite simply, no longer valid: "Here let us stop," he wrote.

While the Farewell Address spoke to the political passions of the moment, it also seemed to offer advice about the future. It is here that the ambiguous language of the address has caused so much confusion. Washington wanted both commercial relations and political isolation. Although such a goal may have seemed desirable, the United States has never been able to avoid political involvement with other countries when it gains commercial ties to them. In 1796, the United States was a fairly weak nation, which relied considerably on Europe for trade and commerce. Washington did not rule out all political alliances, nor did he say that political alliances would never become a necessity in the future. He seemed, rather, to support a policy of isolationism by advocating separation of the interests of the United States from those of Europe.

SIGNIFICANCE

The ambiguity of the Farewell Address, widely considered a statement of political isolationism in political de-

bates over foreign policy, can nevertheless be construed as supporting diverse schools of thought. It was republished in 1809 and 1819 to support the soundness of neutrality in the British-French wars. Echoes of Washington's Farewell Address would be heard in later statements of U.S. foreign policy, beginning with the Monroe Doctrine in 1823.

While it has been used primarily by politicians and policymakers as proof of the desirability of isolationism, it should be remembered that the Farewell Address was a message to the American people of 1796. Furthermore, Washington's concern was as much to bring about a Federalist victory in the upcoming election as it was to guide foreign policy for the nation for the next two centuries. The words of great leaders may be repeated and interpreted to serve a variety of political purposes, as the republication of Washington's Farewell Address in the early nineteenth century demonstrates.

—David H. Culbert, updated by Kelley Graham

FURTHER READING

Bowman, Albert Hall. *The Struggle for Neutrality: Franco-American Diplomacy During the Federalist Era.* Knoxville: University of Tennessee Press, 1974. A detailed study that places the Farewell Address in the larger context of Franco-American relations.

Ellis, Joseph J. *Founding Brothers: The Revolutionary Generation.* New York: Alfred A. Knopf, 2000. Examines how the Founding Fathers met the challenges of the new nation to create a workable government. Focuses on six crucial moments in the nation's early years, including Washington's precedent-setting Farewell Address.

_____. *His Excellency, George Washington.* New York: Alfred A. Knopf, 2004. Ellis, who wrote several books about the Founding Fathers, concentrates here on the personal life and public career of Washington, providing a meticulously researched and accessible biography.

Flexner, James Thomas. *Washington: The Indispensable Man.* Boston: Little, Brown, 1974. A biography that discusses the conflict at the end of Washington's second term: his deep sense of responsibility for the nation and his strong desire to return to private life.

Gilbert, Felix. *To the Farewell Address: Ideas of Early American Foreign Policy.* Princeton, N.J.: Princeton University Press, 1961. A study of the Farewell Address as an intellectual document and the culmination of eighteenth century political thought.

Kaufman, Burton Ira, ed. *Washington's Farewell Ad-

dress: The View from the Twentieth Century. Chicago: Quadrangle Books, 1969. A collection of articles on the Farewell Address and U.S. foreign policy through 1941. Includes the text of the address.

Paltsits, Victor Hugo, ed. *Washington's Farewell Address, in Facsimile, with Transliterations of All the Drafts of Washington, Madison, and Hamilton*. New York: New York Public Library, 1935. All the important drafts of the address and related correspondence are included in this collection, along with a history of its origin and its public reception. Bibliography.

Schwartz, Barry. *George Washington: The Making of an American Symbol*. New York: Free Press, 1987. An exploration of the iconization of Washington, which is key to understanding the lasting impact of his Farewell Address.

Spalding, Matthew, and Patrick J. Garrity. *A Sacred Union of Citizens: George Washington's Farewell Address and the American Character*. Introduction by Daniel J. Boorstin. Lanham, Md.: Rowman & Littlefield, 1996. Analyzes the lessons the address contains for the American people, including advice about how the new nation can cultivate the habits, morals, and civic virtues needed for stable self-government.

SEE ALSO: Sept. 5-Oct. 26, 1774: First Continental Congress; Apr. 19, 1775: Battle of Lexington and Concord; May 10-Aug. 2, 1775: Second Continental Congress; May, 1776-Sept. 3, 1783: France Supports the American Revolution; July 4, 1776: Declaration of Independence; Sept. 19-Oct. 17, 1777: Battles of Saratoga; Feb. 6, 1778: Franco-American Treaties; Mar. 1, 1781: Ratification of the Articles of Confederation; Oct. 19, 1781: Cornwallis Surrenders at Yorktown; Sept. 3, 1783: Treaty of Paris; Sept. 17, 1787: U.S. Constitution Is Adopted; Oct. 27, 1787-May, 1788: Publication of *The Federalist*; Apr. 30, 1789: Washington's Inauguration; Sept. 24, 1789: Judiciary Act; 1790's: First U.S. Political Parties; Dec. 15, 1791: U.S. Bill of Rights Is Ratified; Nov. 19, 1794: Jay's Treaty.

RELATED ARTICLES in *Great Lives from History: The Eighteenth Century, 1701-1800*: Abigail Adams; John Adams; Benedict Arnold; Sir Guy Carleton; Samuel Chase; First Marquess Cornwallis; Thomas Gage; George III; Nathanael Greene; Alexander Hamilton; Patrick Henry; William Howe; John Jay; Thomas Jefferson; Tadeusz Kościuszko; Alexander McGillivray; James Madison; George Mason; Robert Morris; Charles Willson Peale; Comte de Rochambeau; Betsy Ross; Roger Sherman; Gilbert Stuart; George Washington; James Wilson; John Witherspoon.

November, 1796
CATHERINE THE GREAT'S ART COLLECTION IS INSTALLED AT THE HERMITAGE

Constructed as an annex to the Winter Palace where the empress of Russia could obtain privacy, the Hermitage in St. Petersburg evolved, because of Catherine the Great's concerted purchasing efforts, to be a world-renowned museum housing many of Europe's great artistic masterpieces.

LOCALE: St. Petersburg, Russia
CATEGORIES: Art; organizations and institutions

KEY FIGURES
Catherine the Great (1729-1796), empress of Russia, r. 1762-1796
Francesco Bartolomeo Rastrelli (1700-1771), architect who designed the Winter Palace
Johann-Ernst Gotzkowsky (1710-1775), Berlin merchant who developed Frederick the Great's art collection, the first acquired for the Hermitage

Yury Fel'ten (Georg Friderick Velten; 1730 or 1732), architect who helped design and build both the Small and the Great Hermitage
Jean-Baptiste-Michel Vallen de la Motte (1729-1800), French architect

SUMMARY OF EVENT
On November 6, 1796, Catherine the Great died in her bedroom—one of the 1,054 rooms composing the Winter Palace in St. Petersburg. Having taken up residence there in 1762, she was the first Russian monarch to live in the Winter Palace, designed by the famous Italian architect Francesco Rastrelli. The Winter Palace was constructed as a monument to Russia's emergence as a great world power. However, it was also intended as a fitting symbol of Russia's European orientation and cultural refinement. To this end, an annex to the Winter Palace,

called the Small Hermitage, was built in 1764 by the French architect Jean-Baptiste-Michel Vallen de la Motte. The Hermitage was to serve not only as a luxurious refuge for Catherine and her intimates but also as a gallery where Catherine could display her ever-growing collection of art treasures. Between 1764 and 1796, Catherine amassed a collection of more than three thousand paintings and ten thousand drawings, many of them masterpieces, making St. Petersburg a rival of both Paris and Rome.

In 1762, when Catherine took the throne following the orchestrated murder of her husband, Czar Peter III, Russia had only a dozen major Western works of art, purchased in the first quarter of the eighteenth century by Czar Peter the Great. Since Peter dreamed of a first-class Russian navy, merchant marine, and port cities opening Russia's "Window to the West," the majority of his art purchases pictured European ports and seascapes. In contrast, while Catherine wanted as many European artistic treasures as could be obtained, she targeted her purchases toward classical themes, steering away from works that were largely religious in nature. To operate

with opportunistic efficiency, Catherine used a cadre of art connoisseurs, diplomats, and cultural celebrities as her purchasing agents. Among them were Denis Diderot, François Tronchin, Friedrich Melchior von Grimm, and Prince Dimitry Mikhailovich Golitsyn.

Catherine's first major acquisition was a collection of 225 Flemish and Dutch paintings purchased from King Frederick the Great of Prussia, who was facing bankruptcy in the wake of his numerous wars to maintain control of Silesia. Catherine worked through the Berlin financier, Johann-Ernst Gotzkowsky, an adviser to Frederick, to arrange the purchase. Embarrassing to Prussia, the purchase in 1764 was a wonderful addition to the recently opened Small Hermitage. Other private collections from financially strapped aristocrats were identified and purchased en masse: In 1768, Catherine received from Brussels the private collections of the prince de Ligne and Count Karl Coblentz. In 1769, the collection of the Saxon minister Count Heinrich von Bruhl was purchased in Dresden, and in 1770, François Tronchin's collection of 566 paintings by the masters was purchased in Paris. In 1771, Catherine added the collection of G. Braankamp of Amsterdam to her own. In the same year, construction began on a new building to become known as the Great Hermitage, designed by Yury Fel'ten (who had also contributed to the Small Hermitage).

In 1772, Catherine achieved a coup in Paris with the purchase of the world-renowned collection of the French banker Baron Pierre Crozat, which included masterpieces by Anthony van Dyck, Raphael, Titian, and Peter Paul Rubens. Catherine repeated her triumph in 1785 with the purchase of the collection of the Count Baudouin. Catherine's raid on London caused a heated debate in the House of Commons; however, she emerged in 1779 with one of England's greatest collections, the 198-masterpiece gallery (including 15 van Dycks) of Robert Walpole, Great Britain's first prime minister. The purchase of the entire collection meant an instant fortune to Walpole's financially strapped heirs. Catherine commemorated the event by provid-

The Hermitage Museum, c. 1890's. (Geo. L. Shuman and Co.)

The portico of the Hermitage Museum, c. 1890's. (Geo. L. Shuman and Co.)

ing Walpole's grandson with an elegant portrait of herself painted by Alexander Roslin.

While Catherine's agents had the resources of a royal treasury at their disposal, enabling them to purchase entire collections, they also targeted specific pieces at auctions held throughout Europe to add breadth or specific themes, usually of a pastoral or classical nature, to the Hermitage collection. The French Revolution and the subsequent emigration of many French aristocrats (émigrés) provided numerous opportunities for the strategic purchase of art in sets and individual pieces.

Catherine commissioned famous artists of her day, such as Sir Joshua Reynolds, Jean-Baptiste Chardin, and Claude-Joseph Vernet, to add to the Hermitage collection. She also commissioned works by relatively unknown émigré French female artists, such as Marie Anne Collot and Élisabeth Vigée-Lebrun. Moreover, art for Catherine included not only paintings and drawings but also antiquities. In 1787, a large collection of classical busts and reliefs was purchased from the director of the Bank of England, adding to the collection of the Hermitage's classical busts and sculptures. The Crimea, which Catherine annexed in 1783 following two wars against the Ot-

toman Empire, was carefully pruned by archaeologists for Greek and Scythian artifacts to be put on display. Catherine's eclectic artistic interests also included cameos, coins, medals, ceramics, porcelains, and engraved gems (which eventually numbered thirty-two thousand). She also acquired books. Catherine purchased the private libraries of the two leading Enlightenment philosophes, Denis Diderot and Voltaire. The resulting thirty-two-volume collection was also housed in the Hermitage.

The need to accommodate Catherine's cornucopia of art caused the Hermitage to expand into four connected buildings. The final addition was the Hermitage Theater, completed in 1787. There, Russia's elite and foreign dignitaries attending theatrical performances could be entertained in the art exhibition galleries. Catherine, who led Russia to annex more than 200,000 square miles during the course of her reign, nearly doubling its population, presided over an equally impressive growth of her capital city as a major European cultural center.

SIGNIFICANCE

During the first quarter of the eighteenth century, Peter the Great built a new capital of Russia in a marshland.

891

St. Petersburg was intended to create a new identity for Russia as a powerful state with an economic and cultural destiny closely linked to the major states of Europe. During the second half of the eighteenth century, Catherine, a German by birth, devoted great effort to synthesizing and augmenting Peter's work.

In her memoirs, Catherine considered the Hermitage as her little retreat, where she could delight in her things, which were shared largely with the palace mice. However, it is clear that her real joy came from the image her things created. Possession of so much of the great art of Europe enhanced Russia's identity as a sophisticated and culturally advanced European state. The great collection of the Hermitage was part of a royal residence rivaling Versailles in grandeur and elegance. The imperial palace itself was part of a city directed by Catherine to be expanded in a colossal manner according to neoclassical styles of the time. Less than a century old, St. Petersburg would stand as Europe's most modern capital city.

From the start of her reign, Catherine courted leading Enlightenment figures such as Denis Diderot and Voltaire. She used them to project an image of herself as an enlightened "First Servant of the State" ruling according to the rational principles of natural law. The identity of that state was European and culturally advanced. Catherine also embraced new scientific knowledge of the time, such as smallpox vaccination, in part to project a modern image. Catherine's French-speaking court nobles, elegantly dressed in the latest Parisian fashions, completed the remake of Russia's image. The fact that the overwhelming majority of Russians were illiterate and impoverished serfs remained obscured.

Following Catherine's death in 1796, the Hermitage was considered an imperial museum by her son, Czar Paul I (r. 1796-1802), and grandson, Czar Alexander I (r. 1801-1825). Catherine's imperial successors added to the collection and appointed talented museum curators.

Limited public viewing of the collection began in the mid-nineteenth century; however, it was not until after the Revolution of 1917 that the Hermitage became a public museum. Today, visitors can view 120 rooms comprising one of the world's great museums.

—Irwin Halfond

FURTHER READING

Alexander, John T. *Catherine the Great: Life and Legend*. New York: Oxford University Press, 1989. A readable and balanced narrative history of Catherine's life and works. Index and bibliography.

Lincoln, W. Bruce. *Sunlight at Midnight: St. Petersburg and the Rise of Modern Russia*. New York: Basic Books, 2002. As scholarly analysis of the growth of St. Petersburg as Russia's cultural center by a leading Russian historian showing that St. Petersburg was in many ways closer to major European cities than other Russian cities. Index and bibliography.

Steward, James. *Treasures of the Hermitage*. New York: Merrell, 2003. A study of the development of the Hermitage collection; 250 color illustrations, index, and bibliography.

1797
WOLLASTON BEGINS HIS WORK ON METALLURGY

Wollaston and Tennant experimented on platinum ore, discovering the new elements and developing techniques for producing powdered platinum and a malleable, purified platinum metal. Following Wollaston's death, his friend Percival Johnson utilized the same technique for industrial production of platinum, founding the Johnson and Matthey Company, which remains a major producer of platinum group metals.

LOCALE: London, England

CATEGORIES: Geology; chemistry; science and technology

KEY FIGURES

William Hyde Wollaston (1766-1828), English chemist and metallurgist

Smithson Tennant (1761-1815), English chemist and metallurgist

Percival Norton Johnson (1792-1866), English scientist and industrialist

George Matthey (1825-1913), English scientist and industrialist and Johnson's partner

SUMMARY OF EVENT

Archaeologists have discovered platinum inlays in ancient Egyptian tombs. Indigenous peoples in northern Ecuador and Colombia also used the metal, developing methods of sintering platinum to manufacture jewelry around 400 C.E. They continued utilizing platinum until they were conquered by the Spanish in the sixteenth century. Europeans first encountered platinum when Spanish scientist Antonio de Ulloa rediscovered platinum in the form of alluvial "platina" pebbles in the Rio Pinto in Colombia in 1735. Platinum was viewed by the Spaniards as a contaminant in the processing of gold, as it caused metallic gold to become brittle and difficult to refine: They forbade its export to Europe.

In 1745, de Ulloa was detained by the British Royal Navy while en route to Spain, and his notes were temporarily confiscated. De Ulloa was taken to London, where he was befriended by British scientists and made a member of the Royal Society in 1746. British scientists began to study de Ulloa's platina pebbles, and in 1750, William Brownrigg presented evidence to the Royal Society that they were composed of a new metal, "platinum." By 1783, French scientist François Chabaneau was able to produce a malleable platinum ingot.

While a student at Cambridge, Smithson Tennant became interested in platinum metal production. While visiting the chemist Lorenz von Crell in Helmstadt in 1784, Tennant wrote in his diary of learning Count von Sickingen's method for producing malleable platinum, which involved dissolving the ore in aqua regia (a mixture of one part nitric acid to four parts hydrochloric acid), precipitating out platinum powder, and heating and hammering the powder. Throughout Europe, scientists were hampered by the technological inability to generate enough heat to reach the temperature (1,772° Celsius) needed to melt the metal. An alternative, the process of sintering—taking a metal powder, compressing it, and heating it until a solid metal piece is formed (which happens at a temperature below the metal's melting point)—had been known for at least two thousand years.

Tennant and a friend from Cambridge, William Hyde Wollaston, formed a scientific partnership in 1797 to investigate platinum. In late December, 1800, Tennant and Wollaston purchased 5,959 Troy ounces (185 kilograms) of concentrated platinum ore for £795. (Gold and platinum weights are traditionally measured in Troy ounces, rather than the avoirdupois ounces used to weigh most other substances. One Troy ounce equals a weight of about 31.1 grams, as opposed to an avoirdupois ounce, which weighs roughly 28.35 grams.)

Wollaston began treating platina ore with aqua regia to dissolve it. He then added ammonium chloride to the solution, which caused most of the platinum to precipitate. He found that adding zinc caused the residual platinum, some palladium, rhodium, lead, and copper to precipitate as well. Wollaston then took the platinum powder precipitated from his solution, sintered it, and hammered the resulting solid. Using this production technique, now called "powder metallurgy," Wollaston began marketing metallic platinum in 1805, garnering a profit estimated at £30,000. Tennant shared in the platinum profits until his death in 1815. Wollaston's malleable platinum was used to producing boilers that could withstand manufacturing highly corrosive sulfuric acid and in fabricating crucibles for use in specialized chemical reactions.

Manipulating platinum led to several ancillary discoveries: Wollaston discovered palladium sometime before April, 1803, when he offered it for sale as a "new metal" in a Soho shop. He discovered rhodium shortly afterward. Wollaston also found that one by-product of processing platina ore was an insoluble black residue, which he gave to Tennant for further analysis. Studying one hundred Troy ounces of the residue, Tennant first heated some of it with sodium hydroxide and then dissolved the product in water, which yielded an odiferous yellow liquid. When acidified, an odorous white compound, now known as osmium tetroxide, was produced. Dissolving this white compound in water and adding copper, silver, or zinc, Tennant was able to produce another new element, black metallic osmium.

Tennant recovered iridium through a complex series of manipulations of osmium. He fused the black powder with caustic soda, used hydrochloric acid extraction to produce a residue that he again fused with caustic soda, and performed a second hydrochloric acid extraction on the second soda-residue fusion. He was left with red crystals, which he heated until he was left with a white powder that he could not melt. Tennant called this powder iridium. Tennant presented his discoveries of osmium and iridium to the Royal Society in 1804.

Between 1803 and 1821, Wollaston, together with his servant John Dowse, processed an estimated 47,000 Troy ounces of platinum ore, recovering 255 Troy ounces of rhodium and 302 Troy ounces of palladium. Wollaston investigated ways to use palladium, making corrosion-resistant sextants and other graduated scientific instruments out of palladium-gold alloys. Wollaston also made rhodium-tin pen nibs in the 1820's, which were sold for sixpence each.

SIGNIFICANCE

Wollaston made his platinum production process public one month prior to his death in 1828, along with his technique for producing malleable palladium and pure osmium tetroxide. His friend Percival Norton Johnson continued using Wollaston's powder metallurgy methods to produce all five of the then-known platinum group metals (PGM). A sixth PGM, ruthenium, was discovered in 1844 by Karl Karlovich Klaus.

PGMs steadily grew in importance over the nineteenth century, and the Johnson and Matthey Company became the world's major supplier of these specialty metals and their alloys. By 1867, Johnson and George Matthey had exhibited fifteen thousand Troy ounces of platinum products at an international metallurgical exhibition in Paris. In 1874, platinum-iridium alloys were used to produce standard meter and kilogram measures.

In 1908, Sir William Crookes reported on PGM crucibles that Johnson and Matthey had constructed, having

determined that iridium crucibles were as hard as steel, unaffected by mechanical treatment, and resistant to all chemicals except caustic potash. Iridium and iridium-platinum alloy crucibles continue to be manufactured in the twenty-first century.

The physical properties of the PGMs—their resistance to corrosion, high melting points, and roles as catalysts for important chemical reactions—made these metals increasingly important. From their use as catalysts in petroleum refineries to their use in automotive catalytic converters for air pollution control, platinum and palladium are essential to the oil industry. All the PGMs have been used to make electrical contact points because of their resistance to corrosion. Rhodium, ruthenium, iridium, and osmium are often added to the softer and more ductile platinum and palladium to produce a hardened alloy. Iridium has been used as a coating for missile nose cones because of its resistance to heat. Today's Johnson Matthey Company manufactures rhodium-platinum thermocouples for high-temperature use.

—Anita Baker-Blocker

FURTHER READING

Cotton, S. A. *Chemistry of Precious Metals*. London: Blackie Academic, 1997. A monograph concerned with the inorganic chemistry of gold, silver, and the six platinum group metals; contains sixteen hundred references up to the year 1996.

Griffith, W. P. "Rhodium and Palladium: Events Surrounding Their Discoveries." *Platinum Metals Review* 47 (2003): 175-183. Part 1 of a review of the discovery of palladium and its use in metal alloys and as a catalyst in modern air pollution control devices.

_____. "Osmium and Iridium: Events Surrounding Their Discoveries." *Platinum Metals Review* 48 (2004): 182-189. Part 2 of a review of Tennant's partnership with Wollaston in the study of platinum group metals, including discovery of the elements osmium and iridium in the insoluble black powder produced as a by-product of Wollaston's platinum purification process.

McDonald, Donald, and L. B. Hunt. *A History of Platinum and Its Allied Metals*. London: Johnson Matthey, 1982. An authoritative text on the platinum group metals uses through the mid-twentieth century.

Tsuji, Jiro. *Palladium Reagents and Catalysts: New Perspectives for the Twenty-First Century*. Chichester, England: Wiley, 2004. An authoritative text on organopalladium chemistry advances from 1970 to 2003 and the increasingly important role palladium compounds either as stoichiometric reagents or as catalysts in organic synthesis, discusses industrial processes based on palladium-catalyzed reactions.

SEE ALSO: 1709: Darby Invents Coke-Smelting; 1718: Geoffroy Issues the *Table of Reactivities*; 1722: Réaumur Discovers Carbon's Role in Hardening Steel; 1745: Lomonosov Issues the First Catalog of Minerals; June 5, 1755: Black Identifies Carbon Di-

oxide; 1771: Woulfe Discovers Picric Acid; Aug. 1, 1774: Priestley Discovers Oxygen; 1783-1784: Cort Improves Iron Processing; 1789: Leblanc Develops Soda Production.

RELATED ARTICLES in *Great Lives from History: The Eighteenth Century, 1701-1800*: Abraham Darby; John Roebuck; John Wilkinson.

October 4, 1797-September 30, 1800
XYZ AFFAIR

Disagreements between the United States and France over the import of Jay's Treaty and an attempt by French agents to extort a bribe from American negotiators led to an undeclared war between France and the United States.

LOCALE: Paris, France; Philadelphia, Pennsylvania
CATEGORIES: Diplomacy and international relations; wars, uprisings, and civil unrest

KEY FIGURES
John Adams (1735-1826), president of the United States, 1797-1801
Alexander Hamilton (1755-1804), Federalist Party leader and inspector general of the U.S. Army, 1798-1800
Talleyrand (Prince de Bénévent; 1754-1838), French minister of foreign affairs, 1797-1807
Elbridge Gerry (1744-1814), American member of Adams's first mission to France, 1797-1798
John Marshall (1755-1835), American commissioner to France, 1797-1798, U.S. representative, 1799-1800, secretary of state, 1800-1801, and chief justice of the United States, 1801-1835
Charles Cotesworth Pinckney (1746-1825), American minister to France (unrecognized), 1796, commissioner to France, 1797-1798, and major general, 1798-1800
Timothy Pickering (1745-1829), U.S. secretary of state, 1795-1800

SUMMARY OF EVENT
The presidency of John Adams of Massachusetts was not a happy one. Adams inherited all the problems of George Washington but none of his prestige. French-American relations with the French First Republic progressively worsened. Adams also faced dissension within his own

party. Not all Federalists were satisfied when he was chosen as Washington's successor. Alexander Hamilton was known to have opposed Adams and would do so again in 1800. Adams did not help himself by retaining the Washington cabinet, composed of men with no particular loyalty to the new president. The overriding issue was the question of war or peace with France, but hardly less critical was the question of Adams's ability to control his own administration.

In the eyes of the French government, the United States, in signing Jay's Treaty (1794), had repudiated the Franco-American Alliance of 1778. The French charged that the acceptance of the treaty was a non-neutral act, inasmuch as the United States had obviously accepted the British definition of neutral rights at sea. The French decided to break off normal relations with the United States. To give force to this action, the French subjected American vessels on the high seas to the same indignities so recently experienced at the hands of the British. In the year following July, 1796, the secretary of state, Timothy Pickering of Massachusetts, reported that the French had seized 316 U.S. vessels.

In an effort to forestall a complete break between the two nations, President Adams sent a three-man delegation to negotiate with the French. At the time of the mission there was no recognized American representative in France because the French had refused to receive Charles Cotesworth Pinckney (brother of Thomas), whom Washington had sent to France as the successor to James Monroe. Adams chose two distinguished Americans—Elbridge Gerry, a Massachusetts Republican, and John Marshall, a Virginia Federalist—to join with Pinckney in presenting the U.S. position to the French government. The three Americans were in Paris by October 4, 1797.

While Adams and the Federalists were determined to avoid war if at all possible, Adams called upon Congress

"Property Protected à la Françoise": A 1798 British cartoon representing Franco-American relations during the XYZ affair portrays a group of Frenchmen robbing a woman symbolizing America. (Library of Congress)

to look to the defenses of the nation. Bills were introduced calling for the enlargement of the regular army, the creation of a provisional army of fifteen thousand men, the construction of three new frigates for the navy, and tax measures to pay for the preparedness program. The program ran into stiff opposition. The Republicans accused Adams and his party of warmongering and succeeded in defeating the army and tax bills.

The three Americans in Paris made no progress in their negotiations during several weeks in the city. When they were convinced that their mission was a failure, three representatives (the notorious Messrs. X, Y, and Z) from Talleyrand, the French minister of foreign affairs, approached them with certain demands as prerequisites to negotiation: President Adams was to apologize for certain statements in his last message to Congress, and the United States was to pay a sum of 1.2 million livres and make a loan of 32 million florins to the French, which was simply a demand for a bribe. The Americans, with no instructions relative to the payment of such a hugh sum of money, could do nothing but refuse.

Pinckney and Marshall, convinced of the futility of remaining in France, took their departure. Gerry lingered in Paris in the hope of achieving something, but was soon recalled.

When news of this attempt by the French to dishonor the name of the United States was made public, Americans of virtually all political persuasions were united in condemning the insolence of the French. There were demands that the United States take immediate steps to defend its integrity. Some called for war; most shouted the slogan, "Millions for defense but not one cent for tribute." Congress declared that the treaties of alliance and friendship of 1778 with France were void and authorized public and private vessels of the United States to capture French armed ships on the high seas. The United States and France were dangerously close to war.

In the spring of 1798, Congress created a Department of the Navy and appropriated funds to build warships. Preparations were made to raise an army of fifteen thousand men. During the next two years an undeclared war, or Half-War, as Adams called it, was waged against

France. By 1800, the United States Navy, with the aid of hundreds of privateers, had successfully cleared U.S. waters of French cruisers and had even carried the naval warfare into the seas surrounding the French West Indies.

President Adams soon found himself in a difficult position. He was rapidly losing control of his own administration. Alexander Hamilton seemed to have more influence with Congress and the cabinet than did the president. Adams, a good New Englander, was basically opposed to the creation of a large standing army. He emphasized the navy as the United States' first line of defense. Hamilton and his supporters pushed army legislation through Congress. The army was to be commanded by Washington, but until he actually took the field, Hamilton was to be in charge.

Adams opposed Hamilton but could do nothing, since Washington made it clear that he would accept command only on his own terms. Adams, finally recognizing that his cabinet was disloyal, ultimately forced the resignations of Pickering and James McHenry, secretary of war. Adams also learned that the French government was then willing to negotiate seriously. With war fever high among certain Federalists, Adams opted for peace. Without consultation with his cabinet or the Federalist leadership, Adams submitted the name of an envoy to France.

This action precipitated a split in the Federalist Party. Adams did succeed in reopening negotiations with the French, although he was forced to accept a commission of three Federalists rather than the one individual he had nominated. By the time that the three commissioners reached France, Napoleon was First Consul. The settlement reached on September 30, 1800, in the Treaty of Morfontaine (signed the same day as the Convention of 1800) provided for the mutual abrogation of the Franco-American Treaties of 1778, but it also provided that the United States was to receive no indemnity for the French seizures of U.S. merchant shipping. Although not entirely satisfactory to the United States, the agreement did end the undeclared war. The peace was popular with most Americans, but the rift that it caused between the supporters of the president and those of Hamilton seriously injured Adams's chances of reelection in 1800.

SIGNIFICANCE

The XYZ affair would not have achieved the prominence it did had it not become enmeshed in U.S. party politics. Although the XYZ affair is often presented as a case study of U.S. virtue as opposed to Old World corruption, there is evidence that the Americans contributed to the

sordidness of the affair. After having supported the Americans in their struggle for independence, the French had reason to be offended by Jay's Treaty, which favored the British in the war against France. The Federalist Party of President Adams was the party of property. The party as a whole despised and feared revolutionary France. Therefore, some Federalists saw an advantage to keeping the animosity toward France alive, even to the extent of war.

There is reason to question how serious the delegates, all Federalist appointees, were in seeking an accommodation with the French Directory. Were the Americans really surprised by the bribes? Some historians maintain that they were prepared to pay handsomely and that it was merely the greediness of the Directory's agents that offended them. Did the delegates, as Talleyrand later maintained, shut themselves in their hotel rooms and leave before they could be officially received? Were the dispatches written by Federalist John Marshall, released to Congress and the press in April of 1798, deliberately intended to inflame public opinion?

If the Federalists wanted war, Talleyrand was not willing to oblige. The last thing France needed, he warned the Directory, was another enemy. By the fall of 1798, the bribes had been forgotten and French vessels were ordered to respect American neutrality. The relieved Republicans saw the whole affair as a Federalist hoax. Adams was swept from power in the "Revolution of 1800"; the French Directory had suffered the same fate the year before at the hands of Napoleon Bonaparte. The XYZ affair was relegated to history, remembered only by a ringing slogan.

—*John G. Clark, updated by Nis Petersen*

FURTHER READING

Chinard, Gilbert. *Honest John Adams*. Boston: Little, Brown, 1933. A detailed short biography of the second U.S. president, discussing his efforts to deal with an almost treasonable cabinet and the support he received from his wife, Abigail.

DeConde, Alexander. *The Quasi-War: The Politics and Diplomacy of the Undeclared War with France, 1797-1801*. New York: Charles Scribner's Sons, 1966. Summarizes the war in the light of efforts of both the Americans and French to save face.

Elkins, Stanley, and Eric McKitrick. *The Age of Federalism*. New York: Oxford University Press, 1993. A thorough, understandable treatment of the XYZ affair.

McCullogh, David. *John Adams*. New York: Simon &

1790's

Schuster, 2001. This highly acclaimed, meticulously researched biography of Adams includes an explanation of the XYZ affair in chapter 9.

Morison, S. E., H. S. Commager, and W. E. Leuchtenburg. "John Adams' Administration." In *The Growth of the American Republic*. 2 vols. 7th ed. New York: Oxford University Press, 1980. The authors, considered authorities on U.S. history, place the affair in historic perspective and offer some fresh insights.

Palmer, Michael A. *Stoddert's War: Naval Operations During the Quasi-War with France, 1798-1801.* Annapolis, Md.: Naval Institute Press, 2000. Describes how Benjamin Stoddert, first secretary of the navy, led the United States' attack on the French during the undeclared war. Places the war in a European context. Updated edition of a book originally published in 1987.

Rudko, Frances Howell. *John Marshall and International Law: Statesman and Chief Justice.* New York: Greenwood Press, 1991. Examines Marshall's twenty years of experience in international law before his appointment as Chief Justice of the United States. Includes a detailed examination of his negotiations with the French during Adams's administration.

Stinchcombe, William. *The XYZ Affair.* Westport, Conn.: Greenwood Press, 1980. A detailed, documented, standard account of the affair.

SEE ALSO: Feb. 6, 1778: Franco-American Treaties; Sept. 3, 1783: Treaty of Paris; Oct. 27, 1787-May, 1788: Publication of *The Federalist*; 1790's: First U.S. Political Parties; Apr. 20, 1792-Oct., 1797: Early Wars of the French Revolution; Jan. 21, 1793: Execution of Louis XVI; July 27-28, 1794: Fall of Robespierre; Nov. 19, 1794: Jay's Treaty; Mar., 1796-Oct. 17, 1797: Napoleon's Italian Campaigns.

RELATED ARTICLES in *Great Lives from History: The Eighteenth Century, 1701-1800*: John Adams; Elbridge Gerry; Alexander Hamilton; George Washington.

1798
INVENTION OF LITHOGRAPHY

In 1798, aspiring German playwright Alois Senefelder invented a new printmaking technique based on applying ink to an image created by a greasy medium on a porous stone. The unmarked or nonimage areas holding water repelled the ink. This new "chemical printing," later known as lithography (stone writing) transformed both commercial printing and the visual arts.

LOCALE: Munich (now in Germany)

CATEGORIES: Inventions; science and technology; art; communications

KEY FIGURES

Alois Senefelder (1771-1834), Bavarian playwright and printer

Johann Anton André (1775-1842), musician and publisher

Rudolph Ackermann (1764-1834), British-German publisher and inventor

Karl Friedrich Schinkel (1781-1841), German architect and artist

Adolph von Menzel (1815-1905), German artist

Francisco de Goya (1746-1828), Spanish artist

SUMMARY OF EVENT

In the eighteenth century, there were two printing methods, both based on mechanical means for producing the printed image. In the intaglio method, an image is created from ink applied to and retained in lines or marks etched or engraved onto a plate. In relief printing, such as woodblock, ink is applied to a raised surface, which is then pressed onto paper. By the end of the eighteenth century, printing would be revolutionized by a poor playwright.

Born in Prague on November 6, 1771, Alois Senefelder was the son of Franz Peter Senefelder, an actor with the Royal Theatre of Munich. When his father died in 1791, Senefelder gave up legal studies at the University of Ingolstad to support his mother and siblings. He wrote many plays but could not afford a publisher or printer. He began experimenting with engraving copper plates to find an inexpensive way to print his own works.

A coincidental household event in 1796 led to Senefelder's invention of lithography, or chemical printing, in 1798. He had been practicing writing backward and had purchased a flat grinding stone in order to prepare the ink for his writing exercises. When his mother needed to write a list of items for the launderer and did not have any paper or regular ink, he used a greasy ink compound of wax, soap, and lampblack to write the list on the grinding stone. Later, when he was about to wipe away the writing from the stone, it occurred to him to try etching the stone instead of the copper plates he had been using. After applying a mixture of nitric acid and water to the stone, he found that the grease in the written letters had protected them from being eaten away and that the surrounding stone surface was removed, leaving a raised image of the letters.

For the next two years, Senefelder experimented with this printing discovery, and in 1798 he had fully developed chemical printing, an entirely new process based on the chemical principle that greasy substances and water repel each other. He found that because it was very porous, Kelheim limestone from Bavaria was the best stone for printing. The new process could create a wide range of tones, from light grays to the deepest black, and a single stone could produce hundreds of fine proofs. In September, 1799, Senefelder was granted an exclusive license for chemical printing in Bavaria and the electorate.

Aside from printing text, there were many other potential applications of the new technology. In 1799, Johann Anton André, a prominent musician who had just inherited his father's music publishing business in the town of Offenbach, invited Senefelder to join him in the enterprise. In the same year, André signed a publishing agreement with Constance Mozart, the widow of Wolfgang Amadeus Mozart, giving André access to the music of one of the most prolific composers who had ever lived. Among other projects, the technical means to accomplish this monumental task was provided by Senefelder's lithographic presses.

In 1800, André's brother Phillip took Senefelder to London. While his brother was interested in music, Phillip André wanted to explore applications in the visual arts. In 1803, using Senefelder's process, he published *Specimens of Polyautography*, the first collection of drawings made on stone, including pieces by Henry

Fuseli, Thomas Barker, Benjamin West, and others. By this time, the French had begun using the term *lithographie*, or "writing on stone," rather than Senefelder's "chemical printing," to describe the technique, and the French term eventually became standard.

Senefelder was appointed inspector of cartography for the Royal Bavarian Printer in 1809. In 1818, he published a complete account of his invention entitled *Vollständiges Lehrbuch der Steindruckerei* (*A Complete Course of Lithography*, 1819) in Munich and Vienna. King Maximilian Joseph of Bavaria permitted the book to be dedicated to him. The work is divided into two parts: The first provides a history of the invention from 1796 to 1817. The second part covers practical or technical subjects such as acids, presses, paper, and inks. In 1819, the book was translated into French, English, and Italian.

The first English translation had a longer complete title: *A Complete Course of Lithography: Containing*

This nineteenth century engraving shows Alois Senefelder making the accidental discovery in 1796 that would lead him to develop lithography over the next two years. (The Granger Collection, New York)

Clear and Explicit Instructions in All the Different Branches and Manners of That Art—Accompanied by Illustrative Specimens of Drawings, to Which Is Prefixed a History of Lithography, from Its Origin to the Present Time. The publisher was Rudolph Ackermann, a former saddler and coach builder who had established a printshop, the Repository of Arts, in London in 1795. Ackermann was instrumental in popularizing lithography in England.

Senefelder continued to experiment and improve the presses and lithographic process throughout his life. He died in Munich in 1834. Other pioneers of lithography were Karl Friedrich Schinkel, Adolph von Menzel, and Francisco de Goya. A noted Prussian architect, Karl Friedrich Schinkel, was also a painter and lithographer. His lithograph of a Gothic church was one of the best of this early period. Adolph von Menzel was a self-taught artist who took over his father's lithography studio in Berlin in 1830. His prints were considered the most artistically and technically significant lithographs of the time. The celebrated Spanish artist Goya created his first lithograph in 1819. His memorable set of four lithographs about bullfighting was produced in 1825.

SIGNIFICANCE

Lithography revolutionized the field of cartography. Previously, most atlases and maps were produced by engraving, an expensive and labor-intensive process. With Senefelder's transfer lithography technique, cartographers could draw maps on paper, rather than drawing in reverse on stone, and then transfer the image from the paper to the lithographic stone.

Because lithography could produce numerous high-quality copies of an original, it was significant in the development of commercial printing. By the mid-nineteenth century, full-color printing from multiple plates was practical. A growing number of publishers used the process to print popular works for a wide audience. The most famous lithographic publisher was Currier & Ives, which from 1835 to 1907 produced more than seventy-five hundred titles, totaling more than one million prints. These inexpensive prints reflected popular American subjects, including firefighters, famous race horses, hunting scenes, sports, humor, disaster scenes, and sentimental images.

After the mid-1800's, offset printing, a mechanical process developed from Senefelder's chemical printing, became the dominant commercial printing technique. In this process, the source image was printed on a rubber cylinder, which was rotated as it pressed against the paper or other material that received the print. This method's main advantage was that a variety of materials could be used for printing—not only a range of rough and smooth papers but also wood, tin, leather, and cloth. Even after the advent of digital reproduction in the twentieth century, offset printing continued to be used to print high-quality packages, cards, posters, magazines, calendars, books, newspapers, and other printed products.

Late nineteenth century fine artists such as Henri de Toulouse-Lautrec, Paul Gauguin, and Pierre Bonnard created impressive color lithographs. Twentieth century fine artists who worked in this medium included Edvard Munch, Pablo Picasso, Diego Rivera, Henri Matisse, Georges Rouault, Robert Motherwell, Ben Shahn, and Robert Rauschenberg.

—Alice Myers

FURTHER READING

Cohn, Marjorie, and Clare Rogan. *Touchstone: Two Hundred Years of Artists' Lithographs*. Cambridge, Mass.: Harvard University Art Museums, 1998. Catalog of the museums' exhibition of August 15-November 1, 1998. Illustrated. Bibliography and index.

Croft, Paul. *Stone Lithography*. New York: Watson-Guptill, 2003. A practical handbook describing lithography techniques. Illustrated.

Man, Felix H. *Artists' Lithographs: A World History from Senefelder to the Present Day*. New York: G. P. Putnam's Sons, 1970. Includes detailed accounts of Senefelder's life and invention, and the first practical and artistic uses. Illustrated. Glossary and bibliography.

Senefelder, Alois. *A Complete Course of Lithography*. Reprint. New York: Da Capo Press, 1968. An unabridged republication of the first English edition published by R. Ackermann in London in 1819. Includes rare plates from the original German and French editions. Illustrated.

Tonsing, Paul Martin. *The Power of the Press: History and Development of Printing Presses from the Fifteenth to the Twenty-First Century*. Fort Worth, Tex.: P & T, 1998. Covers lithography-stone printing within the context of 550 years of the development of printing presses. Illustrated. Notes and index.

Twyman, Michael. *Breaking the Mould: The First Hundred Years of Lithography*. London: British Library, 2001. Historical account of lithography in the nineteenth century. Illustrated. Maps and bibliography.

SEE ALSO: 1702 or 1706: First Arabic Printing Press; Jan. 7, 1714: Mill Patents the Typewriter; 1737: Revival of the Paris Salon; Dec. 10, 1768: Britain's Royal Academy of Arts Is Founded; 1787: David Paints *The Death of Socrates*.

RELATED ARTICLES in *Great Lives from History: The Eighteenth Century, 1701-1800*: William Blake; Francisco de Goya; Giovanni Battista Tiepolo; Élisabeth Vigée-Lebrun.

1798
MALTHUS AROUSES CONTROVERSY WITH HIS POPULATION THEORY

Malthus published An Essay on the Principle of Population, *developing theories about population explosion, food supply, and environmental concerns that laid the foundation for modern socioeconomic theory.*

LOCALE: London, England

CATEGORIES: Economics; cultural and intellectual history; social issues and reform

KEY FIGURES

Thomas Robert Malthus (1766-1834), English economist and clergyman

William Godwin (1756-1836), English reformer

Marquis de Condorcet (Marie-Jean-Antoine-Nicholas de Caritat; 1743-1794), French revolutionary leader, philosopher, and writer

Daniel Malthus (1730-1800), father of Thomas, an avid adherent of utopian ideas, and a friend of David Hume

SUMMARY OF EVENT

Thomas Robert Malthus, an English clergyman, was perhaps the first professional economist. The son of a middle-class eccentric, he spent most of his life teaching and doing economic research. He taught with other great economists of the time at the staff college of the East India Company, a vigorous and unscrupulous trading company. East India was the source of income for Malthus and many who did not agree with the company's labor and colonialism practices. Malthus's economic thinking was practical in contrast to the dogmatic and rational approach of his friend David Ricardo, who founded the classic school of English economics. Ricardo was an astute stockbroker and businessman who foresaw that an increased population would provide workers for all British businesses, farms, and factories, including his own.

Although he published several important works in the field of economics, Malthus is famous primarily for *An Essay on the Principle of Population, As It Affects the Future Improvement of Society*, which appeared in 1798. In order to understand this work and the impact it had, it is necessary to recall the circumstances at the time it was written. For example, there was then no accurate method of computing the actual population of England, the first census not being taken until 1801. Also, many feared that the population was declining at a time when it was almost universally believed that large populations were desirable.

Malthus had another purpose in writing his book, that of refuting various reformers who had predicted universal progress for the human race. This aspect is made clear from the full title of the work as originally printed: *An Essay on the Principle of Population As It Affects the Future Improvement of Society, with Remarks on the Speculations of Mr. Godwin, M. Condorcet, and Other Writers*. Such speculations were common at a time when the French Revolution, which seemed to spring from such ideas, was still taking place. William Godwin wrote *An Enquiry Concerning Political Justice and Its Influence on General Virtue and Happiness* (1793), in which he asserted the principle of human equality, refuting Malthus.

Godwin's purpose was to justify the inequality found in human institutions according to the laws of the Creator. The marquis de Condorcet wrote on the confrontation between increasing populations and diminishing food supply in his works. Condorcet and Thomas's father Daniel Malthus were both optimistic about the future, believing that birth control and other voluntary checks would keep population numbers within reasonable limits. Thomas Malthus had first come into contact with these ideas through Daniel, who was an avid follower of Jean-Jacques Rousseau. Thomas himself was more conservative, and his remarks frequently reveal a scorn for the French Revolution typical of the English upper and middle classes, who feared that revolutionary fever would spread to England. A large part of Malthus's work is devoted to refuting the claims of Godwin and Condorcet.

The theory put forward by Malthus is based on two propositions: that food is necessary for humans to exist, and that passion between the sexes is necessary and does not essentially change in its intensity. The law says whereas food supplies tend to increase in arithmetic progression, population when unchecked tends to increase in geometric progression. The inevitable result is that, if unchecked, population tends to outrun its means of support. Thus, the ultimate check on population is starvation.

What Malthus wished to consider were the checks that prevented this dire state from occurring. He mentioned two checks: first, the preventative check, or foresight into the difficulties of rearing a family, which inclines people not to have more children than they can support; second, the positive check, or the actual distress and misery that prevent the growth of the population. Malthus was convinced that the second check was more significant than the first. The implication of his view was obvious. Given the constant tendency of the population to increase as a result of passion between the sexes, misery and poverty were impossible to eradicate; society seemed to be condemned to the inevitable treadmill of strain, difficulty, and poverty. Malthus saw no way to alter these tendencies but did suggest three palliatives: Assistance to the poor should be limited because it leads them to reproduce beyond the means of subsistence; encouragement should be given to those who produce food; and education should inculcate the virtue of prudence.

Malthus devoted the remainder of his essay to contradicting the utopian hopes of Godwin and Condorcet. Against Godwin, who believed that the evils in society spring from social and civil inequalities, Malthus argued that such inequalities were natural and stem from the inability of the Earth to support a constantly expanding population. Against Condorcet, who believed that human progress would result from essential changes in human nature, Malthus argued that human nature had always been the same in the past and that no reputable scientific method could postulate significant changes in the future when no grounds for such changes existed in the past.

Malthus was aware that his theory was melancholy; he defended himself against charges of inhumanity by pointing out that his ideas were based on fact, not on personal feeling. Moreover, he did not deny the possibility of human progress altogether; he did believe that limited progress, though unlikely, was possible. His chief aim was to refute those who asserted the inevitability of progress.

SIGNIFICANCE

Three developments allowed the English to change what Malthus had predicted. First, thousands of English citizens and Europeans immigrated to America, Canada, Australasia, and South Africa between 1820 and 1914. Second, as Malthus's essay was being written, the process that was to be called the Agricultural Revolution was beginning, marked by the use of highly improved farming methods. Third, in the two decades previous to Malthus's essay, Britain was entering the first stages of the Industrial Revolution, in which steam, internal combustion, and then electricity were to replace human and animal power.

Malthus's ideas were studied by economists, religious leaders, and politicians. Economist Adam Smith wrote *The Wealth of Nations* (1776), which projected optimism. Smith's writings became the nucleus for the positive views of those who disagreed with Malthus's pessimism about the future of humankind.

Malthus revised his essay for a second edition in 1803. He documented his arguments and abandoned his ideas of precise arithmetic and geometric progressions for the increases in food and population. He also recognized the influence of moral restraint as a preventive check on population growth, but he remained pessimistic concerning the future progress of humankind.

—*Paul T. Mason, updated by Norma Crews*

FURTHER READING

Avery, John. *Progress, Poverty, and Population: Rereading Condorcet, Godwin, and Malthus*. London: F. Cass, 1997. Traces the history of the debate in the late eighteenth and early nineteenth centuries between utopian optimists, such as Condorcet and Godwin, and pessimists, such as Malthus, about the effects of population growth upon society.

Ehrlich, Paul, and Anne Ehrlich. *The Population Bomb*. New York: Simon & Schuster, 1990. Paul Ehrlich has long written on the dangers of overpopulation. Warnings included in this volume are famines, global warming, pollution, and epidemics such as AIDS.

Elwell, Frank W. *A Commentary on Malthus's 1798 Essay on Population as Social Theory*. Lewiston, N.Y.: E. Mellen Press, 2001. An analysis of the essay that seeks to eliminate some of the dogma and misinterpretation surrounding Malthus's theories and present his ideas with more subtlety and complexity. Includes a reprint of the original essay.

Galbraith, John Kenneth. *The Age of Uncertainty*. Boston: Houghton Mifflin, 1977. An overall picture of the workings of economics, those who have made a difference, and changes that have affected the entire world. Witty, many illustrations.

George, Henry. *Progress and Poverty*. New York: Robert Schalkenbach Foundation, 1971. Written in 1879, George's book reveals his total faith in the Malthusian theory. The entire book takes each part of Malthus's essay and proves its probability. A contrast to the works of Ehrlich and Wattenberg.

Halacy, D. S., Jr. *The Geometry of Hunger*. New York: Harper & Row, 1972. Covers the various causes of population explosions, the nutritional gaps in parts of the world, and possible solutions by increasing food production and equalizing distribution. Dated but still useful.

Kennedy, Paul. *Preparing for the Twenty-First Century*. New York: Random House, 1993. A worldly look at scarce resources, new technologies, exploding populations, and health concerns. Questions how the major powers will respond to the needs of the rest of the world.

Rifkin, Jeremy. *Entropy*. New York: Viking, 1980. A scholarly book enlarging on the nineteenth century Entropy Law, or Second Law of Thermodynamics. A contrast to the Malthusian theory.

Ross, Eric B. *The Malthus Factor: Population, Poverty, and Politics in Capitalistic Development*. New York: St. Martin's Press, 1998. A critique of Malthus's theory, tracing how it has been used to defend capitalist economic goals when those goals were confronted by struggles for equality and human progress. Describes the origins of Malthus's theory, its application to land reform and the green revolution, and how the theory was interpreted before and after the Cold War.

Wattenberg, Ben. *The Birth Dearth*. New York: Pharos Books, 1987. Wattenberg notes that the so-called baby boom is over and points out that the resulting "birth dearth" in many of the most technologically advanced countries of the world has long-range implications for world economics and politics.

SEE ALSO: 1720: Financial Collapse of the John Law System; Sept., 1720: Collapse of the South Sea Bubble; Oct., 1725: Vico Publishes *The New Science*; 1739-1740: Hume Publishes *A Treatise of Human Nature*; Mar. 9, 1776: Adam Smith Publishes *The Wealth of Nations*; 1784-1791: Herder Publishes His Philosophy of History.

RELATED ARTICLES in *Great Lives from History: The Eighteenth Century, 1701-1800*: Marquis de Condorcet; William Godwin; David Hume.

April 12, 1798-September 2, 1801
NAPOLEON'S EGYPTIAN CAMPAIGN

Napoleon Bonaparte invaded Egypt with the two goals of disrupting British trade with India and establishing a permanent French colony. Although the campaign was a failure, he successfully manipulated public opinion to enhance his popularity in France.

LOCALE: Egypt
CATEGORY: Wars, uprisings, and civil unrest; expansion and land acquisition

KEY FIGURES
Napoleon Bonaparte (1769-1821), French military commander and later emperor and France as Napoleon I, r. 1804-1814, 1815
Lord Nelson (Horatio Nelson; 1758-1805), British admiral
Talleyrand (1754-1838), French statesman and diplomat
Murad Bey (1750-1801), joint ruler of Egypt
Ibrāhīm Bey (1735?-1817), joint ruler of Egypt
Jean-Baptiste Kléber (1754-1800), French general
Louis-Charles-Antoine Desaix de Veygoux (1768-1800), French general
Ralph Abercromby (1734-1801), British lieutenant general
Jacques-François de Menou (1750-1810), French general
Comte de Volney (Constantin-François de Chasseboeuf; 1757-1820), French traveler and writer
Jean François Champollion (1790-1832), French Egyptologist

SUMMARY OF EVENT
In the late 1780's, Napoleon Bonaparte, after reading a travel account of Egypt by the comte de Volney, conceived the idea of conquering the region. In September, 1797, near the conclusion of his victorious Italian campaign, he advocated the colonizing of Egypt and Malta in a letter to Talleyrand, the French minister of foreign affairs. In response, Talleyrand, who was familiar with

Volney's writings, agreed with Bonaparte's idea. At the time, Bonaparte was also considering an invasion of Britain, but he soon abandoned the notion as unrealistic because of Britain's sea power.

Egypt was a traditional and impoverished country with about 3 million people. Although nominally a province of the Ottoman Empire, it was semiautonomous and ruled by local governors called beys, who belonged to an ancient warrior caste of former slaves called Mamlūks. While often dictatorial, the beys exercised limited control over much of the country. To the dismay of the French, the beys had established close relations with Britain in transporting men and supplies from the Mediterranean Sea to the Red Sea.

On April 12, 1798, the Directory, a group of five Frenchmen holding executive power, secretly issued a decree appointing Bonaparte the commander in chief of an expedition to seize both Malta and Egypt. As justification, the decree claimed that the Mamlūks were closely allied with the British and that they had been regularly perpetrating "horrible cruelties" on French ships in the Mediterranean. The decree further instructed Bonaparte to destroy British settlements in the Red Sea and then to cut a canal across the Suez Isthmus.

When planning and organizing the expeditionary force, called the Army of the Orient, Bonaparte had the assistance of Volney and other knowledgeable people. On May 19, 1798, the army departed Toulon with about thirty-eight thousand troops, accompanied by hundreds of engineers, architects, and scholars in many different fields. The fleet transporting the troops, commanded by Admiral François Brueys, totaled about four hundred ships. Their first stop was at the island of Malta, which they easily captured and reorganized as a French possession. On July 1, the expedition landed in Egypt at Marabut Bay. Within a few days, French soldiers controlled the port cities of Alexandria, Rosetta, and Damietta.

On July 2, Bonaparte published a proclamation addressed to the people of Egypt, asserting that the Egyptian rulers were cruel tyrants who had long injured French merchants. The document promised to end tyranny, to allow wise and learned Egyptians to rule, to promote economic prosperity, and to respect the free exercise of the Islamic religion. Bonaparte gave strict orders for his soldiers to refrain from theft, rape, or the dishonoring of local customs.

On July 11, the main body of the French army left El Rahmanya, on the Nile River, and headed south toward Cairo. The majority of the soldiers marched through the desert, while the rest traveled on a flotilla of barges. By advancing rapidly, Napoleon hoped to defeat the two Mamlūk leaders, Murad Bey and Ibrāhīm Bey, before his own men became demoralized. After traveling 8 miles, the French successfully repelled an attack by Egyptian forces at Shubra Kit. The Egyptians then withdrew to the south.

On July 21, about twenty-five thousand French troops decisively defeated a larger army of probably forty thousand men at Embaba, on the Nile. This conflict is known to

Napoleon leads his troops at the Battle of the Pyramids. (R. S. Peale and J. A. Hill)

history as the Battle of the Pyramids, because it was fought just 10 miles from the Great Pyramid of Giza. The French prevailed because of their advantages in modern equipment, better training and discipline, and a unified command. About one-third of the Egyptian troops were Bedouins, employing traditional tactics and primitive weapons. That night, Napoleon stayed in Murad's house at Giza, and the next day he made a triumphal entry into Cairo.

Things soon began to fall apart for the French invaders, however. On August 1-2, in the Battle of the Nile, the British admiral Lord Nelson found and destroyed most of the French navy at Abū Qīr Bay (Aboukir Bay), cutting off Bonaparte's supply lines. Although General Jean Reynier won a victory over Ibrāhīm Bey's forces at El-Hanka on August 6, General Louis-Charles-Antoine Desaix de Veygoux was unable to catch the mobile forces under Murad's command. In Cairo, Bonaparte's colonial administration succeeded in forcing acquiescence for a few months, but a massive and violent revolt broke out on October 21. The French brutally massacred the insurgents and plundered the al-Azhar Mosque. By then, many French troops were suffering from ophthalmia and outbreaks of the plague.

After the Ottoman government declared war on the French, Bonaparte tried to forestall a Turkish attack by launching defensive invasions of Syria and Palestine in February, 1799. He and General Jean-Baptiste Kléber defeated Turkish troops at Mount Tabor, but they were unable to capture Acre. Returning to Egypt, Bonaparte overcame Mustafā Paşa's Turkish invaders at Abū Qīr on July 25. By then, more than half of Bonaparte's invading army had been buried in Egyptian graves. Recognizing the hopelessness of the situation, Bonaparte decided to abandon the Army of the Orient. On August 23, he and a few of his best generals slipped through the British blockade and sailed for home.

General Kléber, who was left in charge, soon negotiated a surrender to the British on favorable terms, but the British commander of the Mediterranean repudiated the agreement. When fighting resumed, Kléber successfully defeated the main Turkish army at Heliopolis in March, 1800, but he was assassinated by an Egyptian nationalist in June.

Kléber's successor, General Jacques-François de Menou, unpopular and considered incompetent, failed to prevent the landing of a large British army commanded by General Ralph Abercromby. On March 21, 1801, the British won a major victory at Canopus. As Menou quarreled with his officers, British and Turkish forces isolated the French in Cairo and Alexandria. The Cairo garrison surrendered on July 28, and Menou surrendered his forces at Alexandria on September 2, 1801. By the terms of the surrender, the surviving French troops, numbering about eleven thousand, were allowed to return home.

SIGNIFICANCE

For the French, the Egyptian campaign was a military disaster. In addition to a great loss of money and lives, the French navy was decimated, which allowed the British to gain hegemony over the Mediterranean. By returning home before the final defeat occurred, however, Bonaparte managed to escape most of the blame. By 1801, as first consul of a dictatorial government, he was able to control public reporting of the ill-advised adventure, aggrandizing his own role and placing the blame for failure on others.

The French expedition, however, did a great deal to increase knowledge of Egyptian history and culture. In Rosetta, French scholars discovered the famous Rosetta stone inscribed in ancient hieroglyphics, demotic, and Greek, which provided the Egyptologist Jean François Champollion with the key to deciphering hieroglyphics. Bonaparte also established the Egyptian Institute of Arts and Sciences, which would become a center of scholarship.

The invasion had the long-term consequence of promoting significant change in Egypt and elsewhere in the Middle East. The French brought with them many of the elements of modernization, including powerful weapons and printing presses. The defeat of the Mamlūks, moreover, created a vacuum that was soon filled by a powerful leader, Muḥammad ʿAlī Pasha, who would look to Western Europe as a model for building a modern state. The expedition had almost no influence on the later digging of the Suez Canal, in large part because surveyor Jacques Le Père mistakenly concluded that such a project was technically impossible.

—Thomas Tandy Lewis

FURTHER READING

Barthrop, Michael. *Napoleon's Egyptian Campaigns, 1798-1799.* London: Osprey, 1978. Very brief account that is useful as a quick reference for basic facts.

Bierman, Irene, ed. *Napoleon in Egypt.* Ithaca, N.Y.: Cornell University Press, 2003. Ten essays that consider topics like the background of Napoleon's invasion, its impact, al-Jabarti's views, and colonial ideology.

Foreman, Laura, and Ellen Phillips. *Napoleon's Lost Fleet: Bonaparte, Nelson, and the Battle of the Nile.* New York: Discovery Books, 1999. Excellent discussions of the two leaders, Nelson's destruction of the French fleet, and the archaeological excavation of

1790's

drowned relics and treasures at Abū Qīr Bay in 1998. Superb illustrations.

Henry, George A. *At Aboukir and Acre: A Story of Napoleon's Invasion of Egypt*. London, Ont.: Althouse Press, 2002. Excellent source for details about military strategy and battles.

Herold, J. Christopher. *Bonaparte in Egypt*. New York: Harper & Row, 1962. A standard and respected narrative that goes into considerable detail.

Jabarti, Shaykh Al-. *Napoleon in Egypt: Al-Jabarti's Chronicle of the French Occupation, 1798*. New York: Markus Wiener, 1993. Interesting book by a contemporary Arab historian who considered the French invaders "uncouth barbarians" and denounced their religion, morality, government, and civilization.

Lloyd, Christopher. *The Nile Campaign: Nelson and Napoleon in Egypt*. New York: Barnes & Noble Books, 1973. Good short summaries of the two men and their battles, with many original documents and illustrations.

Mackesy, Piers. *British Victory in Egypt, 1801: The End of Napoleon's Conquest*. New York: Routledge, 1995. An account of Sir Ralph Abercromby's expeditionary force to Egypt that dislodged the French presence in Egypt in 1801.

Marshall-Cornwall, James. *Napoleon as Military Commander*. New York: Penguin, 2002. A balanced analysis of Napoleon's military career and his influence.

Meyerson, Daniel. *The Linguist and the Emperor: Napoleon and Champollion's Quest to Decipher the Rosetta Stone*. New York: Random House, 2004. Fascinating narrative account of how the lives of the two Frenchmen converged to produce a revolutionary understanding of the Egyptian past.

SEE ALSO: July 14, 1789: Fall of the Bastille; Apr. 20, 1792-Oct., 1797: Early Wars of the French Revolution; Sept. 20, 1792: Battle of Valmy; July 27-28, 1794: Fall of Robespierre; Mar., 1796-Oct. 17, 1797: Napoleon's Italian Campaigns; Aug. 1-2, 1798: Battle of the Nile; July 19, 1799: Discovery of the Rosetta Stone; Nov. 9-10, 1799: Napoleon Rises to Power in France.

RELATED ARTICLES in *Great Lives from History: The Eighteenth Century, 1701-1800*: Lazare Carnot; Georges Danton; Robespierre.

May-November, 1798
IRISH REBELLION

Motivated by the example of the French and the American Revolutions, Irish nationalists planned rebellion against British control. Although the uprisings were mainly uncoordinated and short-lived, the revolt acted as an inspiration for subsequent generations of Irish Nationalists and, more immediately, set in motion the union between England and Ireland.

LOCALE: Ireland

CATEGORIES: Wars, uprisings, and civil unrest; government and politics; expansion and land acquisition

KEY FIGURES

Wolfe Tone (1763-1798), United Irish leader

Lord Edward Fitzgerald (1763-1798), leader of the Leinster Directory of the United Irishmen

First Marquess Cornwallis (Charles Cornwallis; 1738-1805), lord lieutenant of Ireland, 1798-1801

Beauchamp Bagenal Harvey (1762-1798), lawyer and United Irish leader

Jean-Joseph Humbert (1755-1823), French military commander

Gerard Lake (First Viscount Lake of Delhi; 1744-1808), commander of British forces in Ireland, 1798-1799

James Napper Tandy (1740-1803), United Irish leader

John Murphy (1753-1798), Roman Catholic priest and rebel leader

Henry Joy McCracken (1767-1798), commander of United Irish in County Antrim

Henry Monro (1758-1798), leader of Irish rebel forces in County Down

SUMMARY OF EVENT

The American Revolution and, even more acutely, the French Revolution in 1789 gave a more coherent form and purpose to widespread discontent in Ireland over British domination. In Belfast in 1791, the first United Irish Society was formed by members of the Protestant middle class, the lawyer James Napper Tandy becoming its first secretary. United Irish societies, which were then established throughout much of the country, were dedicated to the principles of liberal democracy as practiced in the Revolutionary United States and in France.

Particularly close ties were forged between the United Irishmen and the French government; these ties strengthened as authorities in Britain in Ireland began cracking down on their activities as subversive and threatening members with arrest. In the face of repressive tactics, some United Irish became more radical, advocating violent rebellion, which they hoped would be assisted by French intervention. Napper Tandy and Wolfe Tone, in particular, became active in plotting such an insurrection with authorities of the Directory—the French government at that time. In Ireland, radical leaders formed provincial or county and city "directories" of their own, so to coordinate the efforts of United Irish agents abroad. By early 1796, the mainly urban, Protestant United Irish were making common cause with the agrarian Catholic Defenders with the potential of creating a powerful rebel army. In December, 1796, a French fleet carrying fifteen thousand troops—under the command of General Lazare Hoche and accompanied by Wolfe Tone—made an abortive attempt to land in County Cork but was frustrated by bad weather.

The long-awaited revolt was set for spring of 1798, but the government at Dublin, warned by informants, took stern measures. The new British military commander in Ireland, General Gerard Lake, who had a reputation for ruthlessness, tried to forestall trouble by rooting out subversives and arresting the leadership of the United Irish Leinster Directory. The most serious loss was that of Lord Edward Fitzgerald, the chair of the Directory, who eluded capture for a while but was shot in the shoulder and apprehended after a fierce struggle on May 19. He eventually died of his wound on June 4, 1798.

The death of Fitzgerald and the imprisonment of his colleagues left the movement without a central, guiding hand, and the uprisings were consequently ill-planned, disorganized, and short-lived. Localized revolts in Counties Kildare, Laois, Offaly, Carlow, and Meath from May 23 to July 14 were soon quelled. In County Antrim, a better-organized force under Henry Joy McCracken enjoyed some initial success, but it was destroyed on June 7 at the Battle of Antrim; several miles away, the United Irish Rising in County Down under Henry Monro was defeated at the Battle of Ballinahinch on June 13. In County Wexford, where fighting broke out on May 26, the scenario was different. The movement there, led by Beauchamp Bagenal Harvey, Father John Murphy, and others, enjoyed spectacular success, took control of the county, and for a brief moment engendered a "Republic of Wexford" (proclaimed May 31-June 26).

The situation was considered serious enough for the British government to dispatch the seasoned general and administrator the first Marquess Cornwallis to Dublin as lord lieutenant.

Without promised assistance from the French government, the rebels in Wexford suffered significant setbacks at New Ross and Arklow before being crushed by Lake's forces at Vinegar Hill on June 21. Shortly thereafter, Harvey, Father Murphy, Monro, and McCracken, among others, were executed. On August 22, the French made an unexpected landing in western Ireland at Killala, County Mayo. Again, there was a heady, initial victory: The French badly routed a British force on August 27 at the Battle of Castlebar (which was dubbed the "Castlebar Races" in recognition of the speed with which the British left the field) and pushed into the Midlands. However, without substantial local support, French general Jean-Joseph Humbert was beaten and forced to surrender to Lake at Ballinamuck, County Longford, on September 8. Irishmen serving in the French ranks were slaughtered.

Tandy and Tone belatedly attempted to effect a landing. Tandy actually made landfall on September 16 at Rutland Island, off County Donegal. Learning of Humbert's surrender and knowing that his force of itself was inadequate, Tandy withdrew. Tone, who sailed with the fleet of French admiral Jean Bompart, actually engaged in action with a British fleet off the northwest coast of Ireland. The British were victorious and captured Tone as he tried to land at Buncrana, in County Donegal, on November 3. Tone was tried, found guilty of treason, and sentenced to hang, but he slit his own throat two days later to "cheat" the hangman. He lingered a week before dying on November 19, 1798.

1790's

SIGNIFICANCE

Tone's death marked the effective end of the rebellion, though partisan bands operating in the Wicklow Mountains remained undefeated and operated against Crown forces until 1803. Though the insurrection achieved little militarily, its political repercussions were significant. British prime minister William Pitt the Younger was able to play on fears that an autonomously governed Ireland might be more vulnerable to future revolts and attacks from foreign powers and successfully pressed for the absorption of the independent Irish parliament into that of Britain. The Act of Union, as this arrangement was termed, was officially consummated on January 1, 1801, and Great Britain and Ireland merged into the United Kingdom.

—*Raymond Pierre Hylton*

FURTHER READING

Elliot, Marianne. *Partners in Revolution: The United Irishmen and France.* New Haven, Conn.: Yale University Press, 1982. A very thorough explanation of the close and tight connection between French Revolutionary ideals and those fostered by the Irish rebels.

Geoghegan, Patrick M. *The Irish Act of Union: A Study in High Politics, 1798-1801.* New York: St. Martin's Press, 1999. Describes, among other things, the galvanizing effect of the 1798 rebellion on William Pitt the Younger's campaign to unite the crowns of Great Britain and Ireland.

Jackson, Alvin. *Ireland, 1798-1998: Politics and War.* Oxford, England: Blackwell, 1999. The author sets great store in depicting the 1798 rising as a key to subsequent long-term political developments in Ireland.

Keogh, Daire, and Nicholas Furlong, eds. *The Mighty Wave: The 1798 Rebellion in Wexford.* Blackrock, County Dublin, Ireland: Four Courts Press, 1996. Gives a detailed description of the action taking place in the Irish county that was most profoundly affected by the rising.

Moody, T. W., and F. X. Martin. *The Course of Irish History.* Cork, Ireland: Mercier Press, 1984. Sets the 1798 risings quite readily into the overall Irish historical context. The time line offered is quite useful.

O'Donnell, Ruan. *The Rebellion in Wicklow, 1798.* Dublin: Irish Academic Press, 1998. Sheds light on the little-known story of rebellion and rebel activities in the mountainous region bordering on the County Dublin and near Ireland's capital city.

Pakenham, Thomas. *The Year of Liberty: The Great Irish Rebellion of 1798.* New York: Random House, 1997. By far the most complete and readable of the general histories of the rebellion, suitable for both scholars and nonacademics.

Tyrrell, John. *Weather and Warfare: A Climatic History of the 1798 Rebellion.* Wilton, County Cork, Ireland: The Collins Press, 2001. An unprecedented approach that makes a case for the decisive nature of meteorological phenomena during the course of the revolution.

SEE ALSO: 1726: Swift Satirizes English Rule of Ireland in *Gulliver's Travels*; Sept. 10, 1763: Publication of the *Freeman's Journal*; Jan. 4, 1792-1797: The *Northern Star* Calls for Irish Independence.

RELATED ARTICLES in *Great Lives from History: The Eighteenth Century, 1701-1800*: First Marquess Cornwallis; William Pitt the Younger; Wolfe Tone.

June 25-July 14, 1798
ALIEN AND SEDITION ACTS

The Alien and Sedition Acts were enacted by a Federalist-controlled U.S. Congress in the hope of not only suppressing the immigrant vote, which had been aligning most often with the Republican Party, but also deporting noncitizens during wartime and noncitizens who were considered a threat to public safety. The Sedition Act, passed in the hope of limiting the power of the Republican press especially, made it a crime to write or publish criticisms of the federal government.

LOCALE: Philadelphia, Pennsylvania

CATEGORIES: Laws, acts, and legal history; government and politics; diplomacy and international relations; communications; organizations and institutions

KEY FIGURES

John Adams (1735-1826), second president of the United States, 1797-1801

William Duane (1760-1835), Republican editor of the Philadelphia *Aurora* who was prosecuted under the Sedition Act

Albert Gallatin (1761-1849), Republican congressman from Pennsylvania who opposed the Alien and Sedition Acts

Thomas Jefferson (1743-1826), vice president of the United States and author of the Virginia Resolutions

Matthew Lyon (1750-1822), Republican congressman who was prosecuted under the Sedition Act

Timothy Pickering (1745-1829), secretary of state and chief enforcement officer of the Alien and Sedition Acts

Harrison Gray Otis (1765-1848), Federalist senator from Massachusetts and one of the chief architects of the Alien and Sedition Acts

SUMMARY OF EVENT

News of the XYZ affair, a major conflict between the United States and France, descended upon the American people and their representatives in Congress like a thunderbolt. It galvanized the government into action on the high seas; it helped unite Americans against the French, just as the initial news of British seizures had united them against Great Britain; it seriously weakened the infant Republican Party, which was associated with Francophilism; and it firmly entrenched the Federalists in power. Even President John Adams, for a time, seemed to relish the thought of leading the United States against its newest antagonist, but Adams regained his sense of moderation in time to prevent a catastrophe. The same cannot be said of certain elements of the Federalist Party, which exploited the explosive situation to strike out at their political opponents.

The Federalist Party, or at least its old guard, deeply resented gains made by the Republican opposition. Many of the Federalist leaders resented the very existence of the other political party. The High Federalists were by no means committed to a two-party system and rejected the idea of a loyal opposition. With the Republican tide at low ebb, these Federalists intended to strike a killing blow at two sources of Republican strength: the immigrant vote and the manipulation of public opinion through the use (and abuse) of the press. In selecting these targets, the Federalists demonstrated an acute awareness of the impact of the press on the growth of political parties, and they intended to use their political power to muzzle the Republican press, while leaving the Federalist press intact. Furthermore, Federalists expressed a deep xenophobia, as they viewed people of foreign birth as threats to the fabric of ordered liberty they believed the Federalists had built and must preserve.

Many Federalists had a long history of antiforeign sentiment. With the United States on the verge of war with France, the Federalists were apprehensive over the loyalty of thousands of French West Indian refugees who had flocked to the United States in an effort to escape the ferment of the French Revolution and its accompanying "terror." The Federalists were further concerned that the refugees who became U.S. citizens generally aligned themselves with the Republican Party. Much the same was true of the Irish, who supported anyone who opposed the English. Such conditions threatened the continued hold of the Federalists on political power in the national government. To deal with such potential subversives, foreign and domestic, the Federalist-controlled Congress passed a series of four acts, known collectively as the Alien and Sedition Acts.

Three of the acts dealt specifically with aliens or immigrants. The Sedition Act declared speech or writing with the intent to defame the president or Congress to be a misdemeanor. The Alien Friends Act permitted the president to deport allegedly dangerous aliens during times of peace. A third act, the Alien Enemies Act, authorized the imprisonment or deportation of aliens in wartime. The Naturalization Act struck at the immigrant

---

ALIEN AND SEDITION ACTS

Congress passed the Alien and Sedition Acts in the summer of 1798, condemning subversiveness not only among immigrants and noncitizens but also among citizens who dared disagree with the federal government. The acts, excerpted here, were adopted without regard for the civil rights outlined in the U.S. Constitution and the Bill of Rights, and were so unpopular that they were repealed after two years.

AN ACT CONCERNING ALIENS.

Sec. 1: That is shall be lawful for the President of the United States at any time during the continuance of this act, to *order* all such *aliens* as he shall judge dangerous to the peace and safety of the United States, or shall have reasonable grounds to suspect are concerned in any treasonable or secret machinations against the government thereof, to depart [be deported] out of the territory of the United States. . . . (June 25, 1798, p. 571)

AN ACT FOR THE PUNISHMENT OF CERTAIN CRIMES AGAINST THE UNITED STATES.

Sec. 1: That if any persons shall unlawfully combine or conspire together, with intent to oppose any measure of measures of the government of the United States, which are or shall be directed by proper authority, or to impede the operation of any law of the United States, or to intimidate or prevent any person holding a place or office in or under the government of the United States, from undertaking, performing or executing his trust or duty. . . shall be punished. . . .

Sec. 2: That if any person shall write, print, utter or publish . . . any false, scandalous and malicious writing or writing against the government of the United States, . . . or to stir up sedition, or to excite any unlawful combinations therein, for opposing or resisting any law of the United States, or any act of the President of the United States, . . . shall be punished. . . . (July 14, 1798, p. 596)

Source: Statutes at Large, 5th Cong., Sess. II, June 25 and July 14, 1798. Library of Congress, U.S. Documents and Debates, 1774-1875. http://memory.loc.gov/ammem/amlaw/lwsl.html. Accessed August, 2005.

1790's

vote. Previously, aliens could become naturalized citizens after residing for five years in the United States. The new act raised the probationary period to fourteen years.

The Sedition Act was by far the most notorious. It imposed heavy fines and imprisonment as punishment on all those found guilty of writing, publishing, or speaking against the federal government. By allowing a defendant to prove the truth of statements as a defense, the Sedition Act was a definite improvement over the English laws of sedition libel. The fact remains, however, that its intent was the repression of political opposition and the annoying Republican press, and the Sedition Act seemed plainly to ignore the First Amendment. Under the law, suits were initiated against the editors of eight major opposition presses. The principal target was the Philadelphia *Aurora*, whose editor, William Duane, was prosecuted under the act. Congressman Matthew Lyon of Vermont received a jail sentence of four months and was fined $1,000 for disparaging remarks he made about President Adams. Some of these suits gave a comic air to the gross abuse of power. One gentleman was fined $100 for wishing out loud that the wadding of a salute cannon would strike President Adams in his backside.

Republican opposition to these laws was immediate. Vice President Thomas Jefferson, himself a Republican, believed that the Alien and Sedition Acts were designed to be used against such leading Republicans as the Swiss-born congressman from Pennsylvania, Albert Gallatin. Republicans were convinced that the Sedition Act was designed to destroy them as an organized political party. The act had passed the house strictly along sectional-party lines. The vote was forty-four to forty-one, with only two affirmative votes coming from south of the Potomac River, where the Republicans were strongest.

SIGNIFICANCE

From the Federalist point of view, the Alien and Sedition Acts were completely unsuccessful in suppressing the opposition. They were resented by many, and it soon became obvious even to those who first supported the new laws that they were as unnecessary as they were ineffective. The handful of "subversives" prosecuted under the Sedition Act hardly compensated for the fact that its existence gave the Republicans another campaign issue. Jefferson through the Kentucky legislature, and Madison through the Virginia legislature, penned immediate responses to the Alien and Sedition Acts. These remonstrances, known as the Virginia and Kentucky Resolves, aroused little enthusiasm at the time but did point out not only some of the basic principles of the Republican Party

but also some striking differences between two streams of thought within the party.

Both resolutions maintained that the Constitution was a compact between sovereign states that granted to the federal government certain narrowly defined powers, while retaining all other enumerated powers. If the states created the Constitution, they had the power to decide when the federal government had overstepped its proper bounds. Jefferson, in the Kentucky Resolves, went much further than Madison in assigning to the states the power to nullify a federal law—to declare it inoperable and void within the boundaries of a state. South Carolina was to do so in 1832, when it nullified the Tariff of 1828. The Virginia and Kentucky Resolves had no immediate effect, but they had spelled out the theoretical position that those advocating states' rights could, and ultimately did, take.

The Alien and Sedition Acts took their place among a growing list of grievances against the Federalist Party. The Alien Acts expired in 1800 and the Sedition Act in the following year. The Naturalization Act was repealed by the Republican-controlled Congress in 1802. The only tangible effect of these measures was to contribute to the defeat of Federalism in 1800. However, the mood that led to their passage was to return in later days.

—*John G. Clark, updated by Edward R. Crowther*

FURTHER READING

Elkins, Stanley, and Eric McKitrick. *The Age of Federalism: The Early American Republic, 1788-1800.* New York: Oxford University Press, 1993. Chapter 15 of this gracefully written document captures the motives and mentalities of the principals responsible for the acts.

McCoy, Drew R. *The Elusive Republic: Political Economy in Jefferson's America.* Chapel Hill: University of North Carolina Press, 1980. Contains an excellent discussion of the competing theories of society and government discussed by Federalists and Republicans.

McCullough, David G. *John Adams.* New York: Simon & Schuster, 2001. The definitive, best-selling biography provides a detailed account of Adams's presidential administration, including the XYZ affair and the adoption and impact of the Alien and Sedition Acts.

Miller, John C. *Crisis in Freedom: The Alien and Sedition Acts.* Boston: Little, Brown, 1951. A thorough and judicious narrative of the passage of, and response to, the Alien and Sedition Acts.

Sharp, James Roger. *American Politics in the Early Republic: The New Nation in Crisis.* New Haven, Conn.:

Yale University Press, 1993. Places the Alien and Sedition Acts in the context of the politics of the 1790's.

Smith, James Morton. *Freedom's Fetters: The Alien and Sedition Laws and American Civil Liberties.* Ithaca, N.Y.: Cornell University Press, 1966. Contains an excellent discussion of the congressional debates concerning the passage of these laws.

Stone, Geoffrey R. *Perilous Times: Free Speech in Wartime from the Sedition Act of 1798 to the War on Terrorism.* New York: W. W. Norton, 2004. This book, written after the September 11, 2001, terrorist attacks on the Pentagon in Washington, D.C., and the World Trade Center in New York City, examines how American liberties have been curtailed during wars or national emergencies. It cites passage of the Alien and Sedition Acts as an example of this restriction and de-

scribes the acts and the trial of Republican congress member Matthew Lyon.

SEE ALSO: Beginning Apr., 1763: The *North Briton* Controversy; Oct. 27, 1787-May, 1788: Publication of *The Federalist*; Sept. 24, 1789: Judiciary Act; 1790's: First U.S. Political Parties; Dec. 15, 1791: U.S. Bill of Rights Is Ratified; 1792-1793: Fichte Advocates Free Speech; Apr. 20, 1792-Oct., 1797: Early Wars of the French Revolution; Nov. 19, 1794: Jay's Treaty; Oct. 27, 1795: Pinckney's Treaty; Oct. 4, 1797-Sept. 30, 1800: XYZ Affair.

RELATED ARTICLES in *Great Lives from History: The Eighteenth Century, 1701-1800*: John Adams; Samuel Chase; Elbridge Gerry; Thomas Jefferson; James Madison; John Wilkes.

August 1-2, 1798
BATTLE OF THE NILE

The Battle of the Nile destroyed the French fleet, isolated more than thirty-five thousand French soldiers in Egypt, and ended Napoleon Bonaparte's attempt to march eastward to India.

ALSO KNOWN AS: Battle of Aboukir Bay
LOCALE: Abū Qīr Bay, near Alexandria, Egypt
CATEGORY: Wars, uprisings, and civil unrest

KEY FIGURES
Napoleon Bonaparte (1769-1821), French military commander and later emperor as Napoleon I, r. 1804-1814, 1815
François-Paul Brueys d'Aigalliers (1753-1798), commander of the French fleet
Lord Nelson (Horatio Nelson; 1758-1805), British rear admiral, and later baron, 1798-1801, vice admiral, 1801-1805, and viscount, 1801-1805

SUMMARY OF EVENT
Napoleon Bonaparte's conclusion of peace with Austria in 1797-1798 brought a temporary cessation of hostilities on the Continent. Only France and Great Britain remained belligerents. However, since France could not control the English Channel long enough to invade the island kingdom successfully, and the British had no sizable army, the war between the two powers had reached a stalemate. Napoleon Bonaparte, then a promising young French general, proposed to the Directory that the best

way to conquer the British would be to attack their trade routes to the East.

On May 19, 1798, he sailed from Toulon at the head of a military expedition bound for Egypt and thence, it was hoped, for India. After stopping at Malta long enough to raise the French flag and reorganize the government, Bonaparte landed his army near Alexandria at the beginning of July. He took the city by assault with little difficulty, and the French army then marched southeast to the Rosetta leg of the Nile and south to Cairo. Within sight of the pyramids at Giza, the Egyptian army was defeated, and Bonaparte occupied the capital on July 24, 1798.

For all practical purposes, Egypt had been conquered. The defeated army split into two sections, one fleeing north along the Nile and the other into Syria, each pursued by French divisions. Napoleon was pleased with this military success and was confident that he would return to France in the fall as he had intended. On August 2, however, he received the startling news that the French fleet, which had convoyed his four hundred transports the length of the Mediterranean, had been annihilated.

Following the capture of Alexandria, the French had used its harbor to unload equipment and supplies. The entrance to the Old Harbor, which was protected by fortifications, was believed to be too shallow to accommodate thirteen ships of the line. So Admiral François-Paul Brueys d'Aigalliers, commander of the French fleet under Bonaparte, sailed 15 miles northeast along the coast to Abū Qīr

1790's

911

The Battle of the Nile. (Francis R. Niglutsch)

Bay (also known as Aboukir Bay). There, he anchored the thirteen ships in line parallel to the shore, with two frigates between the shore and the last ship at each side. He believed that with this positioning he could ward off any possible attack by the British Mediterranean fleet.

Horatio Nelson, then a rear admiral, commanded fourteen British ships of the line. He had attempted to intercept the French armada while it was crossing the Mediterranean, but the two forces had missed each other and Nelson had actually reached Alexandria ahead of his prey. Finding no trace of the French ships, he sailed north along the coasts of Syria and Asia Minor; still unable to sight the French navy, he returned to the Nile Delta. Late in the afternoon of August 1, the British fleet appeared on the horizon north of Abū Qīr Bay. Dispensing with the customary precautions (which would have delayed the battle until the following morning), Nelson ordered his captains to attack the enemy at once.

The French were caught unprepared. A third of Brueys's men were ashore gathering supplies and digging wells. Moreover, the French ships had been an-

chored too far from shore. Brueys's defensive position was based upon the theory that the British would have to attack from the seaward side while they were still under sail; all guns were pointed out to sea with no firepower facing the shore. Nelson quickly summed up this weakness and ordered a number of his captains to position their ships between the French fleet and the shore. The leading British ship, taking a calculated risk that the water would be deep enough, carried out this maneuver successfully; it was soon followed by a second, and then three more which broke through the French line. Before long the French ships were being bombarded from two sides at once, with fire being concentrated on the massive French flagship *L'Orient*, which blew up with extensive loss of life.

The battle raged throughout the night of August 1 and the following morning. The French suffered a major defeat. Eleven battleships were destroyed or captured, and Admiral Brueys was killed. Only two French ships of the line and two frigates escaped, and even these stragglers were later destroyed by Nelson's fleet.

SIGNIFICANCE

In the Battle of the Nile, Nelson received his second serious wound, a gunshot to the forehead, but he gained control of the Mediterranean Sea in a single decisive engagement. The islands of Minorca and Malta were recaptured shortly afterward, while at home the rise of prestige allowed Prime Minister William Pitt the Younger to negotiate the Second Coalition, with the result that Austria, Russia, and Turkey declared war on France.

The defeat of the French fleet trapped more than thirty-five thousand French soldiers in Egypt, and even though Napoleon had a victory on land, remaining there would have been difficult. It was not, however, impossible, and the remaining French ships in the Mediterranean, combined with the Spanish, outnumbered Nelson's fleet. Nevertheless, Napoleon abandoned his troops, escaping on a small vessel. It foreshadowed several instances in his military career when he deserted his armies in the field to flee to safety. Fewer than eight thousand of the French soldiers reached their homeland. Napoleon, however, returned to usher out the Directory and to take his place as one of the three members of the Consulate, then quickly elevated himself to first consul, then, finally, emperor for life. As for the French fleet, the Battle of the Nile represented only the first of a pair of critical defeats administered by Admiral Nelson.

—*John G. Gallaher, updated by Larry Schweikart*

FURTHER READING

Foreman, Laura, and Ellen Blue Phillips. *Napoleon's Lost Fleet: Bonaparte, Nelson, and the Battle of the Nile*. New York: Discovery Books, 1999. Popular history of the battle and the underwater archaeological expedition to recover the remains of *L'Orient* in Abū Qīr Bay. Lavishly illustrated.

Gray, Colin S. *The Leverage of Sea Power: The Strategic Advantage of Navies in War*. New York: Free Press, 1992. Although Gray does not examine Abū Qīr Bay specifically, he nevertheless treats the British-French naval struggle of 1688-1815 in detail, investigating naval strategy and technology, especially as they pertain to the outcome of land warfare.

Herold, J. Christopher. *Bonaparte in Egypt*. New York: Harper & Row, 1962. This remains the classic work on the military campaign in Egypt, including a full chapter devoted to the naval battle. Once again, a pro-British perspective that might be balanced with the broader work of David Chandler, whose 1967 work, *The Campaigns of Napoleon*, claims that the battle, while not immediately decisive, ended Napoleon's long-term objectives.

Knight, Roger. *The Pursuit of Victory: The Life and Achievement of Horatio Nelson*. New York: Basic Books, 2005. An authoritative and complete, scholarly biography of Admiral Nelson.

Lavery, Brian. *Nelson and the Nile: The Naval War Against Bonaparte, 1798*. Annapolis, Md.: Naval Institute Press, 1998. A strategic analysis of the battle, describing the military and political factors that sent Nelson in pursuit of the French.

_____. *Nelson's Navy: The Ships, Men, and Organization, 1793-1815*. Annapolis, Md.: Naval Institute Press, 1989. An excellent investigation into the British Navy in the Napoleonic era.

Mahan, Alfred T. *Influence of Sea Power upon the French Revolution and Empire, 1793-1812*. 2 vols. Reprint. New York: Greenwood Press, 1968. First published in 1892, this is a classic work of scholarship and an outstanding work on the topic, putting the Battle of the Nile in a central position in the decline of French sea power.

Marcus, Geoffrey. *The Age of Nelson: The Royal Navy, 1793-1815*. New York: Viking, 1971. Discusses the Royal Navy, including changes in equipment and administration, more than particular battles, but does contain material on strategy and tactics.

Rodger, A. B. *The War of the Second Coalition, 1798-1801*. Oxford, England: Clarendon Press, 1964. Includes an excellent chapter on the battle and its consequences.

Tracy, Nicholas. *Nelson's Battles: The Art of Victory in the Age of Sail*. Annapolis, Md.: Naval Institute Press, 1996. Detailed account of Nelson's naval career, including the Nile campaign. Describes the conditions of naval warfare in the eighteenth and nineteenth centuries.

Warner, Oliver. *The Battle of the Nile*. London: B. T. Batsford, 1960. A pro-British history of the campaign with particular emphasis on the genius of Nelson. Useful for capturing the mood of each fleet on the eve of battle.

SEE ALSO: Apr. 20, 1792-Oct., 1797: Early Wars of the French Revolution; Mar., 1796-Oct. 17, 1797: Napoleon's Italian Campaigns; Apr. 12, 1798-Sept. 2, 1801: Napoleon's Egyptian Campaign; Nov. 9-10, 1799: Napoleon Rises to Power in France.

RELATED ARTICLE in *Great Lives from History: The Eighteenth Century, 1701-1800*: William Pitt the Younger.

1790's

1799
CODE OF HANDSOME LAKE

The Seneca religious leader Handsome Lake founded the Longhouse religion, which merged Native American and Christian traditions. Both successful and controversial, the Longhouse religion was an attempt to revive indigenous cultures within the context of the contemporary experience of Native Americans.

LOCALE: Western New York State
CATEGORY: Religion and theology

KEY FIGURES

Handsome Lake (Ganeodiyo; c. 1735-1815), Seneca religious leader

Cornplanter (Kayehtwanken, John O'Bail; 1732/1740-1836), Seneca chief and half brother of Handsome Lake

Red Jacket (Sagoyewátha; c. 1756-1830), Seneca chief and nephew of Handsome Lake

Louis Hall (Karoniaktajeh; c. 1920-1993), Mohawk leader of the Warrior Society

Arthur Caswell Parker (1881-1955), Seneca ethnologist and historian

SUMMARY OF EVENT

The Code of Handsome Lake was one of several Native American religions that evolved in reaction to European colonization. These religions often combined traditional Native American beliefs and rituals with the introduction of a Christian-style savior who was said to be able to recapture for Native Americans the better days they had known before colonization. One well-known example of this fusion was the Ghost Dance religion, which was begun by the prophet Wovoka, who had been raised with both indigenous and Christian influences. Tenskwatawa (also known as the Delaware Prophet) also formulated a religion that combined both traditions during the eighteenth century.

Handsome Lake was born at Canawaugus, a Seneca village near contemporary Avon, New York, on the Genesee River. He was a member of the Seneca nation, one of the five nations that had joined together as the Iroquois Confederacy. His personal name was Ganeodiyo; Handsome Lake, a reference to Lake Ontario, is one of the fifty chieftainship lines of the Iroquois Confederacy, a title bestowed on him by clan mothers. He was a half brother of the Seneca chief Cornplanter and an uncle of Red Jacket. Handsome Lake and many other Senecas sided with the British in the French and Indian War and

the American Revolution. George Washington and his subcommanders, principally General John Sullivan, were merciless with Native Americans who supported the British. During the late stages of the revolution, many Seneca communities were laid to waste by scorched-earth marches that destroyed crops, livestock, and homes.

After that war, many Iroquois and other Native Americans who had supported the British were forced into Canada, principally to lands secured by Joseph Brant at Grand River. Others fled westward to join other Native Americans who were still free. Those who remained in their homelands were forced onto small, impoverished reservations, and repeated attempts were made to force them out. It is estimated that by 1794, the Iroquois population had shrunk to approximately four thousand people.

Handsome Lake's revival occurred in an atmosphere of dissension within a fractured Iroquois Confederacy. The course of his life reflected the devastation of his people. Born into a prominent family of the Turtle Clan, Handsome Lake distinguished himself as a leader as a young man, before the American Revolution, when Iroquois society was still largely intact. Handsome Lake's decline began after his birthplace was taken by whites, and he was forced to move to the Allegheny Seneca reservation. The Seneca ethnologist Arthur Parker characterized Handsome Lake as a middle-sized man, unhealthy looking, dissolute, and an alcoholic. After four years lying ill in a small cabin under the care of a daughter, Handsome Lake began having a series of visions. Later, he used these visions to rally the Iroquois at a time when some of them were selling their entire winter harvest of furs for hard liquor, turning traditional ceremonies into drunken brawls, and in winter, often dying of exposure in drunken stupors.

Handsome Lake experienced considerable remorse over his alcoholism but did not stop drinking. In 1799, Handsome Lake experienced a number of visions in which he was taken on a great journey to the sky. During this journey, he was shown a number of personages and events from the past, present, and future. In one of his visions, Handsome Lake met George Washington, who had died that year, and heard him confirm the sovereignty of the Iroquois.

After this series of visions, Handsome Lake stopped his heavy drinking and later committed his code to writing. He persuaded many other Iroquois to stop drinking and to reconstruct their lives. During his own lifetime, Handsome Lake achieved some political influence among the Senecas, but his popularity was limited because of his ideological rigidity. In 1801 and 1802, he traveled to Washington, D.C., with a delegation of Senecas to meet with President Thomas Jefferson and resist the reduction of Iroquois landholdings.

SIGNIFICANCE

Handsome Lake's largest following came after his death. His code combined European religious influences (especially those practiced by the Quakers, which Handsome Lake had studied) with a traditional Iroquois emphasis on family, community, and the centrality of the land to the maintenance of culture. Adherents to his code rejected alcohol and accepted his concepts of social relationships, good, and evil, which closely resemble Quakerism.

The Quaker creed appealed to many Iroquois because the Quakers had been persecuted before coming to America, they had no ornate temples, and they lived frugally and communally, doing their best to respect their Native American neighbors. A nationalistic figure in a religious context, Handsome Lake also borrowed heavily from the Iroquois Great Law of Treaty, popularizing concepts such as looking into the future for seven generations and regarding the Earth as mother, ideas that became part of pan-Indian thought across North America and were incorporated into modern popular environmental symbolism.

With its combination of Old and New World theologies, the Code of Handsome Lake sought to reconcile the gods of Europe and America. It was to be so successful that it both subsumed the ancient religion and halted the spread of Christianity among the Iroquois. The Code of Handsome Lake has continued to be widely followed in Iroquois country as the Longhouse religion. In the late twentieth century, roughly one-third of the thirty thousand Iroquois in New York State attended Longhouse rites.

Although his code remained popular among many Iroquois, others accused Handsome Lake of having sold out to the Quakers and white religious interests in general. Louis Hall, ideological founder of the Warrior Society in Iroquois country, regarded the religion of Handsome Lake as a bastardized form of Christianity grafted onto indigenous traditions. Hall called Handsome Lake's visions "the hallucinations of a drunk." Opposition to these teachings was one plank in an intellectual platform that allowed the Warriors to brand both the Mohawk Nation Council at Akwesasne and the Iroquois Confederacy Council as enemies of the people and to claim that the Warriors were the true protectors of "Mohawk sovereignty." Hall, who died in 1993, regarded Handsome Lake's followers as traitors or "Tontos." Hall's Warriors split bitterly with followers of Handsome Lake over gambling and other issues, leading to violence at Akwesasne, which peaked in 1990 with the deaths of two Mohawks.

—Bruce E. Johansen

FURTHER READING

Deardorff, Merle H. *The Religion of Handsome Lake: Its Origins and Development*. American Bureau of Ethnology Bulletin 149. Washington, D.C.: Smithsonian Institution Press, 1951. Presents a detailed analysis of the Handsome Lake religion from an ethnographic perspective.

Fenton, William N. *The Great Law and the Longhouse: A Political History of the Iroquois Confederacy*. Norman: University of Oklahoma Press, 1998. This meticulously detailed history of the confederacy and its member tribes includes information about the religion of Handsome Lake.

Handsome Lake. *The Code of Handsome Lake, the Seneca Prophet*. New York State Museum Bulletin 163. Albany: State University of New York Press, 1913. Outlines the Handsome Lake religion and discusses the historical circumstances of its creation.

Johansen, Bruce E. *Life and Death in Mohawk Country*. Golden, Colo.: North American Press, 1993. Details conflicts involving followers of Handsome Lake's code and Louis Hall's Warriors at Akwesasne in the late twentieth century.

Parker, Arthur. *Parker on the Iroquois*. Edited by William Fenton. Syracuse, N.Y.: Syracuse University Press, 1968. A detailed description of the Handsome Lake religion by a noted Seneca ethnologist.

Swartzler, David. *A Friend Among the Senecas: The Quaker Mission to Cornplanter's People*. Mechanicsburg, Pa.: Stackpole Books, 2000. Based upon the journal of a Quaker, the book recounts the 1799 Quaker mission to a Seneca village. Describes the Seneca culture, interactions between the Senecas and Quakers, and how Handsome Lake's religion developed in response to these interactions.

Wallace, Anthony F. C. *The Death and Rebirth of the Seneca*. New York: Alfred A. Knopf, 1970. A classic work on the history of the Seneca at the time of Handsome Lake.

Wright, Ronald. *Stolen Continents*. Boston: Houghton Mifflin, 1992. A wide-ranging study of North Amer-

1790's

ica since the voyages of Columbus. Contains extensive treatment of the Iroquois Confederacy; describes Handsome Lake and his religion in the general context of the subjugation of the confederacy after the Revolutionary War.

SEE ALSO: May 28, 1754-Feb. 10, 1763: French and Indian War; Oct. 7, 1763: Proclamation of 1763;

May 24 and June 11, 1776: Indian Delegation Meets with Congress; Oct. 22, 1784: Fort Stanwix Treaty; Oct. 18, 1790-July, 1794: Little Turtle's War.

RELATED ARTICLES in *Great Lives from History: The Eighteenth Century, 1701-1800*: Joseph Brant; Thomas Jefferson; Little Turtle; Alexander McGillivray; Pontiac; Thanadelthur; George Washington.

1799
DISCOVERY OF THE EARLIEST ANESTHETICS

The study of inhalant vapors at the Pneumatic Medical Institute led to Sir Humphry Davy's discovery that nitrous oxide, or laughing gas, could be used to alleviate pain. The gas was the first inhalant used as an anesthetic.

LOCALE: Clifton, Bristol, England
CATEGORIES: Health and medicine; chemistry; biology; science and technology

KEY FIGURES

Sir Humphry Davy (1778-1829), chemist who was the first to describe the effects of nitrous oxide as an anesthetic
Thomas Beddoes (1760-1808), physician and founder of the Pneumatic Medical Institute
James Watt (1736-1819), builder of the first apparatuses to deliver the gases
Joseph Priestley (1733-1804), a clergyman and amateur chemist who discovered nitrous oxide

SUMMARY OF EVENT

The earliest attempts at using agents for relief or prevention of pain date to the first century. The Roman encyclopedist and medical writer Aulus Cornelius Celsus noted the use of poppy seed extracts (opium) as a means of inducing sleep and as a treatment for earache and colic. Literature of the Middle Ages made frequent reference to a variety of narcotics, but several factors prevented the widespread application of such measures.

A common belief was that pain originated with God, and that to mitigate pain was to incur God's wrath. Certainly, some church clerics, and even medical personnel, supported such a belief, but there is little evidence of widespread support for this idea. More critical was ignorance in understanding the concept of dosage in using what were potentially fatal narcotics. A greater level of safety was developed only after an experimental ap-

proach was applied in testing such agents.

The latter part of the eighteenth century was noted for significant advances in chemistry. Among these advances was the discovery of the chemical elements, particularly those associated with atmospheric gases. This led to a better understanding of chemical compounds. Nitrous oxide, a colorless gas often referred to as "laughing gas," was discovered by the English chemist and clergyman Joseph Priestley in 1772, after he had heated ammonium nitrate with iron filings. Priestley, despite having no formal education in chemistry, also discovered oxygen, carbon monoxide, and carbon dioxide. He hoped to use nitrous oxide as a preservative. Though unsuccessful, Priestley did suggest that since the gases he discovered clearly were necessary for life, their use might have medical applications.

In the late 1780's, the English physician Thomas Beddoes attempted to use the newly discovered gases as inhalants in the treatment of disease, believing that some illnesses, such as tuberculosis, might respond to therapy with increased or decreased exposure to various inhalants. In 1798, he founded the Pneumatic Medical Institute in Bristol to study inhalants and disease treatment. James Watt, noted for his work on engines, was hired to build the apparatuses to manufacture the gases. Beddoes also hired a young scientist, Humphry Davy, to oversee the work as superintendent.

Although Davy clearly realized the significance of nitrous oxide for inhalation anesthesia, the procedure's application was overlooked by the medical establishment of the times. After noting the effects of the gas in the relief of pain associated with headaches or inflammations of the gum, the result of tooth decay, Davy resigned his position at the institution in 1801 and was hired as director of the chemical laboratory at the Royal Institution of Great Britain in London (and served as its president from 1820 to 1827). He devoted the remainder of his scientific career to the study of chemistry. The institution he founded produced no significant research on inhalation therapy. Nitrous oxide, although still used on occasion for its anesthetic properties, became better known as an intoxicant that induces a sense of exhilaration.

SIGNIFICANCE

The use of gas to alleviate pain, and its use as a form of anesthesia appropriate for surgery, was not dismissed or forgotten by the medical establishment. During the mid-nineteenth century, Crawford Long, a graduate from what is now the University of Georgia, William Morton, a dentist, and Horace Wells, also a dentist, began testing various gases for their ability to create euphoria or even sleep in prospective surgical patients. Utilizing both nitrous oxide and then ether, each independently applied the ability of these gases to induce sleep, allowing for surgical procedures with a minimum of pain to the patient. Ether proved more useful for invasive surgery, and nitrous oxide was used in treating tooth and gum disease.

—*Richard Adler*

FURTHER READING

Cartwright, F. F. "Humphry Davy's Contribution to Anesthesia." *Proceedings of the Royal Society of Medicine* 43 (1950): 571-578. A biography of Davy as well as a description of his early application of nitrous oxide to anesthesiology.

Davy, Humphry. *Researches, Chemical and Philosophical, Chiefly Concerning Nitrous Oxide or Dephlogisticated Nitrous Air, and Its Respiration.* London: J. Johnson, 1800. Reprint. London: Butterworth, 1972. Davy's work outlining his research on nitrous oxide. Includes illustrations and a bibliography.

Franco, Avelino, et al. *The History of Anesthesia.* Amsterdam: Elsevier Science, 2002. A collection of papers from a symposium that examines the development of anesthesia from antiquity through modern times.

Nuland, Sherwin. *Doctors: The Biography*. New York: Vintage Books, 1988. Nuland provides biographical descriptions of leading figures in the history of medicine.

Waller, John. *Einstein's Luck*. New York: Oxford University Press, 2002. The author explores the myths behind scientific discoveries, including the question of whether religious objections truly existed in the alleviation of pain.

Wolfe, Richard, and Leonard Menczer, eds. *I Awaken to Glory*. Boston: Boston Medical Library, 1994. A collection of essays on the history of anesthesia. Emphasis is placed on the role of Horace Wells and his "rediscovery" of nitrous oxide. The period during which Davy reported his results is also discussed.

Wynbrandt, James. *The Excruciating History of Dentistry*. New York: St. Martin's Press, 2000. An often humorous history of dental practices, as well as the history of anesthesia.

SEE ALSO: 1753: Lind Discovers a Cure for Scurvy; June 5, 1755: Black Identifies Carbon Dioxide; 1757: Monro Distinguishes Between Lymphatic and Blood Systems; 1757-1766: Haller Establishes Physiology as a Science; Aug. 1, 1774: Priestley Discovers Oxygen; 1786-1787: Lavoisier Devises the Modern System of Chemical Nomenclature; 1796-1798: Jenner Develops Smallpox Vaccination.

RELATED ARTICLES in *Great Lives from History: The Eighteenth Century, 1701-1800:* Joseph Black; Henry Cavendish; Edward Jenner; Antoine-Laurent Lavoisier; Joseph Priestley; Benjamin Rush; Lazzaro Spallanzani; Georg Ernst Stahl; James Watt.

1790's

July 16, 1799-July 9, 1804
HUMBOLDT AND BONPLAND'S EXPEDITION

Alexander von Humboldt and Aimé Bonpland's six-thousand-mile expedition through Central and South America was the first major scientific exploration of the region. They made numerous discoveries, describing them fully in their published journals.

LOCALE: New Spain (now Mexico), New Granada (now Colombia, Ecuador, Venezuela), and Cuba
CATEGORIES: Exploration and discovery; environment; science and technology

KEY FIGURES

Alexander von Humboldt (1769-1859), German scholar who sought to unify knowledge by integrating humankind and nature into physical descriptions of the world
Aimé Bonpland (1773-1858), French botanist who traveled with Humboldt and helped write reports

SUMMARY OF EVENT

On July 16, 1799, Alexander von Humboldt and his colleague Aimé Bonpland disembarked at the Venezuelan seaport of Cumaná, where they began an epic journey of scientific discovery and high adventure. Their Latin American odyssey would last five years and cover more than 6,000 miles (9,650 kilometers) in the region. Humboldt, the expedition's leader, was trained in astronomy, botany, chemistry, geology, geography, linguistics, literature, physics, and zoology. He was a firm adherent of the inductive approach to scientific inquiry.

The overall objective of the expedition was to conduct fieldwork for a theory-based physical description of the world and humankind's place in it. Humboldt recruited Bonpland to serve as his assistant. Bonpland's knowledge of botany eclipsed that of most European scholars, including even Humboldt himself. Humboldt was popular among Europe's well-heeled aristocracy for both his broad intellect and his affable wit and charm. Indeed, his reputation was so good that the Spanish crown gave him and Bonpland permission to travel together throughout the Spanish Americas. The Crown issued its consent, in part, because Humboldt promised to evaluate Spain's gold and silver mines in the region. Humboldt also received permission because he was willing to finance the expedition himself.

The array of scientific instruments that Humboldt carried reflects the breadth of the impending investigations. His instruments included barometers for fixing eleva-

tions and quadrants and sextants for determining geographical positions. He also took telescopes, microscopes, chronometers, and compasses, as well as electric batteries, theodolites for surveying land, and hygrometers for measuring water vapor. Other instruments were used for measuring rainfall, oxygen in the air, and the Earth's magnetic field. Humboldt and Bonpland were to make frequent stops to take measurements and collect plant, animal, and mineral specimens as their expedition passed through previously uncharted and most likely uninhabited land. Spanish officials in the few relatively large cities that the explorers visited would provide them with lodging, provisions, and guides for each leg of their journey.

Humboldt and Bonpland began their investigations soon after arriving in Cumaná, from which they went to Caracas, in January, 1800. Caracas was the capital of the Venezuela captaincy general, a semiautonomous division of Spain's colonial province of New Granada. Humboldt and Bonpland scaled Silla de Caracas, a previously unclimbed high peak overlooking the capital, to collect plant specimens. Next, they set off on a southerly trek to confirm the existence of the Casiquiare River, a stream thought to be a tributary of both the Orinoco and Amazon Rivers. The Casiquiare was controversial because it was believed that two rivers could not share the same tributary, as sloping land causes tributaries of different rivers to drain away from one another. However, Spanish missionaries had first reported (mid-sixteenth century) the existence of a canal of sorts that connected the drainage systems of the Orinoco and Amazon. In May, 1800, Humboldt and Bonpland traveled the length of the Casiquiare, proving that it did, indeed, join the Amazon and Orinoco Rivers.

The trip to the Casiquiare took Humboldt and Bonpland across the llanos, or grassy plains that form the midsection of modern Venezuela, to the Amazonas Plain in the southern extremity of Venezuela, the home of the Casiquiare. The explorers followed channels of the Apure, Orinoco, Atabapo, and Negro Rivers, as well as the Casiquiare. They also collected a multitude of previously unrecorded plants. They would eventually also take back to Europe monkeys, birds, and other animals from the region. Both explorers suffered bouts of either yellow or typhoid fever on their way back to Cumaná.

On December 4, 1800, Humboldt and Bonpland traveled to Havana, Cuba, to store their Venezuelan speci-

Alexander von Humboldt encamped near the Orinoco River, after a painting by Edward Ender. (North Wind Picture Archives)

mens. After a brief stay there, they returned to South America to study the Andes region. In March, 1801, they arrived in Cartagena, the great Spanish seaport in what later became Colombia. There, they followed the Magdalena River upstream, then climbed the Andes to Bogotá, Quito, and Cajamarca. Then they descended to Lima, Spain's principal city on the Pacific coast. Along the way, they collected specimens, took measurements, and mapped their progress.

The indefatigable Humboldt also examined the region's geology and mines, in part to satisfy his agreement with the Spanish government to report on mining in Spanish lands. The explorers climbed numerous Andean peaks, including Mount Chimborazo, near Quito. At that time, Europeans believed that Chimborazo, which is 20,561 feet (6,267 meters) high, was the highest mountain in the world. Humboldt and Bonpland themselves ascended to 19,286 feet (5,878 meters)—the highest altitude that any human beings were known to have reached at that time. Along the coast of Peru, Humboldt examined the chemical properties of guano, or bird droppings,

useful as fertilizer. Owing to the dry climate and lack of chemical leaching, he found that Peruvian guano deposits had extraordinarily high concentrations of nutrients. Humboldt also analyzed the chemistry, temperature, and flow of the ocean current that passes by Peru. He named it the Peruvian Current, but modern maps now label it the Humboldt Current in his honor. From Peru, Humboldt and Bonpland sailed to Guayaquil, Ecuador.

In March, 1803, Humboldt and Bonpland sailed from Guayaquil to the Mexican port of Acapulco. At that time, the viceroyalty of New Spain had been at the peak of its prosperity. The explorers conducted fieldwork there for a full year. In March, 1804, they sailed back to Havana to gather the specimens they had collected from Venezuela. By the following summer, they were in Washington, D.C., where they dined with President Thomas Jefferson at the White House. Humboldt and Jefferson became friends and would correspond with each other until Jefferson's death in 1826. On July 9, 1804, Humboldt and Bonpland sailed for France aboard a French frigate.

A magnificently resilient team, Humboldt and Bonpland traveled through many uncharted and physically hostile lands, in which hunger and fatigue were almost constant companions. In the tropical lowlands, they faced stifling tropical heat, hordes of feasting mosquitoes, and torrential floods. In the Venezuelan llanos, they survived parching droughts, wily crocodiles, and hungry jaguars. In the Andes, they teetered atop precarious ridges, battled numbing cold, and climbed dozens of active volcanoes. Even so, the passion of the two scientists to observe, record, and learn was undeterred. While in Venezuela, they even subjected themselves to painful shocks of electric eels as part of a scientific experiment on the passage of electricity through muscles. The physical stamina and unbounded enthusiasm of the two explorers were the key to their expedition's ultimate success.

SIGNIFICANCE

Humboldt and Bonpland collected more than sixty thousand plant specimens and a huge number of exotic New World animals. To document the expedition, Humboldt published a thirty-volume work under the general title *Voyage aux régions équinoxiales du Nouveau Continent* (1807-1834). He included maps and topographic profiles of the region. Bonpland edited several of the volumes and contributed drawings of plant and animal specimens. The tomes would prove invaluable to later explorers, government officials, scientists, and mining engineers. Arguably, volumes 28-30, titled *Relation historique* (*Personal Narrative of Travels to the Equinoctial Regions of America During the Years 1799-1804*, 1814-1821), had the greatest impact on the scholarly world. These volumes are Humboldt's account of the scientific studies that he and Bonpland pursued in South America. They include his insights into social, political, and economic conditions in early nineteenth century Spanish America, as well as his analyses of the interrelationships between the land and its life forms.

Humboldt and Bonpland's expedition sought to answer questions about the interconnections among the phenomena grouped together in rich diversity on the face of the Earth. Although the expedition's most enduring contributions were in the fields of plant geography, meteorology, and climatology, this preoccupation with the interrelationships of all living and inanimate things presaged modern environmental science.

—*Richard A. Crooker*

FURTHER READING

Gaines, Ann. *Alexander von Humboldt: Colossus of Exploration*. Philadelphia: Chelsea House, 1991. A brief but well-written and useful biography of Humboldt.

Helferich, Gerard. *Humboldt's Cosmos: Alexander von Humboldt and the Latin American Journal That Changed the Way We See the World*. New York: Gotham Books, 2004. Analyzes the journey's many contributions to scientific knowledge.

Humboldt, Alexander von. *Personal Narrative of Travels to the Equinoctial Regions of America During the Years 1799-1804*. Translated by Helen Maria Williams. 6 vols. London: Longman, 1814-1821. English translation of volumes 28-30 of Humboldt's *Voyage aux régions équinoxiales du Nouveau Continent*. A facsimile edition of this publication was issued by AMS Press in 1966.

————. *Voyage aux régions équinoxiales du Nouveau Continent*. 30 vols. Reprint. New York: Da Capo Press, 1970-1973. Facsimile reprint of the edition first published in Paris between 1807 and 1834. Humboldt's complete report on the expedition. Includes color reproductions, original drawings, and maps.

SEE ALSO: Apr. 5, 1722: European Discovery of Easter Island; May, 1735-1743: French Scientists Explore the Amazon River; Dec. 5, 1766-Mar. 16, 1769: Bougainville Circumnavigates the Globe; Aug. 25, 1768-Feb. 14, 1779: Voyages of Captain Cook; Dec., 1768-Jan. 10, 1773: Bruce Explores Ethiopia; 1786: Discovery of the Mayan Ruins at Palenque.

RELATED ARTICLES in *Great Lives from History: The Nineteenth Century, 1701-1800:* Louis-Antoine de Bougainville; James Bruce; James Cook; Mungo Park.

July 19, 1799
DISCOVERY OF THE ROSETTA STONE

The discovery of the Rosetta stone provided the key to deciphering hieroglyphics, the ancient Egyptian system of writing, and so recaptured and revealed the rich culture and history of the forgotten civilization.

LOCALE: Rosetta, Egypt
CATEGORIES: Anthropology; communications; historiography

KEY FIGURES

Napoleon Bonaparte (1769-1821), French military commander and later emperor as Napoleon I, r. 1804-1814, 1815
Jean François Champollion (1790-1832), French linguist and Egyptologist
Thomas Young (1773-1829), English physician

SUMMARY OF EVENT

In 1798, Napoleon Bonaparte, general of the French military and a national hero, had defeated most of the enemies of the French Republic except for Britain. He believed that a successful invasion of Britain could not be accomplished until British trade with India was disrupted. To that end, Napoleon planned to conquer Egypt and use it as a military base. Napoleon also had a personal interest in the country and wanted to exploit its wealth, strategic value, and potential for development as a French colony. He decided to take 167 scholars along with his Army of the Orient when he left France for Egypt in May, 1798.

By 1798, foreigners had ruled Egypt for centuries. The Persians conquered Egypt in 525 B.C.E., were driven out by 380 B.C.E., and returned by 343 B.C.E. The Greeks, led by Alexander the Great, conquered Egypt in 332 B.C.E. By the time of Julius Caesar (100-44 B.C.E.), Egypt no longer spoke its own language. Greek eventually gave way to Latin, which was replaced by Arabic. When Napoleon's expedition arrived, Egypt had been under the control of the Ottoman Turks for three hundred years, and the Arabs had ruled for nine hundred years prior to the Turks.

The scholars that Napoleon brought to Egypt included specialists from all branches of the sciences and arts: astronomers, engineers, linguists, painters, draftsmen, poets, musicians, mathematicians, chemists, inventors, naturalists, mineralogists, and geographers. During a three-year period, these scholars recorded massive amounts of information and provided valuable drawings and sketches that helped spark a renewed interest in Egypt. On August 22, 1798, Napoleon established the Egyptian Institute of Arts and Sciences at Cairo, where the scholars conducted research and studied the country's history, industry, and nature.

On July 19, 1799, a soldier named d'Hautpoul, who was working to demolish a ruined wall at Fort Rashid (renamed Fort Julien), discovered a dark gray stone slab with inscriptions on one side. He reported the discovery to Lieutenant Pierre François Xavier Bouchard, who then informed his superior, Michel-Ange Lancret. Lancret recognized one of the three scripts as Greek and another as hieroglyphic. The third script was unknown. Bouchard transported the stone to Cairo so that the scholars at the Egyptian Institute could examine it. The scholars copied the inscriptions using rubbings, drawings, and casts and sent them to other scholars throughout Europe, so they could begin working on translating the hieroglyphics. The scholars named the object the Rosetta stone (*pierre de Rosette*).

The Rosetta stone was a basalt slab, 3 feet, 9 inches long by 2 feet, 4.5 inches wide by 11 inches thick. It

An illustration of the Rosetta Stone on display. (Hulton Archive/Getty Images)

weighed three-fourths of a ton. The stone was damaged, especially the upper portion with the hieroglyphics. The middle section was the unknown language, later identified as demotic script, and the bottom portion was Greek.

In ancient Egypt, there were two types of writing: hieroglyphic, used in formal writing, and hieratic, a cursive form of hieroglyphics—simplified and faster—used for everyday writing. By 650 B.C.E., the hieratic script and language had changed so much that it acquired a new name, "demotic." The last known use of hieroglyphics dated from 394 C.E., at a temple in Upper Egypt. Although they were used for more than three thousand years, by 1799 no one had been able to read or understand hieroglyphics for fifteen hundred years. As a result, ancient Egyptian civilization was a mystery, lost to contemporary knowledge, even though written records of the civilization remained on papyrus scrolls, temples, and monuments.

By Roman times, approximately 250 C.E., Coptic was in use. Coptic was a mixture of demotic and Greek used by Christian Egyptians and marked the first time that vowels were written. Eventually, the Coptic language was replaced, but because it existed in formal Christian religious documents and practices, scholars could understand its spoken and written forms.

The Greek text on the Rosetta stone was a decree by the priests of Memphis, dated 196 B.C.E., commemorating Ptolemy V Ephiphanes, who ruled Egypt from 204 to 180 B.C.E. According to the decree, Ptolemy V restored the economy and peace, reduced taxes, and was a just ruler, so statues were to be erected and festivals held in his honor. The most exciting text, however, was the conclusion, which indicated that the decree would be inscribed in holy (hieroglyphic), native (demotic), and Greek. Since all of the different scripts recorded the same information, the savants believed that the secret of reading hieroglyphics would be quickly and easily solved.

Napoleon left Egypt in August, 1799, to return to France. He took only a few soldiers and some of the scholars back with him, as he needed to travel quickly and did not want to appear to give up the Egyptian military campaign. The campaign had failed once the British cut off the supply line, but Napoleon presented the expedition as a success. With severe economic problems fostering a climate for a governmental coup, Napoleon became part of a triumvirate of consuls governing France. In December, 1804, he declared himself emperor of the French.

The troops and scholars remaining behind in Egypt negotiated with the British to leave in early 1800 but were delayed until late 1801. The British wanted to keep the records and collections gathered by the scholars, but they eventually relented. The British did take the major items, including the Rosetta stone, back to Britain. Several of the scholars de-

---

DECODING THE ROSETTA STONE

The text of the Rosetta stone is dated March 27, 196 B.C.E. Here is an excerpt from the original, unattributed English translation of the stone's text, prepared for the British Museum.

DECREE. . . . WHEREAS KING PTOLEMY, THE EVER-LIVING, THE BELOVED OF PTAH, THE GOD EPIPHANES EUCHARISTOS, the son of King Ptolemy and Queen Arsinoe, the Gods Philopatores, has been a benefactor both to the temple and to those who dwell in them, as well as all those who are his subjects. . . .

WITH PROPITIOUS FORTUNE: It was resolved by the priests of all the temples in the land to increase greatly the existing honours of King PTOLEMY, THE EVER-LIVING, THE BELOVED OF PTAH, THE GOD EPIPHANES EUCHARISTOS . . . to set up in the most prominent place of every temple an image of the EVER-LIVING KING PTOLEMY, THE BELOVED OF PTAH, THE GOD EPIPHANES EUCHARISTOS, which shall be called that of "PTOLEMY, the defender of Egypt," beside which shall stand the principal god of the temple, handing him the scimitar of victory, all of which shall be manufactured in the Egyptian fashion; and that the priests shall pay homage to the images three times a day, and put upon them the sacred garments, and perform the other usual honours such as are given to the other gods in the Egyptian festivals; and to establish . . . a statue and golden shrine in each of the temples, and to set it up in the inner chamber with the other shrines; and in the great festivals in which the shrines are carried in procession the shrine of the GOD EPIPHANES EUCHARISTOS shall be carried in procession with them. And in order that it may be easily distinguishable now and for all time, there shall be set upon the shrine ten gold crowns of the king, to which shall be added a cobra exactly as on all the crowns adorned with cobras. . . .

This decree shall be inscribed on a stela of hard stone in sacred and native and Greek characters and set up in each of the first, second and third rank temples beside the image of the ever-living king.

Source: "Text of the Rosetta Stone." http://pw1.netcom.com/~qkstart/rosetta.html. Accessed November, 2005.

cided to go to Britain in order to retain control over the records and collections that the British had claimed. Eventually, twenty volumes of the *Description de l'Égypte* (description of Egypt) were published between 1809 and 1828, based on the information collected by the scholars. The work covered the monuments, natural history, and modern Egypt as of 1800, and it also included the first comprehensive Western map of Egypt.

SIGNIFICANCE

In early 1802, the Rosetta stone arrived in Britain and was taken to the Society of Antiquaries in London, where plaster casts were made for universities and engravings were distributed to academic institutions throughout Europe. The stone itself was housed in the British Museum by the end of 1802. The Rosetta stone was the first known example of a text written in both a known language and hieroglyphics. Although it was discovered in 1799, it would take twenty-three years before hieroglyphics were translated successfully. The Rosetta stone was vital for launching modern Egyptology, the study of Egyptian antiquities.

Although scholars across Europe worked at translating hieroglyphics, the two main contenders for success were Jean François Champollion of France and Thomas Young of England. Both men came to their conclusions independently, and both contributed greatly to understanding hieroglyphic, hieratic, and demotic writing.

Champollion was in Paris by 1807 at age seventeen and working on a copy of the Rosetta stone inscriptions. He concluded that hieroglyphics were not merely pictorial (representing a thing or idea with a picture) but also phonetic (representing a spoken word or sound). Eventually, he understood the relationship between hieroglyphic, hieratic, and demotic script, and experienced a breakthrough on September 14, 1822. He later established that hieroglyphics were based on pictograms, ideograms, and phonetic symbols, as well as signs used in special ways. Champollion became the first person in more than fifteen hundred years to read hieroglyphics.

Young began his work on hieroglyphics in 1814. He also concluded that not all hieroglyphics were pictorial: Some would indicate plurality or otherwise express numbers. He also determined that demotic script used letters to spell out foreign sounds but was not entirely alphabetic, as some scholars believed. Young's work on hieroglyphics was published anonymously as a supplement to *Encyclopaedia Britannica* in 1819. Although Young's system of deciphering did not work, he was the first scholar to study demotic script seriously, and his work was invaluable in that regard.

Once the ancient Egyptian system of writing was understood, the history of Egypt and its people was revealed to the modern world. A tremendous amount of written material had survived, and it provided a level of insight into Egyptian culture previously unknown. Travel to Egypt, as well as the collection and preservation of ancient monuments and artifacts, became even more important. Continued discoveries in Egypt over the next century yielded remarkable findings about the complexity of ancient Egyptian civilization.

—Virginia L. Salmon

FURTHER READING

Adkins, Lesley, and Roy Adkins. *The Keys of Egypt: The Obsession to Decipher Egyptian Hieroglyphs*. New York: HarperCollins, 2000. An excellent presentation of the history, people, places, and politics involved with hieroglyphics. Illustrations, maps, and index.

Brier, Bob. "Napoleon in Egypt: The General's Search for Glory Led to the Birth of Egyptology." *Archaeology* (May/June 1999): 44-53. Well-written overview of the importance of the work of the French scholars. Illustrations and side article on the Rosetta stone.

Meyerson, Daniel. *The Linguist and the Emperor: Napoleon and Champollion's Quest to Decipher the Rosetta Stone*. New York: Ballantine Books, 2004. Focuses more on the personalities and early lives, but does include background on Egypt and the discovery of the Rosetta stone.

Weissbach, Muriel Mirak. "Jean Francois Champollion and the True Story of Egypt." *21st Century Science and Technology* (Winter, 1999/2000): 26-39. Focuses mostly on Champollion and his system of decipherment. Includes information about the Rosetta stone and its significance.

SEE ALSO: 1719-1724: Stukeley Studies Stonehenge and Avebury; 1748: Excavation of Pompeii; 1786: Discovery of the Mayan Ruins at Palenque; Apr. 12, 1798-Sept. 2, 1801: Napoleon's Egyptian Campaign; Nov. 9-10, 1799: Napoleon Rises to Power in France.

RELATED ARTICLE in *Great Lives from History: The Eighteenth Century, 1701-1800*: William Stukeley.

1790's

November 9-10, 1799
NAPOLEON RISES TO POWER IN FRANCE

Napoleon I rose to power in France through the coup d'état of 18-19 Brumaire, effectively ending France's revolutionary experiment and initiating nearly sixteen years of Napoleonic domination of Europe.

LOCALE: Paris and Saint-Cloud, France
CATEGORY: Government and politics

KEY FIGURES

Napoleon Bonaparte (1769-1821), French military leader and later first consul, 1799-1804, and emperor as Napoleon I, r. 1804-1814, 1815
Talleyrand (1754-1838), French minister of foreign affairs, 1797-1807
Emmanuel-Joseph Sieyès (1748-1836), member of the Directory and Napoleonic co-conspirator
Louis Jérôme Gohier (1746-1830), president of the Directory
Joseph Fouché (c. 1758-1820), French minister of police
Paul-François-Jean-Nicolas de Barras (1755-1829), French member of the Directory
Josephine Bonaparte (1763-1814), wife of Napoleon
Lucien Bonaparte (1775-1840), French politician and brother of Napoleon

SUMMARY OF EVENT

The fall of the Jacobins from power in July of 1794 led to government by the Directory in the following year. The five directors and the two legislative assemblies, the Council of Ancients and the Council of Five Hundred, attempted to steer a middle course and restore order during the final troublesome years of the eighteenth century. Threatened from both the Royalist right and the Jacobin left, the government manipulated elections, put down insurrections, purged its own members, and engaged in political infighting for more than four years. By 1799, France was weary of their ineffective leadership and ready for another change. As a body, the directors were increasingly perceived as weak and corrupt, and their dependence on the army to maintain their authority had grown steadily more essential.

The principal intriguer against the government was also a part of it. Emmanuel-Joseph Sieyès, generally known as Abbé Sieyès despite the fact that he had abandoned Holy Orders, was considered one of the intellectual founders of the French Revolution. During the first phase of the revolution, Sieyès had been a leading spokesman and pamphleteer for the Third Estate, having produced his most famous tract *Qu'est-ce que le tiers état?* (*What Is the Third Estate?*, 1963) in 1789. He was initially active in the National Assembly but prudently became more aloof during the early years of the Republic, as the revolution became more violent. In January of 1793, he voted for the execution of Louis XVI, but his genuine attachment to either the Girondin or Jacobin Party was unclear. After the fall of Robespierre in July of 1794, he served in several positions related to foreign affairs (a pursuit he shared with Talleyrand), and in the fall of 1799, he once again became an influential member of the government.

As a member of the Directory, Sieyès was in a key position to engineer a coup d'état against his unpopular colleagues, especially the complacent President Louis Jérôme Gohier and Paul-François-Jean-Nicolas de Barras, whose name had become a synonym for moral and financial corruption. He was now in a capacity to fulfill a long-held ambition: to give to France what he considered would be a stronger and more ideal constitution. To achieve his end, however, and to neutralize his old political enemies, the Jacobins, he required a military figure of high rank to assure support of the army. Sieyès and his associates approached several generals, but they refused, were considered unreliable, or, in one case, died in battle.

By October, 1799, General Napoleon Bonaparte had successfully evaded the British blockade of Egypt, where he had left his rapidly dwindling army under the command of General Jean-Baptiste Kléber, and returned to France. The Italian campaign of 1796-1797 had already proved that the young general could make both peace and war. Furthermore, Bonaparte had sent back only misleadingly favorable reports about conditions in Egypt. Sieyès was suspicious of his ambitions but invited him to take part in the plot after Talleyrand, who had been minister of foreign affairs but was momentarily without office, presented Napoleon to him as "the man on horseback" who could guarantee the loyalty of the army. After some hesitation, Bonaparte agreed and began to formulate his own plans. His brothers Joseph and Lucien and his most trusted officers, Generals Jean Lannes and Joachim Murat, were taken into the conspiracy, along with Josephine, who was a particular friend of Directors Barras and Gohier and Gohier's wife. As a popular hostess, Josephine's role was to lull those who were not part of the coup into a sense of confidence in her husband.

This Italian cartoon, "The 18 Brumaire, Year VIII," represents France as a sphinx wearing a liberty cap, reclining upon the destruction "she" has wrought. Napoleon, on a platform next to the sphinx's head, unfurls his banner at the head of an army. (Library of Congress)

On 18 Brumaire in the year VIII (November 9, 1799), the Council of Ancients and the Council of Five Hundred were told of a fictional Jacobin plot to overthrow the government. For supposed reasons of safety from the Paris mob, the two assemblies were persuaded to move to the suburb of Saint-Cloud the following day. After Joseph Fouché, the minister of police (who was well aware of the plot but was not an active participant), promised to keep Paris tranquil, Napoleon joined the two assemblies along with a military escort. Some Jacobin members of the two assemblies, realizing that a coup was in progress, attempted to prevent the overthrow of the government.

After badly delivering a rambling speech to the Council of Ancients, which rattled his nerve, Bonaparte went before the Council of Five Hundred, which was already in turmoil. Greeted with cries from the radical deputies of "Outlaw him!" and "Down with the dictator!" he was pushed and shoved by several of the Jacobins. Only the quick action of his younger brother Lucien, who was presiding, prevented collapse of the coup. Ignoring demands to outlaw Napoleon, Lucien left the hall and called on the soldiers to defend his brother and the Republic from "brigands" and "madmen." Inspired by his rhetoric, the troops (led by Napoleon's future brother-in-law, Murat) cleared the room of disorderly deputies. The assemblies met again that same evening, but with most of the members of the Council of Five Hundred absent. The day's actions were covered with a veil of legality, and Bonaparte, Sieyès, and Roger-Ducos were appointed provisional consuls empowered to draw up a new constitution.

925

SIGNIFICANCE

The Constitution of the Year VIII contained the wording of Sieyès but also expressed the political views of Bonaparte. It gave Napoleon virtual dictatorial powers, and the Republic existed only in name thereafter. Napoleon became first consul, and while Sieyès and Pierre-Roger Ducos kept the title of consuls, they were reduced to mere advisers. The power of the legislature was divided among three chambers: the Council of State, whose members were nominated by Bonaparte; the Tribunate, whose members had the power to discuss proposals sent to them by the Council of State; and the Legislative Assembly, whose members, like those of the ancient Spartan assembly, could not discuss proposals but only accept or reject them by vote. The new constitution was based on the principle that "confidence comes from below, power from above," and at the head of the government was Napoleon Bonaparte. As Sieyès himself supposedly remarked shortly after the coup, "Gentlemen, we now have a master."

France passively accepted the new regime. After ten years of revolution and turmoil, most people were willing to support any government that promised order, stability, and peace. That Bonaparte represented such attributes may be seen in the lack of opposition to the coup d'état of 18-19 Brumaire, and the fact that the stock market climbed steadily during the following week. The French Revolution had ended and the Napoleonic era had begun.

—John G. Gallaher, updated by Dorothy T. Potter

FURTHER READING

Bonaparte, Napoleon. *Letters and Documents of Napoleon: The Rise to Power*. Vol. 1. Selected and translated by John Eldred Howard. London: Cresset Press, 1961. Includes a useful collection of Napoleon's speeches, orders, letters, and proclamations from the period of the coup d'état.

_____. *Napoleon on Napoleon: An Autobiography of the Emperor*. Edited by Somerset de Chair. London: Cassell, 1992. This edition of Napoleon's *Commentaries at St. Helena* and his *Memoirs* includes a chapter on Brumaire, with Napoleon's own justifications for the coup.

Doyle, William. *The Oxford History of the French Revolution*. 2d ed. New York: Oxford University Press, 2002. An authoritative and comprehensive account of French history between 1774 and 1802, written by a prominent historian. Includes information on the end of the French Revolution and Napoleon's assumption of power.

Emsley, Clive. *Napoleon: Conquest, Reform, and Reorganization*. New York: Pearson/Longman, 2003. Succinct overview of Napoleon's political career, from his rise to power in 1799 through 1815. Places Napoleon's career within the broad context of European history.

Goodspeed, D. J. *Bayonets at St. Cloud: The Story of the 18th Brumaire*. London: Rupert Hart-Davis, 1965. Goodspeed focuses specifically on the events of 18 Brumaire and the people who supported or opposed Napoleon's seizure of power.

Lefebvre, Georges. *Napoleon: From 18 Brumaire to Tilsit, 1799-1807*. Translated by Henry F. Stockhold. New York: Columbia University Press, 1969. Lefebvre views the coup d'état of 18-19 Brumaire as the logical (though not inevitable) result of the revolution, not merely an isolated event or a turning point.

Markham, Felix. *Napoleon*. New York: New American Library, 1964. Written by a noted historian of the Napoleonic period, this excellent biography is concise and objective, and makes extensive use of a variety of sources.

Orieux, Jean. *Talleyrand: The Art of Survival*. Translated by Patricia Wolf. New York: Alfred A. Knopf, 1974. This richly detailed biography provides insights into the political career of one of the most complex and paradoxical of Napoleon's associates.

Van Deusen, Glyndon G. *Sieyès: His Life and His Nationalism*. Reprint. New York: AMS Press, 1968. First published in 1932, Van Deusen's biography is particularly important, since Sieyès's influence on the events leading up to Brumaire has long been overshadowed by Napoleon's role in the coup d'état.

SEE ALSO: May 5, 1789: Louis XVI Calls the Estates-General; June 20, 1789: Oath of the Tennis Court; July 14, 1789: Fall of the Bastille; Apr. 20, 1792-Oct., 1797: Early Wars of the French Revolution; Jan. 21, 1793: Execution of Louis XVI; July 27-28, 1794: Fall of Robespierre; Mar., 1796-Oct. 17, 1797: Napoleon's Italian Campaigns; Apr. 12, 1798-Sept. 2, 1801: Napoleon's Egyptian Campaign.

RELATED ARTICLES in *Great Lives from History: The Eighteenth Century, 1701-1800*: Georges Danton; Louis XV; Louis XVI; Robespierre; Emmanuel-Joseph Sieyès.

1800
VOLTA INVENTS THE BATTERY

Volta, striving to improve on previous experiments with electricity, designed a battery that used positive and negative poles to charge a wire placed in a wet cell. He refined his battery design three times before 1800, when he is officially credited with inventing the battery.

LOCALE: Como (now in Italy)

CATEGORIES: Inventions; engineering; science and technology

KEY FIGURES

Alessandro Volta (1745-1827), Italian inventor
Luigi Galvani (1737-1798), Italian inventor
William Nicholson (1753-1815), English scientist and inventor
Sir Joseph Banks (1743-1820), English scientist and explorer

SUMMARY OF EVENT

As early as 1600, scientists experimented with ideas of electrical attraction and electrical conductivity in an effort to design a device or machine to capture electricity. Early studies recognized static electricity and current electricity produced by the chemical interaction of positive and negative electrons across a wire. In 1600, Otto von Guericke designed a machine that produced electric sparks, and in England, Francis Hauksbee used static electricity to produce sparks, to the delight of party guests.

In 1752, Benjamin Franklin's discovery of the electrical nature of lightning brought together roughly 150 years of hypothesizing, experimentation, and invention in the application of electricity to scientific studies. Franklin analyzed electrical charges as positive and negative, and he realized that more could be learned about electricity than had been previously known through Ewald Georg von Kleist's Leyden jar, which housed electricity in a glass bottle partially filled with water. The Leyden jar was the first example of a device now called a capacitor, a means of storing electricity. The next major advance in the storage of this type of energy would be made by Alessandro Volta.

Volta showed a lifelong interest in electricity, publishing first a poem on Joseph Priestley's scientific career and his first work on electricity in 1771, at the age of twenty-six. His first invention was a variation on the Leyden jar that used wood instead of water to conduct an electrical charge. In 1775, Volta invented the electrophorus, which used resin to line two metal plates that conducted sparks sufficient to make static electricity. On June 10, 1775, Volta wrote to Joseph Priestley describing his electrophorus.

In 1776, Volta discovered the composition of methane gas and learned of its combustibility when he invented an electrical pistol that shot sparks. This led him to consider how the sparks flying on a wire could be used for signals, a line of thought that predated the telegraph. In 1778, Volta was named to the physics chair at the University of Pavia. As he pursued his scientific studies, he remained connected to British scientists through the efforts of his English-language translator, Tiberius Cavallo, who prepared Volta's essay "On the Method of Rendering Very Sensible the Weakest Natural or Artificial Electricty" for the prestigious *Transactions* of the Royal Society, of which Sir Joseph Banks was president. This essay described the improvements Volta had made to the electrophorus so the new machine could retain or store electricity in greater strength.

In 1793, after carefully studying the experiments of Luigi Galvani, who was calling his work "animal electricity" as he charged the nervous systems of animals including the frog, Volta developed his own idea of "metallic electricity," which he discussed in another essay published in England, "Account of Some Discoveries Made by Mr. Galvani, with Experiments and Observations of Them." Here, Volta reported on his use of metals and carbons and how he conducted electricity using his own moistened tongue. He argued that the metal plates combined with the wet surface electrified the tongue externally and did not, as Galvani believed, stimulate his nerves or his tongue muscle. He asserted that he felt the charge because it was applied to the tongue; it was not generated from inside his body.

Thus, Volta began a series of experiments from 1794 to 1797 during which he tested a variety of metals, learning how positive and negative charges were conducted. By the middle of 1797, he had displaced Galvani's ideas, as well as those of William Nicholson, who in 1788 had invented a device called the "doubler" that he used to conduct and store electricity. Eventually, Volta settled on the design of the first battery for which he is famous: two metal plates (electrodes) vertically set in a liquid solution (electrolyte; acid is used today). The electrolyte conducted electricity between the two electrodes, allow-

1790's

927

A sketch by Alessandro Volta of his battery, published in the Philosophical Transactions *of the Royal Society in 1800.* (Library of Congress)

ing one to become positively charged and one to become negatively charged. The portion of the electrodes protruding from the electrolyte could be placed in contact with a conductive substance such as a wire, either to charge the electrolytic solution or to discharge the electrical energy stored within the solution.

Once Volta was satisfied with the initial results that conducted and achieved a sustainable charge, he shared them in a letter to Sir Joseph Banks, who in turn presented Volta's descriptions to the other scientists in the Royal Society. The first part of Volta's letter to Banks was published in April, 1800; the second part was published in early June, 1800. His ideas were not patented, and it was part of the climate of the times for others to imitate and test and retest new ideas, so Volta soon learned that complementary experiments were conducted by scientists in London, Paris, and Vienna. Chief among these scientists was Nicholson, who began to test the idea of the Voltaic "pile" (the cell that housed the electricity) in salt water, using silver coins to try to conduct electricity. Other scientists continued to support Galvani's idea of "animal electricity," the notion that current was housed

in the nerves of a mammal. Still others tried to show that the function of electric conductivity could be fulfilled with substances other than water. In 1801, a Danish scientist, Hans Christian Ørsted, suggested there was more than one type of current electricity, an extension of Volta's studies.

In September, 1801, Volta went to Paris to promote another version of his battery, which carried a more forceful charge. He was received by Napoleon Bonaparte, who recognized his efforts with a six-thousand-franc stipend. Back in Como, Volta again reworked the battery to improve its charging power. It was not until 1803 that he patented the design of the electric battery, and it is interesting to note the high degree of integrity within the scientific community, as no one else tried to claim Volta's innovative design or discovery as his own.

SIGNIFICANCE

Volta harnessed electricity when he provided a way of producing a continuous electric current. Though he was solving a scientific problem that aroused his curiosity, he left the world with a lasting and major improvement in technology that is widely used in commerce, industry, and households. However, the immediate impact of his invention was to pave the way for the discoveries and applications of electricity and its properties that exploded during the ninteenth century.

Volta's studies would influence Michael Faraday, the English scientist who in the 1810's carried out his research in electrochemistry and electromagnetism. In Paris, in 1801-1802, André-Marie Ampère attended Volta's public lectures on the differences between his theories and those of Galvani. Ampère in the 1820's developed the theories surrounding electrical currents. In 1810, Sir Humphry Davy was indebted to Volta as he experimented with the electrical arc, which led to an early version of the electric light bulb.

—Beverly Schneller

FURTHER READING

Dibner, Bern. *Alessandro Volta and the Electric Battery*. New York: Franklin Watts, 1964. Provides a clear and readable account of Volta's career.

Hamilton, James. *A Life of Discovery: Michael Faraday, Giant of the Scientific Revolution*. New York: Random House, 2002. Mentions Faraday's meeting with Volta in 1814 and quotes from Faraday's travel diaries as he accompanied Sir Humphry Davies in Europe.

Holton, Gerald. *Thematic Origins of Scientific Thought: Kepler to Einstein*. Rev. ed. Cambridge, Mass.: Harvard University Press, 1988. Holton notes that prior to the twentieth century, scientists tried to balance or reconcile various theories, as was the case with Galvani and Volta, while current scientists entertain many theories and do not question their complementarity or lack thereof.

McKenzie, A. E. E. *The Major Achievements of Science: The Development of Science from Ancient Times to the Present*. Cambridge, Mass.: Cambridge University Press, 1960. Devotes a chapter to eighteenth century scientific discoveries and to "field physics," discussing Volta's influence on nineteenth century discoveries.

Pancaldi, Guiliano. *Volta. Science and Culture in the Age of Enlightenment*. Princeton, N.J.: Princeton University Press, 2003. A biographical and critical study of Volta and his times, presenting his discoveries in the context of the eighteenth century.

Rosen, Dennis, and Sylvia Rosen. *London Science: Museums, Libraries, and Places of Scientific, Technological, and Medical Interest*. London: Prion Books, 1994. Discusses the contributions of Sir Joseph Banks and Michael Faraday in particular, mentioning Volta and Faraday's meeting. The book gives an appreciation for the history of science in London culture, especially since it notes the various statutes, memorials, and burial places of prominent London scientists who were influenced by Volta.

SEE ALSO: 1729: Gray Discovers Principles of Electric Conductivity; 1733: Du Fay Discovers Two Kinds of Electric Charge; Oct., 1745, and Jan., 1746: Invention of the Leyden Jar; June, 1752: Franklin Demonstrates the Electrical Nature of Lightning; 1759: Aepinus Publishes *Essay on the Theory of Electricity and Magnetism*.

RELATED ARTICLES in *Great Lives from History: The Eighteenth Century, 1701-1800*: Sir Joseph Banks; Luigi Galvani; Joseph Priestley; Alessandro Volta.

July 2-August 1, 1800
ACT OF UNION FORMS THE UNITED KINGDOM

The English and Irish parliaments passed the Act of Union, creating the United Kingdom of Great Britain and Ireland. The act dissolved Ireland's parliament and unified the Church of England and the Church of Ireland. The act would lead to a history of movements for Irish nationhood and for Catholic emancipation.

LOCALE: England; Scotland; Wales; Ireland
CATEGORIES: Government and politics; laws, acts, and legal history

KEY FIGURES
First Marquess Cornwallis (Charles Cornwallis; 1738-1805), an English military leader who served as viceroy of Ireland and supported Catholic emancipation and union with Ireland

George III (1738-1820), king of Great Britain and Ireland, r. 1760-1820, who denied Pitt's proposal to emancipate the Irish Catholics

Henry Grattan (1746-1820), an Irish patriotic leader and orator who fought for Catholic emancipation and was opposed to union with Great Britain

William Pitt the Younger (1759-1806), prime minister of Great Britain, 1783-1801, who proposed the Act of Union and also the emancipation of the Irish Catholics

Wolfe Tone (1763-1798), an Irish patriot and leader of the Irish rebellion of 1798

SUMMARY OF EVENT
While Great Britain was battling revolutionary France, there was fierce unrest and rebellion in Ireland, leading the prime minister of Great Britain, William Pitt the Younger, to propose the Act of Union.

Although nominally an independent kingdom ruled by the British king, Ireland in the eighteenth century was actually little more than a British colony with a subservient Parliament and government. All political, governmental, religious, legal, social, and economic power was hoarded by the tenth of the nation belonging to the Anglican Church of Ireland as established by law. The Roman Catholic majority, comprising three-fourths of the population, were a subject people, disfranchised, excluded from Parliament and every kind of office on religious grounds, deprived of most of the land, obliged to pay tithes to the established Church of Ireland, and oppressed by law. The Presbyterians in Ulster fared only slightly better.

Discontent arose in Ireland during the reign of King George III. Anglican patriots, led by Henry Grattan and Henry Flood, yearned for an independent parliament, the growing Catholic middle class longed for emancipation, and the peasants desired to be freed from exploitation. During the American Revolutionary War, Ireland had been defended only by a militia organized by nationalists, and a number of concessions had been wrung from Great Britain. In 1782, the Irish parliament won legislative independence, though the British government continued to appoint the executive and retained effective control by corrupting its members. The government of Ireland remained the preserve of a knot of selfish and reactionary aristocrats. About thirty thousand Catholics were enfranchised in 1793 on the same basis as Protestants, but they were still excluded from Parliament and public office—even Presbyterians had been admitted in 1780. Despite Grattan's campaign in Parliament, Catholic emancipation was stubbornly resisted.

Meanwhile, Ireland was not immune to the revolutionary ideas that had triumphed in America and in France. Under the leadership of the Anglican Irish intellectual and patriot, Wolfe Tone, Catholics and Presbyterians, prompted by the French Revolution, joined forces in 1791 to form the Society of United Irishmen, which stood for religious equality and a representative Irish parliament. By 1795, however, all hope of reform had vanished. The United Irishmen, their thoughts drawn to revolution, organized the country on a military basis and appealed to France for aid. A French invasion at the end of 1796 was abortive, and a year later a large invasion fleet was defeated at Camperdown. There followed the disastrous insurrection of 1798. A small French force sent to support the rebels was easily crushed. Tone, who accompanied it, was captured and later committed suicide in Dublin; other leaders of the United Irishmen were imprisoned. Great Britain was committed to a policy of brutal repression, holding down Ireland with an army that eventually numbered 200,000.

At stake were the security of Great Britain against France and Anglican dominance in Ireland. In short, if Great Britain was to win the war with France, a permanent resolution to the Irish upheaval had to be found. William Pitt the Younger had become prime minister of Great Britain in 1783, and he believed, unlike most English, that the only way to solve the problems of Ireland was to extinguish Irish independence in a legislative union of the two kingdoms. The economic idea behind the act recognized the British Isles as a single economic trade entity. The suggestion was so unpopular, however, that the government was prevented from introducing proposed legislation about it to the Irish parliament in 1799. The English parliament passed the Act of Union on

July 2, 1800, but only by corruption on an unprecedented scale: the wholesale promotion and creation of peers, the bestowal of sinecures and pensions, threats of dismissal from office, and the bribing of patrons of parliamentary boroughs at a cost of more than £1 million. The bill passed through the Irish parliament without furor on August 1. Catholic support was secured by a virtual promise of emancipation once the act had been passed. Pitt and First Marquess Cornwallis, the commander in chief and viceroy of Ireland, considered the offer of emancipation essential and could be conceded because in the United Kingdom the Irish Catholics would be outnumbered and outvoted many times by the majority in the British parliament. Most Catholic bishops and priests favored the Union.

SIGNIFICANCE

The Act of Union that created the United Kingdom of Great Britain and Ireland went into effect on January 1, 1801. The imperial Parliament in London was augmented in the House of Lords by four bishops of the Anglican Church of Ireland and twenty-eight Irish representative peers elected by the entire Irish peerage, and in the House of Commons by one hundred Irish members, which brought the total number of members to 658. The Church of Ireland was united with its sister Church of England, but Roman Catholics were still excluded from Parliament. The Irish law courts retained their separate identity. Ireland for the first time enjoyed free trade with Great Britain and the British Empire, perhaps the only gain that Ireland really achieved from the Union. Ireland retained its separate exchequer and national debt and was to share imperial expenses for the following twenty years, when the matter would be reconsidered.

Pitt's promise of Catholic emancipation was not kept, and the Irish felt tricked and betrayed. King George III was convinced that emancipation in any form would violate his coronation oath, and he refused to consider it. Indeed, he referred to anyone who favored emancipation as "his personal enemy." He was supported by many of Pitt's fellow ministers and a majority in Parliament. As a result, Pitt, Cornwallis, and Lord Castlereagh, the chief secretary of Ireland, resigned in March, 1801. Pitt returned to office in 1804 and died twenty months later.

The fight for Catholic emancipation continued, and in 1823, after an intense struggle led by Daniel O'Connell, Parliament passed an act in 1829 that gave Catholics a type of political equality. At this point, O'Connell, popularly known as "The Great Liberator," began the struggle for what was ultimately termed "Home Rule," in an effort both to establish a separate parliament for Ireland and to eliminate the Act of Union. The Catholics in southern Ireland were determined to have the right to Home Rule, but the Protestants in Ulster insisted on maintaining the Act of Union with Great Britain.

Although there were many attempts, it was not until 1914 that the British parliament passed the Home Rule bill. After the start of World War I, however, Home Rule was discontinued. In 1920, Ireland was partitioned, with individual parliaments for both north and south. The Act of Union did not deal with the bitter and intractable problems afflicting Ireland, and they grew more vexing until they were settled by dissolution of the Union in 1921. In 1921, southern Ireland became known as the Irish Free State.

—*James M. Haas, updated by M. Casey Diana*

FURTHER READING

Bolton, G. C. *The Passing of the Irish Act of Union*. New York: Oxford University Press, 1966. A scholarly, challenging, and informative historical account of the Act of Union.

Brown, Michael, Patrick M. Geoghegan, and James Kelly. *The Irish Act of Union: Bicentennial Essays*. Dublin: Irish Academic Press, 2003. Contains eleven essays about the act, including discussions of the role of Ulster Presbyterians in the act's passage and the actions of the Irish House of Commons.

Ehrman, John. *The Younger Pitt: The Years of Acclaim*. New York: E. P. Dutton, 1969. Sheds light on Pitt's economic theory, political intrigue with King George III, and Pitt's struggle for Irish Catholic emancipation.

Foster, R. F. *Modern Ireland: 1600-1972*. London: Penguin Press, 1989. An in-depth account of the Act of Union in chapter 12 provides a perceptive, fact-filled analysis of the act and of Ireland as a whole during this period.

Geoghegan, Patrick M. *The Irish Act of Union: A Study in High Politics, 1798-1801*. New York: St. Martin's Press, 1999. This study of British-Irish relations between 1783 and 1801 examines the connection between the Act of Union's adoption in 1800 and Pitt's resignation as prime minister the following year.

Keogh, Dáire, and Kevin Whelan, eds. *Acts of Union: The Causes, Contexts, and Consequences of the Act of Union*. Dublin: Four Courts Press, 2001. Collection of fourteen essays exploring various aspects of the act, including events leading to its passage, Catholic responses, and public opinion. One chapter describes how the act was depicted in political cartoons. Includes color plates of the cartoons.

Killen, John. *The Decade of the United Irishmen: Contemporary Accounts, 1791-1801*. Belfast, Ireland: Blackstaff Press, 1998. A collection of contemporary sources in which Tone and his writings play a particularly important part.

Lecky, William Edward Hartpole. *A History of Ireland in the Eighteenth Century*. 5 vols. London: Longmans, Green, 1892. Reprint. New York: AMS Press, 1969. Lecky's five-volume work still retains its position as the premier source of information on the Act of Union.

Madden, R. R. *The United Irishmen: Their Lives and Times*. 7 vols. London: J. Madden, 1842-1846. An early, comprehensive account of the political structure and the principal Irish players surrounding the Act of Union, including Henry Flood, Henry Grattan, and Wolfe Tone.

O'Brien, Gerard. *Anglo-Irish Politics in the Age of Grattan and Pitt*. Blackrock, County Dublin: Irish Academic Press, 1987. Sheds light on both sides of the Irish and British schism by addressing the political lives of the Irish orator and independence leader, Henry Grattan, and the British prime minister, William Pitt the Younger, who strove for Irish Catholic emancipation.

Pakenham, Thomas. *The Year of Liberty: The Great Irish Rebellion of 1798*. New York: Random House, 1997. The most complete and readable study of the rebellion, with ample illustrative material.

SEE ALSO: Sept. 10, 1763: Publication of the *Freeman's Journal*; Apr. 19, 1775: Battle of Lexington and Concord; July 14, 1789: Fall of the Bastille; Jan. 4, 1792-1797: The *Northern Star* Calls for Irish Independence; Apr. 20, 1792-Oct., 1797: Early Wars of the French Revolution; Jan. 21, 1793: Execution of Louis XVI; Apr. 12, 1798-Sept. 2, 1801: Napoleon's Egyptian Campaign; May-Nov., 1798: Irish Rebellion.

RELATED ARTICLES in *Great Lives from History: The Eighteenth Century, 1701-1800*: Edmund Burke; Charlotte; First Marquess Cornwallis; Lord Edward Fitzgerald; George III; Henry Grattan; Thomas Hutchinson; William Pitt the Elder; William Pitt the Younger; Wolfe Tone; Robert Walpole.

1790's

Appendixes

TIME LINE

The time line below includes the events and developments covered in the essays in this publication (appearing in small capital letters) as well as more than 250 other important events and developments. Each event is tagged by general region or regions, rather than by smaller nations or principalities, which changed significantly over the century covered in this publication; by this means, the time line can be used to consider general trends in the same region over time. However, because many events, although occurring in one or two regions nevertheless had a global or cross-regional impact, they have been left in strict chronological order to facilitate a better understanding of simultaneous events and their occasional interaction. The abbreviation "c." is used below to stand for "circa."

DATE	REGION	EVENT
18th cent.	Africa/Americas	**EXPANSION OF THE ATLANTIC SLAVE TRADE:** Benefiting from the complicity of European nations, the Atlantic slave trade expanded dramatically during the eighteenth century. This development set the stage for the mass transportation of Africans to the Americas, with more than 70 percent of all slaves arriving in the New World after 1700. Although an antislavery movement emerged in the late eighteenth century, economic influences obstructed its effectiveness.
1701	North America	**Louisiana Becomes a French Province:** Following numerous explorations, France officially established the area drained by the Mississippi, Missouri, and Ohio Rivers as a province.
c. 1701	Africa	**OMAN CAPTURES ZANZIBAR:** Portugal's decline during the 1600's led to cracks in its control of East Africa. Oman took advantage of Portugal's weakness to seize Zanzibar by 1701, effectively ending Lisbon's rule north of Mozambique.
1701	Europe	**PLUMIER PUBLISHES *L'ART DE TOURNER*:** Charles Plumier's *L'Art de tourner* provided the basis for advances in manufacturing at the beginning of the eighteenth century. It cataloged every significant development in the history of lathes and prepared the way for further advances in the art of wood turning.
1701	Europe	**TULL INVENTS THE SEED DRILL:** Jethro Tull's invention of the seed drill revolutionized farming. The drill replaced the wasteful and labor-intensive broadcast method of seeding and paved the way for subsequent advances in mechanized agriculture.
c. 1701-1721	Europe	**GREAT NORTHERN WAR:** The Great Northern War established Russia as the dominant power in the Baltic region and led to Sweden's decline as a great military power in Europe.
1701-1732	Europe	**Decline of Executions for Witchcraft:** From a peak in the sixteenth and seventeenth centuries, executions for witchcraft declined dramatically throughout Europe after the beginning of the eighteenth century.
c. 1701-1750	Europe	**BACH PIONEERS MODERN MUSIC:** Johann Sebastian Bach pioneered modern music, creating a vast library of compositions for keyboard and stringed instruments and ushering in technical innovations that would influence later generations of musicians and composers.
1701-1750	Africa	**Expansion of Asante Influence in West Africa:** With the Battle of Feyiase in 1701, the Asante people began to displace their Denkyira overlords in the region of modern Ghana.

935

DATE	REGION	EVENT
Feb. 4, 1701-Feb. 4, 1703	East Asia	**REVENGE OF THE FORTY-SEVEN RONIN:** After the lord of Ako was disgraced and forced to kill himself, his samurai devised a plan for a revenge killing that took two years to execute. Though they succeeded and were regarded as heroes, the Tokugawa shogunate forced them to commit suicide for defying its authority. Their deed has been celebrated in numerous stories, plays, and films as a model of loyalty and courage in the face of injustice and tyranny.
May 26, 1701-Sept. 7, 1714	Europe	**WAR OF THE SPANISH SUCCESSION:** The death of Spain's King Charles II sparked the first of several eighteenth century wars of succession. The Spanish throne was the nominal source of the conflict, but more at stake was the international balance of power, as every major power in Europe struggled for advantage.
June 12, 1701	Europe	**ACT OF SETTLEMENT:** The Act of Settlement ensured the Protestant succession to the English throne and increased the power of Parliament. As a result of its passage, the Hanover Dynasty was installed as the ruling family of Great Britain in 1714, and the Stuarts were permanently disenfranchised.
July 6, 1701	Europe	**William Kidd Hanged in England:** The notorious pirate had been in Boston in 1699, then sent to England for trial.
July 9, 1701	Europe	**MARSH BUILDS IRELAND'S FIRST PUBLIC LIBRARY:** Narcissus Marsh's library, Ireland's first library open to the public, acquired and preserved several extensive collections of books, including the finest private library at that time in England. The library's founding was revolutionary, given its mission of free and open access to all, which included disenfranchised, and uneducated, Dubliners.
1702	North America	**Founding of Ft. Louis:** The first French settlement on North America's Gulf Coast (later to become Mobile, Alabama) established a settled French presence throughout the Louisiana province.
1702	North America	**New Jersey Established:** After years of bickering between the proprietors of East and West Jersey, the two were combined to form a single colony.
1702 or 1706	Middle East	**FIRST ARABIC PRINTING PRESS:** Arabic-language printing began at Aleppo in Syria in the first decade of the eighteenth century.
May 15, 1702-Apr. 11, 1713	Europe	**QUEEN ANNE'S WAR:** The death of Charles II brought about the War of the Spanish Succession, a struggle for power between all the major nations of Europe, which inevitably spread to their colonial territories. In the portion of the war fought in the Americas, known separately as Queen Anne's War, Great Britain gained territory and commercial concessions and consolidated its status as the world's most powerful empire.
July 24, 1702-Oct. 1, 1704	Europe	**CAMISARD RISINGS IN THE CÉVENNES:** The risings of the Camisards—Protestant peasants in the Cévennes region of southern France—renewed the religious unrest between Catholics and Protestants that had plagued France during the Reformation. This rebellion challenged the absolute authority of the French king and the alliance of church and state.

DATE	REGION	EVENT
1703-1711	Europe	**HUNGARIAN REVOLT AGAINST HABSBURG RULE:** While the Habsburgs battled the Bourbons to gain greater power in Europe, the peasants of Hungary staged a rebellion against their Habsburg king, seeking Hungarian independence from the Habsburg Holy Roman Empire. The failure of the rebellions confirmed the strength of the Habsburgs' empire and the predominance of the Hungarian nobility.
May 27, 1703	Europe	**FOUNDING OF ST. PETERSBURG:** Czar Peter the Great created the city of St. Petersburg on the northwestern frontier of Russia to be a window to the West, a Western-style, modern capital far from the eastward-looking traditions of Moscow.
June 20, 1703	East Asia	**CHIKAMATSU PRODUCES *THE LOVE SUICIDES AT SONEZAKI*:** Chikamatsu's *The Love Suicides at Sonezaki* created a new genre of puppet theater, "domestic" plays in which *chōnin* (ordinary townspeople), rather than the samurai, were presented as tragic heroes.
Dec. 30, 1703	East Asia	**Japanese Earthquake and Fire:** A massive earthquake and fire destroyed much of the capital city of Edo (later Tokyo), killing as many as 200,000 people.
1704	North America	**Appearance of the *News-Letter*:** John Campbell began publishing the weekly *News-Letter*, the first regular newspaper in the American colonies.
1704	Middle East	**Death of Iṣṭifān al-Duwayhī:** This Maronite patriarch had emerged as the first important historian from the Arabic-speaking Christian community in Lebanon.
1704	Middle East	**Hasan Paşa Appointed Governor of Baghdad:** Hasan's appointment established a quasi-hereditary dynasty that brought order to central Iraq and ruled the region throughout the eighteenth century.
1704	Europe	**NEWTON PUBLISHES *OPTICS*:** Sir Isaac Newton's *Optics* established a new theory of light and a more quantitative and experimental style of science.
1704	Europe	**Publication of *The Arabian Nights' Entertainments*:** This edition made the famous tales of Sinbad widely available to Europeans for the first time.
1704	Europe	**Swift Publishes *A Tale of a Tub*:** English author Jonathan Swift famously satirized religious corruption.
1704	Europe	***Weekly Review* Founded:** This important thrice-weekly paper, founded in the midst of the Tory-Whig controversy, was sparked by the War of the Spanish Succession.
1704-1712	Europe	**ASTRONOMY WARS IN ENGLAND:** John Flamsteed was compelled by the queen of England and the Royal Society of London to publish the results of his decades-long observations of star locations. Flamsteed repudiated this unfinished publication of his work and publicly burned most of the available copies. In the end, the conflict would hamper astronomical research in the first two decades of the eighteenth century, despite the catalog's early publication.
1704-1757	Southeast Asia	**JAVANESE WARS OF SUCCESSION:** After decades of growing Dutch influence in Java, uncertainty as to the rightful succession to the dynastic throne of Mataram resulted in a series of wars for the crown. These wars provided the Dutch East India Company with an opportunity, and it seized control of Java.

DATE	REGION	EVENT
Aug. 4, 1704	Europe	**Britain Captures Gibraltar:** English forces seized this strategic fortress, which guarded the entrance to the Mediterranean Sea, in one of the key early allied victories of the War of the Spanish Succession.
Aug. 13, 1704	Europe	**BATTLE OF BLENHEIM:** The Battle of Blenheim marked the greatest military triumph in the War of the Spanish Succession and the first English victory on the Continent since Agincourt in 1315.
1705	Europe	**Blenheim Palace Constructed:** This great English palace was commissioned as a reward and commemoration of the duke of Marlborough's victory at Blenheim, Bavaria, the year before.
1705	Europe	**HALLEY PREDICTS THE RETURN OF A COMET:** Halley's successful prediction of the return of a comet, later named for him, was a stunning confirmation of Sir Isaac Newton's law of gravity and laws of motion. Halley's prediction also established that Comet Halley orbits the Sun.
1705-1712	Europe	**NEWCOMEN DEVELOPS THE STEAM ENGINE:** Thomas Newcomen built the first steam engine, providing the power to operate pumps needed to remove water from coal mines that penetrated the English landscape.
1706	Europe	**Rømer Publishes *Astronomical Observations*:** The last major publication of the pioneering Danish astronomer Ole Rømer.
Feb., 1706-Apr. 28, 1707	Europe	**ACT OF UNION UNITES ENGLAND AND SCOTLAND:** The Act of Union united England and Scotland in the nation of Great Britain, ending centuries of war and animosity between the two countries by forging a single political entity.
May 23, 1706	Europe	**Battle of Ramillies:** John Churchill, the first duke of Marlborough, defeated François de Neufville, the duc de Villeroi, in the War of the Spanish Succession. The English and their allies gained Brussels, Antwerp, Ghent, and Ostend, overrunning Spanish Netherlands.
1707	Europe	**Emigration from the Rhineland Palatinate to England:** The first phase of the German immigration would eventually bring tens of thousands of mainly Calvinists and Lutherans to the American colonies.
1707	Europe	**Fortnum and Mason's Opens in London:** Based upon a growing international trade, this new enterprise successfully catered the best of wines and specialty foods to wealthy English households.
1707	Europe	**Newton Publishes *Arithmetica universalis*:** Sir Isaac Newton presented his theory of equations and observations on algebra developed during the 1670's and 1680's.
1707	Europe	**"Pulse Watch" Invented:** English doctor John Floyer developed the first effective precision diagnostic instrument.
1708	South Asia	**Creation of the United East India Company:** By combining two rival British trading companies, the British government established the strongest European presence on the Indian coast.
1708	Middle East	**Governor of Damascus Becomes Commander of the Annual Damascus Pilgrimage to Mecca:** This arrangement greatly enhanced the prestige and power of the governor's position well into the twentieth century.

DATE	REGION	EVENT
Mar. 23-26, 1708	Europe	**DEFEAT OF THE "OLD PRETENDER":** James Edward—the "Old Pretender," son of James II—sailed to Scotland with an invasion force, but the French fleet assisting him was thwarted, and he returned to France, ending his bid to reclaim the English throne for the Stuarts.
July 11, 1708	Europe	**Battle of Oudenarde:** England's first duke of Marlborough John Churchill and Eugene of Savoy defeated France's duke of Vendôme and the duke of Burgundy, leading to the surrender of Lille and abortive negotiations in the War of the Spanish Succession.
1709	Europe	**Black Death Ravages Prussia:** An estimated 300,000 died in one of numerous recurrences of the plague.
1709	Europe	**DARBY INVENTS COKE-SMELTING:** Abraham Darby developed a coal-based process for smelting iron ore. This process facilitated a major shift in the West from manufacturing predominantly with commonly available organic materials to manufacturing finished products out of mineral components that were themselves industrially produced. Had this shift in the nature of manufacturing not occurred, the Industrial Revolution would never have come about.
1709	Europe	**Fahrenheit Invents the Alcohol Thermometer:** Daniel Gabriel Fahrenheit established his famous Fahrenheit scale, in which the freezing point at sea level is 32 degrees and the boiling point 212 degrees. This early Fahrenheit thermometer led the way to the mercury thermometer a few years later.
c. 1709	Europe	**INVENTION OF THE PIANO:** Bartolomeo Cristofori created the first pianoforte, a keyboard instrument capable of gradations in both volume and intensity of the notes played. His invention inspired others to adapt and improve his fundamental design, which became the basis for modern pianos. As the instruments became more common, composers began to write music specifically for the piano.
1709	Europe	*The Tatler* **Appears in London:** Playwright Richard Steele began publishing this famous journal of politics and social criticism, including essays written by Joseph Addison.
1709-1747	Middle East	**PERSIAN-AFGHAN WARS:** With the weakening of the Ṣafavid Empire during the seventeenth century, Afghan tribes under Persian occupation grew restive. Through a series of conflicts now known as the Persian-Afghan Wars, they asserted their independence and in 1722 decisively defeated the Persian army in the Battle of Gulnabad before seizing the capital city of Eṣfahān.
June 27, 1709	Europe	**BATTLE OF POLTAVA:** Peter the Great's reformed and modernized Russian army secured a major victory over the Swedish army led by Charles XII. The victory marked the ascendancy of Russia over Sweden as a European power and secured the newly founded city of St. Petersburg as a potential capital of the Russian Empire.
Sept. 11, 1709	Europe	**BATTLE OF MALPLAQUET:** The bloodiest battle of the War of the Spanish Succession, which revealed new tactics and attitudes toward warfare. The outcome was a British allied victory, but the battle's grim toll—more than ten thousand dead and twenty thousand wounded—shocked Europe.

DATE	REGION	EVENT
1710	Europe	**Berkeley Publishes** *A Treatise Concerning the Principles of Human Knowledge*: Irishman George Berkeley laid the groundwork for the empiricist school of philosophy.
1710	North America	**Germans Settle at New Bern, North Carolina:** This immigration of 650 Swiss and Germans from the Palatinate into North Carolina began a long process of German immigration that made them the largest European immigrant group of the eighteenth century other than the British.
1710	Europe	**Tory Party Defeats the Whigs in Britain:** In the first clear transfer of power since the Glorious Revolution of 1688, the duke of Marlborough and the Whig ministry were voted out of power, in part because of their perceived association with the Jacobite cause.
Nov. 20, 1710-July 21, 1718	Europe	**OTTOMAN WARS WITH RUSSIA, VENICE, AND AUSTRIA:** Russia invaded Ottoman territory but was humiliated at the River Pruth. The Ottomans, encouraged by their easy victory, decided to attempt to recover territory they had lost to Venice in 1699, but they were defeated when Austria intervened in the conflict.
1711	Europe	**Ascot Races Established:** Queen Anne of England approved support of formalized racing for cash prizes.
1711	Middle East	**Civil War in Egypt:** Mamlūk beys emerged as the most important political force, reducing Ottoman governors to figureheads.
1711	Europe	**Landed Property Qualification Act Passed:** This English law prohibited the election to Parliament of British financiers, merchants, and industrialists.
Mar. 1, 1711	Europe	**ADDISON AND STEELE ESTABLISH** *THE SPECTATOR*: Although it lasted for only two years, Joseph Addison and Richard Steele's Whig newspaper *The Spectator* set the standard for taste and prose style in early eighteenth century London.
Mar. 7, 1711	Europe	*Rinaldo* **Opens at London's Haymarket Theatre:** Debut of the opera featuring music by George Frideric Handel and libretto by Giacomo Rossi.
Sept. 22, 1711-Mar. 23, 1713	North America	**TUSCARORA WAR:** Conflict over land, property, and trade led the Tuscarora Indians to declare war on European colonists in North Carolina. The Tuscaroras were decimated in the war, their society was dispersed, and the way was opened for Carolinian settlers to expand westward.
Dec., 1711	Europe	**OCCASIONAL CONFORMITY BILL:** Stipulated that taking Communion once per year was insufficient to meet the requirement that those holding public office in Britain must take Anglican Communion. The law was an attempt to ensure that only authentic Anglicans could join the government.
1712	North America	**Carolina Colony Divided:** Founded in 1663, the Carolina colony was divided into North Carolina and South Carolina.
1712	North America	**First Sperm Whale Harpooned in Modern Times:** Christopher Hussey's kill sparked a new international trade in sperm oil, spermaceti, whale ivory, and ambergris.
1712	Europe	*The History of John Bull* **Published:** Literature and politics merged when Scottish physician John Arbuthnot satirized the duke of Marlborough and established "John Bull" as a symbol of England.

DATE	REGION	EVENT
1712	Europe	**PHILIP V FOUNDS THE ROYAL LIBRARY OF SPAIN:** A French aristocrat who succeeded to the Spanish throne, Philip was eager to demonstrate his support of institutions that fostered Spanish culture. By founding the Royal Library of Spain, he helped to revive the Spanish Golden Age, which thrived under the Habsburgs. The Royal Library, controlled by the Crown, became the government-run National Library of Spain in 1836.
1712	Europe	**Pope Publishes *The Rape of the Lock*:** Alexander Pope famously satirized the royal court in his mock-heroic poem.
1712	Europe	**STAMP ACT:** Responding to an appeal from Queen Anne to curb the licentiousness of the press, England's Parliament enacted a tax of one-half cent per sheet on periodical publications. The tax became an important source of revenue and was expanded several times during the eighteenth century. As a vehicle for censorship, it was largely ineffective.
Apr. 6, 1712	North America	**NEW YORK CITY SLAVE REVOLT:** A small group of black and American Indian slaves rebelled against mistreatment and restrictive laws, leading to further legal restrictions on slaves—free or not—including the weakening of due process rights and the prohibition against owning or inheriting property. Also, slave owners, before they could free a slave, had to pay a bond to the government as well as an annual allowance for life to each freed slave.
Apr. 13-Aug. 11, 1712	Europe	**SECOND VILLMERGEN WAR:** In Switzerland's fourth and last religious war, Swiss Protestants were victorious, thus gaining constitutional equality as well as political powers commensurate with their majority status and economic wealth.
July 24-25, 1712	Europe	**Battle of Denain:** The French under Claude-Louis-Hector, duc de Villars, defeated Eugene of Savoy and a British-Dutch force during the War of the Spanish Succession.
Aug., 1712	Central America	**MAYA REBELLION IN CHIAPAS:** An anticolonial, indigenous rebellion against Spanish occupation in southern Mexico, initially rooted in religious persecution but later a revolt encouraged by indigenous elites, was unprecedented in its scale, longevity, and leadership structure. The rebellion led to reform of the Mexican Indian labor system by the Spanish and set in motion demands for Mexican independence from Spain.
1713	North America	**Construction of First Schooner:** Built by Andrew Robinson of Gloucester, Massachusetts, this distinctive vessel soon became the model for fleets fishing off the Grand Banks.
1713	Middle East	**Timoni Describes Immunization for Smallpox:** Emmanuel Timoni, a Greek physician in Constantinople, described the method in a letter to London physician John Woodward, who in the following year published Timoni's account in the *Philosophical Transactions of the Royal Society*.
Apr. 11, 1713	Europe	**TREATY OF UTRECHT:** This peace agreement between Great Britain and France concluded Britain's participation in the War of the Spanish Succession. It revised territorial boundaries in North America and Europe, settled dynastic issues, and introduced trade patterns that resulted in Britain's rise to world-power status. The war itself would not end until Austria also negotiated peace in the Treaties of Rastatt and Baden (1714).

DATE	REGION	EVENT
1713	North America	**FOUNDING OF LOUISBOURG:** Following territorial losses in Canada as a result of the Treaty of Utrecht (1713), which ended the War of the Spanish Succession, France chose to establish a new fortress at Louisbourg, on Cape Breton Island, to protect its North American interests.
Aug. 3, 1713	Europe	**FOUNDATION OF THE SPANISH ACADEMY:** The Spanish Academy was founded to regulate the use and development of the Spanish language throughout the Spanish Empire. When Spain lost that empire, the academy continued to function, in concert with the academies of the Spanish language that were established in all former Spanish colonies. These academies, taking their lead from the Spanish Academy, have served to keep the Spanish language unified into the early twenty-first century.
Sept. 8, 1713	Europe	**PAPAL BULL *UNIGENITUS*:** Clement XI issued the papal bull *Unigenitus*, condemning French Jansenist teachings. The bull met stiff opposition among the French clergy, which seriously undermined papal authority.
1714	Europe	**FAHRENHEIT DEVELOPS THE MERCURY THERMOMETER:** Daniel Gabriel Fahrenheit developed sealed mercury thermometers with reliable scales that agreed with each other, revolutionizing the scientific measurement of temperature. By developing a method for calibrating different thermometers to the same scale, he made it possible for different people in different parts of the world to compare temperature measurements accurately and reliably.
1714-1718	Europe	**Ottoman War with Venice and Austria:** The Ottomans, although regaining Morea, could not regain Hungary and lost territory in the Balkans as military power increasingly passed to European states.
1714-1762	Europe	**QUEST FOR LONGITUDE:** John Harrison's chronometer was used to make the first accurate measurement of longitude at sea, revolutionizing ocean exploration and travel. His invention opened new vistas in cartography, astronomy, world commerce, and international timekeeping.
1714-1777	Southeast Asia	**Burmese-Manipuri Wars:** Manipur, an Indian state located on the western border with Burma, engaged in a series of conflicts with Burma during the eighteenth century and evenually sought British assistance in protecting its homeland. British influence in the region increased as a result.
Jan. 7, 1714	Europe	**MILL PATENTS THE TYPEWRITER:** Henry Mill created the first machine for printing individual letters and documents. Queen Anne, recognizing the merits of Mill's innovation, issued a patent guaranteeing his rights to manufacture and sell machines based on his design.
Mar. 7, 1714, and Sept. 7, 1714	Europe	**TREATIES OF RASTATT AND BADEN:** France and the Holy Roman Empire signed the treaties of Rastatt and Baden, respectively, officially ending the War of the Spanish Succession. The treaties supplemented the provisions of the Treaty of Utrecht (1713), which had concluded peace between all the other combatants in the war, but they failed to establish peace between the Holy Roman Empire and Spain.

DATE	REGION	EVENT
Summer, 1714-1741	North America	**FOX WARS:** For almost three decades, the Fox Indians waged war against French settlers and against other Native American tribes, greatly destabilizing North America's Great Lakes region and hampering trade and diplomacy for other inhabitants of the region.
1715	South Asia	**French Conquest of Mauritius:** France seized the Indian Ocean island group from the Dutch, who had held it since the 1630's.
1715	East Asia	**Japan Increases Limits on Foreign Trade:** Alarmed at the trade imbalance with the West, the Japanese government set export limits on copper and reduced to two the number of Dutch ships permitted to trade annually at Nagasaki.
1715-1737	Europe	**BUILDING OF THE KARLSKIRCHE:** The Karlskirche, a votive church commissioned by Emperor Charles VI, represented the supreme architectural achievement of Johann Bernhard Fischer von Erlach, who set his distinctive mark upon the Kaiserstil (the imperial style) of Baroque Vienna.
Feb. 5, 1715	Europe	**James Edward Flees to France:** After Jacobite troops were routed by the Royalist forces of John Campbell, duke of Argyll, James Edward, the Old Pretender, fled to France. The Jacobite cause would be revived by his son, Charles Edward Stuart, the Young Pretender (b. 1720).
Sept. 1, 1715	Europe	**Death of Louis XIV:** The great exemplar of European royal absolutism, Louis XIV died at age seventy-six after seventy-two years on the throne.
Sept. 6, 1715-Feb. 4, 1716	Europe	**JACOBITE RISING IN SCOTLAND:** Supporters of the exiled Stuart Dynasty rose up in Scotland, in an attempt to overthrow the new Hanover Dynasty and place James Edward on the British throne. This Jacobite movement drew enough adherents to pose a serious threat to the Hanoverian monarchy, but it ended in failure because the Jacobites lacked good intelligence, adequate communications, and decisive military leadership.
Nov. 13, 1715	Europe	**Battle of Sheriffmuir:** Royalists under John Campbell, the duke of Argyll, forced the Jacobite army to retreat to Perth, Scotland, prior to the December arrival of James Edward, the Old Pretender.
1716	East Asia	**China Outlaws Christian Teaching:** After an earlier period of relative openness, the incompatibility between Chinese rites and Christian doctrine led the Chinese government to outlaw Christian missionary activity.
1716	North America	**Virginians Settle in the Shenandoah Valley:** Alexander Spotswood led a band of Virginia colonists across the Blue Ridge Mountains.
1717	North America	**German Religious Dissenters Immigrate to America:** German Dunkers, Mennonites, and Moravians began an extensive migration of religious dissenters that would last until the American Revolutionary War. Most settled in Pennsylvania.
1717	Europe	**John Law Secures a Monopoly on Trade and Government in Louisiana:** Having been unsuccessful in attracting French settlers to Louisiana, the French government granted Scottish entrepreneur John Law a twenty-five-year monopoly on trade and government in exchange for establishing at least six thousand white settlers in the region.

DATE	REGION	EVENT
1717	Latin America	**Viceroyalty of New Granada Established:** In order to govern its large New World empire more efficiently, the Spanish government created a new viceroyalty, carved from the viceroyalty of Peru and with its capital in Bogotá.
Aug. 16, 1717	Europe	**Battle of Belgrade:** After a long siege by 180,000 Turkish troops, Prince Eugene of Savoy successfully drove them back with a force of 40,000.
Aug. 20, 1717-Feb. 17, 1720	Europe	**War of the Quadruple Alliance:** France and Britain forced Spain, Austria, and Savoy to accept, with minor revisions, settlements reached at Utrecht and Rastatt that ended the War of the Spanish Succession.
1718	Europe	**BERNOULLI PUBLISHES HIS CALCULUS OF VARIATIONS:** By the early eighteenth century, various approaches had been tried to solve several mathematical problems known since antiquity. Johann I Bernoulli organized much of the earlier material and produced an account that could be followed by a wide range of mathematicians.
1718	North America	**Death of Blackbeard the Pirate:** The pirate Edward Teach, known as Blackbeard, was killed in a battle off the coast of North Carolina, marking the decline of the great age of piracy in North America.
1718	Europe	**First English Banknotes Issued:** After reforms borrowed from the Dutch, including establishment of the Bank of England in 1694, the English issued official banknotes to foster more efficient trade and commerce.
1718	Europe	**GEOFFROY ISSUES THE *TABLE OF REACTIVITIES*:** Geoffroy produced the first systematic treatment of chemical reactivities. He presented a table illustrating these relationships to the French Academy of Sciences, along with a law stating that highly reactive substances will displace less reactive ones in compounds.
1718	Europe	**Montagu Reports on Smallpox Vaccination:** In "Inoculation Against Smallpox," Lady Mary Wortley Montagu, wife of the English ambassador to Constantinople, reported on the practice of variolation, commonly used in the Middle East to prevent severe cases of smallpox.
1718	North America	**New Orleans Founded:** A new commercial city, founded at the mouth of the Mississippi River by Sieur de Bienville, attracted only a handful of French settlers but nevertheless laid the foundation for commercial development.
1718-1730	Middle East	**TULIP AGE:** The last twelve years of the reign of Ahmed III were known to the Turks as *lale devri*, or the Tulip Age, named after the sultan's fascination with the cultivation and display of tulips. It was a period of hedonism and extravagance, artistic and literary florescence, and architectural projects, eventually extinguished by popular religious fanaticism.
June 26, 1718	Europe	**Czarevitch Alexius Petrovich Dies of Flogging:** Fearing rebellion, Peter the Great had his son and heir beaten to death in St. Petersburg.
1719	Europe	**Creation of the Principality of Liechtenstein:** Holy Roman Emperor Charles VI created a new sovereign territory following the purchase of Vaduz and Schellenberg by the Austrian count, Hans Adam von Liechtenstein.

DATE	REGION	EVENT
1719-1724	Europe	**STUKELEY STUDIES STONEHENGE AND AVEBURY:** William Stukeley's systematic method of investigating Stonehenge, Avebury, and related prehistoric stone temple sites produced exceptional notes and drawings that became models for archaeological fieldwork.
Apr. 25, 1719	Europe	**DEFOE PUBLISHES THE FIRST NOVEL:** Daniel Defoe wrote *Robinson Crusoe*, a fact-based, realistically detailed account of a shipwrecked man struggling for survival, the first novel written in English. The genre as a whole would come to be defined in terms of several of *Robinson Crusoe*'s key features, especially its studied focus on character psychology, its association of detail with realism, and its alignment with middle-class values and experience.
1720	Europe	**FINANCIAL COLLAPSE OF THE JOHN LAW SYSTEM:** The fall of Scottish banker John Law's Banque Générale and the collapse of his Mississippi Company in 1720 brought down France's first national bank, ended serious attempts to modernize the state's public financing and tax systems, and indirectly contributed to the massive debts that helped precipitate the French Revolution.
1720	Europe	**Handel Named Director of the Royal Academy of Music:** George Frideric Handel was named director of the London academy and presented his oratorio *Esther* there.
May, 1720-Dec., 1721	Europe	**LAST MAJOR OUTBREAK OF PLAGUE:** On May 20, 1720, a ship carrying victims of plague arrived at the French port of Marseilles. Several days later, an epidemic began in the city. By the time the disease had run its course, fifty thousand people in the city had died, as well as an equal number throughout the countryside. The epidemic represented the last major outbreak of the plague in Europe.
Sept., 1720	Europe	**COLLAPSE OF THE SOUTH SEA BUBBLE:** Fraudulent activities within the South Sea Company—a British concern granted a monopoly on all British trade with South America and the islands of the South Sea in exchange for assuming part of the national debt—along with political corruption and mass mania for speculation, resulted in a major stock market crash and widespread financial ruin.
Dec., 1720	East Asia	**JAPAN LIFTS BAN ON FOREIGN BOOKS:** The Tokugawa shogunate lifted a nearly century-long ban on books containing minor references to Christianity. In harmony with Shogun Yoshimune's policy of promoting "practical learning," the Japanese began to import science and technology books, most of which were well illustrated and were either Chinese translations of European works or books in Dutch. Christian religious books, however, remained banned.
1721	Latin America	**Diamonds Discovered in Brazil:** Once the diamond discovery near Tejuco, Brazil, was authenticated in Europe in 1729, a diamond rush began, greatly altering the character of the region.
1721	Europe/North America	**Regular Postal Service Between England and America:** In a display of British administration and mastery of the sea, regular postal service was established between London and the principal New England cities.

DATE	REGION	EVENT
1721	North America	**Smallpox Epidemic in Boston:** Differences of opinion over the newly learned process of vaccination led to heated debate in the city. The survival rate for those vaccinated proved to be much better than that for those who were not vaccinated.
1721-1742	Europe	**DEVELOPMENT OF GREAT BRITAIN'S OFFICE OF PRIME MINISTER:** The modern concept of the prime minister functioning as the head of Britain's government evolved between 1721 and 1742, with Robert Walpole serving as the first prime minister.
1721-1750	Europe	**EARLY ENLIGHTENMENT IN FRANCE:** During the three decades following publication of Montesquieu's *Lettres persanes* (1721; *Persian Letters*, 1722), French writers produced a growing number of literary, scientific, and philosophical works advocating individual liberty, empirical investigations of all kinds, secular progress, and a skeptical attitude toward religion and tradition.
1722	Europe	**RÉAUMUR DISCOVERS CARBON'S ROLE IN HARDENING STEEL:** René-Antoine Ferchault de Réaumur wrote a treatise on transforming iron ore into steel, revolutionizing metallurgy in France. Réaumur's recommendations and analysis made it possible for France to produce steel for itself and paved the way for the Industrial Revolution.
Apr. 5, 1722	Pacific Islands	**EUROPEAN DISCOVERY OF EASTER ISLAND:** Explorer Jacob Roggeveen discovered a remote, inhabited island about two thousand miles west of the South American continent. The hundreds of massive stone statues and absence of large trees led to centuries of speculation about the island's history, a mystery that scientists have yet to unravel.
1723	Europe	**Bach Appointed Cantor at the St. Thomas School, Leipzig:** After the leading candidate, Georg Philipp Telemann, declined the position, Johann Sebastian Bach auditioned and was hired; the following year he directed the first performances of the *St. John Passion*.
1723	Caribbean	**Coffee First Planted in the New World:** French naval officer Gabriel Mathieu de Cheu planted a coffee plant seedling on the Caribbean island of Martinique, laying the foundation for a new commercial cash crop.
1723	Europe	**Jewish Oaths Permitted in Britain:** In a display of the gradual liberalization of British society, Jews were permitted to take oaths without employing the phrase "On the true faith of a Christian."
1723	Europe	**STAHL POSTULATES THE PHLOGISTON THEORY:** In eighteenth century chemistry, the phlogiston theory—proposed by Georg Stahl—was the dominant model explaining combustion and fermentation. Until the discovery of oxygen, the theory was the basis for all serious chemical experimentation and research. It constituted the first systematic and comprehensive theory of chemistry.
1723-1725	Middle East	**Ottomans Occupy Georgia, Azerbaijan, and Shirvan:** Taking advantage of Afghan attacks in eastern Iran, the Ottoman Empire and Russia partitioned the Caucasus region.

DATE	REGION	EVENT
1724	Europe	**FOUNDATION OF THE ST. PETERSBURG ACADEMY OF SCIENCES:** As part of his program to Westernize and modernize Russian culture, Peter the Great founded an academy of sciences on the model of the British Royal Society and the French Academy of Sciences.
1725	Europe	**FLAMSTEED'S STAR CATALOG MARKS THE TRANSITION TO MODERN ASTRONOMY:** John Flamsteed's catalog, and later atlas showing the locations of the stars, more than doubled the number of stars accurately charted and established a standard used for more than a century by navigators and cosmologists.
1725	Europe	**Russian Academy of Sciences Established:** On his deathbed, Peter the Great established the Russian Academy of Sciences, despite the fact that there were then few Russian scientists of note.
1725-Nov., 1794	Middle East	**PERSIAN CIVIL WARS:** As the Ṣafavid Empire weakened in the seventeenth century, tribal leaders fought one another for control of Persia. Political stability was maintained intermittently under Nādir Shāh and later under the benevolent rule of Karīm Khān Zand. Periods of anarchy nevertheless marked much of the eighteenth century until the establishment of the Qājār Dynasty in 1794 finally brought a stable government to Persia.
Jan. 28, 1725	Europe	**Death of Peter the Great:** By the time of his death after a forty-two-year reign, Peter had transformed Russia into a modern, and sometimes progressive, European power.
Aug. 15, 1725	Europe	**Louis XV Marries Marie:** At the age of fifteen, Louis XV married Marie, daughter of Poland's former king Stanisław I Leszczyński, a marriage that provided few diplomatic complications but to many seemed beneath the dignity of the French crown.
Oct., 1725	Europe	**VICO PUBLISHES *THE NEW SCIENCE*:** Giambattista Vico viewed the state as emerging from primitive origins rather than reasoned philosophical argument, and his "new science" developed this thesis in analyses of both ideas and language.
1726	Latin America	**Montevideo Founded:** The future capital of Uruguay, Montevideo was established at the mouth of the Rio de la Plata by families from Buenos Aires and the Canary Islands who were given lands by the Spanish crown to stem the Portuguese influence in the area.
1726	Europe	**SWIFT SATIRIZES ENGLISH RULE OF IRELAND IN *GULLIVER'S TRAVELS*:** Jonathan Swift's cutting satiric voice harshly criticized the British government and forced England to examine its treatment of its Irish colonial subjects.
1726-1729	Europe	**VOLTAIRE ADVANCES ENLIGHTENMENT THOUGHT IN EUROPE:** After self-exile to England, Voltaire returned to France and introduced advances made by the British in the sciences, religious tolerance, government and political theory, free thinking, and the elimination of aristocratic privilege. British thought thus became a model for the eighteenth century Enlightenment on the Continent.
1727	Europe	**Schulze Studies Silver Salts:** Experiments by German J. H. Schulze established that light, rather than heat, darkens silver salts, laying a foundation for later work in photography.

DATE	REGION	EVENT
May, 1727-1733	Europe	**JANSENIST "CONVULSIONNAIRES" GATHER AT SAINT-MÉDARD:** The Convulsionnaires were a group of Jansenists who gathered at the tomb of one of their members, where miracles seemed to occur. Jansenism had been officially condemned as heretical by the Church in 1713. Thus, for miracles to occur at the tomb of one of the followers of this declared heresy represented a threat to the spiritual authority of the Church.
Oct. 21, 1727	Europe/East Asia	**TREATY OF KIAKHTA:** The Treaty of Kiakhta defined trade between Russia and China for more than a century. It freed the two empires from worrying about each other. Thus, it enabled Russia to concentrate on developing its newly won position as a European power, while in China the Manchu Qing Dynasty could likewise concentrate on consolidating its control over its own far-flung and rapidly growing empire.
Jan. 29, 1728	Europe	**GAY PRODUCES THE FIRST BALLAD OPERA:** With *The Beggar's Opera*, John Gay established a new genre, the English ballad opera, replacing the previous British passion for Italian opera with a new appreciation of native folksongs. His work paved the way for the light operas of the nineteenth century, notably the works of W. S. Gilbert and Arthur Sullivan.
July, 1728-1769	Europe/North America	**RUSSIAN VOYAGES TO ALASKA:** Russian explorers and scientists mounted expeditions to the northern Pacific, surveying and occupying the region. These excursions paved the way for the later Russian settlement of Alaska.
1729	North America	**Franklin Purchases *The Pennsylvania Gazette*:** After years of working for others, Benjamin Franklin purchased his own newspaper with the assistance of partner Hugh Meredith.
1729	Europe	**GRAY DISCOVERS PRINCIPLES OF ELECTRIC CONDUCTIVITY:** Stephen Gray discovered that electricity could flow from one object to another and that, while some materials were conductors of electricity, other materials were insulators of electricity. His meticulous and imaginative experiments transformed the study of static electricity from a parlor amusement to a science.
1729	Europe	**Holy Club Established at Oxford University:** John and Charles Wesley, James Hervey, and George Whitefield met each week to worship, pray, read the classics, and fast, establishing "Methodism" within the Episcopal Church at Oxford.
Nov. 9, 1729, and Feb., 1732	Europe	**TREATY OF SEVILLE:** In 1727, Spain mounted an unsuccessful attempt to recapture Gibraltar from Britain, which had held the peninsula since 1704. The Treaty of Seville ended this military conflict and contributed to the rising power of Britain and the decline of Spain in the eighteenth century.
Nov. 28, 1729	North America	**Indian Attacks in Louisiana:** Following demands that the Natchez Indians relinquish their burial grounds, a war party attacked Louisiana settlers and soldiers, leaving more than two hundred dead and taking several hundred prisoner.
1730	Middle East	**Patrona Hailil Revolt:** In the wake of defeat at the hands of the Persians, Janissaries revolted, attacking many wealthy Turks before being captured and executed.
1730	Europe	**Townshend Introduces Scientific Farming in England:** Learning from Dutch agriculturalists, Charles Townshend introduced the use of turnips as cattle feed, enabling farmers to provide fresh meat year-round.

DATE	REGION	EVENT
1730-1736	Middle East	**Ottoman-Persian War:** Laying siege to Baghdad in 1733, the Ṣafavids secured Ottoman renunciation of previous gains in the Caucasus region.
1730-1739	Caribbean	**FIRST MAROON WAR:** Two groups of rebellious and escaped slaves, as well as their descendants, fought British soldiers to a draw during nearly a decade of fighting in Jamaica, securing for themselves some freedoms but only at the expense of those slaves still in bondage.
Mar. 8, 1730	Europe	**Anna Ivanovna's Coup d'État:** When the Russian czar Peter II died of smallpox on January 30, court intrigues led to the coup d'état by his cousin, who appointed Ernst Johann Biron as grand-chamberlain, initiating a brutal ten-year reign.
1731	Europe	**France Prohibits Barbers from Practicing Surgery:** France forbade barbers from doubling as surgeons (which at this time was still a common practice in Europe), although the law usually allowed barbers to perform minor surgeries such as bloodletting and pulling teeth.
1731	Europe	**Hadley Invents the Reflecting Quadrant:** Mathematician John Hadley's precisely engineered quadrant enabled navigators to determine latitude day or night, proving so successful that it was adopted by Britain's Royal Navy.
July 1, 1731	North America	**Franklin Establishes North America's First Circulating Library:** Benjamin Franklin encouraged members of his Philadelphia intellectual circle to subscribe to a book-purchasing scheme and pool their books for the common good.
1732	North America	***Poor Richard's Almanack* Appears:** Benjamin Franklin's practical advice and agricultural observations made his almanac second only to the Bible as the most widely read book in the American colonies.
c. 1732	Europe	**SOCIETY OF DILETTANTI IS ESTABLISHED:** In response to a growing interest in Greek and Roman antiquities—especially among aristocratic British travelers who had seen them firsthand—the Society of Dilettanti was established in London for the study and discussion of those antiquities. The society helped fund and promote major archaeological expeditions and also contributed to the rise of neoclassicism in British art and architecture.
June 20, 1732	North America	**SETTLEMENT OF GEORGIA:** Georgia became the last of North America's original thirteen British colonies when it was settled in 1732. The philanthropists who settled the colony hoped it would relieve the plight of thousands of destitute debtors and provide a haven for persecuted Protestants from other European countries.
Dec. 7, 1732	Europe	**COVENT GARDEN THEATRE OPENS IN LONDON:** Rivaled only by the Drury Lane Theatre and rebuilt three times after fire damage, Covent Garden Theatre was home to many of the best plays and musical productions of the eighteenth century. It became the foremost opera house in England.
1733	Europe	**British Parliament Passes the Molasses Act:** This legislation was designed to raise revenue in the American colonies by heavily taxing molasses, sugar, and rum imported from non-British colonies; it led to widespread smuggling.

DATE	REGION	EVENT
1733	Europe	**DE MOIVRE DESCRIBES THE BELL-SHAPED CURVE:** Abraham de Moivre was the first person to describe the so-called normal curve, a symmetrical bell-shaped graph that symbolizes probability distribution. This graph of the average distribution of events resolved a serious issue that had been left hanging by the previous generation of mathematicians.
1733	Europe	**DU FAY DISCOVERS TWO KINDS OF ELECTRIC CHARGE:** In extending the electrical experiments of Stephen Gray, Charles-François de Cisternay Du Fay discovered two types of electric charge, which he called vitreous and resinous electricity. He demonstrated the two-fluid theory of electricity: that like charges repel and unlike charges attract. Benjamin Franklin modified this idea with his one-fluid theory, in which an excess or deficiency of the electric fluid was designated positive or negative.
1733	Europe	**KAY INVENTS THE FLYING SHUTTLE:** John Kay's flying shuttle allowed a single weaver to produce fabrics of any width, alleviating the need for two weavers to cooperate on unusually wide fabrics. The invention also leant itself in principle to mechanization, helping to begin the mechanization of the textile industry that constituted the first phase of the Industrial Revolution in England.
1733	Europe	**Voltaire Publishes *Letters Concerning the English Nation*:** Living under Bourbon absolutism, Voltaire praised English representative government.
1733-1734	Europe	**Pope Publishes His *Essay on Man*:** Alexander Pope's poem addressed the human ability to reason, one of the chief concerns of the Enlightenment.
Oct. 10, 1733-Oct. 3, 1735	Europe	**WAR OF THE POLISH SUCCESSION:** When Polish king Augustus II died in 1733, France favored the restoration of Poland's deposed former king, Stanisław I Leszczyński, while the Holy Roman Empire and its allies supported Augustus III's claim to his father's throne. In the resulting War of the Polish Succession, Poland became a pawn through which Western European powers attempted to increase their territory and influence.
Nov. 23, 1733	Caribbean	**SLAVES CAPTURE ST. JOHN'S ISLAND:** Dozens of Amina slaves, originally from the Gold Coast of West Africa, conquered much of St. John in one of the Caribbean region's most successful slave revolts.
1734	Europe	**Comte de Bonneval Begins Modernization of Ottoman Artillery:** French convert to Islam Claude Alexandre de Bonneval, also known as Ahmed Pasha, opened a military engineering school in 1734, inviting opposition from the Janissaries.
1734	North America	**Schwenkenfelders Immigrate to America:** The Schwenkenfelders, a religious group persecuted for their beliefs in Silesia, immigrated to America, settling first in Delaware.
1735	Europe	**British Parliament Passes the Copyright Act:** In an age of increasing public debate in the press, Parliament moved to protect authors from pirated editions of their works. The act was one of the earliest modern laws concerning intellectual property.

DATE	REGION	EVENT
1735	Europe	**HADLEY DESCRIBES ATMOSPHERIC CIRCULATION:** George Hadley, an amateur scientist, described global atmospheric circulation as driven by solar heating and the rotation of the Earth. He was the first person to provide a working explanation for the atmospheric circulation patterns observed in the tropics and subtropics, including the trade winds.
Beginning 1735	Europe	**LINNAEUS CREATES THE BINOMIAL SYSTEM OF CLASSIFICATION:** Carolus Linnaeus designed a hierarchical taxonomic system for naming and classifying plants and animals. His system gave each organism a two-term name that was derived from its unique, or specific, defining characteristics (species name) and its position within the hierarchical system (generic or genus name). Linnaeus's classification system brought an intellectual order to biology that persists to this day.
May, 1735-1743	Latin America	**FRENCH SCIENTISTS EXPLORE THE AMAZON RIVER:** Charles La Condamine and his crew rafted the 3,000-mile-long Amazon River, producing the first scientific accounts of the river and region. In addition to charting the river, he discovered the value of rubber and observed the work of Jesuit missionaries with indigenous peoples.
Aug. 4, 1735	North America	**TRIAL OF JOHN PETER ZENGER:** Zenger published articles criticizing the governor of New York, who had him prosecuted for libel. Zenger was acquitted based on the argument—a novel one at the time—that the truth of an utterance should be a defense in libel cases. The case became a crucial step in the evolution of the freedoms of speech and of the press in Great Britain and subsequently the United States.
1736	Europe	**Concordat Between the Vatican and the Maronite Church:** The Maronite Church accepted the pope's authority in return for the allowance to maintain a distinctive hierarchy, liturgy, canon law, and customs.
1736	Middle East	**End of the Ṣafavid Dynasty in Persia:** The death of ʿAbbās III at the age of six ended the Ṣafavid Dynasty, which had ruled Persia since 1502.
1736	Europe	**Euler Publishes the First Mechanics Text:** Swiss mathematician Leonhard Euler's *Mechanica sive motus analytice exposita* (mechanics or motion explained with analytical science), published nine years after Euler had joined the Russian Academy of Sciences, was the first systematic textbook on mechanics.
1736	Europe	***GENTLEMAN'S MAGAZINE* INITIATES PARLIAMENTARY REPORTING:** Between 1736 and 1746, England's first magazine established a new standard of parliamentary reporting, providing an unbiased—albeit thinly disguised—account of debates in the face of government sanctions.
1736-1739	Europe	**RUSSO-AUSTRIAN WAR AGAINST THE OTTOMAN EMPIRE:** Russia, along with its ally Austria, invaded the Ottoman Empire. This ill-managed and inconclusive aggression ended in a stalemate which left the Russian aggressors determined to build up their army. The Ottomans, believing that their forces were sufficient to maintain their empire, failed to augment them, setting the stage for their defeat at Russian hands later in the century.

DATE	REGION	EVENT
1737	Europe	**British Parliament Passes the Licensing Act:** The measure required that all plays be approved by the Lord Chamberlain and limited the number of theaters in London.
1737	North America	**First City-Paid Police Force in America:** Dissatisfied with the "city watch" in Philadelphia, Benjamin Franklin helped establish a city-paid police force, a precursor to other progressive urban reforms instituted by Franklin.
1737	Europe	**Last Medici Ruler in Tuscany:** With the death of Gian Gastone de' Medici, Austria gave the ducal throne to Franz Stefan, duke of Lorraine and husband of Maria Theresa, heir apparent to the imperial throne.
1737	Europe	**REVIVAL OF THE PARIS SALON:** After two failed attempts to revive the official annual exhibition of art by members of the French Royal Academy earlier in the century, the salon was finally reestablished as a regular event in 1737. This institutionalization of art's public exposure created a cogent and aesthetically reactive public in Paris and a critical literature at once erudite and crudely popular that shaped both taste and art.
Sept. 19, 1737	North America	**WALKING PURCHASE:** Pennsylvania, relying on a questionable deed and practices, acquired a great deal of Lenni Lenape tribal territory. This acquisition led to a greater colonial presence, diminished the prestige of the Lenni Lenape tribe, and enhanced Iroquois dominance over the other tribes of eastern Pennsylvania.
1738	Europe	**BERNOULLI PROPOSES THE KINETIC THEORY OF GASES:** Daniel Bernoulli developed the first systematic theory to explain the behavior of gases in terms of their kinetic (or motion-related) properties. Using a mathematical approach, he established a formal relationship between, on one hand, the many tiny collisions between individual gas molecules and the walls of a container and, on the other hand, the overall pressure exerted on the container by the gas taken as a whole.
1738	Europe	**Excavation of Herculaneum Begins:** Buried by the eruption of Mount Vesuvius in 79 B.C.E., Herculaneum represented one of the great archaeological challenges of the eighteenth century and would continue to be excavated for forty years.
1738	Europe	**Maupertuis Publishes *Sur la figure de la terre*:** French mathematician and biologist Pierre-Louis Moreau de Maupertuis popularized Newtonian mechanics in his report on an expedition to Lapland, confirming the view that Earth is a spheroid flattened at the poles.
May 15, 1738	Europe	**FOUNDATION OF ST. PETERSBURG'S IMPERIAL BALLET SCHOOL:** The St. Petersburg Imperial Ballet School's founding marked the beginning of the great tradition of Russian ballet, which was instrumental in the evolution of dance technique, choreography, and narrative ballets.
Nov. 18, 1738	Europe	**TREATY OF VIENNA:** The Treaty of Vienna was agreed to in the wake of the War of the Polish Succession. It transferred the Kingdom of the Two Sicilies from Austria to Spain and awarded the Duchy of Lorraine and the County of Bar to Stanisław I Leszczyński, the deposed king of Poland.

DATE	REGION	EVENT
1739	North America	**Discovery of the Headwaters of the Arkansas River:** Departing from St. Louis to locate a trade route between Missouri and Santa Fe, French explorers Pierre and Paul Mallet discovered the headwaters of the Arkansas River in the Rocky Mountains.
1739	Europe	**Potato Crop Fails in Ireland:** Cottars began to select potato varieties that provided the highest yields, thus breeding potatoes with little resistance to fungus but setting the stage for later, devastating crop failures.
1739-1740	Europe	**HUME PUBLISHES *A TREATISE OF HUMAN NATURE*:** Although not widely read or well regarded during his lifetime, Hume's first book, *A Treatise of Human Nature*, became a central work in the four-hundred-year tradition of British empiricism.
1739-1741	North America	**WAR OF JENKINS'S EAR:** Great Britain's launch of the War of Jenkins's Ear against Spain brought about the fall of Robert Walpole, the peaceable Whig prime minister, and committed the British government to the use of war as a tool for achieving its imperialistic goals.
1739-1742	North America	**FIRST GREAT AWAKENING:** The First Great Awakening, a spiritual revival in North America, gave birth to religious tolerance and inclusiveness in American society. It influenced the values that would shape the founding of the United States and the framing of the U.S. Constitution a few decades later.
Apr. 7, 1739	Europe	**Highwayman Dick Turpin Hanged:** Richard "Dick" Turpin had been a thief and gang member for more than a decade and was living under the alias John Palmer when he was captured and convicted of stealing horses; most of the legends concerning his career are probably fictional.
Sept. 9, 1739	North America	**STONO REBELLION:** African slaves in South Carolina staged a rebellion that was quickly and brutally suppressed. The revolt demonstrated to white settlers, who were in the minority, the precariousness of their situation in the colonies, and it led them to pass laws designed both to increase their control over their slaves and to decrease discontent among slaves that might lead to future uprisings.
Sept. 18, 1739	Europe	**TREATY OF BELGRADE:** The Treaty of Belgrade ended the Russo-Austrian war against the Ottoman Empire. It checked Austrian expansion into the Balkans for another century and halted Russian expansion southward for a generation.
1740	Europe	**MACLAURIN'S GRAVITATIONAL THEORY:** Colin Maclaurin's prizewinning essay on tides provided an elegant mathematical proof of a key assumption of Newton's gravitational theory. Maclaurin's recognition of the deflecting action of the Earth's rotation also anticipated the more fully dynamical theory of tides that Pierre-Simon Laplace later developed in *Traité de mécanique céleste* (1799-1825; *Celestial Mechanics*, 1829-1839).
1740	North America	**Moravian Immigrants Introduce German Christmas Customs:** Moravians founded Bethlehem, Pennsylvania, introducing customs such as the visit of St. Nicholas (Santa Claus) to the Christmas holiday tradition.

953

DATE	REGION	EVENT
1740-1741	Europe	**RICHARDSON'S *PAMELA* ESTABLISHES THE MODERN NOVEL:** The modern English novel came into its own as a literary form with Samuel Richardson's writing of *Pamela: Or, Virtue Rewarded*. With this work, the episodic method employed by the very first English novels gave way to a plot that focused on a main event, a romantic pursuit, and the realities of contemporary marriage and mores.
May 31, 1740	Europe	**ACCESSION OF FREDERICK THE GREAT:** Frederick the Great ascended the Prussian throne, setting the kingdom on an expansionist and imperialist course. During his reign, Prussia became the dominant Germanic state, significantly changing the balance of power in Europe.
Oct. 20, 1740	Europe	**MARIA THERESA SUCCEEDS TO THE AUSTRIAN THRONE:** In accordance with the Pragmatic Sanction, Maria Theresa succeeded to the Austrian throne upon the death of Charles VI. Although she was one of the greatest of all Habsburg rulers, Maria Theresa's accession began an intense rivalry between Austria and Prussia that eventually led to the eclipse of Austria as a power and the creation of a German empire under Prussian leadership.
Dec. 16, 1740-Nov. 7, 1748	Europe	**WAR OF THE AUSTRIAN SUCCESSION:** For eight years, the nations of Western and Central Europe battered each other over dynastic, economic, and territorial concerns. Austria, Britain, and Piedmont-Sardinia led one side, while France and Spain anchored the other. In the end, the ruling families remained in power, territorial changes were paltry, and economic rivalries continued unabated.
1741	North America	**Edwards Preaches "Sinners in the Hands of an Angry God":** In this sermon, perhaps the most famous of the eighteenth century, Jonathan Edwards of the Massachusetts colony preached Calvinist doctrines in the face of growing opposition from clergy who were increasingly embracing rationalism.
1741	Europe	**LEADHILLS READING SOCIETY PROMOTES LITERACY:** As part of a wide range of reforms of the local lead-mining industry, the creation of the Leadhills Reading Society, a kind of subscription library, helped make the town's lead-mining company a model for the rest of the industrial world. Miners and their families could check out and read the library's books, and then reflect on what they read. The reading society thus promoted both literacy and critical thinking.
1742	Europe	**CELSIUS PROPOSES AN INTERNATIONAL FIXED TEMPERATURE SCALE:** Anders Celsius conducted a series of precise experiments that demonstrated that the melting point of snow or ice and the boiling point of water, when adjusted for atmospheric pressure, were universal constants. He used these results to establish a uniform temperature scale, which allowed the calibration of thermometers worldwide.
1742	North America	**Completion of Faneuil Hall:** Boston merchant Peter Faneuil funded the construction of Faneuil Hall as a meeting house for the city of Boston. It became the site of many rousing speeches as the American Revolutionary War approached.

DATE	REGION	EVENT
1742	Europe	**FIELDING'S *JOSEPH ANDREWS* SATIRIZES ENGLISH SOCIETY:** Originally intended as a retort to *Pamela*, Samuel Richardson's morally strident assessment of eighteenth century social relations, Fielding's *Joseph Andrews* emerged as a sweeping analysis of the foibles of eighteenth century materialism, social snobbery, and moral bankruptcy.
1742	North America	**Franklin Invents the "Pennsylvania Fireplace":** America's great scientist and inventor turned his attention to practical home heating, inventing a fire box, to be set inside a fireplace, that provided for the circulation of warmed air. The invention is now known as the Franklin stove.
1742	North America	**Vérendrye Explores the Dakotas:** Obsessed with discovering the great "Western Sea," Pierre Gaultier de Varennes de La Vérendrye explored southward from Canada, traversing the Dakotas as far as the Yellowstone River.
Apr. 13, 1742	Europe	**FIRST PERFORMANCE OF HANDEL'S *MESSIAH*:** In an attempt to branch out from Italian opera, at which he was an acknowledged master, George Frideric Handel composed *Messiah*, an English concert oratorio that would become his most famous work. The oratorio achieved an effect for which Handel had been searching, combining artistic and popular appeal, and it has withstood both time and revision by other composers.
1743	North America	**Battle of Pamphlets:** Responding to the Jonathan Edwards sermon "Sinners in the Hands of an Angry God," Congregationalist minister Charles Chauncy wrote "Seasonable Thoughts on the State of Religion in New England," initiating a pamphlet war between orthodox Calvinists and more liberal rationalists in New England that would last until Edwards died in 1758.
1743-1744	Europe	**D'ALEMBERT DEVELOPS HIS AXIOMS OF MOTION:** Drawing upon elements of Cartesian and Newtonian thought, Jean le Rond d'Alembert formulated a set of laws describing the behavior of bodies in motion. The laws, all derived completely through mathematical calculation, combined to produce a general principle for solving problems in rational mechanics.
1743-1746	Middle East	**Ottoman-Persian War:** Nādir Shāh of Persia was unable to make gains in Kurdistan but did expand Persian influence in the Caucasus region.
1744	Europe	**Publication of "God Save the King" in London:** Published in 1744 and first publicly performed the following year, this royal anthem had its roots in seventeenth century France and eventually was adopted as the tune for the American patriotic song "My Country, 'Tis of Thee."
1744	Europe	**Sotheby's Auction Houses Established:** London bookseller Samuel Baker auctioned a local library, then turned the business over to his nephew, John Sotheby, in 1767.
1744-1748	North America/Caribbean	**King George's War:** The War of the Austrian Succession spilled over into America, with Anglo-French battles, most notably at sea, from Nova Scotia to the Caribbean.

DATE	REGION	EVENT
Jan. 24, 1744-Aug. 31, 1829	Southeast Asia	**DAGOHOY REBELLION IN THE PHILIPPINES:** The Dagohoy Rebellion was the longest-running successful revolt against Spanish colonizers in the history of the Philippines. The extended conflict was representative of a lasting tradition of resistance to centralized control in the outer Philippines and of the difficulties posed to any government that attempts to overcome that resistance.
1745	Europe	**LOMONOSOV ISSUES THE FIRST CATALOG OF MINERALS:** Soon after returning from scientific studies in Germany, Mikhail Vasilyevich Lomonosov began sorting and cataloging the mineral cabinet of the Kunstkammer in St. Petersburg. His resulting catalog of more than thirty-five hundred mineral specimens was published in 1745.
May 11, 1745	Europe	**Battle of Fontenoy:** French victory under Maurice, comte de Saxe, led to the capture of fortresses in the Austrian Netherlands during the War of the Austrian Succession.
Aug. 19, 1745-Sept. 20, 1746	Europe	**JACOBITE REBELLION:** The attempt by Charles Edward Stuart to launch an invasion on Great Britain through the Highlands of Scotland astounded the world by coming very close to success. However, the withdrawal of the prince's army back into Scotland gave the Hanoverian monarchy the chance to regroup and eventually to crush the Jacobite uprising of Charles Edward Stuart (Bonnie Prince Charlie).
Oct., 1745, and Jan., 1746	Europe	**INVENTION OF THE LEYDEN JAR:** Experimenting independently of each other in different countries, Ewald Georg von Kleist and Pieter van Musschenbroek invented the Leyden jar, the first device that could accumulate and store large amounts of electric energy. Later called a condenser or capacitor, the Leyden jar could conserve an electric charge for future use or experimentation in another location.
1746	Europe	**ROEBUCK DEVELOPS THE LEAD-CHAMBER PROCESS:** John Roebuck found a way to produce sulfuric acid in greater quantities and at a lower price than had been possible previously. His lead-chamber process increased the British supply of sulfuric acid, making it possible to develop new applications and to export the substance for sale to foreign markets.
1746	Middle East	**ZĀHIR AL-ʿUMAR CREATES A STRONGHOLD IN GALILEE:** Zāhir al-ʿUmar seized Acre, resurrecting this Crusader city and fortifying it against Ottoman forces. Ottoman leaders, facing external threats from Russia, were unable to defeat Zāhir and reconquer Acre.
1746-1754	South Asia	**CARNATIC WARS:** The Carnatic Wars established British superiority over the French in India and provided an opening for the British East India Company, allowing it gradually to extend its political control over most of the Indian subcontinent.
1746-1755	Europe	**JOHNSON CREATES THE FIRST MODERN ENGLISH DICTIONARY:** Samuel Johnson's *A Dictionary of the English Language*, the first English dictionary by a major English writer, established a new standard in comprehensiveness and sound lexical judgment.
Jan. 17, 1746	Europe	**Battle of Falkirk:** The Young Pretender, Charles Edward Stuart, led Scottish Highlanders to victory over the British, giving hope to the Jacobite cause, although those hopes were quickly dashed by the defeat at the Battle of Culloden three months later.

DATE	REGION	EVENT
Apr. 16, 1746	Europe	**Battle of Culloden:** The final defeat of the Jacobite rebels and the cause of Prince Charles Edward Stuart, who fled to France in September.
Oct. 20, 1746	South Asia	**Madras Falls to France:** As the War of the Austrian Succession spread to India, France under Joseph-François Dupleix continued its asendancy in southern India by capturing the British fort at Madras.
1747	Caribbean	**Britain Extends Control in the Caribbean:** As the War of the Austrian Succession expanded globally, Britain won a number of victories in the Caribbean under Admirals George Anson and Edward Hawke, threatening the French sugar trade from its Caribbean colonies.
1747	Europe	**MARGGRAF EXTRACTS SUGAR FROM BEETS:** At a time when Europe was dependent on expensive sugar from sugarcane grown using slave labor in the Caribbean, Andreas Marggraf discovered that sugar extracted from a European crop, the beet, was identical to that from sugarcane. His discovery eventually led to the development of a commercially successful sugar beet industry in Europe and North America.
1747	Europe	**Wesley Spreads Methodism in Ireland:** Seeking to model his holiness on the practices of the early Christian Church, Evangelical John Wesley began to spread his "Methodism" to Ireland, making the first of forty-two trips there in 1747.
1747-1773	Middle East	**Wars of Afghan Expansion:** During prolonged conflict with the Ṣafavid Persians and the Indian Marāthās, Afghanistan gained its independence and began to develop a sense of national identity.
1748	Europe	**AGNESI PUBLISHES *ANALYTICAL INSTITUTIONS*:** Maria Agnesi published one of the first introductory textbooks for beginning students in the new field of calculus. By defining the terms in which the new discipline was taught, her text shaped the understanding of a generation of mathematicians. One of the curves discussed in her text is still associated with her name.
1748	Europe	**BRADLEY DISCOVERS THE NUTATION OF EARTH'S AXIS:** After discovering the aberration of starlight in the late 1720's, James Bradley proceeded to catalog the positions of more than three thousand stars between 1727 and 1747. His catalog led him to discover the nutation of Earth's axis as Earth orbits the Sun.
1748	Europe	**EULER DEVELOPS THE CONCEPT OF FUNCTION:** The introduction of algebraic expressions for curves helped mathematicians to analyze geometrical figures. Leonhard Euler's 1748 work marked a change in perspective by putting the function first and the curve second. By inverting the order of the expression, Euler reconceived the very subject matter of mathematics.
1748	Europe	**EXCAVATION OF POMPEII:** The excavation of the intact ancient Roman city of Pompeii, which had been buried under layers of volcanic ash for more than sixteen centuries, caused a sensation among intellectuals and amateurs alike and brought about a revival of interest in the values and styles of the Roman world.
1748	Europe	**MONTESQUIEU PUBLISHES *THE SPIRIT OF THE LAWS*:** *De l'esprit des loix* (1748; *The Spirit of the Laws*, 1750) set a standard for comparative political, cultural, and legal thought in Europe. It laid the foundation for the institution of the social sciences as disciplines more rigorous and distinct from those of the humanities.

DATE	REGION	EVENT
1748	Europe	**NOLLET DISCOVERS OSMOSIS:** Jean-Antoine Nollet discovered that membranes could be selectively permeable and analyzed the process by which a solvent concentrated on one side of such a membrane would pass through it until an equilibrium on either side of the membrane had been reached. Henri Dutrochet later related this process specifically to biological systems and gave it the name "osmosis."
1748	North America	**Settlers Cross the Allegheny Divide:** American colonists traveled beyond the Allegheny divide into territories claimed by France, heightening tensions between France and England.
1748-1755	Middle East	**CONSTRUCTION OF ISTANBUL'S NUR-U OSMANIYE COMPLEX:** The last great work of Ottoman religious architecture, the Nur-u Osmaniye mosque complex assimilated European stylistic influences into the classical Ottoman style. Combining a mosque, school, and library, the complex has functioned since its completion as an important repository and purveyor of Islamic knowledge and faith.
Oct. 18, 1748	Europe	**TREATY OF AIX-LA-CHAPELLE:** The Treaty of Aix-la-Chapelle temporarily ended the set of wars known collectively as the War of the Austrian Succession. Although it merely created a pause in the conflicts between France and England that lasted throughout the eighteenth century, the treaty is noteworthy as a signal of the waning power of the Holy Roman Empire.
1749	North America	**College of Philadelphia Founded:** Benjamin Franklin suggested the founding of the institution of higher learning in Philadelphia that would become the University of Pennsylvania.
1749	Europe	**Fielding Publishes *The History of Tom Jones, a Foundling*:** English author and playwright Henry Fielding published one of the earliest and best-known English novels, set against the backdrop of the Jacobite rebellion of 1745. Samuel Taylor Coleridge regarded the novel as having one of the three greatest plots in all English literature.
1749-1789	Europe	**FIRST COMPREHENSIVE EXAMINATION OF THE NATURAL WORLD:** The comte de Buffon's thirty-six-volume *Histoire naturelle, générale et particulière* (1749-1789; *Natural History, General and Particular*, 1781-1812) represents the first comprehensive and systematic exploration of the natural world. Although Buffon based his conjectures on physical evidence, he was frequently proven wrong by fellow scientists. Despite the work's flaws, Buffon inspired immense respect because of the nature of the undertaking, his systematic approach to his subject, and the high quality of his prose style.
June 10, 1749	Middle East	**SAʿĪD BECOMES RULER OF OMAN:** Aḥmad ibn Saʿīd helped bring an end to the Yaʿrubi Dynasty in Oman. Establishing himself as imam, he founded his own dynastic house, the House of Āl Bū Saʿīd, which has continued to rule into the twenty-first century.
1750	North America	**Battle of Kathio:** This legendary battle is based on oral traditions recounting the moment when the Ojibwe tribe drove the Dakota people from the Thousand Lakes region of northern Minnesota.

DATE	REGION	EVENT
1750	Europe	**British Parliament Passes the Iron Act:** Part of the mercantilistic Trade and Navigation Acts designed to impede the production of finished iron goods in the American colonies, this law encouraged the production of pig and bar iron, which might then be traded for English manufactures.
1750	Europe	**Maupertuis Publishes *Essai de cosmologie*:** French scientist Pierre-Louis Moreau de Maupertuis first suggests the biological concept of survival of the fittest, later made famous by Charles Darwin.
1750	Europe	**TREATY OF MADRID:** The Treaty of Madrid altered the boundary between Portuguese and Spanish South America, formally recognizing that some lands on the western, Spanish side of the original boundary had already become de facto possessions of Portugal. Subsequent treaties reversed and modified the Madrid agreements.
1750	North America	**Walker Finds Cumberland Gap:** Thomas Walker, Virginia land agent and physician, discovered access across the Appalachian Mountains through a gap at 1,665 feet, named for the duke of Cumberland.
1750	Europe	**Westminster Bridge Opens for Traffic in London:** The long-anticipated bridge across the Thames River at Westminster, discussed for almost two centuries and designed by the Swiss engineer Charles Labelye, finally opened for traffic after eleven years in construction.
1750-1792	Central Asia	**CHINA CONSOLIDATES CONTROL OVER TIBET:** Following the murder of Tibet's last king by his Chinese advisers, China consolidated its indirect rule over Tibet in 1751 and strengthened its control over Tibet after defeating the Gurkha invasion of Tibet in 1792.
Mar. 20, 1750-Mar. 14, 1752	Europe	**JOHNSON ISSUES *THE RAMBLER*:** Writing almost all the 208 essays in the semiweekly periodical *The Rambler*, Samuel Johnson established himself as a prominent literary figure in eighteenth century Britain and, through his rigorous examination of literature and human affairs in general, tried to move his readers toward sound judgment and moral wisdom.
1751	Europe	**MAUPERTUIS PROVIDES EVIDENCE OF "HEREDITARY PARTICLES":** The theory of hereditary particles had been competing with other possible explanations of biological reproduction in 1751. However, with the publication of *Système de la nature*, Maupertuis became the first scientist to provide statistical evidence that the existence of particles inherited from both parents could explain specific, empirically observable patterns in the inheritance of physical traits.
1751-1772	Europe	**DIDEROT PUBLISHES THE *ENCYCLOPEDIA*:** The publication of Diderot's *Encyclopédie* (*Encyclopedia*) was one of the great events of the French Enlightenment. A massive work of scholarship designed to assist the triumph of reason, progress, and tolerance, the *Encyclopedia* shaped French intellectual life for several decades.
Aug. 31, 1751	South Asia	**British Seize Arcot:** British troops under Robert Clive seized the French fortress at Arcot, then held off a besieging Indian-French force during September and October to shake French authority in the region.

DATE	REGION	EVENT
1752	North America	**Liberty Bell Cast in Philadelphia:** John Pass and John Stow cast in bronze alloy the 2,080-pound bell that would be hung in the belfry of the Pennsylvania State House.
1752	Middle East	**Sabah Ibn Jābir Becomes Ruler of Kuwait:** Established the Sabah Dynasty, which ruled into the twentieth century.
1752-Mar., 1756	Europe	**MAYER'S LUNAR TABLES ENABLE MARINERS TO DETERMINE LONGITUDE AT SEA:** Johann Tobias Mayer compiled and disseminated tables of astronomical distances, supplemented with mathematical formulas and instructions, to guide navigators to determine longitude at sea. These lunar tables helped sea travelers avoid dangerous areas, reduced the occurrence of shipwrecks and disappearances, and enhanced trade, exploration, and military expeditions.
1752-1760	South Asia	**ALAUNGPAYA UNITES BURMA:** The creation of the Burmese Third Empire by Alaungpaya ushered in the modern era of British colonial affiliation, featuring the exploitation of the production capacities of the Irriwaddy and Salween River Valleys to provide rice exports in the global colonial trade.
June, 1752	North America	**FRANKLIN DEMONSTRATES THE ELECTRICAL NATURE OF LIGHTNING:** By drawing lightning from storm clouds, Franklin's dangerous kite experiment conclusively demonstrated that lightning was a form of electricity. The experiment also offered further proof of his single-substance theory of electricity and showed that this fluidlike static energy could be passed from one object to another.
Sept. 2, 1752	Europe	**England Adopts the Gregorian Calendar:** First proposed in the sixteenth century to correct the length of the mean year in the Julian calendar, the adoption of the Gregorian calendar led to the "loss" of eleven days but became the standard for the Western world.
1753	Europe	**LIND DISCOVERS A CURE FOR SCURVY:** Building upon previous medical accounts and motivated by the medical disasters of long sea voyages, James Lind proved that citrus fruits can prevent and cure scurvy. His results, published in 1753, helped to convince the British court to order the rationing of citrus juice to all sailors, thus dramatically reducing scurvy in the Royal Navy.
Jan. 11, 1753	Europe	**Foundation of the British Museum:** London physician Sir Hans Sloan left initial collections of books, coins, manuscripts, and pictures to the nation, which were enhanced by purchases as a royal foundation charter.
1754	Europe	**BÜSCHING PUBLISHES *A NEW SYSTEM OF GEOGRAPHY*:** In 1754, Anton Friedrich Büsching began publishing a multivolume geographical work, *Neue Erdbeschreibung* (*A New System of Geography*), and by 1792 he had completed ten volumes, mostly dealing with Europe. His work was an advance over previous geographies, because it emphasized measurement and statistics rather than mere description.
1754	Europe	**Chippendale Publishes *The Gentlemen and the Cabinet Maker's Director*:** After opening a London factory for the production of furniture in 1749, Thomas Chippendale produced the best-known eighteenth century guide to furniture design.

DATE	REGION	EVENT
1754	Europe	**CONDILLAC DEFENDS SENSATIONALIST THEORY:** In *Treatise on the Sensations*, Condillac defended a sensationalist theory of understanding, arguing that knowledge forms and develops solely through sensory experience. Condillac's attribution of all human cognition to sensations had an enormous impact on contemporary and subsequent philosophers, especially in France and Italy.
1754	Europe	**Winter Palace Begun in St. Petersburg:** The baroque Winter Palace, designed as the winter home of the Russian czars, began construction under the direction of Italian architect Bartolomeo Rastrelli.
Apr. 17, 1754	North America	**French Troops Halt Virginian Advance:** A land-developing expedition of Virginians under George Washington was defeated while attempting to build a fort at the confluence of the Allegheny and Monongahela Rivers.
May 28, 1754-Feb. 10, 1763	North America	**FRENCH AND INDIAN WAR:** The French and Indian War was the final major European conflict for control of North America before the American Revolution. Great Britain defeated France and its Native American allies, establishing British dominance in the American northeast, but British economic dependence on the American colonies increased in the process.
June 19-July 10, 1754	North America	**ALBANY CONGRESS:** In an attempt to preserve their alliance with the Iroquois and to prepare for war with the French, a congress of colonial delegates drafted a plan to unify the American colonies under a single government. The Plan of Union was rejected by the colonies, and the British government, rather than colonial officials, became responsible for conducting diplomacy with Native Americans.
1755	Europe	**Bakewell Develops Leicester Sheep:** English agriculturalist Robert Bakewell developed the stocky Leicester sheep, one of the first breeds designed for both wool and meat production.
1755	Europe	**Johnson Publishes *A Dictionary of the English Language*:** English author Samuel Johnson published the first edition of the most famous dictionary in the English language.
June 5, 1755	Europe	**BLACK IDENTIFIES CARBON DIOXIDE:** Joseph Black showed that when intensely heated, magnesia alba (magnesium carbonate) and chalk (calcium carbonate) produced "fixed air," a gas, later identified as carbon dioxide, with unique physical and chemical properties.
July, 1755-Aug., 1758	North America	**ACADIANS ARE EXPELLED FROM CANADA:** The British forcibly expelled most of the French population of Nova Scotia, which had been called Acadia when it was under French control. Many French Acadians subsequently returned to Nova Scotia or found new homelands elsewhere, especially in Louisiana.
July 9, 1755	North America	**Battle of Monongahela:** British general Braddock, badly defeated by the French and their Indian allies, demonstrated the unsuitability of British military techniques to the American frontier.
Sept., 1755, and July, 1756	Middle East	**Fire Ravages Istanbul:** Fires in September, 1755, and July, 1756, destroyed much of old Istanbul (formerly Constantinople).

DATE	REGION	EVENT
Nov. 1, 1755	Europe	**GREAT LISBON EARTHQUAKE:** An earthquake of exceptional magnitude devastated the port city of Lisbon, Portugal. The massive destruction wrought by the quake resulted in the systematic rebuilding and modernization of the city, making it the most modern and architecturally advanced capital in Europe. The earthquake also occasioned a critical reexamination throughout Enlightenment Europe of the role of reason in nature and human affairs.
1756	South Asia	**English Prisoners Die in the "Black Hole of Calcutta":** The British public was outraged upon learning that 123 British prisoners had died when forced into a small guardroom by Sūraj-ud-Dowlah as he attacked the city.
Jan., 1756-Feb. 15, 1763	Europe	**SEVEN YEARS' WAR:** The Seven Years' War was both the continuation of a struggle for power in central Europe between Prussia and Austria and a chapter in the ongoing worldwide colonial rivalry between France and Britain. The war established Britain as the dominant world colonial power, and it secured Prussia's status as a major European power, establishing the early framework for the creation of a unified German Empire.
1757	Europe	**Campbell Develops the Sextant:** Expanding Hadley's quadrant by 30 degrees, Royal Naval Captain John Campbell developed an instrument that could measure both longitude and latitude.
1757	Europe	**MONRO DISTINGUISHES BETWEEN LYMPHATIC AND BLOOD SYSTEMS:** Alexander Monro observed a system of fluid absorption associated with lymphatics that appeared to possess its own valvular system. As a result, he correctly argued that the system was unique and separate from the circulatory system for blood.
1757-1766	Europe	**HALLER ESTABLISHES PHYSIOLOGY AS A SCIENCE:** Between 1757 and 1766, Haller published his textbook *Elementa physiologiae corporis humani* (elements of human physiology) in Lausanne and Bern, Switzerland. This comprehensive work established physiology as a science independent of anatomy. Haller's discovery that contractility is a quality inherent in muscles, while sensitivity and pain perception characterize nerve function, laid the foundation of modern neurology.
June 23, 1757	South Asia	**BATTLE OF PLASSEY:** The British East India Company's triumph at the Battle of Plassey led first to British hegemony over Bengal and then to the establishment of the British Raj and to India taking its place as the crown jewel of the British Empire.
Oct., 1757	Middle East	**Bedouin Attack on Damascus Pilgrims:** The worst of frequent attacks, thousands of pilgrims were killed or left to die in the desert.
Nov. 5, 1757	Europe	**BATTLE OF ROSSBACH:** Confronting an advancing allied army of French, German, and Austrian troops that was more than twice the size of his own, Frederick the Great wheeled his soldiers into a position from which they literally destroyed the allied forces. The defeat ended France's advance in the Seven Years' War.

DATE	REGION	EVENT
June 8-July 27, 1758	North America	**SIEGE OF LOUISBOURG:** Nearly fifteen thousand British soldiers under Major General Jeffrey Amherst encircled and bombarded the French Canadian fortress of Louisbourg, gaining victory over the French after seven weeks. Britain's success opened up the St. Lawrence River and exposed Quebec, the center of French power in America, to subsequent British attacks, ultimately resulting in the conquest of Canada.
July 8, 1758	North America	**Battle of Ticonderoga:** In a brave but futile frontal assault on Louis-Joseph de Montcalm's French forces, British troops under Abercromby failed to take Fort Ticonderoga during the French and Indian War.
July 27, 1758	Europe	**HELVÉTIUS PUBLISHES *DE L'ESPRIT*:** A major work in the field of materialist ethics and best seller of the clandestine book trade in prerevolutionary France, *De l'esprit* immediately came under attack by those in church and government who opposed the Enlightenment philosophers. Its author, Claude-Adrien Helvétius, declared self-interest to be the motivating force behind all human actions.
Oct. 14, 1758	Europe	**Battle of Hochkirk:** Austrians under Count Leopold Joseph Daun surprised Frederick the Great and the Prussian army, seizing their artillery and forcing their retreat.
1759	Europe	**AEPINUS PUBLISHES *ESSAY ON THE THEORY OF ELECTRICITY AND MAGNETISM*:** Inspired by Sir Isaac Newton's mathematical explanation of the gravitational force, Franz Maria Ulrich Theodor Hoch Aepinus's *Tentamen theoriae Electricitatis et Magnetismi* (1759; *Essay on the Theory of Electricity and Magnetism*) provided the first systematic, mathematical analysis of the forces of electricity and magnetism.
1759	Europe	**CHARLES III GAINS THE SPANISH THRONE:** Under King Charles III, Spain reached the high point of its "enlightened absolutist" monarchy. Charles initiated far-reaching social, political, and economic reforms, using his nearly absolute power to improve his society and the lives of its people.
1759	Europe	**Guinness Brewery Established:** Arthur Guinness established a brewery in Dublin, Ireland, that would become the largest in the world.
1759	Europe	**WEDGWOOD FOUNDS A CERAMICS FIRM:** Wedgwood's ceramics company developed revolutionary new products and business techniques in response to consumer needs and the new industrial economy, producing affordable, high-quality, functional ware, as well as beautiful ornamental wares in new, refined materials. Also, he instituted new labor and management practices that increased productivity and profit.
1759	Europe	**Wolff Lays Foundation of Modern Embryology:** Careful observations made by German biologist Kaspar Friedrich Wolff established a foundation for the discipline of embryology.
1759-1766	Europe	**CONSTRUCTION OF THE BRIDGEWATER CANAL:** The unique Bridgewater Canal, the first true industrial canal and the first canal to be dug from dry land and to have its own water supply, facilitated the movement of coal and other materials, advancing the Industrial Revolution in Great Britain.

DATE	REGION	EVENT
Jan., 1759	Europe	**VOLTAIRE SATIRIZES OPTIMISM IN *CANDIDE*:** Voltaire published his most famous philosophical tale, a global satire on human corruption that gave birth to the term "pessimism." Its impassioned advocacy of humanitarian principles, religious tolerance, social justice, and realistic confrontation with life's grimness retains its power and relevance more than two centuries later.
Jan. 19, 1759-Aug. 16, 1773	Europe	**SUPPRESSION OF THE JESUITS:** Beginning in 1759, the governments of Portugal, France, and Spain began limiting the activities of the Society of Jesus, eventually expelling the order and seizing its property. In 1773, Pope Clement XIV, under pressure from Jesuit detractors, declared the order abolished.
June 27-Sept. 18, 1759	North America	**Siege of Quebec:** French troops were finally driven from their North American capital following a daring night attack and a battle on the Plains of Abraham (September 13) in which commanders on both sides were killed.
Aug. 1, 1759	Europe	**Battle of Minden:** This battle resulted in a victory for combined British, Hanoverian, Hessian, and Prussian troops over the French army, ending the French threat to Hanover.
Oct. 5, 1759-Nov. 19, 1761	North America	**CHEROKEE WAR:** The colonies of South Carolina and Virginia waged war against the Cherokee Indians, utterly destroying several Cherokee communities. The war ended in an expansion of South Carolina's territory at the Cherokees' expense, and it presaged the Cherokee alliance with the British in the Revolutionary War.
Nov. 20-21, 1759	Europe	**Battle of Quiberon Bay:** The British fleet under Edward Hawke destroyed most the French fleet off the southern coast of Brittany, ending French plans to invade Scotland.
1760's	Europe	**BEGINNING OF SELECTIVE LIVESTOCK BREEDING:** Robert Bakewell, one of the most prominent of the agricultural breeders of the eighteenth century, revolutionized cattle and sheep breeding by using scientific methods to develop new breeds designed to maximize meat production.
1760-1776	Caribbean	**CARIBBEAN SLAVE REBELLIONS:** The ambiguous position of the Maroons (runaway slaves) continued to affect, but not stop, slave rebellions and plots in British Jamaica, as Maroons often worked in alliance with the British. This alliance made clear that the sugar plantations could not function without the help of the Maroons.
Nov. 3, 1760	Europe	**Battle of Torgau:** Frederick the Great drove a numerically superior Austrian army from a heavily fortified position near the Elbe River, suffering more than thirteen thousand casualties in the process.
1761	Europe	**Gainsborough Exhibits at the Society of Artists:** One of the most famous portrait and landscape painters of his day, Thomas Gainsborough was among those who founded and exhibited at Britain's first national arts academy, the Society of Artists, later renamed the Royal Academy of Arts.
1761	Europe	**Rousseau Publishes *The New Héloïse*:** Jean-Jacques Rousseau's great epistolary novel *Julie: Ou, La Nouvelle Héloïse* (1761; *Eloise: Or, A Series of Original Letters*, 1761; better known as *The New Héloïse*) heralded the Romantic movement with its shift from pure reason toward a recognition of the vital role of passion and subjective feeling.

DATE	REGION	EVENT
1761	Europe	**Successful Test of an Improved Chronometer:** Based on John Harrison's design of 1736, an improved chronometer is tested on board HMS *Deptford* on a voyage to Jamaica.
Jan. 14, 1761	South Asia	**Battle of Panipat:** Afghans under Aḥmad Shāh Durrānī crushed the Marāthās north of Delhi, virtually destroying their military power and weakening the region as the British began to expand.
1762	Europe	*THE ANTIQUITIES OF ATHENS* **PROMPTS ARCHITECTURAL NEOCLASSICISM:** James Stuart and Nicholas Revett's *The Antiquities of Athens* shifted the focus of architectural inspiration from ancient Rome to classical Greece and resulted in a uniquely Greek style of neoclassicism often referred to as Greek Revival. The work is considered a landmark in the history of archaeology.
1762	Europe	**France Expels Jesuits:** Suspect both on political and commercial grounds, the Jesuits are expelled from France.
1762	Caribbean	**Widespread British Naval Victories:** British admirals capture Martinique, Grenada, Saint Lucia, Saint Vincent, Havana, and Manila during the latter stages of the Seven Years' War, confirming their naval superiority.
Jan., 1762-Nov., 1766	Europe	**MOZART TOURS EUROPE AS A CHILD PRODIGY:** Wolfgang Amadeus Mozart, a musical prodigy, toured Europe as a child, amazing audiences and winning favor in the courts of Europe; these engagements played a large part in Mozart's later achievements as a world-famous composer.
Apr., 1762	Europe	**ROUSSEAU PUBLISHES** *THE SOCIAL CONTRACT*: In *The Social Contract*, Rousseau responded to the political tyranny of his age by arguing that government derived its legitimacy and power from the free consent of the governed. The text revolutionized political philosophy, contributing to the development of a school of thought known as social contract theory that still exists two and a half centuries later.
Oct. 5, 1762	Europe	**FIRST PERFORMANCE OF GLUCK'S** *ORFEO AND EURIDICE*: Composed when he was already a famous opera composer, Gluck's work with librettist Calzabigi led him to champion revolutionary reforms in opera that have made him a key figure in the transition from the Baroque to the classical and pre-Romantic styles.
1763	Europe	**BAYES ADVANCES PROBABILITY THEORY:** Thomas Bayes's work on the inverse problem in probabilities, which attempted to calculate the probabilities of causes from those of events, helped to advance investigations in the foundations of probability. Bayes's theorem is a major part of subjectivist approaches to epistemology, statistics, and inductive logic.
1763-1767	Europe	**FAMINE IN SOUTHERN ITALY:** In the mid-1760's, food shortages, intensified by insufficient harvests, feudalistic practices, and flawed food distribution systems, resulted in famine conditions, which prompted rural populations to migrate to urban areas. Because charities and governments failed to provide sufficient relief, some famine victims rioted. Several hundred thousand people died either from starvation or diseases exacerbated by unsanitary conditions.

DATE	REGION	EVENT
Feb. 10, 1763	Europe	**PEACE OF PARIS:** In the Peace of Paris, Great Britain, France, and Spain made peace with one another, ending their participation in the Seven Years' War and the French and Indian War. The treaty confirmed the supremacy of the British colonial empire and the virtual destruction of the French overseas empire.
Beginning Apr., 1763	Europe	**THE *NORTH BRITON* CONTROVERSY:** The suppression of John Wilkes's periodical The *North Briton* for alleged aspersions against the British throne resulted in Wilkes's arrest, conviction, and imprisonment for seditious libel, sparking a controversy with major implications for the development of a modern free press and the beginnings of modern lobbying groups.
May 8, 1763-July 24, 1766	North America	**PONTIAC'S RESISTANCE:** A pan-Indian uprising led by Ottawa chief Pontiac presented the greatest threat to British expansion before the American Revolution.
Aug., 1763-Apr., 1765	Europe	**DAVID GARRICK'S EUROPEAN TOUR:** David Garrick, eighteenth century England's most prominent actor and that country's premier theater representative, toured Western Europe, establishing the reputation of English theater throughout Europe. The tour proved to be one of the most significant celebrity events of the century.
Sept. 10, 1763	Europe	**PUBLICATION OF THE *FREEMAN'S JOURNAL*:** The *Freeman's Journal* was the first independent Irish newspaper to survive for more than a few issues, evolving into a newspaper that presented a comprehensive, accurate picture of Irish news. It became famous for the letters collectively known as *Baratariana* and its effective support of the Union Act.
Oct. 7, 1763	North America	**PROCLAMATION OF 1763:** In an effort to avoid further conflict over territorial sovereignty, the British parliament issued the Proclamation of 1763, drawing a frontier line between the American colonies and Native American lands.
Dec. 14 and 27, 1763	North America	**PAXTON BOYS' MASSACRES:** Growing tensions between Pennsylvania backcountry settlers and Native Americans resulted in the massacre of defenseless Susquehannocks. The massacres began a chain of events that resulted in Pennsylvania's declaration of war against several Native American tribes.
1764	Europe	**Beccaria Publishes *On Crimes and Punishment*:** Italian economist Cesare Bonesana, marchese di Beccaria's condemnation of torture and capital punishment becomes a touchstone for modern attitudes toward criminology.
1764	East Asia	**Cao Xueqin (Ts'ao Chan) Dies:** Principal author of the greatest Chinese novel of manners, Ts'ao Chan dies, leaving his masterwork, *Honglou meng* (*Dream of the Red Chamber*), incomplete. It would be published twenty-nine years later.
1764	Europe	**INVENTION OF THE SPINNING JENNY:** The spinning jenny, invented by James Hargreaves in 1764, was the first in a series of inventions that adapted mechanical power to the production of textiles. It laid the foundations for the vast expansion of output achieved by the textile industry in the Industrial Revolution.
1764	North America	**Rhode Island College Founded:** Established in Warren as a Baptist college, this institution would move to Providence and become Brown University in 1804, all the while maintaining nonsectarian principles.

DATE	REGION	EVENT
1764	Europe	**Royal Palace in Madrid Completed:** After twenty-eight years of construction, the royal palace is completed for King Charles III.
Apr. 19, 1764	Europe	**British Parliament Passes the Currency Act:** The measure forbade the American colonies to print paper money, strengthening royal control.
July, 1764	Europe	**VOLTAIRE PUBLISHES *A PHILOSOPHICAL DICTIONARY FOR THE POCKET*:** Combining satire and irony with empirical, rational, and moral arguments, Voltaire attacked superstition, sectarian fanaticism, and intolerance, exposing the atrocities committed in the name of religion. Its aggressive anticlericalism and irreverent treatment of Holy Scripture shocked contemporary readers and provoked virulent public debate.
1765	North America	**First American Medical School Established:** The first formal medical school in the English American colonies is founded at the College and Academy of Philadelphia, later the College of Physicians and Surgeons.
1765	Europe	**Mother Goose Melodies Published:** Boston printer Thomas Fleet published songs sung by his mother-in-law, who put tunes to Charles Perrault's verses, including "Baa Baa Black Sheep," "Georgie Porgie," "Hickory Dickory Dock," "Jack and Jill," and "Little Bo Peep."
1765	Europe	**Walpole Publishes *The Castle of Otranto*:** Usually considered the first gothic horror novel, Horace Walpole's work marked an early stage in English Romanticism.
1765-1769	Europe	**WATT DEVELOPS A MORE EFFECTIVE STEAM ENGINE:** James Watt's improved steam engine ushered in low-cost, efficient steam power for coal mining and manufacturing and permitted the extraordinary development of the Industrial Revolution.
1765-1803	Middle East	**Expansion of Saudi Rule:** ʿAbd al-Azīz ruled as emir during these years, consolidating and expanding control of the peninsula begun under his father Muḥammad ibn Saʿud.
Mar. 22, 1765-Mar. 18, 1766	North America	**STAMP ACT CRISIS:** During the Stamp Act Crisis, the American colonies responded to the first direct tax levied on the colonists with protests and boycotts. The Stamp Act was soon repealed, but the crisis became the first in a series of events that would culminate in the American Revolution.
1766	Europe	**Construction Begins on the Grand Trunk Canal:** English engineer James Brindley's canal connected the Trent and Mersey Rivers, opening a clear route from the Irish Sea to the North Sea.
1766	Europe	**Haller Investigates the Human Nervous System:** Swiss biologist Albrecht von Haller suggested that nerves cause muscles to contract, and that all nerves are connected to the spinal column and brain.
Feb. 24, 1766	Europe	**LORRAINE BECOMES PART OF FRANCE:** In the Treaty of Vienna (1738), which ended the War of the Polish Succession, the deposed king of Poland, Stanisław I, was installed as the sovereign duke of the independent duchy of Lorraine. The treaty stipulated that upon Stanisław's death the duchy would revert to the French crown. Thus, when he died in 1766, Lorraine lost its independence and was absorbed into France.

DATE	REGION	EVENT
Nov. 12, 1766	North America	**FIRST AMERICAN THEATER OPENS IN PHILADELPHIA:** The Southwark Theatre opened in Philadelphia in November of 1766. For the next eight years, it was home to operas, plays, pantomimes, and other performances, including the 1767 debut of the first play by an American author. Works by Americans increased at the Southwark Theatre and at other early theaters after the Revolutionary War, and elegantly designed and better-equipped theaters appeared in greater numbers during the 1790's.
Dec. 5, 1766-Mar. 16, 1769	World	**BOUGAINVILLE CIRCUMNAVIGATES THE GLOBE:** French scientist and statesman Louis-Antoine de Bougainville organized the first successful French expedition around the world. During the voyage, in which he returned the Falkland Islands to Spanish control, he claimed many of the uncharted islands that he discovered for King Louis XV of France.
1767	North America	**American Whalers Venture into the Antarctic:** A fleet of fifty American whaling ships plied the Antarctic, foreshadowing widespread expansion of the whaling industry.
1767	Europe	**Cavendish Reports on Hydrogen:** English scientist Henry Cavendish, examining the action of acids on metals, reported to the Royal Society of London on the inflammable properties of hydrogen.
1767	North America	**Dickinson Publishes Letters from a Farmer in Pennsylvania:** Having previously been part of the Stamp Act Congress in 1765, Philadelphia lawyer John Dickinson spoke out on the nonimportation agreements.
1767	North America	**Mason-Dixon Line Surveyed:** Surveyors Charles Mason and Jeremiah Dixon complete a four-year survey to settle a century-old land dispute between Pennsylvania and Maryland colonies.
1767-1768	Europe	**SPALLANZANI DISPROVES SPONTANEOUS GENERATION:** Lazzaro Spallanzani was among the first to show experimentally that living organisms—such as maggots in rotting meat—could not simply appear out of nowhere. Though his work was not considered conclusive on the subject, it represented the beginnings of a modern view of biology.
1767-1771	Europe	**INVENTION OF THE WATER FRAME:** Richard Arkwright's invention of the water frame increased the supply of high-quality yarn and significantly accelerated the development of the factory system, which was a key component of the Industrial Revolution.
June 29, 1767-Apr. 12, 1770	North America	**TOWNSHEND CRISIS:** Only one year after the conclusion of the Stamp Act Crisis, British laws designed to tighten the empire's economic and political controls on the colonies prompted further American resistance. The Townshend Crisis represented another step on the path to the American Revolution.
Aug., 1767-May, 1799	South Asia	**ANGLO-MYSORE WARS:** The Anglo-Mysore Wars destroyed the power of the last state in the south of India, Mysore, to oppose the British East India Company. At the end of the wars Mysore became an ally of the company as part of the subsidiary alliance system, and the city of Bangalore became an important British military base in the south of India.

DATE	REGION	EVENT
Aug. 10, 1767	Europe	**CATHERINE THE GREAT'S INSTRUCTION:** Catherine the Great issued her Instruction, a series of progressive principles for reforming Russian law and governance. The Instruction was one of the most modern, liberal governmental decrees of the eighteenth century, but it remained merely a theoretical decree, and the reforms Catherine intended never appeared in practice.
1768-May 16, 1771	North America	**CAROLINA REGULATOR MOVEMENTS:** Protesting lack of representation in the western backcountry, the Regulators inspired vigilante insurrections. The movements highlighted the differences between settled colonies and frontier territories and they contributed to the development of an American vigilante tradition.
1768-1773	Europe	**Polish Civil War:** The Confederation of the Bar, an organization of Catholic nobles, gained the support of both France and Turkey in seeking to resist Russian influence, though their failure led to the partition of Poland beginning in 1772.
May 15, 1768	Europe	**France Purchases Corsica:** This Mediterranean island dominated by Genoa from the thirteenth century is now transferred to France.
Aug. 25, 1768-Feb. 14, 1779	World	**VOYAGES OF CAPTAIN COOK:** Three voyages led by James Cook reliably mapped most of the Pacific Ocean, discovered new island archipelagos, led to the British settlement of Australia and New Zealand, and established Great Britain as a leading trading and maritime nation. Cook was also the first sea captain to use citrus fruits to prevent scurvy among mariners.
Oct., 1768-Jan. 9, 1792	Europe/Middle East	**OTTOMAN WARS WITH RUSSIA:** In two hard-fought wars between 1768 and 1792, the Ottoman Empire experienced defeats so decisive that it ceased to be a great power. Russia's rise to power continued, however, as it added vast new territories to its sovereign possessions.
Oct. 30, 1768	North America	**METHODIST CHURCH IS ESTABLISHED IN COLONIAL AMERICA:** The Methodist movement became institutionalized in colonial America with the founding of its first influential congregation and meeting house in New York City, the Wesleyan Chapel. Still standing, the chapel is now called the John Street Methodist Church.
Dec., 1768-Jan. 10, 1773	Africa	**BRUCE EXPLORES ETHIOPIA:** Although James Bruce was not appreciated until the end of his life, his explorations in Ethiopia led to a scientific mapping of much of the Blue Nile. Bruce's numerous naturalistic and scientific observations contributed to the growth of the natural sciences in the eighteenth century.
Dec. 10, 1768	Europe	**BRITAIN'S ROYAL ACADEMY OF ARTS IS FOUNDED:** Great Britain's first large-scale public display of contemporary artworks by British-born artists, including painters Thomas Gainsborough and Sir Joshua Reynolds, led to the establishment of the Royal Academy of Arts in London, Britain's first national arts academy.
1769	Europe	**Blackstone's *Commentaries on the Laws of England* Published:** English jurist Sir William Blackstone published one of the most influential legal treatises of all time, influencing both Britain and America.
1769	Pacific Islands	**Captain Cook Arrives in Tahiti:** English captain James Cook established an observatory in Tahiti and charted the coasts of New Zealand.

DATE	REGION	EVENT
1769	North America	**Discovery of San Francisco Bay:** A scouting party under José Ortega claimed this natural harbor north of Monterey for Spain.
1769	Europe	**Garrick Plays England's First Shakespeare Festival:** David Garrick, England's most famous actor, participated in the first annual revival of William Shakespeare's plays, to be repeated widely throughout the world thereafter.
1769	South Asia	**Great Famine of Bengal:** An estimated 10 million Indians died in the world's worst famine to date.
1769	Europe	**POMBAL REFORMS THE INQUISITION:** The Inquisition in Portugal was transformed from an institution of the Church to secular, state control. It continued its repressive practices, applying them to political opponents of the socioeconomic orthodoxy of the marquês de Pombal's government and its reforms.
1769	Europe	**Russia Occupies Moldavia:** In their campaign against the Ottoman Empire, Russians captured Bucharest.
1769-1776	Middle East	**Futa Toro Jihad:** Muslim Fulbe and Tukolor peoples in what is now Senegal established a theocratic Muslim state, foreshadowing the larger jihadist movements of the nineteenth century.
Apr. 20, 1769	North America	**Pontiac Murdered:** The Ottawa chieftan Pontiac was murdered at Cahokia by another Native American, though there was widespread suspicion that the British were involved.
July 6, 1769	Middle East/Europe	**Battle of Chesme:** Russian Baltic fleet defeated the Ottoman fleet off the coast of Anatolia.
July 17, 1769-1824	North America	**RISE OF THE CALIFORNIA MISSIONS:** Twenty-one Catholic missions, four military installations, and several towns established Spain's claim to Alta, or Upper, California, altering the lives of thousands of American Indians.
Sept., 1769-1778	Southeast Asia	**SIAMESE-VIETNAMESE WAR:** Siamese and Vietnamese leaders fought for control over Cambodia, with each seeking to install their own candidate as Cambodia's new king. The two foreign powers clashed over the issue, until a rebellion in Vietnam forced the Vietnamese army home, leading to a brief peace favoring the Siamese.
Oct. 23, 1769	Europe	**CUGNOT DEMONSTRATES HIS STEAM-POWERED ROAD CARRIAGE:** Nicolas Joseph Cugnot invented a vehicle powered by steam called the steam dray. This three-wheeled carriage, the first of the so-called horseless carriages, could pull up to four tons at a speed of two and one-half miles per hour.
1770	Australia	**Cook Claims Australia for Britain:** Captain James Cook explored the eastern coast of Australia, then known as New Holland, claiming it for the British crown.
1770	Europe/Middle East	**Cretan Rebellion:** Encouraged by Russia, Cretan merchant Ioannis Daskalogiannis rebelled against the Ottoman Empire, which ruthlessly suppressed the rebellion, confirming its power over the mainly Christian population.
1770	Europe	**PUBLICATION OF HOLBACH'S *THE SYSTEM OF NATURE*:** Paul-Henri-Dietrich d'Holbach's *Système de la nature: Ou, Des lois du monde physique et du monde moral* (*The System of Nature*) argued that the source of human misery was an ignorance of nature that was both perpetrated and perpetuated by religion and its superstitious beliefs. The treatise was written to provide a framework of true understanding underpinned by the material mechanisms of nature.

DATE	REGION	EVENT
1770	Europe	**Ramsden Invents the Screw-Cutting Lathe:** English instrument maker Jesse Ramsden's early lathe probably influenced Henry Maudslay's work and had wide implications for the development of industrial machinery.
Mar. 5, 1770	North America	**BOSTON MASSACRE:** British soldiers in Boston fired into an unruly crowd, killing several colonists. The incident arose out of American colonists' fear and distrust of British standing armies in their midst and epitomized the growing colonial unrest of the early 1770's.
1771	Europe	*Encyclopaedia Britannica* **First Published in Edinburgh:** The first full edition of the work was completed three years after the first volume appeared; though full of inaccuracies, it served as the basis of an ongoing educational institution.
1771	Europe	**Serfdom Abolished in Savoy:** Charles Emmanuel III abolished serfdom as he neared the end of his long reign as king of Sardinia-Piedmont.
1771	North America	**West Paints** *Penn's Treaty with the Indians***:** American painter Benjamin West moved toward a new style of realism in art.
1771	Europe	**WOULFE DISCOVERS PICRIC ACID:** Peter Woulfe obtained a solution of picric acid by the action of nitric acid on indigo. The first artificial dye, the substance transformed the textile industry, but its more significant use was as an explosive, adding significant new weapons to the military arsenals of the late eighteenth century.
1771-1802	Southeast Asia	**VIETNAMESE CIVIL WARS:** Three brothers who started the Tay Son Rebellion in the south of Vietnam ended a centuries-long system of divided feudal rule of the country, overthrew the Le Dynasty, and defeated a Chinese invasion before their forces were destroyed by a survivor of the southern lords who unified Vietnam as Emperor Gia Long.
Aug. 5, 1772-Oct. 24, 1795	Europe	**PARTITIONING OF POLAND:** Poland was partitioned, partly annexed, and finally completely absorbed by the more powerful states surrounding it. After the third partition, the nation of Poland no longer existed, as it had become part of the Russian, Prussian, and Austrian empires. Poland would not again become a sovereign state until the twentieth century.
Nov. 2, 1772	North America	**Committees of Correspondence Organized:** Patriots Samuel Adams and Joseph Warren organized the first Committee of Correspondence, soon to be copied throughout the American colonies.
1773	North America	**Boone Leads Settlers into Kentucky:** Daniel Boone led a party of settlers into what would become Kentucky, though they were frightened away by Indian attacks.
1773	Central America	**Destruction of Antigua, Guatemala:** The capital of the Spanish captain-generalcy of Guatemala is destroyed by a powerful earthquake, and a new capital is established in Guatemala City.
1773	Europe	**Dissolution of the Society of Jesus:** Pope Clement XIV dissolves the controversial Catholic order of the Jesuits after they were expelled from most European countries.

DATE	REGION	EVENT
1773	Europe	**GOETHE INAUGURATES THE STURM UND DRANG MOVEMENT:** In reaction to the dryness of Baroque and Enlightenment literature, Johann Wolfgang von Goethe and several of his contemporaries invented an exciting new genre of literature, Sturm und Drang, which proved immensely popular throughout Germany in the 1770's and laid the groundwork for the evolution of neoclassicism and Romanticism.
1773-1788	North America	**AFRICAN AMERICAN BAPTIST CHURCH IS FOUNDED:** An amalgamation of African and European forms of religious worship developed into the African American Baptist Church. The cosmologies and churches fashioned by blacks in the United States helped them survive and transcend the harsh realities of slavery in the South.
Jan. 12, 1773	Antarctic	**Cook Crosses the Antarctic Circle:** The first European explorer to cross the Antarctic Circle, Captain James Cook demonstrated the legendary fallacy of a large southern continent.
Mar. 18, 1773	Europe	**Goldsmith's *She Stoops to Conquer* First Performed:** English playwright Oliver Goldsmith's play is first performed at London's Theatre Royal in Covent Garden.
Sept., 1773-Sept., 1774	Europe	**PUGACHEV'S REVOLT:** A major rebellion in the 1770's seriously threatened the social fabric and political institutions of Russia during the rule of Empress Catherine the Great. The crisis revealed widespread discontent and anger among the population on the southeastern Russian border.
Dec. 16, 1773	North America	**BOSTON TEA PARTY:** A small group of protesters rallied against the British taxation of imported tea by dumping tens of thousands of pounds of tea from anchored British vessels into the Boston Harbor. The largely symbolic uprising had ushered in a series of events that led directly to war and, eventually, American independence.
1774	North America	**Fort Harrod Established in Kentucky Territory:** James Harrod established the first English settlement west of the Alleghenies after sailing down the Ohio River and up the Kentucky River.
1774	Europe	**HANSARD BEGINS REPORTING PARLIAMENTARY DEBATES:** In 1771, the ban on publishing accounts of British parliamentary debates was effectively lifted. Beginning in 1774, limited accounts of Parliament's proceedings began to be published and made available to the public in an officially sanctioned format for the first time. These publications increased the freedom of the British press and helped to institute new standards for an informed British electorate.
1774	North America	**Lee Introduces Shakerism in New York:** An English mystic with a Quaker background, Ann Lee preached celibacy and intense spiritual piety in developing a new religious community northeast of Albany, New York.
Apr. 27-Oct. 10, 1774	North America	**LORD DUNMORE'S WAR:** American colonists on the frontiers of Virginia and Maryland battled Shawnee Indians for control of their land. The Shawnees were defeated and relocated, as European settlers moved into Kentucky.
May 20, 1774	North America	**QUEBEC ACT:** With the passage of the Quebec Act, Great Britain granted limited civil rights to Canadian Catholics and extended the boundaries of Quebec province into the Ohio Valley.

DATE	REGION	EVENT
July 21, 1774	Europe/Middle East	**TREATY OF KUCHUK KAINARJI:** While the Treaty of Kuchuk Kainarji brought only a temporary peace between Russia and the Ottoman Empire, the concessions gained by Russia were more lasting. In particular, Catherine the Great won a permanent foothold on the Black Sea for her empire.
Aug. 1, 1774	Europe	**PRIESTLEY DISCOVERS OXYGEN:** By heating a brick-red compound of mercury, Joseph Priestley produced a gas whose properties of enhanced support of combustion and animal respiration led him to believe that he had discovered an amazing new substance: dephlogisticated air, or oxygen.
Sept. 5-Oct. 26, 1774	North America	**FIRST CONTINENTAL CONGRESS:** A meeting of fifty-six delegates from the American colonies marked the beginning of an independent American government, paving the way for separation from Great Britain.
Dec., 1774-Feb. 24, 1783	South Asia	**FIRST MARĀTHĀ WAR:** This was the first of three major conflicts between the British East India Company and the Marāthās in India, wars that were fought intermittently until 1818. Final victory came to the British and led to the disbandment of the Marāthā army, the abolition of the peshwaship, and the incorporation of the Marāthās into the British subsidiary alliance system.
1775	Europe	**Cook Rewarded for Conquering Scurvy:** Though research into the treatment for scurvy had been conducted for decades, the Royal Society awarded English captain James Cook its Copley Medal for the practical achievement of having sailed with 118 men for more than three years without losing a single man to the disease.
1775	Europe/Africa	**SPANISH-ALGERINE WAR:** Responding to a Moorish siege of Spanish Moroccan possessions by Sultan Mohammed III, King Charles III ordered an invasion of Algiers. Led by Alexander O'Reilly, who commanded a combined military and naval expedition of nearly fifty ships and more than twenty thousand troops, the Spaniards experienced a decisive defeat. The campaign proved a humiliating blow to the Spanish military revival, and it further empowered the Moroccan sultanate.
1775-1790	Europe	**JOSEPH II'S REFORMS:** Holy Roman Emperor Joseph II instituted a series of judicial, ecclesiastical, and social reforms designed to strengthen the Habsburg monarchy and improve the lives of his subjects. Joseph's reforms inspired a liberal tradition that subsequently flowered in the nineteenth century.
1775-1804	Middle East	**Aleppo Revolts:** Ongoing civil conflict and periodic revolts led by the Janissaries demonstrated the growing weakness of central Ottoman control.
Mar. 10, 1775	North America	**Boone Establishes the Wilderness Road:** Departing in the employ of the Transylvania Company, Daniel Boone and a party of thirty North Carolina woodsmen began to clear a road that would be used by tens of thousands of pioneers moving into western Tennessee and Kentucky.
Apr. 14, 1775	North America	**PENNSYLVANIA SOCIETY FOR THE ABOLITION OF SLAVERY IS FOUNDED:** The first antislavery society in America was formed primarily by members of the Society of Friends, or Quakers. The Quakers had formed an abolitionist philosophy that was in line with the religion's belief in equality for all individuals.

Date	Region	Event
Apr. 19, 1775	North America	**BATTLE OF LEXINGTON AND CONCORD:** The American Revolution began with the Battle of Lexington and Concord, in which the British seriously misjudged the resistance of the American colonists.
Apr. 19, 1775-Oct. 19, 1781	North America	**AMERICAN REVOLUTIONARY WAR:** Disaffected American colonists, deciding to wrest their independence from Great Britain, held their own against numerically superior British forces and were able to garner alliances and assistance from France, Spain, and the Netherlands. After more than six years of fighting, the revolutionaries compelled the British government to negotiate the Treaty of Paris of 1783, recognizing the United States of America as an autonomous nation.
Apr. 27-May, 1775	Europe	**FLOUR WAR:** Riots swept the provinces surrounding Paris, caused by the lifting of government controls over the price of grain following the poor wheat harvest of 1774. Ultimately, two French armies quelled the riots; however, the event was indicative of the poverty and poor economic management that would bring about the French Revolution at the end of the following decade.
May 10-Aug. 2, 1775	North America	**SECOND CONTINENTAL CONGRESS:** The second congress of colonial delegates, now a revolutionary body, formed an army, managed the Revolutionary War, began the process of issuing paper money, and took the first steps toward creating a federal government that would bound the individual colony-states in common cause.
June 17, 1775	North America	**Battle of Bunker Hill:** In a battle with significant casualties, American troops were driven from Bunker Hill and Breeds Hill outside Boston in the early days of the American Revolutionary War.
Dec. 31, 1775	North America	**Battle of Quebec:** A small American force hoped to bring Canadian colonies into opposition against Britain in the American Revolutionary War, but failed.
1776	Europe	**Development of the Breech-Loading Rifle:** British army officer Patrick Ferguson invented the first breech-loading rifle to be adopted by the British army.
1776	Latin America	**FOUNDATION OF THE VICEROYALTY OF LA PLATA:** La Plata was established as a viceroyalty of the Spanish Empire, with its capital at Buenos Aires. The new viceroyalty, including territory that originally was part of the viceroyalty of Peru, was established both to decentralize Spanish South America's government and to shift significant military resources to the area south of Brazil, which was threatened by Portuguese and British colonial activity.
1776	Europe	**Potemkin Builds the Russian Black Sea Fleet:** Distinguished Russian admiral and court favorite Grigori Aleksandrovich Potemkin built Russia's first modern Black Sea fleet.
1776	Europe	**Verses to "Rock of Ages" Published:** London editor Augustus Toplady published verses to the hymn "Rock of Ages" in *The Gospel Magazine*.
Jan. 10, 1776	North America	**PAINE PUBLISHES *COMMON SENSE*:** Thomas Paine, who argued against monarchy and for American independence from Britain in a pamphlet that sold out its first edition in a matter of days, became the talk of the American colonies. Many of the American revolutionaries credited the persuasiveness and passion of Paine's arguments for their decision to declare independence.

DATE	REGION	EVENT
Mar. 9, 1776	Europe	**ADAM SMITH PUBLISHES *THE WEALTH OF NATIONS*:** *The Wealth of Nations* marked the culmination of Enlightenment political economy and the advent of modern economics. It became one of the most influential works on capitalism, being used variously as a practical guide, a theoretical description, a defense, and a critique of industrialization and the market.
Mar. 28, 1776	Europe	**FOUNDING OF BOLSHOI THEATRE COMPANY:** Since it was founded by Catherine the Great, the Bolshoi Theatre Company has been preeminent in opera and ballet, and it has staged significant works by Russian playwrights. Its influence has been global, and its name is familiar to most, if not all, arts enthusiasts.
May, 1776-Sept. 3, 1783	Europe/North America	**FRANCE SUPPORTS THE AMERICAN REVOLUTION:** French military and financial support proved indispensable to the United States during the Revolutionary War, and the French played a vital role in the Battle of Yorktown, at which the British surrendered. French diplomacy, however, was less helpful during peace treaty negotiations.
May 24 and June 11, 1776	North America	**INDIAN DELEGATION MEETS WITH CONGRESS:** Representatives of the Iroquois Confederacy attempted to secure neutrality during the Revolutionary War. They believed they had succeeded, but secret American plans to recruit Iroquois mercenaries, as well as a British alliance with the Mohawks, led not merely to Iroquois involvement but to warfare between Iroquois tribes, ultimately causing the dissolution of the confederacy.
July 2, 1776	North America	**NEW JERSEY WOMEN GAIN THE VOTE:** More than a century before securing national woman suffrage, women in New Jersey briefly exercised the right to vote after being given the right in the state's new constitution. In 1807, however, the state legislature changed the suffrage clause to include only adult taxpaying white males.
July 4, 1776	North America	**DECLARATION OF INDEPENDENCE:** The Declaration of Independence announced the beginning of the United States of America to Great Britain and the world, justifying the colonies' decision to secede from Britain and setting forth the political philosophy of the new republic.
Aug. 27-30, 1776	North America	**Battle of Long Island:** British troops under Howe captured southern Long Island, eventually forcing Washington to abandon New York during the early phase of the American Revolutionary War.
Sept. 6-7, 1776	North America	**FIRST TEST OF A SUBMARINE IN WARFARE:** The first submarine, called the *Turtle*, was built in an effort to blow up a British navy ship in the waters of New York Harbor by attaching underwater explosives to the ship's hull. The test marked not only the first submarine journey but also the first time such a vessel, and underwater explosives, had been used in warfare.
Oct. 28, 1776	North America	**Battle of White Plains:** After forcing Washington from Long Island, the British under Howe drove him to winter retreat in Pennsylvania, further demoralizing American troops during the American Revolutionary War.
Dec. 5, 1776	North America	**Phi Beta Kappa Society Founded:** The most distinguished honorary scholarly society in America was established at the College of William and Mary in Williamsburg, Virginia.

DATE	REGION	EVENT
Dec. 26, 1776	North America	**Battle of Trenton:** After a string of defeats in the summer and fall, George Washington recrossed the Delaware River and successfully attacked an outpost of Hessian troops in the pay of the British, lifting morale during the American Revolutionary War.
1777	Europe	**National Library Founded in Prague:** A national library was established in Prague, incorporating the Old Carolinum Library, St. Clementinum College Library, the New Carolinum Library, and a number of private collections.
1777-1791	Europe	**Coulomb's Research in Torsion:** French engineer Charles Coulomb invented the torsion balance and precisely measured electric forces of attraction and repulsion between charged bodies as he explored engineering challenges for the French government.
Jan. 1, 1777	Europe	**FRANCE'S FIRST DAILY NEWSPAPER APPEARS:** The *Journal de Paris*, France's first daily newspaper, was launched on January 1, 1777, and remained in print for sixty-three years. Its pages offered concise information on developments in local and national politics, administrative and police matters, science, health, fashion, art, music, dance, and literature.
Jan. 3, 1777	North America	**Battle of Princeton:** Following success at Trenton, New Jersey, George Washington attacked the British encampment at Princeton, leading to a general British withdrawal from New Jersey for the winter.
July 2, 1777-1804	North America	**NORTHEAST STATES ABOLISH SLAVERY:** Eight northeastern states emancipated their slaves and ended slavery during and in the wake of the American Revolution. Most of the states chose to phase out slavery gradually, and the slave population of the North decreased during the next few decades until abolition was accomplished.
Aug. 6, 1777	North America	**BATTLE OF ORISKANY CREEK:** At Oriskany Creek, American troops coming to break Britain's siege of Fort Schuyler were ambushed by a force of Native Americans and Tories. Although ultimately forced to retreat, the Americans inflicted heavy casualties on the Iroquois, weakening their resolve and laying the groundwork for a British retreat from Benedict Arnold's reinforcements.
Sept. 11, 1777	North America	**Battle of Brandywine:** American troops under Washington were unable to stop British forces from advancing on the American capital of Philadelphia, which was taken on September 26.
Sept. 19-Oct. 17, 1777	North America	**BATTLES OF SARATOGA:** Britain's defeat at Saratoga marked the end of any realistic prospect of British victory in the Revolutionary War. It represented the failure of Britain's plan to divide the colonies in half, isolating New England from the rest of America, and it began the series of events that would culminate with the British defeat at Yorktown.
Nov., 1777-Jan. 1, 1781	Europe	**CONSTRUCTION OF THE FIRST IRON BRIDGE:** In England, the area around Coalbrookdale was one of the foremost iron-producing centers of the world in the eighteenth century. The construction of an iron bridge over the River Severn proved just what could be achieved with the material.

DATE	REGION	EVENT
1778	Pacific Islands	**Cook Explores the North Pacific:** English explorer Captain James Cook explored the Sandwich (Hawaiian) Islands and the northwest Pacific Coast in America, laying British claims to these regions.
Feb. 6, 1778	Europe/North America	**FRANCO-AMERICAN TREATIES:** In the wake of the American victory at the Battle of Saratoga, which suggested that the rebelling colonies had a substantial chance of victory in the Revolutionary War, France recognized the United States and allied with the emerging nation against Great Britain.
June 28, 1778	North America	**Battle of Monmouth:** As British troops retreated in an effort to strengthen their position in the West Indies, George Washington was unable to win a decisive victory, thus enabling the British withdrawal to continue.
July, 1778	Europe	**War of the Bavarian Succession Begins:** Prussia's Frederick the Great invaded Bohemia in response to a potential augmentation of Austrian influence in the region.
Aug. 3, 1778	Europe	**OPENING OF MILAN'S LA SCALA:** Crowning the already rich theatrical life of Italy's most cosmopolitan city, La Scala confirmed Milan as the most important operatic center in Italy.
1779	North America	**City of Louisville Established:** Laid out by Virginia surveyor George Rogers Clark, the town that would become Louisville, Kentucky, was named in honor of French king Louis XVI.
1779	Europe	**CROMPTON INVENTS THE SPINNING MULE:** To invent the spinning mule, Crompton drew on the concepts of James Hargreaves and Richard Arkwright in spinning machinery to create a machine that vastly increased the output of yarn relative to its predecessors.
1779	Europe	**INGENHOUSZ DISCOVERS PHOTOSYNTHESIS:** By studying the relationship between green plants, oxygen, carbon dioxide, and light, Jan Ingenhousz discovered the major, externally observable structures that contribute to the process of photosynthesis. It would remain for later scientists to understand the internal chemical reactions at the heart of the process.
1779-1803	Africa	**FRONTIER WARS IN SOUTH AFRICA:** Three major conflicts occurred when white settlers and indigenous peoples fought over the frontier lands northeast of the South African Cape Colony. Antagonisms had intensified since Dutch farmers first claimed Africans' territory, and war broke out when aggressive settlers and military commandos attempted to seize more land from the Xhosa and other tribes.
Feb. 14, 1779	Pacific Islands	**Cook Killed in the Sandwich (Hawaiian) Islands:** English explorer Captain James Cook is killed by natives on the island of Hawaii.
June 21, 1779-Feb. 7, 1783	Europe	**SIEGE OF GIBRALTAR:** During the American Revolutionary War, Spain and France declared war on Great Britain, and for three and one-half years they laid siege to the British fortress at Gibraltar. However, three convoys loaded with supplies managed to run the blockade, enabling the British on Gibraltar to hold firm, and the "Great Siege" failed.
Sept. 16-Oct. 9, 1779	North America	**Siege of Savannah:** A combined American and French force failed to retake Savannah, Georgia, from British and Loyalist forces during the American Revolutionary War.

DATE	REGION	EVENT
Sept. 23, 1779	North America	***Bonhomme Richard* Captures Royal Navy's *Serapes*:** In the American revolutionary naval battle in which he uttered the famous phrase, "I have not yet begun to fight!" Captain John Paul Jones of the American navy captured the *Serapes*, transferring his men to it when their own ship sank two days later.
1780	North America	**American Academy of Arts and Sciences Founded in Boston:** Proposed by John Adams as a meeting place for the finest minds of each generation, the academy was chartered by the Massachusetts legislature. It would hold its meeting in the Philosophy Chamber at Harvard College.
1780	Europe	**Education Reform in Spain:** Spain's education system was reorganized to allow teaching only by members of the teaching guild. The reforms demonstrated the government's growing interest in education.
1780-1781	Latin America	**REBELLION OF TUPAC AMARU II:** Motivated by a long tradition of economic and social oppression at the hands of the Spanish, Tupac Amaru II led the last great indigenous uprising in Peru before independence from Spain in 1821.
1780-1802	Middle East	**Governorship of Süleyman Paşa:** His rule marked the peak of Mamlūk power in Baghdad.
Apr. 1-May 12, 1780	North America	**Siege of Charleston:** Heartened by Loyalist support in the American South, British troops under Lieutenant General Henry Clinton forced the surrender of Charleston, North Carolina, taking fifty-four hundred prisoners and four hundred guns.
June 2-10, 1780	Europe	**GORDON RIOTS:** The Gordon Riots, which were caused by anti-Catholicism and resentment over the state of the British economy, were inadvertently instigated by Lord George Gordon and illustrated the depths of resentment felt by disenfranchised Londoners toward the wealthy. They also demonstrated the need for better means of controlling mobs.
Aug. 16, 1780	North America	**Battle of Camden:** An American army seeking to reverse the damage following the loss of Charleston, North Carolina, in May, was routed, enhancing British strength in the southern colonies.
Oct. 7, 1780	North America	**Battle of King's Mountain:** American troops killed or captured an entire column of Loyalist troops supporting Lord Cornwallis's invasion of North Carolina, thus forcing its postponement.
Oct. 10-18, 1780	Caribbean	**GREAT CARIBBEAN HURRICANE:** One of the deadliest storms in history struck the eastern Caribbean Islands, killing tens of thousands of people, mostly black slaves. Many of England's and France's lucrative sugar-producing colonies on the islands were severely damaged or destroyed as well. The two European countries had been at war with each other in the Caribbean, and the storm's aftermath affected naval warfare in the region into the following year.
1781	Europe	**KANT PUBLISHES *CRITIQUE OF PURE REASON*:** Immanuel Kant revolutionized philosophy by asking and answering the seemingly simple question, "How is knowledge possible?" His *Kritik der reinen Vernunft* (*Critique of Pure Reason*) is among the most important texts in the history of philosophy, the starting point for both the analytic and Continental traditions that followed.

978

DATE	REGION	EVENT
1781	North America	**Los Angeles Established:** The city was established by Spanish settlers and first called El Pueblo de Nuestra Senora la Reina de los Angeles de Porciuncula.
1781	East Asia	**Muslim Revolt Suppressed in China:** Gao Cong led imperial troops to put down a massive rebellion in Gansu Province.
1781-1784	Europe	**CAVENDISH DISCOVERS THE COMPOSITION OF WATER:** After discovering "inflammable air," or hydrogen, Henry Cavendish investigated its properties and found that pure water formed when hydrogen burned in "dephlogisticated air," or oxygen.
Jan. 17, 1781	North America	**Battle of Cowpens:** An American victory resulted when British troops attempted to destroy an American force of about one thousand that had moved into South Carolina.
Mar. 1, 1781	North America	**RATIFICATION OF THE ARTICLES OF CONFEDERATION:** The Articles of Confederation represented the first attempt of the thirteen American colonies to band together as a single political unit. However, the new states of the Confederation soon discovered that they had retained too much sovereignty for themselves, undermining the unity of the new nation, and they set about creating the Constitution to correct their mistake.
Mar. 31, 1781	Europe	**Herschel Discovers Uranus:** English astronomer William Herschel identified the first planet to be discovered in more than three thousand years.
Oct. 13, 1781	Europe	**Joseph II Issues the Edict of Tolerance:** After closing more than seven hundred monasteries, Holy Roman Emperor Joseph II prescribes new forms of worship and reorganizes the administration of monasteries, with fewer ties to Rome.
Oct. 19, 1781	North America	**CORNWALLIS SURRENDERS AT YORKTOWN:** The entire British field army surrendered to combined American and French forces, marking the military end to the Revolutionary War and confirming once and for all American independence.
1782	Middle East	**Aḥmad ibn Khalīfa Establishes al-Khalīfa Dynasty in Bahrain:** Aḥmad ibn Khalīfa of the Banū ʿUtūb Arabs established a dynasty that ruled into the twentieth century.
1782	Europe	**Newgate Prison Opens in London:** Replacing a prison destroyed in the Gordon Riots of 1780, Newgate would become synonymous with prison austerity.
1782-1798	Europe	**PUBLICATION OF ROUSSEAU'S *CONFESSIONS*:** Jean-Jacques Rousseau's *Les Confessions de J.-J. Rousseau* (*The Confessions of J.-J. Rousseau*) created a new tradition in autobiography, the telling of one's life from a subjective point of view for the purpose of introspective revelation. It was thus influential on all subsequent works, both fiction and nonfiction, in which the main drama occurs in the mind of the storyteller.
1782-1810	Pacific Islands	**WARS OF HAWAIIAN UNIFICATION:** From 1782 to 1810, the rulers of the various Hawaiian Islands clashed in a struggle for power until King Kamehameha I consolidated rule over Hawaii into a single kingdom. As a united kingdom, Hawaii was able to remain independent in the next century, while the other Pacific islands fell to the European imperial powers.
Apr. 6, 1782	Southeast Asia	**Chakri Dynasty Founded in Siam:** Rama I became the first ruler of a dynasty that would rule Siam (Thailand) and parts of Burma and Cambodia for almost two hundred years. He ruled until 1809.

DATE	REGION	EVENT
Apr. 12, 1782	Caribbean	**Battle of the Saints:** British forces under Rodney defeat French fleet under de Grasse in the strait between Guadeloupe and Dominica, restoring British control in the Windward and Leeward Islands.
1783	North America	**LOYALISTS MIGRATE TO NOVA SCOTIA:** The settling of the Loyalists in Nova Scotia helped to preserve Great Britain's remaining North American colonies and played a pivotal part in the establishment of Canada as a separate nation.
1783	Europe/Middle East	**Russia Annexes the Crimean Peninsula:** Russia's conquest marked the first loss of Muslim territory by the Ottoman Empire.
1783	Arctic	**Skaptur Volcano Erupts in Iceland:** In the eruption, 20 percent of the population was killed and the Sun could be seen only when 12 degrees above the horizon.
1783-1784	Europe	**CORT IMPROVES IRON PROCESSING:** Henry Cort developed an economical and quick method for making bar iron (wrought iron) that allowed Britain to go from being an importer to an exporter of this important material needed for industrialization and the military.
Sept. 3, 1783	Europe	**TREATY OF PARIS:** The Treaty of Paris brought the American Revolution to a formal conclusion, as Great Britain officially recognized the United States as an independent, sovereign nation.
Nov. 21, 1783	Europe	**FIRST MANNED BALLOON FLIGHT:** On November 21, 1783, Pilâtre du Rozier and Commandant François Laurent, marquis d'Arlandes, ascended from the Château de la Muette in a hot-air balloon created by the Montgolfier brothers. Their journey over Paris lasted for twenty-six minutes and marked the beginning of human lighter-than-air flight in Europe.
1784	East Asia	**First American Ship Docks at Canton:** Trading ginseng for tea and silks, American investors were richly rewarded and anticipated further development of the China trade.
1784	Europe/North America	**Franklin Suggests Daylight Savings Time:** American scientist, inventor, and diplomat Benjamin Franklin urged France to move clocks ahead one hour in spring in order to maximize hours of daylight, though French farmers resisted.
1784	Europe	**LEGENDRE INTRODUCES POLYNOMIALS:** Adrien-Marie Legendre found, in the course of trying to solve a differential equation, a family of polynomials that satisfied the same kind of properties that ordinary polynomials did. This suggested the use of those polynomials to represent all functions that had certain features, and similar families have been studied by mathematicians and physicists ever since.
1784-1791	Europe	**HERDER PUBLISHES HIS PHILOSOPHY OF HISTORY:** Johann Gottfried Herder's *Ideen zur Philosophie der Geschichte der Menschheit* (*Outlines of a Philosophy of the History of Man*) set the stage for the dialectical thinking of Georg Wilhelm Friedrich Hegel. Dialectics would become a fundamental aspect of nineteenth century German philosophy, particularly in the thought of Friedrich Engels and later the political theory of Karl Marx.

DATE	REGION	EVENT
Apr. 27, 1784	Europe	**FIRST PERFORMANCE OF *THE MARRIAGE OF FIGARO*:** The first performance of Pierre Augustin Caron de Beaumarchais's *The Marriage of Figaro*, a work that reflected the ideals of the Enlightenment and of the impending French Revolution, came after years of struggle with the French court and has remained a symbol of the freedom of the human spirit.
Aug. 13, 1784	Europe/South Asia	**British Parliament Passes the India Act:** Bringing the East India Company under tighter government control, the British government prohibited interference in local politics and made company directors responsible to a Crown board.
Sept. 29, 1784	North America	**HALL'S MASONIC LODGE IS CHARTERED:** Hall's Masonic Lodge became a pillar organization in the African American middle-class community. Serving many of the same functions that mainstream Freemasonry has served among upper-class white communities, members of the so-called African Lodge have helped one another in countless ways for more than two centuries.
Oct. 22, 1784	North America	**FORT STANWIX TREATY:** The Iroquois tribes that had sided with the British in the American Revolutionary War were forced to cede their lands to the United States and move westward. The dismissive negotiating strategy of the American government at Fort Stanwix marked the beginning of its tendency to treat Native Americans as conquered occupants of the United States, rather than as equal, sovereign nations.
1785	Europe	**CONSTRUCTION OF EL PRADO MUSEUM BEGINS:** On the orders of King Charles III, the renowned neoclassical architect Juan de Villanueva began construction of a building for a museum of natural history.
1785	North America	**FIRST STATE UNIVERSITIES ARE ESTABLISHED:** Increased U.S. governmental support made a college education available to a growing middle class.
1785	East Asia	**RITES CONTROVERSY:** Shortly after the introduction of Roman Catholicism to Korea, the government cracked down when Catholics refused to practice traditional Confucian religious rituals. Many of those who persisted in practicing the banned Catholic faith became martyrs.
1785-1788	Europe	**HUTTON PROPOSES THE GEOLOGICAL THEORY OF UNIFORMITARIANISM:** James Hutton's theory that Earth's formation was the result of a cyclic process of erosion and uplift—which, in turn, was the result of the compounding of the ordinary action of water and heat in deep time—was the intellectual precursor of Charles Lyell's uniformitarian geology and a fundamental premise of Charles Darwin's evolutionary theory.
Jan. 7, 1785	Europe	**FIRST CROSS-CHANNEL FLIGHT:** Jean Blanchard and John Jeffries successfully crossed the English Channel in a balloon, demonstrating that travel by air was practical and opening the door to military and scientific observations using balloons.
Apr., 1785	Europe	**CARTWRIGHT PATENTS THE STEAM-POWERED LOOM:** The production of a working power-operated loom was a key step in the mechanization of textile manufacture. Although power looms did not come into general use in England until after 1822, Edmund Cartwright's original model paved the way for future refinements, and the basic design remained unchanged until the middle of the twentieth century.

DATE	REGION	EVENT
May 20, 1785	North America	**ORDINANCE OF 1785:** The Ordinance of 1785 established a system for surveying and selling the vast lands outside the former colonies that were then the property of the U.S. government. It set out the framework for the creation of new states and territories in the newly independent United States.
1786	Central America	**DISCOVERY OF THE MAYAN RUINS AT PALENQUE:** Spanish colonial officials uncovered the spectacular Mayan ruins at Palenque, which had been abandoned in the tenth century. Historians first believed that the technical and artistic abilities of ancient European travelers had inspired and influenced the building of the complex by local peoples. However, the Mayan origins of the site were revealed after the ruins were found, and the origins themselves were uncovered and celebrated by the Mexican indigenous movement of the twentieth century.
1786	North America	**Discovery of the Pribilof Islands:** Russian captain Gerasim Pribilof discovered islands in the Bering Sea, home to an estimated 5 million fur seals.
1786	Middle East	**Ottoman Empire Regains Control of Egypt:** After a long period of Mamlūk control in Egypt, the Ottoman government drove the Mamlūks into upper Egypt but lost authority again by 1791.
1786-1787	Europe	**LAVOISIER DEVISES THE MODERN SYSTEM OF CHEMICAL NOMENCLATURE:** As an important part of the chemical revolution he fathered, Antoine-Laurent Lavoisier, collaborating with other French scientists, devised a rational system of chemical nomenclature in which each substance's name reflected its chemical composition.
1786-1787	East Asia	**TENMEI FAMINE:** The Tenmei era saw the most devastating famine in early modern Japan, a nationwide disaster that took as many as 130,000 lives. Many farming villages were abandoned, and large areas became depopulated. Shogunate officials provided little assistance, and they aggravated the situation through corruption and incompetence. Popular uprisings forced them out of office, bringing not only greater repression but also needed reforms.
Jan. 16, 1786	North America	**VIRGINIA STATUTE OF RELIGIOUS LIBERTY:** Virginia was the first state to legislate religious liberty, which influenced the First Amendment's provision for separation of church and state.
Feb. 2, 1786	Europe	**JONES POSTULATES A PROTO-INDO-EUROPEAN LANGUAGE:** Sir William Jones stunned scholars in Europe and inspired them to review the origin of Western civilization when he suggested that an unknown prehistoric language was the source of classical languages, such as Greek and Latin, as well as Sanskrit.
1787	Europe	**DAVID PAINTS *THE DEATH OF SOCRATES*:** In 1787, the celebrated artist Jacques-Louis David painted *The Death of Socrates*, which epitomized neoclassicism, an artistic movement that grew in reaction to the frivolous and decorative Rococo style. Neoclassical art also reflected the philosophical and moral values of the Enlightenment and the Age of Reason.
1787	Europe	**HERSCHEL BEGINS BUILDING HIS REFLECTING TELESCOPE:** William Herschel's 40-foot-long reflecting telescope was used to discover two of Saturn's moons and to observe nebulae, identified as galaxies such as the Milky Way. The telescope, functional in 1789, remained the largest such instrument for more than fifty years.

DATE	REGION	EVENT
1787-1792	Europe/Middle East	**Ottoman War with Russia and Austria:** Hoping to regain the Crimea, the Ottomans failed, lost territory in Georgia, and were forced to accept the Dniester River as the boundary between the Ottomans and the Russian Empire.
Apr. 12, 1787	North America	**FREE AFRICAN SOCIETY IS FOUNDED:** The Free African Society, the first major secular institution with a mission to aid African Americans, paved the way for later institutions such as the National Association for the Advancement of Colored People (NAACP). The society existed for less than a decade, however, before its membership merged with African American churches and other religious organizations with similar agendas.
July 13, 1787	North America	**NORTHWEST ORDINANCE:** The Northwest Ordinance established the framework for the addition of new states, politically equal to the existing states, to the United States. It marked the rise of federal involvement in the organization of Western lands and the first sectional compromise over the extension of slavery.
Sept. 17, 1787	North America	**U.S. CONSTITUTION IS ADOPTED:** The Constitution of the United States of America replaced the failed Articles of Confederation, creating a new, unified nation under a tripartite federal government.
Oct. 27, 1787-May, 1788	North America	**PUBLICATION OF *THE FEDERALIST*:** This series of essays, designed to convince New York State to ratify the new American Constitution, became classic explications of American constitutional law and history.
1788-Sept., 1809	Europe	**RUSSO-SWEDISH WARS:** As at the beginning of the eighteenth century, Russia and Sweden battled for supremacy in northern Europe at century's end. Russia was victorious, preserving and expanding its imperial ambitions.
Jan. 1, 1788	Europe	***The Times* Begins Publication in London:** Merchant John Walter established England's journal of record.
Jan. 26, 1788	Australia	**BRITAIN ESTABLISHES PENAL COLONY IN AUSTRALIA:** Great Britain established a penal colony in Australia at Sydney Cove not only to overcome inadequate prison facilities at home but also to secure naval resources and create an economic route to Asia.
Feb. 14, 1788	Europe	**MEIKLE DEMONSTRATES HIS DRUM THRESHER:** Andrew Meikle improved mechanical threshing methods by creating a machine that enabled farmers to harvest grain crops efficiently. His invention occurred at a time when demand for agricultural goods was increasing dramatically to feed and clothe growing urban populations employed by industry.
1789	Europe	**LEBLANC DEVELOPS SODA PRODUCTION:** Instead of using organic sources, Nicolas Leblanc discovered an artificial method of making soda (sodium carbonate) from salt (sodium chloride), and his method led to widespread use of soda in industries making soap, glass, and paper, as well as in the bleaching and dyeing industries.
1789	Europe	**Proust Heads Spanish Royal Laboratory:** French chemist Joseph-Louis Proust moved to Madrid to head the Royal Laboratory of Charles IV.
Apr. 30, 1789	North America	**WASHINGTON'S INAUGURATION:** As the first president of the United States, George Washington set lasting precedents for future leaders, helping to define both the qualities befitting a president and the appropriate conduct of presidents while in office.

DATE	REGION	EVENT
May 5, 1789	Europe	**LOUIS XVI CALLS THE ESTATES-GENERAL:** King Louis XVI called the Estates-General, the supreme French legislative body, to meet for the first time in more than 150 years. The disastrous fiscal condition of the French government required new taxes that only the Estates-General could authorize, but those same fiscal problems had caused significant unrest among the bourgeois members of the Third Estate, who were poised to take control of the government.
May 5, 1789-1796	Europe	**French Revolution:** The calling together of the Estates-General on May 5, 1789, set in motion an expanding chain of radical reforms that shattered the ancien régime in France. Many reforms were kept, but the new constitution of 1795 was decidedly reactionary, ending the most radical phase of the upheaval.
June 20, 1789	Europe	**OATH OF THE TENNIS COURT:** The representatives of the French Third Estate swore to accomplish major governmental reform and not to separate—or to allow themselves to be separated—until their goals were achieved. Their oath forced King Louis XVI to accept a truly national assembly, thereby precipitating the French Revolution.
July 14, 1789	Europe	**FALL OF THE BASTILLE:** In the first overt violent act of the French Revolution, a crowd stormed the Parisian prison known as the Bastille, freeing its prisoners and seizing the armaments stored there as well. The Bastille's fall signaled the emergence of the Parisian crowd as a potent political force.
July 28-Oct. 16, 1789	North America	**EPISCOPAL CHURCH IS ESTABLISHED:** In the wake of the American Revolution, a group of former Anglicans created a church based on Anglicanism but no longer associated with Great Britain. The general convention of the Protestant Episcopal Church adopted a church constitution, canons, and liturgy that shaped a uniquely American Episcopal church, independent of its mother Church of England.
Sept. 24, 1789	North America	**JUDICIARY ACT:** The Judiciary Act created a federal court system independent of the legislative and executive branches of the U.S. government. Beyond filling a practical need, the act created the third branch of the American three-branch system and began to apportion power to the judiciary, providing it with a role in the day to day conducting of the national government.
Oct., 1789-Apr. 25, 1792	Europe	**FRANCE ADOPTS THE GUILLOTINE:** The invention of the guillotine made decapitation more humane and gave equality of punishment to all classes. It also made decapitation easier and faster, facilitating the mass executions of the Reign of Terror.
1790's	North America	**FIRST U.S. POLITICAL PARTIES:** Philosophical and practical differences led leaders of the United States to form the first political parties—the Federalists, who generally opposed the Constitution, and the Republicans, who for the most part supported the Constitution—to advance their interests and ideals.
1790's-1830's	North America	**SECOND GREAT AWAKENING:** Beginning in the 1790's, the United States witnessed a spiritual reawakening that gave expression to the new social, political, and economic realities of the late eighteenth century. The Second Great Awakening, coinciding with the first decades of the new nation's existence, established a long-standing American tradition of charity and humanitarianism.

DATE	REGION	EVENT
1790	Europe	**BURKE LAYS THE FOUNDATIONS OF MODERN CONSERVATISM:** The first year of the French Revolution provoked a scathing denunciation in England by the Whig politician Edmund Burke. Although his lengthy *Reflections on the Revolution in France*, published in this year, was not aimed at establishing a systematic political philosophy, Burke nevertheless produced what is widely thought to be the manifesto of modern political conservatism.
1790	Europe	**FIRST STEAM ROLLING MILL:** By the late eighteenth century, steam began to replace waterwheels as the source of power for English mills. Applicable to ironworks, textile mills, and grains processing, the steam-powered rolling mills would result in larger mills, greater efficiency, higher production rates at lower cost, and more flexibility in transportation than small-scale cottage industries could achieve.
Jan., 1790	North America	**HAMILTON'S *REPORT ON PUBLIC CREDIT*:** Alexander Hamilton's report to the U.S. Congress on public credit—which gave high priority to paying interest and principal on the securities constituting the national debt—became the basis for the federal government's economic policy.
Oct., 1790	North America	**NOOTKA SOUND CONVENTION:** After a prolonged dispute over competing Spanish and British claims to the Canadian Northwest, Spain abandoned all settlements there, ceding the region to the British Empire.
Oct. 18, 1790-July, 1794	North America	**LITTLE TURTLE'S WAR:** A coalition of Native Americans in the Ohio Country fought the United States to retain control of their territory. The coalition inflicted the worst battlefield defeat on U.S. Army troops of any Native American force in history, and it prevented the United States from controlling or developing Ohio for four years.
Dec. 20, 1790	North America	**SLATER'S SPINNING MILL:** Slater's mill was the first modern industrial mill in the Americas. It introduced both modern textile-manufacturing techniques and modern business management practices to the fledgling United States.
1791	Europe	**Ball Bearings Patented:** English inventor Philip Vaughan, working on carriage axles, obtained the first patent on modern ball bearings.
1791	Europe	**Brandenburg Gate Completed in Berlin:** Prussian architect Carl Gotthard Langhaus designed the entrance gate to stand for peace, constructing it nearly a mile from the emperor's palace.
1791	North America	**CANADA'S CONSTITUTIONAL ACT:** One of a series of acts that created a constitution for Canada, the Constitutional Act of 1791 divided the territory into Lower Canada and Upper Canada and created a system that attempted to appease the very different political desires and expectations of British and French Canadians.
Feb. 22, 1791-Feb. 16, 1792	North America	**THOMAS PAINE PUBLISHES *RIGHTS OF MAN*:** Thomas Paine's *Rights of Man* was a response to Edmund Burke's *Reflections on the Revolution in France*, in which Burke had heavily criticized the French Revolution and revolutionary causes. Paine gave a theoretical defense of democracy and republican principles and advocated a remarkably modern welfare-state program whose fundamental function was to abolish poverty.

DATE	REGION	EVENT
Aug. 22, 1791-Jan. 1, 1804	Caribbean	**HAITIAN INDEPENDENCE:** Toussain Louverture led a massive slave revolt that resulted in the first black republic in modern times and the second successful revolution for independence in the Western Hemisphere.
Dec. 15, 1791	North America	**U.S. BILL OF RIGHTS IS RATIFIED:** With the ratification of the first ten amendments to the U.S. Constitution, significant limitations were placed upon the powers of the federal government and specific rights and freedoms were granted to individuals and to the states.
1792	North America	**U.S. Mint Begins Decimal Coinage:** The United States begins regular decimal coinage of gold, silver, and copper at a mint in Philadelphia.
1792	Europe	**WOLLSTONECRAFT PUBLISHES *A VINDICATION OF THE RIGHTS OF WOMAN*:** English writer and feminist Mary Wollstonecraft wrote and published the first recognized political work advocating gender equality, especially in education.
1792-1793	Europe	**FICHTE ADVOCATES FREE SPEECH:** Swept up in the ideals of the French Revolution, Johann Gottlieb Fichte and several other young German philosophers argued in the 1790's for increases in individual liberty, including relaxations of censorship.
Jan. 4, 1792-1797	Europe	**THE *NORTHERN STAR* CALLS FOR IRISH INDEPENDENCE:** The *Northern Star* became the mouthpiece of Protestant Irish discontent, fanning the flames of nationalism in the years leading up to the Irish Rebellion.
Mar. 16, 1792	Europe	**DENMARK ABOLISHES THE SLAVE TRADE:** Denmark was the first European nation to outlaw the trade in slaves. Other nations soon followed suit, but neither Denmark nor the other nations outlawed slavery itself at this time. They merely put an end to their colonies' importation of slaves from Africa and elsewhere.
Apr. 20, 1792-Oct., 1797	Europe	**EARLY WARS OF THE FRENCH REVOLUTION:** During the French Revolutionary Wars, the French government, which was committed to spreading antiaristocratic principles, fought against conservative European powers that supported traditional social inequalities and royalist institutions.
Sept. 20, 1792	Europe	**BATTLE OF VALMY:** This first battle of the Wars of the French Revolution might have also been the last had a hastily assembled French army succumbed to a large Prussian-led invading force. Though a minor skirmish, Valmy is considered an important political turning point, since a French defeat might have ended the French Revolution.
Oct. 2, 1792-Apr. 12, 1799	Europe/South Asia	**CHRISTIAN MISSIONARY SOCIETIES ARE FOUNDED:** The evangelical effects of the First Great Awakening and its revival in the Second Great Awakening of the 1790's were widely felt in the establishment of organizations committed to the "conversion of the heathen," most notably the Baptist Mission Society, the London Missionary Society, and the Church Missionary Society.
Nov. 6, 1792	Europe	**Battle of Jemappes:** In the early days of the French Revolutionary Wars, forty thousand French recruits drove Austrian forces from strong positions, reinforcing nationalist morale.

DATE	REGION	EVENT
1793	North America	**WHITNEY INVENTS THE COTTON GIN:** Eli Whitney invented a machine to separate the useful portion of the cotton plant from its seeds and other extraneous materials. The gin revolutionized methods of agricultural production and increased the demand for slave labor in the American South.
1793-Jan., 1794	Europe/East Asia	**MACARTNEY MISSION TO CHINA:** Great Britain sent George Macartney to the court of the Qianlong emperor, who regarded Britain as a vassal state and its people as barbarians. Macartney was to establish diplomatic relations with mainland China and to open new trade opportunities. Although negotiations led to promises, none of them were put into effect, and historians deemed Macartney's mission a failure.
Jan. 21, 1793	Europe	**EXECUTION OF LOUIS XVI:** The trial and execution of Louis XVI placed the Jacobin faction in ascendancy in the French revolutionary government. It helped discredit the revolution among moderate and conservative Frenchmen and stiffened resistance to the revolution abroad.
Feb. 12, 1793	North America	**FIRST FUGITIVE SLAVE LAW:** The U.S. Congress passed a law establishing a procedure for southern slave owners to recover slaves who fled north, aggravating the sectional conflict between free states and slave states.
Mar. 4-Dec. 23, 1793	Europe	**WAR IN THE VENDÉE:** Angered by the execution of Louis XVI, the sale of confiscated Church and émigré lands to the middle classes, the deportation of village priests who did not support the revolution, and the institution of a national draft, the peasantry in Western France revolted. A counterrevolution developed, threatening to topple the First French Republic during the first year of its existence.
July 22, 1793	North America	**MACKENZIE REACHES THE ARCTIC OCEAN:** Alexander Mackenzie, searching for an inland water route to the Pacific Ocean, instead found a river that took him to the Arctic coast of North America. This journey, as well as a subsequent trek across the Rocky Mountains, convinced Mackenzie that there was no commercially viable overland route from the Atlantic Ocean to the Pacific Ocean.
Sept. 7-Dec. 19, 1793	Europe	**Siege of Toulon:** French military under Jacques Dugommier, with Napoleon Bonaparte serving as artillery adviser, forced British, Spanish, and Royalist troops to evacuate, recapturing half of the French fleet that had been taken earlier.
c. 1794-1799	Europe	**PROUST ESTABLISHES THE LAW OF DEFINITE PROPORTIONS:** Through a series of meticulous experiments, Joseph Louis Proust proved that all chemical compounds, whether found in nature or prepared in the laboratory, consist of elements in definite ratios by weight.
June 1, 1794	Europe	***ALLGEMEINES LANDRECHT* RECODIFIES PRUSSIAN LAW:** The *Allgemeines Landrecht*, which codified Prussian civil and criminal laws on the basis of traditional social stratification, contributed to the unification of the various Prussian regions under absolute monarchy. It was thus an important aspect of the growth of Prussia as the central German power and the establishment in the nineteenth century of a German empire.

DATE	REGION	EVENT
July-Nov., 1794	North America	**WHISKEY REBELLION:** A group of dissidents in western Pennsylvania, unwilling to pay a tax on whiskey, engaged in violent protests and attacks upon tax collectors. The response of the federal government demonstrated its willingness and ability to use military force to enforce unpopular laws.
July 27-28, 1794	Europe	**FALL OF ROBESPIERRE:** The fall of French revolutionary leader Robespierre ended the Reign of Terror and allowed the army, now used against the populace, to become the primary force of the French Revolution.
Aug. 20, 1794	North America	**BATTLE OF FALLEN TIMBERS:** In the Battle of Fallen Timbers, the U.S. Army decisively defeated the Native Americans of the Ohio Territory. The resulting Treaty of Greenville secured U.S. control over much of Ohio, and the indigenous peoples were forced to abandon the area.
Nov. 19, 1794	North America/Europe	**JAY'S TREATY:** Jay's Treaty resolved outstanding financial, territorial, and commercial conflicts between Britain and the United States. The treaty led to large-scale settlement of the Northwest Territory, but it opened a rift with France.
1795	North America/Europe	**INVENTION OF THE FLAX SPINNER:** While visiting Great Britain, Robert Fulton invented a flax-spinning machine that would significantly advance the American textile industry.
1795	North America/Europe	**MURRAY DEVELOPS A MODERN ENGLISH GRAMMAR BOOK:** Lindley Murray produced a simple-format English grammar book that was widely adopted by schools in both England and the United States.
1795	Middle East	**Wahabis Conquer Al-Hasa on the Persian Gulf:** Continuing their conquest of central and eastern Arabia, the Wahabis positioned themselves to challenge ruling dynasties for control of the peninsula.
1795-1797	Europe	**PAGANINI'S EARLY VIOLIN PERFORMANCES:** The violin prodigy Niccolò Paganini, who undertook his first concert tour at the age of fifteen, amazed audiences with his feats of agility as well as his passionate stage presence, becoming one of the Romantic era's most famous examples of the emotionally absorbed artist.
May 6, 1795	Europe	**SPEENHAMLAND SYSTEM:** The county magistrates of Berkshire, England, modified an existing system to help poor farmworkers. They linked the amount of money given to the poor to the price of bread, so workers would automatically be given more money as bread became more expensive. Such early indexing schemes became widely adopted and remained in place until a new poor law was enacted in 1834.
July, 1795-Mar., 1796	Caribbean	**SECOND MAROON WAR:** Jamaica's largest community of Maroons (rebellious and escaped slaves) battled British forces for nine months in an uprising prompted by local grievances. The conflict ended when the Maroons agreed to a peace treaty, the terms of which were violated when Jamaica's British governor deported the Maroons to Nova Scotia in Canada. The war marked the last significant Maroon rebellion in Jamaican history.
Oct. 27, 1795	North America/Europe	**PINCKNEY'S TREATY:** Wars in Europe prompted Spain to sign Pinckney's Treaty, recognizing the United States' western boundary claims and ensuring free navigation of the Mississippi River.

DATE	REGION	EVENT
1796	Europe	**LAPLACE ARTICULATES HIS NEBULAR HYPOTHESIS:** Pierre-Simon Laplace published *Exposition du système du monde* (*The System of the World*), in which he demonstrated mathematically that Sir Isaac Newton's laws of motion and gravity could result in a simple cloud of dust transforming over time into the Sun and planets.
1796-1798	Europe	**JENNER DEVELOPS SMALLPOX VACCINATION:** English physician Edward Jenner was the first person to establish the scientific legitimacy of smallpox vaccinations through his experiments and research publications. His campaign to popularize the procedure led to its worldwide use and eventually protected millions from an often fatal disease.
Mar., 1796-Oct. 17, 1797	Europe	**NAPOLEON'S ITALIAN CAMPAIGNS:** Napoleon's lightning strike into Italy secured the region for France; provided a source of revenue, manpower, and resources for the French armies; and further reduced the Austrian forces' ability to stand against the French hegemony in Europe.
May 10, 1796	Europe	**Battle of Lodi:** In pursuit of Austrian troops, Napoleon forced the Austrian rear guard to give up control of a bridge across the Adda River, thus paving the way for the conquest of Milan five days later.
Sept. 19, 1796	North America	**WASHINGTON'S FAREWELL ADDRESS:** George Washington published his final address as the first president of the United States, articulating foreign and domestic policy for the young nation.
Nov., 1796	Europe	**CATHERINE THE GREAT'S ART COLLECTION IS INSTALLED AT THE HERMITAGE:** Constructed as an annex to the Winter Palace where the empress of Russia could obtain privacy, the Hermitage in St. Petersburg evolved, because of Catherine the Great's concerted purchasing efforts, to be a world-renowned museum housing many of Europe's great artistic masterpieces.
1797	Europe	**WOLLASTON BEGINS HIS WORK ON METALLURGY:** William Hyde Wollaston and Smithson Tennant experimented on platinum ore, discovering the new elements and developing techniques for producing powdered platinum and a malleable, purified platinum metal.
Jan. 14, 1797	Europe	**Battle of Rivoli:** Austrian armies attempting to recover their losses in northern Italy were defeated by Napoleon, leading to the invasion of Austria in March.
Oct. 4, 1797-Sept. 30, 1800	North America/Europe	**XYZ AFFAIR:** Disagreements between the United States and France over the import of Jay's Treaty and an attempt by French agents to extort a bribe from American negotiators led to an undeclared war between France and the United States.
Oct. 11, 1797	Europe	**Battle of Camperdown:** An English fleet under Admiral Adam Duncan intercepted a Dutch fleet seeking to join the French in an attack on Ireland, capturing eight ships and ending hopes of a major Irish landing.
1798	Europe	**INVENTION OF LITHOGRAPHY:** In 1798, aspiring German playwright Alois Senefelder invented a new printmaking technique based on applying ink to an image created by a greasy medium on a porous stone. The unmarked or non-image areas holding water repelled the ink. This new "chemical printing," later known as lithography (stone writing) transformed both commercial printing and the visual arts.

DATE	REGION	EVENT
1798	Europe	**MALTHUS AROUSES CONTROVERSY WITH HIS POPULATION THEORY:** Thomas Robert Malthus published *An Essay on the Principle of Population*, developing theories about population explosion, food supply, and environmental concerns that laid the foundation for modern socioeconomic theory.
Apr. 12, 1798-Sept. 2, 1801	Middle East	**NAPOLEON'S EGYPTIAN CAMPAIGN:** Napoleon Bonaparte invaded Egypt with the two goals of disrupting British trade with India and establishing a permanent French colony. Although the campaign was a failure, he successfully manipulated public opinion to enhance his popularity in France.
May-Nov., 1798	Europe	**IRISH REBELLION:** Motivated by the example of the French and the American Revolution, Irish nationalists planned rebellion against British control. However, all did not go as anticipated, and the uprisings were mainly uncoordinated and short-lived. Nevertheless, the revolt acted as an inspiration for subsequent generations of Irish nationalists and, more immediately, set into motion the union between England and Ireland.
June 25-July 14, 1798	North America	**ALIEN AND SEDITION ACTS:** The Alien and Sedition Acts were enacted by a Federalist-controlled Congress in the hope of not only suppressing the immigrant vote, which had been aligning most often with the Republican Party, but also deporting noncitizens during wartime and noncitizens who were considered a threat to public safety. The Sedition Act, passed in the hope of limiting the power of the Republican press especially, made it a crime to write or publish criticisms of the federal government.
July 21, 1798	Middle East	**Battle of the Pyramids:** Napoleon's defeat of the Mamlūk army enabled him to occupy Cairo, but his plans for strategic control were upset by British control of the sea, secured in the Battle of the Nile on August 1-2.
Aug. 1-2, 1798	Middle East	**BATTLE OF THE NILE:** The Battle of the Nile destroyed the French fleet, isolated more than thirty-five thousand French soldiers in Egypt, and ended Napoleon's attempt to march eastward to India.
1799	North America	**CODE OF HANDSOME LAKE:** The Seneca religious leader Handsome Lake founded the Longhouse religion, which merged Native American and Christian traditions. Both successful and controversial, the Longhouse religion was an attempt to revive indigenous cultures within the context of the contemporary experience of Native Americans.
1799	Europe	**DISCOVERY OF THE EARLIEST ANESTHETICS:** The study of inhalant vapors at the Pneumatic Medical Institute led to Sir Humphry Davy's discovery that nitrous oxide, or laughing gas, could be used to alleviate pain. The gas was the first inhalant used as an anesthetic.
1799	Europe	**Founding of the Royal Institution of London:** Scientist Benjamin Thompson, who first proposed that heat was a form of motion, drew up a proposal for the founding of a new scientific institution and helped run it in its early years.
1799	Europe/Africa	**Park Publishes *Travels in the Interior of Africa*:** Following nineteen months of travel, Scottish explorer Mungo Park published his account to great acclaim before embarking on a second expedition in 1805.

DATE	REGION	EVENT
July 16, 1799-July 9, 1804	Latin America	**HUMBOLDT AND BONPLAND'S EXPEDITION:** Alexander von Humboldt and Aimé Bonpland's six-thousand-mile expedition through Central and South America was the first major scientific exploration of the region.
July 19, 1799	Middle East	**DISCOVERY OF THE ROSETTA STONE:** The discovery of the Rosetta Stone provided the key to deciphering hieroglyphics, the ancient Egyptian system of writing, and so recaptured and revealed the rich culture and history of the forgotten civilization.
July 25, 1799	Middle East	**Battle of Aboukir:** Napoleon routed a Turkish army brought from Rhodes by the British, enabling him to return to France to gain direct political power.
Nov. 9-10, 1799	Europe	**NAPOLEON RISES TO POWER IN FRANCE:** Napoleon rose to power in France through the coup d'état of 18-19 Brumaire, effectively ending France's revolutionary experiment and initiating nearly sixteen years of Napoleonic domination of Europe.
1800	Europe	**VOLTA INVENTS THE BATTERY:** Alessandro Volta designed a battery that used positive and negative poles to charge a wire placed in a wet cell. He refined his design three times before 1800, the officially recognized date of his invention.
Jan. 24, 1800	Middle East	**Convention of El Arish:** After returning to France, Napoleon concluded the Egyptian campaigns by seeking to withdraw French troops.
June 14, 1800	Europe	**Battle of Marengo:** French troops under General Louis-Charles-Antoine Desaix de Veygoux and Napoleon routed an Austrian force under General Michael Friedrich von Melas, thus ending the Italian campaign.
July 2-Aug. 1, 1800	Europe	**ACT OF UNION FORMS THE UNITED KINGDOM:** The English and Irish parliaments passed the Act of Union, creating the United Kingdom of Great Britain and Ireland. The act dissolved Ireland's parliament and unified the Church of England and the Church of Ireland. The act would lead to a history of movements for Irish nationhood and for Catholic emancipation.
Dec. 3, 1800	Europe	**Battle of Hohenlinden:** Following victory in Italy, French forces under General Jean Victor Moreau marched into Germany, decisively defeating the Austrians, who soon left the war.

—John Powell

GLOSSARY

Abbey: A self-sufficient religious community of monks or nuns or both, run by an abbot or abbess and sometimes subject to a higher secular authority through feudal obligation. Abbots and abbesses occupied posts that were socially, politically, and spiritually important and powerful. *See also* Monastery, Monk, Nun, Nunnery.

Abolitionists: Men and women who campaigned for a complete end to slavery, led most notably in England by William Wilberforce from the 1770's.

Absolutism or absolute monarchy: A form of government in which monarchs claimed full and absolute authority to rule their lands; generally based upon the concept that monarchs derived their authority from God and thus are responsible only to God.

Agricultural Revolution: The application of new farming and animal husbandry techniques that allowed greater agricultural productivity in the eighteenth century, thus enabling more workers to move into industrial jobs.

Alaafin: A king of the Oyo in Nigeria, Africa.

Allegory: A story, literary work, or play in which characters in the narrative personify abstract ideas or qualities and so give a second level of meaning to the work.

Amir. *See* Emir.

Anglican: Of or belonging to the Protestant Church of England.

Antinomian: Relating to those who believe that Christians, obeying the inward spirit, are exempt from moral law; considered heretical by the Roman Catholic Church.

Apprentice: A person, usually a young male, who agreed to serve an employer for a specified amount of time in return for training in a craft, trade, or business.

Aristocracy: A class of hereditary nobility in Europe, established by royal grants of titles and lands. In the Middle Ages grants were made for military service; by the eighteenth century they often were made for a wide range of services to a monarch. *See also* Gentry, Noble.

Assignants: Government bonds issued by the French government in anticipation of the sale of confiscated Church lands during the French Revolution.

Bannerman: Warriors of Manchu origin in Qing China, granted special economic and social privileges in return for ethnic and imperial loyalty.

Baroque: A style of art, architecture, literature, and music that flourished in seventeenth and early eighteenth century Europe. Baroque is defined especially by its monumental, dynamic, exuberant, grandiose, and theatrical style; its complex and ornate forms; its illusionism; and its tension. *See also* Classicism, Gothic, Mannerism.

Bey: The governor of a province of the Ottoman Empire. Also called "beg." *See also* Sultan, Vizier.

Bishop: The highest-ranking priest within a diocese, responsible for its administration and the guidance of its clergy. *See also* Patriarch, Pope.

Boyar: A Russian noble—of the landed military aristocracy—ranking just below a ruling prince.

Broad Constructionist: Person who accepts the doctrine of implied powers in the Constitution.

Bull: A formal papal letter or document issuing an authoritative statement or policy. Named after the pope's lead seal, or *bulla*.

Bullionism: A fundamental principle of mercantilism that argues that precious metals are the sole source of value, and that they should be concentrated in a national treasury as a source of international strength.

Bushido: The code of conduct of the samurai (Japanese warrior class), stressing martial prowess, discipline, bravery, and unwavering loyalty to one's lord. *See also* Ronin, Samurai, Shogun.

Cabinet: The body of secretaries appointed by a prime minister or president to head executive departments and formulate government policy.

***Cahiers de doléances*:** Petitions for reform drawn up as lists of grievances and submitted to the French crown when the Estates-General met in 1789.

Calculus: A central branch of mathematics first developed during ancient times in Greece and theorized by seventeenth century mathematicians such as Leibniz, Descartes, and Newton. Calculus is concerned, in part, with determining volumes and areas of curved surfaces, with determining the lengths of curved lines, with problems of slopes and areas, and so forth.

Caliph: Islamic ruler claiming both spiritual and secular authority as the successor of the Prophet Muḥammad. *See also* Imam, Islam, Sharif.

Calvinism: The theology based on the teachings of John Calvin in the sixteenth century, which places supreme faith in God and believes in human fallibility and predestination. *See also* Catholicism, Presbyterian, Protestantism.

Canon law: The system of governing the Roman Catholic Church, its bishops, clerics, and laypersons. *See also* Catholicism, Clerics or clergy.

Cardinal: A high official in the Roman Catholic Church, second only to the pope in authority. Cardinals are appointed by the pope, and the college of cardinals is the body that elects a new pope.

Caste system: In India, a system of rigid social hierarchy, rooted in Hindu teachings, in which each person is born into a specific social rank.

Castle: A fortification with a variety of architectural features designed for safety and defense.

Categorical imperative: The internal sense of moral duty that all people possess, according to the philosophical doctrines of German philosopher Immanuel Kant.

Cathedral or cathedral church: The central church in a diocese, the seat of a bishop's cathedra, or throne.

Catholicism: From the Greek *catholicos*, meaning "universal," Catholicism is a branch of Christianity organized in a strict hierarchy and subscribing to a complex body of religious dogma, including belief in transubstantiation, in papal infallibility, and in justification by faith in combination with good works. The two Catholic Churches are the Roman Catholic Church and the Eastern Orthodox Church. *See also* Calvinism, Eastern Orthodox Church, Islam, Judaism, Presbyterian, Protestantism.

Chancellor: The head of the chancery, an officer in a royal household, often a bishop familiar with law, who served as a king's secretary and was responsible for domestic and foreign affairs.

Charter: A document issued by a lord or king, addressed to the public, in which title to property was recorded or, in a charter of franchise, freedom from servitude of a serf or a town.

Christianity: The religion derived from the teachings of Jesus Christ and from the words of the Bible, which is considered sacred scripture. Christianity is practiced by Roman Catholic, Protestant, and Eastern Orthodox bodies. *See also* Catholicism, Eastern Orthodox Church, Islam, Judaism, Protestantism, Presbyterian.

Church: When used alone, "Church" is generally capitalized in reference to the universal Catholic Church. The term is not capitalized when it refers to the building or complex that hosts services. *See also* Cathedral.

Classical economics: The theory that economies operate according to natural, self-regulating laws such as supply and demand, and that government intervention should be strictly minimized.

Classicism: A style of art based on the classical period of the Greeks and Romans. Classicism is marked by its simplicity, proportion and harmony, and restraint. The composition of a work of art or the design of a building is meant to be balanced and harmonious, and the representation of a given "object," especially the human body, is meant to strike a balance between the conflicting demands of realism (the body should look like a "real" body) and idealism (the body should be represented in an ideal, or beautiful, form). *See also* Baroque, Mannerism, Naturalism, Realism.

Clerics or clergy: A general term for all members of the Church, including abbots, monks, priests, friars, bishops, archbishops, cardinals, and others. *See also* Bishop, Cardinal, Monk, Nun, Pope.

Colonialism: The control and subjugation by one power, such as a country or empire, over an area made up of those who become dependent upon that power. *See also* Colony, Governor.

Colony: A territory taken, usually by force, and occupied by peoples of a different, usually distant nation (mostly countries of Western Europe). *See also* Colonialism, Governor.

Commerce: The exchange and buying and selling of commodities, usually on a large scale and between multiple locations. The eighteenth century witnessed increased commerce because of trade between countries and regions of the world, mostly by sea. *See also* Colonialism, Commodity, Consumption, Mercantilism, Physiocrats.

Committee of Public Safety: A twelve-man committee employing dictatorial power and terror to maintain order in Paris during the French Revolution; similar committees operated in other cities.

Committees of Correspondence: Committees formed in the American colonies between 1772 and 1775 to share grievances against the British with other local colonial governments.

Commodity: Any good that circulates as an article of exchange in a money economy. *See also* Commerce, Consumption.

Commoner: One who is not a member of the clergy or of a noble or a royal family. *See also* Peasant, Serf.

Congregational: Of or relating to the Protestant churches that developed in seventeenth century England, which affirmed the critical importance and autonomy of local congregations. Final authority in church matters rested with each congregation. "Congregationalism" is the practice of those who believe in Congregational administration and worship. *See also* Episcopacy, Presbyterian, Protestantism.

Consort: A spouse; when used in conjunction with a royal title, consort becomes the title of a royal spouse, such as queen consort, prince consort, and so forth.

Constitution, British: The collective principles, procedures, and precedents of monarchs, lords, members of Parliament, and other servants of the Crown in governing Great Britain. The constitution is not made up of a single document, nor is it entirely in writing.

Consulate: Form of government replacing the Directory, lasted until 1804. Napoleon was invited to join the Third Consul, but soon became First Consul. *See also* Directory.

Consumption: Satisfying wants and desires through purchasing and using goods and services. The use of these goods results in their transformation, deterioration, or destruction, which ensures that individuals will continue to purchase new goods, thereby maintaining an economy. *See also* Commerce, Commodity.

Convent. *See* Nunnery.

Corvée: A tax of peasant labor in France, requiring labor on roads, bridges, and other public works.

Cossack: The term "cossack" comes from the Turkic for "free warriors." The Cossacks, frontier warriors in southern Russia, lived as free persons. Slaves and peasants fleeing serfdom often would join them. *See also* Hetman, Peasant, Serf.

Count: From the Latin *comes* (companion) and the Middle French *comte*, the French or Continental equivalent of an earl. The office became a noble title, ranked below duke.

Coup d'état: The armed overthrow of a government by its own army.

Coureurs de bois (runners of the woods): Fur traders who explored much of Canada and Louisiana for France, often marrying Native Americans and embracing many aspects of their cultures.

Court: The group of officials, councillors, and hangers-on assembled at the official residence of a monarch or other ruler. European courts contained a mixture of those who wielded real power, those who served the ruler or the ministers, an entourage of people who merely desired to be near power, and practitioners of the arts who enjoyed the patronage of their ruler.

Courtier: A member of a ruler's entourage at court.

Creed: A formal statement of belief, often religious or theological.

Creole: A person of Spanish descent born in the New World. *See also* Indigenous, Mestizo.

Crown: Referring to the sovereign authority of a king, queen, czar, emperor, or empress. *See also* Czar.

Czar: A Russian or other Slavic emperor. The word "czar" is derived from the Roman title "caesar" and suggests a ruler of equal stature to the emperors of imperial Rome.

Daimyo: Great territorial lords in Japan. *See also* Ronin, Samurai, Shogun.

Deacon: A member of the clergy ranking just below priest in the Roman Catholic, Anglican, and Eastern Orthodox Churches. In Roman Catholicism, the deacon is the middle rank of the three major orders, falling between priest and subdeacon in the hierarchy. *See also* Catholicism, Clerics or clergy.

Deccan: Region of India between the Narmada and Krishna Rivers.

Deism: The religious worldview most often associated with the Enlightenment, which stressed rationality, refused to accept the miraculous, and portrayed God as the great impersonal originator of the natural laws of the universe.

Devshirme: A levy of Christian boys, enslaved for training and recruitment to serve in various parts of the administration of the Ottoman Empire. The recruits formed the Janissary corps and also served in the sultan's household. *See also* Janissaries, Sultan.

Diocese: The basic administrative and territorial unit of the Catholic Church. Each diocese is governed by a bishop. *See also* Bishop, Cathedral, Catholicism.

Direct representation: The selection of representatives to an assembly by citizens who vote directly for the delegates who will represent them.

Directory: The form of government that ruled France between 1795 and 1799. Moderate in nature, it safeguarded many revolutionary reforms and was strongly anti-Royalist, but it operated mainly through a narrow franchise of the wealthy and with military support. *See also* Consulate, Estates-General, Thermidorean Reaction, Third Estate.

Divine right: The concept that God bestowed the right to rule upon kings.

Dogma: The body of beliefs and doctrines formally held and sanctioned by a church.

Domestic system of textile production: An economic system in which agents distribute wool, yarn, or other products used to manufacture textiles to laborers working in their homes; the laborers then spin yarn or weave cloth in anticipation of the return of the agent who will transport the finished product. *See also* Putting-out system.

Duke, duchess: From Roman *dux*, a governor, especially of a military jurisdiction; later, a member of nobility who was lord over several counties (headed by "counts"), who could pass the title duke or duchess to offspring. *See also* Count.

Dynasty: A line of rulers who succeed one another based on their familial relationships. *See also* Colonialism, Colony, Empire.

Eastern Orthodox Church: A group of self-governing Catholic churches, such as the Russian Orthodox Church, that split from the Roman Catholic Church in 1054. While the patriarch, or leader, of each branch of Orthodoxy is ranked hierarchically in relation to the others, each branch is essentially self-governing, and the relationship among the various branches is that of a loose federation. *See also* Catholicism, Christianity, Old Believers.

Ecclesiastical: Of or relating to a church.

Edict: An order, command, or proclamation with legal authority.

Emigrés: French aristocrats who fled France during the French Revolution.

Emir: A general title given to Islamic military commanders, rulers, and governors.

Empire: A large realm, ruled by an emperor or empress, which consists of previously distinct political units joined together under a ruler's central authority. *See also* Colonialism, Colony, Dynasty.

Empresario: An agent who received a land grant from the Spanish government in return for settling subjects there.

Enclosure: The consolidation of common lands by British landlords to make agriculture work more efficiently; usually required an act of Parliament.

Encomienda: The grant of indigenous labor for a specified period of time to a landholder by the Spanish crown.

Enlightened despotism: Rule by absolute monarchs who embraced reason and progressive reforms as a means of improving their societies, but who refused to accept the Enlightened doctrine that sovereignty resides in the people. *See also* Divine right, Enlightenment.

Enlightenment: A European worldview progressively developed during the eighteenth century that rejected divine revelation, and a fixed religious and social order in favor of reason, the social contract theory of government, and the desirability and potential for human progress.

Entrepreneur: One who takes risks in business with the hope of making a profit. *See also* Laissez-faire.

Enumerated products: In legislation passed by the British parliament, these were items produced in the American colonies that could only be shipped to approved destinations.

Episcopacy: A system of church governance in which the bishops hold all authority. *See also* Congregational, Presbyterian, Protestantism.

Established churches: A church supported in part by public taxes.

Estates-General: An advisory body to the king of France that represented the three estates (clergy, nobility, commoners). The body did not meet between 1614 and 1789, but was called by King Louis XVI to meet a growing financial crisis. *See also* Directory, House of Commons, House of Lords, Parliament, Separation of powers, Third Estate.

Fatwa: A legal opinion or ruling issued by an Islamic legal scholar, or mufti. *See also* Imam, Mufti.

Free trade: The unrestricted exchange of goods with few or no tariffs. *See also* Commerce, Commodity, Mercantilism.

General will: According to Jean-Jacques Rousseau, the belief that the interests of the community or the nation—expressed in common agreement—form the basis of sovereignty.

Gentry: Landholding families ranked just below the aristocracy in terms of social status. *See also* Aristocracy, Noble.

Girondists: Provincial-based radicals who dominated the early decisions of the government during the French Revolution. They were later ousted by the Jacobins. *See also* Jacobins.

Gold Coast: Coastal area of West Africa, corresponding roughly with the coast of modern-day Ghana. *See also* Ivory Coast, Middle Passage, Slave Coast, Transatlantic slave trade.

Gothic: A style of European architecture between the twelfth and sixteenth centuries, especially, characterized by ornateness, strong vertical lines, and pointed arches. The Gothic style strongly influenced seventeenth and early eighteenth century artists and architects. *See also* Baroque, Classicism.

Governor: The proxy representative of an emperor or central government who rules over a colony or an imperial territory. *See also* Colonialism, Colony, Empire.

Grand duke: The ruler of a sovereign territory called a grand duchy.

Grand prince: The ruler of a Russian city-state. *See also* Czar.

Great Awakening: A religious revival that swept the American colonies during the 1730's, 1740's, and 1790's, splitting many denominations in the process and laying a foundation for unity across the colonies.

Gujarat: Region of western India.

Hadith: A tradition or commentary related to the life or teachings of Muḥammad, used with varying degrees of authority as guides to the application of teachings found in the Qu'rān. *See also* Islam.

Half-War: Undeclared naval war of 1797 to 1800 between the United States and France. Also known as the Quasi-War.

Hanoverians: German, Protestant branch of English royal house sanctioned to rule by the Act of Settlement (1701), in anticipation of the death of Queen Anne, the last Stuart monarch.

Heresy: Making a statement or holding a belief that contradicts established Church dogma. Heresy against the Roman Catholic Church constituted a serious crime subject to severe punishment and even death. *See also* Dogma, Heretic, Inquisition.

Heretic: Someone judged to have committed heresy. *See also* Heresy, Inquisition.

Hetman: A Cossack leader. *See also* Cossack.

Hinduism: The collective term used by Europeans to denote the variety of Indian beliefs and ritual practices.

Holy Roman Empire: A loosely organized state established during the ninth century and incorporating most of the German and north Italian states. Influence in the Holy Roman Empire during the eighteenth century was contested by Prussia and Austria. *See also* Empire.

House: A royal or noble family. *See also* Aristocracy, Dynasty, Empire.

House of Commons: The lower house of the British parliament, comprised of representatives elected by the most wealthy citizens in the country. *See also* Aristocracy, House of Lords, Noble, Parliament.

House of Lords: The upper house of the British parliament, composed of peers representing the aristocratic families of the land. *See also* Aristocracy, House of Commons, Noble, Parliament.

Humanism: Born in fourteenth century Italy and embraced by subsequent centuries, a worldview that centralizes humankind and its values and achievements. In contrast, supernatural or religious worldviews often consider humanity to be inferior or intrinsically depraved. Humanism led to individualism, secular-ism, rational critical thought, and the idea that humankind could triumph over nature. As Humanism blossomed, so did science, revealing physical laws that explained natural phenomena and seemed at odds with biblical and theological explanations of the universe. Humanism also was characterized by a return to classic Greek and Latin (pre-Christian) literature. *See also* Classicism, Enlightenment, Humanistic, Salon.

Humanistic: Relating to a broad concern with the values or tenets associated with Humanism. "Humanistic" applies to beliefs and practices that are more general and less systematic than does "Humanist." *See also* Enlightenment, Humanism, Salon.

Imam: An Islamic religious and political leader. Also, an Islamic ruler in east Africa. *See also* Caliph, Fatwa, Sultan, Ulama.

Indentured servant: A migrant to British colonies in the Americas who agreed to work for a term of four to seven years in return for the cost of passage and training.

Indigenous: A person or thing native to a particular region. "Indigenous" has replaced the terms "Indian" or "American Indian" in many contexts that refer to the early peoples of the Americas. *See also* Creole, Mestizo.

Indirect representation: A system of governing in which representatives of a region or interest are not chosen directly by those they are representing. *See also* Parliament.

Industrial Revolution: The mechanization of Western economies that began with textile production in Britain during the second half of the eighteenth century. *See also* Agricultural Revolution.

Infidel: One who does not believe in a particular religion. *See also* Heresy, Heretic, Jihad.

Inquisition: A Roman Catholic court of religious inquiry charged with discovering and punishing heresy. *See also* Heresy, Heretic.

Invisible hand: Term used by Adam Smith to illustrate the natural law of supply and demand, which works to allocate resources in a given market.

Islam: The religion founded by the Prophet Muḥammad, which, after his death in 632, began to spread throughout the world and contribute to intellectual advancement and the blending of the arts. A person who practices Islam is a Muslim. *See also* Catholicism, Christianity, Jihad, Judaism, Muslim, Protestantism.

Ivory Coast: Coastal area of West Africa, corresponding roughly with the coast of the modern-day Republic of Côte d'Ivoire. *See also* Gold Coast, Middle Passage, Slave Coast, Transatlantic slave trade.

Jacobins: Radical political faction during the French Revolution, predominantly composed of middle-class intellectuals, but who gained support from Parisian artisans and workers. Overthrew the Girondists and dominated the period of the convention between 1792 and 1795. *See also* Girondists.

Janissaries: From the Turkish for "new corps," an elite corps of non-Muslim children, usually Christians from the Balkans, recruited as slaves of the sultan. The Janissaries played a key role in the rise of the Ottoman Empire, with some holding high governmental positions. The corps eventually declined in significance beginning in the early eighteenth century. *See also* Devshirme.

Jesuits: Members of the Roman Catholic Society of Jesus, founded in the mid-sixteenth century, who devote their lives to educational and missionary work. *See also* Abbey, Catholicism, Mission, Missionary, Monastery, Monk.

Jihad: A holy "war" waged by Muslims against those who do not follow Islam, considered by many Muslims a duty imposed by holy law. *See also* Fatwa, Islam.

Joint-stock company: A commercial innovation that enabled companies to raise capital by selling shares to individuals, while limiting individual liability for losses. *See also* Commerce.

Judaism: The religion characterized by belief in one transcendent God who has revealed himself to Abraham, Moses, and the Hebrew prophets. Judaism is practiced in accordance with Scriptures and rabbinic traditions. *See also* Catholicism, Christianity, Eastern Orthodox Church, Islam, Protestantism.

Judicial review: An implied constitutional power by which federal (U.S.) courts review and determine the constitutionality of acts passed by Congress and state legislatures. *See also* Separation of powers.

Kabaka: A king of Buganda in Uganda, Africa.

Kabuki: A popular Japanese drama developed in the seventeenth century by Izumo no Okuni, which combines song, dance, and other varieties of performance. Elaborate, detailed, and ornately costumed and designed, Kabuki plays are based on not only legends and myths but also historical subjects.

King: A male monarch who ruled a large region and under whom ruled subordinate lords. A king's title was usually hereditary and most often for life. *See also* Czar, Dynasty, Empire, Queen, Sultan.

Laissez-faire: French phrase meaning "allow to do." In economics the doctrine of minimal government interference in the working of an economy. *See also* Commerce, Entrepreneur, Mercantilism.

Latitude: The distance between a given point on Earth and the Earth's equator, expressed in angular degrees. *See also* Longitude.

Levellers: A group of Protestant radicals that rose to prominence during the English Civil War at the end of the seventeenth century, demanding legal equality and religious toleration. Many Levellers later adopted Quakerism, which gained prominence in eighteenth century England and the North American colonies. *See also* Old Believers, Protestantism, Quakerism.

Limited (constitutional) monarchy: A system of government in which the powers of the monarch are subject to legislation passed by representative assemblies. *See also* House of Commons, House of Lords, Parliament, Separation of powers.

Longitude: The distance between a given point on Earth and a line (called the prime meridian) that extends, virtually, from the North Pole to the South Pole, expressed in angular degrees. *See also* Latitude.

Mannerism: A style of art preceding that of the Baroque, in which painters expressed often highly emotional subjects through distorted and exaggerated forms and with vivid colors. *See also* Baroque, Classicism, Naturalism, Realism.

Maroon: A runaway or rebellious slave. More specifically, a member of a community of runaway slaves in the West Indies and South America.

Mercantilism: An economic theory first known as "Colbertisme" (after its early proponent Jean-Baptiste Colbert of France) that emerged during the seventeenth century and continued into the eighteenth century. Mercantilism advocated governmental leadership in guiding a nation's economy toward prosperity. *See also* Colonialism, Commodity, Consumption, Laissez-faire, Physiocrats.

Mestizo: In Spanish America, a person of mixed Spanish and indigenous ancestry. *See also* Creole, Indigenous.

Methodism: A pietistic movement within the Church of England led by the brothers John and Charles Wesley, which developed into a separate denomination late in the eighteenth century. *See also* Anglican, Pietism, Protestantism.

Middle Passage: The voyage across the Atlantic Ocean that slaves endured when being taken from West Africa to the New World. *See also* Gold Coast, Ivory Coast, Slave Coast, Transatlantic slave trade.

Minutemen: Companies of colonial militia that began to form in the American colonies in the 1740's. *See also* Patriot.

Mission: A colonial ministry whose task is to convert indigenous peoples to Christianity. *See also* Catholicism, Christianity, Colonialism, Indigenous, Missionary.

Mission system: Chain of missions established by Spain in the American Southwest to convert indigenous peoples to Catholicism. *See also* Catholicism, Christianity, Colonialism, Indigenous.

Missionary: An agent of the Catholic or other Christian church commissioned to travel to a colony or other "distant" location to gain converts from among indigenous populations. *See also* Catholicism, Christianity, Colonialism, Indigenous, Mission.

Monastery: A place where monks or nuns lived a religious life, frequently including a chapter house for meetings as well as sleeping quarters and various other facilities depending on the work of the monastery. *See also* Abbey, Catholicism, Jesuit, Monk, Nun, Nunnery.

Monk: A man who has taken religious vows of self-privation, and who lives in seclusion or semiseclusion from the material world in a monastery or abbey. *See also* Abbey, Catholicism, Clerics or clergy, Jesuit, Monastery, Nun.

Monsoon: Strong and predictable seasonal winds in the Indian Ocean that enabled merchants to engage in regular trade between South Asia and the east coast of Africa.

Mufti: A specialist in Islamic law who is not a public official but a private scholar who functions as a consultant. *See also* Fatwa, Imam.

Mulatto: In Spanish America, a person of mixed African and European descent. *See also* Creole, Indigenous, Mestizo.

Muslim: One who practices the religion of Islam. *See also* Islam.

Mwami: A king of Rwanda, Africa.

Mysticism: The practice of many religious faiths, including Christianity and Islam, which emphasizes the nonrational, spiritual, and felt rather than intellectual aspects of religious truth as an emotional or transcendent experience. *See also* Quietism, Sufism.

Natural rights: As part of Enlightened thought, an understanding that all human beings possessed rights such as life, liberty, property, freedom of speech and religion, and equality before the law, simply by virtue of their humanity. *See also* Enlightenment, Humanism.

Naturalism: An artistic style emphasizing an extremely precise realistic portrayal of an object as it appears in nature. *See also* Realism.

Nawab: A semiautonomous Muslim prince who cooperated with British colonialists in British India.

Neoclassicism: An aesthetic approach based upon Greek and Roman models, emphasizing balance and order. Neoclassicism developed during the eighteenth century in response to the ornamentation of the Baroque period. *See also* Baroque, Classicism.

New Lights: Individuals who experienced emotional, personal conversions during the religious revivals of the Great Awakening. *See also* Great Awakening.

Noble: A member of the landed aristocracy. *See also* Aristocracy, Gentry.

Nun: A woman who has taken religious vows of self-privation, and who lives in seclusion or semiseclusion from the material world. *See also* Abbey, Monastery, Monk, Nunnery.

Nunnery: A home for nuns or other persons living in accordance with religious vows. *See also* Abbey, Monastery, Nun.

Oba: A ruler of Benin in West Africa.

Old Believers: Conservative members of the Russian Orthodox Church who were labeled dissidents for opposing church reforms. *See also* Eastern Orthodox Church, Heresy, Heretic, Inquisition, Levellers, Patriarch.

Ottomans: Turkish rulers of the Islamic world who ruled as sultans from roughly 1281 to 1922. Their conquest in 1453 of the seat of the Byzantine Empire and Eastern Christian Orthodoxy, Constantinople, marked their ascendant power. *See also* Islam, Ṣafavids, Sultan.

Palatinate: A county or principality ruled by a lord whose rights included those of a king, such as the right to coin money or appoint judges. Also, in Germany, the proper name of a principality. *See also* Palatine.

Palatine: The lord of a palatinate or a resident of the (German) Palatinate. *See also* Palatinate.

Papal States: A sovereign Italian city-state, which was based in Rome and ruled by the pope and served as the spiritual seat of his papacy. *See also* Catholicism, Pope.

Parliament: An assembly of representatives, usually a mix of nobles, clergy, and commoners, which functions as a legislative body serving under the sovereignty of a monarch. *See also* Estates-General, House of Commons, House of Lords.

Paşa: The highest title of rank or honor in the Ottoman Empire. The title evolved to include governors of foreign territories and to viziers of a domestic government. *See also* Ottomans, Sultan, Vizier.

Pasha: A man of high rank in northern Africa. *See also* Imam.

Pashalik: A state formed in Mali, northwest Africa, by the Arma, a military caste descended from Moroccan soldiers.

Patriarch: The head of one of the self-governing branches of the Eastern Orthodox Church. *See also* Bishop, Catholicism, Eastern Orthodox Church, Pope.

Patriot: Term applied to Americans during the revolutionary period who believed in the use of force to gain full independence from Great Britain. *See also* Minutemen.

Patron: One who financially or materially supports an artist, composer, poet, or other creative individual.

Patronage: The practice of awarding titles and making appointments to government and other positions to gain political support.

Peasant: The lowest rank of commoner, who works the land in order to subsist. *See also* Aristocracy, Commoner, Noble, Serf.

Peninsulares: Persons born in Spain who settled in the New World.

Persia: A term used by Westerners until the early twentieth century to describe the region always known as Iran to Iranians.

Petit bourgeoisie: The lower middle class. *See also* Aristocracy, Commoner, Gentry, Noble, Sans-culottes, Serf.

Philosophes: French writers and social critics who agitated for progress and popularized the ideas of the Enlightenment. *See also* Enlightenment, Humanism, Salon.

Physiocrats: French economic school that argued against mercantilistic governmental regulations and believed that sound agriculture was essential to the economic well being of a state. *See also* Commerce, Laissez-faire, Mercantilism.

Pietism: A way of Christian worship and belief that promoted religion of the heart rather than of the mind. Pietism is closely associated with the rise of Methodism. *See also* Methodism.

Pilgrimage: Journey to a sacred shrine by Christians seeking to show their piety, fulfill vows, or gain absolution for sins. Other religions also have pilgrimage traditions, such as the pilgrimage to Mecca by Muslims and the pilgrimages made by early Chinese Buddhists to India in search of sacred Buddhist writings. *See also* Christianity, Islam.

Plague: A contagious disease caused by a bacterium, which becomes epidemic and causes a high rate of mortality. Called the Black Death during the Middle Ages, it struck on numerous occasions in various parts of the world during the eighteenth century.

Plantation economy: An economic system organized for producing cash crops such as sugar, cotton, tobacco, rice, coffee, and tea, and most commonly utilizing slave labor. *See also* Commerce, Transatlantic slave trade.

Pope: The spiritual leader of the Roman Catholic Church and temporal ruler of the Papal States. *See also* Bishop, Catholicism, Christianity, Papal States, Patriarch.

Presbyterian: A Protestant Christian church that is mostly Calvinistic in doctrine. "Presbyterianism" is a system of church governance favored as more democratic than Episcopalianism because it is characterized by a graded system of representative ecclesiastical bodies. *See also* Calvinism, Catholicism, Christianity, Congregational, Ecclesiastical, Episcopacy, Presbytery, Protestantism.

Presbytery: The ruling body in Presbyterian churches. Also, the part of a church reserved for clergy who officiate. *See also* Clerics or clergy, Presbyterian, Protestantism.

Presidio: In Spanish America, a military post.

Pretender: Someone who falsely claims to be a rightful ruler.

Privateer: A pirate or pirate ship commissioned or licensed by a government to raid the ships of other nations. Privateers also participated in the slave trade.

Protestantism: A branch of Christianity, incorporating many different churches, which "protests" and rejects Catholic tradition, especially its doctrine of papal infallibility, and believes instead in a religion of all believers who read the Bible for themselves rather than having it interpreted to them by clergy. *See also* Calvinism, Catholicism, Christianity, Clerics or clergy, Ecclesiastical, Episcopacy, Presbyterian, Quakerism.

Puritan: In Protestant England and New England, one who opposed the ceremonial worship and prelacy of the Church of England. "Puritanism" is the belief and practice of Puritans. *See also* Anglican, Calvinism, Catholicism, Christianity, Presbyterian, Protestantism, Quakerism.

Putting-out system: Early system of manufacturing in which merchants furnished households with raw materials that would be processed by workers in their own homes. *See also* Domestic system of textile production, Industrial Revolution.

Quakerism: A Protestant group that began in seventeenth century England, which rejected ritualized forms of worship. Traditional Quaker worship services are not led by ordained ministers and do not involve the recitation of a religious creed. Women play a major role in Quakerism, since Quakers believe that men and women are equally suited to preach the word of God. Quaker religious beliefs are egalitarian and humanitarian. *See also* Levellers, Protestantism, Puritan, Shakers.

Queen: A female monarch who ruled a large region. A queen's title, unlike that of the king—which was usually hereditary—was often gained upon marriage to a king. Some wives of kings were called "consorts," or "queen consorts," instead of "queens." Also, queens would become "regents" if they lived after the death of their husband-kings and were pronounced virtual rulers during the minority of a monarch to be, who was usually the queen's son. *See also* Consort, King, Queen-Mother, Regent.

Queen-mother: A former queen who is the mother of a current ruler. *See also* Queen, Regent.

***Querelles des femmes*:** A literary movement begun in the sixteenth and seventeenth centuries that debated (quarreled over) the subject of women. The movement intensified during the eighteenth century as the findings of the disciplines of anatomy and medicine added further interpretations to the debates.

Quietism: In religion, quietism refers to a mysticism that teaches, among other things, suppression of the will to obtain spiritual peace and perfection. Politically, quietism is the withdrawn or passive attitude or policy toward world affairs. *See also* Mysticism.

***Raison d'état*:** The concept that the interests of the state ("reasons of state"), rather than moral or philosophical concerns, may justify a course of action.

Rajputs: Members of a Hindu warrior caste from northwest India.

Realism: In art, the attempt to depict objects, human figures, or scenes as they appear in real life; that is, with-

out distortion or stylization. "Naturalism" is often used as a synonym for realism. *See also* Mannerism, Naturalism.

Rector: A religious leader. In some Protestant churches, the leader of a parish; in the Roman Catholic Church, the head of a church that has no pastor or a cleric who shares duties with a pastor. *See also* Catholicism, Clerics or clergy, Protestantism.

Recusant: An English Roman Catholic, especially of the sixteenth through eighteenth centuries, who refused to obey the teachings of and participate in the services of the Church of England, thereby committing a statutory offense. *See also* Catholicism, Protestantism.

Regent: One who temporarily governs in place of a monarch or other ruler who is too young or infirm to govern for him- or herself. Oftentimes, a regent is the monarch's mother. *See also* Queen, Queen-Mother.

Regular clergy: Monks and nuns who belong to religious orders and live according to a monastic rule. *See also* Clerics or clergy, Jesuit, Monastery, Monk, Nun.

Regulators: Vigilante groups active in the 1760's and 1770's in the western Carolinas of North America.

Reign of Terror: The period from September, 1793, to July, 1794, when more than twenty thousand people were executed on the orders of revolutionary tribunals, ostensibly to protect the French Revolution.

Republic: A political unit not ruled by a monarch, especially one governed by a group of representatives chosen by and responsible to its citizens. *See also* Parliament.

Rococo: An artistic style that developed in France during the early eighteenth century, emphasizing ornamentation, grace, and lightness, and focusing on the pleasures of the aristocracy. *See also* Aristocracy, Baroque, Classicism, Neoclassicism.

Ronin: A masterless samurai in Japan. Because serving one's master well was the central value of the samurai code of *bushido*, *ronin* were usually considered dishonorable, either because they had failed their lord or because they had willfully rejected the code. *See also* Bushido, Daimyo, Samurai, Shogun.

Royalist: One who favors monarchical government and the power of a ruler. *See also* Directory, Divine right, Tory, Whig.

Ṣafavids: An Islamic empire in Iran (Persia), founded in 1501 and ended in 1722. Shīʿite Islam, developed by the early Ṣafavids, continues to be the dominant religion of Iran into the twenty-first century. *See also* Islam.

Salon: An informal social gathering of artists, writers, and other intellectuals who met in private home. Salons were especially associated with France in the eighteenth century. *See also* Enlightenment, Humanism, Humanistic, Philosophes.

Samurai: A member of the Japanese warrior caste, especially a warrior who served a daimyo and who subscribed to a strict code of conduct called *bushido*. *See also* Bushido, Daimyo, Ronin, Shogun.

Sans-culottes: Meaning "without kneebreeches," the term refers to the lower-middle classes and artisans of Paris associated with the first outbreaks of rebellion during the French Revolution. *See also* Petit bourgeoisie.

Satire: A literary style that uses wit, sarcasm, humor, and such to point out human vices, follies, and immoralities.

Secular: Nonreligious, either in content or in context. Thus, secular can be a simple antonym of "religious," but it can also refer to members of the clergy who live and act in the public sphere rather than spending their lives in religious seclusion in a monastery or abbey.

Secular clergy: Parish clergy who did not belong to a religious order and lived among the people. *See also* Clerics or clergy, Regular clergy.

Separation of powers: System of divided governmental powers, advocated by Montesquieu in his *Spirit of the Laws* (1748). Influential in the development of the U.S. Constitution. *See also* Direct representation, Estates-General, Judicial review, Limited (constitutional) monarchy, Parliament.

Serf: A peasant bound to the land through contract. Serfs were given a parcel of land on which to live and work, but any surplus they produced was owed to their landlord as rent, tax, or tribute. *See also* Commoner, Gentry, Peasant.

Shakers: The followers of Ann Lee, who preached a religion of strict celibacy and communal living. *See also* Jesuits, Quakerism.

Sharia: Islamic holy law. *See also* Caliph, Fatwa, Islam, Ulama.

Sharif: A Muslim who claims descent from the Prophet Muḥammad. *See also* Caliph, Imam, Islam.

Shia: The Muslims of the Shīʿite branch of Islam. *See also* Imam, Shīʿite, Sunni.

Shīʿite: The branch of Islam that holds that Ali and the imams are the only rightful successors of the Prophet Muḥammad and that the last imam will someday return. *See also* Imam, Shia, Sunni.

Shogun: A Japanese military ruler. *See also* Bushido, Daimyo, Ronin, Samurai.

Shogunate system: The system of government in Japan in which the emperor exercised only titular authority while the shogun (regional military dictators) exercised actual political power.

Siege: A military operation in which a city or other territory is cut off from the outside world in order to compel its surrender after food and other supplies are exhausted.

Slave Coast: Coastal region of West Africa along the Bight of Benin and along the coasts of modern-day Nigeria, Benin, and Togo. The area was a major center for the slave trade among African rulers and European nations, from about 1500 to the late eighteenth century. The seventeenth and eighteenth centuries saw increased slave trading, thus the region's moniker. *See also* Gold Coast, Ivory Coast, Middle Passage, Transatlantic slave trade.

Social contract: Theory most eloquently argued by John Locke and Jean-Jacques Rousseau that government gained its authority from the people, who could justly rebel if the "contract" were broken.

Spice Islands: The group of islands that make up the easternmost part of Indonesia. The Spice Islands are so named because the area was the center of the European spice trade. *See also* Mercantilism.

State: An autonomous, self-governing, sovereign political unit. *See also* Estates-General, Parliament.

Succession: The passing of sovereign authority from one person or group to another person or group, or the rules governing that process.

Sufism: Islamic mysticism. A Sufi is one who practices Sufism. *See also* Islam, Mysticism, Quietism.

Sultan: Beginning in the eleventh century, any political and military ruler of an Islamic state or emirate (as opposed to the caliph, the religious authority of the Islamic state). Applied mostly to Ottoman rulers. *See also* Caliph, Ottomans.

Sunni: Muslims who adhere to the orthodox tradition of Islam, which acknowledges the first four caliphs, the religious authorities of Islam, as rightful successors of the Prophet Muḥammad. *See also* Imam, Islam, Shia, Shīʿite.

Swahili: A language spoken in coastal East Africa, combining Bantu and Arabic elements.

Thermidorean Reaction: The reaction against the Reign of Terror and the extreme radicalism of the French Revolution; associated with the establishment of the Directory. *See also* Directory, Reign of Terror.

Third Estate: The branch of the French Estates-General representing all except the nobility and the clergy; served as the basis for the first French republican assembly. *See also* Estates-General.

Tory: In England, the party that supported royal power in the face of challenges by Parliament. Opposed by the Whigs, and one of the two dominant political parties throughout the eighteenth century. *See also* Parliament, Royalist, Whig.

Transatlantic slave trade: The trade in slaves, mostly from Africa, that crossed the Atlantic Ocean from and between East Africa, Europe, North America, and South America. *See also* Middle Passage, Slave Coast.

Transportation: The British policy from the late eighteenth to the mid-nineteenth centuries of shipping persons convicted of the most serious offenses to Australia as an alternative to capital punishment.

Treaty: An agreement or arrangement between, especially, two nations and made by negotiation.

Tributary system: A system in which, from the time of the Han Empire (202 B.C.E.-220 C.E.), countries in East and Southeast Asia not under the direct control of empires based in China nevertheless enrolled as tributary states, acknowledging the superiority of the emperors in China in exchange for trading rights or strategic alliances.

Tsar. *See* Czar.

Tulip Age: A period between 1718 and 1730 when European styles and attitudes became fashionable in the Ottoman Empire.

Ulama: Muslim religious scholars who serve as interpreters of Islamic law. *See also* Caliph, Imam, Islam, Sharia.

Umma: The community of all Muslims, as distinguished from kinship affiliations common in early Middle Eastern lands. *See also* Islam.

Urdu: A Persian-influenced literary form of Hindi, written in Arabic characters and widely spoken along the trade routes of Southern Asia.

Vizier: Title given to high officials of Islamic nations. In the Ottoman Empire beginning around 1453, the viziers were specifically ministers to the sultan. The chief minister was known as the grand vizier, and members of the council that assisted and filled in for the grand vizier were called dome viziers. Use of the title was later expanded to include other important domestic officials, as well as provincial governors. *See also* Bey, Caliph, Imam, Islam, Sultan.

Whig: In seventeenth century England, a political party opposed to absolute royal authority and favoring increased parliamentary power; one of two dominant political parties throughout the eighteenth century. *See also* Parliament, Royalist, Tory.

Writs of assistance: Legal documents that enabled British officials in colonial America to search for smuggled goods.

Zen: A Japanese form of Buddhism based on disciplined meditation and closely associated with the samurai code of *bushido*. *See also* Bushido, Samurai.

—John Powell

BIBLIOGRAPHY

CONTENTS

This bibliography will provide a good starting point for most general areas of research on the eighteenth century. In attempting to cover the history of the world during an entire century, however, it is necessarily selective. Emphasis here has been placed on broad studies, rather than narrowly focused monographs or journal articles. The letters and papers of prominent individuals, such as George Washington, Benjamin Franklin, Jean-Jacques Rousseau, and Sir Isaac Newton, have not been included but are easily located in most good libraries. More recent works have been preferred to older ones, though many of the best older works are also included. Generally speaking, bibliographies from the most recent studies provide a good guide to the monographic and periodical literature available. In any case, the best method of identifying the most recent literature is by making use of dynamic databases such as Article First and Academic Search Premier for periodical literature and Worldcat for books and by consulting ECCB: The Eighteenth Century Current Bibliography (AMS Press). Bucknell University Press publishes an ongoing book series, Bucknell Studies in Eighteenth Century Literature and Culture (http://www.bucknell.edu/News_Events/Publications/University_Press/Books/Book_Series/18th_Century_Studies.html).

Of the many general historical resources that might be helpful in researching eighteenth century themes, two are especially helpful. Peter N. Stearns, ed. The Encyclopedia of World History (Boston: Houghton Mifflin, 2001) is the most detailed and comprehensive compendium of world events, arranged chronologically and extensively annotated to provide an invaluable reference narrative. It is supported by an exhaustive index and an excellent, searchable CD-ROM. Mary Beth Norton et al., eds. The American Historical Association's Guide to Historical Literature (3d ed. 2 vols. New York: Oxford University Press, 1995) is the best comprehensive, annotated bibliography available, covering the most important works in all areas of research for all parts of the world—a tall task but one that specialist section editors achieve remarkably well. Though the work is somewhat dated, it is still an essential point of departure for research into unfamiliar areas.

A good list of web resources on the eighteenth century is maintained by Jack Lynch, associate professor of English at Rutgers University, and can be found at http://andromeda.rutgers.edu/~jlynch/18th/history. html.). A useful Listserv is C18-L: Resources for Eighteenth Century Studies Across the Disciplines (http://www.personal.psu.edu/special/C18/c18-l.htm).

Two important organizations that encourage research in the period are the American Society for Eighteenth-Century Studies (ASECS) and the International Society for Eighteenth-Century Studies (ISECS). ASECS, based at Johns Hopkins University, maintains a website (http://asecs.press.jhu.edu/) with announcements regarding conferences and publications related to contemporary investigations into the period. It also sponsors two journals, Eighteenth-Century Studies *(Johns Hopkins University Press) and* Studies in Eighteenth-Century Culture *(Johns Hopkins University Press), both interdisciplinary in nature. ASECS also works with major research institutions, including the American Antiquarian Society, Boston Athenaeum, Folger Institute, Harry Ransom Humanities Center, Houghton Library, Huntington Library, Keough Institute for Irish Studies, Lewis Walpole Library, Library Company of Philadelphia, McMaster University Library, Newberry Library, William Andrews Clark Memorial Library, and Yale Center for British Art, to fund ongoing research and publication projects. ISECS (http://www.c18.org/so/qqsieds.e.html) promotes international cooperation and is based at the Voltaire Foundation, University of Oxford. It supports conferences, encourages the foundation of local eighteenth-century societies, and distributes the International Directory of Eighteenth-Century Studies, which lists the names of members, with their addresses, research interests, and, where applicable, the institution to which they are affiliated. See also* The Eighteenth Century: Theory and Interpretation *(Texas Tech University Press);* Eighteenth-Century Life *(Duke University Press);* Eighteenth-Century Women *(AMS Press);* Eighteenth-Century Music *(Cambridge University Press);* Eighteenth-Century Fiction *(University of Toronto Press); and* 1650-1850: Ideas, Aesthetics, and Inquiries into the Early Modern Era *(AMS Press).*

GENERAL STUDIES, SURVEYS, AND REFERENCE WORKS

Abernethy, David B. *The Dynamics of Global Dominance: European Overseas Empires, 1415-1980.* New Haven, Conn.: Yale University Press, 2000.

Anderson, M. S. *Europe in the Eighteenth Century.* 4th ed. New York: Longman, 2000.

Bayly, C. A. *The Birth of the Modern World, 1780-1914.* Malden, Mass.: Blackwell, 2004.

Black, Jeremy. *Eighteenth-Century Europe, 1700-1789.* New York: Palgrave Macmillan, 1999.

_____. *Natural and Necessary Enemies: Anglo-French Relations in the Eighteenth Century.* London: Gerald Duckworth, 1986.

_____. *The Rise of the European Powers, 1679-1793.* London: Edward Arnold, 1990.

Black, Jeremy, and Roy Porter, eds. *A Dictionary of Eighteenth-Century World History.* London: Blackwell, 1994.

Cañizares-Esguerra, Jorge. *How to Write the History of the New World: Histories, Epistemologies, and Identities in the Eighteenth Century Atlantic World.* Stanford, Calif.: Stanford University Press, 2001.

Cowie, Leonard W. *Eighteenth-Century Europe.* New York: Frederick Unger, 1963.

Dwald, Jonathan. *The European Nobility, 1400-1800.* New York: Cambridge University Press, 1994.

Frey, L. *Societies in Upheaval: Insurrections in France,* Hungary, and Spain in the Early Eighteenth Century. Westport, Conn.: Greenwood Press, 1989.

Goldgar, Anne. *Impolite Learning: Conduct and Community in the Republic of Letters, 1680-1750.* New Haven, Conn.: Yale University Press, 1995.

Habermas, Jurgen. *The Structural Transformation of the Public Sphere: An Inquiry into a Category of Bourgeois Society.* Translated by Thomas Burger and Frederick Lawrence. Cambridge, Mass.: MIT Press, 1991.

Hall, Thomas. *Ideas of Life and Matters.* 2 vols. Chicago: University of Chicago Press, 1969.

Hampson, Norman. *The Enlightenment.* New York: Penguin Books, 1990.

Held, Julius, and Donald Posner. *Seventeenth- and Eighteenth-Century Art.* Englewood Cliffs, N.J.: Prentice-Hall, 1972.

Horn, D. B. *Great Britain and Europe in the Eighteenth Century.* New York: Oxford University Press, 1967.

Irvine, Jonathan Israel. *Radical Enlightenment: Philosophy and the Making of Modernity, 1650-1750.* New York: Oxford University Press, 2001.

Lindsay, J. O., ed. *The Old Regime, 1713-1763.* Vol. 7 in *The New Cambridge Modern History.* Cambridge, England: Cambridge University Press, 1966.

Melton, James Van Horn. *The Rise of the Public in Enlightenment Europe.* Cambridge, England: Cambridge University Press, 2001.

Northrup, David. *Africa's Discovery of Europe, 1450-1850*. New York: Oxford University Press, 2002.

O'Gorman, Frank, and Diana Donald, eds. *Ordering the World in the Eighteenth Century*. New York: Palgrave Macmillan, 2006.

Parker, Geoffrey, ed. *Hammond Atlas of World History*. 5th ed. Maplewood, N.J.: Hammond, 1999.

Parkinson, G. H. R., and S. G. Shanker, ed. *Routledge History of Philosophy*. 10 vols. New York: Routledge, 2003.

Popkin, Richard, ed. *The Columbia History of Western Philosophy*. New York: Columbia University Press, 1999.

Robinson, Francis. *Atlas of the Islamic World Since 1500*. New York: Facts on File, 1982.

Romaine, Suzanne, ed. *1776-1997*. Vol. 4 in *The Cambridge History of the English Language*. Cambridge, England: Cambridge University Press, 1998.

Schroeder, Paul W. *The Transformation of European Politics, 1763-1848*. Oxford, England: Clarendon Press, 1994.

Stearns, Peter N., and Herrick Chapman. *European Society in Upheaval: Social History Since 1750*. 3d ed. Englewood Cliffs, N.J.: Prentice Hall, 1992.

Thackeray, Frank W., and John E. Finding, eds. *Events That Changed the World in the Eighteenth Century*. Westport, Conn.: Greenwood Press, 1998.

Treasure, Geoffrey. *The Making of Modern Europe, 1648-1780*. London: Methuen, 1985.

Trussler, Simon. *The Cambridge Illustrated History of the British Theatre*. Cambridge, England: Cambridge University Press, 2000.

Wolff, L. *Inventing Eastern Europe: The Map of Civilization on the Mind of the Enlightenment*. Stanford, Calif.: Stanford University Press, 1994.

Woloch, Isser. *Eighteenth-Century Europe: Tradition and Progress, 1715-1789*. New York: Norton, 1982.

Yolton, John W., et al., eds. *The Blackwell Companion to the Enlightenment*. Oxford, England: Blackwell, 1995.

AGRICULTURE AND LAND

Blaxter, Sir Kenneth, and Noel Robertson. *From Dearth to Plenty: The Modern Revolution in Food Production*. Cambridge, England: Cambridge University Press, 1995.

Bourde, André. *The Influence of England on the French Agronomes*. Cambridge, England: Cambridge University Press, 1953.

Chambers, J. D., and G. E. Mingay. *The Agricultural Revolution, 1750-1880*. London: B. T. Batsford, 1966.

Fussell, G. E. *The Farmer's Tools: A History of British Farm Implements, Tools, and Machinery Before the Tractor Came, from A.D. 1500-1900*. London: Andrew Melrose, 1952.

Halacy, D. S., Jr. *The Geometry of Hunger*. New York: Harper & Row, 1972.

Handley, James E. *Scottish Farming in the Eighteenth Century*. London: Faber and Faber, 1953.

Harris, Marshall D. *Origin of the Land Tenure System in the United States*. Westport, Conn.: Greenwood Press, 1953.

Hibbard, Benjamin H. *A History of the Public Land Policies*. New York: Peter Smith, 1960.

Hobhouse, Henry. *Seeds of Change: Five Plants That Transformed Mankind*. New York: Harper & Row, 1986.

Ingen-Housz, Jan. *An Essay on the Food of Plants and the Renovation of Soils*. 1796. Reprint. Oquawka, Ill.: J. Christian Bay, 1933.

_____. *Experiments upon Vegetables: Discovering Their Great Power of Purifying the Common Air in the Sunshine and of Injuring It in the Shade and at Night*. London: Printed for P. Elmsly and H. Payne, 1779.

Linklater, Andro. *Measuring America: How an Untamed Wilderness Shaped the United States and Fulfilled the Promise of Democracy*. New York: Walker, 2002.

Musgrave, Toby, and Will Musgrave. *An Empire of Plants: People and Plants That Changed the World*. London: Cassell, 2000.

Onuf, Peter S. *Sovereignty and Territory: Claims Conflict in the Old Northwest and the Origins of the American Federal Republic*. Baltimore: Johns Hopkins University Press, 1973.

Pattison, William D. *Beginnings of the American Rectangular Land Survey System, 1784-1800*. Chicago: University of Chicago Press, 1957.

Pawson, Henry Cecil. *Robert Bakewell: Pioneer Livestock Breeder*. London: Crosby Lockwood & Son, 1957.

Robbins, Roy M. *Our Landed Heritage: The Public Domain, 1776-1936*. New York: Peter Smith, 1962.

Rogal, Samuel J. *Agriculture in Britain and America: An Annotated Bibliography of the Eighteenth-Century Literature*. Westport, Conn.: Greenwood Press, 1994.

Snell, K. D. M. *Annals of the Labouring Poor: Social Change and Agrarian England, 1660-1900*. Cambridge, England: Cambridge University Press, 1985.

Stanley, Pat. *Robert Bakewell and the Longhorn Breed of Cattle*. Ipswich, England: Farming Press Limited, 1998.

Treat, Payson Jackson. *The National Land System, 1785-1820*. New York: E. B. Treat, 1910. Reprint. Buffalo, N.Y.: W. S. Hein, 2003.

ARCHAEOLOGY AND ANTIQUITIES

Adkins, Lesley, and Roy Adkins. *The Keys of Egypt: The Obsession to Decipher Egyptian Hieroglyphs*. New York: HarperCollins, 2000.

Amery, Colin, and Brian Curran, Jr. *The Lost World of Pompeii*. Los Angeles: J. Paul Getty Museum, 2002.

Cassanelli, Roberto, et al. *Houses and Monuments of Pompeii: The Works of Fausto and Felice Niccolini*. Los Angeles: J. Paul Getty Museum, 2002.

Constantine, David. *Early Greek Travellers and the Hellenic Ideal*. Cambridge, England: Cambridge University Press, 1984.

Dolan, Brian. *Exploring European Frontiers: British Travellers in the Age of the Enlightenment*. London: Palgrave Macmillan, 2000.

Guzzo, Pier Giovanni, et al. *Pompeii*. Los Angeles: J. Paul Getty Trust, 2000.

Harcourt-Smith, Cecil. *The Society of Dilettanti: Its Regalia and Pictures*. London: Macmillan, 1932.

Haycock, David. *William Stukeley: Science, Religion, and Archeology in Eighteenth-Century England*. Woodbridge, Suffolk, England: Boydell Press, 2002.

Kelly, Jason M. *Polite Sociability and Levantine Archeology in the British Enlightenment: The Society of the Dilettanti, 1732-1786*. Santa Barbara: University of California ProQuest Digital Dissertation, 2004.

Lamb, Sydney M., and Douglas Mitchell, eds. *Sprung from Some Common Source: Investigations into the Prehistory of Languages*. Stanford, Calif.: Stanford University Press, 1991.

Meyerson, Daniel. *The Linguist and the Emperor: Napoleon and Champollion's Quest to Decipher the Rosetta Stone*. New York: Ballantine Books, 2004.

Parslow, Christopher Charles. *Rediscovering Antiquity: Karl Weber and the Excavation of Herculaneum, Pompeii, and Stabiae*. New York: Cambridge University Press, 1998.

Piggott, Stuart. *William Stukeley: An Eighteenth-Century Antiquary*. New York: Thames and Hudson, 1985.

Romer, John, and Elizabeth Romer. *The History of Archaeology*. New York: Checkmark Books, 2001.

Schnapp, Alain. *The Discovery of the Past and the Origins of Archeology*. London: British Museum Press, 1996.

Stuart, James, and Nicholas Revett. *The Antiquities of Athens*. New York: Arno Press, 1980.

Stukeley, William. *The Commentarys, Diary, and Common-Place Book, and Selected Letters of William Stukeley*. London: Doppler Press, 1980.

_____. *"Stonehenge: A Temple Restor'd to the British Druids" and "Abury: A Temple of the British Druids."* New York: Garland, 1984.

Van Tilburg, Jo Anne. *Easter Island Archaeology, Ecology, and Culture*. Washington, D.C.: Smithsonian Institution Press, 1994.

THE ARTS

Arruga, Lorenzo. *La Scala*. Translated by Raymond Rosenthal. New York: Praeger, 1976.

Asfour, Amal, and Paul Williamson. *Gainsborough's Vision*. Liverpool, Merseyside, England: Liverpool University Press, 1999.

Aurenhammer, Hans. *J. B. Fischer von Erlach*. Cambridge, Mass.: Harvard University Press, 1973.

Barton, Margaret. *Garrick*. New York: Macmillan, 1949.

Beaumarchais, Pierre-Augustin Caron de. *The Figaro Trilogy*. New York: Oxford University Press, 2003.

Bergdoll, Barry. *European Architecture, 1750-1890*. Oxford, England: Oxford University Press, 2000.

Blair, Sheila S., and Jonathan Bloom. *The Art and Architecture of Islam, 1250-1800*. New Haven, Conn.: Yale University Press, 1994.

Blunt, Anthony, ed. *Baroque and Rococo: Architecture and Decoration*. New York: Harper & Row, 1978.

Bocharnikpva, Yelena, and Mikhail Gabovich. *Ballet School of the Bolshoi Theatre*. Translated by K. Danko; edited by D. Ogden. Moscow: Foreign Languages, n.d.

Borer, Mary. *Story of Covent Garden*. London: Robert Hale, 1984.

Brown, Jared. *The Theater in America During the Revolution*. Cambridge, England: Cambridge University Press, 1995.

Coltman, Viccy. *Fabricating the Antique: Neoclassicism in Britain, 1760-1800*. Chicago: University of Chicago Press, 2005.

Connelly, Frances S. *Modern and the Grotesque*. Cambridge, England: Cambridge University Press, 2003.

Crow, Thomas E. *Painters and Public Life in Eighteenth-Century Paris*. New Haven, Conn.: Yale University Press, 1985.

Doeser, Linda. *The Life and Works of Gainsborough: A Compilation of Works from the Bridgeman Library*. New York: Shooting Star Press, 1995.

Drummond, John D. *Opera in Perspective*. Minneapolis: University of Minnesota Press, 1986.

Dugaw, Dianne. *"Deep Play": John Gay and the Invention of Modernity*. Newark: University of Delaware Press, 2001.

Dunlap, William. *A History of the American Theater*. New York: Harper, 1832. Reprint. New York: Burt Franklin, 1963.

Fried, Michael. *Absorption and Theatricality: Painting and Beholder in the Age of Diderot*. Chicago: University of Chicago Press, 1988.

Glazer, Irvin R. *Philadelphia Theaters, A-Z: A Comprehensive Descriptive Record of 813 Theaters Constructed Since 1724*. New York: Greenwood Press, 1986.

Grout, Donald Jay. *A Short History of Opera*. 2d ed. New York: Columbia University Press, 1965.

Howard, Patricia. *Christoph Willibald Gluck: A Guide to Research*. New York: Garland, 1987.

_____. *Gluck and the Birth of Modern Opera*. New York: St. Martin's Press, 1964.

Howarth, W. D. *Beaumarchais and the Theatre*. London: Routledge, 1995.

Ireland, Joseph N. *Records of the New York Stage from 1750 to 1860*. 2 vols. 1866. Reprint. New York: Benjamin Blom, 1966.

Jacobs, Arthur, and Stanley Sadie. *The Limelight Book of Opera*. 4th ed. New York: Limelight Editions, 1996.

Kennedy, Roger G. *Orders from France: The Americans and the French in a Revolutionary World, 1780-1820*. New York: Alfred A. Knopf, 1989.

Kerman, Joseph. *Opera as Drama*. Rev. ed. Berkeley: University of California Press, 1988.

Lee, Carol. *Ballet in Western Culture: A History of Its Origins and Evolution*. New York: Routledge, 2002.

Leonard, Jonathan Norton. *The World of Gainsborough, 1727-1788*. New York: Time-Life Books, 1969.

Levey, Michael. *Painting and Sculpture in France, 1700-1789*. New Haven, Conn.: Yale University Press, 1993.

Little, David M., George M. Kahrl, and Phoebe deK. Wilson, eds. *The Letters of David Garrick*. 3 vols. Cambridge, Mass.: Harvard University Press, 1963.

Lushin, Stanislav, ed. *The Bolshoi Theatre of the USSR: History, Opera, Ballet*. Translated by Sally Patterson. Moscow: Planeta, 1987.

Metzner, Paul. *Crescendo of the Virtuoso: Spectacle, Skill, and Self-Promotion in Paris During the Age of Revolution*. Studies in the History of Society and Culture 30. Berkeley: University of California Press, 1998.

Millon, Henry A., ed. *The Triumph of the Baroque*. New York: Rizzoli, 1999.

Necipoglu, Gulru. "Anatolia and the Ottoman Legacy." In *The Mosque: History, Architectural Development, and Regional Diversity*, edited by Martin Frishman and Hasan-Uddin Khan. New York: Thames and Hudson, 1994.

Pokrovsky, Boris Alexandrovich, and Yuri Nikolayevich Grigorovich. *The Bolshoi: Opera and Ballet at the Greatest Theater in Russia*. New York: William Morrow, 1979.

Postle, Martin. *Thomas Gainsborough*. Princeton, N.J.: Princeton University Press, 2002.

Rankin, Hugh F. *The Theater in Colonial America*. Chapel Hill: University of North Carolina Press, 1965.

Rosenthal, Michael, and Martin Myrone, eds. *Gainsborough: The Painter in Modern Culture*. London: Tate Gallery, 2002.

Roslavleva, Natalia. *Era of the Russian Ballet*. New York: E. P. Dutton & Company, 1966.

Rosselli, John. *The Opera Industry in Italy from Cimarosa to Verdi: The Role of the Impresario*. New York: Cambridge University Press, 1984.

Rossi, Nick. *Opera in Italy Today: A Guide*. Portland, Oreg.: Amadeus Press, 1995.

Sadie, Stanley, ed. *New Grove Dictionary of Opera*. 4 vols. New York: Grove, 1992.

Scouten, Arthur H., ed. *1729-1747*. Vol. 3 in *The London Stage, 1660-1800*. Carbondale: Southern Illinois University Press, 1961.

Shaw-Taylor, Desmond. *Covent Garden*. New York: Chanticleer Press, 1948.

Soros, S., ed. *James 'Athenian' Stuart*. New Haven, Conn.: Yale University Press, 2006.

Stone, George Winchester, Jr., and George M. Kahrl. *David Garrick: A Critical Biography*. Carbondale: Southern Illinois University Press, 1979.

Stoneman, Richard. *A Luminous Land: Artists Discover Greece*. Los Angeles: J. Paul Getty Museum, 1998.

Surits, Elisabeth, ed. *The Great History of Russian Ballet: Its Art and Choreography*. Richford, Vt.: Parkstone Press, 1999.

Vaughan, William. *Gainsborough*. London: Thames & Hudson, 2002.

Weaver, William. *The Golden Age of Italian Opera: From Rossini to Puccini*. London: Thames & Hudson, 1980.

Wemyss, Francis C. *Wemyss' Chronology of the American Stage, from 1752 to 1852*. 1852. Reprint. New York: Benjamin Blom, 1968.

Wilmeth, Don B., and Christopher Biby, eds. *Beginnings to 1870*. Vol. 1 in *The Cambridge History of Ameri-*

can Theatre. New York: Cambridge University Press, 1998.

Winton, Calhoun. *John Gay and the London Theatre.* Lexington: University Press of Kentucky, 1993.

Woodiwiss, Audrey. *A History of Covent Garden: Covent Garden Through the Years.* London: Conway/ Covent Garden, 1982.

AUSTRALIA

Blainey, Geoffrey. *The Tyranny of Distance.* Melbourne, Vic.: Sun Books, 1970.

Frost, Alan. *Botany Bay Mirages: Illusions of Australia's Convict Beginnings.* Carlton, Vic.: Melbourne University Press, 1994.

Hughes, Robert. *The Fatal Shore: The Epic of Australia's Founding.* New York: Vintage Books, 1988.

King, Jonathan. *The First Fleet: The Convict Voyage That Founded Australia, 1787-1788.* London: Secker & Warburg, 1982.

Martin, Ged, ed. *The Founding of Australia: The Arguments About Australia's Origin.* Rev. ed. Sydney: Hale & Iremonger, 1981.

Rudé, George. *Protest and Punishment: The Story of the Social and Political Protestors Transported to Australia, 1788-1868.* Oxford, England: Clarendon Press, 1978.

Shaw, A. G. L. *Convicts and the Colonies: A Story of Penal Transportation from Great Britain and Ireland to Australia and Other Parts of the British Empire.* London: Faber & Faber, 1966.

Taylor, Peter. *Australia: The First Twelve Years.* Boston: Allen & Unwin, 1982.

BUSINESS, ECONOMICS, AND FINANCE

Aitken, Hugh G. J., ed. *Did Slavery Pay? Readings in the Economics of Black Slavery in the United States.* Boston: Houghton Mifflin, 1971.

Atack, Jeremy, and Peter Passell. *A New Economic View of American History.* 2d ed. New York: W. W. Norton, 1994.

Boyer, George R. *An Economic History of the English Poor Law, 1750-1850.* Cambridge, England: Cambridge University Press, 1990.

Braudel, Fernand. *Capitalism and Material Life, 1400-1800.* Translated by Miriam Kochan. New York: Harper & Row, 1973.

Breen, T. H. *The Marketplace of Revolution: How Consumer Politics Shaped American Independence.* New York: Oxford University Press, 2004.

Brunhouse, Robert L. *The Counter-Revolution in Pennsylvania, 1776-1790.* Harrisburg: Pennsylvania Historical and Museum Commission, 1942.

Carswell, John. *The South Sea Bubble.* Dover, N.H.: Alan Sutton, 1993.

Chancellor, Edward. *Devil Take the Hindmost: A History of Financial Speculation.* New York: Plume, 2000.

Dolan, Brian. *Wedgwood: The First Tycoon.* New York: Viking, 2004.

Dougherty, Peter J. *Who's Afraid of Adam Smith? How the Market Got Its Soul.* New York: J. Wiley, 2002.

Ferguson, E. James. *The Power of the Purse: A History of American Public Finance, 1776-1790.* Durham: University of North Carolina Press, 1961.

Fleischaker, Samuel. *On Adam Smith's "Wealth of Nations": A Philosophical Companion.* Princeton, N.J.: Princeton University Press, 2004.

Floud, Roderick, and Paul Johnson. *The Cambridge Economic History of Modern Britain.* Cambridge, England: Cambridge University Press, 2003.

Galbraith, John Kenneth. *The Age of Uncertainty.* Boston: Houghton Mifflin, 1977.

Garber, Peter M. *Famous First Bubbles.* Boston: MIT Press, 2000.

Goodman, Jordan, and Katrina Honeyman. *Gainful Pursuits: The Making of Industrial Europe, 1600-1914.* New York: Edward Arnold, 1988.

Gordon, John Steele. *Hamilton's Blessing: The Extraordinary Life and Times of Our National Debt.* New York: Walker, 1997.

Hammond, J. L., and Barbara Hammond. *The Village Labourer, 1760-1832.* Reprint. London: Longmans, 1978.

Heilbroner, Robert L. *The Worldly Philosophers: The Lives, Times, and Ideas of the Great Economic Thinkers.* New York: Simon & Schuster, 1953.

Hont, Istvan, and Michael Ignatieff, eds. *Wealth and Virtue: The Shaping of Political Economy in the Scottish Enlightenment.* Cambridge, England: Cambridge University Press, 1983.

Kindleberger, Charles P. *Manias, Panics, and Crashes: A History of Financial Crises.* New York: Wiley Investment Classics, 2001.

Koehn, Nancy. *Brand New: How Entrepreneurs Earned Consumers' Trust from Wedgwood to Dell.* Boston: Harvard Business School Press, 2001.

Law, John. *Money and Trade Considered: With a Proposal for Supplying the Nation with Money.* Reprint. New York: A. M. Kelley, 1966.

Liss, Peggy K. *Atlantic Empires: The Network of Trade and Revolution, 1713-1826.* Baltimore: Johns Hopkins University Press, 1983.

Macht, Carol. *Classical Wedgwood Designs*. New York: Gramercy, 1957.

Mackie, Erin, ed. *The Commerce of Everyday Life: Selections from "The Tatler" and "The Spectator."* Boston: Bedford/St. Martin's, 1998.

Marshall, J. D. *The Old Poor Law, 1795-1834*. New York: Macmillan, 1968.

Mintz, Sidney W. *Sweetness and Power: The Place of Sugar in Modern History*. New York: Penguin, 1995.

Murphy, Antoin E. *John Law: Economic Theorist and Policy Maker*. Oxford, England: Oxford University Press, 1997.

Neeson, J. M. *Commoners: Common Right, Enclosure, and Social Change in England, 1700-1820*. Cambridge, England: Cambridge University Press, 1993.

Nettels, Curtis P. *The Emergence of a National Economy, 1775-1815*. New York: Holt, Rinehart and Winston, 1962.

Ormrod, David. *The Rise of Commercial Empires: England and the Netherlands in the Age of Mercantilism, 1650-1770*. New York: Cambridge University Press, 2003.

Raphael, D. D. *Adam Smith*. Oxford, England: Oxford University Press, 1985.

Rosenband, Leonard N. *Papermaking in Eighteenth-Century France: Management, Labor, and Revolution at the Montgolfier Mill, 1761-1805*. Baltimore: Johns Hopkins University Press, 2000.

Ross, Eric B. *The Malthus Factor: Population, Poverty, and Politics in Capitalistic Development*. New York: St. Martin's Press, 1998.

Rothschild, Emma. *Economic Sentiments: Adam Smith, Condorcet, and the Enlightenment*. Cambridge, Mass.: Harvard University Press, 2001.

Rule, John. *The Vital Century: England's Developing Economy, 1714-1815*. New York: Longman, 1992.

Wallerstein, Immanuel. *Mercantilism and the Consolidation of the European World Economy, 1600-1750*. Vol. 2 in *The Modern World-System*. New York: Academic Press, 1980.

Whigan, Thomas. *The Politics of River Trade: Tradition and Development in the Upper Plata, 1780-1870*. Albuquerque: University of New Mexico Press, 1991.

Williams, Robert B. *Accounting for Steam and Cotton: Two Eighteenth Century Case Studies*. New York: Garland, 1997.

CANADA

Brown, Craig, ed. *The Illustrated History of Canada*. Toronto: Key Porter Books, 2003.

Bruce, Harry. *An Illustrated History of Nova Scotia*. Halifax, N.S.: Nimbus, 1997.

Burt, A. L. *The Old Province of Quebec*. Toronto: McClelland and Stewart, 1968.

Clayton, Daniel W. *Islands of Truth: The Imperial Fashioning of Vancouver Island*. Vancouver, B.C.: UBC Press, 2000.

Coffin, Victor. *The Province of Quebec and the Early American Revolution*. Madison: University of Wisconsin Press, 1896.

Creighton, Donald Grant. *Dominion of the North: A History of Canada*. Cambridge, Mass.: Riverside Press, 1944.

Fillmore, Cathleen. *The Life of a Loyalist: A Tale of Survival in Old Nova Scotia*. Canmore, Alta.: Altitude, 2004.

Gough, Barry M. *First Across the Continent: Sir Alexander Mackenzie*. Norman: University of Oklahoma Press, 1997.

_____. *Northwest Coast: British Navigation, Trade, and Discoveries to 1812*. Vancouver, B.C.: UBC Press, 1992.

Graham, Gerald S., ed. *The Walker Expedition to Quebec, 1711*. Toronto: Champlain Society, 1953. Reprint. New York: Greenwood Press, 1969.

Lawson, Philip. *The Imperial Challenge: Quebec and Britain in the Age of American Revolution*. Montreal: McGill-Queen's University Press, 1989.

Lower, Arthur M. *Colony to Nation: A History of Canada*. Toronto: Longmans, 1946.

MacKinnon, Neil. *This Unfriendly Soil: The Loyalist Experience in Nova Scotia, 1783-1791*. Montreal: McGill-Queen's University Press, 1989.

Mallory, J. R. *The Structure of Canadian Government*. Toronto: Gage, 1984.

Nelson, Paul David. *General Sir Guy Carleton, Lord Dorchester: Soldier-Statesman of Early British Canada*. Madison, N.J.: Fairleigh Dickinson University Press, 2000.

Newman, Richard S. *The Transformation of American Abolition: Fighting Slavery in the Early Republic*. Chapel Hill: University of North Carolina Press, 2002.

Nicholls, David. *Haiti in the Caribbean Context: Ethnicity, Economy, and Revolt*. New York: St. Martin's Press, 1985.

Parkman, Francis. *Count Frontenac and New France Under Louis XIV*. 1877. Reprint. New York: Library of America, 1983.

Plank, Geoffrey. *An Unsettled Conquest: The British Campaign Against the Peoples of Acadia*. Philadelphia: University of Pennsylvania Press, 2003.

Tanguay, J. Fernand, ed. *Canada 125: Its Constitutions, 1763-1992*. Introduction by Gerald A. Beaudoin. Montreal: Éditions du Méridien, 1992.

Treanor, Nick, ed. *Canada*. San Diego, Calif.: Greenhaven Press, 2003.

Walker, James W. *The Black Loyalists: The Search for a Promised Land in Nova Scotia and Sierra Leone*. Toronto: Toronto University Press, 1993.

Winks, Robin W. *The Blacks in Canada: A History*. 2d ed. Montreal: McGill-Queen's University Press, 1997.

CARIBBEAN

Bellegarde-Smith, Patrick. *Haiti: The Breached Citadel*. Boulder, Colo.: Westview Press, 1990.

Brown, Gordon S. *Toussaint's Clause: The Founding Fathers and the Haitian Revolution*. Jackson: University Press of Mississippi, 2005.

Dallas, Robert. *The History of the Maroons*. Vols. 1-2. London: Longman and Rees, 1803.

Dookhan, Isaac. *A History of the Virgin Islands of the United States*. Essex, England: Caribbean Universities Press, 1974.

Dubois, Laurent. *Avengers of the New World: The Story of the Haitian Revolution*. Cambridge, Mass.: Belknap Press of Harvard University Press, 2004.

Fick, Carolyn E. *The Making of Haiti: The Saint Domingue Revolution from Below*. Knoxville: University of Tennessee Press, 1990.

Geggus, David. "The Enigma of Jamaica in the 1790's: New Light on the Causes of Slave Rebellion," *The William and Mary Quarterly*, 3d ser. 44, no. 2 (April, 1987): 274-299.

Gottlieb, Karla Lewis. *The Mother of Us All: A History of Queen Nanny, Leader of the Windward Jamaican Maroons*. Trenton, N.J.: Africa World Press, 2000.

Jamaica Assembly. *Proceedings in Regard to the Maroon Negroes*. Reprint. Westport, Conn.: Negro Universities Press, 1970.

James, C. L. R. *The Black Jacobins: Toussaint L'Ouverture and the San Domingo Revolution*. New York: Vintage Books, 1989.

Knight, Franklin. *The Caribbean: Genesis of a Fragmented Nationalism*. 2d ed. Oxford, England: Oxford University Press, 1990.

Moran, Charles. *Black Triumvirate: A Study of Louverture, Dessalines, Christophe—The Men Who Made Haiti*. New York: Exposition Press, 1957.

Mulcahy, Matthew. *Melancholy and Fatal Calamities: Hurricanes and Society in the British Greater Caribbean*. Baltimore: Johns Hopkins University Press, 2005.

Ott, Thomas O. *The Haitian Revolution, 1789-1804*. Knoxville: University of Tennessee Press, 1973.

Richardson, Ronald Kent. *Moral Imperium: Afro-Caribbeans and the Transformation of British Rule, 1776-1838*. Westport, Conn.: Greenwood Press, 1987.

Rogonzinski, Jan. *A Brief History of the Caribbean: From the Arawak and the Carib to the Present*. New York: Plume, 2000.

Westergaard, Waldemar. *The Danish West Indies, 1671-1917*. New York: Macmillan, 1917.

Zips, Werner. *Black Rebels: African Caribbean Freedom Fighters in Jamaica*. Translated by Shelley L. Frisch. Princeton, N.J.: Markus Wiener, 1999.

DIPLOMACY

Bemis, Samuel Flagg. *The Diplomacy of the American Revolution*. Washington, D.C.: Reprint. American Historical Association, 1957.

_____. *Jay's Treaty: A Study in Commerce and Diplomacy*. 2d ed. New Haven, Conn.: Yale University Press, 1962.

_____. *Pinckney's Treaty: A Study of America's Advantage from Europe's Distress*. Baltimore: Johns Hopkins University Press, 1926.

Bowman, Albert Hall. *The Struggle for Neutrality: Franco-American Diplomacy During the Federalist Era*. Knoxville: University of Tennessee Press, 1974.

Brecher, Frank W. *Securing American Independence: John Jay and the French Alliance*. Westport, Conn.: Praeger, 2003.

Combs, Jerald A. *The Jay Treaty: Political Battleground of the Founding Fathers*. Berkeley: University of California Press, 1970.

Corwin, Edward S. *French Policy and the American Alliance of 1778*. Princeton, N.J.: Princeton University Press, 1916.

Davenport, Frances Gardiner, ed. *1698-1715*. Vol. 3 in *European Treaties Bearing on the United States and Its Dependencies*. Washington, D.C.: Carnegie Institution, 1934. Reprint. Gloucester, Mass.: Peter Smith, 1967.

DeConde, Alexander. *Entangling Alliances: Politics and Diplomacy Under George Washington*. Durham, N.C.: Duke University Press, 1958.

_____. *The Quasi-War: The Politics and Diplomacy of the Undeclared War with France, 1797-1801*. New York: Charles Scribner's Sons, 1966.

Dull, Jonathan R. *A Diplomatic History of the American Revolution*. New Haven, Conn.: Yale University Press, 1985.

Frey, Linda, and Marsha Frey, eds. *The Treaties of the War of the Spanish Succession: An Historical and Critical Dictionary*. Westport, Conn.: Greenwood Press, 1995.

Hoffman, Ronald, and Peter J. Albert, eds. *Peace and the Peacemakers: The Treaty of 1783*. Charlottesville: University Press of Virginia, 1986.

Israel, Fred L., ed. *Major Peace Treaties of Modern History, 1648-1967*. New York: Chelsea House, 1967.

Itzkowitz, Norman, and Max Mote. *Mubadele: An Ottoman-Russian Exchange of Ambassadors*. Chicago: University of Chicago Press, 1970.

Kurat, Akdes Nimet, ed. *The Despatches of Sir Robert Sutton: Ambassador in Constantinople, 1710-1714*. London: Royal Historical Society, 1953.

Montagu, Lady Mary Wortley. *The Turkish Embassy Letters*. Edited by Malcolm Jack. London: Pickering & Chatto, 1993.

Morris, Richard. *The Peacemakers: The Great Powers and American Independence*. Reprint. New York: Harper & Row, 1983.

Rothstein, A. *Peter the Great and Marlborough: Politics and Diplomacy in Converging Wars*. New York: St. Martin's Press, 1986.

Schiff, Stacy. *A Great Improvisation: Franklin, France, and the Birth of America*. New York: Henry Holt, 2005.

Schweizer, Karl W. *War, Politics, and Diplomacy, 1756-1763*. Lanham, Md.: University Press of America, 2001.

EAST ASIA: CHINA, JAPAN, KOREA, AND MONGOLIA

Adshead, S. A. M. *China in World History*. 3d ed. New York: Saint Martin's Press, 2000.

Allyn, John. *The Forty-Seven Ronin Story*. Tokyo: Tuttle, 1970.

Boxer, Charles R. *Papers on Portuguese, Dutch, and Jesuit Influences in Sixteenth and Seventeenth Century Japan: Studies in Japanese History and Civilization*. Westport, Conn.: Greenwood, 1979.

Brandon, James R. *Chushingura: Studies in Kabuki and the Puppet Theatre*. Honolulu: University of Hawaii Press, 1982.

Colcutt, Martin, Marius Jansen, and Isao Kumakura. *Cultural Atlas of Japan*. New York: Facts on File, 1988.

Cranmer-Byng, J. L., ed. *Britain and the China Trade, 1635-1842*. Vol. 3 in *An Embassy to China: Lord Macartney's Journal, 1793-1794*. Selected by Patrick Tuck. London: Longmans, Green, 1962. Reprint. New York: Routledge, 2000.

Gerstle, C. Andrew, ed. *Chikamatsu: Five Late Plays*. New York: Columbia University Press, 2001.

Goodman, Grant Kohn. *Japan and the Dutch, 1600-1853*. Richmond, Surrey, England: Curzon, 2000.

Grayson, James Huntley. *Korea: A Religious History*. New York: Routledge, 2002.

Hall, John Whitney. *Tanuma Okitsugu, 1719-1788: Forerunner of Modern Japan*. Cambridge, Mass.: Harvard University Press, 1955.

Heissig, Walther. *A Lost Civilization: The Mongols Rediscovered*. London: Thames and Hudson, 1966.

Hsu, Immanuel C. Y. *The Rise of Modern China*. 6th ed. New York: Oxford University Press, 2000.

Huang Pei. *Autocracy at Work: A Study of the Yung-cheng Period, 1723-1735*. Bloomington: Indiana University Press, 1974.

Jansen, Marius B. *The Making of Modern Japan*. Cambridge, Mass.: Belknap Press of Harvard University Press, 2002.

_____. *Warrior Rule in Japan*. Cambridge, England: Cambridge University Press, 1995.

Johnson, Hiroko. *Western Influence on Japanese Art*. Amsterdam: Hotei/KIT, 2004.

Kasaya, Kazuhiko, ed. *Dodonaeus in Japan: Translation and the Scientific Mind in the Tokugawa Period*. Leuven, Belgium: Leuven University Press, 2001.

Kato, Suichi. *The Years of Isolation*. Vol. 3 in *A History of Japanese Literature*. Tokyo: Kodansha, 1979.

Keene, Donald. *Chushingura: The Treasury of Loyal Retainers*. New York: Columbia University Press, 1997.

_____. *The Japanese Discovery of Europe, 1720-1830*. Stanford, Calif.: Stanford University Press, 1969.

_____. *World Within Walls: Japanese Literature of the Pre-modern Era, 1600-1867*. New York: Columbia University Press, 1999.

_____, trans. *Four Major Plays of Chikamatsu*. New York: Columbia University Press, 1998.

Norbu, Dawa. *China's Tibet Policy*. Richmond, Surrey, England: Curzon, 2001.

Petech, Luciano. *China and Tibet in the Early Eighteenth Century*. Rev. ed. Leiden, the Netherlands: Brill, 1972.

Pritchard, Earl H. *The Crucial Years of Early Anglo-Chinese Relations, 1750-1800*. 1936. Reprint. New York: Octagon Books, 1970.

Ravina, Mark. *Land and Lordship in Early Modern Japan*. Stanford, Calif.: Stanford University Press, 1998.

Sansom, George Bailey. *The Western World and Japan: A Study in the Interaction of European and Asiatic Cultures.* New York: Random House, 1974.

Screech, Timon. *The Shogun's Painted Culture: Fear and Creativity in the Japanese States, 1760-1829.* London: Reaktion Books, 2000.

Spence, Jonathan. *The Search for Modern China.* 2d ed. New York: W. W. Norton, 1999.

Vlastos, Stephen. *Peasant Protests and Uprisings in Tokugawa Japan.* Berkeley: University of California Press, 1990.

Walthall, Anne, ed. *Peasant Uprisings in Japan: An Anthology of Peasant Histories.* Chicago: University of Chicago Press, 1991.

White, James W. *Ikki: Social Conflict and Political Protest in Early Modern Japan.* Ithaca, N.Y.: Cornell University Press, 1995.

Yamamoto, Tsunetomo. *Hagakure: The Book of the Samurai.* New York: Kodansha America, 2000.

Yu, Chai-Shin, ed. *The Founding of Catholic Tradition in Korea.* Mississauga, Ont.: Korean and Related Studies Press, 1996.

ENGLAND, SCOTLAND, AND IRELAND

Beckett, J. V. *The Aristocracy in England, 1660-1914.* Oxford, England: Blackwell, 1986.

Beer, George L. *British Colonial Policy, 1754-1765.* New York: Macmillan, 1907.

Black, Jeremy, ed. *Britain in the Age of Walpole.* New York: St. Martin's Press, 1984.

_____. *The British Seaborne Empire.* New Haven, Conn.: Yale University Press, 2004.

_____. *The Hanoverians: The History of a Dynasty.* New York: Palgrave Macmillan, 2004.

_____. *Pitt the Elder.* New York: Cambridge University Press, 1992.

_____. *A System of Ambition? British Foreign Policy, 1660-1793.* New York: Longman, 1991.

_____. *Walpole in Power.* Stroud, Gloucestershire, England: Sutton, 2001.

Bolton, G. C. *The Passing of the Irish Act of Union.* Oxford, England: Oxford University Press, 1966.

Brewer, John. *The Sinews of Power: War, Money, and the English State, 1688-1783.* Cambridge, Mass.: Harvard University Press, 1990.

Brooke, John. *The Chatham Administration, 1766-1768.* Vol. 1 in *England in the Age of the Revolution*, edited by Louis Namier. New York: St. Martin's Press, 1956.

Brown, Michael, Patrick M. Geoghegan, and James

Kelly. *The Irish Act of Union: Bicentennial Essays.* Dublin: Irish Academic Press, 2003.

Budge, Ian, and Cornelius O'Leary. *Belfast—An Approach to Crisis: A Study of Belfast Politics, 1613-1970.* London: Macmillan, 1973.

Butterfield, Herbert. *George III and the Historians.* New York: Macmillan, 1957.

Churchill, Winston S. *Marlborough: His Life and Times.* 6 vols. New York: Charles Scribner's Sons, 1933-1938.

Colley, Linda. *Britons: Forging the Nation, 1707-1837.* New Haven, Conn.: Yale University Press, 1994.

Corp, Edward. *A Court in Exile: The Stuarts in France, 1689-1718.* Cambridge, England: Cambridge University Press, 2004.

DeCastro, John Paul. *The Gordon Riots.* London: Oxford University Press, 1926.

Douglas, Hugh. *Jacobite Spy Wars: Moles, Rogues, and Treachery.* Stroud, Gloucestershire, England: Sutton, 1999.

Douglas, Hugh, and Michael J. Stead. *The Flight of Bonnie Prince Charlie.* Stroud, Gloucestershire, England: Sutton, 2000.

Ehrman, John. *The Younger Pitt: The Years of Acclaim.* New York: E. P. Dutton, 1969.

Elliot, Marianne. *Partners in Revolution: The United Irishmen and France.* New Haven, Conn.: Yale University Press, 1982.

Erickson, Carolly. *Bonnie Prince Charlie.* New York: Lillian Morrow, 1989.

Ferguson, William. *Scotland's Relations with England: A Survey to 1707.* Edinburgh: John Donald, 1977.

Flexner, Eleanor. *Mary Wollstonecraft.* New York: Coward, McCann & Geoghegan, 1972.

Foster, R. F. *Modern Ireland: 1600-1972.* London: Penguin Press, 1989.

Franklin, Caroline. *Mary Wollstonecraft: A Literary Life.* New York: Palgrave Macmillan, 2004.

Geoghegan, Patrick M. *The Irish Act of Union: A Study in High Politics, 1798-1801.* New York: St. Martin's Press, 1999.

Gibson, J. *Playing the Scottish Card: The Franco-Jacobite Invasion of 1708.* Edinburgh: Edinburgh University Press, 1989.

Goldgar, Bertrand A. *The Curse of Party.* Lincoln: University of Nebraska Press, 1961.

Gooch, Leo. *The Desperate Faction? The Jacobites of North East-England, 1688-1745.* Hull, Humberside, England: University of Hull Press, 1995.

Hague, William. *William Pitt the Younger.* New York: Alfred A. Knopf, 2005.

Haile, Martin. *James Francis Edward: The Old Pretender*. London: J. M. Dent, 1907.

Hibbert, Christopher. *King Mob and the Story of Lord George Gordon and the Riots of 1780*. London: Longmans, Green, 1959.

Hill, Brian W. *Robert Harley: Speaker, Secretary of State, and Premier Minister*. New Haven, Conn.: Yale University Press, 1988.

Holmes, Geoffrey. *The Trial of Doctor Sacheverell*. London: Eyre Methuen, 1973.

Hopkins, Stephen. *A True Representation of the Plan Formed at Albany*. Providence, R.I.: Sidney S. Rider, 1880.

Hoppit, Julian. *A Land of Liberty? England, 1689-1727*. Oxford, England: Oxford University Press, 2002.

Jackson, Alvin. *Ireland, 1798-1998: Politics and War*. Oxford, England: Blackwell, 1999.

Johnson, Allen S. *A Prologue to Revolution: The Political Career of George Grenville, 1712-1770*. Lanham, Md.: University Press of America, 1997.

Kemp, Betty. *King and Commons, 1660-1832*. London: Macmillan, 1959.

_____. *Sir Robert Walpole*. London: Weidenfeld and Nicolson, 1976.

Keogh, Dáire, and Nicholas Furlong, eds. *The Mighty Wave: The 1798 Rebellion in Wexford*. Blackrock, County Dublin, Ireland: Four Courts Press, 1996.

Keogh, Dáire, and Kevin Whelan, eds. *Acts of Union: The Causes, Contexts, and Consequences of the Act of Union*. Dublin: Four Courts Press, 2001.

Killen, John, ed. *The Decade of the United Irishmen: Contemporary Accounts*. Belfast: Blackstaff Press, 1997.

Kirk, Russell. *Edmund Burke: A Genius Reconsidered*. Wilmington, Del.: Intercollegiate Studies Institute, 1997.

Kishlansky, Mark. *A Monarchy Transformed: Britain, 1603-1714*. Vol. 6 in *The Penguin History of Britain*. London: Penguin Press, 1996.

Langford, Paul. *A Polite and Commercial People*. Oxford, England: Oxford University Press, 1994.

Lecky, William Edward Hartpole. *A History of Ireland in the Eighteenth Century*. 5 vols. London: Longmans, Green, 1892. Reprint. New York: AMS Press, 1969.

Lees-Milne, James. *The Last Stuarts: British Royalty in Exile*. New York: Charles Scribner's Sons, 1983.

Levack, Brian P. *The Formation of the British State: England, Scotland, and the Union, 1603-1707*. Oxford, England: Clarendon Press, 1987.

Little, Crawford. *The Union of Crowns: The Forging of Europe's Most Independent State*. Glasgow, Scotland: Neil Wilson, 2003.

McDowell, Robert Brendan. *Ireland in the Age of Imperialism and Revolution, 1760-1801*. Oxford, England: Clarendon Press, 1979.

McLeod, John. *Dynasty: The Stuarts, 1560-1807*. New York: St. Martin's Press, 1999.

McLeod, Ruairidh H. *Flora McDonald: The Jacobite Heroine in Scotland and North America*. London: Shepheard-Walwyn, 1997.

Magnusson, Magnus. *Scotland: The Story of a Nation*. First American Edition. New York: Atlantic Monthly Press, 2000.

Marlborough, John Churchill, Duke of. *The Letters and Dispatches of John Churchill, First Duke of Marlborough, from 1702-1712*. Edited by Sir George Murray. New York: Greenwood Press, 1968.

Marshall, Dorothy. *English People in the Eighteenth Century*. Temecula, Calif.: Textbook, 2003.

Marshall, P. J., and Alaine Lowe, eds. *The Oxford History of the British Empire: The Eighteenth Century*. New ed. Oxford, England: Oxford University Press, 2001.

Mitchison, Rosalind. *Lordship to Patronage: Scotland, 1603-1745*. London: Edward Arnold, 1983.

Namier, Lewis B., and John Brooke. *Charles Townshend*. New York: St. Martin's Press, 1964.

Neatby, Hilda. *The Quebec Act: Protest and Policy*. Scarborough, Ont.: Prentice Hall, 1972.

O'Brien, Gerard. *Anglo-Irish Politics in the Age of Grattan and Pitt*. Blackrock, County Dublin, Ireland: Irish Academic Press, 1987.

O'Donnell, Ruan. *The Rebellion in Wicklow, 1798*. Dublin: Irish Academic Press, 1998.

O'Gorman, Frank. *The Long Eighteenth Century: British Political and Social History, 1688-1832*. New ed. London: Arnold, 1997.

Pakenham, Thomas. *The Year of Liberty: The Great Irish Rebellion of 1798*. New York: Random House, 1997.

Petrie, Sir Charles. *The Jacobite Movement: The First Phase, 1688-1716*. London: Eyre & Spottiswoode, 1948.

Pittock, Murray. *Jacobitism*. New York: St. Martin's Press, 1998.

Porter, Roy. *English Society in the Eighteenth Century*. 2d rev. ed. New York: Penguin, 1990.

Rae, T. I., ed. *The Union of 1707: Its Impact on Scotland*. Glasgow, Scotland: Blackie and Son, 1974.

Riley, P. W. J. *The Union of England and Scotland: A*

Study in Anglo-Scottish Politics of the Eighteenth Century. Totowa, N.J.: Rowman & Littlefield, 1978.

Robertson, John, ed. *A Union for Empire: Political Thought and the British Union of 1707*. New York: Cambridge University Press, 1995.

Ross, Ian Simpson. *The Life of Adam Smith*. Oxford, England: Oxford University Press, 1995.

Rudé, George F. E. *Wilkes and Liberty: A Social Study of 1763 to 1774*. Oxford, England: Clarendon Press, 1962.

Schama, Simon. *The Wars of the British, 1603-1776*. Vol. 2 in *A History of Britain*. New York: Hyperion, 2001.

Skinner, Andrew S., and Thomas Wilson, eds. *Essays on Adam Smith*. Oxford, England: Clarendon Press, 1975.

Sloan, Kim, ed. *Discovering the World in the Eighteenth Century*. London: British Museum Press, 2003.

Speck, W. A. *The Butcher: The Duke of Cumberland and the Suppression of the Forty-five*. Oxford, England: Basil Blackwell, 1987.

Stone, Lawrence, and Jeanne C. Fawtier Stone. *An Open Elite? England, 1540-1880*. New York: Oxford University Press, 1984.

Thomas, Peter D. G. *John Wilkes: A Friend of Liberty*. New York: Oxford University Press, 1996.

Thomson, George Malcolm. *The First Churchill: The Life of John, First Duke of Marlborough*. New York: William Morrow, 1980.

Trevor, Meriol. *The Shadow of a Crown: The Life Story of James II of England and James VII of Scotland*. London: Constable, 1988.

Trinder, Barrie. *The Darbys of Coalbrookdale*. 4th ed. Chichester: Phillimore, 1993.

West, Richard. *Daniel Defoe: The Life and Strange, Surprizing Adventure*. New York: Carroll and Graf, 1998.

Whatley, Christopher H. *Bought and Sold for English Gold? The Union of 1707*. 2d ed. East Linton, East Lothian, Scotland: Tuckwell Press, 2001.

Whyte, Ian, and Kathleen Whyte. *On the Trail of the Jacobites*. London: Routledge, 1990.

Woodfine, Philip. *Britannnia's Glories: The Walpole Ministry and the 1739 War with Spain*. Rochester, N.Y.: Royal Historical Society/Boydell Press, 1998.

EXPLORATION AND THE SEA

Blumberg, Rhoda. *The Remarkable Voyages of Captain Cook*. New York: Bradbury Press, 1991.

Bruce, James. *Travels to Discover the Source of the Nile.* Edited by C. F. Beckingham. New York: Horizon Press, 1964.

Cohen, J. M. *Journeys Down the Amazon: Being the Extraordinary Adventures and Achievements of the Early Explorers*. London: C. Knight, 1975.

Cook, James. *The Journals*. Abridged edition. Edited by Philip Edwards. London: Penguin Books, 2000.

Dmytryshyn, Basil, E. A. P. Crownhart-Vaughn, and Thomas Vaughn, eds. and trans. *Russian Penetration of the North Pacific Ocean, 1700-1799*. Vol 2. Portland: Oregon Historical Society, 1988.

Fernandex-Armesto, Felipe, ed. *The Times Atlas of World Exploration*. New York: HarperCollins, 1991.

Flenley, John, and Paul Bahn. *The Enigmas of Easter Island: Island on the Edge*. New York: Oxford University Press, 2003.

Francis, Daniel. *Discovery of the North: The Exploration of Canada's Arctic*. Edmonton, Alta.: Hurtig, 1986.

Frost, O. W. *Bering: The Russian Discovery of America*. New Haven, Conn.: Yale University Press, 2003.

Golder, Frank A. *Bering's Voyages*. 2 vols. New York: American Geographical Society, 1922-1925. Reprint. New York: Octagon Books, 1968.

Guadalupi, Gianni, and Anthony Shugaar. *Latitude Zero: Tales of the Equator*. New York: Carroll & Graf, 2001.

Hayes, Derek. *First Crossing: Alexander Mackenzie, His Expedition Across North America, and the Opening of the Continent*. Seattle: Sasquatch Books, 2001.

Lincoln, Margarette. *Science and Exploration in the Pacific: European Voyages to the Southern Oceans in the Eighteenth Century*. Woodbridge, Suffolk, England: Boydell Press, 2001.

Linebaugh, Peter, and Marcus Rediker. *The Many-Headed Hydra: Sailors, Slaves, Commoners, and the Hidden History of the Revolutionary Atlantic*. Boston: Beacon Press, 2000.

Livingstone, David N., and Charles W. J. Withers. *Geography and Enlightenment*. Chicago: University of Chicago Press, 1999.

McGoogan, Ken. *Ancient Mariner: The Arctic Adventures of Samuel Hearne, the Sailor Who Inspired Coleridge's Masterpiece*. New York: Carroll & Graf, 2004.

Mackenzie, Alexander. *Voyages from Montreal on the River St. Laurence Through the Continent of North America, to the Frozen and Pacific Oceans in the Years 1789 and 1793*. Ann Arbor, Mich.: University Microfilms, 1966.

Meany, Edmond S. *Vancouver's Discovery of Puget*

Sound. 1935. Reprint. Portland, Oreg.: Binfords & Mort, 1957.

Nuffield, Edward W. *Samuel Hearne: Journey to the Coopermine River, 1769-1772*. Vancouver, B.C.: Haro Books, 2001.

Pethick, Derek. *The Nootka Connection: Europe and the Northwest Coast, 1790-1795*. Vancouver, B.C.: Douglas & McIntyre, 1980.

Reid, J. M. *Traveller Extraordinary*. New York: W. W. Norton, 1968.

Silverberg, Robert. *Bruce of the Blue Nile*. New York: Holt, Rinehart and Winston, 1969.

Smith, Anthony. *Explorers of the Amazon*. London: Viking, 1990.

Steller, Georg Wilhelm. *Journal of a Voyage with Bering, 1741-1742*. Edited with an introduction by O. W. Frost; translated by Margritt A. Engel and Frost. Stanford, Calif.: Stanford University Press, 1988.

Thomas, Nicholas: *The Extraordinary Voyages of Captain James Cook*. New York: Walker, 2003.

Von Hagen, Victor Wolfgang. *South America Called Them: Explorations of the Great Naturalists—La Condamine, Humboldt, Darwin, Spruce*. New York: A. A. Knopf, 1945.

Wilford, John Noble. *The Mapmakers*. New York: Knopf, 1981.

Williams, J. E. D. *From Sails to Satellites: The Origin and Development of Navigational Science*. Oxford, England: Oxford University Press, 1992.

FRANCE

Bell, David A. *The Cult of the Nation in France: Inventing Nationalism, 1680-1800*. Cambridge, Mass.: Harvard University Press, 2001.

_____. *Lawyers and Citizens: The Making of a Political Elite in Old Régime France*. New York: Oxford University Press, 1994.

Bernier, Olivier. *Louis the Beloved: The Life of Louis XV*. Garden City, N.Y.: Doubleday, 1984.

Brig, Robin. *Communities of Belief: Cultural and Social Tension in Early Modern France*. Oxford, England: Oxford University Press, 1989.

_____. *Early Modern France, 1560-1715*. London: Oxford University Press, 1998.

Campbell, Peter R. *Power and Politics in Old Regime France, 1720-1745*. New York: Routledge, 1996.

Collins, James B. *The State in Early Modern France*. Cambridge, England: Cambridge University Press, 1995.

Cranston, Maurice. *The Noble Savage: Jean-Jacques Rousseau, 1754-1762*. Chicago: University of Chicago Press, 1991.

Crocker, Lester. *An Age of Crisis: Man and World in Eighteenth Century French Thought*. Baltimore: Johns Hopkins University Press, 1959.

Eccles, William J. *France in America*. New York: Harper & Row, 1972.

Ford, Franklin L. *Robe and Sword: The Regrouping of the French Aristocracy After Louis XIV*. New York: Harper and Row, 1955.

Frey, Linda, and Marsha Frey. *Societies in Upheaval: Insurrections in France, Hungary, and Spain in the Early Eighteenth Century*. Westport, Conn.: Greenwood Press, 1987.

Furet, François. *Revolutionary France, 1770-1880*. Translated by Antonia Nevill. Oxford, England: Blackwell, 1992.

Gottschalk, Louis. *Lafayette Comes to America*. Chicago: University of Chicago Press, 1935.

Hardman, John. *Louis XVI*. New Haven, Conn.: Yale University Press, 1993.

_____. *Robespierre*. New York: Longman, 1999.

Hulling, Mark. *Montesquieu and the Old Regime*. Berkeley: University of California Press, 1976.

Jones, Colin. *The Great Nation: France from Louis XV to Napoleon, 1715-1799*. New York: Columbia University Press, 2002.

Jones, P. M. *Reform and Revolution in France: The Politics of Transition, 1774-1791*. New York: Cambridge University Press, 1995.

Knapp, Bettina L. *Voltaire Revisited*. New York: Twayne, 2000.

Lewis, Warren Hamilton. *The Splendid Century: Life in the France of Louis XIV*. Garden City, N.Y.: Doubleday Anchor Books, 1957.

Orieux, Jean. *Talleyrand: The Art of Survival*. Translated by Patricia Wolf. New York: Alfred A. Knopf, 1974.

Price, Munro. *The Fall of the French Monarchy: Louis XVI, Marie Antoinette, and the Baron de Breteuil*. New York: Pan Macmillan, 2002.

Roche, Daniel. *The People of Paris: An Essay in Popular Culture in the Eighteenth Century*. 2 vols. Translated by Marie Evans and Gwynne Lewis. Berkeley: University of California Press, 1987.

Shackleton, Robert. *Montesquieu: A Critical Biography*. Oxford, England: Oxford University Press, 1961.

Shklar, Judith. *Montesquieu*. New York: Oxford University Press, 1987.

Thompson, J. M. *Robespierre*. Reprint. New York: Basil Blackwell, 1988.

Vyverherg, Henry. *Human Nature, Cultural Diversity, and the French Enlightenment*. London: Oxford University Press, 1989.

Wilson, Arthur M. *Diderot*. New York: Oxford University Press, 1972.

_____. *French Foreign Policy During the Administration of Cardinal Fleury, 1726-1743: A Study in Diplomacy and Commercial Development*. Westport, Conn.: Greenwood Press, 1972.

FRENCH REVOLUTION AND NAPOLEONIC ERA

Asprey, Robert. *The Rise of Napoleon Bonaparte*. New York: Basic Books, 2000.

Backzo, Branislaw. *Ending the Terror: The French Revolution After Robespierre*. Translated by Michel Peteram. New York: Cambridge University Press, 1994.

Baker, Keith Michael. *Inventing the French Revolution*. Chicago: University of Chicago Press, 1990.

Bienvenu, Richard T., ed. *The Ninth of Thermidor: The Fall of Robespierre*. New York: Oxford University Press, 1968.

Bonaparte, Napoleon. *Napoleon on Napoleon: An Autobiography of the Emperor*. Edited by Somerset de Chair. London: Cassell, 1992.

Bosher, J. F. *The French Revolution*. New York: W. W. Norton, 1988.

Cobb, Richard, ed. *Voices of the French Revolution*. New York: Simon & Schuster, 1988.

Doyle, William. *Origins of the French Revolution*. 3d ed. New York: Oxford University Press, 1999.

_____. *Oxford History of the French Revolution*. New York: Oxford University Press, 2003.

Dunn, Susan. *The Deaths of Louis XVI: Regicide and the French Political Imagination*. Princeton, N.J.: Princeton University Press, 1994.

Emsley, Clive. *Napoleon: Conquest, Reform, and Reorganization*. New York: Pearson/Longman, 2003.

Godechot, Jacques. *Taking of the Bastille, July 14, 1789*. New York: Charles Scribner's Sons, 1970.

Gregory, Desmond. *Napoleon's Italy*. Cranbury, N.J.: Associated University Press, 2001.

Hardman, John. *The French Revolution Sourcebook*. New York: St. Martin's Press, 1982

Hibbert, Christopher. *The Days of the French Revolution*. New York: Quill/William Morrow, 1999.

Johnson, Paul. *Napoleon*. New York: Viking, 2002.

Jordan, David P. *The King's Trial: The French Revolution Versus Louis XVI*. 25th anniversary ed. Berkeley: University of California Press, 2004.

Lefebvre, George. *The Coming of the French Revolution*. Translated by R. R. Palmer. Bicentennial ed. Princeton, N.J.: Princeton University Press, 1989.

_____. *The French Revolution: From Its Origins to 1793*. Translated by Elizabeth Moss Evanson. New York: Columbia University Press, 1962.

_____. *Napoleon: From 18 Brumaire to Tilsit, 1799-1807*. Translated by Henry F. Stockhold. New York: Columbia University Press, 1969.

Lynn, John A. *Bayonets of the Republic: Motivation and Tactics of Revolutionary France, 1791-1794*. Urbana: University of Illinois Press, 1984.

Markham, Felix. *Napoleon*. New York: New American Library, 1964.

Palmer, Robert R. *Twelve Who Ruled: The Year of the Terror in the French Revolution*. Princeton, N.J.: Princeton University Press, 1941.

Paulson, Ronald. *Representations of Revolution*. New Haven, Conn.: Yale University Press, 1983.

Rudé, George. *The Crowd in the French Revolution*. New York: Oxford University Press, 1959.

_____. *The French Revolution: Its Causes, Its History, Its Legacy After Two Hundred Years*. New York: Grove Weidenfeld, 1988.

Schama, Simon. *Citizens: A Chronicle of the French Revolution*. New York: Alfred A. Knopf, 1989.

Secher, Reynald. *A French Genocide: The Vendee*. University of Notre Dame Press, 2003.

Soboul, Albert. *The French Revolution, 1789-1815: Storming of the Bastille to Napoleon*. Translated by Alan Forrest and Colin Jones. New York: Random House, 1975.

Sutherland, D. M. G. *The French Revolution and Empire: The Quest for a Civic Order*. Malden, Mass.: Blackwell, 2003.

Tilly, Charles. *The Vendee*. Cambridge, Mass.: Harvard University Press, 1964.

Van Deusen, Glyndon G. *Sieyès: His Life and His Nationalism*. Reprint. New York: AMS Press, 1968.

Walzer, Michael, ed. *Regicide and Revolution: Speeches at the Trial of Louis XVI*. Translated by Marian Rothstein. London: Cambridge University Press, 1974.

Wilkinson, Spenser. *The Rise of General Bonaparte*. Brookfield, Vt.: Ashgate, 1991.

HABSBURG EMPIRE AND ITALY

Beales, Derek. *In the Shadow of Maria Theresa, 1741-1780*. Vol. 1 in *Joseph II*. New York: Cambridge University Press, 1987.

Bernard, Paul. *Jesuits and Jacobins: Enlightenment and Enlightened Despotism in Austria*. Urbana: University of Illinois Press, 1971.

Blanning, T. C. W. *Joseph II*. London: Longman, 1994.

Dickson, Peter G. M. *Finance and Government Under Maria Theresa, 1740-1780*. 2 vols. Oxford, England: Oxford University Press, 1987.

Evans, R. J. W. *The Making of the Habsburg Monarchy, 1550-1700: An Interpretation*. 3d ed. New York: Oxford University Press, 1991.

Frey, Linda, and Marsha Frey. *Societies in Upheaval: Insurrections in France, Hungary, and Spain in the Early Eighteenth Century*. Westport, Conn.: Greenwood Press, 1987.

Frigo, Daniela, ed. *Politics and Diplomacy in Early Modern Italy: The Structure of Diplomatic Practice, 1400-1800*. Cambridge, England: Cambridge University Press, 2000.

Gregory, Desmond. *Napoleon's Italy*. Cranbury, N.J.: Associated University Press, 2001.

Henderson, Nicholas. *Prince Eugen of Savoy*. Reprint. London: Phoenix Press, 2002.

Hochedlinger, Michael. *Austria's Wars of Emergence: War, State, and Society in the Habsburg Monarchy, 1683-1789*. New York: Longman, 2003.

Holmes, Gregory, ed. *Oxford History of Italy*. Oxford, England: Oxford University Press, 1997.

Ignotus, Paul. *Hungary*. New York: Praeger, 1972.

Imbruglia, Girolamo, ed. *Naples in the Eighteenth Century: The Birth and Death of a Nation State*. Cambridge, England: Cambridge University Press, 2000.

Ingrao, Charles W. *The Habsburg Monarchy, 1618-1815*. 2d ed. New York: Cambridge University Press, 2000.

Lee, Vernon. *Studies of the Eighteenth Century in Italy*. 2d ed. London: Unwin, 1907.

Lendvai, Paul. *The Hungarians: A Thousand Years of Victory in Defeat*. Translated by Ann Major. Princeton, N.J.: Princeton University Press, 2003.

Macartney, Carlie Aylmer. *Maria Theresa and the House of Austria*. London: English Universities Press, 1970.

McKay, Derek. *Prince Eugene of Savoy*. London: Thames & Hudson, 1977.

O'Brien, Charles H. *Ideas of Religious Toleration at the Time of Joseph II*. Philadelphia, Pa.: American Philosophical Society, 1969.

Parvev, Ivan. *Hapsburgs and Ottomans: Between Vienna and Belgrade, 1683-1739*. New York: Columbia University Press, 1995.

Slottman, William B. *Ference Rákóczi and the Great Powers*. Boulder, Colo.: East European Monographs, 1997.

Sugar, Peter F., Peter Hanak, and Tibor Frank, eds. *A History of Hungary*. Bloomington: Indiana University Press, 1990.

Szabo, Franz A. J. *Kaunitz and Enlightened Absolutism, 1753-1780*. New York: Cambridge University Press, 1994.

Wangermann, Ernst. *The Austrian Achievement, 1700-1800*. New York: Harcourt Brace Jovanovich, 1973.

Wolff, Larry. *Venice and the Slavs: The Discovery of Dalmatia in the Age of Enlightenment*. Stanford, Calif.: Stanford University Press, 2001.

LITERATURE

Andrews, William L., and Henry Louis Gates, Jr., eds. *Slave Narratives*. New York: Library of America, 2000.

Backsheider, Paula R. *Daniel Defoe: Ambition and Innovation*. Lexington: University Press of Kentucky, 1986.

Bate, W. Jackson. *Samuel Johnson*. New York: Harcourt Brace Jovanovich, 1977.

Battles, Matthew. *Library: An Unquiet History*. New York: W. W. Norton, 2003.

Blom, Philipp. *Enlightening the World: "Encyclopédie," the Book That Changed the Course of History*. New York: Palgrave MacMillan, 2005.

Bloom, Edward A., and Lillian D. Bloom. *Addison and Steele: The Critical Heritage*. London: Routledge and Kegan Paul, 1980.

Bond, Richard P. *Studies in the Early English Periodical*. Chapel Hill: University of North Carolina Press, 1957.

Brown, Homer Obed. *Institutions of the English Novel from Defoe to Scott*. Philadelphia: Pennsylvania University Press, 1997.

Brückmann, Patricia Carr. *A Manner of Correspondence: A Study of the Scriblerus Club*. Montreal: McGill-Queen's University Press, 1997.

Burancelli, Vincent. *The Trial of Peter Zenger*. New York: New York University Press, 1957.

Carroll, Denis. *The Man from God Knows Where*. Blackrock, County Dublin, Ireland: Columbia Press, 1995.

Censer, Jack Richard. *The French Press in the Age of Enlightenment*. New York: Routledge, 1994.

Clarke, Bob. *From Grub Street to Fleet Street: An Illustrated History of English Newspapers to 1899*. London: Ashgate, 2004.

Cleary, Thomas. *Henry Fielding: Political Writer*. Waterloo, Ont.: Wilfrid Laurier Press, 1984.

Curtis, Laura. *The Elusive Daniel Defoe*. Lanham, Md.: Rowan and Littlefield, 1984.

Darnton, Robert. *The Business of Enlightenment: A Publishing History of the "Encyclopédie," 1775-1800*. Cambridge, Mass.: Harvard University Press, 1979.

Darnton, Robert, and Daniel Roche, eds. *Revolution in Print: The Press in France, 1775-1800*. Berkeley: University of California Press, 1989.

DeMaria, Robert, Jr. *The Life of Samuel Johnson: A Critical Biography*. Oxford, England: Blackwell, 1993.

Donato, Clorinda, and Robert M. Maniquis, eds. *The "Encyclopédie" and the Age of Revolution*. Boston: G. K. Hall, 1992.

Ferguson, Oliver Watkins. *Jonathan Swift and Ireland*. Urbana: University of Illinois Press, 1962.

France, Peter. *Rousseau: "Confessions."* Cambridge, England: Cambridge University Press, 1987.

Fruchtman, Jack, Jr. *Thomas Paine: Apostle of Freedom*. New York: Four Walls Eight Windows, 1994.

Furbank, Philip Nicholas. *Diderot*. New York: Alfred A. Knopf, 1992.

Girón, Alicia. "The Biblioteca Nacional of Spain." *Alexandria* 6, no. 2 (1994): 91-103.

Gordon, Douglas H., and Norman L. Torrey. *The Censoring of Diderot's "Encyclopedia" and the Re-established Text*. New York: Columbia University Press, 1947.

Hanna, Nelly. *In Praise of Books*. Syracuse, N.Y.: Syracuse University Press, 2003.

Harris, Bob. *Politics and the Rise of the Press: Britain and France, 1620-1800*. New York: Routledge, 1996.

Harris, Michael H. *History of Libraries in the Western World*. Metuchen, N.J.: Scarecrow Press, 1995.

_____. *London Newspapers in the Age of Walpole: A Study of the Origins of the English Press*. Toronto: Associated University Presses, 1987.

Hoover, Benjamin Beard. *Samuel Johnson's Parliamentary Reporting: Debates in the Senate of Lilliput*. Berkeley: University of California Press, 1953.

Hunt, F. Knight. *The Fourth Estate: Contributions Towards a History of Newspapers and of the Liberty of the Press*. London: David Bogue, 1850.

Johnson, Samuel. *The Rambler*. Edited by W. J. Bate and Albrecht B. Strauss. New Haven, Conn.: Yale University Press, 1969.

Kaminski, Thomas. *The Early Career of Samuel Johnson*. New York: Oxford University Press, 1987.

Karl, Frederick R. *A Reader's Guide to the Eighteenth-Century Novel*. New York: Noonday Press, 1974.

Kernan, Alvin. *Samuel Johnson and the Impact of Print*. Princeton, N.J.: Princeton University Press, 1989.

King, Richard Ashe. *Swift in Ireland*. Folcroft, Pa.: Folcroft Library Editions, 1976.

Landau, Sidney I. *The Art and Craft of Lexicography*. New York: Scribner's, 1984.

Laubier, Guillaume de, and Jacques Bosser. *The Most Beautiful Libraries in the World*. New York: Harry N. Abrams, 2003.

Law, William. *Our Hansard: Or, The True Mirror of Parliament*. London: Pitman, 1950.

Lewis, Peter, and Nigel Wood, eds. *John Gay and the Scriblerians*. London: Vision Press, 1988.

Lipking, Lawrence. *Samuel Johnson: The Life of an Author*. Cambridge, Mass.: Harvard University Press, 1998.

Lynch, Jack. *Samuel Johnson's Dictionary: Selections from the 1755 Work That Defined the English Language*. New York: Walker, 2003.

Lynn, Steven. *Samuel Johnson After Deconstruction: Rhetoric and "The Rambler."* Carbondale: Southern Illinois University Press, 1992.

McAdam, E. L., Jr., and George Milne. *Johnson's Dictionary: A Modern Selection*. New York: Random House, 1963.

McCarthy, Muriel, and Ann Simmons. *The Making of Marsh's Library: Learning, Politics, and Religion in Ireland, 1650-1750*. Dublin: Four Courts Press, 2004.

McKeon, Michael. *The Origins of the English Novel, 1600-1740*. Baltimore: Johns Hopkins University Press, 1987.

McMinn, Joseph. *Jonathan's Travels: Swift and Ireland*. Hampshire, England: Palgrave Macmillan, 1994.

Mason, John Hope. *The Irresistible Diderot*. New York: Quartet Books, 1982.

Mitchell, Linda C. *Grammar Wars: Language as Cultural Battlefield in Seventeenth and Eighteenth Century England*. Burlington, Vt.: Ashgate, 2001.

Monaghan, Charles. *The Murrays of Murray Hill*. Brooklyn, N.Y.: Urban History Press, 1998.

Munter, Robert. *The History of the Irish Newspaper, 1685-1760*. Cambridge, England: Cambridge University Press, 1967.

Nicholson, Colin. *Writing and the Rise of Finance: Capital Satires of the Early Eighteenth Century*. Cambridge, England: Cambridge University Press, 1994.

Nisbet, H. B., and Claude Rawson, eds. *The Eighteenth Century*. Vol. 4 in *The Cambridge History of Literary*

Criticism. Cambridge, England: Cambridge University Press, 1997.

Nokes, David. *John Gay: A Profession of Friendship*. Oxford, England: Oxford University Press, 1995.

Novak, Maximillian E. *Daniel Defoe—Master of Fictions: His Life and Ideas*. New York: Oxford University Press, 2001.

Paulson, Ronald. *The Life of Henry Fielding*. Malden, Mass.: Blackwell, 2000.

Ratermanis, J. B., and W. R. Irwin. *The Comic Style of Beaumarchais*. Seattle: University of Washington Press, 1961.

Raymond, Joad, ed. *News, Newspapers, and Society in Early Modern England*. Portland, Oreg.: Frank Cass, 1999.

Reddick, Allen. *The Making of Johnson's Dictionary, 1746-1773*. 2d ed. New York: Cambridge University Press, 1996.

Richetti, John J. *The English Novel in History, 1700-1780*. New York: Routledge, 1999.

Rogers, Deborah D. *Bookseller as Rogue: John Almon and the Politics of Eighteenth Century Publishing*. New York: Peter Lang, 1986.

Rosengarten, Richard A. *Henry Fielding and the Narration of Providence*. New York: Palgrave, 2000.

Sledd, James H., and Gwin J. Kolb. *Dr. Johnson's Dictionary: Essays in the Biography of a Book*. Chicago: University of Chicago Press, 1955.

Thogmartin, Clyde. *The National Daily Press of France*. Birmingham, Ala.: Summa, 1998.

Varey, Simon. *Joseph Andrews: A Satire of Modern Times*. Boston: Twayne, 1990.

Vincent, David. *The Rise of Mass Literacy*. Cambridge, England: Polity, 2000.

Wade, Ira O. *Voltaire and "Candide": A Study in the Fusion of History, Art, and Philosophy*. Princeton, N.J.: Princeton University Press, 1959.

Wallace, Maurice O. *Constructing the Black Masculine: Identity and Ideality in African American Men's Literature and Culture, 1775-1795*. Durham, N.C.: Duke University Press, 2002.

MATHEMATICS

Bliss, Gilbert Ames. *Calculus of Variations*. LaSalle, Ill.: Open Court, 1925.

Dale, Andrew I. *A History of Inverse Probability*. New York: Springer-Verlag, 1991.

Daston, Lorraine. *Classical Probability in the Enlightenment*. Princeton, N.J.: Princeton University Press, 1988.

David, Florence Nightingale. *Games, Gods, and Gambling*. London: Charles Griffin, 1962.

Ehrenfest, Paul, and Tatiana Ehrenfest. *The Conceptual Foundations of the Statistical Approach in Mechanics*. Mineola, N.Y.: Dover, 2002.

Goldstine, Herman H. *A History of the Calculus of Variations from the Seventeenth Through the Nineteenth Century*. New York: Springer-Verlag, 1980.

Hald, Anders. *A History of Mathematical Statistics from 1750 to 1950*. New York: John Wiley and Sons, 1998.

_____. *A History of Probability and Statistics and Their Applications Before 1750*. New York: John Wiley, 1990.

Kline, Morris. *Mathematical Thought from Ancient to Modern Times*. New York: Oxford University Press, 1972.

Pycior, Helena M. *Symbols, Impossible Numbers, and Geometric Entanglements: British Algebra Through the Commentaries on Newton's "Universal Arithmetick."* New York: Cambridge University Press, 1997.

Stigler, Stephen M. *The History of Statistics*. Cambridge, Mass.: Harvard University Press, 1986.

Todhunter, I. *A History of the Mathematical Theory of Probability*. New York: Chelsea, 1949.

Van Brunt, Bruce. *The Calculus of Variations*. New York: Springer, 2004.

MEDICINE

Bertrand, Jean Baptiste, Jean Biraben, and Anne Plumptre. *A Historical Relation of the Plague at Marseilles in the Year 1720*. Whitby, Ont.: McGraw-Hill, 1973.

Black, Joseph. *"On Acid Humor Arising from Foods," and "On White Magnesia."* Translated by Thomas Hanson. Minneapolis, Minn.: Bell Museum of Pathobiology, 1973.

Bown, Stephen R. *Scurvy: How a Surgeon, a Mariner, and a Gentleman Solved the Greatest Medical Mystery of the Age of Sail*. New York: St. Martin's Press, 2004.

Brock, Thomas, ed. and trans. *Milestones in Microbiology, 1546-1940*. Washington, D.C.: ASM Press, 1999.

Carpenter, Kenneth John. *The History of Scurvy and Vitamin C*. Cambridge, England: Cambridge University Press, 1986.

Cuppage, Francis E. *James Cook and the Conquest of Scurvy*. Westport, Conn.: Greenwood Press, 1994.

Defoe, Daniel. *A Journal of the Plague Year*. Rev. ed. Edited by Cynthia Wall. New York: Penguin Books, 2003.

Druett, Joan. *Rough Medicine: Surgeons at Sea in the Age of Sail*. London: Routledge, 2002.

Fisher, Richard B. *Edward Jenner, 1741-1823*. London: Andre Deutsch, 1991.

Franco, Avelino, et al. *The History of Anesthesia*. Amsterdam: Elsevier Science, 2002.

Harvie, David I. *Limeys: The True Story of One Man's War Against Ignorance, the Establishment, and the Deadly Scurvy*. Stroud, Gloucestershire, England: Sutton, 2002.

Hess, Alfred Fabian. *Scurvy: Past and Present*. Philadelphia: J. B. Lippincott, 1920.

McDowell, Julie, and Michael Windelspecht. *The Lymphatic System*. Westport, Conn.: Greenwood, 2004.

McNeill, William. *Plagues and Peoples*. Garden City, N.Y.: Anchor Press, 1976.

Nuland, Sherwin. *Doctors: The Biography*. New York: Vintage Books, 1988.

Porter, Roy. *Blood and Guts. A Short History of Medicine*. New York: W. W. Norton, 2002.

Porter, Roy, and Maurice Kirby. *Disease, Medicine, and Society in England, 1550-1860*. New York: Cambridge University Press, 1995.

Ramsay, William. *Life and Letters of Joseph Black, M.D.* London: Constable, 1918.

Reiss, Oscar. *Medicine and the American Revolution: How Diseases and Their Treatments Affected the Colonial Army*. Jefferson, N.C.: McFarland, 1998.

Solomon, Joan. *Discovering the Cure for Scurvy*. Hatfield, Hertfordshire, England: Association for Science Education, 1989.

Wolfe, Richard, and Leonard Menczer, eds. *I Awaken to Glory: Essays Celebrating the Sesquicentennial of the Discovery of Anesthesia by Horace Wells, December 11, 1844-December 11, 1994*. Boston: Boston Medical Library, 1994.

Wynbrandt, James. *The Excrutiating History of Dentistry*. New York: St. Martin's Press, 2000.

THE MIDDLE EAST: THE OTTOMAN EMPIRE AND ARABIA

Aksan, Virginia H. *An Ottoman Statesman in War and Peace: Ahmed Resmi Efendi, 1700-1783*. Leiden, the Netherlands: E. J. Brill, 1995.

Anderson, M. S. *The Eastern Question, 1774-1923: A Study in International Relations*. Rev. ed. New York: St. Martin's Press, 1996.

Antonius, George. *The Arab Awakening: The Story of the Arab National Movement*. New York: G. P. Putnam, 1946.

Atiyeh, George N., ed. *The Book in the Islamic World: The Written Word and Communication in the Middle East*. Albany: State University of New York Press, 1995.

Avery, Peter, Gavin Hambly, and Charles Melville, eds. *From Nadir Shah to the Islamic Republic*. Vol. 7 in *The Cambridge History of Iran*. Cambridge, England: Cambridge University Press, 1991.

Badger, G. P., ed. *The History of the Imams and Sayyids of Oman, by Salil bin Razik*. London: Darf, 1986.

Barbir, Karl. *Ottoman Rule in Damascus, 1708-1758*. Princeton, N.J.: Princeton University Press, 1980.

Bloom, Jonathan, and Sheila Blair. *Islamic Arts*. London: Phaidon Press, 1997.

Brown, L. Carl. *Imperial Legacy: The Ottoman Imprint on the Balkans and the Middle East*. New York: Columbia University Press, 1996.

Cassels, Lavender. *The Struggle for the Ottoman Empire, 1717-1740*. London: Thomas Y. Crowell, 1967.

Crane, Howard. *The Garden of the Mosques: Hafiz Huseyin al-Ayvansarayi's Guide to the Muslim Monuments of Ottoman Istanbul*. Boston: E. J. Brill, 2000.

Creasy, Edward S. *History of the Ottoman Turks*. Beirut: Khayats, 1961.

Daniel, Elton L. *The History of Iran*. Westport, Conn.: Greenwood Press, 2001.

Gibb, H. A. R., ed. *The Encyclopedia of Islam*. Vol. 11. Rev. ed. Leiden, the Netherlands: E. J. Brill, 1960-2004.

Göçek, Fatma Müge. *East Encounters West: France and the Ottoman Empire in the Eighteenth Century*. New York: Oxford University Press, 1987.

Goodwin, Godfrey. *A History of Ottoman Architecture*. New York: Thames and Hudson, 1987.

Goodwin, Jason. *Lords of the Horizons: A History of the Ottoman Empire*. New York: Picador, 2003.

Hanebuut-Benz, Eva, et al. *Middle Eastern Languages and the Print Revolution: A Cross-Cultural Encounter*. Westhofen, Germany: Verlag-Skulima, 2002.

Hawley, D. *Oman and Its Renaissance*. London: Stacey International, 1984.

Hitti, Philip K. *History of Syria: Including Lebanon and Palestine*. 2d ed. London: Macmillan, 1957.

Holt, P. M., Ann K. S. Lambton, and Bernard Lewis, eds. *The Cambridge History of Islam*. New ed. Cambridge, England: Cambridge University Press, 1977.

Jelavich, Barbara. *History of the Balkans: Eighteenth and Nineteenth Centuries*. New York: Cambridge University Press, 1983.

Joudah, Ahmad Hasan. *Revolt in Palestine in the Eigh-*

teenth Century. Princeton, N.J.: Princeton University Press, 1987.

Kuran, Aptullah. *The Mosque in Early Ottoman Architecture.* Chicago: University of Chicago Press, 1968.

Perry, John R. *Karim Khan Zand: A History of Iran, 1747-1779. Publications of the Center for Middle Eastern Studies,* No. 12. Chicago: University of Chicago Press, 1979.

Quataert, Donald. *The Ottoman Empire, 1700-1922.* New York: Cambridge University Press, 2000.

Risso, Patricia. *Oman and Muscat.* London: Croom Helm, 1986.

Said, Edward. *Orientalism.* New York: Vintage, 1979.

Shaw, Stanford J. *History of the Ottoman Empire and Modern Turkey.* Cambridge, England: Cambridge University Press, 1976.

_____, trans. *Ottoman Egypt in the Age of the French Revolution, by Huseyn Effendi.* Cambridge, Mass.: Harvard University Press, 1964.

Shay, M. L. *The Ottoman Empire from 1720 to 1744 as Revealed in Despatches of the Venetian Baili.* Urbana: University of Illinois Press, 1944.

Smith, Rex. *Studies In the Medieval History of Yemen and South Arabia.* Brookfield, Vt.: Ashgate, 1997.

Stavrianos, L. S. *The Balkans Since 1453.* New York: Holt, Rinehart and Winston, 1963. Reprint. New York: New York University Press, 2000.

Sugar, Peter F. *Southeastern Europe Under Ottoman Rule, 1354-1804.* Seattle: University of Washington Press, 1977.

Ünsal, Behçet. *Turkish-Islamic Architecture in Seljuk and Ottoman Times, 1071-1923.* New York: St. Martin's Press, 1973.

Vine, Peter. *The Heritage of Oman.* London: Immel, 1995.

Vine, Peter, and Paula Casey-Vine, eds. *Oman in History.* London: Immel, 1995.

Wilkinson, John C. *The Imamate Tradition of Oman.* London: Cambridge University Press, 1987.

Wolf, John B. *The Barbary Coast: Algiers Under the Turks, 1500 to 1830.* New York: W. W. Norton, 1979.

MILITARY AND WARFARE

Abbot, Henry L. *Beginning of Modern Submarine Warfare Under Captain Lieutenant David Bushnell.* Edited by Frank Anderson. Hamden, Conn.: Archon Books, 1966.

Alden, John R. *General Gage in America.* Baton Rouge: Louisiana State University Press, 1948.

Alexander, John T. *Emperor of the Cossacks: Pugachev and the Frontier Jacquerie of 1773-1775.* Lawrence, Kans.: Coronado Press, 1973.

Anderson, Fred. *Crucible of War: The Seven Years' War and the Fate of the Empire in British North America, 1754-1766.* New York: Alfred A. Knopf, 2001.

_____. *A People's Army: Massachusetts Soldiers and Society in the Seven Years' War.* Chapel Hill: University of North Carolina Press, 1984.

Anderson, M. S. *The War of the Austrian Succession, 1740-1748.* London: Longman, 1995.

Arnade, Charles W. *The Siege of St. Augustine in 1702.* Gainesville: University of Florida Press, 1959.

Banning, T. C. W. *The French Revolutionary Wars, 1787-1802.* New York: Arnold, 1996.

Beirich, Heidi Ly. "The Birth of Spanish Militarism: The Bourbon Military Reforms, 1766-1808." Unpublished masters thesis. San Diego, Calif.: San Diego State University, 1994.

Bertaud, Jean-Paul. *Army of the French Revolution: From Citizen-Soldiers to Instruments of Power.* Translated by Robert Palmer. Princeton, N.J.: Princeton University Press, 1989.

Black, Jeremy. *Cambridge Illustrated Atlas of Warfare: Renaissance to Revolution, 1492-1792.* Cambridge, England: Cambridge University Press, 1996.

_____. *Warfare in the Eighteenth Century.* London: Cassell, 1999.

Browning, Reed S. *The War of the Austrian Succession.* London: Macmillan, 1995.

Campbell, Leon G. *The Military and Society in Colonial Peru, 1750-1810.* Philadelphia: American Philosophical Society, 1978.

Chandler, David. *The Art of Warfare in the Age of Marlborough.* New York: Hippocrene Books, 1976.

_____. *Blenheim Preparation: The English Army on the March to the Danube—Collected Essays.*

_____. *Marlborough as Military Commander.* London: Penguin, 1973.

Chartrand, Rene. *French Fortresses in North America, 1535-1763: Quebec, Montreal, Louisbourg, and New Orleans.* Toronto: Osprey, 2005.

_____. *Louisbourg 1758: Wolfe's First Siege.* Oxford, England: Osprey, 2000.

Chidsey, Donald Barr. *The Loyalists: The Story of Those Americans Who Fought Against Independence.* New York: Crown, 1974.

Childs, John. *Armies and Warfare in Europe, 1648-1789.* New York: Holmes and Meier, 1982.

Cobb, Richard. *The People's Armies.* New Haven, Conn.: Yale University Press, 1987.

Coggins, Jack. *Ships and Seamen of the American Revolution*. Harrisburg, Pa.: Stackpole Books, 1969.

Commager, Henry, and Richard Morris. *The Spirit of Seventy-Six*. 1975. Reprint. New York: Da Capo Press, 1995.

Cook, Don. *The Long Fuse: England and America, 1760-1785*. New York: Atlantic Monthly Press, 1995.

Deane, John Marshall. *A Journal of Marlborough's Campaigns During the War of the Spanish Succession, 1704-1711*. London: Society for Army Historical Research, 1984.

Dickinson, W. Calvin. *The War of the Spanish Succession, 1702-1713: A Selected Bibliography*. Westport, Conn.: Greenwood Press, 1996.

Dorn, Walter L. *Competition for Empire, 1740-1763*. New York: Harper and Row, 1963.

Dull, Jonathan R. *The French Navy and American Independence: A Study of Arms and Diplomacy, 1774-1787*. Princeton, N.J.: Princeton University Press, 1975.

Edel, Wilbur. *Kekionga! The Worst Defeat in the History of the U.S. Army*. Westport, Conn.: Praeger, 1997.

Edmunds, R. David, and Joseph L. Peyser. *The Fox Wars: The Mesquaki Challenge to New France*. Norman: University of Oklahoma Press, 1993.

Englund, Peter. *The Battle That Shook Europe: Poltava and the Birth of the Russian Empire*. New York: I. B Tauris, 2003.

Esdaile, Charles J. *The French Wars, 1792-1815*. London: Routledge, 2001.

Falkner, James. *Blenheim, 1704: Marlborough's Greatest Victory*. Barnsley, South Yorkshire, England: Pen & Sword Military, 2004.

Foreman, Laura, and Ellen Blue Phillips. *Napoleon's Lost Fleet: Bonaparte, Nelson, and the Battle of the Nile*. New York: Discovery Books, 1999.

Fowler, William M., Jr. *Empires at War: The French and Indian War and the Struggle for North America, 1754-1763*. New York: Walker, 2005.

Francis, David. *The First Peninsular War, 1703-1713*. New York: St. Martin's Press, 1975.

Fremont-Barnes, Gregory. *French Revolutionary Wars*. Botley, Hampshire, England: Osprey, 2001.

French, Allen. *The First Year of the American Revolution*. Boston: Houghton Mifflin, 1934.

Frost, Robert I. *The Northern Wars: War, State, and Society in Northeastern Europe, 1558-1721*. New York: Longman, 2000.

Fuller, J. F. C. *The Decisive Battles of the Western World*. Vol. 3. London: Eyre & Spottiswode, 1955.

Gaff, Alan D. *Bayonets in the Wilderness: Anthony Wayne's Legion in the Old Northwest*. Norman: University of Oklahoma Press, 2004.

Galvin, John R. *The Minute Men, the First Fight: Myths and Realities of the American Revolution*. Washington, D.C.: Brassey's, 1996.

Gardiner, Robert. *Fleet Battle and Blockade: The French Revolutionary War, 1793-1797*. London: Chatham 1997.

_____, ed. *Navies and the American Revolution, 1775-1783*. Annapolis, Md.: Naval Institute Press, 1996.

Gerolymanto, André. *The Balkan Wars: Conquest, Revolution, and Retribution from the Ottoman Era to the Twentieth Century*. New York: Basic Books, 2002.

Glover, Michael. *General Burgoyne in Canada and America: Scapegoat for a System*. London: Gordon & Cremonesi, 1976.

Gray, Colin S. *The Leverage of Sea Power: The Strategic Advantage of Navies in War*. New York: Free Press, 1992.

Graymont, Barbara. *The Iroquois in the American Revolution*. Syracuse, N.Y.: Syracuse University Press, 1972.

_____, ed. *Fighting Tuscarora: The Autobiography of Chief Clinton Rickard*. Syracuse, N.Y.: Syracuse University Press, 1973.

Griffith, Paddy. *The Art of War in Revolutionary France, 1789-1802*. London: Greenhill Books, 1998.

Griffith, Samuel B., II. *The War for American Independence: From 1760 to the Surrender at Yorktown in 1781*. Urbana: University of Illinois Press, 2002.

Griswwold, Wesley S. *The Night the Revolution Began: The Boston Tea Party, 1773*. Brattleboro, Vt.: S. Greene Press, 1972.

Gunton, Michael. *Submarines at War: A History of Undersea Warfare from the American Revolution to the Cold War*. New York: Carroll & Graf, 2003.

Hallahan, William H. *The Day the Revolution Ended: 19 October 1781*. New York: Wiley, 2004.

Hamilton, Edward P. *The French and Indian Wars: The Story of Battles and Forts in the Wilderness*. Garden City, N.Y.: Doubleday, 1962.

Hargrove, Richard J., Jr. *General John Burgoyne*. Newark: University of Delaware Press, 1983.

Hattendorf, John B. *England in the War of the Spanish Succession: A Study of the English View and Conduct of Grand Strategy, 1702-1712*. New York: Garland, 1987.

Herold, J. Christopher. *Bonaparte in Egypt*. New York: Harper & Row, 1962.

Hibbert, Christopher. *Redcoats and Rebels: The American Revolution Through British Eyes.* New York: W. W. Norton, 1990.

Hutchinson, Robert. *Jane's Submarines: War Beneath the Waves from 1776 to the Present Day.* London: HarperCollins, 2001.

Jennings, Francis. *Empire of Fortune: Crowns, Colonies, and Tribes in the Seven Years' War in America.* New York: W. W. Norton, 1988.

Kennett, L. *The French Armies in the Seven Years' War.* Durham, N.C.: Duke University Press, 1967.

Ketchum, Richard M. *Saratoga: Turning Point of America's Revolutionary War.* New York: H. Holt, 1997.

_____. *Victory at Yorktown: The Campaign That Won the Revolution.* New York: Henry Holt, 2004.

Lavery, Brian. *Nelson and the Nile: The Naval War Against Bonaparte, 1798.* Annapolis, Md.: Naval Institute Press, 1998.

_____. *Nelson's Navy: The Ships, Men, and Organization, 1793-1815.* Annapolis, Md.: Naval Institute Press, 1989.

Lawford, James P. *Britain's Army in India: From Its Origins to the Conquest of Bengal.* London: G. Allen & Unwin, 1978.

Leach, Douglas E. *Arms for Empire: A Military History of the British Colonies in North America, 1607-1763.* New York: Macmillan, 1973.

Lee, E. Lawrence. *Indian Wars in North Carolina, 1663-1763.* Raleigh: North Carolina Department of Archives and History, Division of Archives and History, 1997.

Lenman, Bruce. *Britain's Colonial Wars, 1688-1783.* New York: Longman, 2001.

Lumpkin, Henry. *From Savannah to Yorktown: The American Revolution in the South.* Columbia: University of South Carolina Press, 1981.

Lynn, John. *The Wars of Louis XIV.* London: Longman, 1999.

Mackesy, Piers. *The War for America, 1775-1783.* Cambridge, Mass.: Harvard University Press, 1964.

Mahan, Alfred Thayer. *The Influence of Sea Power upon History, 1660-1783.* New York: Barnes and Noble Books, 2004.

_____. *Influence of Sea Power upon the French Revolution and Empire, 1793-1812.* 2 vols. Reprint. New York: Greenwood Press, 1968.

Marcus, Geoffrey. *The Age of Nelson: The Royal Navy, 1793-1815.* New York: Viking, 1971.

Marshall-Cornwall, James. *Napoleon as Military Commander.* London: B. T. Batsford, 1967.

Marston, Daniel. *The French-Indian War, 1754-1769.* Oxford, England: Osprey, 2002.

Mintz, Max M. *The Generals of Saratoga: John Burgoyne and Horatio Gates.* New Haven, Conn.: Yale University Press, 1990.

Morrissey, Brendan. *Saratoga, 1777: Turning Point of a Revolution.* Illustrated by Adam Hook. Oxford, England: Osprey, 2000.

Nester, William R. *"Haughty Conquerors": Amherst and the Great Indian Uprising of 1763.* Westport, Conn.: Praeger, 2000.

Palmer, Dave R. *1794: America, Its Army, and the Birth of the Nation.* Novato, Calif.: Presidio Press, 1994.

Palmer, Michael A. *Stoddert's War: Naval Operations During the Quasi-War with France, 1798-1801.* Annapolis, Md.: Naval Institute Press, 2000.

Parker, Geoffrey. *The Military Revolution: Military Innovation and the Rise of the West, 1500-1800.* 2d ed. New York: Cambridge University Press, 1996.

Parkman, Francis. *The Conspiracy of Pontiac and the Indian War After the Conquest of Canada.* 7th ed. Boston: Little, Brown, 1874.

Parrish, Thomas. *The Submarine: A History.* New York: Viking, 2004.

Rodger, A. B. *The War of the Second Coalition, 1798-1801.* Oxford, England: Clarendon Press, 1964.

Roider, Karl A., Jr. *The Reluctant Ally: Austria's Policy in the Austrian-Turkish War, 1737-1739.* Baton Rouge: Louisiana State University Press, 1972.

Rothenberg, Gunther E. *The Art of Warfare in the Age of Napoleon.* Bloomington: Indiana University Press, 1980.

_____. *Napoleon's Great Adversaries: The Archduke Charles and the Austrian Army, 1792-1814.* Bloomington: Indiana University Press, 1982.

Schwartz, Seymoor. *The French and Indian War, 1754-1763: The Imperial Struggle for North America.* New York: Simon & Schuster, 1994.

Scott, Samuel F. *From Yorktown to Valmy.* Boulder: University Press of Colorado, 2003.

Showalter, Dennis. *The Wars of Frederick the Great.* New York: Longman, 1996.

Steele, Ian K. *Warpaths: Invasions of North America.* New York: Oxford University Press, 1994.

Syrett, David. *The Royal Navy in European Waters During the American Revolutionary War.* Columbia: University of South Carolina Press, 1998.

Tebbel, John W. *The Battle of Fallen Timbers, August 20, 1794.* New York: Franklin Watts, 1972.

_____. *Turning the World Upside Down: Inside the American Revolution.* New York: Orion Books, 1993.

Tracy, Nicholas. *Nelson's Battles: The Art of Victory in the Age of Sail.* Annapolis, Md.: Naval Institute Press, 1996.

Tyrrell, John. *Weather and Warfare: A Climatic History of the 1798 Rebellion.* Wilton, County Cork, Ireland: Collins Press, 2001.

Van der Vat, Dan. *Stealth at Sea: The History of the Submarine.* Boston: Houghton Mifflin, 1995.

Warner, Oliver. *The Battle of the Nile.* London: B. T. Batsford, 1960.

Watt, Gavin K. *Rebellion in the Mohawk Valley: The St. Leger Expedition of 1777.* Toronto: Dundurn Press, 2002.

Weigley, Russell F. *The Age of Battles: The Quest for Decisive Warfare from Breitenfeld to Waterloo.* Bloomington: Indiana University Press, 1991.

Williams, Glyn. *The Prize of All the Oceans: Commodore Anson's Daring Voyage and Triumphant Capture of the Spanish Treasure Galleon.* New York: Viking Penguin, 2000.

Wood, W. J. *Battles of the Revolutionary War, 1775-1781.* New York: Da Capo Press, 1995.

MUSIC

Bucchianeri, E. A. *Handel's Path to Covent Garden: A Rocky Journey.* Bloomington, Ind.: 1st Books Library, 2002.

Buelow, George J. *A History of Baroque Music.* Bloomington: Indiana University Press, 2004.

Bullard, Roger A. *Messiah: The Gospel According to Handel's Oratorio.* Grand Rapids: Wm. B. Eerdmans-Lightning Source, 1993.

Burrows, Donald. *Handel: "Messiah."* New York: Cambridge University Press, 1991.

Featherstone, J. Scott. *Hallelujah: The Story of the Coming Forth of Handel's "Messiah."* Eugene: ACW Press, 2001.

Gutman, Robert W. *Mozart: A Cultural Biography.* New York: Harcourt Brace, 1999.

Hindemith, Paul. *J. S. Bach: Heritage and Obligation.* New Haven, Conn.: Yale University Press, 1952.

Hogwood, Christopher. *Handel.* London: Thames & Hudson, 1984.

Kolneder, Walter. *Amadeus Book of the Violin: Construction, History, and Music.* Pompton Plains, N.J.: Amadeus Press, 1998.

Kupferberg, Herbert. *Basically Bach: A Three Hundredth Birthday Celebration.* New York: McGraw-Hill, 1985.

Larsen, Jens Peter. *Handel's Messiah: Origins, Composition, Sources.* New York: W. W. Norton, 1957.

Luckett, Richard, and Diane Sterling. *Handel's "Messiah": A Celebration.* New York: Harvest/HBJ Book, 1995.

Marshall, Robert L. *The Music of Johann Sebastian Bach: The Sources, the Style, the Significance.* New York: Schirmer Books, 1989.

Myers, Robert Manson. *Handel's "Messiah": A Touchstone of Taste.* New York: Octagon Books, 1971.

Pearce, Charles E. *Polly Peachum: The Story of Lavinia Fenton and "The Beggar's Opera."* Reprint. New York: Benjamin Blom, 1968.

Robbins Landon, H. C. *Handel and His World.* Boston: Little, Brown, 1984.

Roth, Henry. *Violin Virtuosos from Paganini to the Twenty-First Century.* Los Angeles: California Classics Books, 1997.

Sadie, Stanley, ed. *New Grove Dictionary of Music and Musicians.* 2d ed. 29 vols. Oxford, England: Oxford University Press, 2001.

Schweitzer, Albert. *J. S. Bach.* Rev. ed. Translated by Ernest Newman. London: A. & C. Black, 1952.

Williams, Peter. *The Life of Bach.* New York: Cambridge University Press, 2004.

Wolff, Christoph. *Johann Sebastian Bach: The Learned Musician.* New York: W. W. Norton, 2000.

NATIVE AMERICANS

Auth, Stephen F. *The Ten Years War: Indian-White Relations in Pennsylvania, 1755-1765.* New York: Garland, 1989.

Carter, Harvey Lewis. *The Life and Times of Little Turtle: First Sagamore of the Wabash.* Urbana: University of Illinois Press, 1987.

Chouinard, Jeffrey. *Mouths of Stone: Stories of the Ancient Maya from Newly Deciphered Inscriptions and Recent Archaeological Discoveries.* Durham, N.C.: Carolina Academic Press, 1995.

Clark, Jerry E. *The Shawnee.* Lexington: University Press of Kentucky, 1993.

Cook, Sherburne Friend. *The Conflict Between the California Indian and White Civilization.* 4 vols. Berkeley: University of California Press, 1943.

Corkran, David H. *The Cherokee Frontier: Conflict and Survival, 1740-1762.* Norman: University of Oklahoma Press, 1962.

Dowd, Gregory Evans. *A Spirited Resistance: The North American Indian Struggle for Unity, 1745-1815.* Baltimore: Johns Hopkins University Press, 1991.

_____. *War Under Heaven: Pontiac, the Indian Nations, and the British Empire*. Baltimore: Johns Hopkins University Press, 2002.

Fenton, William N. *The Great Law and the Longhouse: A Political History of the Iroquois Confederacy*. Norman: University of Oklahoma Press, 1998.

Gosner, Kevin. *Soldiers of the Virgin: The Moral Economy of a Colonial Maya Rebellion*. Tucson: University of Arizona Press, 1992.

Graymont, Barbara. *The Iroquois*. New York: Chelsea House, 1988.

Grinde, Donald A., Jr., and Bruce E. Johansen. "Mohawks, Axes, and Taxes." In *Exemplar of Liberty: Native America and the Evolution of Democracy*. Los Angeles: American Indian Studies Center, University of California, Los Angeles, 1991.

Hagen, William T. *The Sac and Fox Indians*. 2d ed. Norman: University of Oklahoma Press, 1980.

Hamilton, Charles, ed. *Cry of the Thunderbird*. Norman: University of Oklahoma Press, 1972.

Hatley, Tom. *The Dividing Paths: Cherokees and South Carolinians Through the Era of Revolution*. New York: Oxford University Press, 1993.

Hays, H. R. *Children of the Raven: The Seven Indian Nations of the Northwest Coast*. New York: McGraw-Hill, 1975.

Hemming, John. *The Conquest of the Incas*. New York: Harcourt Brace Jovanovich, 1970.

Hughes, Nigel. *Maya Monuments*. Woodbridge, Suffolk, England: Antique Collectors' Club, 2000.

Jennings, Francis. *The Ambiguous Iroquois Empire*. New York: W. W. Norton, 1984.

_____, ed. *The History and Culture of Iroquois Diplomacy: An Interdisciplinary Guide to the Treaties of the Six Nations and Their League*. Syracuse, N.Y.: Syracuse University Press, 1985.

Johansen, Bruce E. *Life and Death in Mohawk Country*. Golden, Colo.: North American Press, 1993.

Johnson, F. Roy. *The Tuscaroras*. Vols. 1-2. Murfreesboro, N.C.: Johnson, 1967.

Josephy, Alvin M., Jr. *Five Hundred Nations: An Illustrated History of North American Indians*. New York: Alfred A. Knopf, 1994.

Kraft, Herbert C. *The Lenape-Delaware Indian Heritage, 10,000 B.C.-A.D. 2000*. Stanhope, N.J.: Lenape Lifeways, 2001.

Lightfoot, Kent G. *Indians, Missionaries, and Merchants: The Legacy of Colonial Encounters on the California Frontiers*. Berkeley: University of California Press, 2005.

Macleod, Murdo J., and Robert Wasserstrom, eds. *Spaniards and Indians in Southeastern Mesoamerica: Essays on the History of Ethnic Relations*. Lincoln: University of Nebraska Press, 1983.

Merritt, Jane T. *At the Crossroads: Indians and Empires on a Mid-Atlantic Frontier, 1700-1763*. Chapel Hill: University of North Carolina Press, 2003.

Murphy, Lucy Eldersveld. *A Gathering of Rivers: Indians, Metis, and Mining in the Western Great Lakes, 1737-1832*. Lincoln: University of Nebraska Press, 2000.

Oliphant, John. *Peace and War on the Cherokee Frontier, 1756-1763*. Baton Rogue: Louisiana State University Press, 2001.

Parker, Arthur. *Parker on the Iroquois*. Edited by William Fenton. Syracuse, N.Y.: Syracuse University Press, 1968.

Pencak, William A., and Daniel K. Richter, eds. *Friends and Enemies in Penn's Woods: Indians, Colonists, and the Racial Construction of Pennsylvania*. University Park: Pennsylvania State University Press, 2004.

Richter, Daniel K., and James H. Merrell. *Beyond the Covenant Chain: The Iroquois and Their Neighbors in Indian North America, 1600-1800*. With a new preface by Daniel K. Richter and James H. Merrell; foreword by Wilcomb E. Washburn. University Park: Pennsylvania State University Press, 2003.

Ringle, William M. and Thomas C. Smith-Stark. *A Concordance to the Inscriptions of Palenque, Chiapas, Mexico*. New Orleans: Middle American Research Institute, Tulane University, 1996.

Ross, Thomas E. *American Indians in North Carolina: Geographic Interpretations*. Southern Pines, N.C.: Karo Hollow Press, 1999.

Sandos, James A. *Converting California: Indians and Franciscans in the Missions*. New Haven, Conn.: Yale University Press, 2004.

Schele, Linda, and David Freidel. *A Forest of Kin: The Untold Story of the Anicient Maya*. New York: W. Morrow, 1992.

Snow, Dean R. *The Iroquois*. Cambridge, Mass.: Blackwell, 1994.

Stavig, Ward. *The World of Tupac Amaru: Conflict, Community, and Identity in Colonial Peru*. Lincoln: University of Nebraska Press, 1999.

Swartzler, David. *A Friend Among the Senecas: The Quaker Mission to Cornplanter's People*. Mechanicsburg, Pa.: Stackpole Books, 2000.

Sword, Wiley. *President Washington's Indian War: The Struggle for the Old Northwest, 1790-1795*. Norman: University of Oklahoma Press, 1985.

Tanner, Helen Hornbeck, ed. *Atlas of Great Lakes Indian History*. Norman: University of Oklahoma Press, 1987.

Thomas, David Hurst, et al. *The Native Americans: An Illustrated History*. Atlanta, Ga.: Turner, 1993.

Waldman, Carl. *Encyclopedia of Native American Tribes*. New York: Facts on File, 1988.

Wallace, Anthony F. C. *The Death and Rebirth of the Seneca*. New York: Alfred A. Knopf, 1970.

Wallace, Paul A. W. *Indians in Pennsylvania*. Harrisburg: Pennsylvania Historical and Museum Commission, 1981.

Washburn, Wilcomb E., ed. *History of Indian-White Relations*. Vol. 4 in *Handbook of North American Indians*, edited by William C. Sturtevant. Washington, D.C.: Smithsonian Institution Press, 1988.

White, Richard. *The Middle Ground: Indians, Empires, and Republics in the Great Lakes Region, 1650-1815*. New York: Cambridge University Press, 1991.

Wilson, Edmund, and Joseph Mitchell. *"Apologies to the Iroquois" with "A Study of the Mohawks in High Steel."* Syracuse, N.Y.: Syracuse University Press, 1992.

Winger, Otho. *Last of the Miamis: Little Turtle*. North Manchester, Ind.: O. Winger, 1935.

Wright, Ronald. *Stolen Continents*. Boston: Houghton Mifflin, 1992.

PHILOSOPHY

Aarsleff, Hans, ed. *Condillac: Essay on the Origin of Human Knowledge*. Cambridge, England: Cambridge University Press, 2001.

Adler, Hans, and Ernest A. Menze. *On World History: Johann Gottfried Herder*. New York: M. E. Sharpe, 1997.

Adorno, Theodor. *Kant's "Critique of Pure Reason."* Stanford, Calif.: Stanford University Press, 2001.

Ameriks, Karl. *Kant and the Fate of Autonomy: Problems in the Appropriation of the Critical Philosophy*. Cambridge, England: Cambridge University Press, 2000.

Avery, John. *Progress, Poverty, and Population: Rereading Condorcet, Godwin, and Malthus*. London: F. Cass, 1997.

Baier, Annette C. *A Progress of Sentiments: Reflections of Hume's "Treatise."* Cambridge, Mass.: Harvard University Press, 1994.

Becker, Carl Lotus. *The Heavenly City of the Eighteenth Century Philosophers*. New Haven, Conn.: Yale University Press, 2003.

Bedani, Gino. *Vico Revisited*. Oxford, England: Oxford University Press, 1989.

Burke, Edmund. *Reflections on the Revolution in France*. Edited by L. G. Mitchell. London: Oxford University Press, 1999.

Capaldi, Nicholas. *David Hume: The Newtonian Philosopher*. Boston: Twayne, 1975.

Carrithers, David W., Michael A. Mosher, and Paul A. Rahe, eds. *Montesquieu's Science of Politics: Essays on "The Spirit of the Laws."* Lanham, Md.: Rowman & Littlefield, 2001.

Cullen, Daniel. *Freedom in Rousseau's Political Philosophy*. DeKalb: Northern Illinois University Press, 1993.

Dicker, Georges. *Kant's Theory of Knowledge: An Analytical Introduction*. New York: Oxford University Press, 2004.

Evrigenis, Ioannis, and Daniel Pellerin. *Johann Gottfried Herder: Another Philosophy of History and Selected Political Writing*. Indianapolis: Hackett, 2004.

Flew, Antony. *Hume's Philosophy of Belief*. London: Routledge and Kegan Paul, 1961.

Forster, Michael. *Johann Gottfried Von Herder: Philosophical Writings*. Cambridge, England: Cambridge University Press, 2002.

Gardner, Sebastian. *Kant and the "Critique of Pure Reason."* London: Routledge, 2000.

Grimsley, Ronald. *Jean d'Alembert, 1717-1783*. Oxford, England: Clarendon Press, 1963.

Hankins, Thomas L. *Jean d'Alembert: Science and the Enlightenment*. Oxford, England: Clarendon Press, 1970.

Hanna, Robert. *Kant and the Foundations of Analytic Philosophy*. New York: Oxford University Press, 2004.

Hartnack, Justus. *Kant's Theory of Knowledge: An Introduction to the "Critique of Pure Reason."* Indianapolis: Hackett, 2001.

Hine, Ellen McNiven. *A Critical Study of Condillac's "Traité des systèmes."* The Hague: Martinus Nijhoff, 1979.

Holbach, Paul-Henri Thiry d'. *System of Nature*. Manchester, England: Clinamen Press, 2000.

Horowitz, Irving Louis. *Claude Helvetius: Philosopher of Democracy and Enlightenment*. New York: Pain-Whitman, 1954.

Hume, David. *An Enquiry Concerning Human Understanding: A Critical Edition*. Edited by Tom L. Beauchamp. Oxford, England: Clarendon, 2000.

_____. *An Enquiry Concerning the Principles of Morals: A Critical Edition*. Edited by Tom L. Beauchamp. Oxford, England: Clarendon, 1998.

_____. *A Treatise of Human Nature.* Edited by David Fate Norton and Mary J. Norton. New York: Oxford University Press, 2000.

Johnson, Oliver A. *The Mind of David Hume: A Companion to Book I of "A Treatise of Human Nature."* Chicago: University of Illinois Press, 1995.

Keohane, Nannerl. *Philosophy and the State in France: The Renaissance to the Enlightenment.* Princeton, N.J.: Princeton University Press, 1980.

Knight, Isabel F. *The Geometric Spirit: The Abbé de Condillac and the French Enlightenment.* New Haven, Conn.: Yale University Press, 1968.

Kors, Alan Charles. *D'Holbach's Coterie: An Enlightenment in Paris.* Princeton, N.J.: Princeton University Press, 1976.

Kuehn, Manfred. *Kant: A Biography.* New York: Cambridge University Press, 2001.

La Vopa, Anthony J. *Fichte: The Self and the Calling of Philosophy, 1762-1799.* Cambridge, England: Cambridge University Press, 2001.

Livinton, Donald W., and James T. King. *Hume: A Reevaluation.* New York: Fordham University Press, 1976.

Mali, Joseph. *The Rehabilitation of Myth: Vico's "New Science."* Cambridge, England: Cambridge University Press, 1992.

Manuel, F. E. *The Eighteenth Century Confronts the Gods.* Cambridge, Mass.: Harvard University Press, 1959.

Mooney, Michael. *Vico in the Tradition of Rhetoric.* Princeton, N.J.: Princeton University Press, 1985.

Mossner, Ernest C. *The Life of David Hume.* 2d ed. Oxford, England: Clarendon Press, 1980.

Norton, David Fate. *David Hume: Common-Sense Moralist, Sceptical Metaphysician.* Princeton, N.J.: Princeton University Press, 1982.

O'Neal, John C. *The Authority of Experience: Sensationalist Theory in the French Enlightenment.* University Park: Pennsylvania State University Press, 1996.

Pompa, Leon. *Vico: A Study of "The New Science."* 2d ed. Cambridge, England: Cambridge University Press, 1990.

Qvortrup, Mads. *The Political Philosophy of Jean-Jacques Rousseau: The Impossibility of Reason.* Manchester, England: Manchester University Press, 2003.

Rosenfeld, Sophia. *A Revolution in Language: The Problem of Signs in Late Eighteenth-Century France.* Stanford, Calif.: Stanford University Press, 2001.

Sassen, Brigitte, ed. *Kant's Early Critics: The Empiricist Critique of the Theoretical Philosophy.* Cambridge, England: Cambridge University Press, 2000.

Savile, Anthony. *Kant's "Critique of Pure Reason": An Orientation to the Central Theme.* Malden, Mass.: Blackwell, 2005.

Sedgwick, Sally S., ed. *The Reception of Kant's Critical Philosophy: Fichte, Schelling, and Hegel.* Cambridge, England: Cambridge University Press, 2000.

Smith, David. *Helvétius: A Study in Persecution.* Oxford, England: Clarendon Press, 1965.

Smith, Norman Kemp. *A Commentary to Kant's "Critique of Pure Reason."* New York: Palgrave Macmillan, 2003.

Yolton, John W., ed. *Philosophy, Religion, and Science in the Seventeenth and Eighteenth Centuries.* Rochester, N.Y.: University of Rochester Press, 1990.

POLITICAL THOUGHT

Aldrich, John H. *Why Politics? The Origin and Transformation of Political Parties in America.* Chicago: University of Chicago Press, 1995.

Aldridge, A. Owen. *Thomas Paine's American Ideology.* Newark: University of Delaware Press, 1984.

Allen, W. B., and Kevin A. Cloonan. *The Federalist Papers: A Commentary—"The Baton Rouge Lectures."* New York: P. Lang, 2000.

Amar, Akhil Reed. *The Bill of Rights: Creation and Reconstruction.* New Haven, Conn.: Yale University Press, 1998.

Ayling, Stanley Edward. *Edmund Burke: His Life and Opinions.* New York: St. Martin's Press, 1988.

Ben-Atar, Doron, and Barbara B. Oberg, eds. *Federalists Reconsidered.* Charlottesville: University Press of Virginia, 1998.

Berkin, Carol. *A Brilliant Solution: Inventing the American Constitution.* New York: Harcourt, 2002.

Blakemore, Steven. *Intertextual War: Edmund Burke and the French Revolution in the Writings of Mary Wollstonecraft, Thomas Paine, and James Mackintosh.* Cranbury, N.J.: Associated University Presses, 1997.

Brenner, Lenni. *The Lesser Evil.* Secaucus, N.J.: Lyle Stuart, 1988.

Broadus, Mitchell, and Louise P. Mitchell. *A Biography of the Constitution of the United States: Its Origin, Formation, Adoption, Interpretation.* New York: Oxford University Press, 1965.

Callahan, Kerry P. *The Articles of Confederation: A Primary Source Investigation into the Document That Preceded the U.S. Constitution.* New York: Rosen Primary Source, 2003.

Claeys, Gregory. *The Political Thought of Thomas Paine.* Winchester, Mass.: Unwin Hyman, 1989.

Cohler, Anne. *Montesquieu's Comparative Politics and the Spirit of American Constitutionalism*. Lawrence: University Press of Kansas, 1988.

Dietze, Gottfried. *"The Federalist": A Classic on Federalism and Free Government*. Baltimore: Johns Hopkins University Press, 1960.

Epstein, David F. *The Political Theory of "The Federalist."* Chicago: University of Chicago Press, 1984.

Fennessey, R. R. *Burke, Paine, and the Rights of Man: A Difference of Political Opinion*. The Hague: Martinus Nijhoff, 1963.

Foner, Eric, ed. *Thomas Paine: Collected Writings*. New York: Library of America, 1995.

Freeman, Michael. *Edmund Burke and the Critique of Political Radicalism*. Chicago: University of Chicago Press, 1980.

Gerber, Scott Douglas, ed. *The Declaration of Independence: Origins and Impact*. Washington, D.C.: CQ Press, 2002.

Hamilton, Alexander, John Jay, and James Madison. *The Federalist*. Annotated by Jacob E. Cooke. Middletown, Conn.: Wesleyan University Press, 1961.

Hampson, Norman. *Will and Circumstance: Montesquieu, Rousseau, and the French Revolution*. Norman: University of Oklahoma Press, 1983.

Kelly, Christopher. *Rousseau's Exemplary Life: The "Confessions" as Political Philosophy*. Ithaca: Cornell University Press, 1987.

Kenyon, Cecelia M., ed. *The Antifederalists*. Indianapolis: Bobbs-Merrill, 1966.

Kesler, Charles, ed. *Saving the Revolution: The Federalist Papers and the American Founding*. New York: Free Press, 1987.

Levine, Andrew. *The General Will: Rousseau, Marx, Communism*. New York: Cambridge University Press, 1993.

Levy, Leonard W., and Dennis J. Mahoney. *The Framing and Ratification of the Constitution*. New York: Macmillan, 1987.

Lewis, John D., ed. *Anti-Federalists Versus Federalists: Selected Documents*. San Francisco: Chandler, 1967.

Lewis, Thomas T., ed. *The Bill of Rights*. 2 vols. Pasadena, Calif.: Salem Press, 2002.

McCoy, Drew R. *The Elusive Republic: Political Economy in Jefferson's America*. Chapel Hill: University of North Carolina Press, 1980.

McDonald, Forrest. *"Novus Ordo Seclorum": The Intellectual Origins of the Constitution*. Lawrence: University Press of Kansas, 1985.

McWilliams, Wilson Carey, and Michael T. Gibbons, eds. *The Federalists, the Antifederalists, and the American Political Tradition*. New York: Greenwood Press, 1992.

Maier, Pauline. *American Scripture: Making the Declaration of Independence*. New York: Random House, 1997.

Medina, Vicente. *Social Contract Theories: Political Obligation or Anarchy?* Savage, Md.: Rowman & Littlefield, 1990.

Peck, Robert S. *The Bill of Rights and the Politics of Interpretation*. St. Paul, Minn.: West, 1992.

Peters, William. *A More Perfect Union: The Making of the United States Constitution*. New York: Crown, 1987.

Portis, Edward B. *Reconstructing the Classics: Political Theory from Plato to Marx*. Chatham, N.J.: Chatham House, 1994.

Potter, Kathleen O. *"The Federalist's" Vision of Popular Sovereignty in the New American Republic*. New York: LFB Scholarly, 2002.

Putnam, William Lowell. *John Peter Zenger and the Fundamental Freedom*. Jefferson, N.C.: McFarland, 1997.

Rakove, Jack N. *Original Meaning: Politics and Ideas in the Making of the Constitution*. New York: A. A. Knopf, 1996.

Rutland, Robert A. *Birth of the Bill of Rights, 1776-1791*. Chapel Hill: University of North Carolina Press, 1955.

Sack, James J. *From Jacobite to Conservative*. New York: Cambridge University Press, 2002.

White, Morton Gabriel. *Philosophy, "The Federalist," and the Constitution*. New York: Oxford University Press, 1987.

PRUSSIA AND THE GERMAN STATES

Asprey, Robert B. *Frederick the Great: The Magnificent Enigma*. New York: Ticknor & Fields, 1986.

Duffy, Christopher. *The Army of Frederick the Great*. 2d ed. Chicago: Emperor's Press, 1996.

_____. *Prussia's Glory: Rossbach and Leuthen, 1757*. Chicago: Emperor's Press, 2003.

Dwyer, Philip G., ed. *The Rise of Prussia, 1700-1830*. New York: Longman, 2000.

Fay, Sidney B. *The Rise of Brandenburg-Prussia to 1786*. Rev. ed. by Klaus Epstein. New York: Holt, Rinehart and Winston, 1964.

Fischer-Fabian, S. *Prussia's Glory: The Rise of a Military State*. Translated by Lore Segal and Paul Stern. New York: Macmillan, 1981.

Fraser, David. *Frederick the Great: King of Prussia.* New York: A. Lane, 2000.

Friedrich, Karin. *The Other Prussia: Royal Prussia, Poland, and Liberty, 1569-1772.* New York: Cambridge University Press, 2000.

Gagliardo, John G. *Germany Under the Old Regime, 1600-1790.* New York: Longmans, 1991.

Hagen, W. *Ordinary Prussians: Brandenburg Junkers and Villagers, 1500-1840.* New York: Cambridge University Press, 2002.

Hahn, H. G. *German Thought and Culture from the Holy Roman Empire to the Present Day.* Manchester, England: Manchester University Press, 1995.

Holborn, Hajo. *1648-1840.* Vol. 2 in *A History of Modern Germany.* New York: Alfred A. Knopf, 1964.

Koch, H. W. *A History of Prussia.* New York: Longman, 1978.

MacDonogh, Giles. *Frederick the Great: A Life in Deed and Letters.* London: Weidenfeld and Nicolson, 1999.

Redman, Alvin. *The House of Hanover.* Reprint. New York: Funk & Wagnalls, 1969.

Ritter, Gerhardt. *Frederick the Great: A Historical Profile.* Translated, with an introduction, by Peter Paret. Berkeley: University of California Press, 1968.

Scott, H. M., et al. *The Emergence of the Eastern Powers, 1756-1775.* Cambridge, England: Cambridge University Press, 2001.

Sheehan, James J. *German History, 1770-1866.* Oxford, England: Oxford University Press, 1993.

Weill, H. *Frederick the Great and Samuel von Cocceji.* Madison: University of Wisconsin Press, 1961.

RELIGION

Addison, James Thayer. *The Episcopal Church in the United States, 1789-1931.* New York: Charles Scribner's Sons, 1951.

Anderson, John L. *Night of the Silent Drums.* New York: Charles Scribner's Sons, 1975.

Andrews, Dee E. *The Methodists and Revolutionary America, 1760-1800: The Shaping of an Evangelical Culture.* Princeton, N.J.: Princeton University Press, 2000.

Aveling, J. C. H. *The Jesuits.* Briarcliff Manor: Stein and Day, 1982.

Barthel, Manfred. *The Jesuits: History and Legend of the Society of Jesus.* Translated by Mark Howson. New York: Morrow, 1984.

Bellew, Christopher Brent. *The Impact of African-American Antecedents on the Baptist Foreign Missionary Movement, 1782-1825.* Lewiston, N.Y.: Edwin Mellen Press, 2004.

Bridenbaugh, Carl. *Mitre and Sceptre: Transatlantic Faiths, Ideas, Personalities, and Politics, 1689-1775.* New York: Oxford University Press, 1962.

Brockway, Robert W. *A Wonderful Work of God: Puritanism and the Great Awakening.* Bethlehem, Penn.: Lehigh University Press, 2003.

Bucke, Emory Stephens, ed. *The History of American Methodism.* 3 vols. New York: Abingdon Press, 1964.

Chorley, E. Clowes. *Men and Movements in the American Episcopal Church.* New York: Charles Scribner's Sons, 1950.

Chung, David. *Syncretism: The Religious Context of Christian Beginnings in Korea.* Albany: State University of New York Press, 2001.

Cleveland, Catherine C. *The Great Revival in the West, 1797-1805.* 1916. Reprint. Gloucester, Mass.: Peter Smith, 1959.

Cordara, Giulio Cesare. *On the Suppression of the Society of Jesus: A Contemporary Account.* Translated by John P. Murphy. Chicago: Loyola Press, 1999.

Costo, Rupert, and Jeannette Henry Costo, eds. *The Missions of California: A Legacy of Genocide.* San Francisco, Calif.: Indian Historian Press, 1987.

Cragg, G. R. *The Church and the Age of Reason, 1648-1789.* New York: Atheneum, 1961.

Cross, Whitney W. R. *The Burned-Over District: The Social and Intellectual History of Enthusiastic Religion in Western New York, 1800-1850.* Ithaca, N.Y.: Cornell University Press, 1950.

Denzinger, Heinrich J. D. *The Sources of Catholic Dogma.* St. Louis: Herder, 1957.

Doyle, William. *Jansenism: Catholic Resistance to Authority from the Reformation to the French Revolution.* New York: St. Martin's Press, 2000.

Duncan, Thomas Bentley. "Pombal and the Suppression of the Portuguese Jesuits: An Inquiry into Causes and Motives." Unpublished master's thesis. Chicago: University of Chicago, 1961.

Englehardt, Zephyrin. *The Missions and Missionaries of California.* 4 vols. Santa Barbara, Calif.: Mission Santa Barbara, 1929.

Fauske, Christopher J. *Jonathan Swift and the Church of Ireland, 1710-1724.* Dublin: Irish Academic Press, 2002.

Fitts, LeRoy. *A History of Black Baptists.* Nashville, Tenn.: Broadman Press, 1985.

Fitzmier, John R. *New England's Moral Legislator: Timothy Dwight, 1752-1817.* Bloomington: Indiana University Press, 1998.

Gaustad, Edwin S. *The Great Awakening in New England*. New York: Harper & Row, 1957.

Gawthrop, Richard L. *Pietism and the Making of Eighteenth-Century Prussia*. Cambridge, England: Cambridge University Press, 1993.

Geiger, Maynard J. *The Life and Times of Fray Junipero Serra, OFM*. 2 vols. Washington, D.C.: Academy of American Franciscan History, 1959.

George, Carol V. R. *Segregated Sabbaths: Richard Allen and the Emergence of Independent Black Churches, 1760-1840*. New York: Oxford University Press, 1973.

Goen, Clarence C. *Revivalism and Separatism in New England, 1740-1800: Strict Congregationalists and Separate Baptists in the Great Awakening*. Hamden, Conn.: Archon Books, 1969.

Hatchett, Marion J. *The Making of the First American Book of Common Prayer, 1776-1789*. New York: Seabury Press, 1982.

Holmes, David L. *A Brief History of the Episcopal Church*. Valley Forge, Pa.: Trinity Press, 1993.

Howe, Mark De Wolfe. *The Garden and the Wilderness: Religion and Government in American Constitutional History*. Chicago: University of Chicago Press, 1965.

James, Sydney V. *A People Among Peoples: Quaker Benevolence in Eighteenth Century America*. Cambridge, Mass.: Harvard University Press, 1963.

Johnson, Charles A. *The Frontier Camp Meeting: Religion's Harvest Time*. Reprint. New introduction by Ferenc M. Szasz. Dallas, Tex.: Southern Methodist University Press, 1985.

Johnson, Paul C., et al., eds. *The California Missions: A Pictorial History*. Menlo Park, Calif.: Lane, 1985.

Jones, George Fenwick, ed. *The Salzburger Saga: Religious Exiles and Other Germans Along the Savannah*. Athens: University of Georgia Press, 1984.

Kreiser, Robert. *Miracles, Convulsions, and Ecclesiastical Politics in Early Eighteenth Century Paris*. Princeton, N.J.: Princeton University Press, 1978.

Lambert, Frank. *The Founding Fathers and the Place of Religion in America*. Princeton, N.J.: Princeton University Press, 2003.

_____. *Inventing the Great Awakening*. Princeton, N.J.: Princeton University Press, 1999.

Latourette, Kenneth Scott. *A History of Christianity*. San Francisco, Calif.: Harper, 1953.

Lincoln, C. Eric, and Lawrence H. Mamiya. *The Black Church in the African American Experience*. Durham, N.C.: Duke University Press, 1990.

Luccock, Halford, and Paul Hutchinson. *The Story of Methodism*. New York: Abingdon-Cokesbury Press, 1949.

Luchettik, Cathy. *Under God's Spell: Frontier Evangelists, 1722-1915*. New York: Harcourt Brace Jovanovich, 1989.

McEllhenney, John G., ed. *United Methodism in America: A Compact History*. Nashville, Tenn.: Abingdon Press, 1992.

McLoughlin, William G. *Revivals, Awakening, and Reform: An Essay on Religion and Social Change in America, 1607-1977*. Chicago: University of Chicago Press, 1978.

McManners, John. *The Clerical Establishment and Its Ramifications*. Vol. 1 in *Church and Society in Eighteenth Century France*. London: Oxford University Press, 1999.

Mansfield, Stephen. *Forgotten Founding Father: The Heroic Legacy of George Whitefield*. Nashville, Tenn.: Highland Books/Cumberland House, 2001.

Mapp, Alf J., Jr. *The Faith of Our Fathers: What America's Founders Really Believed*. Lanham, Md.: Rowman & Littlefield, 2003.

Marsden, George M. *Jonathan Edwards: A Life*. New Haven, Conn.: Yale University Press, 2003.

Marshall, Paul Victor. *One Catholic, and Apostolic: Samuel Seabury and the Early Episcopal Church*. New York: Church, 2004.

Maxson, Charles H. *The Great Awakening in the Middle Colonies*. Chicago: University of Chicago Press, 1920.

Morner, M., ed. *The Expulsion of the Jesuits from Latin America*. New York: Knopf, 1965.

Murray, Jocelyn. *Proclaim the Good News: A Short History of the Church Missionary Society*. London: Hodder and Stoughton, 1985.

Nash, Gary B. *Quakers and Politics: Pennsylvania, 1681-1726*. Princeton, N.J.: Princeton University Press, 1968.

Neill, Stephen. *A History of Christian Missions*. 2d ed. Harmondsworth, Middlesex, England: Penguin Books, 1994.

Noll, Mark A., ed. *Religion and American Politics: From the Colonial Period to the 1980's*. New York: Oxford University Press, 1990.

Norwood, Frederick A. *The Story of American Methodism*. Nashville, Tenn.: Abingdon Press, 1974.

Pastor, Ludwig. *History of the Popes from the Close of the Middle Ages*. Vol. 33. Translated by Ernest Graff. St. Louis: Herder, 1923-1969.

Perciaccante, Marianne. *Calling Down Fire: Charles*

Grandison Finney and Revivalism in Jefferson County, New York, 1800-1840. Albany: State University of New York Press, 2003.

Peterson, Merrill D., and Robert C. Vaughan, eds. *The Virginia Statute for Religious Freedom: Its Evolution and Consequences in American History*. New York: Cambridge University Press, 1988.

Phillips, C. H. *The History of the Colored Methodist Episcopal Church in America*. 1898. Reprint. New York: Arno Press, 1972.

Posey, Walter B. *Frontier Mission: A History of Religion West of the Southern Appalachians*. Lexington: University Press of Kentucky, 1966.

Rhoden, Nancy L. *Revolutionary Anglicanism: The Colonial Church of England Clergy During the American Revolution*. New York: New York University Press, 1999.

Richey, Russell E. *Early American Methodism*. Bloomington: Indiana University Press, 1991.

Sernett, Milton C. *Afro-American Religious History: A Documentary Witness*. Durham, N.C.: Duke University Press, 1985.

Stanley, Brian. *The History of the Baptist Missionary Society, 1792-1972*. Edinburgh: T & T Clark, 1992.

Stout, Harry S. *The Divine Dramatist: George Whitefield and the Rise of Modern Evangelicalism*. Grand Rapids, Mich.: Wm. B. Eerdmans, 1991.

Thomas, George W. *Revivalism and Cultural Change: Christianity, Nation Building, and the Market in the Nineteenth-Century United States*. Chicago: University of Chicago Press, 1989.

Trinterud, Leonard J. *The Forming of an American Tradition: A Re-examination of Colonial Presbyterianism*. Philadelphia: Westminster Press, 1949.

Van Kley, Dale K. *The Religious Origins of the French Revolution: From Calvin to the Civil Constitution, 1560-1791*. New Haven, Conn.: Yale University Press, 1996.

Wald, Kenneth D. *Religion and Politics in the United States*. 2d ed. Washington, D.C.: Congressional Quarterly Press, 1992.

Ward, Kevin, and Brian Stanley, eds. *The Church Mission Society and World Christianity, 1799-1999*. Grand Rapids, Mich.: W. B. Eerdmans, 2000.

Washington, James Melvin. *Frustrated Fellowship: The Black Quest for Social Power*. Paperback ed. with new preface by Quentin H. Dixie and a new foreword by Cornell West. Mercer, Ga.: Mercer University Press, 2004.

Wigger, John H. *Taking Heaven by Storm: Methodism*

and the Rise of Popular Christianity in America. New York: Oxford University Press, 1998.

Wright, Jonathan. *God's Soldiers—Adventure, Politics, Intrigue, and Power: A History of the Jesuits*. New York: Doubleday, 2004.

RUSSIA AND POLAND

Alexander, John T. *Autocratic Politics in a National Crisis: The Imperial Russian Government and Pugachev's Revolt, 1773-1775*. Bloomington: Indiana University Press, 1969.

_____. *Catherine the Great: Life and Legend*. New York: Oxford University Press, 1989.

Anderson, M. S. *Peter the Great: Profiles in Power*. 2d ed. New York: Longman, 1995.

Ascherson, Neal. *The Struggles for Poland*. New York: Random House, 1987.

Avrich, Paul. *Russian Rebels, 1600-1800*. New York: Schocken, 1972.

Barratt, Glynn. *Russia in Pacific Waters, 1715-1825*. Vancouver: University of British Columbia Press, 1981.

Beik, William. *The Modernisation of Russia, 1676-1825*. New York: Cambridge University Press, 1999.

Black, Lydia T. *Russians in Alaska, 1732-1867*. Fairbanks: University of Alaska Press, 2004.

Bushkovitch, Paul. *Peter the Great*. Lanham, Md.: Rowman & Littlefield, 2001.

Cooper, Leonard. *Many Roads to Moscow: Three Historical Invasions*. New York: Coward-McCann, 1968.

Cracraft, James. *The Revolution of Peter the Great*. Cambridge, Mass.: Harvard University Press, 2003.

Curtis, Mina Kirstein. *A Forgotten Empress: Anna Ivanova and Her Era, 1730-1740*. New York: Ungar, 1974.

Davies, Norman. *Heart of Europe: The Past in Poland's Present*. New ed. Oxford, England: Oxford University Press, 2001.

De Madariaga, Isabel. *Catherine the Great: A Short History*. New Haven, Conn.: Yale University Press, 2002.

Dixon, Simon. *Catherine the Great*. New York: Longman, 2001.

Dukes, Paul. *Catherine the Great and the Russian Nobility: A Study Based on the Materials of the Legislative Commission of 1767*. London: Cambridge University Press, 1967.

_____. *The Making of Russian Absolutism, 1613-1801*. 2d ed. New York: Longman, 1990.

Fedorowicz, J. K., ed. *Republic of Nobles: Studies in Polish History to 1864.* Cambridge, England: Cambridge University Press, 1982.

Florinsky, Michael T. *Russia: A History and an Interpretation.* Vol. 1. Reprint. New York: Macmillan, 1973.

Hughes, Lindsey. *Russia in the Age of Peter the Great.* New Haven, Conn.: Yale University Press, 1998.

Kamenskii, Aleksandr Borisovich. *The Russian Empire in the Eighteenth Century: Searching for a Place in the World.* New York: M. E. Sharpe, 1997.

Lincoln, W. Bruce. *Sunlight at Midnight: St. Petersburg and the Rise of Modern Russia.* New York: Basic Books, 2000.

Lord, Robert. *The Second Partition of Poland.* Cambridge, England: Cambridge University Press, 1915.

Lukowski, Jerzy. *The Partitions of Poland: 1772, 1793, 1795.* London: Longman, 1999.

Lukowski, Jerzy, and Herbert Zawadzki. *A Concise History of Poland.* Cambridge, England: Cambridge University Press, 2001.

Montefiore, S. S. *Potemkin: Catherine the Great's Imperial Partner.* New York: Vintage, 2005.

Reddaway, W. F., et al. *The Cambridge History of Poland, 1697-1935.* New York: Octagon Books, 1978.

Scott, H. M. *The Emergence of the Eastern Powers, 1756-1775.* New York: Cambridge University Press, 2001.

Starr, S. Frederick, ed. *Russia's American Colony.* Durham, N.C.: Duke University Press, 1987.

Sutton, John L. *The King's Honor and the King's Cardinal: The War of Polish Succession.* Lexington: University Press of Kentucky, 1980.

Wandycz, Piotr S. *The Lands of Partitioned Poland, 1795-1918.* Seattle: University of Washington Press, 1974.

SCANDINAVIA AND THE LOW COUNTRIES

Bain, Robert Nisbet. *Charles XII and the Collapse of the Swedish Empire, 1682-1719.* Freedport, N.Y.: Books for Libraries Press, 1964.

Derry, T. K. *A History of Scandinavia.* Minneapolis: University of Minnesota Press, 1979.

De Vries, Jan. *The First Modern Economy: Success, Failure, and Perseverance of the Dutch Economy, 1500-1815.* Cambridge, England: Cambridge University Press, 1997.

Hatton, R. M. *Charles XII of Sweden.* New York: Weybright and Talley, 1968.

Israel, Jonathan Irvine. *The Dutch Republic: Its Rise, Greatness, and Fall, 1477-1806.* Oxford, England: Clarendon Press, 1995.

Jespersen, Knud J. V. *A History of Denmark.* Translated by Ivan Hill. New York: Palgrave Macmillan, 2004.

Nordstrom, Byron. *Scandinavia Since 1500.* Minneapolis: University of Minnesota Press, 2000.

Schama, Simon. *The Embarrassment of Riches: An Interpretation of Dutch Culture in the Golden Ages.* Berkeley: University of California Press, 1987.

Westergaard, Waldemar. *The Danish West Indies, 1671-1917.* New York: Macmillan, 1917.

SCIENCE

Andrade, E. N. da C. *Sir Isaac Newton: His Life and Work.* New York: Macmillan, 1954.

Andrewes, William J. H., ed. *The Quest for Longitude: The Proceedings of the Longitude Symposium, Harvard University.* Cambridge, Mass.: Collection of Historical Scientific Instruments, Harvard University, 1996.

Armitage, Angus. *William Herschel.* Garden City, N.Y.: Doubleday, 1963.

Asimov, Isaac. *The History of Physics.* New York: Walker, 1966.

Bensaude-Vincent, Bernadette, and Isabelle Stengers. *A History of Chemistry.* Cambridge, Mass.: Harvard University Press, 1997.

Bernal, J. D. *A History of Classical Physics from Antiquity to the Quantum.* New York: Barnes & Noble, 1997.

Blunt, Wilfrid. *Linnaeus: The Compleat Naturalist.* Princeton, N.J.: Princeton University Press, 2001.

Bodanis, David. *Electric Universe: The Shocking True Story of Electricity.* New York: Crown, 2005.

Brock, William H. *The Chemical Tree: A History of Chemistry.* New York: W. W. Norton, 2000.

Buffon, Georges-Louis Leclerc. *Natural History, General and Particular.* Translated by William Smellie. Bristol, England: Thoemmes Press, 2001.

Cartwright, David E. *Tides: A Scientific History.* Cambridge, England: Cambridge University Press, 1999.

Chang, Hasok. *Inventing Temperature: Measurement and Scientific Progress.* Oxford, England: Oxford University Press, 2004.

Christianson, David. *Timepieces: Masterpieces of Chronometry.* New York: Firefly Books, 2002.

Christianson, Gale E. *In the Presence of the Creator: Isaac Newton and His Times.* New York: Free Press, 1984.

Clow, A., and N. C. Clow. *The Chemical Revolution.* Freeport, N.Y.: Books for Libraries, 1970.

Cohen, I. Bernard. *Benjamin Franklin's Science.* Cambridge, Mass.: Harvard University Press, 1990.

_____. *Revolution in Science.* Cambridge, Mass.: Harvard University Press, 2000.

Cohen, I. Bernard, and George E. Smith, eds. *The Cambridge Companion to Newton.* New York: Cambridge University Press, 2002.

Conant, James Bryant. *The Overthrow of the Phlogiston Theory: The Chemical Revolution of 1775-1789.* Cambridge, Mass.: Harvard University Press, 1967.

Cook, Alan. *Edmond Halley: Charting the Heavens and the Seas.* Oxford, England: Clarendon Press, 1998.

Crawford, Deborah. *King's Astronomer William Herschel.* New York: Julian Messner, 2000.

Dale, Andrew I. *Most Honourable Remembrance: The Life and Work of Thomas Bayes.* New York: Springer, 2003.

Dash, Joan. *The Longitude Prize.* New York: Farrar, Straus and Giroux, 2000.

Dean, Dennis R. *James Hutton and the History of Geology.* Ithaca, N.Y.: Cornell University Press, 1992.

Dibner, Bern. *Alessandro Volta and the Electric Battery.* New York: Franklin Watts, 1964.

Djerassi, Carl, and Roald Hoffmann. *Oxygen.* Weinheim, Germany: Wiley-VCH Verlag, 2001.

Donovan, Arthur. *Antoine Lavoisier: Science, Administration, and Revolution.* Cambridge, England: Cambridge University Press, 1996.

Dreyer, John Louis Emil, ed. *The Scientific Papers of Sir William Herschel.* Dorset, England: Thoemmes Continuum, 2003.

Dunn, Kevin M. *Caveman Chemistry.* Parkland, Fla.: Universal, 2003.

Fara, Patricia. *An Entertainment for Angels: Electricity in the Enlightenment.* New York: Columbia University Press, 2002.

_____. *Newton: The Making of a Genius.* New York: Columbia University Press, 2002.

_____. *Sex, Botany, and the Empire: The Story of Carl Linnaeus and Joseph Banks.* New York: Columbia University Press, 2003.

Farber, Paul Lawrence. *Finding Order in Nature: The Naturalist Tradition from Linnaeus to E. O. Wilson.* Baltimore: Johns Hopkins University Press, 2000.

Fellows, Otis E., and Stephen F. Milliken. *Buffon.* New York: Twayne's, 1972.

Fix, John D. *Astronomy: Journey to the Cosmic Frontier.* New York: McGraw-Hill, 2001.

Forbes, Eric G. *The Birth of Scientific Navigation: The Solving in the Eighteenth Century of the Problem of Finding Longitude at Sea.* London: National Maritime Museum, 1974.

Ford, R. A. *Homemade Lightning: Creative Experiments in Electricity.* New York: McGraw-Hill, 2002.

Fränmyr, Tore, ed. *Linnaeus: The Man and His Work.* Canton, Mass.: Science History, 1994.

Galston, Arthur W. *Life Processes of Plants.* New York: Scientific American Library, 1994.

Gibbs, F. W. *Joseph Priestley: Revolutions of the Eighteenth Century.* Garden City, N.Y.: Doubleday, 1967.

Gillipsie, Charles Coulston, Robert Fox, and Ivor Grattan-Guinness. *Pierre-Simon Laplace, 1749-1827: A Life in Exact Science.* Princeton, N.J.: Princeton University Press, 2000.

Glass, Bentley, et al. *Forerunners of Darwin, 1745-1839.* Baltimore: Johns Hopkins University Press, 1959.

Gleick, James. *Isaac Newton.* New York: Pantheon Books, 2003.

Golinski, Jan. *Science as Public Culture: Chemistry and Enlightenment in Britain, 1760-1820.* Cambridge, England: Cambridge University Press, 1992.

Gould, Stephen Jay. *Time's Arrow, Time's Cycle: Myth and Metaphor in the Discovery of Geological Time.* Cambridge, Mass.: Harvard University Press, 1987.

Govindjee, J. T. Beatty, H. Gest, and J. F. Allen, eds. *Discoveries in Photosynthesis.* Berlin: Springer, 2005.

Greenberg, John L. *The Problem of the Earth's Shape from Newton to Clairaut: The Rise of Mathematical Science in Eighteenth-Century Paris and the Fall of "Normal" Science.* Cambridge, England: Cambridge University Press, 1995.

Gribbin, John. *The Scientists: A History of Science Told Through the Lives of Its Greatest Inventors.* New York: Random House, 2004.

Guerlac, Henry. *Antoine Laurent Lavoisier: Chemist and Revolutionary.* New York: Scribner, 1975.

Hall, A. Rupert. *Isaac Newton: Adventurer in Thought.* New York: Cambridge University Press, 1996.

Hall, Nina, ed. *The New Chemistry.* Cambridge, England: Cambridge University Press, 2000.

Hamilton, James. *A Life of Discovery: Michael Faraday, Giant of the Scientific Revolution.* New York: Random House, 2002.

Hankins, Thomas L. *Science and the Enlightenment.* New York: Cambridge University Press, 1985.

Hawking, Stephen, ed. *On the Shoulders of Giants: The Great Works of Physics and Astronomy.* Philadelphia: Running Press, 2002.

Heilbron, J. L. *Electricity in the Seventeenth and Eighteenth Centuries: A Study in Early Modern Physics.* Mineola, N.Y.: Dover, 1999.

Holton, Gerald. *Thematic Origins of Scientific Thought:*

Kepler to Einstein. Rev. ed. Cambridge, Mass.: Harvard University Press, 1988.

Home, Roderick W. *The Effluvial Theory of Electricity*. New York: Arno Press, 1981.

Hoskin, Michael A. *The Herschel Partnership: As Viewed by Caroline*. Cambridge, England: Science History, 2003.

Howse, Derek. *Greenwich Time and the Longitude*. London: Philip Wilson, 1997.

_____. *Nevil Maskelyne: The Seaman's Astronomer*. Foreword by Astronomer Royal Sir Francis Graham-Smith. Cambridge, England: Cambridge University Press, 1989.

Hutton, James. *"System of the Earth," 1785, "Theory of the Earth," 1788, "Observations on Granite," 1794, Together with Playfair's Biography of Hutton*. Darien, Conn.: Hafner, 1970.

Jaffe, Bernard. *Crucibles: The Story of Chemistry*. New York: Dover, 1998.

Josephson, Paul. *Physics and Politics in Revolutionary Russia*. Berkeley: University of California Press, 1991.

Jungnickel, Christa, and Russell McCormmach. *Cavendish: The Experimental Life*. Lewisburg, Pa.: Bucknell, 1999.

Kuhn, Thomas. *The Structure of Scientific Revolutions*. 3d ed. Chicago: University of Chicago Press, 1996.

Lechevalier, Hubert, and Morris Solotorovsky. *Three Centuries of Microbiology*. New York: Dover, 1974.

Lindzen, Richard S. *Dynamics in Atmospheric Physics*. New York: Cambridge University Press, 1990.

Lubbock, Constance A. *The Herschel Chronicle: The Life-Story of William Herschel and His Sister, Caroline Herschel*. Cambridge, England: Cambridge University Press, 1933.

McCann, H. Gilman. *Chemistry Transformed: The Paradigmatic Shift from Phlogiston to Oxygen*. Norwood, N.J.: Ablex, 1978.

McIntyre, Donald B., and Alan McKirdy. *James Hutton: The Founder of Modern Geology*. Edinburgh: Stationery Office, 1997.

McKenzie, A. E. E. *The Major Achievements of Science: The Development of Science from Ancient Times to the Present*. Cambridge, England: Cambridge University Press, 1960.

McKie, Douglas. *Antoine Lavoisier: Scientist, Economist, Social Reformer*. New York: Da Capo, 1980.

Middleton, W. E. Knowles. *A History of the Thermometer and Its Use in Meteorology*. Ann Arbor, Mich.: UMI Books on Demand, 1996.

Monmonier, Mark. *Air Apparent: How Meteorologists Learned to Map, Predict, and Dramatize Weather*. Chicago: University of Chicago Press, 2000.

Nash, Leonard K. *Plants and the Atmosphere*. Cambridge, Mass.: Harvard University Press, 1952.

Newton, Isaac. *Opticks: Or, A Treatise of the Reflexions, Refractions, Inflexions, and Colours of Light*. New York: Dover, 1952.

Niccolò Guicciardini. *Reading the "Principia": The Debate on Newton's Mathematical Methods for Natural Philosophy from 1687 to 1736*. Cambridge, England: Cambridge University Press, 1999.

Nicolson, Marjorie Hope. *Newton Demands the Muse: Newton's "Opticks" and the Eighteenth Century Poets*. London: Archon Books, 1963.

Nye, Mary Jo. *Before Big Science: The Pursuit of Modern Chemistry and Physics, 1800-1940*. New York: Twayne, 1996.

Pancaldi, Giuliano. *Volta: Science and Culture in the Age of Enlightenment*. Princeton, N.J.: Princeton University Press, 2003.

Poirier, Jean Pierre. *Lavoisier: Chemist, Biologist, Economist*. Philadelphia: University of Pennsylvania Press, 1996.

Porter, Roy. *The Greatest Benefit to Mankind*. New York: W. W. Norton, 1998.

_____, ed. *Eighteenth Century Science*. Vol. 4 in *The Cambridge History of Science*. New York: Cambridge University Press, 2003.

Quill, Humphrey. *John Harrison: The Man Who Found Longitude*. New York: Humanities Press, 1966.

Repcheck, Jack. *The Man Who Found Time: James Hutton and the Discovery of the Earth's Antiquity*. Cambridge, Mass.: Perseus Books, 2003.

Roger, Jacques. *Buffon: A Life in Natural History*. Translated by Sarah L. Bonnefoi. Ithaca, N.Y.: Cornell University Press, 1997.

Ronan, Colin A. *Edmond Halley: Genius in Eclipse*. Garden City, N.Y.: Doubleday, 1969.

Rosen, Dennis, and Sylvia Rosen. *London Science: Museums, Libraries, and Places of Scientific, Technological, and Medical Interest*. London: Prion Books, 1994.

Rossi, Paoli. *The Birth of Modern Science*. Translated by Cynthia De Nardi Ipsen. Malden, Mass.: Blackwell, 2001.

Schaaf, Fred. *Comet of the Century: From Halley to Hale Bopp*. New York: Springer-Verlag, 1997.

Schofield, Robert E. *The Enlightened Joseph Priestley: A Study of His Life and Work from 1773 to 1804*. University Park: Pennsylvania State University Press, 2004.

Sidgwick, J. B. *William Herschel: Explorer of the Heavens*. London: Faber & Faber, 1953.

Simmons, John. *The Scientific One Hundred: A Ranking of the Most Influential Scientists, Past and Present*. Secausus, N.J.: Carol, 1996.

Sobel, Dava. *Longitude: The True Story of a Lone Genius Who Solved the Greatest Scientific Problem of His Time*. New York: Walker, 1995.

Strathern, Paul. *Mendeleyev's Dream: The Quest for the Elements*. New York: Berkeley Books, 2000.

Tanford, Charles. *Franklin Stilled the Waves*. Durham, N.C.: Duke University Press, 1989.

Terrall, Mary. *The Man Who Flattened the Earth: Maupertuis and the Sciences in the Enlightenment*. Chicago: University of Chicago Press, 2002.

Thackray, Arnold. *Atoms and Powers: An Essay on Newtonian Matter-Theory and the Development of Chemistry*. Cambridge, Mass.: Harvard University Press, 1970.

Thrower, Norman J. W., ed. *Standing on the Shoulders of Giants: A Longer View of Newton and Halley*. Berkeley: University of California Press, 1990.

Tompkins, Peter, and Christopher Bird. *The Secret Life of Plants*. New York: Harper & Row, 1973.

Tweedle, Charles. *James Stirling: A Sketch of His Life and Works, Along with His Scientific Correspondence*. Oxford, England: Clarendon Press, 1922.

Uglow, Jennifer S. *The Lunar Men: Five Friends Whose Curiosity Changed the World*. New York: Farrar, Straus and Giroux, 2002.

Vucinich, Alexander. *Science in Culture: A History to 1860*. Stanford, Calif.: Stanford University Press, 1963.

White, Michael. *Isaac Newton: The Last Sorcerer*. Philadelphia: Perseus Books, 1997.

Whittaker, Edmund. *A History of the Theories of Aether and Electricity*. New York: Dover, 1989.

Wilmoth, Frances, ed. *Flamsteed's Stars: New Perspectives on the Life and Work of the First Astronomer Royal, 1646-1719*. Suffolk, England: Boydell Press, 1997.

SLAVERY AND THE SLAVE TRADE

Aitken, Hugh G. J., ed. *Did Slavery Pay? Readings in the Economics of Black Slavery in the United States*. Boston: Houghton Mifflin, 1971.

Alpers, E. A. *Ivory and Slaves in East Central Africa to the Later Nineteenth Century*. London: Heinemann, 1975.

Aptheker, Herbert. *American Negro Slave Revolts*. Rev. ed. New York: Columbia University Press, 1969.

Blackburn, Robin. *The Making of New World Slavery*. New York: Verso, 1997.

Campbell, Stanley. *The Slave Catchers: Enforcement of the Fugitive Slave Law, 1850-1860*. Chapel Hill: University of North Carolina Press, 1970.

Conyers, James L., Jr., ed. *Black Lives: Essays in African American Biography*. Armonk, N.Y.: M. E. Sharpe, 1999.

Cranton, Michael. *Testing the Chains: Resistance to Slavery in the British West Indies*. Ithaca, N.Y.: Cornell University Press, 1982.

Curtin, Philip D. *The Atlantic Slave Trade: A Census*. Madison: University of Wisconsin Press, 1969.

Davis, David Brion. *The Problem of Slavery in the Age of Revolution, 1770-1823*. Ithaca, N.Y.: Cornell University Press, 1975.

_____. *The Problem of Slavery in Western Culture*. Ithaca, N.Y.: Cornell University Press, 1966.

Dirks, Robert. *The Black Saturnalia: Conflict and Its Ritual Expression on British West Indian Slave Plantations*. Gainesville: University Presses of Florida, 1987.

Finkelman, Paul. *Slavery and the Founders: Race and Liberty in the Age of Jefferson*. 2d ed. Armonk, N.Y.: M. E. Sharpe, 2001.

_____. *Slavery in the Courtroom: An Annotated Bibliography of American Cases*. Washington, D.C.: Library of Congress, 1985.

Fogel, Robert William. *Without Consent or Contract: The Rise and Fall of American Slavery*. New York: W. W. Norton, 1989.

Fogel, Robert William, and Stanley L. Egnerman. *Time on the Cross: The Economics of American Negro Slavery*. Boston: Little, Brown, 1974.

Frost, J. William, ed. *The Quaker Origins of Antislavery*. Norwood, Pa.: Norwood Editions, 1980.

Grant, R. G. *The African-American Slave Trade*. Hauppauge, N.Y.: Barron's, 2003.

Hall, Neville. *Slave Society in the Danish West Indies*. Edited by B. W. Higman. Baltimore: Johns Hopkins University Press, 1992.

Harris, Leslie M. *In the Shadow of Slavery: African Americans in New York City, 1626-1823*. Chicago: University of Chicago Press, 2003.

Hart, Richard. *Slaves Who Abolished Slavery*. Volume 2. Mona, Jamaica: Institute of Social and Economic Research, University of the West Indies, 1985.

Hoffer, Peter Charles. *The Great New York Conspiracy*

of 1741: Slavery, Crime, and Colonial War. Lawrence: University Press of Kansas, 2003.

Horton, James Oliver, and Lois E. Horton. *In Hope of Liberty: Culture, Community, and Protest Among Northern Free Blacks, 1700-1860.* New York: Oxford University Press, 1997.

Jordan, Winthrop. *White over Black: American Attitudes Toward the Negro, 1550-1812.* Chapel Hill: University of North Carolina Press, 1968.

Klein, Herbert S. *The Atlantic Slave Trade.* New York: Cambridge University Press, 1999.

Lepore, Jill. *New York Burning: Liberty, Slavery, and Conspiracy in Eighteenth-Century Manhattan.* New York: Alfred A. Knopf, 2005.

Litwack, Leon F. *North of Slavery: The Negro in the Free States, 1790-1860.* Chicago: University of Chicago Press, 1961.

Lustig, Mary Lou. *Robert Hunter, 1666-1734.* Syracuse, N.Y.: Syracuse University Press, 1983.

McDougall, Marion G. *Fugitive Slaves, 1619-1865.* 1891. Reprint. New York: Bergman, 1969.

Monaghan, Tom. *The Slave Trade.* New York: Raintree Steck-Vaughn, 2003.

Nash, Gary B. *Race and Revolution.* Madison, Wis.: Madison House, 1990.

Nash, Gary B., and Jean R. Soderlund. *Freedom by Degrees: Emancipation in Pennsylvania and Its Aftermath.* New York: Oxford University Press, 1991.

Newman, Richard S. *The Transformation of American Abolition: Fighting Slavery in the Early Republic.* Chapel Hill: University of North Carolina Press, 2002.

Olwell, Robert. *Masters, Slaves, and Subjects: The Culture of Power in the South Carolina Low Country, 1740-1790.* Ithaca, N.Y.: Cornell University Press, 1998.

Rawley, James A. *The Transatlantic Slave Trade: A History.* New York: Alfred A. Knopf, 1981.

Segal, R. *Islam's Black Slaves.* New York: Farrar, Straus and Giroux, 2001.

Sobel, Mechal. *Trablin' On: The Slave Journey to an Afro-Baptist Faith.* Westport, Conn.: Greenwood Press, 1979.

Soderlund, Jean R. *Quakers and Slavery: A Divided Spirit.* Princeton, N.J.: Princeton University Press, 1985.

Thomas, Hugh. *The Slave Trade.* New York: Simon & Schuster, 1997.

Thompson, Vincent Bakpetu. *The Making of the African Diaspora in the Americas, 1441-1900.* New York: Longman, 1987.

Walvin, James. *Black Ivory: A History of British Slavery.* Washington, D.C.: Howard University Press, 1994.

_____. *Making the Black Atlantic: Britain and the African Diaspora.* London: Cassell, 2000.

Ward, J. R. *British West Indian Slavery, 1750-1834: The Process of Amelioration.* Oxford, England: Clarendon Press, 1988.

White, Shane. *Somewhat More Independent: The End of Slavery in New York City, 1770-1810.* Athens: University of Georgia Press, 1991.

Wiecek, William M. *The Sources of Antislavery Constitutionalism in America, 1760-1848.* Ithaca, N.Y.: Cornell University Press, 1977.

Wood, Peter H. *Black Majority: Negroes in Colonial South Carolina from 1670 Through the Stono Rebellion.* New York: W. W. Norton, 1974.

Zilversmit, Arthur. *The First Emancipation: The Abolition of Slavery in the North.* Chicago: University of Chicago Press, 1967.

SOUTH ASIA: INDIA, AFGHANISTAN, PAKISTAN, AND BURMA

Bayly, Susan. *Caste, Society, and Politics in India: From the Eighteenth Century to the Modern Age.* Cambridge, England: Cambridge University Press, 2001.

Cannon, Garland. *The Life and Mind of Oriental Jones: Sir William Jones, the Father of Modern Linguistics.* Cambridge, England: Cambridge University Press, 1990.

Cannon, Garland, and Kevin Brine, eds. *Objects of Enquiry: The Life and Contributions of Sir William Jones, 1746-1794.* New York: New York University Press, 1995.

Didwell, Henry. *Dupleix and Clive.* London: Methuen, 1920.

Dupree, Louise. *Afghanistan.* Princeton, N.J.: Princeton University Press, 1980.

Ewans, Martin. *Afghanistan: A Short History of Its Peoples and Politics.* New York: Harper Collins, 2002.

Fernandes, Praxy. *The Tigers of Mysore: A Biography of Hyder Ali and Tipu Sultan.* New Delhi: Viking, 1991.

Franklin, Michael J., ed. *Sir William Jones: Selected Poetical and Prose Works.* Cardiff: University of Wales Press, 1995.

Gordon, Stewart. *The Marathas, 1600-1818.* Cambridge, England: Cambridge University Press, 1993.

Gupta, Brijen K. *Sirajuddaullah and the East India Company.* Leiden, Netherlands: E. J. Brill, 1966.

Habib, Irfan, ed. *Confronting Colonialism: Resistance and Modernization Under Haidar Ali and Tipu Sultan.* New Delhi: Tulika, 1999.

_____. *State and Diplomacy Under Tipu Sultan: Documents and Essays*. New Delhi: Tulika, 2001.

Harvey, Robert. *Clive: The Life and Death of a British Emperor*. New York: St. Martin's Press, 1998.

Kadam, V. S. "Franco-Maratha Relations." In *French in India and Indian Nationalism*, edited by K. S. Mathew. Vol. 1. Delhi: B. R., 1999.

Kantak, M. R., ed. *The First Anglo-Maratha War: The Last Phase, 1780-1783 A.D.* Pune, India: Deccan College Post-Graduate and Research Institute, 1989.

Koenig, William J. *Burmese Polity, 1752-1819: A Study of Kon Baung Politics, Administration, and Social Organization*. Ann Arbor: Center for South and Southeast Asian Studies, University of Michigan, 1990.

Lafont, Jean Marie. "Observations on the French Military Presence in the Indian States, 1750-1849." In *Indo-French Relations*, edited by K. S. Matthew and S. Jeyaseela Stephen. Delhi: Pragati, 1999.

Lockhart, Laurence. *The Fall of the Safavid Dynasty and the Afghan Occupation of Persia*. Cambridge, England: Cambridge University Press, 1958.

_____. *Nadir Shah: A Critical Study Based Mainly upon Contemporary Sources*. London: Luzac, 1938.

Marshall, P. J., ed. *The Eighteenth Century in Indian History: Evolution or Revolution?* Oxford, England: Oxford University Press, 2005.

Marshall, P. J., et al. *Bengal: The British Bridgehead—Eastern India, 1740-1828*. Cambridge, England: Cambridge University Press, 1988.

Murray Alexander, ed. *Sir William Jones, 1746-1794: A Commemoration*. Oxford, England: Oxford University Press, 1998.

SOUTHEAST ASIA AND THE PACIFIC

Aung-Thwin, Michael A. *Mists of Ramanna: The Legend That Was Lower Burma*. Honolulu: University of Hawaii Press, 2005.

_____. *Myth and History in the Historiography of Early Burma: Paradigms, Primary Sources, and Prejudices*. Athens: Ohio University Center for International Studies, 1998.

_____. *Pagan: The Origins of Modern Burma*. Honolulu: University of Hawaii Press, 1985.

Chandler, David. *A History of Cambodia*. 2d ed. Boulder, Colo.: Westview Press, 1992.

Chapuis, Oscar. *A History of Vietnam*. Westport, Conn.: Greenwood Press, 1995.

Cribb, Robert. *Historical Atlas of Indonesia*. London: Curzon Press, 1997.

Daws, Gavin. *Shoal of Time: A History of the Hawaiian Islands*. New York: Macmillan, 1968.

Grant, Glen. *Fornander's Ancient History of the Hawaiian People*. Honolulu: Mutual, 1996.

Hall, D. G. E. *A History of South-East Asia*. 4th ed. New York: St. Martin's Press, 1981.

Kuykendall, Ralph S., and A. Grove Day. *Hawaii: A History from Polynesian Kingdom to American State*. Rev. ed. Englewood Cliffs, N.J.: Prentice-Hall, 1961.

Li, Tana. *Nguyen Cochinchina*. Ithaca, N.Y.: Cornell University Press, 1998.

Ricklefs, M. C. *A History of Modern Indonesia Since c. 1200*. Stanford, Calif.: Stanford University Press, 2001.

Taylor, Jean Gelman. *Indonesia: Peoples and Histories*. New Haven, Conn.: Yale University Press, 2003.

Terwiel, B. J. *A History of Modern Thailand, 1767-1942*. St. Lucia: University of Queensland Press, 1983.

Wyatt, David K. *Studies in Thai History*. Reprint. Chiang Mai, Thailand: Silkworm Books, 1996.

Zaide, Gregario. *Dagohoy: Champion of Philippine Freedom*. Manila: Enriquez, Alduan, 1941.

SPAIN, PORTUGAL, AND THE IBERIAN EMPIRES

Alden, Dauril. *Royal Government in Brazil: With Special Reference to the Administration of the Marquis of Lavradio, Viceroy, 1769-1779*. Berkeley: University of California Press, 1968.

Bethell, Leslie, ed. *Colonial Brazil*. Cambridge, England: Cambridge University Press, 1986.

Bevan, Bryan. *King James the Third of England: A Study of Kingship in Exile*. London: Hale, 1967.

Boxer, Charles. *The Golden Age of Brazil, 1695-1750: Growing Pains of a Colonial Society*. Berkeley: University of California Press, 1962.

Brooks, Charles B. *Disaster at Lisbon: The Great Earthquake of 1755*. Long Beach, Calif.: Shangton Longley Press, 1994.

Burkholder, Mark, and Lyman L. Johnson. *Colonial Latin America*. 4th ed. Oxford, England: Oxford University Press, 2001.

Dynes, Russell Rowe. *The Lisbon Earthquake in 1755: Contested Meanings of the First Modern Disaster*. Newark: Disaster Research Center, University of Delaware, 1997.

Fausto, Boris. *A Concise History of Brazil*. Cambridge, England: Cambridge University Press, 1999.

Font Obrador, Bartolome. *Fr. Junipero Serra: Mallorca, Mexico, Sierra Gorda, Californias*. Palma, Mallorca, Spain: Comissio de Cultura, 1992.

Frey, Linda, and Marsha Frey. *Societies in Upheaval: Insurrections in France, Hungary, and Spain in the Early Eighteenth Century.* Westport, Conn.: Greenwood Press, 1987.

Harvey, Maurice. *Gibraltar.* Kent, England: Spellmount, 1996.

Herr, Richard. *The Eighteenth Century Revolution in Spain.* Princeton, N.J.: Princeton University Press, 1958.

_____. *Rural Change and Royal Finances in Spain at the End of the Old Regime.* Berkeley: University of California Press, 1989.

Hills, George. *Rock of Contention: A History of Gibraltar.* London: Robert Hale, 1974.

Hull, Anthony H. *Charles III and the Revival of Spain.* Washington, D.C.: University Press of America, 1980.

Jackson, Sir William G. F. *The Rock of the Gibraltarians: A History of Gibraltar.* Cranbury, N.J.: Associated University Presses, 1987.

Kamen, Henry. *Empire: How Spain Became a World Power, 1492-1763.* New York: Harper Collins, 2003.

_____. *Golden Age Spain.* 2d ed. New York: Palgrave Macmillan, 2004.

_____. *Philip V of Spain: The King Who Reigned Twice.* New Haven, Conn.: Yale University Press, 2001.

_____. *Spain's Road to Empire: The Making of a World Power, 1492-1763.* New York: Penguin Putnam, 2002.

Lewis, James E., Jr. *The American Union and the Problem of Neighborhood: The United States and the Collapse of the Spanish Empire, 1783-1829.* Chapel Hill: University of North Carolina Press, 1998.

Lynch, John. *Bourbon Spain, 1700-1808.* Cambridge, Mass.: Basil Blackwell, 1989.

Maxwell, Kenneth. *Pombal: Paradox of the Enlightenment.* Cambridge, England: Cambridge University Press, 1995.

Pendle, George. *Argentina.* New York: Royal Institute of International Affairs, 1955.

Stein, Stanley J., and Barbara H. Stein. *Apogee of Empire: Spain and New Spain in the Age of Charles III, 1759-1789.* Baltimore: Johns Hopkins University Press, 2003.

Tandeter, Enrique. *Coercion and Market: Silver Mining in Colonial Potosi, 1692-1826.* Albuquerque: University of New Mexico Press, 1993.

Wallwork, J. F., and J. S. Kirkman. *The Portuguese in East Africa.* Nairobi, Kenya: n.p., 1961.

TECHNOLOGY, INVENTION, AND INDUSTRIALIZATION

Andrews, Mildred Gwin. *The Men and the Mills: A History of the Southern Textile Industry.* Macon, Ga.: Mercer University Press, 1987.

Ashton, T. *Iron and Steel in the Industrial Revolution.* 3d ed. Manchester: Manchester University Press, 1963.

Baines, Edward. *History of the Cotton Manufacture in Great Britain.* Reprint. New York: Augustus M. Kelley, 1966.

Balen, Malcolm. *The King, the Crook, and the Gambler: The True Story of the South Sea Bubble and the Greatest Financial Scandal in History.* New York: Fourth Estate, 2004.

Batchelder, Samuel. *Introduction and Early Progress of the Cotton Manufacture in the United States.* Boston: Little, Brown, 1863. Reprint. Clifton, N.J.: August M. Kelley, 1972.

Blanchard, Jean-Pierre. *First Air Voyage in America.* Bedford, Mass.: Applewood Books, 2002.

Brig, Asa. *The Power of Steam: An Illustrated History of the World's Steam Age.* Chicago: University of Chicago Press, 1982.

Britton, Karen Gerhardt. *Bale o' Cotton: The Mechanical Art of Cotton Ginning.* College Station: Texas A&M University Press, 1992.

Cameron, Edward H. *Samuel Slater: Father of American Manufactures.* Freeport, Maine: Bond Wheelwright, 1960.

Cardwell, D. S. L. *The Norton History of Technology.* New York: Norton, 1995.

_____. *Turning Points in Western Technology.* New York: Neale Watson Science History, 1972.

Chapman, S. D. *The Cotton Industry in the Industrial Revolution.* London: Macmillan, 1972.

Christopher, John. *Riding the Jetstream: The Story of Ballooning, from Montgolfier to Breitling.* London: John Murray, 2002.

Cossons, Neil, and Barrie Trinder. *The Iron Bridge: Symbol of the Industrial Revolution.* London: Moonraker, 1979.

Deane, Phyllis. *The First Industrial Revolution.* London: Cambridge University Press, 1965.

Dickinson, H. W. *James Watt and the Steam Engine.* Oxford, England: Clarendon Press, 1927.

Fitton, R. S. *Arkwrights: Spinners of Fortune.* New York: St. Martin's Press, 1989.

Fitton, R. S., and A. P. Wadsworth. *The Strutts and the Arkwrights.* Reprint. New York: Augustus M. Kelley, 1968.

Freethy, Ron, and Marlene Freethy. *The Bridgewater Canal.* Bolton, Lancashire, England: Aurora, 1996.

Freytag, Dean A. *The History, Making, and Modeling of Steel*. Milwaukee, Wis.: William K. Walthers, 1996.

Gillipsie, Charles Coulston. *The Montgolfier Brothers and the Invention of Aviation, 1783-1784: With a Word on the Importance of Ballooning for the Science of Heat and of Building the Railroad*. Princeton, N.J.: Princeton University Press, 1983.

Green, Constance McLaughlin. "The Invention of the Cotton Gin." In *Eli Whitney and the Birth of American Technology*. Boston: Little, Brown, 1956.

Hadfield, Charles. *British Canals: An Illustrated History*. London: Newton, Abbott, and Charles, 1966.

Hyde, Charles K. *Technological Change and the British Iron Industry*. Princeton, N.J.: Princeton University Press, 1977.

Lakwete, Angela. *Inventing the Cotton Gin: Machine and Myth in Antebellum America*. Baltimore: Johns Hopkins University Press, 2003.

Landes, Davis S. *Revolution in Time: Clocks and the Making of the Modern World*. Rev. ed. Cambridge, Mass.: Belknap Press of Harvard University Press, 2000.

_____. *The Unbound Prometheus: Technical Change and Industrial Development in Western Europe from 1750 to the Present*. London: Cambridge University Press, 1960.

MacLeod, Christine. *Inventing the Industrial Revolution: The English Patent System, 1660-1800*. Cambridge, England: Cambridge University Press, 1988.

Malet, Hugh. *The Canal Duke: A Biography of Francis, Third Duke of Bridgewater*. Manchester, England: Manchester University Press, 1977.

Mantoux, Paul. *The Industrial Revolution in the Eighteenth Century: An Outline of the Beginnings of the Modern Factory System in England*. Chicago: University of Chicago Press, 1983.

Marion, Fulgence. *Wonderful Balloon Ascents: Or, The Conquest of the Skies*. Whitefish, Mt.: Kessinger, 2004.

Marsden, Ben. *Watt's Perfect Engine: Steam and the Age of Invention*. New York: Columbia University Press, 2002.

Miller, David Philip. *Discovering Water: James Watt, Henry Cavendish, and the Nineteenth Century "Water Controversy."* Burlington, Vt.: Ashgate, 2004.

Mokyr, Joel. *The Lever of Riches: Technological Creativity and Economic Progress*. New York: Oxford University Press, 1990.

More, Charles. *Understanding the Industrial Revolution*. New York: Routledge Press, 2000.

_____, ed. *The British Industrial Revolution: An Economic Perspective*. 2d ed. Boulder, Colo.: Westview Press, 1999.

Muter, Grant. *The Building of an Industrial Community: Coalbrookdale and Ironbridge*. Chichester, Sussex, England: Phillimore, 1979.

Nahum, Andrew. *James Watt and the Power of Steam*. East Sussex, England: Wayland, 1981.

Pawson, Eric. *The Early Industrial Revolution: Britain in the Eighteenth Century*. New York: Harper and Row, 1979.

Pursell, Carroll W. *The Machine in America: A Social History of Technology*. Baltimore: Johns Hopkins University Press, 1995.

Raistrick, Arthur. *Industrial Archaeology: An Historical Survey*. London: Eyre Methuen, 1972.

_____. *Quakers in Science and Industry*. New York: Augustus Kelley, 1968.

Rolt, L. T. C. *James Watt*. New York: Arco, 1963.

Rowland, K. T. *Eighteenth-Century Inventions*. New York: Barnes & Noble, 1974.

Ruddock, E. C. *Arch Bridges and Their Builders, 1735-1835*. Cambridge, England: Cambridge University Press, 1979

Schiffer, Michael B. *Draw the Lightning Down: Benjamin Franklin and Electrical Technology in the Age of Enlightenment*. Berkeley: University of California Press, 2003.

Smiles, Samuel. *Industrial Biography: Iron Workers and Tool Makers*. Reprint. McLean, Va.: IndyPublish.com, 2002.

Sutcliffe, Andrea. *Steam: The Untold Story of America's First Great Invention*. London: Palgrave Macmillan, 2004.

Thompson, E. P. *The Making of the English Working Class*. 2d ed. Harmondsworth, Middlesex, England: Penguin, 1982.

Usher, Abbott P. *A History of Mechanical Inventions*. Cambridge, Mass.: Harvard University Press, 1966.

Van Gelder, A. P., and H. Schlatter. *History of the Explosives Industry in America*. New York: Arno, 1972.

Wood, Cyril J. *The Duke's Cut: The Bridgewater Canal*. Stroud, Gloucestershire, England: Tempus, 2002.

UNITED STATES

General Studies

Alexander, James. *A Brief Narrative of the Case and Trial of John Peter Zenger, Printer of the "New York Weekly Journal."* Edited by Sidney N. Katz. Cambridge, Mass.: Harvard University Press, 1963.

Beard, Charles A. *Economic Origins of Jeffersonian Democracy*. New York: Macmillan, 1915.

Becker, Carl L. *The Declaration of Independence: A Study in the History of Political Ideas*. 2d ed. New York: Harcourt, Brace, & World, 1951.

Brasseaux, Carl A. *The Founding of New Acadia: The Beginnings of Acadian Life in Louisiana, 1765-1803*. Baton Rouge: Louisiana State University Press, 1996.

Braud, Gerard-Marc. *From Nantes to Louisiana: The History of Acadia, the Odyssey of an Exiled People*. Translated by Julie Fontenot Landry. Lafayette, La.: La Rainette, 1999.

Burt, Alfred L. *The United States, Great Britain, and British North America from the Revolution to the Establishment of Peace After the War of 1812*. Reprint. New Haven, Conn.: Yale University Press, 1968.

Cayton, Andrew R. L. *The Midwest and the Nation: Rethinking the History of an American Region*. Bloomington: Indiana University Press, 1990.

Chernow, Ron. *Alexander Hamilton*. New York: Penguin Press, 2004.

Clarke, Thomas D., and John D. W. Guice. *Frontiers in Conflict: The Old Southwest, 1795-1830*. Albuquerque: University of New Mexico Press, 1989. Reprinted as *The Old Southwest, 1795-1830: Frontiers in Conflict*. Norman: University of Oklahoma Press, 1996.

Cohen, Warren, ed. *Cambridge History of American Foreign Relations*. 4 vols. New York: Cambridge University Press, 1993.

Cooper, William J. *The American South: A History*. 2 vols. New York: McGraw-Hill, 1990.

Darling, Arthur B. *Our Rising Empire, 1763-1803*. New Haven, Conn.: Yale University Press, 1940.

Dershowitz, Alan. *America on Trial: Inside the Legal Battles That Transformed Our Nation*. New York: Warner Books, 2004.

Doughty, Arthur G. *The Acadian Exiles: A Chronicle of the Land of Evangeline*. Toronto: Glasgow, Brook, 1916.

Ellis, Joseph J. *Founding Brothers: The Revolutionary Generation*. New York: Alfred A. Knopf, 2000.

Ferling, John. *A Leap in the Dark: The Struggle to Create the American Republic*. New York: Oxford University Press, 2003.

Forbes, Esther. *Paul Revere and the World He Lived In*. Boston: Houghton Mifflin, 1942.

Franklin, Benjamin. *Autobiography of Benjamin Franklin*. New York: Buccaneer Books, 1984.

Hoeveler, J. David. *Creating the American Mind: Intellect and Politics in the Colonial Colleges*. Lanham, Md.: Rowman & Littlefield, 2002.

Isaacson, Walter. *Benjamin Franklin: An American Life*. New York: Simon & Schuster, 2003.

Jefferson, Thomas. *Writings*. New York: Library Classics, 1984.

Jennings, Francis. *The Founders of America*. New York: W. W. Norton, 1993.

Jillson, Calvin, and Rick Wilson. *Congressional Dynamics: Structure, Coordination, and Choice in the First American Congress, 1774-1789*. Stanford, Calif.: Stanford University Press, 1994.

Johnson, Andrew J. *The Life and Constitutional Thought of Nathan Dane*. New York: Garland, 1987.

Johnson, George Lloyd. *The Frontier in the Colonial South: South Carolina Backcountry, 1736-1800*. Westport, Conn.: Greenwood Press, 1997.

Kaye, Harvey J. *Thomas Paine and the Promise of America*. New York: Hill and Wang, 2005.

Lanton, Thomas S., and Michael G. Sherman. *George Washington*. Washington, D.C.: CQ Press, 2003.

Lucas, Christopher J. *American Higher Education: A History*. New York: St. Martin's Press, 1994.

Ludlum, David. *Early American Hurricanes*. Boston: American Meteorological Society, 1963.

McCullogh, David. *John Adams*. New York: Simon & Schuster, 2001.

McDougall, Walter A. *Freedom Just Around the Corner: A New American History, 1585-1828*. New York: HarperCollins, 2004.

Marsden, George M. *The Soul of the American University: From Protestant Establishment to Established Nonbelief*. Oxford, England: Oxford University Press, 1994.

Morgan, Edmund S. *Benjamin Franklin*. New Haven, Conn.: Yale University Press, 2002.

Nash, Gary B. *Forging Freedom: The Formation of Philadelphia's Black Community, 1720-1840*. Cambridge, Mass.: Harvard University Press, 1988.

Pangle, Lorraine Smith, and Thomas L. Pangle. *The Learning of Liberty: The Educational Ideas of the American Founders*. Lawrence: University Press of Kansas, 1993.

Powell, William. *North Carolina Through Four Centuries*. Chapel Hill: University of North Carolina Press, 1989.

Reichley, A. James. *The Life of the Parties: A History of American Political Parties*. New York: Free Press, 1992.

Rudko, Frances Howell. *John Marshall and Interna-

tional Law: Statesman and Chief Justice. New York: Greenwood Press, 1991.

Schwartz, Barry. *George Washington: The Making of an American Symbol.* New York: Free Press, 1987.

Stahr, Walter. *John Jay: Founding Father.* London: Hambledon, 2005.

Thelin, John R. *A History of American Higher Education.* Baltimore: Johns Hopkins University Press, 2004.

Tolles, Frederick B. *James Logan and the Culture of Provincial America.* Boston: Little, Brown, 1957.

Tucker, Robert W., and David C. Hendrickson. *Empire of Liberty: The Statecraft of Thomas Jefferson.* New York: Oxford University Press, 1990.

Westmayer, Paul. *A History of American Higher Education.* Springfield, Ill.: Charles C Thomas, 1985.

Colonial America

Cashin, Edward J., ed. *Setting Out to Begin a New World: Colonial Georgia.* Savannah, Ga.: Beehive Press, 1995.

Crane, Werner W. *The Southern Frontier: 1670-1732.* 1929. Reprint. Ann Arbor: University of Michigan Press, 1956.

Ettinger, Amos A. *James Edward Oglethorpe: Imperial Idealist.* Hamden, Conn.: Archon Books, 1968.

Ferguson, Russell J. *Early Western Pennsylvania Politics.* Pittsburgh: University of Pittsburgh Press, 1938.

Franz, George W. *Paxton: A Study of Community Structure and Mobility in the Colonial Pennsylvania Backcountry.* New York: Garland, 1989.

Gipson, Lawrence H. *The Coming of the Revolution, 1763-1775.* New York: Harper & Row, 1954.

_____. *The Rumbling of the Coming Storm, 1766-1770: The Triumphant Empire.* Vol. 9 in *The British Empire Before the American Revolution.* New York: Alfred A. Knopf, 1965.

Goodfriend, Joyce D. *Before the Melting Pot: Society and Culture in Colonial New York City, 1664-1730.* Princeton, N.J.: Princeton University Press, 1992.

Kammen, Michael. *Colonial New York: A History.* New York: Charles Scribner's Sons, 1975.

Kars, Marjoleine. *Breaking Loose Together: The Regulator Rebellion in Pre-Revolutionary North Carolina.* Chapel Hill: University of North Carolina Press, 2002.

Kelley, Joseph J., Jr. *Pennsylvania: The Colonial Years.* Garden City, N.Y.: Doubleday, 1980.

McConnell, Michael N. *A Country Between: The Upper Ohio Valley and Its Peoples, 1724-1774.* Lincoln: University of Nebraska Press, 1992.

Morgan, Edmund S., and Helen M. Morgan. *The Stamp Act Crisis.* Chapel Hill: University of North Carolina Press, 1995.

Pomfret, John. *Colonial New Jersey: A History.* New York: Charles Scribner's Sons, 1973.

Robinson, W. Stitt. *The Southern Colonial Frontier, 1607-1763.* Albuquerque: University of New Mexico Press, 1979.

Schwartz, Sally. *"A Mixed Multitude": The Struggle for Toleration in Colonial Pennsylvania.* New York: New York University Press, 1987.

Shannon, Timothy J. *Indians and Colonists at the Crossroads of Empire: The Albany Congress of 1754.* Ithaca, N.Y.: Cornell University Press, 2000.

Sosin, Jack M. *Whitehall and the Wilderness: The Middle West in British Colonial Policy, 1760-1775.* Lincoln: University of Nebraska Press, 1961.

Spalding, Phinizy, and Harvey H. Jackson, eds. *Oglethorpe in Perspective: Georgia's Founder After Two Hundred Years.* Tuscaloosa: University of Alabama Press, 1989.

Stagg, Jack. *Anglo-Indian Relations in North America to 1763 and an Analysis of the Royal Proclamation of 7 October, 1763.* Ottawa, Ont.: Research Branch, Indian and Northern Affairs Canada, 1981.

Thomas, P. D. G. *British Politics and the Stamp Act Crisis.* Oxford, England: Clarendon Press, 1975.

_____. *The Townshend Duties Crisis: The Second Phase of the Revolution, 1767-1773.* Oxford, England: Clarendon Press, 1987.

Weslager, C. A. *The Stamp Act Congress.* Newark: University of Delaware Press, 1976.

Revolutionary Period

Ammerman, David. *In the Common Cause: American Response to the Coercive Acts.* Charlottesville: University Press of Virginia, 1974.

Bailyn, Bernard. *The Ideological Origins of the American Revolution.* Cambridge, Mass.: Belknap Press of Harvard University Press, 1967.

Brown, Richard D. *Revolutionary Politics in Massachusetts: The Boston Committee of Correspondence and the Towns, 1772-1774.* Cambridge, Mass.: Harvard University Press, 1970.

Burnett, Edmund C. *The Continental Congress.* New York: Macmillan, 1941.

Fischer, David. *Paul Revere's Ride.* New York: Oxford University Press, 1994.

Foner, Eric. *Tom Paine and Revolutionary America.* New York: Oxford University Press, 1976.

Hansen, Harry. *The Boston Massacre: An Episode of Dissent and Violence*. New York: Hastin House, 1970.

Henderson, H. James. *Party Politics in the Continental Congress*. New York: McGraw-Hill, 1974.

Jacobson, David L. *John Dickinson and the Revolution in Pennsylvania, 1764-1774*. Berkeley: University of California Press, 1965.

Jameson, J. Franklin. *The American Revolution Considered as a Social Movement*. Princeton, N.J.: Princeton University Press, 1926.

Jensen, Merrill. *The Founding of a Nation: A History of the American Revolution, 1763-1776*. London: Oxford University Press, 1968.

Knollenberg, Bernard. *Growth of the American Revolution, 1765-1775*. New York: Free Press, 1975.

_____. *Origin of the American Revolution, 1759-1766*. New York: Macmillan, 1960.

Labaree, Benjamin W. *The Boston Tea Party*. New York: Oxford University Press, 1964.

Langguth, A. J. *Patriots: The Men Who Started the American Revolution*. New York: Touchstone, 1988.

Main, Jackson T. *The Social Structure of Revolutionary America*. Princeton, N.J.: Princeton University Press, 1965.

Martin, James Kirby. *In the Course of Human Events: An Interpretive Exploration of the American Revolution*. Arlington Heights, Ill.: Harlan Davidson, 1979.

Middelkauff, Robert. *The Glorious Cause: The American Revolution, 1763-1789*. New York: Oxford University Press, 1982.

Montross, Lynn. *The Reluctant Rebels: The Story of the Continental Congress, 1774-1789*. New York: Harper & Row, 1950.

Morris, Richard B. *The American Revolution Reconsidered*. New York: Harper & Row, 1967.

Morrissey, Brendan. *Boston, 1775: The Shot Heard Around the World*. Westport, Conn.: Praeger, 2004.

Morton, Brian N., and Donald C. Spinelli. *Beaumarchais and the American Revolution*. Lanham, Md.: Lexington Books, 2003.

Raphael, Ray. *A People's History of the American Revolution: How Common People Shaped the Fight for Independence*. New York: New Press, 2001.

Smith, Page. *A New Age Now Begins: A People's History of the American Revolution*. 2 vols. New York: Penguin Books, 1976.

Stinchcombe, William C. *The American Revolution and the French Alliance*. Syracuse, N.Y.: Syracuse University Press, 1969.

Stone, Geoffrey R. *Perilous Times: Free Speech in Wartime from the Sedition Act of 1798 to the War on Terrorism*. New York: W. W. Norton, 2004.

Thomas, Peter David Garner. *Tea Party to Independence: The Third Phase of the American Revolution, 1773-1776*. Oxford, England: Clarendon Press, 1991.

Tuchman, Barbara. *The First Salute: A View of the American Revolution*. New York: Alfred A. Knopf, 1988.

Ubbelohde, Carl. *The Vice-Admiralty Courts and the American Revolution*. Chapel Hill: University of North Carolina Press, 1960.

Wills, Garry. *Inventing America: Jefferson's Declaration of Independence*. Garden City, N.Y.: Doubleday, 1978.

Wood, Gordon S. *The Radicalism of the American Revolution*. New York: Alfred A. Knopf, 1992.

Young, Alfred E. *The Shoemaker and the Tea Party: Memory and the American Revolution*. Boston: Beacon Press, 1999.

Early Republic

Banning, Lance. *Conceived in Liberty: The Struggle to Define the New Republic, 1789-1793*. Lanham, Md.: Rowman & Littlefield, 2004.

Casto, William R. *The Supreme Court in the Early Republic: The Chief Justiceships of John Jay and Oliver Ellsworth*. Columbia: University of South Carolina Press, 1995.

Clouse, Jerry A. *The Whiskey Rebellion: Southwestern Pennsylvania's Frontier People Test the American Constitution*. Harrisburg: Bureau of Historic Preservation, Pennsylvania Historical and Museum Commission, 1994.

Conley, Patrick, and John Kaminski, eds. *The Constitution and the States: The Role of the Original Thirteen in the Framing and Adoption of the Federal Constitution*. Madison, Wis.: Madison House, 1988.

De Pauw, Linda G. *The Eleventh Pillar: New York State and the Federal Constitution*. Ithaca, N.Y.: Cornell University Press, 1966.

Elkins, Stanley, and Eric McKitrick. *The Age of Federalism: The Early American Republic, 1788-1800*. New York: Oxford University Press, 1993.

Emord, Jonathan W. *Freedom, Technology, and the First Amendment*. San Francisco, Calif.: Pacific Research Institute for Public Policy, 1991.

Farrand, Max. *The Records of the Federal Convention of 1787*. 4 vols. New Haven, Conn.: Yale University Press, 1966.

Gilbert, Felix. *To the Farewell Address: Ideas of Early American Foreign Policy*. Princeton, N.J.: Princeton University Press, 1961.

Goebel, Julius, Jr. *Antecedents and Beginnings to 1801.* Vol. 1 in *History of the Supreme Court of the United States.* New York: Macmillan, 1971.

Hoadley, John F. *Origins of American Political Parties, 1789-1803.* Lexington: University Press of Kentucky, 1986.

Jensen, Merrill. *The Making of the American Constitution.* Princeton, N.J.: Van Nostrand, 1964.

Kammen, Michael. *A Machine That Would Go of Itself.* New York: Alfred A. Knopf, 1986.

Kaufman, Burton Ira, ed. *Washington's Farewell Address: The View from the Twentieth Century.* Chicago: Quadrangle Books, 1969.

Konig, David Thomas. *Devising Liberty: Preserving and Creating Freedom in the New American Republic.* Stanford, Calif.: Stanford University Press, 1995.

McCloskey, Robert G. *The American Supreme Court.* 4th ed., rev. by Sanford Levinson. Chicago: University of Chicago Press, 2005.

Marcus, Maeva, ed. *Origins of the Federal Judiciary: Essays on the Judiciary Act of 1789.* New York: Oxford University Press, 1992.

Miller, John C. *Crisis in Freedom: The Alien and Sedition Acts.* Boston: Little, Brown, 1951.

_____. *The Federalist Era, 1789-1801.* New York: Harper and Brothers, 1960.

Morris, Richard B. *Forging of the Union, 1781-1789.* New York: Harper & Row, 1987.

Morris, Thomas D. *Free Men All: The Personal Liberty Laws of the North, 1780-1861.* Baltimore: Johns Hopkins University Press, 1974.

Onuf, Peter S. *Statehood and Union: A History of the Northwest Ordinance.* Bloomington: Indiana University Press, 1987.

Reuter, Frank T. *Trials and Triumphs: George Washington's Foreign Policy.* Fort Worth: Texas Christian University Press, 1983.

Ritz, Wilfred. *Rewriting the History of the Judiciary Act of 1789.* Norman: University of Oklahoma Press, 1990.

Schwartz, Bernard. *A History of the Supreme Court.* New York: Oxford University Press, 1993.

Sharp, James Roger. *American Politics in the Early Republic: The New Nation in Crisis.* New Haven, Conn.: Yale University Press, 1993.

Slaughter, Thomas. *The Whiskey Rebellion: Frontier Epilogue to the American Revolution.* New York: Oxford University Press, 1986.

Smith, Richard Norton. *Patriarch: George Washington and the New American Nation.* Boston: Houghton Mifflin, 1993.

Spalding, Matthew, and Patrick J. Garrity. *A Sacred Union of Citizens: George Washington's Farewell Address and the American Character.* Lanham, Md.: Rowman & Littlefield, 1996.

Stinchcombe, William. *The XYZ Affair.* Westport, Conn.: Greenwood Press, 1980.

Warren, Charles. *The Supreme Court in United States History.* 2 vols. Boston: Little, Brown, 1932.

Wiecek, William M. *Liberty Under Law: The Supreme Court in American Life.* Baltimore: Johns Hopkins University Press, 1988.

Williams, Frederick D., ed. *The Northwest Ordinance: Essays on Its Formulation, Provisions, and Legacy.* East Lansing: Michigan State University Press, 1988.

Wood, Gordon. *The Creation of the American Republic, 1776-1787.* New York: W. W. Norton, 1969.

WOMEN'S STUDIES

Agnesi, Maria Gaetana, et al. *The Contest for Knowledge: Debates Over Women's Learning in Eighteenth-Century Italy.* Chicago: University of Chicago Press, 2005.

Cleary, E. J. *The Feminization Debate in Eighteenth-Century Britain: Literature, Commerce, and Luxury.* London: Palgrave McMillan, 2004.

Davis, Natalie Zemon, and Arlette Farge, eds. *Renaissance and Enlightenment Paradoxes.* Vol. 3 in *A History of Women in the West.* Cambridge, Mass.: Belknap Press of Harvard University Press, 1993.

Erickson, Carrolly. *The Girl from Botany Bay.* Hoboken, N.J.: John Wiley & Sons, 2005.

Gunther-Canada, Wendy. *Rebel Writer: Mary Wollstonecraft and Enlightenment Politics.* Dekalb: Northern Illinois University Press, 2001.

Hesse, Carla. *The Other Enlightenment: How French Women Became Modern.* Princeton, N.J.: Princeton University Press, 2003.

Jones, Vivian, ed. *Women in the Eighteenth Century: Constructions of Femininity.* New York: Routledge, 1990.

Landes, Joan B. *Visualizing the Nation: Gender, Representation, and Revolution in Eighteenth-Century France.* Ithaca, N.Y.: Cornell University Press, 2003.

Lorence-Kot, Bogna. *Child-Rearing and Reform: A Study of Nobility in Eighteenth-Century Poland.* Westport, Conn.: Greenwood Press, 1985.

Norton, Mary Beth. *Liberty's Daughters: The Revolutionary Experience of American Women, 1750-1800.* Boston: Little, Brown, 1980.

Petschauer, Peter. *The Education of Women in Eigh-*

teenth-Century Germany. Lewiston, N.Y.: Edwin Mellen Press, 1989.

Smith, Bonnie. *Changing Lives: Women in European History Since 1700*. Lexington, Mass.: D. C. Heath, 1988.

Stone, Lawrence. *The Family, Sex, and Marriage in England, 1500-1800*. New York: Harper and Row, 1977.

Taylor, Barbara. *Mary Wollstonecraft and the Feminist Imagination*. New York: Cambridge University Press, 2003.

Todd, Janet. *Mary Wollstonecraft: A Revolutionary Life*. New York: Columbia University Press, 2000.

Trager, James. *The Women's Chronology*. New York: Henry Holt, 1994.

Turner, Cheryl. *Living by the Pen: Women Writers in the Eighteenth Century*. New ed. New York: Routledge, 1994.

Ulbrich, Claudia. *Shulamit and Margarete: Power, Gender, and Religion in a Rural Society in Eighteenth Century Europe*. Translated by Thomas Dunlap. Boston: Brill Academic, 2004.

Wilson, Kathleen. *The Island Race: Englishness, Empire, and Gender in the Eighteenth Century*. New York: Routledge, 2002.

Wollstonecraft, Mary. *A Vindication of the Rights of Woman*. Edited by Carol H. Poston. New York: W. W. Norton, 1988.

—John Powell

ELECTRONIC RESOURCES

WEB SITES

The sites listed below were visited by the editors of Salem Press in July, 2005. Because URLs frequently change or are moved, the accuracy of these sites cannot be guaranteed; however, long-standing sites—such as those of university departments, national organizations, and government agencies—generally maintain links when sites move or upgrade their offerings.

GENERAL

Eighteenth Century Resources

http://andromeda.rutgers.edu/~jlynch/18th/index.html

Jack Lynch, an associate professor of English at Rutgers University, has compiled this extraordinarily comprehensive list of Web links about the eighteenth century—the best site available for this period. The site contains a search engine enabling users to quickly locate Web resources about a specified topic. Users also can search for Web links by accessing several broad subject areas, such as art and architecture, music, literature, science and mathematics, philosophy, and religion. The section listing history Web sites is especially useful for its wide range of information about British and American history.

The European Enlightenment

http://www.wsu.edu:8080/~dee/ENLIGHT/
    ENLCONT.HTM

This list of links to information about seventeenth and eighteenth century thought is part of *World Civilizations: An Internet Classroom and Anthology*, produced by Washington State University. The European Enlightenment page links to information about philosophy, the Industrial Revolution, the changing status of women, and absolute monarchy. It also features links to a glossary of Enlightenment terms and concepts, and excerpts of works by Voltaire, Jean-Jacques Rousseau, and Adam Smith.

History World International

http://history-world.org/

A wealth of information about history from the Neolithic period to the present. Users can access the "Contents A-Z" page for a list of pages with information about the Americas, art and architecture, Asia and the Middle East, Europe, science, world religions, and other general topics. The "Europe" section includes overviews of the Age of Enlightenment and the French Revolution, and articles tracing the influence of Goethe and Johann Sebastian Bach. The "Science" section includes a discussion of Benjamin Franklin and electricity, while the "World Religions" section contains information about the rise of Methodism.

WebChron: Web Chronology Project

http://campus.northpark.edu/history/Webchron/

The Web Chronology Project was created by the History Department at North Park University in Chicago, and it contains a series of hyperlinked time lines. The chronologies trace developments in the United States, Africa, Middle East, India, China, and Russia and Eastern Europe. Other chronologies provide information about Islam, Christianity, Judaism, art, music, literature, and speculative thought in the Western tradition.

AFRICA

African Slave Trade and European Imperialism

http://Web.cocc.edu/cagatucci/classes/hum211/time
    lines/htime line3.htm

This is the third part of a five-part African time line created by Cora Agatucci, professor of English at Central Oregon Community College. The time line offers an overview of African history between the fifteenth and early nineteenth centuries, including information on the Asante Empire, the Kingdom of Dahomey, and the slave uprising in Haiti. The site is especially useful for its information on the Atlantic slave trade, African resistance to slavery, and the African diaspora.

Internet African History Sourcebook

http://www.fordham.edu/halsall/africa/
    africasbook.html

A page in the *Internet History Sourcebooks Project*, a highly-regarded collection of primary source materials compiled by Paul Halsall of Fordham University.

1045

Internet African History Sourcebook contains information about African history, including documents regarding African societies, the impact of slavery, and European imperialism.

Oloudah Equiano, or Gustavus Vassa, the African
http://www.brycchancarey.com/equiano/

Comprehensive site about Equiano, a Nigerian-born slave who purchased his freedom and eventually moved to London, where he became active in the abolition movement. The site includes excerpts from Equiano's best-selling book, *The Interesting Narrative Life of Oloudah Equiano, or Gustavus Vassa, the African* (1789), as well as a biography, portraits, and a map of Equiano's travels.

ART AND ARCHITECTURE

Art History Resources on the Web: Part 11, 18th Century Art
http://witcombe.sbc.edu/ARTH18thcentury.html

Chris Witcombe, a professor of art history at Sweet Briar College in Virginia, has compiled this extensive list of Web sites about art history. This page of the site deals specifically with eighteenth century painting, sculpture, and architecture, featuring almost three hundred links to information about Canaletto, Gainsborough, Watteau, Hogarth, William Blake, Sir Joshua Reynolds, Goya, and other artists, sculptors, and architects of the period.

A Digital Archive of American Architecture: 18th Century
http://www.bc.edu/bc_org/avp/cas/fnart/fa267/
    fa267_18.html

Professor Jeffery Howe of Boston College has compiled this slide collection of eighteenth century American architecture, which includes examples of buildings created in the Georgian and federalist styles, and slides of period houses, churches, and public and commercial structures.

A Digital Archive of Architecture: 18th Century Architecture
http://www.bc.edu/bc_org/avp/cas/fnart/arch/
    18arch_europe.html

Another page in Jeffery Howe's Web site, featuring examples of eighteenth century European architecture, including additions to Versailles and buildings in Vienna and London.

Metropolitan Museum of Art: Time Line of Art History
http://www.metmuseum.org/toah/splash.htm

The museum's Web site describes itself as a "chronological, geographical, and thematic exploration of the history of art from around the world, as illustrated especially by the Metropolitan Museum of Art's collection." The time line for the period from 1600 to 1800 contains art works, maps, and chronologies organized by regions of the world, including North America, Europe, Central America and Mexico, Africa, Oceania, and several areas of Asia. The site also features numerous pages devoted to specific topics, including European Art in the Baroque and Rococo eras, and African, Asian, and Islamic art.

WebMuseum, Paris: Famous Art Works Exhibition
http://www.ibiblio.org/wm/paint/

This Web collection of European and American paintings from 1250 through the twentieth century includes two pages specifically about eighteenth century art: "Baroque, 1600-1700," and "Revolution and Restoration." Each page contains links to information about specific artists, including Claude Lorraine, Fragonard, Constable, Goya, Watteau, Benjamin West, and Copley. Additional information about artists is accessible through the "Artist Index," an alphabetical listing of artists whose work is featured on the site.

World Art Treasures
http://www.bergerfoundation.ch/

A collection of 100,000 slides compiled by art historian Jacques-Edouard Berger and the foundation bearing his name. The site includes a separate section containing slides of eighteenth century art, and other pages with paintings by Caneletto, William Blake, Goya, Hogarth, and Watteau.

ASIA

The British Presence in India in the Eighteenth Century
http://www.bbc.co.uk/history/state/empire/
    east_india_01.shtml

Part of the British Broadcasting Company's Web site, this page contains an essay by Professor Peter Marshall, professor emeritus at King's College, London University, about the East India Company's presence in India. It also features a bibliography.

Internet East Asian History Sourcebook

http://www.fordham.edu/halsall/eastasia/
eastasiasbook.html

This site provides primary source materials tracing the historical and cultural developments in China, Japan, and Korea, including information about European exploration and the activities of the East India Company.

Manas: India and Its Neighbors

http://www.sscnet.ucla.edu/southasia/index.html

Vinay Lal, associate professor of history at the University of California, Los Angeles, created this Web site with a vast array of information about the history, politics, and culture of India. The section entitled "British India" includes information about the fortunes of the East India Company in eighteenth century India, and the beginnings of British rule following the Battle of Plassey in 1757.

Tokugawa Japan, 1603-1868

http://www.wsu.edu:8000/~dee/TOKJAPAN/
TOKJAPAN.HTM

This section of _World Civilizations: An Internet Classroom and Anthology_, created by Professor Richard Hooker of Washington State University, focuses on Tokugawa Japan, with information about daily life, Neo-Confucianism, and kabuki.

AUSTRALIA

Australian Government Culture and Recreation Portal: European Discovery and Settlement of Australia

http://www.cultureandrecreation.gov.au/articles/
australianhistory/

Australian Government Culture and Recreation Portal: Convicts and the European Settlement of Australia

http://www.cultureandrecreation.gov.au/articles/
convicts/

These two pages in the Australian government's Web site describe Captain James Cook's expedition to Australia in 1770, and the subsequent British colonization of the country by convicts and other European settlers. The pages contain numerous links to additional sites providing information about Cook and other explorers, European settlement, convicts, and aboriginal life.

AUSTRIA

Internet Modern History Sourcebook: Enlightened Despots

http://www.fordham.edu/halsall/mod/
modsbook11.html

This page, featuring primary source materials about government in the age of Enlightenment, includes information about Empress Maria Theresa of Austria.

CANADA

Canada

http://canada.gc.ca/acanada/
acPubHome.jsp?font=0&lang=eng

This site, created by the Canadian government, includes a wealth of information about the country's history, culture, society, and government. There is a time line of military history, which includes information about the eighteenth century, and an online version of the _Dictionary of Canadian Biography_, featuring authoritative articles about prominent Canadians.

The Canadian Encyclopedia

http://thecanadianencyclopedia.com/
index.cfm?PgNm=Homepage&Params=A1

The Canadian Encyclopedia provides authoritative information on what the site describes as "all things Canadian." The "Feature Articles" section contains numerous articles offering an introduction to historical topics. These articles include biographies of important Canadians, including eighteenth century figures Pontiac and Alexander Mackenzie, and articles about culture, sports, exploration, the military, and society. An extensive time line chronicles significant events throughout Canadian history.

oCanada.ca: Canadian History, 18th Century

http://www.ocanada.ca/history/history_18.php

The _oCanada.ca_ Web site contains a time line listing significant events in Canadian history, including this page featuring a chronology of events occurring in the eighteenth century.

Pathfinders and Passageways: The Exploration of Canada

This Web site, produced by the Library and Archives Canada, is described in **EXPLORATION** (below).

ECONOMICS

The History of Economic Thought
http://cepa.newschool.edu/het/

Created by the Department of Economics at the New School for Social Research, this site features biographical information and excerpts of texts from more than five hundred economists who can be accessed via an alphabetical index. Adam Smith, Jeremy Bentham, Étienne Bonnet de Condillac, Denis Diderot, and Benjamin Franklin are among the eighteenth century thinkers featured here.

McMaster University Archive for the History of Economic Thought
http://socserv2.socsci.mcmaster.ca/~econ/ugcm/3ll3/

An extensive collection of texts about economics, organized by author. The site includes the writings of Adam Smith, Jeremy Bentham, Tom Paine, David Hume, François Quesnay, and Jean-Jacques Rousseau, among other eighteenth century thinkers.

EXPLORATION

Australian Government Culture and Recreation Portal: European Discovery and Settlement of Australia

This site, which includes information about James Cook's discovery of Australia, is described in **AUSTRALIA** (above).

History of Exploration: 17th - 18th Century
http://www.historyworld.net/wrldhis/
PlainTextHistories.asp?groupid=
2092&HistoryID=ab90

This page in the *History of Exploration* Web site contains information on the eighteenth century exploration of Canada, the Pacific Islands, Australia, and Africa.

Pathfinders and Passageways: The Exploration of Canada
http://www.collectionscanada.ca/explorers/index-e.html

Created by the Library and Archives Canada, the site chronicles the many people who discovered and explored the country. It includes three pages devoted to eighteenth century exploration, plus additional pages about prominent explorers of the period, including Alexander Mackenzie, James Cook, George Vancouver, Thanadelthur, and Vitus Jonassen Bering.

FRANCE

Internet Modern History Sourcebook: French Revolution
http://www.fordham.edu/halsall/mod/modsbook13.html

This page of Web links is part of *Internet Modern History Sourcebook*, a compilation of primary source materials organized by Paul Halsall of Fordham University. The *French Revolution* page links to documents related to the revolution, including the Tennis Court Oath and the Declaration of the Rights of Man. There are also links to Web sites with information about Napoleon and the Napoleonic wars.

Liberty, Equality, Fraternity: Exploring the French Revolution
http://chnm.gmu.edu/revolution/

A user-friendly guide to the French Revolution, featuring twelve essays that provide an overview of the causes, events, and legacy of the conflict. The Web site also contains 245 political cartoons and other images; 330 documents, such as memoirs, reports, newspaper articles, and eyewitness accounts, chronicling the revolution; and an extensive time line of events.

Marie Antoinette
http://www.royalty.nu/Europe/France/
MarieAntoinette.html

Part of the *Royalty.nu* Web site, this page provides a biography of Marie Antoinette, including information about the French Revolution and her execution. It also features a bibliography, with materials about Marie Antoinette, Louis XVI, Marie's court and times, and the French Revolution.

Napoleon Bonaparte Internet Guide
http://www.napoleonbonaparte.nl/

A guide to help users readily access what its creator describes as "the best Napoleonic sites in the world." There are hundreds of links to sites about Napoleon, the Napoleonic era, and other topics, as well as articles about Napoleon.

GERMANY

Internet Modern History Sourcebook: Enlightened Despots
http://www.fordham.edu/halsall/mod/modsbook11.html

This page, featuring primary source materials about government in the age of Enlightenment, includes information about King Frederick II, described as a "model of an Enlightenment despot." It also contains information about the decline of the Holy Roman Empire and the rise of Prussia.

GREAT BRITAIN

Britain's Prime Ministers

http://www.britannia.com/gov/primes/

Contains a page of biographical information about each prime minister, from Robert Walpole through Tony Blair. Each page also lists significant historical events that occurred during each prime minister's term in office.

The British Presence in India in the Eighteenth Century

http://www.bbc.co.uk/history/state/empire/
    east_india_01.shtml

Part of the British Broadcasting Company's Web site, this page contains an essay by Professor Peter Marshall, professor emeritus at King's College, London University, about the East India Company's presence in India. It also features a bibliography.

England Time Line: The Stuarts and Civil War, 1603-1713

http://www.bbc.co.uk/history/time lines/england/
    stu_james_vi_i.shtml

England Time Line: The Georgians, 1714-1836

http://www.bbc.co.uk/history/time lines/england/
    geo_georgian_britain.shtml

These pages are part of the British Broadcasting Company's time line of English history. They feature information about significant people and events of the period, related links, and multimedia games.

Monarchs

http://www.britannia.com/history/h6f.html

An informative, easy-to-use site containing biographies and portraits of the queens and kings who have ruled England since 829.

Scottish History: The Enlightenment and Industrial Revolution

http://www.bbc.co.uk/history/scottishhistory/
    enlightenment/index.shtml

The British Broadcasting Company's Web site contains a section on Scottish history, including these pages about Scottish Enlightenment thinkers, Scotland's contributions to the Industrial Revolution, and Scottish radicalism in the eighteenth and nineteenth centuries.

LITERATURE

The Cambridge History of English and American Literature: An Encyclopedia in Eighteen Volumes

http://www.bartleby.com/cambridge/

An exhaustively comprehensive examination of all forms of writing in Great Britain and the United States, including literature, legal and church writing, journalism, children's literature, and philosophy. Volumes nine through eleven contain essays about various aspects of eighteenth century English literature, including information about Samuel Johnson, Alexander Pope, Edmund Burke, Daniel Defoe, and Jonathan Swift. Volume fifteen focuses on literature from the colonial and revolutionary United States, including the works of Jonathan Edwards, Thomas Paine, and Benjamin Franklin.

Eighteenth Century E-Texts

http://andromeda.rutgers.edu/~jlynch/18th/etext.html

Jack Lynch, associate professor of English at Rutgers University, has compiled this amazingly extensive collection of hundreds of electronic texts. The texts are arranged alphabetically by author, and cover a wide time range—from the period of John Milton to that of Lord Byron. Many of the texts are in English, including some works translated from other languages, while other texts are in German, French, and other original languages. The site includes works by William Blake, Robert Burns, Daniel Defoe, Thomas Jefferson, Benjamin Franklin, Phyllis Wheatley, Jonathan Swift, Johann Wolfgang Goethe, Mary Wollstonecraft, Samuel Johnson, Alexander Pope, Voltaire, Jean-Jacques Rousseau, and Friederich Schiller.

SAC Lit Web: Restoration and Eighteenth Century English Literature Index

http://www.accd.edu/sac/english/bailey/18thcent.htm

A page in *San Antonio College LitWeb*, a compendium of biographical and bibliographical information about English literature. *Restoration and Eighteenth Century English Literature Index* provides links to pages about authors whose works were published between 1660 and 1784, including Jonathan Swift, Alexander Pope, Samuel Johnson, Fanny Burney, Ann Radcliffe, Oliver Goldsmith, and Henry Fielding. Each author page lists that author's major works and provides links to related Web sites.

Voice of the Shuttle: Restoration & 18th Century
http://vos.ucsb.edu/browse.asp?id=2738

Voice of the Shuttle is an excellent collection of Web resources about the humanities compiled by professors at the University of California, Santa Barbara. This page contains links to English-language essays, literary criticism, and examples of prose, poetry, and drama from a long list of British authors.

The William Blake Archive
http://www.blakearchive.org/main.html

A hypermedia archive of Blake's prints, paintings, and poems, sponsored by the Library of Congress, with support from the National Endowment for the Humanities and several universities. Includes a biography, chronology, and glossary, with search engines and detailed instructions describing how to use the site.

MATHEMATICS

The MacTutor History of Mathematics Archive
http://www-groups.dcs.st-and.ac.uk/~history/index.html

A very comprehensive Web site, created and maintained by the School of Mathematics and Statistics at the University of St. Andrews, Scotland. The site features biographies of prominent mathematicians which can be accessed by either an alphabetical or chronological index. It also contains information about math history, with separate pages explaining important mathematical discoveries and concepts.

Mathematicians of the Seventeenth and Eighteenth Centuries
http://www.maths.tcd.ie/pub/HistMath/People/
   RBallHist.html

This page, part of a Web site maintained by the School of Mathematics at Trinity College in Dublin, links to biographical information about prominent mathematicians. The biographies are adapted from *A Short Account of the History of Mathematics* by W. W. S Rouse Ball (4th ed., 1908). Leonhard Euler, Jean le Rond d'Alembert, and Joseph-Louis Lagrange are among the eighteenth century mathematicians included here.

MILITARY HISTORY

Military History Encyclopedia on the Web
http://www.historyofwar.org/main.html

Compiled by three British professors, this Web-based encyclopedia features articles about wars and battles throughout history. The information can be assessed with several indexes, including alphabetical listings of wars, battles, biographies, and countries. The French and Indian and Seven Years' Wars are among the conflicts discussed here.

MUSIC

Carolina Classical Connection: An Index of Classical Music Web Site Links
http://www.carolinaclassical.com/links.html

A wide variety of music-related Web sites, with biographical information on composers, descriptions of musical genres and types of compositions, and encoded music files. The page with links to the Baroque period includes information on Johann Sebastian Bach, George Frideric Handel, Antonio Vivaldi, and other composers of the early eighteenth century; the page of Classical period links features information about late eighteenth century composers, such as Wolfgang Amadeus Mozart, Christoph Gluck, and Franz Joseph Haydn.

The Classical MIDI Connection: The Baroque Period
http://www.classicalmidiconnection.com/cmc/
   baroque.html

The Classical MIDI Connection: The Classical Period
http://www.classicalmidiconnection.com/cmc/
   classica.html

A collection of music "midi" files. "Midi," or musical instrument digital interface, is a digital technology that allows electronic musical instruments and computers to communicate with one another and enables people to listen to music on their computers. The site has an alphabetized list of composers with links to midi files of their music. A separate page is devoted to the music of the Baroque era, featuring information about Johann Sebastian Bach and Antonio Vivaldi; another page contains midi files of Classical period music from composers such as Christoph Gluck, Franz Joseph Haydn, and Wolfgang Amadeus Mozart.

J. S. Bach Home Page

http://www.jsbach.org/

A well organized overview of Johann Sebastian Bach's life and music. The site features a biography, bibliography, portraits of the composer, a complete list of his works, and a list of recommended recordings. There is also an extensive list of links to other Bach-related Web sites, as well as links to sites with midi files of Bach's music.

The Mozart Project

http://www.mozartproject.org/

The site, in its own words, provides information about "the life, times, and music of Wolfgang Amadeus Mozart." It contains an illustrated biography, lists of compositions organized by date and musical genre, selected essays, a bibliography, and links to related resources, including Web sites with sound files of Mozart's music.

Music History 102: A Guide to Western Composers and Their Music from the Middle Ages to the Present

http://www.ipl.org/div/mushist/#baro

Created by the highly regarded Internet Public Library, this site provides an overview of music in six eras, biographical information about significant composers, and sound files created with Real Audio Players software. Two of the site's pages highlight music from the eighteenth century: the page about the Baroque Age (c. 1600-1750), with information about Johann Sebastian Bach, George Fredric Handel, and Antonio Vivaldi, and the page about the Classical Period (1750-1820), with information about Franz Joseph Haydn, Wolfgang Amadeus Mozart, and Christoph Gluck.

PHILOSOPHY

The Internet Encyclopedia of Philosophy

http://www.utm.edu/research/iep/

A collection of articles written by philosophy professors, including information about French and English Deism, German Idealism, the Encyclopedists, Cesare Beccaria, Johann Gottlieb Fichte, Jeremy Bentham, and George Berkeley.

Internet Modern History Sourcebook: Enlightenment

http://www.fordham.edu/halsall/mod/modsbook10.html

A compilation of full texts and excerpts of writings providing the philosophical, religious, economic, and political thought of Denis Diderot, Voltaire, Montesquieu, Adam Smith, Jean-Jacques Rousseau, Immanuel Kant, David Hume, Jeremy Bentham, George Berkeley, and other eighteenth century authors.

Philosophy Pages

http://www.philosophypages.com/

A comprehensive and easily accessible site aimed at students of the Western philosophical tradition. Users can access information via a dictionary of philosophical terms and names, a survey of the history of Western philosophy, and a time line. *Philosophy Pages* also provides links to other philosophy Web sites and essays examining the ideas of several major philosophers, including Immanuel Kant, Jean-Jacques Rousseau, David Hume, and George Berkeley.

Stanford Encyclopedia of Philosophy

http://plato.stanford.edu/contents.html

A collection of articles about various aspects of philosophy, which can be accessed through an alphabetical table of contents. Includes articles about Scottish philosophy in the eighteenth century, George Berkeley, David Hume, Immanuel Kant, and Montesquieu.

RELIGION

Baʿal Shem Tov Foundation

http://www.baalshemtov.com/

The foundation's Web site provides information about Rebbe Baʿal Shem Tov, the founder of Hasidic Judaism. Site pages include a biography, explanations of the rebbe's teachings, a bibliography, stories about Baʿal Shem Tov, and links to related Web sites.

Jonathan Edwards.com

http://www.jonathanedwards.com/

A collection of Edwards's sermons and other writings. The site also contains a chronology of his life, biographical sketches, overviews of his theology, and a bibliography of materials about Edwards and the Great Awakening.

Methodist Archives and Research Centre

http://rylibWeb.man.ac.uk/data1/dg/text/method.html

Established by the Methodist Church of Great Britain, this online archive contains primary and secondary texts written by John Wesley, George Whitefield, and other theologians. Users also can access an exhibit on

Wesley's life and legacy and links to other Web sites about Methodism.

Religion in Eighteenth century America
http://www.loc.gov/exhibits/religion/rel02.html

Religion and the American Revolution
http://www.loc.gov/exhibits/religion/rel03.html
These two pages are part of *Religion and the Founding of the American Republic*, a Web site accompanying an exhibit at the Library of Congress. The first page describes various aspects of eighteenth century religion, including the appearance of churches, Deism, and the rise of American evangelism during the Great Awakening, with information about George Whitefield, Jonathan Edwards, and the Presbyterians, Baptists, and Methodists. The second page describes the role of religion and the problems of American Anglicans during the American Revolution.

RUSSIA

Internet Modern History Sourcebook: Enlightened Despots
http://www.fordham.edu/halsall/mod/modsbook11.html
This page, featuring primary source materials about government in the age of Enlightenment, includes information about Peter the Great, the rise of Russia, and the reign of Catherine the Great.

SCIENCE, TECHNOLOGY. AND MEDICINE

Eighteenth Century Inventions, 1700-1799
http://inventors.about.com/library/inventors/bl1700s.htm
About.com has created a time line of inventions, with links to additional information about some of the inventors and inventions of the eighteenth century. Jethro Tull's seed drill, Thomas Newcomen's steam engine, and Gabriel Fahrenheit's thermometer are among the inventions included.

Eric Weisstein's World of Science
http://scienceworld.wolfram.com/
This online reference has been compiled by a research scientist and former professor of astronomy. It contains comprehensive encyclopedias of information about astronomy, chemistry, mathematics, and physics. There also are brief biographies and portraits of noteworthy scientists, including Luigi Galvini, Alessandro Volta, Joseph Priestley, James Watt, Comte de

Buffon, William Herschel, and other eighteenth century figures.

History of Western Biomedicine
http://www.mic.ki.se/West.html#West3
Compiled by the Karolinska Institutet in Sweden, this site contains links to information about medical and scientific history. The section entitled "Modern Period, 1601-   " includes a list of sites about eighteenth century scientific and medical developments, including the chemical revolution, Captain Cook and the scourge of scurvy, and Edward Jenner and the discovery of vaccination.

Lavoisier's Friends
http://historyofscience.free.fr/Lavoisier-Friends/
A bilingual English-French Web site designed to publicize the work of the man whom many consider the father of modern chemistry. Contains an extensive biography, explanations of Lavoisier's scientific discoveries, and a bibliography.

THEATER

Theatre Database: 18th Century Theatre
http://www.theatredatabase.com/18th_century/
The pages on this site link to biographical information about playwrights and actors, including Joseph Addison, Hannah Cowley, Johann Wolfgang von Goethe, Oliver Goldsmith, Gotthold Ephraim Lessing, and Friedrich Schiller. There are also Web links to pages about eighteenth century American theater.

TRADE AND COMMERCE

African Slave Trade and European Imperialism
This site about the Atlantic slave trade is described in **AFRICA** (above).

The Bubble Project
http://is.dal.ca/~dmcneil/bubble.html
Created by a team of scholars at Dalhousie University, the site provides a historical overview, essays, and Web links about the South Sea Bubble, a major stock market crash in England in 1720.

Internet Modern History Sourcebook: Industrial Revolution
http://www.fordham.edu/halsall/mod/modsbook14.html
A list of Web links providing information about the

agricultural revolution of the seventeenth and eighteenth centuries, the revolution in textile manufacturing, and the growth and development of steam power.

The Open Door Web Site: The Industrial Revolution

http://www.saburchill.com/history/chapters/IR/
    001.html#The

The Open Door Web Site was created by teachers to make British history available to their students online. The site includes a series of pages about the changing nature of agriculture and industry in Britain during the eighteenth and nineteenth centuries, including information about the textile industry and iron and steel manufacture.

Textile Industry

http://www.spartacus.schoolnet.co.uk/Textiles.htm

Created by Spartacus Educational, a British company that provides Web-based information for teachers and students, this site chronicles the development of the British textile industry in the eighteenth and nineteenth centuries. It includes information about the inventions of James Watt, Matthew Boulton, James Hargreaves, and John Kay, and about textile entrepreneurs, such as Richard Arkwright. The site also contains descriptions of life in a textile factory and interviews with factory workers.

UNITED STATES

American Memory: Documents from the Continental Congress and the Constitutional Convention, 1774-1789

http://memory.loc.gov/ammem/bdsds/bdsdhome.html

This site, created by the Library of Congress, contains more than two hundred and seventy broadsides with information about the work of the Continental Congress and the drafting of the U.S. Constitution. Broadsides were large sheets of paper with printed information that were widely disseminated during the eighteenth century. The broadsides can be accessed by a list of subjects, such as U.S. Revolutionary history, the currency question, and politics and government of the Old Northwest. The site also features early printed versions of the Constitution and the Declaration of Independence.

American Memory: George Washington Papers at the Library of Congress, 1741-1799

http://memory.loc.gov/ammem/gwhtml/gwhome.html

The Library of Congress has digitized its massive collection of Washington's correspondence, letterbooks, diaries, journals, reports, and other papers, and made them available on this Web site. The site also contains a detailed time line of Washington's life and an essay about Washington's work as a surveyor and mapmaker.

American Revolution.org

http://www.americanrevolution.org/

A gateway providing extensive information about the American Revolution, including a lengthy list of links to related historical sites, electronic versions of books, and scholarly essays.

Archiving Early America

http://earlyamerica.com/

A digital archive of historical documents, newspapers, maps, and other materials from the eighteenth century. The site is chock full of information, including period biographies and autobiographies of Benjamin Franklin, George Washington, Paul Revere, and Daniel Boone; biographies of notable women of early America; digitized copies of the Declaration of Independence, Bill of Rights, and U.S. Constitution; period documents representing milestone historic events; and brief films about Franklin, Washington, Revere, and the American Revolution.

Avalon Project at Yale Law School

http://www.yale.edu/lawWeb/avalon/avalon.htm

A collection of digitized documents relevant to the fields of law, history, economics, politics, diplomacy, and government. A separate page entitled "18th Century Documents" features numerous legal and political documents originating in the United States, including charters and constitutions for the American colonies, the Stamp Act, Declaration of Independence, Federalist Papers, Thomas Paine's *Rights of Man* and *American Crisis*, and papers of George Washington, Thomas Jefferson, and other Founding Fathers.

Benjamin Franklin: A Documentary History

http://www.english.udel.edu/lemay/franklin/

Franklin scholar Leo Lemay has created this chronology, extensively documenting the significant events in Franklin's life and placing his life within the context of the era's politics.

A Chronology of American Slavery: 1619-1789

http://innercity.org/holt/slavechron.html

The first page of a three-page chronology, tracing the history of slavery during the seventeenth and eighteenth centuries.

Internet Modern History Sourcebook: American Independence

http://www.fordham.edu/halsall/mod/modsbook12.html

This is one of the sourcebooks, or collections of primary source materials, compiled by Paul Halsall of Fordham University. The *American Independence Sourcebook* includes a wide range of primary source materials about eighteenth century American history, including documents about the original colonies, the American Revolution, American foreign policy prior to 1898, the establishment of the American state, Native Americans, and slavery.

Thomas Jefferson Digital Archive

http://etext.lib.virginia.edu/jefferson/

A compendium of electronic information about Jefferson compiled by the University of Virginia. The site includes letters, manuscripts, and other digitized texts written by or to Jefferson; *The Jefferson Cyclopedia*, containing Jefferson's views on government, politics, law, religion and other subjects; and a collection of Jefferson's quotes. There also is an electronic text of B. L. Rayner's *Life of Thomas Jefferson*, a biography published eight years after Jefferson's death.

WOMEN

The Bluestocking Archive

http://www.faculty.umb.edu/elizabeth_fay/archive2.html

An archive of texts related to the Bluestockings, a mid-eighteenth century group of British women who held "conversations" with men to encourage the pursuit of literary and intellectual interests.

The English Bride: The Eighteenth Century Gentlewoman's Guide to Marriage

http://www.umich.edu/~ece/student_projects/wedding_bride/index.html

This is one of several Web sites about eighteenth century England created by and for literature students at the University of Michigan. The site describes marriage laws and customs of the period, including advice on how to snag a baronet, a gentleman's view of marriage, and information on bridal fashion and marriage ceremonies.

The Hannah Snell Home Page

http://www.users.bigpond.com/ShipStreetPress/Snell/

An account of Hannah Snell, an eighteenth century British woman who disguised herself as a man and served in the Royal Marines.

Make Your Way as a Woman in Eighteenth Century England

http://www.umich.edu/~ece/student_projects/make_your_way/index.html

Another site designed by and for literature students at the University of Michigan. The site provides an overview of how English women lived, describing the lives of a single woman and a wife and mother. There is also information about two common career paths for eighteenth century women: domestic service and prostitution.

The Penn State Archive of Women Writing Before 1800

http://www.hn.psu.edu/Faculty/KKemmerer/18thc/women/main.htm

The archive features works by women poets that were previously unavailable to the public. It contains separate pages for each poet, with links to examples of her poetry.

Women Artists: Self-Portraits and Representations of Womanhood from the Medieval Period to the Present

http://www.csupomona.edu/%7Eplin/women/womenart.html

California State University, Pomona, sponsors this Web site about women artists and their depiction of women. The site features portraits and brief biographies of women artists and is arranged chronologically, with one page devoted to seventeenth and eighteenth century artists, and another page featuring information about artists of the eighteenth and nineteenth centuries.

Women of the American Revolution

http://www.americanrevolution.org/women.html

This site, adapted from the book of the same name by Elizabeth F. Ellet (1848), contains biographical information and portraits of notable women, including Abigail Adams, Martha Washington, and Flora MacDonald. This information is part of American Revolution.org (see **UNITED STATES** above).

SUBSCRIPTION WEB SITES

The following sites are posted on the World Wide Web but are available to paying subscribers only. Many public, college, and university libraries subscribe to these sources; readers can ask reference librarians if they are available at their local libraries.

GENERAL

Oxford Reference Online

http://www.oxfordreference.com

A virtual reference library of more than one hundred dictionaries and reference books published by Oxford University Press, *Oxford Reference Online* contains information about a broad range of subjects, including art, architecture, military history, science, religion, philosophy, political and social science, and literature. The site also features English-language and bilingual dictionaries, as well as collections of quotations and proverbs.

Oxford Scholarship Online

www.oxfordscholarship.com

Oxford Scholarship Online currently contains the electronic versions of more than 980 books about economics, finance, philosophy, political science, and religion that are published by the Oxford University Press. The site features full texts of these books, advanced searching capabilities, and links to other online sources.

ART

Grove Art Online

www.groveart.com

This authoritative and comprehensive site provides information about the visual arts from prehistory to the present. In addition to its more than 130,000 art images, the site contains articles on fine arts, architecture, China, South America, Africa, and other world cultures, as well as biographies and links to hundreds of museum and gallery Web sites.

BRITISH ISLES

Oxford Dictionary of National Biography

http://www.oxforddnb.com/

The online version of the recently revised *Oxford Dictionary of National Biography* is a highly authorita-

tive reference source of biographical information. According to the site's description, the dictionary contains "50,000 biographies of people who shaped the history of the British Isles and beyond, from the earliest times to the year 2001."

HISTORY

Daily Life Through History

http://dailylife.greenwood.com/mkting/
        history_product.aspx

The site, created by Greenwood Press, describes the religious, domestic, economic, material, political, recreational, and intellectual life of people throughout history. It contains information from *The Greenwood Encyclopedia of Daily Life* and other sources, and features maps, illustrations, chronologies, and primary documents.

MUSIC

Grove Music Online

www.grovemusic.com

The online version of the highly regarded *The New Grove Dictionary of Music and Musicians* features thousands of articles on musicians, instruments, musical techniques, genres, and styles. In addition to its articles and biographies, the site provides more than five hundred audio clips of music, and links to images, sound, and related Web sites.

SCIENCE

Access Science: McGraw-Hill Encyclopedia of Science and Technology Online

http://www.accessscience.com

An online version of *McGraw Hill Encyclopedia of Science and Technology* and *McGraw Hill Dictionary of Scientific and Technical Terms*, containing the information found in the latest editions of those books. Users can access biographies, articles, and science news.

ELECTRONIC DATABASES

Electronic databases usually do not have their own URLs. Instead, public, college, and university libraries subscribe to these databases and install them on their Web sites, where they are only available to library card holders or specified patrons. Readers can check library Web sites to see if these databases are installed or can ask reference librarians if these databases are available.

GENERAL

Gale Virtual Reference Library
The database contains more than eighty-five reference books, including encyclopedias and almanacs, allowing users to find information about a broad range of subjects.

BIOGRAPHY

Biography Resource Center
The database, produced by Thomson Gale, includes biographies of more than 320,000 prominent people from throughout history and throughout the world.

Wilson Biographies Plus Illustrated
Produced by H. W. Wilson Co., this database offers more than one hundred and twenty thousand biographical profiles, more than 32,000 images, and bibliographies of prominent people throughout history.

HISTORY

History Reference Center
A product of EBSCO Information Services, the History Reference Center is a comprehensive world history database. It contains the contents of more than 750 encyclopedias and reference books, the full text of articles published in about sixty history periodicals, thousands of historical documents, biographies, photographs, and maps, and historical film and video.

History Resource Center: U.S.
This database, produced by Thomson Gale, provides primary source documents, reference materials, and articles about United States history from colonial times to the present.

MagillOnHistory
Available on the EBSCO platform, Salem Press's MagillOnHistory offers the full contents of its ongoing Great Lives from History series as well as its Great

Events from History and entries from its many history and social science encyclopedias, such as the award-winning *Ready Reference: American Indians* and its decades series, *The Fifties*, *The Sixties*, and *The Seventies*. Full-length essays numbering in the thousands are designed to cross-link coverage of historical events and biographies of the movers and shapers of the world, from ancient times to the twenty-first century.

World History FullTEXT
A joint product of EBSCO Information Services and ABC-CLIO, this database offers a global view of history contained in the full texts of more than one hundred fifty books. Information is available on a wide range of topics, including anthropology, art, culture, economics, government, heritage, military history, politics, regional issues, and sociology.

World History Online
Facts On File, Inc., has created this reference database of world history, featuring biographies, time lines, maps, charts, and primary source documents.

LITERATURE

Literature Resource Center
Literature Resource Center, produced by Thomson Gale, includes biographies, bibliographies, and critical analyses of authors from a wide range of literary disciplines, countries, and eras. The database also features plot summaries, the full text of articles from literary journals, critical essays, plot summaries, and links to Web sites.

MagillOnLiteraturePlus
Available on the EBSCO platform, MagillOnLiteraturePlus contains more than 160 volumes of information. Salem Press's comprehensive integrated literature database incorporates the full contents of its many title- and author-driven series and is continuously growing as new titles are added. As of 2005, these included *Masterplots* (series I and II), *Cyclope-*

dia of World Authors, *Cyclopedia of Literary Characters*, *Cyclopedia of Literary Places*, *Critical Surveys of Literature*, *Magill's Literary Annual*, *World Philosophers and Their Works*, and *Magill Book Reviews*. Updated quarterly, the database examines more than thirty-five thousand works and more than ten thousand writers, poets, dramatists, essayists, and philosophers. Most essays are several pages in length, and nearly all feature annotated bibliographies for further study. Essays feature critical analyses as well as plot summaries, biographical essays, character profiles, and authoritative listings of authors' works and their dates of publication.

—*Rebecca Kuzins*

CHRONOLOGICAL LIST OF ENTRIES

1700's

18th cent.: Expansion of the Atlantic Slave Trade
c. 1701: Oman Captures Zanzibar
1701: Plumier Publishes *L'Art de tourner*
1701: Tull Invents the Seed Drill
c. 1701-1721: Great Northern War
c. 1701-1750: Bach Pioneers Modern Music
Feb. 4, 1701-Feb. 4, 1703: Revenge of the Forty-Seven Ronin
May 26, 1701-Sept. 7, 1714: War of the Spanish Succession
June 12, 1701: Act of Settlement
July 9, 1701: Marsh Builds Ireland's First Public Library
1702 or 1706: First Arabic Printing Press
May 15, 1702-Apr. 11, 1713: Queen Anne's War
July 24, 1702-Oct. 1, 1704: Camisard Risings in the Cévennes
1703-1711: Hungarian Revolt Against Habsburg Rule

May 27, 1703: Founding of St. Petersburg
June 20, 1703: Chikamatsu Produces *The Love Suicides at Sonezaki*
1704: Newton Publishes *Optics*
1704-1712: Astronomy Wars in England
1704-1757: Javanese Wars of Succession
Aug. 13, 1704: Battle of Blenheim
1705: Halley Predicts the Return of a Comet
1705-1712: Newcomen Develops the Steam Engine
Feb., 1706-Apr. 28, 1707: Act of Union Unites England and Scotland
Mar. 23-26, 1708: Defeat of the "Old Pretender"
1709: Darby Invents Coke-Smelting
c. 1709: Invention of the Piano
1709-1747: Persian-Afghan Wars
June 27, 1709: Battle of Poltava
Sept. 11, 1709: Battle of Malplaquet

1710's

Nov. 20, 1710-July 21, 1718: Ottoman Wars with Russia, Venice, and Austria
Mar. 1, 1711: Addison and Steele Establish *The Spectator*
Sept. 22, 1711-Mar. 23, 1713: Tuscarora War
Dec., 1711: Occasional Conformity Bill
1712: Philip V Founds the Royal Library of Spain
1712: Stamp Act
Apr. 6, 1712: New York City Slave Revolt
Apr. 13-Aug. 11, 1712: Second Villmergen War
Aug., 1712: Maya Rebellion in Chiapas
1713: Founding of Louisbourg
Apr. 11, 1713: Treaty of Utrecht
Aug. 3, 1713: Foundation of the Spanish Academy
Sept. 8, 1713: Papal Bull *Unigenitus*

1714: Fahrenheit Develops the Mercury Thermometer
1714-1762: Quest for Longitude
Jan. 7, 1714: Mill Patents the Typewriter
Mar. 7, 1714, and Sept. 7, 1714: Treaties of Rastatt and Baden
Summer, 1714-1741: Fox Wars
1715-1737: Building of the Karlskirche
Sept. 6, 1715-Feb. 4, 1716: Jacobite Rising in Scotland
1718: Bernoulli Publishes His Calculus of Variations
1718: Geoffroy Issues the *Table of Reactivities*
1718-1730: Tulip Age
1719-1724: Stukeley Studies Stonehenge and Avebury
Apr. 25, 1719: Defoe Publishes the First Novel

1720's

1720: Financial Collapse of the John Law System
May, 1720-Dec., 1721: Last Major Outbreak of Plague
Sept., 1720: Collapse of the South Sea Bubble
Dec., 1720: Japan Lifts Ban on Foreign Books
1721-1742: Development of Great Britain's Office of Prime Minister
1721-1750: Early Enlightenment in France
1722: Réaumur Discovers Carbon's Role in Hardening Steel
Apr. 5, 1722: European Discovery of Easter Island
1723: Stahl Postulates the Phlogiston Theory
1724: Foundation of the St. Petersburg Academy of Sciences
1725: Flamsteed's Star Catalog Marks the Transition to Modern Astronomy

1725-Nov., 1794: Persian Civil Wars
Oct., 1725: Vico Publishes *The New Science*
1726: Swift Satirizes English Rule of Ireland in *Gulliver's Travels*
1726-1729: Voltaire Advances Enlightenment Thought in Europe
May, 1727-1733: Jansenist "Convulsionnaires" Gather at Saint-Médard
Oct. 21, 1727: Treaty of Kiakhta
Jan. 29, 1728: Gay Produces the First Ballad Opera
July, 1728-1769: Russian Voyages to Alaska
1729: Gray Discovers Principles of Electric Conductivity
Nov. 9, 1729, and Feb., 1732: Treaty of Seville

1730's

1730-1739: First Maroon War
c. 1732: Society of Dilettanti Is Established
June 20, 1732: Settlement of Georgia
Dec. 7, 1732: Covent Garden Theatre Opens in London
1733: De Moivre Describes the Bell-Shaped Curve
1733: Du Fay Discovers Two Kinds of Electric Charge
1733: Kay Invents the Flying Shuttle
Oct. 10, 1733-Oct. 3, 1735: War of the Polish Succession
Nov. 23, 1733: Slaves Capture St. John's Island
1735: Hadley Describes Atmospheric Circulation
Beginning 1735: Linnaeus Creates the Binomial System of Classification
May, 1735-1743: French Scientists Explore the Amazon River
Aug. 4, 1735: Trial of John Peter Zenger

1736: *Gentleman's Magazine* Initiates Parliamentary Reporting
1736-1739: Russo-Austrian War Against the Ottoman Empire
1737: Revival of the Paris Salon
Sept. 19, 1737: Walking Purchase
1738: Bernoulli Proposes the Kinetic Theory of Gases
May 15, 1738: Foundation of St. Petersburg's Imperial Ballet School
Nov. 18, 1738: Treaty of Vienna
1739-1740: Hume Publishes *A Treatise of Human Nature*
1739-1741: War of Jenkins's Ear
1739-1742: First Great Awakening
Sept. 9, 1739: Stono Rebellion
Sept. 18, 1739: Treaty of Belgrade

1740's

1740: Maclaurin's Gravitational Theory
1740-1741: Richardson's *Pamela* Establishes the Modern Novel
May 31, 1740: Accession of Frederick the Great

Oct. 20, 1740: Maria Theresa Succeeds to the Austrian Throne
Dec. 16, 1740-Nov. 7, 1748: War of the Austrian Succession

1750's

1760's

Jan., 1762-Nov., 1766: Mozart Tours Europe as a Child Prodigy

Apr., 1762: Rousseau Publishes *The Social Contract*

Oct. 5, 1762: First Performance of Gluck's *Orfeo and Euridice*

1763: Bayes Advances Probability Theory

1763-1767: Famine in Southern Italy

Feb. 10, 1763: Peace of Paris

Beginning Apr., 1763: The *North Briton* Controversy

May 8, 1763-July 24, 1766: Pontiac's Resistance

Aug., 1763-Apr., 1765: David Garrick's European Tour

Sept. 10, 1763: Publication of the *Freeman's Journal*

Oct. 7, 1763: Proclamation of 1763

Dec. 14 and 27, 1763: Paxton Boys' Massacres

1764: Invention of the Spinning Jenny

July, 1764: Voltaire Publishes *A Philosophical Dictionary for the Pocket*

1765-1769: Watt Develops a More Effective Steam Engine

Mar. 22, 1765-Mar. 18, 1766: Stamp Act Crisis

Feb. 24, 1766: Lorraine Becomes Part of France

Nov. 12, 1766: First American Theater Opens in Philadelphia

Dec. 5, 1766-Mar. 16, 1769: Bougainville Circumnavigates the Globe

1767-1768: Spallanzani Disproves Spontaneous Generation

1767-1771: Invention of the Water Frame

June 29, 1767-Apr. 12, 1770: Townshend Crisis

Aug., 1767-May, 1799: Anglo-Mysore Wars

Aug. 10, 1767: Catherine the Great's Instruction

1768-May 16, 1771: Carolina Regulator Movements

Aug. 25, 1768-Feb. 14, 1779: Voyages of Captain Cook

Oct., 1768-Jan. 9, 1792: Ottoman Wars with Russia

Oct. 30, 1768: Methodist Church Is Established in Colonial America

Dec., 1768-Jan. 10, 1773: Bruce Explores Ethiopia

Dec. 10, 1768: Britain's Royal Academy of Arts Is Founded

1769: Pombal Reforms the Inquisition

July 17, 1769-1824: Rise of the California Missions

Sept., 1769-1778: Siamese-Vietnamese War

Oct. 23, 1769: Cugnot Demonstrates His Steam-Powered Road Carriage

1770's

1770: Publication of Holbach's *The System of Nature*

Mar. 5, 1770: Boston Massacre

1771: Woulfe Discovers Picric Acid

1771-1802: Vietnamese Civil Wars

Aug. 5, 1772-Oct. 24, 1795: Partitioning of Poland

1773: Goethe Inaugurates the Sturm und Drang Movement

1773-1788: African American Baptist Church Is Founded

Sept., 1773-Sept., 1774: Pugachev's Revolt

Dec. 16, 1773: Boston Tea Party

1774: Hansard Begins Reporting Parliamentary Debates

Apr. 27-Oct. 10, 1774: Lord Dunmore's War

May 20, 1774: Quebec Act

July 21, 1774: Treaty of Kuchuk Kainarji

Aug. 1, 1774: Priestley Discovers Oxygen

Sept. 5-Oct. 26, 1774: First Continental Congress

Dec., 1774-Feb. 24, 1783: First Marāthā War

1775: Spanish-Algerine War

1775-1790: Joseph II's Reforms

Apr. 14, 1775: Pennsylvania Society for the Abolition of Slavery Is Founded

Apr. 19, 1775: Battle of Lexington and Concord

Apr. 19, 1775-Oct. 19, 1781: American Revolutionary War

Apr. 27-May, 1775: Flour War

May 10-Aug. 2, 1775: Second Continental Congress

1776: Foundation of the Viceroyalty of La Plata

Jan. 10, 1776: Paine Publishes *Common Sense*

Mar. 9, 1776: Adam Smith Publishes *The Wealth of Nations*

Mar. 28, 1776: Founding of Bolshoi Theatre Company

May, 1776-Sept. 3, 1783: France Supports the American Revolution

May 24 and June 11, 1776: Indian Delegation Meets with Congress

July 2, 1776: New Jersey Women Gain the Vote

July 4, 1776: Declaration of Independence

Sept. 6-7, 1776: First Test of a Submarine in Warfare

1780's

1790's

GEOGRAPHICAL INDEX

List of Geographical Regions

ETHIOPIA

EUROPE

Category Index

List of Categories

AGRICULTURE
1701: Tull Invents the Seed Drill, 7
1747: Marggraf Extracts Sugar from Beets, 316
1760's: Beginning of Selective Livestock Breeding, 427
1763-1767: Famine in Southern Italy, 446
1786-1787: Tenmei Famine, 722
Feb. 14, 1788: Meikle Demonstrates His Drum Thresher, 753
1790: First Steam Rolling Mill, 786
1793: Whitney Invents the Cotton Gin, 828
May 6, 1795: Speenhamland System, 870

ANTHROPOLOGY
Apr. 5, 1722: European Discovery of Easter Island, 165
c. 1732: Society of Dilettanti Is Established, 205
1748: Excavation of Pompeii, 325

1749-1789: First Comprehensive Examination of the Natural World, 338
1786: Discovery of the Mayan Ruins at Palenque, 716
Feb. 2, 1786: Jones Postulates a Proto-Indo-European Language, 727
July 19, 1799: Discovery of the Rosetta Stone, 921

ARCHAEOLOGY
1719-1724: Stukeley Studies Stonehenge and Avebury, 138
Apr. 5, 1722: European Discovery of Easter Island, 165

ARCHITECTURE
1715-1737: Building of the Karlskirche, 125
1719-1724: Stukeley Studies Stonehenge and Avebury, 138
c. 1732: Society of Dilettanti Is Established, 205

HEALTH AND MEDICINE

HISTORIOGRAPHY

INVENTIONS

LAWS, ACTS, AND LEGAL HISTORY

SCIENCE AND TECHNOLOGY, AGRICULTURE

SOCIAL ISSUES AND REFORM

WOMEN'S RIGHTS

Great Events from History

Indexes

Personages Index

SUBJECT INDEX